REPORT

OF

THE DEBATES

IN THE

CONVENTION OF CALIFORNIA,

ON THE

FORMATION OF THE STATE CONSTITUTION,

IN SEPTEMBER AND OCTOBER, 1849.

BY J. ROSS BROWNE.

WASHINGTON:
PRINTED BY JOHN T. TOWERS.
1850.

PROCLAMATION OF THE GOVERNOR,

Recommending the formation of a State Constitution, or a plan of a Territorial Government.

Congress having failed at its recent session to provide a new government for this country to replace that which existed on the annexation of California to the United States, the undersigned would call attention to the means which he deems best calculated to avoid the embarrassments of our present position.

The undersigned, in accordance with instructions from the Secretary of War, has assumed the administration of civil affairs in California, not as a *military* Governor, but as the executive of the existing civil government. In the absence of a properly appointed civil Governor, the commanding officer of the Department is, by the laws of California, *ex officio* civil Governor of the country, and the instructions from Washington were based on the provisions of these laws. This subject has been misrepresented or at least misconceived, and currency given to the impression that the government of the country is still *military*. Such is not the fact. The military government ended with the war, and what remains is the *civil* government recognized in the existing laws of California. Although the command of the troops in this Department and the administration of civil affairs in California, are, by the existing laws of the country and the instructions of the President of the United States, temporarily lodged in the hands of the same individual, they are separate and distinct. No military officer other than the commanding General of the Department, exercises any civil authority by virtue of his military commission, and the powers of the commanding General as *ex officio* Governor are only such as are defined and recognized in the existing laws. The instructions of the Secretary of War make it the duty of all military officers to recognise the existing civil government, and to aid its officers with the military force under their control. Beyond this, any interference is not only uncalled for but strictly forbidden.

The laws of California, not inconsistent with the laws, Constitution and treaties of the United States, are still in force, and must continue in force till changed by competent authority. Whatever may be thought of the right of the people to temporarily replace the officers of the existing government by others appointed by a provisional Territorial Legislature, there can be no question that the existing laws of the country must continue in force till replaced by others made and enacted by competent power. That power, by the treaty of peace, as well as from the nature of the case, is vested in Congress. The situation of California in this respect is very different from that of Oregon. The latter was without laws, while the former has a system of laws, which, though somewhat defective, and requiring many changes and amendments, must continue in force till repealed by competent legislative power. The situation of California is almost identical with that of Louisiana, and the decisions of the Supreme Court in recognizing the validity of the laws which existed in that country previous to its annexation to the United States, were not inconsistent with the Constitution and laws of the United States, or repealed by legitimate legislative enactments, furnish us a clear and safe guide in our present situation. It is important that citizens should understand this fact, so as not to endanger their property and involve themselves in useless and expensive litigation, by giving countenance to persons claiming authority which is not given them by law, and by putting faith in laws which can never be recognized by legitimate courts.

As Congress has failed to organize a new Territorial Government, it becomes our imperative duty to take some active measures to provide for the existing wants of the country. This, it is thought, may be best accomplished by putting in full vigor the administration of the laws as they now exist, and completing the organization of the civil government by the election and appointment of all officers recognized by law. While at the same time a convention, in which all parts of the Territory are represented, shall meet and frame a State constitution or a Territorial organization, to be submitted to the people for their ratification, and then proposed to Congress for its approval. Considerable time will necessarily elapse before any new government can be legitimately organized and put in operation; in the interim, the existing government, if its organization be completed, will be found sufficient for all our temporary wants.

A brief summary of the organization of the present government may not be uninteresting. It consists 1st, of a Governor, appointed by the Supreme Government; in default of such appointment the office is temporarily vested in the commanding military officer of the Department. The powers and duties of the Governor are of a limited character, but fully defined and pointed out by the laws. 2d. A Secretary, whose duties and powers are also properly defined. 3d. A Territorial or Departmental Legislature, with limited powers to pass laws of a local character. 4th. A Superior Court (*Tribunal Superior*) of the Territory, consisting of four Judges and a Fiscal. 5th. A Perfect and sub-Perfects for each District, who are charged with the preservation of public order and the execution of the laws; their duties correspond in a great measure with those of District Marshals and Sheriffs. 6th. A Judge of First Instance for each District. This office is by a custom not inconsistent with the laws, vested in the 1st Alcade of the District. 7th. Alcades who have concurrent jurisdiction among themselves in the same district, but are subordinate to the higher judicial tribunals. 8th. Local Justices of the Peace. 9th. *Ayuntamientos* or Town Councils. The powers and functions of all these officers are fully defined in the laws of this country, and are almost identical with those of the corresponding officers in the Atlantic and Western States.

In order to complete this organization with the least possible delay, the undersigned, in virtue of power in him vested, does hereby appoint the first of August next as the day for holding a special election for Delegates to a general Convention, and for filling the offices of Judges of the Superior Court, Prefects and sub-Prefects, and all vacancies in the offices of 1st Alcade (or Judge of First Instance,) Alcades, Justices of the Peace, and Town Councils. The Judges of the Superior Court, and District Prefects are by law executive appointments, but being desirous that the wishes of the people should be fully consulted, the Governor will appoint such persons as may receive the plurality of votes in their respective districts, provided they are competent and eligible to the office. Each District will therefore elect a Prefect and two sub Prefects, and fill the vacancies in the offices of 1st Alcade (or Judge of First Instance) and of Alcades. One Judge of the Superior Court will be elected in the Districts of San Diego, Los Angeles and Santa Barbara; one in the Districts of San Luis Obispo and Monterey; one in the Districts of San Jose and San Francisco; and one in the Districts of Sonoma, Sacramento, and San Joaquin. The Salaries of the Judges of the Superior Court, the Prefects and Judges of First Instance, are regulated by the Governor, but cannot exceed, for the first, $4,000 per annum, for the second, $2,500, and for the third, $1,500. These salaries will be paid out of the civil fund which has been formed from the proceeds of the customs, provided no instructions to the contrary are received from Washington. The law requires that the Judges of the Superior Court meet within three months after its organization, and form a tariff of fees for the different Territorial Courts and legal officers, including all Alcades, Justices of the Peace, Sheriffs, Constables, &c.

All local Alcades, Justices of the Peace, and members of Town Councils elected at the special election, will continue in office till the 1st January, 1850, when their places will be supplied by the persons who may be elected at the regular annual election which takes place in November, at which time the election of members to the Territorial Assembly will also be held.

The general Convention for forming a State constitution or a plan for Territorial government, will consist of 37 Delegates, who will meet in Monterey on the first day of September next. These delegates will be chosen as follows:

The District of San Diego will elect two delegates, of Los Angeles four, of Santa Barbara two, of San Luis Obispo two, of Monterey five, of San Jose five, of San Francisco five, of Sonoma four, of Sacramento four, of San Joaquin four. Should any District think itself entitled to a greater number of Delegates than the above named, it may elect supernumeraries, who, on the organization of the convention, will be admitted or not at the pleasure of that body.

The places for holding the election will be as follows: San Diego, San Juan Capistrano, Los Angeles, San Fernando, San Buenaventura, Santa Barbara, Nepoma, San Luis Obispo, Monterey, San Juan Baptiste, Santa Cruz, San Jose de Guadalupe, San Francisco, San Rafael, Bodega, Sonoma, Benecia; (the places for holding election in the Sacramento and San Joaquin Districts, will be hereafter designated.) The local Alcades and members of the Ayuntamientos or Town Councils, will act as Judges and Inspectors of elections. In case there should be less than three such Judges and Inspectors present at each of the places designated on the day of election, the people will appoint some competent persons to fill the vacancies. The polls will be open from 10 o'clock, A. M. to 4 P. M., or until sunset, if the Judges deem it necessary.

Every free male citizen of the United States and of Upper California, 21 years of age, and actually resident in the district where the vote is offered, will be entitled to the right of suffrage. All citizens of Lower California who have been forced to come to this territory on account of having rendered assistance to the American troops during the recent war with Mexico, should also be allowed to vote in the district where they actually reside.

Great care should be taken by the Inspectors that votes are received only from bona fide citizens actually resident in the country. These Judges and Inspectors previous to entering upon the duties of their office, should take an oath faithfully and truly to perform these duties. The returns should state distinctly the number of votes received for each candidate, be signed by the Inspectors, sealed, and immediately transmitted to the Secretary of State for file in his office.

The following are the limits of the several Districts:

1st. The District of San Diego is bounded on the south by Lower California, on the west by the sea, on the north by the parallel of latitude including the mission San Juan Capistrano, and on the east by the Colorado river.

2d. The District of Los Angeles is bounded on the south by the District of San Diego, on the west by the sea, on the north by the Santa Clara river, and a parallel of latitude running from the head waters of that river to the Colorado.

3d. The District of Santa Barbara is bounded on the south by the District of Los Angeles, on the west by the sea, on the north by Santa Inez river, and a parallel of latitude existing from the head waters of that river to the summit of the coast range of mountains.

4th. The District of San Luis Obispo is bounded on the south by the District of Santa Barbara, on the west by the sea, on the north by a parallel of latitude including San Miguel, and on the east by the coast range of mountains.

5th. The District of Monterey is bounded on the south by the District of San Luis, and on the north and east by a line running east from New Year's point to the summit of the Santa Clara range of mountains, thence along the summit of that range to the Arroya de los Leagas, and a parallel of latitude extending to the summit of the coast range, and along that range to the District of San Luis.

6th. The District of San Jose is bounded on the north by the straits of Carquenas, the bay of San Francisco, the Arroya of San Francisquito, and a parallel of latitude to the summit of Santa Clara mountains, on the west and south by the Santa Clara mountains, and the District of Monterey, and on the east by the coast range.

7th. The District of San Francisco is bounded on the west by the sea, on the south by the Districts of San Jose and Monterey, and on the east and north by the bay of San Francisco, including the islands in that bay.

8th. The District of Sonoma includes all the country bounded by the sea, the bays of San Francisco and Suisun, the Sacramento river and Oregon.

9th. The District of Sacramento is bounded on the north and west by the Sacramento river, on the east by the Sierra Nevada, and on the south by the Cosumnes river.

10th. The District of San Joaquin includes all the country south of the Sacramento District, and lying between the coast range and the Sierra Nevada.

The method here indicated to attain what is desired by all, viz: a more perfect political organization is deemed the most direct and safe that can be adopted, and one fully authorized by law. It is the course advised by the President, and by the Secretaries of State and of War of the United States, and is calculated to avoid the innumerable evils which must necessarily result from any attempt at illegal local legislation. It is therefore hoped that it will meet the approbation of the people of California, and that all good citizens will unite in carrying it into execution.

Given at Monterey, California, this third day of June, A. D. 1849.

B RILEY,
Brevet Brig. Gen. U. S. A., and Governor of California.

Official—H. W. HALLECK,
Brevet Capt. and Secretary of State.

PROCEEDINGS OF THE CONVENTION.

SATURDAY, SEPTEMBER 1, 1849.

In pursuance of Gov. RILEY's Proclamation of the 3d of June last, the Convention for forming a State Constitution for California, met in Colton Hall, in the town of Monterey, at 12 M. on Saturday, the 1st of September, 1849.

The following Delegates appeared and took their seats, viz:

District of San Jose.—Kimball H. Dimmick, J. D. Hoppe, Joseph Aram, Antonio M. Pico.

District of Monterey.—H. Wager Halleck, Thos. O. Larkin.

District of Sonoma.—Robert Semple.

District of San Joaquin.—J. McHenry Hollingsworth.

District of San Luis Obispo.—Henry A. Tefft.

District of San Diego.—Henry Hill.

On motion of Mr. HALLECK, Kimball H. Dimmick, Esq., was appointed Chairman, *pro tempore.*

On motion of Mr. DIMMICK, Henry A. Tefft, Esq., was appointed Secretary, *pro tempore.*

Whereupon, it appearing that a quorum was not present, on motion of Mr. HALLECK, the Convention adjourned to meet again on Monday, September 3, 1849, at 12 M.

MONDAY, SEPTEMBER 3, 1849.

The Convention met pursuant to adjournment. Prayer by the Rev. S. H. Willey.

The minutes of Saturday's meeting were read and approved.

THE CHAIR announced the receipt of a communication from the Governor, through the Secretary of State, transmitting the election returns from the various Districts of California, together with the names of the Delegates elected. The communication was read by the Secretary of the Convention, as follows:

STATE DEPARTMENT OF CALIFORNIA,
MONTEREY, SEPTEMBER 3, 1849.

Hon. K. H. Dimmick, Chairman of the Convention:

SIR: I have the honor to transmit herewith by direction of the Governor, all the returns which have been received up to this date, of the election of delegates in the several districts for the general Convention. These papers are numbered from 1 to 51 inclusive. As they are originals, and contain the vote for district and town officers, as well as for delegates to the Convention, it is hoped that they will be preserved with care, and returned to this office as soon as your honorable body shall have completed its organization.

It appears from the returns that the following regular delegates are elected from the several districts, viz:

From San Diego.—Miguel de Pedrorena, Henry Hill.

From Los Angeles.—S. C. Foster, J. A. Carrillo, M. Dominguez, A. Stearns.

From Santa Barbara.—P. La Guerra, J. M. Cabarruvias.

From San Luis Obispo.—H. A. Tefft, J. M. Cabarruvias.

From Monterey.—H. W. Halleck, T. O. Larkin, C. T. Botts, P. Ord, L. Dent.

From San Jose.—J. Aram, K. H. Dimmick, J. D. Hoppe, A. M. Pico, E. Brown.

From San Francisco.—E. Gilbert, M. Norton, W. M. Gwin, J. Hobson, W. M. Steuart.

From Sonoma.—J. Walker, R. Semple, L. W. Boggs, M. G. Vallejo.

From Sacramento.—J. R. Snyder, W. E. Shannon, W. S. Sherwood, J. A. Sutter.

San Joaquin.—It appears from the returns from this district, that in the town of Stockton, (for reasons stated in the report of the Judges and Inspectors of election) the election was held on the 16th instead of the 1st of August. Counting all the votes polled in the district, including the town of Stockton, it appears that the four delegates elected are, J. M. Hollingsworth, S. Haley, B. S. Lippincott, C. L. Peck.

But if only the votes polled on the 1st of August are to be counted, *i. e.*, if the vote of Stockton be excluded, the four delegates elected are, J. M. Hollingsworth, S. L. Vermuile, M. Fallon, B. F. Moore.

This question is left for the decision of your honorable body, which is deemed the proper judge of the election returns and qualifications of its own members.

As the relative population of the several districts has materially changed since the issuing of the proclamation of June 3d, calling for the election of delegates to this Convention, the Governor would respectfully recommend that additional delegates be received from some of the larger and more populous districts. It should, however, be remembered, that, at the time of holding the election, (on the 1st day of August last,) many of the legal voters were absent from the middle and southern portions of the country; so that the number of votes actually polled, will not serve as a perfect criterion by which to judge of the true relative population of the different districts. It is hoped that, by mutual concessions, all these questions may be amicably arranged, and that a spirit of harmony and good will may prevail in your councils. You have an important work before you—the laying of the corner-stone of the State structure; and the stability of the edifice will depend upon the character of the foundation which you may establish. Your materials are good; let it never be said that the builders lacked skill in putting them together!

By order of the Governor:

H. W. HALLECK,
Brevet Capt. and Secretary of State.

The Chair stated that there appeared to be a question as to the regularly elected delegates from the District of San Joaquin. It would be for the Convention to decide who were the members elected.

Mr. Semple observed that he would offer, as soon as he could put it in writing, a resolution accepting the whole vote of the district, and admitting the four delegates having the highest number of votes. From the best information he could collect, he understood it to be a very fair and full election, notwithstanding it had been postponed from the day first designated, to a later period. He presumed the principal object in view was, that the mass of the people should be fully and fairly represented in this Convention; and he trusted the House would pursue the most liberal course in admitting the additional members.

Mr. Gwin asked if the gentleman (Mr. Semple,) would introduce his motion in writing. He had an amendment to offer.

Mr. Semple then submitted the following resolution:

Resolved, That the whole vote from the San Joaquin District be received, and the members elect be invited to take their seats.

Mr. Gwin would move an amendment to the resolution. To admit all of the members *now present* from the San Joaquin District, without contest as to the number of votes cast, or where they were cast. He considered that the district was entitled to a much larger representation than the number now here claiming seats. He considered it nothing but an act of justice that the the District of San Joaquin should be fully and fairly represented in the original organization of this body; and he contended that every member who had received a respectable number of votes, was entitled to a seat in the Convention. San Joaquin was clearly entitled to ten members. If there were not ten other persons voted for, who had received more votes, these members were duly elected by the people, and had a right to participate in the organization of the Convention. He was authorized to say that the returns presented to the House were not correct—that a full statement of the vote polled, had not reached the Secretary of State.

Mr. Halleck was opposed to both the resolution and amendment. He thought the difficulty might be obviated by the appointment of a committee of one delegate from each district, with authority to report to the Convention the number of delegates regularly elected in each district, and the names of the persons entitled to seats. It was quite probable complete returns had not been received. Additional returns to the Secretary's office might possibly come in during the day. The only data upon which the Governor could base his estimate, were the returns themselves. The committee could meantime examine into those already received, and be prepared to report at the next meeting of the Convention.

Mr. Botts was of opinion that the first question in the meeting of a Convention was, as to the certificates of election. What certificate of election had been presented here? He presumed none that could be so called, except the official communication of the Governor, which states that certain gentlemen, naming them, have been duly elected according to the official returns. These gentlemen, and these only, have a *prima facia* right to sit in this body. He was very unwilling, during the pendancy of this question, to admit any others than the members so designated. He hoped all the facts in relation to the postponement of the election and the grounds upon which these gentlemen claimed seats, would be placed in possession of the House, and that for this purpose, a committee on privileges and elections would be appointed.

Mr. Gwin then submitted his amendment to Mr. Semple's, as follows:

Resolved, That all persons present who were voted for on the 1st and 16th of August, in the San Joaquin District, as members of this Convention, be admitted to seats.

Mr. Halleck said that his colleague (Mr. Botts,) had suggested an amendment to the amendment proposed by him, having in view the appointment of a committee on privileges and elections. With the permission of that gentleman, he would introduce the following as a substitute for the original amendment:

Resolved, That a committee on privileges and elections, to consist of one member from each district, be appointed by the Chair, and that they report to this Convention this day, the number of delegates which, in their opinion, ought to be received from each district, and the names of the persons who are deemed entitled to seats according to the apportionment so recommended.

Mr. Semple, being the proposer of the original resolution, said he would withdraw it, and accept with pleasure the amendment last read.

Mr. Gwin having no objection to the appointment of this committee, withdrew his own amendment. He did not think, however, that the whole day should be lost in waiting for the report of the committee, and would therefore propose that the members present from the San Joaquin District, claiming seats, should be admitted to participate in the organization of the House.

Mr. Botts asked his colleague (Mr. Halleck) what was intended by this resolution. As it reads, it seemed to confound two very distinct questions. Was the committee to report what number of regular delegates from each district were to be admitted, or supernumerary delegates?

The Chair stated that the resolution read, "the number of delegates."

Mr. Botts suggested that this matter be made the subject of two resolutions. He deemed it important that the question should be divided as to the regular and supernumerary delegates, and would therefore make a motion to that effect.

Mr. Halleck amended his resolution so as to read, "according to their recommendations as to the number to be received."

Mr. Norton said that this was a matter involving a great deal of investigation, and would occupy a great deal of time to report upon. It would be entirely impracticable for the Committee to report as early as three o'clock. Another point: the question as to the District of San Joaquin should stand upon its own basis. It should be decided one way or the other, and not considered in connexion with other districts. This would give rise to much confusion, and greatly retard the business of the House. He was in favor of the appointment of a committee of one delegate from each district, or such a committee as might be deemed proper, to take this question alone into consideration, and report upon it to the House at as early a period as practicable.

Mr. Sherwood did not for his part see the object of having several committees. It was most desirable that the Convention should organize at once and proceed to business without delaying from day to day the question as to what members were entitled to seats. If in the first place one committee was appointed to investigate the election of delegates from the District of San Joaquin, and settle that question; and then another in regard to San Francisco, and another for Sacramento, the result would be that the Convention could not proceed to business short of three or four days. He was in hopes there would be no delay; but if two or three committees were to be appointed, the time of the House would be unnecessarily consumed. He was in favor of one committee, consisting of a delegate from each district. It was desirable that there should be a full and fair representation from each district. He thought the committee could report by 2 or 3 o'clock.

Mr. GILBERT said that the only districts upon which it was necessary the committee should report, were San Joaquin, San Francisco, and Sacramento. In regard to all the other districts, he regarded the question as settled by the action of the people themselves, under the recommendation of the Governor's proclamation. From none of those districts did it appear that there were supernumerary delegates claiming seats. He would therefore move that the duties of the Committee be explicitly prescribed with reference to these districts. He believed that two or three supernumeraries had been elected in the District of San Jose; but he understood there would be no attempt made by them to claim seats. He regarded the representation made by the proclamation as fair and equitable, with regard to every district, except the three named. He, therefore, thought it best that the Committee should be instructed to report the names of the regularly elected delegates from these districts, who were entitled to seats in the Convention, without reference to the other districts.

Mr. GWIN said his colleague (Mr. Gilbert) was mistaken in one particular. There were five delegates elected in San Diego, three supernumeraries and two regular delegates. There was no reason why they, as well as the supernumeraries from San Jose, should not apply for their seats. It was not probable they would, but the question ought to be decided in advance. He believed there was also a supernumerary elected in Los Angeles. He thought the resolution as it stood covered the whole ground, and hoped it would be adopted.

Mr. GILBERT observed, that if such was the fact, it altered the case. He was guided by the Governor's message in making the statement, and presumed a clerical error had been committed. If San Diego claimed additional members, as well as the other districts, the resolution as it stood was correct and proper.

Mr. HALLECK said that the two districts of San Louis Obispo and Santa Barbara had elected the same individual. He would probably be here this afternoon, and would select from which district he would be received. From the other district one of the supernumeraries should be chosen to fill his place. That fact had influenced him in offering the resolution in its present form.

After some further discussion, Mr. Halleck's resolution was adopted.

Mr. FOSTER offered the following resolution, which was unanimously adopted:

Resolved, That the chair invite Mr. W. E. P. Hartnell to act at present as interpreter to the Convention.

On motion of Mr. SHERWOOD, the reporters present were invited to take seats within the bar.

The CHAIR then announced the following as the Committee on Privileges and Elections, namely:

San Diego—Henry Hill. *Los Angeles*—S. C. Foster. *Santa Barbara*—P. La Guerra. *San Luis Obispo*—H. A. Tefft. *Monterey*—H. W. Halleck. *San Jose*—J. Aram. *San Francisco*—M. Norton. *Sonoma*—M. G. Vallejo. *Sacramento*—J. R. Snyder. *San Joaquin*—J. McH. Hollingsworth.

Whereupon, on motion of Mr. GWIN, the Convention took a recess till 3 o'clock, P. M.

AFTERNOON SESSION, 3 O'CLOCK, P. M.

The Convention met pursuant to adjournment.

Mr. HILL, from the Committee on Privileges and Elections, reported progress and asked for further time.

Whereupon, on motion of Mr. GWIN, the convention adjourned to meet again at 8 P. M.

EIGHT O'CLOCK, P. M.—The Convention met pursuant to adjournment.

Mr. HILL, from the Committee on Privileges and Elections, submitted the following report;

Your Committee, appointed by the President to ascertain and report to the Convention "the number of delegates which in their opinion ought to be received from each district, and the names of the persons which they deem entitled to seats according to their recommendations as to the number to be received," would respectfully report to your honorable body, that from the best information to be obtained by your committee, the district of San Diego is entitled to two delegates, Los Angeles, four; Santa Barbara, two; San Luis Obispo, two; Monterey, five; San Jose, five; San Francisco, eight; Sonoma, four; Sacramento, eight; and San Joaquin, eight.

And the following named persons having received the greatest number of votes in the respective districts, are entitled to seats, viz:

San Diego.—Miguel de Pedrorena, Henry Hill.

Los Angeles.—S. C. Foster, J. A. Carillo, M. Dominguez, A. Stearns.

Santa Barbara.—P. La Guerra.

San Luis Obispo.—Henry A. Tefft, J. M. Cabarruvias.

Monterey—H. W. Halleck, T. O. Larkin, C. T. Botts, P. Ord, L. S. Dent.

San Jose.—J. Aram, K. H. Dimmick, J. D. Hoppe, A. M. Pico, E. Brown.

San Francisco—E. Gilbert, M. Norton, W. M. Gwin, J. Hobson, W. M. Steuart, W. D. M. Howard, F. J. Lippitt, A. J. Ellis.

Sonoma—J. Walker, R. Semple, L. W. Boggs, M. G. Vallejo.

Sacramento.—J. R. Snyder, W. S. Sherwood, L. W. Hastings, J. S. Fowler, W. E. Shannon, J. A. Sutter, J. Bidwell, M. M. McCarver.

San Joaquin—J. McH. Hollingsworth, C. L. Peck, S. Haley, B. S. Lippincott, T. L. Vermuile, M. Fallon, B. F. Moore, Walter Chipman.

And your Committee, having no further business before them, most respectfully beg leave to be discharged.

Mr. GWIN moved that the report be recommitted to the committee, with instructions to report in favor of the admission of every member voted for by a respectable constituency, and now present, claiming a seat. He would reduce his motion to a more definite form in writing. According to this report the district of San Joaquin had but three members on this floor. It was well known to the Convention, that the main communications of this country were of a character not to be relied upon; that San Joaquin was a very remote district; and that the members that were not here, could not get the information contained in the report in time to participate in the deliberations of this body. It was to be borne in mind, that the district of San Joaquin was larger than any other portion of California represented by twenty members on this floor; that the number of voters was greater. He did not wish to excite sectional prejudices, but when a manifest act of injustice was about to be committed, it was due to the occasion to speak his opinions freely. One of the gentlemen excluded (Mr. Wozencraft) represented a mining district into which a large emigration was pouring through Fort Smith and San Antonio. It was notorious that not less than twenty thousand American citizens were now on the road; and when you send that member back to inform his constituency that he shall not have a seat on this floor, it is proper you should look boldly in the face the consequences. It was not for the native Californians we were making this Constitution; it was for the great American population, comprising four-fifths of the population of the country. In this report that majority has been cut off from a representation in the Convention. A member who had received upwards of eight hundred votes was to be excluded, while there were members on this floor who had received less than one hundred. It was important that a Constitution should be sent forth which would meet the approval of the great majority of the people. If a constitution was submitted to them in which they considered their rights violated, it would be indignantly rejected by their votes. These gentlemen had been elected by a large and respectable constituency of American citizens. Were they to be rejected and sent back, after incurring extraordinary expense and subjecting themselves to the greatest inconvenience in coming here? He would wage a war of extermination against such an act of injustice. His only object was to insure a successful issue for the labors of the Convention. He considered that when a man was sent here as a delegate, he was entitled to all the privileges of the body until the question of representation was settled. He therefore moved the adoption of the following order:

On motion, it is ordered by the Convention, that the report of the Committee on Privileges and Elections be recommitted, with instructions to report in favor of the election as a delegate of this Convention, of any person present who has received one hundred votes for the same, from any district in California where any election has been held, without reference to the day on which the election may have been held.

Mr. Hill explained the motives which had actuated the Committee in arriving at the conclusions contained in the report. He did not believe the Committee with the facts before them could have come to any other conclusion.

Mr. Shannon gave a statistical synopsis of the number of delegates which he considered each district entitled to, with a view of showing that, on the basis assumed by gentlemen from the San Joaquin district, that of Sacramento was entitled to a larger representation than she claimed under the proclamation of Governor Riley.

On motion of Mr. Gwin, those persons excluded from their seats as well as those admitted to seats, by the report, were invited to take seats within the bar, and to participate in the debate.

Messrs. Jones, Wozencraft, and Moore, thereupon entered and addressed the Committee in relation to their claims.

Mr. Jones considered it a poor privilege, to which every prisoner at the bar was entitled, that of defending his rights. He did not come here to subject himself to the discretion of any committee. He came to represent a large and respectable constituency, by whom he was elected, and he claimed a seat in this Convention, not as a matter of sympathy, but as a matter of right. His reputation, he trusted was above committees. In the absence of full election returns, he contended that the word of a gentleman who was deemed worthy of the confidence reposed in him by his constituents, was sufficient to establish his right to a seat in this Convention—at least until the arrival of complete returns. Mr. Jones proceeded at some length to sustain the position which he had assumed.

Mr. Wozencraft entered into an elaborate defence of the grounds upon which he claimed a seat in this Convention. He had been urged by his friends, much against his will, to submit his name as a candidate. It was known to many present that he had received a large vote in the district of San Joaquin, there being no opposing candidate. He came here knowing he had received this vote, and without the slightest expectation of being refused a seat. He had subjected himself to a great sacrifice of time and money in the hope of being enabled to serve that constituency who had conferred the honor of election upon him. He had agreed to every honorable compromise proposed by gentlemen on the floor, and had studiously avoided everything calculated to lead to dissention. It was his sincere hope that the difficulty would be amicably adjusted, and that the House would proceed to business in a spirit of harmony and concession. Whatever might be its decision he would abide by it, confident that it would be actuated by no other than just and patriotic motives.

Mr. Moore briefly defended his claim, stating that the vote which he had received in the San Joaquin district greatly exceeded that of his colleague (Mr. Wozencraft.) He did not claim any priority or preference on that account, but merely submitted the fact, in common with others, to show that he did not come here without some ground for supposing that he was entitled to a seat.

Mr. BOTTS proposed to amend the resolution (Mr. Gwin's) by striking out all after the word "resolved," and inserting the following: "That the report be recommitted to the Committee with instructions to report what members, in addition to those returned by General Riley in his message, are entitled to seats in this Convention, with the facts and circumstances attending their election." He had seen a good deal of parliamentary bodies, and had read a great many reports made by Committees, but never such a report as that made to this House. It was, to say the least of it, the briefest and most unsatisfactory report that ever came under his observation. The Convention was called upon to vote upon a question in which it was utterly in the dark. This Committee was raised to ascertain the facts that the House might vote understandingly. Where were the facts? It was utterly impossible to vote without them. A great mistake had been committed. In every parliamentary body something must be taken for granted; some start must be given. As a constituent part of every election, was the returning officer. By the adoption of the proclamation of Governor Riley, the people made it their act, and as such it was in full force and effect. General Riley was made, by the adoption of that proclamation, the returning officer of this Convention. The judges and magistrates of election were directed to make sealed returns to the office of the Secretary of State. The inference is conclusive, that the certificates of election were to issue from that department. It has been done. That statement has been made to this House. According to all parliamentary usage, the persons therein named, and no others, have a *prima facia* right to seats on this floor.

Messrs. HILL and TEFFT sustained the position taken in the report, and defended the action of the Committee.

Mr. BOTTS finally withdrew his proposed amendment.

Messrs. MCCARVER, SHANNON, GWIN, SHERWOOD, HALLECK, BOTTS, PRICE, GILBERT, and SEMPLE continued the debate, chiefly in relation to the representation of the respective districts which they represented.

Mr. GILBERT regretted exceedingly that the recommendation of the Governor in regard to the supernumerary delegates in the different districts should have brought about the confusion which existed in the Convention. He was certain that the recommendation was made with the best motives, and having in view the best ends. He was also satisfied that the Committee, in their report on this case, had done what they conceived to be their duty, and though he regretted that they had not given full statistics opposite the name of each delegate, yet the principal which they had acted upon, of taking the highest number of votes cast for each delegate, as the data upon which to base his election, was the proper one. The only evidence of a right to a seat in this body, was the election returns, which alone could prove that the delegate claiming admittance had received a majority of the votes of his district over and above a certain number of men who had received a minority of those votes. For the purpose of keeping the questions at issue as distinct as possible, be submitted the following amendment to the motion of the gentleman from San Francisco (Mr. Gwin:)

Resolved, That so much of the report of the committee on Privileges and Elections as relates to the districts of San Diego, Los Angeles, Santa Barbara, San Luis Obispo, Monterey, San Jose, and Sonoma, be received and adopted by this Convention.

Mr. GWIN accepted Mr. Gilbert's amendment as a substitute for his motion, and moved to amend by adding the following:

Resolved, That J. M. Jones and O. M. Wozencraft, of San Joaquin district; P. O. Crosby and John McDougal, of Sacramento district; W. D. M. Howard, Rodman M. Price, A. J. Ellis and Francis J. Lippitt, of the district of San Francisco, are all duly elected delegates of this Convention, and that they be now admitted as such.

Mr. GWIN withdrew his amendment to allow Mr. Botts to submit the following:

That the district of San Diego shall be entitled to 2 delegates, Los Angeles 4, Santa Barbara 2, San Luis 2, Monterey 5, San Jose 5, San Francisco 10, Sonoma 4, Sacramento 15, San Joaquin 15.

A debate of considerable length here arose in relation to the representation of the different districts, in which Messrs. GWIN, MCCARVER, SHANNON, SHERWOOD, PRICE, and BOTTS took part.

The previous question was called, but the House refused to sustain the call.

The question was then taken on the amendment offered by Mr. Botts, and it was rejected.

The question was then taken on the resolution of Mr. Gilbert, and it was adopted.

On motion of Mr. Gwin, so much of the report of the Committee as was not included in the resolution of Mr. Gilbert was rejected.

The Convention then adjourned to 9 A. M. to-morrow.

TUESDAY, SEPTEMBER 4, 1849.

The Convention met pursuant to adjournment. The minutes of yesterday were read and approved.

The Chair stated that the roll would be called according to the communication of the Secretary of State, the delegates therein mentioned being those entitled to seats according to the message of Governor Riley.

Mr. Botts said that he came so near the mark last night, that he was encouraged to let fly another shaft at the target of reconciliation. He proposed to move the reconsideration of the vote of last night, by which the amendment of Mr. Gilbert was adopted, fixing a certain representation of the southern districts. His object was to introduce the following resolution, which he was inclined to think would command the votes of this House, and settle this vexed question :

Resolved, That the representation in this Convention from the several districts shall be apportioned as follows: San Diego, two; Los Angelos, five; Santa Barbara, three; San Luis Obispo, two; Monterey, five; San Jose, seven; San Francisco, nine; Sonoma, six; Sacramento, fifteen; San Joaquin, fifteen.

He did not think the question needed further debate, and would therefore be content to move a reconsideration of the vote on Mr. Gilbert's resolution.

The question was taken on the reconsideration, and it was carried.

Mr. Botts then offered his resolution as an amendment.

Mr. Gwin hoped there would be a direct vote on this amendment.

Mr. McCarver desired to offer an amendment providing that a majority of the members from each district shall control the absent votes. If this plan was adopted, he thought it would prove satisfactory; but if not, the amendment was a mockery. He had seen such a course taken in conventions several times.

Mr. Sherwood sustained the proposition of Mr. McCarver.

Mr. Carillo felt a diffidence in addressing the assembly, from his ignorance of the English language. He claimed its indulgence, therefore, as he was compelled to speak through an interpreter. He had seen the representation presented in the amendment offered by Mr. Botts, and he was surprised to find that Los Angelos was put upon a level with Monterey. It was well known that Los Angelos had double the number of inhabitants. He likewise perceived that Santa Barbara had only three members. He hoped Mr. Botts would amend his resolution by giving to Los Angelos and Santa Barbara the number of representatives to which they were entitled. In his opinion Santa Barbara ought to have a number equal to Monterey, and Los Angelos seven members.

Mr. Hill moved an additional amendment, as follows:

That the district of Los Angelos be entitled to seven delegates instead of five; and Santa Barbara five instead of three.

Mr. Tefft hoped the amendment would be taken into consideration and adopted.

Mr. Botts said, if it was in his power he would accept the amendment. He would, however, vote for it.

The question was then taken on the amendment of Mr. Hill, which was adopted.

The question recurring on Mr. Gilbert's resolution as amended by Mr. Botts,

Mr. Gwin remarked that it seemed to have been an understanding among those who had compromised this question, that it was intended each district should have the strength to which it was entitled, whether all the members were prese not. In order to test the sense of the Convention on this subject, he would, in accordance with the wishes of the members from San Joaquin and Sacramento, submit a proposition to the effect that the majority of the members from each district present may vote for absentees from their respective districts.

Mr. NORTON objected to any such proceeding. He thought a proposition of this kind should not be offered for the purpose of riding it in upon another proposition which might possibly meet the wishes of the House.

Mr. HALLECK also objected. The Convention would never be able to get through its business, if each delegation was to vote for absent members. If a few members from one district was to cast fifteen or twenty votes by proxy on any question, members from other districts would naturally and justly object to such a proceeding. He thought it absolutely essential to the progress of business that each member should do his own voting, and that the delegation from each district should be distinctly determined. If one member who was present to-day, should be sick to-morrow, he did not think other members had a right to vote for him.

Mr. SHANNON considered the proposition extremely objectionable. It was the very worst principle that could be adopted. The precedent would be most injurious. For his own part, if he had to vote for any absentee, he wished at least to have the power of attorney.

Mr. SHERWOOD presumed if the grounds of the motion were properly understood, his colleague (Mr. Shannon) would not object. It was generally admitted that the people of Sacramento were entitled to a much larger representation than either San Joaquin or San Francisco. In order to give San Francisco the votes which it claimed, and at the same time give Sacramento and San Joaquin the number of votes to which they were entitled, this proposition was made. The ratio of representation was to be fixed upon by the Heuse, and it was important that it should be done on the most liberal terms.

Mr. HILL thought the House was losing time in this discussion.

The CHAIR was of opinion that the discussion was not appropriate to the question before the House.

Mr. SEMPLE understood the question to be on the amendment of Mr. Botts as amended by Mr. Hill. The primary question before the House, therefore, was, whether this ratio of representation shall be agreed upon. He intended voting for this amendment, as he believed it to be a fair apportionment. One additional word. It was utterly unprecedented in any Convention held in any State, or in any parliamentary body, to vote by proxy. Where there were different nations to be represented, such a practice might be tolerated, but he hoped there was a general feeling in this Convention against the principle.

Mr. GWIN did not wish to be misunderstood on this question. His only object, as stated in the first instance, was to give the districts of Sacramento and San Joaquin their full complement of votes. He did not desire that members present should vote for absent members; but if an increase was made in other districts, he claimed the right of those districts to an additional representation. He held that the Convention could with perfect propriety give to Sacramento and San Joaquin the power to cast fifteen votes. It was not bound by the action of any other body. It was a body composed of the original representatives of the people. He did not introduce, nor did he favor any proposition to do wrong to any portion of California; but these two mining districts, having the largest population, should have the largest representation. It was simply from a desire to facilitate the organization of the House that he had submitted the proposition.

The question then recurring on the amendment of Mr. Botts as amended by Mr. Hill, it was adopted.

Mr. BOTTS offered the following resolution:

Resolved, That a committee of three be appointed to report forthwith to this Convention the names of the additional delegates referred to in the foregoing resolution, who have received the greatest number of votes in their respective districts.

Mr. HALLECK suggested a slight alteration to the resolution. That this Committee should report the names of the persons who had received the highest number of votes from their respective districts according to the apportionment agreed upon by the House. If any person claiming a seat should not be included, the question would come up on his case, and be decided on its own merits.

Mr. BOTTS accepted the amendment. The question recurring on the resolution, as amended, it was adopted.

Mr. HALLECK stated that he had received a few moments since some additional election returns.

On motion, they were received, and ordered to be laid before a committee.

The CHAIR appointed, as such Committee, Messrs. Shannon, Hoppe, and Dent.

Mr. SEMPLE suggested that there was a good deal of business to transact, which might be done during the sitting of this Committee. It was important to determine what officers were necessary. This could be done while the Committee was preparing its report.

Mr. NORTON thought it hardly fair to go into any business whatever until it was first ascertained who were entitled to seats. It would then be time to go into the election of officers.

Mr. SEMPLE said, that if the House proceeded according to any established rules, it had no right to determine on the sitting of members until it was fully organized. It was necessary that there should be some members at least to proceed to business before this question could be determined. He did not mean to say that it was absolutely necessary for the House now to commence confining itself to rules before it was organized, but to facilitate business under present circumstances, having gone so far astray from all parliamentary custom, he thought it advisable to determine what officers were necessary, and to elect them without further delay.

Mr. GWIN believed the gentleman was entirely mistaken. It was well known that for weeks and weeks the Congress of the United States was in session under just such a temporary organization, on the famous Jersey question. He considered the present organization of the Convention perfectly legitimate. He hoped there would not be a solitary step taken, except on the admission of members, until every member entitled to a seat was admitted.

Mr. GILBERT read a portion of Cushing's Manual on this subject, [page 10, section 6,] which he thought settled the question.

On motion of Mr. GWIN, the House took a recess of one hour.

AFTERNOON SESSION, 2 O'CLOCK, P. M.

The Convention met pursuant to adjournment.

Mr. SHANNON, from the Special Committee appointed this morning, made a report, which, on motion of Mr. Gwin, was adopted; viz:

Your Committee has the honor of reporting the following as the "names of the persons who have received the highest number of votes in the several districts, equal to the apportionment adopted by the resolution of to-day," and additional to those already returned as elected by the Governor, to this Convention, viz;—

Los Angeles—Hugo Reid, Luis Rubideaux, Manuel Requerra.

Santa Barbara—Manuel Imeno, Jacinto Rodriguez, Amitasio Carillo.

San Jose—Pedro Sansevaine, Julian Hanks.

San Francisco—W. D. M. Howard, Francis J. Lippitt, A. J. Ellis, R. M. Price.

Sonoma—Richard A. Mawpin, James Clyman.

Sacramento—L. W. Hastings, John Bidwell, John S. Fowler, M. M. McCarver, John McDougal, E. O. Crosby, W. Blackburn, Jas. Queen, R. M. Jones, W. Lacy, C. E. Pickett.

San Joaquin—B. F. Lippincott, S. Haley, C. L. Peck, B. F. Moore, M. Fallon, B. Ogden, J. M. Jones, T. L. Vermuile, O. M. Wozencraft, George A. Pendleton, Jeremiah Ford, Colonel Jackson, B. L. Morgan, Walter Chipman.

Mr. GILBERT moved that the Convention now proceed to the election of a President.

Mr. SEMPLE suggested the propriety of first determining what officers were necessary to complete the preliminary organization of the Convention.

Mr. BOTTS said that the election of President was first in order.

Mr. McCARVER moved that the election be conducted by ballot.

Mr. HOBSON submitted the following:

1. In the election of officers of this Convention a majority of all the votes given shall be necessary to a choice.

2. In voting for the officers, where several candidates are presented, the lowest on the list shall be dropped until a selection is made.

3. In the election of officers of this Convention members shall vote by ballot.

Mr. McCARVER insisted on his motion.

Mr. BOTTS hoped that it would not be the pleasure of the House to vote by ballot. He thought it a principle that should be observed here, that it was a representative body, and that those who were represented had a right to know the manner in which members disposed of their votes. They were not here casting their own votes, but the votes of others. He preferred calling by name the individual for whom he voted, when representing the will of others. He therefore proposed to amend the resolution by striking out the word ballot, and insert *viva voce*.

Mr. SHERWOOD preferred the adoption of the original resolution. The remarks of the gentleman were true, as a general rule. But in the selection of officers where there was no principle involved, and where there might be personal feeling, it was usual to vote by ballot. He hoped the gentleman would withdraw his amendment.

Mr. BOTTS could not consent to withdraw the amendment. He did not believe there would be any personal feeling. As to the principal, he could tell gentlemen there was frequently a great deal of principle involved in the election of officers. His constituents had a right to know his vote, and he insisted upon his amendment.

The question was then taken, and the amendment was rejected.

The question then recurring on the original resolution,

Mr. NORTON moved that three tellers be appointed to count the votes, which was agreed to.

Mr. CARILLO said there were certain members from below, who were entitled to seats under the resolution adopted by the House. He moved that they be sent for.

The CHAIR stated that there was no officer to send for them.

Mr. HALLECK moved that the Convention take a recess till 3 o'clock, in order that the absent members who were in town might be sent for. Adopted.

AFTERNOON SESSION, 3 O'CLOCK, P. M.

The roll was read. Messrs. Norton, Snyder and Jones were announced by the Chair as tellers appointed under the motion of Mr. Norton.

A discussion as to which resolution had precedence having arisen,

The CHAIR stated that the question before the House was on the adoption of the amendment offered by Mr. Hobson to the resolution of Mr. McCarver.

Mr. McCARVER objected to the amendment on this ground: That it was fixing the rules of the House by resolution. It also prevented persons from becoming candidates, who might possibly be the ultimate choice of the Convention. The candidate having the least number of votes could never be reconsidered. This was forestalling all further action, and was different from any custom with which he was acquainted.

Mr. SEMPLE also objected to the amendment. He thought it was not customary to withdraw the hindmost candidate. The usual plan was to continue to ballot until some member received a majority of the votes.

Mr. Botts considered this objection unfounded. The member dropped would have a right to be renominated.

Mr. McCarver was of opinion that in passing this resolution a rule of the House was adopted, and the candidate under that rule could not become a candidate again.

Mr. Halleck moved to strike out the second article of Mr. Hobson's proposition, which was agreed to.

The question recurring on the proposition as amended, it was adopted.

The Convention then proceeded to the election of a President.

On motion, Messrs. Norton, Snyder, and Jones were appointed tellers.

Upon counting the ballots, it was announced to the Convention, by the tellers, that Robert Semple, of the district of Sonoma, was duly elected President.

Messrs. Sutter and Vallejo were appointed a committee to escort the President to his seat.

PRESIDENT'S ADDRESS.

Fellow-citizens of the House of Delegates of California: While, with an open heart, I feel grateful for the honor conferred upon me, yet I must say that I feel a regret that it has not fallen into abler hands. I shall expect a due feeling of forbearance on your part. What services I am capable of rendering shall be rendered freely and impartially. So far as the duties of the President of this Convention shall devolve upon me, I shall use every effort to perform them with as much moderation as I can, and as nearly as practicable with justice and attention to the right.

We are now, fellow-citizens, occupying a position to which all eyes are turned. The eyes not only of our sister and parent States are upon us, but the eyes of all Europe are now directed toward California. This is the preliminary movement for the organization of a civil government, and the establishment of social institutions. You are called upon, by your fellow-citizens, to exert all your influence and power to secure to them all the blessings that a good government can bestow upon a free people. It is important, then, that in your proceedings you should use all possible care, discretion, and judgment; and especially that a spirit of compromise should prevail in all your deliberations.

It is to be hoped that every feeling of harmony will be cherished to the utmost in this Convention. By this course, fellow-citizens, I am satisfied that we can prove to the world that California has not been settled entirely by unintelligent and unlettered men. I am sure that the present population of California is well calculated to strike the world with, at least, a degree of that admiration which our rapid progress in wealth and prosperity has done. Although the progress of California in point of wealth, has been beyond all previous anticipations, yet her progress in population has been still greater. So far from this population consisting of persons who had nothing to do at home, it has drained from the States many of the best families and most intelligent men in the country. The knowledge, enterprise and genius of the old world will reappear in the new, to guide it to its destined position among the nations of the earth.

Let us, then, go onward and upward, and let our motto be, "Justice, Industry, and Economy."

On motion of the President, an invitation was extended to Governor Riley to a seat on the floor of the House.

Mr. Sherwood offered the following resolution, which was adopted:

Resolved, That the Convention elect one Secretary, two Assistant Secretaries, a Reporter, a Sergeant-at-Arms, and a Doorkeeper.

Mr. Price moved that the rules of the House be suspended, and nominated Mr. Hartwell as Interpreter and Translator. Adopted, *viva voce.*

The House then proceeded to elect a Secretary and Assistant Secretaries; whereupon Wm. G. Marcy received a majority of votes, and was declared duly elected Secretary.

Caleb Lyon received a majority of votes as First Assistant Secretary, and was declared duly elected.

J. G. Field received a majority of votes as Second Assistant Secretary, and was declared duly elected.

On motion of Mr. Gwin, a committee of three were appointed to report upon the subject of a Reporter for the Convention. Messrs. Gwin, Dent, and Gilbert, were selected as such committee.

The House then proceeded to the election of a Sergeant-at-Arms; whereupon, Mr. Houston, having received a majority of the votes, was declared duly elected.

On motion of Mr. Gwin, the rules were suspended, and Cornelius Sullivan was elected Doorkeeper, *viva voce*.

Mr. Vallejo moved that a Clerk be appointed to assist the Interpreter and Translator.

Mr. Price moved the following resolution, which was adopted:

Resolved, That the President appoint a Committee of three to call upon the clergy of Monterey, and request them to open this Convention each day with prayer.

Committee—Messrs. Price, Larkin, and Norton.

Mr. Gwin then offered the following resolution:

Resolved, That a select committee, composed of two delegates from each district, be appointed by the President, to report the plan or any portion of the plan of a State Constitution for the action of this body.

On motion of Mr. Price, the above resolution was made the special order of the day for to-morrow.

A motion for adjournment was made and lost.

Mr. Price offered the following resolution:

Resolved, That a Clerk be appointed to the Interpreter and Translator.

Adopted.

On motion of Mr. Gwin, the rules of the House were suspended, and Mr. W. H. Henrie elected (*viva voce*) to the office of Clerk to the Interpreter and Translator.

Mr. Gwin then submitted the following resolution, which was adopted:

Resolved, That the parliamentary law as laid down in Jefferson's Manual, so far as applicable, be the law of the Convention, until otherwise ordered.

The Convention then adjourned until 10 o'clock, A. M. to-morrow.

WEDNESDAY, SEPTEMBER 5, 1849.

The Convention met pursuant to adjournment. Prayer by the Rev. Padre Antonio Ramirez.

Mr. Gwin inquired whether there was a quorum present.

The Chair stated that, by a resolution passed yesterday settling the ratio of representation in the several districts, the whole number of members who should be here was fixed at sixty-nine. It would then require thirty-six to form a quorum for the transaction of business, which was about the whole number present. In all regularly organised legislative bodies, it would be beyond their reach to change this order of things; but the Convention was an original meeting of the people, through their representatives, to form a system of laws, and its organization was legitimately under its own control. He thought some provision should be made to facilitate business. It would now require too much time to send emissaries throughout the country to compel the attendance of the members elected.

Mr. Gwin said it was for that very reason that he made the inquiry. He was perfectly confident that no instance could be given of any deliberative body transacting business without a quorum of its own members. The report of the Committee named the persons elected. It would be impossible to get over the difficulty, by requiring the attendance of these members. There was but one remedy that he could see—to give the power to those present to represent the absent members of their respective districts. Then the House could always have a quorum.

Mr. Halleck was opposed to any proceeding of this kind. Although the House might give the votes of a whole district to two or three members of that district, it would be altogether improper, if not impracticable, to make those members serve for fifteen person in forming a quorum. This difficulty he anticipated at the outset, and had mentioned it to the members, when the committee fixed the number for each district. To adopt the plan suggested would only get the House into still greater difficulty. There would be several additional members present in a few days, and with them he thought a quorum could be formed.

Mr. Gwin said if the gentleman would suggest a remedy he would cheerfully agree to it. He was not personally in favor of the plan which he had thrown out, but it occurred to him as the only alternative within their reach.

Mr. Dimmick observed that there was a quorum now present, and he hoped the House would proceed to business.

Mr. Crosby moved that the officers and members of the Convention first take the oath to support the Constitution of the United States.

Mr. Botts moved to postpone the order of the day for that purpose.

Mr. Gwin was willing to waive, but not postpone the order.

The Chair deemed it necessary that the body should first be organized. It was for the House to determine whether or not that course should be adopted. It was either organized, or not organized. The question would be whether the members should take the oath before proceeding to business as an organized body. Which was put and determined in the affirmative.

Mr. Gwin suggested that the President be sworn by some legal officer of the city. He thought the Judge of the Supreme Court, who was present, could do it, and then swear in all the other members. The Judge or Alcade should perform this duty.

The Chair said if it was the will of the House, the Secretary of State could swear in the President, and the President could then administer the oaths to the members as a body.

Which was adopted; and the President of the Convention was duly sworn by the Secretary of State; after which the President administered the oath to the members.

ORDER OF THE DAY.

Mr. Gwin's resolution being the order of the day, was then taken up and read.

Mr. Halleck wished to propose a substitute, for the purpose of getting an expression of the sense of the House on two points. He had very little doubt as to the result; nevertheless, as many wished their views to be known on that subject, he desired to make the two points separate and distinct. It was with respect to a State or a Territorial form of government. He therefore moved that the resolution be so worded as to give a direct expression of opinion on each point, whether the plan of a State Government was desired, or whether the Convention should propose to Congress a plan of a Territorial Government.

Mr. McCarver said, that if the question was whether any other than a State Government should be considered, he was willing the vote of this House should be taken to decide it, but he was not willing to sit here and take any other plan into consideration.

The Chair stated that the question was on the amendment of Mr. Halleck.

Mr. Gwin could not agree to accept this amendment as a substitute for his resolution, because it embodied precisely the same thing. The resolution submitted by him was open to discussion. If there be any objection to a State Constitution, the questien of a Territorial Government is thrown open.

Mr. HALLECK's only object was to separate the two questions.

Mr. GWIN did not think there was a member on this floor in favor of a Territorial Government.

Mr. McCARVER proposed moving the question, whether this body proceed to form a State or Territorial Government.

The CHAIR considered the question embodied in the resolution.

Mr. HASTINGS was opposed to the resolution last offered, and in favor of the resolution providing for the organization of a State Government. If it was a State Government it would not be a Territorial Government.

Mr. GILBERT, in order to cover the whole, moved the following as an amendment to the amendment of Mr. Halleck:

1. *Resolved*, That it is expedient that this Convention now proceed to form a State Constitution for California.

2. *Resolved*, That a Committee consisting of —— members from each district be appointed by the Chair to prepare a draft or plan for a Constitution for the State of California; and that such Committee be instructed to report to this Convention, with as little delay as possible, such articles or sections of said draft or plan as may have been passed in Committee from time to time.

Mr. HALLECK accepted Mr. Gilbert's proposition as a substitute for his amendment.

Mr. GWIN accepted the first resolution offered by Mr. Gilbert as a substitute for his second resolution, and in order to have a direct vote, called the previous question.

The CHAIR stated that the previous question was on the original resolution, that being the order of the day.

Mr. HASTINGS moved to amend the resolution by inserting two from each district instead of one.

The CHAIR stated that the motion to add an additional member was within the reach of the House at any time.

Mr. GWIN accepted the amendment of two instead of one.

Mr. FOSTER suggested that the resolution to appoint a Committee be put in such shape as to give the opinion of the House directly on the subject of the form of government. Some members were in favor of a Territorial Government. For one, he was opposed at present to entering into a State Government. He desired, and so did others, to have the vote separate and distinct. It appeared to him that Mr. Halleck's amendment to the resolution accomplished the object.

Mr. GWIN renewed his call for the previous question; but the motion giving rise to discussion, he finally withdrew it.

Mr. CARILLO said the first question ought to be, whether California was to remain a Territory, or be formed into a State. Whatever determination there might be on that subject, he thought a Committee ought to be appointed to report upon it, that members might record their votes on that question alone, if they so desired it. Any step taken contrary to this plan would only involve the Convention in difficulty.

Mr. WOZENCRAFT did not perceive what right the House had to enter into any question of that kind. The delegates of this Convention were elected for a special purpose—to form a State Constitution. They were not required to give any expression of opinion as to any other form of government.

The CHAIR stated that Governor Riley, in the recommendation contained in his proclamation, referred to a Territorial as well as a State Government.

Mr. TEFFT thought there was another reason why the two questions should be separated. If gentlemen were honest in stating that the two resolutions would have the same effect, it was yielding nothing to comply with the wishes of those who desired to record their vote in favor of a Territorial Government. He was compelled, in compliance with the wishes of his constituents, to vote for a Territorial Government. He considered it due to members who voted under such instructions, that the direct question should be put, whether the Convention should proceed to form a State or a Territorial Government.

Further dicussion having taken place, Mr. GILBERT called for the reading of the two resolutions (Mr. Gwin's and his own in juxta position.) The Secretary read the resolutions.

Mr. Botts cordially approved of the sentiments expressed in the resolution of Mr. Gilbert; but strange to say, they led him to entirely different conclusions. He (Mr. Botts) wanted to see the whole subject discussed by the Convention in Committee of the Whole. He desired that every member should participate in the discussion. He was aware it was the wish of the gentleman that this Committee should return immediately with a plan of a Constitution to be laid before the House. But what does the resolution authorize this Committee to do? What power does it give the Committee? The very difficulty which the gentleman sought to avoid was involved in the adoption of the Constitution so reported. For his own part, he would vote for the resolution which provides for the taking of the test question at once, whether it should be a Constitution for the State or a Territorial Government. He would then offer an amendment providing that the House go directly into Committee of the Whole for the consideration of a Constitution for that State or Territory; and for precisely the same reasons that the gentleman from San Francisco had offered his resolution, requiring the Committee to report the plan of a Constitution in detached portions.

Mr. Gilbert said his chief motive was the desire to save time—the wish to shorten the sitting of this Convention to the least possible limit. In all the Conventions of which he had read, a great deal of time had been lost by parcelling out different departments of the Constitution to different Committees. It was the case in the late Convention of New York. They had some ten different Committees. When all the reports were before the House, it took them two months to settle upon a plan of a Constitution. It was found that the different reports had no co-relative sympathy, and it was almost utterly impossible to unite them. This Committee, which he proposed, could hold its meetings during the intervals between the sittings of the Convention, and report from time to time such portions of the Constitution as they had adopted. The House could, meantime, be engaged in debating the articles before it in Committee of the Whole. He wished it distinctly understood that his object was to save time.

Mr. Carillo stated that he represented one of the most respectable communities in California, and he did not believe it to be to the interest of his constituents that a State Government should be formed. At the same time, as a great majority of this Convention appeared to be in favor of a State Government, he proposed that the country should be divided by running a line west from San Luis Obispo, so that all north of that line might have a State Government, and all south thereof a Territorial Government. He and his colleagues were under instructions to vote for a Territorial organization. He took this view, because he believed it to be to the interest of his constituents. And although a gentleman belonging to this body had stated, that it was not the object of the Convention to form a Constitution for the Californians, he begged leave to say, that he considered himself as much an American citizen as the gentleman who made the assertion.

Mr. Gwin said he was very glad that the gentleman had afforded him an opportunity of stating precisely what his meaning was. He had been very much misunderstood on this point. What he said was, that the Constitution which they were about to form was for the American population. Why? Because the American population was the majority. It was for the protection of the California population—government was instituted for the protection of minorities—this Constitution was to be formed with a view to the protection of the minority: the native Californians. The majority of any community is the party to be governed; the restrictions of law are interposed between them and the weaker party; they are to be restrained from infringing upon the rights of the minority.

The Interpreter having translated this explanation,

Mr. Carillo expressed himself perfectly satisfied. He had nothing further to say, except that he conceived it to be to the interests of his constituents, if a Territorial Government could not be formed for the whole country, that the country should be so divided as to allow them that form, while the northern population might adopt a State Government if they preferred it.

Mr. FOSTER, although acting under instructions similar to those of his colleague, did not believe that a majority of his constituents wished a separation. There was no doubt they desired a Territorial Government, but he believed they would prefer to bear their share of the burden of a State Government rather than divide the country.

Mr. DIMMICK wished to say a word before the question was put. He represented a portion of the California population in this House. The idea was prevalent that the native Californians were opposed to a State Government. This he did not conceive to be the case. He was satisfied from the conversations he had had with them, that they were nearly unanimous in favor of a State Government. As to the line of distinction attempted to be drawn between native Californians and Americans, he knew no such distinction himself; his constituents knew none. They all claimed to be Americans. They would not consent to be placed in a minority. They classed themselves with Americans, and were entitled to be considered in the majority. No matter from what nation they came, he trusted that hereafter they would be classed with the American people. The Constitution was to be formed for their benefit as well as to that of the native born Americans. They all had one common interest at stake, and one common object in view: the protection of government.

Mr. GWIN would not be misunderstood by any interpretation given to his remarks on this floor or elsewhere. It was notorious that the citizens of the United States were known as Americans here; and when he spoke of Americans, he spoke of citizens of the old States of the Union, now in California. He knew no distinction prejudicial to the interests of either. He had attempted to draw none. He spoke of them as a matter of numbers; that the citizens from the old States of the Union formed the majority here, and this Constitution was for the protection of the class forming the minority.

Mr. DIMMICK desired to say that his constituents claimed no protection under the Constitution of California, which was not guarantied to them by the treaty of peace.

The question being then taken on the first part of Mr. Gilbert's proposition, the result was as follows:

YEAS—Messrs. Aram, Botts, Crosby, Dent, Dimmick, Ellis, Gwin, Gilbert, Hoppe, Hobson, Halleck, Hastings, Hollingsworth, Jones, Larkin, Lippencott, Moore, McCarver, Norton, Ord, Price, Sutter, Snyder, Sherwood, Shannon, Semple, Vallejo, Wozencraft—28.

NAYS—Messrs. Foster, Hill, Reid, Stearns, Pico, Tefft, Carillo, Rodriguez—8.

The question as to there being a quorum present having arisen, and being decided in the negative by the President,

On motion of Mr. DENT, the Convention took a recess for half an hour.

AFTERNOON SESSION, 2 O'CLOCK, P. M.

The Convention met pursuant to adjournment.

The CHAIR remarked that it was desirable to have some known and settled rules for the government of the House. It was not practicable for each member to determine at any time which was the best rule. The House should establish proper regulations, and abide by them. It was true, it had been irregularly organized. The Territory of California was obtained from another government, differing very materially from ours. We were to make something out of nothing; to construct organization and form out of chaos. The object was to produce a good fundamental system of laws; and to accomplish this it was absolutely necessary to adopt some fixed rule of action. All business should be suspended until the house was properly organized. It was now in confusion. By an act of the Convention, it would seem that the number of members was fixed at seventy-three; thirty-eight would, therefore, be necessary to form a quorum. It would be impracticable to alter a decision once made without a quorum. If such action were admissable, five members might proceed to form rules and regulations, and even laws. There appeared to be but one way to get out of the difficulty. By some misunderstanding, it was supposed that by the adoption of the report of the special committee appointed yesterday, the Convention consisted of seventy-three members. This committee was to report the names of the additional delegates duly elected in their respective districts. The journal does not declare what members were duly elected. They were therefore not members of this House until some authority made them so. The journal afforded no evidence of additional action of the Convention on the subject. Under this omission, it was within the power of the House to proceed now and declare who were the duly elected members. He thought the difficulty might be obviated by some course of this kind.

A discussion here arose on the subject of a quorum, and the rules necessary for the action of the House, during which several propositions were offered but not entertained.

On a call of the House, the President declaring a quorum present,

Mr. Gwin moved to reconsider the report of the Committee on Privileges and Elections, and offered the following resolution:

Resolved, That the report of the Select Committee appointed by order of the House to report upon the number of votes received in the several districts by persons who were candidates for seats in this body be adopted; and Hugo Reid, Jacinto Rodriguez, Francis J. Lippitt, A. J. Ellis, R. M. Price, L. W. Hastings, M. McCarver, John McDougal, E. O. Crosby, B. F. Lippincott, B. F. Moore, I. M. Jones, and O. W. Wozencraft, are duly elected and hereby admitted as members of this body.

Adopted, *viva voce*.

A motion to adjourn having been made—

Mr. Gwin said he hoped the House would first dispose of the resolution in regard to the appointment of a Select Committee on the Constitution, in order that it might report some material upon which the Convention could proceed at its next meeting.

Mr. McCarver moved to amend Mr. Gilbert's amendment to Mr. Gwin's resolution by striking out all after the word "Resolved," and insert the following:

That the Convention do now resolve itself into a Committee of the Whole, and take into consideration the Constitution of the State of Iowa, as a basis for the Constitution of California.

Mr. Gwin remarked, that the motion of the gentleman rendered it proper that he should make an explanation. Before he (Mr. Gwin) was elected a member of this Convention, a consideration of very great importance occurred to him—the difficulty that would be encountered during the labors of the Convention from the absence of a printing press. It would be admitted, that it was indispensable that every member should have before him the precise words upon which he was called upon to vote. He had exerted himself to have a press here, but found it impracticable. He then took the responsibility, in consideration of the great public necessity of the case, and after consultation with several members, to print a copy of the Constitution of Iowa, in order that every member might have it before him, and write on the margin any amendment that might occur to him. He had intended, if the Committee had been appointed, to have proposed this paper as a basis; and if it met the approval of the Committee, he would then have moved to come into Committee of the Whole. No member would be committed to any part or provision. He had selected the Constitution of Iowa, because it was one of the latest and shortest.

Mr. Botts most heartily approved of the suggestion of the gentleman from San Francisco. It placed business before the House at once. As to any particular Constitution, it made no difference. This paper was well printed, and could be taken in hand without further delay. He suggested to the mover of the proposition the propriety of withdrawing the resolution originally offered by him, in order to permit this to go directly before the House.

Mr. GWIN would be glad to do so if it met the wishes of the House. With the consent of his colleague, he would therefore propose to withdraw it.

Mr. GILBERT could not consent to withdraw his amendment.

Mr. SHERWOOD was of opinion that there would be enough to do in discussing propositions consolidated by a Committee, without bringing the whole matter before the Convention at once. It was desirable to have the cream of the whole—the best material of the Constitutions of the thirty States.

Mr. HALLECK asked gentlemen who approved of this idea of taking up an entire Constitution in Committee of the Whole, whether from the experience of the last few days they considered the whole body better calculated to do business than a small committee.

Mr. GILBERT remarked that, although in introducing his amendment, he did it to avoid the complicated machinery of a number of committees, he did not suppose any member would be in favor of destroying altogether that principle of legislative action. It was an established usage in legislative bodies, that matters of great importance should come before the House through a committee. This committee must digest the material for the action of the House. He apprehended that when the report of the proposed committee came up for consideration, there would be enough amendments, propositions, and debates to satisfy all. He was opposed to adopting any one constitution as a basis, unless it came through a committee. Let this committee take all the constitutions and report what they deemed best. Each member could then, in Committee of the Whole, propose such amendments as he thought proper. It appeared to him that there was no other judicious mode of proceeding.

Mr. GWIN said there was still one difficulty. He was not opposed to a committee where there were ordinary facilities, but he wanted to know what was to be done with the report of this committee? Were the members to act upon one copy of the report? It was impossible for business to progress this way. If there was a printing press it would be the proper course, but no deliberative body, within his knowledge, ever passed a measure without first having it laid before each member for his examination.

Mr. GILBERT thought the gentleman overrated the difficulty of getting copies of this report for the use of the members. It would possibly consist of not more than half a page at a time, which could be copied by the clerks.

Mr. DIMMICK did not see how business could be expedited by adopting, as a basis, the Constitution of Iowa. It would have to be translated into Spanish, and a sufficient number of copies made for those who only spoke that language. If, on the other hand, the committee reported, article by article, a plan of a Constitution, it could be translated, copied, and laid upon the tables of the members at the opening of each day's session. He approved of Mr. Gilbert's resolution.

Mr. BOTTS would like to know how the House could understandingly vote upon a particular section, when it was ignorant of what was to follow. Nothing appeared to him more impolitic than the introduction, by piecemeal, of sections upon which others, behind, might be dependent. All must be acted upon together. A section, objectionable in itself, in one part of the Constitution, might, in another, be made beneficial.

Mr. PRICE said there seemed to be great difficulty in the minds of gentlemen in relation to the mode of getting to work at the business of making a Constitution. He had a resolution which he thought would be acceptable to the House. He hoped it would also be satisfactory to his colleague, (Mr. Gilbert.)

Resolved, That a Select Committee, composed of one delegate from each district, be appointed by the President, to report upon the best mode of proceeding to make a State Constitution, for the action of this body.

Mr. GILBERT preferred that the question should come at once between Mr. Gwin's resolution and his own. As to the difficulty referred to by gentlemen in relation to reporting, from time to time, different portions of a Constitution, it was not to be supposed that the House was to act finally and irrevocably upon each provision as it came up. It would first be considered in Committee of the Whole. The entire Constitution would afterwards come up in the House, and be open to amendment, section by section.

Mr. PRICE objected to making one general committee, as contemplated by the resolution of Mr. Gilbert. The work of the Convention should be subdivided. He believed five or seven standing committees should be made. By adopting this plan, he thought the form of a Constitution could be thrown together much quicker than by putting the whole labor on one committee. It was with this view that he moved the appointment of a committee to report upon the best mode of proceeding.

The question was then taken on Mr. Price's amendment, and it was rejected.

On motion of Mr. BOTTS, the Convention adjourned till 10 o'clock to-morrow morning.

THURSDAY, SEPTEMBER 6, 1849.

The Convention met pursuant to adjournment. Prayer by the Rev. Mr. Willey.

Journal of yesterday's proceedings were read, amended, and adopted.

Mr. LARKIN offered the following resolution:

Resolved, That Messrs. P. La Guerra, and J. M. Cabarruvias, now at the bar of this House, have produced to this House satisfactory evidence of having been duly elected members of this Convention from the districts of San Lüis and Santa Barbara, and that they be requested to come forward and be qualified as such. Adopted.

Whereupon Messrs. Cabarruvias and De La Guerra were sworn in by the President and took their seats.

Mr. LIPPITT then stated that he was absent when the members were sworn in yesterday, and requested that the oath be administered to him; which was accordingly done by the President.

On motion of Mr. GWIN, an invitation to take seats upon the floor of this House was extended to Col. Weller, Judge Hastings, and Col. Russell.

On motion of Mr. HALLECK, Manuel Dominguez was sworn in by the President, and took his seat.

Mr. GWIN reported, as chairman of the Committee on the appointment of a Reporter, against the publishing of the proceedings by the Convention.

He then moved a suspension of the rules, and nominated Mr. J. Ross Browne as Reporter to the Convention, who was elected, *viva voce.*

Mr. GWIN moved a reconsideration of the vote upon the resolution declaring it expedient to establish a State Government, which was received, and ordered to be laid on the table subject to call.

On motion of Mr. PRICE,

Resolved, That the President appoint two Pages for the Convention.

ORDER OF THE DAY.

Mr. PRICE stated that he had drafted a resolution asking for the appointment of six standing committees by the President, to take into consideration the different portions of the Constitution. There might be special committees appointed from time to time if necessary; but these standing committees would always be ready to perform any duty imposed upon them by the House in Committee of the Whole. He believed the business of the Convention would be done quicker by the adoption of this resolution than by any other mode yet suggested. There appeared to be three distinct propositions before the House: One to go at once into Committee of the Whole, and debate, section by section, the entire Constitution. In addition to the same resolution, it was proposed yesterday to take as a basis one of the State Constitutions. Mr. Gilbert's resolution proposes to appoint one general committee, to report from time to time the plan of a Constitution. He would not detain the House by going into a discussion of the merits of these different propositions, but would content himself by stating, that after consultation with several of the members, he was of opinion the following resolution would meet with general favor. He moved it as an amendment to Mr. Gilbert's amendment to Mr. Gwin's resolution:

Resolved, That six standing committees, of five members each, be appointed by the President, to take into consideration and report upon the following articles of a Constitution, to be submitted to this Convention, viz:

1st. Enacting clause and Bill of Rights.
2d. Legislative Department and qualification of electors.
3d. Executive and Executive powers.
4th. Judicial Department.
5th. Mode of amending and revising.
6th. General provisions and schedule.

Mr. HALLECK was opposed to this plan, and preferred the amendment of Mr. Gilbert as better calculated to facilitate the business of the Convention. He knew of no instance of the appointment of a number of committees, where a body of this kind had been enabled to get through its labors short of two or three months. There was no reason to suppose that six committees would get through any sooner here than in other Conventions. Great labor would be required in combining the reports of these different committees. Confusion and difficulty would be the inevitable result. Moreover, there would be various omissions, as in the case of the Constitution of New York. He did not know of any State Constitution that contained more admirable provisions than that; nevertheless, there was no Constitution in the States so imperfect; and this fact arose, not from the want of talent in the Convention, but from the appointment of a large number of committees. He was aware that there were numerous aspirants for the position of chairman to the proposed committee, but he thought that matter might be decided by the House.

Mr GWIN said the gentleman's remarks presented a most irresistible argument against the proposition which he advocated. The very fact referred to by him showed the impracticability of doing business in the mode proposed, without a printing press. The experience of forming thirty Constitutions of the States—the result of seventy years of labor—was to be thrown aside, and this Convention was to enter into a new field, to draft a new Constitution. The gentleman had shown the absolute necessity of taking one of these Constitutions as a basis. There would then be no necessity for either one standing committee or six special committees. The entire Constitution could be discussed in Committee of the Whole. He did not care which Constitution was taken up. It would be infinitely better to take any one of them than appoint a committee to report upon a form section by section. It was with the intention of proposing in committee to lay the printed copy, already referred to, before the House, that he had offered his original resolution. That Constitution was one of the latest and briefest. He wanted nothing better than to form a Constitution from the thirty Constitutions of the Union. Had some standard or plan been taken as a basis, the Convention would now be at work upon it.

Mr. BOTTS rose to protest against the haste apparent in every quarter of the House, to proceed headlong in this important matter of forming a Constitution. He appealed to members to consider the circumstances under which they were here. It was to perform the most solemn of trusts—to decide upon the fundamental principles of a Government. This great question of securing to mankind the prosperity and happiness which can only result from a good Government, now agitates the world. It occupies the minds of sages, and the discussion of it fills volumes. Yet gentlemen come here under the expectation of making a Constitution almost in a single day. He had been present as a spectator in one or two Conventions of the old States. He was struck with the contrast presented by this; for highly respectable as it was, he could not but be impressed with the absence of those gray hairs which he had seen in assemblies of this solemn character in the older States. He hoped to see a good Constitution formed, but it would take time to make it. He was well aware that gentlemen, in coming here, sacrificed much—that all were desirous of returning home without delay. Business in California was very profitable, and it was natural that gentlemen should wish to get back to their money bags; but he would oppose the spirit of patriotism to the spirit of mammon. There was something in the very word patriotism calculated to inspire men to make sacrifices. It was true houses were built in a single night in San Francisco; it was a go-ahead place; but he feared, if this Constitution was built in the same way, it would bear about the same relation to an enduring political structure that a shanty in San Francisco bore to a great monument of architectural skill. Gentlemen complained that the time of the House was consumed in useless discussion; that nothing had been done; no vote taken. Suppose you ascend a hill in the morning, and come down again in the evening, without being able to get over, have you done nothing? Have you not discovered that you cannot get over in that way? Delay is the characteristic of hasty legislation. A word with regard to the propositions before the House. By the first, proposing the appointment of one large committee, you can only have a portion of the intelligence of this body to engage in the formation of a Constitution. Is there any to spare? Mr. Price's proposition employs the whole intelligence of the Convention. He (Mr. Botts) was in favor of having as much wisdom as possible engaged in this business, and would therefore vote for the amendment offered by Mr. Price.

Mr. NORTON sustained Mr. Gilbert's proposition. He thought it would be the only means of advancing the work before the Convention. It was a great object to expedite business. The people sent delegates here to form the organic law of what would soon, he trusted, be a great State of the American Union. The proposition of Mr. Gilbert seemed to him to indicate the most practicable mode of proceeding. The Committee thus appointed could report, in whole or in part, a form to be acted upon in Committee of the Whole. He was not prepared to say they could form a Constitution better than those of the several States; but the Committee could select from them such provisions as were most applicable to this country, and by combining the wisdom of the whole, make a better Constitution than could be accomplished in any other way. The experience of Conventions proved that where several Committees were appointed on the several articles of the Constitution, men of different opinions necessarily presided over them, who deemed themselves bound to sustain their respective Committees. In the present case the objection would be peculiarly striking, where so many were assembled together coming with conflicting prejudices from different States of the Union.

Mr. GWIN observed that he had lived in three of the old States. He had carefully examined all the State Constitutions, and he preferred the Constitution of Iowa to that of any other State. He had no sectional prejudices to gratify here.

Mr. NORTON did not refer particularly to Mr. Gwin. That gentleman was not the only member of this House. Such prejudices existed, and that was sufficient.

Mr. HASTINGS said that all appeared anxious to effect the same great object, but arrived at different conclusions. It was very important that the work should be commenced at once; yet it was argued that it should not be hastily commenced, because the object was an important one. He considered that an excellent reason for beginning it without delay. They were not without a guide; there was one book to which they had access, containing the Constitution adopted by the wisdom of the age in which the framers lived—sanctioned by long experience—pronounced superior to any ever adopted in the known world. If the lawyer appears at the bar to argue his cause, he knows well where to find the best book extant on human rights and human government—the Constitution of the United States. The record of the debates on that Constitution embraced the principles of all the State Constitutions. The best plan would be to take up that great instrument as a guide, and proceed to form a Constitution for the State of California.

By adopting this as a standard, one committee could be appointed, which could accomplish all the work. He was opposed to a number of Committees. He considered one sufficient, and he would prefer a small one. But if gentlemen insisted upon having all the intelligence of the House concentrated in that Committee, he would not object to two members from each district, although he thought a smaller number would accomplish the work sooner. He was in favor of Mr. Gilbert's proposition.

The question was then taken on Mr. Price's amendment, and it was rejected.

The question then recurring on Mr. Gilbert's amendment—

Mr. Gwin rose to a question of order, whether his resolution and that of Mr. Gilbert were not precisely the same in effect.

Mr. Gilbert explained that the Committee proposed by him might report from time to time such articles or sections of a plan as might be passed upon in Committee.

Mr. Gwin asked if his was not precisely the same in effect—to report the plan, or any portion of the plan of a State Constitution. He made it a question of order.

The Chair decided that where two resolutions were the same in substance and effect, the amendment could not be properly considered as before the House. It was the opinion of the chair that these two propositions did not vary in effect.

Mr. Gilbert appealed from the decision of the Chair.

Mr. Halleck asked if an appeal could be debated.

The Chair decided in the negative.

Mr. Gilbert called for the yeas and nays on the appeal, which was ordered.

Yeas—Messrs. Aram, Carillo, Cabarruvias, Crosby, Dimmick, Dominguez, Ellis, Foster, Gwin, Hoppe, Hobson, Hastings, Jones, La Guerra, Larkin, Lippitt, Moore, McCarver, Ord, Price, Pico, Rodriguez, Reid, Sutter, Snyder, Shannon, Sherwood, Stearns, Vallejo, Woozencraft—30.

Nays—Messrs. Gilbert, Halleck, Hollingsworth, Lippincott, Norton, and Teft—6.

The question then recurring on Mr. Gwin's resolution, it was adopted.

On motion, the blank was filled with the word two.

Mr. Shannon offered the following resolution:

Resolved, That a Select Committee of five members be appointed by the President to frame and report to this House, at as early a period as practicable, the necessary rules for its government.

Adopted.

On motion of Mr. Gwin, the House took a recess of half an hour to allow the Chair an opportunity of appointing the Standing Committee.

AFTERNOON SESSION, 1 O'CLOCK, P. M.

The Convention re-assembled pursuant to adjournment.

The President announced the following as the Standing Committee on the Constitution:

Messrs. Gwin and Norton, of San Francisco; Hill and Pedrorena, of San Diego; Foster and Carrillo, of Los Angelos; De La Guerra and Roderiguez, of Santa Barbara; Tefft and Cabarruvias, of San Luis Obispo; Dent and Halleck, of Monterey; Dimmick and Hoppe, of San Jose; Vallejo and Walker, of Sonoma; Snyder and Sherwood, of Sacramento; Lippencott and Moore, of San Joaquin.

Committee on Rules and Regulations.—Messrs. Shannon of Sacramento, Butts of Monterey, Price of San Francisco, Jones of San Joaquin, and McCarver of Sacramento.

Mr. Gwin moved that the Secretary of the Convention have power to employ a clerk or clerks, if such are necessary, and to report to the Convention the name or names of the person or persons he proposes to appoint, for its approval. Adopted.

On motion of Mr. Price,

Resolved, That the Committee to frame a Constitution is hereby authorized to employ such number of Clerks as may be necessary, and that the Committee are instructed to bring in a copy of their report for each member of the House.

Mr. Price offered the following resolution:

Resolved, That the President appoint a committee of three to wait on Gov. Riley, and inform him that the Convention is fully organized and ready to receive any communication from him that he may be pleased to make.

Mr. GWIN objected, and the resolution was laid over.

On motion, the hour of the assembling of the Convention was fixed at 10 A. M. until otherwise ordered.

The Convention then adjourned.

FRIDAY, SEPTEMBER 7, 1849.

The Convention met pursuant to adjournment. Prayer by the Rev. Padre Ramirez.

Mr. E. Brown, from the District of San Jose, appeared, was sworn, and took his seat.

Mr. BOTTS offered the following resolution. He thought it proper that the officers of this Convention should know precisely upon what they were to depend:

Resolved, That a committee of five be appointed to inquire and report to this body the proper mode of providing for the payment of the expenses of this Convention, and that they report the proper per diem, or other allowance, to be made to the officers in the employment of this House.

Adopted.

Messrs. Botts, Halleck, Vallejo, Brown, and Price, were appointed by the President as such committee.

Mr. NORTON, on behalf of the Committee on the Constitution, begged leave to state that the Committee had had the subject under consideration, and during the brief time allowed it, had not been able to prepare any written report. There had been, in Committee, a great degree of unanimity on the adoption of the first portion of a Constitution; and it was prepared to report this morning, verbally, if the House desired it, a bill of rights. The Committee were of opinion that the preamble should be postponed until after the form of a Constitution had been agreed upon.

Mr. HASTINGS moved that the Committee be permitted to report, when one copy of their report was ready. Adopted.

Mr. NORTON, the Chairman of the Committee, then reported as follows:

The Select Committee appointed to report a plan, or any portion of "a plan of a State Constitution," having had the same under consideration, respectfully report the following proposed articles:

ARTICLE I.

Declaration of Rights.

I. No member of this State shall be disfranchised or deprived of any of the rights or privileges secured to any citizen thereof, unless by the law of the land, or the judgment of his peers.

II. The right of trial by jury shall be secured to all, and remain inviolate forever. But a jury trial may be waived by the parties in all civil cases in the manner to be prescribed by law.

III. The free exercise and enjoyment of religious profession and worship, without discrimination or preference, shall forever be allowed in this State to all mankind; and no person shall be rendered incompetent to be a witness on account of his opinions on matters of religious belief; but the liberty of conscience hereby secured, shall not be so construed as to excuse acts of licentiousness, or justify practices inconsistent with the peace or safety of this State.

IV. The privileges of the writ of *habeas corpus* shall not be suspended, unless when, in cases of rebellion or invasion, the public safety may require its suspension.

V. Excessive bail shall not be required, nor excessive fines imposed, nor shall cruel and unusual punishments be inflicted, nor shall witnesses be unreasonably detained.

VI. No person shall be held to answer for a capital, or otherwise infamous crime, (except in cases of impeachment, and in cases of militia, when in actual service; and the land and naval forces in time of war, or which this State may keep with the consent of Congress in time of peace; and in cases of petit larceny, under the regulation of the Legislature,) unless on presentment, or indictment of a grand jury; and in any trial, in any court whatever, the party accused shall be allowed to appear and defend in person and with counsel, as in civil actions.

No person shall be subject to be twice put in jeopardy for the same offence, nor shall he be compelled, in any criminal case, to be a witness against himself; nor be deprived of life, liberty, or property without due process of law; nor shall private property be taken for public use without just compensation.

VII. When private property shall be taken for any public use, the compensation to be made therefor, when such compensation is not made by the State, shall be ascertained by a jury, or by not less than three commissioners appointed by a Court of Record, as shall be prescribed by law. Private roads may be opened in the manner to be prescribed by law, but in every case the necessity of the road, and the amount of all damage to be sustained by the opening thereof, shall be first determined by a jury of freeholders, and such amount, together with the expenses of the proceedings, shall be paid by the person to be benefitted.

VIII. Every citizen may freely speak, write, and publish his sentiments, on all subjects, being responsible for the abuse of that right, and no law shall be passed to restrain or abridge the liberty of speech or of the press. In all criminal prosecutions or indictments for libels, the truth may be given in evidence to the jury; and if it shall appear to the jury that the matter charged as libellious is true, and was published with good motives, and for justifiable ends, the party shall be acquitted; and the jury shall have the right to determine the law and the fact.

IX. No law shall be passed, abridging the right of the people peaceably to assemble and to petition the government, or any department thereof; nor shall any divorce be granted, otherwise than by due judicial proceedings; nor shall any lottery hereafter be authorized, or any sale of lottery tickets allowed within this State.

X. Any citizen of this State who may hereafter be engaged, either directly or indirectly, in a duel, either as principal or accessory before the fact, shall forever be disqualified from holding any office under the Constitution and laws of this State.

XI. All laws of a general nature shall have a uniform operation.

XII. The military shall be subordinate to the civil power. No standing army shall be kept up by the State in time of peace, and in time of war no appropriation for a standing army shall be for a longer time than two years.

XIII. No soldier shall, in time of peace, be quartered in any house, without the consent of the owner, nor in time of war, except in the manner prescribed by law.

☛ XIV. No person shall be imprisoned for debt, in any civil action in mesne, or final process, unless in cases of fraud; and no person shall be imprisoned for a militia fine in time of peace.

XV. Foreigners, who are, or who may hereafter become, residents of this State, shall enjoy the same rights in respect to the possession, enjoyment, and descent of property, as native born citizens.

XVI. This enumeration of rights shall not be construed to impair or deny others, retained by the people.

By order of the Committee. MYRON NORTON, *Chairman.*

Mr. GWIN offered the following resolution:

Resolved, That this House resolve itself into a Committee of the Whole House, at half-past 12 o'clock this day, to take under consideration the report of the Select Committee appointed to report a Constitution, or any part thereof; and that the Secretary and Assistant Secretaries be required to prepare copies of said report for the use of the members.

With regard to this resolution, Mr. GWIN would merely state that the first eight sections of the report submitted by the chairman of the Select Committee, were from the Constitution of New York; all the others were from the Constitution of Iowa. There were several manuscript copies of the first part, and printed copies of the last, which would enable the Convention to proceed to business at the hour designated.

Mr. HALLECK stated that the committee did not consider this article (the declaration of rights) complete; but they had agreed upon it in a spirit of compromise, and with a determination to go forward with the work this morning. If other members united with the committee in this effort, he thought the object could be accomplished.

Mr. ORD moved to amend Mr. Gwin's resolution by laying the report on the table, and making it the special order of the day for Monday, at 10 o'clock, A. M. Rejected.

Mr. JONES suggested that a portion of the House did not understand the language of this bill of rights. They required time to have it translated. Besides, it was desirable that the House should have time to examine other Constitutions.

Mr. GWIN stated that a translation had already been made.

Mr. BOTTS was not, for his part, prepared to cast any vote that this important committee should dictate to him. He found, this morning, that the whole power of making this Constitution was consigned to the hands of twenty members; the rest were completely emasculated. No doubt there would be great unanimity here, as there was in committee. They bring in a Constitution which they voted for in committee. As a matter of course they will vote for it again. What object is there, then, in sitting here? Simply to form a quorum to enable the great committee to make a Constitution. The people of California have sent some forty members here for that purpose, but sixteen or seventeen of them, who are present, are disfranchised. They are to have no part or voice in the formation of this Constitution. Where are the eloquent champions of the rights of San Joaquin and of Sacramento?

Mr. SHERWOOD remarked that this Committee, although composed of twenty members, did not assume to make a Constitution. No such power was delegated to them. In conformity with the resolution under which they were appointed, they merely discharged the onerous duty imposed upon them of reporting to the Convention what they deemed to be the best plan of a government for California. The gentleman from Monterey is one of the members to decide whether the results of the labors of this Committee are worthy to be laid before the people for their sanction. It is for the purpose of giving work to the Convention, that this material is reported by the Committee.

Mr. GWIN then withdrew his resolution and substituted the following in its place:

Resolved, That the report of the Select Committee be referred to the Committee of the Whole House, and be made the special order for to morrow, at 10 o'clock.

Mr. SHERWOOD moved to amend Mr. Gwin's resolution, by providing that the House resolve itself immediately into a Committee of the Whole, to take into consideration the reported Bill of Rights.

After debate, the amendment was withdrawn.

The question upon the adoption of Mr. Gwin's resolution was then put to the Convention, and carried.

The President then stated that the Secretary had submitted to him for the approval of the Convention, the names of Messrs. J. F. Howe, John E. Durivage, and J. S. Robb, as Clerks.

The President submitted a communication from J. Ross Browne, Reporter to the Convention, which was referred to the Committee on Reporting.

On their own application, Messrs. Halleck and Vallejo were excused from the Committee of five on Expenses of the Convention, and Messrs. Crosby and Larkin were substituted.

On motion of Mr. SHERWOOD, the Convention adjourned.

SATURDAY, SEPTEMBER 8, 1849.

Convention met pursuant to adjournment. Prayer by the Rev. Mr. Willey.

On motion of Mr. GWIN, the daily calling of the roll of members was dispensed with, until otherwise ordered by the Convention.

On motion of Mr. SHANNON, Mr. McDougal, a member from Sacramento, and on motion of Mr. VALLEJO, Mr. Walker, a member from Sonoma, were sworn by the President to support the Constitution of the United States, and took their seats as members of the Convention.

The Journal of yesterday was read, amended on motion of Mr. Botts, and then approved.

Mr. BOTTS submitted the following resolutions:

Resolved, That a "Bill of Rights," if appended to a Constitution at all, should only be declaratory of general fundamental principles.

Resolved, That the object of a Constitution is to organize a government, prescribing the nature and extent of the powers of the several departments thereof, and that to engraft any legislative enactment on a Constitution, is anti-republican, and contrary to the character and genius of such an institution.

If he (Mr. Botts) understood the origin of a bill rights, it was this. When the colonies, which now compose a portion of the United States of America, felt themselves aggrieved by the arbitrary action of the British Government, they started questions that were then new in the world, with regard to the great rights of mankind. They promulgated these important truths in the form of a declaration of rights, embodying the principles which they avowed. The object of the Constitution was to sustain those rights. Their design was to lay down a great, broad principle of human government. The first, or general declaration, is called a bill of rights; and the second, embracing a special system of government, is known by the term Constitution. It is the true meaning of these two terms that this Convention should recognise. Perhaps it is altogether unnecessary that we should refer to these general principles of government here. Do not forget them. Cherish them as you would your heart's blood; but why append them to this Constitution? If it is the wish of the House, there is no objection to promulgating them still further, and giving them the sanction of this Convention, but let the bill of rights be kept to its legitimate object. The proposed bill is objectionable. It embraces legislative enactments. The crime of duelling, for instance, is taken up, and, instead of a general declaration that duelling is an evil and ought to be prohibited, leaving it to the people to prohibit it in such manner as they may deem proper, we undertake to prescribe the mode for them. They do not require us to perform this duty. We are sent here to prepare for them a system by which they can enact laws for themselves. No civilized people pretend to pass laws without at least making them run the gauntlet of two Houses, differently constituted—often requiring them to pass through the final revision of a single individual, called a President or Governor. When a Convention assumes to pass laws and impose them upon the people, it constitutes itself an oligarchy. If you take notice of one species of crime, can you neglect another? Do you not usurp the power of designating crime? Where will be the end? If you undertake to prohibit duelling, will you have no reference to gambling? Or, if you entertain these two minor evils, will you omit the great crime of murder? You go, then, through all the evils of society. If you entertain crime, will you not entertain the subject of usury? Gentlemen may refer to Constitutions without number, adopted in the United States, with these very features engrafted on them, but that is no reason why we should adopt the faults of others. We should rather profit by their experience. By the adoption of this resolution, instructing the committee to confine itself to the legitimate object for which it was appointed, some hopes may be entertained of progressing with the business of the Convention; but if we undertake to enact laws on all subjects, it will be impossible to get through in less than four months.

Mr. Sherwood called for the special order of the day; and, after debate, it was decided by the Chair that the special order was the first business before the Convention.

Mr. Botts moved a reference of his resolution to the Committee of the Whole. The motion was decided in the negative.

COMMITTEE OF THE WHOLE.

On motion of Mr. Gwin, the Convention resolved itself into Committee of the Whole, Mr. Lippett in the chair, and took up the special order of the day, being the "Declaration of Rights," yesterday reported by the Select Committee appointed to report "a plan or part of a plan of a State Constitution."

Mr. Shannon moved the following as the first and second sections of the bill of rights:

Sec. 1. All men are by nature free and independent, and have certain inalienable rights, among which are those of enjoying and defending life and liberty, acquiring, possessing, and protecting property, and pursuing and obtaining safety and happiness.

SEC. 2. All political power is inherent in the people. Government is instituted for the protection, security, and benefit of the people; and they have the right at all times, to alter or reform the same whenever the public good may require it.

Mr. NORTON stated, on behalf of the Committee, that in making this report, they did not intend that it should comprise the whole bill of rights. The Committee was forced, by the action of the House, to come in without proper time for deliberation and reflection, and report something. It was the understanding of every member that they were to have the privilege of introducing other sections. The first and second sections, introduced by the gentleman from Sacramento, (Mr. Shannon,) he believed the committee had agreed should be incorporated in the bill of rights. It was the proper place for them. The declaration of the sovereignty of the people, emanates from the foundation of our Republic. It has been adhered to ever since, and, he trusted, would be adhered to in all time to come.

Mr. HALLECK suggested whether it would not be expedient, as the bill of rights introduced by the Committee was imperfect, and new sections must come in, to proceed to act upon those reported. Such additional sections as were deemed necessary, might then be moved. It would afterwards remain to determine upon the relative order in which they should appear.

Mr. JONES proposed, as an amendment, to strike out the first section of the bill now before the Committee, and insert the first section of the Constitution of Iowa.

The CHAIR observed that an amendment to any part, except what was directly before the House, was not in order.

The question recurring on the first section, proposed by Mr. Shannon,

Mr. JONES moved to strike it out.

Mr. BOTTS was in favor of the amendment suggested by Mr. Jones, He considered the first section superfluous. It merely secures to the citizens of the State certain privileges, of which this Convention has no power to deprive them. It is only by their own act that they can be legally dispossessed of those privileges.

Mr. SEMPLE rose barely to say, that he was opposed to striking out this article. He considered it an essential principle to be incorporated in a bill of rights. It takes precedence of all others, and places those that follow it in a higher point of view. He trusted it would be retained.

After some discussion on the order of amendments, the question was taken on the first section proposed by Mr. Shannon, and it was adopted; the question then being on the second section,

Mr. ORD moved an amendment, which he stated was a literal copy of the second section of the bill of rights of Virginia. There was some difference between the phraseology of this section and that of the section before the Committee. It was in the following words:

2. That all power is vested in, and consequently derived from the people; that magistrates are their trustees and servants, and at all times amenable to them.

Mr. SHANNON had carefully examined the Constitutions of the different States, Virginia included, and had been unable to find a more terse, comprehensive, and appropriate section than that which he had proposed. He did not perceive what Mr. Ord's amendment added to it, or in what respect it was superior.

Mr. ORD explained the difference.

Mr. BOTTS thought Iowa had the advantage in this case. She said all in one clause that was contained in the two clauses proposed. He would vote against the amendment of his colleague (Mr. Ord.)

The question then being on Mr. Ord's amendment, it was rejected.

The question was then taken on the second section proposed by Mr. Shannon, and it was adopted.

The next question was on the first section of the report of the committee, viz:

3. No member of this State shall be disfranchised, or deprived of any of the rights or privileges secured to any citizen thereof, unless by the law of the land, or the judgment of his peers.

Mr. Botts moved to strike out the word "member," and insert "citizen." He considered the whole section superfluous, but desired that it shouid appear in the most acceptable form.

Mr. Norton suggested the word "inhabitant," which amendment was accepted by Mr. Botts.

Mr. Halleck observed that the clause was properly worded. The term "inhabitant" would apply to a certain class of people who were not entitled to the rights of citizens, but who were entitled to protection as inhabitants.

Mr. Jones objected to any such interpretation. The reading of the section is, "no *member* of this State shall be disfranchised." That is to say, no *citizen* having certain rights, such as the right of voting, shall be deprived of them. You cannot deprive an Indian of a right to vote, when he has no such right. It applies to the full rights of a citizen. A citizen cannot be partly a citizen. This section requires to be analyzed. "No member," &c. Now a member of a State must have the rights and privileges of a citizen thereof; because if he has not, the article gives them to him. An Indian cannot be deprived of the rights secured to a white man without due process of law. The word disfranchised is applied to citizens in contra-distinction to foreigners. A man who is not franchised cannot be disfranchised; a foreigner in the United States, who is not a citizen, cannot be disfranchised. The provision is superfluous, and he (Mr. Jones) would not support it.

Mr. Sherwood supposed the word "member" referred not only to Indians, negroes, and Africans, but to citizens; and that the word disfranchised referred particularly to citizens. "No member," either a citizen or a foreigner, Indian, negro, or African, "shall be disfranchised." A citizen being the only member who who could be disfranchised, is therefore referred to by that word. A citizen of the State of New York, by the commission of certain crimes specified in the statute books, is disfranchised by law. This is intended to secure to him all the rights to which he is entitled, unless by his own act he is disfranchised.

Mr. Hastings. There is another view of this question. Whether it is designed or not, the adoption of this section of the bill of rights would secure to certain classes, Indians and Africans, (if Africans are ever introduced here,) precisely the same rights that we ourselves enjoy. There is no clause in relation to the introduction of slaves or any other class of men. If you provide that no member of this State shall be deprived of the rights and immunities of a citizen, it is to be presumed that such member enjoys those privileges and immunities. If you declare that no man shall be decapitated for a certain crime, it may reasonably be presumed that he has a head. It must be clear, therefore, that that section proposed to be amended, was not designed by the mover to produce an effect of this kind. The word "inhabitant" would not be proper. Indians are inhabitants, but they do not enjoy those privileges in any portion of the United States; they are disfranchised. Yet we declare here, that they shall not be disfranchised without due process of law.

Mr. Botts thought the objections of the gentleman who had just taken his seat, to the word "inhabitant," were based upon an erroneous impression of the word "disfranchised." Every inhabitant of this State is franchised. It is not the elective franchise that is meant. The term embraces the general rights of a freeman. All classes of men possess rights and privileges. An Indian has rights— he has a right to his life. There can be no objection to the word "inhabitant." If the gentleman is correct, and the inhabitant has no rights, of course he cannot be deprived of them. He (Mr. Botts) would vote against the whole section, because he considered it entirely superfluous.

Mr. Ord could not agree with his colleague (Mr. Botts) as to the meaning of the word "disfranchise." The popular meaning of the word "franchise" is the right of suffrage. It is derived from the French, and it would be well to be sure of the precise meaning. Words are things. If this is true, we are giving to all inhabitants, whites, Indians, blacks, and mulattoes, the right of suffrage. The Constitution of New York has the word "member." Member and inhabitant mean different things. A member of a State, is a citizen. If gentlemen had left the word citizen, it would be more appropriate, and he would be disposed to vote for the amendment.

Mr. Jones said that, in France the word franchise is used to express a political right. In the Constitution of Louisiana it is used in the same sense. It refers to the right of suffrage.

Mr. Ord quoted from Webster's dictionary: *Franchise*, n. *Exemption from any onerous duty; privilege; immunity; right granted; a district to which a privilege or exemption belongs;* v. *To enfranchise—to make free.* It is a word derived from the French, and means simply the right of suffrage, and nothing more. This amendment, which it is proposed to substitute for the first article of the report of the Committee, is, therefore, out of place here. It relates to certain rights which come properly under the provisions of the legislative department. It should be left to the Committee to be inserted in that part of the Constitution. He moved to lay it on the table.

Mr. Dent differed from his colleague (Mr. Ord) on one point. If the word "disfranchised" has reference to the right of suffrage and nothing more, what is the meaning of the words following—"or deprived of any of the rights or privileges secured to the citizens thereof." It appears from this, that the word must have reference to the whole community, and not to a particular class entitled to special privileges; for this class is afterwards defined by the term citizen.

Mr. Botts rose to rescue a good old English word from the hands of the enemy. In the days of the Anglo-Saxons, a man who had been a serf, was made *frank* or *free*. The word has reference to freedom. It may be well enough to declare, that we shall not deprive the inhabitants of this State of their franchise or freedom, except by the law of the land; but there does not appear to be any necessity for making such a declaration, inasmuch as they cannot be deprived of such rights in any other way. The gentleman from San Joaquin (Mr. Jones) refers to the word as used in Louisiana. Does he mean to say, that because a man fights a duel in that State, he is deprived of the privilege of voting, and no other privilege? Is that the only punishment? The meaning must extend beyond the right of suffrage; for the man who commits crime is not only deprived of that right, but of many others.

Mr. Gwin had some doubts as to the propriety of using this word. He thought the shortest way of settling the question was to reject the amendment.

Mr. Botts suggested that if a gentleman was obliged to take a dose of physic, he had a right to make it as palatable as possible. He intended to vote against the whole section. To save time, however, he would withdraw his amendment.

Mr. Gwin moved to reject the first section.

Mr. Halleck. This is a very excellent provision. It is drawn up to cover certain rights. The object is this. There are two members of a community—one has several rights, another but a single right. Neither of these members shall be deprived of the one right or of the several rights, unless by the law of the land or the judgment of his peers. The person possessing but a single right cannot deprived of it except in the same way with the individual who has several rights.

Mr. Gwin could not see how a man could be disfranchised of any of his rights except by the law of the land or the judgment of his peers.

Mr. Wozencraft would vote for Mr. Botts' amendment, and against the whole. He thought it was the shortest way of accomplishing the object.

Mr. Botts stated that he had withdrawn his amendment.

Mr. Price could see no necessity for telling people in a bill of rights that their rights are secured to them by law. They understand that very well.

Mr. Gwin asked if there was any Constitution, of all the States, containing anything about franchise, except that of New York.

Mr. Ord had looked over the whole thirty Constitutions, and had found none.

Mr. NORTON said it was taken verbatim from the Constitution of New York.

Mr. MCCARVER thought it a matter of no importance where it came from. He was opposed to its adoption. We designate in this Constitution who are entitled to the right of franchise. Having given that right, no one under our system of government can be deprived of it except by law.

Mr. SHANNON was of opinion that the section defined itself.—"No member shall be disfranchised or deprived of any of the rights or privileges secured to any citizen." This does not refer to the single right of voting or the elective franchise. It includes all the rights and privileges secured to citizens. There can be no understanding here as to the previous existence of those rights. It is for the very purpose of creating a fundamental law of the land to determine them, that this Convention is now assembled.

Mr. NORTON had but a word to say in regard to this section. It is admitted that there is nothing improper in it. Objection is made to it on the ground that all American citizens know they possess these rights and privileges, without a formal statement of the fact. It is necessary, however, that not only citizens should be protected in the enjoyment of their rights, but all who are inhabitants of the State. Besides a large proportion of the citizens of California have had no opportunity heretofore of knowing so much about the rights and privileges of American citizens, and the protection given to all classes under our laws, as they are now about to have. It is necessary that they should see upon the face of this Constitution that their rights are to be secured to them. It will be a guarantee that they will not be deprived of such rights except by the law of the land or the judgment of their peers. There are foreigners in this country who are entitled to the protection of our laws. That of itself is a consideration of great importance. If there is no harm in this provision, and it can do the least possible good, it should be permitted to remain in the Constitution.

Mr. GWIN objected to it, not because it was improper, but because everything inserted in this Constitution should be proper, and not negative. Louisiana had the same descriptive population unacquainted with our laws. He would also refer to Arkansas, Missouri, and Florida. Is there anything of the same kind in their Constitutions? Because it happens to be in one Constitution, it is not necessary to put it in ours. It is a precedent that should not be established.

Mr. SEMPLE. Suppose we pass this provision in the bill of rights, will it not cramp our action hereafter? Other sections must come up defining who are entitled to certain rights. Here you declare that no citizen shall be deprived of any of his rights or privileges unless by due process of law. Particular classes must necessarily be deprived of the right of suffrage. You proceed in another section to deprive them of that right. This is not due process of law. If such a provision is necessary at all, it cannot properly be introduced in this part of the Constitution. It must be incorporated in that portion which defines the classes entitled to the right of suffrage. He (Mr. Semple) would therefore vote for the rejection, with the view of considering the proposition in its appropriate place.

Mr. DIMMICK was in favor of having this in the bill of rights, and for this reason. That nothing should be introduced into the Constitution or the laws of this country, which would disfranchise any person, who, under a particular law, has the right of citizenship. He had heard gentlemen say that under the Mexican law, there is a class who have the right of elective franchise, and he knew they were in favor of prohibiting them from the enjoyment of this right. He considered the bill of rights the proper place for this section. In another part of the Constitution it would be easy to determine who were entitled to the right of suffrage, without reference to this.

Mr. GWIN wished to know what class under the Constitution of Mexico did the gentleman refer to. Was it the Indian population?

Mr. DIMMICK stated that the Indians could not vote; but that there was a portion of the population having Indian blood in their veins who were entitled to that privilege.

Mr. Botts renewed his amendment.

Mr. Price moved to strike out the latter clause—"except by the judgment of his peers."

Mr. Ord was not quite satisfied that the meaning of the word franchise was thoroughly understood. It seemed to him that the latter part of the clause covered the whole ground. The word "disfranchised" might be stricken out altogether, leaving the other portion of the section to stand. He therefore moved the following:

3. No inhabitant of this State shall be deprived of his rights or privileges, unless by the law of the land or the judgment of his peers.

Mr. Jones expressed surprise at one argument urged in favor of this section; that the original citizens of this country require to be told that they are entitled to the rights of citizenship. He believed it was no more necessary to tell them that than it was to tell him. It might be a very charitable concession to award to them in a bill of rights the privileges of citizenship; but he would remind gentlemen that these privileges were already guarantied to them by the treaty of peace and by the Constitution of the United States. It was unnecessary to patent their rights by a declaration of this kind.

The question was then taken on the amendment of Mr. Ord, and it was rejected.

The question was then taken on the amendment of Mr. Botts, and it was rejected.

The question recurring on the first section as reported by the Committee,

On motion of Mr. Gwin, it was stricken out.

The Committee then rose, reported progress, and asked leave to sit again. Report accepted and leave granted.

Mr. Shannon, from the Committee on Rules of the House, submitted a written report, which, on motion of Mr. Gilbert, was laid on the table, subject to call on Monday morning at 10 o'clock.

Mr. Botts desired to draw the attention of the House to a state of things that existed with regard to the Secretaries. They were up until twelve o'clock every night, preparing manuscript copies of the reports for the House. There was no printing press. This was a burden that ought not to fall upon the shoulders of these gentlemen. He therefore moved the following resolution:

Resolved, That when copies of reports are ordered by this House, that the Secretary shall be authorized to contract for the same, making an immediate report of the terms of the contract to the President of the Convention for his approval.

The resolution was adopted.

On motion of Mr. Gwin, the House then took a recess till 3 o'clock.

AFTERNOON SESSION, 3 O'CLOCK, P. M.

The Convention met pursuant to adjournment.

The House then resolved itself into Committee of the Whole on the special order of the day.

The question came up on the second section of the report of the Committee, and it was adopted, viz:

3. The right of trial by jury shall be secured to all, and remain inviolate forever. But a jury trial may be waived by the parties in all civil cases, in the manner to be prescribed by law.

Mr. Botts thought this the place in which Virginia might appear most appropriately. One of the most eloquent and beautiful clauses in the Constitution of Virginia, was the following, in the bill of rights. He proposed it as a substitute for the third section reported by the Committee:

That religion, or the duty which we owe to our Creator, and the manner of discharging it, can be directed only by reason and conviction, not by force or violence; and, therefore, all men are equally entitled to the free exercise of religion, according to the dictates of conscience; and that it is the mutual duty of all to practice Christian forbearance, love, and charity toward each other.

Mr. HALLECK remarked that this left out a very important provision contained in the article from the Constitution of New York, in regard to witnesses appearing in court.

Mr. NORTON was decidedly opposed to the amendment. He could see no objection to the section as reported by the Committee. It is plain and explicit. It not only guarantees to every man his rights in matters of religion, but protects the community from any violation of the peace, and from all acts of licentiousness calculated to impair the well-being of society, or infringe upon the dignity of the State.

Mr. BOTTS remarked, that under the clause reported by the Committee, a declaration might be made that the Roman Catholic religion is inconsistent with the safety of the State. He wanted to prohibit the Legislature from making such a declaration. He wanted a bill of rights to declare, what the bill of rights of Virginia does, in the most appropriate and beautiful language—the right of man to worship in his own way. The one does it—the other does not.

Mr. SHERWOOD said that the gentleman from Virginia, (Mr. Botts,) was evidently not acquainted with the history of the new sects in the State of New York, or he would see the propriety of the restrictions contained in the section reported by the Committee. There have been sects known there to discard all decency, and admit spiritual wives, where men and women have herded together, without any regard for the established usages of society. It was for this reason that the clause was put in the Constitution of New York. No such thing as an attempt to limit the Roman Catholics to any fixed rules of worship was intended; but it was deemed necessary that society should be protected from the demoralizing influence of fanatical sects, who thought proper to discard all pretentions to decency.

The question was taken on the amendment of Mr. Botts, and it was rejected.

The question was then taken on the proposition of the Committee, and it was adopted, as follows:

4. The free exercise and enjoyment of religious profession and worship, without discrimination or preference, shall forever be allowed, in this State, to all mankind; and no person shall be rendered incompetent to bear witness on account of his opinions on matters of religious belief; but the liberty of conscience hereby secured shall not be so construed as to excuse acts of licentiousness, or justify practices inconsistent with the peace or safety of this State.

The question being on the fourth section reported by the Committee,

Mr. BOTTS moved to amend it by introducing, after the words "public safety," the words "in the opinion of the Legislature," as follows:

The privilege of the writ of *habeas corpus*, shall not be suspended, unless when in cases of rebellion or invasion, the public safety, IN THE OPINION OF THE LEGISLATURE, may require its suspension.

Mr. McCARVER was opposed to leaving to the Legislature the power to suspend the writ of *habeas corpus*. It would be very inconvenient, in cases of great emergency, to wait until the Legislature could convene. In most of the States, the sessions are annual, and in some they occur only once in two years. There is not likely to be any abuse of this power. The emergency must be shown. It must be established that the public safety requires the suspension. No executive officer would undertake to exercise the power, unless compelled to do so by the necessity of the case.

Mr. NORTON was clearly of opinion that the proposed amendment was no improvement upon the original section. The only way the writ of *habeas corpus* can be suspended, is by the Executive of the State. He is the only person who can declare the country under martial law; and this power of suspending the writ is given to him for obvious reasons. It would be impossible, in many cases, for the Legislature to be convened at a proper time. It is only in cases of invasion, or any sudden emergency, involving the public safety, that the Executive officer is called upon to exercise this power.

Mr. BOTTS felt that it was a very idle business to attempt to amend the report of this mammoth Committee. He was aware that a majority of those present were always ready to support it. Nevertheless, he begged that gentlemen would consider for a moment what they were doing. Did they know what it was to suspend the writ of *habeas corpus?*—to declare martial law, and leave the power in the hands of a single individual? It is nothing less than to make a Dictator of that individual. He can at his will and pleasure arrest citizens of the State. It is the bulwark of the British Government. You put every man at the will of the Executive. You disfranchise every man. A few moments ago, you declared every man to be free, and yet, now, at the pleasure of a single individual, he can be deprived of his liberty. This is worse than a monarchy. If an invasion happens, you are that moment a slave, under an absolute monarchy. Is it the desire of gentlemen to place their constituents in this position?

Mr. GWIN read from the Constitution of the United States the following clause:

"The privilege of the writ of *habeas corpus* shall not be suspended, unless when in cases of rebellion or invasion the public safety may require it."

Mr. SHANNON thought the gentleman's principles (Mr. Botts') beautiful enough in theory, but he was afraid they would be found rather inconvenient in practice. Instances have occurred where the suspension of the writ of *habeas corpus* has been actually necessary—as in the case of General Jackson. Circumstances sometimes occur to require the exercise of this power, where nothing but the most extreme emergency would justify it. Above all, it is a provision in the Constitution of the United States.

Mr. WOZENCRAFT conceived that the question was not as to the necessity of this power, but as to the propriety of placing it in the hands of the Executive. He preferred giving it to the Legislature, as less liable to abuse it.

Mr. ORD had very serious objections to the section reported by the Committee, and moved the following amendment, which was accepted by Mr. Botts:

The privilege of the writ of *habeas corpus* shall not be suspended, except in such cases and in such manner as the law shall provide; and only then in cases of actual rebellion, invasion, or when the public safety may require it.

Mr. DIMMICK considered the last amendment quite as objectionable as the first. He was in favor of fixing this matter definitely in the Constitution, and not leaving it to the Legislature. A very serious objection, is the fact that the Legislature cannot provide for emergencies which it knows nothing about. How can it anticipate under what circumstances the public safety may be in danger? In cases of rebellion or invasion, it would be impossible for the Legislature to become acquainted with the facts, and provide proper measures, in time to meet the difficulty. The Executive, from his position, has a better opportunity of acquiring this knowledge in advance, and without waiting for the action of the Legislature, he has power under this provision to take such immediate measures as the public safety may require.

Mr. TEFFT urged the necessity of proceeding cautiously in this matter. It was one of incalculable importance, involving the best interests of the people. Were gentlemen willing to strike out upon this new tack, and leave this sacred writ in the hands of every new Legislature that might think proper to alter it. He appealed to their good judgment to let it stand as it stands in the Constitutions of twenty-nine States of the Union.

Mr. BOTTS remarked that, while he was represented as the enemy of this sacred writ, he went further than its dearest friends. They were willing that it should be suspended at the pleasure of a single individual; he was unwilling that it should be suspended at all. He would go for prohibiting any power from suspending it—either the Executive or the Legislature; but if such a provision was to be incorporated in the Constitution, he desired to have it in the least objectionable form.

The question was then taken on the amendment, and it was rejected.

The fourth section, as reported by the Committee, was then adopted.

The question being on the fifth section of the report,

Mr. McCarver moved to strike it out. He wanted no legislative enactments in a bill of rights.

The motion to strike out was decided in the negative, and the section was adopted without debate.

The sixth section was then read, and also adopted without debate.

The 7th section, reported by the Committee, being under consideration, viz:

When private property shall be taken for any public use, the compensation to be made therefor, when such compensation is not made by the State, shall be ascertained by a jury, or by not less than three commissioners, appointed by a court of record, as shall be prescribed by law. Private roads may be opened in the manner to be prescribed by law; but in every case the necessity of the road, and the amount of all damage to be sustained by the opening thereof, shall be first determined by a jury of freeholders, and such amount, together with the expenses of the proceeding, shall be paid by the person to benefitted.

Mr. Ord said he considered such a section entirely out of place in the Constitution. It should be upon the statute books. He therefore moved to strike it out and substitute the following:

The power of suspending laws, or the execution of the laws, ought never to be exercised, but by the Legislature, or by authority derived from it, to be exercised in such cases as this Constitution or the Legislature may provide for.

Mr. Jones wished a division of the question on the motion to strike out, and the proposed substitute. He was opposed to the section reported by the Committee. The subject of private roads comes peculiarly within the province of the Legislature. The pages of the Constitution should not be encumbered with regulations in regard to local improvements. It is a subject belonging to the statute books.

Mr. Shannon was also opposed to interfering with the regulation of private roads.

Mr. Halleck stated that the object of this section was to carry out that of the preceeding section. The two are intimately connected. "Nor shall private property be taken for public use, without just compensation." There are cases, such as those enumerated, which it was thought necessary to provide for. He need not tell gentlemen of the abuse of the legislative power in New York. This very article resulted from it. It was there determined in Convention that the abuse of power on this subject by the Legislature, was such as to require this restraint. The section, as reported, may not be well worded; but there seems to be an obvious necessity for some provision of this kind.

Mr. Gwin was of opinion that the section should be stricken out.

Mr. Botts. Is this in the Constitution of New York? If so, I shall vote for it. I have a very great desire to be in a majority, for the novelty of the thing. I confess, however, that I can seen no connexion between a McAdamised road and a bill of rights.

The question being taken on the first clause of Mr. Ord's proposed amendment, it was decided in the affirmative, and the section ordered to be stricken out.

The question then recurring on the second clause of Mr. Ord's amendment, to insert as above, Mr. Ord withdrew the same.

The question was then taken on the following section, and it was adopted, viz:

8. Every citizen may freely speak, write, and publish his sentiments on all subjects, being responsible for the abuse of that right; and no law shall be passed to restrain or abridge the liberty of speech, or of the press. In all criminal prosecutions or indictments for libels, the truth may be given in evidence to the jury; and if it shall appear to the jury that the matter charged as libelous is true, and was published with good motives, and for justifiable ends, the party shall be acquitted; and the jury shall have the right to determine the law and the fact.

The ninth section, as reported by the Committee then came up, viz:

No law shall be passed abridging the right of the people peaceably to assemble and to petition the government, or any department thereof; nor shall any divorce be granted, otherwise than by due judicial proceedings, nor shall any lottery hereafter be authorized, or any sale of lottery tickets be allowed within this State.

Mr. SHANNON moved to strike out all after the word "thereof." He did not approve of mixing up in a bill of rights, lottery tickets, divorces, and the right of the people to peaceably assemble and petition the Government. He objected to the theory of creating a bill of rights to legislate on the future Government of this State. California is yet a Territory. While taking the first step in the first movement to form the first fundamental law of the new State, it would be improper to insert legislative enactments for her government, five, ten, or twenty years hence. He proposed the following (being the 20th section of the bill of rights of Iowa) as a substitute for the entire section:

The people have the right freely to assemble together to consult for the common good, to make known their opinions to their representatives, and to petition for redress of grievances.

MR. BOTTS suggested, instead of *petitioning* for the redress of grievances, that the people have a right to *demand* it. The bill of rights has already declared that all power is inherent in the people. Shall the people petition their own servants and public trustees? It is high time to discard the phraseology which belongs to the old system of petitioning a superior power. The same power that enables the people to govern themselves, surely gives them a right to *remedy* their grievances.

Mr. ORD moved to amend the amendment by inserting instead thereof, the following as a substitute therefor:

The people have a right, in an orderly and peaceable manner, to assemble and consult upon the common good, give instructions to their representatives, and to request of the legislative body, by the way of addresses, petitions, or remonstrances, redress of the wrongs done them, and of the grievances they suffer.

Mr. ORD subsequently withdrew his amendment.

Mr. JONES moved to amend the amendment of Mr. Shannon, by substituting therefor the 20th section of the bill of rights of the Constitution of the State of Iowa, in the words following:

The people shall have the right freely to assemble together to consult for the common good, to instruct their representatives, and to petition the legislature for redress of grievances.

Mr. Jones' amendment to the amendment of Mr. Shannon was agreed to, and as thus amended, the substitute for the original section was then adopted.

On motion of Mr. GWIN, the Committee rose, reported progress, and obtained leave to sit again.

On motion, the House then adjourned.

MONDAY, SEPTEMBER 10, 1849.

The Convention met pursuant to adjournment. Prayer by Rev. Senor Antonio Ramirez.

Journal of yesterday was read and approved.

On motion, the Report of the Select Committee on "Rules and Orders for the government of the Convention," was taken up and read.

Mr. GWIN moved to strike out the 30th rule, and to substitute therefor the 127th rule of the House of Representatives of the United States, as follows:.

No standing rule or order of the House shall be rescinded or changed without one day's notice being given of the motion therefor. Nor shall any rule be suspended, except by a vote of at least two-thirds of the members present. Nor shall the order of business, as established by the House, be postponed or changed, except by a vote of at least two-thirds of the members present.

The question being taken, the motion was decided in the affirmative.

The report of the Committee, thus amended, was then adopted.

Mr. MOORE submitted the following, which was adopted:

Resolved, That a committee of five members be appointed to report to this Convention, at as early a day as practicable, a plan for taking the enumeration of the inhabitants of the State of California.

The PRESIDENT appointed, as the Committee under the foregoing resolution, Messrs. Moore, Sutter, Hill, Ord, and Reid.

Mr. GWIN submitted the following, which, on motion of the same gentleman, was ordered to lie over:

Resolved, That a committee of three be appointed by the President to report a plan to defray the expenses of the State Government, to be adopted by this Convention.

On motion, the Convention then resolved itself into Committee of the Whole. Mr. Lippett in the Chair.

The tenth section of the report of the Committee being under consideration, as follows:

Any citizen of this State who may hereafter be engaged, either directly or indirectly, in a duel, either as principal or accessory before the fact, shall forever be disqualified from holding any office under the Constitution and laws of this State.

Mr. SHERWOOD spoke in favor of the section, and Messrs. PRICE, MCCARVER, HASTINGS, SHANNON, and BOTTS against it, on the ground that it was properly the subject of legislative action.

The question being taken on the section, it was rejected by a vote of 12 to 18.

The eleventh, twelfth and thirteenth sections of the report were then adopted, as follows:

11. All laws of a general nature shall have a uniform operation.

12. The military shall be subordinate to the civil power. No standing army shall be kept in up by the State in time of peace, and in time of war no appropriation for a standing army shall be for a longer time than two years.

13. No soldier shall, in time of peace, be quartered in any house, without the consent of the owner, nor in time of war, except in the manner prescribed by law.

Mr. MOORE submitted, as an additional section, the following, which was adopted:

14. As all men are entitled to equal political rights, representation should be apportioned according to population.

The question was then taken on the fourteenth section of the Committee's report, and it was adopted, viz:

14. No person shall be imprisoned for debt in any civil action on mesne or final process, unless in cases of fraud; and no person shall be imprisoned for a militia fine in time of peace.

Mr. HASTINGS submitted the following as an additional section:

15. No bill of attainder, *ex post facto* law, or law impairing the obligation of contracts, shall ever be passed.

Which was agreed to by a vote of 21 to 8.

The 15th section of the report of the Committee being under consideration, viz:

Foreigners who are, or who may hereafter become, residents of this State, shall enjoy the same rights, in respect to the possession, enjoyment, and descent of property, as native-born citizens.

Mr. JONES moved to substitute the word "inheritance" for the word "descent," and to insert the word "permanent" before the word "residents."

Mr. LARKIN moved to amend the amendment, by striking out the word "residents," and inserting the word "citizen." The motion was decided in the negative.

Mr. HILL moved to amend the amendment of Mr. Jones, by striking out the word "permanent" before the word "resident," and substituting therefor the words "*bona fide*," which was agreed to.

Mr. SEMPLE moved to strike out the entire section. The motion was decided in the negative, yeas 11, nays 25.

Mr. Jones' amendment, as amended, was then agreed to; and the section, as amended, was adopted.

Mr. SHANNON moved to insert, as an additional section, the following:

Neither slavery nor involuntary servitude, unless for the punishment of crimes, shall ever be tolerated in this State.

Mr. CARVER moved to amend the amendment, by adding thereto the following:

Nor shall the introduction of free negroes, under indentures or otherwise, be allowed.

After debate as to the propriety of a division of the two questions, Mr. CARVER withdrew his amendment.

Mr. Shannon's amendment then being first in order, Mr. HALLECK, after debate in reference to the particular portion of the Constitution which the provision should appear in, moved that "a declaration against the introduction of slavery into California shall be inserted in the bill of rights," Mr. Shannon temporarily withdrawing his amendments to enable Mr. Halleck to make the motion.

The motion of Mr. Halleck was decided in the affirmative.

Mr. SHANNON then again submitted his amendment, and after further debate as to the expediency of submitting the question to the people in a separate article, the proposed section was *unanimously adopted.*

On motion, the Committee rose, reported progress, and obtained leave to sit again.

Mr. WOZENCRAFT submitted the following, which was considered and adopted:

Resolved, That a Committee of three be appointed to receive proposals for the printing of the proceedings of this Convention in Spanish and English, with instructions to receive all bids, and report to the House.

The President appointed, as the Committee under this resolution, Messrs. Wozencraft, Price, and Hastings.

Mr. NORTON, from the Committee appointed to report "a plan or a portion of a plan for a State Constitution," made a further report in writing, being Article II of the proposed Constitution; which was read, and on motion referred to the Committee of the Whole.

Mr. BOTTS submitted a resolution, that when Spanish copies are ordered of any papers before the Convention, the Secretary shall be authorized to contract for the same, as in the case of English copies ordered under a previous resolution.

The President decided that the previous resolution referred to, embraced all necessary authority, and that the Secretary was already fully empowered by that resolution to contract for Spanish as well as English copies.

On motion, the Convention then adjourned.

TUESDAY, SEPTEMBER 11, 1849.

The Convention met pursuant to adjournment. Prayer by the Rev. Mr. Willey Journal read and approved.

Mr. GWIN called for the consideration of his resolution offered yesterday, providing for the appointment of a committee to report the ways and means of defraying the expenses of the State Government which might be adopted by this Convention. A question as to the order of business arose, and it being decided that the resolution was in order,

Mr. GWIN said that his sole object in offering the resolution, was to collect necessary and important information. It was absolutely essential that the House should ascertain how the means of supporting this government after its adoption, are to be obtained. Other means must be provided to pay the expenses, than by taxing the people of California. The Government of the United States should bear the expenses of the State government for a number of years after its adoption. Fourteen of the thirty States of the Union—all the new States, except Texas—have had the benefit of territorial government. The expenditure of public money in sustaining territorial governments has been immense. There never was a Territory, except California, that had not large appropriations to sustain it. When Louisiana was purchased from France, the first thing after the ratification of the treaty was a territorial government. The same was the case with Florida, a Territory purchased from Spain under very similar circumstances to this country. Florida had the benefit of twenty-four years territorial government, during which period she received forty millions of dollars. Mississippi had the benefit of seventeen years; Alabama nineteen; Louisiana (which was infinitely more capable of paying the expenses of a government) nine years; Tennessee six; Kentucky ten; Ohio three; Indiana sixteen; Illinois, nine with Indiana, and nine as a separate Territory, making eighteen; Michigan thirty-one; Missouri eighteen; Arkansas thirty-five, seventeen years alone, and eighteen in connexion with Louisiana and Missouri; Iowa eight, and Wisconsin twelve. The object of the resolution is, to report upon these facts, and if the statistics can be obtained here to ascertain how much has been paid out of the public treasury, to sustain these Territories, and to show that the Congress of the United States is bound to appropriate, out of the tax collected here, sufficient to support this State government, until other means can be obtained, without imposing onerous burdens upon the people. It is not intended that the resolution should, in any way, direct or control the future action of the House. The means of sustaining this government must be procured; and it is desirable, that all the information necessary to be had on the subject, should be obtained at the earliest practicable period.

Mr. Halleck moved to amend the resolution, by striking out after the word "report," the words "a plan to defray the expenses," and to substitute therefor the words "on the ways and means of defraying the expenses."

The amendment was accepted by Mr. Gwin, and the resolution adopted.

The President appointed as said Committee, Messrs. Gwin, Hobson, and Stearns.

On motion of Mr. Gwin, the Convention resolved itself into Committee of the Whole, Mr. Lippitt in the Chair.

Mr. Hastings moved the following as an additional section:

As the true design of all punishment is to reform and not to exterminate mankind, death shall never be inflicted as a punishment for crime in this State.

Mr. Hastings. I do not know, sir, what favor this question may meet with here—whether it will have a single supporter but myself. It has, however, found many supporters at home, in the United States; I believe, in every State of the Union. And, sir, the time is fast approaching when this great principle will be engrafted into the laws of all the different States. My opinion is, that this new State should adopt it, and that it should be incorporated in the bill of rights. It is evident to my mind that we have not the right to take human life. I arrive at this conclusion from these premises: First, we have no rights, as a Government, other than those derived from the people themselves. If it be true, then, that the people have not that right, they cannot transfer it. What, as individuals of the community, they do not possess, they cannot transfer to the Government. No individual, sir, has the right to take human life, unless in self-defence. We acknowledge this as a starting point. It is conceded as a general principle. If an individual is assailed by an enemy, and his life endangered, he slays his assailant. He is acquitted by the laws; he is justified by the community. But if he take the life of a fellow-man without such provocation, he cannot be pursued by his fellow-man, and, in cold blood, slain. No individual possesses this right, and hence no individual can transfer the right to a Government. Life is taken; the party is arraigned long after the act is committed. The Government, in cold blood, pursues, arrests, and murders the criminal. Why can the Government, the representative of individuals, do this, when the individuals themselves cannot do it?—when it is admitted that no right can be delegated by individuals which they do not possess?

But, sir, I will not detain the House. I merely wish an expression of opinion on the subject, and I hope the article will be adopted. Perhaps I am hoping against hope; yet I must say, that in practice, as well as in theory, the principle of taking human life, as a punishment for crime, is wrong. Our books are full of instances of innocent persons being executed, who are charged with the crime of murder, and, eventually, it is ascertained, entirely to the satisfaction of the law, that the party executed was innocent. What remedy has the Government? What remedy has he? He is dead. This occurs to me as a very forcible argument why this system of punishment should never be introduced into any civilized community. Numerous instances might be given, but I take these general grounds as sufficient for my present purpose, which is to show that the principle is wrong. It will be asked, what substitute I propose? What are we to do with our criminals? What are we to do with murderers, the highest grade of criminals? Sir, imprison them for life. Let them reform. Do not exterminate your fellow-men; reform them. It is asked, where are your prisons? I maintain that the absence of prisons does not make the principle right. It is our business to make these prisons. We shall soon have facilities for accomplishing this object. Then we can carry into practice that which I propose. Until then, we may be subject to some inconvenience. But is it not better that we should be subject to a temporary inconvenience, than to a permanent evil?

Some would argue, undoubtedly, that the great object of punishment is to deter—to prevent the commission of crime. That is true; it is one great object; but a greater one, or at least as great, is to reform. These are the two great objects—to prevent the commission of crime, and to reform the criminal. The latter object is defeated if death be inflicted as a punishment. It may be argued that the infliction of death would deter to a greater extent, from the commission of crime, than imprisonment during life. Sir, I do not conceive this to be the case. Let every man put it to his own heart, and view the subject for himself, and should he ever be so unfortunate as to be convicted of murder, whether innocent or guilty, (for he may be convicted, although innocent,) I venture to say he would greatly prefer the punishment of death to imprisonment during life. I hope this article may be incorporated in the bill of rights. With these remarks, I submit it to the House.

Mr. McCarver seconded the resolution, not because he believed the House would adopt it, or that it could be adopted here, but because he considered the question entitled to a fair consideration. If the gentleman (Mr. Hastings) would devise a plan by which criminals could be properly punished in this country, he would go with him; but as California is situated at present, it is impracticable. The construction of penitentiaries would be enormously burdensome. In Iowa prisons were built, but the State could not defray the expense, and was obliged to set the prisoners at liberty. As to the right to take human life, it is very questionable whether we have that right; but as it has been a practice ever since the world was created, perhaps it would be as well to let it rest awhile longer. It may be that it is a good old principle established by the experience of ages. He would vote against the resolution, not because he was opposed to it, but because he considered it impracticable to accomplish the object under existing circumstances.

The question was then taken on the proposed section, and it was rejected.

Mr. Ord submitted the following as an additional section:

Sec. 16. That perpetuities and monopolies are contrary to the genius of a republic, and shall not be allowed; nor shall any hereditary emoluments, privileges, or honors, ever be conferred in this State.

Mr. Semple could not permit the proposed section to pass without a few remarks. It involves a question of great importance—the equal rights of mankind. It should be in the Constitution. Monopolies should be prohibited. No class of men should continue from generation to generation, to enjoy privileges given to them by the Legislature, which are not conferred under general law. The principle of monopolies includes banking privileges. The Legislature should have no power to grant charters or privileges to certain men to the exclusion of others. He was opposed to the banking system, as not only contrary to republican principles, but injurious to the people.

Mr. Halleck thought the subject properly came in another part of the Constitution.

Mr. Jones considered the proposed section one of much importance. It contains a declaration of great general principles, and involves great consequences. A provision prohibiting banking or other incorporations would come very well under the general provisions. But a declaration of the genius of a Republic in relation to those equal rights which we claim for all citizens, would come more appropriately in the bill of rights. A declaration of principle may be either positive or negative. There have been introduced into this bill of rights many negative declarations; but this is a great positive principle—that no man shall have any rights which are not possessed by the citizens generally.

The question was then taken on the proposed section, and it was rejected.

Mr. Ord offered the following:

Sec. 16. Every person has a right to bear arms for the defence of himself and the State.

Mr. McCarver moved to amend by saying, "provided they are not concealed arms." He did not think, however, that this was a proper subject for the Constitution. No attempt should be made to prevent the Legislature from regulating matters of this kind.

Mr. Sherwood was of the same opinion. To make a positive declaration that a man has not this right would be null and void, inasmuch as it would be in opposition to the Constitution of the United States, which provides that "a well regulated militia, being necessary to the security of a free State, the right of the people to keep and bear arms, shall not be infringed."

Mr. Botts was surprised that the gentleman from New York (Mr. Sherwood) should object to any provision here, because it was contained in the Constitution of the United States. After taking half-a-dozen provisions from that Constitution, word for word, such an objection came with rather a bad grace. He (Mr. Botts) would himself prefer having this provision under the legislative head. A bill of rights is a general declaration; the Constitution is a specific declaration. It is an admitted rule of construction that the bill of rights, or preamble, is of inferior force, and succombs to the Constitution. If there be in the Constitution a clause which conflicts with the bill of rights, the latter falls to the ground. He (Mr. Botts) desired to see all great principles involving the rights of citizens brought into direct operation in the body of the Constitution. He saw no necessity for mere declarations which could have no force or effect. For this reason he had voted against the subject of monopolies; and for the same reason he would vote against this.

Mr. Sherwood was not aware of having voted in the bill of rights for any provision which was directly secured to the people of California by the Constitution of the United States. But if he had done so, it was with the good example before him of the gentleman from Monterey, who had voted for a provision in regard to the law of attainder. That provision he would find in the Constitution under the limitation of the powers of Congress. It was introduced here to limit the powers of the Legislature. But Mr. Ord's proposition directly touches the rights of every citizen.

The question was then taken, and both the amendment, and amendment to the amendment, were rejected.

Mr. Ord submitted the following amendment as an additional section.

Sec. 17. The right of the people to be secure in their persons, houses, papers, and effects, against unreasonable seizures and searches, shall not be violated; and no warrant shall issue but on probable cause, supported by oath or affirmation, particularly describing the place to be searched, and the papers and things to be seized.

Mr. Jones moved to amend the latter part of the amendment by inserting "persons" instead of "papers," so as to read, "and the persons and things to be seized."

Mr. Hastings presumed it was a mere clerical error. Papers and things would just amount to "things and things."

Mr. Ord accepted the amendment.

Mr. Gwin said this section, as amended, was word for word from the Constitution of the United States, 4th article.

Mr. McCarver objected to it in the bill of rights. He thought it properly belonged to another part of the Constitution.

The question was then taken on the proposed amendment, and it was adopted.

Mr. Ord offered the following as an additional section:

Sec. 18. Treason against the State shall consist only in levying war against it, adhering to its enemies, or giving them aid and comfort. No person shall be convicted of treason, unless on the evidence of two witnesses to the same overt act, or confession in open court.

Mr. Botts proposed to strike out the latter clause, commencing "No person shall be convicted of treason," &c. He thought treason should stand on the same footing with any other crime, and should be proved to the satisfaction of a jury. It is well known, and is often the case, that circumstantial evidence is the strongest in the world. It was said by one of the ablest jurists, that it is that kind of evidence which cannot lie. By this clause two witnesses are required to prove the overt act, when it can be proved without any. It is a provision which might often prevent crime from being punished. Besides, if you do not punish a man except upon the evidence of two witnesses, for treason, why will you permit him to go to the gallows for murder, except upon that evidence? The principle is either true or false. If you adopt it in one case, why not adopt it in all? Yet is there a member of this House who would be in favor of saying no crime shall be punished except upon the evidence of two witnesses? It is a strong incentive to crime to say in this Constitution, that treason, the greatest of crimes, shall have this advantage over all others; and that the prisoner may go scot free, unless this provision is complied with. He (Mr. Botts) would read a sentence from Blackstone in relation to the punishment of high treason.—[*See Blackstone on high treason.*]

Mr. Gwin considered the Constitution of the United States better authority than Blackstone.

The question was then taken on the amendment of Mr. Botts, to strike out the latter clause, and decided in the negative.

The original amendment was then adopted.

Mr. McCarver had an amendment which he desired to offer as an additional section. It was in the following words:

Sec. 19. The Legislature shall, at its first session, pass such laws as will effectually prohibt free persons of color from immigrating to and settling in this State, and to effectually prevent the owners of slaves from bringing them into this State for the purpose of setting them free.

He deemed this necessary because the House had already made a provision prohibiting the introduction of slavery, the object of which he thought would be defeated by a system already in practice. He had heard of gentlemen having sent to the States for their negroes, to bring them here, on condition that they should serve for a specified length of time. He was informed that many had been liberated with this understanding. After serving a few years, they were to be set loose on the community. He protested against this. If the people of this Territory are to be free against the curse of slavery, let them also be free from the herds of slaves who are to be set at liberty within its borders. He wished to have the sense of the House on this question. If the subject was neglected now, it would soon be necessary to alter the Constitution. In Illinois, this question was laid before the people in a separate article, and a majority of twenty thousand of the voters of that State supported it. Have we not greater reason to fear the introduction of free negroes here, than they had in Illinois? The slave owner, possessed of a hundred negroes, can well afford to liberate them, if they engage to serve him for three years. What is to support them after that? Are they to be thrown upon the community? He believed that if any State in the Union required protection from this class of people, it was California. It is the duty of gentlemen to make provision in this Constitution against the introduction of negro labor, as well as prohibit the introduction of slavery.

Mr. Wozencraft said:

Mr. President: We have declared, by a unanimous vote, that neither slavery nor involuntary servitude shall ever exist in this State. I desire now to cast my vote in favor of the proposition just submitted, prohibiting the negro race from coming amongst us; and this I profess to do as a philanthropist, loving my kind, and rejoicing in their rapid march toward perfectability.

If there was just reason why slavery should not exist in this land, there is just reason why that part of the family of man, who are so well adapted for servitude, should be excluded from amongst us. It would appear that the all-wise Creator has created the negro to serve the white race. We see evidence of this wherever they are brought in contact; we see the instinctive feeling of the negro is obedience to the white man, and, in all instances, he obeys him, and is ruled by him. If you would wish that all mankind should be free, do not bring the two extremes in the scale of organization together; do not bring the lowest in contact with the highest, for be assured the one will rule and the other must serve.

I wish to cast my vote against the admission of blacks into this country, in order that I may thereby protect the citizens of California in one of their most inestimable rights—the right to labor. This right is not only valuable, but it is a holy commandment—"by the sweat of thy brow shalt thou earn thy daily bread." I wish to inculcate this command, and encourage labor. I wish, so far as my influence extends, to make labor honorable; the laboring man is the *nobleman* in the true acceptation of the word; and I would make him worthy of his high prerogative, and not degrade him by placing him upon a level with the lowest in the scale of the family of man. I would remove all obstacles to his future greatness, for if there is one part of the world, possessing advantages over another, where the family of Japhet may expect to attain a higher state of perfectability than has ever been attained by man, it is here, in California. All nature proclaims this a favored land. The assertion that we would be unjust in excluding that part of the human race from coming here, has no foundation in reason. We must be just to ourselves—by so doing we avoid injustice to others. In claiming the right to labor we do not deny the same to others. The African is well fitted for labor, you would say. Why deny him our field? Sir, we do not deny him the right to labor; we are willing that he should have the boundless wastes of his native land for his field—a region where the all-wise Creator, in his wisdom, saw fit to place him; but we are not willing that he should be placed in our field, where, instead of good to either party, evil would come to both. We are not only reasonable but we are just. No one will deny that a free black population is one of the greatest evils that can afflict society. We know it to be so. We have witnessed enough to know it and deplore it. There is not an advocate for the admission of blacks that would be willing to take the negro by the hand in fellowship—that would be willing to extend to him the right of suffrage—that would be willing to admit him on a footing in our political or social confederacy. Is it just, then, to encourage by our silence the emigration of a class of beings who at best are dead weights in society—resting on our social institutions like an incubus of darkness?

I desire to protect the people of California against all monopolies—to encourage labor and protect the laboring class. Can this be done by admitting the negro race? Surely not; for if they are permitted to come, they will do so—nay they will be brought here. Yes, Mr. President, the capitalists will fill the land with these living laboring machines, with all their attendant evils. Their labor will go to enrich the few, and impoverish the many; it will drive the poor and honest laborer from the field, by degrading him to the level of the negro. The vicious propensities of this class of population will be a heavy tax on the people. Your officers will have to be multiplied; your prisons will have to be doubled; your society will be corrupted. Yes, sirs, you will find when it is too late that you have been saddled with an evil that will gall you to the quick, and yet it cannot be thrown off. You can prevent it now, by passing this section. It should be done now. Do not wait for legislative enactment—the Legislature may, and doubtless will, pass laws effectually to prevent blacks from coming, or being brought here, but it will be an extended evil even at that date. When this Constitution goes forth without a prohibitionary clause relative to blacks, you will see a black-tide setting in here and spreading over the land; you will see a greater curse than the locusts of Egypt. This is no fancy sketch—it is a plain assertion, based on a just knowledge of things, which requires no gift of prophecy to foresee. If you fail to pass this bill you will have cause to revert to my assertions.

The future, to us, is more promising than that of any State that has ever applied for admission into the Union. The golden era is before us in all its glittering splendor; here civilization may attain its highest altitude; Art, Science, Literature will here find a fostering parent, and the Caucasian may attain his highest state of perfectibility. This is all before us. It is within our reach; but to attain it we must pursue the path of wisdom. We must throw aside all the weights and clogs that have fettered society elsewhere. We must inculcate moral and industrial habits. We must exclude the low, vicious, and depraved. Every member of society should be on a level with the mass—able to perform his appropriate duty. Having his equal rights, he should be capable of maintaining those rights, and aiding in their equal diffusion to others. There should be that equilibrium in society which pervades all nature, and that equilibrium can only be established by acting in conformity with the laws of nature. There should be no incongruities in the structure; it should be a harmonious whole, and there should be no discordant particles, if you would have a happy unity. That the negro race is out of his social sphere, and becomes a discordant element when among the Caucasian race, no one can doubt. You have but to take a retrospective view, and you need not extend your vision beyond our own land to be satisfied of this fact. Look at our once happy republic, now a contentious, antagonistical, discordant people. The Northern people see, and feel, and know, that the black population is an evil in the land, and although they have admitted them to many of the rights of citizenship, the admixture has acted in the political economy as a foreign, poisonous substance, producing the same effect as in physical economy—derangement, disease, and, if not removed, *death*. Let us be warned—let us avoid an evil of such magnitude.

I will trespass on the patience of the House no further, Mr. President, than to express the wish that this clause may become an article in the Constitution.

Mr. Gwin said that this was clearly a legislative feature of the Constitution, and should come up in the legislative department.

Mr. McCarver had no objection to letting it come up in another part of the Constitution, but as other provisions of a similar character had been placed in the bill of rights, he thought that was the proper position for it. He would, however, withdraw it, with the understanding that it should come up for consideration in the legislative department.

Mr. Ord had another amendment to offer, providing that no power of suspending the laws shall be exercised, unless by the Legislature or its authority. It was the same in substance as the amendment which he had offered the other day.

Mr. Botts objected to the proposition. He was opposed, in the first instance, to giving either the Executive or the Legislature the power to suspend the writ of habeas corpus, but he preferred, of the two evils, that this power should not be placed in the hands of a single individual. He hoped he was not forbidden to doubt even the propriety of some of the provisions in the Constitution of the United States. What would be the interpretation of this clause, if adopted in this Constitution? That the laws of this State, which are, in part, the Constitution, may be suspended by the Legislature; that the Constitution itself may be suspended. Of course, it cannot be the laws passed by the Legislature that are referred to, because the Legislature has a right to suspend or repeal its own laws. It is unnecessary to say that the Legislature has power to suspend its own laws. The right to make laws gives it the right to suspend or repeal them. What other laws of the land are there, which nobody but the Legislature can suspend. There is but one other set of laws—those contained in your Constitution. It is, therefore, inevitable that the Legislature may suspend the laws of this Constitution.

Mr. Price asked if the gentleman (Mr. Ord) would withdraw the amendment, and let it come in as a section at the final passage of the Constitution.

Mr. Ord thereupon withdrew his amendment.

Mr. Ord submitted the following as an additional section, which was rejected:

Sec. 19. All persons shall, before conviction, be bailable, by sufficient sureties, except for capital offences, where the proof is evident or the presumption great.

Mr. Ord offered the following, which was rejected:

That no free Government, or the blessing of liberty, can be preserved to any people, but by a firm adherence to justice, moderation, temperance, frugality, and virtue; and by a frequent recurrence to fundamental principles.

The last section of the report being now under consideration, as follows:

20. This enumeration of rights shall not be construed to impair or deny others retained by the people.

Mr. Gwin moved to amend by striking out and inserting the following, from the bill of rights of Arkansas:

This enumeration of rights shall not be construed to deny or disparage others retained by the people; and to guard against any encroachments on the rights herein retained, or any transgression of any of the higher powers herein delegated, we declare that everything in this article is excepted out of the general powers of Government, and shall forever remain inviolate; and that all laws contrary thereto, or to the other provisions herein contained, shall be void.

Mr. BOTTS proposed to amend the amendment. As his present proposition was the only definite one which he had offered in this bill of rights, he hoped it would be treated with some degree of indulgence. It was not to be found in the bill of rights of New York, or Iowa, or Arkansas; there was that objection to it, but he believed the spirit of it was broached in them all.

As constitutions are the instruments by which the powers of the people are delegated to their representatives, they ought to be construed strictly, and all powers, not expressly granted, should be taken to be reserved.

He (Mr. Botts) considered the original section picked up by the Committee extremely imperfect. He imagined the Committee had found it somewhere in the Constitution of New York or Iowa.

Mr. HALLECK stated that it was the closing article of the bill of rights of Iowa.

Mr. BOTTS suggested that it was probably the people of Iowa who got it in that way. He submitted to the House, whether this devotion to the particular States from which gentlemen happened to come, was proper here. No man reverenced the feeling more than himself—attachment to the place of his nativity. But may not this feeling be carried too far? Should not gentlemen on this floor remember that they are no longer cititizens of New York, or Missouri, Iowa, or Michigan, but citizens of California. This Convention should not reject the experience of others that had gone before it. It should draw wisdom from the spirit and meaning of all their constitutions, but not servilely copy them. He did not see why this Convention was not as capable of being original as any other that had ever met. He hoped gentlemen would not make a constitution like an old woman's spencer—composed of shreds and patches. If the amendment which he proposed did not meet the views of the House, let them alter the phraseology, but let there be at least one original section in the Constiution.

Mr. SEMPLE said: There is one important principle involved in the amendment, which requires some expression of opinion. It should be borne in mind, that there is a marked difference between the Federal Constitution, and that of a State. The Constitution of the United States, is a delegation of power from a confederation of sovereign and independent States. By the consent of the whole, each State is limited to a certain extent; and such powers as are not expressly prescribed in the Constitution, are reserved to the people. As it is impossible for the people, individually, to regulate taxes, organise towns and villages, and make and amend laws, they form a Legislature to conduct these operations for them. That Legislature is amenable to them, for the faithful discharge of its duties, either annually or biennially. No other state sovereignty can interfere with these rights. If the Legislature abuse its powers by passing injurious or objectionable laws, the people form a new Legislature to repeal or amend them. But for the general welfare of all, each State has delegated to the confederacy a portion of its sovereignty. If this were not so, any one of them would have power to levy war. They reserve, however, all rights pertaining to the regulation of their local affairs, as States. The General Government has no power to interfere with them in their individual capacity. Congress is therefore prohibited, by the Constitution, from infringing upon these reserved powers. Its duties are to regulate navigation and commerce with foreign nations, to supervise the affairs of the Republic, to declare war, and impose taxes for the support of the Government. All power which is not expressly forbidden by the Federal Constitution, is left to the people and their representatives in their State capacity. He (Mr. Semple) was opposed to all encroachments of the General Government on the rights of the States. And when gentlemen talk about restricting the Legislature from the exercise of any rights reserved to the people by the Constitution of the United States, it is assuming a power not delegated to this Convention. Are we to say how many sheriffs, and how many coroners are to be in the State? If so, why have a Legislature at all? It is impossible to direct your State Legislature what it shall do. You can only say what it shall not do—you can only embody certain fundamental principles of government in your Constitution for the protection of minorities and the well-being of the mass—majorities can protect themselves. All measures not expressly prohibited in the Constitution, are fair subjects of legislative action. He was opposed to the amendment on these grounds.

Mr. Botts wished to know if the gentleman from Sonoma (Mr. Semple) meant to deny the right of the people to maintain their own power? If such a doctrine was maintained on this floor, it should be recorded on the journal. But he (Mr. Botts) thought he knew that gentleman too well in private life, to suppose that upon calm consideration, he would oppose, by his vote, the principle embodied in the last amendment. The gentleman maintains that all power is in the hands of the people, and if they have not parted with it, it is there still. No, sir; all power is in the hands of the people, whether they have delegated it to others or not. The government is subservient to the Constitution, and the ministers of that government are the servants of the people. They have no power except what they derive from the people. All the power committed to their hands is delegated to them through the Constitution. If it does not come through the Constitution, it does not come all. The Constitution is the message of the people to their servants, and what they do not grant in that way, they do not grant at all.

Mr. McCarver thought it would be very easy to make a constitution here that would take away one man's property and give it to another. The bill of rights declares what powers the people have, and the Constitution of the State consists of restrictions, not of delegated powers. The difference between the Federal Constitution and that of a State, is, that the people of the States in whom all power is inherent, have delegated a certain portion of their State sovereignty to the General Government. The Constitution of the United States, therefore, consists of expressed delegated powers. The Constitution of a State is a constituiion of restrictions. By accepting it, the people agree not to exercise the powers therein expressly prohibited. It is a constitution of restrictions that we should form here. It is not questioned that the people have a right to pass such laws as they please; but the powers not enumerated here, remain in the hands of the people and their agents. He (Mr. McCarver) could see no necessity for the amendment. The bill of rights, already adopted, declares that all power is inherent in the people, and this covers the whole subject.

Mr. Gwin said if he understood the gentleman from Sonoma, (Mr. Semple,) the doctrine broached by him, that the people in their legislative capacity have a right to violate the Constitution, was such as he could not sanction. He would like to see any man go back to his constituents after recording his vote in favor of such a monstrous doctrine.

Mr. Semple claimed to make a few additional remarks. Although he had as high a regard for the will of his constituents as any gentleman on this floor, he wished it distinctly understood that he contended for the doctrine that the people have a right to do anything which is not a violation of the Constitution; and so long as he could record his vote against any declaration to the contrary, he would do so. Whenever he was refused that liberty, he would resign his seat and tell the people he could serve them no longer. He held that whenever the State of California is admitted as a State, her right to legislate for herself is beyond the reach of any other power; that it is beyond the reach of Congress; that Congress is inferior to the State Legislature, because the Legislature is the direct emanation of the people; that Congress is limited in its powers, while the Legislature is no further limited than by the desire of the people. He would glory in recording his vote upon the principle that the Legislature of California, when formed, is the superior power, and not to be dictated to by any other power than that of the people who constituted it. The difference between the Constitution of the United States and that of a State is exemplified in the very article under discussion. The Federal Constitution is a limited Government, granted by certain sovereignties—that is to say by the sovereign people in their sovereign capacity. The State Legislature, under the specified restrictions imposed upon it by the people themselves, is a direct emanation from the people, and is annually or biennially responsible to them at the ballot-box. Here is where the powers of the State Government are limited. This Convention is not called upon to tell the people what they shall do, but what they shall not do. By the adoption of the Constitution, formed by their delegates, imposing certain restrictions upon them, they make it their act. We are sent here to tell them that because they are a majority they are not to infringe upon great general rights and great general principles. What says your bill of rights? It says, in the first place, that the people are the sovereigns. It then goes on to specify certain inalienable rights, and to provide that those rights shall not be infringed upon. The people agree, by adopting the Constitution, that so long as they are members of the community they will not infringe on those special rights; but they reserve the control over all others not restricted by the Constitution. He (Mr. Semple) was always opposed to the exercise of any power by Congress which is not expressly delegated to it by the Constitution of the United States. No member of this body went further than he did for a strict construction of the Constitution. He went for a strict construction of all Constitutions. He was willing, in forming this Constitution, that the powers not herein expressly delegated should be withheld. But by whom? By the State, or by the people in their individual capacity. It must be by the people in some capacity—either individual or legislative. He would be proud to record his vote against any restriction upon the people of California, except where they chose to impose restrictions upon themselves. In every respect, where restrictions are not made, they possess and have a right to exercise all the power. This is the doctrine of State rights. It is the pure doctrine of the right of a sovereign State to enjoy all power which she has not, by her own action, restricted. The will of the sovereign is the law. The people of the State say they will not make certain laws. How do they say it? By this Constitution. Wherever they have not thus restricted their own power, they have a right to enact such laws as they please. He (Mr. Semple) was ever ready to maintain this doctrine on this floor or before his constituents.

Mr. Gwin remarked that all the amendment declares is, that the powers not delegated are reserved. If it went beyond that he would be unwilling to vote for it. This is merely to protect the people from the violation of their rights. The Constitution of the United States has no reference to the question under consideration. There is nothing in this clause but a great declaration—that all power not specially delegated to the legislature is reserved to the people. It has nothing to do with Congress—no reference either directly or indirectly to it. It is a declaration embraced in every Constitution in the United States, and he (Mr. Gwin) would be unwilling to vote for a Constitution that did not contain it.

Mr. Semple asked what Constitution contained it?

Mr. Gwin said that he believed that it was in all.

Mr. Halleck, in behalf of the Committee, (the chairman of which was absent,) stated that the article from the Constitution of Iowa was selected on account of its brevity. It was to be found in four other Constitutions of the States, nearly in the same words. He thought it could not be improved, and hoped that it would be adopted.

Mr. Hastings said it occurred to him that there was no necessity for further discussion on this subject, inasmuch as there appeared to be no necessity for the article at all. Why declare that all rights not herein enumerated are reserved to the people? Would it not be true without such a declaration? Does the mere assertion make it any more true? Gentlemen seem to be afraid that if they omit one right the people will loose it altogether. He would not attempt to explain his conclusions, lest they might be misunderstood; and would therefore vote for any amendment to leave the article out.

The question was then taken on Mr. Botts' amendment, and it was rejected.

Mr. Semple said he was perfectly satisfied to vote for the amendment offered by Mr. Gwin.

Mr. Gwin hoped the gentleman would pardon him. He really thought he was opposed to the amendment.

Mr. Botts had just that objection to it—that two gentlemen having precisely opposite opinions could consistently vote for the same amendment.

Mr. Semple did not perceive, upon a more careful examination of the amendment, that there was any difference of opinion after all between himself and the gentleman from San Francisco.

Mr. Sherwood thought the report of the Committee covered the whole ground.

The question was then taken on the amendment offered by Mr. Gwin, and it was rejected.

The question recurring on the original section, being the 16th, as reported by the Committee, it was adopted.

On motion of Mr. Gwin, the Committee then rose and reported the bill of rights to the House.

The Chair stated that the question would be on the adoption of the report.

Mr. Gwin said it was not intended that the bill of rights should be adopted now. He proposed that it should be recommitted to the Select Committee for the purpose of having it made complete and perfect for the future vote of the House, section by section, when the votes would be taken by yeas and nays.

Mr. McCarver thought it necessary to make some disposition of it; and he presumed the proper course would be to let it remain in the House, to be called up at any future time.

On motion of Mr. McCarver, the report was received and laid upon the table, subject to call.

Mr. Botts offered the following resolution, which was unanimously adopted:

Resolved, That the officiating clergy of this House be admitted to the privileged seats of the House.

On motion, the Convention then adjourned to 12 o'clock to-morrow.

WEDNESDAY, SEPTEMBER 12, 1849.

In Convention, prayer by Rev. Senor Antonio Ramirez.

The journal of yesterday was read and approved.

On motion of Mr. Gilbert, it was

Resolved, That an Engrossing Committee, to consist of three members, be appointed by the Chair.

The President appointed as the Committee, Messrs. Gilbert, Dent, and Tefft.

On motion of Mr. Hastings, it was

Resolved, That a Committee of five be appointed by the President, to report to this Convention, what, in their opinion, should constitute the boundary of the State of California.

The President appointed, as the Committee, Messrs. Hastings, Sutter, Reid, La Guerra, and Rodriguez.

Mr. McCarver submitted the following resolution:

Resolved, That a Committee of —— be appointed, to report on that portion of the schedule to be appended to the Constitution, which relates to districting, fixing the number of members for both branches of the Legislature, and for the apportionment of the same.

Mr. McCarver said it was true the schedule was to be appended to the Constitution, yet it seemed to him there was no reasonable ground for not allowing it to go before a separate committee. It would not conflict with the duties of any other committee, and some of the members of the House not engaged upon the business of the Select Committee already existing, could prepare a schedule for the House.

Mr. Dimmick desired that the proposed committee should consist of one member from each district. He thought the districts should be all represented.

Mr. McCarver preferred a small committee.

Mr. Sherwood hoped the gentleman from Sacramento (Mr. McCarver) would not press his motion. The Select Committee on the Constitution had already laid over a number of articles for the schedule. He did not think it would be expedient to form another committee.

Mr. Gwin differed entirely from the gentleman last up. The resolution offered by Mr. McCarver had reference to the apportionment which had never come up in the Select Committee. It was no portion of the duty of that Committee to report a schedule. They might report certain provisions to be embraced in the schedule, but he did not think it was their duty to report a schedule, which is a separate and distinct portion of the labors of the Convention. It evidently did not seem proper that one committee should have the whole labor to perform, while other members were going about doing nothing.

Mr. Jones moved to amend the resolution by providing that a committee be appointed to report a schedule for the Convention, without reference to any particular portion. His only object was to make it the duty of this committee to report all the legitimate material of a schedule for the action of the House.

Mr. Sherwood said, that as there seemed to be considerable doubt as to what belonged to the Constitution and what should be embraced in the schedule, he thought the schedule should be referred to the Select Committee. If another committee was appointed, the Constitution would be garbled and incomplete.

Mr. Gwin was in favor of the resolution, and opposed to the amendment offered by the gentleman from San Joaquin (Mr. Jones.) The original resolution referred a distinct question to a separate committee. The question of the apportionment was one of vital importance. It should have the fullest consideration from a committee unembarrassed by other duties.

Mr. Halleck would merely ask one question, whether the committee proposed could do anything till the number of members was designated in the body of the Constitution.

Mr. McCarver was not satisfied that the people of his part of the country would be willing to accept any report that the Select Committee might choose to make. It was the largest committee he had ever heard of, in a body of this character. Gentlemen who supported a measure in this committee, would be very apt to support it in the House; and having the majority, it would of course prevail. There could be no impropriety in appointing a small committee, as proposed in the resolution. When that committee made its report, there would be no member to say, you supported that measure in committee, and, therefore, must go for it now.

Mr. Noriego remarked, that the gentleman from Sacramento (Mr. McCarver) founded his argument on the ground, that each member of this grand committee, consisting of two delegates from each district, felt himself bound to sustain in the House whatever had been acted upon in committee; that consequently, having a majority in the House, they would carry any measure they thought proper to propose. He (Mr. Noriego) ventured to assert that the members of that Committee considered themselves as free to give their votes on any subject in the House, as they did in committee. Whatever they objected to there, they would as freely object to here.

Mr. Shannon said it appeared to him that this matter of the apportionment properly belonged within the body of the Constitution itself, and should not, therefore, be taken out of the hands of the Select Committee and consigned to another. He contended that even if the House thought proper to appoint another committee, this subject should be embodied in the Constitution, and not in the schedule. It would be impossible to know what to do, or what to place in this schedule until the Select Committee had reported. He called the attention of the gentleman from San Francisco (Mr. Gwin) to some precedents on this subject, as he seemed so extremely anxious to follow precedents. In the Constitution of New York, the districting of the State forms the 5th article. It is not placed in any schedule. In the Constitution of Louisiana, the boundaries of the State form the very first article. In the Constitution of South Carolina, the State is districted in the third article. He believed the rule was almost universal. It was the case in most of the constitutions throughout the States. A majority of them, or if not a majority, (because in some States there is not a word said about establishing the limits,) at least in those States which he presumed would be the best authority with the gentleman from San Francisco, (Mr. Gwin,) the boundaries, as well as the districting of the State, are embraced in the body of the Constitution itself, and not left to the schedule.

Mr. Jones. The gentleman from Sacramento (Mr. Shannon) has made one unfortunate quotation at least, for the Constitution of Louisiana contains a schedule in which the first representation is a portion. It is in the 8th article of the the schedule. The gentleman has most strangely hit upon, perhaps, the only two Constitutions which do not apportion the first representation in the schedule, where there is any apportionment made. He refers to the different constitutions of the States, and asks if a majority of them do not contain the clause districting the States and apportioning the representation, in the body of the Constitution. I have myself looked over the constitutions slightly within the past few minutes, and I find that Maine, Pennsylvania, Delaware, Kentucky, Tennessee, Indiana, Louisiana, Illinois, Alabama, Missouri, Michigan, and Arkansas, all have formed these schedules, and all have temporarily apportioned the representation of the State in the schedules. I admit that this is a mere temporary thing—that the schedule has nothing to do with the organic law of the State. Its object is well expressed by the schedule of Louisiana, that "no inconvenience may arise from the change from a Territorial to a State Government." These sudden changes are always apt to produce confusion and inconvenience, and it is deemed necessary to make some provision for them, in the form of a schedule. The organic law of the State is the Constitution, properly so called. In the meaning of terms, then, the schedule is not the Constitution, or a part of the Constitution, and does not fall within the province of the Select Committee. By the resolution appointing that committee, they were instructed to report upon a plan, or any portion of a plan, of a State Constitution. The schedule is not a part of a State Constitution; it is not the organic law. If the gentleman will examine one or two of these Constitutions, he will find that the first portion of the schedule is under the head of ordinance. No man will say an ordinance is a part of the Constitution. It falls peculiarly within the schedule. The districting of the State, perhaps, would fall within the limits of the Constitution; but the first apportionment should be within the schedule. Certainly, I do not wish to deprive this Committee of any of the powers which have been delegated to it by this Convention. I am not disposed to find fault even with my friend from Sacramento, (Mr. Shannon,) who clamed fifteen votes for his district. Yet, though I am willing to listen to the suggestions of this Committee on the general provisions of the Constitution, when it comes to the apportionment of the State, I want the eight votes of Sacramento on this floor; I want the six votes of San Joaquin, and the eight votes of San Francisco. It is for that reason that I support the proposition to make a small committee, which will not consider itself bound to support its own propositions, to the exclusion of all others; but which will come before the Convention with any suggestions it may think proper to make, as a very small portion of this body. I have heard members of this Committe call upon members on this floor to support every measure reported by the Committee, and I have heard them denounced because they did not think proper to do so. I have one great reason to give for the position which I shall take here. That reason is contained in a statement which I hold in my hand. Without pressing it upon the attention of the House, I would merely state, that by it I am prepared to prove that 740 votes will rule this House, against 4,429 votes, which are entitled to be represented here. I am prepared to adopt no such principle—a principle which, in the words used the other day on this floor, would emasculate my district.

Mr. Tefft. Gentlemen seem to mistake entirely the ground upon which this resolution is based. It is the duty of the Select Committee to apportion the number of representatives. This special committee is to apportion the districts, and say how many representatives each district is to be entitled to. This certainly will clash with the duties of the Committee already existing, because it is the business of that Committee to state the number of members that shall be sent to the Legislature; to fix the size and general organization of the legislative department of the Government. That seems to me a sufficient reason why this resolution should not be acted upon now. Until the report of the general Committee on that subject is made, it would be folly to appoint a special Committee to work entirely in the dark. As to the fling made at the committee by the gentleman who last spoke, I consider his remarks entirely unwarranted, and unworthy of notice. I would call his attention to the following quotation from Junius: "There are men who never aspire to hatred—who never rise above contempt."

Mr. Jones. I call npon the gentleman to put that down in writing. I think, Mr. President, that any gentleman who is the subject of offensive remarks in a parliamentary body, has a right, with or without the permission of the House, to claim that those remarks shall be put down in writing, that the House may take such notice of them as they think proper. Such, I believe, is the rule of all parliamentary bodies. I wish them placed upon the journal.

The Chair. There certainly is a rule prohibiting personal remarks from being made by any of the members. It was hoped by the Chair that all such remarks would have been avoided; but where offensive remarks are made, they may, at the request of the gentleman, be placed upon the journal, by permission of the House. The Chair is unwilling, himself, to have these remarks entered upon the journal of the House.

Mr. Jones. I am merely referring, Mr. President, to that general rule which protects members of a parliamentary body from gross and insulting remarks from any member. I rise to claim the protection of the House from such remarks, and, I believe, the first thing to be done is to require the Secretary to put those remarks down. I call upon the Secretary to put them down.

Mr. Gwin. I believe the general practice is to declare the remarks out of order. The gentleman using the offensive remarks is called to order, and the House decides whether he has exceeded the parliamentary limits.

Mr. Lippett. With the permission of the House, I will read, from Cushing's Manual, a passage applicable to this case. (Mr. Lippett then read the usage as laid down by Cushing) The above is the course of proceeding established by writers of the greatest authority, and ought uniformly to be pursued. It might, however, be improved by the member objecting to the remarks, requiring that the words shall be written down at once, and have them entered upon the minutes.

The President. The Chair will adopt the latter suggestion.

Mr. Tefft. I do not intend to retract or apologise for anything I said. I had no idea a simple quotation would have raised such commotion in the House. The gentleman had taken occasion to do what he had no right to do, to question the motives of every member of the Committee. I have been laboring under sickness for some days, and did not wish to enter into any long argument on the matter.

Mr. Hastings. Is the House to pause until this matter is disposed of, or are we to proceed?

The Chair is of opinion that this difficulty must be disposed of before the House can proceed to business.

Mr. Jones. I will read the remarks, as I have written them down. I read them for correction: "The gentleman from San Luis Obispo says that the remarks of the gentleman from San Joaquin do not deserve to be noticed, and that he would call his attention to the following passage from Junius—'there are men who never rise to hatred, or reach beyond contempt.'"

Mr. TEFFT. If the gentleman was better acquainted with the works of Junius, he would not make that as a quotation.

Mr. JONES. I am better acquainted with the duties of a gentleman than with the language of Junius. Let the gentleman state the words himself.

Mr. JONES. I will state the words if the House desire it, but not at the instance of the gentleman.

Mr. NORIEGO desired that those who did not understand the English language might be excused from giving any vote on this subject. The question appeared to be respecting certain English words, which they did not understand, and they desired to be excused from voting.

On motion, the Spanish delegation were accordingly excused from voting.

Mr. TEFFT. I want the words written precisely as I said them. I referred to the gentleman's reflections on the course taken, and which probably would be taken, by the Select Committee on the Constitution, and I stated that his remarks were worthy of the following passage from Junius: "There are men who never aspire to hatred—who never rise above contempt."

Mr. BOTTS offered a resolution prohibiting members from indulging in personalities, and requiring them in such cases to apologize to the House. He thought gentlemen had gone entirely too far in impugning the motives of members. In the present case, both the gentleman who made the imputation, and the gentleman who threw it back, ought to apologize to the House. He had been opposed to this Committee himself from the beginning; he had fought it tooth and nail; he had called it the great Committee and the mammoth Committee; but if he had cast any personal reflection upon the motives of members who composed it, he hoped the House would pardon him. He was not aware of having done so. He was ready to set the good example, if he had expressed himself improperly, of asking pardon of the House, which he now did in advance.

Mr. SHANNON suggested that the resolution be offered as an addition to the rules of the House.

The CHAIR was of opinion, that the rules of the House already existing were sufficient to sustain the object of the resolution. Where two members are out of order, an apology from both is due to the House. If in the opinion of the House, the gentleman who impugned the motives of the Committee, and the gentleman who threw back the imputation, were both out of order, it was their duty upon being called upon, to make an appropriate apology to the House.

Mr. GWIN concurred in the remarks of the gentlemen from Monterey (Mr. Botts) on this subject. He (Mr. Gwin) had seen the bitterest hatred and most ferocious controversy spring from a smaller matter than this. Every gentleman here should bear in mind that this body is assembled for a great national object; and should be cautious not to wound the feelings of a fellow-member. He hoped it would be a settled principle that no matter how much excitement—how much difference of opinion might exist, (for it was impossible to form a Constitution without severe collisions, in the heat of debate,) all personalities would be avoided. If there are collisions, let them be mental and not personal collisions. He was sure the gentleman who had made use of the words deemed offensive, would not hesitate to say, that if he had misconstrued the remarks of the member from San Joaquin (Mr. Jones,) he would withdraw them. It is usual in cases of this kind, when one member takes exceptions to the remarks of another, for that member to demand an explanation from the gentleman who makes those remarks. If the gentleman from San Luis Obispo had applied to the gentleman from San Joaquin to know whether he intended a personal reflection upon this Committee, and that gentleman had replied that he did, then the offensive words might probably be applicable. That gentleman, however, took it for granted, without demanding any explanation, that the gentleman from San Joaquin was impugning the motives of the Committee.

Mr. Tefft doubted very much whether there was any gentleman on this floor more anxious than he was to maintain good order and friendly relations between the members. He insisted upon it that he had not now transgressed that principle. He had borne many reflections upon his native State; but he had always kept his seat, in deference to those who were older and more experienced, and whose views he desired to hear in preference to giving his own. In calling the attention of the House to the remarks of the member from San Joaquin, he did not conceive that he had gone beyond the legitimate bounds of debate. If it was the opinion of the House that he had done so, he would cheerfully apologize to the House, but not to the gentleman, who, he conceived had impugned the motives of the Committee. If it was not the intention of that gentleman to impugn the motives of the Committee, then, of course, the offensive quotation was not applicable to him.

Mr. Jones asked if it was possible that he, as a member from San Joaquin, in opposing the principle of allowing smaller districts an equal vote with his own in the formation of this Constitution, should be considered as impugning the motives of any person, or insulting any committee? Was it possible that the right of speech was so far prohibited on this floor, that he could not advocate the principle incorporated in the bill of rights without having it said that he was impugning the motives of the members of this House who did not happen to represent so large a population as he did? It was upon the broad principle that the representation here should be according to population, that he had based his remarks; and he had said what he believed to be true, and what he must believe to be true until convinced to the contrary. It had been said upon the floor of this House, and out of the House, that members of this Committee had been called upon to sustain by their votes the reports of the Committee. If such was the case, and he believed it to be true, were the people of San Joaquin to be told that they had no right to protest against such a principle as this? He considered it to be one of their first rights, that they should not be cheated out of their representation in the Convention. He would not say that it was intended by the appointment of this Committee to do this, but he maintained that no course should be adopted in the House which would have that effect. He conceived that he had not done injustice to the Committee, because, if fault there was, the whole tenor of his remarks was to attribute the fault to the Convention. He did not consider that he had injured the feelings of any gentleman on that Committee. If there was any member who, perhaps, had a right to feel himself aggrieved, it was the gentleman from Sacramento, (Mr. Shannon,) but he (Mr. S.) was too much of a gentleman to rise in his place and——

Mr. Botts here called the gentleman from San Joaquin to order.

The President stated that he had seen with deep regret the effect of some very trivial disorders. He had heard the Committee on the Constitution spoken of in various ways. Sometimes it had been called the mammoth committee, which was by no means a respectful term; sometimes, the almighty committee, an equally disrespectful term; and various other epithets of opprobrium had been applied to it. Under the impression that the members of this body had too a high a respect for themselves to cast such reflections upon the Committee as would give offence, the Chair was disposed to allow the fullest liberty of speech, not incompatible with the dignity of the House. He regarded these remarks as made in a spirit of pleasantry, and with no intention of giving offence. But it was now evident that too much liberty had been taken with the Committee, and he hoped that both the gentlemen (Messrs. Jones and Tefft) would follow the example of the gentleman from Monterey, and apologize to the House.

Mr. Botts objected to this view of the matter. He had never apologized to the House for having called this a mammoth committee; but if the House said that there was anything personal in calling it a mammoth committee, he would amply apologize now.

The Chair did not think it was personal.

Mr. SHERWOOD said that, in regard to the difficulty before the House, it seemed to him it could be adjusted in the simplest way imaginable. If the gentleman from San Joaquin did not intend to impugn the motives of the Committee, he has liberty to make that statement to the House. The gentleman from San Luis Obispo would undoubtedly meet it by the withdrawal of the offensive remarks.

Mr. GWIN. The gentleman from San Joaquin, as he conceives, has been grossly insulted by the gentleman from San Luis Obispo. Is he to get up here and make an apology before that insult is withdrawn? It is the duty of the House to make these members settle the difficulty here. There should be no after settlement out of doors—no bloodshed resulting from what has transpired. The majesty and the power of the House should be brought to bear upon this case, and it should be settled before these gentlemen are permitted to leave their seats.

The CHAIR was of opinion that the gentleman from San Louis Opispo had apologized to the House.

Mr. GWIN said an apology to the House was not an apology to the gentleman who conceived himself insulted.

Mr. LIPPETT concurred with his friend from Sacramento (Mr. Sherwood.) He did not see any difficulty in regard to this matter. The member from San Luis Opispo has already stated to the House that the occasion of his making the offensive remarks was his understanding that the Committee to which he belonged had been attacked, and the motives of the members impugned by what fell from the gentleman from San Joaquin. The object, therefore, of the offensive remarks, was to throw back this imputation. Now, it certainly does not appear that there was any intention on the part of the gentleman from San Joaquin to cast any reflection upon the motives of that Committee. It would be a very simple matter then, for the gentleman from San Luis Obispo to state distinctly and formally to the House, that if the gentleman from San Joaquin did not intend, by anything he said, to impugn the motives of the Committee, he would withdraw his remarks. The gentleman from San Joaquin makes that statement; the gentleman withdraws his remarks, and the whole difficulty is settled.

Mr. WOZENCRAFT remarked, that the gentleman from San Joaquin had already denied having intended any personal remarks to the Committee. It was not necessary to call upon him again.

Mr. MOORE hoped his friend (Mr. Jones) would not require any apology here. If there was any misunderstanding let it be settled out of doors. He (Mr. Moore) would not trouble the House, if insulted, by asking any apology here.

Mr. GWIN said it was for that very reason he wanted it settled here. In all deliberative bodies, when a difficulty occurred, it was usual to close the doors. Having had some little experience in legislative bodies, he knew the importance of settling questions of this kind before they were permitted to go beyond the House. Another thing he wished to protest against, and that was, the sacredness of committees. He desired that there should be unlimited debate on all questions. This mammoth Committee was able to defend itself. But personalities should be avoided.

Mr. SHERWOOD thought this matter might easily be settled in the mode indicated. He desired that it should not be permitted to go out of the House. He trusted that withont further words the gentleman from San Joaquin would state exactly what he intended by his remarks.

The CHAIR said the gentleman had already made that statement.

Mr. GWIN then moved that the gentleman from San Luis Obispo be required to withdraw the offensive words.

Mr. TEFFT said it was strange that he should be called upon to apologize to the gentleman, after having explained the motive which actuated him in using those words. If the gentleman from San Joaquin did not impugn the motives of the Committee, then the quotation had no bearing upon him. It was only applied to him on that ground.

Mr. Lippett moved that the House receive this statement as satisfactory.

Mr. Price wished to know before this vote was taken, whether this reconciliation was entirely satisfactory to these gentlemen—whether there was anything left upon their minds for an out-door settlement. He had not yet heard distinctly the perfect withdrawal of the offensive words, and the perfect acceptance of such withdrawal by the other gentleman.

Mr. Jones said the gentleman had apologized to the House, but not to him. He did not take that as an apology.

Mr. Halleck remarked, that when the words were read as originally stated, the gentleman from San Luis Obispo had disclaimed applying them to the gentleman from San Joaquin, if that gentleman did not impugn the motives of the Committee. As he (Mr. Jones) disclaimed having made this imputation, then the offensive words were clearly withdrawn, and the difficulty was settled.

Mr. Gwin wished to know if the withdrawal of the remarks was satisfactory to the gentleman from San Joaquin. [Mr. Jones said it was.] He wished to know also, if the statement of the gentleman from San Joaquin, that he intended no personal imputation on the motives of the Committee, was satisfactory to the gentleman from San Luis Obispo? [Mr. Tefft replied that it was.] He (Mr. Gwin) then moved that the reconciliation be accepted by the House, which motion was adopted, and the difficulty was thus amicably adjusted.

The question then recurring on the resolution of Mr. McCarver—

Mr. Botts said he would vote against it. The apportionment was, to his mind, one of the most important features of the Constitution. It was well known that he was opposed to the original formation of the Committee of twenty. (He hoped there was nothing personal in that.) But since it had been the pleasure of the House to form that Committee, he did not see how any portion of its work could, with propriety, be taken out of its hands. He voted for the provision a few days since, that representation should be according to population. He conceived that in doing so, he was giving instructions to this very Committee, to apportion the representation of this State upon that principle. It had been well objected here, that it is utterly impossible that this single portion of the forming of the Constitution can be taken out of the whole and submitted to the action of a separate committee, whilst so much depending upon it is in the hands of another. This is a portion that most requires concert and co-operation. He hoped it would not be the pleasure of the House to adopt the resolution.

The question was then taken, and the resolution was rejected.

Mr. Norton, from a majority of the Committee on the Constitution, made a report, which was received and referred to the Committee of the Whole.

Mr. Gwin made a minority report from the same committee, which was received and referred to the same committee.

COMMITTEE OF THE WHOLE.

The House then resolved itself into Committee of the Whole, Mr. Lippett in the Chair, on so much of the report of the Committee on the Constitution as relates to the right of suffrage.

The first section of the report of the Committee being under consideration, as follows:

Sec. 1. Every white male citizen of the United States, of the age of twenty-one years, who shall have been a resident of the State six months next preceding the election, and the county, in which he claims his vote twenty days, shall be entitled to vote at all elections which are now, or hereafter may be, authorized by law.

Mr. Gilbert moved to amend as follows:

After the words "United States," and before the word "of," insert, "and every male citizen of Mexico, who shall have elected to become a citizen of the United States, under the treaty of peace, exchanged and ratified at Queretaro, on the 30th day of May, 1848."

Mr. Gilbert said he would read from the Treaty of Peace, a couple of sections which explained in full the reasons which induced him to offer the amendment:

Art. VIII. Mexicans now established in territories previously belonging to Mexico, and which remain for the future within the limits of the United States, as defined by the present treaty, shall be free to continue where they now reside, or to remove at any time to the Mexican Republic, retaining the property which they possess in the said territories, or disposing thereof, and removing the proceeds wherever they please, without being subjected, on this account, to any contribution, tax, or charge whatever.

Those who shall prefer to remain in the said territories, may either retain the title and rights of Mexican citizens, or acquire those of citizens of the United States. But they shall be under obligation to make their election within one year from the date of the exchange of ratifications of this treaty; and those who shall remain in the said territories after the expiration of that year, without having declared their intention to retain the character of Mexicans, shall be considered to have elected to become citizens of the United States.

In the said territories, property of every kind, now belonging to Mexicans not established there, shall be inviolably respected. The present owners, the heirs of these, and all Mexicans who may hereafter acquire said property by contract, shall enjoy, with respect to it, guaranties equally ample as if the same belonged to citizens of the United States.

Art. IX. The Mexicans who, in the territories aforesaid, shall not preserve the character of citizens of the Mexican Republic, conformably with what is stipulated in the preceding article, shall be incorporated into the union of the United States, and be admitted at the proper time (to be judged of by the Congress of the United States) to the enjoyment of all the rights of citizens of the United States, according to the principles of the Constitution; and, in the meantime, shall be maintained and protected in the free enjoyment of their liberty and property, and secured in the free exercise of their religion without restriction.

It seemed to him (Mr. Gilbert) that the section, as reported by the Committee, providing that "every white male citizen of the United States shall be entitled to the elective franchise," did not cover the whole ground. We wish to give every Mexican citizen residing in California, who becomes a citizen of the United States, the free right to vote. Under the 9th article of the treaty it would seem that they are not in fact American citizens, but require some further action of Congress to make them citizens of the United States. That article says: "shall be incorporated into the union of the United States, and be admitted at the proper time, (to be judged of by the Congress of the United States,) to the enjoyment of all the rights of citizens of the United States, according to the principles of the Constitution." If the Congress of the United States had done its duty to this country, it would have passed a law at the last session, admitting these citizens to all the powers and privileges of citizens of the United States. But, as it failed to do so, he (Mr. Gilbert) deemed it absolutely essential, in order to prevent any difficulty, that the amendment which he offered should be inserted in this clause. The meaning of the word "white," in the report of the Committee, was not generally understood in this country, though well understood in the United States; but that objection would be removed by the adoption of his amendment.

Mr. Botts said he had risen almost at the same time with his friend from San Francisco (Mr. Gilbert) to offer an amendment nearly, but not quite, indentical with that proposed by him. It was clear that by the adoption of the clause reported by the Committee, citizens of Mexico would be excluded from voting before they were made citizens of the United States by the Congress of the United States. His amendment was to insert the word "white" before "male citizens of Mexico."

Mr. Norton said he was instructed by the Committee to introduce an amendment to the first section. The reason why he did not do so, was because the amendment of Mr. Gilbert seemed to him to accomplish the object. He would read the amendment: after the words "United States," and before the word "of," to insert the words, "and every person who was a citizen of California after the 1st of May, 1848."

Mr. Botts said that the Committee had made a report; they could not order it to be altered. If any amendment was made to it, it must be made by the gentleman himself, (Mr. Norton.) He (Mr. Botts) wanted to come to the main principle—that unless provision is made for these persons the clause does not admit them. The gentleman from San Francisco (Mr. Gilbert) had left out an exceedingly important word. He (Mr. Botts) proposed to amend the amendment by inserting the word "white" before the words "male citizen of Mexico." He hoped it would be the will of the House that no citizens of the United States should be admitted to the elective franchise but white citizens. All he asked was that citizens of Mexico who had become citizens of the United States should be placed upon the same footing with ourselves; that white citizens alone should be admitted to the right of suffrage. He was sure there would not be any objection on their part to this course.

Mr. Noriego desired that it should be perfectly understood in the first place, what is the true signification of the word "white." Many citizens of California have received from nature a very dark skin; nevertheless, there are among them men who have heretofore been allowed to vote, and not only that, but to fill the highest public offices. It would be very unjust to deprive them of the privilege of citizens merely because nature had not made them white. But if, by the word "white," it was intended to exclude the African race, then it was correct and satisfactory.

Mr. Botts had no objection to color, except so far as it indicated the inferior races of mankind. He would be perfectly willing to use any words which would exclude the African and Indian races. 't was in this sense the word white had been understood and used. His only object was to exclude those objectionable races—not objectionable for their color, but for what that color indicates.

Mr. Gilbert hoped the amendment proposed by the gentleman from Monterey (Mr. Botts) would not prevail. He was confident that if the word "white" was introduced, it would produce great difficulty. The treaty has said that Mexican citizens, upon becoming citizens of the United States, shall be entitled to the rights and privileges of American citizens. It does not say whether those citizens are white or black, and we have no right to make the distinction. If they be Mexican citizens, it is sufficient; they are entitled to the rights and privileges of American citizens. No act of this kind could, therefore, have any effect. The treaty is above and superior to it.

Mr. Gwin would like to know from some gentleman acquainted with Mexican law, whether Indians and negroes are entitled to the privileges of citizenship under the Mexican Government.

Mr. Noriego understood the gentleman from Monterey (Mr. Botts) to say that Indians were not allowed to vote according to Mexican law.

Mr. Botts said that, on the contrary, it was because he believed they were, that the had offered the amendment. He wished to exclude them from voting.

Mr. Gwin asked the gentleman from Santa Barbara (Mr. Noriego) whether Indians and Africans were entitled to vote according to Mexican law.

Mr. Noriego said that, according to Mexican law, no race of any kind is excluded from voting.

Mr. Gwin wished to know if Indians were considered Mexican citizens?

Mr. Noriego said that so far were they considered citizens, that some of the first men in the Republic were of the Indian race.

Mr. Gwin had learned from the gentleman from Santa Barbara (Mr. Stearns) that there were twenty thousand Indians in Mexico. He wished to know whether these twenty thousand Indians were allowed to vote?

Mr. Foster said that, according to Mexican law, very few of the Indian race were admitted to the right of suffrage. They are restricted by some property qualification, or by occupation or mode of livelihood. But they are considered Mexican citizens according to the Constitution.

Mr. Hastings remarked that if, by the treaty of peace, these persons are all entitled to vote, they could not be excluded by this Convention from the enjoyment of that right. If they are not entitled to vote according to Mexican law, and hence according to the treaty, we should not allow them to vote. It would be a most injurious measure to permit the Indians of this country to vote. There are gentlemen who are very popular among the wild Indians, who could march hundreds up to the polls. There is no distinction between an Indian here and the remote tribes. An Indian in the mountains is just as much entitled to vote as anybody, if Indians are entitled to vote. But men who have Indian blood in their veins are not for that reason Indians. There are, perhaps, many persons resident in this country who have Indian blood, but who are not considered Indians. If the motion was in order, he (Mr. Hastings) would move to defer further action upon this matter until the law of Mexico on the subject could be procured. There was no necessity for haste in passing this section.

Mr. Dimmick trusted the motion would prevail, to defer the consideration of the subject. He held different opinions from some of the gentlemen who had spoken, as to the Mexican law in relation to the citizenship of Indians. He had supposed that Indians, in order to be entitled to the rights of citizenship in Mexico, were obliged to go through some form of naturalization, by which they became citizens. He arrived at this fact from having seen papers in the possession of Indians, who had received grants of lands, in which they went through certain forms of naturalization. He trusted the Convention would not act hastily in this matter; for he would be very unwilling to see the Indians of this country brought to the polls to vote in our elections. At the same time, where there was here and there a good Indian, capable of understanding our system of government, he had no objection to making such provision as would entitle him to vote.

Mr. Tefft had obtained some information in regard to this matter. He was disposed to differ from the gentleman from San Jose, (Mr. Dimmick.) The Mexican laws define, in the first place, what is a Mexican citizen; "any person born of Mexican parents, or under Mexican laws;" they declare that all Mexicans shall vote, having an income of $100 in labor, lands, &c. He (Mr. Tefft) would like to have further time to look into the Mexican laws, and, therefore, hoped the subject would be postponed. He desired that the House should act advisedly, and according to the treaty of peace.

Mr. Botts had no objection to deferring the consideration of the clause. He had no doubt in his mind that the statement made by the gentleman from San Luis Obispo (Mr. Tefft) was correct. But there was one doctrine urged here, that really astonished him—that the treaty of peace between the United States and Mexico, or any other treaty, could prescribe to this Convention what persons it should make voters in the State of California! The Congress of the United States could not do it. Were gentlemen not aware of that fact? They ought to be shouting hozannas to liberty, now that they were informed of it. The States of this Union are free and sovereign. They prescribe for themselves the right of suffrage. Gentlemen need not look to the treaty of peace for authority; it is competent for the people of this country to declare that no man, unless he have black hair and black eyes, shall vote. If that treaty had said, that none but the citizens of Mexico should vote, the Constitution of the United States prescribes that you shall fix your own elective qualifications. It particularly guards you against the abuse of the powers exercised by Congress.

Mr. Gwin had been endeavoring to get all the information possible on this subject. He had ascertained the fact, that by the passage of the amendment of his colleague, (Mr. Gilbert,) Indians would be permitted to vote. He found, that in the Constitution of Texas, (a State somewhat similar in the character of its population to this country,) there is the following restriction:

"Every free male person who shall have attained the age of twenty-one years, and who shall be a citizen of the United States, or who is, at the time of the adoption of this Constitution by the Congress of the United States, a citizen of the Republic of Texas, and shall have resided in this State one year next preceding an election, and the last six months within the district, county, city, or town, in which he offers to vote, (*Indians not taxed, Africans, and descendants of Africans, excepted,*) shall be deemed a qualified elector," &c.

He did not think the descendants of Indians should be excluded, but the pure uncivilized Indians should not be permitted to vote. It was stated to him, by an officer of the army, that in California there are a hundred tribes of Indians; that a few white persons control them; and that they would vote just as they were directed. He did not wish to limit the portion of the population that was in the habit of voting—those having property qualifications—but the restriction should be distinctly understood and defined. He would be in favor of saying, "Indians, but not the descendants of Indians."

Mr. Botts accepted the suggestion of the gentleman from San Francisco (Mr. Gwin;) instead of the word "white," to insert, "and every male citizen of Mexico, Indians, Africans, and the descendants of Africans excepted."

Mr. Gilbert rose to say a word or two in reply to the remarks of the gentleman from Monterey (Mr. Botts.) He was willing to go as far as that gentleman in defence of State rights, and as far as any member in the House to protect the States from encroachments on the part of Congress, but he differed from him in the reading of this treaty, and in the reading of the Constitution of the United States. He would call the gentleman's attention to the 6th article of the Constitution, section 2d:

"This Constitution, and the laws of the United States which shall be made in pursuance thereof, and all treaties made, or which shall be made, under the authority of the United States, shall be the supreme law of the land; and the Judges in every State shall be bound thereby, anything in the Constitution or laws of any State to the contrary notwithstanding."

This treaty is therefore the supreme law of the land. It appeared to him that nothing could more definitely settle the question. We cannot go beyond this treaty, and disfranchise any man who is admitted under the treaty to the rights of citizenship. Perhaps, so far as regards the election of Governor and State officers, we might prescribe the rules of voting; but we cannot, in this instance, where the Constitution guaranties certain rights to these persons, who have become citizens of the United States under the treaty, deprive them of those rights. The only question here is in regard to the proper time when they shall be entitled to vote, and the object of the amendment is to fix the time beyond doubt. He wished to make no invidious distinctions as to color, but to abide by the treaty of peace and the Constitution of the United States.

Mr. Hastings said that, upon further reflection, he presumed the gentleman from Monterey (Mr. Botts) would observe that if we do not recognize this treaty, no treaty of peace exists. We are then at war with Mexico. We have no treaty to protect us. We are protected by no authority whatsoever but that of physical force. We came here under this treaty; gentlemen sit in this Convention under this treaty; it is in virtue of this treaty alone that we are possessed of this territory. If we carry our principle of State rights so far as to say we are wholly independent, and need not regard treaties of the United States, why not, with the same propriety, carry it further, and say we need not regard the Constitution of the United States? If we violate the stipulations of this treaty, we violate the Constitution. The gentleman from Monterey (Mr. Botts) asserts that we have a right to declare that no man shall vote unless he have black hair and black eyes. This is a principle of State rights that cannot be maintained in the present case. We must include every citizen of Mexico which the treaty of peace admits to the right of citizenship. It is impossible to arrive at any other conclusion, unless we violate the treaty. If the principle be well founded, that we may exclude certain persons who are made citizens by the adoption of the treaty, and hence who are entitled to be regarded as citizens, may we not, with the same propriety, exclude every native Californian? We cannot do it. We dare not exclude one human being who was a citizen at the time of the adoption of that treaty. Every man who was a citizen then, is a citizen now, and will be while he lives in California, unless he declares his intention to remain a citizen of Mexico. Our Constitution must, therefore, conform to the treaty, or it is null and void.

Mr. Botts thought the doctrines which he had just heard urged were at least novel. He had heard many federal doctrines, but never any like these. He saw plainly, after all that was said about not having Whigs or Democrats here, that it was a shallow device. A new party had come up—one beyond the extreme of federalism; a party that contends that there is a power in the Executive of the United States to make a treaty contrary to the provisions of the Constitution. Were there any three men on this floor ready to record their names in support of this doctrine? But he desired that his own position should be well understood. He maintained that this treaty, so far as he knew, is binding in every clause, because it does not contradict the Constitution of the United States; it does not prescribe who shall be our voters. If it had made those citizens of Mexico directly citizens of the United States, it would not have said that they should be voters of the State of California. He granted, for the sake of argument, that these Indians are citizens of the United States, because they were citizens in Mexico. The question is still open whether they shall be voters. There are thousands of citizens of the United States who are not voters. Gentlemen should not confound the words. It does not follow that if a man be a citizen of the United States he shall be a voter. Was it necessary for him (Mr. Botts) to speak two minutes to put down forever the monstrous doctrine that the treaty-making power can transcend and set at naught the Constitution of the United States; and, least of all, that a citizen of the United States must necessarily be a voter?

Mr. Gwin said that in Virginia there are thousands who spend their lives and die without ever having the privilege of voting. There is a property qualification required there, as also, he believed, in some other States of the Union. As the gentleman (Mr. Botts) said, we could exclude all these Californians from the privilege of voting; but that is not our intention. It would not be right or just. This is a very important question. If we permit every Mexican citizen to vote, under our free and liberal system of voting, we would enlarge the vote immensely to what it was under the former Government here. For instance, there were certain laws, under the Mexican Government, that no man should vote unless he could read and write. We are to declare who shall have a right to vote. We only exercise the same privilege that was exercised by the previous Government. Indians should be excluded, but not the descendants of Indians. It must be by special enactment if they are permitted to vote.

Mr. Hastings asked if the treaty did not design that those citizens referred to should be entitled to all the privileges of free citizens of the United States.

Mr. Gilbert said that according to the principles of the Constitution they should be admitted to all the rights and privileges of free citizens of the United States.

Mr. Hoppe had a different construction of this clause of the Constitution from some of his friends in the House. His friend from San Francisco (Mr. Gwin) observed that there was a property qualification in some of the States. He (Mr. Hoppe) admitted that; but at the same time it should be remembered that the States of the Union, and that of California, were admitted into our Republic in a different manner. California was admitted by a treaty between the United States and Mexico. Now we have taken a solemn obligation that we will support the Constitution of the United States. That treaty gives the right to every Mexican citizen, who becomes thereby a citizen of the United States, to enjoy the freedom and privileges which we enjoy. What does the Constitution say? It says that all treaties made under the authority of the United States shall be the supreme law of the land. Suppose we pass a law prohibiting Mexican citizens from the full enjoyment of the free elective franchise. What will be the effect? When this Constitution is presented to the Congress of the United States it will be rejected, because it is in direct conflict with the treaty of peace and the Constitution of the United States. He (Mr. Hoppe) was prepared to vote in favor of Mr. Gilbert's proposition. He thought the House was fully satisfied on the subject.

Mr. DIMMICK differed from most of the gentlemen who had spoken on this question. He admitted that the spirit of the treaty of peace, if made in accordance with the Constitution of the United States, and not in violation thereof, is the strongest law that could be adduced; that it is stronger than any Constitution we can form here, and which the people might adopt. But upon looking at this treaty he found that it says that Mexican citizens shall be received at a suitable time to all the rights of citizens of the United States. What are the rights of citizens of the United States? Are we to admit them to rights superior to those which we enjoy ourselves? Does any one pretend to assert that we are under obligations to do this? Does it necessarily follow that the right of suffrage is one of these rights? He contended not. It is not necessarily the right of a citizen. He believed that the States in their sovereign capacity have a right to make their own regulations in respect to this matter. The right of suffrage is not possessed by all citizens; it is not a general right. We admit these Mexicans subject to the same restrictions to which American citizens are subject. We are not necessarily compelled to make Indians citizens, entitled to the elective franchise, when many of our own citizens in the United States are not entitled to such privilege. He (Mr. Dimmick) would go as far as any gentleman on this floor, to admit to all the privileges of citizenship such of them as are capable of understanding our institutions, and who are responsible and orderly citizens; but he would be very unwilling to admit the wild Indian tribes of California to the right of suffrage. He did not think such a thing was ever contemplated by the treaty. Those Indians who have become civilized, and who were entitled by the Mexican Government to hold lands and pay taxes, are not objectionable. They should be allowed the elective franchise; and as for the mixed race, descended from the Indians and Spaniards, he certainly was in favor of permitting them to enjoy the right of suffrage as liberally as any American citizen. It is no objection to them that they have Indian blood in their veins. Some of the most honorable and distinguished families in Virginia are descended from the Indian race. It was the proudest boast on the floor of Congress of one of Virginia's greatest statesmen, that he had Indian blood in his veins. At the same time, it is absolutely necessary to embody in this Constitution such a restriction as will prevent the wild tribes from voting. He believed that these Indian tribes were never Mexican citizens in the full sense of the word; that it was necessary, according to Mexican law, for them to receive naturalization papers before they could enjoy that privilege. He would like to ascertain the fact, whether the Mexican laws declared these Indians free. He was under the impression that they were held in some kind of peonage or servitude. He could not vote or act understandingly until he knew more of the Constitution and laws of Mexico.

Mr. GWIN said it was very important that this matter should not be misunderstood. The question raised by gentlemen as to the Constitution of the United States, is not applicable. Louisiana was purchased precisely as the United States purchased California. The very same words, in regard to citizenship, that you find in the treaty with Mexico, are in the treaty with France. Yet when Louisiana formed a State Constitution, she put a restriction upon the right of suffrage; she declared that only such and such persons should vote; and if she violated the Constitution of the United States, she did so according to this construction. In the old Constitution of Louisiana, it is provided, that no person shall be a representative who, at the time of his election, is not a free white male citizen of the United States, &c. So much for the representative; now for the voter. Recollect that Louisiana was purchased from France, and that all the rights were guarantied by treaty to the citizens of Louisiana that are now guarantied to the citizens of California. There was a great mixture of population in Louisiana as there is here. The Constitution of that State says: "In all elections held by the people, every free white male, who has been two years a citizen of the United States, who has attained the age of twenty-one years, and resided in the State two consecutive years next preceeding the election, and the last year thereof in the parish in which he offers to vote, shall have the right of voting," &c.

In regard to the property qualification, it should be strictly guarded. Gentlemen had heard of the celebrated Plaquemine vote. Vast numbers of votes were created there by buying up the public domain, and transferring it to parties who paid the taxes on it. They were then voters. It was certainly within the power of this Convention to impose such limitations as it thought expedient. He (Mr. Gwin) was disposed to adopt the suggestion of the gentleman from Los Angelos (Mr. Foster,) who proposed that those Indians, and those only, who had the right of suffrage in Mexico, should be entitled to the same privilege here.

On motion of Mr. SHERWOOD, the Committee, without taking the question, rose, reported progress, and asked leave to sit again.

The House then adjourned to 8 o'clock, P. M.

AFTERNOON SESSION, 8 O'CLOCK, P. M.

On motion, the House resolved itself into Committee of the Whole, Mr. Dimmick in the chair, on the report of the Committee on the Constitution relative to the right of suffrage.

The consideration of Mr. Bott's amendment to the amendment of Mr. Gilbert was taken up as follows :

To insert after the word "Mexico," and before the word "who," the words "Indians not taxed, Africans and the descendants of Africans excepted."

Mr. DENT said it appeared to him, that if the treaty of peace between the United States and Mexico destroyed the right of this House to prescribe the qualifications of the voters of California, a treaty could, upon the same principle, compel us to pass such regulations as it thought proper to prescribe. It could, in other words, destroy the sovereignty of the State. California makes application for admission into the Union on the same footing, and on the same conditions, with other States. She applies, as a sovereign and independent State, exercising undoubted control over matters of this character. No law that the Government of the United States has made, can interfere with her in the exercise of this right, without depriving her of her sovereignty. He could not believe that the Government of the United States, at the time of the adoption of this treaty, contemplated establishing the qualifications of voters here ; he could not believe that it contemplated the destruction of the sovereignty of California.

Mr. JONES had been absent during the debate to-day, and had therefore been unable to follow the subject. According to his construction of the treaty, all those who were citizens of Mexico at the time of the adoption of that treaty, were to become citizens of the United States within one year, if they did not remain citizens of Mexico. By article 8th, it is provided that—

"Mexicans now established in Territories previously belonging to Mexico, and which remain for the future within the limits of the United States, as defined by the present treaty, shall be free to continue where they now reside, or remove at any time to the Mexican Republic, retaining the property which they possess in the said Territories, or disposing thereof, and removing the proceeds wherever they please, without their being subjected, on this account, to any contribution, tax, or charge whatever. Those who shall prefer to remain in the said Territories, may either retain the title and rights of Mexican citizens, or acquire those of citizens of the United States."

They may either retain the title and rights of Mexican citizens, or acquire those of citizens of the United States. The treaty goes on to define the method by which they shall acquire the title and rights of citizens of the United States, in these words :

"But they shall be under the obligation to make their election within one year from the date of the exchange of ratifications of this treaty ; and those who shall remain in the said Territories after the expiration of that year, without having declared their intention to retain the character of Mexicans, shall be considered to have elected to become citizens of the United States."

The clause might possibly be subject to two constructions. It might be said, that by choosing to become citizens of the United States they so became, or that they showed a disposition to become so. He (Mr. Jones) thought the 9th article settled the question:

"The Mexicans who, in the Territories aforesaid, shall not preserve the character of citizens of the Mexican Republic, conformably with what is stipulated in the preceding article, shall be incorporated into the Union of the United States, and be admitted at the proper time (to be judged of by the Congress of the United States) to the enjoyment of all the rights of citizens of the United States, according to the principles of the Constitution; and in the meantime, shall be maintained and protected in the free enjoyment of their liberty and property, and secured in the free exercise of their religion without restriction."

Now, the treaty provides, that they shall be incorporated into the Union, and be admitted at the proper time. They must make application for admission. You do not admit citizens into the Union, and makes them citizens of States by treaty. This is a union, not of men, but of States. It has been well said to-day, that a man might be a citizen of the United States, and still not have the right to vote. It is not Congress that decides—it is the State. The Constitution gives to the States the right to determine who shall be voters. The State of Virginia denies to a great portion of its citizens the right of voting. The State of Louisiana, until lately, did the same. The State of Massachusetts requires that a man shall pay a stated tax in order to have the right. He (Mr. Jones) held that the citizens of Mexico, as recognized by the treaty of peace and the Constitution of the United States, are fully represented on this floor, that they have, in accordance with their privilege, voted for members of this Convention, and are, therefore, as much represented as other American citizens; and that the Constitution has given to the Convention the right to declare what shall be the qualification of voters in this State.

Mr. Hastings asked whether the Mexican law had been obtained on this subject.

Mr. Jones stated that he had the Constitutions of 1824 and 1836. The Constitution, however, of 1843, established different rights of Mexican citizens, and consequently would govern all previous laws.

Mr. McCarver could see nothing in the treaty to give this class of citizens the right of suffrage. This Convention was perfectly competent to allow or deny them that right whenever it thought proper. The usual mode is to require from those who desire to become citizens the oath of allegiance.

Mr. Tefft was in favor of Mr. Gilbert's amendment. He thought it covered the whole ground. It permitted all those persons to vote who enjoyed that privilege under the Mexican laws. Very few Indians were allowed to vote under Mexican law. He was quite satisfied this amendment would meet with the approbation of those interested in the matter.

Mr. Hoppe said that his reason for moving to strike out the words "not taxed," was, that the whole Indian race should be excluded from the elective franchise.

Mr. Sherwood presumed the motion to insert would render a motion to strike out unnecessary. If the words were not inserted, they would be stricken out.

Mr. Wozencraft wished gentlemen to reflect, that there are Indians by descent, as well as full-blooded Indians. He supposed the majority of the members on this floor were not willing to deprive the descendants of Indians of the elective franchise. Many of the most distinguished officers of the Mexican Government are Indians by descent. At the same time, it would be impolitic to permit the full-blooded Indians who held property to vote. Those who held property, would, of course, be taxed. Capitalists could, for special purposes, make them purchasers of property. He was, therefore, in favor of the amendment as first proposed—to exclude all Indians.

Mr. Botts desired to have the sense of the House in regard to the words "not taxed." He was willing to accept that amendment, if it was the wish of the House; but not otherwise.

The CHAIR stated that the proper course would be, to take the question on the amendment as it originally stood, and then on the words "not taxed," as an additional amendment.

Mr. HOPPE remarked, that in the district of San Jose there were not less than two hundred Indians who would become taxable. Was it proper that they should vote? The consequences of such a provision would be most injurious.

Mr. GWIN said the gentleman from San Jose (Mr. Hoppe) could accomplish his object by withdrawing his amendment, until the vote was taken on the amendment of Mr. Botts.

Mr. NORIEGO desired to say a word in reply to the gentleman from San Jose, (Mr. Hoppe) who stated that there were at least two hundred Indians in that district, who would become taxable. He (Mr. Noriego) requested that gentleman to place himself in the position of one of those Indians. Suppose he had to pay an equal tax with all other persons, to sustain the expenses of the State? Would it not be most unfair to deprive him of equal privileges, when he had to bear an equal burden? The gentleman, he hoped, would readily perceive the great injustice of such a provision in the Constitution.

The question was then taken on the amendment offered by Mr. Botts, to Mr. Gilbert's amendment, and it was adopted.

The question then being on the motion to strike out the words "not taxed,"

Mr. DENT observed that it might be a weakness in him, but he had always entertained a peculiar deference for the Indians. They were the original proprietors of the soil. From them we derived it, and from them we derived many of the blessings which we now enjoy. They have already been deprived of their original independence. Why should we pursue them, and drag them down to the level of slaves? It appeared to him that the Indians should enjoy the right of suffrage, and that they should not be classed with Africans. He hoped the amendment of Mr. Gilbert, would remain without further alteration.

Mr. MCCARVER would vote for striking out the clause allowing Indians who paid taxes the right to vote. He believed the privilege would be greatly abused. Many men who wished to carry an election, would pay the taxes of the ranche, and induce the Indians to vote as he directed. He was in favor of giving this class of people all the protection of our laws, but not the right of suffrage. As a general thing, the Indian is illiterate, and incompetent to judge of the questions presented in an election. If he pays taxes, he has an equivalent for it—the protection of the law. By giving him the right to vote, he would in nine cases out of ten, be placed in the power of crafty and designing men.

The question was then taken on the motion to strike out the words "not taxed," and decided in the affirmative—ayes, 25; noes, 15.

Mr. TEFFT said he could not in justice to his own feelings, allow the motion to pass, without expressing, with the gentleman from Monterey, (Mr. Dent) the deep sympathy which he felt for this unhappy race. It might be a prejudice that had grown with his growth, and strengthened with his strength; but from his earliest youth, he had felt something like a reverence for the Indian. He had ever admired their heroic deeds in defence of their aboriginal homes, their stoicism, their wild eloquence and uncompromising pride. He was much pleased, when a resident of Wisconsin, to see incorporated in the Constitution of that State, a provision allowing Indians the privilege of voting. He hoped this question would be considered calmly and dispassionately in all its bearings, and that gentlemen would not, by acting hastily, exclude all Indians, absolutely and entirely, from the right of suffrage. Were gentlemen aware, that, because a man is two-thirds Indian, he is not an Indian? Had they considered well the feeling that would go abroad among the native population of California, if injustice was done to this class of people? Has not injustice enough already been visited upon the Indian race? They have been driven back from the haunts of civilization into the wilderness—

driven from one extremity of the land to the other; shall they now be driven into the waves of the Pacific? Shall we deprive them of the advantages of civilization? Shall we prohibit them from becoming civilized? Surely the prejudice against color does not extend so far! He did not desire that the Tulas, and other savage tribes should vote, but it is not difficult to draw a line of distinction between these wild Indians, and those who are accustomed to habits of civilization. He considered that this native population was better entitled to the right of suffrage than he was, or a thousand others who came here but yesterday.

Mr. MOORE preferred retaining the words "all free white male citizens." He could not think that any white man would object to this clause.

Mr. SHANNON moved further to amend the amendment of Mr. Gilbert, by striking out all after the word following, and inserting "Indians not taxed, Africans, and descendants of Africans excepted. His amendment was the same as that of Mr. Botts, but he proposed inserting it in a different place.

Mr. MCCARVER said the gentleman was out of order. The House could not vote upon the same question twice. The House by its vote has already refused to incorporate these words in the section.

The question of order giving rise to discussion,

Mr. GILBERT said he thought that, in offering the amendment this morning, he had sufficiently explained the grounds upon which he did so. To illustrate his design more clearly, he would read again the 9th article of the treaty, [*see Art.* 9.] He contended that under this article, native Californians or Mexicans now established in California, have not yet been properly admitted into the United States by act of Congress. They are, no doubt, American citizens, entitled to all the rights and privileges of any other American citizens here, but he moved the amendment to prevent any difficulty that might arise at any future period under this article of the treaty. He particularly stated at the time, that he did not wish to draw any invidious distinctions as to who should be permitted to vote, whether Indians, Africans, or their descendants. He was quite willing to leave that to the Convention. But he contended that it was absolutely necessary to insert either the amendment which he proposed or something like it. He considered that "every white male citizen of the United States," was not sufficiently explicit, and did not cover the ground.

Mr. SHERWOOD disagreed with his friend from San Francisco (Mr. Gilbert) in regard to the construction which he put upon the right of citizenship. A person may be a citizen of the United States, formerly a citizen of Mexico, but not necessarily a citizen of the new State of California, so far as regards the right of voting. We are now attempting to establish the qualifications of voters, and we say that a great many good citizens of the United States shall not be voters. Have we not the same right to say that those who were previously citizens of Mexico, but who under the treaty became citizens of the United States, shall not vote? If we can debar those who have been previously citizens of the United Sates from this privilege, surely we can debar those who have been previously citizens of Mexico from the same privilege. We do it in virtue of the right always exercised by the States, to determine the qualifications of their voters. We say unless a man be a resident so many months, he shall not be a voter. We may make it a property qualification. These restrictions would of course debar a great many citizens of the United States from the elective franchise. Gentlemen will not undertake to say, that because a person was a citizen of Mexico previous to the treaty, and under the treaty comes into the United States and becomes a citizen thereof, he has a right to vote, no matter what may be the restrictions imposed upon other citizens of the State, or of the United States? In forming a new State, it is clear that we have a right to determine the qualifications of our voters; but we have no right to deprive any man of the common rights of citizenship. We cannot deprive the Indian, or even the free negro of the right to hold property. It is a right that appertains to all freemen. But we can say who shall and who shall not elect the officers of the government. We have a right to govern the State. Will gentlemen undertake to say that the wild Indians, who never heard of a Government or a Legislature, and who might possibly have been by the laws of Mexico, entitled to vote, should be entitled to privileges under our laws, superior to those enjoyed by the citizens of our own Union?—that because they are admitted under a treaty of peace, they shall not be subject to restrictions in regard to the elective franchise which we impose upon ourselves? Or that we have not the right to impose such additional restrictions upon them as we think proper? He hoped gentlemen would see how preposterous the idea was without further discussion of the question.

He objected to the amendment: "Indians, Africans, and the descendants of Africans, excepted." What is meant by the descendant of an Indian, or the descendant of a negro? Did the gentleman who offered the proposition mean to say that a man who has the least taint of Indian or negro blood shall not vote? He had never heard such a doctrine in the States. The word descendant means a person who descends in regular line. He may be of mixed blood or full blood. There is nothing specific in the term "descendant." He (Mr. Sherwood) did not believe the Committee could adopt any better form than the words "white male citizen." If the word "descendant" is more definite than "white," he would like to know in what particular. We do not debar the Spanish, or the French, or the Italians from voting by the use of this word. They are darker than the Anglo-Saxon race, but they are white men. He was in favor of the distinct expression, "every white male citizen," as used in the thirty different Constitutions of the Union.

Mr. Semple was of opinion that every Constitution in the States makes some provision of this kind. He had a very distinct recollection of the words, "negroes, mulattoes, and Indians excepted," in the Constitution of Kentucky." They had Indians there as well as here, and they were invariably considered free. They never had been made slaves of, nor had they ever been allowed the privilege of voting. He would suggest the same principle here. He was opposed to taxing them without giving them all the rights enjoyed by others. It is one of the principles laid down in the Declaration of Independence, that taxation and representation shall go together. If, then, we levy a tax on the Indian, either a capitation tax or a tax on his property, he should by all means be represented. He (Mr. Semple) believed that, although we might exclude the native Indian, it was beyond the reach of this Convention to exclude those who might be descended from the Indian race. He saw no better way of settling the difficulty than by adopting the word "white" before male citizen, which is sufficiently explained in the courts of the United States.

Mr. Gilbert remarked that in so far as the word "descendant" was concerned, to which the gentleman from Sacramento (Mr. Sherwood) objected, he wished it understood that it was not a portion of his amendment; and he agreed with that gentleman that if we strike out the whole of this section as it stands, it is not necessary to insert in the proposed section the words of the gentleman from Sacramento (Mr. Shannon.) It would certainly be of no importance, if this section was to stand "every white male citizen of the United States," to insert Indians, Africans, and the descendants of Africans excepted." Those words were altogether unnecessary. His (Mr. Gilbert's) intention, in proposing an amendment to the clause, was to prevent any question arising hereafter, from the wording of the treaty of peace, by which Mexican citizens might be debarred the privilege of voting. He objected to the words "white male citizen" on the ground that they were not sufficiently explicit. They might be very well understood in our courts, but it was necessary that every citizen should understand the provisions of this Constitution, without going into court to have them explained. It was only by adopting his amendment that the words proposed by Mr. Shannon became important. Without it, it would be nonsense to adopt them. If his (Mr. Gilbert's) amendment was not adopted, the words of the report ought to stand.

Mr. HOPPE moved to strike out the words "not taxed" from the proposed amendment.

The CHAIR stated that the question having already been taken and decided on that portion of the amendment, it could not be brought up again. It was, therefore, out of order, and not before the House.

Mr. SHANNON insisted upon his right to have the question taken on the amendment as a whole.

The CHAIR decided that the words "not taxed" were out of order.

The question was then taken on Mr. Shannon's amendment, modified in accordance with the decision of the Chair, and decided in the negative.

The question being on the amendment offered by Mr. Gilbert,

Mr. LARKIN proposed to insert "Indians and Africans, and the descendants of Africans to the fourth generation excepted."

Mr. BOTTS cordially approved of the proposition. It would make certain that which would probably be uncertain. Even in our courts there is some uncertainty on this subject. He thought it well that this assembly should determine the meaning of any doubtful term which it might use.

Mr. SHERWOOD was of opinion that no other construction could be placed upon the word white than this: if an Indian is more than half Indian, he is an Indian; if he is more than half white, he is white. With respect to Africans, he believed that all after the fourth generation are considered white in most of the States.

Mr. MOORE asked who was to determine, on the day of election, the various grades of color?

The question recurring on Mr. Gilbert's amendment, as amended, it was adopted—ayes 20, noes 20—the Chairman giving the casting vote in the affirmative.

The question then being on the filling up of the blanks,

Mr. NORTON moved to insert "six" in the first blank.

Mr. SEMPLE moved the word "twelve." He believed the rule was to put the question first on the highest number.

Mr. CROSBY suggested that the next election ought to be embraced in this section.

Mr. ELLIS remarked that there would be very few to vote if twelve months was the time fixed upon.

Mr. SEMPLE said it was well known to almost every member of this Convention that there are a vast number of persons who come to California for no other object than to remain one working season and dig gold. They are in the mines, and expect to remain but a single season. About the 1st of November your annual election comes on. These persons, who have only been in the country three or four months previous to that date, who are on the very eve of leaving California, are qualified voters. Is this just towards the permanent population of California? Is it politic to permit persons to vote who come here with the avowed intention of digging gold to carry it away and spend their wealth elsewhere? What interest have they in the welfare of the State? All persons who are residents of California, no matter when they arrived, at the time of the reception of the Constitution, are, of course, and should be, entitled to vote. The provision, therefore, making twelve months residence necessary, would not affect a single person who was here previous to the adoption of the Constitution. It would only operate upon those who come into the country after the adoption of the Constitution, and become a permanent portion of the population. It seemed to him that twelve months was short enough a period to entitle them to the privilege of voting. If his own brother was to come here, he would be unwilling to see him participate in the elections any sooner. It is a necessary protection to the ballot-box that no man shall vote unless he is willing to remain in the country twelve months.

Mr. HALLECK would merely call attention to a single point. This section of the Constitution, as reported, does not affect the first election. It has reference only to the second and those that follow. The time of residence necessary for the first election must be defined in the schedule, not in the body of the Constitution.

Mr. GWIN was astonished that the gentleman from Sonoma, (Mr. Semple,) should insist upon twelve months. There was not a State in the Union that required so long a time. The gentleman is in favor of every man who is now a citizen of California voting on the Constitution, but he excludes hereafter all persons who may become citizens, because they are not citizens for twelve months. He (Mr. Gwin) had heard much said about persons after acquiring wealth, returning to spend it elsewhere; but he believed it was seldom the case. People generally invest their money where they earn it. Every inducement should be held out to emigrants to remain here, and one of the strongest inducements would be the enjoyment of the right of suffrage. Where thousands come, it is common to see but very few leaving. He would vote for three, four, five, or six months. He thought six months ought to be the limit, but he would prefer three.

Mr. HASTINGS said that two considerations were involved in the proposition of the gentleman from Sonoma (Mr. Semple.) The first seemed to be, that in forming this Constitution, we return it to the same people who elected us as delegates. Are we to declare in the Constitution, that they shall not vote upon its adoption? Most members on this floor occupy their seats in virtue of votes given by constituents, who have resided here less than three months. When this Constitution comes before them for their ratification, they are not entitled to vote. But we are relived from this difficulty, because there is to be inserted in some other portion of the Constitution a clause saying, that the people are entitled to vote at the first election. Will it not be argued, as it was when the proposition to appoint a committee for the purpose of reporting a schedule was made, that the schedule in which this provision is to be made, is a portion of the Constitution? We cannot say twelve months here and two months there. We should insert in this article itself, the words, "after the first election." He therefore submitted a motion to that effect. Such limitation of time could then be made as the House thought proper.

Mr. DENT said it appeared to him, that Gen. Riley had settled this matter in his proclamation. All who are privileged to vote at the first election are made known in the words of that proclamation. This Constitution will not be a law until it first receives the sanction of a majority of the people, and is ratified by Congress.

The question was then taken on filling the first blank with the words, "twelve months," and decided in the negative, 15 to 22.

Mr. BOTTS proposed "nine months." Rejected, 13 to 24.

Mr. NORTON moved "six months." Adopted, yeas 30, noes not counted.

Mr. NORTON moved to fill the second blank (in relation to a residence in the county) with the words "thirty days."

Mr. HILL moved "ninety days." Rejected.

The question was then taken on Mr. Norton's motion and it was decided in the affirmative.

On motion of Mr. HOPPE the first section was further amended by inserting after the word "county," "or district."

The first section, as amended, was then adoped, by yeas 26, noes 10, as follows:

SEC. 1. Every white male citizen of the United States, and every male citizen of Mexico, (Indians, Africans, and descendants of Africans excepted,) who shall have elected to become a citizen of the United States under the treaty of peace exchanged and ratified at Queretaro, on the 30th day of May, 1848, of the age of twenty-one years, who shall have been a resident of the State six months next preceding the election, and the county or district in which he claims his vote, thirty days, shall be entitled to vote at all elections which are now, or hereafter may be, authorized by law.

The following sections were then adopted without debate, viz:

2. Electors shall, in all cases except treason, felony, or breach of the peace, be privileged from arrest on the days of elections, during their attendance at such election, going to, and returning therefrom.

3. No elector shall be obliged to perform militia duty on the day of election, except in time of war or public danger.

The question then coming up on the fourth section of the Committee's report, Mr. GILBERT moved the following:

4. For the purpose of voting, no person shall be deemed to have gained or lost a residence by reason of his presence or absence while employed in the service of the United States; nor while engaged in the navigation of the waters of this State, or of the United States, or of the high seas; nor while a student of any seminary of learning; nor while kept at any almshouse, or other asylum, at public expense; nor while confined in any public prison.

The amendment was rejected without debate, and the section of the Committee adopted, viz:

4. No person in the military, naval, or marine service of the United States, shall be considered a resident of this State by being stationed in any garrison, barrack, or military or naval place or station within this State.

Mr. BOTTS moved to amend the report of the Committee, by inserting between the 4th and 5th sections the following:

No person living in California, who has left his family elsewhere, shall be considered as a resident of California.

Mr. HALLECK wished to know if the persons, to whom the gentleman had reference, were not included under the head of "idiots and insane persons," in the 5th section.

Mr. WOZENCRAFT thought it rather unfair that a gentleman who enjoyed the blessing of having his family here, should be so hard upon those who, like himself, had left theirs at home. The gentleman (Mr. Botts) ought to be content with his good fortune, without compelling others to take a trip home to the United States for their families before they could enjoy the privilege of electors, at the risk of losing it after all by absence from the State.

Mr. BOTTS had really supposed that there would not be a dissenting voice to this very plain proposition. As to the difficulty of the gentleman from San Joaquin, (Mr. Wozencraft,) he would answer him as others had been answered—we will provide for him in the schedule. In serious earnest, the object of the amendment was to have some guarantee, that persons who are to assist in making our laws will remain in the country long enough to be subject to the operation of those laws. He did not wish any man to have a vote in the formation of a law, and then leave the country to let that law operate on others. The peculiar condition of California renders such a provision most desirable. There should be a community of interest among those who are privileged to vote. The fact that people leave their families elsewhere when they come here, is some evidence, at least, that they do not intend to remain.

Mr. SUTTER protested against this proposition. It would be very hard, if he should, after his long residence here, be deprived of his right to vote because his family was elsewhere.

Mr. ELLIS thought one more provision ought to be introduced—that all single men should be married in three months.

The question was then taken on amending the report, by inserting the additional section, as proposed, and the amendment was rejected.

The question being on the 5th section reported by the Committee, it was adopted, as follows:

5. No idiot or insane person, or persons convicted of any infamous crime, shall be entitled to the privilege of an elector.

Mr. PRICE moved to insert the following between the 5th and 6th sections:

Laws shall be made for ascertaining, by proper proofs, the citizens who shall be entitled to the right of suffrage hereby established.

The question being taken, it was rejected.

The question was then taken on the last section of the report of the Committee, and it was carried, viz:

6. All elections by the people shall be by ballot.

Thereupon, on motion, the Committee rose and reported the "right of suffrage" to the House with sundry amendments.

On motion, the report was received, and ordered to lie on the table.

On motion, the House adjourned.

THURSDAY, SEPTEMBER 13, 1849.

The Convention met pursuant to adjournment. Prayer by Rev. S. H. Willey.

The journal of yesterday was read, amended, and approved.

Mr. Gwin submitted certain maps of California, which were referred to the Committee on the Boundary.

Mr. Shannon submitted the following, which was adopted, viz:

Resolved, That the Secretary of the Convention return to the Governor all election papers and returns transmitted by him to this body, but that copies of the same be retained by the Secretary of the House.

The Convention then resolved itself into Committee of the Whole, Mr. Dimmick in the chair, upon the report of the Committee on the Constitution.

The question being taken on the first section, it was adopted, as follows:

The powers of government of the State of California shall be divided into three separate departments, the Legislative, the Executive, and the Judicial; and no person charged with the exercise of powers properly belonging to one of these departments, shall exercise any function appertaining to either of the others, except in the cases hereinafter expressly directed or permitted.

The question was then taken on the next section, and it was adopted:

LEGISLATIVE DEPARTMENT.

Sec. 1. The legislative power of this State shall be vested in a Senate and Assembly, which shall be designated the Legislature of the State of California, and the style of their laws shall commence in the following manner: "The people of the State of California, represented in Senate and Assembly, do enact as follows."

The second section being then under consideration, as follows:

2. The session of the Legislature shall be ——, and shall commence on the first Monday in January next ensuing the election of its members, unless the Governor of the State shall, in the interim, convene the Legislature by proclamation.

Mr. Gwin moved that the blank be filled with the word "biennial."

Mr. Norton moved the word "annual."

Mr. Semple had no idea that we should be able to make a Constitution here, which would last twenty or thirty years without alteration. The peculiar condition of the country is such as to render modification in legislation necessary, to meet the progressive changes of circumstances that must take place. He believed that the Legislature, by meeting only once in two years, would not be able to prepare such a code of laws as would be sufficient for California. For a few years, at least, it should meet annually. If a proviso was inserted, that after the first five years, the sessions should be biennial, then there might possibly be no objection. Gentlemen should remember that we have no organized code of laws. We are changing from one form of government very different from ours, to another, requiring a complete legislative reorganization. The Legislature must establish an entire code of laws. It will be impossible to keep members of the Legislature more than two or three months at the seat of Government. The rapid progress of affairs in this country, and the great value of time, would render a longer session impracticable. The first winter the Legislature will pass some of the most necessary laws, and probably the next improve and increase the code. If the people find that annual meetings of the Legislature are oppressive, they can very easily change to biennial.

Mr. GWIN said his motion had direct reference to one great question—the enormous expense entailed upon the public, by frequent elections and frequent legislatures. He knew by experience that the legislative action of all new bodies is hasty, and if we expected to have a correct system of laws, we would be compelled to establish a commissioner or commissioners to prepare a system for the consideration of the Legislature. It is impossible for us to adopt a system of laws, by frequent sessions of the Legislature. In the present state of the country, the expense of frequent elections will be so extraordinary, as to give rise to great inconvenience. The power of convening the Legislature, in all cases of necessity, rests with the Governor. It can be assembled when required. Experience has shown the evils of excessive legislation. Laws should be well tested before changes are made. All the new States have biennial Legislatures. We commence with Texas—a Territory somewhat similar in the character of its population to this. The sessions of its Legislature are biennial. So also, with Louisiana, Mississippi, Arkansas, Tennessee, Illinois, Missouri, Iowa, Wisconsin, and Michigan. All the new border States have biennial sessions. Look at the difference in the expense there and here. A member of the Legislature gets but two dollars a day in Iowa. The Legislature is not permitted to sit more than fifty days, at that rate. If its sessions are prolonged beyond that period, the members get but one dollar a day. It has been well demonstrated by experience, that in new States, the hasty passage of laws is a source of great evil. Of all the States in the confederacy, California requires most an efficient system of laws, and she is the last State that should multiply the expenses of government, by having frequent meetings of the Legislature. The Government, in the most economical form, will be expensive enough.

Mr. WOZENCRAFT said he had a resolution to offer which he thought would meet the difficulty of the gentleman from Sonoma (Mr. Semple.) He notified the House that at a suitable time, he would submit a resolution for the appointment of a commission of three persons to form a code of laws, to be submitted to the Legislature at its first session. He was in favor of biennial sessions. He thought they would be sufficient, and would avoid the difficulty arising from excessive legislation.

Mr. NORTON did not see that we had any power to appoint such a commission as the gentlemen proposed. What authority had members of this Convention to appoint three persons to form a code of laws for the Legislature? He thought it absolutely essential that the sessions of the Legislature should be annual. We have no laws here. It has been impossible to ascertain what the law is, or to enforce it. The Mexican system, as retained under the existing civil government, is repugnant to the feelings of American citizens. It is too late for them to learn any other system than that to which they have been accustomed. The Legislature of California will therefore have a great deal of work to do. It is said that in new States, there is great danger of hasty legislation. He would ask if there is as much danger in the case of a Legislature that meets once a year, as in that of one that meets once in two years? If the business of two years is crowded into one session, is there not more danger of imperfect legislation, than when there are two sessions within the same period, to perform the same work? It is very desirable that the Legislature should meet and proceed at once to form a system of laws, so that the people may know what laws they are living under. This cannot be done in a country like this, so rapidly increasing in population and wealth, at one meeting of the Legislature. Another Legislature must soon convene, to complete the work of the last, and provide new laws to meet the exigencies of events. Gentlemen say there will be great expense in meeting once a year. What of that? Our means will be proportionate to the expense. We have great wealth here. If it is necessary at all to have a Legislature, we have the means to pay for it. We are not the people to say, we cannot have such a government as we require, because we are too poor to pay for it.

Mr. Halleck agreed with the gentleman last up, (Mr. Norton,) in regard to annual sessions. If there is a country in the world, at the present time, that requires the Legislature to meet at least once a year, it is California. Let us suppose that, by our Constitution, when it is adopted by the people, we call a session of the Legislature on the 1st day of January next. In all probability, as the gentleman from San Francisco (Mr. Gwin) said, we may have hasty legislation. This is a very strong reason why we should have a remedy as soon as possible. Are we to wait two years before we can correct the laws made by that body? Or shall another body be called into session the next year to correct these evils? Has not every citizen already felt the great inconvenience of the want of legislative power, to make new laws, to provide for the peculiar circumstances of the country? The people should have the power of convening the Legislature at least once a year, to meet the extraordinary changes that must take place. We have been constantly told on this floor, that there is an immense emigration directing its course into California. That emigration will be for the next four or five years, floating about from one portion of the country to another. Laws made by one Legislature for the government of one portion of the Territory, may be rendered unnecessary, and new laws for the government of other portions may be required in less than two years. Let us suppose that all this emigration should be fixed in the valley of the Sacramento or San Joaquin. A Legislature passes laws for the government of that people. In six months after, the mines in the southern portion of the country draw the flood of emigration in that direction. Are we to wait two years before the Legislature can meet to provide for that portion of our population? Why throw upon the Governor the responsibility of judging what is necessary to be done? If you think proper, you may limit the duration of the session to a certain number of days or months, but they should at least be annual.

Mr. Botts believed that, for the first time, he was about to find himself in the majority. He would endeavor to make sure of it, by adding a few remarks to those just made. For his own part he was in favor of the annual meeting of the Legislature. He had one great test to which he submitted all these questions—the principles of the Democratic party. When he subjected the gentleman's biennial proposition to that test, he found it wanting. He was very well aware that there would be hasty legislation. The people of California are fallible; they will make mistakes; but when they do they want the opportunity to correct them. They will not be content that any one man power should govern them in retracting or improving the laws which they may make. Suppose the Governor should think a very good law passed by the people in their legislative capacity, an oppressive one? He has power to convene the Legislature at any time, thereby subjecting the people to great inconvenience, and, probably, serious injury. He is to judge of the necessity. We are told that annual meetings of the Legislature are expensive. Why should we be threatened continually with this dreadful bugbear of expense? It is true legislation is expensive in California. So is everything else. But the people are the most wealthy in the world, and the best capable of defraying these expenses. The quantity of the circulating medium, which is the bullion of the country, is greater than in any other State of the Union. When this ceases to be the case, everything will come down to a proportionate standard. The same relative proportion exists between the expense of legislation here and elsewhere. If prices are higher nominally, there are more abundant means of meeting them. The people of California should not be debarred from the privilege of being constantly heard in their legislative assembly on the plea of want of pecuniary means to defray the necessary expenses. It appeared to him (Mr. Botts) a little singular, that gentlemen who were so devoted to precedents—who were so afraid of novelties—who hugged the shore and never ventured out to sea—who always recommended some clause or provision, because it was to be found somewhere else, should now recommend the latest and newest and most untried policy. The biennal provision is one of recent enactment. He called upon gentlemen who were opposed to novelties and untried experiments, to go with him for the old settled principle of annual legislation.

Mr. McCarver said that the only objection he had to annual sessions of the Legislature was this: there are no lands owned and occupied as yet in California, except a few large tracts. To place an ordinary tax on these lands would make it very oppressive. A capitation tax to defray the expense of annual sessions would probably be equally objectionable. It is revolting to man to be obliged to pay for his head. For these reasons, he thought it would be better to meet biennially. The system had been adopted in the new States, and it was found to work admirably.

Mr. Botts wished to know if the gentleman meant to say that his constituents would rather pay two dollars and a half, if it was called a tax upon the man, than two dollars for his head.

Mr. McCarver merely referred to the general principle as objectionable.

Mr. Semple rose to pledge his constituents for their share of taxation. He was sent here by them to assist in making such a Constitution as would protect them in all their rights and property. Whatever tax was put upon them by their own act, they would never complain of. It would be easy to make the sessions of the Legislature biennial, when the necessity of such a change was demanded by circumstances.

Mr. Shannon would not say a word but for the allusion of the gentleman from Sonoma, (Mr. Semple,) to the people of that district. His (Mr. Shannon's) constituents, the people of Sacramento, were as willing and as able as any in California to pay taxes. They wanted a good government, no matter what the expense might be, and he believed they would require annual sessions of the Legislature.

Mr. Snyder stated that he had before him a map of California, and that he understood an effort would be made in this House to establish, as the boundary line of the State, the entire territory known as California. Now if the boundary line should take in the whole of California, there would be certain members from the Salt Lake region, who never would be able to get home if the Legislature met annually. At the close of the session they might start homeward, but they would be compelled to turn back before they got beyond the Sierra Nevada, in order to be at the seat of government in time for the next session.

Mr. Gilbert said it seemed to him that this question of annual and biennial sessions was one that admitted of very little doubt in favor of annual sessions. One of the essential reasons why this Convention was assembled here, was to provide the means of proper legislation. His colleague from San Francisco, (Mr. Gwin,) cited the examples of the new States in favor of biennial sessions. From a speech made by that gentleman a day or two since, it would seem that these new States enjoyed from seven to thirty years experience under Territorial forms of government. There was comparatively but little change to make in their laws. That very fact would go to show the absolute necessity of annual Legislatures here. It is notorious that the laws now in force, are repugnant to the feelings, education, and habits of the great majority of the people. These laws cannot be discontinued, and such laws enacted in their place as the wants of the people may require, by biennial sessions of the Legislature. It appeared to him that nothing but annual sessions would answer the demands of the community. It might not be necessary to continue the annual meetings more than four or five years, but it should be left to the people to determine upon the expediency of a change, at the expiration of that time.

Mr. Gwin did not wish to trespass upon the patience of the House, but as he was contending for an important principle he desired to reply to some remarks which had been made during the debate. When he spoke of hasty legislation he did not intend to be understood as stating that one Legislature would meet this year, and another would meet next year to repeal its acts. Legislatures meet for other purposes—to provide for the increasing wants of the community. It is not the hasty action of a preceeding Legislature that is repealed; it is the accumulation of laws that requires a remedy. If all the laws of all the States of this Union, that have been passed and repealed, were collected together, they would fill this hall. The world is governed too much. We have too many laws. If he (Mr. Gwin) had happened to come from Virginia, the gentleman from Monterey (Mr. Botts) would not have been so indignant. There is no danger of not having laws enough. The great danger is that we shall have too many. It was probable the first Legislature would have to remain in session a long time, in order to pass such laws as would meet the demands of the community. His only desire was to have a good system of laws established. It was with this view that he proposed a commission to digest, in advance, a code of laws for the action of the Legislature, and he desired that the first Legislature that met after the adoption of the Constitution should have full and ample time to provide for the wants of the country. If this system of biennial sessions is so inexpedient, how is it that it has been adopted in most of the States? As to the system of laws referred to as growing up under the Territorial form of government, it was well known that the first session of a State Legislature is always the longest. After that, the less legislation, unless to meet pressing emergencies, the better. We are not to legislate for a wandering and changing population. The miners will have their home, and there will not be that fluctuating population which gentlemen imagine. People who come here will find it to their interest to become permanent residents of the country. He would not attempt to argue the question, however, for he had no feeling on the subject. It merely occurred to him that it would be to the interest of the people to be subjected to as little expense as possible, and to have no more legislation than was actually necessary.

Mr. Sherwood said that this question was a matter of principle with him. Economy should be studied by wealthy people as well as poor. If he was satisfied that the proposition of the gentleman from San Francisco (Mr. Gwin) would be more economical, and better calculated to promote the interests of the people, he would most cordially sustain it; but he did not believe such to be the case. The gentleman (Mr. Gwin) was opposed to accumulating laws. What effect would biennial sessions have in preventing the accumulation of laws? If the Legislature of California met once in two years, instead of sitting one month, it would probably remain in session two months. The amount of laws passed would be about the same; and so far as the question of economy is concerned, there would be nothing gained in that respect. For public convenience annual sessions would be preferable. We are an anomalous people. There is no State in the Union like California Rapid as has been the progress of the Western States, they are left far behind by the new Territory of the Pacific. Towns and cities spring up here in a month. The population is subject to extraordinary changes. It may number five thousand now in a certain district, and a year hence fifteen thousand. We have no pre-existing laws that can form the basis of our legislation. With all this new material in the country—without any previous territorial organization—we have to assemble together a Legislature to enact laws suitable to the condition of the country. It cannot be supposed that the wants of the people, at the outset, can be thoroughly understood by the first body that meets. The proposition to appoint a commission to prepare a code of laws should not be brought up now. Whatever may be its merits, it is entirely irrelevant to this question. Each Legislature that meets, for a few years to come, will undoubtedly have enough work to perform, allowing it annual sessions, to provide for the wants of the people. Suppose this House was transformed into a legislative body, who upon this floor is prepared to make the necessary laws for California—to lay out roads—to determine what public officers shall be appointed—to provide for all the local wants of the community. This is a matter that requires experience. It cannot be done at once. Most of the

the people here are new comers, and those who will be sent to the Legislature from among them will require time to learn the wants of the districts which they represent. It is, therefore, absolutely necessary that the Legislature should meet at least once a year for a few years—leaving it to the people, when they become more settled, to establish biennial sessions if they think proper. In regard to representation, if we meet but once in two years, there will be no representative apportionment for two years to come. To prevent that, we require annual sessions. Undoubtedly they will be short, and not expensive; because, in this Constitution, it seems to be the intention of the House to make it the duty of the Legislature to pass general laws, as far as practicable, instead of special laws for particular purposes; which will greatly shorten legislation.

Mr. Brown believed he would be in the minority on this question. It was a subject upon which he was very decided. Not only did he consider the question of economy involved in this case, but a question of much higher importance—public interest. Annual meetings of the Legislature would, in his opinion, be most injudicious as well as most expensive. If the Legislature passed laws every twelve months, those laws would have to go before the people. They would probably be in operation but six months when a new code of laws would be established. Sufficient time should be given to test all legislative enactments. He was convinced that the sudden changing of laws is a source of great public inconvenience, and is always attended by serious loss to individuals. It requires time and experience to demonstrate the necessity of legislative reform. Laws may be objectionable in the beginning, from imperfect administration, but after being fairly tested they may prove most beneficial. If, within two years, experience establishes the propriety of reform, the laws can then be repealed or amended; but six months is an insufficient time. The gentleman from San Francisco, (Mr. Gilbert,) urged this facility of speedily repealing laws as a strong argument in favor of annual sessions. He (Mr. Brown) considered it one of the greatest objections. It is impossible to get laws fairly in operation before the people in less than six months after their enactment, and six months would surely be too short a time to test these laws. In regard to the question of expense, it is the worst policy a State can adopt to establish an expensive system of government. No matter what may be the wealth of California, if her mountains were of pure gold, it would be inexpedient in her to lavish money in the commencement of her career as a State. It is impossible to say with certainty how long the mineral resources of California may hold out. We believe them to be inexhaustible, but it is only a matter of belief. Heavy taxation is always oppressive and unpopular. The question of taxation is one that involves the best interests of the community. It should be touched with a careful hand. Gentlemen boast of the wealth of their constituents in particular districts. It is not a matter to be considered here, whether this distriet or that is the richest. In forming this Constitution it is necessary to consider that it is not made for the benefit of particular localities, but for the whole people. He had no doubt there would be a general willingness on the part of the citizens of California to defray the necessary expenses of a good government; but it was for this Convention to adopt such a course of policy as would promote the permanent interests of the State. He believed, upon full consideration of the question, that on the score of economy and public convenience, biennial sessions of the Legislature would be most expedient, and he would therefore vote for the proposition of the gentleman from San Francisco, (Mr. Gwin.)

Mr. McCarver desired to offer a resolution providing that the Legislature shall meet annually for the first three years, and after that biennially. It seemed to him that would cover the objections of gentlemen who apprehended inconvenience from the want of laws at the present time.

Mr. Halleck suggested that the motion should be put on the longest time, which was the biennial sessions.

6

Mr. WOZENCRAFT objected to the proposition of the gentleman from Sacramento, (Mr. McCarver.) He thought it would only increase the difficulty. The facilities for getting to the seat of government after a few years would be much greater than they are at present.

The question was then taken on filling the blank with the word "biennial," and decided in the negative.

Mr. NORTON'S motion to insert "annual" was then adopted; and the question being on the second section, it was adopted, as follows:

SEC. 2. The sessions of the Legislature shall be annual, and shall commence on the first Monday in January next ensuing the election of its members, unless the Governor of the State shall in the interim convene the Legislature by proclamation.

The third section was then read, as follows:—

SEC. 3. The members of the Assembly shall be chosen by the qualified electors of their respective districts on the Tuesday next after the first Monday in November, whose term of office shall continue —— years.

Mr. TEFFT moved to fill the first blank with the word "annually;" the second blank with the word "one," and to strike out the letter "s" in the word "years" at the close of the section.

Mr. PRICE desired to see as few elections in this country as possible. He considered every two years often enough to elect members of the Legislature. There is always excitement in elections. When too frequent, they are prejudicial to the industrial habits of the community. He moved that the blank be filled so as to provide that elections shall be held every two years.

Mr. SHERWOOD said it occurred to him that the day fixed for the election of President of the United States was the Tuesday succeeding the first Monday in November. All our elections should be held on that day. He wished to be sure of this before the passage of the section.

Mr. SEMPLE informed the gentleman that it was on the Tuesday succeeding the first Monday in November. He moved further to amend the section by adding after the word "November," "unless otherwise directed by the Legislature."

The amendment was adopted, and the question then being on the adoption of the section as amended, it was adopted, as follows:

3. The members of the Assembly shall be chosen —— annually by the qualified electors of their respective districts, on the Tuesday next after the first Monday in November, unless otherwise directed by the Legislature, whose term of office shall continue one year.

The question then coming up on the fourth section of the report, as follows:

4. Senators and members of Assembly shall be citizens of the United States, and be duly qualified electors in the respective counties and districts which they represent.

Mr. BOTTS thought some provision was necessary to make this section perfect, inasmuch as there seemed to be a good deal of doubt whether a certain portion of the population here were entitled to the rights of citizenship without a special act of Congress. He desired to see all participate in the first election. This requires that, in addition to the qualification of elector, a man must be a citizen of the United States. If, however, those who were most interested in the matter had no objection to the section, he would not press any amendment.

Mr. GWIN thought the difficulty could easily be remedied. The qualification of an elector is that "every white male citizen of the United States," &c. It is an essential qualification. It would be easy to strike out citizen of the United States, and say, Senators and members of the Assembly shall be qualified electors.

Mr. BOTTS moved to strike out the words "citizens of the United States and be."

Mr. PRICE moved to amend by striking out the words "United States," and inserting "of the State of California," so as to read; "Senators and members of the Assembly shall be citizens of the State of California," &c.

Mr. MCCARVER did not see the necessity of inserting "California" here. It seemed to him that they would be citizens of California as a matter of course.

Mr. PRICE would modify his amendment so as to read: "Senators and members of the Assembly shall have been citizens of the State two years" in order to be qualified electors. His object was to give electors a higher qualification than members of the Assembly.

The question was then taken on Mr. Price's amendment, as modified, and decided in the negative.

Mr. PRICE moved "one year" a resident of the State. Rejected.

Mr. SHANNON could see no occasion for the introduction of any thing of this kind here. There could be no substantial reason for striking out the words "citizen of the United States." They were usual, he believed, in all the Constitutions of the States. There could be no objection on the score that it would leave out any of the original inhabitants of California. A previous article has fixed the qualifications of voters. No person can be a citizen of California, without first being a citizen of the United States.

Mr. DENT supposed a person could.

Mr. SHANNON remarked that supposition would not answer. Facts were necessary.

Mr. DENT said that, according to the clause of the Constitution which was debated last night, he believed persons were sometimes entitled to the elective franchise in States, who could not be considered as citizens of the United States.

Mr. SEMPLE was of a similar opinion, and referred to the case of Illinois, which, for many years, made citizens of the State who were not previously citizens of the United States.

Mr. SHANNON was not altogether convinced that this was the case. It was certain, however, that a great majority of the Constitutions of the United States contained these words.

The question was then taken on the motion to strike out the words "citizens of the United States and be," and decided in the affirmative.

The question then recurring on the 4th section, as amended, it was adopted, as follows:

4. Senators and members of Assembly shall be duly qualified electors in the respective counties which they represent.

The fifth section being under consideration, as follows:

5. Senators shall be chosen for the term of four years, at the same time and place as members of Assembly. No person shall be eligible to the office of member of Assembly except he shall have attained the age of twenty-one years, nor to that of Senator except he shall have attained the age of twenty-five years.

Mr. GWIN moved to strike out the word "four," and insert the word two, which was adopted.

Mr. PRICE moved to strike out all after the word "Assembly." His reason for this motion was, that in the previous section the qualifications of a representative were fixed, and therefore he considered the latter clause of the present section useless. The age of a representative is fixed at twenty-one years, and that of a Senator at twenty-five. He considered the people as the best judges of these matters, and preferred leaving the age of their representatives unrestricted. It would be just as well to say Senators and Representatives shall not be over a certain age as to say they shall not be under a certain age. In fact it would be much better sense, for a young man may correct his errors, but in the case of an old man, there is no remedy.

Mr. BOTTS not only seconded this motion, but would endeavor to support it. There had been much discussion in the world as to what that period of life is at which a man arrives at the age of discretion. The common law has fixed it at twenty-one years, and the civil at twenty-five. It must be either one or the other. In the case of the legislator, it seems that the more general rule of twenty-one years is to prevail. Could any gentleman explain what there is in the Senate to make a member an immature man who was a mature man in the House below? He is competent to be a legislator in the lower House, but if you carry him up a day older in the Senate, he is unfit to legislate. He (Mr. Botts) was aware that this provision was to be found in perhaps all the Constitutions; but he was opposed to retaining an absurdity because it was to be found elsewhere. This lower House is to have the right of originating bills. It is, therefore, the more important branch. But, in this provision, he who is fit to exercise the greater powers is unfit to exercise the lesser. This is an old aristocratic principle. He (Mr. Botts) had caused some pleasantry in the House on account of his reverence for gray hairs; but he hoped he would not be misunderstood now. It may be that a gentleman at twenty-one is not a proper representative, but if the people desire to have a gentleman at twenty-two, they can best judge as to his qualifications for the position, and should be entitled to elect him to the Senate.

Mr. McCarver was not satisfied as to the propriety of striking out this clause, and allowing the people to elect persons to the Senate without reference to their age. He was in favor of leaving everything to the people, as a general rule, but as Constitutions are restrictions imposed upon the people by their own consent, and as this seemed to be a reasonable and proper restriction, he preferred letting it remain in the Constitution. He thought those gray hairs to which gentlemen so often alluded, were peculiarly appropriate in a body of so grave a character as the upper House of the State Legislature. When the young and inexperienced members of the lower House passed laws, he desired that those laws should be reconsidered and amended by older and wiser heads. It is but reasonable to suppose that maturity of judgment is acquired by the experience that age affords, and for this reason, as well as because it was a principle well tested, he would vote against the motion before the House.

Mr. Shannon did not know what right this Convention had to put restrictions on the people. It was a body elected by their votes to carry into effect their wishes, not to prevent them from exercising their rights as freemen. He was decidedly in favor of the amendment. He wished the question of age left to the free judgment of the people. Let them send whom they please, either to the House or the Senate. They are best qualified to judge as to the capability of members. He had the pleasure, shortly before he left the United States, of listening to a debate in the Convention of New York on this subject. The result of it was, that in the new Constitution of that State, all restrictions of this kind were left out. He trusted the same republican policy would be adopted here.

The question was then taken on Mr. Price's motion to strike out all after the word Assembly, and decided in the affirmative, 15 to 10.

Mr. Price moved to amend by inserting in place of the words stricken out, the following:

And no person shall be a member of the Senate or Assembly who has not been a citizen and inhabitant of the State one year, and of the county for which he shall be chosen six months next before his election.

Mr. Gilbert rose to a question of order. A proposition had already been voted upon which covered the same ground.

Mr. Botts thought nothing would facilitate the business of the Convention more than a strict observance of the rules. He would therefore suggest to the Chair that any amendment substantially the same as one already voted upon, was excluded under the rules.

The Chair was of opinion that this became an original proposition when offered as an amendment to a distinct and separate section.

The question was then taken, and the amendment was adopted—15 to 11.

Mr. Gwin moved that the Committee rise and report progress. His object was to move a call of the House, in order to have a full vote and reconsider the motion last adopted. It was absurd to attempt to do business where so few members were present.

The Committee then rose, reported progress, and asked leave to sit again.

Mr. Gwin moved a call of the House, which was ordered, and twenty-six members answered to their names.

On motion, the Sergeant-at-Arms was directed to proceed, and require the attendance of the absent members.

On motion, the Committee took a recess till half-past 2 P. M.

AFTERNOON SESSION, $2\frac{1}{2}$ O'CLOCK, P. M.

On motion, a call of the House was ordered, and twenty-two members answered to their names.

On motion of Mr. Gwin, the Sergeant-at-Arms was directed by the President to require the attendance of the absentees.

Mr. Gilbert moved an adjournment until 8 P. M., but the motion was decided in the negative.

Mr. Hoppe submitted the following:

Resolved, That a committee of two be appointed by the President to obtain the names, age, native State, profession, or occupation of each member of this Convention, and how long each gentleman has been a resident of California.

The Chair decided that the resolution was not in order, and that the gentleman could accomplish his object without the action of the House.

On motion, the House resolved itself into Committee of the Whole (Mr. Botts in the Chair) on the 3d Article of the Constitution.

Mr. Gwin moved further to amend Section 5th of Article III, on the "Distribution of Powers," by striking out the entire section.

A question of order here arose as to whether the substance of this section as it stood, was embodied in the previous section; when, after some discussion, Mr. Gwin withdrew his amendment, and the section as amended by Mr. Price, was adopted, viz:

5. Senators shall be chosen for the term of two years, at the same time and place as members of the Assembly. And no person shall be a member of the Senate or Assembly who has not been a citizen and inhabitant of the State one year, and of the county for which he shall be chosen six months next before his election.

On motion, the committee then rose, reported progress, and obtained leave to sit again.

The Convention then adjourned to 8 P. M.

NIGHT SESSION, 8 O'CLOCK, P. M.

On motion, the House resolved itself into Committee of the Whole on the report of the Committee on the Constitution.

The sixth and seventh Sections of Article III, on the Distribution of Powers, were taken up, and adopted without debate, as follows:

6. The number of Senators shall not be less than one-third nor more than one half the members of the Assembly, and at the first session of the Legislature after this Constitution takes effect, the Senators shall be divided by lot, as equally as may be, into two classes. The seats of the Senators of the first class shall be vacated at the expiration of the first year, so that one-half shall be chosen annually.

7. When the number of Senators is increased, they shall be annexed to one of the two classes, so as to keep them as nearly equal as practicable.

The eighth Section being under consideration, as follows:

8. Each House shall choose its own officers, and judge of the qualifications, elections, and returns of its own members. A contested election shall be determined in such manner as shall be directed by law.

Mr. Price said there seemed to be some clashing in this section between the first and last clause. Each House shall be the judge of the qualifications and returns of its own members, as provided for in the first part. The second part gives no force or effect to the section. He therefore moved to strike out all after the word "members."

Mr. Norton said that, although the necessity of this clause might not have occurred to the gentleman, (Mr. Price,) it had occurred to the framers of nearly all the Constitutions throughout the States of the Union. Each House should, of course, be the judge of its own members, qualifications, and officers; but the manner of determining a contested election should be fixed by law. The Legislature, by this clause, determines the manner by law. It is perfectly consistent with the preceding clause, and simply directs the Legislature to provide the manner in which contested elections shall be decided. It is not only proper but absolutely necessary.

Mr. Price would like the gentleman to give him a better reason for retaining this clause, than the fact that it is to be found in the various Constitutions. He (Mr. Price,) professed to understand the English language, and he really could not see that there was any necessity for words which added nothing to the section in substance. It amounts to very much the same thing as giving power to the Legislature to form a law by which contested elections shall be decided, after you have already provided that the Legislature shall decide the elections and qualifications of its own members.

Mr. Norton. This clause does not only provide for contested elections of the members of the Legislature; there may be contested elections in regard to the Governor, or Sheriff, or different county officers. It provides that the Legislature shall determine by law the manner in which these contested elections shall be decided. It is necessary to have some system of action laid down for the Legislature, so that proper notice may be given to the person holding the seat or office, and the person claiming it, and the manner in which the witnesses shall be summoned and examined, may be determined.

Mr. Crosby remarked that if this last clause was adopted, the Legislature might pass laws that could settle the election of members for succeeding Legislatures. If its adoption therefore, was insisted upon, he would suggest the propriety of amending it so that all contested elections, except for members of the Legislature, shall be settled by laws passed by the Legislature, and that contested elections of members shall be decided by no law except the decision of the body in which those persons claim seats.

Mr. Price said that if a contested election in relation to Governor should come up, this clause has no bearing upon it. It simply provides that the laws shall direct and determine the manner in which a contested election (having reference to elections to the Legislature) shall be decided. He had no objection, if it was thought necessary, to make a separate section containing a general provision for all elections, except of members of the Legislature; but he did not think it should be included in this section.

The question was then taken on the amendment, and it was rejected.

The question recurring on the 8th section, as reported by the Committee, it was adopted.

The following sections were then taken up in order, read, and adopted without debate:

9. A majority of each House shall constitute a quorum to transact business, but a smaller number may adjourn from day to day, and may compel the attendance of absent members in such manner and under such penalties as each House may provide.

10. Each House shall determine the rules of its proceedings, and may, with the concurrence of two thirds of all the members elected, expel a member.

11. Each House shall keep a journal of its own proceedings and publish the same; and the yeas and nays of the members of either House, shall, at the desire of any three members present, be entered upon the journal.

12. Members of the Legislature shall, in all cases except treason, felony, and breach of the peace, be privileged from arrest; nor shall they be subject to any civil process during the session of the Legislature, nor for fifteen days next before the commencement and after the termination of each session.

13. When vacancies occur in either House, the Governor, or the person exercising the functions of Governor, shall issue writs of election to fill such vacancies.

14. The doors of each House shall be open, except on such occasions as, in the opinion of the House, may require secrecy.

15. Neither House shall, without the consent of the other, adjourn for more than three days, nor to any other place than that in which they may be sitting.

16. Any bill may originate in either House of the Legislature; and all bills passed by one House may be amended by the other.

The 17th Section being under consideration, as follows:

17. Every bill which may have passed the Legislature shall, before it becomes a law, be presented to the Governor. If he approve it, he shall sign it; but if not, he shall return it with his objections to the House in which it originated, which shall enter the same upon the journal, and proceed to reconsider it. If, after such reconsideration, it again pass both Houses, by yeas and nays, by a majority of two-thirds of the members of each House present, it shall become a law notwithstanding the Governor's objections. If any bill shall not be returned within ten days after it shall have been presented to him (Sunday excepted) the same shall become a law in like manner as if he had signed it, unless the Legislature, by adjournment, prevent such return.

Mr. JONES moved to amend the section by inserting the word "three," instead of "ten."

Mr. NORTON thought it was usual to give the Governor ten days to prepare his veto. It would be almost impossible to write it out in three days.

Mr. JONES said that many of the States allow five days. In the Constitution of Iowa the limit is three days. It is well known that most of the important bills are passed within the last ten days of the session. If the Governor has a right to pass a pocket veto on bills, he has within himself an absolute and uncontrollable veto power. The Governor is always found where the Legislature sits. He knows all the reasons for the passage of the law; and is advised of all the initiatory steps which have been taken. Why then should he not be able within three days to form an opinion upon almost any measure which might be passed through the Legislature? It is the case in Congress that the most important bills are passed at the close of the session, and would be much more likely to be the case in a State Legislature, where the bills are local and much less important. He (Mr. Jones) was democratically opposed to giving the Governor any power to pass a pocket veto upon the people.

Mr. NORTON said the gentleman's arguments would be very good if he did not base it altogether upon the assumption that the Governor would be a corrupt man. No Governor would dare to veto a bill in this manner. If a bill passed during the last few days of the session of the Legislature was radically wrong, the Governor would, in virtue of his power, veto it; but no Governor would assume the responsibility to veto a bill in this manner. If it is to be assumed that the Governor will violate his oath of office, then he should be deprived of the veto power altogether. He should either have no such power at all, or sufficient time to present his views, in the exercise of that power.

Mr. SHANNON suggested five days instead of three.

Mr. JONES accepted the amendment.

The question was then taken on striking out the word "ten" and substituting "five," and decided in the negative.

The 17th Section, as reported by the Committee, was then adopted.

Mr. DENT offered the following:

No bill shall become a law unless it receive the sanction of a majority of all the members of both Houses.

There might be a quorum which would consist of little more than a quarter of all the members. He thought no bill should become a law unless it received the sanction of a majority all the members of both Houses.

Mr. GWIN said this might be a very good regulation, but it was utterly impracticable under existing circumstances. It would be impossible to tell when a majority was voting. Hence the provision would be a dead letter in the Constitution.

Mr. JONES remarked that, if he remembered rightly, the Constitution of New Jersey said "persons present." He did not see how it was practicable at all times to ascertain whether there was a majority of all the members elected—especially in this country, where it was necessary to act with locomotive speed.

Mr. Semple had the Constitution of Illinois before him, which provides that all bills before they become laws shall be passed on the yeas and nays, and that the yeas and nays shall show a majority vote of all the members elected to both Houses. It seemed to him that the propriety of such a rule was evident. In the brief experience of this Convention, important measures had been carried when there was a bare quorum present. Although this might be admissable in Committee of the Whole, it was objectionable when measures of importance came up for final action. Very important bills might be passed in the Legislature by some understanding among the members, which would be directly contrary to the wishes of the people. He had seen it done He had seen members invited out on some pretence, for the purpose of getting bills passed. It seemed to him the best course that could be adopted to avoid what gentlemen were so apprehensive of—too much legislation. Where the propriety of a measure is at all doubtful, it is better that this restriction should prevail.

Mr. Halleck said that, from the peculiar character of our population in California, it would be very difficult for the first two or three Legislatures to get together more than a majority of the members elected. If we require the vote of a majority of those elected on every bill before it becomes a law, it may readily be anticipated that the Legislature will be obliged to home, or sit and talk to the walls. He thought it would be very impolitic, for this reason, to introduce the proposed section.

The question was then taken on Mr. Dent's proposition, and it was rejected.

The question being on the adoption of the 18th Section, viz:

18. The Assembly shall have the sole power of impeachment; and all impeachments shall be tried by the Senate. When sitting for that purpose, the Senators shall be upon oath or affirmation; and no person shall be convicted without the concurrence of two-thirds of the members present.

Mr. Jones moved to amend by inserting, in place of "Assembly," the words "House of Representatives." It was the ordinary phraseology, and he thought it would be better.

Mr. Norton stated that the word Assembly was used in the preceding sections, and could not be altered here without changing the whole so as to correspond.

Mr. Jones therefore withdrew his amendment, and the section, as reported by the Select Committee, was adopted.

The 19th Section was then read, as follows:

19. The Governor, ——— shall be liable to impeachment for any misdemeanor in office; but judgment, in such cases, shall extend only to removal from office and disqualification to hold any office of trust or profit under the State; but the party convicted or acquitted shall, nevertheless, be liable to indictment, trial, and punishment according to law. All other civil officers shall be tried for misdemeanors in office in such manner as the Legislature shall provide.

Mr. Halleck proposed that the blank should be passed over for the present, as it would be necessary, before filling it, to determine what officers should be created.

Mr. McCarver saw no impropriety in creating those officers now, and filling the blank.

Mr. Norton said the blank could not filled until the Constitution was formed.

Mr. Dimmick moved to insert the word "honor" before trust or profit; which was adopted.

The filling of the blank was then postponed, and the question recurring on the section as amended, it was adopted.

The 20th and 21st Sections were adopted without debate, as follows:

20. So Senator or member of Assembly shall, during the time he shall have been elected, be appointed to any civil office of profit under this State, which shall have been created, or the emoluments of which shall have been increased during such term, except such offices as may be filled by elections by the people.

21. No person holding any lucrative office under the United States or this State, or any other Power, shall be eligible to the Legislature. *Provided*, that officers in the militia, to which there

is attached no annual salary, or local officers and postmasters, whose compensation does not exceed five hundred dollars per annum, shall not be demed lucrative.

The 22d Section being under consideration, as follows:

22. No person who may hereafter be a collector or holder of public moneys, shall have a seat in either House of the Legislature, or be eligible to any office of trust or profit under this State, until he shall have accounted for and paid into the treasury all sums for which he may be liable.

Mr. PRICE moved that the section be stricken out. He could see no good that could arise from it, and it might be the means of depriving an honest and worthy man of a seat in the Legislature. Many an honest man may be owing the State. It may be from no dishonesty on his part, but from various calamities beyond his control. He (Mr. Price) did not see that this section afforded any protection to the Government—that there was any principle or restriction in it worthy of a place in the Constitution.

Mr. NORTON thought it a matter of very serious importance that persons holding office should be made accountable for the money placed in their hands. It is no small matter that the Government should be protected against dishonest men. Many public officers hold large amounts of money. The people should know where that money goes. If it has been fraudulently disposed of, the officer who commits the fraud should be ineligible to office. The gentleman says that a person holding public funds may be unfortunate in business, and unable to settle his accounts at the proper time. If so, he has no business in the Legislature. He should stay at home, and endeavor, by strict attention to business, to meet his liabilites. He has no business engaging in political contests.

Mr. WOZENCRAFT wished to know what object a defaulting officer would have in running for the Legislature, unless to propose and probably carry such measures as would free him from his indebtedness. He considered it a very important provision; that the door should be closed against persons of this character.. Every member had seen the effects of the immense defalcations in the States, and should profit by past experience.

Mr. PRICE did not wish to be misunderstood in his remarks on this question. There was no member who would go further than he would in relation to accountability; but he saw nothing in this section to afford protection to the people of California. If any man is a defaulter in this country, the people know it. He is a marked man. If he has their money in his pocket, they know it, and they can act accordingly. He never can be supported by the people for any public office. But he (Mr. Price) contended that a man, by a series of calamities, may be indebted to the State, and at the same time bear as good a character, and be as well entitled to the respect and confidence of his fellow-citizens, as any person in the State. Yet, by this provision, a man who has not lost the respect and confidence of his fellow-citizens, is to be deprived of a seat in the Legislature, and rendered ineligible to any office of trust or profit. The people are competent to judge who shall represent them.

Mr. McCARVER was decidedly in favor of the section. It is impossible for the people always to know whether public officers have settled their accounts. It should be made a constitutional requirement, so that they may be well advised of it at the time of election. No man should be allowed to be returned as an officer of the Government, if he be a defaulter. He (Mr. McCarver) was satisfied the community would be in favor of this measure.

The question was then taken on the 22d Section as reported, and it was adopted.

Mr. McDOUGAL thought there was some misunderstanding about this vote. The motion was to strike out the section, and the question was taken on its adoption. If the Chair decided that the section was adopted, he appealed from the decision.

Mr. SHANNON asked whether it was the decision of the Chair that, when a motion to strike out a section is made, that motion cannot be received, but that, in its place, the original question on the passage of the section must be put. If so, it would give rise to a great deal of misunderstanding.

THE CHAIR stated that the first question after the reading of the section, was, "Shall this section pass?" The motion to strike out was unnecessary, because if the House refused to adopt the section, it would of course be rejected or stricken out.

Mr. McDOUGAL appealed from this decision. Whereupon, the question on the appeal was put, and the decision of the Chair sustained.

Mr. PRICE moved a reconsideration of the vote on the passage of the section, in order to allow the gentleman rrom Sacramento (Mr. Shannon,) an opportunity of submitting an amendment.

The question was taken, and the House refused to reconsider the vote on the adoption of the section.

The 23d Section was then read, and adopted without debate, as follows:

23. No money shall be drawn from the treasury, but in consequence of appropriations made by law.

The 24th Section being under consideration, as follows:

24. The members of the Legislature shall receive for their services a compensation to be ascertained by law, and paid out of the public treasury; but no increase of the compensation shall take effect during the term for which the members of either House shall have been elected.

Mr. SEMPLE had always held the opinion that where time is concerned, it should not reach back beyond the adoption of the Constitution; but in this instance there is an obvious necessity for adding a proviso. The section itself is very good and should be adopted; but by amending it a little, it would obviate a difficulty upon his mind, and he had no doubt, upon the minds of other members. He referred to the necessity of this Convention making provision for the compensation of the first Legislature.

Mr. WOZENCRAFT suggested the propriety of saying "fixed," instead of "ascertained" by law.

Mr. CROSBY enquired of the gentleman (Mr. Wozencraft,) whether the compensation of the next Legislature was to be fixed in the schedule.

Mr. WOZENCRAFT said it was.

Mr. DENT supposed it would be much to the interest of the first Legislature that this matter should be settled by this Convention. He wished to know if the schedule was to be a portion of the Constitution, and whether it was to have the force of law. If the schedule had not that force, the compensation of members of the first Legislature would not be provided for.

Mr. GWIN read the 18th Section of the Constitution of Michigan, from which this section was copied, as follows, omitting the last clause:

The members of the Legislature shall receive for their services a compensation to be ascertained by law, and paid out of the public treasury; but no increase of the compensation shall take effect during the term for which the members of either House shall have been elected; and such compensation shall not exeeed ——— dollars a day.

The question being on the amendment of Mr. Wozencraft to insert "fixed" instead of "ascertained," it was carried, and the section as amended was adopted.

The 25th and 26th Sections were then adopted without debate, viz:

25. Every law enacted by the Legislature, shall embrace but one object, and that shall be expressed in the title; and no law shall be revised or amended by reference to its title, but in such case the act revised, or section amended, shall be re-enacted and published at length.

26. No divorce shall be granted by the Legislature.

The 27th Section being under consideration, as follows:

27. No lottery shall be authorised by this State, nor shall the sale of lottery tickets be allowed.

Mr. PRICE moved to strike out this section. He believed it to be exceedingly impolitic to prohibit the drawing of lotteries in this country. It might be made a source of great revenue to this State, and however objectionable the principle was, yet he believed it was better in some cases to legalize immoral acts than to have them done in secret. He was opposed to restricting future Legislatures in relation to this matter. He thought it should be left to the people to prohibit lotteries or not, as they deemed expedient. He regarded the propriety of this policy as too palpable to require an elaborate argument. He wished gentlemen to reflect before they forever prohibited lotteries in California. He was opposed to the system himself, and would be sorry to see it legalized; but he believed it was a necessary evil in California at this time. Three hundred thousand dollars could be raised annually by the State for the privilege of lotteries. This would be a great relief under the embarrassing position that the State will be placed in when the new government goes into operation, owing to the difficulty of organizing a perfect system of taxation. It would be a very essential relief to the people, and would defray the expenses of their Legislnture until better means of obtaining the full amount of taxes necessary to defray the expenses of the government are established.

Mr. McCarver thought it very strange if the people of this golden region could not defray the expenses of a State government without entering into a legalized system of gambling. If the government that authorizes the sale of lottery tickets, and the purchasers of those tickets were not direct gamblers, they certainly were on the road to professional gambling.

Mr. Hoppe looked upon this as a very important question. He admitted the fact stated by his friend from San Francisco, (Mr. Price,) that the State of California would probably receive from the privilege of lottery-drawing, three hundred thousand dollars annually; and he admitted that it was a very desirable acquisition of revenue. But there is another question involved in the adoption of this section—a question of far greater importance than money. It concerns the well-being of society, and the permanent industrial interests of the State. The system is not only objectionable in itself, but it is peculiarly objectionable in this country, where the temptation to gamble is so great. The effects are most deeply felt by those who are least able to sustain them. It penetrates to the domestic circle; it destroys the happiness of families, and falls with a peculiar weight upon the widow and the orphan. He appealed to this House not to sanction a principle so fatal to the best interests of society, by striking out the section.

Mr. Shannon said he would sustain the motion of the gentleman from San Francisco, (Mr. Price,) in accordance with the principle which he had advocated when the subject of lotteries was brought up in the bill of rights. He thought it should be left to the Legislature. He did not conceive that there was a greater amount of wisdom, including the gray hairs, in this Convention, than there would be in the future Legislatures of the State; nor was it proper to prevent those bodies from adopting such measures of general policy as they might deem expedient. He desired to leave the Legislature untrammelled. It was sufficient to lay down the broad fundamental principles of a republican form of Government, without assuming to deprive the people of the right to pass such laws, not inconsistent with those principles, as they thought proper.

Mr. Dent was opposed to the amendment. He believed the State should be prohibited from indulging in a practice which was condemned in individuals. The State should not be permitted to derive its nourishment from the destruction of its members. If the practice is objectionable in individuals, it is still more so in a Government, which professes to be the guardian of individuals, and the protector of their interests. He thought other means of obtaining revenue for the support of the Government could be resorted to, more honorable than a legalized system of gambling.

Mr. Price admitted that he was entirely floored by the remarks of his friend from San Jose, (Mr. Hoppe,) who had posted him up on morals. He (Mr. Price) contended that the people of California are essentially a gambling people at this period, and it was no use to back out of that position. Every public house in California has its monte and faro tables, licensed by law, wherever there is law. Hundreds are to be seen at these houses casting their money on the chance of the game. He wished to know if lotteries were more immoral than establishments of this kind. Had the gentleman (Mr. Hoppe) denounced these gambling houses amongst his constituents? He (Mr. Price) might be taking a very impolitic ground to assume this position; but he felt assured it was to the interest of this country, at the present period, to gather all the means within her reach for revenue. It has been remarked that this is a rich country; that the people are able to pay $300,000 without resorting to a system of this kind for support; but he could tell the gentleman when they fixed a heavy tax upon the people they would find greater difficulty in collecting it than they imagined. He believed there was no people in the world who could bear taxation with more difficulty at this time than the people of California. The present state of the country forbids the collection of taxes. The people are a moving, floating population. You see them, but you cannot find them. Three hundred thousand dollars a year would be a very considerable sum in our treasury. He desired to send the Constitution to the people of this country in its most simple form; he wished it to go forth unembarrassed by onerous restrictions. Let the people judge for themselves, and pass such laws as circumstances may require.

Mr. Halleck agreed with the gentleman from San Francisco, (Mr. Price,) as to the propriety of permitting the people to legislate for themselves; but at the same time the object of this Convention is to limit the powers of the Legislature; and it appeared to him that this very clause fixes a very important limit upon those powers. We may be a gambling community, but let us not in this Constitution create a gambling State. If money is necessary for the support of the State government, let us not raise it by means which even the gentleman himself, (Mr. Price) admits to be immoral. In nearly all the new Constitutions you will find this clause. It was not contained in the old Constitutions, but in most cases where they have been amended it has been introduced. In the old Constitution of New York, to which reference has been made in the course of debate, no prohibition was inserted. Many gentlemen present would remember the famous case of Yates and McIntyre, which involved not only individuals of the State in ruin, but was the occasion of serious embarrassment to the State government itself. The result so clearly established the evils of the lottery system, that the Convention of New York, in 1846, inserted a clause in the very first article of the new Constitution, (see Sec. 10.) prohibiting lotteries and the sale of lottery tickets. It appeared to him (Mr. Halleck) that this prohibition was one of the best that could be inserted in the article limiting the powers of the Legislature.

Mr. Moore said he had received no instructions from his constituents directing him to prescribe the particular amusements at which they should pass their time; when they should go to bed, or when they should get up. He came here to lay down the broad and general principles of religious freedom.

Mr. Dimmick agreed with the gentleman, (Mr. Moore,) that this Convention met here for the purpose of making a Constitution on the broad principles of religious freedom, but he had yet to learn that the exclusion of a clause which prohibits gambling is religious freedom. It might be contended that gambling is religious freedom, inasmuch as it takes the largest possible liberties known in any community where religion exists; but it would require a very free interpretation of the gentleman's remarks to bring the practice of gambling within the ordinary bounds of religion. He trusted it would be a long time before he became a moral man, entitled to membership in any church, by reason of his proficiency in the art of gambling. It was a new theory of morals, which he thought should be omitted in this Constitution. The gentleman from San Francisco, (Mr. Price,) proclaimed this a gambling community. He (Mr. Dimmick) was not ready to accept the remark as applicable to his constituents. He trusted such a thing could not be said of all the districts of California, though it might be appropriate as applied to the district which the gentleman represented, and perhaps some other districts. It might possibly be expedient to license gambling in certain parts of the country, but not lotteries. Other modes, such as have always been customary in the country, might be sanctioned. But, for his own part, he preferred that gambling of every description should be prohibited. Whatever might have been usual in other Constitutions, it was time for this Convention to present to the people of California a Constitution which would prohibit any injurious or immoral practice. Gentlemen assert that we are not here to make laws. He would ask are we not here to make a Constitution—the strongest law known under our system of government. That Constitution only requires the sanction of the people to become the fundamental law of the country. Other laws, passed by the Legislature, will be subservient to it. He trusted the new State, which was to occupy so prominent a position in this confederacy, would not, for her own credit, adopt an immoral system of taxation as a source of revenue. The best policy for governments, as well as individuals, is a strict adherence to legitimate and honorable means of support. Whatever temporary benefit may be derived from a contrary policy, the evils of a departure from this great principle are certain to be felt sooner or later. In the case of governments, the inevitable consequences are, an extravagant and reckless system of legislation; an undue spirit of speculation, and a general derangement of the permanent interests of the State. With individuals, it encourages habits of idleness, and a distaste for those industrial pursuits best calculated to promote the weath and prosperity of the mass. The question of revenue is of very trifling importance, compared with the deep and lasting injury which institutions of this kind must inflict upon the community. The lottery system is the same as all other gambling—a system of cheatery. The chances are against the purchaser of the ticket—otherwise the institution could not be sustained. All the revenue is obtained from these chances, which are against the buyer. Shall this State, which is to introduce our great republican principles of government to the nations of the Pacific, derive its means of support from the ruin of individuals? Shall the State of California give its sanction to an institution which can only be sustained by producing degradation, poverty, and crime? He trusted not. He sincerely hoped this prohibition would be incorporated in the Constitution. He appealed to the good judgment of this House, forever to prohibit the Legislature from adopting a measure so injurious in its tendency; so degrading to the honor of a republican State; so destructive of the best interests of the people, both in their social and political relations; and so universally condemned at this period by the deliberate judgment of the American people.

The question was then taken on the 27th Section as reported by the Committee, and it was adopted.

The 28th and 29th Sections were then passed without debate, as follows:

28. The enumeration of the inhabitants of this State shall be taken under the direction of the Legislature in the years one thousand eight hundred and fifty two, and one thousand eight hundred and fifty five, and at the end of every ten years thereafter; and these enumerations, together with the census that may be taken under the direction of the Congress of the United States in the year one thousand eight hundred and fifty, and every subsequent ten years, shall serve as the basis of representation in both Houses of the Legislature.

29. The number of Senators and members of Assembly at the first session holden after the enumerations herein provided are made, be fixed by the Legislature, and apportioned among the several counties and districts to be established by law, according to the number of white inhabitants. The number of members of Assembly shall not be less than twenty-four nor more than thirty-six, until the number of inhabitants in this State shall amount to one hundred thousand; and after that period at such ratio that the whole number of members of Assembly shall never be less than thirty nor more than eighty.

The 30th Section reported, being under consideration, as follows:

30. When a Congressional, Senatorial, or Assembly district shall be composed of two or more counties, it shall not be separated by any county belonging to another district; and no county shall be divided in forming a Congressional, Senatorial, or Assembly district.

Mr. PRICE inquired of the Chairman of the Committee, (Mr. Norton) where this section came from.

Mr. NORTON said it came from the Select Committee on the Constitution.

Mr. PRICE inquired if the Chairman of the Committee assumed to himself, as Chairman, the authorship? He would like to know whether the section could be found in any of the Constitutions, and if so, in what Constitution?

Mr. HALLECK stated that it was from the Constitution of Iowa.

Mr. PRICE could not see the use of encumbering the Constitution of California with sections of this kind. If there was no Legislature ever going to be formed, it might be very well to provide for the districting of the counties; but what this House had to do with it, he could not perceive. He moved, therefore, to strike the section out.

Mr. SEMPLE called the gentleman's attention to a system known as *gerrymandering* in the States, and explained the effects of that system. He was in favor of the section; he considered it a necessary provision in the Constitution to provide against political frauds of this kind, and if there never had been such a provision reported before, he thought the Committee would deserve credit for originating so excellent a provision.

The question was then taken, and the section was adopted.

On motion, the Committee rose, reported progress, and obtained leave to sit again.

On motion, the House adjourned to 10 o'clock, A. M., to-morrow.

FRIDAY, SEPTEMBER 14, 1849.

The Convention met pursuant to adjournment.

Prayer by Rev. Senor Antonio Ramirez.

Journal of yesterday read and approved.

Mr. BOTTS, from the Select Committee to whom was submitted the subject of the proper mode of paying the expenses of the Convention, and the proper *per diem*, or other allowance, of its officers, made a report in writing, accompanied by certain correspondence which had taken place between the Committee and Brevet Brigadier General Riley, Governor of California, in which General Riley stated that he would pay, so far as the means in his possession would permit, the necessary expenses of the Convention; and submitting a communication addressed by him to General Persifer Smith, containing a statement of the manner in which this fund was collected; together with a minority report from the same committee; which were ordered to lie on the table for further consideration.

Mr. ORD moved that forty-three copies of the report, not including the correspondence, be prepared for the use of the Convention. The motion was decided in the negative.

On motion of Mr. SHERWOOD, it was ordered that twenty copies of the report, without the correspondence, be prepared for the use of the Convention.

A motion to prepare copies of the correspondence for the use of the Convention was decided in the negative.

Mr. GWIN moved to reconsider the vote by which twenty copies of the report, without the correspondence, had been ordered to be furnished. The motion was decided in the negative.

On motion, the Convention adjourned to 3 o'clock, P. M. to-morrow.

SATURDAY, SEPTEMBER 15, 1849.

The journal of yesterday was read and approved.

Mr. GWIN moved to take up the report of the Committee of the Whole on the bill of rights, with a view to action on the amendments.

At the suggestion of Mr. SHANNON, Mr. GWIN withdrew his motion.

Mr. CARILLO rose to address the Convention, and the Interpreter and Interpreter's Clerk being absent, Mr. Foster, a member from Los Angelos, was requested to interpret the remarks of Mr. C.

Mr. CARILLO complained of incompetency and disrespectful language on the part of the Interpreter's Clerk—whereupon

Mr. BOTTS moved the following:

Resolved, That on the complaint of Mr. Carillo, a member of this House, of indignity offered to him, in his seat, by the Interpreter's Clerk, the said Clerk be removed.

The resolution was adopted.

On motion of Mr. HOPPE, Judge White was requested to act, temporarily, as Assistant Interpreter to the Convention.

On motion of Mr. SHANNON, the report of the Finance Committee was taken up, viz:

Report of the minority of the Committee of five on the payment of the expenses of the Convention, and the per diem or other allowance of its officers:

The Committee, to whom was referred the subject of the proper mode to be adopted to pay the expenses of the Convention, and who were directed to report the proper per diem or other allowance of its officers, have had the same under consideration and beg leave to report:

That the officers of this Convention are entitled to a per diem allowance, as follows:

Secretary, $28 00; Assistant Secretary, $23 00; Sergeant-at-Arms, $22 00; Copying Clerks, $18 00; Doorkeeper, $12 00; Page, $4 00; Reporter, $50 00; Chaplain, $16 00; Interpreter, $24 00; Interpreter's Clerk, $21 00.

And the Committee further report that, in the opinion of your Committee, the most feasible and proper mode of paying the expenses of the Convention is in the schedule to provide that the first Legislature that meets under this Constitution shall make early provision for it.

Mr. HALLECK moved that the report be recommitted, with instructions to report the daily pay of the Secretary and Translator at $16, and of the other officers of the Convention in proportion.

Mr. BOTTS was opposed to the resolution. He thought it would only produce delay. He could not, for his own part, come to a correct conclusion as to what ought to be the per diem allowance of these officers, until he knew the source from whence their pay was to come, and the time at which it was to be paid. He thought it exceedingly important that that part of the report should be taken up first. The purpose of the minority report was to decide this question at once, so that there would be some ground to proceed upon in fixing the compensation of the officers. It was unnecessary to require the Committee to report again. The two reports fixed the same rate of pay; they were exactly similar in that respect. They arrived at this conclusion in the following manner. Each member put down the amount which he thought proper. The aggregate salary for each officer was written down, and divided by five—the number of members composing the Committee. The amount thus arrived at was adopted. He did not believe that when it was taken into consideration the manner in which labor is paid for in California, though the amount seemed very large, that it would be found extravagant, or at all out of proportion. He had enquired among merchants who employ clerks in San Francisco, and he found that this Convention was giving, at the rates fixed in the report, little more to a temporary Secretary or clerk, who was employed only for a few weeks, than was paid in San Francisco to clerks who were employed by the year. The Committee were of opinion that the State was entitled to be served with as good talent as any merchant. It was in consideration of these facts that the Committee went so far beyond the proposition of the gentleman from Monterey, (Mr. Halleck.) In justice to these gentlemen he thought the people of California should be required to pay them as liberally as they would be paid by private individuals. The Convention had no right to draw upon the patriotism of its officers; gentlemen might draw upon their own patriotism if they wished, and make their pay as low as they pleased; they could readily afford to do that when they had all the honor; but the case was different with the clerks, who had none of the honor and most of the labor.

Mr. JONES could not see what vast difference the lower estimate of the gentleman from Monterey, (Mr. Halleck) would make. It would not amount to more than a hundred dollars a day at the most. Moreover, he thought this body should remember that these gentlemen are not residents of Monterey. They have sacrificed their prospects elsewhere, and lost time in coming here, and it would be but simple justice to pay them liberally.

Mr. SNYDER addressed the Committee as follows:

There are many matters touched upon in that and the accompanying correspondence, which deeply interest us; and particularly that portion which relates to the collection of customs in this country, and the manner in which the money so collected has been appropriated.

I ask the indulgence of this Convention to make a few remarks, which, I think, will not be inappropriate at this time, relative to the financial affairs of this country, and the treatment received from the Government of the United States.

The question of the expenses of this Convention, referred to in the report of the Committee, very naturally suggests that it is high time the Government of the United States should awaken to a sense of its duty towards the distant Territory of California.

There was a time, Mr. President, when emigration to this country was encouraged by a *certain power*, if not directly, indirectly.

I speak, sir, from personal knowledge in regard to this matter, for I was influenced by a gentleman in this country to come to California. Aye, sir, he is now in this very house. You well know, sir, we were here but little over one short year before it was understood that despatches had arrived for Capt. Fremont, then on his way to Oregon. Be that as it may, he returned after accomplishing half his journey, and in a very short time the American flag was seen floating within the walls of this town. I will not say, Mr. President, nor need I dwell upon the fact how the Government of the United States rewarded that young man—how he was placed between the jealous fire of older and more subtle officers.

I will only here assert that the action of the Home Government was, in his case, and in that of the country which he aided to annex to our confederation, in every respect consistent. They condemned the devoted soldier, and they no less showed their disregard of the rights of Americans, by a total refusal to provide means to pay the expenses incurred in bringing this territory into the line of our government limits.

Sir, California has been abused by the General Government. The citizens who cast themselves on the hostile shores of the Pacific, have been abused; and chief among them is that young man, who, perilling all for his country, stood shoulder to shoulder with the daring few who crossed the rocky ridges between this and the old States, to add another bright star to our already glorious Confederation.

How appropriate are the words of Byron to this case!

"He who ascends the mountain tops shall find
The loftiest peaks most wrapt in clouds and snow;
He who surpasses or subdues mankind,
Must look down upon the hate of those below;
Though high above the sun of glory glow,
And far beneath the earth and ocean spread,
Round him are icy rocks, and loudly blow,
Contending tempests on his naked head,
And thus reward the toils which to these summits led."

It is true, sir, that the great Government of the United States, of which we claim to be a part, should be rebuked by California! Not only the emigrants to their country, but the foreign residents and native Californians, have suffered from the negligence of the home Government. I do not make these remarks because I now love my country and her institutions less, but because I love that freedom of speech guarantied by our forefathers more. And I glory in the privilege which allows the poorest man in our Republic to condemn his rulers when they act unjustly, as they have done toward California.

Judging from its acts, it would indeed seem, sir, that Congress believed the assertion of the representative from the little State of Delaware, that there "were not five men in this territory capable of forming a Government for it," and, of course, that there was, in his opinion, as few capable of judging how far their rights were outraged by neglect. This, sir, is the voice from little Delaware, uttered in that august assembly to which we, the forty members of this Convention, are about to submit a petition for admittance into the Union. We hope that the distinguished mouthpiece of little Delaware did not entirely exhaust the wisdom of his State or its representative, by this sage remark. However insulting it may be to this great territory and its inhabitants, we can have no quarrel with the little State of Delaware, for we have here a country which could put both the little State and its wisdom in its pocket, and forget in its vastness that such small things were there.

Now then, Mr. President, I will come to the matter which is more immediately connected with what I most wish to say.

We have had the report of the Committee on Finance, and the letter of Gov. Riley relative to the means of paying the expenses of this Convention, and he feels a delicacy in giving a decisive answer to the inquiries of the Committee. This does not at all astonish me. I am too well acquainted with the liberal policy and generosity of Gov. Riley, to suppose for one moment that he would hesitate to pay the expenses of this Convention, were his instructions sufficiently full from his Government.

No sir! The niggardly policy adopted by the Government of the United States towards California, puts it out of her power to keep up such a civil government as this country should have, to say nothing about supporting the citizens of California in establishing a State Government after using the thousands they have collected from customs in California. I would ask, what has become of the revenue collected in California? although, sir, as' we have not laws like our Territories at home, you may ask what right we have to make inquiries. It is an old saying, sir, "that he that dances must pay the fidler;" and "it is a poor rule that will not work both ways." Have we not a right to make the fidler play that tune we like best? Has that revenue been appropriated in accordance with certain stipulations in the Constitution of the United States? Certainly, if they tax us, they should give us something in return. Sir, at this very time, there is an officer of the United States Navy surveying and bouying out the channels of San Pablo and Suisun Bays, and who pays for it? Sir, the people, by *subscription*. I handed a paper around among the citizens of Sacramento city for subscriptions: what did they say? We cannot pay out any more of our money for the Government until we get what they already owe us.

Still, sir, we must go on as we have done, paying the expenses of the Government ourselves, fighting on our own hook, for the honor of it! I beg pardon—for the honor of the Government of the United States.

Sir, in the Report of the Committee on Finance, in regard to the payment of the expenses of this Convention, the Governor refers to the very delicate situation in which he is placed. There is no person who sympathi-es with him more deeply than I do; and little do I care whether I receive one cent or not to defray my expenses.

Sir, there are now gentlemen in this Convention who have travelled many miles to get here; and many of these gentlemen, who are now serving their country gratuitously, (as they have done before,) have accounts against the Government for supplies furnished during the war, to troops of the United States Government.

I can point to a gentleman now present, who holds claims against the Government of the United States to the amount of from twelve to fifteen thousand dollars; and there are many more of a similar character.

In this very town, sir, there is, to my certain knowledge, a large bundle of musty papers, claims against the Government of the United States to the amount of $100,000, which, in a few more years, will no doubt be interesting objects for antiquarian research.

All nations are reaping the benefits of the discovery of the gold; and first on the list stands out, in bold relief, the United States. To whom are they indebted for the discovery? To the pioneer veteran, Capt. J. A. Sutter, through whose generosity and benevolence, protection and assistance have been afforded to the travel worn emigrants who had toiled through many a weary day, and had passed many an anxious night upon the barren waste of a desolate country.

I need not say how they have been recompenseed for the toils and dangers they encountered in opening the road to the stores of wealth that are now drawn from the inexhaustible placers of California. Neglect, gross neglect, has been their reward.

What has been the sacrifice? Look upon the bleached bones of the starved emigrants which now lie scattered in the valley of the Sierra Nevada, where, hemmed in by mountains of impassable snow, they wasted from day to day, struggling with feeble hope against dark despair, until one by one, they drooped and died, leaving but few to tell the sad tale of their suffering.

O! let us draw a veil over the mournful picture, and hope, if nothing else, that a little sympathy may be created for the poor emigrant.

Sir, I hope the time is not far distant when the Government of the United States will cease to neglect a country from which her people, and all other nations, are draining such an immense amount of wealth.

Mr HALLECK said, as he offered the resolution, he supposed he was bound to defend it. The object of the resolution was to avoid the difficulties which gentlemen apprehended. If the expenses of this Convention were limited to a small amount, he had no doubt they would be paid; but it was necessary that the rate of salaries should be economical. If the expenses exceeded the proper bounds, he was certain they would not be paid, and the result would be, that it would have to be left to the next Legislature to provide for them. There would be great difficulty in obtaining the adjustment of back claims in this way. If the salaries of officers were to be fixed at twenty-two to twenty-eight dollars a day, what was the salary of the members to be fixed at? He had heard thirty dollars a-day mentioned. What would be said of members of this Convention when they went back to the people with a bill of seventy thousand dollars a month for making a Constitution? A hall is furnished, together with stationery, lights, and all the minor articles necessary for the use of the House. For the officers and pay of members alone, we demand seventy thousand dollars. He was very confident it could not be paid in any other way than by a tax fixed by the next Legislature. He did not know what General Riley would do. He had not heard a word from him on the subject. But he knew this much, that if General Riley sent a bill with these rates of pay to Washington, it would be sent back, and he would have to pay it out of his own pocket. He had had something to do with public accounts for some time, and he knew that it was very difficult to get vouchers through the Treasury of the United States. Within the last ten days, he had had offers from five or six competent persons to do similar work at the rates fixed in the resolution. He found no difficulty in getting competent persons at that salary. Again: if we fix the salaries of officers and members of this Convention at this price, can we fix the salaries of officers and members of the next Legislature at a less price? If we, with every thing furnished, expend seventy thousand dollars a month, what amount of money must be appropriated for the expenses of the Legislature? Can it be obtained in California by any system of taxation that may be adopted? No sir: we send the bill to the general Government, and ask Congress to make an appropriation for its payment. Congress will never grant such an expenditure. Let the expenses of this Convention, then, be fixed on moderate terms, so that they can be paid as we go along; let us set an example of economy to the Legislatures that may follow us. We are a new State; we have rich gold mines, and a growing commerce; we have abundant sources of wealth; but we have not facilities for collecting taxes. If an example of extravagance is to be followed by the next Legislature, there is no difficulty in predicting that the members of that Legislature will sit but one session. He (Mr. Halleck,) was of opinion that the salaries should be fixed now, and would therefore withdraw his resolution.

Mr. Botts referred to the report of the Committee as proving that instead of being an extravagant estimate, these gentlemen receive probably less than was ever paid in similar offices in the United States. Terms are altogether relative. When a Secretary receives $28 in one place, and $8 in another, we are to look at what can be purchased with these sums where they are paid. It should be borne in mind that, when his cook costs him $10 a month in the one place, and $100 in the other, the highest price is paid to the Secretary in the United States. As to the impossibility of collecting taxes—these taxes are to be paid by the farmers, shoemakers, carpenters, lawyers, and doctors. Now, a blacksmith at home, is very well content to make $2 a day. In this country he makes $20, and he is just as well able to pay a dollar tax here as twenty cents in the United States. The rates of pay fixed in the report are not out of proportion with the usual rate of wages. Gentlemen should not be alarmed at the high sound these amounts have. They should refer to the rate of wages here in other departments of labor. But he would say nothing more on that subject. He hoped it would be the pleasure of the House to determine the pay of the officers. He thought it proper, however, that the House should first take up that part of the report relating to the manner of obtaining the means. It is necessary to determine whether this fund with which General Riley proposed to pay the expenses of the Convention is tangible or not. By an examination of the official correspondence, it would be found that General Riley studiously reserves the right which he (Mr. Botts,) could not for one, accord to him, in effect to decide what are the necessary expenses of this Convention. In other words, if you apply to him to pay these expenses, he holds the right to veto the rate of salary which you may deem proper to adopt, by saying that is unnecessary. General Riley is an old soldier and a gallant one; and he (Mr. Botts,) would sever his right arm from his body before he would bring the blush of anger to his cheek. It was not to him personally he applied his remarks, but to a higher and greater authority. He found, upon glancing at the correspondence, that the President of the United States had dared to give orders for the disposal of the civil fund. Every feeling prompted him to repel any proposition founded upon this state of things. Could any man doubt the illegality of such an order? Is there not a clause in the Constitution of the United States providing that no monies shall be drawn out of the public treasury, except in consequence of appropriations made by law? With such a clause staring them in the face, were gentlemen willing to ask any individual to do an act so clearly illegal? He was told expressly that these are the civil funds of the United States. Every member of this House was well aware that Congress has made no appropriation by which this money can be paid out of the Treasury of the United States for this purpose. It was a violation of the Constitution on the part of the President of the United States to give such an order. Will you aid or abet in this act? Will you have any hand in receiving or disposing of this money, which you can only get by a violation of the Constitution? The alien and sedition law was nothing to this. In the whole history of our Government, there never has been such a flagrant violation of the Constution, as that which is brought to your knowledge in this correspondence. That fund is, and must of necessity be, in the Treasury of the United States; it cannot be otherwise. He hoped it would not be urged upon him that it had never been in the Treasury. From the moment that money belonging to the United States comes into the hands of a collecting officer, it is in the Treasury. Deny it, and the people's money is at the disposition of every receiving and disbursing officer in the country. There never comes a dollar but comes through their hands. General Riley does undoubtedly what he was ordered to do; but that order was illegal, and you are aiding and abetting in an illegal act when you consent, much more propose to receive any portion of this fund. In the first place, he (Mr. Botts,) could not admit for one moment, that this Convention should appear at the footstool of any individual, and humbly ask that he should dole out to them such expenses as he deemed necessary. In the next place, he considered this whole affair an unclean thing; that the Executive of the United States had violated every obligation he had given to support the Constitution, and that this Convention would be equally culpable in accepting any portion of this fund. He designed to take no part in the difficulties which had arisen between General Riley and General Smith upon this subject; he had not a word to say about it; but whether it came from General Riley, or General Smith, or the President of the United States, he could not consent to touch cne cent of this money. As to the pay of members of this House, it would be more decorous and consistent with the dignity of the Convention, in his opinion, to leave others to fix that matter. It was just and proper that the pay of the officers should be fixed; but with regard to the members, he proposed to introduce in the schedule a clause providing that the first Legislature shall fix the rate and provide for the pay of members of this House. He thought there was no other mode of paying the officers than that usually adopted by similar bodies in the States—to refer it to the first Legislature. If it was the opinion of the House that, in consequence of the delay and inconvenience to which they would necessaraily be subjected, their salaries should be increased, he was prepared to allow them more.

Mr. Jones remarked that such was the discursive character of this debate, that he apprehended the original resolution had been forgotten. There was one great objection he had to the course of the majority of this Committee in getting the money from the hands of the civil government here. He thought it a greater objection than that argued by his friend from Monterey, (Mr. Botts.) The objection was this: that it does not appear to be known whether there is any money there or not. We are told that if you give the officers of this Convention about what they could dig with their picks at the mines, they may in all probability be paid. He (Mr. Jones) did not suppose that an officer representing the Government of the United States here—an officer high in command—and whose reputation was above reproach, would attempt to hold the reins of government so far in his hands as to attempt to guide this Convention, by saying that he would regulate the pay of the officers himself, and thereby bring it within such bounds as he deemed proper.

Mr. BOTTS said he intended no reflection upon the officer high in command. He had simply opposed the principle giving the right to any officer, or any power in existence, to dictate to this Convention what should be its necessary expenses.

Mr. JONES alluded to the general tendency of the gentleman's remarks. The great objection urged in other quarters of the House seemed to be that this was an enormous tariff of prices brought in by the Committee—that it could never be paid. In the estimate made by the Committee, some twenty dollars a day must have been allowed for the pay of members, besides travelling expenses. This he considered altogether too high. As one member of this Convention, he preferred that the Congressional price should be the utmost paid to members of this Convention. A Senator of the United States receives eight dollars a day and eight dollars for every twenty miles. He (Mr. Jones) thought that price amply sufficient for members of this Convention. It would greatly decrease the estimate of the Committee. The whole expense for the month would not probably exceed some thirty thousand dollars. When General Riley, acting as the civil head of this Territory, stated to the Committee that he could not say whether he would be able to pay it all, it was in reply to a communication from the Committee asking whether he would pay the expenses, and was evidently not intended to control the action of this Convention. In relation to the pay of officers, he (Mr. Jones) contended that this House was in honor bound to pay them as much as they could receive in other parts of this Territory; not at the rates they could obtain in the old States, where living is so much cheaper. Any one of these gentlemen, by pursuing his occupation in the mines, might readily have gained sixteen dollars a day; and great expense has been incurred by them in coming here. He considered it quite as hard work leaning over a desk, as wielding the pick and shovel in the mines. These officers must be paid. We cannot do without their services. We, as members, have all the honor and glory, and may possibly submit to serve without any pecuniary consideration; but there is no particular honor—no extraordinary glory attached to the office of a copying clerk. He (Mr. Jones) was willing not to demand one cent for his services, if this State objected to pay it; but it was altogether a different matter with officers of the Convention. There was one gentleman—the Sergeant-at-Arms—who had lost from his ordinary occupation some fifteen days in coming here. The pay of that officer would not amount at the end of the session to what he would have earned at his pick and shovel. Here was a copying clerk who had travelled hundreds of miles, by land and water, to get here; his pay was eighteen dollars a day, without anything for his travelling expenses. It was the same case with all the officers. He would, therefore, most heartily support the estimate of the Committee; he thought it very reasonable. But another branch of the subject had been taken up by his friend from Monterey, (Mr. Botts.) Shall we touch this money at all, which we suppose to be in the hands of General Riley? Won't it burn our fingers, or soil them, or create some extraordinary sensation throughout the community? Would it be at all proper to pay those gentlemen out of a fund placed at the disposal of the civil Government, by the President of the United States, unless we can find authority in the Constitution of the United States to justify the President in adopting this course? Now he (Mr. Jones) contended that if the Government of the United States does legally possess this Territory it is legally bound to support it.

Mr. BOTTS asked the gentleman to distinguish between the Government and the President.

Mr. JONES resumed. The only right we can have is the incidental right of the treaty-making power. We are the conquering power, and make the treaty. If we acquire territory by cession, we do it under the treaty-making power, and not by express grant of the Constitution. He acknowledged this was a nice question, requiring deep reflection. It had come suddenly before the House, and he was altogether unprepared to discuss it; but he would endeavor to give some idea of the principles which he thought should be recognized by his friend from Monterey as thoroughly democratic. That theory is, that we govern this country not by the Constitution of the United States, but by virtue of the treaty-making power, and by the right of sovereignty. If by virtue of the treaty-making power we (the Government of the United States) came into possession of this territory, and it is left without support, we are bound to provide for it. We cannot, under the law of nations conquer a country, or become the possessor of an entire territory, without providing some sort of government for it. We cannot deprive that territory of its legitimate government, and not establish another in its place. Suppose General Riley had received no authority to expend a cent for the support of this territory, what would have been its situation? It would have been a community without law—without government—without the right to receive a single cent to support a government. Such a policy would have been a high crime against the law of nations. It would have merited the reproach of all mankind. The Congress of the United States failed to perform its duty; the executive branch of the Government, under the treaty-making power, was therefore bound to supply this absolute necessity of a conquered country.

Mr. Botts asked if the gentleman meant to say that a clear and plain clause of the Constitution could be violated by the Executive, or by any other branch of the General Government.

Mr. Jones. A clear and plain clause of the Constitution, and the whole spirit of the Constitution, and the whole spirit of the Government of the United States, were violated when Texas was acquired, and when this country was conquered. He did not think there was a single gentleman in this House who really and candidly believed that the Constitution of the United States gave the slightest color of authority to the acquisition of any foreign territory whatever to the United States. He did not believe the framers of the Constitution ever contemplated such a thing. But he had no disposition to go into that question. This country was now in possession of the United States. It must be provided with law—with a government. It is necessary to establish some system of government, to prevent the inhabitants from reverting to an absolute state of barbarism. If, therefore, the General Government is bound to furnish us with the protection of laws, it is bound to furnish us with the means to pay for the establishment of a Government. He had endeavored to answer the arguments of the gentleman from Monterey, merely to show that this was at least a doubtful question, and that it was unwise to bring it up on this floor. It does not pertain to the business of this Convention. It is a question between the Government of the United States and its Executive head; and between that Executive head and the civil officer who has charge of the Government of California. If it is not plainly a question of receiving stolen money, he had no objection to receive this money. Where it is a matter of doubt, and where the instructions of the Government will sustain its officer here, he did not see that this Convention was called upon to interfere, one way or the other. He did not believe the people required that they should settle the question here, as to whether the Executive was justifiable in giving certain instructions to General Riley. Will the gentleman from Monterey propose a better mode of paying the officers of the Convention? Shall we pay them by subscription, or taxation, or in the schedule? As to the proposition of the gentleman to provide in the schedule that a tax shall be levied at some future time to pay these gentlemen, it is unjust as well as impracticable. The officers are here under heavy expenses, and without means. They must be paid. They are working for this Convention, and are entitled to their wages as they perform their work; and if members were all as well satisfied as he was that the payment of this money by General Riley would be legal and proper, it would be paid.

Mr. HALLECK observed, in relation to the instructions as to the use of the civil fund here for the payment of officers of the civil Government, that they were instructions from the former, not the present administration.

Mr. GWIN asked if they did not apply distinctly to the country when it was in a state of war.

Mr. HALLECK was understood to say that their application was not limited to any particular period.

Mr. PRICE said that, representing as he did, the majority of the Committee that made the report, he felt bound to say a few words in relation to it. The rate of pay fixed in the report for the officers of the Convention, was a matter of a good deal of discussion in the Committee; and in coming to their conclusions, they took the standard of wages which they believed to be usual in this country at the present period, and graduated the pay of these gentlemen in accordance with that standard. They believed that the laborer was worthy of his hire. They wanted the Convention first to decide upon the rate of pay that these officers are to receive, that they might be able to make an estimate which they could send to General Riley, so as to get a direct reply from him, stating whether he would be able to pay the amount fixed by this Convention. He (Mr. Price,) did not believe that General Riley wanted any higher voucher for the payment of these officers, than the vote of this Convention. He had some little experience in the settlement of accounts with the Treasury of the United States, and he knew that the Government of the United States never could ask any higher authority—any higher approving power than the vote of this Convention. He could not believe for a moment that General Riley would attempt to exercise any authority or control over the vote of this House. He did not believe that he would say these gentlemen shall receive more or less than the amount fixed by the Convention. He did not believe General Riley had ever thought of fixing any other rate of pay, by the term necessary expenses. The meaning intended to be conveyed was, to the limited amount that the civil fund now in his hands might justify. As he (Mr. Price) understood it from the correspondence, he (General Riley) was willing to go to that extent. Now, the wages of a mechanic at this day in California average from $12 to $16 a day—that is an uncontrovertible fact; and it may just as well be, that we enlighten the Government at Washington upon this point—that we make known to them through this Convention, the high rate of wages here. It will be the most striking mode in which they can receive it. The Committee had had a due sense of economy in fixing these rates; they believed them to be entirely just and proper, and they hoped the House would sustain them in their estimate. We have nothing to do with the right, or the inquiring as to the right of General Riley to dispose of the civil fund in his hands. The Congress of the United States will pay, and is bound to pay the expenses of this Convention. Now, if the merchants of San Francisco, perchance the clients of the honorable gentlemen from Monterey, (Mr. Botts,) have any claim upon these funds, their rights cannot be impaired in this way, by General Riley defraying the expenses of the Convention; for if the funds have been illegally collected, he is the Government officer, and the Government is bound by his acts; and these funds will be paid back. The course pursued by General Riley cannot change or alter the rights of these claimants. He (Mr. Price,) trusted that this estimate of the Committee might be thought, as a majority of the Committee thought, the proper rate of compensation, and that the House would immediately act upon it, and give instructions to the Committee for further action, if it was deemed necessary.

Mr. MCCARVER thought gentlemen were taking grounds that should not be taken by this Convention in relation to obtaining the means of defraying its expenses. He could not see in what way it devoled upon this body to inquire how General Riley came by the funds which he has in his posssession, or to ascertain by what authority he proposes defraying the expenses of the Convention. The citizens of California sent delegates here for a special object—to form a Constitution. If any individual proposes to come forward and pay the expenses, there is no necessity for entering into any inquiry as to the manner in which he obtained the means, nor is it the duty of this House to discuss questions of that kind. It is enough to know that General Riley is an honest, high-minded gentleman, holding a high position here. If he has acted improperly, or if the President of the United States has acted improperly, it is between him and the President, and between the President and the Congress of the United States to settle it. The proper place to try him for malfeasance in office is in the United States. We have no right to go behind his instructions, and question the Executive authority. He (Mr. McCarver) did not believe that the Governor had any right to exercise any control or authority over this House. Intimation is given to us that, if the expenses are brought within certain limits, they will be paid; if not, they will not be paid. It mattered not to him (Mr. McCarver,) whether General Riley paid a portion or the whole of the sum necessary for that purpose. The action of this House should be entirely independent of any thing General Riley has said. It should regulate the salaries of its own officers, and is fully competent to do it on its own responsibility. It is not for this Convention to inquire what amount General Riley will pay, and then graduate the salaries of the officers accordingly. Let the rates of pay be determined unconditionally and directly, so that those gentlemen may know what they are to receive.

Mr. Wozencraft said that this report was laid on the table yesterday, with the understanding that that portion should be taken up which relates to the per diem allowance of the officers. If he had supposed that the minority report, or that part relating to the manner of providing for the payment of the expenses of the Convention, would have come up, he would have moved for its indefinite postponement. We have no business to take into consideration here, whether the existing civil officer of this Territory has or has not the power to pay these expenses. This question is foreign to the legitimate object of the Convention, and leads to endless debate. He now moved to divide the question as to the rate of salaries and the subject of the civil fund, and indefinitely postpone the latter.

Mr. Sherwood. I desire to make a few remarks on this subject, although the question has been very fully discussed. There seem to be two reports from this Committee—the majority and minority report; one assuming the ground, founded upon a correspondence with Governor Riley, that we can obtain the means of paying the expenses of the Convention, mostly, if not entirely, out of the funds now in possession of the civil Government of California. The minority report, on the contrary, assumes the ground that we should not ask Governor Riley for these funds, but leave the payment of the expenses entirely to a future Legislature. Almost necessarily, this minority report opens the question as to the power of Governor Riley to pay out any portion of the money in his possession. For myself, I do not think this question should have been brought up here. There should have been no discussion as to his power in this Convention; and although the minority of the Committee have seen fit to make a report founded upon th s correspondence, I entirely disagree with that report in regard to the question of power; at the same time I do not think it should have been brought before the House. In the first place, we are the representatives of the people, assembled under a call from the Civil Governor of the Territory. We came here for a specific object—to form a Constitution; and without knowing whether this Constitution will be adopted by the people or not, we cast about us to ascertain how we can pay the ordinary expenses of the Convention.

We have certain officers for whom, if no provision be made now, and the Constitution be rejected by the people, no compensation will be received by them, unless it be defrayed personally by us. The people of California, if they reject our labors here, are not bound by any law to meet the expenses of the Convention. They could make a subscription and pay the necessary sum in that way; but the question now is, as to the payment of our officers at this time, for I apprehend they would scarcely be willing to look to a future Legislature for their compensation. We have, through our Committee, applied to the Governor. That officer states that he has a civil fund under his control; and for the information of the Convention has laid before us a document in which he defends the right to collect the money in the manner that it has been collected for the purpose of a civil fund. In a state of war we have collected imposts. We did it in the last war with Mexico; California came into the possession of our troops. It is to be pre-supposed that after war shall have ceased, the Government of the mother country will provide a Government for the conquered territory. A year and a half, perhaps, have elapsed; a long session of Congress has closed, and yet no more than during and after the close of the war has Congress provided for the government of its conquered territory, afterwards acquired by treaty. It was competent for the military officer, under the instructions of the Secretary of the Treasury, to collect imposts during the war. From the want of action by Congress after the war closed, the same course was necessarily pursued, and it was perfectly justified by the absence of contrary instructions from the Government; and until there was some direct action of Congress authorizing a different course, it was the duty of the military officer in California to collect the revenue as it was collected during and after the war. About a million of dollars has been thus collected—a very small portion of which has been expended upon a Government for the people of California, for they have been without courts, without proper legal tribunals, almost without a form of government. The civil Governor now says to this Convention that he has a fund collected in this way by imposts, and that he has expended it to defray the necessary expenses of the Government, and will continue to do so while he holds the office, until he has contrary instructions from the Departments in Washington. I think in this he has acted wisely and properly, and will be justified not only by the people of California, but by the Congress and people of the United States. Congress neglected, after a protracted discussion on a question with which they had nothing to do, to provide a Government for this Territory. Foreign ships with foreign cargoes have come into our ports here, and the civil Government has received the duties which, under the revenue laws of the United States, must be received on foreign goods. What would have been the result had he decided otherwise, during the interegnum between the termination of the war and the present time, or up to the period when the revenue laws for this Territory were passed by Congress. Your English ships, your Chinese ships, your Chilian and Sandwich Island ships would have cast anchor in the harbor of San Francisco, and their cargoes would have rotted there; or otherwise those cargoes would have been admitted into this Territory, carried across into other States, and no revenue whatever would have been derived from them. The people of this Territory needed those goods. The merchants paid these duties as they would have done under a law of Congress; as they do now under the revenue law passed during the last session. They were bound to pay duties by the general laws of the United States, which prohibit the introduction of foreign goods into any part of our territory without the payment of imposts. The people of California, however, paid the duty in the end. The miners, and the people who live throughout the country, who own land and have families—in short the whole population of California eventually paid those duties, not the merchants. The merchant, if he paid 20 per cent. upon his goods, charged the 20 per cent. and his profits besides. It was the people of California that paid this whole fund; and yet, at the same time, they have been furnished by Congress with no laws to govern them. As a necessary inference these duties belong to them. If Congress had furnished a Territorial Government, with officers and courts for the Territory of California, then the duties received here on foreign imports would have gone into the Treasury of the United States, and Congress, by law, would have appropriated them to defray the expenses of a Territorial Government. But, in the absence of law, these revenues belong to the people of California—to the people of the future State—to enable them to carry on their government, to erect their public buildings, and pay all the expenses incident to the organization of a State Government. General Riley has loaned out to the General Government a portion of these revenues If we are admitted as a State; if this Constitution is adopted by the people; if the proper men are sent to the Congress of the United States, they will insist upon this half million loaned by General Riley being returned to the people of California. The people paid the duties, and it belongs to them. The General Government neglected to provide them with the protection of laws—with any of the advantages afforded by a Territorial Government. In the absence of this action on the part of the home Government, it justly and properly belongs to them as a fund for the accomplishment of that which the General Government neglected to do. But, after all the discussion on this question, it comes down to the point which I conceive to be that upon which the House is now to decide. I do think that the report of the Committee in regard to the pay of the officers is a little too high. I admit the justice of the remarks made by the different gentlemen, that the cost of living is much higher here than in the United States; that the cost of labor is higher; and consequently I would pay them the wages that are paid throughout the country. We must not be governed by the wages paid throughout the United States—that is evident. The people of this Territory would say we had done injustice to these gentlemen if we were guided by that standard. The cost of living, the price of board, rent, lodging, &c., is much higher here than in the old States. I think that the people of California who will adopt this Constitution, as I trust they will, are willing to pay them good fair wages; but we must not, as has been said, set the example of extravagance here. Though we pay well, we should not squander the public funds. We should not lay ourselves liable to the imputation of having acted from motives which will create distrust with our constituents when we go home, by paying to ourselves and to the officers a higher amount than public opinion will justify; an imputation that would taint even the Constitution that may go from our hands to them. Although I would be liberal and pay them fair prices, yet, I think, with all deference to the opinions of the Committee, we shall be compelled to reduce the estimate. When we come to strike out and fill up the blanks, the Convention can fix upon the amount which they think best. I am in favor of fixing the highest salary at one ounce. It is the value of daily labor in the mines. It is all that can be got here. It is all that can be got ordinarily any where in the country. I trust the other officers will be paid very nearly the same. There is, as I understand, but little difference in the duties performed; at any rate not such as to require any great difference in the salaries. It is usual in paying the officers of the older States to pay from the highest to the lowest—those elected by the House as well as those appointed by its authority—about the same price. I think we should not vary from that rule.

Mr. Wozencraft had a word to say to gentlemen who were in the habit of preaching economy. This House was spending day after day at an enormous expense in discussing questions which had no reference to its duties. He was an economist himself, and he thought the best economy would be for the Convention to confine itself to its legitimate business. He believed the estimate of salaries was reasonable enough, and he was prepared to vote for it.

Mr. Gwin said he would give his reasons why the motion of the gentleman from San Joaquin (Mr. Wozencraft,) should be adopted. In the first place, he did not think that this question as to General Riley's power, ever should have come up before this Convention. It was no part of the duty of members of this House to discuss it. Every word that had been said on the subject was out of order. It was to form a Constitution that this Convention was assembled—not to determine whether the present civil Governor of California had acted in accordance with instructions, or whether these instructions were in accordance with the Constitution of the United States. If General Riley has a fund out of which he is willing to pay the expenses of this Convention, the fact that he has that money, and is willing to advance it, is sufficient for this Convention. It is not necessary to go beyond that fact. Before the Convention adjourns, it should be stated by resolution that, if any amount he may advance out of that fund should involve him in difficulty, that the faith and honor of the people of California are pledged to protect him. What the delegates of this Convention say as to the legality of the manner in which that fund may have been collected or may be disposed of, can have no effect on the subject. He could assure gentlemen that if they were to vote here that General Riley had exceeded his powers or had not exceeded them, it would not make the slightest difference. It would be looked upon as absolutely nothing by those before whom this question will eventually come. The gentleman from Monterey (Mr. Botts,) was altogether mistaken in saying that the President of the United States had ever committed himself on the subject of these duties. He called upon him (Mr. Botts,) for his authority. It could not be found; it did not exist. For no President of the United States ever would have done, or sanctioned the doing of what General Riley has been forced by necessity to do. Look to the public documents and to this communication from the Governor, (which is one of the most important documents that has appeared for a long time in this country,) and if you will find a single word where the President of the United States has authorized the collection of these duties, you will find a question in the Congress of the United States infinitely more exciting than the removal of the deposites from the Bank of the United States, which convulsed this country some years ago; for the President has sworn strictly to execute the laws under the Constitution. There is not a man who lives, can pretend that any law of the United States has ever authorized the collection of these duties. But it was no sinecure upon those who collected them. He did not wish to be misunderstood on this question. There was no doubt but that the people of California claimed this fund, and had a right to it; and if justice was done them, they should have it.

Mr. Botts threw himself on the indulgence of the House to reply to some of the remarks which had been made. He contended that this money was in the Treasury of the United States; that without an act of Congress, it could not be paid out; that Congress had never appropriated it to pay the expenses of this civil Government. He had called upon his fellow-members to show him any law for it. When he asked for bread, they gave him stones. Gentlemen asserted that this subject was not properly before the House. He (Mr. Botts,) contended that General Riley himself, by this correspondence, in which he states that his instructions authorize him to make this use of the civil fund, had put the question directly before him, and compelled him to vote upon it. It was said we were not here to discuss General Riley's action. Such was not the case. If a breach of the Constitution is involved in the payment of this money, it properly comes before the House in receiving it. He did not wish to convey any thing disrespectful by the comparison ; but if an individual was to come to him and offer him the use of a hundred dollars which he had stolen, or frauduently obtained, and which fact was known to the receiver, would it be proper to take it? It became this Convention, on the same principle, to consider whether this fund was constitutionally obtained, as in the other case it became him to consider whether the money proffered was honestly gotten. He had taken an oath to abide by the Constitution of the United States, and to defend and adhere to it as a member of this Convention. A direct case of a violation of the Constitution was brought before him in this correspondence. Was he not bound by his solemn oath to protest against this fraud upon the people? He would take this money with the greatest pleasure, and say nothing about it, if gentlemen would only show him that it was not a violation of the Constitution. But what were the facts? The Congress of the United States was directly requested by the President of the United States in July last to take this matter into consideration, and form a government for California. The Congress of the United States solemnly deliberated on this subject, refused to form a government, and solemnly declared that they would make no appropriation for the support of this Territory. The gentleman from Sacramento (Mr. Sherwood) went into a long discussion to show what would have been the fatal consequences if this money had not been collected as it was, by imposing duties on the foreign cargoes that arrived in the ports of California. He (Mr. Botts) would take General Riley's own word for that. It was in the hands of a collecting officer of the Government, and therefore in the Treasury of the United States. It was obtained either legally or illegally ; but it is in the Treasury of the United States, and cannot be paid out without special act of Congress. He was told by the gentleman from San Francisco, (Mr. Gwin,) to quiet his conscience about this matter—to submit to it ; that the money was not collected by the authority of the President, or by any authority except that of necessity, and hence it was not in the Treasury of the United States. It was done altogether by the law of necessity. Now he (Mr. Botts) had sworn to support the laws of the United States, not the law of necessity. He had heard enough of that law. It is the tyrant's policy. Take that and the responsibility doctrine, put the two together, and the Constitution of the United States is not worth a cent. He trusted, in conclusion, that it would be the pleasure of gentlemen either to assist him in rejecting the use of this fund, or enlighten him so that he could receive it without violating the oath which he had taken to support the Constitution.

On motion, the House adjourned.

MONDAY, SEPTEMBER 17, 1849.

Prayer by Rev. Mr. Willey.

Journal of Saturday read and approved.

On motion, the report of the Finance Committee was taken up ; the following resolution, submitted by Mr. Wozencraft, being first in order:

Resolved, That the subjects placed before the Committee be so divided that the report be received, and the communication from the Governor be indefinitely postponed.

On motion of Mr. Wozencraft, it was ordered that the vote be taken separately on the two clauses of the resolution.

The question being taken on the first clause of the resolution, it was decided in the affirmative.

Mr. Wozencraft moved that so much of the report as was included by the clause of his resolution just agreed to, be adopted, with the exception of the per diem allowance to the interpreter, and that that be increased to $28.

Mr. Hastings submitted the following amendment, as a substitute for Mr. Wozencraft's motion:

The per diem pay of the Secretary, Assistant Secretary, Translator, Interpreter, Clerks, and Members, (excepting the President,) be twenty-five dollars; that of the President and Reporter be fifty dollars; that of the Sergeant-at-arms be twenty dollars; that of the Doorkeeper, sixteen dollars; and that of the Page, four dollars.

And the question being on Mr. Hastings amendment, it was decided in the negative.

Mr. Shannon submitted the following amendment, as a substitute for Mr. Wozencraft's proposition:

The per diem allowance, &c., of the officers and members of this Convention shall be as follows: one Secretary, $20; one Interpreter, $20; two Assistant Secretaries, $18 each; one Engrossing Clerk, $18; two Copying Clerks, $16 each; one Sergeant-at-Arms, $16; one Doorkeeper, $12; one Page, $4; one Reporter, $40; one Chaplain, $16; one Interpreting Clerk, $16; forty-three Members, $16 each; travelling allowance of members, at the rate of $16 for every twenty miles travel.

And the question being on the amendment, it was decided in the negative.

The question recurring on the motion to increase the Interpreter's per diem to $28, it was decided in the affirmative.

Mr. Norton moved further to amend by providing that the per diem allowance of Mr. Howe, in consideration of his performing the duties of Engrossing Clerk, shall be the same as the Assistant Secretaries.

And the question being on the amendment, it was decided in the affirmative.

On motion of Mr. Jones, the per diem of the Reporter was excepted from the report of the Committee, for future consideration.

The question then recurring on the report of the Committee as amended—

Mr. Sherwood asked the yeas and nays; which being ordered, they resulted as follows:

Yeas—Messrs. Aram, Botts, Brown, Crosby, Dent, De la Guerra, Dominguez, Hill, Hobson, Hastings, Jones, Larkin, Lippett, Moore, McCarver, Ord, Price, Pico, Rodriguez, Reid, Sutter, Snyder, Stearns, Tefft, Vallejo, Wozencraft, President—27.

Nays—Messrs. Dimmick, Ellis, Given, Gilbert, Halleck, Hollingsworth, Lippincott, McDougall, Norton, Sherwood, Shannon, Walker—12.

So the report, as amended, was adopted, and the per diem allowance of the officers of the Convention fixed at the following rates:

Secretary, $28; Assistant Secretaries, $23; Engrossing Clerk, $23; Sergeant-at-Arms, $22; Copying Clerk, $18; Interpreter, $28; Interpreter's Clerk, $21; Chaplain, $16; Doorkeeper, $12; Page, $4.

The question then being on the second clause of Mr. Wozencraft's resolution, he modified the same, so as to provide that the *consideration* of the correspondence, and not the correspondence itself, be "indefinitely postponed."

The question being taken on the second clause of Mr. Wozencraft's resolution, as modified, it was decided in the negative.

Mr. Ellis moved the following, which was decided in the negative:

Resolved, That the consideration of so much of the reports of the majority and minority of the Committee on Finance, as relates to the ways and means of paying the expenses of this Convention, be laid upon the table.

On motion of Mr. Dent, it was—

Resolved, That so much of the report of the Committee, relating to the communications of General Riley, as relates to the ways and means of obtaining the fund for paying expenses, be referred back to the Committee, and the said Committee be instructed to make the necessary arrangements with General Riley for paying the expenses of this Convention; and also be instructed to report on the proposition of the Reporter, J. Ross Browne, for furnishing printed copies of his reports.

Mr. Botts, at his own request, was excused from further service on the Finance Committee, and Mr. Walker was appointed by the President to fill the vacancy.

On motion of Mr. JONES, the House then resolved itself into Committee of the Whole, Mr. Botts in the Chair, on the report of the Committee on the Constitution.

COMMITTEE OF THE WHOLE.

The 31st Section of the report of the Committee being under consideration, as follows:

31. Corporations may be formed under general laws, but shall not be created by special act, except for municipal purposes, and in cases where, in the judgment of the Legislature, the objects of the corporation cannot be attained under general laws. All general laws and special acts passed pursuant to this section, may be altered from time to time, or repealed.

Mr. JONES moved to strike out the 31st section, and if in order, the four following, and to insert in lieu thereof, the section 2d of the 9th Article of the Constitution of Iowa, with an amendment, which he would submit in writing.

Mr. GWIN said that, inasmuch as he had made a minority report on this subject, he hoped the gentleman (Mr. Jones,) would withdraw his motion, so as to permit him to offer the following amendment. He moved to strike out from the 31st to the 36th sections, inclusive, of the majority report, and insert as follows:

SEC. 1. No corporate body shall be created, renewed, or extended, with the privilege of making, issuing, or putting in circulation any bill, check, ticket, certificate, promissory note, or other paper, or the paper of any bank, to circulate as money. The Legislature of this State shall prohibit by law, any person or persons, association, company, or corporation, from exercising the privileges of banking, or creating paper to circulate as money.

2. Corporations shall not be created in this State by special laws, except for political or municipal purposes; but the Legislature shall provide, by general laws, for the organization of all other corporations, except corporations with banking privileges, the creation of which is prohibited. The stockholders of every corporation or joint stock association, shall be personally and jointly responsible for all its debts and liabilities of every kind. The State shall not, directly or indirecly, become a stockholder in any corporation. All general laws and special acts passed pursuant to this section, may be altered from time to time, or repealed; and all corporations shall have the right to sue, and shall be subject to be sued, in all courts, in like cases as natural persons.

Mr. SHERWOOD inquired if it was in order to move to strike out five or six sections, when only one was under consideration.

The CHAIR presumed that the whole report was before the Committee, and that it was in order to propose a substitute for several sections, having direct reference to the same subject.

The point of order giving rise to discussion,

Mr. GWIN said he would simply move to strike out the 31st section, and insert the amendment which he had just read. If adopted, the other sections of the report would necessarily be stricken out.

Mr. JONES remarked that the first section proposed by the Committee provided that no corporation should be created by special act, unless the Legislature saw fit to create it. He understood that to be the full scope and meaning of the section. The clause to which he had reference, was in the following words: "Corporations may be formed under general laws, but shall not be created by special act, except for municipal purposes, and in cases where, in the judgment of the Legislature, the objects of the corporation cannot be attained under general laws." In any case whatever, where, in the opinion of the Legislature, the object cannot be attained under general law, corporations therefore can be granted. Take this clause on its own bottom, and it would allow, and in fact, soon suggest the incorporation of banks. He wished, for that reason, to introduce the discussion of the whole subject at once. He did not think this article could stand upon its bottom. Every member in the House would at once see the absurdity of prohibiting the Legislature from passing acts of this kind, unless it thought proper to do so. He was willing to submit the article to a vote upon that construction; it carried its absurdity upon its face; but if the debate was to be opened, it was necessary to know how far this clause was to be affected by subsequent sections.

Mr. Norton. I imagine the gentleman is mistaken in the view which he takes of this section. He does not give it a fair interpretation. It does not say, nor does its meaning bear the import that corporations shall not be created by special act, except the Legislature see fit to create them. The section is plainly expressed, and states what it means. Corporations may be formed under general laws, but shall not be created by special act, except for municipal purposes, and in cases where, in the judgment of the Legislature, the object of the corporations cannot be attained under general laws. If, under this section, the Legislature grant a charter for a corporation by special act, where the object of the corporation can be attained under general laws, that act of the Legislature is unconstitutional. The question of constitutionality will be for the courts to decide. In regard to this whole subject of corporations, it was expected by the Committee that it would give rise to a good deal of discussion; and knowing the opinions of the House respecting institutions of this kind, especially banking corporations, we endeavored to report such provisions as would cover the whole ground. With this view, the Committee selected from the different Constitutions such provisions as they deemed necessary to prohibit the Legislature from granting charters to banking corporations, or giving any corporations whatever the right to issue paper money, or any equivalent for a paper currency. Under these sections, nothing can circulate as money, except gold and silver. It was the opinion of the majority of the Committee, as it is of the majority of the House, that corporations for banking purposes should be prohibited. The substitute proposed for the different sections reported by the Committee, prohibits the creation of any corporation whatever, by special law, and also prohibits banking, and the issuing, and putting into circulation, any bills, checks, promissory notes, or paper to circulate as money. The report of the Committee also prohibits banking corporations and the circulation of bank paper as a medium of currency; but the Legislature has power to grant charters for corporations when the object of such corporations cannot be attained under general law. The only difference between the two in effect is with regard to the liability of corporations. I am not tenacious myself about this article. Let it be worded as gentlemen think best. I go as far as any one in making corporators liable for the debts of the corporations; but inasmuch as the report of the Committee does not vary essentially from the substitute moved in its place, I hope the House will not reject the report, and adopt a substitute which does not materially differ from it.

Mr. Lippett. I agree entirely with the view taken by my friend from San Joaquin, (Mr. Jones,) that the clause of this section, which intends to limit the Legislature, is perfectly nugatory, or will be so in effect. I am opposed to giving the Legislature the power, in any case, to pass special acts for corporations. For this reason alone, I should vote for the amendment. But even if I were in favor of granting such power to the Legislature in cases where the object of the corporation could not be attained under general laws, I would object to the section as it now reads, on the grounds stated by the gentleman from San Joaquin—that the language of the clause makes the limitation perfectly nugatory. The Chairman of the Committee (Mr. Norton,) states that special acts passed by the Legislature where the object could be attained under general laws, would be unconstitutional, and that the courts would decide the question of constitutionality. I think not. If such a question were raised in any court of law, it could not be entertained. From the very reading of the clause, the question of constitutionality is left to the decision of the Legislature itself. The Constitution, by leaving it to the discretion of the Legislature, settles the question; and it cannot be brought into court. If that clause was stricken out of the 31st section, so that it would read "Corporations may be formed under general laws, but shall not be created by special act, except for municipal purposes," then it might be competent for a court of law to sit and hear arguments on the question; but as it stands, the right to decide is taken out of the hands of the court. The very fact of the passage of the law, makes it conclusive that, in the judgment of the Legislature, the object of the corporation could not be attained otherwise than by special act.

Mr. JONES. I must say it is very difficult to discuss one part of this subject without going into a discussion of the whole. It is almost a matter of impossibility to state what effect that particular article will have, if we cannot discuss what effect the succeeding article is to produce. But, I am, as a general principle, against the creation of corporations by special act. I think the power is always liable to be abused. I have seen a corporation under the name of the Sun Insurance Company, in New Orleans, for the sale of pork. You might with this authority, with all these prohibitions and constructions staring you in the face, incorporate a body for the purpose of moulding tallow candles, and that corporation could next day issue bank notes. There is no prohibition here, as in the Constitution of Iowa, against the issuing any bill, ticket, check, or promisory note, to circulate as money. The only prohibition in all the articles reported by the Committee is against the circulation of bank bills. A bank bill is a specific, determinate object. It is well known that a bank bill is not a check or certificate of deposite. Neither one of these would come under that definition. Suppose a corporation were to be created by special act for the purpose of moulding tallow candles, would it not be competent for that corporation to issue paper payable at par?

Mr. HALLECK. I call the gentleman's attention to another section, which says there shall be no corporations for banking purposes.

Mr. JONES. Does the gentleman call a tallow-candle corporation, a corporation for banking purposes? They have a right to use their credit. A corporation for banking purposes is a well known object; that object is to discount paper, to receive deposites and issue notes. But I presume any corporation has a right to issue its notes, or, if money be deposited in its hands, it has a right to issue certificates of deposite. Now I wish to call the attention of the gentleman to the reading of this article on banks: "The Legislature shall have no power to pass any act granting any charter for banking purposes; *but associations may be formed under general laws for the deposite of gold and silver.*" This is the most imperfect and objectionable bank I know of. If it has power to receive gold and silver, it has a right to issue certificates of deposite; it has a right to make them payable to bearer, and consequently make them bank paper, and circulate them as money. The gentleman will certainly not deny that if I deposite the sum of one hundred dollars in one of these associations, I can take a certificate of deposite payable to bearer. None of the usual guards of the banking system are attached to this. You create here the most irresponsible sort of a bank. It is not necessary for such an establishment to have capital in order to receive deposites. You do not compel it to have capital. It goes on and makes money on borrowed capital. Such is the scope and inevitable result of any special act creating corporations. If an individual has funds of his own to work upon, sufficient for his commercial and trading purposes, he does not want to work upon the capital of other people; if he has not, I do not desire that the Legislature should give him the privilege of using other people's money. This question will come up more fully hereafter for argument. In relation to the 31st section, I contend that the objections against it have not by any means been answered; that if you leave it entirely to the Legislature to determine upon the propriety of granting charters by special act, the rest of the section is nugatory and void; there is no limitation; and a general power is given to the Legislature to pass any special act it may think proper.

Mr. SHERWOOD. This section which it is proposed to strike out, was taken literally from the Constitution of New York. Previous to the adoption of that Constitution there were various projects for corporations before the Legislature every session; sometimes as many as eight or ten for railroads, and sometimes two or three for the formation of Cemetery corporations or Insurance Companies.

Many of these corporations were meritorious in their character and objects; but the result was that half the time of the Legislature was occupied in examining their respective claims and granting charters. This had become an evil so great that it was at length deemed necessary by the people of the State, in Convention, to put a provision in the Constitution making it the duty of the Legislature to pass general laws, by complying with which, any association of individuals might form themselves into a corporation. There were other considerations that operated in bringing about this clause in the Constitution; the desire to extend to every one the privilege of forming associations for any beneficial purpose, whether by the combination of capital or otherwise, where the object could be attained under general law. It is necessary in certain cases that corporations should be passed by special act. They cannot be brought under a general head. There are instances where but one corporation of the kind, for a charitable purpose, is offered to the Legislature. The subject may never come up again; hence the necessity of providing that, where the object cannot be accomplished by general law, special acts may be passed by the Legislature. What has been the experience of New York? The Legislature, in compliance with this provision of the Constitution, has passed a general law permitting railroad companies to be formed. Instead of numerous applications every winter for corporations, this great item of expense is cut short; and the general law is upon the statute book allowing any number of persons to form railroad associations, insurance companies, cemetery associations, or other corporations. This provision of the Constitution was complied with by the Legislature at the first session after its adoption. As occasion requires, where general laws could be passed, they have passed them—showing conclusively that they regard this clause as binding. The judgment of the people would be against them if they did not comply; their own oaths of office would be against them. I have heard no complaint, since the article was adopted, of the Legislature granting special charters where the object could be accomplished under general laws. It is not my design to discuss the questions embraced in the other sections, until we come to them in their proper order; but I think it clear that some discretion should be left to the Legislature to pass special grants of charter where the object is meritorious and cannot otherwise be obtained.

On motion, the Committee rose and reported progress.

The Convention then took a recess of one hour.

AFTERNOON SESSION, 3 O'CLOCK, P. M.

Mr. Julian Hanks, a member from San Jose, came forward, took the oath, and was admitted to his seat.

On motion of Mr. Jones, the House then resolved itself into Committee of the Whole, Mr. Botts in the Chair, on the report of the Committee on the Constitution, the question being on Mr. Gwin's amendment.

Mr. Halleck. I have a very few words to say on this subject. I would call the attention of the House to one point. There are articles on the subject proposed in the amendment in the original report of the Committee. The gentleman's minority report proposes to substitute several articles for one. I object to it on that ground. I also object to it on the ground that the articles reported by the majority of the Committee are far better, and the same object may be attained under one of the articles reported by the majority, and that is, to prohibit the circulation of any check, bill, promissory note, or paper. Why strike out one section of the report of the Committee, and then substitute for it an amendment which is afterwards carried in that report? It seems to me to be an unprecedented proceeding. It divides the whole subject. If it is possible to attain the object directly, why not attain it directly, according to the rules of the House? If we wish to limit the powers of the Legislature as is proposed in this substitute, let the question come under the proper section of the majority report—the section prohibiting the circulation of bank notes; and then if we choose, we can insert, as an amendment, all these prohibitions as to tickets, checks, bills, promissory notes, and other papers. I go for the report of the majority, because I think it infinitely superior to the sections reported by the minority, in the definition and limitation of the powers of corporations.

Mr. SEMPLE. This is a subject upon which I have looked with a great deal of interest. I have been almost from boyhood opposed to every principle of banking. This settled conviction against the system has induced me to express my opinions freely to members out of the House; and I am pleased to say I have not found a single member who, like myself, is not opposed to the banking principle. There is, therefore, no necessity for discussing this subject, or occupying our time in reiterating arguments which have so often been used before, and which have become established truths in political economy. I would much prefer, if the report of the Committee is not properly worded, or sufficiently guarded, taking it up on its own merits, and so amending it as to make it suit the wishes of the House. I can see no necessity for entertaining ourselves here making long speeches, when not one solitary member is in favor of the banking system. The object of every member seems to be to avoid incorporating any privilege in this Constitution for its establishment. There are some, I admit, who have but little knowledge of the baneful influence of this system, and who have not thought much upon the subject; but the general feeling is against it. Let us make the wording of the section as explicit as we deem necessary. I will read a portion of the 31st article, and give my views respecting it. "Corporations may be formed under general laws." This is proper. No person can object to it. It is evident that corporations must be formed for certain purposes. The article continues—"But shall not be created by special act, except for municipal purposes, and in cases where, in the opinion of the Legislature, the object cannot be attained under general law." Leave out a portion of this clause, and it will read: "Except for municipal purposes, in cases where the object cannot be attained under general law." This gives it a very different aspect. Are not all the objections of the most strenous opponents of the banking system answered by omitting this clause? I am satisfied there will be no difficulty in altering the report to meet the wishes of every gentleman on the floor. Either the report of the Committee, or the amendment of the gentleman from San Francisco, (Mr. Gwin,) will answer the purpose of a basis; but as there seems to be a difficulty in getting at the latter, I propose that we shall take up the Committee report on its own merits. The main question is, can an association, under this article, go before the Legislature and get a special act for creating a bank of deposite? This seems to be the point at issue. If the object which every member of the Convention desires, and which the people throught the country desire, is not accomplished by these words, the restrictions can be made more explicit.

Mr. JONES. I would suggest that the 2d section of the article in the Constitution of Iowa, includes exactly the same subject as the 31st section of the report of the Committee. I moved it this morning, but withdrew it at the request of the gentleman from San Francisco, (Mr. Gwin.) I now move it again. It includes all that is in the report of the majority, and is much more to the point, viz:

Corporations shall not be created in this State by special laws, except for political and municipal purposes; but the General Assembly shall provide, by general laws, for the organization of all other corporations, except corporations with banking privileges, the creation of which is prohibited. The stockholders shall be subject to such liabilities and restrictions as shall be provided by law. The State shall not, directly or indirectly, become a stockholder in any corporation.

Mr. GILBERT. Do I understand the gentleman as proposing this as a substitute for the 31st section? I think it can only be offered as a substitute for the substitute proposed by the gentleman from San Francisco, (Mr. Gwin.)

After some discussion as to the order of amendments, Mr. Jones withdrew his proposed amendment.

The question then recurring on Mr. Gwin's amendment, Mr. PRICE said:

There is no subject, Mr Chairman, that has been, or can come, before this House, that has more importance or influence upon the future well-being of the State of California than this. Sir, it is pregnant with the greatest amount of good or evil. And if I have been desirous at any time to fasten my views upon this House, I am an hundred fold more desirous to convert those who hold different opinions from me on this subject; for my mind was never more decided that we should prohibit the Legislature, by our Constitution, from creating, by general or special acts, corporations to carry on any species of banking.

The Constitution of the State of New York, from which the substance of the sections now under consideration is taken by the Committee, will not, I trust, be considered a guide to us.—We are representing a country and people existing under very different circumstances from what the people of the State of New York were, when they made their revised Constitution. The people of that State sent their representatives in 1846, to revise and amend their old Constitution, which gave the most unrestrained power to their Legislature to charter banks, and these powers had been used to an unlimited extent. The number of banks existing in the State of New York at the time (1846) of the adoption of the banking system—which it is now proposed by your Committee to engraft on the Constitution which we are forming for the future State of California—was very great, I believe some hundreds. I have no statistics to give me the exact number, but the amount of bank notes in circulation at the time is stated to be about $105,000,000. Now, sir, how very different are the circumstances under which we are assembled, representing as we do the people of a young and virgin territory, without banks, and whose great natural wealth is unparalled. Her very soil is abundant and prolific in the hard metallic currency, and is now daily adding three hundred thousand dollars to the positive wealth of the country and of the world. This gives us currency enough, and will more than pay for the supplies that are to be brought to us; and there is no occasion for us to resort to a fictitious currency, such as paper money, with its train of evils, as exhibited in the old States.

Sir, this is an original question with us. Let us appreciate our position, and act accordingly. The Convention of the State of New York in 1846, were not free to act upon this great principle. They were saddled with a banking system, which had the immense amount of $105,000,000 paper money in circulation, which it would have been ruinous to their citizens to have contracted or curtailed. They could not go as far as we can, although such was the desire expressed throughout the debate on this subject in that Convention. They meant to reform and restrict banking privileges by the general laws which they passed. But, I trust, sir, that the fact of these sections being found in the New York Constitution, or any other State Constitution, will have no influence here with us, who are dealing with this subject for the first time. It is most important that we start right. With the experience we all have, it surely will be our own fault if we do not start right.

We are called upon, sir, and the people expect that this Convention will interpose its power as a shield to protect the commercial and laboring classes from the frauds and abuses resulting from the substitution of the credit and paper money of legalized banking associations, for the metallic currency of the world. The people of California want no extraordinary privileges, they only ask for a sound currency—a currency produced from their soil—to secure the stability of trade. Let us provide then the strongest constitutional guards against the vicissitudes which we know the people of the United States have suffered. Ay, sir, and this is the time and place to cut off the head of this monster serpent, paper money, which, I fear, may creep in and sting us, if we adopt the report of the Committee. Our enlightened knowledge on this subject makes us unanimous in the opinion that no bank charters, no paper money, either of individuals or corporations, ought to circulate as currency. It is only for us to consider whether the sections reported by the Committee permit, by their general provisions, the Legislature to incorporate any association that may, hereafter, put in circulation paper money. I am afraid, sir, that by the section such a construction might be given. The associations authorized to receive deposites of gold and silver must issue certificates of deposit, and these certificates might be made a currency. At any rate, it might be attempted and supported by the many ingenious lawyers we have among us. Sir, it is upon this ground that I oppose this section; it behooves us to act on this subject distinctly and emphatically, and leave no room for misconstruction. Let us say what we mean, that corporations shall never be chartered by the Legislature with banking privileges, such as receiving or holding gold or silver on deposite. I go for the strongest and fullest restrictions; and I believe I am acting understandingly. We have the wisdom and experience of the old States of the Union to direct us in steering our bark of State clear of the shoals and breakers that have created such wonderful commercial revolutions in the different States.

This question, sir, is one of great importance, not only to ourselves, but to the whole Union, owing to our circumstances, position, and commercial relations—foreign and domestic. Our commercial capital, San Francisco, is, in my opinion, destined to be the centre of the exchanges of the world, and is destined to supply the world with a large share of its currency. With our great natural wealth, we can never want currency. We will soon have a mint; let us not, then, allow any special privileges to corporations or associations to compete with, or paralyze, individual enterprize and industry. The people of California are peculiarly a laboring people—they are miners, sir, who live by the pick and shovel, and "by the sweat of their brow, earn their bread." But, we have another large class of citizens, I mean those engaged in commercial pursuits, who are characterized by the greatest enterpize, and who also require this constitutional restriction to prevent what I am so much opposed to under sanction of law, the raising up of any priviledged class, or set of men, that may consolidate capital, and thereby monopolize individual capital, which I fear may be done under this section of the report of the Committee. Our people, sir, will be most happy and most content to abide by the laws of trade, and require no false credit or artificial regulation. In short, sir, I believe the broad doctrine of free trade and free banking as most applicable to their condition. I am an advocate of this great principle, and it is my highest ambition to see the government we are now establishing for this country put in motion by this enlightened lever, which will raise us to the highest pinnacle of power.

I shall move the amendment necessary to carry out these views at the proper time. Of the two propositions before the House, I greatly prefer the substitute, or minority report, to the report of the majority.

Mr. Hastings. I find that the proposition to amend is so complicated, and presented in such manner, as to confuse and distract the whole matter. It appears at one time to amend one section, and at another all the sections at once. The gentleman introduces his proposition in this form to give a wide scope to the discussion. That is one of the objections I have to it—the scope is too wide. Let us narrow it down. I am not disposed to encourage the introduction of any amendment which will bring up at once the entire report of the committee on the subject. If I could see the whole thing in a few words, I would be willing to vote upon it, but we find in many words in the amendment the same thing set forth precisely that we find in one section of the report of the committee. In the 34th article we find that the committee have distinctly and positively prohibited banking, and in three short lines, which would not exceed a line and a half in print. These are the words: "The Legislature shall have no power to pass any act granting any charter for banking purposes." We find in the proposed amendment six, and perhaps more lines, all amounting to the same thing. It appears that there is no rule of the House on this subject, but when this portion of the report of the committee was brought before the House, it was moved to be received and taken up article by article. This is not taking it up article by article. It is taking up the entire report, so far as relates to corporations, altogether.

Mr. Gwin said that if his motion to insert a substitute for the 31st section prevailed, the other sections, as they came up, would be stricken out as a matter of course—the whole ground being covered by his substitute.

Mr. Lippett quoted the usages of parliamentary bodies in regard to amendments, and explained their application to the question under consideration.

Mr. Jones. I have no desire to exhaust the patience of the House by saying anything more on this question; but I conceive it to be so important a subject that I would be willing, and I wish, that the gentlemen who favor the majority report should have every opportunity to discuss it fully and thoroughly. I cannot well conceive how the question can come up on striking out this single section (the 31st) without bringing up those very points embodied in the succeeding sections. The clause upon which this debate has principally turned is in the 31st section. I conceive that it gives to the Legislature the power of passing all special acts, which in their judgment may seem proper. Gentlemen who sustain the majority report say there is no difference between the two. I can see a very material difference. In the 31st section they say the Legislature shall have power to create, by special act, corporations for municipal purposes, when, in their judgment, the object cannot be attained under general law. In the 32d section they say: "Dues from corporations shall be secured by such individual liability of the corporators and other means as may be prescribed by law." In the 33d: "The term corporations, as used in this article, shall be construed to include all associations and joint-stock companies having any of the powers or privileges of corporations, not possessed by individuals or partnerships; and all corporations shall have the right to sue and shall be subject to be sued, in all courts, in like cases as natural persons." In the 34th section: "The Legislature shall have no power to pass any act granting any charter for banking purposes; but associations may be formed under general laws for the deposit of gold and silver." Now, compare the two and see the difference. The minority report says:

SEC. 1. No corporate body shall be created, renewed, or extended, with the privilege of making, issuing, or putting in circulation, any bill, check, ticket, certificate, promissory note, or other paper, or the paper of any bank, to circulate as money. The Legislature of this State shall prohibit by law, any person or persons, association, company, or corporation, from exercising the privileges of banking, or creating paper to circulate as money.

2. Corporations shall not be created in this State by special laws, except for political or municipal purposes, but the Legislature shall provide, by general laws, for the organization of all other corporations, except corporations with banking privileges, the creation of which is prohibited. The stockholders of every corporation or joint stock association, shall be personally and jointly responsible for all its debts and liabilities of every kind. The State shall not, directly or indirectly, become a stockolder in any corporation. All general laws and special acts passed pursuant to this section, may be altered from time to time or repealed; and all corporations shall have the right to sue and shall be subject to be sued in all courts in like cases as natural persons.

Now, associations mean corporations. We say that no such corporations shall be formed. There is not a single article where the difference is not direct and positive. I dislike to be obliged to get up here and discuss these articles one by one, to show that they are distinct and separate. I wish the chairman of the committee would explain to this House the reasons why these articles should be adopted, and show where the restrictions are, show us why we should allow the Legislature to pass these special acts. I am sorry the gentleman did not think proper to take advantage of the opportunity which was afforded when these articles came up, to say something definite in their defence, in order that we who oppose the indecisive and dangerous words, and still more dangerous principles, should not have been compelled to open this debate, and bring forward our objections in the first place. Now, I must bring forward here, because it cannot be done in any other place, one or two of these objections to the provision allowing those corporate associations. I ask the gentleman whether the section providing for the incorporation of associations for the deposit of gold and silver, would not permit these associations to issue paper certificates of deposit. I say if they can enter into any speculation, and take this money deposited in their hands and use it for the purpose of trade, and issue certificates of deposit, probably at par, it is, to all intents and purposes, a bank, and the worst sort of bank. Where is their stock? What are the individual speculators liable for? You bind them by a bond? What is a bond? Cannot any lawyer pick a flaw in a bond? Give me private and individual responsibility. The whole system is different from the minority report. I am prepared to go to any extent against banks in this country. The inhabitants are against them; public opinion everywhere is against them. We have a metallic currency here, which is worth all the banks in the world.

Mr. GWIN. It seems to be the determination of the gentlemen who compose the Select Committee, and by whom the majority report was made, not to discuss this question. It is proper, sir, that I should give the reasons that actuated me in making the minority report, and show why it should be adopted by this House. I believed that public sentiment was such as to render it impracticable for any provision to be introduced in this Constitution which would countenance, in the remotest degree, the banking system.

Mr. NORTON. I rise to a question of order. I insist upon it that the Committee have introduced no article in favor of banking, or giving the power to the Legislature to create banks in any form.

Mr. GWIN. If I do not prove it, then my argument is worth nothing. I do not intend to consume the time of this House, by going into a discussion of the bank question. That question, sir, has been settled. Public opinion throughout the United States is against the banking system. All I want to show is that there are dangerous provisions in these articles granting privileges to corporations of this character.

It is useless, Mr. Chairman, to fight shy any longer on this question, which has no other effect than to waste the time of the House. The whole question of corporations and banking is open for discussion by my motion. It is to strike out and insert what? An article in which is inserted all that will, if it is adopted, appear in the Constitution on the subject of corporations and banking.

I was somewhat surprised, Mr. Chairman, that the Chairman of the Committee did not put this construction on my motion, and proceed to defend the position of the majority of the Committee, as embodied in the report on the subject of corporations; this is the usual course in all parliamentary bodies with which I am acquainted. The Chairman of a Committee, making a majority report upon an important subject, opens the debate, giving the reasons why the Committee came to the conclusion that induced them to present the subject in the shape it appeared before the House. The minority then have the privilege of reply, and presenting their reasons for differing with the majority. I had a right to expect that the Chairman would pursue this course, but I waive it, with a single remark in reply to his assertion, that the difference between the majority and minority reports are merely verbal. There never was a greater mistake; they are as widely separated as if the Pacific lay between, as I will proceed to show.

It is with most unaffected reluctance, Mr. Chairman, that I engage in the discussion of this question at all. I did hope that it had been completely settled by the advancing spirit of the age, and that no member of this body would bring forward any proposition which could in any form introduce the banking system into this country, and insist upon its insertion in the Constitution which we are about to adopt. But I am mistaken, and am called on most reluctantly to buckle on my armor, worn in many a hard-fought battle on this subject, and which I hoped was laid aside forever, and battle for the rights of the people, against monopoly and the legalized association of wealth to appropriate the labor of the many for the benefit of the few. * * * *

I will waste but little time on those sections of the report granting the power to create corporations, and leave the discussion that will no doubt take place on them, to the members of the legal profession, who will participate in this debate, and point out their defects. Yet I cannot permit the occasion to pass without entering my protest against the discretion given to the Legislature on this subject. The Legislature is to be the sole judge of the necessity of passing special acts for incorporations. Constitutional restrictions are not worth a straw, if they can be set aside in this way. I hope and believe that portion of the section will be stricken out, and what I propose in the minority report may be adopted in its stead. Nor am I satisfied with the section making stockholders liable only for the amount of stock they may hold in the corporation. I have so altered my substitute as to make them liable for the whole of its debts, in proportion to the amount of stock held by each party. If one man hold a hundred shares, he shall be liable for ten times the amount of the debts of the concern as the man who holds but ten shares; but there shall be a direct liability for all the debts. Without this there is no safeguard for the people against fraud. Precautions should also be taken against the fraudulent transfer of stock to irresponsible persons. A man familiar with the affairs of a corporation, aware of its approaching bankruptcy to which he may have contributed and been enriched by it, may go scot free if no guards are placed upon transfers.

But I will not go into the detail of the New York system of corporations proposed to be incorporated in our Constitution, but must declare my opposition to it as unsuited to this country. There is no similarity in the positions and conditions of New York and California. In the former, corporations are the institutions of ages, and have become an indivisible portion of its system of government. What has been incorporated in the Constitution of that State is not to lay the basis of a system of corporations suited to a new country like ours, but to restrict and restrain what has existed for more than half a century. Do you suppose we should find any thing of the kind in the New York Constitution, if her condition had been as ours is. Never, sir! The object of the framers of that Constitution was to correct and restrain a system that could not be eradicated with safety to the State.

In what respect does our position assimilate to that of New York, that we should so closely adhere to her fundamental law in forming our Constitution. In none whatever. We are a new people, creating from chaos a government; left free as air to select what is good, from all republican forms of government. Our country is like a blank sheet of paper, upon which we are required to write a system of fundamental laws. Let the rights of the people be guarded in every line we write, or they will apply the sponge to our work.

I now come to what I conceive to be the banking system, to be established by these sections of the Committee's report. Sir, the Committee speaks out in the boldest language when it places some restrictions upon banking; it is then the bank shall not do this, and the bank shall not do that; but when they wish to steal from the people the nucleus around which a monied oligarchy may be built up in the country, the subject is approached—let me say with all due respect to the Committee, whose motives I in no wise impugn—in real petit larceny style; aye, with the cringing sycophancy of the beggar asking alms while filching your purse from your pocket.

The word *bank* never appears once, no, not even *corporation; that* might alarm the people. Association is the magic word that is to remove every objection, and do away with every scruple. Sir, it is a shallow device, and will deceive no one. It reminds me of the celebrated exchequer brought before Congress after John Tyler had vetoed the United States Bank Bill. Mr. Sargeant, the Chairman of the Committee of Ways and Means, of the House of Representatives, in introducing the bill, announced with great form and ceremony that the word *bank* could not be found in it; that it was no bank, but simply an exchequer, for the convenience of the Government in managing its finances, and where the people might safely make their deposits; in other words, an association for the deposit of gold and silver. Sir, if that exchequer had become a law, we would now have in full operation, a mammoth National Bank, and if the power there granted is incorporated in our Constitution, in its present unrestricted state, we may soon look for a mammoth State exchequer, more dangerous to the liberties of the people than any foreign enemy that can approach our shores.

Bank notes are prohibited with great parade, but not a word is said against bank certificates of deposit, with which the country may become flooded, and will be, if this section is not stricken out.

Sir, no one familiar with the banking system as it existed in the United States from 1836 to 1840, can have forgotten how the country was flooded with post notes, corporation and individual tickets, and in many instances, certificates of deposit, precisely similar to those which these associations are authorized to issue.

It would be a curious spectacle to exhibit before this Convention the various kinds of paper in circulation, as money, during that memorable period. I have seen collected, as a matter of curiosity and amusement, upwards of one hundred, and if I had them here, they would be the only argument required to nip this whole system in its bud. The devices to gull and deceive the people were so many and varied that none could be so blind as not to see that the slightest authority or countenance given in this Constitution, to associations which can assume banking privileges of any kind, will, in times of high speculative excitement, lead to enormous abuses, alike destructive to the happiness and prosperity of the country.

The Committee have not even attempted to restrict the power to issue certificates of deposit, thus in effect expressly sanctioning it. In this cunningly devised bill, this was no omission or oversight, for the whole scheme bears evidence on its face of having been got up carefully, emasculating the section in the New York Constitution, by striking out all that might alarm the members of this body.

It may be said that no danger can result from the passage of this section; that the restrictions upon banking are so great that it will be impossible to abuse the power granted. Believe it not. How do they expect to make money to put the expensive machinery into operation? How is the costly lot in the centre of the city—the fine fire proof houses—fire-proof vaults—fire proof safes, to be paid for? The President, Cashier, Teller, Book-keepers, Messengers, &c. &c., to be supported simply upon the per centage charged upon the gold and silver deposit, for you will be gravely told that these associations will charge a per centage upon deposits, and thus make money to sustain themselves. Nothing can be more fallacious. Banks, bankers, and merchants, the world over, never charge for deposits; in fact, they seek them, and in many instances, if the amount is large, pay an interest upon them. My friend and colleague near me, Mr. Hobson, has at times on deposit in his commercial establishment in San Francisco, upwards of one hundred thousand dollars in gold dust, and the gentleman from Monterey, Mr. Dent, says he has had from thirty to forty thousand dollars on deposit, in his store in the mines, and all without expense to the owners. Some difficulties have doubtless heretofore existed, but they are lessening daily, and very soon deposits of gold dust and coin will be eagerly desired by safe and responsible persons.

But the great depository for California must be the Mint, which will no doubt, next winter, be located at some commercial point, probably with branches in the mines. It is the true policy of the United States to coin every dollar of gold taken from the mines, and one of the first acts of Congress in legislating for this country, will be the establishment of a Mint. It is folly to create associations for the deposit of gold and silver in California; the chief, if not the only product of the country is gold in its uncoined state; it is like asking for associations to receive wheat, corn, and hogs in Ohio. The thousands and tens of thousands engaged in gold digging, want no such associations. It will benefit those only who live by their wits, and not the hard-handed gold digger, who by his labor, enriches the country. Let us guard against infringing on the rights of the people, by legalizing the association of capital to war upon labor. This is the only country on the globe where labor has the complete control of capital. Let it remain so if we would be free, independent, and prosperous. If there are to be banks in the country, let us have private bankers, who, if they abuse the confidence of the people, can be punished by the law, indicted, and put in the penitentiary. The safest banking we ever had in the United States was that of Stephen Girard. Who ever lost a dollar by depositing with him? while thousands were beggard by the bankruptcy of the United States Bank. Look at the great bankers of Europe, the Rothschild's, the Baring's, the Brown's, and others who control the finances of the world—do they ask for the privilege of corporate powers to receive on deposit gold and silver? But why say more? We certainly cannot retrogade on this subject. States may continue to tolerate the system of banking from necessity; it is so mixed with their systems of government, they cannot eradicate it without danger to the body politic; but no new country should, for a moment, entertain the proposition of incorporating it in her fundamental law—it would be folly and madness to do so. The plea of necessity will not avail. Look at Havana, with a commerce of millions annually, that never has had a bank or paper money. Look at New Orleans, the largest exporting city in the Union, where banks are prohibited in the State Constitution, and as the charters of those now in existence expire, the system will be eradicated for ever. Look at the exchanges of the world carried on by private individuals, and can any man have the hardihood to say we want such associations in this country as this section of the bill tolerates? I hope not. Sir, I have seen our countrymen as wild on the subject of banking, as they now are about our gold mines. I have seen the people going by thousands to get loans from the banks, as they are now rushing to our banks of gold. Misery, ruin, and destruction to the citizens, and prostration of the public credit follows the banking era of 1834, '35, '36, and '37. The private wealth and public prosperity which it was predicted would result from the system, like dead sea fruit, burned to ashes on the lips, while our banks of gold, if left unrestricted by improper legislation, will yield a rich reward to the laborer for his toil, and ensure to the country a permanent prosperity.

Mr. SHERWOOD. I am in favor of the report of the Select Committee, although the articles reported by that Committee are rather longer than the amendment offered by the gentleman from San Francisco (Mr. Gwin.) I consider them more explicit in regard to what is meant by corporations, and the mode of forming them, their powers, and the restrictions thrown around them. In regard to banks, I perfectly agree with him that this country does not need the banking system. I have not the horror, however, of a well regulated banking system, as it exists in the State of New York, which the gentleman seems to entertain towards banks of every description. The gentleman was raised in a part of the country where, unfortunately, sufficient guards were not thrown around corporations of this character, and private individuals, by hundreds and thousands, have suffered in consequence. In the State of New York the later laws organizing banks have been general laws. Now no bank is formed there unless its whole capital is paid in, in the stocks of the State, or of the United States, dollar for dollar; and these stocks, which are as good as the faith of the State of New York or the people of the United States can make them, are deposited with the Comptroller of the State. Dollar for dollar in bank bills is issued to the corporator. Such is the foundation of the present banking system in New York. Nearly all of the charters of the old safety fund banks have expired. The existing system has been found to work well in that State ; but, as I have said before, there is no necessity for a banking system in this country. I trust there never will be ; and with that view of the subject, I would of course go against any provision in the Constitution which, by possibility, could be construed as a grant of power to the Legislature to introduce any such system. The gentleman says that the Constitution of New York may do very well for New York, but that the system of banking there is an entirely different thing from what we need here. That is true ; perfectly agree with him ; but I think he is unfair in using that argument on the assumption that the Committee reported in favor of banks. We have examined different Constitutions in committee, and from the latest, or about the latest Constitution of one of the oldest States of the Union—a State which has had sad experience on the subject of banking—we have selected a clause in regard to corporations. The Convention that assembled three years since in the State of New York, was got together by the voice of the people, on the subject of corporations and the dangers attending them. The result was, that the most stringent restrictions were thrown around the Legislature on this subject, The powers of the Legislature were strictly confined to the passage of general laws of incorportion, except for municipal purposes, and then only when the object could not be attained under general law. The Legislature, under this limitation, has faithfully complied with the requirements of the Constitution. A precise definition of what is meant by corporation is given. It is every association with powers granted by the Legislature not possessed by individuals or common partnerships. We, in the same manner, have introduced a provision defining what shall be considered corporations, and how they shall be created, saying that the Legislature shall have no power to create banks. We then go on, and, in another provision, say that the Legislature shall create no institution which shall issue bank bills of any description. Can the gentleman then find any room for the man of straw which he has pictured to the House ? In this country, it is true, we have what is coin all over the world—gold and silver. This is and always will be our circulating medium. But the gentleman knows—merchants know—every man knows—that wherever there is a large amount of the precious metals, there must be a place of deposit. The gentleman is also aware that if he desires to send a hundred thousand dollars to Louisiana, he must either buy a bill of exchange or get a certificate of deposit, and if he gets that he will be very apt to select the association which will have the most credit to deposit his money with and draw his certificate from. We say here that the Legislature may create associations for the deposit of gold and silver. This is not a special act. It is for every man who has money. It is not confined to the particular favorites of the Legislature. It is a general law. I have no horror for general laws of that description. What is the law now here in regard to deposits? An individual deposits with me a thousand dollars. I have no iron safe. My store burns up, and the money with it. I charge him nothing for receiving his money on deposit. He cannot, according to the common law, collect it from me, because I have received no consideration. Now, sir, as our commerce extends, as our population increases, as the gold is dug from the earth in augmenting quantities, as the wealth of the country is enhanced from every source, I am in favor of giving to the Legislature the power to create a general law, by which any association of men can receive money on deposit, and give a certificate therefor. I am not afraid of such bank bills. The gentleman will not fear such bank bills, any more than a bill of exchange on Louisiana or New York. It is a settled principle that the people will use the currency they like best. You cannot force a currency upon them. If a man has money which he does not want to carry about him, he will deposit it in a place of security, and get a paper for it which he he can carry conveniently. I see none of those terrible phantasies which disturb the mind of the gentlemen from San Joaquin and San Francisco. The raw-head and bloody bones does not appear before me, because the soul and body are not here. We have given no banking power to the Legislature. We have said expressly that they never shall charter a bank; they never shall allow any association with corporate powers to issue bank bills. Would the gentleman prevent an individual or an association from issuing a certificate of deposit? If he would prevent an association from issuing a certificate founded upon a thousand dollars put into its vaults, would he not as soon refuse his colleague from San Francisco, (Mr. Hobson,) the right to issue a certificate of deposit for a thousand dollars offered by an individual to be placed in his safe, even if the money was offered for nothing? I can see no distinction. The Legislature has power by this article to create—not banks to swindle the community, or to cheat those who deposit money in their vaults, or buy stock—but those necessary associations for the deposit of gold and silver, without which, the community of this country, where the amount of the precious metals is so large, would be subject to serious inconvenience. They must deposit their money somewhere, and it is better that they should have some known and reliable public association to deposit with, than irresponsible private establishments, from which they could obtain no indemnification in case of loss. There is nothing in this provision to touch the fears of the most timid; and I cannot perceive why the gentleman should see the fearful visions which he pictures to us, when he knows distinctly, that the Committee are opposed to banks in this country. He says the Committee have carefully kept out of view the word bank—that it never once appears in the articles reported—as if they desired banks under a specious covering. The gentleman has no authority for such an imputation. There has been no concealment on the part of the Committee, but a straightforward desire to get up a Constitution which the people would approve—to deprive the Legislature of all power to create banking institutions. Suppose we refuse the Legislature the power to regulate the depositing of gold and silver. In five years from now, the population of California may be a million; the commerce fifty millions. Would we not, with this commerce, and this population, present a strange spectacle to the world? No legalized depositories for our money; no power in the Legislature to create them; a positive denial of the right to issue paper as medium of currency, which is right and proper. but also a denial of the right of the people to deposit their capital, which is gold and silver, and obtain for the legitimate purposes of business, certificates of deposit or bills of exchange. In conclusion, Mr. President, if we strike out this provision, we deny to the Legislature a power which the people desire, which the currency of the country renders necessary, which can be attended by no possible danger, and which must have a beneficial influence in augmenting the wealth of the community, and promoting the facilities of commerce.

After further discussion on the order of amendments, Mr. GWIN, in order to prevent further difficulty on the subject, withdrew his amendment.

Mr. LIPPITT then moved to amend the 31st section by striking out the words, "and in cases where, in the judgment of the Legislature, the objects of the corporation cannot be attained under general laws."

Mr. PRICE. Before this question is taken, I wish to say a few words in reply to the gentleman from Sacramento, (Mr. Sherwood,) whose views and mine are diametrically opposed in relation to the system proposed in the 34th section of granting general privileges to associations to receive deposits of gold and silver. Now, sir, we have the practical operation of affairs in California for the last nine months as a guide. The commercial operations of this country are already very extensive, and the people have not asked for any such privileges yet. They find that they can conduct their affairs very well without associations of this kind. I am opposed to granting any privileges here which are not required by the community, and which can only have the effect of consolidating capital.

Mr. NORTON. I call the gentleman to order. He is not speaking to the amendment.

Mr. PRICE. I believe I am entirely in order, sir. I take the broad ground that the country does not require any general law, as proposed by the 34th section. We have tried the experiment of depositing without the aid of legislative action, in San Francisco, to the amount of several millions of dollars, and I am not aware that there has been any loss or any inconvenience resulting from the manner in which these deposits are made. The gentleman (Mr. Sherwood) tells us of the necessity of legalized associations to receive deposits and carry on the exchanges of this country. We are clearly at issue on this point, for so far as my observation of affairs in this country extends, (and I have had some experience in monetary transactions here,) I believe it to be not only needless to create establishments of this kind, but I believe they would have a most pernicious effect upon the business interests of the community. In regard to exchanges, I do not see what facilities these institutions would afford to the people.

Mr. SHERWOOD. Does the gentleman mean to say that domestic exchanges are not needed here at all.

Mr. PRICE. I say this provision will not facilitate them. I say that exchanges of every kind, domestic and foreign, can be conducted by individuals; and that no grant should be given to corporations to do this business for individuals. We have already places of deposit in San Francisco; there are individuals there who have constructed safe places of deposit for gold dust or coin, as may be brought to them. Now, sir, it is proposed here to give the Legislature power to pass a general law by which persons may associate, under legislative sanction, to compete with these individuals who have already done this business without any enactments of this kind. I have seen enough to satisfy me that all such privileges have a pernicious tendency, and would be more particularly injurious in California than any other part of the world, because they are less required and less known. Places of deposit, sir, will keep pace with the requirements of the country, and I trust that no section which has the shadow of a banking institution in it, or which can bear the shadow of a construction under which corporations of this character can grow up, will be adopted by this House.

Mr. HALLECK. I was with the majority of the Committee who reported this article. On a careful examination of the subject, I have found reasons why I think some verbal amendment, such as that suggested by the gentleman from San Francisco, (Mr. Lippitt,) ought to prevail. I do not think that particular clause, which he proposes striking out, will be necessary in California. I shall therefore vote for the amendment.

On motion of Mr. Shannon, the Committee then rose, reported progress, and obtained leave to sit again.

On motion, the Convention then adjourned to 12 o'clock, to-morrow.

TUESDAY, SEPTEMBER 18, 1849.

In Convention. Prayer by the Rev. Antonio Ramirez. Journal of yesterday read, amended, and approved.

Mr. Hill announced the arrival of his colleague from San Diego, Miguel de la Pedronena, and moved that he be qualified and authorized to take his seat. Whereupon, Mr. Pedronena was duly sworn and admitted to his seat.

Mr. Hill then moved that Mr. Wm. H. Richardson who was one of the five delegates elected in the District of San Diego, be also sworn, and allowed to take his seat.

Mr. Botts said that the gentleman could not take his seat unless the existing resolution fixing the representation of the several districts was rescinded.

Mr. Gilbert said that the resolution made the apportionment of two members from San Diego.

Mr. Tefft was willing to admit as many members from San Diego as that district was justly entitled to; but he could not see how any, in addition to the two already admitted, could be admitted under the rules of the House.

Mr. Shannon regarded the vote of the House upon that resolution as perfectly null and void; that they went beyond any right that they possessed, in declaring that such a district should have so many and no more members. He believed he expressed his opinion at the time of its adoption as strongly as he could, and he had seen no cause since to change that opinion. The bad effects of such a course were now evident. The House was in difficulty. The people of San Diego, under the proclamation of General Riley, had elected five delegates, and this Convention had said they should have but two delegates. The people of San Joaquin had elected ten delegates; the Convention said they were entitled to fifteen. He thought the gentleman from San Diego (Mr. Richardson) had a perfect right to come upon this floor, and be admitted as a member.

Mr. Gwin said that this was to be found in a portion of the proceedings of the House, under which they got into a difficulty about a quorum. He recollected that he had moved a reconsideration of the vote on the resolution, and it was his understanding that the reconsideration was carried.

Mr. Gilbert explained the circumstances of the vote of the Convention on that subject. The apportionment finally agreed upon by resolution allowed to San Diego only two members; consequently no other gentlemen could be admitted, unless that resolution was rescinded.

Mr. Gwin said that if the journal proved such to be the case, he would move that the resolution be rescinded, and that the gentleman be admitted.

Mr. Tefft did not wish the House to proceed without a proper understanding of this matter. He was in favor of admitting the gentleman, and would vote for the proposition of the gentleman from San Francisco, (Mr. Gwin.) But he denied that the House should not contradict itself by its own action.

The Secretary then read from the journal the order of the House fixing the representation from San Diego at two members.

Mr. Gwin moved that this order be so amended as to admit the member now claiming his seat, (Mr. Richardson.)

The Chair inquiried if there were not other members from other districts claiming seats.

Mr. Hill stated that there were none to his knowledge, except from San Diego.

Mr. Dimmick said that if this representation was to be increased, he would state, as the Chair had made the inquiry, that there were other members from San Jose who would also claim their seats.

Mr. Tefft did not see any better way of settling the difficulty than to take the claims of the gentleman who appeared to take his seat, and settle the case at once, on its own merits.

Mr. Shannon moved a suspension of the rules of the House for the purpose of reconsidering the order allowing the District of San Diego but two members.

The Chair stated that it would require a vote of two-thirds to suspend the rule.

Mr. Gwin offered the following resolution :

Resolved, That the action of the Convention apportioning delegates to the several districts, be so far rescinded as to admit William Richardson, a delegate elect from the District of San Diego, to his seat as such.

Mr. Lippitt remarked that a good deal was said the other day by his friend from Monterey (Mr. Botts) about the elective franchise. He thought that gentleman would not dispute that, whenever a citizen is elected by the people to any body whatever, that the fact of his election of itself proves that he has acquired a franchise of which he cannot legally be deprived. Any member who has been elected by his fellow-citizens, and who has received his certificate of election, possesses a franchise in the rights acquired under that election. It is therefore perfectly competent for the House to entertain a motion that the person elected, be allowed to take his seat. The House has no right to refuse him admission or deprive him of his franchise, which they would do, if they denied him his seat, whatever may have been the previous action on the subject. He considered that action of the House null and void, and would therefore vote in favor of whatever method was proposed, in order to meet the difficulty, and accomplish the object he had in view.

Mr. Botts did not intend to enter into any argument on this subject. He thought that the oldest politician might learn something new in regard to parliamentary rules in this body. He called the attention of the Convention to the proclamation of the Governor, fixing the ratio of representation in the first place. Until this House reconsidered and annulled the resolution which it had adopted, it was utterly impossible to admit any delegate from San Diego, other than the two admitted under its existing decision. The proclamation left this matter to the decision of the House. He did not consider that either the proclamation or the Convention could deprive any man of a franchise given to him by the people, but the people having in the first place adopted the proclamation, it became their act, and the House having formed certain rules in accordance with the powers conferred upon it, could not adopt an order, and then proceed to violate that order. It would be necessary to rescind it before any additional members were admitted from the District of San Diego.

Mr. Gwin, to prevent further debate, moved the previous question ; but at the request of Mr. McCarver, he withdrew it.

Mr. McCarver said that the House must suspend its rules before it proceeded in this matter ; and to suspend the rules, would require one day's notice.

Mr. Shannon moved a suspension of the rules so as to admit a motion to reconsider the vote fixing the apportionment of the several districts.

The motion was decided in the affirmative, two-thirds of the members present, voting in favor thereof.

Some discussion as to the order of proceeding here took place, when the President decided the question of reconsideration to be first in order.

Mr. Shannon submitted the following :

Resolved, That the House now proceed to reconsider their action on so much of the apportionment of delegates as relates to the District of San Diego.

Mr. SHANNON subsequently modified his resolution so as to embrace a reconsideration of the entire action of the Convention on the subject of apportionment.

And the question being on the adoption of the resolution, as modified, it was decided in the negative.

Mr. GWIN submitted the following:

Resolved, That William Richardson, a member elect from the District of San Diego, be admitted to his seat.

Mr. CARVER moved an indefinite postponement of the whole subject.

The President decided that all further action was precluded by the refusal of the Convention to reconsider the vote fixing the apportionment of the several districts.

Mr. HILL submitted the following:

Resolved, That a committee of five be appointed by the President, to ascertain and report to this House who are or shall be delegates from San Diego.

And the question being on the adoption of the resolution, it was decided in the affirmative—yeas 19, nays 9.

The President appointed as said committee, Messrs. Tefft, Stearns, Wozencraft, Jones, and Sherwood.

On motion of Mr. CROSBY, the President filled a vacancy on the Committee on Finance, occasioned by the absence of Mr. Price, by the temporary appointment of Mr. Aram.

Mr. HASTINGS, from the Committee on the Boundary, made the following report, which was received, read, and referred to the committee of the whole:

Mr. President: The committee, to whom was referred the subject of the boundary of the State of California, in accordance with a resolution of this House requiring the appointment of a committee of five to report what, in their opinion, should constitute the boundary of the State of California, have had the same under consideration, and beg leave to report the following.

Your committee are of the opinion that the present boundary of California comprehends a tract of country entirely too extensive for one State, and that there are various other forcible reasons why that boundary should not be adopted by this Convention. The area of the tract of country included within the present boundary is estimated to be four hundred and forty-eight thousand six hundred and ninety-one (448,691) square miles, which is nearly equal to that of all the non-slaveholding States of the Union, and which, deducting the area of Iowa, is greater than that of the residue of the non-slaveholding States.

Your committee are of opinion that a country like this, extending along the coast nearly a thousand miles (1,000) and more than twelve hundred miles into the interior, cannot be conveniently or fairly represented in a State Legislature here, especially as a greater part of the interior is entirely cut off from the country on the coast by the Sierra Nevada, a continuous chain of lofty mountains, which is covered with snow, and is wholly impassable nearly nine months in the year.

Your committee are also of the opinion that the country included within the boundary of this territory as now established, must ultimately be divided and sub-divided into several different States, which divisions and sub-divisions (should the present boundary be adopted) would be very likely to divest the State of California of a valuable portion of her sea coast. Your committee are therefore of the opinion that a boundary should now be fixed upon which will entirely preclude the possibility of such a result in future. Another important reason which has aided very much in producing the conclusion to which your committee have arrived, is predicated upon the fact that there is already a vast settlement in a remote portion of this territory, the population of which is variously estimated to be from fifteen to thirty thousand human souls, who are not represented in this Convention, and who, perhaps, do not desire to be represented here.

The religious peculiarities of these people, and the very fact of their having selected that remote and isolated region as a permanent home, would seem to warrant a conclusion that they desire no direct political connection with us, and it is possible, and highly probable, in the opinion of your committee, that measures have been, or are now being taken by these people, for the establishment of a Territorial Government for themselves.

For the above and foregoing reasons, your committee are of the opinion that the following should constitute the boundary of the State of California, viz:

Commencing at the northeast corner of the State at the intersection of the parallel of latitude forty-two degrees north with the parallel of longitude one hundred and sixteen west; thence south, upon and along that parallel of longitude to the boundary line between the United States and Mexico, established by the treaty of peace ratified by the said Governments at Queretaro, on the 30th day of May, 1848; thence west, upon and along the said boundary line, to the Pacific ocean; thence, in a northerly direction, following the course of the Pacific coast, to the said parallel of forty-two degrees north latitude, extending one marine league into the sea from the southern to the northern boundary, and including all the bays, harbors, and islands adjacent to the said coast; and thence, east from the said coast, at latitude forty-two degrees north, upon and along that parallel of latitude to the place of beginning.

All of which is respectfully submitted. L. W. HASTINGS, *Chairman.*

On motion, the House then adjourned to 8 o'clock P. M.

NIGHT SESSION, 8 O'CLOCK P. M.

Mr. NORTON, from the Committee on the Constitution, reported the "Executive Department," which was received, and referred to the committee of the whole.

On motion of Mr. Botts, the House then resolved into

COMMITTEE OF THE WHOLE,

Mr. SHERWOOD in the Chair, on the report of the Committee on the Constitution.

The amendment offered by Mr. Lippett, yesterday, being under consideration, as follows:

To strike out after the word "purposes," "and in cases where, in the judgment of the Legislature, the objects of the corporations cannot be attained under general laws."

Mr. BOTTS said: I rise Mr. Chairman, to support that amendment. I think, sir, that we have arrived at an era in the discussion of this Constitution. The questions that have hitherto been presented to this Convention, although grave in their character, are nothing at all in practical importance, compared with the question now under consideration. Those points which have been the main subjects of discussion in the original declaration of rights, although in themselves of momentous importance as great fixed principles, may be regarded as fit subjects for declamation; for it does not matter a great deal in my opinion whether they are embraced in this Constitution or not; they have become established truths. But, sir, we have now come to a question of the most vital importance to the interests of the community—a question of direct and practical importance, and one which will be brought home to every man in his daily business relations. I hope we will consider it with all the gravity and deliberation that its character demands. This Convention should be willing to spend one or two days if necessary, in the full consideration of the subject. Sir, there is not a gentleman on this floor, who has a constituency at home, who will not be made to feel the effects of his decision on this question. For my own part, I must apologize to the House in advance, for the crude remarks which I am about to make. The subject has been brought up in such a manner as to prevent me from reducing my ideas to anything like a systematic arrangement. I am in favor of this amendment simply for this reason: that the object of the original section as reported, being to limit the power of the Legislature in the creation of corporations, the clause giving a discretionary power to the Legislature, entirely destroys that effect, and grants all the power which it is evidently the object of the section to deny. Corporations may be formed under general laws, says the section, but shall not be created by special act, except for municipal purposes, and in cases where, in the judgment of the Legislature, the object of the corporation cannot be attained under general law. That is to say, the Legislature shall not erect corporations of a particular character, unless they choose to do so. Now, sir, my object is, and I suppose it was the object of the Committee, to prohibit the Legislature from erecting these particular corporations, whether they choose to do it or not; and yet from the section, it is perfectly clear that the discretion is left with the Legislature. Whatever law they may pass, is constitutional, because the question as to the necessity of the law is left to the judgment of the Legislature. There is not a judge in the land who will not be compelled to tell you that any law erecting corporations under this clause, is rendered constitutional by the act of the Legislature. There is no check contained in the section. If, therefore, we are to have this section at all, I would greatly prefer it with the clause stricken out as proposed by gentleman from San Francisco, (Mr. Lippett.) But I would prefer even to the gentleman's amendment, prohibiting the Legislature from granting any exclusive privileges to corporations at all, by special act, or any immunities not possessed by the citizens of the State generally. Corporations as they were originally known to the Roman law, had several beneficial properties. One was the power of succession, by which the property of the corporation does not become subdivided into the hands of the heirs, but remains subject to the rules of the corporation. Another was, to sue and be sued in their corporate capacity, instead of being regarded as a partnership merely of individuals. These were the useful properties of these corporations as known to the Roman law. The institution as it was known when adopted by the common law, had engrafted upon it this doctrine: that to establish a corporation was the great prerogative of the crown; and it followed soon with the numerous other prerogatives of the crown, that it was claimed by the crown; and certain great privileges and immunities were given to these corporations. This is the evil which we have followed so nearly in our own country, and of which we have such grevious cause to complain. I propose now to deny the Legislature the power of creating them for the purposes which we do not desire, and to give it the privilege of creating them for all useful purposes. The Legislature should not be permitted to grant exclusive privileges to these corporations; they are then not only harmless, but they are useful. If it be the will of the House to adopt the amendment, and the section as amended, I shall propose to follow it up by another proposition, instead of the one that comes afterwards. But at present, my object is merely to put the House in possession of the principles which I propose. I am opposed to any corporations with exclusive privileges, and especially to banking corporations. My chief object, therefore, is to crush this bank monster. I do not believe that any system you can devise here that does not secure the existence of a circulating medium of paper money, will ever put down banks. I repeat the proposition, for it may seem a very singular one to some members. To put down banks, you must give the people a paper circulating medium. For twelve years, more or less, my mind has been given to the consideration of this subject. In the year 1836-7, I witnessed the desolating operations of the banking system in the United States. My mind has been intent on the subject ever since. The result of my observation and reflection has been this—that in a mercantile community, some circulating medium more portable than gold and silver is absolutely necessary to its existence. Sir, you must give to the people a good circulating medium of paper currency, or they will have a bad one for themselves. You may make all the provisions in the world that you choose; but if you leave a loop-hole, this insinuating serpent, a circulating bank, will find its way through, because of the absolute necessity of the community for a paper currency. How is it then that we are to effect the object?

[Here Mr. Botts read a paper, the substance of which was understood to be, that it should be the duty of the Treasurer of the State to open a place of deposit for gold and silver, and to issue certificates, of suitable denominations, dollar for dollar on the amount deposited, payable on demand, which certificates were to circulate as money, being secured by actual deposits with the Treasurer, and for which the State was to be held responsible.]

The greatest genius of the age, a bank man of the very purest water, declared upon the floor of the Senate, that the greatest evil with which a country could be afflicted, was an irredeemable circulating paper medium. I do not believe that statesman ever said a wiser or truer thing; I do not believe that any bank paper that the ingenuity of man can devise which is not covered dollar for dollar by actual capital, can be other than the ruinous system to which Mr. Webster alluded. I do not believe it is possible to pay three dollars with one. There may be some gentlemen on this floor who have had experience in that experiment; but I consider it the hardest matter in the world. Now, sir, that is the foundation of all your circulating banks. I grant you there are times, when these banks have the full faith and confidence of the community, when they can redeem with a certain portion of gold and silver; but when a foreign debt is to be paid, which has usually to be paid with the products of the country; when these products fall short, when your corn crop or tobacco is deficient, there then occurs what is called a run upon the banks. Individuals who have their debts to pay abroad, unable to purchase cotton or tobacco unless at a very high rate, find it cheaper to export gold and silver. They come upon the banks, and if, by force of circumstances, the scarcity in the crops should be general, the banks must necessararily fail, being unable to pay three dollars with one. The consequence is, ruin and desolation are spread throughout the country. But it is not worth my while here to expatiate on the evils of bank paper. It has been stated, and I hope it is true, that a majority of this House are opposed to the system. I hope every gentleman on this floor feels as deeply as I do the ruinous effects of bank paper. I hope there is not a member present who disguises his opinions, or desires to steal through this House a bank in disguise.

But, Mr. Chairman, I fear that, without being aware of it, this vigilant enemy is near them; they may find bank men in this country, and they are the sharpest and cunningest of men. I call upon every anti-bank man in this House to weigh well every word used here. For I tell you, sir, these banks can creep through an auger hole; they can get into this country through the smallest place you ever saw in your life; and I will endeavor to show you, when I come to the proper place, that there is a clause in this bill which will admit the enemy I speak of into our midst. Mr. Chairman, I believe that the framers of the Constitution of the United States were not less aware than we are of the injurious character of bank paper. I think you will admit, if you look at the published debates of that Convention, that there was as much unanimity there as there is here on that subject. But they unfortunately fell into the error into which I am afraid we will fall, if we are not extremely careful. They thought when they had provided that gold and silver coin should constitute the legal tender, that they had forever crushed this bank monster. It did not occur to them that any man would take bank paper when he might require gold and silver coin. But they forgot the superior portability of the paper money would induce men to do what seemed so much against their interest. Let us not forget this fact, sir, in forming our Constitution. Let us remember that we must have a paper circulating medium; that it is impossible for any individual to carry in his pocket twenty thousand dollars of gold and silver from one point to another, especially in this country where the means of conveyance are so indifferent. Let us remember more, Mr. President; what will be the result of permitting, as some gentlemen propose to do, every individual in this community to issue his own individual paper, and put it in circulation as money, depending upon his own credit for the successful result of the speculation. Sir, this question of currency is a very delicate one; it ought not to be trusted in the hands of the community. It is peculiarly the subject of legislation; it requires the protection of Government to keep the fountain pure and healthy. If you throw open this subject of a circulating medium, as I know it is the desire of many gentlemen to do; if you permit every individual in the community to issue his own paper notes for circulation as a currency, what wlil be the consequence? You will have fifty or a hundred different currencies in the country. It is a rule in political economy, and none better established, that when there are several currencies existing, the worst will always be in circulation; for the simple reason that, if you have a debt to pay, and you have two currencies in your pocket, either of which will pass, you will always pay out the worst and keep the best, and what you will do every other man in the community will do. The worst currency will therefore, unfortunately, be in circulation, and the probability is that there will be constant failures, and all those concurrent disasters resulting to the community from an irredeemable and depreciated circulating medium. For my own part, sir, I am so far a bank man, that if this privilege is not to be denied to individuals; if individuals are to be allowed to interfere and tamper with the currency of the country; if you will not restrain them by legislative enactment, I know of but one other way, and that is the restraint imposed upon them in the United States, which is better than none, bad as it is; the restraint of a corporation imposed upon them by the Legislature. Sir, you have never attempted this experiment yet. Let it not be said that there are portions of the United States in which individuals have been permitted to emit their own paper, and make it the circulating medium. Wherever it has been done, individuals have been overshadowed by large associations, the emission of whose paper has expelled the minor paper. This must be the inevitable result. If you remove the check upon the issue of paper as a currency by corporations, you must go one step further, and remove the evil itself. You must not only prohibit corporations from doing it, but also individuals. Why not as much an evil in the one case as in the other? What are the evils proceeding from the emission of paper money by corporations which would not exist if that corporation were a partnership, or single individual? I cannot see, for my life, how these evils would be lessened in that way. However, I am free to admit that the remarks which I am making would be more appropriate when we come to that particular part of this portion of the Constitution which treats of corporations in general, and banking corporations in particular. For the present I shall confine myself simply to the point presented in the clause under consideration. I propose to amend it by prohibiting the Legislature from granting any particular privileges or immunities to any corporations whatever. This is not merely a different wording, it is substantially a different thing; because that clause, even with the amendment of the gentleman from San Francisco, (Mr. Lippett,) does allow the Legislature to make corporations by special laws, but it does not do what I propose. I want to make a general law for all corporations; I want to prohibit the Legislature from ganting to any corporation any peculiar privileges or immunities; that is to say, if a railroad should be proposed from Monterey to San Francisco, a general law incorporates the company, or the company becomes a corporate body under a general law. Let them make the road as fast as they see fit; but do not permit the Legislature to grant them the sole privilege of this railroad for the next forty, fifty, or hundred years, as the case may be. We have all seen how unwisely this power has been used; how likely it is to be abused. I could produce instances of thousands of evils resulting from its abuse by the Legislature. I propose, therefore, to inhibit it altogether. I propose to pass a general law which will save all the expense of constant legislation on this subject Limited partnerships may be permitted—corporations may be permitted; but what shall be the nature of those corporations? Simply those useful principles which belonged to them in their original simplicity. To that original simplicity I would return. I would bring back corporations to what they were under Roman law, and what they ought always to have remained. You have then a creature that is useful to you as a servant, instead of being to you a tyrant master. By this section, as amended, corporations may be created by special act for municipal purposes. With respect to this clause, I have only to say that I have seen myself some of the most tyrannical violations of the rights of the people result from these charters for municipal corporations. I have seen a despotic government created in the powers granted to municipal corporations. My desire is that the character of these institutions shall not be inconsistent with the republican principles laid down in our Constitution; and that the powers of these corporations, if granted at all, shall be strictly limited to municipal purposes. I have seen the most complete and despotic power given by this provision. I have seen a majority in the Legislature compel the minority to subscribe to some magnificent scheme of internal improvement. I have seen men beggared against their will in this way. For this reason I desire that these powers shall be confined strictly to municipal purposes.

Mr. Norton. I do not propose to discuss at length all the questions suggested by the gentleman, (Mr. Botts.) I have no particular objection to the amendment proposed by my colleague, (Mr. Lippett,) to the section under consideration. I thought when the report was made, and I still think, that the section as it stands is not only just but a very proper one. It provides for the passage of general laws granting corporate privileges, and in some cases where, in the judgment of the Legislature, the object of the corporation cannot be attained by general laws, although it may be perfectly legitimate and proper, it provides that special acts may be passed. I do not believe, sir, that a body of men coming directly from the people are going to do what they know the people do not desire. They are too closely connected with the people themselves; they come too directly from the people, and are going to return too directly to them, to do anything that in their opinion, and in the opinion of the people, is not to the interest of the community and perfectly correct in itself. I have no doubt that under this section every object of a corporation that can be attained under general laws will be so attained, and that it would be very seldom special acts of the Legislature, granting corporate powers, would be passed. But I believe such cases may arise. This was the opinion of the Committee, and this was the reason why the section was introduced. But if, in the judgment of this House, it is inexpedient to give the Legislature any power to pass special acts, I would then be willing to take the section as it stands, so amend it, and let it be passed. I am not so much afraid, as some gentlemen seem to be, of these corporations. I do not believe that they are an injury to the public; on the contrary, I believe them to be a most essential benefit, for the purpose of developing public enterprise, facilitating improvements, carrying on business, and affording investments for capital, when a greater amount is required than can be commanded by single individuals or limited partnerships, as in the case of railroads, turnpikes, insurance companies, cemeteries, and numerous other beneficial purposes. At the same time I am in favor of having these corporations so created as to render them perfectly safe. I believe the section introduced in the report of the Committee, guarded as it is, will be entirely safe. I go for throwing around them all necessary restrictions. But, sir, I am decidedly opposed to the proposition of the gentleman from Monterey, (Mr. Botts.) In the first place, I see no possible good that can result from it. You declare here in the organic law of the land, that the people shall have the power to associate together for the purpose of doing any legitimate act. They have that power without declaring it in your Constitution. The gentleman from Monterey supposes a case. We wish to build a railroad from Monterey to San Francisco. I consider in that instance that it would be necessary to have an act of incorporation, granting privileges not possessed by individuals, so that the corporation might take land belonging to individuals for the use of this road, by paying them a proper equivalent. Let private individuals attempt to do this; they cannot go on your land and take an acre or foot of it unless you are willing to dispose of it. A great public benefit would therefore be defeated. Under a general law of incorporation they can take this land by paying the proper equivalent for it; and it is perfectly right, for the public good, that they should possess this power. In such cases it is necessary, and it may be necessary in a great many more. This provision does not give to corporations, or to any particular set of men, exclusive powers. Corporations are created under general laws passed by the Legislature. It is not any particular set of men who obtain the privilege. Any persons who choose may get together and form a corporation, under general laws, with these privileges. It is perfectly right that they should possess these powers; they are conferred upon corporations for the benefit of the people; they enable persons of limited means to combine and accomplish great public works by a consolidation of capital. If you place around them such restraints as will render them safe, I can see no possible reason for prohibiting institutions of this sort. The gentleman has given us a lengthy argument on banking. There is nothing in this report to favor the system of banking. No man has advocated the banking the system on this floor. I now disclaim any intention on the part of the Committee to introduce, secretly, any clause in the Constitution that will favor that system. It is not necessary to repeat the arguments which have been urged upon that subject.

Mr. Botts. I expressly disclaimed any remarks of that kind, in reference to this clause. I said that banks might steal into our Constitution in spite of the vigilance of the Committee.

Mr. Norton. I did not intend to say you made any reflection upon the Committee. In regard to restricting the powers of municipal corporations, to which the gentleman referred, I believe the subject is fully covered in section 37:

"It shall be the duty of the Legislature to provide for the organization of cities and incorporated llages, and to restrict their powers of taxation, assessment, borrowing money, contracting debts, and loaning their credit, so as to prevent abuses in their assessments, and in contracting debts, by such municipal corporations."

That covers the whole ground. It gives the Legislature the privilege of incorporating, for municipal purposes, towns and villages, and at the same time so to restrict their powers as not to render them oppressive upon the people. I believe then, with general laws for the purpose of granting corporate privileges, these institutions will not only be a great benefit to the corporators themselves, but to the people at large; and that they will not favor any set of men. All persons who choose can employ their capital in this way for their own benefit, and for the benefit of the people at large.

Mr. Jones. I merely rise to say that I am in a quandary, and while the amendment is being translated for the Spanish gentlemen, I will endeavor to explain what it is. I must protest against the course of my friend from Monterey, (Mr. Botts,) in making his speech this evening. If he had made it this morning it would have been all right. I think I have discovered in this article, reported by the Committee, a very fine opening for a small bank. Now, in pursuance of this idea, I have even gone so far as to draw up a fac simile of one of my bank bills over a certificate of deposit. If the bank could be got up on this principle, I have no doubt it would be a very respectable fiscal agent.

[Here Mr. Jones exhibited an etching of a bank bill, designed in pursuance of the power which he contended was conferred upon him under this clause.]

This is a bank bill to all intents and purposes, although it professes to be nothing more than a certificate of deposit. It is a very excellent and beautiful circulating medium; and any number of gentlemen, under the head of an association for the deposit of gold and silver, might very well make and issue such a circulating medium. No court in the country could condemn them for it.

Mr. Shannon. I call the gentleman to order. He is not speaking on the subject before the House. The debate is on the 31st section, and not upon the section which comes up afterwards, relating to the establishment of associations for the deposit of gold and silver.

The Chair stated that, owing to the latitude of debate customary in Committee of the Whole, it had not attempted to impose any restraint upon gentlemen who had availed themselves of the privileges usual in bodies of this kind. The Chair considered that as one part of the subject had a direct bearing upon the other parts, it was not out of order to discuss the whole.

Mr. Gwin had always supposed that the object of a Committee of the Whole was to allow the fullest and widest discussion on all subjects appertaining to the business of the House. He desired that every gentleman should have liberty to speak his sentiments fully and freely, without the restraints necessarily imposed, when the subjects have been thoroughly discussed in Committee, and come up for final action in the House.

Mr. Jones. I hold the whole system to be embodied in the different sections. The adoption of one leads necessarily to the adoption of another. I am compelled, in discussing the subject, to take up the entire system. If I hold the system to be radically wrong, I hold that I have a right to attack it either at the tail or the head. If I choose to expose the absurdity of the beginning, I have a right to expose the absurdity of the end. I was going to remark that I thought I had seen in the amendment of the gentleman from San Francisco, (Mr. Lippett,) a complete knockdown to all speculations; but a section comes up in the rear of it, which destroys all its force. Now I have this to say, I will take this circulating medium which I hold in my hand, and make it pass, throughout the State, to all intents and purposes as bank paper, and no Court of Justice will decide it to be illegal or unconstitutional. It will be the worst and most irredeemable bank paper ever inflicted upon a community. I can see no difference between certificates of deposit and bank paper. I should think the man who would vote for these certificates, would vote for a bank.

Mr. TEFFT called for the question.

Mr. BOTTS said he did not believe the House was prepared for the proposition which he had submitted in the course of his remarks. He would therefore withdraw it, with the intention of offering it in the House instead of the Committee, leaving a few days for reflection.

The question was then taken on Mr. Lippett's amendment, and it was adopted.

The question recurring on the section as amended, it was adopted, as follows:

31. Corporations may be formed under general laws, but shall not be created by special act, except for municipal purposes. All general laws and special acts, passed pursuant to this section, may be altered from time to time or repealed.

The question was then taken without debate on the 32d and 33d sections, and they were adopted, as follows:

32. Dues from corporations shall be secured by such individual liability of the corporations, and other means, as may be prescribed by law.

33. The term corporations, as used in this article, shall be construed to include all associations and joint stock companies having any of the powers or privileges of corporations not possessed by individuals or partnerships. And all corporations shall have the right to sue, and shall be subject to be sued, in all Courts in like cases as natural persons.

The 34th section being under consideration, as follows:

34. The Legislature shall have no power to pass any act granting any charter for banking purposes; but associations may be formed under general laws for the deposit of gold and silver.

Mr. GWIN moved to strike out all after the word "purposes," to the end of the section. He had a substitute to propose, but to avoid embarrassing the question would not submit it until the last section came up for consideration.

Mr. NORTON. I would simply remark, before the vote is taken, that the object of this section is to afford protection to deposits of gold and silver. I, as an individual, may keep an office of deposit, receive gold and silver, and issue my certificates of deposit. No Legislature, no Constitution, can prevent me. Associations may do the same thing, and you cannot prevent them. Your laws can prevent them, for they have a right to do it. The object of the section is to give to the Legislature the power of providing, in such manner as it may deem best, for the protection of persons in the deposit of gold and silver. Now, if laws can be passed affording this protection, rendering the depositories perfectly secure, it is much better than to depend upon individuals, upon whom no restriction is placed by the Legislature. This is all that the section attempts to attain.

Mr. GWIN. It covers a great deal more ground than that. Banks can grow up under it—banks of the worst kind; and for this reason I move to strike it out. I have heard one argument in favor of it, which may be worthy of notice. It is said that after we grow up to be a large commercial community, say in two or three years hence, such associations will be absolutely essential to the transaction of business. Sir, long before this necessity exists the people of California will meet in Convention and make another Constitution. In the mean time, when there is no pressing necessity for associations of this kind, I think it of the utmost importance that such a provision, upon which there is so great a difference of opinion, should not appear in this Constitution. I have heard a good deal of the exchanges of the country, and the necessity of these associations to carry them on. Look at the Island of Cuba, sir; at Havana, where they collect eleven millions annually. The income of that city is eleven millions; and yet they have nothing of the kind there—nothing in the shape of banking. The State that includes the great commercial emporium of the valley of the Mississippi has inserted in her late Constitution a provision prohibiting such associations forever. It is my solemn conviction that banking institutions may spring up under this section. I look upon it as a duty that we owe to the country to strike it out. If the people want it hereafter they will put it in another Constitution. Let us not do it; let us be as nearly unanimous in regard to this Constitution as we can. There is a solemn conviction on the minds of the members of this Convention that any thing that gives the slightest shadow of power to create banking institutions would be most injurious in its consequences. Let us, in accordance with that conviction, exclude from our Constitution whatever may, by possibility, produce that effect.

Mr. Tefft. I am convinced there is an honest difference of opinion in regard to this matter. I believe that each member on this floor has the good of California in view. The Committee, I am sure, had no intention of reporting in favor of the banking system. There was a general feeling on the part of the members against permitting banks of any kind to be created under the powers granted to the Legislature. I entertained the belief when the subject first came up, and I still hold the same opinion, that the powers granted under this section cannot be abused. I believe such associations to be actually necessary in this country at the present period; that we need not wait for any future period to render them necessary. The fact that associations for the deposit of gold and silver now exist, is sufficient proof that they are necessary. They will continue to exist; they must continue as long as the community requires them. I look upon this clause as merely affording the additional security of legislative protection to the individuals depositing their gold and silver. I should most assuredly vote for the rejection of this article, did I believe for a moment that bank paper could be issued under it; but as I do not believe such to be the effect, I feel constrained to vote for retaining it as a necessary provision of the Constitution.

Mr. Halleck. I agree with the gentleman last up, as to the necessity of this provision. The Committee were unanimous in their desire to prohibit banks for the circulation of bank paper, properly so called. When this article was introduced, I made inquiries of persons engaged in business as to the necessity of some legislative action on this point, and the propriety of providing for it in the Constitution. I was informed that such necessity did exist; and I believe the general feeling of the business community would be in favor of it. I shall therefore vote against the amendment striking out the last clause of this section. If it be necessary, in order to prevent the circulation of bank notes springing out of this clause, to add further restrictions, let us do it. It can very easily be done. There is an obvious necessity for these associations. They exist already; and it is proper they should be put under the direction of law, for the security of persons making deposits. If we pass the section as it stands, we can easily introduce after it such prohibitions against the circulation of paper of any description as the House think proper.

Mr. Jones. I shall detain the House but a few moments on this section. I think it hardly fair that two or three should speak on one side without something being said on the other side. The latter clause of this section contains, in my opinion, a system quite as dangerous to this country as banks. What responsibility are they to have? What is to prevent these associations from speculating on the money in their possession? We are told that there will be guaranties provided by law. Sir, I don't want to trust it to the Legislature. If we do, why not trust the whole subject—why put these restrictions upon the Legislature? Why not submit the whole banking system to the discretion of the Legislature? We are guarding here against bad Legislatures; we are not making provisions for good ones. If we supposed them to be as wise and virtuous as they are represented to be by some gentlemen, we would put no restrictions upon them whatever. I want to see restrictions effective, and not merely nominal. We are told that associations for the deposit of gold and silver must be governed by law—that this subject requires legislative protection. Sir, it is governed by law; the best kind of law: it is governed by the law which says that a man shall pay his debts, or loose his property and perhaps his personal liberty. But you build up an institution by special act; you build a man's reputation up by special act; you say he is entitled to receive deposits. Sir, a man who has wealth and standing does not require legislative enactments to make the community trust him. These deposits, if you leave them alone, will go where they ought to go; they will go into the safest and most reliable places that can be found. You are not required to set men up by legislative enactment. Will you say that these associations shall not issue certificates of deposit. How in the name of Heaven will these deposits be proved, unless by certificates? Will you say that they shall not word them so and so, put a picture on one corner, and make them look as much like bank bills as they please? You can do no such thing. They must become a circulating medium. These associations must enter into commerce, otherwise they cannot be supported. There is not a man in the community who would pay two or three per cent. to have his money kept and guarded. But these depositories—these traders upon borrowed capital—these men of small means combined together under legislative sanction will pay for these deposits. They will solicit them at a premium. They will not permit them to be idle in their vaults—for they cannot afford it. On the contrary, they will engage in active speculation. If they are unfortunate, they will appeal to this section and say they are individually liable to the amount of their stock. Sir, I want a man to be liable under the law as it exists. I want a man who owes a debt to be compelled to pay it. I don't want him to pay five thousand when he owes fifty thousand, pocket the forty-five thousand, and leave his creditors to suffer for their credulity.

The question being on the amendment of Mr. Gwin, to strike out the latter clause of the section, it was decided in the negative, by ayes 18, noes 19.

The question then recurring on the adoption of the 34th Section,

Mr. Gwin offered the following amendment as a portion of the same section:

"And the Legislature shall pass penal enactments for the punishment of the officers and stockholders of any association that may be formed under the authority herein granted, or any other person or persons who shall be convicted of making, issuing, or putting in circulation, any bill, check, ticket, certificate of deposit, promissory note, or other paper, or the paper of any bank, to circulate as money."

Mr. Semple. I had not intended to make any further remarks on this subject, under the impression that it was sufficiently discussed. I voted to strike out the latter clause of this section, but there I must stop. I cannot support this amendment. I am in favor of all necessary restrictions to prevent any thing like banking; but I think the present restriction would be utterly impracticable. If we form associations, it will be absolutely necessary that they should issue certificates. We must have these evidences of deposit to put in our pockets, and sue them upon if they refuse to pay. If the managers of these associations choose to put pictures upon their certificates of deposit; if they put the goddess of justice on one corner, and a grizzly bear on another, I would be unwilling to make it a penal enactment, not because I am in favor of the circulation of this sort of money, but because it would be utterly impracticable to prevent the issue of these certificates. If I had ten thousand dollars which I desired to deposit with a friend, or association, or corporation, I should certainly require some memorandum acknowledging the deposit; and when I had that, it would be very hard indeed if I should not have the privilege of selling it, without subjecting myself to penal law. Such a restriction would be impracticable. Suppose I have no other means? I must sell it to pay my necessary expenses, or dispose of it in some shape or other. I carry it to some gentleman in town and ask him to give me the money for it. But, for doing this, I am liable to be put in the penitentiary. If it be the disposition of the Convention to permit these associations at all, they must be permitted to issue certificates of deposit. I voted against all the preceding articles because I want no banks or bank paper; but this section would be an absurdity with the restriction proposed.

Mr. Gwin. I am sorry the gentleman flinches so soon in the argument. If it is not intended to pass the certificate of deposit for money, there is no restriction. No man maintains that it should be used as a currency. If, therefore, it is not intended to make a currency of it, what objection can there be to provide in this section that no paper shall ever circulate as money, and if it is done, that it shall be a penal offence. Gentlemen talk about depositing gold and silver and receiving certificates as indispensable proof of the deposit. Why, sir, deposits to the amount of millions of dollars are made without certificates. If you want to use your money elsewhere, you get a bill of exchange. The commercial business is carried on by bank books. There is not one out of a hundred cases where certificates are issued. In this country a man can carry enough of gold to pay his expenses, without such papers. If it is the intention of gentlemen, by inserting this section, to prohibit the circulation of paper money, the clause which I propose will be actually necessary to carry out the object; but if certificates of deposit are to be used as they have been used under similar associations, if they are to be passed as money, they will vote for the section as it stands. Those familiar with the banking era of 1834, '35, and '36, know that certificates of deposit and post notes were circulated to the amount of millions of dollars, for the purpose of avoiding the law. There were several banks in the District of Columbia whose charters expired in 1839. The most extraordinary exertions were made to re-charter them. At one time they even attempted to accomplish the object by tacking a provision for their continuance to the appropriation bill. When the charters expired, they transferred over to trustees the whole of their assets, and now they are transacting business as they did before, although they have no authority under the law to issue bank paper. The greatest caution is necessary to prevent associations of this kind from encroaching upon the rights of the people. I trust, sir, that every member of this Convention who does not intend that paper money shall be issued, will vote in favor of the amendment.

Mr. Botts. I have seen the result of a trial in a court of justice upon exactly such a penal clause as is proposed by my friend from San Francisco, (Mr. Gwin.) I have seen a penal law which prohibited an individual from issuing his promissory note, check, or bond, for the purpose of circulating as money It turned, as it ought to have turned, simply upon the intent. All the circumstances under which these shinplasters were issued went to the jury. The individual had issued his checks in printed form, in great numbers, and of small denominations. From these circumstances it was evident they were intended to circulate as money, and the individual was accordingly fined. They could come to no other conclusion. The paying of a washerwoman's bill, or board bill, or any other, such as the gentleman from Sonoma (Mr. Semple) referred to, is not such a circumstance as would lead to this conclusion. But there may be circumstances, and they do exist, such as every gentleman here seems desirous to provide against. I look upon that clause, as it stands, as fraught with evil. It is the wooden horse introduced by the Greeks within the walls of Troy, from the body of which will come forth thousands of armed men. Sir, I fear the Greeks when they proffer gifts, and I very much fear there are Greeks in the midst of us.

Mr. Tefft. I consider the gist of that amendment, as offered, a fair test of my sincerity. I am entirely and absolutely opposed to the circulation of any sort of bank paper. But if I do not misunderstand the effect of the amendment I shall certainly oppose it. I was in Wisconsin when the first Convention was called to form a Constitution for that State. In that Convention there were some of the strongest anti-bank men I ever knew, and a clause was inserted in the Constitution providing against the circulation of any kind of bank paper. They made it a penal offence for any person to have in his possession a bank bill, or attempt to pass it. That Constitution was rejected by the people. Another Convention was called, and that Convention inserted in the Constitution an article precisely similar, omitting the penal offence. Now, I am willing to go as far as the gentleman from San Francisco, or any other gentleman, in prohibiting banks or the circulation of bank paper, but I cannot vote for the amendment making it a penal offence to pass a certificate of deposit. The question of currency is one of momentous import. It should never have been made a party question in the States—subject to the fluctuating influences of political factions. The financial policy of a country is too intimately associated with the best interests of the people to be rudely touched. It is only by carefully observing the different systems which have been in operation that we can arrive at a just estimate of what it is our true interest to adopt. I am very sure, sir, that no member of this Convention can be blind to the disastrous results of the banking system, where it has been subjected to the test of experience, as in the late era of our banking history. Nor do I believe, whatever opinions gentlemen may have held in the parent States, that there is any latent desire on the part of any member of this Convention to introduce the system into this country. I think there is no dissimulation on this subject, for if ever there was a country on the face of the earth designed by the Creator to have a metallic currency it is this. We have not been so richly gifted with the precious metals for the purpose of introducing a fictitious medium of circulation. It is not for us to turn from those resources which nature has placed within our reach, and enter upon a policy so clearly in opposition to our interests. But, in attempting to effect the object which we all have in view, we should carefully avoid running into the other extreme of excessive and onerous restrictions, which, from the necessity of the case, can only result injuriously to the commercial interests of the people. No legislation which goes beyond judicious limits, or makes it a penal offence to exercise rights so generally acknowledged, can have a beneficial effect; nor will it in any degree tend to lessen the evil which it is our desire to avoid. The absolute necessity of permitting the transfer of these certificates of deposit, for the legitimate purposes of business, and the impracticability of administering penal laws for the punishment of persons who may so dispose of them, are sufficient reasons, in my opinion, why this amendment should not be adopted.

Mr. SEMPLE. I do not wish to detain the House, but I desire to be fully understood on this subject. With regard to the manner in which business is transacted in the Island of Cuba, it is the custom there for every merchant, who has reputation enough, to receive deposits. I know no better way to explain the operation of the system than to state my own experience. I visited Cuba in company with a family—a sick gentleman and his lady. Our money consisted of gold and silver and Alabama bank bills. The bank bills were worth nothing there. We went to one of the best merchants, deposited our specie with him, and told him that some of the money we wanted in a large amount to pay our expenses home, but the most of it we wanted to defray our immediate expenses. He gave us certificates of deposit as low as five dollars—some of ten, twenty, and fifty dollars, for temporary use. With these we paid our board and ordinary expenses. The whole check for the large amount which we required for expenses home was given in duplicate. The certificates only went as far as his acquaintance reached. We passed them seventeen miles out in the country where we had occasion to use them. That is the system upon which business is conducted in Cuba. They never had a bank, and never carried on banking. In this country, if we have associations of deposit, we must have certificates. The gentleman (Mr. Gwin) says this is done by bank books. That is in cases where the same individuals or firms make deposits almost every day. But suppose I arrive at New York a stranger, and want to deposit my money. I have no bank account, and do not desire to open one. I take a certificate of deposit and put it in my pocket. This I believe is the course usually pursued. Another thing: I have seen the banks in Alabama give certificates of deposit to be sent to the East—not drafts, but pure certificates. A laboring man who worked for me wanted to know how he was to send seventy or eighty dollars to his wife in Philadelphia. I went to the bank with him, but the teller said the amount was too small for a draft. To accommodate the man, he took the money and gave him a certificate of deposit, which certificate was cashed by a bank in Philadelphia. Now, sir, if you make it a penal offence for a man to carry a certificate of deposit in his pocket, I think it will be a very dangerous provision. This Constitution will be rejected by the people. I think I shall vote against it myself when I get home. He may or may not intend to circulute it as money. The only proof of his intention is the fact that he has the certificate in his pocket. I contend, that to make this a penal offence would not only be unjust and impolitic, but would jeopard the Constitution itself.

Mr. Gwin. I do not intend that the vote shall be taken on my amendment under a misapprehension. Every person who has any knowledge of commercial affairs knows that what the gentleman from Sonoma (Mr. Semple) refers to in the Island of Cuba is a mere matter of convenience in the absence of banks. It is the commercail way of transacting business, and as a certificate of deposit in a commercial point of view, it has no bearing upon the point at issue. It is not circulating it as money to transfer it from one portion of the country to another. It is purely a commercial transaction; it is commercial paper for commercial purposes. But if the gentleman deposits $1,000 and takes out a thousand dollars in five and ten dollar notes, expressly to circulate as money, and puts them in circulation throughout this country, then it is money, and that is what this amendment is intended to cover. As to the necessity of these associations for the benefit of the commercial community, it is notorious that they are not wanted. In San Francisco there are associations now, that, instead of charging for the deposit of gold and silver, are willing to pay a premium on deposits. No commercial community requires any legislative interference with their manner of depositing. What the gentleman speaks of as to the convenience, in the case to which he alludes in Alabama, refers merely to a bank check. It is not money, and it is not circulating it as money to send it from Alabama to be paid in Philadelphia. This amendment is to prohibit the circulation of certificates of deposit as money.

Mr. Halleck. Several gentlemen who have agreed to these sections as they were first offered by the Committee, and who are very anxious to obviate the objections which have been made, have proposed an amendment very slightly differing from the amendment of the gentleman from San Francisco, in order that there may be unanimity not only in the Committee, but in the House and out of the House, on this subject. I now offer it as an amendment to his amendment, putting in the restrictions which he has there, but not making it a penal offence. This amendment is to commence after the words as they now stand in the section, as follows:

But no such association shall make, issue, or put in circulation, any bill, check, ticket, certificate, promissory note, or other paper, or the paper of any bank, to circulate as money.

Mr. Botts. I should like to know, if that amendment is adopted, what would be the result if any individual should issue paper under these circumstances. I suppose you would say it was a violation of the Constitution: that is the only restraint or punishment so far as I can see. I submit it to gentlemen who honestly want some restraint, if that satisfies them?

Mr. Hastings. The gentleman will see, upon a little further reflection, in what position that individual would place himself. He violates the Constitution, it is true; but he is subject to any law that the Legislature may enact to punish him. The Legislature may make it penal. We are forming an organic law of the State, and not passing penal enactments. The Legislature may pass such laws as it deems necessary to sustain the provisions of the Constitution. We are not legislating; nor were we legislating, as the gentleman from Monterey justly contended, when we were debating the bill of rights. Has the nature of our duties changed because we have arrived at another part of the Constitution? I think such a doctrine as that will hardly be maintained. I am prepared to vote for the amendment as it now stands.

The question being on Mr. Halleck's amendment to the amendment offered by Mr. Gwin, it was adopted.

Mr. Gwin's amendment, as amended, was then adopted.

The question then recurring on the 34th section, as amended—

Mr. Dimmick. It seems that we have now arrived at the main question before the House. I am opposed to the adoption of that article. It introduces a provision which I consider dangerous and unnecessary. The business of the country has been transacted very well so far, without associations of this kind, created by legislative enactment. Private individuals have accomplished all that is intended, or can be done, by such associations as are now to be incorporated by the Legislature. Individuals at the present time receive money on deposite and issue certificates; which amount to nothing more, in my opinion, than evidence in the possession of the holder that he has at such a place deposited so much money. What will your incorporated associations do more than this? The individual brings his money and deposits it; he will receive a certificate, which is evidence of the deposit. Now, sir, I contend that an individual can receive money on deposit cheaper than an association. He is not compelled to devote all his time to this business. An association must have its officers; its President, Cashier, Teller, and such others as may be necessary. These officers must have large salaries for their support; for people who enter into associations of this kind do so to make money. When all these items of expense are combined, the result will be that a proportionate tax must be levied on the money deposited. Individuals in San Francisco, I am informed, now tax in proportion to the money deposited, where they receive it simply on deposit; but where they have the privilege of investing it in their business transactions, they charge nothing. In the latter case, if the money is destroyed, the person who deposits it loses it in consequence of there being no consideration; but in the other case, where he pays for his deposit, the individual who receives it would be held accountable, because he undertakes it for a consideration. I conceive, sir, that individual enterprise can do more than these corporations, which it is intended shall be authorized by law. The object can be accomplished on better terms, because their expenses are less, and the community will always know where to find the most reliable places of deposit without legislative interference. Why then encumber the Constitution with grants of power which can have no beneficial effect? I consider that this clause is only an encumbrance to the Constitution, and shall therefore vote against its adoption.

The section, as amended, was then read by the Secretary and adopted, as follows:

34. The Legislature shall have no power to pass any act granting any charter for banking purposes; but associations may be formed under general laws for the deposit of gold and silver. But no such association shall make, issue, or put in circulation, any bill, check, ticket, certificate, promissory note, or other paper, or the paper of any bank, to circulate as money.

The question being on the adoption of the 35th section, viz:

35. The Legislature shall have no power to pass any law sanctioning, in any manner, directly or indirectly, the issuing of bank notes of any description.

Mr. Hastings said it contained, substantially, the same prohibition as that which had just been adopted. He therefore moved to strike it out.

Mr. Halleck was also of opinion that the two sections covered the same object, and therefore concurred in the propriety of striking out the latter.

Mr. Hastings compared them; and, the question being taken, the 35th section was stricken out.

Mr. Wozencraft offered the following in lieu of the section stricken out:

35. The Legislature of this State shall prohibit, by law, any person or persons, association, company, or corporation, from exercising the privileges of banking, or creating paper to circulate as money.

Mr. Jones. I voted in favor of striking out the 35th section for the express purpose of proposing that which my colleague has anticipated me in. The Committee has at length got itself into the predicament of having prohibited the Legislature from granting any charter for banking purposes; and, at the same time, tacitly allowing any person or persons, associations or companies, except those particular associations named in the article just passed, to exercise any of the privileges of banking. I claim to understand English when it is read to me plainly; and I think if gentlemen will closely examine this section they will find that interpretation to be a just one. There is no prohibition against banking, in so far as it refers to associations for other purposes. I ask for the reading of the whole section, as amended and passed.

The Secretary thereupon read the 34th section.

The question then being on the 35th section, as proposed by Mr. Wozencraft, it was adopted.

The 36th section of the report of the Committee being under consideration, as follows:

36. The stockholders of every corporation or joint stock association shall be individually responsible to the amount of their respective share or shares of stock in any such corporation or association for all its debts and liabilities of every kind.

Mr. Jones moved to strike out the section and insert the following; which was adopted, viz:

36. Each stockholder of a corporation or joint stock association shall be individually and personally liable for his proportion of all its debts and liabilities.

The 37th and 38th sections were then passed, without debate, as follows:

37. It shall be the duty of the Legislature to provide for the organization of cities and incorporated villages, and to restrict their powers of taxation, assessment, borrowing money, contracting debts, and loaning their credit, so as to prevent abuses in their assessments and in contracting debts by such municipal corporations.

38. In all elections by the Legislature the members thereof shall vote *viva voce*, and the votes shall be entered upon the journal.

Mr. Ord then offered the following:

No person, while he continues to exercise the functions of a clergyman, priest, or teacher of any religious persuasion, society, or sect, shall be eligible to the Legislature.

Mr. Norton. You might as well say a lawyer should not have a seat in the Legislature.

Mr. Jones. If this question is to be debated, I move the Committee rise and report progress.

The motion was decided in the negative.

Mr. Shannon. I voted the other day against introducing restrictions of this character in the Constitution. We have no right to dictate to the people what shall be the professional character of their representatives. I am in favor of leaving it to themselves to determine from among what classes or professions they shall select persons to represent them in the Legislature. If they think fit to select a priest, let them do so if they choose. Why, sir, you are assuming despotic powers when you attempt, through your Constitution, to tell the people they shall not select their own candidates. This was one of the restrictions contained in the old Constitution of New York; but which, with all other restrictions of that character, was stricken out by the Convention of 1846. It was regarded there as an anti-republican principle and totally inconsistent with the spirit of our institutions. Upon this broad principle, that the people of the State have a right to select their representatives from whatever profession or class of society they choose, I shall oppose the introduction of the proposed section.

Mr. Hastings. I move to amend it by inserting the words "Lawyers, physicians, or merchants." If ministers of the gospel are to be excluded, we must act impartially and exclude other classes of men.

Mr. Shannon. Will the gentleman be so good as to introduce "miners" in his list?

Mr. Hastings. I think, sir, that a minister of the gospel would make a better legislator than a lawyer—far less troublesome, at all events; and probably quite as good as a merchant. I am opposed to the principle of allowing ministers of the gospel to legislate for me—unless the people elect them. They must be the judges of these things. If there is any prohibition against ministers, or priests, it should extend to all other professions. A good honest preacher, who has the morals of the community at heart, would make one of the best legislators in the world. To prevent further discussion, however, I withdraw my amendment.

The question was then taken on the proposed section, and it was rejected.

Mr. GWIN. I have one word to say in regard to an absent member of this House. General McCarver, who is now absent on account of sickness, has been two or three days watching for the 37th section to come up, so that he could offer his free negro amendment. It is a subject in which he takes a deep interest, and I hope the Committee, without proceeding any further, will now rise.

The motion was adopted, and the House then adjourned till 12 o'clock to-morrow.

WEDNESDAY, SEPTEMBER 19, 1849.

The Convention met pursuant to adjournment. Prayer by the Rev. T. D. Hunt. The journal of yesterday was read and approved.

Mr. STEUART, a member from San Francisco, elect, appeared, was sworn, and took his seat.

Some conversation here occurred on a motion of Mr. Shannon, relative to the absence of two members without leave; but the motion was finally withdrawn.

Mr. NORTON, from the Committee on the Constitution, made a report in writing, being Article VI, on "the militia," Article VII, on "State debts," Article IX, on the "mode of amending and revising the Constitution;" which, on motion of Mr. GILBERT, was received, and referred to the Committee of the Whole.

On motion of Mr. McCARVER, the House then resolved itself into Committee of the Whole, Mr. Jones in the Chair, on the report of the Committee on the Constitution.

COMMITTEE OF THE WHOLE.

Mr. McCARVER then moved the following section:

39. The Legislature shall, at its first session, pass such laws as will effectually prohibit free persons of color from immigrating to and settling in this State, and to effectually prevent the owners of slaves from bringing them into this State for the purpose of setting them free.

Mr. McCARVER. This is the article which I offered to the House some time ago. I withdrew it at the suggestion of several gentlemen who thought it would be more appropriate in another part of the Constitution.

I have no doubt, sir, that every member of this House is aware of the dangerous position in which this country is placed, owing to the inducements existing here for slaveholders to bring their slaves to California and set them free. I am myself acquainted with a number of individuals who, I am informed, are now preparing to bring their slaves here upon indentures and set them free. I hold it to be a correct doctrine, sir, that every State has a right to protect itself against an evil so enormous as this. No population that could be brought within the limits of our Territory could be more repugnant to the feelings of the people, or injurious to the prosperity of the community, than free negroes. They are idle in their habits, difficult to be governed by the laws, thriftless, and uneducated. It is a species of population that this country should particularly guard against. I believe large numbers will be brought here and thrown upon the community in a short time, unless we take urgent measures to prohibit their introduction. No measure would be more effectual, in my opinion, than this provision in our fundamental law. If it does not produce the desired effect, the Legislature can pass such penal enactments as will enforce it. In Illinois an effort of this kind was made, and finding they were unable to carry the measure in the Convention, they left it to the vote of the people of the State whether it was to be appended to the Constitution or not. What was the result? A majority of twenty thousand of the voters of the State were in favor of it. And, sir, I am of opinion that a greater number of votes would be given in favor of it here, because the dangers to which this country is exposed, from the superior inducements presented, would be so much greater. They have not gold mines such as we have here, in Illinois. Even the slaveholding States have made provisions to prevent the immigration of free negroes within their borders. If they have that privilege, it surely will not be denied to us. I have been informed by gentlemen that they have received letters from the States, stating that in a short time from this hundreds of negroes would be brought here for the purpose of being liberated after they have worked a short time in the gold mines. What will be the result? Do you suppose the white population of this country will permit these negroes to compete with them in working the mines? Sir, you will see the most fearful collisions that have ever been presented in any country. You will see the same feeling, only to a much greater extent, that has already been manifested against the foreigners of Chili. It is the duty of the Legislature to provide against these collisions. The opportunity is now presented. I am satisfied that every gentleman in this House will see the propriety of such a measure. I believe it to be equally as essential to the prosperity of this country as the prohibition of slavery. The evil would be greater than that of slavery itself. I therefore submit the proposition to the kind consideration of the House, in the hope that it may become a part of the Constitution.

Mr. Semple. This is a subject upon which I had reflected very seriously before coming to Monterey. During the month between the election and the assembling of this Convention, I took a great deal of pains to enquire among my constituents whether such a measure would meet with their approbation. I found no man in my district who did not approve of it; and I have been informed, since my arrival here, that it is altogether likely, if this measure is not adopted in the Constitution, we will have free negroes brought in very soon by thousands. The few who are now here cannot be regarded as an evil of any great extent. They are not sufficient in number to be a disadvantage to the community. But that portion of our population will be immensely large if emancipated slaves—not free negroes—not freemen—but emancipated slaves, directly from the slave States, are permitted to be introduced. Sir, it would be one of the greatest curses that could be entailed upon California. Let us look at the inducements and see whether these fears are without foundation; let us see what is the probable value per annum of an able bodied negro man in the Southern States. They hire there at from sixty to a hundred dollars a year. I have known them to hire there for as much as two hundred; but never more. I was raised in a slave State; and I believe they more frequently hire at a less sum than sixty dollars, than over that amount. Let gentlemen reflect for a moment, and see how many of these negroes are producing their absolute value—paying interest on cost. The life estate is from four to six hundred dollars. Physicians fees and occasionally other expenses have to be deducted out of their hire—so that the income from this sort of property at the present period is very small. Suppose you pay seven hundred dollars to get a slave here, and set him free, on condition that he shall serve you for one year. He produces, according to the ordinary rates in the mines, from two to six thousand dollars. There are many of our Southern friends who would be glad to set their negroes free and bring them here, if they produced only half of that amount. When the terms of the contract have expired what would these slaves do? They would become a burthen on the community. And I can assure you, sir, thousands will be introduced into this country before long, if you do not insert a positive prohibition against them in your Constitution—an immense and overwhelming population of negroes, who have never been freemen; who have never been accustomed to provide for themselves. What would be the state of things in a few years? The whole country would be filled with emancipated slaves—the worst species of population—prepared to do nothing but steal, or live upon our means as paupers. I do not see any objection to passing this resolution. There is no opposition to it throughout the country. It will be a strong recommendation to the Constitution, and give it many votes in the community which may not otherwise be cast for it.

Mr. Shannon. I presume, Mr. Chairman, that I shall stand nearly alone in a minority on this subject, but I cannot let it pass without at least expressing some of my sentiments. Sir, I am opposed to the resolution. I oppose it, in the first place, because I think it a most singular one. Does the gentleman, my colleague from Sacramento, suppose that any slaveholder in the United States will bring slaves to the territory of California for the purpose of setting them free? Why, sir, the slaveholder can set them free at home. What object can he have in bringing them first to California, and then setting them free? As this Constitution has been adopted, so far, almost by the unanimous vote of this Convention, the position in which he stands is this: it is not at his option to set them free here; the moment they touch this soil they are free by the fundamental law of the land. No matter whether the slaveholder brings them here with the understanding, or under the contract, that after they shall have served a certain time in the mines they shall be free; they are free the moment they touch the soil of California. Why, then, introduce this prohibition? What effect can it have? It is perfectly worthless, and stands null, void, and unmeaning in that relation. You can, if you choose, pass it as a section, but it has no meaning. I am most decidedly opposed, sir, to the introduction of any thing of this kind in the Constitution, because I do contend that free men of color have just as good a right, and ought to have, to emigrate here as white men. I think, too, that the necessities of the territory require them; the necessities of every State in the Union require them. They are required in every department of domestic life; they form a body that have become almost necessary for our domestic purposes; and I see no reason why this Convention should introduce an article here depriving the people of California of the services of a class of men who are required by the people of every State in the Union, and regarded as absolutely essential to the comfort and convenience of domestic life. For this, among other reasons, I shall vote against the resolution. I do not want the people of California to be cut off from the services of any particular body of men. It matters not if they were baboons, or any other class of creatures. I do not speak now, Mr. Chairman, upon the rights of men, of whatever color, as citizens or men. I leave out that consideration entirely, and speak of this as a matter of expediency. I think the latter part of the resolution is entirely out of place, and is perfectly dead and worthless—"and to effectually prevent the owners of slaves from bringing them into this State for the purpose of setting them free." They can set them free at home, sir, without bringing them here for that purpose. It is hardly to be supposed that they would subject themselves to the cost of transporting their slaves two or three thousand miles for the purpose of emancipating them, when they can do it at home. For this reason, because I think it null and void and of no earthly import, I am opposed to the latter clause; and, for the reasons already stated, I think the first part should not be introduced.

Mr. McCarver. In relation to the gentleman's objections to the latter part of the resolution, I do not see how he arrives at the conclusion that it is nugatory or void of effect. It is certain that when the slaveholder sees in the Constitution of California a prohibition against the introduction of slavery, he would, in bringing his slaves here, bring them to set them free. The object of the latter part of the section is to prevent the slaveholder from bringing his slaves here to be set free by the laws of California. The gentleman cannot conceive what object the slaveholder would have in going to this expense. If he could make a profitable speculation by working them in the mines for a limited period there would be a very strong inducement; and the very fact that such speculations have been and are about to be commenced, sufficiently demonstrates that they are considered lucrative. The first view I took was that we should pass a law prohibiting colored persons from being brought here under indentures; but that did not cover the whole ground so well as my present resolution. What is the condition of some of the States? Kentucky, I am told, is now holding a Convention for the purpose of setting at liberty their slaves. How many of my friends there would be glad to come here and get the value of their negroes, before the acts of that Convention would set them free; and how many enquiries have those slaveholders made of individuals here by letters, as to whether such a thing would be tolerated in this country. There are gentlemen in this House, sir, who have a certain knowledge that persons in the States are in the act of bringing their slaves out for the purpose of setting them free. If the gentleman can provide a way by which we can protect and feed these negroes, and provide laws that would control them, it would greatly lessen my objections; but they have never been able to provide these laws in the slaveholding States, or where those negroes are permitted to reside. I go as far as any gentleman to provide for the admission of all classes of men, where it does not entail upon us injury or endanger the prosperity of the country. But when herds of negroes from the slaveholding States are to come in, then I think it is proper that we should take measures to prevent them. And now is the time, while we are forming this Constitution. Let us make them know that we do not want their slaves or free negroes, and that we are determined to make laws effectually to prevent them from coming among us.

Mr. Sherwood. The gentleman from Sacramento (Mr. McCarver) has stated that some provision of this kind is contained in most of the State Constitutions of the United States. I should like to know what Constitutions they are?

Mr. McCarver. It is a provision of the Constitution of Illinois, and most of the States have made laws for the same purpose—the prohibition of free negroes.

Mr. Wozencraft. I am not surprised that a debate has taken place on this question. The subject was brought up some time since, and I supposed at the time that it would give rise to considerable difference of opinion. I am prepared myself to vote without further agitation of the subject. I voted in favor of the clause introduced in our Constitution prohibiting the introduction of slavery. I think it equally important that we should exclude the African race; and, strange as it may appear, I wish to do this from philanthropic motives. I think it better for that race that they should be excluded. I must say that the gentleman's remarks (Mr. Shannon's) were of the most latitudinarian character when he asserted that in all the States negroes are necessary for society; that they are indispensable to domestic comfort and happiness. Why, sir, of all the States that I have any knowledge of, either free or slave States, it is admitted by all, whether philanthropists for blacks or for all mankind, that the free negro is one of the greatest evils that society can be afflicted with. Many of the States have had sad experience in this sort of population, and have made provisions against their introduction. Ohio has tried the experiment of free black population. I know an instance there where a quantity of the best land was bought for them, improved and ready for cultivation. The result was, as stated by the gentleman from Sonoma, (Mr. Semple,) that instead of tilling the soil, they went to stealing, and were soon thrown on the community for support. I think, if we wish to protect the citizens of California in any thing, we should protect them in the right to labor—one of the most inestimable of all rights. We should protect them against the monopolies of capitalists who would bring their negroes here. We should protect them against a class of society that would degrade labor, and thereby arrest the progress of enterpise and greatly impair the prosperity of the State.

Mr. Dimmick. We have introduced into our bill of rights a clause permitting foreigners to exercise the same rights in reference to holding lands and enjoying the political privileges of this country which we enjoy ourselves. I shall not discuss that matter. It stands as a self-evident fact—as an axiom asserted in our bill of rights. Now it is proposed to do what? Not to extend to a greater degree this freedem to foreigners; not to extend political freedom further to any class; but to say that a certain class of Americans born in the United States—their forefathers born there for many generations—shall be excluded from entering this Territory at all! I am not so strenuous, sir, as to this being done by legislative enactment if the people deem it necessary or expedient; but I am clearly opposed to a provision of this kind in the Constitution, on the ground of principle and consistency. What will be said of our Constitution if we assert one thing in our bill of rights—extend the privileges of our free institutions to all classes, both from foreign countries and our own, and then in another exclude a class speaking our own language, born and brought up in the United States, acquainted with our customs, and calculated to make useful citizens. We even debar them from the privilege of entering upon our soil. The two provisions are inconsistent. If we adopt the proposition of the gentleman from Sacramento, (Mr. McCarver,) we should strike out the article in our declaration of rights. I have none of the fears of the African here, which gentlemen seem to entertain. It is said that many States have passed laws excluding free negroes from their limits—I have seen no such laws. It is true some of the States have passed laws on this subject, and one Constitution has been adopted requiring the Legislature to provide against the admission of free negroes; but none, so far as I know, to exclude the negro population already in the State. There existed an obvious necessity for these prohibitory regulations in the States, to which gentlemen have not thought proper to refer. In the slave States, the citizens owning slaves are deprived of the right by law of emancipating their slaves within the borders of the State. Many slaveholdors wishing to emancipate their slaves, but unable to do it in the States in which they resided, took them into free States and set them free; and the old and decripid, and those unable to support themselves, were thrown upon the charitable institutions of the free States. The community had, therefore, a necessity for such laws to protect itself against this class of population. But what necessity exists here? Are the slaveholders going to remove their slaves to a State thousands of miles distant, at an enormous expense—an expense equal to the value of the slaves, for the purpose of setting them free. If they wish to set them free, they can do it at much less expense. But we are told that free negroes will be brought here under indentures. I have yet to learn that there is any law of California by which a freeman can be indentured. The moment they enter our limits they are subject to our laws, and cease to be slaves. If colored boys in the States are indentured to the age of twenty-one and brought here before the expiration of the indenture, I suppose the indenture would be recognized; they would be required to serve to that period. But at the age of twenty-one they would undoutedly become free. I do not believe there is any danger of being overrun with free negroes. It is well known, that by the laws of the several States, where a person brings his slaves from a slave to a free State, they are free. No man would bring his slaves here for the purpose of working in the mines when he knows they are free the moment they enter our limits. The argument deserves no consideration. I for one, sir, am opposed to inserting this provision in the Constitution. I prefer that we should adopt and send forth to the world a free and liberal fundamental system of government. We occupy a peculiar position. We are forming a Constitution for the first State of the American Union on the shores of the Pacific. The eyes of the world are turned towards us. The Constitution which emanates from our hands is to be subjected to the scrutiny of all the civilized nations of the earth. The spirit of freedom is inspiring mankind throughout the world, to throw off the shackles of despotic systems of government. Let it not be said that we, the first great republican State on the borders of the Pacific, who should set the example of an enlightened policy to the nations of the Pacific; who have it within our power to spread the blessings of free institutions even to the remotest shore of the Eastern world—let it not be said that we have attempted to arrest the progress of human freedom. Let this Constitution go forth from this Convention and from the new State, a model instrument of liberal and enlightened principles. It will be time enough when the evils with which gentlemen say we are threatened, are demonstrated by experience, to provide against them. If the Legislature should at any future period, find that our interests are endangered by any particular class of population, there will then be justifiable reasons for excluding them. But in the absence of this proof, let our organic law be consistent with the declarations embraced in our bill of rights. Let Africans be placed upon the same footing with natives of the Sandwich Islands, Chilians, and Peruvians, and the lower classes of Mexicans. You permit those classes to come here and enjoy the political rights which we enjoy ourselves. Why should we adopt a proscriptive rule with reference to another class speaking our own language, fully as intelligent as they are, possessed of as much physical energy, and better acquainted with our habits and customs? I have no partiality for the negro race. I have the same personal antipathies which other gentlemen avow; but I desire that we should act with consistency. Unless there is an absolute necessity for such a provision demonstrated by actual proof, I do insist that it should not be embraced in our Constitution. Let the Legislature do as they have done in Ohio, Indiana, and other free States, if they find it necessary to protect the community against this class of men. Do gentlemen mistrust the Legislature? Do they anticipate that we are to have a Legislature so corrupt that it will have no regard whatever for the interests of the State? I trust not, sir. I trust that the Legislature will be a body of men equally as much interested in the welfare of the people—equally as intelligent and capable of guarding the interests of California, as this Convention. We have no right to presume to the contrary; and until the danger is evident, such law should not be passed; such a provision should not be inserted in this Constitution—a provision illiberal in its object, and in direct conflict with the great common privileges which we have extended to all mankind in our declaration of rights.

Mr. Hastings. I shall not detain the House; but to me this is a very dark subject. I have some doubts as to the manner in which I shall vote. Perhaps, when it is known upon what my doubts are founded, some gentleman will be kind enough to enlighten me. Mr. Chairman, it is a fundamental declaration made by us in our bill of rights, or whether made by us or not it is true, that all men are free and entitled to certain rights, privileges, and immunities. If this ever reaches the ears of the African race, it occurs to me that they will conceive this country to be a very favorable asylum for the oppressed; especially when they find that upon that broad principle we have added another, that neither slavery nor involuntary servitude shall ever be allowed in this State. It appears to me I can see them now by thousands on their way here; but when they arrive they are met at our portals and told that they are coming to the wrong place. They are informed that this is not the place where slavery does not exist; where all men are free and independent. It is true we said so, but we did not mean it. You are coming to the wrong place. Now, sir, why say one thing and mean another? By the adoption of this resolution the free negro is excluded. This is the difficulty which occurs to me now. If any gentleman will remove it, I shall be prepared to vote for the adoption of the resolution. I am prepared to do so any how, because there are various reasons which have occurred to me why negroes should not be introduced into this Territory, as slaves or freemen. But if they are introduced at all, I think they had better be introduced as slaves, for a free negro is the freest human being in God's world. Let us not receive them at all; but if we do, let us receive them as slaves. There are hundreds of reasons why their introduction should be prohibited, but I think those reasons are sufficiently obvious, and I shall not detain the House by entering into any argument on the subject.

Mr. McDougal offered the following substitute:

The Legislature of this State shall at its first session create enactments against the introduction into this State of any negro or negroes who has or have been slaves previously in any of the States of this Union, or of any other country, and who are brought here under bonds or indentures of servitude.

Mr. Botts enquired of the Chairman of the Committee on the Constitution, whether the Committee proposed to introduce any provision in the Constitution with respect to the common law. He thought this matter should be left in the hands of the Committee, and he desired to know whether they intended reporting upon it, and if so in what part of the Constitution.

Mr. Norton said that the Committee had not had the subject under consideration at all.

On motion of Mr. Sherwood, the Committee then rose, reported progress, and obtained leave to sit again.

On motion, the House took a recess till 4 o'clock.

AFTERNOON SESSION, 4 O'CLOCK, P. M.

On motion of Mr. Gilbert, the House resolved itself into Committee of the Whole, (Mr. Jones in the Chair,) on the report of the Committee on the Constitution.

The consideration of the motion of Mr. McCarver, as proposed to be amended by Mr. McDougal, being first in order,

Mr. Shannon said: I cannot conscientiously allow this proposition to pass, without answering some of the arguments which have been urged in support of it. I regret that old Sacramento should be divided on this question; but although there may be a division among her representatives here, it will not prevent me from adhering to what I conceive to be the opinions and sentiments of my constituents. By what course of argument my colleague from Sacramento (Mr. Hastings) arrived at his conclusions, I am unable to say. He must reconcile that matter with his constituents as he thinks proper. The gentleman, although he declared that he was in doubt upon this question—that it was a dark subject—one he could not see through—yet declared that he was determined to vote one particular way, no matter what reasons might be urged in favor of a different course. With him, and with all who express such a determination, I wish to have nothing to do. It is useless to attempt to convince them. I called this morning before the Convention adjourned upon my colleague, (Mr. McCarver,) to inform me what States and what number of States contained in their Constitutions provisions excluding free negroes. He answered me that it was contained in the Constitution of Illinois, and also that there had been legislative enactments in several of the States—in all, or nearly all, of the slaveholding States, against their admission.

Very well. I have not taken time, I have not even attempted to look into it. I take it upon the gentleman's own authority, and say it is so. But, Mr. Chairman, how was it introduced into the Constitution of Illinois? It was not adopted by the Convention.

Mr. McCarver. It is certainly in the Constitution of Illinois. It was put there by the people.

Mr. Shannon. Precisely what I am coming at. That measure, or clause, could not pass in the Convention that formed the Constitution of Illinois; and, as a compromise, it was submitted directly to the people as a distinct resolution for the people to decide upon. It was not introduced in the Constitution as passed by the Convention. The people decided in favor of it in the manner in which my colleague has stated. Leave it so here if you choose. Leave it to the people to prohibit the introduction of free negroes if they deem it expedient to do so. But, under present circumstances, I have the authority on my side that it ought not to be introduced in the Constitution of California—not only of the Constitution and Convention of Illinois, but of every State in the Union, that it should be left to the Legislature. The gentleman has substantially stated this himself. It is not contained within the Constitution of any State in the Union except that of Illinois, and there it was inserted after having received the separate and distinct vote of the people of that State. This authority, I know sir, has a tremendous influence with gentleman here—the authority of the various Constitutions of the States—the gray hairs of the States—the precedents afforded by other Conventions. But why should such a measure as this be adopted in this country, even by enactments of the Legislature? It is very properly introduced in the slave States to which the gentleman, my colleague, has referred. The admission of free negroes would be injurious to the system of slaveholding—it would strike a decided blow at the peculiar institutions of those States. But we have no such system here, sir. We have forever excluded slavery. We have determined by the unanimous vote of this Convention that California shall not be a slaveholding State—that involuntary servitude shall not exist within its limits. I submit it to the Convention if the argument is entitled to any weight, as applied to this country. The slave States, for the protection of their peculiar institutions, exclude free negroes; but we have no peculiar institutions—our State is free from the curse of slavery; and upon the broad principle which we have adopted, of admitting all freemen of all nations, we cannot consistently exclude any race.

I have another reason for opposing the measure proposed by my colleague, (Mr. McCarver.) Coming, as I do, from the State of New York, one of the free Sta es—knowing that many men of color there are most respectable citizens; that they are men of wealth, intelligence, and business capacity; men of acknowledged mental ability; men who have, to some extent at least, considerable influence in their different communities, and who have all the rights and privileges of citizens of that State—I cannot agree to exclude them here from the rights which they possess there. I cannot sustain any measure which will disfranchise them of any of the privileges or immunities which they possess at home. I think it is not consistent with the great principles which we have already declared. The substitute of my friend, (Mr. McDougal,) relieves me from this difficulty. I greatly prefer it to the original resolution, and between the two I should certainly vote for that of Mr. McDougal. I would not feel satisfied in voting to disfranchise any citizen of New York, Massachusetts, Ohio, Pennsylvania, or any of those Eastern or Northern States; and I certainly have strong scruples against disfranchising even those from the Southern States, where there is no provision contained within the Constitutions of those States prohibiting them from the enjoyment of such rights. For these reasons, Mr. Chairman, I shall oppose any proposition excluding these classes of men. I merely rose to answer the arguments of my colleague from Sacramento, (Mr. McCarver,) so far as relates to the States containing this provision in their Constitutions. I have found that there is but one Constitution that contains it; I have found that the Convention which formed that Constitution would not adopt it as a provision, but submitted it as a separate measure to the people of the State. The people chose to adopt it. If the people of the State of California choose to adopt a similar measure, very well. I am in favor of leaving all these doubtful measures of policy to the people—placing no restrictions upon them beyond the broad general principles of a liberal and enlightened Constitution.

Mr. Tefft. One word in relation to this matter of freemen. I am not fully prepared to advocate the passage of the resolution offered by the gentleman from Sacramento, (Mr. McCarver,) but I am decidedly in favor of some action in regard to this matter. I am opposed to the introduction into this country of negroes, pœons of Mexico, or any class of that kind; I care not whether they be free or bond. It is a well established fact, and the history of every State in the Union clearly proves it, that negro labor, whether slave or free, when opposed to white labor, degrades it. That is the ground upon which I oppose the introduction of this class of persons. It is said that we have declared in our Constitution, and should adhere to that declaration, that all men are by nature free and independent, entitled to certain inalienable rights. Most assuredly I believe that to be so. I believe that all men are free and equally entitled to the enjoyment of liberty and independence. But does it follow that we are to allow certain objectionable classes of men to emigrate here and settle in California. What is a sovereign State? An association of men having the same interests—a family of brothers bound together by the same social and political ties. When the State proclaims all men free and equal, does it follow that all men are to be admitted into this family? I contend, sir, that the declaration means neither more nor less than this: they are free to remain at home; but they are not free to come here and degrade white labor—free to disturb the social and political harmony of the State. It is a very strange argument that these persons are a necessary evil—that they are absolutely indispensible to carry on the ordinary operations of life. I maintain that this is not so. Let us look forward a few years and see what would be the probable result if we permit the introduction of this class of population.

Here are thousands upon thousands of enterprising, able, and intelligent young men, leaving their homes and coming to California. They cannot all devote themselves to digging gold in the placers here; they will be compelled to turn their attention to other branches of industry; and if you do not degrade white labor there will not be the slightest difficulty in obtaining white men to labor. But there will be a difficulty if they are to work with negroes. Men, sir, who are every way competent to sit in the halls of this Convention, to assist in forming laws for California, are now working in the placers. There are men of intelligence and education, laboring there with the pick and shovel—men who, at home, were accustomed to all the refinements of life. No new State in the Union has ever had a population of so enterprising and intelligent a character. They are working willingly, and they do not consider it a degradation to engage in any department of industry which will afford an adequate renumeration. But will this state of things continue—will this class of population continue to work cheerfully and willingly if you place them side by side with the negro? They would be unable, even if willing, to compete with the bands of negroes who would be set to work under the direction of capitalists. It would become a monopoly of the worst character. The profits of the mines would go into the pockets of single individuals. The labor of intelligent and enterprising white men who, from the want of capital, are compelled to do their own work, would afford no adequate renumeration. We declare that all men are free and entitled to the enjoyment of certain inalienable rights. Gentlemen hold us to that point and ask can we consistently prohibit the negro race from coming among us and doing as they please. Allow me to ask in return, what consistency would there be in declaring that all men are free, and then deny our own white citizens the privilege of laboring, and subject them to the influence of monopolies which would not only degrade their labor, but amount in effect to a prohibition of the right to labor; for I contend, sir, that no man can or will labor, unless he is renumerated by the result. If you destroy that result, you deprive him of his freedom and render him a slave in the strongest sense of the term. Gentlemen say that negroes in any considerable numbers are not going to be brought here. I cannot think so. I claim to know something of the feeling of slaveholders. There are many in the slave States who would deem it a blessing if they could get rid of their slave property. And where would there be a better opportunity than this? But, sir, we are told if they desire to set them free they can do so at home; they need not subject themselves to the expense of bringing them here for that purpose. Surely gentlemen must admit that if they can make nothing by setting them free at home, and have very strong reasons to suppose that they can receive not only the value of the negroes, but considerably over it, by bringing them here and working them in the mines for a limited period, they will adopt the more profitable course. The slaveholder agrees that the negro shall be free on condition that he serve him for three years after leaving home. What a bright prospect for the negro! Instead of being a slave for life, he and his family are to be free in consideration of three years' labor. I ask gentlemen to reflect upon these inducements, and candidly consider whether there is not a strong probability of this threatened evil. What will be the result when these engagements have expired—when these herds of emancipated slaves are set free upon the community? As the gentleman (Mr. Hastings) has said, when negroes are free, they are the freest of all human beings; they are free in morals, free in all the vices of a brutish and depraved race. They are a most troublesome and unprofitable population. And yet the gentleman from Sacramento presumes to tell this House of the wealth, ability, and influence of the negroes in the State of New York! I have always lived in a free State, sir, and I have always seen that, of all classes of population, the free negroes are the most ignorant, wretched, and depraved.

Mr. Shannon. I presume to tell the gentleman from San Luis Obispo that he has not seen everything in the States in which he resided.

Mr. Tefft. I say that the statement made by the gentlemen is not warranted by the facts. I contend that they do not understand, and cannot appreciate the blessings of freedom. I assert it as a well established fact; and the condition of the free negroes in the free States warrants me in making the assertion. I am utterly opposed to allowing them to come here and settle in California, either as freemen or slaves. Efforts have been made to make better men of them; but I ask every reasonable man if these efforts have not most signally failed. Gentlemen are no doubt acquainted with many instances where grants of lands have been made to them, and the result of which has proved an entire failure. Grants were made to them in Canada. Many citizens, from mistaken notions of philanthropy, assisted in taking runaway negroes, and carrying them into Canada to make them free. What has been the result? I lived in New York close by the line, and I know this to be the fact: that where these communities of free negroes are located on the lands granted to them, they are an idle, worthless, and depraved population. Instead of tilling the soil, they have taken to stealing; they are too indolent to work, and too depraved to be governed by ordinary laws. I have no prejudice against the negro because of his color. I object to their introduction here, because the experience of other States has proved that they are the worst possible class of beings we could have among us—the most idle, disorderly, and unprofitable. I do not believe, sir, that their nature will undergo a change by coming here. I do not believe that they will be in California what they never yet have been in any of the old States. But my strongest objection is, that they will degrade white labor, and for this reason alone I would oppose their introduction into this Territory.

Mr. WOZENCRAFT. The amendment of the gentleman from Sacramento, (Mr. McDougal) has been overlooked in the consideration of the original proposition. I cannot consent to vote for that amendment. He makes a distinction between those negroes or colored gentlemen who have always been free, and those who have always been slaves. I think it hardly necessary to divide the subject in that way; it is rather a nice distinction. I wish to vote against the admission of all colored men of the African race. I am not capable of distinguishing between the respective merits of the two classes. Permit me now to notice a remark of my friend from Sacramento, (Mr. Hastings.) He asks some gentleman to relieve him in regard to the doubts which he entertains as to the consistency of a provision of this kind, after the broad declaration in our bill of rights, that all men are free and entitled to the privileges of freemen. If I can in the least remove that troubled cloud that hangs over his mind, I will endeavor to relieve him.

Mr. HASTINGS. No, sir, you have already relieved me. I beg you will not trouble yourself to go into an argument—I am relieved, sir—perfectly relieved.

Mr. WOZENCRAFT. I must explain, nevertheless; it can do the gentleman no harm. I stated this morning that if we desired that the African should remain free, we had better enact laws to prevent them from coming here. For, depend upon it, sir, so soon as they come among us, though we have a clause prohibiting slavery, they will be slaves to all intents and purposes. The African will always be subservient to the Caucasian. It is his nature to be so—he must be so. If we wish to avoid placing them in a position of servitude, we must exclude them. We must never bring them in competition with our own labor, for if we do, they cannot maintain an equality with the white man; and they will either become slaves in effect, or we must give up our white labor. They are an evil that will grow and become fastened upon us. I see no act of injustice to any class of men in prohibiting them from coming here; on the contrary, I conceive that we are simply doing justice to ourselves. I shall vote against the amendment and in favor of the original resolution.

Mr. DIMMICK. Of all lands threatened with evils, California seems to be the most unfortunate. One gentleman tells us that these vagrant negroes, this miserable herd of thieves, are capable of getting the means to come to California. Another gentleman, or perhaps the same one, intimates that they will work in the mines with all the industry of which man is capable; that they are of industrious habits, and will toil honestly for the precious gold. Another tells us they will be brought here by their masters who now hold them in servitude, when our Constitution says they are free the very moment they arrive. A section is now offered as an amendment by which these negroes, now held as slaves, and who may be brought here under bonds to labor, not as slaves, but as apprentices, shall be excluded; and that is objected to on the same grounds. Now, sir, it is well known that the negroes of the States are incapable of getting to this country. Their habits of life, their indolence, and deficiency in force of character, render this almost impracticable. I am not in favor of their coming here; and if we make any addition to what has already been adopted prohibiting slavery, let it be the resolution submitted to the House to prevent them from coming under bonds of apprenticeship. There is no fear that they will come in any other way, or that they will come at all, unless brought by their masters. I think that resolution covers the whole ground. We have nothing else to guard against. I know that negroes have been induced to run away from the Southern States and seek refuge in Canada, where they obtained their freedom. But what has that to do with

California. Can they be induced to run away from those States, with any hope of reaching this distant country. Will they undertake to cross the vast and inhospitable regions that intervene between the old States and this remote Territory? Gentlemen are not serious in their fears of such a thing. Then why should we submit this exciting question to Congress, as contained in the amendment originally proposed? Why should we make any provision in the Constitution relative to free negroes? But gentlemen say it is absolutely essential that we instruct the Legislature as to the laws which they must pass on this subject. Sir, it is not necessary that we should instruct the Legislature. The Legislature can enact laws on this subject without our intervention. I consider it unnecessary to encumber the Constitution with provisions which can have no force or effect; it is nothing less than this—a profession of mistrust in the judgment and good sense of the first Legislature that shall assemble in our State. If negroes are being brought into this country, as gentlemen seem to fear, the Legislature will know as much about the matter as we can presume to know, and it will be competent for that body to enact such laws as the occasion may require. I do not stand here either as an advocate for the admission of free negroes, or as opposed to it. But, sir, I came here to present to the people a Constitution free and liberal in its principles; to leave all legitimate subjects of legislation unembarrassed by our action; and to place no unnecessary restrictions upon the future Legislatures that may assemble in this State. I hope and believe that if a Legislature assembles in January next, under this Constitution, they will at that time be ready to pass enactments prohibiting the flooding of this country with free negroes, or negroes under indentures. But we should keep the Constitution free from every thing calculated to provoke discussion and hostility in the halls of Congress. Let it go to the old States in a form so unobjectionable that the free soil man, as well as the slaveholder, can look upon it with approbation. I do not speak of the propriety or impropriety of the principles involved in this question; but I object to any provision calculated to do no good, and the effect of which would be to encumber the Constitution and deprive the Legislature of its legitimate powers of legislation.

Mr. Steuart. I am just recovering from a severe attack of illness, and it was only a short time since that I thought it would be at all practicable for me to take part in your deliberations. At the present moment I feel entirely incompetent to enter into this discussion, but I must beg leave to give one or two reasons which actuate me in the vote which I intend to give on this important question. Sir, I came to California from a State which has had no little experience in this matter. If there is any State in the Union that has a right to speak on the subject of free negroes, it is the State of Maryland. While other States have been talking Maryland has been acting. In the gloomiest period of her financial difficulties, when her people were struggling under a load of taxation to meet their engagements, and every honest man of every party was doing his utmost to shield the State from the stain of repudiation, Maryland for twenty years taxed her citizens to the amount of $30,000 per annum for the purpose of colonization. We had felt deeply and painfully the evils of emancipation in that State. I grieve to touch upon the sufferings of her citizens, under the evils to which they were subjected. It is in vain that they attempted to remove the difficulty by colonization. It was found to be, like the old saying, baling the ocean with a ladle. It is not my purpose, Mr. Chairman, to detain this assembly by entering into the troubles of that State on this subject—indeed I have not the physical ability to do so if I were so disposed. I will content myself by merely stating that I have in my possession letters, received by the last steamer, from gentlemen prominent in the State of Maryland, informing me, and asking my advice as the effect, of their intention to come here in the spring with a large number of negroes, to be emancipated on the condition of serving them six or twelve months in the mines. I concur most cordially with every remark this evening in regard to the effect that slavery has upon free labor.

Coming from a slaveholding State, I know its baneful influence. I know it is utterly impossible to unite free and slave labor. I have tried the experiment, and I feel justified in saying that such a thing is impracticable. I mention these facts to meet the arguments of gentlemen who say that it will be the duty of the Legislature to meet this difficulty, and that we should have nothing to do with it. Sir, it is our duty to declare the intention of the people of California in this Constitution; and let us do it at once. Let us declare to those gentlemen who are about engaging in this enterprise at home, that they cannot bring their negroes here on any condition or under any pretence whatever. Let us not pass it over and thereby impose upon the Legislature and people of California the onerous duty of providing ways and means to get rid of this class of population, after they shall have come here and become an evil almost impossible to remove. I think, however, that there is still a better way of accomplishing the object than either of those proposed; and I beg leave to offer as a substitute for both propositions, the following. If it meets with opposition from a single individual I shall not press it. It makes it the duty of the Legislature to pass prohibitory enactments, thereby giving notice on the face of this Constitution that such laws will be put in force.

It shall be the duty of the Legislature, as soon as may be, to pass such laws as may be necessary to prevent negroes and mulattoes from coming to and settling in the State of California, and shall declare null and void every indenture conditioned for the manumission, or freedom, of such negro or mulatto, or in consideration of any service to be rendered in California.

The Chair considered the amendment out of order, as a substitute for the two propositions before the House.

Mr. Steuart proposed that it should be offered as a substitute for Mr. McDougal's amendment. If adopted, the original proposition would then as a matter of course be stricken out.

Mr. Botts. I am very much in favor of the exclusion of free negroes from this country; but at present I would only suggest to the gentleman from Sacramento, (Mr. McCarver,) whose resolution, or that of the gentleman from San Francisco, (Mr. Steuart,) I prefer to the amendment, (Mr. McDougal's,) that the wording should be somewhat in this wise: These objectionable individuals shall not be allowed to enter the State of California under such penalties as the Legislature may hereafter impose. My object would be to prevent the coming in of any, either those who have always been free or those who have always been slaves. I think the House will see that there is a difference in the effect that would be produced. It would be, perhaps, going too far to provide the penalty in the Constitution. But by your Constitution inhibit them from coming in, and leave the penalty to the Legislature.

Mr. Semple. It has been the pleasure of gentlemen to place a good deal of weight upon precedents in this matter. I know of no authority, sir, which I hold above that of the people. I have received special instructions from at least more than half of the voters in my district on this subject. It is the very best authority I can have; I know of no other entitled to so much consideration as that of the people themselves. Whatever might be my individual feelings, having been specially instructed by my constituents, I conceive that I have no right to place my own personal wishes in opposition to theirs. We should prevent the difficulty now. It is a duty which we owe to the people; it is a duty we owe to our fellow citizens in the States, who are about to send out negroes. We should not wait till the country becomes full of a population that we have no desire should remain here. I would rather keep three men, inimical to my interests, out of doors, than one inside. The gentleman from San Francisco (Mr. Steuart) tells you that his friends in Maryland ask his advice as to whether they can bring their negroes here, and what will be the probable effect. What is his duty, if we omit a provision of this kind in the Constitution? To write to his friends, and tell them that they can have this privilege—that there is no law against it; that they can bring as many of their negroes here as they please; that at six months labor they will pay a higher price here than they can sell their slaves for in Maryland. Now, sir, I maintain that we owe it to ourselves and to our fellow-citizens at home, to show them in this Constitution that their slaves are not wanted here; that they cannot be introduced into this country; that it is the determination of the people to exclude them. I have my eye, sir, on a certain gentleman in Louisiana, and I will risk it that if you allow him to come here and dig gold with his slaves, he will set free within your borders at least a thousand. He resides in the vicinity of Lake Ponchartrain. There are many others similarly situated with regard to their slaves. Now is the time to act. I think my authority is good, that it is the general desire of the people to exclude them. I have taken some pains to ascertain the feeling on this subject in other districts besides my own. In San Jose, I did not find a single individual who did not give me the same instruction—go on, it is your duty to do it—keep them out. If this Convention refuse to place this provision in the Constitution, if the vote should be against it, I give notice now that I will ask the same disposition to be made of it that was made in the Convention of Illinois. There was a strong and exciting contest there on this subject. The abolitionists ruled it out; and the privilege of submitting it to the people for their decision only passed by two votes. It was however agreed, after a prolonged struggle, that the people should decide it. What was the result? Sir, a majority of twenty thousand voted in favor of it. That article in the Constitution of Illinois, of which this is a copy, it is proposed to place in our Constitution, requiring the Legislature at their first session to pass such laws as will accomplish the object. That will be time enough. Those who came in the last steamer, and others who came previously, are free by the adoption of our Constitution. They are here, and it is not right or just to drive them out of the country. They came without any possibility of notice. But, Mr. Chairman, insert this provision in the Constitution, requiring the Legislature to pass laws prohibiting all others from coming, and the notice commences from the adoption of the Constitution, and the enactment will be passed at the first sitting of the Legislature. In God's name, I say, let us make California a place where free white men can live. It is probably the richest country in the world. It is for you to determine whether the population shall be free and independent, or whether they shall be idle and dissolute. Already thousands of free white men have poured into this country; they are here, an intelligent and enterprising population, and they will labor in the mines while they can get an adequate remuneration. But bring negro labor in competition with them, and you will soon see the disastrous results. You degrade white labor—you place the intelligent and enterprising citizen under the control of monopolists; you deprive him of all that encourages him to industry and makes labor profitable. Let us keep our institutions pure; and let our progress be onward. Let us elevate society here to the highest degree that can possibly be attained by man. We have the means, the natural resources, and the proper character of population to effect this great object. With judicious legislative enactments we can do it. I appeal to gentlemen not to sacrifice the best interests of their country on the plea of domestic convenience, or the imaginary necessity of negro labor for the comfort and happiness of domestic life. If they are to be admitted here at all, let us make slaves of them. If you refuse to do this, sir, and insist upon their admission, I shall vote against that clause in your declaration of rights which excludes slavery from this State. I look upon slavery as one of the worst evils, but I consider a free negro population a greater evil still; and of the two evils I shall certainly choose the least.

Mr. STEUART. I regard the acts of this body as abstract in their character. We are merely called upon to fix the land-marks of the future legislation of California. In regard to the suggestion of the gentleman from Monterey, (Mr. Botts,) I presume, sir, that the power given or the power denied to the Legislature to allow certain things to be done, carries with it the co-relative power of fixing certain penalties. The second clause, providing that no slave or negro shall be manumitted in California who shall be brought here by his master, has reference not only to their being brought here for the express or avowed purpose of being manumitted for value received or services rendered, but to any person coming here to travel with his negro, and with no intention of residing here—that after coming here he shall not be compelled to manumit his slave.

Mr. GILBERT. I have listened with much attention to this debate, and I may say that I have felt no little anxiety as to the result. That aniexty induces me at this late hour, to offer a few remarks upon the question under consideration. It has been the misfortune of this House to have several hobbies. In the first place, the hobby of the apportionment; then the Indian hobby; then the bank or association hobby—all of which have been ridden. Last of all, we have the free negro hobby—the worst, in my opinion. I think, sir, that some of the pictures presented to our view by gentlemen on this floor, are drawn from the imagination, and have no substantial existence in fact. We are told that the slaveholders will manumit their slaves and bring them to this country to dig gold; that they will give up their plantations, however lucrative may be their business, and sacrifice their property to accomplish this object; that they will do all this, when they see staring them in the face, in the Constitution of California, that no slavery shall exist here. I do not believe this; it is not credible. There may be exceptions. Some few may do it under particular circumstances—those having a few slaves who are attached to them, servants who have lived in their families a long time; these may be manumitted and brought here; but that there is any probability of the number being great, I deny. This view of the question, which gentlemen urge upon us with so much vehemence, is overrated. If you insert in your Constitution such a provision or any thing like it, you will be guilty of great injustice—you will do a great wrong, sir—a wrong to the principles of liberal and enlightened freedom; a wrong to the education and feelings of the American people; a wrong to all the rights of government. You have said in the beginning of your bill of rights, that all men are by nature free and independent, and have certain inalienable rights. You go on to say that all men have the right of pursuing and obtaining safety and happiness; and yet, sir, at the bottom of this you propose to say that no free negro shall enter this territory—that he, a freeman, shall not enjoy the right which you award to all mankind. You have not only said this, but you have said that slavery shall not exist here. You have prohibited slavery, and thereby acted in accordance with the dictates of the whole civilized world. Look at the people of Europe. For what are they battling—for what are they shedding their blood? It is to maintain their rights—it is for liberty they contend. Are we to attempt here to turn back the tide of freedom which has rolled across from continent to continent? Are we to say that a free negro or Indian, or any other freeman, shall not enter the boundaries of California? I trust not, sir. Under the former action of this House; under the feelings and principles that have been maintained upon this floor, it would be unjust. Neither slavery nor involuntary servitude, unless for the punishment of crime, shall ever be tolerated in this State; and yet you say a free negro shall not enter its boundaries. Is it because he is a criminal? No, sir—it is simply because he is black. Well might it be said in the words of the revolutionary writer: "You would be free, yet you know not how to be just." It has been asserted that our constituents expect us to put such a provision in the Constitution. Gentlemen who know this may be right in advocating it; but I do not believe my constituency expect it, nor do I believe it is the desire of a majority of the people of California. I therefore oppose it. But, sir, we must go a little further than our constituents in settling this question. The people will consider our acts in this Convention, and if they ratify them, those acts will go before the Congress of the United States; and not only there, but before the great public of the United

States, and before all the nations of the world. Does any gentleman here believe, sir, that there is a man who has ever contended upon the floor of Congress for free soil and free speech, and for the universal liberty of mankind, who will sanction a Constitution that bears upon its face this darkest stigma? Even here in California, I do not believe such a provision would be sanctioned or approved. If it should be approved here, it will never be approved there. I tell you, gentlemen, you jeopard the interests of California far more by inserting this in your Constitution than by any other measure you can introduce. But I have another objection to it. I find on glancing at the Constitution of the United States, under article 4th, section 2d, that—

"The citizens of each State shall be entitled to all the privileges and immunities of citizens in the several States."

I contend, sir, that it is an immunity and privilege of a citizen of one State to remove from that State to another—to remove also his goods and chattles and effects; and no law that we can pass can prevent him from doing it.

Mr. McCarver. Are free negroes citizens of the States?

Mr. Gilbert. In the State of New York and in most of the Eastern States they are. I will not say that in the Southern States they are considered as citizens, though they are citizens under the spirit and meaning of the Constitution. But gentlemen apprehend that we are in danger of being overwhelmed by free negroes and manumitted slaves. I have said that I do not believe it; but admitting their fears to be well grounded, I think the evil should be provided for by the Legislature when circumstances demonstrate the necessity of such provision. It is certainly within the province of the Legislature to correct evils of this character. It is their province and theirs alone; and I should prefer leaving the subject for legislative enactment. We go beyond the bounds of ordinary constitution—making, when we attempt to introduce into ours a provision of this character. But, sir, if the matter is to be pressed upon the House—if we must come to action upon it, I shall deem it my duty to move that it be referred back to the Committee on the Constitution, and that they be instructed to report in favor of submitting it separately to the people. Entertaining the feelings that I do upon this matter, and I grant that my prejudices against negroes are as strong as any man's can be, for my whole education has tended to make them repugnant to me, yet I am not willing to go this far, and say that a free negro, or any other freeman, shall not enter California. Besides, if we wish to be just here; if, as gentlemen say, we must protect this community from vagrants, murderers, assassins, thieves, and all sorts of criminals, we are doing but half the work. Look at the miserable natives that come from the Sandwich Islands and other Islands of the Pacific; look at the degraded wretches that come from Sydney, New South Wales—the refuse of population from Chili, Peru, Mexico, and other parts of the world. Why do you not insert a provision preventing them from polluting the soil of California? If your object is to protect the community from the evils of a bad population, why not include these in your prohibition? Most of them are as bad as any of the free negroes of the North, or the worst slaves of the South. Do not be partial in this matter. You are treading upon the United States' Constitution itself. You must beware how you conflict with its provisions. If, therefore, this matter is to be pressed, I shall move that the whole subject be referred back to the Committee on the Constitution, with such instructions as the House may think proper to give it; but I desire, if a majority of the House be in favor of making it a portion of the Constitution, that it should be submitted to the people for a separate vote. I believe our Constitution will be rejected if you make it a provision which cannot be separated from it; I believe it will not be sanctioned by the people here; and even if sanctioned by them, that it will be rejected by that revisory power which it must pass at Washington. Sir, if there is one consideration more than another that would tempt me to forego all my feelings and principles, it would be that of securing to California, with as little delay as possible, a proper form of State Government.

Mr. Botts asked what was the question before the House.

The Chair stated that it was on the amendment of Mr. Steuart.

Mr. Shannon. I did not think the question would have been sprung so soon upon the House. It seems to me, sir, that it has been decided by the unanimous vote of this Convention that no slavery shall exist in the State of California. A portion of the amendment under consideration, (Mr. Steuart's,) which by-the-by I thought he had withdrawn, declares what? It most directly and positively annuls a section introduced and passed unanimously in the bill of rights; it declares that the Legislature shall pass laws as soon as possible, preventing the emancipation of any slaves introduced into the territory of California. As I understand it, the slaves of the gentleman's friends in Maryland, of whom he has spoken, can be brought here and introduced under that provision, but they cannot be manumitted within our limits. It protects these slaveholders; it gives them the right to hold their slaves in defiance of the section which this House has so unanimously adopted in the bill of rights.

Mr. Steuart. I understand the mover of the original resolution is willing to accept my proposition. I stated expressly in reference to this clause, to which the gentleman from Sacramento (Mr. Shannon) objects, that it is merely designed to cover the case of individuals who may desire to travel with their negro servants through the State—that while it gives those who have no intention of settling here with their slaves that right, they are prohibited from setting them free here or introducing and retaining them as slaves.

Mr. McCarver. I have no objection to it as an amendment. I wish my proposition to remain before the House; but if the House think proper to accept the amendment in preference to mine, I shall be satisfied. I did not withdraw my original resolution, nor do I now withdraw it.

Mr. Shannon. I wish to know how this matter stands. I desire that the effect of the amendment proposed by the gentleman from San Francisco, (Mr. Steuart,) should be distinctly understood.

Mr. Dimmick. Before this question is decided, I wish to correct one statement made on this floor. I desire that there shall not go forth a wrong impression from the district of San Jose. Some gentleman, not representing that district, has taken occasion here to state that he is instructed, or in other words requested, by the people of San Jose, to advocate the adoption of this section, or a section involving these principles. Sir, I beg leave to state that such is not the wish of the people of San Jose. I profess to know something of the voice of that district. There were, perhaps, individuals in the district who wished to have such a provision incorporated in the Constitution, but they do not wish it now, or at least the number is very small. I speak knowingly when I say a large portion of that district do not desire such a provision. I believe there are none but a portion of the population from the States. The native inhabitants of the country do not desire it. I do not wish to be misrepresented here, or to have an impression go forth that I am misrepresenting the will of the people of San Jose. I rise, therefore, to correct that impression. I would make one remark more. If this is to be put upon the statutes, I would suggest to the gentleman the propriety of forbidding the slaveholders from bringing their negroes here, rather than the negroes from coming themselves. The resolution before the House is directed against the negro, who is utterly helpless, and who is brought here by the slaveholder. If such a provision is to be incorporated in the Constitution, it would better please me, and seem more appropriate, to direct the prohibition against the slaveholder.

Mr. Hoppe. I beg leave to detain the House a few minutes. I am a delegate from the district of San Jose, and I beg leave to differ (honestly, I hope) from my colleague on this subject. We have no doubt received our vote from the same people, who elected us to seats upon this floor. I have no particular instructions to vote for or against the introduction of free negroes; but, so far as I am acquainted with the feelings of our district, I consider myself authorized to say that two-thirds of the Americans in that district will go against the introduction of free negroes. I speak it honestly. The feeling is against it. As to the Spanish population, I confidently believe that a full majority will be opposed to the introduction of free negroes among them. That, sir, is my candid impression. I will support the resolution as offered by my friend from San Francisco, (Mr. Steuart.) I believe it will meet the exigencies of the case; and will effectually prevent the introduction of free negroes—a class which would always be a curse to California. I have a rising family here, sir, and I expect to end my days in California; but I never wish to have free negroes for servants, or for any other purpose. I have been educated and reared in the slave States, and have held slaves nearly all my life. I have lived in the free States for a short period, and I have seen riots of the most sanguinary and deplorable character arise from the habitation of negroes among the whites. The two races can never intermingle without mutual injury. I refer especially to the great riot in Cincinnati in 1835. Look at the bloodshed that occurred there. Negroes from all parts of the State were engaged in the conflict, and there was an enormous destruction of property and loss of life. Riots took place also in Illinois, followed by the same melancholy results. What have the people of Illinois done? They have seen the evil consequences that grow out of the intermingling of free negroes with whites, and they have adopted a provision prohibiting their introduction into the State. Let us now, before we are overrun with that race, exclude them from our boundaries, and we shall avoid those evils which have been experienced by the other free States.

The question was then taken on Mr. Steuart's amendment, and it was rejected.

The question being next on Mr. McDougal's amendment, it was also rejected.

The question then recurring on Mr. McCarver's proposition, it was adopted.

On motion, the Committee rose and reported progress.

On motion, the House then adjourned to 12 o'clock to-morrow.

THURSDAY, SEPTEMBER 20, 1849.

The Convention was called to order by the President, pursuant to adjournment.

Prayer by Rev. Senor Antonio Ramirez.

Mr. Gwin stated that there was not a quorum present, and moved that the Convention adjourn, and that the fact that a quorum was not present be entered upon the journal.

Mr. Gwin subsequently modified his motion so as to provide merely that the Convention will take a recess, until 7 o'clock P. M.

The question being taken thereon, it was decided in the affirmative—yeas 9, nays 9—the President giving the casting vote in the affirmative.

And the Convention took a recess accordingly.

NIGHT SESSION, 7 O'CLOCK, P. M.

The Convention met pursuant to adjournment. The journal of yesterday was read, amended, and approved.

Mr. Gwin gave notice of a motion to amend the rules.

Mr. Jones gave notice of a motion to amend the rules.

Mr. Crosby, from the Committee on Finance, to whom was referred back so much of the report of said Committee as relates to the communications of Governor Riley on the ways and means of obtaining the funds for paying the expenses of the Convention, and also to report on the proposition of Mr. J. Ross Browne, to furnish printed copies of his report, made a report in writing, stating the form in which it was necessary to make out the accounts, and recommending the Convention to take a number of printed copies of the Debates in Engligh and Spanish, which was read; and on motion of Mr. GWIN, laid on the table for further consideration.

Mr. TEFFT submitted the following:

Resolved, That until otherwise ordered, the following be a standing rule of this Convention, viz.: This House of Delegates shall hereafter meet at 10 o'clock in the morning, and at 8 o'clock in the evening.

Mr. McDOUGAL moved to amend the same by striking out the words "and at 8 o'clock in the evening," and the motion was decided in the affirmative, 19 to 16.

Mr. BROWN moved further to amend, by striking out "10," and inserting "9."

Whereupon, Mr. TEFFT on leave, withdrew his motion.

Mr. NORTON, from the Committee appointed to prepare a plan or portion of a plan of a State Constitution, made a further report in writing, being Article VI, on the "Judicial Department," and Article VIII, on "Public Instruction;" which was read, and on motion, referred to the Committee of the Whole.

Mr. COBARRUVIAS submitted the following, which was agreed to:

Resolved, That the consideration of the report just presented, be deferred until it shall have been translated into Spanish.

Mr. DIMMICK gave notice that he would in due time, present a minority report on the "Judicial Department," from the Committee appointed to prepare a plan or portion of a plan of a State Constitution.

Mr. TEFFT from the Committee appointed to ascertain and report to this House who are or shall be the delegates from San Diego, made a report in writing, sustaining the previous action of the House, which was read.

Mr. MOORE moved to lay the report on the table, and the motion was decided in the negative.

Mr. MOORE submitted the following, which the President decided to be out of order:

Resolved, That William Richardson be admitted to a seat in this Convention, satisfactory proof having been produced that the people of San Diego did, in pursuance of a resolution adopted by them, elect five delegates, to give in this body whatever vote might be agreed upon as the proper apportionment for the district.

Mr. GWIN submitted the following:

Resolved, That William Richardson be allowed to occupy a seat on this floor, and to be heard by himself or by ourselves, in defence of his right to a seat in this Convention as a delegate from the District of San Diego.

The question being on the adoption of the resolution, it was decided in the affirmative, and Mr. Richardson took a seat on the floor of the Convention.

Mr. GWIN stated that Mr. Richardson desired to be heard by counsel, and had requested that the further consideration of the report might be postponed until tomorrow.

Mr. McDOUGAL moved that Mr. Richardson be permitted to have access to the report and to the papers in the hands of the Committee, and that he be required to present in writing any communication which he may desire to make.

The motion was decided in the negative.

On motion of Mr. JONES, the further consideration of the report was postponed and made the special order for to-morrow at 10 o'clock.

On motion of Mr. JONES, the Convention resolved itself into Committee of the Whole, (Mr. LIPPETT in the Chair,) on the 4th article, being the Executive Department of the Constitution.

On motion of Mr. GWIN, the 3d article being the Legislative Department of the Constitution, was laid aside to be reported to the House.

The first section of the report was adopted without debate, viz:

Sec. 1. The supreme executive power of this State shall be vested in a chief magistrate, who shall be styled the Governor of the State of California.

The 2d section being under consideration, as follows:

Sec. 2. The Governor shall be elected by the qualified electors at the time and place of voting for members of the Assembly, and shall hold his office two years from the time of his installation and until his successor shall be qualified.

Mr. Gilbert wished to offer an amendment to this section—to strike out all after the word "office," and before the word "and," and insert "for two years from the first day of January, next ensuing his election." He apprehended it was the object of the Committee that there should be a concurrence between the election of Governor and the assembling of the Legislature; but he found upon referring back to the Legislative Department, that this would not be the case as the section stands.

The second section of article III, says:

The sessions of the Legislature shall be annual and shall commence on the first Monday in January next ensuing the election of its members, unless the Governor of the State shall in the interim convene the Legislature by proclamation.

In section 4th of the present report, it is provided that—

The returns of every election for Governor shall be sealed up and transmitted to the seat of Government, directed to the Speaker of the Assembly, who shall, during the first week of the session, open and publish them in the presence of both Houses of the Legislature, &c.

In that case, of course, the Governor could not take his seat or act as Governor until after the assembling of the Legislature. He (Mr. Gilbert) would therefore give notice of a motion to amend the second section of the report by inserting instead of the first Monday, the second Monday in January, and to amend the fourth section of the report under consideration, by striking out the whole section and inserting the following:

The returns of every election for Governor and other State officers shall be sealed up and transmitted as soon as practicable thereafter, to the seat of Government, directed to the Secretary of State, who shall, on or before the fifteenth day of December next ensuing, publish the same in one or more public newspapers. The person having the highest number of votes for Governor or other office, respectively, as the case may be, shall be declared duly elected; but in case any two or more persons have an equal and the highest number of votes for Governor or other office, respectively, the Legislature shall choose by ballot at its first session thereafter, one of said persons so having an equal and the highest number of votes for Governor or other office, respectively, as the case may be.

By the adoption of these amendments, the Legislature will assemble on the 2d Mondary of January, which will be in no case sooner than the 8th day of the month. The gubernatorial election will have been decided by the Secretary of State on the 15th of December, and the Governor will have an opportunity of preparing his messsage for the Legislature by the first of January. He thought it necessary in that view of the case, that these last amendments should be made. As the section stands, it would make it incumbent on the retiring Governor to send in a message at the opening of the Legislature. Such, he apprehended, was not the wish of the people or of the House. Coming into office, the new Governor should have the privilege of laying down the principles that are to govern him during his term of office, and at the same time, a new Legislature may come in of the same political views, and it is desirable that there should be unity of action between the Executive and Legislative Departments of the Government.

Mr. Gwin said that if that amendment was to be adopted, the gentleman, (Mr. Gilbert,) had better report an entire new article on the subject, because the whole system depends upon each part, and goes through the report. It is sustained by the experience of many of the States. In case of a contested election of Governor under this proposition, how is the decision to be made, or by what power? It is decided here by the Legislature. If he is to be sworn before the Legislature meets, his election cannot afterwards be contested.

Mr. GILBERT remarked, that in case of a tie, he should expect the question to remain till the Legislature should act upon it. If the Legislature could not decide it, it would of course go back to the people. He was not aware of the course pursued in any of the States in reference to this matter, except the State of New York, which has a board of canvassers, consisting of the officers of the State.

Mr. BOTTS. I congratulate myself that I have arrived at a point for once, when I can give my full assent to the report of the Committee; and I only regret that I cannot at the same time sanction the practice of New York. I hope it will not be the will of the House to approve of the doctrines proposed by the gentleman from San Francisco, (Mr. Gilbert.) It is to my mind a most important point. As I understand it, the difference between the two questions is this: To whom shall the power of deciding these elections be left, whether to the Legislature or to a subordinate executive officer of this Government?

Mr. GILBERT. The gentleman mistakes entirely. I will read the substitute which I propose for the 4th section. (See amendment to section 4.)

Mr. BOTTS. Just exactly as I supposed it to be. Who has the highest number of votes. That is the question, and that great and important question is to be settled by your Secretary of State.

Mr. GILBERT. It is to be settled by the official returns.

Mr. BOTTS. The Secretary of State is to decide who has received the highest number of votes, and if the Legislature is to act at all, it is only to register the decree of the Secretary of State. He is to decide upon the legality of the returns. I consider that to be a question of very great importance. It is scarcely necessary to multiply words on the subject. I think when my friend from San Francisco, (Mr. Gilbert) sees that such a question will necessarily have to be decided by such an officer, that he will withdraw the amendment. At any rate, I wish to impress upon the House the effect of this amendment. The question of the legality of the returns must of necessity, under this resolution, be decided, and that without appeal, by an officer who, I presume, it is not contemplated should hold such a position as to entitle him to this power. He is called upon to decide not only upon the legality of the election, but upon the legality of the returns. We have known questions of the most important character to arise in the United States on this subject. In the celebrated New Jersey case, it was one of the most important questions presented before the House of Representatives as to what were the legal returns. It was a question that agitated Congress and the country for weeks, and produced a most extraordinary and exciting debate in the House. And yet this question, which the House of Representatives could hardly decide, the gentleman proposes to leave to an executive officer!

Mr. GILBERT. Of course the question upon this amendment has no necessary relation to the others that I have offered. If it be adopted or not, it does not materially change the report. It is a mere question of words in this section. But in so far as relates to the remarks of the gentleman from Monterey, (Mr. Botts) I must say I have arrived at an entirely different conclusion. It is very possible that the Secretary of State might be a very bad man; but I cannot think there is any danger of his making false returns.

Mr. BOTTS. I do not fear that the Secretary of State would be a worse man than any other. I am afraid of all men. I do not say he would make a false return; but I fear to trust him with the decisions of the legality of such an important question as the election returns of the Governor—one of such vital importance to the people.

Mr. GILBERT. I am willing to leave it to the House.

The question was then taken on Mr. Gilbert's amendment to the second section, and it was rejected.

The question recurring on the adoption of section 2d,

Mr. Halleck said: I must call attention to one point that did not strike me in Committee, and that is, that a difficulty may arise as to the succession in office. Suppose a question should occur in regard to the votes, and a month, to the 1st of February, should be occupied in coming to a decision upon it. The Governor holds on to that time. The time of the installation of the new Governor may thus pass beyond the time of the meeting of the Legislature, and that might go on for several years.

Mr. Gwin. The Legislature will settle all matters of that kind. It is a duty that is incumbent upon it. I do not see how we can remedy the difficulty unless the system be entirely changed.

Mr. Shannon offered the following amendment: to strike out all from the word "and" to the word "and," and insert in its place, "and shall hold his office two years from the first day of January following his election, and until his successor shall be qualified."

Mr. Gilbert. I rise to a question of order; if that is not substantially the same as the amendment which I offered, and which has just been rejected.

Mr. Halleck. I call the attention of the gentleman to the fact that the last part of the amendment is different from that offered by the gentleman from San Francisco.

The Chair decided that the amendment did not differ substantially from the amendment just acted upon.

The question recurring on the 2d section as reported, it was adopted.

The question being on the 3d section,

Mr. Wozencraft moved the following as an additional section, to come in between sections two and three of the report:

A Governor, after having served two consecutive terms, shall be, and is hereby, declared ineligible for a third.

Mr. Shannon. Coming back again to the old ground; throwing restrictions around your Legislature and people that you have no right to impose upon them. Is this Convention any wiser than the future Legislatures to assemble here, or are the people any wiser now than they will be years hence. I desire to see no restriction, that we can possibly avoid, thrown around the Legislature; and I desire still more to see no restriction thrown by this Constitution over the people. I desire to see them left as unhampered as we can possibly leave them. It is now proposed that we shall declare that whether they choose or not to elect any man they see fit to the office af Governor, they cannot do it, because this Constitution prohibits it. I regard it as a most improper restriction. I certainly cannot vote for it, nor can I vote in favor of the limitation in the third section of the report, requiring the candidate to be twenty-five years in order to be eligible to the office of Governor.

Mr. Wozencraft. I was very much in hopes this section would pass without debate. I think one of the great principles of a republican government is rotation in office. As to hampering the people with restrictions, the only restriction here is in regard to succession. The same person may be elected a dozen times, if he lives long enough.

Mr. Norton. I can see no necessity for this provision. There is an obvious necessity in the case of some offices for such restriction—that of Sheriff, for instance—a person who is supposed to have by virtue of his office an immense deal of influence throughout the country; and who has large sums of money in his possession. If he should be eligible a second term, he might use his influence, or the money in his hands, for the purpose of procuring his re-election. The people will settle this matter about the Governor. If they want a certain man to continue as Governor, they will have him; if not they will reject him.

Mr. Wozencraft. He may come in for a life time, under this provision, but not in successive terms. There is no other restriction but that of successive terms.

The question was then taken, and the proposed section was rejected.

The third section of the report being under consideration, as follows:

3. No person shall be eligible to the office of Governor, (except at the first election,) who has not been a citizen of the United States and a resident of this State two years next preceding the election, and attained the age of twenty five years at the time of said election.

Mr. McDougal moved to amend so as to make the section read "ten years a citizen of the United States or of California."

Mr. Dimmick. I trust, sir, that this amendment will not be adopted; for it certainly does appear to me to operate hard upon portions of the people of California. There are persons in this territory whom I consider justly entitled to be elected to the highest offices within the gift of the people, which this amendment would exclude. I mean the native Californians, whom I consider equally as well entitled to hold office as the American population. If it can be so modified as to include only those who become naturalized under the naturalization laws, I have no objection to the amendment; but when I see a proposition brought forward that will cut off the native-born citizens of California, I hope it will not be the pleasure of the Convention to adopt it.

Mr. Norton. I have the same objections. This amendment will not only cut off all the native Californians, but all those persons not residents of the United States who were here residing in this country before California became a part of the United States

Mr. McDougal. At the time I offered this amendment, I did not reflect for a moment upon the objections that the gentlemen have urged against it. I see that their objections are good and valid. In casting my eye over the section, I thought only of the necessity of requiring that none but a citizen of the United States should be eligible to the office of Governor. I will therefore amend my motion so as to read, "citizens of the United States, or of California, for the last ten years."

Mr. Botts. I am afraid the gentleman is running from one extreme to the other. He will shut us all off if we have to be citizens of California ten years.

Mr. McDougal explained that it was "of the United States or California."

Mr. Tefft. I consider the resolution still objectionable. There may be in California English or Scotch people, who have not been residents ten years. It would deprive them of all right to the office of Governor.

Mr. Dimmick. I still find the proposition objectionable, for the same reason that I did at first. It is well known that there are many citizens in California, who were citizens of Mexico, who have not been in this country ten years. I think there are some upon this floor, born in Mexico, who were Mexican citizens, but who have not lived in this country quite ten years. I am certain there are many worthy citizens in this territory who come under this head. Emigrating here when this country was their own, they surely ought to be entitled to every right and privilege enjoyed by all who have been here the same length of time. I consider therefore that the amendment still operates unjustly towards a portion of the citizens of California, and I shall vote against it.

Mr. Shannon. I wish to put a case to my colleague from Sacramento, (Mr. McDougal.) I should dislike very much to have any of the Sacramento delegation rendered ineligible to the office of Governor. Now, the gentleman's friend and my friend, (Captain Sutter,) if we choose to nominate him as a candidate for that position, would come directly under this clause, and be rendered ineligible. He has not been a citizen of the United States, I believe, ten years; neither has he been a citizen of California quite ten years. Under the treaty he became a citizen of California; but not being a citizen either of the United States or of California ten years, he is excluded by this section. If there is any thing to get Captain Sutter out of this dilemma, there are still others who at home are eligible to the office of Governor, who by coming here are rendered ineligible.

Mr. McDougal. I certainly think gentlemen take a wrong view of this amendment. It strikes me that each gentleman thinks himself specially referred to. In answer to the case put by my colleague, in relation to Captain Sutter, I can state that he is not cut off by this resolution. He has been a citizen of California over ten years, and of the United States previously six years. I offer this amendment making it requisite for the incumbent—the Chief Magistrate of the State—to reside ten years in the United States or California, from the fact that it requires at least that residence to understand our institutions and the principles of our government. No foreigner can come in here and become thoroughly Americanized under ten years. I think it should be a constitutional requirement that he should be here at least that period before he is eligible to so high and resonsible a position. If there is any objection to requiring him to be a resident ten years, there is the same objection to requiring him to be a resident of this State previous to the election. Both stand upon precisely the same footing; and it was in that view of the case I offered the amendment.

Mr. Dent. If I recollect right, it appears to me that at an early day in the session, it was decided that persons might be citizens either of Mexico or of the United States, without necessarily having the privilege of voting in this State. I know that such is the case; but lest there may be some doubt in the House relative to the truth of my position, I will read an extract from the treaty of peace between the United States and Mexico which establishes the fact:

"The Mexicans who, in the territories aforesaid, shall not preserve the character of citizens of the Mexican republic, conformably with what is stipulated in the preceding article, shall be incorporated into the Union of the United States, and be admitted at the proper time, (to be judged of by the Congress of the United States,) to the enjoyment of all the rights of citizens of the United States, according to the principles of the Constitution; and in the meantime shall be maintained and protected in the free enjoyment of their liberty and property, and secured in the free exercise of their religion, without restriction."

Now it is admitted, I believe, that all negroes who came into California previous to the treaty, or lived in California at the time of its adoption, were considered in the light of Mexican citizens, but not having the privilege of voting. If such is the fact, all of the African race living in California at that time would be included as citizens, and would of course be entitled to aspire to the position of Governor. I propose therefore that we substitute in place of "citizen of the United States or of California," "shall be a qualified elector of the State of California."

Mr. Botts. I am opposed to the amendment of the gentleman, (Mr. McDougal.) I have not that prejudice against foreigners which seems to inspire some of the members of this House. I certainly desire that the individual who is to administer this Government shall understand the character and nature of our institutions; but I deny the fact that ten years' residence is necessary to acquire that knowledge. These principles are based upon truths that are not confined to the United States; they are known throughout the world. Wherever civilized man exists, the nature and character and celebrity of those institutions are well understood. It is not a fact that persons on the other side of the Atlantic know nothing about our institutions; they are well known, sir, well understood. In my opinion, that celebrated French writer, De Tocqueville, has given the most satisfactory evidence that he understood them perhaps as well as nine-tenths of our own countrymen. That these great principles are not only known and preached but practiced, by that class of individuals whom this resolution would exclude, is proved by the fact that they leave their native land—that they sunder all those ties of kindred—give up all that love of country which is so natural to the heart of man, to come to our shores—thereby evincing their high appreciation of our institutions. They present, if any thing, stronger claims to understand and appreciate them than any which we have had it in our power to give; and it may be, that that just such an individual as this resolution would have a tendency to exclude, would command the votes of seven-eights of the people to that office. Why then adopt a provision that would produce the effect of nullifying the wishes of our constituents? I shall certainly oppose this resolution. I do not know but I am favor of the amendment of the gentleman from Monterey, (Mr. Dent,) which goes still further than the report of the Committee.

Mr. DENT read his proposed amendment, as follows:

No person shall be eligible to the office of Governor (except at the first election) who has not the qualifications of an elector, and been a resident of this State two years next preceding the election, and attained the age of twenty-five years at the time of said election.

The question was then taken on the amendment, and it was rejected.

The question was then taken on Mr. McDougal's amendment, and it was rejected.

Mr. SHANNON moved to strike out all after the word election, being the words "and attained the age of twenty-five years at the time of said election."

The motion was decided in the negative.

The 3d section was then adopted without amendment.

The 4th section being under consideration, as follows:

4. The returns of every election for Governor shall be sealed up and transmitted to the seat of Government, directed to the Speaker of the Assembly, who shall, during the first week of the session, open and publish them in the presence of both Houses of the Legislature. The person having the highest number of votes shall be Governor. But in case any two or more have an equal and the highest number of votes, the Legislature shall, by joint ballot, choose one of said persons so having an equal and the highest number of votes for Governor.

Mr. GILBERT said: If now in order, I would move the amendment which I have already referred to, and which I will now explain to the House. I would state that if the section be adopted as it stands in the report, the Legislature will commence on the first Monday in January, and the returns of the election of Governor will have to go before the Legislature; consequently there will be no Governor until the Speaker of the Assembly shall have declared who is Governor. There will be an interregnum between the meeting of the Legislature and the decision of the election. My substitute is designed to obviate this difficulty; that the going out of office of the Governor and the assembling of the Legislature shall be consistent. I deemed some provision of the kind absolutely necessary. I am not tenacious that the Secretary of State should be the canvassing officer of the election; there may be a board consisting of all the State officers; but it is necessary that the Governor should go into office on the first day of January. He would then have eight days to prepare himself for the duties of his office, and to render to the Legislature a proper report or message; under the proposed state of things the Legislature assembles on the 1st day of January, and you have the old Governor in office. He delivers a message to the Legislature, whereas, I think the new Governor should have that privilege, and not be obliged to sit out a part of that Legislature without the right to present to it any exposition of his views. You might make a canvassing board consisting of the Attorney General, Surveyor General, Comptroller, or other State officers, if the remarks of the gentleman from Monterey (Mr. Botts) have frightened the House. You will find if you refer further to the report, that these officers are, in the first instance, to be elected by the Legislature, and thereafter by the people. I now move that section 4th be stricken out, and the following be substituted:

4. The returns of every election for Governor and other State officers shall be sealed up and transmitted as soon as practicable thereafter, to the seat of Government, directed to the Secretary of State, who shall, on or before the fifteenth day of December next ensuing, publish the same in one or more public newspapers. The person having the highest number of votes for Governor or other office, respectively, as the case may be, shall be declared duly elected; but in case any two or more persons have an equal and the highest number of votes for Governor or other office, respectively, the Legislature shall choose by joint ballot, at its first session thereafter, one of said persons so having an equal and the highest number of votes for Governor or other office, respectively, as the case may be.

Mr. Crosby. I hope this amendment will prevail, as it seems to be of the highest importance that the Governor and the Legislature should go into office at the same time. Almost always the same policy is agreed to by the Governor and the Legislature, and it is desirable there should be a co-relative agreement in the commencement of their operations. In addition to the persons named as canvassing officers, perhaps it would be well to have the Supreme Chief Justices added, or have them alone, without the State officers.

Mr. Gilbert. I believe that in the State of New York all the State officers constitute the board.

Mr. Gwin. I hope this amendment will not be adopted. My colleague seems to think it of great importance that the new Governor should make a speech. There is no difficulty about that as the matter stands. The retiring Governor presents his valedictory—the new Governor his inaugural address.

Mr. Sherwood. After hearing the remarks of my friend from San Francisco on the right, (Mr. Gilbert,) I am decidedly in favor of the proposed substitute. I think the Governor and other State officers should be aware of the election previous to the hour of their installation. It seems proper that any officer who has received the vote of the people of the State should know, previous to his installation, whether he is elected or not; and that we should not require officers to come to the seat of Government to inquire whether he has received a majority of the votes, and wait for the Legislature to tell him.

Mr. McDougal. I would suggest to my friend from San Francisco, (Mr. Gilbert,) the propriety of an addition to his amendment. There is no provision, either in the amendment or in the original report, designating who shall seal up and transmit these election returns to the seat of government.

Mr. Gilbert. That will be provided by law.

Mr. Halleck. I will remark that that subject will be reported upon hereafter by the Committee.

Mr. Botts. I would simply inquire if it be designed in the resolution that this officer—the Secretary of State—is merely to count the votes as they are sent in, and declare the result, or is a discretionary power left with him to decide whether they are legal or illegal?

Mr. Gilbert. The returns that come to him will come from the duly elected canvassers in the several districts, and of course he will take no returns unless they come under that authority. The Speaker of the Assembly must act upon the same returns; the Assembly and Legislature must act upon the same returns; they cannot act upon any others. If these returns are false the Legislature will make a mistake, and be placed just in the same position as the Secretary of State. The gentleman has conjured up a danger that has no existence in reality. As a further answer to the objections of the gentleman from Monterey, (Mr. Botts,) I would remind him that the substitute provides that the returns shall be published fifteen days before the meeting of the Legislature.

The question was then taken on the proposed substitute and decided in the negative.

The fourth section, as reported, was then adopted.

The question being on the fifth section, viz:

5. The Governor shall be commander-in-chief of the militia, the army, and navy of this State.

Mr. McDougal moved to amend by adding at the end of this section, "except when they shall be called into service by the United States."

Mr. McCarver thought the gentleman's amendment was needless. Who would be commander-in-chief if the Governor was not? The Governor should be commander-in-chief. The Government of the United States, in case of necessity, makes a call upon him, and he furnishes the required forces.

Mr. SHANNON read from the second article, section 2d, of the Constitution of the United States, as follows:

"The President shall be commander-in-chief of the army and navy of the United States, and of the militia of the several States, when called into the actual service of the United States," &c.

Mr. McDOUGAL could see no necessity then for the section, unless it contained the exception which he had proposed.

Mr. NORTON remarked that it was usual to have such an article in the Constitutions of the States, and he considered the amendment entirely out of place.

The fifth section was then adopted, without amendment.

Sections 6, 7, 8, 9, and 10, of the report, were then adopted without debate, viz:

6. He shall transact all executive business with the officers of Government, civil and military, and may require information in writing from the officers of the executive department upon any subject relating to the duties of their respective offices.

7. He shall see that the laws are faithfully executed.

8. When any office shall from any cause become vacant, and no mode is provided by the Constitution and laws for filling such vacancy, the Governor shall have power to fill such vacancy, by granting a commission which shall expire at the end of the next session of the Legislature, or at the next election by the people.

9. He may, on extraordinary occasions, convene the Legislature by proclamation, and shall state to both Houses, when assembled, the purposes for which they shall have been convened.

10. He shall communicate by message to the Legislature, at every session, the condition of the State, and recommend such matters as he shall deem expedient.

The question being on the 11th section, viz:

11. In case of a disagreement between the two Houses with respect to the time of adjournment, the Governor shall have power to adjourn the Legislature to such time as he may think proper, provided it be not beyond the time fixed for the meeting of the next Legislature.

Mr. HASTINGS moved to strike it out. The motion was decided in the negative, and the section was adopted.

Sections 12, 13, 14, 15, 16, and 17, of the report, were then adopted without debate, as follows:

12. No person shall, while holding any office under the United States or this State, exercise the office of Governor, except as hereinafter expressly provided.

13. The Governor shall have the power to grant reprieves, commutations, and pardons, after conviction, for all offences except treason, and cases of impeachment, upon such conditions, and with such restrictions and limitations as he may think proper, subject to such regulations as may be provided by law relative to the manner of applying for pardons. Upon conviction for treason, he shall have power to suspend the execution of the sentence until the case shall be reported to the Legislature at its next meeting, when the Legislature shall either pardon or commute the sentence, direct the execution of the sentence, or grant a further reprieve.

He shall communicate to the Legislature at the beginning of every session, every case of reprieve, commutation, or pardon granted, stating the name of the convict, the crime of which he was convicted, the sentence, and its date, and the date of the commutation, pardon and reprieve.

14. There shall be a seal of this State, which shall be kept by the Governor, and used by him officially, and shall be called the great seal of the State of California.

15. All grants and commissions shall be in the name and by the authority of the people of the State of California, sealed with the great seal of the State, signed by the Governor, and countersigned by the Secretary of State.

16. A Lieutenant Governor shall be elected at the same time and places and in the same manner as the Governor; and his term of office and his qualifications of eligibility, shall also be the same. He shall be the President of the Senate, but shall only have a casting vote therein. If during a vacancy in the office of Governor, the Lieutenant Governor shall be impeached, displaced, resign, die, or become incapable of performing the duties of his office, or be absent from the State, the President of the Senate shall act as Governor until the vacancy be filled, or the disability shall cease.

17. In case of the impeachment of the Governor or his removal from office, death, inability to discharge the powers and duties of the said office, resignation or absence from the State, the powers and duties of the office shall devolve upon the Lieutenant Governor for the residue of the term, or until the disability shall cease. But when the Governor shall, with the consent of the Legislature, be out of the State in time of war at the head of any military force thereof, he shall continue Commander-in-chief of all the military force of the State.

The 18th section of the report being under consideration, as follows:

18. A Secretary of State, a Comptroller, a Treasurer, an Attorney General, and Surveyor General, shall be chosen in the manner provided in this Constitution, and the term of office and eligibility of each shall be the same as are prescribed for the Governor and Lieutenant Governor.

Mr. Gilbert moved to strike out the words "a Comptroller." He thought it absolutely necessary that we should have as few State officers as possible. He could see necessity for having a Comptroller. Such an officer was not required here where our public improvements and the amount of public funds would be so limited for several years.

Mr. Sherwood hoped the motion would not prevail. The Comptroller is auditor of public accounts, and is a very important officer in that light. As for public improvements, he trusted we would have some before long.

Mr. McCarver suggested that the Secretary of State be required to perform the duties of Comptroller.

Mr. Gilbert said that the business of the Comptroller was simply to audit the accounts of the State Treasurer. In some States there is a Committee of the Legislature to audit the accounts of the Treasurer. In the State of New York a Comptroller is absolutely necessary. The Treasurer in that State is a mere Cashier. The Comptroller is the principal officer. But in California for many years we shall not need an office of this kind. He hoped the House would strike it out and provide, if necessary, for a board of officers of both Houses of the Legislature.

Mr. McCarver thought this matter should be left to the Legislature. It is usual in legislative bodies in the States to have frequent settlements with the auditor of public accounts, by a committee appointed for that purpose.

Mr. Botts hoped the motion would not prevail. He was in favor of retaining this officer, not only because the Constitution of New York has a Comptroller in it, but because his duties are extremely important. In some of the States they are so important as to be divided between two—a first and second Comptroller. A most wholesome and useful check is created by the union of the two officers; the one is a check upon the other. It is absolutely necessary to have some officer to keep a check upon the public accounts.

The question was taken on Mr. Gilbert's motion to strike out the words "a Comptroller," and decided in the negative.

The 18th section was then adopted.

The 19th section being under consideration, viz:

19. The Secretary of State shall be appointed by the Governor, by and with the advice and consent of the Senate. He shall keep a fair record of the official acts of the legislative and executive departments of the Government, and shall, when required, lay the same, and all matters relative thereto, before either branch of the Legislature, and shall perform such other duties as shall be assigned him by law.

Mr. Dent moved to strike out all of the first sentence after the word "be," and insert thereof the words "elected by the people."

Mr. Halleck suggested that if this amendment was adopted, another should be passed also, providing that the Secretary of State shall not be required to keep the records of the Governor, if he is not to be a confidential officer, appointed under his authority.

The question was then taken on the amendment, and it was rejected.

The 19th section, as reported, was then adopted.

The 20th and 21st sections of the report were adopted, without debate, as follows:

20. The comptroller, treasurer, attorney general, and surveyor general, shall be chosen by joint-ballot of the two Houses of the Legislature, at their first session under this Constitution; and thereafter shall be elected, at the same time and places, and in the same manner as the governor andl ieutenant governor.

21. The governor, lieutenant governor, secretary of state, comptroller, treasurer, attorney general, and surveyor general shall each, at stated times during their continuance in office, receive for their services a compensation which shall not be increased or diminished during the term for which they shall have been elected, but neither of these officers shall receive for his own use any fees for the performance of his official duties.

The 22d section of the report being under consideration, as follows:

22. The governor may suspend from office the secretary of state, comptroller, treasurer, surveyor general, and attorney general during the recess of the Legislature, until thirty days after the commencement of the next session of the Legislature, whenever it shall appear to him that such officer has in any particular violated his duty, and he shall appoint a competent person to discharge the duties of the office during such suspension, and within ten days after the meeting of the Legislature, or after such suspension; if made during the session, the governor shall lay before that body his reasons for such suspension, and the Legislature shall determine by joint ballot whether the officer so suspended shall be removed or restored to office.

Mr. Botts said he thought he would vote for everything brought up to night; but he could not vote for this. It was putting into the hands of the Governor most extraordinary powers. Whilst he was not prepared to debate, he was certainly prepared to vote against it.

The question was then taken, and the 22d section was adopted.

On motion, the Committee then rose, reported the 3d and 4th articles to the House, with sundry amendments, and had leave to sit again.

On motion, the House adjourned to 10 o'clock A. M. to-morrow.

FRIDAY, SEPTEMBER 21, 1849.

The Convention met pursuant to adjournment. Prayer by Rev. S. H. Wiley. Journal of yesterday read and approved.

Mr. Gwin offered the following resolution:

Resolved, That the proposition f J. Ross Browne to print and publish, for the use of the State, 1,000 copies in English, and 250 copies in Spanish, of a stenographic report of the proceedings of this Convention, for $10,000, be and is hereby accepted; and the President of the Convention is hereby authorized to enter into the necessary arrangements with Mr. Browne for the security and payment of said appropriation.

Mr. Gwin remarked that it was a matter of importance to the reporter that this proposition should be acted upon without further delay. He regarded it as extremely important that a correct official record of the proceedings of this Convention should be published, both in English and Spanish. He thought the proposition reasonable enough; and, as it seemed to be the only feasible mode of accomplishing the object, he moved the adoption of the resolution.

Mr. Crosby stated that the Committee had taken a great deal of pains to ascertain whether this sum was as low as it could possibly be done for, and they were clearly of the opinion that the proposition was more favorable than any other that had been presented. Almost the entire expense of printing these Spanish copies is additional; or, in other words, after printing the English edition, it would cost the same to have it translated into Spanish and an edition of two hundred and fifty copies printed in that language.

Mr. Lippitt called for the reading of Mr. Browne's proposition, which was ordered.

Mr. McCarver would vote for the adoption of the resolution; but, at the same time, he would greatly prefer that each member should have one copy of the Report instead of the number specified. It would not look so much like voting themselves books at the people's expense.

Mr. Botts had no great desire to see the debates of this Convention reported at all. He conceived that questions of the greatest magnitude had been discussed under circumstances of hurry and haste; and that the debates, if correctly reported, would leave the members of the Convention in a very unenviable attitude before the country. He had no sort of fancy for having the debates laid before the country. He did not think, from the difficulties experienced by every gentleman who had spoken, owing to the want of books for reference, time for preparation, and a systematic order of things, that they were calculated to do credit to California. But it was not to that point he wished to call the attention of the House. If this Convention adopted the resolution, the Reporter was, from that moment, entitled to receive ten thousand dollars. Had the Committee on Finance that much money in their pockets to pay him with?

Mr. CROSBY explained that the Reporter would be paid in the same manner as other officers of the Convention.

Mr. BOTTS opposed the appropriation of the civil fund for paying the expenses of the Convention, on the ground that neither General Riley nor the President of the United States, had a right to dispose of it, and that it could not be legally so appropriated without special act of Congress. (See debate on this subject, page 95.)

After further discussion, the question recurring on the adoption of Mr. Gwin's resolution, Mr. GILBERT called for the yeas and nays, which were ordered, and resulted as follows:

YEAS—Messrs. Aram, Brown, Crosby, De la Guerra, Dimmick, Dominguez, Foster, Gwin Hoppe, Halleck, Hastings, Hollingsworth, Jones, Lippitt, Lippincott, Moore, McCarver, Pedrorena Rodriguez, Reid, Snyder, Shannon, Stearns, Steuart, Tefft, Vallejo, Walker, President—28.

NAYS—Messrs. Botts, Dent, Ellis, Gilbert, Hill, McDougal, Norton, Sherwood, Wozencraft—9.

On motion of Mr. GWIN, the Committee proceeded to the consideration of the special order, being the report of the Committee appointed to ascertain and report who are or shall be delegates from San Diego.

The report, on motion, was read. Whereupon, Col. John B. Weller appeared as counsel for Mr. Richardson, and advocated at length his claim to a seat in this Convention, as a member elect from the District of San Diego.

Further discussion ensued, by Messrs. Hill, Halleck, Tefft, Botts, Pedrorena, and Shannon.

Col. Weller replied—when Mr. GWIN submitted the following:

Resolved, That William H. Richardson be admitted to his seat as a member of this Convention, and that, in all votes taken in this House, the District of San Diego shall be entitled to but two votes; a majority of the delegates from that district to give the vote; but the dissenting member, on any vote by yeas and nays, shall have the privilege of entering his dissent on the journal.

The President ruled that the resolution could not be entertained, as the Convention had already decided as to the manner of casting the votes in Convention, and had also fixed the apportionment for San Diego at two members. A reconsideration of the vote fixing the apportionment of the several districts, and declaring the manner in which the votes shall be cast in this Convention, would be necessary, before the resolution would be in order, as no resolution could be entertained in contravention of the law of the Convention. As the Convention had already decided that the vote therein shall not be given by districts, but by the members individually, the law of the Convention cannot be disregarded until changed in due process by the action of this body.

From this decision Mr. GWIN appealed, and proceeded to state his reasons for so doing.

The question being—Shall the decision of the Chair stand as the judgment of the Convention, it was decided in the affirmative.

Mr. GWIN requested that the decision of the President should be reduced to writing and entered upon the journal, and the Secretary was directed by the President to take down the words, and enter them accordingly.

Mr. GWIN also asked and obtained leave to have entered upon the journal a protest by himself against the decision of the President.

The question then recurring on the adoption of the report, Mr. WOZENCRAFT asked to be excused from voting, but the Convention refused so to excuse him.

Messrs. HILL and PEDRORENA were excused from voting on the question of adoption. Mr. GWIN asked the yeas and nays on the adoption of the report, and they were ordered. The question was then decided in the affirmative, as follows:

YEAS—Messrs. Aram, Botts, Brown, Cobarruvias, Crosby, De la Guerra, Dimmick, Dominguez, Foster, Gilbert, Hanks, Hoppe, Halleck, Hastings, Hollingsworth, Jones, Lippitt, Lippincott, McCarver, Norton, Pico, Rodriguez, Reid, Sherwood, Shannon, Stearns, Steuart, Tefft, Vallejo, Walker, Wozencraft, President—32.

NAYS—Messrs. Ellis, Gwin, Moore, McDougal, Ord—5.

Mr. ELLIS submitted the following:

Resolved, That hereafter the claims of all persons to become members of this body, except such persons as have already been declared members by a vote of this Convention, shall be declared out of order, and shall not be entertained by this House.

On motion of Mr. MOORE, the Convention took a recess until 7½ o'clock, P. M.

EVENING SESSION, 7½ O'CLOCK, P. M.

On motion of Mr. GWIN, the Convention resolved itself into Committee of the Whole, Mr. Botts in the Chair, on the report of the Committee on the Constitution.

Article VI of the report of the Committee was then adopted, without debate, as follows:

ARTICLE VI.—*Militia.*

SEC. 1. The Legislature shall provide, by laws, for organizing and disciplining the militia, in such manner as they shall deem expedient, not incompatible with the Constitution and laws of the United States.

2. The Legislature shall provide for the efficient discipline of the officers, commissioned and non-commissioned, and musicians, and may provide by-laws for the organization and discipline of volunteer companies.

3. Officers of the militia shall be elected or appointed in such manner as the Legislature shall, from time to time, direct, and shall be commissioned by the Governor.

4. The Governor shall have power to call forth the militia, to execute the laws of the State, to suppress insurrections, and repel invasions.

Article VII of the report of the Committee then coming up—

Mr. SHERWOOD moved to strike out the word "one," before the words "hundred thousand dollars," and insert the word "five."

By this section we prevent the Legislature from creating a debt of over one hundred thousand dollars, in the aggregate, without submitting it to a vote of the people. He was in favor of submitting the question of creating a large debt to the people, but it may be necessary in carrying on the expenses of the Government to borrow temporarily more than that sum. In the State of New York there is a provision of a similar nature in the Constitution, but the amount is one million instead of a hundred thousand. In his opinion it might be necessary at some period—probably at the very first session of the Legislature, before a tax can be levied and collected, in order to keep the wheels of Government in motion—to borrow more than a hundred thousand dollars as a temporary loan. He would make it five hundred thousand. The expenses of this State would be larger than those of any other State, and this sum might be required.

Mr. NORTON said that the Committee were not particular in regard to the sum, but they thought it necessary to specify some definite amount. He thought himself that the circumstances of the country required that the sum should be increased, so that the Legislature should have the power to raise such an amount as might be indispensably necessary.

Mr. SHERWOOD stated further that it was, in the view of the Committee, deemed proper to reconsider this question, and fix the amount at a larger sum than that reported; but from some circumstance or other it was not reconsidered.

Mr. GWIN was utterly opposed to the amendment, to increase the amount of State debt to $500,000. If we could not carry on our State Government without contracting a debt of that magnitude, we were certainly starting wrong. This was a provision of the utmost importance. He hoped the report of the Committee would be received, or if the amount was to be increased that it would be in a very small ratio. He was opposed to the principle of permitting the Government to create a public debt at all, and would not go beyond the report of the Committee.

Mr. MCCARVER was of opinion that $100,000 was sufficient to pay the expenses of State Government. Iowa went into existence prohibiting the borrowing of over a hundred thousand dollars; and he did not see why we should not do so.

Nearly all the lands of Iowa were public lands and were not taxable by the State. He was of opinion that the sum should not at all events be over $300,000. If we went beyond that we created an indebtedness that might probably be entailed upon our posterity; and he was altogether opposed to the principle of borrowing money and making others pay it. The interest in a short time would amount to as much as the principal. It was impossible to borrow money here short of six to ten per cent. He believed that two, or, at furthest, three hundred thousand dollars would be sufficient. He would be willing to vote for that, but not one cent beyond it.

Mr. HASTINGS observed that the gentleman seemed to labor under the impression that, if the sum of $500,000 was inserted instead of $100,000, a debt to that extent must necessarily be created. He conceived it was discretionary with the Legislature, and that probably no debt at all would be created. If it was necessary to provide for obtaining money when required, it was highly important that we should so form our Constitution that the Legislature might be able to meet the contingency. He would be willing to rely upon the good judgment of the Legislature. It could not reasonably be presumed that the Legislature would create a debt to the full amount of the authority given it unless the public necessities demanded it.

Mr. SHERWOOD said that it would not probably be necessary to borrow money at all after the first organization of the Government. It would be necessary to raise some fund to put the wheels of government in motion; and to do that would certainly require over a hundred thousand dollars.

The question being on Mr. Sherwood's amendment to insert "five hundred thousand," it was rejected.

Mr. LIPPITT moved to insert "three" instead of "one."

The question being on this motion, it was adopted.

Mr. HILL moved to amend the latter part of the section so as to read "and such law shall be published in at least one newspaper in each Judicial District, if one is published therein, throughout the State, for three months next preceding the election at which it is to be submitted to the people," which was agreed to.

Article VII, as amended, was then adopted, viz:

ARTICLE VII.—*State Debts.*

The Legislature shall not in any manner create any debt or debts, liability or liabilities, which shall singly or in the aggregate, with any previous debts or liabilities, exceed the sum of three hundred thousand dollars, except in case of war, to repel invasion, or suppress insurrection, unless the same shall be authorized by some law for some single object, or work, to be distinctly specified therein, which law shall provide ways and means, exclusive of loans, for the payment of the interest of such debt or liability as it falls due, and also to pay and discharge the principal of such debt or liability within twenty years from the time of the contracting thereof, and shall be irrepealable until the principal and interest thereon shall be paid and discharged; but no such law shall take effect until at a general election it shall have been submitted to the people, and have received a majority of all the votes cast for and against it at such election; and all money raised by authority of such law shall be applied only to the specific object therein stated, or to the payment of the debt thereby created, and such law shall be published in at least one newspaper in each Judicial District, if one is published therein, throughout the State, for three months next preceding the election at which it is submitted to the people.

Article IX was then taken up and passed, without debate, as follows:

ARTICLE IX.—*Mode of Amending and Revising the Constitution.*

SEC. 1. Any amendment or amendments to this Constitution may be proposed in the Senate or House of Representatives; and if the same shall be agreed to by a majority of the members elected to each of the two Houses, such proposed amendments shall be entered on their journals, with the yeas and nays taken thereon, and referred to the Legislature then next to be chosen, and shall be published for three months next previous to the time of making such choice; and if in the Legislature next chosen as aforesaid such proposed amendment or amendments shall be agreed to by two-thirds of all the members elected to each House, then it shall be the duty of the Legislature to submit such proposed amendment or amendments to the people, in such manner and at such time as the Legislature shall prescribe; and if the people shall approve and ratify such amendments, by a majority of the electors qualified to vote for members of the Legislature voting thereon, such amendment or amendments shall become part of the Constitution.

2. And if at any time two-thirds of the Senate and House of Representatives shall think it necessary to revise or change this entire Constitution, they shall recommend to the electors, at the next election for members of the Legislature, to vote for or against a Convention; and if it shall appear that a majority of the electors voting at such election have voted in favor of calling a Convention, the Legislature shall, at its next session, provide by law for calling a Convention, to be holden within six months after the passage of such law, and such Convention shall consist of members not less in number than that of both branches of the Legislature.

On motion of Mr. WOZENCRAFT, the Committee then rose, reported Articles 6, 7, and 9, to the House with sundry amendments, and had leave to sit again.

The House then, on motion of Mr. MCDOUGAL, resolved itself into Committee of the Whole, Mr. Botts in the Chair, on the report of the Committee on the Boundary.

A sufficient number of copies of the report not being prepared for the use of the members,

The Committee, on motion, rose and reported progress, and obtained leave to sit again.

Mr. GWIN moved to take up the bill of rights, as reported to the House, and commence its consideration.

Mr. NORTON thought it proper that the entire Constitution, as passed in Committee of the Whole, should be before the House, before any portion of it was taken up for final action.

Mr. HALLECK called attention to the fact that each article, as finally acted upon, must be given to the translator after a very careful revision, so that Spanish copies could be made for the use of the Spanish delegates at the same time with the English copies.

Mr. BOTTS hoped the bill of rights would not be taken up to-night. He moved that the House adjourn till 10 o'clock to-morrow.

Mr. GILBERT suggested that the bill of rights should have its first and second reading, which was merely formal.

Mr. NORTON hoped that the House would adjourn, in order to afford the Committee on the Constitution an opportunity of holding a meeting.

The House then adjourned.

SATURDAY, SEPTEMBER 22, 1849.

In Convention. Prayer by the Rev. Padre Antonio Ramirez.

The Journal of yesterday was read and approved.

The rules of the House were then amended, in pursuance of notice given by Messrs. Gwin and Jones.

Mr. DIMMICK, from the Committee on the Constitution, made a minority report on the subject of the Judiciary, which was read and referred to the Committee of the Whole.

On motion of Mr. BOTTS, the Secretary was authorized to take such measures as he might deem proper to secure the papers and records of the Convention.

On motion of Mr. MCDOUGAL, the House then resolved itself into Committee of the Whole, Mr. Lippitt in the Chair, on the report of the Committee on the Boundary.

The question being on the adoption of the report of the Committee, which proposes the following as the boundary, viz:

Commencing at the northeast corner of the State, at the intersection of the parallel of latitude forty-two degrees north with the parallel of longitude one hundred and sixteen degrees west, thence south upon and along that parallel of longitude to the boundary line between the United States and Mexico, established by the treaty of peace ratified by the said Governments at Queretaro on the 30th day of May, 1848; thence west upon and along the said boundary line to the Pacific ocean; thence in a northerly direction following the course of the Pacific coast to the said parallel of forty-two degrees of north latitude, extending one marine league into the sea from the southern to the northern boundary, and including all the bays, harbors, and islands adjacent to the said coast; and thence east from the said coast at latitude forty-two degrees north, upon and along that parallel of latitude to the place of beginning.

Mr. McDougal said: This question is so important that I would suggest some course of action, on the part of the Committee of the Whole, for the purpose of order and convenience in the despatch of business. I understand that there are a variety of opinions in relation to the proper boundary of this State. I therefore suggest that gentlemen who intend to introduce propositions on the subject present their various amendments. Let these amendments be copied by the Clerk, and copies furnished at the earliest practicable moment for the use of the members. I differ, myself, from the Committee that made this report, as to the line therein proposed. I shall therefore offer an amendment; and, as I presume others will come up, I hope the course which I have suggested will be pursued. For the present, without explaining the line which I propose as a boundary, I will simply present my amendment:

That the boundary of the State of California shall include all that tract of country from the 105th degree of longitude west from Greenwich to the Pacific coast, and from the 32d to the 42d degree of north latitude, known as the territory of California; also, the harbors, islands, and bays adjacent and along the Pacific coast; also, to extend three English miles into said Pacific ocean and along the coast thereof from the 32d to the 42d degree of latitude north; but if Congress should not grant or adopt the boundary herein set forth, then the boundary to be as follows, viz: commencing at the point of intersection of the 42d degree of north latitude, and of the 120th degree of longitude west from Greenwich, and running south on the line of said 120th degree of west longitude until it intersects the 38th degree of north latitude; thence running in a straight line in a southeasterly direction to the boundary line between the United States and Mexico as established by the treaty of May 30th, 1848, and at a point where the 116th degree of west longitude intersects said boundary line; thence running west and along said boundary line to the Pacific ocean, and extending therein three English miles; thence, running in a northeasterly direction and following the direction of the Pacific coast to the 42d degree of north latitude, to the place of beginning; also, all the islands, harbors, and bays along and adjacent to the Pacific coast.

Mr. Semple. I desire to make a few remarks, which I think may be of some service to the House on this subject. I conceive that our object is not so much to define the particular line of boundary, provided it does not run west of the range of California mountains, known as the Sierra Nevada; that it is not important about the territory on the other side, but that the great object now is to secure the admission of California as a State into the Union. There may be other questions which involve great difficulty, connected with this boundary, in the Congress of the United States. It would therefore seem proper for California to define her northern and southern boundary, and leave her eastern boundary open, subject to the action of Congress, with a proviso, that Congress shall not extend the boundary west of the Sierra Nevada. It is evidently not desirable that the State of California should extend her territory further east than the Sierra Nevada. That is the great natural boundary; better than military fortifications, to secure us from any danger from the interior. Beyond that we do not desire; but if Congress think proper to include it, it would probably be our policy to abide by that decision. It seems to me that this course is the proper one. Let us establish our northern and southern lines, and our western line, including the bays along the coast, and lands lying between the crest of the Sierra Nevada and the Pacific, and leave the Eastern line to the discretion of Congress. It would be a great drawback to this country to be left three or four years without a State Government, while Congress is debating our boundary. We must therefore, as a primary consideration, adopt such a course as will be least calculated to produce dissension in the halls of Congress. If we secure this valley lying between the Sierra Nevada and the Pacific it is all we desire. It is the limit formed by nature for this State. But if it is at all likely, after the Constitution is carried to Washington to be ratified, that a definite eastern boundary would delay our admission as a State, it is an important matter that we leave it to be settled there. Those great and exciting questions which have distracted Congress for years ought not to be brought up there by any course which we may pursue. This is the true policy of California. In almost all the other States, which have been admitted into the Union, the only material difficulty has been in regard to boundaries. It was the cause of the difficulty between Missouri and Iowa, Michigan and Ohio. In one instance, in the latter case, the military were called upon to settle the boundary line. This is the consequence of asking too much territory. If we ask for little, it seems to me that Congress would be willing to grant it; and we might insert a proviso in our Constitution that, if Congress desires to add the territory east of the Sierra Nevada, hereafter that portion may be introduced with the consent of the Legislature of California. It is a very doubtful question what is the disposition of Congress in regard to our eastern boundary. But I think it should be left to the discretion of Congress. When settled by Congress, it will be as definitely settled as if we had fixed it in our Constitution. It is said by members of Congress that one portion of the Union refused to settle the question, in regard to California, at the last session, on principle; another portion as a point of honor. It would appear that each party is determined never to yield on this question. If we can avoid exciting these sectional prejudices, it will be greatly to our interest. It is highly desirable that we should have a regularly organized Government, and I think this is the best course to effect that object.

The Chair thought it desirable, before the House proceeded any further in this discussion, that every member should clearly understand the different eastern boundaries proposed by the report and the amendment.

[The Chair then read the report and amendment in juxta-position.]

Mr. Halleck. I have a proposition which I wish to offer as a substitute for the whole. I was not aware that the subject was to be brought up this morning; and I have drawn up my proposition very hastily here at my desk. It is as follows:

[Here Mr. Halleck read a proposition with a proviso, but withdrew it to allow Mr. Gwin to submit the following, which he accepted as a portion of his amendment, as it accomplished precisely the same object which he had in view.]

Mr. Gwin then offered the following amendment to the amendment, viz:

The boundary of California shall be as follows: beginning at the point on the Pacific ocean south of San Diego, to be established by the Commissioners of the United States and Mexico, appointed under the treaty of 2d February, 1848, for running the boundary line between the territory of the U. S. and Mexico, and thence running in an easterly direction on the line fixed by said Commissioners as the boundary to the Territory of New Mexico; thence northerly on the boundary line between New Mexico and California, as laid down on the "Map of Oregon and Upper California from the survey of J. C. Fremont, and other authorities, drawn by Charles Preuss, under the order of the Senate of the U. S., Washington city, 1848," to the 42d degree of north latitude; thence due west, on the boundary line between Oregon and California, to the Pacific ocean; thence southerly along the coast of the Pacific ocean, including the islands and bays belonging to California, to the place of beginning.

Mr. Halleck then submitted his proviso, which he stated was taken nearly verbatim from the Constitution of Florida:

But the Legislature shall have power by the votes of two-thirds of both Houses to accede to such propositions as may be made by the Congress of the United States, upon the admission of the State of California into the national confederacy and Union, (if they shall be deemed just and reasonable,) to limit the eastern boundaries of the State to the Sierra Nevada, and a line drawn from some point in that range to some point of the Colorado or Gila rivers, and to organize, by Congress, a Territorial Government for that portion of California east of these boundaries, or to admit it into the Union as a distinct and separate State. And the Legislature shall make declaration of such assent by law.

Mr. Gwin accepted the proviso as an amendment to his amendment. He regarded this question of boundary as the most important that had to be settled in this Convention. He thought that more important results proceeded from it than from any other. He had devoted much attention to the subject of the boundary, knowing the difficulties which would arise in connexion with it. He had maps which he had laid before citizens of California who are well versed in this matter, and they informed him that the boundary which he proposed was that recognised by the Government of Mexico, and he believed it would be recognised by the Government of the United States, and in fact had been recognised by the official documents and maps published by order of Congress. He believed that we should in the first place fix the boundary definitely in this Constitution, so as not to leave open the question which had heretofore prevented California from having a government; but as this was a fair subject of negotiation between the two high contracting parties, and as Congress had a right to determine what our boundary should be, and might refuse to sanction the proposed boundary, then it was competent for Congress and the Legislature, under this proviso, to change it by their joint action. Any other course he thought would give rise to a great deal of difficulty in Congress.

If we include territory enough for several States, it is competent for the people and the State of California to divide it hereafter. This a privilege guarantied by the Constitution of the United States. He looked upon it as a matter of great importance that the boundary should include the entire territory, so that there could be no question hereafter. It was true this proposition embraced an immense unexplored region; that it brings in the Mormon settlement on the Salt Lake. But the Mormons have already applied for a government, and if they do not desire to remain in the State of California, it is very easy for them to form a separate government. He was informed that they were already breaking up, and would in a short time dissolve their association. At all events, we should not jeopard our admission into the Union by omitting them. If they desire it, they can have a government of their own.

The Chair stated that the question would be on the amendment of Mr. McDougal.

Mr. McCarver. I am decidedly of opinion that it is the duty of this House to fix some permanent line as the boundary of California. It is the duty of the State of California and the United States, as the two high contracting parties, to fix the boundary; and I believe it is the duty of this Convention to designate some particular limits, so that the people may know where the boundary is. There has been much collision between the Government and the new Territories that have recently been admitted into the Union; not so much because they were claiming too great an extent of territory, but because the Government wished to shape it in a particular manner. We may find the same difficulty here. We may find an attempt on the part of the Government, if we leave this an open question, to make two States bordering on the Pacific. It is our duty to refuse to come into the Union as Iowa did, unless Congress accedes to the boundary which we deem proper to adopt. A similar difficulty may take place in California. The amendment just read (Mr. Gwin's) fixes an indefinite boundary. I am of opinion that it is greatly too large, and that it leaves the boundary in an indefinite form, and in a condition that will hereafter produce agitation in Congress. It is not at all probable that the Government at home will demand such a boundary. It is true that the proviso which the gentleman accepts as a part of his proposition may have a tendency to quiet that difficulty, but it leaves the question open, to be settled hereafter by the Congress of the United States and the people of California in their legislative capacity. Is it not calculated to bring up the slavery question again? Here are two States possibly to be hereafter made out of California. There is certainly too much territory for one. The whole question as to slavery in one of these States is therefore to be brought up again. If we leave it for Congress to settle, they may divide the territory east and west instead of north and south. I contend that we should clearly and definitely settle the question of slavery for that portion of California that we expect shall remain permanently the State of California, and should not extend our boundary beyond that part over which we intend to extend our laws.

Mr. Shannon. The proposition of the gentleman from San Francisco, (Mr. Gwin,) including the entire boundary of the territory known as California, has been read. I have prepared here, sir, an amendment, which I shall offer at the proper time, after the present amendment and substitute have been disposed of. The amendment which I propose to offer leaves out a great portion of the territory of California as included within the proposition of the gentleman (Mr. Gwin;) and as he has already claimed and received the favor of the House to read his amendment, I shall claim the same privilege. My amendment is in these words:

Resolved, That the boundary of the State of California, be the following: Commencing at the point where the one hundred and twentieth (120) parallel of longitude west from Greenwich intersects the forty-second degree of north latitude (forming the southern boundary of the Territory of Oregon;) thence following said one hundred and twentieth parallel, southerly, to its intersection with the thirty-eighth degree of north latitude; thence in a southeasterly direction to the point where the thirty-fifth degree of north latitude crosses the river Colorado; thence southerly, following high water mark on the east bank of said river, to the boundary line established by the late treaty between the United States and Mexico, dated at Queretaro, May 30th, 1848; thence westerly along and upon said line to Pacific ocean; thence following the course of said Pacific coast to the parallel of forty-two degrees north latitude, extending one marine league into the sea from said coast, and including all the bays, harbors, and islands adjacent to said coast, to said forty-second degree, and thence easterly along and upon said parallel of latitude to the place of beginning.

The advantages of this line I deem very great; for the reason that it will include every prominent and valuable point in the territory; every point which is of any real value to the State, including also the river Colorado, and that point which will be so important at our southern extremity as a port of entry and depot for the trade carried on between the interior provinces of Mexico and the lower portion of the State of California. Including these points, and all the rest included in the boundary reported by the Committee, it possesses another advantage; it brings the State within reasonable limits—very nearly the same limits proposed by my colleague from Sacramento (Mr. McDougal;) that is—following the crest of the Sierra Nevada. But it makes a more distinct and perfect boundary line, and possesses the further advantage of giving regularity to the width of the State. If you observe, it follows nearly in a parallel line along the coast. It makes the territory nearly of an equal width at the northern and southern points. It follows the coast in its southeast bend, nearly in a parallel direction. As to the proposition now before the House, (Mr. Gwin's,) I cannot but regard it as one of the most objectionable that could possibly be adopted by this Convention. I consider that it is indispensably necessary that we should have more fixed limits to the new State of California. I believe, if we do not, it will occasion in the Congress of the United States a tremendous struggle. Leaving an immense extent of territory at the east, to be included or not at the discretion of Congress, it will certainly leave open a subject for contest. The slaveholding States of the South will undoubtedly strive their utmost to exclude as much of that territory as they can, and contract the limits of the new free State within the smallest possible bounds. They will naturally desire to leave open as large a tract of country as they can for the introduction of slavery hereafter. The Northern States will oppose it because that question is left open—the very difficulty which it is our policy to avoid. This is an immense territory which the gentleman proposes to include. It is very unwieldy and could never be subjected to the operation of our laws. A great portion of it can be of no advantage to us. A vast deal of it is an immense unexplored region—a barren waste. The northeastern portion of it is, as the gentleman states, settled now by a large population of people, whose religious tenets certainly form a great barrier to their introduction among the people of California. I know not upon what authority the gentleman states that these settlements are now breaking up—that therefore no difficulty can occur hereafter on that ground. Mr. Chairman, these settlements are only forming. They are day by day acquiring strength, and becoming more permanently fixed as a great community; they are rapidly increasing in wealth, population, and stability. They may, after some time, become an immense and unwiedly body, with numbers of elders striving for the control and influence of the sect; and when all these different influences become struggling against each other, they may break up. But now it is not the case, nor is it likely that it will ever be so; for they are not contracted within narrow bounds as they were in the United States. They have an immense extent of territory, which as they divide they can extend themselves over, and form new settlements; and that, sir, I take it, will be the natural course of events with them. But the great difficulty with them is, that they have no representation in this Convention. How can you force them to come within the State of California? Will not the objection be a valid one, that they have no representation here. They will say: we had no hand in forming this Constitution which you endeavor to force upon us, and we will not submit to it. It seems to me that such an objection would be most just and proper. And the gentleman sees it too, from the fact that he endeavors to get over the difficulty by suggesting the probability of their breaking up hereafter, and abandoning their settlements. But we are told that they are already leaving there in great numbers. Very well, sir. They are and have been for the last eighteen months; they have been coming to the gold mines and working hard; but when they do so, you almost invariably find that they return back to their homes, carrying with them a great portion of the wealth of California, to enrich them there and render their stability more certain. But even suppose they would quietly submit to the government which we are establishing here. Just imagine a member of the Assembly or of the Senate, starting from the Salt Lake settlement and traveling three or four months to reach the Legislature of California, and traveling three or four months back to reach his constituents. The only way in which I can see that we could get over that difficulty, would be to provide for a perpetual legislature here; otherwise it would be impossible for them ever to keep up their proper representation. For these reasons, Mr. Chairman, I shall certainly oppose the introduction of any territory as a part of the State of California that would render the State so unwiedly as this; while, at the same time, I shall oppose any proposition that leaves out any important point which may be valuable to the State hereafter.

Mr. Hoppe. I have not made up my mind fully, Mr. Chairman, whether it will be best to include the whole of California as laid down upon this map, (Fremont's,) or to have a fixed boundary defined; but from what knowledge I have of the country, and what I have seen, I think if there is any definite boundary to be made, that that proposed by the Committee is decidedly preferable to any other yet proposed—taking the longitude of 116. Any person who has been over the tract of country northeast knows that it is nothing but an isolated desert, until you get to the region of the Salt Lake. The land on this side of the desert is naturally separated from that on the other side, and should be kept so. On the western side of this boundary line, 116° W. longitude, there is a great deal of desirable land before you reach the base of the Sierra Nevada. It is supposed by many that it embraces a good deal of valuable mineral land; but if we make the Sierra Nevada the dividing ridge we have no protection from the territory beyond. Depredations will be committed within our limits. How will you reach the offenders by process, when all they have to do is to withdraw a short distance on the other side. They are then out of reach. We want some line beyond this range of mountains. My friend from Sacramento (Mr. Shannon) stated that he desired to include the Colorado, because there might be valuable seaports there. I think we should leave out the Colorado altogether. The Mormons have settled there, and if they can make a good seaport of it, it will be valuable to the interior, and be of decided advantage to us also in our southern trade. If the question comes up, unless my mind should be made up to include the whole of the territory of California, I shall vote in favor of 116° west longitude as our eastern boundary line. I believe there is no other that would suit us so well; and I hope gentlemen will take its advantages into consideration.

Mr. Botts. I entertain very different views on this subject from most of the gentlemen who have addressed the House. I think it is true, with my friend from San Francisco, (Mr. Gwin,) that this is an exceedingly important question, and one that we should exercise due deliberation in considering. There is but one question, in my mind, in forming this Constitution, that I would condescend to consider with any reference to the views of Congress. It is the only one that they have a right to exercise any control over in this Constitution; and that question is contained in the clause now under consideration. All other provisions in our Constitution affect ourselves, and ourselves only, and we have a right to shape them as we think proper; but the question of boundary affects the interests of others whom Congress holds in charge. It is for this reason that I like so much the character of the amendment proposed a little while ago by the gentleman from Monterey, (Mr. Halleck,) leaving it to Congress to reduce the boundary to certain limits, if such course be deemed advisable. This is the only proper subject of negotiation between the people of California and the Congress of the United States. I say, then, with respect to this eastern line, I am willing after the Spanish fashion, to leave it to those *buenos humbres* in Congress and our Legislature to decide. Let us define the line; let us, upon our part, claim a line, but let us provide also that that line may be altered by those two high contracting parties. I would not insist upon two-thirds of the Assembly; I would desire that it should be decided by a majority of the Assembly of the State of California, together with a majority of the Congress of the United States—our Assembly against their Assembly. When these two agree, the line determined upon by them should be our eastern boundary. There is one point upon which I entertain very different views from most of the gentlemen on this floor; and that is, that we can be accommodated or benefited in the slightest degree by having a very extensive territory in California. This thing is better understood at home than here, and the difficulty will be in obtaining what we ought to desire—small and contracted limits. We claim a representation in the Senate of the United States equal to that of any other State in the Union. The question will be there, for how small a territory do you claim this power? Do you remember, Mr. Chairman, that the little State of Delaware, because of her size, is the most powerful State in the Union? Do you remember that her ratio of representation in the Senate of the United States is infinitely greater than that of any other State in the Union?—a fact that formed an almost insuperable obstacle to the adoption of the Constitution of the United States. Sir, the difficulty will be to contract and not to expand your limits; and, if you are seeking power for your State, your object ought to be to make it as small as possible. I wish we could get it divided into two or three States, as some gentleman suggests. Instead of having two votes with the hundred and twenty thousand people here, we would have six votes in the Senate of the United States. But there is no danger of this. They are too vigilant at home to permit anything of this kind. It is upon this subject that we ought to be particularly guarded. Inasmuch as it is a fair subject of negotiation, I would not propose the original resolution of the mover, (Mr. Gwin,) but would suggest a modification of it somewhat in this wise: The eastern boundary shall follow the Sierra Nevada as far as that range of mountains extends on Fremont's map, and thence in a diriect line to the mouth of the Gila. That may be the very boundary proposed by some of the gentlemen who have submitted propositions, but I merely throw it out casually as a suggestion. It is a boundary which, I understand, would include a very important portion of country in the lower part of the State. But if Congress should desire to include a greater extent of territory than that, it can only be done by the joint action of Congress and the Legislature of California. My object is, to secure to the inhabitants of this country just as much power as I believe they are entitled to in the public councils of the nation; and I am not willing that all that extent of country embraced between the Pacific ocean and the boundary laid down in Fremont's map, as proposed in the amendment, on the east, should be represented in the Senate of the United States by only two members. Sir, the extent of country laid down by the first part of the proposition (Mr. Gwin's) is probably about fifty times as great as that proposed by other members here. Suppose Congress should adopt that line? There is no power in your Assembly to alter the line so adopted. It becomes the law of the land, and a part of the Constitution. But whilst I permit that to be done, if the Congress of the United States insist upon it, it can only be done under the approval and joint consent of Congress and the State of California. If it is to be forced upon us at all, let us only have it upon a joint vote of the two parties. Let us fix the line which we think ought to be the true and proper line of the State of California. The question then occurs, which is the true and proper line; what is the line which it is to our interest to adopt? Is there a gentleman on this floor who hesitates between the two lines—the original, reported by the Committee, or that afterwards proposed by the gentleman from Monterey, (Mr. Halleck?) Can the extreme eastern line command half a dozen votes? I propose to amend the proposition of the gentleman from Monterey, by adopting some much more limited line for the eastern boundary than that proposed by him. My proposition would be, after fixing this limited boundary: "But this boundary may be altered by the Congress of the United States, if that alteration is confirmed by a vote of the Assembly of California." I do not see why we should require a two-thirds vote on this question. It is a fair subject of negotiation between the parties. It does not require a two-third vote on the part of Congress, and I do not see why it should require it here. I suggest to the gentlemen who favor the narrow line, that it is a very important matter that you modify the resolution so as to make your expression of opinion state fairly and clearly the desire of this House. I shall go for the principle embodied in the amendment, while I am opposed to the details.

Mr. Hastings. Before voting upon this matter it is important that we understand what is proposed by the various gentlemen who have made propositions. The Committee, Mr. Chairman, propose the boundary which is now before the House. In view of certain facts which I do not believe are in possession of many of the members of this House, the Committee was constituted mostly, if not entirely, of persons who are acquainted not only with this side of the Sierra Nevada, but with the other side also. The Committee were of opinion that it was important to reduce the territory as much as possible; but, at the same time, important to include all of the most valuable portions of the country. We found that to fix the boundary of the Sierra Nevada, and follow the crest of that chain of mountains as the line, would intersect the ocean to the northward of San Diego; and that the parallel of 116 deg. longitude would strike the boundary on the south, but sixty miles or one degree to the eastward of San Diego. Even the boundary as reported by the Committee throws the whole territory into a triang lar form, running to a point at the south. This was done because it was understood by the Committee that the territory on the south, in the vicinity of the Rio Colorado, was entirely worthless, and the river not navigable there. We therefore preferred to fix a boundary there, including as little as possible of that sterile region. But at the north where the territory becomes wider, it was extended for the purpose of including a valuable portion of the country—a portion of the country with which every member of the Committe was well acquainted. In the first place, it includes the country immediately east of the Sierra Nevada, extending about two hundred and fifty miles from the base, and including the rivers and streams of the snowy region. Upon those rivers and streams we find often agricultural lands well adapted to grazing purposes, and in all respects a valuable agricultural region. This tract of country extends along the Sierra Nevada on the eastern side as far as parallel of longitude 116, and includes what is called Savan, Trout river, Meriot river, and various lakes and settlements in that territory. Beyond that parallel of longitude is nothing but one vast sterile plain to the Great Salt Lake, now occupied by the Mormons. This consideration induced the Committee to propose the eastern boundary at 116 deg. It occurs to me that it is the only practicable and the best boundary that can be or has been proposed. If the boundary is fixed upon the Sierra Nevada, a valuable portion of the country is rejected. If, on the other hand, the entire country is included, then the objections are immovable. I can scarcely enumerate them all. The gentleman from San Francisco (Mr. Gwin,) who proposes this boundary, remarks that it is important that we leave this question of the eastern boundary unsettled; but, in the next breath, he proposes to fix it.

Mr. Gwin. I said it was important we should settle it.

Mr. Hastings. I understand the gentleman to propose that we should include the entire territory, and then fix it, if Congress chooses, by including a smaller boundary. I do not regard that as a settled boundary; it extends to the vast chain of the Rocky mountains. By the nearest route to the coast, it is fifteen hundred miles. This is a fact known in Congress as well as in California. The boundary which the gentleman proposes, includes all the territory from the Pacific coast to the Rocky mountains and New Mexico. It is urged that we ought to include this entire territory and leave it open, in order not to interfere with a question of vast importance which has agitated Congress for some time past. Sir, we ought to interfere with that question. We ought to settle it. Congress cannot within any reasonable space of time settle it. We would have had a Territorial Government now could Congress have settled that exciting question. If we leave this question of boundary open, we leave the question of slavery open. If we fix the boundary, we fix that question also. We relieve Congress on that important point. We leave the question out by deciding it for ourselves. Sir, if you leave that question with Congress again, I can assure you that for years we shall have no government here with the sanction of the Government of the United States. But gentlemen maintain that it is very important to include the whole territory, if possible, because if we settle the question of slavery now for the entire territory it is forever settled; and Congress would be very much obliged to us for doing it; but if we do not include the whole territory, the question will be brought up again in Congress, and that very fact would give rise to endless discussion when we apply for admission. Now, sir, if we propose a thing of this kind, I know the result. I know the South will insist that we have no right, as a State here, to present our claims to Congress for a State Government extending over a country as large in extent as all the Northern States of the Union. The South will readily see that the object is to force the settlement of this question. The South will never agree to it. It raises the question in all its bitterness and in its worst form before Congress. On the other hand, if we propose to settle the question for ourselves, in reference to a territory which is not too extensive for a State, Congress cannot for a moment hesitate to sanction our action. I can assure gentlemen that the new State of California will not be permitted to settle the great question of slavery for a territory of such vast extent as that proposed—an extent of territory as large as all the non-slaveholding States of the Union. Will the South permit it? No, sir. It will be insisted by the South that we have been urged to do it by influences brought to bear upon us from the North. We will never be admitted in that way as a State. The gentleman (Mr. Gwin) remarks that, in reference to including the whole territory, it is no objection that the Mormon settlements are formed in the interior. Now, sir, it occurs to me as a very serious objection. While the Mormon settlements exist there, we cannot be admitted into the Union with that boundary; because they are a portion of the people of the United States prepared to adopt our institutions and establish a government for themselves. They have already applied to Congress to establish a Territorial Government for them. Suppose these two propositions are brought up before Congress at the same time; we applying for a State Government, and they for a Territorial Government; both propositions coming from the same territory. Can we be admitted into the Union claiming the same territory, at the same time that they call for a Territorial Government over it? No, sir; for the Mormons will insist, and justly too, that they had nothing to do with the formation of our government—that they had no representation in this Convention, and never gave their assent to the Constitution which we attempt to impose upon them. How would the Congress of the United States look upon it? Would they say to the Mormons, you were bound to take part in the formation of that government; if you did not, it was your own fault. Certainly not. The answer would be, you are as well entitled to a government for yourselves as the territory on the coast. We will grant governments to both; but we cannot grant to California this enormous extent of territory which she claims. I repeat, Mr. Chairman, that if you leave this boundary question open, you leave open the question of slavery; and if you do, sir, we get no boundary at all, and cannot have a State Government for three or four years. If we fix the boundary within reasonable limits, and Congress receives our proposition, the question of slavery is settled. Why not at once say at what point the boundary shall be? What possible cause to hesitate will Congress have if we claim no more than is sufficient for a State? I am very sure that, if gentlemen who favor the boundary of the gentleman from Monterey (Mr. Halleck) were acquainted with the country east of the Sierra Nevada which it excludes, but which is included in the report of the Committee, that they would greatly prefer the latter. I have traveled all over it, sir, and the Committee are well acquainted with that country. We have a vast mineral region as well as agricultural, on this side of the Sierra Nevada; but I am of opinion the other side affords probably equal agricultural resources and as much gold as this. The line proposed by the Committee includes all that is valuable and no more. The Committee were very cautious to include as little as possible, and yet omit no portion of the territory that was deemed valuable.

Mr. Gwin. As this is a very important question, and several amendments have been proposed this morning, and it is important that the House should understand them before they are voted upon, I propose that the subject be laid aside, and that the Secretary be directed to prepare copies of the amendments to be laid before the members, so that when the subject comes up again we may be prepared to act upon it.

Mr. McDougal. I hope the motion will prevail.

Mr. Botts. I am of the gentleman's opinion that we had better not take the question this morning; but I do not see why we should yet dispose of it. I am ignorant of the character of the country proposed to be included, and have not made up my mind definitely as to the proper boundary. There may be gentlemen here who are prepared to throw some light on the subject. If it appears that nobody has anything further to remark upon it, I shall be very willing that the Committee rise and report progress.

Mr. Gwin. My object is this. We are to debate certain propositions which different gentlemen have made. Before we can do so understandingly, we must have these propositions on our tables in writing, in order to comprehend them properly.

Mr. Botts. There may be other gentlemen who would be glad to make remarks upon this subject, and throw some light upon it. I am not prepared myself to do so. If there are none, I concur with the gentleman.

On motion of Mr. Gwin, the Committee then rose and reported progress.

On motion of Mr. Halleck, the House resolved that when it adjourn it would adjourn to 10 o'clock A. M. on Monday next.

Mr. Gwin then moved that the House now go into consideration of the amendments, adopted in Committee of the Whole, to so much of the report of the Committee on the Constitution as is styled the "Bill of Rights."

After some discussion, as to the propriety of taking up the Bill of Rights before the entire Constitution was passed through Committee of the Whole, the motion was rejected.

Mr. Gwin, from the Committee of Ways and Means of defraying the expenses of the State Government, made a report, which, on his motion, was laid on the table to be read on Monday next.

On motion, the House then granted Mr. Ellis ten days' leave of absence.

On motion, the House then adjourned.

MONDAY, SEPTEMBER 24, 1849.

In Convention. Prayer by the Rev. Mr. Willey. Journal of Saturday read and approved.

Mr. Norton, Chairman of the Committee on the Constitution, reported the article on miscellaneous provisions; which was read and referred to the Committee of the Whole.

Mr. Shannon, on leave, made some verbal amendments to his proposition, and introduced a proviso prohibiting Congress from dividing the State of California by running any line east and west.

Mr. Gwin, on leave, made some verbal amendments to his amendment.

On motion of Mr. Wozencraft, Mr. Vermuele, a member elect from San Joaquin, was introduced, sworn, and admitted to his seat.

On motion, the House then resolved itself into Committee of the Whole, Mr. Lippitt in the Chair, on the report of the Committee on the Boundary.

After some discussion as to the order of amendments, the Chair decided that Mr. Gwin's amendment, with the proviso offered by Mr. Halleck and accepted by Mr. Gwin, was before the House.

Mr. Jones said that he hoped the gentleman from Monterey, (Mr. Halleck,) would explain the object of the two-third rule adopted in his proviso. We might, through the absence of one-third of the members of the Legislature, be kept out of a State Government for years. He could not see what object the gentleman had in view by requiring that two-thirds of the members of the Legislature accede to a proposition passed by a majority in Congress. He was clearly in favor of a majority himself, ever since Mr. Van Buren was knocked in the head by the two-third rule.

Mr. Halleck said that it was because the first portion of the proviso was taken from the Constitution of Florida, and not a word of objection was made to it by Congress. Congress admitted the State with that provision, and he thought that was a sufficient reason.

Mr. Jones said it was his understanding of the matter that, if our boundary was not accepted by Congress, Congress should make a proposition to us, and we should accept it or reject it as we pleased. He thought that the State Government should at least have its boundaries well defined; but in relation to the precedent of Florida, as far as the proposition goes, Congress had nothing to say. If Florida chose to impose a two-third rule upon her own Legislature, it was not a subject for the consideration of Congress. He preferred having a majority against a majority, and then any reasonable proposition made by Congress would certainly be accepted by the State Legislature; but this one-third are certainly the most stubborn part of the Legislature. If in order, he would therefore move to strike out that portion and insert a majority.

Mr. HALLECK had no objection if the original mover of the amendment chose to accept it.

Mr. GWIN accepted the amendment; and the Secretary then, by order of the Chair, read the three propositions before the Committee, viz: the report of the Committee on the Boundary; the proposition of Mr. McDougal, and the proposition of Mr. Gwin, with Mr. Halleck's proviso.

Mr. McCARVER wished to offer an amendment to the proposition of the gentleman from Monterey, (Mr. Halleck.)

The CHAIR stated that it would not be in order, as there were three propositions before the Committee. If the gentleman chose to accept the amendment, it could be introduced in that way.

Mr. McCARVER said he desired to shape it so that the Legislature should not entertain any proposition from Congress, fixing a boundary line. He thought if the boundary was left open, Congress might cut this State in two by running a line east and west—which he was decidedly opposed to.

Mr. HALLECK remarked that no line could come west farther than the Sierra Nevada under this proposition.

Mr. McCARVER said it was his desire to fix a permanent boundary line. He wished to amend the proposition so that neither Congress nor the Legislature could change that line.

Mr. HALLECK. I will endeavor to explain the object of the united proposition. In the first place, the boundary includes all of Upper California, as has always been recognized by Mexico and by the Congress of the United States, so far as any action has been had on that subject. By the treaty with Mexico and the discussions with Mexico previous to the treaty, and the maps that have been published of California since that time, and all the orders which have proceeded from our Government, these limits have been acknowledged and recognised as the limits of Upper California. The first part of the proposition embraces such limits as have always been heretofore recognised as the territory of Upper California. It is asked what is the object of embracing the whole territory? As was said the other day, it closes forever this agitating question of slavery in all the territory this side of the Rocky mountains. But objections are urged against including those limits—that we include more territory than we are capable of governing. Before taking up these objections, let me state one other point in connexion with this boundary. It is known that there is a large number of Americans settled beyond the Sierra Nevada, a peculiar class of people, it is true, but nevertheless American citizens. Large numbers of American citizens are travelling from the United States to the portions of California this side of the Sierra Nevada—the portion which is to be included in the State Government. Numerous questions are arising and will continue to arise, in that portion of the country, between the members of this large emigration. These questions must be decided somewhere. Probably half a dozen or a dozen murders have taken place during the past year in that country. Where are these persons to seek justice, if we limit California to the Sierra Nevada, or to a meridian of longitude a few degrees beyond. All cases that occur beyond that limit cannot be tried in any court, because there is no government in that country, and if we leave this question of slavery open in that portion of the territory, there will be no government for the next five years, and these people will be obliged to resort to lynch law for the punishment of crime. Now it is said that Congress will not agree to so large a State, unless some provision is introduced that these limits may be narrowed down. Such objection I have heard from very high authority, and I have no doubt it is a valid one. It is therefore proposed to remove that objection by introducing a proviso to that effect. Then it is said that we ought not to include that portion of the territory in our government, because it is not represented here. I think this objection will disappear when we consider it. In the first place, it was impossible to get a representation here; we would have been obliged to put off this Convention five or six months longer. That portion of the country is without the limits of the organized districts of California, and there are sufficient precedents in all the States of the Union, for excluding portions of the territory of the State not included in organized districts of that State. Those members who are acquainted with the history of New York will recollect that the county of Hamilton for many years was excluded under the old Constitution from taking any part in the deliberations of the Legislature, because it was beyond the organized portions of the State; and even now it has no representation. I do not consider that a valid objection. Other examples of other States were mentioned to me yesterday; and I have no doubt every gentleman can recollect examples in the history of his own State. Another objection which I have heard to this proviso is, that we do not become a State until the Legislature and Congress agree upon those limits. Such is not the case. The very object of putting it in this form was to make us a State with the whole boundary and whole limits immediately, but to give Congress the power afterwards to limit our boundary to a smaller State. Suppose this amendment and proviso should pass and be approved of by the people of California; that it should go to Congress, and they should admit California into the Union with this Constitution and this amendment and proviso. Is not California a State instantly on the ratification of the Constitution; a State, too, with the entire boundary as defined in that amendment? But then Congress, together with the Legislature of California, may limit these boundaries, and organise, if they choose, a Territorial Government for that portion of the country beyond the Sierra Nevada, or beyond the line through the great desert. Many think it more expedient to make the boundary line in the great desert itself, instead of the coast of the Sierra Nevada. This can be done under the present proposition and proviso, by joint agreement between Congress and the Legislature. It possesses this advantage over the boundary reported by the Committee—that while that line comes this side of the mouth of the Gila river and within forty or fifty miles of San Diego, cutting off a portion of the southern part of Upper California, if I remember right, that is already inhabited—throwing without the limits of California a portion of the people who have always belonged to California and have taken part in its government—by this proviso, the boundary line cannot come this side of the mouth of the Gila, nor this side of the northern part of the Sierra Nevada. There is no danger then of the State being divided by a line of latitude, as apprehended by the gentleman from Sacramento, (Mr. McCarver,) which I think would be very objectionable. It is not my purpose to go into any detailed argument. I merely rose to make this brief explanation of the effect of the united proposition, as I understand it. I have endeavored to draw up the proviso so as to obviate all the objections that I have heard on the other side of the House.

Mr. SEMPLE. I desire to state my views in regard to this proposition. At the proper time, I will offer an ordinance which is equally competent and will ensure the same general result. If we make no boundary for California at all, the Congress of the United States will fix the boundary. They are under particular obligations to give us all that California ever had; they will have no right to dismember this territory. If this be the case, then we will take the entire boundary to New Mexico. I say then, if we pass an ordinance determining that, in the formation of the new State, they shall not come east of a certain line, it will accomplish the same object proposed by the gentlemen from Monterey and San Francisco, (Mr. Halleck and Mr. Gwin.) In the first instance, the Constitution of the United States provides that—"New States may be admitted by Congress into this Union; but no new State shall be formed or erected within the jurisdiction of any other State, nor any State be formed by the junction of two or more States, or parts of States, without the consent of the Legislatures of the States concerned, as well as of Congress." This, then, gives the power to form new States, with the consent of the Legislature, either within the jurisdiction of one State already existing, or a new State to be admitted. I deny, then, that Congress has a right to dismember California without her consent; and I doubt very much whether we ourselves possess the right to dismember the territory without the consent of Congress. I contend that Congress must admit us with our whole boundary, or reject our Constitution claiming that boundary. The gentleman from Monterey (Mr. Halleck) has fully answered the objections which may be urged against including the whole boundary of California. I think the House is decided in opinion that we should take it all in.

It is a duty we owe to the emigrants passing the deserts, and the people residing there, to take care of them until they are otherwise provided for. I shall certainly vote for the amendment. I never can consent to have this State divided east and west, so as to have our coast cut in two. It is well in the formation of the State to provide permanently against any danger upon that point. You will find in the admission of Maine that there was just such a proposition made there originally. It will be recollected by the House, that none of the original States had their boundaries defined. Virginia claimed all the territory from the Atlantic to the Western ocean. They knew just as little about the extent of her boundary west as we do about the extent of our boundary east. The boundary of Virginia once included the very territory that we now occupy. If you look at the old charter of Virginia, you will find that she runs to the great Western ocean. In the territory of Massachusetts, Maine was included. It was a district of Massachusetts; and the gentleman will observe in the preamble of the act admitting Maine, that it was constituted an independent State by an act of the Massachusetts Legislature, which was ratified by Congress as provided in the Constitution; and she barely passed an act of four lines and a half, saying Maine was a member of the Union. It would seem, therefore, that in the admission of this State we would be doing ourselves injustice to dismember California. In proposing to do this, we should bear in mind another consideration. It will be recollected that not many years ago there was a very considerable trade carried on between San Diego and the interior of Mexico, and that there still exist strong inducements for a lucrative commerce with the interior provinces of Mexico. The State of California ought to have the means of throwing out military escorts for the protection of that portion of the country. It is important that it should be protected. It is a matter of justice to the southern part of California that we should include a sufficient portion of the territory south to protect our trade there. From this time, when the port of San Diego is open to the vessels of the United States, there will be an immense trade carried on to the interior States of Mexico. The Indian tribes inhabiting that portion of the country are almost invariably hostile and disposed to commit murders and robberies on the traders. If the State is so extended in that part of the territory as to throw out military defences, you will find that much smaller parties can carry on that interior trade, and that it will be greatly facilitated. Suppose we include the whole territory recognised as California, and in a few years we find that southern trade profitable to the State, is it likely she would consent to dismember that portion of her territory? It is proper we should claim it, when we can get the whole just as readily as we can a part. Congress has no right to dismember us; and if she does, it can only be with the consent of our Legislature. I trust, therefore, that the amendment will prevail, including originally the entire territory of California, giving Congress the power to accept that, but not to dismember the State or reduce these limits, unless with the consent of the Legislature.

Mr. MCCARVER. The gentleman's position is not tenable. What was the position of Louisiana? It stood in the same position as California. The territory included not only Louisiana but

Arkansas; Missouri included the new State of Iowa and a portion of the Territory of Nebraska. Has anybody ever questioned the right of Congress to divide these territories? I venture to say that the very first question that gentlemen propose to settle by leaving an open boundary, will be the obstacle that will keep us out of the Union—the question of slavery. It is a very desirable thing, and as an individual opposed to slavery, I desire to settle it; but do gentlemen suppose that the South will acquiesce in this arrangement—that they will permit us to settle the question of slavery in a territory as large as all the slaveholding States of the Union? It is the duty of the people of California to fix their boundary definitely. We want our two Senators in the Senate chamber to maintain the interests and supply the wants of California; we want our Representatives in Congress as early as we can. What prevented Congress from providing a Territorial Government for California at the last session? It was nothing else but the slavery question; and we should avoid anything calculated to keep us from taking our position in the Confederacy at as early a period as practicable. Now, sir, I am decidedly of opinion that this will be a barrier against the admission of California into the Union; and that we may be detained several years while they are debating this question in the halls of Congress. I deem it absolutely essential that we should fix a permanent boundary north, south, east, and west. We should leave no boundary open; we should leave no question open that would be the means of keeping us out of the Union. The boundary proposed in the report of the Committee is a reasonable one. It gives us a moderate sized State, such as cannot be objected to in Congress. I shall sustain that or some boundary of a similar character. But I am decidedly in favor of submitting to Congress a fixed and permanent boundary, which I am confident they will not reject. That boundary is as advantageous as any I have heard suggested, and unless I see a better one, I shall vote for it.

Mr. Hastings. As the joint proposition of the gentleman from San Francisco and the gentleman from Monterey, is now before the House, I wish to examine the effect and object designed to be accomplished by it, and what the result of its adoption would be. The object is to establish a State Government here as speedily as possible, and to effect the consumation of that State organization at once. But, sir, that object is wholly defeated if we include all this territory, for the reason that I mentioned yesterday, and for the reason that my colleague, (Mr. McCarver,) has urged this morning, and which I shall not repeat. It is clear to my mind that this proposition raises the question of slavery; it is also clear that that question is settled beyond dispute, if we establish a reasonable boundary. Congress has not, in that event, the right or power to interfere with us; no right to say whether slavery shall or shall not be introduced. But if we include the whole territory, Congress has that right. We have a very low estimate of the sagacity of the South, if we suppose they will overlook this point. They will naturally say: You, a few Californians on the other side of the continent, assume to settle the great question of slavery for a tract of territory which must ultimately constitute thirteen or fourteen States of the Union. What an important position you assume—what an important object you attempt to accomplish! No, California, you cannot be made the tool to accomplish an object like this. East, west, and north, and south, combined, will oppose it. We cannot—we should not attempt this. But, sir, there is another reason why we defeat ourselves—why we cannot, with this boundary, obtain admission into the Union. It is this: that a proposition from a vast population of that region east of the great desert, is now or will soon be before Congress, calling for the establishment of a Territorial Government. It is the Mormon population of the Salt Lake. Their proposition will probably be presented to Congress at the same time with ours. What must Congress do? Can they give us all that territory, a portion of which is demanded by these people who actually occupy it. No, sir; they cannot; they can only reasonably say: Your proposition cannot be entertained. You have no right to include all that territory. It contains a vast population as much entitled to respect as you are, amounting to thirty or forty thousand souls, twelve or fifteen hundred miles remote from your seat of Government—out of the reach of your laws or authority, and impossible for them to be represented in your Legislature. We must consider their rights and interests as well as yours. They ask that we shall grant them a Territorial Government. You ask a State Government. We are willing to do both, but we are not willing to include the Mormons in the proposition of the State of California. Theirs is a distinct proposition, originating from a distinct population, having distinct interests. This, sir, would be an insuperable obstacle to our admission. But here I come to a proposition contained in the proviso, which admits that all this may be true; that there are very strong reasons why we ought not to include the whole territory, but says we are willing, since it is useless to insist upon including the whole territory, to accept such boundary, including such extent of territory as Congress may choose to fix, provided they do not extend it westward beyond certain limits. Now, it is contended that the great object is to acquire speedy admission into the Union; but instead of making a proposition to Congress, we ask Congress to make a proposition to us, and say that our Legislature will probably accede to it. The proposition is now to come from Congress, and we, through our Legislature, must accede to it before we are a State. Whereas, on the other, if we make a proposition, fixing the boundary ourselves, the moment Congress accedes to it, our boundary is permanently established, and no further proposition is necessary. Everybody must see that it is a rare specimen of independence in California to dictate to Congress, that if they do not think proper to give us all the territory for a State Government, they may form a Territorial Government on the other side. This proviso says: "and to organize a Territorial Government for that portion of California east of this boundary, or to admit it into the Union as a separate State." This is valuable information for Congress. When they have fixed upon the boundary of California, they can go on and form a government for another Territory if they please. The design of the proposition may be, to fix the question of slavery; but I can hardly imagine that the gentleman who introduces it, can suppose that when Congress proposes a boundary to us, that we have settled the question of slavery for that vast territory. This view is fallacious. It cannot be maintained. But admit that we settle the question of slavery for the State of California, what do we do beyond this State? What right have we tell to Congress that beyond it they may form a Territorial Government. I do not know how we are to settle the question of slavery, when Congress is to settle all beyond our boundaries. Now a word in regard to the advantages which we derive from establishing an absolute and definite boundary. If we establish a boundary absolutely, which we have beyond doubt a right to do, Congress must admit us with that boundary, provided we do not include territory sufficient for an independent republic. The proposition then comes directly from us. When ratified by Congress, all is done. We are a State of the Confederacy. The act is consummated; no further action is necessary. Congress would view it in this light: Here comes a direct proposition from the people of California, reasonable in itself, and claiming only what they have a right to claim. They have settled the question of slavery within their own limits; those limits do not embrace too much territory. We have no right to refuse our sanction to it. On the other hand, we find that Congress would be at a loss. They would say: We have every disposition to do all we can for the people of California, but they ask us to fix their boundary—to make them a proposition; they have said nothing, unless it be, that they want territory amply sufficient for an independent republic—independent of the United States and of the world. Now, sir, I contend that by making a direct proposition, and fixing the boundary definitely, we at once come into the Union beyond all doubt. We claim to exercise no authority in settling the great questions which Congress has been unable to settle. For these reasons, and many others, I shall oppose the joint proposition, and sustain the report of the Committee. I am satisfied, having been upon the ground and viewed the territory myself, that it includes all that is valuable beyond the Sierra Nevada, and is liable to none of the objections which have been urged against the amendment of the gentleman from San Francisco, or the proviso of the gentleman from Monterey.

Mr. BOTTS. I had thought this morning that nothing could have called me upon my feet to-day; but, sir, I should be recreant to every principle of justice that I have ever supported, if I could sit in silence and listen to propositions that have been made upon this floor. On Saturday I was inclined to leave the decision of this boundary to the Congress of the United States; but I hope I am not one of those who may not receive enlightenment from discussion; that I am not one of those fixed and immoveable human beings who, when they lay down a proposition, will never vary from it. I have been enlightened here to-day. I have been taught by an open avowal of a member on this floor, what is the object and intention with which this extreme eastern boundary is to be fixed, and the disposition of it left to Congress. Mr. Chairman, I have looked upon it, and do look upon it, that the spirit which has animated a certain portion of the Union, inducing them to claim the right of settling this question of slavery in the Congress of the United States, as a most unrighteous, unholy, and unconstitutional spirit. And, sir, I am not ready to pander on this floor to such a spirit, either directly or indirectly. I understand now from one of the gentlemen that constitute the new firm of Gwin & Halleck—the gentleman from Monterey, who avows at last the reason for extending this eastern boundary beyond the natural limits of California, that it will settle, in the United States, the question of slavery over a district beyond our reasonable and proper limits, which we do not want, but which we are to take in for the purpose of arresting further dispute on the subject of slavery in that territory. It has been well asked if the gentleman can suppose that Southern men can be asleep when such a proposition is sounded in their ears. Sir, the avowal of this doctrine on the floor of this House, necessarily and of itself, excites feelings that I had hoped might be permitted to slumber in my breast while I was a resident of California. But it is not to be. This harrowing and distracting question of the rights of the South, and the aggressions of the North—this agitating question of slavery, is to be introduced here. Sir, let me be where I will, I will never introduce it; but where the subject is introduced, I shall discuss it boldly and freely. Why not, upon the same principle, settle this question for Congress and for the Southern people over a still greater extent of territory. Why not indirectly settle it by extending your limits to the Mississippi. Why not include the Island of Cuba, a future acquisition of territory that we may one day or other attain, and forever settle this question by our action here. Sir, if I were upon the floor of Congress, and such a proposition were made, I should indignantly pronounce against it. I am willing, sir, and no man more willing, within what may be the proper limits of the territory in which I live, to exclude slavery, because I consider it to be a great evil. But that is a question entirely different. Enemy as I am to slavery, I think that no man with feelings of justice, will refrain from reproving this doctrine at once—a doctrine which is entirely different from the question of slavery—that any man, or any set of men, have a right, except the people of the Territories themselves, to settle this question. I was not aware, sir, until I was pressed to give to this subject of leaving open for the consideration of Congress the boundary of this State, a favorable consideration—I did not see what has been pointed out to me since; that by either fixing this boundary ourselves to the extent proposed eastward, or by leaving it open to Congress to reduce it, that it would be acknowledging a right, which I deny that Congress possesses, much less a right on the part of the people of California or their delegates in this Convention. I deny that Congress has any such right or power to settle for the people of the South or North this question of slavery. I admit it to be a right of the people of the Territory to erect themselves into a State, and settle it for themselves; and if gentlemen could show me that the boundary proposed were the proper and politic boundary of California, I am ready to vote for it; I am ready to apply to it a declaration that we have already made, that no slavery shall exist within its limits; but when gentlemen urge upon me as an argument, to adopt that boundary because it excludes slavery from an immense extent of territory; not because it is the proper boundary of California, not because it is desirable to the State of California, but because it will settle the slavery question for the whole of the Southern people; and that against the will of the inhabitants of that portion of the Union who are not represented here, the millions of people there, who desire to have the institution of slavery amongst them; when we are told that this may be, and that we here now may adopt that boundary and prevent the people of the South who may come there, from exercising their rights and determining the question for themselves—when I am urged to do this, sir, I cannot give my consent to it.

Mr. Chairman, I have always been opposed to this extreme eastern boundary for reasons that I gave here yesterday. I thought then that it might be left to the Congress of the United States. I desired then, as I desire now, to secure for the State of California political power. I desire to secure to the people political power. I am willing to give up the shadow for the substance. I do not care about having it said that California is a very large State, with a very small ratio of representation. I would like to secure to every ten thousand men, if I can get it, a representation in the Congress of the United States. I know I cannot do this, but I would like to secure it to as small a portion of population as possible. This was the great difficulty in the adoption of the Federal Constitution—the power that was conferred upon the small States of the Union. The large States of the Union opposed it; and I am sorry to say that my native State (Virginia) should have been so recreant to republican principles as to have opposed it. The large States did not desire that equal sovereignty should be allowed to the smaller States, and the consequent power that it gave to the smaller States. And, sir, a provision of the Constitution that has been read here, was made expressly to avoid this power, which gentlemen do not seem rightly to comprehend. That no State should separate itself into two States, and therefore be entitled to four representatives in the Senate, instead of two, without the consent of Congress. I have been endeavoring to show you that real power consists in making your limits as small as possible; and thinking as I do now, that we have got the Congress of the United States in a tight place; that they are compelled to admit us unless there be something exceedingly objectionable—so objectionable, sir, as this extreme eastern boundary, together with the declaration of the purpose for which it is intended, Congress is bound to take us—admit us, boundary and all. I say, therefore, I am willing to take advantage of this circumstance; it is a legal and proper advantage—and to secure to as small a portion of this community as I can, this sovereign power of representation in the Senate of the United States. I am, therefore, now inclined to lay down the dictum to Congress—to prescribe to them even this question of boundary; to make it the *sine qua non* of our admission. I guarantee that they accept us with it, if there is nothing more objectionable—provided you do not make your State too small—provided you do not include so small a portion of territory as they shall think would give you too much power. I am inclined, therefore, to go with my friends of the Committee and other gentlemen on this floor, fixing definitely a boundary; but in that boundary, I shall vote for as small a reasonable extent of territory as the nature of circumstances will permit. I was forcibly struck with the remarks of the gentleman from Sonoma, (Mr. Semple,) as illustrating my opinions with respect to the advantages of a small boundary. He tells you that we ought to have an extensive boundary that we may establish forts and arsenals and standing armies. I think that would be difficult to do. I cannot see upon what ground the gentleman desires that the State of California should take to herself the right to secure a good road to the United States. I suppose the next proposition will be to extend this State to the Mississippi, so that the State of California shall make a railroad. Do you not see the fallacy of this argument in favor of an extensive border. Do you not see that the smaller the boundary the greater the power? You have a less burden of expense—you have a less border to protect. Mr. Chairman, I shall vote against all propositions to open this matter to the consideration of Congress; and so far as I have yet seen, I shall probably be inclined to vote for the narrowest limits that may be proposed as the confines of this State, under the impression that although it may be objectionable to Congress because of the power it gives us, yet we have a right to secure to ourselves as much power as possible, provided we do not make inordinate demands.

Mr. McDougal. Before the question is taken on the amendment of the gentleman from San Francisco, (Mr. Gwin,) I should like to give my views on the subject. If I understand that amendment, it embraces the whole of the Territory of California as ceded by Mexico to the United States; to be embodied as one State; to be under the government of the Constitution that we are about to present to our fellow citizens in Congress. I am opposed to it; and I will give my reasons for opposition as plainly as I can. I am no speaker, sir; I have never in my life undertaken to deliver any kind of argument in a deliberative body; and I trust my views will be at least understood, if not properly expressed.

Mr. Chairman, when we send our Constitution to Congress for ratification, and ask to be admitted as a State into this Confederacy, Congress has no right to consider the local and internal regulations which we have adopted for our government; they simply look over them to see that there is no violation of the Constitution of the United States. But there is one question which they have a right to consider, and to that question their attention will necessarily be drawn. It is the line which we may adopt for our boundary as a State. They have a right not only to consider it, but to dictate to us what shall be our limits. According to all usage, when any American population settles in territory belonging to the Union, the privilege has been given to them to select the boundary line of their State. It is a matter of courtesy and custom, not a right. And when Congress comes to consider the line that we may present to them for our State limits, they will think us very modest indeed, to claim for ourselves, as a State, an extent of territory equal to half of this Union. The gentleman, sir, proposes an area of territory some four hundred and odd square miles. I make it that six hundred square square miles is included in the territory granted to us by Mexico by the treaty of peace. It is very nearly equal to the whole of the non-slaveholding States of the Union. Do you suppose the North or South either, are so blind as to give us that country as one State—equal to all they possess themselves? If we present our Constitution to them with this boundary, placing the question on this ground—claiming all this territory—they will throw it back to us. They will say: We cannot give it to you, gentlemen. You claim more territory than you can govern—more than you have any right to govern. They are certainly not blind to their own interests. It is objectionable to both the South and North—to the North because, in the course of time when this vast country becomes populated by its natural increase as well as the emigration flowing from all parts of the world into our country—it will, if you include this whole vast territory, give you a power in the legislative halls of Congress to control this Union, and peradventure the people may alter their Constitution. The people may change their notions about slavery after they get hold of the territory; they may assemble in Convention and adopt slavery. It leaves this hole open. You at once acquire the sole control over this Confederacy for time immemorial. We do not wish to give you this power because other subjects as important as that of slavery may arise in this Government, and you would have power alone to control them. And another very good reason which they might urge with a great deal of plausibility. Suppose this State should have this immense population; this immense representation. Suppose, like South Carolina, she should undertake to act independently and recede from the Confederacy; she could do it, having the physical and all other powers to do it. If, therefore, we adopt this line, I am very sure it will be sent back to us. We will have to call another Convention, and adopt other lines to suit the views of Congress. In the meantime we have no law. We are in the same chaotic condition that we are now in. And that is the very thing, Mr. Chairman, if the secret was known, which I apprehend they want to do. They want a Constitution presented to Congress so objectionable that it will be thrown back for another Convention. Gentlemen have risen on this floor and stated that they had received letters from the South; and that they knew of many others, who want to bring their slaves here, and work them for a short period in the mines and then emancipate them. If this Constitution is thrown back upon us for re-consideration, it leaves them the opportunity of bringing their slaves here. It is what they desire to do; to create some strongly objectionable feature in the Constitution, in order that they may bring their slaves here and work them three months. They will even then get more than they can get for them in the States. I look upon that as the result if we send our Constitution to Congress with a boundary so objectionable as this. We will have herds of slaves thrown upon us—people totally incapable of self-government; and they are so far from our mother country, that we can never get rid of them; and we will have an evil imposed upon us that will be a curse to California as long as she exists. The Sierra Nevada, Mr. Chairman, presents to my mind a most proper and feasible boundary line for our State. Following the course of the crest of that line from the north to the south, taking the waters as they flow to the east and to the west, all that country where the water commences to flow to the west, is what my proposition includes; and that gives us an area of country double as large as any other State in the Union. If you cast your eye on the map, you will see three distinct divisions marked by nature in the Territory of California. One is the great basin of the Salt Lake. It is bounded on the west by the Sierra Nevada, and by the Rocky Mountains on the east, and by a range of unexplored mountains in the 38th parallel of latitude on the south—three grand natural divisions. For these reasons, Mr. Chairman, and others that I cannot now think of, I consider the eastern boundary line as proposed by the gentleman from San Francisco, (Mr. Gwin,) extremely objectionable, and think it would be very impolitic to include all the territory of this country. I hope it will be at once rejected; and that we will adopt some positive line, which will not be objectionable to the South or North, and which will receive the sanction of Congress, that we may at once be admitted as a State into this Union. We are told that the South wants us as a body, in our deliberations, to settle forever the question of slavery. Well, sir, I for one, would be glad to see that subject settled, and the only way I can see that we can settle it, would be to adopt a reasonable and positive line as our boundary. If we adopt any other, we leave the question still open for agitation, and we avoid that which some gentlemen think we will obviate by adopting the whole territory as one State.

Mr. Sherwood. As to what ought to be our future boundary, I concur fully with several gentlemen who have expressed the opinion that the crest of the Sierra Nevada, or some line of longitude near it should be the future permanent boundary of this State; and if that was the only question before the House, I should, without hesitation, vote for the proposition which embraces these limits. But there are other questions which ought to influence our action. We are here now in

September, 1849, without a government; at least we are without any government sanctioned by Congress or by the people of this Territory. A session of Congress has passed, and no laws regulating the rights of property here, or the rights of citizens, have been passed. We have all seen—many of us have mingled in the discussions which have occurred in the United States in regard to California; we all know why Congress neglected to make a government for this Territory. We are a part of the people of the United States; we are governed by the same influences that govern them; we are men of a like nature. There has sprung up in the parent States a question in regard to the future government of California and its domestic institutions. The power of Congress on this subject has been discussed throughout the States, and it has caused the greatest excitement; it has in my opinion been needlessly discussed. But, nevertheless, it is a question that agitates the whole people of the United States. It is one which we have heretofore settled in Committee of the Whole, so far as regards the territory to be embraced within the limits of this State—I refer to the question of slavery. We have forever prohibited slavery within our limits. Members of Congress, when they go to the capitol at Washington, are governed by what they suppose to be the views of their constituents. We are governed, in like manner, by what we conceive to be the opinions of those who sent us here; and if the great question is to come up before the people of the United States which has heretofore governed the action of Congress and the election of the President, we may reasonably suppose the members of Congress will be governed in their future action by the views of their constituents. A very large portion of the last session was consumed in the discussion of the Wilmot proviso. The result was that the two great parties—neither desiring the other to get the advantage—did not act in regard to a government here; they refused, by neglect or by positive vote, to furnish us with a government. We obtained from Mexico the territory of Upper California and New Mexico. It is a matter of discussion now in the United States, whether the people of California desire slavery or not; at any rate, it is a matter in discussion between the North and South—between the politicians of each section of the Union. As we have had no government from Congress during the last session, so if we do not embrace in our limits here as much as heretofore belonged to California, the discussion of the same question will be open in regard to that portion of California which we throw out.

As a friend of the Union, and speaking to men whom I believe to be actuated by similar motives, I say that if possible we should take that bone of contention from the Congress of the United States and from the discussions of the people. The sentiments of the people of the North are decided; the sentiments of a large portion of the people of the South are equally decided upon this question; and if it is left open, you will find, three years hence, at the election for President, the question whether or not there shall be slavery in the territory acquired from Mexico, and you will find California and New Mexico without a Territorial Government. There are aspirants for power on each side. Neither of them desire to take the responsibility to settle the question alone, and it will be constantly a subject of agitation from this time hence. Party politicians will urge upon the people of the North that Congress should pass a proviso preventing slavery in California and New Mexico. Politicians in the South will urge upon their representatives the rejection of any such proviso. And we shall either be left without a government from Congress, or we must form a government ourselves, independent of Congress. No man here desires to see such a result; we all came here with a sincere desire to form a Constitution which will obtain the sanction of Congress. And now, if by taking in the whole of California to the New Mexican line, we can throw that question out of Congress, and keep it from discussion before the people, and thus remove the bone of contention between the North and the South, we should then do an act that may render certain that this Union cannot be dissolved. We are not here aware of all the feelings that control the people of the Eastern States; we are not aware here, or are not sufficiently sensible, of the evil consequences of the discussion which last year agitated the Union from one end to the other. That question is still discussed—it still produces discord among those who are bound together by the strongest social and political ties. In the State from which I came (New York) there was much division of opinion upon the question, whether Congress should pass a proviso prohibiting slavery in all the territory acquired from Mexico—a very large portion of the people believing that Congress had no power to interfere, but that it was the right of the people of the territory to decide in regard to it; they believed also that it was useless for Congress to touch the subject; that to do so would divide one great party, and partially the other, which exist, in the Eastern States. Over one hundred thousand votes were cast on each side. A candidate was nominated for the Presidency, expressly on the ground that he was in favor of the Wilmot proviso. The feelings of the people were avowed; and the excitement continues still, and will continue, unless arrested by some mediating power; and no man from the South, because the South are in a minority of votes, can be elected to the Presidency in future. And mark this, sir; when no man from the South can be elected to the highest office in the gift of the people; when a Northern candidate is elected, and his officers are appointed from his own party in the North, the South bearing no responsibility in the Government, receiving no advantage from it, will of course no longer feel itself a part of the Union, and the Union is, in effect, dissolved, by the very fact that two parties are created with a sectional line, where the majority on the one side prevents the other side from obtaining the emoluments or bearing any of the responsibility of the Government. I say, sir, from that moment, the Union is dissolved. Now, if we in this Convention, can so far settle the question as to keep it out of Congress, we are bound to do it; and in my opinion, the Congress and people of the United States, aside from that question, care very little whether we go to the Sierra Nevada or to the line of New Mexico. In view then, of these considerations, I would say go to the extreme limit of California as it exists now, and as it always existed under the Spanish and Mexican Governments; and put in a proviso which will meet the opinions of certain gentlemen here who think that Congress will not admit us with so large an extent of territory—that they may cut us off if they so desire it, to the Sierra Nevada, which we all admit to be the natural boundary. We say by that, that they shall not cut from our southern limits or northern limits any portion of territory, but simply reduce our boundary, if it be deemed expedient, to the Sierra Nevada. I know not but that Congress may say, if we do not embrace the territory east of that line, that the Government of the United States will not desire to pay the expenses of a Territorial Government, and that they (Congress) would prefer that it should belong to California until it acquires sufficient population to require admission as a State. There is another argument why we should leave the boundary open to negotiation. We have very little definite information as to how far the Sierra Nevada extends south—or where the line would extend if you adopt the crest of that range of mountains. It may be that a line of longitude would be better; and in order to give time for the State to adopt such measures as will bring forth information on this point, I think we should adopt the whole. With these views, I hope it will be the pleasure of the House to adopt that course. I am in favor of the amendment of the gentleman from San Francisco, (Mr. Gwin,) with the proviso of the gentleman from Monterey, (Mr. Halleck.)

Mr. SNYDER. Much has been said, Mr. Chairman, in regard to the boundaries proposed by different gentlemen. It must be acknowledged that a vast portion of the country east of the Sierra Nevada is utterly useless. I perceive a disposition existing amongst a majority of the members to go for the whole Territory of California or none, which by the way, would appear exclusively American, did I not know that some of my native California friends are in favor of it. Gentlemen have said that if we do not take in all of California, that room will be left for future debate in Congress in regard to the question of slavery. And if we do not settle upon a definite boundary, we leave the door open to accomplish the very object that California wishes to avert. I therefore urge the necessity of establishing a boundary that cannot be objected to. We should endeavor by all means in our power, to prevent all discussion in Congress in regard to our admission into the Union. We have been waiting anxiously for a long time for a government. It is well known, sir. All over the world is it known. And never has the world presented such a picture; a people at peace with nations, occupying a proud and lofty position, an intregal part of the great American Union, without a civil government. I hope we may act together with union and harmony, and what we do, let it be well done, that no member of this Convention need be ashamed of it hereafter. I have heard but very few arguments adduced in favor of the whole of Upper California as our State. We did not come here to settle questions that may arise in the Congress of the United States, but to establish a government for California, and settle questions for and amongst ourselves, that the home Government have refused to do. I cannot see that we gain any thing by extending our limits on the east further than the Sierra Nevada, which is the natural boundary of the State, sufficiently large for all the purposes of the people who will inhabit it for hundreds of years. No good results can be derived from a further extension of the boundary. For, as the report of the Committee says, the Sierra Nevada is almost impassable for nearly nine months in the year—and I know that when it is at all passable, it is with great difficulty, either with wagons or pack mules. I would like to know what use the country on the eastern side of the mountains could be to us, even if it were possible to pass them with ease. There is no territory there of any value to this State. Interminable plains of artemesia, vast bodies of salt water a great part of the year, and immense deserts. Truly a valuable acquisition! If any gentlemen, with their slaves, wish to inhabit the country of the Great Basin, let them have it, and I wish them all the happiness that man can enjoy amidst deserts of sand and salt lakes. We have within the region of country between the Sierra Nevada and the Pacific ocean, the only lands in Upper California that are fit for the habitation of a community of people. It is true that the Mormons have a settlement at the great Salt Lake; but are they cut off from all civilized communities, and even now many of their people are dissatisfied with their situation, and some have already come to this part of the country. The lands along Bear river are the only agricultural lands within the whole of the boundary of Upper California, save the country west of the Sierra Nevada, and a large portion of the Bear river lands are in the Territory of Oregon. It is true there are some delightful spots on the eastern slope of the Sierra Nevada, but they are like the green spots spoken of in the desert; and I would not hesitate to say that the men who would settle there would be found equally as verdant, and probably would not present so fine a picture.

Let us draw a definite line for the boundary on the east, and contend for it. We have no neighbors who can be injured by it; no white men live within a thousand miles of us, and why should we hesitate to adopt at once that line—the Sierra Nevada—that God and nature intended for us. I can see no advantage in the proposition to take in all and leave Congress to settle the line, admitting that they give nothing less than the country west of the Sierra Nevada. The proposition to take in all the country west of the Sierra Nevada, and no more nor less, I think decidedly better. Mr. Chairman we will suppose a case. Our Constitution is sent to the United States, with the whole boundary of Upper California with a proviso by which Congress has the privilege of diminishing it. Then, sir, suppose that the members in Congress from the Southern States should say, If the boundary is not permanently established, why should we not come in for a share of these rich mineral lands. If the Mason and Dixon line was run out to the Pacific ocean, where would it strike? Very near Monterey. Ah! what a beautiful State would that part of the country to the southward of Monterey make for the Southern portion of the people of the United States. Nearly the whole mass of the native Californians in the country would be included in the Southern portion. Would the Southern people desire to come here with their slaves? Yes, sir. There are many of them on their way now. It is a well known fact that cotton has not paid a good price since the days of the Brandon Bank; and I am certain that any Southern gentleman would prefer moving here with his slaves. I would be very happy to see Southern gentlemen settling in California; but we do not want their dark appendages. I am no abolitionist or amalgamationist. I lived in the South about two years, and I only oppose the introduction of slaves from the fact that the institution could not exist here in connection with white labor. Are not the whites already at war with the hordes from South America that are filling the mining districts. Numbers have been ordered off from the north and middle forks of the Rio de los Americanos. And even when the gold was first discovered, disputes arose between parties who lived in the mining districts, and those bringing Indians from other districts. The free white man will not labor side by side with the slave, unless forced.

It is a matter of vast importance to the people of this Territory that our Constitution should go to Congress with a boundary for the State that no fault can be found with. It is of vital importance that this State Government, when fully formed, should immediately go into operation. We are able, and have an undoubted right to do so; and should the United States not receive us into the Union, are we not able to take care of ourselves? And does such an event render it incumbent upon us to pause where we stand for one moment. No, sir. We have taken the first step towards establishing a government, and I say *let it be done, and done speedily!* Some gentlemen have preferred leaving the eastern boundary open. If, upon the presentation of our Constitution in Congress, any debating should arise, they may not immediately admit us; and to prevent and difficulty occurring in regard to an open boundary, I am opposed to taking no more territory than we actually require, so that no objection can be raised in Congress regarding the boundary. This I conceive to be the only debatable matter that can be taken hold of. Let the members of the Legislature be elected, and all the necessary officers for the State Government filled. If we are capable of forming a government at all, we are as well prepared to do so now as we will be in two years hence. Delay is dangerous, and will give opportunities to flood the country with slaves, for there are slaves now on their way here. I wish to see the officers of the State, when elected, immediately enter upon the duties of their respective posts (or as soon thereafter as p acticable,) that the machinery may be immediately in full operation. We are not obliged to wait the action of Congress. California is a peculiar country, and contains a population equally as strange. From all parts of the world are the eager gold hunters wending their way here; almost every sail that whitens the Pacific, contains a beating heart, and a mind fevered by the exciting reports, spread about California. The laborer, the mechanic, the lawyer, the preacher, the politician, and the statesman, are all removing bag and baggage to California. Who would make suit for poor California a few years ago in her sober garb? There were none but early adventurers, the hardy pioneer, in her sylvan groves. But in her now rich attire, a thousand admiring suitors are ever ready to attend her wants. Well may the people watch her interests with a jealous eye. How much has already been said about the emigration from all parts of the world daily pouring into this country to obtain our gold; for what purpose? To improve and embellish the country? To pay taxes for supporting a government? No, sir. To carry the produce of their labor into other countries. As well might a man come into my wheat field and carry away from my wheat stack the produce of my farm. I may appear to be deviating from the matter under consideration. But I contend that all these questions have a definite bearing upon our labors. What effect the discussions of this Convention may have upon the home Government, we have yet to learn. But I hope every man in this Convention is fully aware of the position he occupies. The people of California have sent you here to make a Constitution for them. They doubtless have full confidence in your abilities and integrity, or they never would have sent you. In making this Constitution, they expect you to settle many important questions relative to the interests and wants of the people of this country; and amongst these is a most important one—the boundary. I trust it may be definitely determined by your vote, and determined with a view to the true interests of California.

Mr. McCarver. I desire to ask if gentlemen suppose that this Convention is able to settle a question which all the talent and wisdom in Congress could not settle? I believe that both parties in Congress would be willing to leave this matter to the inhabitants of California so far as regards the territory that properly comes within the limits of this State; but my colleague from Sacramento (Mr. Sherwood) argues that we should settle it to the full extent of the territory acquired from Mexico, known as California. Not a gentleman here seems to be willing to admit that Congress will sanction a line extending to New Mexico; and the very fact that they give Congress the privilege of reducing it, shows that they prefer the lesser boundary. The only object, therefore, is to settle the question of slavery beyond that line. No member desires that we should embrace it within our limits as a State; this is the only point at issue. I ask gentlemen to reflect on the proposition they make. Is it at all likely that Congress will permit a handful of men on the remote shores of the Pacific, to determine for them this question over an extent of territory equal to the whole South? I ask what do we gain by leaving an indefinite boundary? So far as I can see, we only open the door of debate. It is impossible for me to arrive at any other conclusion. Sir, we want the wing of the great American eagle over us at as early a period as practicable. We desire to remain no longer an isolated people; and I conceive that a definite and permanent boundary is the only means by which we can acquire the protection of Government. The same feeling will exist in the next Congress that existed in the previous Congress in relation to the Wilmot proviso. Do gentlemen suppose that we, a mere atom of sand in the wilderness, can accomplish that which has baffled the wisdom of the whole nation? How can we go to our constituents, and with what face can we tell them we have formed a Constitution, but we have adopted no boundary!—that we left it to Congress and the Legislature. Sir, they sent us here to determine a boundary—it is the most important part of our duty. If we leave it to the Legislature to determine our boundary, why are we here? The object of a Constitution is to impose restrictions on the Legislature; to form a State, and to provide a fundamental system of laws within its prescribed limits. Let us form this Constitution and adopt a definite boundary, and when that Constitution receives the sanction of the people, our limits are permanently established. I will therefore vote in favor of a permanent boundary embracing a reasonable extent of territory.

Mr. SHERWOOD. The gentleman (Mr. McCarver) says he is in favor of a permanent boundary. How is he going to get a permanent boundary by fixing it upon the Sierra Nevada? Is he sure that Congress will not cut us off on the south? If the gentleman has that assurance from a majority of the members of Congress, I should like to see it. I hope he will produce it. In my opinion, if a majority of Congress are determined to settle the question of slavery, they will give us the whole territory. If it is objected to by Mr. Calhoun or any other gentleman who is in favor of slavery over a part of California, it will be answered that it is too expensive to establish a Territorial Government on the eastern side of the Sierra Nevada; that that territory is for the most part a desert waste, and may rest with California as a part of the State without being expensive to the people of California; but that it would be quite a burden in thirty or forty years at an annual expense to the Treasury of the United States of one or two hundred thousand dollars a year—a large portion of which we would have to pay ourselves. In regard to preventing our admission into the Union by extending the boundary to New Mexico, we expressly say to Congress, that if they will not give us that, they may cut us down to the Sierra Nevada. If we cut ourselves down now, gentlemen on the other side will say we have acted very foolishly in not embracing the whole territory, and thus throwing out of the councils of the nation the subject of all the difficulty. If we are admitted into the Union, and become a constituent part of the great confederacy—a new star in the galaxy of stars, we shall always, I trust, have the same desire to keep the Union together; to preserve it in spirit and substance, as we had when we were residents of the older States.

Mr. SEMPLE. I feel under some obligation to repeat a conversation which has a direct bearing upon this matter. There is a distinguished member of Congress who holds his seat from one of the States of the Union, now in California. With a desire to obtain all the information possible in relation to the state of things on the other side of the mountains, I asked him what was the desire of the people in Congress; I observed to him that it was not the desire of the people of California to take a larger boundary than the Sierra Nevada; and that we would prefer not embracing within our limits this desert waste to the east. His reply was: "For God's sake leave us no territory to legislate upon in Congress." He went on to state then that the great object in our formation of a State Government was to avoid further legislation. There would be no question as to our admission by adopting this course; and that all subjects of minor importance could afterwards be settled. I think it my duty to impart this information to the Convention. The conversation took place between Mr. Thomas Butler King and myself.

Mr. BOTTS. I have remarked it as a singular fact that we have reports daily and almost hourly, of some important information that has been received from some particular source; letters that have arrived, conversations that have occurred; something that some gentleman has heard Mr. Thomas Butler King say. Now, sir, I take it that Mr. Thomas Butler King, nor no other single individual, is the exponent of the wishes of the Congress of the United States. He is but one man on the floor of that Congress. He gives but one vote, and that vote it is not in his power to give whilst he remains in the State of California. No, sir, not even that vote, either directly himself, or indirectly through his friend upon this floor. Sir, I take it that if Mr. Thomas Butler King did know, and had a right to tell us what were the opinions of the Congress of the United States, it would be for us to consider rather what our own opinions are, than those of Congress, upon this subject. Therefore I exclude the whole testimony as totally irrelevant to this matter. It is not for Mr. Thomas Butler King, or any other man, to preclude Congress from the consideration of this subject, by saying that they do not want to consider it. The assertion amounts to nothing, and can have no effect here. I hope Congress will not enter into a discussion of the slavery question, for I think it is entirely beyond their province; but I do not wish a measure passed here with the express intention of giving them an opportunity of doing what they have no right to do—to determine a question wholly without their province. Yet if I understand this extreme eastern boundary, the whole object of it is to bring it directly within the province and power of Congress; to give them the opportunity of doing that which the Constitution of the United States has forbidden them to do. Is not this the intended effect of this measure? Congress and a small body of people in California may exclude the institution of slavery from a portion of territory of the United States other than that occupied by the people of California. Now, sir, I deny this right. I hold the doctrine that the people of the State have a great natural right to exclude slavery from their own limits;

but, sir, I deny that by an unnatural extension of their limits, they could, even with the consent of Congress, exclude slavery from territory that does not belong to them. I see that this doctrine is discarded by a great many members on this floor, but I could not help taking a note of one remark of the gentleman from New York—I beg his pardon, the gentleman from Sacramento, (Mr. Sherwood.) The most extraordinary reason I ever heard given, was the reason he gave for the extension of that limit. Mr. Chairman, if I understand it, it was this: That the government of this waste country would be a most extensive one, the judiciary system would have to be extended over it, and it was so expensive that it would be a pity to burden the Treasury of the United States with it; that Congress would object to it on that account, and we might as well take it in and pay the expenses ourselves.

Mr. SHERWOOD. The gentlemen misunderstood my remarks. I said that the whole machinery of a Territorial Government from the Governor downwards, including the judiciary, would be more expensive for forty or fifty years, than Congress would desire to make it; but that the State of California, with almost the same number of officers that it would take to govern to the Sierra Nevada, might at the same time extend her laws over the territory to the eastward without additional expense; and that Congress might urge this as a reason against the admission of California without that boundary.

Mr. BOTTS. I understand the gentleman's argument now to be, that Congress will say, if we do not include this in our limits, that the government of this territory on the eastern side is too expensive for them, and we must take it upon our own shoulders, otherwise they will not admit us. I think I would have a ready reply to Congress: Your resources enable you much better to undertake the expenses of this government than the resources of the State of California. You can better afford to make the appropriation than we can. I will grant you, sir, that the burden of government would be less, because it would be a much more imperfect government for the people, but it is not the less an appropriation. Does the gentleman forget that all the great sources of revenue to come from imports levied in California, go into the Treasury of the United States?

Mr. SHERWOOD. We intend to have a portion of it.

Mr. BOTTS. I know nothing about the intention of the gentleman; but he tells you that the burden of this government will be less. I deny it, if you give to this people a government that they will be entitled to; if you do not force them to come a most extraordinary distance to the seat of government, you will be obliged to locate your seat of government somewhere that is as attainable to them as to us; and then, sir, the burden of that government will be felt by every citizen of this country who is compelled to travel to it. You must extend your judiciary system over that part of the country. A tax collector must go among them. These men do not travel for nothing. You must have many additional judges. A judge would probably be two, four, or five months in travelling to and fro upon his circuit. Then he would have to come and sit in your court of appeals. Is this all to be done without expense? Let any gentleman run over the whole organization of government, and see if it is possible to extend it over this country without expense. Mr. Chairman, the gentleman has produced by his remarks probably one of the strongest arguments that could be addressed to this House against this eastern boundary.

But there is another. I believe it is the desire of many members of this Convention to secure for the passage of this Constitution, when it is submitted to the people, as many votes as they can. I do say that the adoption of that eastern boundary, with the avowed intention as expressed on this floor on the question of slavery, must secure against it the vote of every Southern man in this country who has left a brother or friend at home. I know they are comparatively few; but, sir, there are others that will unite with them. There are Northern men who look upon the inhabitants of the Southern portion of this Union as their friends and brothers, entitled to privileges that they are not to be deprived of by any course of this sort. I know that the two together will form a strong body of opponents to this Constitution, and united with other opponents to the Constitution on other grounds, they will form such a body as will prevent the possibility of its receiving the approval of the people.

Mr. McCARVER. I move to rise and report progress.

Mr. SHERWOOD. I beg leave to make a single remark in answer to that portion of the gentleman's remarks where he referred to my argument that Congress might object on account of the expense of the Territorial Government. I contend that if we govern that portion as a portion of this State, we must govern it in proportion to population. If it is five thousand or ten thousand, they will certainly have to pay their proportionate share of taxes. In the other case, if they are governed by Congress, we will also have to pay a considerable portion of the expense.

On motion, the House then took a recess till half-past seven.

NIGHT SESSION, 7½ O'CLOCK, P. M.

Mr. NORTON. This question, Mr. Chairman, is a very important one. I consider the proposition of my colleague from San Francisco, (Mr. Gwin,) the only one that we can act upon legitimately and in good faith. It becomes us not only to act upon the question as regards the present, but the future. We are to determine what now is, and what is to be, the future limits of the State of California; and I contend, sir, as a first principle, that we are not at liberty either to take one acre of land more than now belongs to California, or to yield one acre that now belongs to it. There is no power delegated to us, and we can assume no power to yield an acre of the domain included within the established limits of California. It becomes us, then, to decide whether or not we should claim here, as the representatives of the people, that territory which has always been considered as Upper California, or throw aside either the half of it or a portion of it. I do not believe myself, sir, that it lies within us to dismember the State. I believe if we are entitled to any thing at all—if we came here here to form a Constitution for California—we came to form a Constitution for the whole of California, not a portion of it. Gentlemen may talk of the disadvantages that may arise from the immense extent of territory of the Salt Lake and the people who have settled there ; they may talk of other portions of California inhabited by white men or Indians ; but are we to say here that California is circumscribed within certain limits heretofore not known, or are we to take it as it has always been known and as it still exists ? I insist, sir, that we have no right to say that California is not the California which we took her to be when she became part and parcel of the United States. As I understand it, she is described within certain limits ; those limits laid down upon the official maps of the Government of the United States. A certain degree of northern latitude and a certain degree of southern latitude, (the latter to be decided upon by the U. S. and Mexican Commissioners ;) the western line no one can dispute ; and in regard to the eastern, I contend, sir, that we are entitled every foot of land that has heretofore been considered part of California, and that we can recognise no other line. We have been elected and have received instructions to represent here the interests of California—not any portion of it. We might as well run a dividing line from east to west through this whole territory, and say we are sent here to represent Northern or Southern interests. We cannot go beyond these instructions. I care not if there are thirty thousand people on the Salt Lake who are not represented here. Is that our fault ? We represent California, and if any portion of the people neglect or refuse to send delegates to this Convention, we are not responsible for it. It is our duty to form a Constitution that will be acceptable to the people at large. This Constitution is to govern us for years, and it behooves us that we do not betray the people who sent us here—that we do not abuse our trust; that we do not go home and tell them we have said in this Constitution that a portion of California is not California, and we have formed no government for it. If the inhabitants of the Salt Lake do not see fit to send their representatives to our Legislature, no matter whether it takes them four months or six to arrive at our capital, it is not our fault. If they have sent to the Congress of United States asking to have a Territorial Government, I care not. Leave Congress to decide that question. We will appear on the floor of Congress as soon as they will ; and Congress, with the whole matter before them, with all the light they can ask or obtain, will decide upon the facts. I do not fear the action of Congress ; no matter what sectional questions, interests, or prejudices may divide that body, I fear not. I am satisfied that the people of California will ultimately—I do not say they will obtain it now or within a very short time—but ultimately our rights will be recognized.

California is not a new territory, although she seems to be considered so by many here. Heretofore she was but little known ; she was regarded as an isolated part of the earth. No one thought of California ; no one thought of emigrating here ; no one ever thought, previous to the last two years, that she would ever amount to anything. But within the last twelve months, behold what a change ! The eyes of the world are turned towards her. The people from every spot of God's earth are starting here, impatient to make it their future home—some to acquire wealth and carry it away. Sir, she has been considered, as I heard remarked to-day, in the light of a courtezan ; she had a disreputable character ; no one courted her, no one had any regard for her ; but since her rich treasures have been developed on the slopes of the Sierra Nevada, she has become a most beautiful mistress. The whole world are worshipping at her feet. Is it any portion of California ? No, sir, it is the whole of California ; and I ask members of this Convention, as the representatives of the people, if they can point to any portion of California on the map and say there is California, and the rest of it we know nothing about. Gentlemen may say that a certain portion of the territory is worthless. Have we any right to make that an objection ? If the country east of the Sierra Nevada was as rich in mineral wealth or agricultural rescurces as the western slope, would gentlemen come here and say, we will relinquish that wealth ! No, sir ; they dare not, they would not be willing to do it, nor would they have the right. Whatever that region may be, a barren waste or a land of promise, we have no right to relinquish it. It may hereafter, as I understand the proviso, be divided by the joint action of Congress and the Legislature ; but it cannot now be dismembered by us. We have heretofore said that slavery shall not exist within the limits of this Territory ; we have also said that free negroes shall not be allowed to come within our borders. It is necessary in order to carry out both of these principles, that we should settle at once, in this Convention, what are the limits of California ; and I maintain that we have no power delegated to us to recognize any other than those already established by the treaty. The Southern States may bring any number of slaves within the Territory of California ; you may say to the owners, you have no right to bring slaves or free negroes here. They will ask you, where is California ; what are its limits ; what extent of territory composes your State ? Who is going to answer that question ? You can say nothing but that California is here, somewhere on the Pacific coast—no man knows where. Can you prevent such men from bringing slaves within its borders ? Can you prevent free negroes from coming within its borders ? No, sir, you must have some known and recognized limits, and those limits have already been determined. I admit this gives us an immense territory—

one that is unwieldy, and if it should become populous, it would be almost out of the question to manage it; but at the same time it is not supposed that a great portion of this territory will ever become populous or even be populated at all, except by the wild tribes of Indians that now inhabit it. But should this be the case, we give the Congress of the United States, with the concurrence of the Legislature, the power to reduce it, while at the same time we inhibit them from dividing the territory so as to deprive us of a single foot of the sea coast. That is of immense importance to us. The southern extremity—the bay of San Diego, is destined ere long, to become an important commercial point. The bay of San Francisco is, and will hereafter be the great commercial point of the western hemisphere. I believe, sir, it will soon become the great metropolis of the western world. Nature has done much for it, and man is doing more. Between San Francisco and San Diego are commercial points bays, and harbors that will be of immense importance hereafter, although they may not now be. It is necessary we should look to all this in fixing the boundaries of our State; and more particularly to this portion of the territory than what lies beyond the eastern slope of the Sierra Nevada—a territory unexplored, and of which we know comparatively nothing. It may be rich in agricultural and mineral wealth, we know nothing to the contrary. Should we, I ask you, give away this great extent of territory before we know what it is? Should we give away perhaps millions of wealth? It all belongs to us; we are entitled to it, and it properly comes within the limits of California. No man knows whether it is worthless or not. If we find out in the course of time that it is of no value, we can easily, under this proviso, or under the provisions of the Federal Constitution, get rid of it. I have every confidence in the Congress of the United States; its action may be tardy, and it may have done us injustice heretofore; but, sir, if this thing is rung in her ears for years and years to come, we shall obtain our rights some time or other. I am willing to place the whole question of our eastern boundary between Congress and the Legislature of our own State. The people of California and of the United States will be aroused, and, sir, when the people are aroused, Congress takes great care what she does. The whole people of the United States are awake upon this question. They know what is due to California and what her rights are. It does not rest entirely with the people of California to declare and maintain her rights. The people of every State in the Union are interested in this question; and such a noise will be raised around the doors of Congress as to compel it to give us what we are justly entitled to—the protection of Government.

Mr. Hastings. I understand that my friend, Captain Sutter, desires to speak on this question. The House, I have no doubt, will be much pleased to hear him.

Mr. Sutter. I speak English so imperfectly that I shall only make a single remark. Gentlemen who have passed through these deserts and travelled over these mountains, may know something about it; but it is impossible for gentlemen who have come by the way of Cape Horn, to imagine what a great desert it is, and know how impolitic it would be to the State of California to embrace within its limits such a country. Except a small slip of the great Salt Lake, which is worth something to the people who are living there, but there is such an immense space between us and that part of the country, that I consider it of no value whatever to the State of California. I believe our limits ought to be just as much as agreed upon by the Committee, with the exception of an amendment which I think it requires to facilitate the trade of the people of San Diego with Sonora and New Mexico, to include that portion, to the confluence of the Gila and Colorado rivers, which it omits. This is all I have to say.

Mr. McCarver. I wish to examine the postion of the gentleman from San Francisco, (Mr. Norton,) who has just taken his seat, and see how it would place the Constitution of the United States. Suppose the Convention which formed the Constitution of Louisiana, had occupied the ground that the gentleman takes. The two countries stand upon the same footing. Louisiana, as obtained by treaty from France, embraced territory enough for several States. Suppose the Convention insisted upon it that the whole territory belonged to them. Would it not have been a monstrous doctrine, would it not have been scouted by every intelligent man in the United States? They would laugh at such a doctrine in Congress, that Louisiana had a right to establish the whole territory as her boundary, merely because it was known as Louisiana; that it was the only proper limits, and that they could recognize no other. We occupy a similar position here. We have a tract of country purchased either by the blood or treasure of the United States, known as California. It stands in precisely the same position as Louisiana stood. Do gentleman suppose that Congress would have suffered Louisiana to settle that question of slavery for the whole territory known as Louisiana. Equally idle is the assumption that Congress will stand by and allow a handful of citizens in California to settle the slave question. The position is preposterous. I am astonished, sir, to hear it advocated on this floor. It is a monstrous doctrine. It does not enter my mind that Congress will entertain such a proposition. The South, sir, is not asleep on that subject; Congress is not asleep on that subject. They will inquire whether we are more competent to settle the question of slavery than they are. The very fact that we provide that the Legislature shall settle this question, is evidence that we think Congress will not acquiesce in it. If we insert such a provision, our admission into the Union will be defeated. I am in favor of the report of the Committee, with a slight alteration at the southern point for the benefit of the southern districts.

Mr. Tefft. There are periods in the proceedings of every delibrative body, when calm investigation should follow the excitement of debate; and if that period has at any time arrived, I believe it is the present. I consider this question of the boundary decidedly the most important that has yet been debated. I think it is due to every member that he should express himself calmly and dispassionately, and have the privilege of having his opinions called preposterous, or his doctrines monstrous. As delegates of this Convention, I consider it our first duty to inquire the situation in which we find California; then to inquire what are the acknowledged limits of California; and if we define the boundaries of the State, to define them without the slightest reference to the future limits which we may include. Let us first inquire what are the proper boundaries of California without reference to the question of slavery. From the investigation that I have given the subject, I am decidedly in favor of the proposition of Messrs. Gwin and Halleck. I believe that under the circumstances in which we find the country it is the only course we can take. I question the authority of this Convention, as delegated to them by the people, to decide upon any other eastern boundary line than that marked, as clearly as can be, between the Territory of New Mexico and California. If we draw any other line, we run the risk of its being changed by the Congress of the United States. Then I ask what course is there for us but to take California as she was when she became a part of the United States. The objections to taking this portion are rather questionable. Gentlemen say it is a barren waste, entirely worthless; that it ought to be left to the action of Congress. With all deference, I dissent from these opinions. I think it is a matter entirely foreign to our deliberations what may be the character of the country east of the Sierra Nevada. I see no just or proper course for this Convention to pursue other than to take the established boundaries of California as they exist. I have perfect confidence in the action of Congress in regard to this matter. Congress may have been dilatory in her course towards California, but it does not follow that she will be so in future. There are other important questions before Congress When the people are determined that justice shall be done to California, it follows that it must be done. The proposition before the House at this time, I consider one that will meet the approbation of our friends at home, and be most likely to obtain the sanction of Congress.

Mr. Halleck. I do not wish to delay the action of the Committee on this question; but I think the Convention will bear me witness that I have always endeavored to facilitate the proceedings of this body. I conceive that this is a question of so much importance, that we had better delay than give it hasty action. As has been said by nearly every gentleman who has spoken this evening, I regard it as the most important question that has yet come up for discussion, and the longer we delay it, the better it will be for the final action and success of our Constitution. I hope for this reason that we may not come to a final decision this evening. I think it is a subject upon which we ought very carefully to deliberate, and that we ought to examine very attentively the propositions that have been brought up. The proposition now before the Committee has been facetiously called the proposition of the new firm. I can only say in regard to it that it has been and will be my course in this body to look to the propositions alone, and not to the sources from which they eminate. If one has come from a doubtful source, I should not reject it for that reason. It may be a good proposition notwithstanding the character of the source. Now as to this new partnership, corporation, association, or bank, it was entirely unintentional. Certainly the partners in the firm never had any previous knowledge or understanding about it, and if it has proceeded from members who, upon certain other other propositions before this Convention have been in opposition, is that any reason for opposing it. I think if members have opposed each other here, they have done it honestly, and if they are united upon this proposition without any previous concert of views, it is an argument rather in favor of than against it. I agree perfectly with gentlemen who have said we have no right to divide California; and that in forming a Constitution, we must form it for California as she now exists, not for a portion of California. It would in my opinion be a very dangerous proceeding. Do not members of this body remember seeing in the discussions of the past winter in Congress the result of every effort made to divide California, and fix the slavery question for one part of the territory, and leave it open at the other? Both parties of the Union opposed strenously, every such effort; and I fear both of these factions would oppose any effort of the kind, even coming from this body. As to the question of the power of this body to form a Constitution for all California, I think it has already been sufficiently answered by the fact that this Convention is called to represent California, not a section of it, but the whole country. It is true that a small portion of the country has not been represented here from the fact that it could not be, because it was beyond the districts. Every State furnish precedents of the same kind. With even greater propriety may it be said that a large portion of American emigrants on their way to California are not represented here. If the Mormon settlements onthe Salt Lake have been left out in this Convention, may it not be said that the twenty thousand emigrants that are now travelling over the desert plains on the northern and southern routes, coming like the waves of the Pacific, into California—may it not be said that they are not represented? Let us look at the proposition of this new firm. What is it? In the first place, it says that this Constitution is to be the Constitution of Upper California. What is Upper California, or rather California as we have acquired it from Mexico? Unfortunately, it does not include all Upper California, for by the treaty of Hidalgo, we did not obtain all Upper California. There is quite a considerable strip—one of considerable importance as every person who has examined it, will bear me witness, that properly belongs to California—which has been left to Mexico. When the news reached Mexico that we had not included Lower California, or even Upper California, according to the old dividing line between Upper and Lower California, there was great rejoicing among our enemies.

This I understand to be the first part of this proposition; taking upon ourselves no power to divide this Territory, or to include any more than belongs to us by the treaty with Mexico; but recognizing the line between California and the United States as laid down in the official maps published by Congress, and receiving the authority of Congress as to what constitutes the boundaries of California. Then providing that, with the assent of Congress, and with the assent, not of this body—for we have no power to give it—but of the people of California through their representatives in the Legislature, they may fix upon new boundaries if they desire it, subject to certain conditions. Let us look at the first part of the proposition. I would call the attention of those who object to including the entire territory of Upper California, if this provision does not satisfy every objection which they have made. Congress, in concert with the Legislature of California, has the power to divide it, and reduce it to smaller limits. It may be said, and has been said, that that power is already given by the Constitution. But we wish to go further than that; we wish to leave that power with the Legislature and with Congress now. If the portion of California west of the Sierra should become of sufficient importance to be divided, then we need not say anything about it in our Constitution. The Constitution of the United States says how it is to be done. With the consent of California, Congress may divide that portion of the State into two States. But we wish to determine this boundary sooner. If California, as it now exists, includes more than we want as a State, we wish to provide for a separation of it. How is it to be done? By taking some line, either the line of the Sierra Nevada as far south as you choose, and then running a line, not cutting California into two parts, but preventing that portion from coming south of the Gila river. (Here see the proposition as submitted.) That must leave all that portion of California to the new State; or this proposition goes further. Instead of taking the line of the Sierra Nevada, which is conceived to be very objectionable by some gentlemen, as a portion of the country east of it is deemed valuable, and should be included in the State, we say the Legislature and Congress may form a different line—fix it any point between the Sierra Nevada and the Salt Lake, but preventing them from coming any further west than the mouth of the Gila river, as heretofore. There is another object in this. In the map which we have before us, and in the other maps published by Congress, in Disturnell's map, they include in California a portion that never properly belonged to it; a portion that New Mexico has always claimed and always governed. Nevertheless, Congress has said these are the boundaries of California. Leaving this question out by this proviso, Congress can either organize a new Territorial Government for that portion of California, or make a State Government, or she can organize it with New Mexico for a Territorial Government. Leave it then for Congress, with the concurrence of this State, to settle that question. The proposition of the gentleman from San Francisco, (Mr. Gwin,) to which this proviso is an amendment, amounts to almost the same thing as the amendment, except that this fixes definitely the second line if we do not take the first. We must take one or the other line. There is, otherwise, no chance for negotiation—no chance for an understanding with Congress, or even an investigation to see whether that line does not exclude from the Territory beyond it a portion that would be very desirable to include. We say that it is necessary to have a fixed line in order that Congress shall act. We fix the boundary that Congress itself has given us. We then say to Congress, you can agree upon another line with the concurrence of our Legislature. That I conceive to be far the safest mode; and it seems to me that it accords perfectly with the opinions of the gentleman from Sacramento, (Captain Sutter,) who says, that the country beyond is almost worthless. If it is, we certainly can exclude it under the proposition now before the House. There is full power given to the Legislature to draw a new line, and exclude it immediately after this goes into effect. I think this proposition does not endanger the rejection of the Constitution by Congress. I consider it the most likely of all the propositions to secure the approval of Congress. It seems to me very strange, Mr. Chairman, that we have threats of the rejection of the Constitution from different parts of this House, based upon points directly opposite. It is urged by one side that this proposition has been sprung upon this House as coming from the North, and to deprive the South of her rights; whereas, it is said on the other side that it is designed to continue the existing Government in this country, in order that the South may introduce her slaves. When such objections come from different parts of the House, it strikes me as a good reason, that the best policy is, to take an intermediate course, which is not liable to either objections. But the point that I consider most important is, that if we include only this side of the Sierra Nevada, or adopt one of the proposed lines excluding all that portion east of it, we deprive that country of all government for the next five, or perhaps ten years. This is a result which I, for one, wish to avoid. There are large bodies of emigrants passing over that country; and as I said this morning, offences against law and order, and crimes of a serious nature are committed on the road. Are we, by fixing a certain boundary this side of that Territory, to cut them off from our protection—to deprive them of redress on their arrival here; and leave crimes unpunished, or force people to resort to the Indian mode of revenge, or lynch law, as has been the case sometimes in California. No, sir, I would hope not. I call upon gentlemen to consider this question, and to give to this people, if possible, some form of government, until Congress, in connexion with the Legislature of California, can form for them a Government. This strikes me as one very important point. It has not been sufficiently urged upon this body. Is it not a strong argument in favor of such a measure, that it has been advocated by the extreme South and extreme North—the two extremes of our country. And without bringing names before this House, do we not know that in Congress and out of Congress, in California and out of California, that the leading men in the national councils have urged, and advised, and begged California to pursue this course—to settle this question of slavery forever. I think it was with great impropriety that the names of individuals were brought into this debate. But as they have been brought in, let them have their weight. I have received no letters or information from any source, (for I never had a correspondence with a politician in my life;) but verbal reports have been in circulation here, and letters have been shown from different leading politicians in the United States pointing out to us that the result of a Constitution for only a part of California may be the same result as was produced by an attempt to organize only one portion of California into a State, and unite the other with New Mexico; to leave the question unsettled.

I believe this proposition will secure the reception of our Constitution. I am very confident it will receive the support of the Administration, and of all the moderate men of the South. I am confident it will secure the support of the North; and with these three bodies, there can be no doubt of its success.

Mr. Shannon. I should be doing myself injustice, having presented a proposition that I intended should stand upon its own merits, not to say something upon this matter before the House decides the question. I have listened silently to the remarks of every gentleman who has spoken here upon it; and I have endeavored to draw knowledge and instruction from these remarks in regard to every branch of the subject, so that I might know whether I was right or wrong. Every argument which has been offered here, whether by the gentleman from Monterey, (Mr. Halleck,) or the gentleman from San Francisco, (Mr. Gwin,) or gentlemen from any other districts, has in my opinion, tended uniformly to the same result—that the best course we can pursue, is to settle upon the boundary presented in my proposition. There has been enough said by every gentleman who has spoken—particularly to-night, as to the importance of this question. For my own part, sir, I regard it as the most important that has yet come before this Convention. It is so on more than one account. The gentleman from Montery (Mr. Halleck,) has made it important not only as guarding the rights and protecting the interests of the thousands who are coming westward—men whom we know not of—shielding them, affording them protection and comfort—but in the same overflowing benevolence of heart, he is determined that this matter shall include also the settlement of that great question which has agitated the United States, and which has shaken the Union to its centre for years; that here in this Convention we shall settle not only the boundary line for those whom we represent and for those whom we do not represent, but put an end to all further agitation throughout the Union on the subject of slavery. I never supposed this Convention possessed powers so great, or importance so immense as that. I certainly never imagined there was so much responsibility resting upon my shoulders as an humble member from Sacramento. There are five propositions before the House. The first is the proposition of the Committee on the Boundary. That proposition seems to be, as it deserves to be unless amended, universally discarded. While at the north, it includes an immense extent of waste and barren country, at the south it runs almost up to the Pacific coast, and leaves out points most important for that section of the country. But let me say a word as to a matter upon which I think gentlemen who have been arguing in favor of taking in the whole of California, have rather been changing ground. During the most of the day, the principal argument seemed to rest upon the propriety or possibility of obtaining admission into the Union. It seemed to depend entirely upon the slave question. But to-night it has changed ground, and the right of the people of California to fix any boundary within the furthest limits of territory known as California, is denied. Sir, I maintain that the people have that right. They have a right to come within the acknowledged limits of the territory, and fix such boundaries, through their representatives in this Convention, as they choose. They can establish such lines as they think proper. I refer you for authority to the action of the people of Louisiana. You will find there, that in their first Constitution, in defining the boundaries, they took from the whole territory of Louisiana, a portion sufficient, as they thought, to make the State of Louisiana. They did not include the whole territory as obtained by treaty from France. The case stands precisely the same with us. You will find this precedent in the very first article of the Constitution of Louisiana. I claim the same right for the people of California. We have the authority of the gray hairs here, sir, to which we should all reverentially bow.

Another instance is to be found in the Constitution of Missouri. No territory had been previously rejected by any act of Congress. The manner of fixing the boundaries there is precisely similar to what I have presented to the House—following degrees of latitude and taking meridianal lines of longitude. I hardly believe that gentlemen will maintain any longer that the people of California have no right to fix their own boundaries. This territory was purchased—how and in what manner? It was purchased from Mexico and received into the Union, not as Mexican Territory, not as California territory, but as territory of the United States. It belonged to the United States Government the moment it was purchased. and was therefore entitled to the same privileges which have been enjoyed by other territories. It is for the people of California to say around what portion of it they shall fix their boundary lines. The old gray hairs, sir, of the States, sustain me in that position. Upon this the gentlemen have been changing ground. We have, then, five propositions before the House. The first is, the proposition of the Committee; next is, the proposition of the gentleman from San Francisco, (Mr. Gwin,) united with the proposition of the gentleman from Monterey, (Mr. Halleck.) Now, sir, I do not know whether they call this a partnership concern or not; but that, together with the proposition of my colleague, (Mr. McDougal,) can, I suppose, be classed together. The only place where they differ is in regard to the proviso, and upon that they seem determined to make a stand. Let us see precisely upon what they do stand. The chief argument which has been urged in favor of the extreme boundary, has been, not as to the necessity, not the convenience, not the benefit to be derived from it, not the necessity of including it, but the probability of its passing the Congress of the United States, and the authority of a gentleman from Congress, that if such a proposition was adopted, it would pass. Sir, I claim for the dignity of the new State of California, that dictation of this kind should not receive a very favorable reception in this House; that we should not listen to the propositions of gentlemen in this matter, however high their characters at home, who shall come here and say to this Convention, gentlemen pass such and such boundaries for the State of California, and you will probably be able to pass through Congress, and become a sovereign and independent State. If you don't do so, there is danger at hand; you cannot pass. Sir, this is not only an insult, but it is a threat held out; and I call upon this Convention to have some regard for their own dignity, and for the dignity of the State of California by promptly rejecting such authority. But who are these authorities? Are they men who have become, by long life or service in this country, so deeply interested in the welfare of California, that the weal of the new State is alone the dearest object of their aspirations? Or are they not rather the agents of interested parties, not of Congress? For they do not speak the will of Congress; a single man cannot speak the will of Congress. And when the President of this Convention stated this afternoon the expression of Mr. Thomas Butler King—"*For God sake leave no territory in California to dispute about*"—when he (Mr. Thomas Butler King) spoke it, I presume he did not speak the sentiments of the entire Congress of the United States. The secret of it is this: that the Cabinet of the United States have found themselves in difficulty upon this question, they are in difficulty about the Wilmot Proviso, and Mr. Thomas Butler King—it may be others—is sent here, in the first place, for the purpose of influencing the people of California to establish a State Government, and in the next place to include the entire Territory. Sir, it is a political quarrel at home into which they wish to drag the new State of California. For my own part I wish to keep as far away from such rocks and breakers as possible. Let the President and his cabinet shoulder their own difficulties. I have no desire to see California dragged into any political quarrel. Are these the high authorities to which we should so reverentially bow? I think not. I believe they speak but their own sentiments, or his own sentiments, or the sentiments of the cabinet. Besides, sir, I always wish to watch a political agent. I would always be careful of men of that description. And however my sentiments may accord with those of Mr. Thomas Butler King, or those of any other good Whig of the United States, I suffered a severe lesson enough in one campaign, to pay but little attention to political parties. I allude, sir, to the campaign of Henry Clay in 1844. I have lived long enough in California to regard first her interests in preference to the interests of any political party or parties. This, then, is the authority upon which the main argument has been urged to-day for including the entire territory. But, even in direct opposition to the opinions of Mr. Thomas Butler King, I think that even with the proviso of the gentleman from Monterey, (Mr. Halleck,) this proposition defeats the very object which we wish to attain, and brings up the very difficulty which we wish to avoid. The proviso commits the whole matter directly to the discretion of Congress, and affords all the material of party discord. Suppose this Constitution, including the boundary, goes before Congress. There are two great political parties there who have been for years past fighting like tigers in their cage. Every day, every hour, but increases the ferocity with which they struggle upon this question of slavery. When this proposition comes before them, Southern members—those from the slaveholding States—will see that it strikes from beneath their feet an enormous tract of country into which they desire to introduce slavery hereafter. Add to that the further argument of the enormously extensive territory that it includes; and then add to that the further argument, that a large portion of that territory has not been represented in this body—that the feelings and wishes of the population are not known, and I think you leave open ground enough for them to build an argument upon that will defeat your Constitution; that you at least, bring all those difficulties which gentlemen hope to avoid, directly to bear against it; a result which every gentleman here, I have no doubt, honestly seeks to avoid. These are arguments which you cannot get over. It is true, sir, that the boundary is enormous. No man here wishes to include the whole of it. We are told by these very gentlemen that it is too large. It is unwieldy; it includes an enormous barren tract of country—an immense desert waste; but say they, we will bring it all in, not for the purpose of retaining it within the State of California, but for the purpose of settling the slave question at home. We don't intend to keep it. Permit me to inquire, sir, how will this settle it? If you do not retain it, the struggle must commence again at some point or other. The very fact of demanding such an extent of territory, will cause it to open in all its bitterness in the halls of Congress; and let me tell you, sir, if you once cause this struggle to re-commence upon grounds so strong as this, it will be interminable. Another reason, and one which ought to appeal to us in strong terms here, is the fact that the population in the northeast portion of the territory are unrepresented here. Gentlemen say that we could not reach them and have returns within six months. My friend from San Francisco, (Mr. Norton,) repeated and re-repeated the declaration that it was not our fault if these people were not represented. Whose fault was it then? We are to acknowledge them as a portion of the population of this territory; we include them within our limits, and then say it is not our fault! Can they have the gift of prophecy that they can know without some information reaching them that a Convention is held here, and that they should have their delegates here? I say, sir, it is our fault; and when we are so in fault, should we not do them the justice to leave them out—to leave them free to form a government for themselves, if they think proper. It is an act of gross injustice to force upon them the Constitution and limits which you prescribe here. But, sir, my venerable friend and colleague from Sacramento, (Mr. McCarver,) has stated another strong reason—the perfect worthlessness of this immense extent of territory, or at least, a great portion of it. The fact that the population residing in that territory, could not be represented here in our annual Legislatures, owing to its remoteness from the seat of Government, is a sufficient argument of itself against including it. If we cannot send to them and have a representation here in a reasonable time, I would ask gentlemen to explain to me how their yearly representatives are going to come here and return to their homes? These remarks include, also, the proposition of my colleague from Sacramento, (Mr. McDougal.) The proviso of the gentleman from Monterey, (Mr. Halleck,) leaves to the joint action of Congress and the Legislature of California, the fixing of the eastern boundary line, in case Congress does not see fit to adopt the one here proposed.

Mr. Charman, these gentlemen need not tell me that this must close the question which has heretofore prevented us from having a government here, when at the very same time, they provide the means of opening it. The two ideas are diametically opposed—they cannot exist together. If the one closes the door, the other opens it. I leave it to the common sense of gentlemen, if this is not so. The object of the proposition of the gentleman from San Francisco is defeated by the proviso of the gentleman from Monterey. For these reasons, Mr. Chairman, I go against fixing any boundary line with any proviso, admitting and giving to Congress the right to move it wherever they see fit. The next proposition to which I would refer, is the boundary proposed by the Committee. That boundary commences at the intersection of the 116th meridian of west longitude, and 42d degree of north latitude, and includes more than one-half the width of the entire territory of California at the north, while at the southern part it runs to less than one degree. It has the same fault as the proposition of the gentleman from San Francisco, (Mr. Gwin,) including too much territory, only in a slighter degree. It includes an enormous tract of country, which, from the best information we can obtain, is entirely useless. It gives us an extent of territory nearly as unwieldly and unmanageable as if we included the whole; while at the southern portion of the country, a source of trade to that portion of California, which has already proved extremely valuable, and which will be greatly enhanced in value when our commerce is fully opened in that direction. I speak of the trade with the interior provinces of Mexico, passing the Colorado river, together with the navigation of the Colorado, to whatever extent that navigation can be carried. I cannot, therefore, agree with the report of the Committee. It includes too much territory that is useless, and omits too much that is valuable.

The proviso of my colleague from Sacramento, (Mr. McDougal,) that in case Congress shall not ratify the boundary including the entire limits of California, then that the summit line of the Sierra Nevada shall form the eastern boundary, I consider, of all the boundaries, the most objectionable. It leaves out valleys, rivers, streams, places which may afford immense wealth upon the eastern side of the summit. It is a kind of boundary which must always be indistinct and difficult to determine under the very best circumstances; but here it is most peculiarly so. However well-determined, however plain and distinct the summit line of the Sierra Nevada may be as far south as it is here laid down in the map of Col. Fremont, you will see that it crosses it only as far south as the 35th degree of N. latitude. It leaves a great stretch of country at the southern boundary. Now, I am not aware what the character of that chain of mountains may be, but I think there are gentlemen from the southern part of the country who will sustain me in this, that below that, all southeast and south, there is not a chain of mountains that could be followed as a distinct line. The whole country there is a region of mountains, shaken down as it were on the face of the earth at random. There is no regular summit line that could possibly be followed. Then you have there a most indirect line, you have no boundary at all. But even if you could find a line of boundary there, it has the same objection which the line proposed by the Committee has—that it leaves out a most important portion of territory in the southern part of California, and gives to the State a sort of three cornered form—a shape most awkward and ungainly. In making up a State we should look a little to the formation.

The proposition which I offer, it seems to me, removes every difficulty of this kind. Commencing at the intersection of the 120th meridian of west longitude, and the 42nd degree of north latitude, it runs southerly in a direct line about half a degree east of the Sierra Nevada, and always running sufficiently east to include this entire range, until it strikes the meridian at their southeast bend, about the 38th degree of north latitude, then it takes a direct line from that intersection till it strikes the Colorado at a point where the 35th degree of north latitude crosses it; thence down the eastern bank of that river to the boundary line established between the United States and Mexico; and thence following the report of the committee. This secures to us, in the first place, all that is valuable in the territory. In the next place, it fixes the boundary within such reasonable limits that Congress can make no objection to it. It settles the question of slavery within our own territory, and leaves to Congress a matter which ought to be entirely foreign to us—the question of slavery in any further territory. It will be sustained, too, on the ground that a great portion of this territory beyond those limits is so barren that for years it will not be settled to any extent, so that it can become a State or a Territory. If this is a fact, as it probably is, in reference to the territory which we leave out at our southern extremity, it will be years before the question of slavery can be raised upon it. In the boundary of this State, therefore, as here defined, we obtain the cordial assent of the North. I do not desire to draw party lines in this House, but as other gentlemen have started this division between North and South, I feel justified in stating the advantages of the present proposition. We unite the North upon it. And why? Because they have here a new State—a free State; and with it they gain one or two Representatives and two Senators. This is certainly a strong inducement to the North, the additional power that it gives them in the halls of Congress. I can see no use in undertaking to settle a question here which I have no doubt the lapse of one or two years will settle. The increase of population in the territory beyond the Sierra Nevada will be very great this coming year. They can exclude slavery for themselves if they desire it; and to that the South will not object. The South has always maintained the doctrince of the right of the States to determine this question for themselves, and they will not be disposed to deny it now. In conclusion, Mr. President, I think, in every view of the case, it would be impolitic to adopt this extensive boundary, and that, to secure a favorable reception for our constitution, we should fix upon a reasonable line, embracing every portion of California that is valuable for a State, and excluding all beyond that, making a permanent and judicious boundary to which none can object.

Mr. CARILLO addressed the Convention, through the interpreter, as follows:

So far as I understand the question before the House, it is as to what are the proper limits of Upper California. In the year 1768, the Spanish Government formed certain limits for this country. Afterwards, when the Spanish possessions here fell into the hands of the Mexicans, the Government of Mexico always recognised and respected that as the boundary of Upper California. I am of opinion that the proposition of the gentleman from San Francisco (Mr. GWIN) adopts the proper boundary as fixed by old Spain. I see no reason why it should not continue to be recognised still. Quite enough has been said on this subject. Members of this Convention are sent here by the people of California, not to form a State Government for any particular portion of the territory, but for California. The only question is, what is California? It is the territory defined as such by the Government of Spain, and always recognised as such by the Mexican Government. I do not cenceive that this Government has any right whatever to take the least portion away that has been ceded by the Gorvernment of Mexico. You have no right to deprive the inhabitants of any portion of California of the protection of government. Your duty is to form a constitution for what really is, and always has been, California. If you do not, your descendants hereafter will have good cause to complain that you have done them injustice. This State, in a very short time, may become one of the richest States in the Union, and contribute as much to the honor, power, and glory of the United States as any State in the confederacy. For these reasons, and many other that I do not deem it necessary to urge at present, I hope you will take the vote on the merits of the case without further discussion. For my own part, I am in favor of the joint proposition of Messrs. Gwin and Halleck.

Mr. BOTTS. I would not, Mr. Chairman, at this late hour of the evening, and after the long, able, and eloquent speech of the gentleman from Sacramento, (Mr. Shannon,) trouble the Committee, if it were not that I think I can, in a few brief remarks, present this subject in a light in which it has not yet been discovered. Let us go back if you please, for a moment, to first principles. Let us consider how we are here and for what we are here. Let us remember that we assemble here as no other convention ever assembled in the United States. As has been said elsewhere, our condition is an anomalous one. We meet here under no express law; we meet here with no previous legislation; we meet here to produce order out of chaos; we meet here, sir, under what is sometimes called a proclamation, and what is sometimes called a suggestion from General Riley. Be it one or the other, it is the basis of our action here. Now, sir, if you will refer to that document which has been adopted as a basis by this very people from whom we came and whom we represent, you will find that this question is already settled for us. You will find that the districts of Sacramento, San Joaquin, Sonoma, San Francisco, Santa Barbara, Los Angeles, and San Diego, that these districts, be what they may, are the portions that are represented here and have started to establish a government. Now, sir, I ask you this question: Is it possible that this people can establish a government for others than themselves? Can they give us power that they themselves do not possess? Can they make a government for any other people on the face of the earth than for themselves? I would like to ask you, sir, if this be so, in which of these districts lies the Salt Lake with its thirty thousand inhabitants. Yes, sir, I am told there are thirty thousand freemen in this extent of country east of the Sierra Nevada, which you propose to include in your limits. Are they in the District of Sonoma, or Sacramento, or Monterey?—thirty thousand freemen unrepresented. Do you know, sir, by what vote of my constituents I sit upon this floor? I will tell you. I received ninety-six votes—I, who am modestly requested to legislate for thirty thousand people I never saw, am sent here by ninety-six votes. My colleague, it is true, who makes this proposition, received some twenty or thirty more; and as for the remainder of my colleagues, I believe they are even worse off than I am. And yet we are called upon to form laws for thirty

13

thousand freemen upon the Salt Lake. For my own part, I have not the face to do it. I cannot undertake to do it. This is not a small or immaterial portion either of country or of human beings—an extent of country that probably exceeds ours some fifty times, and in population probably one-half of our own—a reasonable estimate; and yet, sir, this is the country and this the people over whom we propose to extend our laws. Suppose this thirty thousand people of the Salt Lake were to send to Congress a remonstrance, which, if they have the souls of freemen, they will do, am I to be told that their remonstrance will not be listened to? They have had no part in the formation of this Constitution. Do you mean to say it would form no valid claim upon the Congress of the United States, so far as to extend their protection over them as not to give to this Constitution their sanction? If it be true that those are the real natural limits of California, I say dissolve this Convention, call another, and summon from every portion of it delegates to be elected by the people of those portions. Is not that fair? Is there a man within the sound of my voice that will not say it is just and proper. I was struck with the remarks of a gentleman on this floor this evening, who argued as a reason for extending our Government over that country, that it must remain for the five or six years next ensuing without a government at all. Let us see what it is you propose to do for this people. If an individual upon or near that eastern line should be charged with a crime, as I understand it, he will be dragged some six hundred miles from his home, across barren wastes and dreary mountains, to your courts of justice, to be tried upon the charge, for it seems it is not proposed to establish courts of justice in that country. Sir, it is not to the tender mercy of such a gentleman I would commit friends of mine. It is the mercy that the wolf shows to the lamb. I will not detain the House by either repeating the very powerful arguments that have been addressed to them on this subject, or by adding others that might have been advanced. I will simply remark that I have received no high authority to speak the sentiments of the Administration, or of this great man or that great man. I deny their right to be heard here either directly or by proxy. But, sir, I tell you what I will propose to speak, and that is the sentiments of the Southern people of this Union; not because I have had any letters from that portion of the country, or any other, intimating what course I should pursue, but because I know the character and feelings of the people. I know their hatred of oppression, and determination to insist upon their rights at all hazards. And I tell you, sir, that if you send a Constitution to the Congress of the United States with that eastern boundary line, together with the doctrine avowed upon this floor of your determination to settle the question of slavery for that entire territory as well as the portion that properly comes within your limits as a State, you will wake up indignation in every Southern breast that you will find it impossible to extinguish. I have but one word more. It is in respect to a brief allusion of my own to the creation of this new firm, (Messrs. Gwin & Halleck.) Why, sir, the gentleman, my colleague, is much too sensitive on this subject. It was the Chair, if I am not mistaken, that first announced the resolutions under the firm of Messrs. Gwin & Halleck. That was the first intimation I had of this copartnership, coalition, corporation, confederacy, or bank. I never meant to impugn the motives of the sources whence this resolution came. I said not a word about it. I did not know myself that there had been, until the gentleman told me, former hostility between these parties. I see one of the gentlemen is here who is capable of responding, if necessary. Now, I simply want to know this: If the firm were originally united in argument and opinions upon this subject?

Mr. Gwin. Mr. Chairman, after the long discussion we have had this evening and throughout the day upon this question, I confess I am thoroughly exhausted, and will offer but very few remarks. Before I commence I should like to ask the gentleman from Sacramento (Mr. Shannon) what was the remark that he made in regard to Louisiana and Missouri—whether he stated that the State of Louisiana picked out her own territory, and that Missouri was admitted without having had a Territorial Government?

Mr. Shannon. I said that the people of Louisiana, in defining the boundaries of the State, took from the whole territory, as obtained by treaty from France, a portion sufficient for the State of Louisiana; and I referred to the first article of the constitution of that State as affording a precedent of the right of States to establish their own boundaries. I said that in the State of Missouri no portion of the territory had been rejected by any act of Congress previous to the State organization.

Mr. Gwin. I thought it probable I might have misunderstood the gentleman; I merely made the inquiry because I have some knowledge on that question that differs from the gentleman's first statement, which I think he has now modified.

I desire to make a few remarks in answer to the gentleman from Monterey (Mr. Botts) in regard to the extent of this territory, and the objection which he urges that the representation in this Convention does not cover this boundary. If the gentleman was at all familiar with the history of all the new States, where there are Indian tribes, he would know perfectly well that nearly every constitution and every State was formed where there was not, in some instances, one-half of the territory included in the regularly organized counties of the State. It was so in the State of Mississippi. For fifteen years more than half of her territory was unrepresented, and not regarded as within the organized limits of the several counties of the State. So also with the State of Alabama; and nearly every Western State occupied the same position. They formed State Governments including tribes of Indians, without that portion of the population being represented in the Conventions of the States. If I have been correctly informed, there are a hundred tribes of Indians in the gorges of the Sierra Nevada, speaking forty or fifty different languages. I am told there are vast numbers of Indians in the southeast portion of California, somewhat under the control of the authorities of New Mexico. Now, sir, I believe it has been the practice of all the States heretofore, when they formed their State limits, never to have any reference to that portion of the territory occupied by the Indian tribes, but to extend the government over them as they would over those portions which were represented in Convention.

In regard to the extent of this territory, as proposed to be included, a great deal has been said, especially by the gentleman from Monterey (Mr. Botts.) Now that gentleman knows perfectly well that the "Old Dominion" formerly occupied a great deal larger territory than this. The State of Virginia at one time covered an extent of territory far beyond that which California will contain within the whole boundary which has been proposed. So far as the extent of territory is concerned, we can suffer no inconvenience. As it populates, provision may be made for the inhabitants who will occupy those portions now unsettled. I do not intend to occupy much time in the discussion of this question, but will proceed briefly to answer some remarks in regard to the Mormon settlements. Gentlemen proclaim against the injustice of forcing a government upon them. Great stress is laid upon the fact that they are not represented here. Why, sir, there is no proposition on the part of the State of California to force the Mormons to become a part of this Government. We do not propose to extend the laws of the State or any district to them. We do not propose to send tax collectors or government officers there. We await their own action. If they wish the benefits of the Government we are about to establish, let them send a petition to have representatives allotted to them, and judicial districts established. If they desire the protection of our laws, let them send to us, and it will then be a matter of inquiry on the part of our State Government.

But have they any right to complain? Are we not the majority? Does any one pretend to say, in this House or elsewhere, that the districts of California established under the proclamation do not contain a population that is not here represented? Have not thousands reached the country since we were elected? As a minority are they not bound to submit to the will of the majority? Sir, are we not here forcing a State Government upon a portion of the people of California whose delegates have, by their recorded votes, stated the fact that their constituents are unanimously against a State Government, and in favor of a Territorial organization. Do you not expect and require that they shall sustain this Government and become a part of it? If not, let us require their delegates to retire from this Convention, apply to Congress for a Territorial Government, and exclude them from our State boundary. Gentlemen affect to believe that in taking in a large extent of territory not represented here, and from which no opposition to our action has become known to us, we are doing a great act of injustice to those people; when, at the same moment, we have here before us the direct protest against a State Government of a portion of the inhabitants of this territory who are represented. But do we stop—do we refrain from committing this act of injustice? No, sir; we go on and include them; we never think of excluding them. They bear the expense of a State Government, while they prefer a Territorial Government; but rather than submit to a separate organization, or run the risk of getting no Government at all, they waive their objection and act with us.

The constitution of Michigan was formed by a political party. The Democratic party of Michigan determined to form a State Government; the Whig party protested against it. This is my recollection of the case. If I am in error I hope some gentleman will correct me. Thus a single party formed a State Government, the other party refusing to go to the polls or participate in it. Yet it was recognised as a legitimate Government by the Congress of the United States; and their Senators and Representatives took their seats. What was the result? The minority, upon whom a State Government was forced, acquiesced. It was not the less binding upon them because they did not participate in its formation; nor was it the less binding because they actually took part against it.

Sir, it is a new doctrine that every man must be represented within the borders of the new State; a new doctrine, never known or preached before. It is said here, and I have been informed myself, that the Mormons have petitioned Congress to give them a Territorial Government. I take it for granted that this is true. I admit, and argue from it. If they have petitioned for a Territorial Government, have they any right to complain of the Government which we are about to establish? They want the benefit of government; and do they suppose that if the Congress of the United States had established the Government that it was proposed to create here, at the last session, that they would have given them a separate Government? There never was more than one proposition on the subject, and that was to give a Territorial Government to all California; one Territory, not a western one for us, and an eastern one for them. If the people of California could not get a Territorial Government, how can the Mormons expect to get it? What superior claims have they? All they ask for is the protection of government. What injury do we inflict upon them in forming a State Government, which, if they want protection, affords it to them as well as to us. Especially, if we are to judge from what has occurred at the two sessions, it is impossible for them to get a Territorial Government from Congress. But if they are more fortunate than we have been, then Congress will alter our boundary, excluding them from our limits, which we would greatly prefer.

It is well known that the Mormons are a peculiar class of people; that they are a religious sect, professing principles peculiar to themselves. They sought their present location for the express purpose of getting out of the reach of government; to establish a system of their own; and they have located at an isolated point which cannot maintain a large population. We do not ask them to pay taxes or support this Government. We do not ask them to send their representatives here. If they remain there peaceably, if they want protection from the Indians, let the Government of the United States send its forces and protection to them. If they want representation, let them send their memorial here and ask for it.

If I understood the gentleman from Sonoma, (Mr. Semple,) he stated this morning, that if we establish no boundaries, Congress will be forced to admit us with the boundaries we now have. I cannot admit the argument. I do not look upon it, that if we were to send our constitution to Congress they are forced to give us all of the boundary that we have described, or that they are forced to give it to us if we do not describe it. I think gentlemen are laboring under a great mistake in regard to the power of Congress on this subject when they assume that, if we pronounce a certain line as the boundary of California, it shall be the boundary, notwithstanding any objection of Congress. I have not the remotest idea that the Congress of the United States would give us this great extent of boundary if it was expected that it should remain one State. And when gentlemen say that they never will give up one inch of the Pacific coast, they say what they cannot carry out. So far as I am concerned, I should like to see six States fronting on the Pacific in California. I want the additional power in the Congress of the United States of twelve Senators instead of four; for it is notorious, sir, that the State of Delaware, smaller than our smallest district, has as much power in the Senate as the great State of New York. It is not the passage of a bill through the House of Representatives that makes a law; that bill has to go through the Senate, and in that body the State of Delaware has as much power as the State of New York. And the past history of our country, sir, developes the fact that we will have State upon State here—probably as many as on the Attantic side—and as we accumulate States we accumulate strength; our institutions become more powerful to do good and not to do evil. I have no doubt the time will come when we will have twenty States this side of the Rocky Mountains. I want the power, sir, and the population. When the population comes, they will require that this State shall be divided.

Mr. Botts. Will the gentlemen who propose this line tell us what proofs there are on record, anywhere, that it was ever adopted or ever known as the original boundary line of California—that it has ever been recognised as such by the Congress of the United States?

Mr. Gwin. The only information I have on the subject is that which I obtain from the official documents of the United States, the great umpire to whom we must submit this question. They have published officially certain maps and laid down certain boundaries. I take it for granted that Congress will recognise them. They are official, so far as the Government of the United States is concerned, and I have conversed with gentlemen in California who tell me that it is the precise boundary laid down by Mexico.

Mr. Botts. I have conversed with the oldest inhabitants, and they have assured me that no such line exists.

Mr. Gwin. I care not what the Mexican authorities say the boundary is; but I know what the United States say it is—one branch of Congress, at least, and the other branch will not deny it. It is laid down in three different and distinct maps—one accompanying the President's message, giving the area and extent of every State of the Union; and the other printed by order of the Senate. All the official information from our own Government makes this the boundary of California. There was some reference made in the course of debate to the case of Maine and Massachusetts, Kentucky and Virginia, as affording a precedent for the division of California into smaller limits than her entire boundary. That was a mere question between States. It did not concern the Government of the United States, except so far as to ratify the action of the States. For instance, Massachusetts contained within its borders the present State of Maine. By mutual consent they agreed to separate. It was the same with Kentucky and Virginia. Congress merely gave its assent, as provided under the fourth article of the Constitution. But the whole Territory of California belongs to the United States. We should bear it in mind that the General Government bought this country, and paid for it. Not to take into consideration the hundred millions of dollars expended out of the public treasury in carrying on the war, the sum of fifteen millions has to be paid for the Territory of California and New Mexico. It is not to be supposed that the General Government is to be controlled or forced into any course of policy to meet our inordinate demands. We say within a certain amount of territory negotiation shall be open; but we do not say we will refuse to accept any other proposition on the part of Congress. If we do, we throw the gauntlet down to a power that has the control of this question. Congress has the power to say what our territory shall be; and when we say, you shall come only to such a line, we make an issue which we cannot sustain.

The proviso of the gentleman from Monterey, (Mr. Halleck,) was added at his suggestion. I prefer sending my proposition as I offered it. We should not mutilate our Constitution on this subject. We send it to a great power. Gentlemen deny the right of Congress to interfere with the subject of our limits. If Congress has not the power to designate what we shall be, why do we send our constitution there? I was opposed to any other boundary but that of California as recognised by the Governments of the United States and Mexico, for another reason, and I consider it a very important one, that if we leave a portion of territory out, we would necessarily open a question which we here should not interfere with. We all know what 36 deg. 30 min. is. It is the great bone of contention. North of that there is no contest. South of it there is a contest. If gentlemen will look where this line strikes the Pacific, they will see that not a solitary vote was cast by a delegate in this Convention south of that line, except those cast against a State Government. The Representatives here from that region are unanimous in their votes against the establishment of a State Government. If we include the Territory these Delegates represent on the coast, why exclude the barren waste beyond, where no white man lives? We take away the substance and leave the shadow. Let us take the whole terrirory or stop at that line. If we stop at that line, we mutilate the Convention by excluding the members south of it. When we speak of the necessity of having the whole Pacific coast, and especially my friend from Sacramento, (Mr. McCarver,) who says we must have it *all*, we should take into consideration this question. The gentleman (Mr. McCarver) speaks of the miserable waste land which it is proposed to include, as a great objection. Sir, having been to Oregon, he ought to have borne in mind that there is a good deal of territory between this and Oregon unexplored—some of the most difficult country to pass through this side of the Rocky Mountains. If you send to Congress a constitution fixing limits to this State, and not including California as it has always been recognised, it is more probable that Congress may look at that portion of the map and also at the votes represented in favor of a Territorial Government. They would cut off all the northern line down to 39 deg., add it to Oregon, and all south of 36 deg 30 min., and make a Territorial Government of it. Gentlemen who want all the Pacific coast should look to this, that if the slave question is not settled by our meeting here, Congress will say, such are your boundaries and you must abide by them.

Sir, the gentleman alluded to Iowa this morning, and stated that the Government of the United States had been compelled to grant her eventually such boundaries as she demanded. The question with Iowa was this: She formed a State Constitution and laid it before Congress. Now, bear it mind, that most of the new States came into existence by express authority of Congress. We have none. The very authority that was granted to Iowa, and which was asked for in the Congress of the United States to permit us to form a State Government, was refused. Sir, sixty out of ninety days of the last session was occupied in the discussion of this great question, and they refused to pass a bill to permit us to do what we are sitting here now to do—to form a State Government for California. In regard to Iowa, by authority of the Congress of the United States, she formed a State Constitution, defining certain limits. What did she do? She rejected those limits. Then what did she do? Did she come in in defiance of Congress? By no means; she waited quietly under her Territorial Government until Congress thought proper to admit her; then, and not until then, did she come in as a State. That is the way they do things on the other side of the mountains. When Louisiana came up, what did Congress say before she permitted her to talk about a Constitution at all? That State, sir, was admitted in the Union by act of Congress in 1812. Before her admission, conditions were prescribed, requiring that the laws which the State should pass, and its records of every description, should be preserved in the English language.

You will see something of that kind when you go there, because there are portions of California whose records are published in a different language from our own. They will require that these records shall be in the same language as ours. Congress may require us to insert the same provision in regard to the public lands. Sir, if we look through the history of Territorial Governments and the States that have been admitted from Territorial Governments, you will find that the Congress of the United States assumes a power and control which that body will not lightly surrender. I know, sir, that we are in a peculiar situation; and as my friend from Sacramento (Mr. McCarver) stated this morning that Congress is in a tight place, and to get clear of the difficulty will probably go farther than they ever did before. But there is a certain point beyond which they cannot go and do justice to the people of the United States whom they represent. Sir, a gentleman from Sacramento (Mr. McDougal) stated this morning that probably there were parties on this floor who wished to make boundaries so objectionable, including territory so large, that Congress would reject it; that these gentlemen had friends who have negroes over the way, to whom they were anxious to extend the opportunity of bringing them out here. Did the gentleman allude to me in that remark?

Mr. McDougal. I am not aware that the gentleman has any friends who own negroes that they wish to bring here.

Mr. Gwin. I am glad to hear the gentleman did not allude to me. So far as I am concerned, I have no fear but that the Constitution which we are about to send to Congress will be accepted, if it has no objectionable provisions; if we do not insert in it that which may be offensive in language, or in restrictions upon the Government of the United States, which we have no right to impose, and which may force them to reject it altogether.

I have been called upon, sir, to give my sentiments in regard to the question that caused these difficulties— that has prevented California from having a government. The boundary which I have proposed here, I never for a moment thought would be open to question. I would scorn to propose a boundary that would deprive of their rights a portion of the people of this Union. If there is any portion of this country south of 36 deg. 30 min. adapted to slave labor and slave cultivation, I have never heard of it. The mines are all north of it; south of it, except in a few spots, it is a barren waste. If any portion of the people south of that line, or those likely to settle there, favor the introduction of slavery, let it be included. If not, why provide for that which can never happen? I have no fears but if we send our Constitution to Congress with this boundary, and with no other objectionable features, it will be adopted, to include the Pacific coast and to the Sierra Nevada, if not the whole territory.

Sir, I hear great complaints against the Government of the United States here. It does no good. We all know that we ought to have had a government; that such a case never existed before in the history of any Government, that such a great country as this should have been neglected as it has been. But gentlemen should recollect that there must have been great cause to have produced such a result. This question, sir, which agitates the Union, may be looked upon by some here as a mere abstract question; but as has been said by a distinguished gentleman, whose name has been used here: "to the North it is a sentiment; to the South, a point of honor." We all know what a point of honor is in Governments. A point of honor may dissolve our Confederacy. It has dissolved nations. If we make a Constitution with unexceptionable features, and send to the Congress of the United States a State Government for the Territory of California as she is known and recognised, I am not afraid of injustice being done us. We may be cut down in our eastern boundary to the Sierra Nevada. I do not expect, nor do I desire that California shall contain all the territory which we include in our boundary. I want to see many States in it as our population increases.

Mr. Chairman, I have stated that we should have had a Government; that we have been treated as no civilized people ever were before by any free Government. But there have been causes, uncontrollable, to have produced this; and for remarks to emanate from this body, all of which will be published, denouncing the Government of the United States, is not the way for us to obtain that action there which I hope we will obtain. I believe the time has arrived to settle the question that agitates the Union, or it is in danger. I believe we can do it if wisdom and moderation govern our action; and I have made it my object, while participating in the formation of this Constitution, to make one that would have that tendency in the Congress of the United States. As to gentlemen quoting high authorities in the United States, and reading partisan newspapers to prove that there is no excitement on the question of slavery, no man who looks deliberately at the state of feeling at home can be blind to the fact that the whole public are aroused on this question; that they are preparing for a conflict. Let us allay this excitement; leave no room to bring it up in the consideration of your Constitution.

This has been the cause of my taking so deep an interest in this boundary question, believing it to be one of transcendent importance As to the celebrated partnership between the gentleman from Monterey (Mr. Halleck) and myself, it was by the merest accident I made any proposition at all. I had no knowledge of the proposition which the gentleman from Monterey (Mr. Halleck) was about to present. I came into this whole discussion very unexpectedly to myself. I have not at any time urged my views upon the House. Not liking any of the propositions which had been submitted, I offered this as a substitute for a part of the proposition of the gentleman from Monterey, (Mr. Halleck,) believing that it would accomplish the object had in view, and he accepted it. This is the beginning and the end of the copartnership or coalition between us.

Mr. Shannon. I did not expect to have said one additional word on this question; but, sir, there is a secret out. I wish to say something in relation to it, but not to night. I rather would urge the committee to rise. Before doing so, however, I would ask the gentleman from San Francisco (Mr. Gwin) if there has ever been an instance in which the Constitution of the State, or the boundaries of the State, were not finally admitted by the Congress of the United States, not even excepting Iowa? For it seems to me that, after all, it was Congress that submitted to include her boundaries. I shall content myself for the present by moving that the committee rise and report progress.

The motion was decided in the negative.

Mr. Shannon. I introduced this morning a proviso against dividing the State of California north and south, which I afterwards withdrew. The gentleman (Mr. Gwin) has just held it out that if we do not include this entire territory, Congress will have the right to run Mason and Dixon's line, or any other line, through our territory. That is another strong argument why we should define a particular boundary. The gentleman can point to no instance in which the boundaries of a new State, particularly defined within the Constitution presented to Congress, has not finally been accepted by Congress. He made one reference and failed in that, for he admitted that Congress had finally to admit the State of Iowa as she at first defined her bouudaries. Now, sir, if we are to follow precedents, and show a proper deference for the gray hairs of the States, it is our policy to fix a permanent boundary, and it follows that the State of California will be admitted.

Mr. Hastings hoped the question would not be taken to-night, as several gentlemen were absent who desired to vote on it.

Mr. Halleck explained that the question was on the amendment of the gentleman from San Francisco (Mr. Gwin) as amended by himself.

After some discussion it was decided that the question should be put, so as to test the sense of the Committee in regard to which proposition it preferred—the joint proposition of Messrs. Gwin and Halleck, or the amendment of Mr. McDougal, and it was decided in favor of the former by Ayes, 16; Noes, 13.

Mr. Shannon moved as an amendment his propositon.

The Chair decided it to be out of order, inasmuch as the House had, by the vote just taken, determined to accept the proposition of Messrs. Gwin and Halleck.

Mr. Botts asked if the Chair was very sure of the correctness of this decision? Were they all substitutes for the report of the Committee? Was this body entitled to consider no other proposition than that of Messrs. Gwin and Halleck?

Some discussion took place on this point of order; an appeal was taken from the decision of the Chair, and the decision of the Chair was sustained.

Mr. McDougal. I am exceedingly anxious to get through this matter, and I hope it may be settled to-night. We have two propositions before the House—one from a committee, and one from a celebrated firm or co-partnership. There are some features in the report of the committee that I do not like, but still my objections are not insuperable. The committee agree in their report that they ought not to go beyond the Sierra Nevada, because it is an interminable barrier, and destroys any political relation between the two countries. But in the face of this argument they draw a line in fixing their boundary two hundred and fifty miles beyond the crest of the Sierra Nevada, taking in, according to the description of the Chairman, a most beautiful portion of the Territory of California. The chairman of the commiittee states that it is a fine agricultural country, and affords ample resources for a large population. If this be true, it will be at once filled up by the hardy yeomanry of our country. It will present a population of several thousand very soon. But the Sierra Nevada forms a barrier to the extension of our laws over them Then why adopt it? You leave them without any government. They must adopt a government for themselves. This is the line proposed by the committee. Their argument is good as far as the snowy ridge, beyond that it fails; but if we are to have the alternative left to vote for that line, or include the whole territory, I shall vote for the alternative proposed by the committee. In regard to the line of the firm (Messrs. Gwin and Halleck) I see many objections. It is very loosely and carelessly drawn up. They have no ocean line. They simply take the land line of the ocean. It is usual to have a water line to which the jurisdiction of the State shall extend. That is a material objection. They then, in the same amendment or substitute, define the eastern line as laid down in the official maps and the treaty of peace. I think by that construction we might run through Minesota, Missouri, and Lake Superior. We have no specific boundary. If we adopt this grand and indefinite line, running up northerly, perhaps to the Russian or British boundary, and easterly to Lake Superior, it is but reasonable to presume that both the North and South will reject us. They will send our Constitution back with this message—Gentlemen, define a modest boundary and we will admit you.

It is said, Mr. Chairman, that we have had an emissary here—a political emissary, from the present Administration, the powers that be at Washington—to urge upon California to relieve them of the Wilmot proviso; and it seems that the only way we can relieve them, is by adopting the whole territory as one State. If the President of the United States does not wish to shoulder the responsibility of the Wilmot proviso, he ought certainly never to occupy the chair that he does; certainly he ought not to throw upon us the task of relieving him. All we want, is a reasonable extent of territory for a State. Leave the balance for legislation by Congress. If, in adopting the proper limits of our State, we do not relieve the subject of slavery for the territory beyond it, we are not to be held accountable for it. It is for the North and South to determine it in Congress. The territory embraced within the smallest proposed line is double the extent of any State in the Union. Why do we desire more? It will give us no additional power. There are some upon this floor, Mr. Chairman, who appear to think that the whole of this territory belongs to us; that Congress has nothing to say in relation to it; that we should dictate to them where our line shall be, and they shall not take from us one inch. I wonder if the confederacy of the United States did not pay her blood and treasure for every foot of this territory. We are assuming extraordinary powers when we say we have the exclusive control over the public property. Surely gentlemen forget that every State in the Union assisted in the purchase of this territoty. Now we all know what the American people are; they propagate very rapidly; and if we adopt this extreme line, we would soon present a phalanx that would rule all the States of the Union. They are not going to give us a club to break their own heads with; they would send back our Constitution, and say, gentlemen, adopt some reasonable bounds, and we will admit you. What would be the consequence? We would have to call another Convention to define another boundary. It would take more than a year. In the mean time you have a vast multitude of people here from every portion of the world, without law or government. Already, and before I left the Sacramento, there were coming in from the slave States persons with their slaves to go to the mines. Doubtless by this time there are hundreds more. If we adopt this line, we will find the whole cotton plantations of the South depopulated of their negroes; they will work a few months in the mines, and then be told that they are free. It is an evil that California can never get rid of, if we have any delay in the reception of this Constitution by Congress. I speak this seriously. Mark my words, it will be the result, if this Constitution comes back for amendment. The gentlemen from San Francisco (Mr. Gwin) makes a great flourish here about something that Louisiana has done; then he quotes from Iowa and Michigan what they have done. I do not conceive that there is anything in the argument. Their history and condition are entirely different from ours. We stand here in a peculiar attitude, different from any other State ever admitted into the Union. If these States had any difficulty about the extent of their boundaries they did not mind waiting two or three years. Congress was near to them, and could come to some understanding with them in a short time. But we stand here, several thousand miles distant from the seat of Government, with an immense population from every part of the world. We have no laws to govern them. It is absolutely essential to our political existence that we have some substantial laws to govern this immense mass of beings who are within our borders—people who have lived under every variety of law and government, and many of them under no government at all. The protection of government is required to keep them from reverting to an absolute state of barbarism; and, sir, it is my earnest desire to secure it for them without delay. If ever there was a period when delay would be fatal to us, it is now. I trust the committee in its action on this question will take these facts into consideration.

The question was then taken on the amendment of Mr. Gwin, as amended by Mr. Halleck, to the original report of the committee, and it was adopted, by ayes 19, noes 4—as follows:

The boundaries of California shall be as follows: beginning at the point on the Pacific ocean south of San Diego, to be established by the Commissioners of the United States and Mexico, appointed under the treaty of 30th May, 1848, for running the boundary line between the territories of the United States and those of Mexico, and thence running in an easterly direction, on the line fixed by said Commissioners as the boundary, to the territory of New Mexico; thence northerly on the boundary line between New Mexico, the territory of the United States, and California, as laid down on the "Map of Oregon and Upper California, from the surveys of John Charles Fremont and other authorities, drawn by Charles Preuss, under the order of the Senate of the United States, Washington city, 1848," to the 42d degree north latitude; thence due west, on the boundary line between Oregon and California, to the Pacific ocean; thence southerly along the coast of the Pacific ocean, including the islands and bays belonging to California, to the place of beginning.

But the Legislature shall have power, by the votes of a majority of both houses, to accede to such propositions as may be made by the Congress of the United States, upon the admission of California into the national confederacy and Union, (if they shall be deemed just and reasonable,) to limit the eastern boundary of the State to the Sierra Nevada, and a line drawn from some point in that range to some point on the Colorado or Gila river, or to limit such eastern boundary to a line running from some point on the 42d degree of north latitude, between the Great Salt Lake and the Sierra Nevada, to some point on the Colorado or Gila river, as aforesaid, and to organize by Congress a Territorial Government for that portion of California east of this boundary, or to admit it into the Union as a distinct and separate State, and the Legislature shall make declaration of such assent by law.

On motion, the committee then rose, and reported its action to the House, which report was received and laid upon the table.

On motion, the House then adjourned.

TUESDAY, SEPTEMBER 25, 1849.

In Convention. Prayer by the Rev. Padre Antonio Ramirez. The journal of yesterday was read and approved.

Mr. Hastings offered the following resolution:

Resolved, That this House adjourn *sine die* on or before 12 o'clock, M., on Saturday next.

He did this because it would give the Committee sufficient time to transact all the business before it, and he thought by having an understanding as to the exact time when it would adjourn, the business could be concluded, and the members return to their homes. He believed the principal business was finished; and that the Committee on the Constitution had concluded its labors, with the exception of the schedule.

Mr. Jones protested against the resolution. The Convention had not, by any means, decided the most important questions before it; and if it was tied down to a certain time, there might be haste in its action, which would be felt for some time to come.

Mr. DIMMICK believed that a majority of the members were ready to vote upon all questions that might come up hereafter. He trusted the resolution would be adopted; and that gentlemen would shape their debates accordingly. For one, he was anxious to get through the business and go home; and he believed the majority of the delegates shared the same anxiety. The most important question to be decided was the judiciary system. This would not require debate; it would only be necessary to consider it calmly and deliberately, and then vote upon it.

Mr. HALLECK moved to amend the resolution by saying Monday at 12 o'clock, so as to give the Convention Saturday night. By adjourning on that day the Southern members would still have time to go home in the steamer.

Mr. LIPPITT, for one, would be obliged to record his vote against the resolution. It was the first instance on record, he believed, of a Convention adjourning in this way. Such things were common in Legislative bodies; but the members of this Convention were not sent here to form acts which might be rescinded or repealed in a few months. They were sent here to form a permanent Constitution; to settle the great principles upon which legislation itself should be conducted in this State for all time to come. He thought that a few days more or less, upon questions of such momentous importance, not only to ourselves, but to the millions who are to occupy this country hereafter, was of no sort of consequence when compared with the importance of the object. He thought it clear that the tendency and necessary effect of the adoption of such a resolution fixing a day so near, must be to hurry measures of great importance through in an imperfect form, and prevent that deliberate exercise of judgment so necessary in forming a fundamental law of government. If there was any thing that should be deliberately done, it was the revision of the Constitution as partly adopted in Committee of the Whole. Much time had been spent in debate. Reason had not had full scope owing to the mists of excitement. Now was the time, after the excitement of debate, when reason should have its full sway, undisturbed by prejudice or feeling. For these reasons, he thought it inexpedient to fix a day of adjournment, and would therefore oppose the resolution.

Mr. HASTINGS accepted the amendment of the gentleman from Monterey, (Mr. Halleck,) fixing the time on Monday.

Mr. DIMMICK said that some of his friends wished him to make a suggestion. The business of the Convention could be finished by Monday, and then if any gentleman wished to make long speeches, they could do so after the adjournment.

Mr. LIPPITT reminded the House that the Schedule had yet to come up, and there were questions in it which would necessarily give rise to much debate.

Mr. JONES referred also to the fact that there was a rule of the House which could not be reconsidered without one day's notice, requiring an entire day for the final reading of the Constitution.

Mr. GWIN gave notice of rescinding that rule.

Mr. JONES moved to lay the resolution on the table.

The motion was decided in the affirmative by ayes 18, noes 16.

Mr. DIMMICK gave notice that Mr. Pedro Sansevane, a delegate elect from San Jose, was present, and being entitled to take his seat under the report of the Committee on Elections, he asked that Mr. Sansevane be sworn and permitted to take his seat.

Mr. SANSEVANE was accordingly sworn, and took his seat.

Mr. WOZENCRAFT offered the following resolution, which was adopted:

Resolved, That the Committee on Finance be instructed to report on the compensation of members of this Convention.

Mr. GWIN said he made a report some days since, from the Committee of Ways and Means. He now moved that it be taken up and read, which was agreed to, and the report was read by the Secretary as follows:

The Committee appointed to report on the ways and means of defraying the expenses of the State Goverment to be adopted by this Convention, beg leave to submit the following report:

That the position of California is anomalous and different from that which any portion of the United States ever occupied. Like Louisiana and Florida, it is a purchase; but while they had the benefits of Territorial Governments, California has been left without any. A question of exciting interest and importance in the United States has so divided Congress that all attempts to establish a government for this country have failed, and the necessity is forced upon California of forming a State Government in her present unprovided state. This is no fault of the people of California, nor should they be oppressed by it. The United States, up to the present time, have always provided governments for their Territories, and paid from the national treasury the expenses incident to the building up of a State in an unsettled country. Why should this be denied California? No portion of the territory of the United States ever more needed the paternal care of a Territorial Government. We are without public buildings, court houses, jails, roads, bridges, or any works of internal improvement. The prices of building materials and labor of every class are excessively high; we are without a dollar belonging to the people, nor can we raise one but by levying taxes, which no population were ever in a worse condition to bear. In the lower portions of the Territory, commencing partially in the District of San Jose, and extending to the Mexican boundary, the laborers have abandoned their ranches and gone to the mines. Hence the owners of property in this section of the Territory are nearly ruined, by having to abandon their farms for want of laborers, and are losing their herds for want of persons to attend them.

Ranches that yielded an income equal to six per cent., or $100,000, three years ago, now produce nothing. The discovery of the gold mines has inflicted the deepest injury on this portion of the Territory, where but two years since were concentrated its wealth and population. The smallest amount of taxes that would justify the appointment of an assessor and collector would be oppressive to these people, already reduced to poverty, and their ranches going to ruin for want of laborers, and no one can state the time when a different result may be realized.

In the upper and more recently populated districts the vast majority of the people have no property to be taxed, except the gold they dig out of the earth, and which would be difficult, if not impracticable, to reach by taxation. In the towns that have sprung up, something might be collected; but like all new communities they make the most of their limited capital, and taxes would be severely felt by them. It is difficult to raise by taxation in these towns where is concentrated most of the active capital of the country, an amount sufficient to support a municipal government, the expenses are so great to get competent persons to hold the offices, administer justice, and collect the revenue. When laborers and mechanics can command for their services from ten to twenty dollars per day, competent persons to collect and disburse the revenue must be well paid. These, in a Territorial Government, would be dispensed with, which is one of the great advantages which would accrue to the people of California under such a form of government.

The Committee have not access to the proper statistics, to lay before you a general statement of the amount each of the States, who have had a Territorial Government, received in support of such form of government from the Treasury of the United States. This is much to be regretted, as it would be an irresistible argument in favor of the plan the Committee feel called upon to propose to the Convention to provide ways and means to support the Government we are about to form.

The Committee have attached to their report a statement of the number of years that each of said States, fourteen in number, had the benefit and protection of a Territorial form of Government, in some cases extending to more than thirty years.

Without having time to go further into the subject, the Committee recommend that a memorial be prepared to be laid before Congress, with the Constitution we may adopt, showing the necessity we are under of calling on that body to provide for the support of a State Government, by the donation of a portion of the public domain, or by appropriating from the moneys collected in California from the customs and sale of the public lands such amount as may be necessary for that object.

This proposition, in the opinion of the Committee, for reasons herein stated, is based upon a principle of right, and should be insisted upon as such.

In the opinion of the Committee, any system of taxation at present might fail in the object of revenue, and they believe that, when the necessity or policy for adopting this measure may arise, the Legislature will be the proper authority to provide for the case.

All of which is respectfully submitted. W. M. GWIN.

The undersigned, a member of the Committee, finds great difficulty in organizing the "ways and means" best adapted to the present peculiar and unprecedented circumstances in which the State is placed, but would recommend as the most eligible plan, that the Legislature be empowered to raise the proper revenue for defraying the State expenses by levying an Income Land Property Tax, which shall not exceed one quarter per cent.; as likewise a Poll Tax, which shall be left to the Legislature to decide upon, both in relation to the amount as well as the manner of carrying out the same. A. STEARNS.

On motion, the House then resolved itself into Committee of the Whole, Mr. Lippitt in the chair, on Article VIII, on Education, as reported by the Select Committee on the Constitution.

COMMITTEE OF THE WHOLE.

The first section was read as follows:

SEC. 1. The Legislature shall provide for the election by the people of a superintendant of public instruction, who shall hold his office for three years, and whose duties shall be prescribed by law, and who shall receive such compensation as the Legislature may direct.

Mr. SEMPLE had an addition which he wished to append to the report.

Mr. MCDOUGAL thought this a proper subject for legislative action. He would therefore move an amendment, that it be left to the Legislature to elect these superintendants.

Mr. McCarver was decidedly in favor of placing every thing in the hands of the people, and particularly the subject of School Commissioners.

Mr. McDougal withdrew his amendment, and the question being on the 1st section as reported, it was adopted.

The 2d section then coming up, as follows, viz:

2. The Legislature shall encourage by all suitable means the promotion of intellectual, scientific, moral, and agricultural improvements. The proceeds of all lands that may be granted by the United States to this State for the support of schools which may be disposed of; and the 500,000 acres of land granted to the new States under an act of Congress distributing the proceeds of the public lands among the several States of the Union, approved A. D. 1841; and all estates of deceased persons who may die without leaving a will or heir; and also such per cent. as may be granted by Congress on the sale of lands in this State, shall be and remain a perpetual fund, the interest of which, together with all the rents of the unsold lands, and such other means as the Legislature may provide, shall be inviolably appropriated for the support of public schools throughout the State: *Provided*, That the Legislature may, if the exigencies of the State require it, appropriate to other purposes the revenue derived from the 500,000 acres of land granted by Congress to new States, A. D. 1841; and also the rents and profits of all other unsold lands not granted by Congress for the support of education.

Mr. Botts. I move to strike out the proviso. It seems to me to be inconsistent with the previous portion of the section. In one part you say that the proceeds of these lands shall be inviolably appropriated to the support of public schools. Yet, then turn round and say, provided the Legislature shall not enact laws to the contrary. Either the first clause or the last should be stricken out. It is an absurdity in its present shape. The exigencies of the State, you say, may require it. You leave the Legislature to judge of what are the exigencies of the State. The main object of the provision, I presume, is to prohibit the Legislature from appropriating this fund to any thing else. I cannot see how a friend of this school fund could vote for this proviso.

Mr. Sherwood. The object of the Committee in putting in this proviso was not to prevent the formation of a munificent fund for the support of education, but in case the terms of the act of Congress of 1841, granting five hundred thousand acres of land to the new States, shall not be altered by Congress, that the State should have the power to locate these lands where they please. If that location covered half a mile or a mile on each side of every river in California, it would give to the State the title to all the principal mining portions of the territory. This being the case, it is evident that the State Government would have to make some use of these lands on the rivers for the purpose of contributing to the support of the State, from which they would derive some revenue. This proviso does not touch all thelands that are granted by Congress for the purpose of schools. Sections of lands are located in each township by Congress, for the support of schools. It barely refers to the rents and profits that may be derived from any lands. The Committee thought that this should be left open to the Legislature, because if you devote it all to the support of education, it might make too large a fund for the support of education. At any rate, it might deprive the State of the means of supporting itself without too onerous a taxation, because the rent from the gold mines might be conceived to be all that is necessary to impose on the persons engaged in digging the gold.

Mr. McCarver. The Congress of the United States will never admit a State into the Union, nor never has, since the origin of the territorial system, when Ohio came into the Union, without making it a condition that the 16th section should be reserved and set apart for school purposes. I do not recollect the amount that is set aside for the benefit of a State when it comes into the Union. Some few of the States, Iowa the first, I believe, determined that this fund should be placed in the hands of a School Commissioner and held sacred for the purposes of education. The General Government acquiesced in it, and allowed them this privilege. Now, sir, if we can locate in the gold mines and procure a fund sufficient to educate our children without calling upon the parents to do so, we should do it. I am deciedly in favor of placing every farthing that we can, and secure it by constitutional provision, in the hands of this community for the purpose of educating our children. Nothing will have a greater tendency to secure prosperity to the State, stability to our institutions, and an enlightened state of society, than by providing for the education of our posterity. Some of the ablest men we have in the United States are men from the poorest origin, who have had their minds opened to the advantages of knowledge by public schools. Educate the children of this country, and you will find in the halls of the Legislature of California men, able statesmen too, of the poorest origin. I am in favor of securing every blessing to be derived from this fund that Congress is willing to give us.

Mr. Crosby. I would suggest to the gentleman who moved to strike out this proviso, that he limit the amount to which the income of these public lands shall go. He might say one hundred thousand dollars, or any other fixed amount that that the House might desire.

Mr. Semple. I had not supposed that there would be much debate on the subject of the school clause in this committee, from the very fact that it seems now to be the almost universal feeling of every American to promote and encourage the system by all possible means. As to the proposed limitation, I ask you whether you have ever seen a school fund sufficiently large to answer every purpose, or secure too great a spread of knowledge ?

Mr. Crosby. I made the suggestion under the statement of my colleague, (Mr. Sherwood,) that if these lands were located in the gold mines the fund derived from them might rise to such an enormous amount that it might be doing other parts of the State injustice to appropriate all this revenue to school purposes.

Mr. Semple. From the clause here reported, it seems to me that the whole school fund will be placed under the direction of the school commissioners and Legislature. This is a subject upon which I have thought probably more than upon any other subject that has ever engrossed my attention. I regard it as a subject of peculiar importance here in California, from our location and the circumstances under which we are placed, the immense value of our lands, and the extent and wealth of the country. I think that here, above all places in the Union, we should have, and we possess the resources to have, a well-regulated system of education. It is the duty of members of this House to unite together and secure that reputation, character, and ability in our public teachers which can only be obtained by a liberal and permanent fund. It is the basis of a well-regulated school system that it shall be uniform throughout the State ; that any surplus funds collected in one district shall not be appropriated in that district, but that the aggregate fund from all the districts shall be appropriated strictly to school purposes, and distributed equally throughout the State. It is important then, although these articles have been well digested by Iowa, that we look into the subject carefully, and see that our school fund is well secured ; that it is under the management of its friends ; that proper means be taken to secure responsible commissioners for the faithful and legitimate appropriation of this fund. Although there are fanatics in the United States on the subject of education, I think it a question of extreme importance ; there cannot be too large a fund for educational purposes. Why should we send our sons to Europe to finish their education ? If we have the means here we can procure the necessary talent ; we can bring the President of the Oxford University here by offering a sufficient salary. We should, therefore, carefully provide that this fund shall be used for no other purpose. Education, sir, is the foundation of republican institutions ; the school system suits the genius and spirit of our form of government. If the people are to govern themselves they should be qualified to do it ; they must be educated ; they must educate their children ; they must provide means for the diffusion of knowledge and the progress of enlightened principles.

Mr. Sherwood. I regard the education of the youth of this country as highly as the gentleman from Sonoma (Mr. Semple) or any other member upon this floor ; but when I am acting for the people of this country, I desire to act for all alike. The gentleman says that he would not limit the fund for education. Suppose the committee had brought in a provision that all the taxes to be levied in this State should be appropriated to the support of education. It is a notorious fact that now in California there are but very few children; that the great mass of the inhabitants are males, without families here. Suppose the committee had brought in a provision to that effect, would not your wheels of government stop? And yet the gentleman would not limit the fund. The proviso is intended to prevent the stopping of the wheels of government. The General Government has always appropriated a certain section in every township for the purposes of education. This proviso does not touch it. It remains inviolate. But lest we should be enabled only to raise one tax from the mineral lands within the five hundred thousand acres granted to the new States by act of Congress, this proviso was inserted that, under certain exigencies, it shall go towards the support of the civil government. If you have five hundred thousand people, and four hundred thousand are engaged in the mines, that four hundred thousand enjoy the fruits of your government. Should they not assist in supporting your government? And yet, if these lands are located there, if you tie up the Legislature, you cannot gain a tax from these people—certainly not two taxes. It was to leave this question open in regard to this five hundred thousand acres that the proviso was inserted. I am entirely unacquainted with what the Legislature will do in regard to taxation. It is an open question how they will raise their revenue in the mines. That they must raise some revenue there for the support of the Government is perfectly evident. You cannot tax the lands south of San Jose sufficiently to gain all our revenue. The residents cannot pay a tax sufficient to support your Government, because labor is so high that they will be unable to make their lands pay this tax. I am for a munificent fund, and I trust our Senators and Representatives in Congress will obtain, through their influence, from Congress, a grant of another five hundred thousand acres of land for the support of schools in this State. In this article, which the proviso does not touch, all other funds and property that the Legislature can appropriate to the subject of education are to be so appropriated.

Mr. Botts. I do not think I have been understood by the House in the few remarks that I made on this subject. I have a tender solicitude for the character and reputation of this Convention, and it is for that reason that I have endeavored to blot from the clause introduced in the report of the committee all evidence of the haste and hurry with which we have adopted this constitution. That was one great motive that induced me to urge upon this House the striking out of the inconsistent proviso in the last part of this section—either that or the first—so that this five hundred thousand acres of land shall be left altogether at the disposal of the Legislature, or that we tell the Legislature distinctly what shall be done with it. All I ask is, do one thing or the other clearly and distinctly. I hope that every acre of that land may be one solid mine of gold. I am in the habit, sir, of expressing my ideas in as few words as possible, and I hope my remarks may be sufficiently understood without saying any thing more.

Mr. Jones. I rise, sir, to propose an amendment. I propose to strike out the word "inviolably" before the word "appropriated," and insert after the word "appropriated" the words "previous to the year 1855." I think this amendment will effectually do away with all inconsistency upon the face of the clause; and I further think that both the clause itself and the proviso should be retained. I think the motives of the committee were very proper, for this is a case where we are to legislate for the present as well as the future. We have now to govern men, not children. We have a government of men to support which will be costly and burdensome to the State, and we are called upon by the exigencies of the case, until at least a certain time, to appropriate whatever funds may be appropriated by the General Government, to the support of our State Government. I do not think the school fund is needed particularly at the present period. There are but few children now here, and it is not probable the number will be great for some time to come.

Mr. Botts. Does the gentleman propose that we, who have children, shall wait until he and all others who have none shall procure such appendages?

Mr. Jones. Not at all, sir. But I do not think such a fund as this is necessary to support one or two children who may be in each district. I am in favor of public education as much as any man upon this floor. I think that the Committee, in view of the number of children which we shall have here in the course of time, have very properly placed the whole fund at the disposal of the common schools; but I make this amendment so that the Legislature, until that period, shall have the right to appropriate to the exigencies of the Government whatever fund may not be necessary for school purposes.

The question was then taken on the amendment of Mr. Jones, and it was rejected.

The question was then taken on the motion of Mr. Botts to strike out the proviso, and it was decided in the affirmative by ayes 18, noes 17.

The question recurring on the section as amended, it was adopted.

The 3d section being under consideration, as follows:

Sec. 3. The Legislature shall provide for a system of common schools, by which a school shall be kept up and supported in each district at least three months in every year; and any school district neglecting to keep up and support such a school may be deprived of its proportion of the public fund during such neglect.

Mr. Hastings moved to insert the word "six" instead of "three," so as to read "six months in every year."

Mr. Gwin hoped the motion would not prevail. The limit of three months was put in to meet a defective system in the management of the school fund in some of the States. The school fund arising from the 16th section has been entirely squandered and lost, from a want of a proper administration of the fund. If you say six months, it might be rendered impracticable to keep up the system.

Mr. Hastings. I hope, Mr. Chairman, that the amendment will be adopted, for I know, sir, from experience, that the people will not go beyond whatever we adopt in the Constitution. In several States of the Union this provision is adopted, requiring the schools to be kept up three months in the year. Nine months in the year they are idle. If there is a probability of our having a fund entirely too large, let us have schools to dispose of that fund nine months in the year. The people will not go beyond what we require them to do.

Mr. Dimmick. I trust this amendment will not be adopted, for I conceive that three months is sufficient for all purposes here. This is a new country; many of our townships will be unable, at first, to keep up a school for a longer term. It seems to me, sir, that it would operate unjustly on them. In a large portion of the old States, where they have become settled and permanent, three months is all that is required. Gentlemen need not fear but that the Legislature will provide that the whole fund shall be appropriated to its legitimate object; but it you require schools to be kept up at least three months, that will answer every purpose. If you go farther than this, thinly populated townships will be unable to support a school for a length of time without drawing the money from their own pockets. Many a township would have but two children. Much of the country south of this is laid off in large ranches. The residents of these ranches cannot, at first, support schools without great expense; and I fear, if we place such a restriction upon them as this, they will give up the school system altogether.

Mr. Hastings. How will this operate hard upon them? They are to keep up a school provided the Legislaiure furnish the means to enable them to do it. If the Legislature does not provide the means, then of course, if they have schools, they must defray the expense themselves. But, by this article, the Legislature is to provide the means; and, if it does not do so, the people are not obliged to keep up a school. We propose to establish a system of schools which requires that a school shall be kept up in each district at least six months in the year. This is fair and proper. If schools are to be kept up at all, they should be subject to this requirement, in order to do any good.

Mr. Gwin. The manner in which the Legislature provides the means is this: they sell lands in each district to keep up the system. In every township, they have two sections. Heretofore, it has been the practice of Congress to give a section in every alternate township. When a Territorial Government was established over Oregon, some able men contended for four sections for each township, and they succeeded in getting two for each township. I will read an eloquent extract from the report of the Secretary of the Treasury (Mr. Walker) on this subject:

"My last report recommended the grant of one section of land for schools in every quarter township in Oregon. This grant in each of the new States, of one section of the public lands in each township, was designed to secure the benefit of education to all the children of that township. This object has failed to a great extent, because one section in the centre of a township six miles square is too distant from many other sections to furnish a school to which all can resort, and because, as a pecuniary provision, it is inadequate. The grant, however, of one section for every quarter township would be sufficient, whilst the central location would be adjacent to every other section in such quarter township, bringing the school-house within the immediate vincinage of every child within its limits. Congress, to some extent, adopted this recommendation, by granting two school sections in each township, instead of one, for education in Oregon; but it is respectfully suggested that, even thus extended, the grant is still inadequate in amount, whilst the location is inconvenient, and too remote for a school which all can attend. This subject is again presented to the attention of Congress, with the recommendation that it shall be extended to California and New Mexico, and also to all the other new States and territories containing the public domain. Even as a question of revenue, such grants would more than refund their value to the Government, as each quarter township is composed of nine sections, of which the central section would be granted for schools, and each of the remaining eight sections would be adjacent to that granted. These eight sections thus located, and each adjoining a school section, would be of greater value than when separated, by many miles, from such opportunities; and the thirty two sections of one entire township with these benefits would bring a larger price to the Government than thirty five sections out of thirty-six where one section only so remote from the rest was granted for such a purpose. The public domain would thus be settled at an earlier period, and, yielding larger products, thus soon augment our exports and our imports, with a correspondent increase of revenue from duties. The greater diffusion of education would increase the power of mind and knowledge applied to our industrial pursuits, and augment in this way also the products and wealth of the nation. Each State is deeply interested in the welfare of every other; for the representatives of the whole regulate by their votes the measures of the Union, which must be more happy and prosperous in proportion as its councils are guided by more enlightened views, resulting from the more universal diffusion of light, and knowledge, and education."

These townships will have two sections. I do not think it is right that these school sections should lose the privilege of the fund arising out of their own neighborhood. I think it is very important that it should remain as it is, and not be subjected to the discretion of the Legislature.

The question was then taken on the amendment of Mr. Hastings, and it was rejected.

The question recurring on the 3d section, as reported, it was adopted.

The 4th section being under consideration, as follows:

Sec. 4. The clear proceeds of all the fines collected in the several counties, for any breach of the penal laws, shall be exclusively applied in the several counties in which said money is paid or fine collected among the several school districts of said counties, in the proportion of the number of inhabitants in each district, to the support of common schools, or the establishment of libraries, as the Legislature shall from time to time provide by law.

Mr. McDougal moved to amend by striking out the word "inhabitants," and inserting the word "children." There might be a district with inhabitants, but without a child in it, and there might be another composed entirely of families.

Mr. Botts reminded the gentleman that it sometimes occurred that grown-up men wanted education as much as children. He hoped the amendment would not prevail.

Mr. SEMPLE said it seemed to him that the fund collected throughout the State should be distributed in proportion to the number of children in each district; that fines and penalties arising from breaches of the law should be paid to the school commissioner, who should have supervision of the whole system of education, and whose duty it should be to regulate the proper appropriation of these funds. This section provides that these funds shall be distributed in a district when the wants of that district may require it. This has been the case in Kentucky and other States. Each district should be allowed a proper proportion.

Mr. WOZENCRAFT moved to strike out the 3d section altogether, with a view of offering a substitute.

The CHAIR decided that the motion would not now be in order.

Mr. WOZENCRAFT said his substitute was to this effect: that this fund arising from the proceeds of fines, as herein stated, shall be appropriated for institutions of public charity—for the support of one or more hospitals. He thought this was a much better channel to turn it into than that proposed. He knew of no country where there was likely to be a greater amount of suffering than in this, from sickness and distitution.

Mr. BOTTS said he would vote against the amendment of the gentleman from Sacramento, (Mr. McDougal,) for this reason, that the provision of the committee was a much simpler, and came to exactly the same thing. When you have a number of inhabitants you have a number of children.

The question was then taken on the amendment, and it was rejected.

The question being on the adoption of the 3d section, as reported—

Mr. WOZENCRAFT said he would simply state that, if all the members had seen as much as he had of the suffering condition of people in this country from the want of some charitable institution, they would see the necessity of the article which he had suggested.

Mr. GWIN hoped such a proposition would not prevail. The establishment of hospitals was a matter that required a large amount of money. He appealed to every lawyer whether the nett proceeds arising from fines amounted to much. This was a small fund, which, when added to the immense school fund, might be useful in forming libraries. The Legislature should have the power to establish hospitals; but let the members of this Convention not attempt to do a thing which it would be impossible to accomplish with so small a fund as that collected from fines.

Mr. WOZENCRAFT admitted that it was but a small fund; but he expected to get other means from other sources. By getting this. it would not exclude every other resource.

Mr. ORD said: In regard to the amount to be expected from this source, the Legislature will establish penalties for the infraction of any of its laws. It is in their discretion, instead of punishing by imprisonment, to punish by fines. The revenue derived from fines for the next five years will, I think, be very large. Therefore I differ in toto from the gentleman from San Francisco, (Mr. Gwin.) It is frequently left to the discretion of juries to punish by fine *and* imprisonment, or by fine *or* imprisonment. If juries know that this fund is to be devoted to the support of institutions of charity, they will punish by fine in many instances, instead of imprisonment; and this fact will be continually in view before them in the infliction of punishments.

Mr. HASTINGS. In reference to striking out this article, I would like to have it stricken out, but not for the same reason. I think it is perfectly useless, either for school purposes or hospital purposes. No revenue can be derived from this source. To draw upon criminals for charitable purposes seems to me a course which we ought not to pursue. If we depend upon that for our schools, we will have none; and the same objection applies to hospitals. Those who violate laws are generally men who care but little about fines; they are persons who seldom have the means to pay fines.

Mr. SHANNON. The remarks of the gentleman from Monterey, (Mr. Ord,) although I do not concur in the object, have brought my mind to this conclusion: that punishment by fine will bring a very large fund. With all my anxiety, which is as great as that of any gentleman on this floor, for the support of common schools, and my desire to furnish a munificent fund for that purpose, still may it not be inexpedient to limit a fund, which may be very large, to that particular purpose. No person knows how large it may be. I am perfectly willing that it should be exclusively devoted to the support of schools when the necessities of the country require it; but, when no such necessity exists, I think the surplus should be placed at the disposal of the Legislature, to meet the wants of any other department of the Government that may require it. I am in favor of devoting it to educational purposes, when the wants of the community demand it; but, before that necessity exists, the Legislature should not be prohibited from appropriating it to meet such exigencies as may arise from the want of sufficient revenue for the support of the Government.

Mr. BOTTS. The proposition of the gentleman from San Joaquin (Mr. Wozencraft) infringes upon a principle which I have frequently avowed in this Convention. I do conceive, sir, that there is no subject that more appropriately comes within the province of the Legislature than that of public charity. I have uniformly voted against all these directions to the Legislature as to what they shall do with the different subjects that come under the general head of charity or morality. I propose to give the Legislature power to legislate upon them untrammelled, because it better represents the feelings and wishes of the people on these local subjects. It is a body coming fresh from the people, and it is to be supposed that it understands their desires and necessities. It is only upon some great and absorbing subject, such as education, that I will consent to lay down rules for the Legislature. I am not willing to prescribe what it shall do on the subject of roads, asylums, or hospitals. As to the clause under consideration, I think there is reason in the roasting of eggs. I think we have already carried this subject of appropriations far enough. We have made a most munificent appropriation, if the gentleman from Sacramento (Mr. Sherwood) be right in his notions of the mineral wealth of that portion of the country; an appropriation beyond example. There are other expenses of the Government to be provided for. Let us leave some remnant of the income of the State to meet these expenses. Gentlemen here seem to think that no person commits crime but very poor people, who are unable to pay their fines. Crime, sir, is not confined to the poorer classes. I deny the doctrine that persons of wealth commit no offences against the law. They are no more moral than other people. This fund may be very large. I would leave it at the disposition of the Legislature, having already sufficiently restricted that body in regard to the school fund.

The question was then taken on striking out the 4th section, and it was decided in the affirmative by ayes 17, noes 11.

Mr. SEMPLE moved the following, in place of the section just rejected:

SEC. 4. All funds collected from any source, intended for purposes of education, shall be paid into the educational fund, and shall be appropriated throughout the State, according to its number of children, in such manner as may be directed by law. *Provided,* that no private donation shall be directed from the purpose for which the donor intended such donation.

Mr. GWIN. I hope no such provision will be incorporated in this Constitution. It goes directly in the teeth of the grant made by Congress of those school lands. The whole system of education would be changed. Every thing is to go into this great maelstroom, when we ought to have district school funds. Congress appropriates certain lands in certain townships for the purpose of school funds in these townships. Let the Legislature be restricted, in not imposing upon weak townships for the benefit of rich ones.

Mr. SEMPLE. It does seem to me the gentleman's last remark is very inapplicable to the present question. I propose here to put all the wealth of the rich townships into this general fund, so that the poor ones may get a share of it. In regard to the question of constitutionality, my own opinion is that there is no law enacted by Congress which prohibits the State of California from making a general school fund. Suppose your 16th section falls upon a very poor piece of land, and your next falls upon a very valuable section; one gets nothing, the other gets far more than its share; the one is benefited, the other receives no benefit whatever from his grant. The 16th section, in many instances, is worth nothing, whereas the township may be a very productive one, with a considerable number of inhabitants. The children receive no benefit from the grant, because there are no revenues derived from it to support a school. Suppose you place the general fund in one great maelstroom, as the gentleman calls it, there is a general head accountable for his stewardship. You know where to go in order to find what disposition has been made of your school funds; but if you appropriate money in this and that township, there is no accountability.

Mr. Gwin. The gentlemen is disingenuous in his remarks in regard to what I said. He talks about one township that is worthless and the adjoining one rich. He takes the fund arising from a mineral district and gives it to another. Where are the children in this country? In the towns and cities. The gentleman's own district, Sonoma, will probably have little or no school lands, because the lands there are covered by private claims. The whole of his system is wrong. The school fund that we will have here is in that section of the country that is now unsettled. We ought to hold out inducements to people to settle in these unsettled districts. If we get what we are entitled to from Congress, these school sections will amount to millions of acres. I hope the gentleman's proposition will be rejected.

Mr. Halleck. If the proposed section pass it annuls all the preceding sections of the report. It entirely overthrows the whole system embodied in the report. It would be necessary to refer the subject back to the committee. Moreover, I consider it in direct conflict with the laws of Congress.

Mr. Semple. I beg the House to listen to the preceding section, and see if my proposition is at all inconsistent with it. [Here Mr. Semple compared the two in juxta-position.] It seems to me that there is no contradiction here. The proposition which I make carries out the object of that provision.

Mr. Tefft. I shall oppose the proposition of the gentleman from Sonoma, (Mr. Semple.) In the State of Wisconsin this subject has been agitated more than all others. I tell the gentleman, and every member of this House, that it is necessary there should be in each county a county system of schools. I am opposed to placing this immense fund in the hands of any one man. We must have a county system applicable to that county. It is the case in Wisconsin and all the new States. The general Superintendent has the general supervision; but all the funds arising in the county are under the control of the county officers, who are at their own homes, and are interested in the legitimate and proper disposition of these funds.

Mr. Halleck. I think the gentleman's system is in total violation of the established rules in the Atlantic States. I will not detain the House by any remarks, for I conceive the objections to be perfectly evident.

Mr. Semple. The gentleman from San Luis Obispo (Mr. Tefft) objects because this fund, he says, is to be appropriated by one individual. If he will examine the proposition he will find that the fund is to be appropriated exclusively by the Legislature.

The question was then taken on the proposed section, and it was rejected.

The fifth section was then adopted without debate, as follows:

5. The Legislature shall take measures for the protection, improvement, or other disposition of such lands as have been or may hereafter be granted by the United States, or by any person or persons, to this State, for the use of a University; and the funds accruing from the rents or sale of such lands, or from any other source, for the purpose aforesaid, shall be and remain a permanent

fund, the interest of which shall be applied to the support of said University, with such branches as the public convenience may demand for the promotion of Literature, the Arts and Sciences, as may be authorized by the term of such grant. And it shall be the duty of the Legislature, as soon as may be, to provide effectual means for the improvement and permanent security of the funds of said University.

Mr. SEMPLE offered an additional section, making a donation of certain lands for educational purposes, in the vicinity of the town of Benicia. He observed that, as there appeared to be some objection to introducing names in the Constitution, he would so amend his proposition as to leave out the names of the owners of these lands.

The question being on the adoption of the additional section proposed—

Mr. SEMPLE further remarked that the original proprietors of these lands were now present.

Mr. HALLECK begged leave to correct the gentleman. The original proprietors were a company of Mexican soldiers. He presumed they were not present now.

Mr. SEMPLE explained the nature of the donation. He did not ask any appropriation whatever out of the treasury. It was merely a private donation for educational purposes.

Mr. McDOUGAL remarked that the gentleman from Benicia (Mr. Semple) was a great public benefactor. He had devoted a great deal of time and incurred much expense in building up the town of Benicia, and making a ferry there for the accommodation of the public. It had been a source of great expense to him, and now he asked that the Government of California should bear a part of it.

Mr. BOTTS. I do not doubt that the motives of the gentleman (Mr. Semple) are perfectly disinterested; but I think he has mistaken the means of arriving at a good object. It seems to me that the gentleman had as well make his will at once, bestow these lands, and ask this Convention to act as a court of record. If the House will observe, the arrangement which he desires to make is already provided for in the last clause which has been adopted. The gentleman will be one of these donors whom the last clause takes care of. But I rise principally to call attention to a very important point connected with this proposition. It may produce a result which perhaps the gentleman does not intend. The solemn sanction of this House is given to a claim that may be a very doubtful one. I do not believe this is the object for which these gentlemen come here, and seek to obtain the sanction of this House; but I am not prepared to say that they have an inalienable and inherent right to these lands. I have not looked into the question. It may be that they have no title at all. I hope the gentleman will reconsider his proposition and take it back.

Mr. SEMPLE. I will take the gentleman's advice, and withdraw the proposition.

On motion the Committee then rose, reported progress, and had leave to sit again.

The House took a recess until half past 3 o'clock P. M.

AFTERNOON SESSION, HALF PAST 3 O'CLOCK, P. M.

The Convention met pursuant to adjournment.

On motion of Mr. SHANNON, (the President not being present,) Mr. F. J. LIPPITT took the Chair temporarily.

Mr. WOZENCRAFT introduced the following, and on his motion it was referred to the Committee of the Whole, viz:

Public Charities.—The Legislature shall at an early day provide for the erection of one or more suitable building or buildings, to be designated and used as a public hospital or hospitals, to be located at such place or places as shall the best subserve the good and welfare of suffering humanity; and shall provide for the support and maintenance of the same, out of such funds as are not otherwise appropriated.

On motion of Mr. Sherwood, the House then went into Committee of the Whole, Mr. Lippitt in the Chair, on the report of the Committee on the Constitution.

COMMITTEE OF THE WHOLE.

Mr. Crosby moved that the article on the Judiciary be taken up.

Mr. Halleck was of opinion that the proper course would be to take up the majority report, and then decide the question as to which report should be acted upon; which would be best arrived at by a motion to strike out the first section of the majority report, and insert the first section of the minority report. To take up the minority report first and consider it would be very unfair, and would be doing injustice to the Committee. That minority report had never been submitted to the Committee, and the majority report had received the sanction of all the members except one.

Mr. Crosby had no objection to taking that course.

Mr. Gilbert rose to a question of order. The motion of the gentleman from Sacramento (Mr. Sherwood) was to go into Committee of the Whole on the report of the Committee on the Constitution—consequently that report must have precedence of all others.

The majority report was then taken up and read, as follows:

The Committee appointed to report "a plan or a part of a plan of a State Constitution," having had the same under consideration, respectfully further report the following:

Article V.—*Judicial Department.*

Sec. 1. There shall be a Supreme Court, having general jurisdiction in law and equity.

Sec. 2. This Court shall consist of four judges, each of whom shall be elected at the general election by the qualified electors of the judicial district in which he resides, provided that the Legislature shall, at its first session, elect the judges of the Supreme Court by joint vote of both Houses. These judges shall hold their office for the term of four years. On the organization of the court, the judges shall be classified by lot, so that one shall go out of office every year.

Sec. 3. The State shall be divided into four judicial districts, in each of which circuit courts shall be held at stated periods by one of the judges of the Supreme Court.

Sec. 4. There shall be a Court of Appeals formed of any three of the judges of the Supreme Court; but no judge shall sit in the Court of Appeals in any case upon which he has given a judicial opinion in the Circuit Court. In case of the absence or disability of any of the judges of the Supreme Court from the Court of Appeals, their places shall be supplied in the manner to be prescribed by law.

Sec. 5. The Legislature shall have power to increase the number of judges of the Supreme Court, and the number of judicial districts; and whenever it shall deem expedient, it may provide by law for the separation of the Court of Appeals from the Circuit Court, and for the election of the circuit judges by the qualified electors of each judicial district. And when such separation shall be made, the Court of Appeals shall consist of three judges, who shall be elected by the qualified electors of the whole State. They shall hold their office for the term of six years, and be so classified that one shall go out of office every two years; and when such separation is made, the circuit judges shall also hold their office for the term of six years.

Sec. 6. The Supreme Court shall have the power to issue all writs and processes necessary to do justice to parties, and exercise a supervisory control, under such regulations as may be prescribed by law, over all inferior judicial tribunals, and the judges of the Supreme Court shall be conservators of the peace throughout the State.

Sec. 7. The Legislature shall provide for clerks of the Court of Appeals and Circuit Courts, and shall fix by law their duties and compensations.

Sec. 8. There shall be elected in each of the organized counties of this State one county judge, who shall hold his office for four years. He shall hold the County Court and perform the duties of surrogate or probate judge The county judge, with two justices of the peace, to be designated according to law, shall hold courts of sessions with such criminal jurisdiction as the Legislature shall prescribe, and shall perform such other duties as shall be required by law.

Sec. 9. The County Court shall have jurisdiction in cases arising in justices' courts, and in special cases, as the Legislature may prescribe, but shall have no original civil jurisdiction, except in such special cases.

Sec. 10. In the temporary absence or disability of the county judge, his place in criminal cases shall be supplied by the senior justice of the peace of the county.

Sec. 11. The times and places of holding the terms of the Court of Appeals, and of the general and special terms of the Circuit Court, within the several districts, and of the Courts of Oyer and Terminer, shall be provided for by law.

Sec. 12. No judicial officer, except justices of the peace, shall receive to his own use any fees or perquisites of office.

Sec. 13. The Legislature may authorize the judgment decrees and decisions of any local and inferior court of record of civil jurisdiction, established in a city, to be removed directly into the Court of Appeals.

Sec. 14. The Legislature shall provide for the speedy publication of all statute laws, and of such judicial decisions, as it may deem expedient, and all laws and judicial decisions shall be free for publication by any person.

Sec. 15. Tribunals for conciliation may be established with such powers and duties as may be prescribed by law; but such tribunals shall have no power to render judgment, to be obligatory on the parties, except they voluntarily submit their matters in difference, and agree to abide the judgment, or assent thereto in the presence of such tribunal, in such cases as shall be prescribed by law.

Sec. 16. The Legislature shall determine the number of justices of the peace to be elected in each county, city, town, and incorporated village in the State, and fix by law their powers, duties, and responsibilities. It shall also determine in what cases appeals may be made from the Justices' Courts to the County Court.

Sec. 17. The judges of the Supreme and District Courts shall severally, at stated times during their continuance in office, receive for their services a compensation to be paid out of the treasury, which shall not be increased or diminished during the term for which they shall have been elected. The county judges shall also, severally, at stated times, receive for their services a compensation to be paid out of the county treasury of their several counties, which shall not be increased or diminished during the term for which they shall have been elected.

Sec. 18. The supreme and district judges shall be ineligible to any other office during the term for which they shall have been elected.

Sec. 19. The style of process shall be: "The people of the State of California," and all prosecutions shall be conducted in the name and by authority of the same.

All of which is respectfully submitted.

MYRON NORTON, *Chairman.*

The minority report was then read.

The first section of the report of the Committee being under consideration, Mr. Ord offered a substitute for the whole report, which was read.

Mr. Ord said he offered this substitute because he thought the judicial system proposed by the Committee was unsuited to the wants and the condition of the people of California. His first objection was that it was too complicated. There were four tribunals proposed by the Committee: 1st, the Supreme Court; 2d, the Circuit Court; 3d, the County Court; 4th, the Magistrates' Court. He regarded that as a serious objection. Another objection: He thought the system an expensive one; that it would be found, when put in practice, extremely costly. A third objection was, that it would give rise to delays in the administration of justice—delays which he was sure every citizen of California was anxious to avoid.

Mr. Tefft. I think it well to consider the points at issue between the several reports. Let us bring the matter down to a single point, and confine the debate to that issue—the difference between the majority and minority reports. The same holds good in regard to the amendment of the gentleman from Monterey, (Mr. Ord.) The Committee had in view to report to this house, if possible, a judicial system, which should be entirely adequate to the present wants of California—simple and economical, at the same time possessed of express powers which would enable it, without any change of the Constitution, to meet the prospective wants of the people of California. We hope we have succeeded in presenting to the house such a judicial system. I believe there is an honest difference of opinion in regard to the chief point at issue. In fact, with that exception, the two systems are nearly identical. They only differ in regard to the number of officers and judges. We want a judicial system which is adequate to meet the present wants of California, combining simplicity and economy, and which can be so altered at any time as to meet the future wants of the community. The question is, whether we shall adopt a system which has less officers, fewer judges, and which is to be carried out afterwards when circumstances may require a change, or one which has a greater number of officers, will cost more, and cannot be changed.

The report of the majority provides for a Supreme Court, a District Court, a system of County Courts, and Justices of the Peace. To avoid expense, the District Court judges are to act as Supreme judges. Here we make judges act as supreme judges and circuit judges. I think this is good policy at this time. It is adequate to the present wants of the country, and more economical than the others proposed. In the next place, we provide for a system of County Courts—a county judge who is to set as surrogate or judge of probate. The proposition of the gentleman from Monterey (Mr. Ord) requires that the clerks of the Circuit Court shall be elected by the people, and not appointed by the judge. We provide, on the other hand, in this report, that the clerk of the County Court shall act as clerk of the Circuit Court in the district in which that court is held. If the gentleman's system prevails, it will be very necessary that we should have in each county a judge of probate or surrogate. That will be another office created, because, in the report of the Committee, the county judge fills and discharges the duties of that office. I wish to look at this thing calmly and dispassionately, and to avoid unnecessary delay. If the proposition of the majority of the Committee possesses these advantages over the others, which I think it does, let us adopt it at once. Let us, at all events, confine ourselves to the point at issue, and not branch out into unlimited debate on incidental or extraneous subjects. I regard this as the only difference. We have labored long and arduously to form a judicial system adequate to the present wants of California, combining simplicity and economy, and at the same time calculated to meet the increasing wants of the community.

Mr. Dimmick. I agree with the gentleman last up in some respects; but, for one, I am in favor of the plan reported by the minority of the Committee. As far as it goes, it changes nothing in the lower courts. It is proposed as a substitute for the first six sections of the majority report. I consider it accomplishes something which in the majority report is incomplete. That system was formerly adopted by many of the old States. It was the manner in which they first established courts; but it was found insufficient and incompetent to do the business in an effectual and permanent manner. The whole of the States except one, so far as my knowledge extends, have changed from the old system to another; and in one State at least it was the cause of their calling a Convention to alter the Constitution. Let us examine it for a moment. Suppose we have four judges for the trial of cases. As this system provides, three judges of the Supreme Court constitute a Court of Appeals. Now we have four judicial districts in California. Suppose a case is tried by one of those judges in the northern district, and a decision is had in that trial. The case is appealed, and the second judge in the northern district agrees with the first. The two other judges, being the majority reverse, that decision. Suppose I bring another similar case in the Southern district, and I get a decision exactly as that case was decided by each of the northern judges. That case is carried up, and comes before the two judges in the north, who reverse that decision. I have then two decisions reversed. Such a system as that would give rise to endless delay and litigation. There is no stability in it. I therefore felt bound as a member of the Committee to introduce a different system. That is not all; there are many other objectionable features in it; one of which is the union of the two courts with the same judges. It is a system which has been exploded in all the States except one. I now move an amendment to the amendment of the gentleman from Monterey, (Mr. Ord,) to substitute the first section of the minority report in lieu of his amendment.

Mr. Shannon proposed to amend that section by inserting: "The Legislature may also establish such municipal and other inferior courts as may be deemed necessary."

Mr. Dimmick. I accept the amendment. The phrase municipal and other inferior courts pleases me. I was about to remark upon the economy of this system. The objection on that point, in regard to the system proposed by the majority, is this: Judges from the north and south are to be convened at the capital as a matter of course, or some other prominent point, for the hearing of appeals. Now, sir, a judge, under this regulation, must necessarily leave the lower, or it may be the upper part of California, and travel a great distance. Suppose he leaves the southern part of the State and has to travel to this point, or farther north. It would be a journey of fourteen to eighteen days; and it would take the same length of time to return. There would be more than one month lost by that judge going to and returning from the point where he is to hear the appeal. Should your court meet once, twice, or three times a year, there would be from three to six months every year lost in travelling to and returning from the court; and if half the time of these judges is lost in travelling, the other half can only be left to the trial of original cases. In the system which I propose, it will not be necessary for the same judges to sit in the two different courts; consequently, when the judge tries his case, he does not have to travel. His salary may be less. But it may be argued that there are more officers in the court which I propose. There may be one or two more; but the majority saw the failure of their plan in relation to these judges acting in both courts, and to meet the advantages of my system they inserted, after the articles were drawn up, a provision that the Legislature, whenever it deems it expedient, may provide by law for the separation of the Court of Appeals from the Circuit Court, and for the election of the circuit judges by the qualified electors of each judicial district. This, when brought into effect, is similar to the system embodied in the minority report. The fact that they have introduced it shows that it must become the permanent judicial system. It is to be organized and brought into effect by the Legislature at some future period. Now, sir, I conceive it to be of the highest importance that our judicial system should be made permanent in the first instance; that it should not be established with any view to a change at some future period; that when practitioners in these courts bring in their cases they may know where they are to end. This will prevent endless litigation, which would be the consequence if you have the courts vascillating; here to-day and there to-morrow; different judges on the same Court of Appeals, and the prospect of a change at any moment it may suit the wishes of the Legislature. I do not desire, Mr. Chairman, to trespass upon the patience of the House. I shall be satisfied with the decision of the Convention on this subject.

Mr. Crosby. I hope the substitute of the gentleman from San Jose (Mr. Dimmick) will be adopted, for I am clearly of opinion that it is a more advantageous plan than that reported by the majority. I consider it, as the gentleman remarks, of the highest importance that, in the organization of this new State, our judiciary should be fixed and permanent; that we may know what to rely upon in bringing our suits. It has been my fortune, or misfortune, to see the practice under the new Constitution of the State of New York. From June to December we had more conflicts of decision in the Supreme Court, (which was precisely organized like this, with the exception that it was extended a little further, having eight circuits,) in that short space of time, more conflicts of decision than we had for years and years before, under the old system, where there were separate judges for the different courts. I think the proposition of the gentleman from San Jose is more feasible and advantageous in every respect, and I shall vote for its adoption.

Mr. Botts. We are considering the first section of the report of the Committee. I am quite at a loss to vote. If I vote for the substitute of the gentleman from Monterey, (Mr. Ord,) which, as I heard it read, struck very favorably upon my ear, under the rules of this House, it is not open for amendment. I would like that proposition with certain amendments.

Mr. Ord. I should be pleased to receive amendments.

The Chair stated that, according to the rules, amendments could not be made to it at this time.

Mr. Semple moved that the Committee suspend the rules, and take up all three propositions at once.

A discussion here arose as to the rules, in which various points of order were raised, but without coming to any decision. The Committee, on motion, rose and reported progress.

On motion, the House then took a recess till 8 o'clock P. M.

NIGHT SESSION, 8 O'CLOCK P. M.

Mr. CROSBY offered the following resolution:

Resolved, That a committee of five be appointed with instructions to report upon the three plans for a judiciary now before this body.

He moved this for the purpose of uniting those different propositions, and so concentrating the best points of each, as to have a system reported to the House which would combine these advantages, and be liable to none of the objections urged against them now. He thought this might be the means of facilitating the action of the House, and would probably prevent much confusion and avoid a long debate, which seemed likely to arise if the propositions now before the House were all taken up and discussed.

Mr. McDOUGAL. I was about submitting a proposition of the same kind. My views differ slightly from those of my colleague. I move to amend his resolution so that instead of a committee of five we make a committee of ten, to be composed of the lawyers of this House. There is a fine large room below in which they can discuss all the legal technicalities, settle all the knotty points, and then bring in something upon which we can act without further difficulty. I am always in favor of letting the lawyers fight these abstruse points alone.

Mr. McCARVER. I cannot conceive what advantage we are to derive from this proposition. The members of this committee may adhere to the different plans, and we may have as much confusion and trouble as ever. For my part, unless the gentleman shows me some better grounds for creating such a committee, I shall go for the House fighting this battle themselves.

Mr. GWIN. I have great respect for the gentleman's (Mr. Crosby's) opinions, but I do not think it advisable to appoint this committee. Five lawyers have already had this subject in hand. I think the House will be better able to settle it than any committee.

Mr. HALLECK. This whole subject was before the Committee of twenty. The result is the different systems presented. Finally, this majority report was agreed to by all the members except one. I think the House had better go on and determine on these reports. If we appoint the committee it will require a delay of at least a day before we can proceed with the consideration of this subject.

Mr. BOTTS. I tell you what was done in the Convention that formed the Constitution of the United States. Members of the Convention offered resolutions on the subject, which were voted upon, expressive of the sense of the House. Many sets of resolutions were offered in this way, and after the subject had been fully debated, it was referred back to a Committee. After we have seen these various propositions, they might be referred back to the Committee, which might then make such a report as they had reason to believe would meet the sanction of the House.

The question was then taken on the resolution, and it was rejected.

On motion, the House then resolved itself into Committee of the Whole, Mr. SHANNON in the Chair, on the report of the Committee on the Constitution.

COMMITTEE OF THE WHOLE.

The article on the Judiciary being under consideration—

Mr. BOTTS said: My choice lies between the first section of the minority report and the first section of the report of the Committee. I shall detain the House but a few moments in stating my views—raising my objections upon each particular paragraph as it comes up for consideration.

Mr. McCarver. I rise to a point of order. My understanding is, that the first section alone is under consideration.

Mr. Botts. I believe the point of order which the gentleman is about to raise is, that the gentleman from Monterey is about to be out of order. Mr. Chairman, it is to exactly that first section that I am about to object; and if the gentleman had only waited, I would have told him, in my own poor way, the reasons why I prefer the first section of the minority report in lieu of it. It will not do for gentlemen to attempt to trammel us within a narrow limit of debate. It is necessary, in discussing this subject, that I should refer to other parts of the report.

Mr. Gwin. If the gentleman will give way, I will offer a suggestion by which I think the question may be opened entirely. It seems to me that the whole difficulty turns upon a single point. If the decision of the House is to strike out the fourth section of the majority report, with a view to adopting the minority report, the system falls, because that is the section combining the Supreme and District Courts.

Mr. Botts. I would agree with the gentleman who proposes to open the way to this question, but the Chairman tells me it is open. I was about to give my reasons why I prefer the first section of the minority to the first section of the majority report. It is because it is the forerunner and introducer of certain other sections which would not so appropriately come up in the majority report. The other contains this proposition: that the final and Appellate Court shall be distinct from the District Court. To me that is a most important point. If you will notice the report of the majority, it admits this proposition by a provision for the future separation of the Appellate from the District Court; it sanctions it as a good principle. I need not enter into the reasons fully why these courts should be distinct, for I conceive they are admitted by all; but one main substantial reason is this: When I take a case to the Appellate Court, I want an impartial court. I know, sir, what the law of consistency is. It pervades the mind of man. We all know the obstinate character of man; we all know that upon this principle is founded the objections to a juror who has ever expressed an opinion upon the subject before the court. What is the case with respect to a District Court? It is very true, sir, that you acknowledge the principle which I maintain, when in your fourth section, you disqualify a district judge who has given a judicial opinion upon any case in the Circuit Court from sitting in the Court of Appeals upon that case. But do you remember that the other judges have also, in all probability, if not decided the case, decided the principle below? And when I carry such a case up, do I carry it to an impartial court? No, sir; and there are many other reasons why these two courts should be kept separate and distinct. I want for that final court a degree of experience, talent, and wisdom, which I cannot expect to command in the inferior courts. I want the very highest order of legal ability to sit in that court. This great principle is admitted to be the true one by the very Committee who brought in that report, and they provide for carrying it into effect in a few years; but we are told by the gentleman from San Luis Obispo, (Mr. Tefft,) who is a most unflinching supporter of the report of the Committee, that the wants of the country do not require it at present. What am I to understand from that, sir? That we can afford for the present to do without that system which the report itself admits, in the abstract, is the best. What is there in the circumstances of the country to destroy the principle? One principle must be better than the other. What is there that enables us to dispense with this better principle in favor of the worse one? I know none; I cannot understand what grounds there can be for such a proposition. If the gentleman means to say (which is altogether a mere secondary consideration) that it is a cheaper system, that is another matter; but if the gentleman admits that the other is a better system, the cheaper does not weigh a feather in my mind. I have fought this cheaper principle throughout; I have opposed it on all occasions, because I believe it to be the dearest when properly considered. I stand here to ascertain which is the best system; and, in my opinion, that is the cheapest system of justice which is the best. For these reasons, I prefer the opening clause of the minority to the first section of the majority report; and for these reasons I shall vote for it, intending to vote also for the other clauses that hang upon it.

Mr. Jones. It appears to me that we have a sort of triangular duel here, in which, of course, the supporters of each report have to fight two other propositions. Now, I claim to consider in reference to the whole system of judiciary certain fixed principles and so far as any one of these reports agrees with these principles, I am willing to sustain it. I hold, first, sir, that this is a subject which should not be lightly treated or hastily decided by this Convention. I consider it one of the most important questions yet submitted to the Convention—touching the honor and welfare of the State and the prosperity and happiness of the people in perhaps a greater degree than any other yet discussed. Your Legislative and your Executive departments might be faulty in design, the principles of liberty might be discarded and denied by the despot upon the throne, and the evils would be less felt than those under a bad judiciary system from the despot of the law, at the firesides of the people. I hope the members of this body will discard their usual locomotive speed, and endeavor to consider the propositions before the House with a due sense of their importance; and I claim the right which has heretofore been granted by the Chair, not to consider one section alone, but the whole system as embodied in the different sections. Will you tell me the quality of a watch by examining one of its wheels? We must look at the whole machinery, we must examine into the general principles. In regard to the propositions before the House, what is the first requisite of a system of judiciary? It is not that it should be cheap, but effective. If it is not an effective system it is not cheap; it is no system at all. The requisites of an effective system are simplicity of construction and a speedy administration of justice. I am compelled to differ greatly from the report of the majority of the Committee. I do not think, above all things, that their system is an effective one. It is complicated in its machinery, and will work badly. It has left out a great many wheels that should be there, and has a great many in that should not be there. The minority report is better, but I must differ from that also in certain points. I fall, then, upon the system of my friend from Monterey, (Mr. Ord.) I believe that to be the best yet presented, with the amendments which may be proposed. I have said that the report of the majority of the Select Committee contained a great deal too many wheels. Some gentleman told us today that it established four different tribunals. If I am not mistaken there are six: there are general jurisdictions and special jurisdictions, limited and original jurisdictions, supervisory and criminal jurisdictions. The very first section would stagger a systematic lawyer, when it says that the Supreme Court shall have general jurisdiction. I have heard of a great many jurisdictions; I have heard of original and appellate, separate and concurrent, of limited and universal, but I never heard of a general jurisdiction. Is it intended to include all the jurisdictions in the category? Does it mean that it shall be original and appellate; that it shall be universal and special; that it shall be limited and concurrent? Does it include every thing which comes within the term jurisdiction? Now, sir, I have a plain way when I wish to say anything of saying it, and I take it that the Committee has the same way. If they say general jurisdiction, I take it at what they said. There are altogether too many tribunals. I see they have a Supreme Court, a Circuit Court, a Court of Appeals, a County Court, a Justices' Court, Courts of Oyer and Terminer, and Tribunals for Conciliation. They give these courts special, limited, general, and universal jurisdiction. By the 11th section they provide for the holding of a Court of Oyer and Terminer, without having provided any where for the establishment of such a court. I should like to know if gentlemen understand what this Court of Oyer and Termines is intended for? wherein its jurisdiction will differ from the other Courts? I should not only like to understand it myself, but should like every member of the House to understand it; and

I doubt whether such a translation has been presented to the Spanish gentlemen here as they will understand. I am therefore opposed to this report. It contains too many courts; it asserts a principle which I have always denied—that is, the principle of special jurisdiction. I will not give my vote in favor of any Court having special jurisdiction. The principle is a bad one.

Sir, I have practised in a State where there was a court of special jurisdiction, where these very County Courts were organized with probate jurisdiction, and I refer to gentlemen here from the State of Louisiana, if there was not a special Convention to abolish that court in that State. Its evils were so great that it was actually deemed necessary to call a Convention for the purpose of getting rid of them—the very same courts here proposed having a special jurisdiction. I say this report contains too much and too little. It has omitted very many necessary things in a system of judiciary. There is no provision for a chief justice; none for impeachment; none for district attorneys, sheriffs, and coroners; none for the jurisdiction of district courts; none for the qualification of judges; none for the jurisdiction of justices of the peace; none for the removal of officers; all impeachments seem to have been placed at the power of the Legislature. Now, I do not wish to place our judiciary at the mercy of the Legislature. I do not believe that the Legislature should have the right to say that a judge of the Supreme Court should be deprived of his office. I think a mode of impeachment should be prescribed by the Constitution; and as to the qualification of judges, shall the Legislature say who is to be judge? I think the direct qualification of judges should be established in the Constituiion. Then there is the jurisdiction of the District Courts. I never saw a system which did not establish that jurisdiction in the system itself. I have said that I prefer the minority report. I do prefer it infinitely to the majority report, but at the same time I cannot agree to it entirely. It establishes these same County Courts, with special jurisdiction, against which I fought for years in another State, and against which I hope I will have a majority in this Convention to fight with me. Now, I wish to inquire whether it is intended to try in this special court contested cases. I presume it is not. I have heard that it is merely intended to transact such probate business as is not opposed—such as granting letters of administration, settling accounts, &c. Now, Mr. Chairman, the first thing we should decide upon is a simple system of courts. Why not say that the clerk of each county shall be empowered to grant letters of administration and settle accounts where there is no contest? The system which, above all others, I would support would be a system of three courts alone—such a system as that of my friend from Monterey, (Mr. Ord.) A Supreme Court with appellate jurisdiction only, a District Court with universal jurisdiction beyond a certain sum, and a Justices' Court with universal jurisdiction to a settled sum. When one wishes to bring a suit, it is easy for him to know whether his account is over or under $300. He can easily ascertain what court he should go before. Let us therefore establish three simple courts, so organized as to hold their jurisdiction within a certain limited sum. You have there all the officers that are necessary. The Supreme Court, which sits the whole year round for the decision of appellate cases, and which can transact all the appellate business of the State. You have district judges who, instead of spending two, three, or four months from their own districts, to transact the business of another court, are distinct and separate. You have for your justices the ordinary conservators of the peace. You have in your clerks, officers of the court amply sufficient to transact all the unopposed probate business of the country. Where is there a single wheel wanting in the machine? When we have enough let us not take any more. When we have tribunals sufficient, do not call up tribunals to complicate the judicial system of the State. We want simple courts, for, as a population in this country from every portion of the Union and from all parts of the world, we are accustomed to different systems of judiciary and different systems of law. Let us have a system which all the people can understand; and, if we adopt a simple judicial system, I think we will have a simple system of laws.

Mr. WOZENCRAFT. I am satisfied of one fact, that we cannot expedite business by debate. I move now that the Committee rise, in order that an appointment may be made of five or six persons by the Chair for the purpose of perfecting a plan to be reported to this House immediately.

The Committee then rose and reported progress.

On motion of Mr. BOTTS, the Secretary was directed to furnish each member with a copy of the judiciary system offered by the gentleman from Monterey, (Mr. Ord.)

Mr. CROSBY suggested that the proposition of the gentleman from San Joaquin was the same as he had offered in the early part of the evening.

Mr. SHERWOOD. I am satisfied that the movement is made for a very laudable object—that of bringing these three systems proposed together in one report; but I do not believe, from what experience I have had in committee, that any special committee can produce a report which can prevent more discussion than what we will have on the propositions now before the House. I have made up my mind in regard to the matter myself, and after this discussion I think every gentleman will be prepared to make up his mind and vote. After looking the ground carefully over, I am satisfied that there can be no compromise in the matter; that the House, after a full and free discussion, must choose between the propositions. I am opposed therefore to its going into any committee. I know that discussion is to be had, and that many gentlemen who are not lawyers have doubts on their minds in regard to which of these propositions should be adopted; but I think they will have the same doubts if this new committee brings in a proposition. The same views will then be advanced that are now advanced.

Mr. HASTINGS. It is my opinion that this matter will be greatly facilitated by the appointment of a committee. What is now before the House is an undigested medley of propositions. We find the two systems, as reported, confused. That of the minority would be a very good one had they continued it, but they have not thought proper to continue it; they have left off at a certain point and taken up the majority report. From whatever Constitution that system was taken, I think it would have our favor if they had gone through with it. A special committee could easily digest this matter, and make a report to the House which I have no doubt would be generally approved.

Mr. MCCARVER. I am in favor of referring it back to the Committee on the Constitution, with instructions. The sense of the House in relation to these different propositions can be given in the instructions.

Mr. JONES moved that a committee be appointed, with instructions to report in favor of three courts.

Mr. SHERWOOD. I cannot consent to vote for any such instructions, knowing the condition of this country and the difficulty of getting witnesses and jurors far from home. I would not be in favor of trying criminal cases, which under the instructions must be tried in a District Court, in the mining districts of this State. They would have to go from fifty to two hundred miles; you could not get your witnesses that distance. You must have a County Court near to the residence of these persons. I am in favor of a County Court, which the gentleman would exclude. When a murder or robbery is committed, if you wish to punish the criminal, you must have his trial where the witnesses against him will attend; but where the witnesses daily labor is one ounce, or sixteen dollars, you cannot get him to go any great distance to wait upon the court. You must have, as near as possible, justice administered where the crime is committed. Even all City Courts are excluded by his instructions, when most of the legal business will have to be performed in the City Courts.

Mr. JONES. I think my friend from Sacramento founds his argument upon a false supposition; that is, that these District Courts will be held in one particular place, and cannot be held in any other place.

Mr. HASTINGS. I would suggest this amendment: "Three courts, and such other courts as the Legislature shall think proper to create."

Mr. JONES. I accept it. These District Courts, Mr. President, are not necessarily held in one place alone, during the entire year. A District Court in the district of San Joaquin would not be held at Stockton during the entire year; it would go to every one of the principal mines, and there would be a court there once or twice, or four times, during the year. These witnesses whom the gentleman speaks of would be brought into that court at their own doors. Would this County Court be open all the time? Will the gentleman not give them particular terms? Where is the difference in convenience. Such is the object and intention of separating these courts. It is to give the district judges sufficient time to hold their courts at all the different places in the district. We have contended here, according to the report of the majority, that it is impossible for the district judge to do justice to his district and hold the Appellate Court. I certainly cannot agree to the necessity of these County Courts.

Mr. GWIN. I move to go into Committee of the Whole on the judiciary bill; and upon that question I call for the yeas and nays.

Mr. HALLECK. I wish to call the attention of the House to this point. It is proposed here to refer these three reports, as they are called, to a Select Committee, or back to the Committee on the Constitution. I should think it would be very improper to refer it back to the Committee on the Constitution. That Committee, with the Constitution of every State in the Union before it, has been at work three days on this report, and I think, when they have come to an almost unanimous decision, it would be altogether improper to send back the subject to them, and ask them to come to a reverse decision. As to a Select Committee, if they make a report, does it exclude all these propositions before the House? They would all be in order when this report comes in. Instead of three reports to choose from we would then have four. That Committee cannot take this subject into consideration, perfect a judicial system, and make their report in less than twenty-four hours; and the same length of time will be required to make copies of it for the use of the members. I really think the motion of the gentleman from San Francisco (Mr. Gwin) ought to prevail; that we should go into Committee of the Whole, take this question up, and decide it to-night or to-morrow. Otherwise, we certainly cannot get through until next week; and I do not believe we will be able to keep a quorum here beyond Tuesday.

Mr. HASTINGS. I shall oppose referring this to a Select Committee. I would suggest that we take all the various Constitutions and make such a Judiciary system from them as we please.

Mr. BOTTS. I believe, Mr. President, that I am inclined to make as much haste as any member of this House, and the object, the great object I have in referring this matter to a Select Committee, is to get them to examine more carefully than I could, from a casual reading in this House, a set of sections or articles that I believe to be valuable, and which I think would meet the wishes of the House.

Mr. TEFFT. I ask for the reading of the motion; and I beg leave to say that I am utterly opposed to this being referred back to the Committee on the Constitution.

Mr. SHERWOOD. I have a good many reasons against giving these instructions. I believe every county should pay its own criminal expenses; and that the proper court is the County Court. I will not go into the reasons, for I think the House is prepared to vote on this question.

Mr. LIPPITT. Before the vote is taken, I will simply give notice that, if the resolution now before the House is rejected, I shall offer another resolution, that the fifth article, as reported by the Committee on the Constitution, be referred back to the Committee, with instructions to remodel it so as to provide for the establishment of a Court of Appeals separate and distinct from the Circuit Court, and with certain other amendments. I am satisfied with the report of the Committee as it stands, with the exception that the first four or five sections I conceive to be faulty, in not providing for a separate Court of Appeals. The alteration which I propose will extend from the first to the fifth section. It is very certain that if the resolution is voted upon as it now stands, that vote will be a test vote. I have no particular desire that it should be made so, and, at the suggestion of any member, I would be willing to modify the resolution so as to make it a mere question of expediency.

Mr. Botts. Would it not be well to divide the question as to the appointment of this Committee and the instructions?

The Chair stated that the question before the House was on the appointment of a Select Committee of five.

The question was then taken and decided in the negative, by ayes 16, noes 19.

Mr. Lippitt then moved his resolution.

Mr. Hastings wished to inquire what was the necessity of pursuing a course of this kind? Could not the House amend the majority report in the manner suggested as well as the Committee?

Mr. Sherwood hoped the resolution would not be pressed. It would not facilitate the action of the Convention.

Mr. Jones understood the gentlemen (Mr. Lippitt) that he was satisfied with the report of the Committee, except where it connected the two courts—at least with the first five sections. He would ask him if he was satisfied with the 11th section. Those who chose to vote for it might do so; but, so far as he was concerned, he could not sanction it. He was in favor of no such section. He was opposed to the whole system. He moved to amend the resolution by instructing the Committee to report in favor of the establishment of three courts.

Mr Lippitt said this would defeat the very object he had in view.

The question was then taken, and the resolution was rejected.

On motion of Mr. Gwin, the House then resolved itself into Committee of the Whole on the Judiciary Bill.

COMMITTEE OF THE WHOLE.

Mr. Sherwood. I believe we are exactly in the same position as we were when the Committee last rose. I am in favor of the majority report with a few amendments, which I conceive it is in the power of any member to make, if the report be adopted in substance. There may be some one or two changes in effect, which I think would obviate the difficulty. In the first place, it creates a court of four judges, called the Supreme Court. Any three of these judges form a Court of Appeals. Each of these four judges is made a chief judge also, and at home is assigned a special portion of the State—a judicial district. If a case is appealed from his decision to the Supreme Court, the three other judges form a Court of Appeals to decide upon it. This at first forms the Supreme Court and Court of Appeals of the State. The Committee were desirous, as much as possible, of decreasing the expenses of the administration of the laws, and therefore proposed but one set of judges to perform the duties of the two highest courts. The Committee were aware that the expenses of the Government would be great in this country; that the salaries of these officers must be high, because their duties were arduous, and because the judges would have to be selected from the first legal characters in the State. At first, they supposed that this court would be all that was necessary; but, at the same time, they give the power to the Legislature, if they desire a separate and distinct Circuit Court with all its expenses, to create such court. It was a matter of economy with the Committee, and their plan does not differ in effect from the minority report, because the Legislature can separate the Circuit from the Supreme Court at its very first session, if it be thought desirable. They also, in the majority report, provide for a County Court and the election by the people, of a county judge, who shall, at the same time be surrogate, and vested with probate powers. They provide, also, for the election of justices of the peace by the people, who are to hold the court nearest to the residence of the persons who bring the suit. The justice of the peace is selected from the smallest subdivision of the district, and as it is desirable in a country like this where the expense of travelling is so great, and where time is so valuable, that justice should be administered, if possible, at his own door, of course a Justices' Court cannot be objected to. Next to that comes the County Court, which has cognizance of appeals from the Justices' Court. It will only be necessary to carry cases of great moment from the County Court to the Circuit Court. The Legislature are to decide what shall be the jurisdiction of the County Courts. Viewed then, as a matter of expense, I conceive that the majority report of the Committee (which received the sanction, I believe, of all the members except one) is preferable; and in presenting this Constitution to our constituents, it is most desirable, inasmuch as our expenses here have been very large, and as the expenses of the State Government—the Legislature, the Governor, the State officers, the Judiciary, and every other branch—must be very high, that we present a Constitution which makes as little machinery as the State can get along with, and with no more cogs in the wheels than are actually necessary. If you make fewer officers and less expense, the Constitution will receive more votes. In one or two or three years, if the people demand a Circuit Court separate from the Supreme Court, then the Legislature can provide for the separation. For the present, I think four able and distinguished jurists are entirely sufficient to perform the duties of these two courts. I fear nothing from these three judges. They act independently; their judgments are separate and distinct.

I will not proceed further in discussing this question. There are many reasons why I prefer the majority report to either of the reports in question. I think its advantages go through the entire system. It elects its clerks and officers, which is not provided for in at least one or perhaps both of the other plans presented to the House.

Mr. Dimmick, by permission of the House, made some amendments to his proposition.

Mr. Lippitt. I wish to state the reason of the vote which I shall give on these propositions. I prefer, as a whole, the majority report of the Committee. There are certainly sections proposed by the gentleman from San Jose (Mr. Dimmick) and the gentleman from Monterey (Mr. Ord) which I would prefer, but I find myself obliged to vote for some system as a whole. I am compelled to select at once one of these three systems. I am satisfied with the report of the Committee, with the single exception, that there is no Court of Appeals separate from the Circuit Court provided for. I have already tested the opinion of the House on this matter, and I find they are not willing to instruct the Committee to provide for the separation. For that reason, I shall vote against every proposition before the House in its present form.

Mr. Botts. I wish to know what would be the effect of rejecting the proposition of the gentleman from San Jose, (Mr. Dimmick.)

The Chair stated that the question would then come up on the amendment of the gentleman from Monterey, (Mr. Ord.)

Mr. Crosby. I hope there may be some compromise. The principal question at issue is the propriety of a separate Supreme Court and District Court.

Mr. Botts. I offer this resolution as a test question:

Resolved, That in the opinion of the Committee the Supreme Court of Appeals should be separate and distinct from the District Courts.

The question was then taken, and the resolution was adopted.

The Chair stated that the amendment of the gentleman from San Jose (Mr. Dimmick) was before the House.

Some discussion took place here as to the order of reports. Several propositions were made to facilitate the action of the House, when finally, without coming to any decision, the Committee rose and reported progress.

Mr. SHERWOOD moved that a Committee of three be appointed with instructions, in conformity with the resolution adopted in Committee of the Whole, to make the two courts separate, and to bring in a report on the different propositions modeled on that plan, by to-morrow morning at 12 o'clock.

Mr. HILL suggested a Committee of five instead of three.

Mr. SHERWOOD thought three would perform the business more expeditiously and with less discussion.

The question was then taken on the highest number, "five," and decided in the negative.

A Committee of three was then appointed, consisting of Messrs. Norton, Dimmick, and Jones.

On motion, the House then adjourned till 10 o'clock to-morrow morning.

WEDNESDAY, SEPTEMBER 26, 1849.

The Convention met pursuant to adjournment. Prayer by the Rev. S. H. Willey.

The journal of yesterday was read, amended, and approved.

Mr. VALLEJO offered the following, which, being objected to, lies over for one day, viz:

Resolved, That three Commissioners be elected by ballot to draft a code of laws for the State of California; to report at the first session of the Legislature to be elected under this Constitution.

Mr. NORTON, from the Special Committee on the Judiciary, made a report; which was read and referred to the Committee of the Whole.

The House then resolved itself into Committee of the Whole, Mr. BOTTS in the Chair, on the report of the Select Committee on the Judiciary.

The question was taken on the first and second sections of the report, and they were adopted without debate, as follows:

SEC. 1. The judicial power of this State shall be vested in a Supreme Court, in District Courts, in County Courts, and in Justices of the Peace. The Legislature may also establish such municipal and other inferior courts as may be deemed necessary.

SEC. 2. The Supreme Court shall consist of a Chief Justice and two Associate Justices, any two of whom shall constitute a quorum.

The question being on the third section, viz:

SEC. 3. The Justices of the Supreme Court shall be elected at the general election by the qualified electors of the State, and shall hold their offices for the term of six years, from the first day of January next after their election: *Provided*, That the Legislature shall at its first meeting elect a Chief Justice and two Associate Justices of the Supreme Court by joint vote of both Houses, and so classify them that one shall go out of office every two years. After the first election, the Justice in commission shall be the Chief Justice.

Mr. HASTINGS moved to amend by striking out the proviso. He desired that the election of justices and other officers should be left to the people. The people are as well qualified to judge of these officers as the Legislature. Great abuse would be created by having the Legislature control this matter.

Mr. NORTON. The Committee are as much in favor of the election of judges by the people as the gentleman. I believe a great majority of the members of this House are in favor of leaving the election of these officers to the people. But it is well known that, under the peculiar organization and condition of this country at present, it would be almost impossible at an election coming off as soon as the next election necessarily must, that the people could have time to ascertain and fix upon the best men to be elected as judges of the Supreme Court. The people who are now resident in this country are to a great extent strangers to each other. They hardly know their next door neighbors, and it is scarcely to be expected that, under such a state of things, they should be prepared so soon to elect the proper persons to these responsible offices. The Legislature, it is but reasonable to suppose, will be composed of men acquainted with the wants of the country; they will assemble after this first election, and they will be qualified by their acquaintance with the people and the country to select the proper persons to compose our judiciary. It is only at the first session that they are to be elected in this way. For this reason, the Committee deemed it expedient to insert the proviso. After the first session of the Legislature, the people will have become more settled and better acquainted with their prominent men, and they can then elect their own judicial officers. It would be impracticable to make an efficient judiciary at the first general election.

The question was then taken, and the amendment was rejected.

The section as reported was then adopted.

The fourth section being under consideration, Mr. LIPPITT moved to insert after the word "thereof," and before the word "shall," the words "as well as all district and county judges;" which motion having passed, the section as amended was adopted.

Mr. NORIEGO suggested that the jurisdiction of the Appellate Court should be limited to the sum of $200.

Mr. JONES moved a reconsideration of the vote on the adoption of the section, in order to test the sense of the House on the proposed limitation.

Mr. LIPPITT. I believe that according to parliamentary usage whenever a motion is made for reconsideration it is in order to go into the consideration of the whole question. I would simply say, in relation to the amendment proposed, limiting cases to $200, that sometimes questions of the utmost importance—questions of the utmost difficulty—which have embarrassed the highest courts in our country, have turned upon a less amount than $200 or even $50. I therefore do not think it would be advisable, on the whole, to limit the appellate jurisdiction of the highest court to any amount whatever. Cases have occurred, and no doubt will occur again, where questions involving principles of the utmost importance have come up upon a paltry matter in amount, involving only ten or twenty dollars.

Mr. NORIEGO. Among many of the reasons which I have for proposing the amendment, the principal one is, that very often there are rich persons who do not care so much about the decision of the case on account of the amount involved in it, but who make use of their wealth to carry out their caprices; and who thereby compel these judges, who ought to be occupied in higher matters, to attend to these trivial disputes, merely to gratify the whims and caprices of certain men who may be possessed of property. If the door is left open to appeal in this way, there would be no end to it. I have known persons to appeal merely on the subject of a calf, and send it up to the Supreme Court of Mexico, not on account of the value of the article, but to gratify a malicious feeling towards the opposite party. I therefore desire that there shall be some limitation; the judgments will then be properly attended to. It is very true that often great principles are involved in very small amounts; but I do not consider that this tribunal has the deciding of principles. Its province is to decide the law.

Mr. LIPPITT. In regard to the caprices of men, I would remark that there is a check in the costs. Under any proper system of laws, the costs are thrown upon the appealing parties. That will operate as a very powerful check in preventing any abuse of the right of appeal.

The question on the reconsideration of the vote adopting the fourth section was then taken, and decided in the affirmative, by ayes 15, nays 13.

The question being on the fourth section, as amended,

Mr. NORIEGO moved to amend by inserting after the word "cases" and before the word "in," the words "where the matter in dispute exceeds $200."

Mr. JONES. I am in favor of the proposed amendment. I do not believe that cases, however small in importance or sum, should be brought before the Supreme Court; that sums of five, ten, or fifty dollars, which the desire of litigation might induce any individual to bring before the Supreme Court, should occupy its time and attention. We all know that there are individuals in a community who care for no cost or delay, and they will push the smallest case to the greatest extreme. I wish to prevent them from taking up the time of the Supreme Court; its time and attention should not be occupied by such small matters. Picture to yourself three supreme judges presiding over some petty case which some petty justice of the peace has decided. I certainly am not in favor of putting questions of this kind before a supreme tribunal. But I would make an exception. I would say where any tax, toll, or impost shall be decided. That should be an exception. There may be great questions at issue in that case. Let any case of tax, toll, or impost, therefore, be decided by the supreme judicial tribunal. In cases of municipal fines, you might have such a fine as would act with great hardship upon some of the inhabitants; it might be only $100. This should be decided by the Supreme Court.

Mr. LIPPITT. I am decidedly opposed to the amendment for two reasons. The first I have already stated—that all cases under $200 are not petty cases. There are many cases under that sum which involve most important principles, and require the highest legal wisdom of the country to settle. The second reason is, that it will work oppressively upon the poor if this amendment is adopted. They will bring the great mass of suits in cases under $200; it is the poor who will be the litigants. Then, sir, if this amendment is adopted, you allow the rich man, in all his suits, to go before the highest tribunal; to avail himself of the highest legal wisdom of the land. At the same time, you tell the poor man he shall have the benefit of only one Court of Appeals; that he shall not have the benefit of any higher tribunal than the District Court. It is taken for granted that the ultimate Court of Appeals is a wiser, and will decide more correctly than the inferior courts. Our system, which we are about to establish, supposes that as a principle. I contend, therefore, that the poor have just as much right to carry up their disputes, and have them settled by the most competent tribunals, as the richest man in the land.

Mr. MCCARVER. I am in favor of all of this section except the latter part. The part that my friend from San Francisco (Mr. Lippitt) objects to, I am decidedly in favor of, for the very fact that it stops all unnecessary litigation, and prevents the lawyers of the county, who wish to figure in the Supreme Court, from bringing in every petty case that may occur. I am also opposed to that part of the amendment that provides for an appeal of criminal cases to the Supreme Court. If we adopt that system, we may take it for granted that every case will go to the Supreme Court. Who would suffer himself to be hung in thirty days when he has an opportunity of going to a higher court, with the prospect of a different decision? The State is at the expense of keeping this individual until his case can be brought into the Supreme Court and decided by that tribunal. I am in favor of having a fair trial before a jury; and whenever they have decided the case, if they say hang him, then hang him in thirty days, and do not give him an opportunity to escape. I do not desire that men shall get clear, after they have been found guilty before a jury of their peers, by any quibble of the law. I wish to see them justly tried, and if found guilty, then justly and properly punished.

Mr. SHERWOOD. I am utterly surprised to hear such a sentiment advanced by my colleague. He denies to a man who may have been convicted because some techinal point may have compelled the conviction, and who may be as innocent as he who suffered on the cross, the privilege of appearing before a higher tribunal! Public sentiment throughout the world is gaining ground against punishment by death. Although I do not go that far, yet I am for affording an innocent man the last possible chance of preserving his life. If we, upon our Constitution, place the provision that a man shall not have the chance to go to a higher tribunal, what will be the common opinion of the world? That we are more barbarous than the heathen. I say, sir, if a man has a chance for his life, take it not away from him. If he is innocent, and can prove it, or if the court has wrongly construed, through prejudice or any other cause, the law, give him a chance to go to a higher tribunal. If you hang him by the neck till he is dead, and then it shall appear that his appeal was good and sound, my colleague would say that he regretted there was not a chance for a trial before a higher tribunal. You cannot recall the slumbering dead from the grave. And yet, within the Constitution—the law which is to govern us for all time, unless the Legislature and people get together another Convention, which I trust will not be necessary for many years—you have fixed this unchristian principle; you hang many men who afterwards may be proved to be innocent. I trust we will not prove ourselves, in the opinion of the world, so blood-thirsty as this. I have known, in the State from which I came, cases where innocent men would have been hung, but for an appeal, when it was afterwards clearly proved that they were innocent; and the only means of proving their innocence was not by bringing in new proof in the Supreme Court, but by appealing on account of wrong decisions, which were made by prejudiced men. In the Supreme Court new evidence is not granted. If an appeal is made, it is made upon some wrong decision. I am in favor of granting every opportunity to the accused, of avoiding the punishment of death if he is innocent; if he is guilty, he will be punished notwithstanding the appeal.

Mr. Norton. I am decidedly opposed to the first part of the amendment. I am willing to allow appeals in criminal cases where they amount to felony. That, I think, should be provided for. The argument of the gentleman from Sacramento (Mr. Sherwood) shows that such should be the case. I am opposed to the remainder of the amendment upon the grounds given by my colleague, (Mr. Lippitt,) and also upon another ground. It has been stated that this right of appeal is liable to abuse; that men of wealth would carry cases to the highest tribunal, where the poor could not go. I do not consider this argument to be well founded. If a decision in the court below is radically right, the party against whom the decision is made, no matter what may be his wealth, if he goes to the highest tribunal of the land, has the case again decided against him. The cost is thus thrown upon him, and he bears the whole burden of the suit. It is he who is injured, and not the poor man. But, sir, if a case is decided by the court below wrongfully, no matter whether against the rich man or the poor man, he should have the right to go to the highest tribunal to get justice, if he cannot get it below. If he gets a wrong decision against him in a matter not amounting to $200, he should have the same right to go to a higher tribunal and have that decision reversed, as he would if it amounted to more than $200. He should have the right in all cases—the poor man as well as the rich. If he is aggrieved in one court, his rights should be protected in another.

Mr. Hastings. I shall feel myself compelled to oppose the amendment as it now stands, although having on a former occasion opposed the infliction of death as a punishment for crime, I would of course here favor any measure that would have that effect. But the other portions of the amendment I cannot support. It strikes fatally at another unfortunate class of men—the poor. By this provision, the poor are deprived of the privilege of maintaining their interests to the same extent that the rich are. Let us suppose a case. The amount involved is $199; the parties are both poor. The court is prejudiced, and decides against the party in favor of whom the decision should have been given. A friend advises the injured party to appeal. He replies that he cannot, because the Constitution of the State prohibits him. But his friend is a rich man, and proposes to advance the money—still the Constitution interferes. This amendment ought not to prevail for another reason. So far from encouraging litigation, the section, as it stands, allowing the right of appeal in all cases, avoids that result. We suppose that a case is pending in court; it is decided unjustly and cannot be appealed. Now, this same question involves, perhaps, the interests of fifty men in the community, who cannot appeal their cases. If these parties could come forward and say to the parties whose suit is in court, let this case go up; we will pay part of the expense in order to settle a great principle by which we are all willing to abide. Your case will decide ours, and prevent all litigation. I maintain, therefore, that every party, whether rich or poor, ought to be entitled to the benefits of appeal to the highest tribunal.

Mr. Noriego. No doubt this question is a very difficult one to determine. The gentleman has stated various examples. Now I propose, in a contra position, to state one or two others of a different kind. It is said that this provision operates unjustly on the poor—that they cannot appeal, because they have not the means—that the rich man can carry his case to the highest tribunal, while the poor man is denied that privilege. There are many classes of men who have money, but who have not the capacity to carry on their affairs as they ought. These classes the lawyers pounce upon like vultures upon dead bodies; and although the lawyers know they cannot succeed in their suits, they urge them to go on. This is one reason why I offer the amendment. I think these classes require protection from the ingeunity of men who derive their income from the litigation which they are enabled to produce. What do they care how long the suit lasts, or what it will cost, provided they make money by it. There are in California a great many persons who are not in want of money, but who are totally unacquainted with the technicalities of the law, and have not sufficient sagacity to guard against the abuses to which this right of appeal in petty cases would subject them.

Mr. Lippitt. The whole scope of the gentleman's argument seems to be that certain classes in California, either poor men or ignorant men, would be left open to the ingenuity of dishonest lawyers. I can only say that it is perfectly impracticable, by any legislation, or any amendment, or any Constitution, to guard clients against that class of men. It would puzzle more than a Yankee legislator to do it.

Mr. McCarver. I admit there is a great deal of sagacity in that class of men, and that it requires considerable wisdom to guard against them—particularly when they are engaged in forming the organic law of the State. I fully agree with the gentleman from Santa Barbara, (Mr. Noriego,) in his opinion. I have seen cases carried to the Supreme Court under the amount of eight or ten dollars, and carried on till the costs reached a thousand dollars. The poor man is often persuaded to take an appeal, and finally is mulcted in the costs, and ruined forever. I go for the amendment, with the exception of the provision which I objected to a little while ago, with respect to appeals in criminal cases, where the parties have been duly tried and found guilty. I think the best way is to hang them. It will be the most effectual way of preventing them from escaping.

Mr. Hastings. In order to get a direct vote on this subject, if it is susceptible of division, I call for a division.

Mr. Jones. I have only to remark that the most frequent cases under $200 are cases of wages, the hire of servants and laborers. The next most frequent cases are small debts due persons in commercial business. If you give two courts an appellate jurisdiction over cases of this kind, there will be an immense delay in the collection of debts. The poor man goes to work for the rich man, who does not pay; the poor man carries his case up; the rich man is able to pay the expense, and will carry it to any extent.

Mr. Lippitt. The poor man need not appeal unless he chooses.

Mr. Brown. It frequently happens that the poor man is compelled to follow the rich man, if he cannot get justice in any other way. The argument of the gentleman from Santa Barbara (Mr. Noriego) is excellent, and I fully concur with him on this subject.

Mr. Ord. I will state the result of my experience. It probably differs from that of the two lawyers on the other side of the House—that nine-tenths of the cases under two hundred dollars are brought by poor men. They are the plaintiffs; they go to the court and seek redress; and if you give the right of appeal in all cases, whatever the amount in controversy, the rich man can take his appeal; he can keep the poor man out of his wages until it is decided by the Supreme Court. It may cost the poor man ten times the amount of the original claim. I therefore differ in opinion from the gentleman across the way, as to the result of this limitation. I shall vote for the amendment of the gentleman from Santa Barbara, (Mr. Noriego.)

Mr. Hastings. My experience is just the reverse. It is true that it is the poor man who is under the necessity of instituting suit as a general thing—perhaps for compensation for his daily labor; but what is the result if you deprive him of the right of appeal. He enters his suit in the County Court, if you please, against an immensely wealthy man. This court is probably under the immediate influence of wealthy men, and without intending injustice to the poor man, they decide the case against him. The rich man's influence operates almost unconsciously upon the members of the court. He is a prominent man in the county, and his name has a controlling power over the County and Circuit Courts. But give the poor man the privilege of going further, and he goes to a Court that is beyond the influence of the wealthy man.

Mr. Lippitt. My own professional experience certainly confirms the view just stated to the House. It is a new view, and a very strong one. I have always found that the influence of the poor man is much greater in the higher than in the lower courts. The relative influence of the rich and poor differs in the lower courts. In the highest tribunals there is no difference made between them, in ordinary cases. If the amendment is adopted, I think that the operation of it will be rather against the poor than the rich. The whole amendment amounts, as I view it, to this: for all time to come, as long as this Constitution lasts, it prohibits the application of the best talent and fairest judgment to all disputes under $200. It tells the poor that they shall not enjoy the advantages, as long as this Constitution endures, of the best law and justice, but must take up with the second rate. I shall therefore vote against the amendment.

Mr. Jones. Does the gentleman remember that these persons have a right to juries in the first court and second court. If twelve of their peers decide against them, it is not probable that injustice will be done them.

Mr. Dimmick. I ask the gentleman who it is that introduces and shuts out testimony before these twelve men. It is the justice of the peace. He decides what testimony shall be introduced before the court; and he it is who brings the facts before these twelve men. I concur with the remarks of the gentleman from Sacramento, (Mr. Hastings,) who has well spoken of the influence which the rich man has upon the courts of his neighborhood. I have seen that influence in my course of life, and I know how often it prejudices the judgment of men. But here is one thing in favor of the poor man—the lawyer, when he sees that his client is right, does not ask whether he has money or not. If he knows he is right, and can succeed in gaining his suit, he does not ask whether he has property or not; he knows what the result of the suit will be, and will not advise the poor man to take the appeal, unless he has good cause for believing that it will be decided against the rich man.

Mr. Vermeule. In illustration of my vote to support the right of appeal in all cases, I would simply state what I conceive to be a few practical common sense views. In the first place, in order to show that the influence of the rich man in the court below is overwhelming, I would ask who controls the elections and appointments of its officers? It is not the tenants of the houses in the village, but the owners. With regard to the long course of litigation which my colleague from San Joaquin (Mr. Jones) supposes will be the result of permitting the right of appeal in all cases, does it follow that the poor man can always get that appeal? If the judge below is an honest man, he will not get the appeal unless it is a just one.

Mr. Lippitt. It will be the duty of the Legislature to limit the right of appeal.

Mr. Vermeule. I believe in abstract principles. I believe in their justice. If a principle be good in the abstract it must be good in practice; and I believe the right of appeal is a righteous abstract principle.

Mr. Ord. One word in reply to the gentleman across the way, (Mr. Hastings.) I think, with regard to the opinion that he expressed different from my own as regards the decisions of lower courts of justice, that probably two of the gentlemen on that side have practiced in a State where these judges are not elected by the people.

Mr. Norton. They were elected by the people—the gentleman is mistaken.

Mr. Ord. No, sir; you had but one, and that was the lowest judicial officer in your State—justices of the peace. I believe neither of the gentlemen has practiced under that system. I have practiced under a system where justices of the peace were elected by the people; and I think that the objection urged against the decisions of the lower courts is not a valid one. I think that the people of the district will take care that they elect men who will not be swayed by rich men. I should be sorry to suppose that the people would, in the exercise of that right, elect men of so little integrity as to be influenced by men of wealth.

Mr. Vermeule. One suggestion. If the right of appeal be admitted in these small cases, will not the fact, that a supervisory power is vested in the Supreme Court over the inferior courts, make the judges of the inferior courts more careful and correct in their decisions?

Mr. Hastings. It seems to me that the gentleman from Monterey (Mr. Ord) did not carry out his argument. The justice of the peace is elected by the influence of these wealthy men. Perhaps he occupies the house belonging to one of them. He finds one great obstacle, when the case is brought before the court, in arriving at what is termed justice. When he is required to read the law, he cannot distinctly see it; the golden spectacles is drawn over his eyes. The great man controls the district in which this small man resides. Hence the prejudiced decisions, from which the poor man cannot appeal.

Mr. Ord. If I believed that these justices of the peace, and other judges who are elected by the people, could be swayed by one or more rich men, I would vote against the principle which we have adopted, of making them elective by the people. I think the gentleman's argument strikes at the whole elective system of the judiciary.

Mr. Jones. I am willing to admit an amendment—that in all cases where the justice of the peace is elected, and occupies the house or houses of the plaintiff, or in all cases where he is elected by one man in the district, then, that this provision shall be null and void.

Mr. Tefft. Has not every member of the House who has practiced law, without reference to the States, seen gross and rank injustice done where the amount was less than $200? I think the proposition is a preposterous one.

Mr. Hastings. I call for a division in reference to civil and criminal cases.

Mr. Norton. I believe that the latter part of the amendment is entirely unnecessary, and the other is too preposterous to be introduced.

Mr. Lippitt. I think a division of the question is unnecessary.

Mr. Jones. The object of the part of the amendment in relation to criminal jurisdiction is to give the Supreme Court appellate jurisdiction upon questions of law in criminal cases. As to trying questions of fact tried in the courts below, the Supreme Court has nothing to do with that; and as to the gentleman's ideas of preposterosity—that this proposition is too prepostorous to be considered for a moment—in more than half the States of the Union, the appellate jurisdiction of the Supreme Court is limited. I am very much mistaken if there are more than two States where it is not limited. Therefore, this preposterous proposition is a preposterosity of twenty-eight of the States of the Union.

Mr. Lippitt. I hope the question will not be divided. If the first part of the amendment is stricken out, the second part will not be required. If it is the desire of the House, however, I withdraw the objection.

The Chair then stated that the question would be upon the first portion of the amendment offered by the gentleman from Santa Barbara, (Mr. Noriego,) which was taken, and the result was ayes 15, noes 16.

On motion, there was a re-count, and it was decided by ayes 17, noes 18.

On motion, Mr. Semple and Mr. Hoppe were appointed tellers, and the question being again taken, it was decided by ayes 18, noes 17—so the first portion of the amendment was adopted.

The question was then taken on the latter portion of the amendment, and it was adopted.

The question recurring on the section as amended,

Mr. Norton moved to strike it out, with the intention of moving a section in its place. It was of no use in its present form.

Mr. Lippitt. I would suggest to my colleague that he reserve this motion till the final action of the House.

Mr. Norton. I would rather see the motion prevail here. I wish to strike out the section as it stands, with the intention of offering it as it originally stood.

Mr. Jones. I rise to a question of order. I do not believe the gentleman has any such right under the rules.

Mr. Lippitt. The object of the gentleman cannot be attained in that way.

Mr. Brown. I am not surprised at the excitement this question has made. The interests it effects are important to two classes in this House; the one are going to be deprived of very important employment or greatly benefited by the decision; and the other must of course pay the profits.

The Chair did not think it exactly in order to charge any gentleman or class of gentlemen on this floor with personal motives.

Mr. Brown. I do not wish to be understood in that way. Perhaps my mode of expressing myself is not as distinct as it might be. There is an interest—a general interest in the decision of this question; and whenever we take an interest in any question, I think our views are apt to be tinctured in some degree by our profession or employment. I hope I shall not be considered as impugning the motives of any individual or class, by advancing this principle. There are private interests which affect every man to some extent. I consider this a question which involves these interests. Those who have made the law their study, and who gain their living by it, have opinions influenced, no doubt unconsciously, by the interests of that profession. Others form different opinions based upon different considerations. The question is one of very great importance. The experience of fifty years has shown me that lawsuits are unprofitable to the litigants; they are usually attended with costs, loss of time, ill feeling, and many other evil results to both parties. It is well, therefore, in my opinion, to embrace such features in our judiciary system as will operate as a check upon litigation. I conceive that it is not to the benefit of the community that these decisions should be carried from court to court at their expense. The community must suffer for it in the end, for whatever retards or diminishes the productive industry of the poeple individually, must operate to their disadvantage as a body. I am opposed to the principle of holding out inducements for appeals in every petty case that may arise.

Mr. Vermeule. I would ask the gentleman if he does not see here in this body some lawyers who are in favor of, and some against the amendment. There certainly appears to be as much division of opinion among legal gentlemen as among others in this question, so that they cannot be justly charged with having their own interests in view.

Mr. Brown. I do not intend to be understood as making that charge. I said that the views of all men are tinctured more or less by the character of their employment.

Mr. Vermeule. I am perfectly satisfied with the gentleman's explanation. Lawyers are a very useful body of men, and when this Constitution goes forth to the world it will be greatly indebted to them for the part they took in its formation.

Mr. Price. I am gratified with the result of the vote upon this amendment. I am satisfied that it is important to check appeals. The restriction I think is a just and proper one. I have seen the greatest injury result to parties from these appeals in small cases. In relation to the influence spoken of here, of the rich over the poor, in controlling the decisions of the magistrates' or lower courts, I do not believe it has any existence. I have seen quite the reverse; my experience has been, that the rich man never had the chance in the lower court that the poor man has had. The poor man appears there with the sympathies of the community; and the jury and the court consider the ability of the one to pay, and the inability of the other to lose. I know that wealth is a very powerful inducement, and I believe it controls the judgment of the courts in many cases; but I consider when these magistrates are elected by the people themselves, as provided in this Constitution, that no improper influence can be brought to bear against the poor man; and particularly in California, where there is to be a greater equality of wealth than in any other State of the Union. I trust, sir, that the amendment will be engrafted permanently upon this Constitution. I believe it is of vital importance to the well-being of the community, and I hope that, upon reflection, my colleague (Mr. Norton) will withdraw his motion to strike out this section as it now stands.

Mr. McCarver. I hope the House will not strike out the provision which we have adopted. I have nothing to say as regards the impugning of the motives of the lawyers; but I can say this: that in almost every case of litigation which I ever had in my life, I was persuaded by the counsel that I would succeed if I took an appeal to the Supreme Court. The counsel almost invariably persuades the party complaining that he will gain his suit by an appeal, and when the matter comes up before the court, he usually finds himself defeated. The claimant is of course disposed to believe in the justice of his own case, and suffers the appeal to be taken, to his ruin. I think it is the duty of this Convention to protect the community against this abuse. I do not believe there are lawyers here that have any such object in view; but so far as I have been concerned in litigation, I have always found it the case that the counsel advises this course; and as one of the citizens of the community, and as a guardian of the interests of those who sent me here, I believe it to be my duty to support this restriction. Whenever the yeas and nays are called, I will be proud to record my vote in favor of it.

Mr. Shannon. I have heard some curious arguments brought forward on this subject. I have heard distinctions drawn between one class of the community and another; I have seen lines drawn between the rich and the poor; between one profession and another; personal allusions made and thrown back. I think, sir, that a debate of this kind ought to be brought to an end as soon as possible. I see no cause for such distinctions here; and I thank my friend from San Joaquin (Mr. Vermeule) for meeting them, so far as the profession to which I belong is concerned. Still, Mr. Chairman, I must oppose the motion of the gentleman (Mr. Norton) to strike this section out, without any reference whatever to rich or poor; to the inability of the poor man to carry his suits up to the ultimate tribunal, or to the ability of the rich man. I am in favor of including this provision upon what I regard as a principle of common justice. It is a very proper and necessary limitation. I do not think it is right, that every petty suit, from five dollars up, should go through two or three or four courts, and go before the Supreme Court, for the grave consideration and discussion of that tribunal. You will find that the decisions of the justices of the peace, made immediately at home, close by the doors of the parties concerned, where the facts are known, are generally correct. I am perfectly willing to leave these petty suits to be settled by these decisions. They have the right of appeal to the District Court in cases of errors of law. For these reasons, I shall vote in favor of the amendment of the gentleman from Santa Barbara, (Mr. Noriego) and against the motion of the gentleman from San Francisco (Mr. Norton) to strike out the section.

Mr. Price. I wish to place one view before the House, and it is this: that, in my observation, the court of last appeal always feels a higher responsibility in its decisions, and is more likely to be correct than where appeal is made in the lower courts. It has a higher responsibility and generally gives better satisfaction, because its judgments are made up with greater deliberation and care.

Mr. CROSBY. One word. I think the profession will bear me witness that the gentleman's experience has proved entirely contrary to theirs. If any influence is brought to bear upon these courts, it is generally upon the court of last resort. An inferior court is always tenacious of its decisions, and takes care that these decisions are made so that they will not be reversed.

Mr. JONES. If the motion to strike out prevails, no part or portion of the section can hereafter be introduced. Now there are various parts of this section necessary to the judicial system proposed. How will the House proceed then, if the motion to strike out prevails?

Mr. NORTON. I withdraw the motion for the purpose of putting and end to this debate.

The fourth section, as previously amended, was then adopted, viz:

SEC. 4. The Supreme Court shall have appellate jurisdiction in all cases when the matter in dispute exceeds $200, or concerns the legality of any tax, toll, or impost, or municipal fine, and to all criminal cases amounting to felony, on questions of law alone. And the said court, and each of the justices thereof, as well as all district and county judges, shall have power to issue writs of *habeas corpus* at the instance of any person held in actual custody. They shall also have power to issue all other writs and process necessary to their appellate jurisdiction, and shall be conservators of the peace throughout the State.

On motion of Mr. LIPPITT, the Committee then rose, reported progress, and had leave to sit again.

Mr. NORIEGO expressed a desire to have a recess until 7 o'clock, in order that the translator might have an opportunity of translating the report now before the House.

Mr. HILL alluded to the fact that several members spoke of leaving in the next steamer for the southern districts, and that it was desirable to get through the business of the Convention before its arrival.

Mr. BOTTS hoped no such consideration as that would influence the House in its action.

The CHAIR expressed the opinion that it was highly improper for any member or any delegation, to talk about abandoning their seats until the object for which the people sent them here was accomplished. It was to be hoped that the subject would not be alluded to again.

On motion, the House then adjourned till 7 o'clock.

EVENING SESSION, 7 O'CLOCK P. M.

On motion of Mr. CROSBY, the House resolved itself into Committee of the Whole, Mr. LIPPITT in the chair, on the report of the Special Committee on the Judiciary.

Sections five and six were then adopted, as follows:

SEC. 5. The State shall be divided by the first Legislature into a convenient number of districts, subject to such alteration from time to time, as the public good may require; for each of which, a district judge shall be appointed by the joint vote of the Legislature at its first meeting, who shall hold his office for two years from the first day of January next after his election; after which, said judges shall be elected by the qualified electors of their respective districts at the general election, and shall hold their office for the term of six years.

SEC. 6. The District Courts shall have original jurisdiction in law and equity, in all civil cases where the amount in dispute exceeds $200, exclusive of interest. In all criminal cases not otherwise provided for, and in all issues of fact joined in the Probate Court, their jurisdiction shall be unlimited.

Section seven being under consideration—

Mr. McDOUGAL offered to amend by inserting after the word "election" and before the word "of," the words "by the people."

Mr. GWIN. Will the gentleman provide that sheriffs and coroners shall also be elected by the people?

Mr. McDougal. Most assuredly. I propose that the Legislature shall provide for the election of all officers of their courts by the people.

Mr. Shannon. I would ask if the proposition of the gentleman is not provided for in some other part of the report of the Committee?

Mr. Norton. The Committee supposed that it was a necessary inference that the election would be by the people. It was not thought necessary to insert the words, but I have no objection to them.

The section as amended, was then adopted, viz:

Sec. 7. The Legislature shall provide for the election, by the people, of a clerk of the Supreme Court and County Court clerks, district attorneys, sheriffs, coroners, and other necessary officers, and shall fix by law their duties and compensation. County clerks shall be ex-officio clerks of the District Courts in and for their respective counties.

Mr. Norton. I would now state that the majority report contains the remainder of the sections nearly word for word, commencing at the eighth section.

Sections 8, 9, 10, 11, 12, 13, 14, 15, and 16, were then adopted without debate, as follows:

Sec. 8. There shall be elected in each of the organized counties of this State, one county judge, who shall hold his office for four years. He shall hold the County Court, and perform the duties of surrogate or probate judge. The county judge, with two justices of the peace, to be designated by law, shall hold Courts of Sessions, with such criminal jurisdiction as the Legislature shall prescribe; and he shall perform such duties as shall be required by law.

Sec. 9. The County Court shall have such jurisdiction in cases arising in Justices' Courts and in special cases, as the Legislature may prescribe, but shall have no original civil jurisdiction, except in such special cases.

Sec. 10. The times and places of holding the terms of the Supreme Court and the general and special terms of the District Courts within the several districts shall be provided for by law.

Sec. 11. No judicial officer except justices of the peace, shall receive, to his own use, any fees, or perquisites of office.

Sec. 12. The Legislature shall provide for the speedy publication of all statute laws, and of such judicial decisions as it may deem expedient, and all laws and judicial decisions shall be free for publication by any person.

Sec. 13. Tribunals for conciliation may be established, with such powers and duties as may be prescribed by law; but such tribunals shall have no power to render judgment to be obligatory on the parties, except they voluntarily submit their matters in difference, and agree to abide the judgment, or assent thereto in the presence of such tribunals, in such cases as shall be prescribed by law.

Sec. 14. The Legislature shall determine the number of justices of the peace to be elected in each county, city, town, and incorporated village of the State, and fix by law their powers, duties, and responsibilities. It shall also determine in what cases appeals may be made from Justices' Court to the County Court.

Sec. 15. The justices of the Supreme Court and judges of the District Courts, shall severally, at stated times, during their continuance in office, receive for their services a compensation to be paid out of the treasury, which shall not be increased or diminished during the term for which they shall have been elected. The county judges shall also, severally, at stated times, receive for their services a compensation to be paid out of the county treasury of their respective counties, which shall not be increased or diminished during the term for which they shall have been elected.

Sec. 16. The justices of the Supreme Court and district judges, shall be ineligible to any other office during the term which they shall have been elected.

Mr. Ord then moved the following as section 17, viz:

Sec. 17. Judges shall not charge juries with respect to matters of fact, but may state the testimony and declare the law.

Mr. Botts. I presume the object of the gentleman is to prevent a custom which I understand prevails in some portions of the world—to prevent the judge from arguing the case before the jury in what is commonly called the summing up. If that be the object, I think it is wholly defeated by the amendment as it now stands; because, if the judge is permitted to state the testimony, he can state it exactly in that objectionable way which it is intended to avoid. It sometimes happens that the judge, in summing up the testimony, takes advantage of this privilege to become a party to the suit before the court. I do not know that such a practice is common in our own country, but it is in England, and is a very reprehensible one. I think great injustice may proceed from it. The judge may give to the jury that prejudiced view of the case which may bias his own feelings on the subject; and I think it very proper that one in his high position should not be allowed to exert that influence one way or the other. If this practice is carried out, it would be only necessary to know what is the opinion of the judge to ascertain what is the opinion of the jury. I think the proposed section should be amended so as to prohibit the judge from making any statement of the kind. The jury hear the testimony, and know as well as he does what it means.

Mr Ord. The proposed section is taken from the Constitution of Tennessee. It is rather difficult to distinguish the difference between stating the facts and recapitulating the testimony. It is usual for the judge to state that such and such are the facts proved. The amendment prevents him from making such a statement to the jury; he merely states what is the testimony. I accept the suggestion of the gentleman. Let the judge merely state or expound the law.

Mr. Sherwood. I hope no such amendment will prevail. Juries are differently constituted; in some cases all are well informed men; in other cases a portion of the jury are not so well informed. In the highest bodies upon earth, there are men of genius who have carried away the majority by the influence of their eloquence. It is said that when Fisher Ames made his celebrated speech upon the treaty between John Jay and the British Minister, a member who took part in the opposition, moved an adjournment of the House, from the fact that the impression made by the speech was so strong that the House could not come to a just decision at that time. There are men of talent in the legal profession who may be employed upon both sides of the case. They may leave doubts upon the minds of the jury both as regards the law and the facts. It is necessary, therefore, that there should be an impartial umpire, who should state the facts as adduced in the testimony, as well as the law. Leave the jury to decide upon the facts; but leave the judge at liberty to state them as they appeared in the testimony. I never knew a judge who attempted to re-state facts in his court, proven by creditable witnesses, where, if he made a mistake, the opposite counsel did not correct him. The minutes are kept by the counsel. If the judge makes a mistake, it is at that moment corrected. There is no fear that this umpire will give a wrong statement to the jury. After one, two, or three able and eloquent counsel have addressed the jury for many hours, I think it is very proper that the judge should re-state the facts as presented in the testimony, leaving the jury to form their own conclusions.

Mr. Gwin. The gentleman (Mr. Ord) mentions the Constitution from which he got this section. I am a native of that State, and have some knowledge of the manner in which the section got into that Constitution. It originated from the acts of two of the judges. They were impeached on the very charge of having abused the power of making charges to the jury. The case involved the State in great expense, and caused great excitement throughout the country. I look upon it as a most important provision, and I hope it will be adopted.

Mr. Tefft. I think if the gentleman from Monterey (Mr. Botts) would discriminate between the words *charge* and *declare* in the section, he would arrive at different conclusions. I hope this provision will prevail. I do not desire that the judge should have power to charge juries, but that he may have the privilege of *declaring* to the jury the law and the facts. It would be a singular feature in this Constitution to declare that he should not have that power. Declaring the facts is a very different thing from the old system of charging the jury, or requiring the jury to find a certain verdict. The section as it stands I conceive to be perfectly proper, and shall vote for it.

Mr. Norton. I am opposed to the amendment of the gentleman from Monterey, (Mr. Botts.) I consider that it takes away from the judge the power which he must necessarily possess, if he charges the jury at all. That there have been judges who have abused this power is true. Many gentlemen, I presume, upon this floor, have seen instances of it; but, sir, it has been customary during all time for judges to have this power of charging the jury. It is necessary after the testimony has been discussed and presented in various aspects by the counsel, that the jury, in order to deliberate upon the subject, and come to a proper understanding, should have from the judge upon the bench, a clear and succinct statement of the whole case, together with his opinion in regard to the question of law involved. It would be almost impossible for the judge to declare the law and charge the jury, unless he is at liberty to refer to the testimony. I agree with the gentleman from Monterey as to the propriety of prohibiting the judge from becoming a party in any case; but I am opposed to taking away from him the right of referring to and stating the testimony. This, I believe, is all the gentleman wishes to get at; that the judge shall be inhibited from arguing upon the testimony. He, may, in his charge to the jury, state that such a witness swore so and so, and go on to state the testimony; and then leave it to the jury to decide upon the weight of that testimony; but the judge shall not himself argue the case upon the testimony, and decide what has been proved and what has not been proved. As far as that, I am willing to go with the gentleman, but no further. When you take away the entire power of the judge to state what the witness swore to, you take away the whole power of charging the jury upon matters of law, because he cannot do that without incidentally referring to the testimony.

Mr. Botts. Every lawyer and every gentleman understands, that in all cases arising in courts of law, there are questions of two distinct and separate characters; one concerning the law, and the other concerning the facts; and as I understand it, sir, it is a most wholesome and useful division of these two points that is generally recognized. It has been the object of the great common law of England to separate these two subjects, so divisible in their nature, and turn them over to the consideration of two distinct and separate tribunals—if I may so say—the judge to decide the law, and twelve unlawyered men to decide the facts; and the opinion of the common law is, that the jury are better judges of the facts than he who sits upon the bench; that twelve men are more competent to judge of the facts than any one man can be; and that the law and the facts are distinct and separate things. It is an invasion of this principle whenever the judge undertakes to judge the facts; he invades the principle as much as if the jury should express an opinion upon the law. It is against this invasion of the principle that I contend. The judge should not have the right to express an opinion upon the facts. Here it is proposed that, in accordance with a very bad custom that prevails across the water, that the judge shall give his statement of the facts to the jury; in other words, his view of the facts. I ask if this House is willing to sanction such a principle. What can it avail? If the judge gives a correct statement of the facts, it must be mere a repetition of the statement of the witnesses. Have not twelve men, with twenty-four ears, heard as much as any one man can hear with two ears? Have they not already heard the testimony?—listened to it as attentively as ever the judge did? What, then, is the object of this proposition, unless it be to permit the judge to lend his coloring to the facts. Gentlemen admit that to be improper. Why then, give an improper power to the judge? But, sir, is it true that the judge cannot lay down the law without referring to the particular facts in the case, or without expressing an opinion upon what facts have been proved to the jury? If you will only put me on the bench, with all its influence, and permit me to instruct the jury upon what facts have been proved upon the trial, I will venture to assert, that in nine cases out of ten, the jury shall bring in just the verdict I wish. Permit me to state the facts, sir, and you give me the power to mould the verdict to suit myself. The gentleman (Mr. Norton) admits that the judge may do this; that he has that kind of influence, and that it is most improper that he should exercise it; but he says he cannot exercise it in making a statement of the facts. Such is not the case; the gentleman does not sustain the argument. Certainly, to repeat the words of the witnesses verbatim, cannot be the object of the gentleman, for that would be a most useless as well as impracticable provision. I hope it will be the pleasure of the House to render the section even more valuable than it is, by striking out that portion of it which opens the door to enter on the subject of facts at all, leaving the jury the unbiassed and uninfluenced judges of the facts, and leaving to the judges the question of law.

Mr. Sherwood. I agree with the gentleman that the jury should have an unbiassed and uninfluenced statement of the facts; and if there is any person who can give to the jury such a statement, it is the judge. He is heard, not as the prisoner or defendant on the one side, or as the prosecutor or plaintiff on the other; he is the impartial umpire of the law, selected by the State. He is influenced by no possible prejudices; and when he states facts to the jury, the gentleman from Monterey knows very well if they are not to the letter true, he is immediately interrupted by the counsel upon the side against which his statement appears; he is corrected on the spot, and the jury have no misstatement from the judge, because all the facts are before them and the counsel, as well as before him. The memory of the jury is brought back to the facts, and upon their minds no false impression is left; but if you deny to the judge any such power, if you prevent him from reciting the facts, what is the result? I need not go further than the members of this body to prove what would be the result, in reading the journal of this Convention. Can we all remember, even from day to day, the proceedings of the previous day? and gentlemen here are considered to be intelligent, educated men, with good memories. Much less can you suppose that every jury in the State can remember the proceedings of a whole trial, four or six days, when they have not pen, ink, and paper before them, to note the lengthy discussions and objections interlarding the evidence of the witnesses. If you refuse to this impartial umpire a recital of the facts after a long trial, and after the eloquent speech of the District Attorney, you probably send an innocent man to the scaffold. I think it is but justice to the prisoner at the bar, that the judge should recite the facts, and then charge the jury as to the law alone, leaving it to the jury and the counsel to determine whether he stated them fairly or not.

Mr. Hastings. I feel disposed to sustain the amendment of the gentleman from Monterey, (Mr. Botts.) I am led to this course from the fact of the many abuses I have witnessed, which it is the design of the amendment to prevent. It has been argued that the court cannot lay down the law without a direct or indirect allusion to the facts. Let us first determine what is the duty of the court. Its duty is to declare what the law is. The judge has nothing to do with the facts or the testimony; it is the business of the jury to take them into consideration. If he is permitted to state the testimony, he necessarily takes the place of counsel, because the testimony is the very thing about which the counsel is contending. The legitimate power of the judge is the law; he should never be permitted to interfere with the facts. I shall therefore support the amendment.

Mr. Shannon. It seems to me this is bringing up an old time-honored question. The gentleman from Monterey (Mr. Botts) argues principally upon the assumption that the judge will not be an honest judge; that he will be in fact rather a poor sample of an impartial umpire. He also urges strongly the adoption of this amendment on the ground that it would be easy for him, as a judge, having the right to state the facts to the jury, to change the opinions of that jury. I am perfectly willing, Mr. Chairman, to accord to the gentleman the high opinion which he seems to have of his own ability, but I think this position goes rather to defeat his own argument. The jury can resist the arguments of the counsel—they are proof against the eloquent appeals of the counsel; but they cannot resist the statement of facts by the gentleman from Monterey. They are honest enough for every thing else; but when it comes to the statement of the judge, their honesty takes flight. They are completely carried away by the ability of the gentleman from Monterey. Their integrity of character is destroyed altogether when he pronounces his statement. Up to that period, they have been honest men, with a good reputation in the community, but they are now overcome by the seductive coloring given to the facts by the gentleman from Monterey. Now, Mr. Chairman, I regard this feature in this system as necessary and proper, and I hope it will be ratained. I think it is precisely the feature which will best maintain the independence and impartiality of juries.

Mr. Vermeule. I hope this amendment will prevail; that, in the Constitution of this State, judges may be prohibited from charging juries as to the facts; that their powers may be limited to declaring the law. If our judges, who are presumed to be men of superior minds, have not such a degree of integrity as to enable them to declare the testimony without giving it a prejudicial coloring, your counsel cannot check them. You may not have a watchful counsel. I prefer having this check in the Constitution.

Mr. Botts. I would just ask you, Mr. Chairman, if the observations of the gentleman from Sacramento (Mr. Sherwood) do not convince you as to the effect which this power given to the judge would have upon the testimony; and it is this: that, in the event of a feeble counsel on one side, and an able attorney for the commonwealth, the whole influence of the judge might be brought to bear against the prisoner; or you may reverse the case. Suppose you have an indifferent attorney for the commonwealth and the best ability that can be procured for the prisoner, justice may be defeated. Now, sir, I have but one word more to add with respect to this time-honored custom. I do not consider that we are to adopt every thing that has been customary with our ancestors for four or five thousand years past, There was a circumstance that occured once in a certain county of Virginia—I believe it was Culpepper county. As it was related to me, it will illustrate this principle. It was there the old time-honored custom to carry corn to mill, with the corn in one end of the bag, and a very large stone to balance it, in the other. A gentleman from a more civilized part of the world, meeting a boy on the road under such circumstances, and understanding what was the object in carrying the stone in the bag, suggested to him the idea that it would be perhaps as well to throw out the stone and divide the corn, putting an equal quantity in each end of the bag. The lad was forcibly struck with the argument; he did so divide the corn; and then he returned to his father, and suggested to him the improvement which he had learnt. The old gentleman gravely deliberated upon it for some time; at length he shook his head and said: this is a breach of the old time-honored custom; it may all be very well, but we don't know; we had better stick to the old custom, which has been well tested by the experience of our forefathers. So he sent his corn to the mill with the stone in the bag as usual. Now, sir, this is the effect of your time-honored customs. Let us lay aside these prejudices. Let us consider the bare merits of the case; if these customs are good, preserve them; if they are bad, discard them. The custom of permitting judges to charge the jury, if it be a time-honored custom, it is a very bad one, and should be discarded at once.

Mr. Sherwood. I beg the indulgence of the House for one remark. I do not know in what court the gentleman has practised—certainly it must have been a different court from any I have ever been in. I agree with him, that we are not to take every thing because it is old, although the gentleman the other day, urged upon the Convention not to infringe upon the time-honored usage in regard to the *habeas corpus*. I go with him in discarding all usages that are not beneficial in the judgment of the Convention. He says that the case I adduced is an argument on his side of the question; that an eloquent attorney and a weak counsel for the prisoner might produce the conviction of the prisoner. This seems to me rather to prove the necessity of an impartial umpire. He reverses the case, and supposes that the counsel for the prisoner is an able man, and that the District Attorney is a weak man. Then, sir, it requires, to further the ends of justice, a succinct and clear recital by the judge, to bring the facts before the minds of the jury. In either case, the counsel have the right to object to the charge on the spot. As to the amendment of the gentleman who submits the proposed section, (Mr. Ord,) that the judge shall charge only as to the law, leaving the facts to be decided by the jury, there can be no dispute. It is a custom so time-honored, that even the gentleman from Monterey, (Mr. Botts,) who may be opposed to some time-honored usages, cannot deny that it should be adopted. That the judge shall charge as to the law, not as to the facts, and that the jury shall decide upon the facts, is a principle which, I believe, is now commonly recognized.

Mr. Dimmick. I am opposed to introducing into our Constitution sections which are more properly matters of legislative action. Our object is to establish in this article a fundamental judiciary system, and it is not necessary that we incorporate these trivial incidents which belong to the statute books of the State, or the books of the common law. I am not opposed to time-honored customs or old laws; but I desire to see them in their legitimate places. Because one or two States have seen the evils resulting from a violation of these rules of law—because one or two of their judges have been impeached, and an excitement has has been produced among the citizens—is that a reason why we should adopt them here. I do not believe that any danger can arise from permitting the law to stand as it is. If there is, the Legislature can provide the remedy. For this reason, I shall vote against both the proposed section and the amendment.

The question was then taken on Mr. Botts' motion, and decided in the negative.

The 18th section, as submitted by Mr. Ord, was then adopted.

Mr. Crosby. I should like to offer another section to come in last; that the common law shall be the law in all cases not otherwise provided for.

Mr. Norton. This question will give rise to a great deal of discussion. It can come up under the miscellaneous provisions.

Mr. Crosby. I withdraw the amendment for the present.

The 18th section of the report of the Committee was then adopted, as follows:

Sec. 18. The style of all process shall be, "The people of the State of California," and all prosecutions shall be conducted in the name and by the authority of the same.

On motion, the Committee then rose, and reported the article on the Judiciary, which, on motion, was laid upon the table.

On motion of Mr. Gwin, the House then resolved itself into Committee of the Whole, Mr. Lippitt in the chair, on so much of the report of the Committee on the Constitution as relates to "Miscellaneous Provisions."

The first section thereof being under consideration, as follows:

Sec. 1. The first session of the Legislature shall be held in the Pueblo de San Jose, which place shall be the permanent seat of Government until removed by law: *Provided*, however, that two-thirds of all the members elected to each House of the Legislature shall concur in the passage of such a law.

Mr. Halleck offered the following as a substitute:

The first session of the Legislature under this Constitution shall be held at Monterey, and the subsequent sessions at the permanent seat of Government, which shall be the Pueblo de San Jose, unless otherwise directed by a majority of all the members elected to each House of the Legislature.

Mr. Halleck. I offer this as a sort of compromise. By this amendment, the first session of the Legislature under this Constitution is to be held at this place, and the subsequent sessions at San Jose, which is to be the permanent seat of Government until otherwise directed by the Legislature. If the first Legislature should meet in the latter part of November or in the early part of December, as proposed by many, it would be difficult for the people of San Jose to provide, at so early a date, a suitable place for that body to meet in; whereas, this entire building, I am authorized to say, is placed at the disposal of the Legislature for that purpose; and there are other buildings in Monterey which are suitable as public offices, and which will be occupied as such until the capital is moved from this place. I think, moreover, that the friends of the removal of the capital to San Jose, ought to have a little consideration for Monterey, and not take it away instantly. They should at least give us time to prepare for the change. This place has been the capital of the country, with the exception of a few years, ever since 1781; and to provide for the instant removal from the old capital of the country by so summary a process as this, requires at least some consideration. It is true, that the accommodations in Monterey, from circumstances entirely beyond the control of the inhabitants, for the members of this Convention, have been very scanty, but that difficulty will be remedied between this and the latter part of November. I think the friends of the removal of the capital, and especially the delegates from San Jose, ought to be content that the next session of the first Legislature will go to the place designated in the resolution as the permanent capital of the State. For these reasons, I hope the substitute may pass; and that it may even receive the approval of the members from San Jose themselves. If the members from Monterey are willing to unite with them and vote for the removal to that place of the capital after the first session of the Legislature, I think they should show us a little encouragement. Moreover, the records and archives of the Government are at this place, and they cannot be removed until after the new Government goes ito operation. The existing Government cannot remove, according to the laws of California, any of its offices or papers until the capital shall be changed by law, and the capital cannot be changed until after the Constitution goes into effect—so that if the first Legislature meets at San Jose before the organization of the new Government, (and I suppose very probably the new Government will go into operation on the first of January next,) it will meet at a place distant from the public archives. Without intending to delay the House by any discussion, I hope, for these reasons, that the substitute will prevail.

Mr. Dimmick. I deeply sympathise with the gentleman from Monterey, (Mr. Halleck;) but, sir, I do not agree with him in his argument. Monterey is at one side of the geographical centre of the country—far distant from the centre of population. If the seat of Government has been here since the year 1781—some sixty years—Monterey having enjoyed that privilege during that long period, is it any reason why she should have it still longer. Because she has had the privilege for a long time, must she continue to have it? The gentleman's agument amounts substantially to this: that, if a thing has been wrong for a long time, it should continue to be wrong. I say, sir, let the capital be put at its proper place at once; let it be where it is designed to be permanently. The gentleman from Monterey says, here is a building which he is at liberty to offer. Very well. We have a building at San Jose too, strange as it may seem; and we hope to have more; and if this Legislature is to meet there, I am authorized to say, by the people of the place, that a room shall be furnished free of expense, as good as this. I do not rise here to complain of the building or accommodations in Monterey, but simply to state that the people of San Jose have offered a suitable building and the best accommodations the place can afford, to the first Legislature.

Mr. Dent. I rise to a rule of order. I do not believe any proposition of this kind has been received by the House.

Mr. Dimmick. I would not have stated it unless the gentleman from Monterey (Mr. Halleck) had rendered it necessary by his statement.

Mr. Halleck. I would ask the gentleman if this is merely held out as a bribe; that the citizens of San Jose will do this now, but not hereafter?

Mr. Dimmick. I am not prepared to say that the people of San Jose have offered a bribe as yet; but they have offered between twenty and thirty acres of ground as a site for the State capitol.

Mr. Halleck. I did not consider it as a bribe offered for the first session.

Mr. Dimmick. No, sir, nor for any session. The building to be occupied as a capitol now, will be completed in time for the first session. I am authorized to say that it will be ready, free of expense, for the accommodation of the Legislature for the first session, no matter when it meets, whether in November, December, or January—so there is no excuse as to the shortness of time. The gentleman seems to think the delegates from Monterey deserve some return if they vote with the delegates from San Jose. The time was when, if such a proposition had been made, it might have been acceded to, but it is now too late. If the capital is not moved there the first session, I am not prepared to say what the people of San Jose will do a year or two or three years hence.

Mr. Hoppe. I deem it only necessary to make a few observations relative to the seat of Government. I feel somewhat interested on account of my constituents, and will offer but a few plain statements. Every gentlemen will, of course, judge for himself as to the advantages of the proposition. In the first place, for the satisfaction of the Convention, I will present to them a plan of the Pueblo of San Jose. The whole square for the capitol, should it be located there, contains thirty-one or two acres. It embraces sixty lots, and the same description of property is selling at this time for a thousand dollars a lot in that neighborhood. The town of San Jose, by a resolution of the 8th of September, unanimously resolved to appropriate that square to the State of California, provided the capital was moved from Monterey there at the first session of the Legislature. I present also to this Convention a plan of the house, now nearly completed, built by my friend Don Pedro Sansevane. This house is seventy feet in length, which is nearly equal to this; thirty-five feet in width, nearly ten feet wider than this; and twenty-one feet high. The front is precisely the same as this. It will be completed in four weeks. Another consideration which is more striking than any that I have presented is this: that San Jose is the geographical centre between the northern and southern parts of the country. By reference to Disturnel's map of Oregon and California, you will find that it is four degrees and forty minutes north of San Diego, and four degrees and forty minutes south of the forty-second degree of north latitude, which throws it exactly in the centre. It is desirable that the seat of Government should be in the central part of the State. Monterey is fifty-two miles south of the central line. Another consideration: we must suppose that the native Californians in the south will have their members in our legislative halls, and I think they would choose at once San Jose in preference to any other point, from the fact there are a number of native Californians there, and it would be more agreeable to them to be among their countrymen and relatives. I presume the mind of every member of this house is made up that it is the proper place. A moment's reflection will convince any gentleman who is in doubt that San Jose is the most eligible and advantageous point.

Mr. Botts. Strange as it may seem to you, Mr. Chairman, and to this house, member as I am from the district of Monterey, I do not consider that I am instructed to vote for Monterey. I consider myself perfectly at liberty to vote for the seat of Government at San Jose, or any other point of the territory that I think best. I believe our constituents permit us to vote for the good of the whole territory. When any gentleman can show me here any good and sufficient reason for removing the capital of the State from its present location, I declare myself ready and willing to vote for that place. Now, sir, I grant you there have been some tolerably potent arguments used here this evening. We have had a beautiful map introduced, a plan of a beautiful building presented to us. But this is not exactly fair; this thing has been sprung upon the people of Monterey. They did not know that maps were to be prepared and buildings to be drawn. Sir, if you will wait a week, I will pledge the people of Monterey to furnish you with one of the most beautiful architectural specimens of a building you ever saw. Is it seriously proposed, sir, that you shall remove the capital of the Commonwealth upon such grounds as this? Are these the only reasons that gentlemen have to present here for the removal of the capital of this country? The gentleman (Mr. Hoppe) does say something about the centrality of the place. I thought then he had at length got to the merits of the question; but, sir, he touched it only. Centrality of position is one great reason. I do not maintain that there is a great deal of difference between the centrality of San Jose and Monterey; but if there be a difference at all, it is certainly in favor of Monterey. I do not want to see maps. The central place is that which is most accessable to the greatest number of population. I it was on the extreme verge of the territory, and was more accessible than a other to the greatest number, it would be the most central point. That point I believe to be Monterey. It is accessible from the sea; it is accessible by land from the north and from the south; and it is a fact, that this Legislature will not meet before you have steamers running from San Francisco to Monterey, and from Monterey to the ports below. Now, it is very evident that the members from the lower districts will come in these steamers; no man will travel on horseback when he can get on board a steamer. In regard to the members from the northern districts, they will find it most convenient to come down in the steamers navigating the bays and rivers to San Francisco, which is the great depot for these vessels. What would be the difference between coming to Monterey or going to San Jose? It requires but a day to arrive at either place. For all these two great classes Monterey is infinitely more accessible. What reason, then, do gentlemen give for moving the seat of Government at all? The question is not upon the permanent removal of the seat of Government, for that question is to be left to the Legislature to determine. I do not know upon what ground the Legislature is to be restricted to the point of San Jose. I would greatly prefer that it be left entirely to the Legislature. Do you not see that, in the constantly recurring course of events, the proper locality will be in one place, and that as railroads and canals spring up, another more accessible point will soon be in a different place? Who can tell us here what ought to be the seat of Government in this country in one, two, or three years hence? In California great changes are produced in a year. I am opposed to any proposition limiting this Legislature to any point in the territory. I am prepared to vote alone for the meeting of the next Legislature, and not for a capital, at any fixed point.

Mr. Price. I rise to move an amendment to the substitute proposed by the gentleman from Monterey, (Mr. Halleck;) to strike out the word "Monterey," and insert "San Francisco." I think this will be acceptable to the Convention. There is now some chance for a compromise. A great deal of sectional and local feeling has arisen on this question. I am not authorized by my constituents to offer a lot of ground or a building for the accommodation of the Legislature, but I know that legislative halls will be furnished by the citizens of San Francisco, and grounds upon which to erect a permanent building, if the people of this State see fit to make that their capital. The gentleman who has preceded me (Mr. Botts) has made a good argument in favor of San Francisco. He tells you that it is the great centre of navigation; that the vessels from the north and the south will be running there constantly—its population and trade being more there than any other part of the country; members of the Legislature while there can attend to other business; the accommodations are better than at any other place in the country; and with a view to the first meeting of the Legislature, whatever may be the future determination of the people, it strikes me as decidedly the most desirable place. When I first came down here to join this Convention, I had to come in the steamer from San Francisco with sixteen delegates, who had congregated at San Francisco for the purpose of coming to Monterey. They were obliged to come to this remote place, where no other business can be attended to than their official duties. I rise altogether in a spirit of conciliation. I desire to compromise the difficulty between San Jose and Monterey by locating the capital at San Francisco, which I believe every gentleman will admit is the most accessible and therefore the most central point.

Mr. McCarver. I am decidedly opposed to the last amendment, and I am not certain that I can support either of the other propositions. We ought to be careful that our action upon this subject will be satifactory to the people. I am opposed to San Francisco for this reason: that it has too much mercantile influence for a legislative body; there is too much of the subsidizing influence to control the votes of members. The consideration that the gentleman from San Francisco (Mr. Price) brings forward as to the convenience of having the seat of Government where members can attend to other than their official business, is a strong objection in my mind. The people do not elect them to attend to other business. They are elected for a special object; and if they cannot afford to devote their time to that object, they had better not run for the Legislature. I am opposed to the removal of the capital to San Jose, from this fact: that the Convention has been called here; the public documents are here, and it may be inconvenient to have them removed; a suitable building is offered to the Legislature, already furnished, and with suitable accommodations; we do not depend upon chance; no additional expense will be incurred; we know precisely what the conveniences are; and I think, taken altogether, the advantages of Monterey, at least for the first session, are very great. I am opposed to locating the seat of Government, at present, any where. It should be left to the Legislature to locate it in the Great Salt Basin, or some other place that may shortly be the centre of our territory.

Mr. TEFFT. My opinions coincide substantially with those of the gentleman who has just taken his seat; and in order to meet the views of that gentleman, I am requested by my colleague, and other southern gentlemen, to state that the most appropriate place for the capital is San Luis Obispo. We have there a most beautiful Mission, which is at the service of the State.

Mr. SHANNON. I have something here which I have no doubt will settle all this difference. I know it involves a principle which must unite one large portion of the House. I do it, sir, in the same spirit of compromise in which the gentleman from San Francisco (Mr. Price) has moved the insertion of that place in the amendment. I give notice that I shall move, at the proper time, to strike out the words fixing the place, whatever they may be, and insert in lieu thereof, "at some point east of the Sierra Nevada range of mountains, in the Great Basin, as near to the central point defined in the Constitution as possible."

Mr. VERMEULE. In the selection of the seat of Government, or any other act of equal magnitude, I think the main considerations are, public necessity and public convenience; and to these ends must give way all private or corporate views. I am myself in favor of the Pueblo of San Jose as the capital of this country. I believe it to be more accessible, more salubrious in climate, and possessing greater facilities for the Legislature than any other point near the centre of our territory. I do not look lightly upon the very liberal donation which the gentleman from San Jose offers to this Convention; it certainly paves the way for what we require at a seat of Government. But so far as the first session of the Legislature is concerned, an insuperable obstacle has been presented by the gentleman from Monterey, (Mr. Halleck.) The public archives and records are kept here, and cannot be removed until the Government is organized and adopted. I think that the present agitated state of the country with regard to property, and the necessity of frequent reference to these records, would render such a movement extremely inexpedient. Besides, I ask you, would it not be more in accordance with republican usage, to leave the question of the seat of Government to the people, after the first Legislature?

Mr. SEMPLE. In speaking upon this amendment, I would barely give notice, that if Benecia should be substituted as a compromise, I shall feel under the necessity of voting for it. I am clearly of opinion that the seat of Government should not be too great a commercial emporium; and although that may be regarded as an objection to Benecia—inasmuch as it is becoming a place of great commercial importance—I will only say, that if the members of this Convention desire to make it the seat of Government, I have lots there which the Government can have by paying for them; and they can also have a building there very soon, provided they build it on those lots after they have paid for them. But I am opposed to the location at San Francisco. For the present, if any location is made, I am decidedly in favor of the Pueblo of San Jose. It has many advantages over all others. In a very short time we shall have the means of going from Benecia to San Jose in four hours. I shall vote against the amendment of the gentleman from San Francisco, (Mr. Price.) I do not think it compromises the question. Benecia would certainly have the preference over San Francisco, but she is about to become a place of great commercial importance, which may be objectionable. I believe Benecia is the head of ship navigation. It is more easily approached, and affords greater convenience for vessels than any other point. It will be remembered that there is now a ferry boat there—a horse-boat—and people by land can approach it very easily. When we get our steamboats in motion, we will advance rapidly.

Mr. SHANNON. Can the gentleman give us any statistics of the various improvements and the number of departures by land and water daily?

Mr. SEMPLE. I was just coming to that part of the subject, but I shall reserve my remarks for another occasion.

Mr. WOZENCRAFT. The gentleman proposes Benecia, and states that that remarkable place is the head of ship navigation. Now, sir, it is well known that Stockton is the head of ship navigation. It possesses a great many advantages over Benecia, and I should not be surprised if the future Legislature would locate the seat of Government there.

Mr. COBARRUVIAS. You are now debating a very interesting question—where the capital of California shall be. I do not believe you can fix upon a more eligible place than Santa Barbara, both because of its eligible position and salubrity of climate. I hope the Convention will take its advantages into consideration.

The question was then taken on the amendment of Mr. Price to insert "San Francisco" instead of "Monterey," and it was decided in the negative.

Mr. GWIN. I shall vote against the substitute proposed by the gentleman from Monterey, (Mr. Halleck.) There is not a single man in my district who prefers Monterey even for the first session. I look upon San Jose as the proper place for the seat of Government. If that is to be the seat of Government, let us have it at once. I have seen more time wasted on questions of the seat of Government than perhaps any others. If you leave this open, it will give rise to interminable discussion. I consider San Jose the best location both for the present and the future. The argument, so far as the archives are concerned, amounts to absolutely nothing. If we have a Government, we will have the archives; if we have the archives here, we can have them there. We ought to have one seat of Government, and one only. If San Jose has the advantage over Monterey, and is to be the permanent seat of Government, we should have it there at once.

Mr. DENT. I shall vote for the substitute for two very important reasons: the first of which is, that I am so instructed by my constituents; and the second is, because I deem it the proper place for the capital. I do not believe there is a single individual within the district of Monterey but who is in favor of having the capital at this place; and I do not consider that their wishes should be overlooked by their representatives in this Convention. I fully agree with them that this is the proper place. In case, however, we should not be able to retain it here, I sincerely hope the gentlemen who advocate its removal to San Jose, will receive the proposition of my colleague to have it remain here during the first session of the Legislature. I think the reasons which I have urged, are sufficient to warrant me in taking this ground. The fact that the public records are here, and cannot be removed at present, is another very forcible reason. Gentlemen speak of the upper part of the country as the great central point in regard to population. It should be borne in mind that the prospects of this district are very promising; that discoveries of gold mines are being made; and the probability is, that its mineral resources, when fully developed, will be found equally as attractive as those of the upper portions of country. Population is moving south. The climate is more salubrious than it is above, and every day new inducements are springing up for emigration in this direction. If Monterey is not to be the permanent seat of Government, I hope at least, that the substitute of my colleague will be adopted, providing that the capital shall not be removed until after the first session of the Legislature.

Mr. Cobarruvias moved to amend, by striking out all after the words "San Jose."

Mr. Halleck. I have but a few words to offer in relation to the substitute before the House. With due deference to the opinions and remarks of the gentleman from San Francisco. (Mr. Gwin,) I would call his attention to one fact. Look at the constitutions of the different States as made by the Conventions? Did they not generally provide for the capital at the first session of the Legislature, and insert a provision requiring the Legislature afterwards to provide for it? Such has been the course of a majority of the States beyond the Rocky Mountains. One remark more: We have everything here that will be necessary for the use of the Legislature, and I really believe we ought not to make the expenses of this Government greater by removing it immediately to another place, where most if not all the expense would be additional, and where any building erected in the next two months must be temporary. The Legislature should have time to erect permanent buildings at the place to which the capital is to be removed.

Mr. Vermeule. The only obstacle to my vote in favor of San Jose is removed by the statement of the gentleman from San Francisco, (Mr. Gwin,) who says we can get these public documents; and by the admission of the gentleman from Monterey, who, by implication, does not deny it.

Mr. Hastings. I am in favor of the immediate removal of the seat of Government to San Jose, because it is the most central point. The people of Monterey have had it here quite long enough; unless, indeed, we are to be governed altogether by time-honored customs.

Mr. Price. As I failed in my effort, I am bound to take sides in this fight one way or other. I am decidedly in favor of San Jose. Under our Constitution the State officers are to be elected. These State officers are to be located at the seat of Government; they must carry their families there; they must obtain houses there, and locate themselves permanently. For a temporary meeting of the Legislature they would have to incur a vast amount of inconvenience and expense to do this. I think it is the best policy to fix the seat of Government permanently at this time—to settle this question for the people at once. If anything is left at all, I fully concur with the gentleman from San Joáquin, (Mr. Vermeule,) that every future change should be left to the people; and if that was the question before the House, I should certainly vote for it. I am in favor of San Jose being permanently and at once the seat of Government.

Mr. Aram. I think that this Convention should decide on some point as the permanent location for the seat of Government. Judging from the past, we have illustrations enough to satisfy us of the great importance of locating permanently at some central point. In Ohio they located their capital at Chillicothe. Afterwards sectional divisions and interests grew up; they abandoned Chillicothe and moved it to Zanesville. It remained there a few years, and subjected both places to great expense, and was a source of great expense to the State. Afterwards other interests drew it to the centre of the State, Columbus, where it ought to have been in the first place. Have we no reason to expect that, unless we select some central point, we will incur the same expense—perhaps a million of dollars? It is very probable that unless we do adopt that policy, and fix it permanently at this time, we will have to undergo even greater expense and inconvenience than any of the States have experienced from changes of this kind. San Jose is the geographical centre of this State; it has none of the objectionable features of a commercial town. Being further inland than San Francisco or Monterey, it possesses the additional advantage of greater security in case of invasion. History records many instances of the capital of the country being torn down, and the public archives being destroyed. San Jose is central and salubrious—accessible from all parts of the country; and within a very short time there will be small steamboats plying to the Embarcadera, which is within six miles of the town. Maps of the plan of the town have not been exhibited here for show—it is a reality. And let me tell you that Washington square is now composed of some sixty lots that would sell for a thousand dollars apiece. I feel perfectly confident that San Jose will eventually be the capital; and I am willing to let the matter rest with the people, for I believe they will be nearly unanimous in favor of that point.

The question was then taken on the motion to strike out the words "unless otherwise directed by a majority of both Houses of the Legislature," and it was decided in the negative.

The question was then taken on Mr. Halleck's substitute, and it was rejected by ayes 15, noes 23.

The first section, as reported, was then adopted—ayes 23, noes 14.

On motion, the Convention then rose and reported progress.

Mr. PRICE then offered the following, which was adopted:

Resolved, That a committee of three be appointed to receive designs for a Seal for the State of California, to select one from those offered, if appropriate, and report the same to this Convention.

The CHAIR then announced Messrs. Price, Sherwood, and McDougal, as such committee.

The House then adjourned.

THURSDAY, SEPTEMBER 27, 1849.

The Convention met pursuant to adjournment. Prayer by Rev. Senor Padre Antonio Ramirez. Journal of yesterday read and approved.

Mr. STEUART offered the following resolution, which, being objected to, lies over one day, viz:

Resolved, That a Committee of three be appointed to prepare and publish an address to the people of California, asking their early consideration of the Constitution submitted for their approval; and urging the attendance of every qualified voter at the polls, at the elections appointed to be held, in order that a full and fair expression of the public voice may be had upon questions involving the peace, happiness, and prosperity of the whole people.

On motion, the Convention then resolved itself into Committee of the Whole, Mr. BOTTS in the chair, on the report of the Committee on the Constitution.

The 2d section of the article on Miscellaneous Provisions being under consideration, as follows:

SEC. 2. Any citizen of the State who shall, after the adoption of this Constitution, fight a duel with deadly weapons, with a citizen of this State, or send or accept a challenge to fight a duel with deadly weapons, either within this State or out of it, with a citizen of this State, or who shall act as second, or knowingly aid or assist in any manner those so offending, shall be deprived of holding any office of profit, and of enjoying the right of suffrage under this Constitution.

Mr. DENT. No clause that you can introduce in the Constitution will prevent a man from fighting a duel, if it be in defence of his honor. There are few men who will not risk their lives when their honor is at stake. If a man be forbidden to hold office because he has too much respect for his honor, we place him in a degraded position. It may be said that it is a false sense of honor, but there may be circumstances in every man's life to induce him, if he possess one particle of manliness or one principle of liberty, to defend his honor at the risk of his life. If we we had in the Constitution of the United States a clause like this, Hamilton, Randolph, Jackson, Clay, and Benton, would have been dropped from the roll of American statesmen. Their eminent services would not have been known to the public. For this reason, I am in favor of striking out this clause from the Constitution, and I sincerly hope that other members will sustain me.

Mr. SHERWOOD. There was a remark dropped from the gentleman who last spoke, (Mr. Dent,) which, I think, should claim the attention of this House as one of great force. It was, after urging in favor of duelling, that it might be from a false sense of honor that persons engaged in a duel. If this Convention say that it is a false of honor that drives a man to shoot his neighbor—if the people of California say so—then duels should be prevented here. The gentleman named a distinguished statesman in connection with this subject, the circumstances of whose death have caused as great an opposition to the practice of duelling in some of the States of the Union, as perhaps to any other evil known in civilized communities. How would Hamilton have shone in the councils of the nation had it not been for this practice? Under the impression that his honor was assailed, he sent a challenge, and he went out to the field. His life, in the very meridian, was cut short. It is in the observation of every gentleman here, that the most trival circumstances have caused the death of the most distinguished men. Circumstances of no moment in themselves, where the practice of duelling has been encouraged, or where it has been upheld by law, have cut them off from the earth. Jackson, to be sure, fought a duel; but is it any credit to him that he killed his opponent. I hope that will not be used on this floor as an argument in favor of the practice. If the law had discountenanced it, probably he would not have been challenged, or have sent a challenge. His name would have been as high and as bright as it is now, and a life would have been saved. I have no doubt that the last days of a duelist who slays his fellow man are wretched. Now this question is before the Convention, and a formal vote is to be passed upon it. I trust we shall not set such an example as to countenance the practice in any way. If you say that a man shall be deprived of the right of suffrage for fighting a duel, you interpose a check that may have a most beneficial effect. If I am insulted, I know how to obtain redress. In the States where duelling is prohibited by law, I know of no difficulty that a man of honor has in sustaining his honor. You hear of no duelling, as a general thing, in the Northern States. If this clause was not reported by the Committee, I should move it, for I sincerely believe it should be in the Constitution. I wish the character of the citizens of California to be as high as that of the citizens in any of the States of the Union—that the law of order shall be as high; that we shall not obtain the character that belongs to the citizens of some portions of the Union. Where duelling is most practised, you see other evils; you see street fights every day. The very fact that duelling is permitted, seems to encourage all kinds of sanguinary conflicts between man and man. It is known to all of us, that in some of the Southern States—one in particular—a character has attached itself to the citizens that is not very enviable; and it is from the fact that duelling has not been prohibited by law. But it is a striking fact that the people of those States, in later years, have come to the conclusion that their position was not very enviable, and in all their late Conventions to form new constitutions, they have adopted a clause similar to this. They have seen the most blood-thirsty conflicts; they have seen their best citizens shot down for nothing at all. Men's passion, under a southern sun, become easily excited; they will not withdraw. The difficulty in suppressing the practice is therefore greater there than in the more northern climes.

It is no mark of courage for one man to shoot another in a duel. I have known great cowards to fight duels. Nor does it sustain a man's honor. The experience of all the northern States of the Union, proves that the honor of men can be sustained without fighting duels.

Mr. Shannon. I wish to explain the reason why I shall vote in favor of the amendment of the gentleman from Monterey (Mr. Dent) to strike this section out. I have no doubt but that the disposition of the House will be to reject the amendment. I regret that the gentleman took the ground in defence of the propriety of duelling——

Mr. Dent. I did not mean to defend the propriety of duelling, but the propriety of keeping it out of the Constitution. I said that a man might be placed in circumstances that all the considerations of position, all the prohibitions of the law would not deter him from fighting; and that it would be injustice to deprive ourselves of the services of such a man. I am opposed to having such a clause in the Constitution.

Mr. Shannon. Still I regret that the gentleman has thought proper to urge upon this floor any thing in support of his motion, which might go towards showing the occasional necessity even of duelling, or be construed as any excuse for it whatever. For my own part, no one can more abhor the practice than I do; and none can have a stronger belief in its evil consequences, or in the falseness of that sense of honor by which it is attempted to be justified. But, Mr. Chairman, I take the ground that the Constitution of the State is not the place for legislation of this kind. A constitution is a general system of laws—an instrument not designed to contain enactments which are properly the subject of legislation or regulations concerning the acts of individuals. It lays down the great landmarks; it embodies the great principles upon which the government of the State is to be founded. I opposed this provision when it was introduced in the bill of rights, and for the same reason that I now oppose it. I shall vote for the amendment of the gentleman from Monterey (Mr. Dent) to strike it out.

Mr. Gwin. This provision reported by the Committee is verbatim the same that exists in the Constitution of Louisiana, adopted in 1845. It is well known to every member of this House that, for the last half century, Louisiana has been the duelling ground of the new world—it certainly has been for the great valley of the Mississippi. There have been more duels fought in the State of Louisiana than any other State of the Union; and after long experience, the last Convention assembled to revise their Constitution, deliberately adopted the section now under consideration, and made it a part of the fundamental law of the land. If we are to benefit at all by experience, the experience of that State certainly should have some weight with this body. If you go through the cemetry of New Orleans, you will see the whole earth covered with tombstones of the victims of honor. It is a wonderful and a melancholy sight. It is said to have been the practice of the French population to go out almost every morning to fight with small swords or pistols. The practice of duelling has not sprung up here in California yet, and it is to be hoped that it never will. If, by our action here, we can have any influence in preventing it, we should certainly exercise that influence. I must, with all due deference, express my astonishment that this motion should come from a gentleman who is on the Supreme Court of the State—a conservator of the peace; an officer of the State, who should be the last to go against inserting in the Constitution a provision against duelling. Sir, I have all my life lived in States where duelling was countenanced; and I have had sad cause to know and feel its evil consequences. It is one of the most important provisions in our Constitution that this practice shall be forever prohibited here. I hope this Convention will insert the section, and make it, by an overwhelming vote, a part of the fundamental law. Go through the Southern States and you will see it now in their Constitutions every where. When I first went to Mississippi eight or ten years ago, whenever a man got into a warm political contest, he went about with pistols. They revised their Constitution seventeen or eighteen years ago, and although they did not insert this provision, they required the Legislature to insert it, in the 2d section of the 7th article, viz:

"The Legislature shall pass such laws to prevent the evil practice of duelling, as they may deem necessary, and may require all officers, before they enter on the duties of their respective offices, to take the following oath or affirmation: 'I do solemnly swear, (or affirm, as the case may be,) that I have not been engaged in a duel, by sending or accepting a challenge to fight a duel, or by fighting a duel, since the first day of January, in the year of our Lord one thousand eight hundred and thirty three, nor will I be so engaged during my continuance in office. *So help me God.*'"

No man could occupy an official position in that State until he took this oath; and it was with the utmost difficulty that some of the most distinguished citizens afterwards, in violating that law, could get an act of the Legislature passed to exonerate them. Opposite where I live, in Vicksburg, on the other side of the river, there have been hundreds of duels fought, and many valuable lives sacrificed. Let us not omit such a valuable provision! We are a peculiar and isolated people. No part of the Union could be more injuriously affected by duelling than this, where there is so large a mixed population.

Mr. McCarver. I am in favor of this provision in the Constitution. I have contended in this House, not only upon that subject, but many others, that the Bill of Rights was not the proper place for it. I therefore opposed putting it there, with the view of having it inserted in the body of the Constitution, where it should remain, and where it is a part of the organic law of the State. I believe that no man, who has been either directly or indirectly engaged in the murder of his fellow man, should be permitted to represent a great free people, or enjoy the elective franchise in a civilized country.

The Chair reminded the House that any motion to amend the paragraph would take precedence of a motion to strike out. If there were any amendments to be offered, therefore, they must be offered before the vote was taken on striking out.

Mr. Dent. I should be perfectly willing to introduce a clause to this effect: that no man shall be entitled to hold office under the Government, who gives an insult to his fellow man; for where insults are given, duelling is the inevitable result. The proudest names on the roll of American statesmen are proof of this fact. Such men as Hamilton and Clay, and others whom I have named, are men possessed of sufficient credit to back out of fighting, if it was necessary. I say that under peculiar circumstances a man would be damned in the estimation of the public if he did not fight. Who is to reap the disadvantages of refusing these men who have participated in duelling the right to hold office? We are ourselves—the people of the State. The gentleman from San Francisco, (Mr. Gwin,) has declared his surprise that such a motion should emanate from me. Now, sir, I here pledge my honor, that if such a clause is introduced in the Constitution of California, and I should be upon the bench, I shall, to the very best of my ability, carry out that provision of the Constitution. I do not think the gentleman was right in alluding to me in my official capacity. I say there are circumstances which may render a duel necessary. A large man may impose upon a smaller one, in such manner that he can obtain no reparation in law. I have sworn to support the Constitution of the United States, and I find no provision there to sanction the principle of depriving a man of the right of suffrage because he fights a duel. I deem it but just that such a clause should be expunged from the Constitution of this State. Besides it will not prevent the practice. A man who is willing to risk his life when his honor is assailed, will risk all the rights of citizenship under this prohibition. If death, or the prospect of death, has no influence upon him, certainly the prospect of being deprived of the rights to hold office will not.

Mr. Steuart. I regret, very much, sir, that this clause has been introduced at all in the provisions of the Constitution. I need not say that I am always disposed to prevent an evil practice, and that I detest most heartily the practice of duelling; but I would be a hypocrite if I did not say that there are circumstances which compel men to resort to this mode of contest. I deem it entirely useless to attempt to restrain men by mere laws from engaging in duels, as long as they are not restrained by the general feeling of the community. Public opinion must be the restraint, and it is the only effectual restraint. I have always thought that laws of this kind have a baneful tendency—that they only add to the difficulty; but if it should be the determination of the Convention to introduce this provision in the Constitution, I most certainly desire, under the decision of the Chair, that an amendment shall be made to the section. I see no reason why the words "with any citizen of this State" should be adopted. Why a citizen of this State? I would move, therefore, that they be stricken out. If he is restrained from raising his arm in defence of his honor against a citizen of this State, I see no reason why he should not be prohibited from wreaking vengeance against a foreigner.

Mr. Gwin. As I was in some degree instrumental in having this section drawn up, I feel bound to defend it. Although I have been often twitted upon this floor as having a great deference for precedents, still I adhere to this: that when we have the deliberate judgment of those who have great experience on any subject, we are bound to pay deference to their opinions; and I say that there is no State which has had more experience on the subject of duelling than Louisiana. That is the great point of the southern portion of the Union where citizens of all the States assemble, and it was believed that, inasmuch as this Constitution was made for the State of Louisiana, that it should contain this restriction, and after a great deal of discussion and deliberation, this section was inserted. California being a point to which the citizens of all nations will be directed, it is peculiarly desirable that we should have a provision of this kind in our Constitution; and it might materially effect this article, if, in their collisions with the citizens of other countries, they should not be left entirely to the Legislature; for this does not prohibit the Legislature from making enactments on the subject. Let us confine our operations to the people of California, inasmuch as we are forming the Constitution for them. It is intended to operate upon our own citizens. I am sorry that the gentleman from Monterey (Mr. Dent) should have supposed that my reference to his bringing in this proposition to strike the section out, should be of a personal character. It was a mere matter of taste, in my view, and I thought, as what he says here and what we do here, will go elsewhere, that it would not look so well that a judge of the Supreme Court should be the first to move that a provision prohibiting duelling should be stricken out. I believe he is perfectly honest in his opinions on this subject. And inasmuch as it has been stated that this is a proper subject of legislation, I wish to make this statement: that when it was supposed this legislative restriction would prohibit duelling in Mississippi, we have seen instances where men in high positions have been enabled, by the influence that they could bring to bear upon the Legislature, to relieve themselves from the effects of the law. There is now a gentleman from that State, a Senator in Congress, who, by an act of the Legislature, was relieved from the disability. I want a man when he fights a duel with a citizen of California, or aids or abets in a duel, to be forever prohibited from holding office here. When that provision was carried into effect in Mississippi, they all went over to Louisiana; but whether a citizen of California fights a duel here or elsewhere, he is prohibited from holding office. At this advanced period of the world, it is not necessary to say a word against this remnant of the dark ages. It is no evidence of bravery, for the greatest cowards engage in it. I say it should be discountenanced and put down; and I know that law does put it down, for I have seen it. When you insert this provision in your Constitution, the fundamental law of the land, that a man is branded when he fights a duel, he quits it. In Tennessee, where it was made a penitentiary offence, it was abandoned. We have the best evidence that the law has a beneficial influence in suppressing this great evil; and I hope the deliberate sense of the House will be in favor of incorporating this section in our Constititution.

Mr. Shannon. There is certainly no better way of striking at the practice of duelling, than that contained within this section, because it strikes at the very root of the evil. This deprivation of a citizen of all political rights, touches directly that honor which incites him to fight a duel. But my argument against this section has been upon the propriety of introducing it in the Constitution at all. There is now another matter before the House—the amendment of the gentleman from San Francisco, (Mr. Steuart.) I shall vote for that amendment. I think if we adopt such a provision at all, we should make it do full justice to other men—to the citizens of other States, who are our common fellow-citizens. Let us not say that the citizens of our sister States can be shot down, can be murdered with impunity, or at least without the guards here imposed upon the citizens of this State.

Mr. Moore. There is one advantage to be derived from this provision, if you place it in the Constitution. It will at least afford men a pretext for not engaging in duels.

Mr. McCarver. I do not think it right that the citizens of California should be deprived of all the rights of citizenship, and persons who come within our State should have the right to call out any of our citizens and shoot them down—that they should have the right to hold office, when our own citizens do not possess that right.

Mr. Jones. It appears, Mr. Chairman, that the whole House is in favor of the amendment, (Mr. Steuart's,) and therefore it would be very useless for me to say any thing against it. But I must add my mite to oppose a proposition which would throw a citizen of this State, hand and foot, at the mercy of any stranger of any nation who chooses to come among us. I do not want to see them put upon an unequal footing. We are making a Constitution for the advantage of our own citizens, and not for the advantage of foreigners. I do not want foreigners to have the right to insult our citizens with perfect security and impunity; that we should lose our dearest rights of citizenship, and they lose nothing. They may hereafter become citizens of this State after having, in duels, slain its citizens. There is no prohibition against them. They may sit in our Legislature, and even at the head of our Government. I consider that it would be doing injustice to the citizens of this State to establish any such distinction. We should stand upon the same footing with them that they stand upon with us. If they lose no rights or franchise, we should lose none; and I should hesitate long to vote for a proposition that binds us hand and foot.

Mr. Wozencraft. The provision now before the House strikes alone at those men who aspire to office; at the same time it leaves the great mass of the citizens the privilege of fighting duels whenever they please. Why should you put restrictions alone upon men who occupy, or aspire to occupy, certain positions?

Mr. McDougal. It strikes me that this provision itself puts the matter in all the lights in which it can be viewed. Any citizen of this State, after the adoption of the Constitution shall, if he fight a duel, be deprived from holding any office. It is not clear but that a citizen of this State may fight a duel with a citizen of another State, or of France, or England; or he may go to Washington and fight all the Senators and Representatives, provided they are not citizens of this State; but if he meets there a citizen of California, they must be friendly. It won't do for them to fight, because if they do they cannot hold office when they get home. A man who commits a crime in this State is to be disfranchized; a man who commits a crime anywhere else is also to be disfranchised. Foreigners may come into this State and fight as many duels as they please among themselves, and with us too, but they may become citizens in twenty-four hours after the duel is fought; and they may occupy the Supreme bench or the gubernatorial chair. But, sir, this thing is carried still further, in another section which follows; the party who has committed the crime is compelled to be a witness against himself, and swear that he has committed the crime. Who ever heard of anything like this? If Louisiana has done it, she has done wrong. It would be a stain upon our Constitution to insert such a provision, when we have declared in another part of the Constitution that no man shall be a witness against himself. Both articles ought to be stricken out, for they are both ridiculous. The Legislature ought to do just what they please about it. No Legislature can make a party a witness against himself; nor can any Legislature pass a law contradicting itself, as this does.

Mr. Sherwood. The first article which has been read on the subject of dueling is the one under consideration. The article after that, compelling a man to take a certain form of oath, is separate and distinct. My own opinion is, that to strike out the words "with a citizen," accomplishes the object. It prevents a duel between a person not a citizen and a person who is a citizen of this State; that is, a citizen of this State is disqualified if he fights with a person not a citizen of the State. It prevents duelling entirely, so far as disqualification to hold office can present it. With that amendment, and without adopting the next section, I think we can cover the whole ground.

Mr. Hastings. I pronounce this clause unconstitutional. The article proposed to be introduced produces this effect: The party is tried in the State in which he fights the duel, and is amenable to the laws; he is acquitted, and returns here to this State, where he is again subjected to punishment without trial. The Constitution provides that no person shall, after acquittal, be tried for the same offence again. Can that individual return here, after having been duly tried and acquitted for this offence in one State, and be disfranchised here without a trial? The article goes even further; the individual who fights a duel here is not allowed a hearing at all—he has no trial—he is disfranchised at once. There is no evidence brought to bear upon the case. It is in conflict with the provisions of the Constitution of the United States, and again with the provisions of our own Constitution.

Mr. Wozencraft moved to amend by inserting after the words "of this State" the words "who shall have been convicted of fighting such duel."

Mr. Price. I did hope that this question was settled when it came up in the Bill of Rights. It was there objected to, and I regret to see it introduced again. I am clearly of opinion that no clause should be introduced in this Constitution fixing a penalty to an offence. We have here a clause against duelling imposing one of the highest penalties known under our system of Government—disfranchisement, prohibition from holding office. You bring the offender down, sir, to a level with the veriest criminal, whilst the fact of his having fought a duel does not degrade him in the estimation of his fellow-men. I would leave this for your future Legislature. We have not the grave-yard of Louisiana here; we have not yet merited the reproach of being known as a duelling people, and I trust we never will. But it is a stain upon the people of California to engraft upon this Constitution a prohibition against duelling. It is saying to them that they want this restraint, when they have shown no evidence that they require it. There is an inconsistency in this which I should regret to see our Constitution contain.

Mr. Lippitt. I am very glad my colleague (Mr. Price) has brought forward these views precisely in the way he has. I do not mean to go into a discussion of the subject, but it is exactly for the reasons stated by the gentleman himself that I shall vote for the section; and it was for these reasons that the section was introduced. And I presume that, for the same reasons, that a majority of the members of this Convention have made up their minds to vote for it. What does he state? He says that any citizen who has committed this offence—for I believe there is not a gentleman here who does not admit either directly or indirectly that it is an offence against society and against God——

Mr. Moore. I would like to be considered as not in that category.

Mr. Price. I should like also to be excepted.

Mr. Lippitt. Very good. The gentleman tells you that he does not wish to have any provision made by law punishing as a crime that which does not involve any social degradation. That is precisely why we are called upon to introduce such a provision in our Constitution. It is the reason why ordinary laws passed by the Legislature have not accomplished the object. Owing to these false notions of honor, which have come down to us from barbarous times, the commission of this offence, I am sorry to say, does not involve social degradation; and as the gentleman observes, one man may in a duel bathe his hands in his brother's blood and still hold up his head as a man—still be considered the same righteous, honorable, just citizen that he has always been. He loses no character by the act; for precisely that reason, owing to the vitiated state of public opinion, the crime of duelling differs from all other offences known to our code, and for that reason we cannot leave it to the Legislature. All other crimes to which a stigma is attached, we can leave to ordinary laws passed by the Legislature; they are sufficient to put a stop to the evil. Why do not constitutions impose certain penalties against murder, or robbery, or any other infamous offence? Because public opinion stigmatises those offences with infamy, and they are arrested by ordinary laws, which is the object designed to be accomplished.

Mr. Price. It does seem to me that my colleague is misrepresenting his constituents. He tells them things which must, shall, and will be done; and he admits in his argument that he is opposing public opinion, and hence he is arguing that we are here to restrict and not to act in accordance with the wishes of our constituents. I contend, sir, that it is our highest duty to carry out public opinion on this and all other subjects.

Mr. Lippitt. One word with respect to misrepresenting my constituents. I have received no instructions from them to vote against any constitutional provision; and I would only add, that if I had received any such instructions, I should resign my seat in this body before I would carry them out by voting to strike out a clause against duelling.

Mr. Semple. Duelling itself is, so far as I am individually concerned, unconstitutional. My constitution forbids it, and I have resolved never to fight a duel if I can honorably get out of it. A few remarks as to the propriety of such a measure; In the first place, the penalty here in this clause is the highest punishment that I know of. Now, I have an instinctive dread of death. I dislike the idea of dying; but give me my choice, whether I shall be branded with infamy, prohibited from holding any office from under the Government, from that of governor down to a tax gatherer, and never more have the privilege of chosing at the ballot-box the men who shall preside over me, and I should choose death in preference. The idea of hanging is a little more elevated, but to me more honorable and more to be desired than such a punishment as this. I would dislike very much to fight a duel, because I might be killed. I consider that one of the strongest objections to the practice. To me it is a constitutional objection; but I think to be shot down, or to be hung, is preferable to disfranchisement. I am opposed to disproportionate punishments. The man who is convicted of the highest crime known to our laws—the murder of his brother—is only hung, nothing more; barely hung by the neck till he is dead. But for fighting a duel, carrying or sending a challenge, aiding or abetting in any manner—even for knowing that a duel is fought, you inflict a higher punishment than you do upon the man who has committed murder.

I say, Mr. Chairman, that the very object of punishment is to prevent crime. Why wreak vengeance upon a man who has committed a crime, unless it have the effect of preventing it. In all time past, it has been found that an equitable gradation of punishment has had the best tendency to prevent the commission of crime. When Draco made laws, he was called the bloody law-maker. And why? Because even the slightest deviation from right, he maintained, deserved death; and when he had inflicted death, he could do no more. If Draco had known the privilege of going to the ballot-box—the glorious privilege of exercising the rights of a freeman—he would have made some gradation in hispunishment. He would have made disfranchisement a greater punishment than death. If you embody this in your Constitution, it is beyond the reach of the Legislature; you say to the Legislature and the people of California, we, your representatives in this Convention, have declared that you shall abide by this clause, and you shall never alter it unless you begin at the foundation and call another Convention. I am decidedly opposed to duelling, Mr. Chairman; I think it is a wrong mode of settling a difficulty; but I am opposed, also, to such an inordinate punishment; a punishment so infamous that two generations will not wipe it out. I say, then, pause before you act; reflect upon the stain that you are about to inflict upon your fellow-citizens; remember that even the crime of treason cannot, under the Constitution, work corruption of blood or forfeiture, except during the life of the person so attainted. I am opposed to both the amendments. The original clause as reported is greatly superior to them, but I would like, if it is adopted at all, to have a punishment proportionate to the offence.

Mr. Lippitt. The gentleman from Sonoma (Mr. Semple) says he is opposed to this provision only for the reason that the punishment proposed is too great for the offence. Let us take his own premises, and see what they amount to. He told us that he would prefer being hung by the neck at thirty days notice, to deprivation of the right of suffrage. There are the premises. What is the conclusion? Is it not known to every member of this Convention that almost, if not every State in the Union, has on its statute book, and has had ever since the organization of the State, laws inflicting this very punishment of hanging by the neck, in order to repress the very crime in question; and that these laws have remained a perfect dead letter on the statute book? If the penalty of death has not been sufficient to repress the offence, then we must increase it. We must establish a higher grade of punishment; and if we are compelled to have recourse to this punishment, deprivation of the right of suffrage, we can only do it in the Constitution. We cannot permit the Legislature to pass any law which will impair the right of suffrage. It is one of those rights that is established by the Constitution, and cannot be impaired except by constitutional provision.

Mr. McCarver. On the very ground upon which the gentleman from Sonoma (Mr. Semple) opposes this provision—the deprivation of the right of suffrage—I am in favor of this high penalty. Suppose an individual calls out his friend and shoots him down, and suppose another murders a citizen for his money, what difference is there in effect between the two cases. They have both committed murder; the object was different, but the result is the same. In either case, a citizen of the State is slain. The one murderer is hung; the other is merely deprived of a political right. The gentleman says that the penalty of death is not so great. Why, sir, when a man is hung, he is disfranchised; he can no more exercise the rights of citizenship. He is deprived both of his life and his political rights; whereas, the other is deprived of his political rights only; he is permitted to live and profit by his punishment. But the man who is put to death is forever deprived of that opportunity. I am in favor of putting a restriction in the Constitution to disfranchise any man of his political rights who shall attempt to murder his fellow man.

Mr. McDougal. Did I understand my colleague (Mr. McCarver) to say that a man after he is hung is disfranchised? I desire to know whether he is serious in that belief, because it is a very important point, and it is well we should all understand it. I confess I have very great doubts on the subject myself; and I should like to have some opportunity of coming to a correct decision upon it. In the remarks which I made at the commencement of this discussion, I hope I may not be considered as an advocate of duelling, for I certainly am not; and I will go as far as any member of this House in fixing a penalty against it. I would fix a penalty against it as against the violation of any moral law; but, Mr. Chairman, I cannot give my vote to disfranchise any person who shall be guilty of duelling, if he has fought it in the ordinary way. If the Committee wish to prevent the crime of fighting, why do they not make a gradation, and take the whole subject up from first to last. They simply define one mode of fighting. There are forty other modes. Why exclude one and fix a penalty upon another. If you deprive a citizen of this State from holding any office of trust or profit within the gift of the people, for fighting a duel in defence of his pride or honor, that pride and that sense of honor will seek revenge in some other way if he does not choose to be disfranchised. It is against the very laws of nature for him to act otherwise. He will have satisfaction in some other way. Suppose if this law goes into effect, and one of our worthiest citizens finds himself insulted, he does not wish to be disfranchised or deprived of his right to hold office which the citizens may desire to confer upon him, he goes into the street with his gun, and fires upon his assailant or opponent, irrespective of the danger to other persons. You force him into the street to attack his foe, and as is often the case, the wound is inflicted upon others. This is the inevitable result; you place a man in a position which causes him to take a mode of settling his difficulties which endangers not only the life of his opponent, but the lives of others. I say let the punishment be such as will not produce this effect; let it be simply a fine. If fighting a duel be a violation of the laws of

God, his own conscience alone is affected by it. Do not place our citizen upon a level with the degraded culprit coming from the penitentiary; do not deprive him of the glorious right of suffrage. The advocates of the section reported by the Committee and of the various amendments, presume that every man that goes out to fight a duel must certainly kill somebody or die himself; and they have painted terrible pictures here, brought up grave-yards, and blood flowing in the dust, and various sanguinary spectacles. Why, sir, I do not suppose, in all the history of duelling, that there is one case in twenty that results in death. I venture to say, that in the aggregate of duels, there are more legs and arms hurt than lives taken, and far more cases than either, where there is no damage done at all. It is a presumption that I do not admit. But if gentlemen who consider themselves bound to fight, choose to stand breast to breast and shoot one another, they had better be out of society and out of the world. Such a class of men are not wanted here. Let them take their own course and we will get rid of them the sooner.

Mr. Crosby gave notice that if the amendment before the House was rejected, he would introduce an amendment leaving the punishment entirely to the Legislature, but recognizing in the Constitution a dissent from the custom. He thought it would satisfy the scruples of those who were opposed to carrying the penalty to the extent provided in the clause as reported.

The question was then taken on Mr. Steuart's amendment, to strike out the words a "citizen of thisState," wherever they occur, and the amendment was adopted.

Mr. Wozencraft then offered the amendment of which he had previously given notice.

Mr. Gwin gave notice that if this amendment was adopted, he would move to strike out the section, and insert the provision on this subject from the Constitution of Iowa.

Mr. Hoppe was opposed to the amendment on the ground that it gave foreigners the advantage over citizens of the State. He moved to strike it out, and insert an amendment requiring the Legislature to pass such laws as effectually to prevent all persons, not citizens of the State, as well as citizens, from engaging in duels within its borders.

Mr. Lippitt rose to a question of order. He desired the Chair to state which of the amendments was before the House.

The Chair decided that the question was on the adoption of the amendment offered by Mr. Wozencraft.

The question was then taken, and the amendment rejected by ayes 14, noes 20.

Mr. Crosby then moved his proposed amendment.

Mr. Sherwood suggested that his colleague withdraw the amendment, and let the question be taken on the original article.

The question was then taken on the original section, as amended by Mr. Steuart, and it was adopted as follows:

"Any citizen of this State who shall, after the adoption of this Constitution, fight a duel with deadly weapons, or send, or accept a challenge to fight a duel with deadly weapons, either within this State or out of it, or who shall act as second, or knowingly aid or assist in any manner those thus offending, shall be deprived of holding any office of profit, and of enjoying the right of suffrage, under this Constitution."

Section 3 then coming under consideration as follows:

"Sec. 3. Members of the Legislature, and all officers, before they enter upon the duties of their offices, shall take the following oath or affirmation: I (A B) do solemnly swear (or affirm,) that I will faithfully and impartially discharge and perform all the duties incumbent on me as ———, according to the best of my abilities and understanding, agreeably to the Constitution and Laws of the United States, and of this State; and I do further solemnly swear (or affirm,) that since the adoption of the present Constitution, I, being a citizen of this State, have not fought a duel with deadly weapons within this State, nor out of it, with a citizen of this State, nor have I sent or accepted a challenge to fight a duel with deadly weapons, with a citizen of this State, nor have I acted as second in carrying a challenge, or aided, or advised, or assisted any person thus offending. *So help me God.*"

Mr. HALLECK moved to strike out the whole section, and insert the following, viz:

"SEC. 3. Members of the Legislature, and all officers, executive and judicial, except such inferior officers as may be by law exempted, shall, before they enter on the duties of their respective offices, take and subscribe the following oath or affirmation:

'I do solemnly swear (or affirm, as the case may be,) that I will support the Constitution of the United States, and the Constitution of the State of California, and that I will faithfully discharge the duties of the office of ———, according to the best of my ability.'

"And no other oath, declaration, or test, shall be required as a qualification for any office or public trust."

Mr. HALLECK said this substitute was the most simple he could find on the subject in any of the Constitutions.

Mr. McDOUGAL was opposed to it on the ground that the section as reported was necessary to carry out the object of the preceding section.

The question was then taken on the substitute, and it was adopted.

The question was then taken, without debate, on sections 4, 5, 6, 7, 8, 9, 10, 11, and 12, and they were passed, as follows:

SEC. 4. The Legislature shall establish a system of county and town governments, which shall be as nearly uniform as practicable, throughout the State.

SEC. 5. The Legislature shall have power to provide for the election of a board of supervisors in each county; and these supervisors shall jointly and individually perform such duties as may be prescribed by law.

SEC. 6. All county officers whose election or appointment is not provided for by this Constitution, shall be elected by the respective counties, or appointed by the board of supervisors or other authorities, as the Legislature shall direct. All city, town, and village officers, whose election or appointment is not provided for by this Constitution, shall be elected by the electors of such cities, towns, and villages, or some division thereof, or appointed by such authorities as the Legislature shall designate for that purpose; and other officers whose election or appointment is not provided for by this Constitution, and all officers whose offices may hereafter be created by law, shall be elected by the people or appointed, as the Legislature my direct.

SEC. 7. When the duration of any office is not provided for by this Constitution, it may be declared by law, and if not so declared, such office shall be held during the pleasure of the authority making the appointment; but the duration of any office not fixed by this Constitution, shall never exceed four years.

SEC. 8. The political year shall begin on the 1st day of January, and the fiscal year on the 1st day of July.

SEC. 9. Each county, town, city, and incorporated village, shall make provision for the support of its own officers, subject to such restrictions and regulations as the Legislature may prescribe.

SEC. 10. The credit of the State shall not, in any manner, be given or loaned to or in aid of any individual, association, or corporation; nor shall the State directly or indirectly become a stockholder in any association or corporation.

SEC. 11. Suits may be brought against the State in such manner, and in such courts, as shall be directed by law.

SEC. 12. No contract of marriage, if otherwise duly made, shall be invalidated for want of conformity to the requirements of any religious sect.

Mr. HALLECK asked the consent of the House to receive the reading of an additional section. It was drawn up to satisfy the opinions of the southern members in regard to taxation:

All lands liable to taxation in this State shall be taxed in proportion to their value; and this value shall be appraised by officers elected by the qualified electors of the district, county, or town in which the lands to be taxed are situated.

Mr. ORD moved to amend by striking out the word "lands" after the word "all," and insert the words "immoveable and moveable property;" to strike out the word "there" before the word "value," and insert the word "its," and to strike out all after the word "the" and before the word "situated," and insert the words "said property is."

Mr. HALLECK said that this had reference to lands particularly. There were other provisions in relation to other kinds of property.

Mr. SHERWOOD thought the amendment of the gentleman from Monterey (Mr. Ord) would not operate very well in this country. Suppose the gentleman had a hundred thousand dollars in gold dust in Sacramento, and he lived here? It would be impracticable to carry it out in respect to personal property.

Mr. Ord. I believe my amendment is not understood by the House. Assessors, in making their assessments of property, will make general assessments; they will make assessments of all the property at a ranch. As to the instance of a bag of gold dust, it will be very difficult, whatever law you may form, to draw taxation from property of that kind. I think, with regard to assessments, that the rule should be uniform.

Mr. Halleck. There is a custom in California of sending cattle to ranches in one district from other districts, but I do not wish the question of cattle, or other questions of moveable property, to mix up with this. You cannot conveniently send lands from one district to another. I wish this to refer to lands merely, and if gentlemen want such a provision as that suggested by the gentleman from Monterey, (Mr. Ord,) they can put it in a new article.

The question was then taken on Mr. Ord's amendment, and it was rejected.

Mr. Price could see no use in the section proposed by the gentleman from Monterey, (Mr. Halleck,) and therefore no reason for inserting it in the Constitution. The operation of taxation would go on without it, and other provisions of the Constitution provided that it should be uniform.

The question was then taken, and the additional section proposed by Mr. Halleck was adopted.

The question being on the thirteenth section—

Mr. Lippitt said it was a subject of great importance, and as there appeared to be scarcely a quorum present, he hoped the Committee would rise and report progress.

The Committee then rose and reported progress.

On motion, the House took a recess till 7 o'clock, P. M.

NIGHT SESSION, 7 O'CLOCK, P. M.

On motion of Mr. Sherwood, the Committee appointed to report a plan for taking the State census were instructed to report to-morrow.

On motion, the House then resolved itself into Committee of the Whole, Mr. Shannon in the Chair, on so much of the report of the Committee on the Constitution as relates to miscellaneous provisions.

The thirteenth section of the report being under consideration, as follows:

Sec. 13. All property, both real and personal, of the wife, owned or claimed by her before marriage, and that acquired afterwards by gift, devise, or descent, shall be her separate property, and laws shall be passed more clearly defining the rights of the wife, in relation as well to her separate property as that held in common with her husband. Laws shall also be passed providing for the registration of the wife's separate property.

Mr. Lippitt. I have a substitute to propose for this section. It is in the following words:

"Laws shall be passed more effectually securing to the wife the benefit of all property owned by her at her marriage, or acquired by her afterwards, by gift, demise, or bequest, or otherwise than from her husband."

It is not my intention at present to enter into any argument upon this question. I would only state, generally, that I am opposed to the section as it stands, because I think it a matter of great importance, and goes to change entirely the nature of the married relations. The relative rights of property of husband and wife, I think, are matters involving laws that can more safely be entrusted to the action of the Legislature, than introduced at once into one Constitution, and form part of the fundamental irrepealable law of the land. I think that we tread upon dangerous ground when we make an invasion upon that system which has prevailed among ourselves and our ancestors for hundreds and hundreds of years. The married relation is one from which flow all other relations. It lies at the very foundation of society; the well-being, happiness, and morality of society, and

17

of every individual in it, depend more upon the nature of that relation than any other. I think it a dangerous subject of experiment. I do not say that the experiment is not worth trying; I am inclined to admit that there are abuses connected with the present marriage system which need correction. What I contend against is, trying the experiment in our Constitution. This Constitution is irrepealable until the people choose to meet in Convention again. It is not so with the statute—with the law passed by the Legislature. If the law is found to be a bad one, or does not work well, if its tendency is to produce mischief, it is easy to repeal it; a majority of the Legislature can always repeal. You may make a bad law, and you can repeal it, or have it amended in a few months time. Not so with the Constitution. This provision, if we insert it here, will be the fundamental law of the land. It will not be, in fact, trying any experiment at all; it will be adopting it at once without experiment. It will be rash and headlong, and we do not know to what consequences it may lead. I therefore hope that the section may be stricken out, and that the substitute which I have offered in its place may be adopted.

Mr. Tefft. It is not my intention, on this occasion, to enter into any discussion as regards the two systems of civil and common law; neither is it my intention to argue here upon the rights of women in general, and married women in particular; but I feel bound to notice the objections of the gentleman from San Francisco, (Mr. Lippitt,) and his amendment. This is undoubtedly a matter of great importance. It is a matter upon which we cannot otherwise than expect a difference of opinion in this House. It was said this evening that this was an attempt to insert in our Constitution a provision of the civil law. Very well—suppose it is; there are gentlemen in this House wedded to the common law; I am myself greatly attached to it; but that does not prevent me from seeing many very excellent provisions in the civil law. The gentleman (Mr. Lippitt) terms this an invasion. I do not regard it in that light; but I think that to strike this section out would be a very decided invasion upon the people of California. This very section not only stands upon the statute books of many of the old States, but is inserted in the Constitution of some of them. It is our duty to give a favorable consideration to any proposition which does not do marked and radical wrong to any class in California, and which deeply concerns the interests of the native Californians. It would be an unheard of invasion, not to secure and guaranty the rights of the wife to her separate property; and of all classes in California, where the civil law is the law of the land, where families have lived and died under it, where the rights of the wife are as necessary to be cared for as those of the husband, we must take into consideration the feelings of the native Californians, who have always lived under this law. We come then to the actual right of the wife to the protection of her property. I do not pretend to look far into the future, no farther than other men, but any cool, dispassionate man, who looks forward to California, as she will be in five years to come, who does not see that wildness of speculation will be the characteristic of her citizens, as it has been for some time past, is not, I think, gifted with the power of prophecy. I claim that it is due to every wife, and to the children of every family, that the wife's property should be protected; and I am not willing to trust to the Legislature in this matter. It is the common cry to leave all these things to the Legislature, assuming that we are to have a Legislature that will look upon those matters as we do. I say that we have not only the right to embrace a provision of this kind in our Constitution, but that it is our duty. This is a matter in which not only the native Californians, but many of the new residents in this country, feel a deep interest. I do contend, sir, that every wife has a right, a positive right, to the entire control of her private and personal property. I do not, and cannot see, that it will create dissensions in families, or that it makes separate and distinct interests between man and wife. It does not interfere with the rights of those whom this law is not designed to restrain.

The industrious business man, with his frugal wife, is not in any way affected by it; but if an idle, dissipated, visionary, or impractical man, brings his family to penury and want, then I say it is our duty to put this provision in the Constitution for the protection of that family who are helpless, and who have no other means of subsistence. I see a disposition on the part of the House to oppose this provision. Representing, as I do, a constituency entirely of native Californians, because the few Americans in my district are identified with them and may classed as native Californians, I am compelled, not against my wishes, for my wishes coincide with theirs, to advocate it on this floor. I believe that much opposition to the protection of the separate property of the wife arises from a degree of false pride on the part of man; placing it in the position of a distinct and separate interest on the part of the wife, and regarding any thing that can bear such a construction as a reproach upon himself. I look upon the marriage contract as a civil contract. I consider that the wife's interest is the husband's interest; and whatever can afford protection and security to her, must necessarily be to his adtage as well as hers. I trust, in consideration of the peculiar necessity which must exist here for such a provision, owing to the inducements for wild and hazardous speculations, and the probability of frequent and sudden losses which would otherwise involve families in ruin; in consideration, also, of the native population of California, who have always lived under this system, that it will become a part of our fundamental law.

Mr. Halleck. I am not wedded either to the common law or the civil law, nor as yet, to a woman; but having some hopes that some time or other I may be wedded, and wishing to avoid the fate of my friend from San Francisco, (Mr. Lippitt,) I shall advocate this section in the Constitution, and I would call upon all the bachelors in this Convention to vote for it. I do not think we can offer a greater inducement for women of fortune to come to California. It is the very best provision to get us wives that we can introduce into the Constitution.

Mr. Botts. Feeling as unwell as I do to-night, I had hoped that the gentleman from San Francisco (Mr. Lippitt) who I understood would open this debate, would so far have been the exponent of my own sentiments as to have enabled me to be silent on this subject. But he has not taken the ground that I would have taken, and which I hope some other gentleman will advocate. I trust it is by no such light and trival arguments as those which have just been advanced to the House, that this important question is to be settled. Before I go further, Mr. Chairman, I would deprecate the distinction that has been drawn here between one portion of the inhabitants of California and another. I do not, in discussing any question in this body, stop to consider the claims of particular classes. All distinctions should be lost among us; I consider that we are all Californians. The question then is, what is best—what is most desirable for the great majority of the people of California? I not only object to this clause, but I object to the amendment. I believe there is but one proper course to pursue, and I shall vote for any amendment that will accomplish that object—to expunge it altogether from the Constitution. I object to it on the general principle so often avowed in this Convention, that it is a legislative enactment; but I would object, also, to see it upon our statute books, because I think it is radically wrong. In my opinion, there is no provision so beautiful in the common law, so admirable and beneficial, as that which regulates this sacred contract between man and wife. Sir, the God of nature made woman frail, lovely, and dependant; and such the common law pronounces her. Nature did what the common law has done—put her under the protection of man; and it is the object of this clause to withdraw her from that protection, and put her under the protection of the law. I say, sir, the husband will take better care of the wife, provide for her better and protect her better, than the law. He who would not let the winds of heaven too rudely touch her, is her best protector. When she trusts him with her happiness, she may well trust him with her gold. You lose the substance in the shadow; by this provision you risk her happiness forever, whilst you protect her property. Sir, in the marriage contract, the woman, in the language of your protestant ceremony, takes her husband for better, for worse; that is the position in which she voluntarily places herself, and it is not for you to withdraw her from it. I beg you, I entreat you, not to lay the rude hand of legislation upon the beautiful and poetical position in which the common law places this contract. There is not only much of poetry and beauty in it, sir, but there is much of sound sense and reason in it. This proposition, I believe, is calculated to produce dissention and strife in families. The only despotism on earth that I would advocate, is the despotism of the husband. There must be a head and there must be a master in every household; and I believe this plan by which you propose to make the wife independent of the husband, is contrary to the laws and provisions of nature—contrary to all the wisdom which we have derived from experience. This doctrine of woman's rights, is the doctrine of those mental hermaphrodites, Abby Folsom, Fanny Wright, and the rest of that tribe. I entreat, sir, that no such clause may be put in this Constitution. It is not desirable to introduce into every household that state of things which must ensue from the enactment of such a clause. It is often the case that the union takes place between a man of little or no property, and a woman of immense landed estate. But do you mean to say that, under such circumstances, the husband must remain a dependant upon his wife? a dependant upon her bounty? would you, in short, make Prince Albert's of us all?

Mr. Chairman, I am so very unwell that I find it utterly impossible to give expression to the opinions that I entertain upon this subject. I hope that the suggestions which are here thrown out may serve as a basis for some gentleman who coincides with me in opinion, to make such an elaborate argument upon as I find myself entirely incompetent to offer at this time.

Mr. Lippitt. I am sorry that I am not able myself to make the elaborate argument which my friend (Mr. Botts) desires. I presume the House will recollect that the object of the amendment is to give power to the Legislature to try the experiment which many of us think ought to be tried. I must confess that, for one, I am wedded to the common law. I am wedded to it as a member of this Convention, as representing a portion of the people, and as a citizen of California; and if I were in the Legislature, I should be, as a member of the Legislature, and for this reason: that the common law, and no other law, is the law under which nine-tenths of the people now in California were born and educated; it is the only law which is known, the only law which her lawyers and judges know, and which we have access to. For this reason it must be the law of the land hereafter, whether it is established this month or next, this year or next. I do not wish to make any distinctions between the native and the American population of California. I will go on that point just as far as my friend from San Louis Obispo, in doing everything, by legislative enactment, to preserve all the rights of the native population, and as far as I would in protecting the rights and interests of my own countrymen; but this Convention cannot cover one-tenth part of the ground which my friend wishes to have covered in order to protect their rights. It will be a matter of very great difficulty to determine what laws shall be passed hereafter in our Legislature in order to protect all the rights of the California population, without sacrificing the rights of the great American population. It is very certain we have all got to come under one uniform code of laws. The general rights of property must be considered with reference to the great mass of the population—the Americans; the smaller party, the Californians, must yield. But the rights of property in reference to man and wife, and a thousand other matters, are totally different at present. The Americans have been living under the common law; the Californians have been living under the civil. It is useless to disguise the fact, that in course of a few months, the question has to be settled under what code of laws the people are to live. The great mass must live under the common law. It would be unjust to require the immense mass of Americans to yield their own system to that of the minority. There will have to be a great deal of legislation in order to cover all this ground; a very small portion of it can be covered by the insertion of any constitutional provision. In order to carry out the views of my friend from San Luis Obispo, we may as well at once pass another section making the whole civil law the law of the land. It would be impossible in any other way to carry out the system. There is another objection to this enactment. It is contrary to general and well-established principles that any community, or any branch of a community, can long exist where there is more than one head. This enactment certainly goes to conflict with this great law of nature. It introduces a separation of interests; and where there is a separation of interests, there must of necessity exist a contrariety of interests. I recollect reading of an English case in one of the courts, where the trustees of the wife sued her husband for the use of her carriage in riding to the theatre one evening. The suit was decided against him. This goes to show, that where you have a separation of property and interests in the marriage contract, the moment there is any unkind feeling, you may depend upon it, it will be kindled into a flame—it will soon show itself, and destroy the happiness of the couple. An old French philosopher (Chaupart was his name) lays it down, that all mankind are divided into two classes: those who have better appetites than dinners, and those who have better dinners than appetites. I am inclined to think that all wives may be divided into two classes: those who wear the breetches, and those who do not. If that be so—if there are two classes of wives—those who submit, and are under the influence of their husbands, in all matters, and those who set up against his influence, then, sir, with respect to the first class, I say that such a constitutional provision would be perfectly nugatory. You may introduce it into your statute book or your Constitution—you may make it the law of the land—you may give the right and control of separate property to the wife—but every wife who habitually yields to her husband, will yield to him in all cases relative to the disposition of that property, and the husband will have the control of it, just as if no such enactment existed. If, on the other hand, the wife is of that class which does not yield, I think it is evidence that the very existence of such a right would only tend to increase and foment every dissension, no matter how trifling the cause may have been in the first place. I have lived some years in countries where the civil law prevails, and where precisely such a separate right of property is given to the wife. I have seen, therefore, something of the working of the principle. I have lived in Paris, and I was assured by respectable inhabitants there, that it was an ascertained fact, that two-thirds of the married couples in Paris were living separately—the husband living separate from the wife. If there is any country in the world which presents the spectacle of domestic disunion more than another, it is France, where this principle is carried most completely into effect. There the husband and wife are partners in business—there you find precisely the point of difference between myself and my friend from San Luis Obispo—the principle of setting the wife up as an equal, in every thing whatever, to the husband—raising her from the condition of head clerk to partner. The very principle, Mr. Chairman, is contrary to nature, and contrary to the real interests of the married state. But there is another consideration, and that is, that there is no necessity, at least not the necessity that is supposed, under the common law, for any such enactment or incorporation of the civil law; because, Mr. Chairman, in every case where the wife has property before her marriage, it is competent for the parties, by an ante-nuptial contract, under our system, to provide for that separate property and separate control. It is done in every country where the marriage contract prevails, especially where the property owned by the wife is large; so that whenever the parties please, they can so make their contract as to secure to the wife all the benefits that can result from the provision which is proposed to be inserted in the Constitution; and where that is not done—that is, where the wife has no considerable property, or where the parties do not choose to make such contract, it is evidence that they do not desire it; and they are certainly the parties most interested. There is another consideration which has not been adverted to. We must be careful how we undertake to repair a building by taking away one part from it. The whole building may fall down, if we do not understand the construction of it—the relative support given to it by the different parts. If we are going to incorporate such an enactment as this upon our established system, we must take care to make such provisions as will not impair the rights of the husband. Under the marriage contract, as it exists, the husband becomes liable the moment he is married for every cent of his wife's debts, which she may contract. Upon what does the law found this liability? On this very ground; that the husband at the time of the marriage, immediately becomes the owner of all his wife's property—all her tangible personal property. He is supposed to come into possession of his wife's property, and hence the common law makes him liable for her debts. No matter what the amount may be, the law throws the liability upon him. If we introduce any such provision, we must look to the rights of the husband, and introduce another to free him from this liability, after we have taken from him the control of his wife's property. We must also look to the rights of the creditor in this matter—they have some rights too. We must take care how we introduce a constitutional enactment which, for ever and ever, until this Constitution is altered or amended by the people, puts the creditors of the husband completely in the power of the husband himself, if he is a dishonest man. How does the section read? It declares that the Legislature shall pass laws providing for the registration of the wife's separate property. It is a matter of absolute necessity that that should be done, otherwise the creditors of the husband are completely at his mercy. As the section stands, there is no obligation imposed upon the Legislature to pass a registration law before this enactment goes into operation. Suppose the Legislature does not pass this registration law, what will be the consequence? If the husband is a dishonest man, gets in debt, and cannot or will not pay his debts, he has only to pretend, when a bill or execution is sent against his property, that it belongs to his wife—that it is her separate property. There is a law-suit to ensue. It is throwing impediments against the collection of debts. There is nothing in the section which declares that it shall not go into operation until the Legislature shall pass a registration law. If the Legislature should pass such a registration law, it would diminish the obstacle; but we do not know whether the Legislature will pass any such law for the first, second, or tenth session; and if they do pass it, we cannot now tell what kind of a law it may be. Meantime, creditors are certainly, if not deprived of the power of collecting their debts, put completely at the mercy of every dishonest man who has a wife, and can say that the property belongs to her. But after all, what is the object of the amendment which I propose as a substitute? Precisely the object which my friend from San Luis Obispo, (Mr. Tefft,) agrees with me in. It says, let us try the experiment—let us see how it works; let the Legislature pass the enactment, because if it does not work well they can repeal it. If we insert such a provision in this Constitution, it may be found to operate badly, and then we place ourselves in the position of having adopted an objectionable provision, which must remain the law of the land so long as the Constitution adopted by this Convention exists.

Mr. Dimmick. It will be remembered that this section proposed in the Constitution is, and always has been, the law of this country. When we propose, therefore, to put it in the Constitution, we are not stepping upon untried ground. We are only reiterating that which is already the law of the country. For this reason, I am in favor of making it a constitutional provision. It is no experiment in this country. The main reason which the gentleman from San Francisco, (Mr. Lippitt,) has so urgently presented against this provision, is that the common law will soon be the established law of this country. If that is to be so, it will make a great change over the laws as they now exist, and will materially affect the rights of women, unless we incorporate a portion of it so far as relates to this subject. Women now possess in this country the right which is proposed to be introduced in the Constitution. Blot it out, and introduce the common law, and what do you do? The wife who owns her separate property loses it the moment the common law prevails, and it is to avoid taking away that right of control over her property that I would wish to see this provision engrafted in the Constitution. Instead of an argument against its introduction, I think the gentleman has advanced a very strong reason in favor of it. He told us it was introducing a principle which could not work prosperously in any community. Has it worked any evil in California? It may not work well in Paris, but we are now to consider the experience, character, and condition of California, not the nations of Europe. The only country I have ever lived in where the civil law prevails is California, where I have resided for the brief period of three years. I admire many provisions of the civil law. I am, however, in favor of the adoption of the common law, but while we adopt that, there are certain provisions of the civil law which I prefer, and when we adopt it in the Constitution, it is no more an invasion of the common law than certain local enactments of the State. The time was, sir, when woman was considered an inferior being; but as knowledge has become more generally diffused, as the world has become more enlightened, as the influence of free and liberal principles has extended among the nations of the earth, the rights of woman have become generally recognized. At the time the common law was introduced, woman occupied a position far inferior to that which she now occupies. As the world has advanced in civilization, her social position has been the subject of increased consideration, and by general consent of all intelligent men, she is now regarded as entitled to many of the rights in her peculiar sphere which were formerly considered as belonging only to man. This part of the common law is one of those portions belonging to the dark ages, which has not yet been expunged by the advance of civilization, Sir, I cannot see any of the evils which the gentleman fancies he sees in introducing into this Constitution, or making it a permanent law of the country, a provision for the protection of the wife's property. It has been found to work well here; it works well now; why should it operate worse if we adopt other portions of the common law? It is true, that under the common law, when a man marries a wife he becomes responsible for the debts of that wife; but I would not shield her property from her own debts. No man is compelled to pay the debts of his wife when she has property of her own. I have yet to learn that there is any principle in the common law which releases her property from this liability, or impairs the contract heretofore existing between her and her creditors. If she had property previous to her marriage, that property is still liable for her debts, and the marriage contract does not release it from that liability. We are told, Mr. Chairman, that woman is a frail being; that she is formed by nature to obey, and ought to be protected by her husband, who is her natural protector. That is true, sir; but is there any thing in all this to impair her right of property which she possessed previous to entering into the marriage contract? I contend not. In justice to her and to her family, who may become dependent upon her, these rights should not be impaired.

Mr. Jones. Following after my able friend from San Jose, (Mr. Dimmick,) and being on the same side of the question, I feel some difficulty in giving expression to my views. I shall say but few words on the subject, and, if it were not for hints thrown out from time to time, I should certainly, in my present exhausted state of health, say nothing. But, sir, to this complexion has it come at last: but yesterday the gentleman from Monterey (Mr. Botts) inquired if there was to be an article introduced to adopt the common law, and but to-day the gentleman from San Francisco, (Mr. Lippett,) another member of the bar, arose in his seat and said this was a strange admixture, some horrible principle of the civil law, that gentlemen were going to incorporate in this Constitution. Here is to be the battle-ground, and here will I meet the gentlemen. I have yet to learn that at this present sitting the common law is the law of the land—that its principles have been adopted, except perhaps by the San Francisco Legislature. That may possibly be; but that this is an invasion upon any existing law in this country, I deny. With the permission of the gentleman, I will translate the principle: The property of the wife owned or claimed by her before marriage, and acquired afterwards by gift, devise, or descent, shall be her separate property, and laws shall be passed more clearly defining the rights of the wife in relation, as well to her separate property, as that held in common with her husband.

Now, does this section of the Constitution introduce any invasion into the common law of this land. No, sir, it but enforces what is the law of the land, and the principle which I shall sustain here. These nice distinctions of the common law, what are they? What is the principle so much glorified, but that the husband shall be a despot, and the wife shall have no right but such as he chooses to award to her. It had its origin in a barbarous age, when the wife was considered in the light of a menial, and had no rights. But in this age of civilization, it has been found that the wife has certain rights. State after State has adopted this principle. The barbarous principles of the early ages have been done away with from time to time. For forty or fifty years the States of the American Union have been trying to modify and simplify this principle of the common law. Sir, I want no such system; the inhabitants of this country want no such thing; the Americans of this country want no such thing. They want a code of simple laws which they can understand; no common law, full of exploded principles, with nothing to recommend it but some dog latin, or the opinions of some lawyer who lived a hundred years ago; they want something that the people can comprehend. The gentleman forgets that the law is the will of the people properly expressed, and that the people have a right to understand their own will and derive the advantage of it, without going to a lawyer to have it expounded. It is absurd to require them to apply for legal advice to learn how they are to collect a debt of fifty dollars. Where is this common law that we must all revert to? Has the gentleman from Monterey got it? Can he produce it? Did he ever see it? Where are the ten men in the United States that perfectly understand, appreciate, and know this common law? I should like to find them. When that law is brought into this House—when these thousand musty volumes of jurisprudence are brought in here, and we are told this is the law of the mass—I want gentlemen to tell me how to understand it. I am no opponent of the common law, nor am I an advocate of the civil law. Sir, I am an advocate of all such law as the people can understand. Whether I find it in that book or this, I say let us give to the people, who have been chained down for hundreds of years, the right and privilege of understanding their own laws. I would make the laws of this Territory, if possible, so plain, simple, and comprehensible, that every man in the Territory could go into a court of justice and defend himself; and he has just as much right to do that as to defend himself in a street fight. The member from Monterey (Mr. Botts) intimated that if this Committee of the Whole did not introduce an article proposing the common law, he would do it. When that resolution is introduced, I will meet the gentleman at Phillippi. I put one question to the gentleman from Monterey. Whom does he represent upon this floor in abolishing the law of the land, and substituting a law which the ninety-six votes by whom he was elected, never heard of?

Mr. Botts. Will the gentleman permit me to interrupt him? I was called to order here the other night for something that it was supposed I was going to say out of order. He is reprehending me for something he supposes I am going to do. Would it not be well to reserve his strictures until the article is introduced?

Mr. Jones. I understood the gentleman here and elsewhere to express his entire support of such an article. The question which I asked was a sort of answer, in a plain way, to what had been adduced here as argument. If gentlemen have a right to get up here and advocate a principle, and I have no right to get up here and oppose it, I might as well take my seat. But I will confine myself to the question before the House. What, under the laws of this country and under the laws of all civilized nations, is the marriage contract? Does it merge in the husband every right of woman? Has she no right whatever? Does she become annihilated because she enters into this contract, or does she preserve certain rights? Are we to adopt laws which make man a despot of woman, and give woman no right because she has no representation? Sir, I consider the marriage contract as a civil partnership—a civil contract. It is not that sacrament which the gentleman would make it; and as to all this talk about the poesy of the marriage contract, I did not come here to advocate poesy. Gentlemen preach poesy to me; let them convince me by any principle of reason that there should be this merging, this annihilation of the woman, let them convince me that the wife should have no rights, and that the law should give her no protection, it will have a much stronger influence upon my feelings than these rhapsodies about poesy. Sir, the marriage contract is a civil contract—not a sacrament. It is recognized and prescribed by law, and every single one of its conditions is a legal matter; it is not a part of the conventional law; it is part of the municipal law of the country. The law must prescribe the rights of the contracting parties. You cannot say that one party consents to have all its rights annihilated, all its property lost, by this contract of marriage.

Sir, the member from San Francisco (Mr. Lippitt) says that there are two classes of wives—those who wear the breeches, and those who do not. I admit the distinction; and where the woman wears the breeches, and intends to wear them, she will take advantage of this common law right and secure her property; but, sir, it is to those who do not wear the breeches—it is to those gentle and confiding creatures who do not think of contracts—that the protection of the law is designed to be given. A man marries a woman of this kind, and owes debt after debt. She knows nothing of it; she does not stop to inquire whether he owes debts or not. No, sir, she enters into this contract blindly confident. There is a true poesy in the confidence with which the woman yields herself to man, believing him to be all that is upright and honorable. Now, would it not be a very poetical idea for one of these gentle and confiding creatures to ask the man to whom she had given her heart and pledged her hand, whether he owed his tailor or shoemaker? how many small bills he had outstanding? whether he was in the habit of being dunned or not? Is she to say to him: let us go before a notary, sir, you to whom I have given my heart and hand; let us draw up a certain contract; I want certain lands and tenements secured by marriage contract. Is not that a regular knock-down to poesy? Let the law secure to this class of women their rights, for they have no power themselves to secure them. I would never, under the common law, unite myself to a woman of wealth who would want me to draw up a marriage contract before the notary public. This much for the rights of women.

Sir, I suppose from the course that has been pursued here, and from the manifestations which I have seen of the sense of this House, that the common law is to be visited upon this country. Very well, sir; I can stand it; I have practised under it and can comprehend it; but do not, I entreat you, make women the subject of its despotic provisions.

Mr. Norton. I am in favor of the section as reported by the Committee, and being so, am of course, opposed to the substitute of my colleague, (Mr. Lippitt.) I regret that, during this discussion, gentlemen should have made this a question between the common and the civil law. It is taken for granted that if we adopt this section, or that of my colleague, we are going to adopt the civil or the common law. I insist that that question has nothing to do with it; and that the whole course of argument, whether we are to adopt common or civil law is totally irrelevant to the question under consideration. The question before the Committee is, whether or not we shall adopt a certain section as introduced here, providing for the security of property, both real and personal, of the wife. The gentleman from

San Jose (Mr. Dimmick) tells you that all of this is secured by the civil law, and that the civil law is the existing law of the land. If that law is adopted as the law of the land, there will be no necessity whatever for this provision ; if not, and if the common law should be established hereafter, as I hope it will be, it is necessary, if we attempt at all to provide for the security of the wife, that we should adopt some such article as this. I believe, sir, that we should do this as a matter of necessity. Every one here can relate to you instance after instance where the property of the wife has been sacrificed through the idle habits, carelessness or dissipation of the husband ; and is it not necessary, forming a new State as we are about to do, that we should protect the wife against such contingencies as this ? We are peculiarily situated here ; in a country where wealth is acknowledged to be abundant, and where lucrative speculations are made every day; but no man can tell how long he can stand upon the pinnacle of wealth that he has reared for himself. No man can tell how soon he may tumble down from that lofty height to which he has risen within the last two years ; and if, in the meantime, he takes to himself a partner, it is necessary that she should be protected against the recklessness of speculation. Gentlemen say that this is an invasion upon a great principle—an invasion upon the common law—an invasion against a time-honored custom. I care not, sir, if it is all this ; if members of this Convention are satisfied that the principled embodied in the section is a good and valid principle, it matters not to me how long the custom has existed, or how great may be the invasion, I will go heart and hand for the adoption of the principle. We should be satisfied that the principle embodied here is a correct one ; and the experience of every man who has lived as long as I have, (though there are many who have lived a great deal longer,) shows full well the necessity of this provision. We are sent here to form a Constitution for what I trust will soon be a great and glorious and prosperous State ; and I think it is not only incumbent upon us to make such provisions in our Constitution as will protect the stronger sex, but such as will also protect frail and lovely woman. I think, sir, that in doing this, we are doing no more than what is due to her ; but I trust we shall hear no more distinctions drawn in this discussion between the common and the civil law.

The gentleman from San Joaquin (Mr. Jones) would make you believe that the common law is inexplicable and incomprehensible—that it is so musty from its long existence, that no man can tell what it is. I believe, sir, that there are gentlemen on this floor who are somewhat conversant with the common law ; who have explored the musty volumes of the common law, and dug out of them great and glorious principles ; principles upon which the Constitution of the United States is founded ; principles which are now the fundamental law of twenty-nine of the thirty States of this Union. For gentlemen to say here that we have no right to adopt the common law—that it is unintelligible, that it is written in dog latin or some other dead language, and that no man knows what it is—I trust, sir, that under the writings of Blackstone, Kent, and of all common law writers, through all the reports of the various States of the Union—the large field of learning—that we have such a common law, that he who runs may read. It is entirely useless here to go against the common law. Nine-tenths of all the population of this country are its warmest advocates. They have been born and brought up under its glorious protection ; they have learned it from their boyhood ; they understand its provisions, and have been protected under its influence. And, Mr. Chairman, these are not the men to throw away the early predelictions of their youth, to discard what they know to be good, and embrace something that they know not of; and are these men to be told that, because the civil law may have heretofore existed in this country, that it shall forever exist ? No, sir ; according to a principle that we have adopted in our Bill of Rights, the people are sovereign ; and they have a right to alter their organic law—alter their whole system of jurisprudence—do away with it, and establish another in its stead. And whenever it shall be the wish of a majority of the people of this country in a legitimate way to provide for the establishment of one system or the other, no man can dispute but they have that right. But, sir, the whole discussion between the common and the civil law is inapplicable to the question under consideration. The section now before the House is one providing for the rights of the wife against the misconduct or misfortune of the husband. The man when he takes to himself a wife, knowing this to be the law of the land, cannot say, with any degree of fairness, that her separate property should not be so taken care of—that no matter whatever misfortune should happen to him, her property shall not go to the common wreck. He has no right to object to it. No matter what may become of the husband, the wife should be protected; her property should be sacred to her; and whatever she may be willing to do for her husband thereafter, she can do. But, under this provision, if, upon the celebration of the marriage, the wife desires to convey all her property to her husband, she can make such disposition of it. Gentlemen contend here that it will cause a disunion in families; that it will be a source of dissention between the husband and the wife during the whole time that they live together. I do not believe any such thing. If this is provided for by the law of the land, the husband when he marries a wife, knows full well the rights that belong to her. If whatever property she is possessed of should remain vested in her, and not subject to his control, he knows beforehand that such is the case, and he has no cause to complain. But if, under the common law, a marriage should be celebrated, and it should be the desire of the parents to enter into an ante-nuptial contract, these are the occasions which create difficulties between the husband and wife; these cases are not expressly provided for by the law, but in an ante-nuptial contract, and hence they give rise to all these difficulties. I believe that it is essentially necessary that the wife's property should be so protected. I expect myself, sir, at some future time, to take to myself a wife. She may be possessed of some little property, and I am not sure but that if it is not secured to her, I may squander it.

Mr. Botts. I have lately given to this House sufficient proof that any thing I shall say to-night, will probably be very crude; but, sir, my pulse would have to cease altogether before I could remain silent under such doctrines and propositions as have been broached here. I find, sir, that the burden of this defence is resting altogether upon the shoulders of myself and the gentleman from San Francisco, (Mr. Lippitt.) I anticipated as much. That you may know how it is, Mr. Chairman, that the common law views this contract, I will read you the words of one of the oldest commentators upon it: "By marriage" says Blackstone, "the husband and wife are one person in law." (See Blackstone in full on this subject.) This is but another mode of repeating the declaration of the Holy Book, that they are flesh of one flesh, and bone of bone. That is the principle of the common law, and it is the principle of the bible. It is a principle, Mr. Chairman, not only of poetry, but of wisdom, of truth, and of justice. Sir, it is supposed by the common law that the woman says to the man in the beautiful language of Ruth: "Whither thou goest I will go; and where thou lodgest, I will lodge; thy people shall be my people, and thy God my God." This, sir, is the character of that holy ceremony which gentlemen have considered as a mere money copartnership. Sir, it is this view of that contract that has produced that peculiar and lovely English word *home*, which it has been said no other people on the face of the earth know. It arises from the very peculiar light in which the English law looks upon this social relation. Bear that in mind, you who love your homes. I tell you, Mr. Chairman, that if you introduce this clause, you must take care to carry along with it a speedy and easy and effectual way of procuring divorces, for they will come as sure as you live, as a necessary consequence. That very moment that you set up two heads in one family, you sow dissentions which lead to applications for divorces, and your courts and Senate chambers will be filled with them.

There was one statement of my friend from San Francisco, (Mr. Lippitt,) that under the common law, ante-nuptial contracts were frequent. So far as my experience goes, they are any thing but frequent. The man who lacks the spirit of a man so far as to enter into such a contract, is a rara avis. I have known such cases; it was the sort of cases where a man who had been unfortunate in life or reduced in circumstances, was about to make a union with a lady of wealth. It was for the purpose of protecting the property from his former creditors, that this ante-nuptial contract was entered into. But so far as my experience goes, it is a very unfrequent thing to find an individual who will, of his own consent, agree to put himself in this humble position. The love and affection of which the gentleman talks can never, I believe, accompany this arrangement. If there is one thing more than another upon which this high affection hangs, it is the dependency of the wife; it is that she is frail and weak and tender, that she calls for all the sympathies of man; and she has them. Sir, if she had a masculine arm and a strong beard, who would love her? She had just as well have them as a strong purse; she is rendered just as independent by the one as the other, and as little loveable.

It has been my fortune this night, for the first time in my life, to hear the common law reviled; yes, sir, that which has been the admiration of all ages, and of the able and wise and learned of all climes, has been in this House, this night, spoken of with contempt and derision. Sir, I would as soon think of slandering the mother to whom I owe my life, as I would the common law to which I owe my liberty. Do you remember, Mr. Chairman, that it is to the common law that you owe the writ of habeas corpus, to which you have already paid the tribute of respect?

Mr. Jones. The writ of habeas corpus is contained in the first Justinian.

Mr. Botts. It has been said by some of the greatest civil lawyers in the world that the superior freedom of the English was attributable to the practical operation of the common law of England. This is the reason why, of all who live under monarchies, they are the freest people on earth. It is our boast to have derived our descent from them; it is our boast to have borrowed this system from them, and made it the basis of our free institutions. And yet, it is this that is made the subject of common reviling and common sneering. Sir, I believe the greatest republican that ever lived, considering the lights under which he lived, was the greatest common law writer of the world, Sir Edward Coke. The gentleman tells you that there are not ten men that understand the principles of the common law; and if he had not himself asserted afterwards that he understood them, I should not have supposed from the way he spoke that he was one of the ten. He tells you that the civil law is so compact and so brief—this is exactly my objection to it, it is so brief that the people cannot find it. The dictates of Draco were said to be written in blood; but that was not the only difficulty; they were hung so high that nobody could read them. The worst law on the face of the earth is the law that resides in the breast of the judge. The great beauty of the common law is that it is so expanded, so full and complete, that it fits all cases, and leaves nothing in the breast of the judge. If the gentleman had understood the common law a little better he would have known that, while he was reviling, he was paying it the greatest compliment. But, Mr. Chairman, to leave this subject, which is extraneous to the matter under debate, and has been lugged in by the gentlemen across the way without reason, without rhyme, without poetry, I come back to the subject before the House. There are only one or two considerations that I desire to present. I want to know to whose benefit is this provision to enure? What is the provision? That a married woman shall enjoy the use and control of her own property without any regard to the acts and doings of her husband; that is to say, that the husband and wife together may enjoy my property and yours, and become possessed of thousands and thousands, leaving us beggars; and then, sir, under this system, while they are indebted to us together for that which they here jointly used and occupied, under the pretence of this clause, they may leave us pennyless while they revel in luxury. I ask you, sir, what honest woman could avail herself of this clause? I ask you what honest woman could see the creditor knocking at the door appealing for the payment of what is justly due to him, and send him away? Who is it then that it benefits? The fraudulent husband and the colluding wife; who, after they have enjoyed the benefit of what gentlemen call speculation, seek to defraud honest men of their means. What are these speculations that gentlemen allude to? They are money put upon the hazard of a die. Suppose the die turns up the wining face, who gets the benefit of it? Is it not the woman who is incorporated with the husband. When he speculates, both speculate; when he gambles they both gamble; and when he becomes indebted they both become indebted. From every debt, from every gambling act, every speculation, if it is successful, the wife reaps the advantage; if it is unsuccessful she should bear her share of the misfortune. This is the doctrine of an honest woman. The proposition amounts simply to this: that if the husband's speculation turns out well, both husband and wife are to enjoy the benefit of it; but if it fails, the loss is to fall upon the creditor. You ask us to secure speculators in all their enterprises, at the expense and risk of the community; you propose that we shall introduce a provision in this Constitution to ensure all people who choose to hazard their means against loss. But, sir, you cannot make an honest woman dishonest if you would; you may seek to do it by constitutional provision, or by legislative enactment, but her great spirit will burst through all your bonds, and she will come to the husband's rescue, and so long as she has a single cent she will pay his debts. Thank God you cannot by any of your laws crush that spirit of integrity which abides in the breast of woman.

The question was then taken upon striking out the 13th section of the report, and inserting Mr. Lippitt's substitute, and it was decided in the negative.

The 13th section was then adopted.

The 14th section being under consideration, as follows:

Sec. 14. The Legislature shall have power to protect by law, from forced sale, a certain portion of the property of all heads of families. The homestead of a family not to exceed three hundred and twenty acres of land, (not included in a town or city,) or any town or city lot or lots in value not to exceed —— dollars, shall not be subject to forced sale for any debts hereafter contracted, nor shall the owner, if a married man, be at liberty to alienate the same, unless by consent of the wife, in such manner as the Legislature may hereafter point out.

Mr. McCarver said he thought the Legislature had that power already without any constitutional provision. He therefore moved to strike out the words "have power to."

Mr. Botts moved to amend by adding the following proviso: Provided, That the creditor who needs the money of the debtor to purchase a homestead, shall be entitled to recover it.

Mr. Semple. It seems to me that the amendment of the gentleman from Monterey is very reasonable. I have observed these exemption laws, and am honestly of opinion that it is not right to exempt this homestead property. It should be susceptible of proof that the debtor whom you propose to protect, is absolutely more in need of the exemption than the creditor. I think it but fair that if you protect one man, you should also protect another, who is in the same situation.

Mr. Tefft. It certainly is a matter of great surprise to me that a gentleman of such liberal and enlightened principles as he who offers to give his horse-ferry at Benicia to the public, should entertain such views as these. This is only following out a principle of exemption adopted every where now in this enlightened age—that a man's means of living should be preserved to his family.

The question was then taken on Mr. Botts' proviso, and it was rejected.

Mr. Tefft moved to insert after the word city, the word two thousand dollars.

Mr. Botts. Suppose a man should own a lot in a city worth $5,000, and he should owe a debt of $2,000; can you sell his lot? I think this law as it is here framed is exceedingly incomplete, and we had better give it up altogether. The case which I have mentioned does not come within this clause. The house alone is worth $5,000. What provision does the law make in this instance? If we make a law at all, let us make it a good and complete one.

Mr. Steuart. I move to strike out all after the word "families." The section as it then stands will cover every case that properly comes before the Legislature.

Mr. Lippitt. I shall be in favor of that, because it leaves the matter to the Legislature and people. It belongs to the people, through their representatives in the Legislature, to say how far the Legislature shall go in this matter.

Mr. Steuart. I am really in earnest when I say I am not physically able to sustain my proposition. I think this clause will protect every interest of the Legislature. The object of this House is to give to the people certain fundamental principles upon which the Legislature is to act. I am astonished when I hear gentlemen here so strenuous in their advocacy of the protection of the poor from the rich, that they should advocate a section that will go farther to defeat the adoption of this Constitution than perhaps any that has yet been proposed.

Mr. McCarver. I think there is no provision of the Constitution which would better meet the approbation of the mass of the people than this.

Mr. Halleck. I concur with my friend from San Francisco (Mr. Steuart) as to the propriety of this section not being adopted as it stands; but I believe, with the addition of two words, so as perfectly to express the meaning of the section, that it will be acceptable to the House. If the amendment before this House does not pass, I shall propose an amendment.

Mr. Wozencraft. I am in favor of the amendment of the gentleman from San Francisco, (Mr. Steuart,) for I think it is a legitimate subject of legislative action. There is certainly property much more important to a man than his homestead. Why do not the Committee go further, and specify his tools, his implements upon which his very existence depends? In the State of Tennessee, the articles are specified. This Committee may bring in a bill as long as that which we may expect in the famous schedule. Why not, then, at once commit it to the hands of the Legislature, and let them say what shall be protected from seizure?

The question was then taken on Mr. Steuart's amendment, and it was rejected.

Mr. Halleck. I now move to insert after the word "lot," the words "said land or lots not to exceed in value two thousand dollars."

Mr. Wozencraft. I propose an amendment to the amendment; that these articles shall be included after the words specifying the value, "together with his mechanical tools and farming utensils, household furniture, two cows, two yoke of oxen, and five sheep." In all seriousness, Mr. Chairman, I offer it. I do think it is due to the section itself, if gentlemen wish to put it through in complete form, that it should be so. What would be a man's household, his home to him, if that home was stripped of every thing in it? What protection do you give to a man in his humble home, if you deprive him of the means of earning a subsistence?

Mr. Botts. I would remark that, if this amendment is lost, I hope my friend from San Joaquin (Mr. Wozencraft) will present it to the House at the proper time, and ask the yeas and nays upon it. We will then test the sincerity of gentlemen who profess to be friends of the poor.

The question was then taken on Mr. Wozencraft's amendment, and it was rejected.

Mr. Sherwood. I regret now that I did not vote for the amendment of the gentleman from San Francisco (Mr. Steuart.) I see the difficulty which has since been suggested. I cannot perceive how it is possible with this provision of the Constitution, as no law of the Legislature can go behind the Constitution, to divide the city or town lot which exceeds in value $2,000. It may be worth $20,000. I do not see how it is possible for the Legislature to take from this homestead $2,000 out of the $20,000. It had better be left to the Legislature to make such guards in relation to it as they deem expedient. I would simply make it the duty of the Legislature to pass laws for the protection of the homestead.

Mr. Hoppe. I am sorry I voted against the amendment of my friend from San Francisco, (Mr. Steuart,) and that it was not adopted. I would, if the amendment of the gentleman from Monterey (Mr. Halleck) is not adopted, move this, which I think covers the whole ground: "homestead and other property." I would observe that there is other property more valuable to the head of the family than his homestead.

Mr. Tefft. I think the Legislature have the power to do this without saying it in the Constitution.

Mr. Halleck. I wish to remark this; I want the amendment which I offer to pass merely as an amendment. I am not in favor of the original section. I desire to make it as perfect as it can be, in case the House think proper to adopt it.

Mr. Lippitt. I am willing to vote for the amendment of the gentleman for that purpose. If the section is to be adopted, I wish it to be in the least objectionable form.

The question was then taken on Mr. Halleck's amendment, and it was adopted.

Mr. Sherwood. There is no possible way that the Supreme Court can divide at present a lot such as I have mentioned in value, $20,000, or a ranch of three hundred acres, if it is a homestead, although it may be much more valuable than $2,000; but if the Supreme Court could decide it, any attempt to prevent the sale of that valuable property by the Legislature is unconstitutional. I think the majority of the House agree that a homestead should be free from sale on execution from a debt; and as we are changing year after year in this new State, as the value of property is changing, it may be necessary year after year for the Legislature to amend the acts of the previous year. Each Legislature will, or ought to know, more than its predecessors; it is to be presumed of course that experience will be gained by future Legislatures; and I think we had better leave the subject open to them, simply directing them to preserve a certain portion of the homestead.

On motion, the vote on Mr. Steuart's amendment was reconsidered.

The question was then taken on the amendment, and it was adopted.

The question being on the adoption of the section, as amended—

Mr. Tefft moved to insert the word "homestead" before property.

Mr. Botts. I understand the reason the gentleman goes in favor of this section is that the Legislature will be opposed to the object in view, and the provision is therefore necessary in order to compel the Legislature to do it. Now, sir, if the Legislature, which certainly reflects the will of the people, object to it, if we anticipate such a result, it certainly forms a strong ground of objection.

Mr. Tefft. I would ask why, if gentlemen have such implicit confidence in the Legislature, they voted in favor of prohibiting the practice of duelling and other restrictive clauses.

Mr. Botts. The reason is that we don't understand the word Constitution.

Mr. Lippitt. I think it belongs to the members of the Legislature coming directly from the people to say what amount, and precisely what articles, shall be exempted. The word "homestead" is indefinite. It may include a homestead to the value of $100,000, or any other amount. If we insert homestead, we might as well insert cattle, sheep, bottles of wine, and all other kinds of property.

The question was then taken on Mr. Tefft's amendment, and it was adopted.

The section as amended was then adopted, as follows:

Sec. 14. The Legislature shall protect by law, from forced sale, a certain portion of the homestead and other property of heads of families.

Mr. Wozencraft. I now wish to introduce in this bill the resolution which has been before the Committee for the last two days, relative to the establishment of hospitals. It is in the following words:

The Legislature shall at an early day provide for the erection of one or more suitable building or buildings, to be designated and used as a public hospital or hospitals, to be located at such place or places as shall best subserve the good and welfare of suffering humanity; and shall provide for the support and maintenance of the same, out of such funds as are not otherwise appropriated.

Mr. SHERWOOD. I can go for considerable legislation in the Constitution, but I cannot go quite so far as this. I think that the Legislature ought to entertain all those feelings of charity for suffering humanity that we do; and if they do, and if it is the desire of their constituents, they will unquestionably raise money enough to provide for the insane, or blind, or sick.

Mr. WOZENCRAFT. I was much in hopes this would pass without a word of debate, and certainly without a word of opposition. I think it strange that the gentleman over the way, (Mr. Sherwood,) has no compunctions of conscience in prohibiting the Legislature from relieving suffering humanity. There are many clauses introduced into the Constitution of minor importance compared with this. We certainly ought to provide measures of relief for those who are stricken down by disease. If there is any land where an establishment of this kind is required, it is California. A great class of persons who have come to California, or are now coming, are exposed to all the vicissitudes of the climate—a climate most trying to the human constitution; and in a country where there is no shelter for the sick, no spot upon which they can lay their heads, I think the sufferings of this class of people appeal to us in the strongest manner.

Mr. HASTINGS. It is too late in the day, and certainly too late in the night for us to question the propriety of this species of legislation. We have been erecting sundry castles in the air, and why not erect the castle proposed by the gentleman from San Joaquin? Let us go on; let us legislate! Gentlemen seem to labor under the idea that we are never to have a Legislature. Then let us go on and make laws complete for black and white, for male and female, for the lame, halt, and blind. We have provided for the living in every possible form; now let us provide for the dying and the dead.

Mr. WOZENCRAFT. I have but one word to say. This is not a castle in the air; it purports to be nothing more than a structure upon earth for the purpose of relieving suffering persons on earth. It is true we have done much for all classes, but there is still another class whose claims are greater than any who have been provided for—the sick and the destitute. Let us suppose a case—such a case of suffering as I have myself often seen here. A poor destitute man, who has been left sick on the way side, is taken by some charitable teamster to the nearest town. The charitable citizens of that place he probably calls upon to provide him with some place upon which he can lay his head; he asks nothing more; he merely seeks a place of shelter, where nature may produce a restoration of his health. But they can give him no encouragement, they have no room for him. If he complains, he is told, do not say so, we have an excellent Constitution; there are plenty of places to put you in if you steal, where you will be boarded for nothing. If you die, we will take care of your children. Is there anything airy in that?

Mr. HASTINGS. Yes, sir, very. It looks to me as much like building castles in the air as any proposition I ever heard of.

The question was then taken on the proposed section, and it was rejected.

Mr. LIPPITT. I have a very short section to offer here:

No perpetuities shall be allowed.

It is to prevent perpetuity of lands from families to families. It is upon perpetuities that aristocracies are built up. Democracy would soon be overturned if this was allowed. The principle is so well established that all our courts of law have made it a rule, in the absence of any statute upon the subject. Whenever they could possibly put any such construction upon any deed or instrument they have deemed themselves bound to do it.

The section was adopted.

Sections 15, 16, 17, and 18 were then adopted without debate, as follows:

SEC. 15. Every person shall be disqualified from holding any office of profit in this State who shall have been convicted of having given or offered a bribe to procure his election or appointment.

Sec. 16. Laws shall be made to exclude from office, serving on juries, and from the right of suffrage, those who shall hereafter be convicted of bribery, forgery, perjury, or other high crimes. The privilege of free suffrage shall be supported by laws regulating elections, and prohibiting, under adequate penalties, all undue influence thereon from power, bribery, tumult, or other improper practice.

Sec. 17. Absence on the business of this State, or of the United States, shall not forfeit a residence once obtained, so as to deprive any one of the right of suffrage, or of being elected or appointed to any office under this Constitution.

Sec. 18. A plurality of the votes given at an election, shall constitute a choice, where not otherwise directed in this Constitution.

Mr. Noriego offered the following:

All laws, decrees, regulations, and provisions emanating from any of the three supreme powers of this State, which from their nature require publication, shall be published in English and Spanish.

Mr. Norton. I believe a section has already been adopted, providing that all laws, &c., shall be published in Spanish as well as in English.

Mr. Botts. We must take care what we are doing here. If I understand the resolution, as I heard it read, it is to engraft in the Constitution that all laws shall be published in Spanish and English. That is a necessity so clear that the Legislature must at once perceive and provide for it; but we cannot but foresee here, that the day will soon arrive when every man in the State will understand the English language. If you engraft this upon the Constitution, you impose an immense and permanent expense upon the people—an expense for which there will be no necessity in a few years. The Legislature will provide for the translation and publication of these laws in Spanish as long as it is necessary. It is one of those things that are vacillating, and should not be put in the permanent fundamental law of the land.

Mr. Noriego. The reason why I make this proposition is, that since this country has been under the American Government, in general all decrees have been published in English. In Santa Barbara, there has been no interpreter at all, and I myself, though my knowledge of the English language is imperfect, have been compelled to translate several public documents. I desire to put it in the Constitution for this reason: that however natural and obvious it may appear that the Legislature should take care of it, the experience of three years has proved that such things may be neglected. The proposition may seem of trival consequence to some; but to me, and those whom I represent, is one of very great importance. The present inhabitants of California will not learn the English language in three or four years; their children may do it; but at present, all laws ought to be published in a language which the people understand, so that every native Californian shall not be at the expense of procuring his own interpreter; and moreover, you will bear in mind that the laws which will hereafter be published, will be very different from those which they obeyed formerly. They cannot obey laws unless they understand them. I do not believe that in six years the adult Spanish population will be able to speak English; but in twenty years they may; and by that time it is very probable that the present Constitution will be altered.

Mr. Tefft moved to amend, by providing that these laws and decrees shall be published in Spanish for a certain number of years.

Mr. Gwin. In support of the section offered by the gentleman from Santa Barbara, I would state that it has been nearly fifty years since Louisiana came into the Union, and they have published laws there in English, French, and Spanish, ever since.

Mr. Lippitt, I am in favor of inserting this provision as drawn up by the gentleman from Santa Barbara. I have no doubt the Legislature will do it; but in order to satisfy the California population, I think it well to insert this provision in the Constitution. No inconvenience will grow out of it. In the course of ten or twenty years, everybody will speak English, and it will then be a very easy matter to have the Constitution altered in that respect. There is this especially in favor of it—that it will satisfy the minds of the whole California population.

Mr. Botts. I withdraw any opposition to the measure. I did not know the practice in Louisiana; and only looked at it connection with this Constution as a transient provision introduced into an instrument made for an indefinite period. I hope my motives will not be misunderstood. But I have one word to say in relation to my friend from Santa Barbara. I solemnly protest against his taking what has been done here for the last three years, as a specimen of the actings or doings of the people of the United States in their political capacity.

Mr. Noriego. When I mentioned that the laws and decrees had been published merely in English hitherto, I had no wish to wound the feelings of the gentleman or any person whatever. I merely referred to actual facts.

Mr. Botts. I will merely add, that the Government which existed here for the last three years, was not the republican Government that we hope to exist here soon. The gentleman must not judge of the character of our American institutions from that. It was a mere military, despotic government, not recognized by the people.

Mr. Dimmick. The proposition is so reasonable that I trust it will be unanimously adopted.

The question was then taken, and the proposed section was unanimously adopted.

On motion, the Committee then rose, reported the article with sundry amendment, and had leave to sit again.

Mr. Norton, from the Committee on the Constitution, laid before the Convention the following:

The Chairman of the Select Committee is requested to ask instructions from the Convention, as to whether the government established by this Constitution shall go into operation from and after the day of its ratification by the people, or not until official news is received of the admission of California into the Union as a State. M. NORTON, *Chairman.*

In order to obtain the sense of the Convention, Mr. Norton offered the following:

Resolved, That the government established by this Constitution shall go into operation as soon as practicable after the ratification of said Constitution by the people."

On motion, the subject was laid on the table, and the House then adjourned.

FRIDAY, SEPTEMBER 28, 1849.

The Convention met pursuant to adjournment. Prayer by the Rev. S. H. Willey.

The Journal of yesterday was read and approved.

Mr. Wozencraft, from the Committee on Printing, made a report, which was read and laid on the table.

The following resolution, offered yesterday by Mr. Norton, was then taken up for consideration:

Resolved, That the government established by this Constitution shall go into operation as soon as practicable after the ratification of said Constitution by the people.

Mr. Botts. It is with great reluctance, Mr. President, that I undertake the discussion of the important questions involved in this resolution. They are questions novel in their character, momentous in their consequences, and deeply interesting to every American citizen. And yet, sir, what are the circumstances under which we are called on to vote upon it. Last night, at 11 o'clock, we were furnished with the first notice of its introduction, and this morning, at 10 o'clock, we are called to the discussion of it. It must be remembered, too, that we are here without the opportunities of reference that are usually afforded; I believe I should hardly be exaggerating were I to say that there are not fifty volumes of law or history in all Monterey; nevertheless, with such poor opportunity as has been afforded me, and out of such slender materials as I could command, I will endeavor to weave an argument in support of the resolution offered by my friend, who is absent from the House. I am not unmindful of the impatience so frequently manifested by this body—of the railroad speed with which we are expected to travel through our labors. I have not forgotten that memorable night on which, under whip and spur, we passed twenty-eight of the most important sections in our Constitution in little less than two hours. I well remember the approbation this style of legislation secured, and I will endeavor to conform to the manifest wishes of the House, by being as brief as the nature of the subject will admit.

Under ordinary circumstances, this resolution itself, much less any defence of it, would appear to be a work of supererogation. The resolution would seem to contain the statement of a self-evident proposition. But, sir, this proposition, plain as it may appear, has been denied; denied in this hall and elsewhere; in this hall by implication, and out of doors flatly and plainly. It has been asserted that the Constitution that we shall make, and the people of California may ratify, is but the cold statue of Pygmalion, until the Promethean heat has been breathed into it by the Congress of the United States. It has been asserted that there is a government, and that there are laws now existing in this country, that can be superseded only by the legislative action of the Union. It is this doctrine that I propose calmly, deliberately, and dispassionately to investigate. The most tangible and the most authentic assertion of this doctrine is to be found in the proclamation of General Riley, under which we were convened. In reviewing this document, I shall exercise the unquestioned and unquestionable right of every representative of the people, aye, sir, the right of every individual of the people, to examine narrowly and discuss freely the acts of their servants. I shall not, nor have I ever, indulged in personalities of any kind, so far as an avoidance of them is compatible with a full, free, and unlimited discussion of the doings and sayings of men in their public capacities. When the two become, as they sometimes do, inseparably connected, I will not shrink from my duty in considering the one, because it may involve feelings of delicacy in regard to the other.

General Riley is a noble old soldier; he is what, in my opinion, it is a much higher honor to be—he is a devoted friend of the rights of man. But he neither seeks nor claims the title of statesman; he is content with that of hero. I will read you the first column of his proclamation:

"Congress having failed at its recent session to provide a new government for this country, to replace that which existed on the annexation of California to the United States, the undersigned would call attention to the means which he deems best calculated to avoid the embarassments of our present position.

"The undersigned, in accordance with instructions from the Secretary of War, has assumed the administration of civil affairs in California, not as a *military* Governor, but as the executive of the existing civil government. In the absence of a properly appointed civil Governor, the commanding officer of the Department, is, by the laws of California, *ex officio* civil Governor of the country, and the instructions from Washington were based on the provisions of these laws. This subject has been misrepresented, or at least misconceived, and currency given to the impression that the government of the country is still *military*. Such is not the fact. The military government ended wiih the war, and what remains is the *civil* government recognized in the existing laws of California. Although the command of the troops in this Department, and the administration of civil affairs in California, are, by the existing laws of the country, and the instructions of the President of the United States, temporarily lodged in the hands of the same individual, they are separate and distinct. No military officer other than the commanding General of the Department exercises any civil authority by virtue of his military commission, and the powers of the commanding General as *ex officio* Governor are only such as are defined and recognized in the existing laws. The instructions of the Secretary of War make it the duty of all military officers to recognize the existing civil government, and to aid its officers with the military force under their control. Beyond this any interference is not only uncalled for but strictly forbidden.

"The laws of California, not inconsistent with the laws, constitution, and treaties of the United States, are still in force, and must continue in force, till changed by competent authority. Whatever may be thought of the right of the people to temporarily replace the officers of the existing government appointed by a provisional Territorial Legislature, there can be no question that the existing laws of the country must continue in force till replaced by others made and enacted by competent power. *That power, by the treaty of peace, as well as from the nature of the case, is vested in Congress.* The situation of California in this respect is very different from that of

Oregon. The latter was without laws, while the former has a system of laws, which, though somewhat defective and requiring many changes and amendments, must continue in force till repealed by competent legislative power. The situation of California is almost identical with that of Louisiana, and the decisions of the Supreme Court in recognizing the validity of the laws which existed in that country previous to its annexation to the United States, where not inconsistent with the Constitution and laws of the United States, or repealed by legitimate legislative enactments, furnish us a clear and safe guide in our present situation. It is important that citizens should understand this fact, so as not to endanger their property and involve themselves in useless and expensive litigation, by giving countenance to persons claiming authority which is not given them by law, and by putting faith in laws which can never be recognised by legitimate courts."

Here, then, we have it clearly and distinctly asserted, that a government exists, and that laws are in force in California which must continue in force until repealed by competent legislative powers; and that that power is necessarily the Congress of the United States. Let us see how far this doctrine, which we are told is that of the Secretary of War, comports with the opinions expressed by other members of the cabinet, and how far it is sustained by principles of law and republicanism. In his message of July, 1848, the President of the United States says:

"The war with Mexico having terminated, the power of the Executive to establish or to continue temporary civil governments over these Territories, which existed under the laws of nations whilst they were regarded as conquered provinces in our military occupation, has ceased. By their cession to the United States, Mexico has no longer any power over them; and, until Congress shall act, the inhabitants will be without any organized government. Should they be left in this condition, confusion and anarchy will be likely to prevail."

Says General Riley and the Secretary of War, an organized government exists; says the commanding officer of the one and the superior of the other, there is no organized government. What a division upon this important subject there must have been in the cabinet of Mr. Polk, when the President expresses one opinion to Congress, and the Secretary forwards his instructions in direct opposition to them. Nevertheless, the President seems to adhere to his first opinions with a good deal of tenacity. In his December message, he says:

"Upon the exchange of ratifications of the treaty of peace with Mexico on the thirtieth of May last, the temporary governments which had been established over New Mexico and California by our military and naval commanders, by virtue of the rights of war, ceased to derive any obligatory force from that source of authority; and having been ceded to the United States, all government and control over them under the authority of Mexico had ceased to exist. Impressed with the necessity of establishing Territorial Governments over them, I recommended the subject to the favorable consideration of Congress in my message communicating the ratification of peace, on the sixth of July last, and invoked their action at that session. Congress adjourned without making any provision for their government. The inhabitants, by the transfer of their country, had become entitled to the benefits of our laws and Constitution, and yet were left without any regularly organized government. Since that time, the very limited power possessed by the Executive has been exercised to preserve and protect them from the inevitable consequences of a state of anarchy. The only government which remained, was that established by the military authority during the war. Regarding this to be a *de facto* government, and that by the presumed consent of the inhabitants it might be continued temporarily, they were advised to conform and submit to it for the short intervening period before Congress would again assemble and could legislate on the subject. The views entertained by the Executive on this point are contained in a communication of the Secretary of State, dated the seventh of October last, which was forwarded for publication to California and New Mexico, a copy of which is herewith transmitted."

Here he repeats the old assertion that there is no regularly organized government in California. "Regarding, says the President, the military government established during the war as a *de facto* government, and that, by the presumed *consent of the inhabitants*, it might be continued temporarily, they were *advised* to conform and submit to it for the short intervening period before Congress would again assemble and could legislate on the subject."

Now mark: the President considers the despotic military government established during the war, consisting of a military Governor alone, in whom were concentrated the legislative, executive, and judicial departments, as the *de facto* government, which may continue to exist by the consent of the people. Gen. Riley, and, as he says, the Secretary of War, conceive that the existing government is *civil* not *military*; that the political law of Mexico is still in force in this country; and that the political organization of the Mexican system is restored, and cannot be abolished except by an act of Congress, regardless of the wishes or opinions of the inhabitants. Here is a direct conflict between two high functionaries. Let us see how the other members of the Cabinet sided in the dispute. Mr. Buchanan, the Secretary of State, addresses a letter, dated October 7, 1848, to a certain Mr. W. V. Voorhies, then in Washington, about to come to California in an official capacity connected with the Post Office Department, in which he says: "the President has instructed me to make known, through your agency, to the citizens of the United States inhabiting that territory, his views respecting their present condition and future prospects." And here I stop to ask how it was that, if the Cabinet recognized the existence of a civil officer in California higher than Mr. Voorhies, they should, forgetful of all etiquette, both military and civil, presume to communicate with the people through any other than their Governor? I resent this indignity to their Governor, if indeed he be such, in the name of the people of California.

Mr. Halleck. Will the gentleman allow me to interrupt him? That communication was not only sent overland, with the expectation of reaching here a long time previous to the arrival of Mr. Voorhies, but the *de facto* Governor of California was directed to publish it before Mr. Voorhies arrived. Mr. Voorhies was directed to give it to the Governor on his arrival here, and did so. The other copy however was first received.

Mr. Botts. If we had a civil governor here, how dare the President put such a slight upon that governor and upon the people, as to address the people of California through an inferior and subordinate agent?

Mr. Gwin. I would inform the gentleman that Mr. Voorhies was the only officer of the United States through which that communication could be sent. There was no other officer here up to that time.

Mr. Botts. I do not think my colleague is so sensitive in regard to the honor of California as I am, or he would more readily perceive the objections that I have to this communication. It is not the source through which it came to the Governor of California, but it is that it was not addressed to the Governor of California. It commences "My dear Voorhies." That is what I object to. It does not matter when it came here. It is the address and character of the letter; addressed to an inferior functionary. I believe it is a well established principle of etiquette, both in military and civil departments, that you communicate with the highest authority.

Mr. Halleck. The gentleman from Monterey does not seem to know quite so much about this matter as he would have us think. Not only was the letter sent to the Governor here, but an apology was sent with it, that if the other letter did not arrive with the Governor, he (Mr. Voorhies) was to take this and circulate it among the people. It is usual both in civil and military matters to send the communication directly to the highest officer, and then others are sent to subordinate officers in case the first should not arrive.

Mr. Botts. I will not be blamed for my ignorance, for I could know nothing but this paper; and certainly it bears a very different sort of statement. I am glad an apology was made to California, and I only wish the people of California had had an opportunity of knowing of that apology before. I am happy, sir, to be the humble means through which California is to hear that apology. I will not refer again to the beginning of the letter which I hold in my hand; it is fraught with information upon the subject; but I will confine myself more properly to that portion of it which bears upon the particular subject under discussion. I call your particular attention to this letter, because we are now told that it was expressly intended that the Governor of California should make it known as the sentiments of the administration. It is, in short, if I understand it, instructions to the Governor of California Mr. Buchanan in the course of this letter remarks:

"In the meantime, the condition of the people of California is anomalous, and will require on their part the exercise of great prudence and discretion. By the conclusion of the treaty of peace, the military government which was established over them under the laws of war, as recognized by the practice of civilized nations, has ceased to derive its authority from this source of power. But is there, for this reason, no government in California? Are life, liberty, and property, under the protection of no existing authorities? This would be a singular phenomenon in the face of the world, and especially among American citizens, distinguished as they are above all other people for their law abiding character. Fortunately they are not reduced to this sad condition. The termination of the war left an existing government—a government *de facto*—in full operation; and this will continue, with the presumed consent of the people, until Congress shall provide for them a Territorial Government. The great law of necessity justifies this conclusion. The consent of the people is irresistibly inferred from the fact, that no civilized community could possibly desire to abrogate an existing government, when the alternative presented would be to place themselves in a state of anarchy, beyond the protection of all laws, and reduce them to the unhappy necessity of submitting to the dominion of the strongest."

Here is a repetition of the repeated doctrine of the President, of a *de facto military* government, continued and existing only at the will of the people. The question that Mr. Buchanan raises is this, what is the natural and legal inference to be derived from the *inaction* of the people of California? He answers, an implied assent to the continuance of the government they found in existence at the close of the war, be it what it may. The proposition, and the argument by which it is maintained, are based upon the supposed passiveness of the people. Indeed by the very terms of the proposition itself, the power of the people to relieve themselves from anarchy by passive submission to the *de facto* government, or by the establishment of an organized civil goverment, is plainly stated. This then is in direct opposition to the views of the honorable Secretary of War and General Riley. But whilst the documents which admit this right are before us and the world, the sole authority upon which the opposite doctrine rests, is locked up in the office of the so-called Secretary of State of California. We have never seen these extraordinary instructions of the Secretary of War, nor do I know, for we have not been told, whether they came from the last or the present administration. This doubt casts, in my opinion, a shade upon the reputation of one of the best democrats and ablest members of Mr. Polk's Cabinet; and I will never believe, until I have seen it with my own eyes, that Wm. L. Marcy ever counselled or abetted a doctrine so repugnant to the spirit of our free and liberal institutions. Not that I mean to doubt the veracity of the gentleman who intimates that he has received these instructions, but it is possible that if he would condescend to submit what he has received to the inspection of the public, he and the public might differ as to the interpretation of this instrument, a thing not very unusual as between the governors and the governed. To say the least of it, then, we have the high authority of Messrs. Polk and Buchanan to oppose the supposed opinion of the Secretary of War. Leaving the one to counterbalance the other, we will proceed to examine the doctrine upon its intrinsic merits.

In General Riley's proclamation, we find the principle stated as follows:

"The undersigned, in accordance with instructions from the Secretary of War, has assumed the administration of civil affairs in California, not as a *military* Governor, but as the Executive of the existing civil government. In the absence of a properly appointed civil Governor, the commanding officer of the department is, by the laws of California, *ex-officio* civil Governor of the country; and the instructions from Washington were based on the provisions of these laws."

We are informed, then, that General Riley has been sent amongst us as "the Executive of the existing civil government in California." If he were sent for that purpose alone, he might well return to those that sent him, and inform them that he found no civil government in California—that none such had existed for years, and that the *de facto* or existing government which the treaty of peace extinguished, was of a character purely military, and that in fact, from that time to the present, no government, either *military* or *civil*, had existed in California. What, sir, is meant by the term government? I apprehend it may be defined to be the supreme power to whom is entrusted the authority to legislate and adjudicate and execute. Can it be pretended that any such authority has been established since the declaration of peace? It is not even pretended that there is or has been an organized *existing* government authorized to exercise the functions of legislation in California. Hence, this great essential being confessedly wanting, it is absurd to talk about the existing government in California. Indeed, in this very document (I mean the proclamation of General Riley) we are told that the Congress of the United States alone possesses the power to legislate for California. In that body, then, resides the existing government of California; and by that body, as we all know, General Riley has been invested with no civil functions. But after assuming that a civil government actually exists in California, General Riley informs us that he claims to exercise the powers of civil Governor, not in consequence of any authority derived from the only body who, in his opinion, are entitled to govern California, but from an act of that Mexican Congress that has ceased to possess any power or authority in this country. That is to say, to the right of the people to form a government, he opposes the power of the Congress of the United States; and to sustain his own position and what he calls the existing government, he quotes the authority of the Congress of Mexico. Such opposite and conflicting arguments are the inevitable result of doctrines so false and preposterous. If the people of California are precluded from exercising the powers of self-government by reason of the controlling authority vested in the Government of the United States, *a fortiori*, says every republican, must every one else be precluded from the power of administering the government of California, except those deriving their authority from the legally constituted agents of the Government of the United States? Those agents are the legislative and executive departments—the one to create, and the other to fill the offices. It is not pretended that either have acted upon the subject. But it is contended, that under some undefined thing that is called the "law of nations," all the laws in force in a ceded province at the moment of cession, remain in force until they are repealed by the government to whom it is ceded. That most sound and thoroughly practical writer, Jeremy Bentham, has sufficiently exposed the nonsense which has so long been palmed upon the world as "the law of nations." But let us see what is the doctrine of the Supreme Court of the United States upon the subject. In the case, Am. Ins. Co. vs. Canter, 1 Peters, Chief Justice Marshall, in delivering the opinion of the Court, speaks as follows:

> "The usage of the world is, if a nation be not entirely subdued, to consider the holding of conquered territory as a mere military occupation, until its fate shall be determined at the treaty of peace. If it be ceded by the treaty, the acquisition is confirmed, and the ceded territory *becomes a part of the nation* to which it is annexed, either on the terms stipulated in the treaty of cession, or on such as its new master shall enforce. On such transfer of territory, it has never be held that the relations of the inhabitants with *each other* undergo any change. Their relations with their former sovereign are dissolved, and new relations are created between them and the government which has acquired the territory. The same act which transfers their country, transfers the allegiance of those who remain in it; and the law which *may be denominated* POLITICAL *is necessarily changed*, although that which regulates the intercourse and general conduct of individuals remains in force *until altered* by the newly-created power of the State."

Now, sir, I would ask, what is the nature of the law which may be denominated political, that is necessarily abolished by the act which transfers the country? Is it not that class of laws, which, in contradistinction to the *municipal*, defines the character and powers of the officers of the Government and the relation of individuals; and is not that law of Mexico, which it is asserted provides for the civil supremacy of the commanding officer of the department in a certain contingency, precisely one of that class of laws which the Supreme Court declares to be abrogated by the act of cession? Here, then, we have the decision of the Supreme Court, which was ratified and repeated in a subsequent decision, directly opposed to this assumption of power by General Riley.

But we are gravely assured that the law of Mexico provides, that in the absence of a civil Governor, the civil authority devolves upon the military commander of the department, *ex-officio*. I can only say that I have failed in all my inquires to discover any such enactment. But if there be such an enactment, it must necessarily refer to the commander of the military forces of Mexico, and, if I mistake not, this is a position which he who fought so bravely for a "yellow sash," would not assume for the privilege of administering any government upon the face of the earth. Is not this point sufficiently clear? Is it necessary to trace its consequences, and show how inimical it is to all the acknowledged rights of man? Why, sir, the military commander of a department who, by this doctrine is the absolute master of a hundred thousand American citizens, may, by accident, be the corporal of a guard. It is enough to look at the Mexican laws and see what are the powers and attributes of the Governor of this department, to turn the stomach of every freeman against this revolting doctrine.

So much for the "existing government" of California, and the position of this country in the absence of congressional action. We come now to the consideration of another even graver and more important point than this. What legal effect can the legislation of the Congress of the United States have upon this Constitution that we are in the act of forming? This painful question I am not anticipating, because upon its solution depends the one immediately raised by the resolution before us, as to the proper time for putting into operation the government we are creating. For my own part, however repugnant the doctrine may be to the opinions of some of the ablest and best men that the world has ever seen, I must frankly avow, that I hold the Congress of the United States possesses no legal authority over this country in its present condition. We are an unorganized community, not referred to in the Constitution of the United States, and entirely without its pale. But, to bring ourselves within its influence, which is the ardent desire of every true-hearted American, it is necessary that we should, by a political organization, become a State; and under the provision of the Constitution of the United States, be admitted as a "new State," into that glorious Confederacy that is the admiration of the world. I utterly deny and repudiate the fashionable doctrine of Territorial Governments, as abhorrent to free principles, and altogether without any authority to be derived from the Constitution of the United States. I am well aware, sir, that in this position I may be met by the authority of the Supreme Court; but it is this doctrine of the Supreme Court that I propose to investigate and controvert. Before I enter upon this subject, I would call your attention to the history and character of the bench that have promulgated this decision. This bench, it will be remembered, was composed of that batch of judges appointed by the elder Adams at the close of his administration, which has been dignified in history by the soubriquet of "midnight." When the Federal party had, by the sentence of the people, been expelled from the legislative and executive departments of the Government, Mr. Adams secured them in the stronghold of the judiciary, by the appointment of men to the bench of the Supreme Court, who, whatever their other qualifications may have been, possessed, for him, the essential one of open, avowed attachment to the doctrines and principles of the Federal party. That bench, as jurists, have never had their superiors in America; and he, their presiding officer, he who was so long their pride and their glory, for talents and legal abilities, will rank with the brighest ornaments of the English court, whilst in the virtues of the heart he had hardly a compeer in the four quarters of the globe. The mere *legal* opinions of John Marshall have been confirmed by the admiring assent of the legal world; but the *political* decisions of that court have long ago been reversed by that appellate tribunal, mightier than the mightiest, the voice of the people. This reversal is expressed too plainly to be mistaken, in the acknowledged discomfiture of the party who maintained the principles to which these decisions belong; and it will be no great while, I venture to predict, before this reversal will be more formally registered by the present bench, which more, truly represents the political opinions of the country than ever did its predecessors.

With this reference to the history, the character, the party prepossessions and prejudices of the late Supreme Court of the United States, I will proceed to examine the doctrine of Territorial Governments, as laid down by that body. Let us remember that one great distinction between the two parties that agitated the country was this. The Federal party, called Whigs at the present day, instinctively the advocates of governmental power, by a liberal, or, as I would say, strained construction of the Constitution, claimed for the Congress of the United States much more extensive powers than the straight-laced Republicans or Democrats of the present day, were willing to allow them. We shall see how this destructive feature worked in the present case. In the case of the American Ins. Co. *vs.* Canter, 1 Peters, before referred to, the Court lay down the broad ground that the control of Congress over the inhabitants of acquired territory is supreme, despotic, and unlimited; and this extraordinary, anti-republican, and unholy claim, is based upon a clause in the Constitution of the United States. It is a slander upon the liberty breathing spirit of that instrument to say so; it would subvert the very end and object of its creation, which was to uphold, not destroy, the liberties of mankind. Let an unsophisticated enquirer read that instrument through, and I apprehend he would be much at a loss to discover the clause from which the Supreme Court derived this power for the Congress of the United States. Would he not be surprised to hear that it was the one which simply declares that "the Congress shall have power to dispose of and make all needful rules and regulations respecting the territory and other property belonging to the United States?" After hunting, with argus eyes, through the whole instrument, for something to support this favorite theory of government prerogative, they candidly confess that this is all they can find. Remember that this is a great substantive power, opposed to the whole tenor and spirit of the Constitution, and one so despotic and so anti-republican in its character, that it can hardly expect any of the benefits of implication, at the hands of a freeman at least. The authority which contradicts the Declaration of Independence, and disfranchises a people, and reduces them to the condition of serfs and vassals, must be clearly, distinctly, and unequivocally granted. Let us see whether, under this rule, the clause in question supports the inference drawn from it. The word territory is *now* used in two senses; the first, material in its nature, to signify landed property; and the other, political, to denote the peculiar organization that has been instituted for the people inhabiting the territorial or landed property of the United States. The latter is metaphorical, and by a very common figure of speech, derived from the former. The first, or material sense, was certainly the only one known to the framers of the Constitution, because the second is a term applied to a creation subsequent to the adoption of the Constitution. At that time there was no such thing as a Territory, in the sense of a Territorial Government; the word had no such meaning, and therefore it never could have been used in that sense. The claimants of this power create a new thing—steal an old word to express it—and then claim all the perquisites of the old word for the new thing. The public lands are the *territory* of the United States, and this clause authorises the Congress to dispose of and make all needful rules and regulations respecting it, and the *other property* of the Union. It surely requires a Federal stretch of imagination to discover any other meaning it. But let us understand the word territory in the sense in which the Supreme Court supposes it to have been used—that is to say, the inhabitants of the territory instead of the territory itself. It would then read: the Congress shall have power to *dispose* of and make all needful rules and regulations for the government of the inhabitants of the territory of the United States. If under this clause Congress can govern the people of a territory, it may unquestionably "dispose" of them, as of "other property" of the United States. And, as there is no limit nor measure to this disposing power, they may constitutionally sell them like sheep in the shambles, at so much a head, whenever they can find a purchaser, and the wants of the Government may require it. All this they have a right to do with the *territory*, forts, arsenals, ships, horses, mules, and "other property" of the United States. If human beings are included in the clause at all, they are put upon the same footing as "other property," and are as much liable to be disposed of as they are to be regulated. The proposition, except for the source from whence it comes, is not worthy of a moment's notice. The Court itself seems rather to distrust the sufficiency of this argument, and seeks therefore to bolster it up by a claim from another source—they allude to the treaty-making power and the inherent rights of sovereignty. If there is one position of the Federal party more false and more dangerous than another, it is the extent to which they carry the treaty-making power of the United States. Treaties are binding only when they are made in pursuance, at least not in opposition, to the spirit and object of the Constitution. If they controvert the one or oppose the other, they are null and void; and it behooves all those upon whose action the execution of the treaty depends, to watch and carefully guard this sacred instrument from desecration by this insidious means. It is a monstrous doctrine, subversive of all the checks and balances established against the abuse of power, that to the Executive and Senate, Congress is bound to surrender its conscience and its judgment, and simply register the decrees of this bloated branch of the Government. A treaty that ties any portion of the human race hand and foot, and surrenders them to the despotic authority of a government in which they are not represented, is *malum in se*, and therefore void; is repugnant to the dictates of christianity and the established principles of freedom; is subversive of the chartered liberties of mankind, and is therefore to be spurned and contemned by every christian and every freeman. The doctrine of America is, that the liberties of the human race are not the subject of traffic or of *treaty;* the law of England denies that a man can barter away his own liberty, and we deny, *a fortiori*, that any government can sell or *cede* away the liberty of its subjects. Any treaty expressly providing for the effect implied by the Supreme Court, made in the present age, would tarnish the reputation of the most despotic monarch in civilized Europe. So much for the doctrine of cession. That of conquest rests exactly upon the same basis. Is it possible that the supreme judicial tribunal of that republican government, which has been a pillar of light to the groping children of freedom in the Eastern hemisphere, has sanctioned the doctrine that the liberties of a people may be subverted by force of arms; and that a nation may be lawfully reduced to bondage by the right of conquest? Why, sir, to conquer and reduce to slavery the negro of Africa, has been declared by the enlightened nations of the earth to be a crime equal to that of piracy itself; is the enslaving a white man less criminal than that of a negro? Remember, sir, the dismemberment of the Republic of Cracow; remember the curses, loud and deep, that were heaped upon the doers of that foul deed, and do not forget that under the doctrine of the Supreme Court, this was all legal, right, and proper, because this little republic was overthrown, dismembered, and parcelled out by *conquest* and by *treaty*—the only *legitimate* means of reducing mankind to slavery. The opinion of the Supreme Court intends that, or it means nothing.

The inherent right of sovereignty is the antiquated, obsolete, *Dei gratia* doctrine of the European monarchies, applied, not the people themselves, but to their special and limited agents. I leave it to its fate.

It is upon these grounds, sir, that I hold, and have ever held, that the Congress of the United States had no warrant or authority for the passage of the bill to collect revenue in California—that in doing so, they transcended the powers with which they are invested, and violated every principle of republican freedom. Much has been said here about the political aspirations of the honorable members of this House; but, for my own part, I have no higher ambition than one day to stand before the Supreme Court of the United States, as it is at present constituted, to argue the unconstitutionality of that infamous bill. Why, sir, it was an act infinitely less unjust than this, that, in olden time, stirred men's blood, and lighted a flame in the rebellious Colonies, that nothing but freedom and independence ever extinguished. This right of absolute government claimed for the Congress of the United States, and supported by the decision of the Supreme Court, involves exactly the question between Great Britain and the Colonies. To proves this, needs no more than a few quotations from Story's commentaries on the Constitution. Vol. 1, p. 181, we find the following:

"The principal grounds on which Parliament asserted the right to make laws to bind the colonies in all cases whatsoever, were, amongst others, that the Territories were dependencies of the realm, and that the legislative power over the colonies is supreme and sovereign."

Mr. Tory, Justice Blackstone, v. 1, 107, foreshadowing the doctrine of the Supreme Court, insists that the American Colonies are principally to be deemed conquered or ceded countries, and therefore he asserts, "the common law of England which secures the liberty of the subject, has no force there; they being no part of the mother country, but distinct, though dependent dominions." "This doctrine of Mr. Justice Blackstone," says Judge Story, book 1, p. 139, "may will admit of serious doubt upon general principles." And yet the same Judge Story declares, that the same doctrine, even carried to a greater extent by the Supreme Court, when applied to the limited government of the United States, is unquestionably correct. Hear what the Congress of the nine colonies assembled at New York in October, 1765, had to say upon this subject of taxation without representation. They say, "it is inseparably essential to the freedom of a people, that no taxes be imposed on them but with their own consent, given personally or by their representatives." Judge Story tells us that, in the early stages of the discontent, the general powers of Parliament over the Colonies was not denied; but that subsequent events drove them to a more close and narrow survey of the foundation of parliamentary supramacy; doubts were soon infused into their minds; and from doubts they passed by an easy transition to a denial, first of the power of taxation, and next of all, authority whatever to bind them by its laws. And exactly the same fate, I venture to predict, awaits a more close and narrow survey of the doctrine that the Congress of the United States can bind by its law, the unrepresented people of a Territory. The doctrine and the argument in both cases are precisely the same; they have been settled, at least for us, by that Revolution of which we love to boast; and I will not trouble you further with a discussion of them.

I commenced, sir, with the doctrine of the Secretary of War; I will conclude with that of the Secretary of the Navy, as I find it reported in the newspapers of the day. I knew William Ballard Preston well—he is my foster brother—twenty years ago we drew milk together from the breast of the same *alma mater;* and my heart leaped with pleasure when I found these sentiments of political freedom flowing from his lips, as clear and pure as the waters of one of the gushing rills of his native mountains. Upon the discussion of the Territorial Bill, Mr. Preston is made to say—

"A people kept in territorial bonds, are under oppression. Our fathers intended to bring every American into the Union. It was a broad, wide platform,; popular sovereignty resides with the people. The principle is that the trust with us must be surrendered at the first moment of time. Before this bill could go into operation, there will be a population there of two hundred thousand souls, twice or thrice as large as any State ever was when she came into the Union. Who is there who can stand back, and refuse to surrender the trust on any grounds—personal, political, or partisan? None can, and none ought. The bill but holds that truth, which is seen and felt all over the earth—the great truth, that popular constitutional government is the great sustaining machine of the age, possessing within it all the virtue, all the strength, and wisdom necessary for its creation, its solidity, and its permanence. He submitted to no master to direct its force, no king or ruler to control its action, but left it to the people—the source of legitimate power. Let the people themselves determine the character of their local institutions.

"There was never a field so wide and long for a patriot to die on as the present one. Let them forget party and sectional differences. At the North and at the South there are extremes, but there is a middle ground, a great republican party. He did not mean of whigs and democrats. Their principles are embodied in this bill. There is a republican highway, in which we all may walk in peace. If this proposition be carried, that the people of these territories are entitled to govern for themselves, will gentlemen of the North attach the Wilmot proviso? The clause of the Constitution which guarantees to every State a republican form of government does not authorize Congress to interfere with the formation of a State government. To say that Congress has the power to prescribe, is to declare that the people shall not enact for themselves. The very proposition which they would prescribe, subverts the free principles of the Constitution. The idea that there is a right to control the creation of a State at all, is a power which assumes to alter, amend, or change. But this idea that this guarantee subjects the constitution of a State to the action of Congress, is in precise opposition to the principles on which the Constitution was formed. That was a guarantee to each State against all interference. It was a guarantee that each State that had a republican form of government should not be subject to the control of the other States."

For the reasons I have given, I conclude then, sir, that there is no existing government in California; that the right to institute one is inherent in the people; that, by the exercise of this right, they can alone prepare themselves for admission into the Confederacy of the United States; that until they become a member of the Union, Congress have no authority whatever to legislate for the people of California, and that, from the moment of its ratification, this Constitution becomes the supreme law of the land, and the government it creates the only one that ought to be recognized in California. I shall therefore vote for the resolution

Mr. HALLECK. I have no disposition to prolong this discussion, or reply in any way to the remarks of the gentleman from Monterey. I think we have enough else to do, without attempting to reconcile conflicting decisions of the Supreme Court, or to reconcile any conflicts of opinion between the present and the past Cabinets. If the instructions from the Secretary of State, Mr. Buchanan, conflict with the instruction of the Secretary of War, Mr. Marcy, let them reconcile the matter themselves; if there was a division of opinion in that Cabinet on this subject, let them settle it. If the instructions from Mr. Clayton and Mr. Crawford, officers of the present Cabinet, conflict with the opinions of Mr. Preston, as known in Congress, and there be a division in the present Cabinet, let them settle it. If General Riley, in his course here, has acted contrary to his instructions, let the powers that sent him here, and the powers that instructed him, hold him responsible for it. I have no desire at all to go into any discussion on that subject. If we attempt to discuss the question as to the correctness of the decisions of the Supreme Court, I think it will take us a long time to get at the bottom of it. In my mind, the question before the House narrows itself down to this point, and it is the point presented in the resolution of the Committee. Is it politic for us to set the wheels of the new Government in motion as speedily as possible after the ratification of the Constitution by the people, or is it politic for us to wait until it is ratified by Congress? I, for one, shall vote to put the new Government in operation as soon as may be convenient—the question of convenience to be decided hereafter. I am very certain (I give it only as my opinion) that no opposition will be made, either from Washington, or any party here, to that course.

Mr. JONES had certain doubts in his mind as to the unqualified right of any territory belonging to the government of the United States to establish a State Government and put it in operation without the sanction of the General Government. With regard to the municipal laws of the State, he thought that right could not be disputed, but he was not prepared to assert the absolute sovereignty, independent of any control or action on the part of the General Government, of a State claiming admission into the Union. This was a very important question, and one which he had not studied with that care which its importance demanded. He would like to bring out the views entertained on the subject by gentlemen better acquainted with it than himself, and for that purpose would propose a series of questions.

Mr. MCCARVER quoted Mr. Calhoun's opinion, as follows:

Resolved, That it is a fundamental principle in our political creed, that a people, in forming a Constitution, have the unconditional right to form and adopt the Government which they may think best calculated to secure their liberty, prosperity, and happiness; and in conformity thereto no other condition is imposed by the Federal Constitution on a State, in order to be admitted into this Union, except that its Constitution shall be 'republican,' and that the imposition of any other by Congress would not only be in violation of the Constitution, but in direct conflict with the principle on which our political sostem rests."

Mr. SNYDER. I will not say a great deal on this subject. I am no lawyer; neither have I ever studied such questions. But there is one thing that I want to impress upon the minds of this Convention. What right had our forefathers to say that they were free and independent? What right had they to establish a republican government? If they, as a body of people, declared that they had certain rights and privileges, and founded a government upon those principles, have not the people of California the same right to make a State as a body of free people, and to enact such laws as they think will benefit them? You have been all talking here for a long time, and what does it amount to? You have not arrived at the point yet; nor will you arrive at it while you do nothing but talk from day to day, at the public expense. It would be much better for you to come to some conclusion in regard to this matter. In regard to State rights and the rights of the people, I would refer you to what our forefathers did. The question is, whether we have a right to go immediately into operation as a State government or not; and the conclusion I have come to is this: that if our forefathers had a right to declare themselves independent and establish thirteen States, I think we have a right to establish one.

Mr. LIPPITT. I believe in what my friend from Sacramento (Mr. Snyder) has said. But this very principle has been denied by our most eminent jurists for thirty or forty years. It has been denied in a decision, which has been quoted to us, by the Supreme Court of the United States. They have undertaken to say, that American citizens, when they leave the confines of their own State lose all the rights of American citizens; that they lose not only those rights, but the rights of freemen, because it is the right of freemen to make their own government, and they no longer possess that right. For the very reason that this principle has been denied, I call upon gentlemen not to come to a hasty decision upon this subject. Time should be left for reflection, and we should if possible come to the right conclusion; for our action upon this subject will go forth to the people and to the Congress of the United States. I would also observe that the mover of the resolution is not in his seat; I believe he wishes to make some remarks upon it. I desire to make a few as to the legal question myself. Therefore, I move to lay it on the table for the present.

Mr. JONES. I think my friend from Sacramento (Mr. Snyder) entirely mistakes the object and intention of this resolution.

Mr. SNYDER. If I misunderstand the object and intention, I do not misunderstand the language of the resolution.

Mr. JONES submitted a series of written questions on the subject, and said: The object of these questions is to draw forth debate. I believe myself that the people of the territory have an undoubted right to exercise certain acts of authority in relation to their municipal Government; that in the absence of any action on the part of the General Government, they have a right to establish a municipal Government, and pass such laws for their own protection as the Congress of the United States have neglected to pass. But as to the entire right of sovereignty, the absolute independence of the State, I consider that a very doubtful question. I do not wish to go at present into any discussion of abstract principles, but this may become a very important question. If Congress should refuse to give us the protection of government, I would be perhaps as willing as any man to establish a municipal Government here; but to declare ourselves independent of the Government of the United States—I would not go to such a length. I do not believe we have the right to declare ourselves wholly and totally independent of the Government of the United States. So far as regards our municipal laws, I think we have a right to decide for ourselves. This is the right which I wish to investigate. I am not prepared to discuss the question myself. These are nice and delicate questions, which demand the attention which the gentleman from Monterey (Mr.

Botts) has devoted to them. They are questions which do not perhaps necessarily demand our action, but which may become of immense importance hereafter. Above all things I must beg not to be understood as denying the right of the people of this territory to establish a State Government properly. I do not deny it; but I consider their entire and absolute independence at least questionable.

Mr. Lippitt. I move to lay the resolution on the table.

Mr. Hastings. I hope this resolution will not be laid on the table. If the object is to obtain further discussion on this subject, I do not see the necessity of that course. I think the minds of members are fully made up. I do not believe there are three members in this House who are opposed to the adoption of the resolution. Why not take the question now? Is it supposed that Congress will deny our right to establish a State Government here, if we make no unreasonable demands? We have made none as yet. Let us vote down the motion to lay on the table, and adopt the resolution at once.

Mr. Lippitt. I do not wish to lose time, and therefore I propose to take up something else for the present.

Mr. McCarver. I am in favor of disposing of this resolution now. That we can do it I have no doubt. My own mind is satisfied on the subject, and I believe there will be no opposition to the resolution. The arguments have been very good, as to our right to establish a State Government. I believe there is not a member here who is not willing to settle this question at once, and decide that the government shall go into immediate effect upon the ratification of this Constitution by the people. I believe we are all sent here to form a government, not to be indefinitely postponed, but to go into immediate effect.

Mr. Lippitt. I do not see what we can gain by refusing to lay it on the table. It can be taken up at any time. I only ask an hour or two for consideration. It may become a matter of vital importance, that not only this resolution should appear on the records of the Convention, but that the reasons for it should also appear; that it may be known upon what grounds we, the representatives of the people, decided this question. The chairman of the Committee gives as a reason for desiring this action on the part of the House, that the Committee are at a loss to decide without advice; that there is a division of opinion among them as to whether this Constitution should go into effect when the people choose, or whether they should wait until Congress chooses. The question of the sovereignty of the people is raised by this report of the Committee. It is precisely on that point that the Committee come into the House and ask for instructions. I say now, sir, that it is not only absolutely essential that we should give them these instructions, but that we should put it in the proper ground, and let the Government of the United States and General Riley, or any other general or military commandant, or corporal, know that the representatives of the people in this Convention have solemnly declared not only that this Constitution shall go into effect immediately on its adoption, but that they consider they have the right to say so; to fix themselves the time when this Constitution shall become the law of the land, in virtue of the sovereignty that resides in them. That, Mr. President, is the reason why I consider that it is extremely desirable that this motion to lay on the table should prevail. Who can say what course General Riley is instructed to take? Who can say what course his successor in office may take? Suppose, at the time fixed by us for the going into operation of this Constitution, that there should be an opinion prevailing here that the people of California have not the right, and, suppose the officer in authority should take the ground taken by the Supreme Court and by the proclamation of General Riley himself; (and certainly the supposition is not unreasonable;) I say we are bound to suppose the military government here will take the view already given to the world in that proclamation, and given by the Supreme Court of the United States, and laid down by our eminent jurists. Suppose, then, when the question comes up, it is thought inexpedient, or for some reason or other, they do not wish to have this Constitution go into effect, and they deny the power of this Convention to pass such a resolution, what will they do? They may tell you, gentlemen excuse us; we are the Government of California until Congress, according to the decisions of the Supreme Court and according to the decisions of the most eminent jurists, admits you as a State into the Union. We cannot allow you, under these decisions, to govern yourselves without the sanction of Congress; you cannot put your Constitution into effect. But, sir, unless this Convention sends to the people of California and of the world, not only the resolution and decision that her Constitution shall go into effect at such a time, but also gives the reasons for it, all of which will be published, I doubt very much whether any American military commandant, be he general or corporal, will dare to take the responsibility, without throwing himself upon the Government at Washington. It will be entirely another matter if we, the representatives of the people, solemnly take it upon ourselves, as freemen, to decide this question for ourselves, in spite of the decisions of the Supreme Court, in spite of the proclamation of General Riley and of the President of the United States and the opinions of certain jurists. It is an extremely delicate question, and requires the greatest caution. I therefore hope the motion to lay it on the table will prevail. In the meantime the House may take up something else.

Mr. HILL. I hope if any gentleman desires to speak, that this question will not be forced.

Mr. JONES. I would like to make one remark as a suggestion before the question is taken. This I think is more a question of expediency with us than of abstract right. We all know the opinions of members of Congress on this subject; and we all know that, while sectional questions dividing the North and the South were discussed, and while the power of Congress over the territories was imputed by the one to the Constitution, and by the other to the treaty-making power, that there was scarcely a single member upon the floor of Congress who did not absolutely assert that Congress had the right of sovereignty over the territories to some extent. It was a matter upon which there was no doubt. Now, I say, that while we have carefully avoided in this Constitution the introduction of a single article which would give Congress a pretext for delaying its sanction to the Constitution, we should not now, by the broad assertion of some right of independence and of sovereignty, which will not be admitted on the floor of Congress, delay the admission of our State for years to come. I am most anxious to see our government go into operation immediately. But can we not, by some more cautious wording of this resolution, avoid the assertion of independent sovereignty? It is not probable that Congress will acknowledge this right to that extent. This is a great question of expediency. I did not come here to argue abstract principles of right; but having so far most carefully avoided any course which would give a pretext to Congress to delay our admission, I think we should not now jeopard our own interests by the assertion of an important principle, which is at least a matter of doubt. I am sorry to see the extent to which sectional feeling has been carried in Congress on the subject of slavery; but that will be the great source of all difficulty. A government will have to be established in New Mexico. One of the two great parties on this question will take advantage of this fact to delay our admission, in case of any pretext given in this Constitution, until that territorial government is established. It is therefore expedient that we look at this question in every point of view before we come to a decision.

Mr. MCCARVER. If I understand this question, we go with a Constitution that does not claim this absolute and independent sovereignty. We only ask to exercise the functions of a State. If the Government refuse to admit us into the Union as one of the Confederacy, we may then exercise the sovereignty of an independent State. We do not now claim the right to collect the revenue of the Union, nor to regulate post-offices, nor to exercise any of the functions which have been ceded by the thirteen States to the General Government; we only claim to exercise the rights and powers of a State.

Mr. LIPPITT. I do not rise to discuss this question. I wish merely to call for the yeas and nays, and to state the reasons why I rise for that purpose. I have already said that I only ask that the resolution be laid on the table, in order to express more fully the views of the representatives of the people of California; to have these principles more fully illustrated; that the reasons why we adopted the resolution should be more clearly laid down. If the Convention refuse to lay on the table, the effect I conceive will be, that it will naturally be presumed by the people that we wish to shirk this question which has been decided against us.

Mr. McDOUGAL. I would simply make one remark; that in voting to lay this matter on the table, I do not wish to shirk any responsibility which the gentleman from San Francisco (Mr. Lippitt) has charged upon those who think proper to oppose his motion.

Mr. LIPPITT. The gentleman misunderstands my meaning. I meant to say that if we refused to give this subject a full and deliberate consideration, it would seem to the people as if the Convention had endeavored to shirk the question. I do not charge such a motive upon any gentleman here.

Mr. McDOUGAL. I understand, then, that an inference would be drawn; that it would seem to the people as if we desired to shirk the responsibility. This is a question which I have not taken into consideration, and I do not intend to speak upon it; but I desire to state, that so far as I am concerned, I am ready, in recording my vote, to stand any responsibility which it may bring upon me.

Mr. HALLECK. We are all perfectly willing to vote without any further speeches.

The question was then taken on Mr. Lippitt's motion to lay the resolution on the table, and decided in the negative, by ayes 18, noes 20.

Mr. LIPPITT then moved a recess until three o'clock, which was agreed to.

AFTERNOON SESSION, 3 O'CLOCK, P. M.

Mr. SHERWOOD asked if the resolution which was last up, was now the order of proceeding.

The CHAIR stated that it was.

Mr. SHERWOOD was informed by several gentlemen who intended addressing the House on this subject, that they were willing to reserve their arguments until the subject came up in the schedule.

Mr. LIPPITT gave notice that if the question was taken now without debate, he would offer a resolution on the subject when it should come up again for consideration.

The question was then taken, and the resolution was adopted unanimously.

Mr. WOZENCRAFT, from the Committee on Printing, asked for instructions in regard to printing the Constitution.

Mr. GWIN moved that the Committee be instructed to make the necessary arrangements to have the Constitution and accompanying documents printed, so as to have them laid before the people.

Mr. SHERWOOD suggested that the bidders should specify the time when the printed copies would be ready.

Mr. GILBERT moved that the Committee be instructed to report on Monday morning; which motion was agreed to.

On motion of Mr. HALLECK, the Bill of Rights, as reported by the Committee of the Whole, was then taken up for consideration.

The first section, as reported, was adopted.

The question being on concurring with the Committee in striking out the second section—

Mr. LIPPITT asked why that section was stricken out?

Mr. NORTON said it was stricken out because it was considered unnecessary. The Committee adopted the first two sections, and this section was not then considered necessary. He voted in favor of keeping it in, and he still believed that it ought to be in the Bill of Rights.

Mr. SHANNON thought he had opposed the striking out of the section in Committee of the Whole, and he could not now see any reason why its introduction would not be perfectly proper. There was certainly nothing contained in it that was in any manner opposed to the principles contained in either of the sections. He thought there was considerable confusion in the Convention when it was stricken out, and that it was not fully understood.

Mr. BOTTS said he voted in favor of striking out that section when it was before the Committee of the Whole. He would now vote for retaining it as a provision of the Constitution. He did not know then that it would be proposed to deprive any man of his franchise; but having since seen, that by the duelling clause, a man is to be deprived of his franchise, he thought the two ought to go together.

Mr. GWIN said that the question was fully discussed in Committee of the Whole, and he was opposed to having it now introduced. There could be no reason for the adoption of this section which was not presented in Committee.

Mr. PRICE hoped the House would adhere to the report of the Committee of the Whole, in striking out this section. He could see no necessity for it. The principles contained in it were fully embraced in the two preceding sections.

The question being on concurring with the report of the Committee of the Whole, it was decided in the affirmative, by ayes 23, noes 17.

The House then took a recess till 7 o'clock.

NIGHT SESSION, 7 O'CLOCK, P. M.

Mr. CROSBY, from the Committee on Finance, made a report, fixing the pay of the members of the Convention at $16 per diem, and $16 for every twenty miles travel; and that of the President at $25 per diem.

Mr. BOTTS offered the following substitute:

Resolved, That the Legislature of the State of California shall be authorized to provide by law for the payment of the members of this Convention.

Mr. SHERWOOD was not quite sure that there would be a Legislature at all.

Mr. HALLECK moved to lay the whole subject on the table, for this reason: that it would be necessary to determine in the schedule what would be the pay of the members of the Legislature; and it would be improper to fix the pay of members of this House first, and then determine the pay of members of the Legislature at a different rate.

Mr. PRICE thought the two questions had no necessary connection. They were distinct and independent.

The question was then taken on Mr. Bott's resolution, and the yeas and nays having been called and ordered, the result was as follows:

Yeas.—Messrs. Botts, Gilbert, Gwin, Hill, McDougal, Vallejo, Wozencraft.—7.

Nays.—Messrs. Aram, Brown, Carillo, Covarrubias, Crosby, Dent, Dominguez, Foster, Hanks, Hoppe, Hobson, Halleck, Hastings, Hollingsworth, Jones, Larkin, Lippitt, Lippincott, Moore, McCarver, Norton, Price, Pico, Snyder, Sherwood, Stearns, Steuart, Tefft, Vermeule, Walker, President.—31.

So the resolution was rejected.

Mr. JONES then offered the following amendment:

Resolved, That the pay of the members of this Convention shall be eight dollars per day, and eight dollars for every twenty miles travel, going and returning.

Mr. McDOUGAL asked if an amendment to the amendment would be in order.

The CHAIR replied that it would.

Mr. McDOUGAL then moved to insert the word "Buncombe" in the resolution.

Mr. JONES called the gentleman to order.

19

Mr. Wozencraft hoped his colleague would withdraw the motion.

Mr. McDougal could not consent to withdraw his motion.

Mr. Jones entered into a calculation to show that the expenses of this Convention, for the members alone, according to the report of the Committee, would be $1,625 a day.

Mr. Sherwood thought the House understood arithmetic as well as the gentleman from San Joaquin.

Mr. Lippitt felt it his duty to state the reason why he should vote for the amendment of the gentleman from San Joaquin. He thought the question in regard to the per diem allowance of members was, whether they should vote themselves merely a nominal allowance, or one that would indemnify them for loss of time and sacrifices made in business; and he was opposed to voting a sum which was neither one nor the other. He thought it would be more delicate and consistent with the dignity of the Convention to vote a mere nominal allowance—the pay of members of Congress. If the other principle was to be adopted, $16 a day, or twice $16, would not be sufficient to indemnify the members.

Mr. Shannon would not only second the amendment of his friend (Mr. McDougal) but sustain it. He thought the proposition of the gentleman (Mr. Jones) ought to go before the people of San Joaquin with that amendment attached to it.

Mr. Gwin asked if he understood the President as entertaining that amendment? It was totally irrelevant, and, according to his knowledge of the rules, could not be entertained,

Mr. McDougal said if the gentleman could not see the relevancy of the amendment he must be a very dull man. It was as plain as any proposition possibly could be: to insert the word "Buncombe" after the word "that," so as to read, "That for Buncombe, the pay of the members of this Convention shall be eight dollars per day, and eight dollars for every twenty miles of travel." Nothing could be plainer than that. He had hoped that the question would be taken silently on the report of the Committee, but as such did not seem to be the disposition of the House he deemed it appropriate to offer the amendment.

Mr. Gwin asked if the Chair decided that it was in order to offer that amendment?

The Chair did not feel at liberty to reject any proposition made in good faith, and decided that this amendment was in order.

Mr. Gwin appealed from the decision of the Chair.

The question being on the appeal,

Mr. McDougal said he could see very plainly that the gentleman from San Joaquin wished to withdraw his proposition. He would therefore withdraw his amendment.

Mr. Jones objected to the withdrawal.

The question was then taken on permitting Mr. McDougal to withdraw his amendment, and it was decided in the affirmative.

The question recurring on Mr. Jones' resolution,

Mr. Covarrubias moved the following amendment:

Resolved, That it being the duty of every citizen to serve his country gratuitously when the circumstances require it, the delegates of this Convention shall receive no compensation whatever for their services.

Mr. Norton could not see the necessity of such a resolution. Any of the members who felt any compunctions of conscience in receiving money for their services could very easily refuse it.

Mr. Vermeule thought the mover of the resolution was right in his views, provided existing circumstances required such a course; but as there did not appear to be any necessity of the kind at present, he was disposed to sustain the report of the Committee. The amount per diem was about the wages of a mechanic; the proposition of his friend from San Joaquin (Mr. Jones) was a great deal less. He did not think that the people would think any thing more of the delegates of this Convention if they accepted less pay than common laborers receive; nor did he think that existing circumstances required the course indicated by the mover of the last amendment.

On this amendment of Mr. Covarrubias, the yeas and nays were called for by Mr. Jones, and being taken, resulted as follows:

YEAS.—Messrs. Covarrubias, De La Guerra, Dimmick, Gilbert, Lippincott, McDougal, Pedrorena, Price, Sutter, Sansevaine—10.

NAYS.—Messrs. Aram, Botts, Brown, Carrillo, Crosby, Dent, Dominguez, Gwin, Hanks, Hill, Hoppe, Hobson, Hastings, Hollingsworth, Jones, Larkin, Lippitt, McCarver, Norton, Pico, Rodriguez, Snyder, Sherwood, Shannon, Stearns, Steuart, Tefft, Vallejo, Vermeule, Walker, Wozencraft, President—32.

Mr. WOZENCRAFT suggested the following amendment: That all members who wished a lower sum than that reported by the Committee, should be authorized to receive it.

Mr. SHERWOOD moved the previous question.

Mr. GWIN inquired of the chairman of the Committee if the gentleman who represented Los Angelos, and who resided in Monterey, were to receive mileage.

Mr. CROSBY stated that the Committee was not instructed to make any distinction.

Mr. McDOUGAL remarked that the previous question had been called and seconded by two members.

Mr. GWIN asked the vote of the House on this amendment: That the payment of constructive mileage should be prohibited.

Mr. LIPPITT thought that the Convention could never get through, if that subject was to be taken up and discussed. It would consume an immense amount of time to undertake to lay down rules for the guidance of the presiding officer on this question.

The CHAIR was of opinion that there was no guide in relation to constructive mileage, except the act of Congress.

The question then recurring on the adoption of the report—

Mr. BOTTS asked a division of the question, so that the vote should first be taken first on the pay and mileage of the members, and then on the per diem of the President, and it was so ordered.

The yeas and nays were ordered on the first clause of the paragraph as divided, and it was adopted by yeas 32, nays 13, as follows:

YEAS.—Messrs. Aram, Brown, Carrillo, Crosby, Dominguez, Foster, Hanks, Hill, Hoppe, Hobson, Hastings, Hollingsworth, Larkin, Lippitt, Moore, McCarver, Norton, Pedrorena, Price, Pico, Rodriguez, Snyder, Sherwood, Shannon, Stearns, Sansevaine, Steuart, Tefft, Vermeule, Walker, Wozencraft, President—32.

NAYS.—Messrs. Botts, Covarrubias, Dent, De Da Guerra, Dimmick, Gilbert, Gwin, Halleck, Jones, Lippincott, McDougal, Sutter, Vallejo—13.

The question being on the other branch of the report—

Mr. GWIN said that it having been usual in all deliberative bodies to pay the President double what the members receive, in consequence of the additional expenses to which he is subject, and the first portion of the report having fixed the salary of the members at $16, he would vote for that portion which fixed the salary of the President at $25.

The PRESIDENT said he wished his name to appear in the affirmative on that question. He was not willing that the members of this body should vote for their pay, and he himself not share the responsibility.

The question then being on the clause fixing the President's per diem, it was amended on motion of Mr. VERMEULE, by adding thereto the words "and mileage as above."

The yeas and nays being then taken on this clause, as amended, the result was follows:

YEAS.—Messrs. Aram, Botts, Brown, Carrillo, Crosby, Dent, De La Guerra, Dominguez, Foster, Gwin, Hanks, Hill, Hoppe, Hobson, Hastings, Hollingsworth, Jones, Larkin, Lippitt,

Norton, Pedrorena, Price, Pico, Rodriguez, Sherwood, Stearns, Sansevaine, Steuart, Tefft, Vallejo, Vermeule, Walker, President—33.

NAYS —Messrs. Covarrubias, Dimmick, Gilbert, Halleck, Lippincott, McCarver, McDougal, Sutter, Snyder, Shannon—10.

The question then recurring on the report, as amended, it was adopted.

On motion of Mr. HALLECK, the Bill of Rights was then taken up.

The third section, as reported, was adopted.

The question being on the fourth section—

Mr. BOTTS said: If it will not create too great an excitement among that portion of the members who seem to think it little short of treason to reverse any thing done in Committee of the Whole, I would move to amend this section by striking out all after the word "belief." The section, as reported, is in the following words:

4. The free exercise and enjoyment of religious profession and worship, without discrimination or preference, shall be allowed in this State, to all mankind; and no person shall be rendered incompetent to bear witness on account of his opinions on matters of religious belief; but the liberty of conscience hereby secured, shall not be so construed as to excuse acts of licentiousness, or justify practices inconsistent with the peace or safety of this State.

I move to insert the clause from the Bill of Rights of Virginia, which I once had the honor of proposing in lieu of this very clause. I remember the effect produced upon this House by the reading of that eloquent and beautiful clause; and I remember that the House seemed inclined to adopt it; but the great chairman of the great Committee seemed struck aback with it. The latter clause of the section, as reported, I propose to strike out, because it is contradictory. You have no guaranty in your Bill of Rights for religious liberty. It is left wholly to the Legislature. The gentleman from Sacramento (Mr. Sherwood) objected to striking it out, because it was thought necessary in the Constitution of New York. He spoke of certain sects there, (the Mormons, I believe,) in a very harsh manner, and said it was introduced to prevent licentious practices. I entertain very different opinions of the Mormons. I believe we have no right to prescribe the forms of worship of any religious sect; they are all amenable to the laws of the land, and it is not our province to exclude any class from worshiping God as their conscience may dictate.

Mr. NORTON. I do not desire to enter into a very lengthy discussion on this subject. I had hoped that my friend from Monterey would not urge this question. I had at one time supposed that I had made him a convert to the New York faith, but he has retrograded and gone back upon his old fighting ground, with the intention of opposing everthing coming from the State of New York. I deem this provision a very important protection to the community; and if gentlemen here remember the remarks made by the gentleman from Sacramento, (Mr. Sherwood,) they will see the necessity of retaining it.

Mr. SHANNON. I will correct the gentleman from Monterey as to one portion of his remarks. In referring to certain sects in New York, my colleague from Sacramento (Mr. Sherwood) did not intend his remarks for the Mormons. I am in favor of introducing the section from the Constitution of Virginia—not entirely in place of the orignal section, as reported, but we can make an excellent and beautiful section by combining the two, so that a portion of the first shall contain the principles and rights, and a portion of the last the reasons for asserting those principles and rights.

Mr. HASTINGS. I think the latter clause of the section, as reported, should be stricken out. The whole object is effected by the first clause. Religious liberty is secured. Beyond that you contradict what you have said above, and you put it in the power of your courts to decide whether the exercise of any peculiar religious belief is compatible with the public safety and morality or not. Now any religious sect may become a little excited; they may be somewhat noisy and zealous in their mode of worship; it is competent for the court to decide that they must worship in a different manner. First we secure religious liberty to the full extent; next we deny religious liberty beyond a certain extent. This is inconsistent with the principles which we have avowed. I trust either the whole section or the latter clause will be stricken out.

Mr. TEFFT. I do not wish to see this section stricken out. We secure religious liberty so far as is consistent with decency and public order. No man ought to desire more.

Mr. WOZENCRAFT. I do not remember how I voted in Committee of the Whole; but I think the language of the section from the Constitution of Virginia is very beautiful and appropriate.

Mr. VERMEULE. I am in favor of retaining the latter part of the clause in the original section. I cannot see the incongruity of the two, which has appeared to the gentleman from Monterey. The sense of the section is this: that it guaranties the free exercise and enjoyment of religious worship, provided it does not amount to licentiousness, or a breach of the peace. You give the free right of speech to all classes, and yet you say it must not be indulged in to the extent of libel. The two cases stand upon the same footing. I hope the entire section will be retained.

Mr. BOTTS. What I wish to impress upon gentlemen is, that crime is not religion, and that there are laws for the punishment of crime. Those laws are sufficient in themselves to protect the community from licentious practices or breaches of public order.

The question was then taken on the motion to strike out, and it was decided in the negative.

The fourth section, as reported, was then adopted.

The fifth and sixth sections, as reported, were then adopted.

Mr. NORTON. I have a section which I wish to introduce here, somewhat in connection with the section just passed:

SEC. 7. All persons shall be bailable by sufficient sureties, unless for capital offences, when the proof is evident or the presumption great.

It has been thought by some that the section which we have just adopted covers this entire ground; but in my opinion it does not. This section is a part of the common law, and as we have not adopted the common law, and perhaps may not, I think it very necessary that such a section should be introduced, so that in all cases, except capital offences, where the proof is evident or the presumption great, the party accused shall be entitled to bail. An innocent man may be kept in prison and refused bail, without such a provision as this.

Mr. HASTINGS. I shall be opposed to this section unless the latter clause be stricken out. It is very indefinite, and may lead to acts of injustice and partiality. "Where the proof is evident or the presumption great." This is left to the courts to decide. Both great and small courts are to determine this matter. They may decide it in their own way. Some would pronounce the presumption great; others would pronounce it small. It seems to me that the clause had better be stricken out.

Mr. LIPPITT. I cannot agree with my friend from Sacramento, (Mr. Hastings.) It is impossible to leave it to any other than the court itself, by whose order the arrest is made. It must be left to the discretion of that court. We cannot lay down here a general rule to provide for every possible variety of circumstances.

The question was then taken on striking out the latter clause of the section, and it was decided in the negative.

The question recurring on the proposed section, it was adopted.

The next question being on the seventh section, as reported, it was adopted.

Mr. NORTON. I have another section which I desire to propose in connection with the section just adopted. That section is from the Constitution of the United States. The section which I propose is also from the Constitution of the United States, next to it. The first says:

"No person shall be held to answer for a capital, or other infamous crime, (except in cases of impeachment, and in cases of militia, when in actual service; and the land and naval forces in time of war, or which this State may keep, with the consent of Congress, in time of peace; and in cases of petit larceny, under the regulation of the Legislature,) unless on presentment or indictment of a grand jury; and in any trial, in any court whatever, the party accused shall be allowed to appear and defend in person, and with counsel, as in civil actions. No person shall be subject to be twice put in jeopardy for the same offence, nor shall he be compelled, in any criminal case, to be a witness against himself; nor be deprived of life, liberty, or property, without due process of law; nor shall private property be taken for public use without just compensation."

This does not cover the whole ground; it does not say that he shall have counsel, or that he shall be confronted by two witnesses on compulsory process. It is very necessary in criminal prosecutions, where the prisoner is poor, and has not the means of obtaining counsel and witnesses, that all these facilities should be given by the court, so that the poor man shall not be tried without every advantage that the rich man enjoys. The additional section which I propose is as follows:

"In all criminal prosecutions the accused shall enjoy the right to a speedy and public trial, by an impartial jury of the district or county wherein the crime shall have been committed; and to be informed of the nature and cause of the accusation; to be confronted with the witnesses against him; to have compulsory process for obtaining witnesses in his favor, and to have the assistance of counsel in his defence."

Mr. Sherwood. I think the Legislature would adopt this without any constitutional provision. We are descending too much into detail.

Mr. Price. It seems to me that we now have more sections in the Bill of Rights than any other State in the Union; and, without giving proper time for reflection, I think it would be inexpedient to introduce this new section in this hurried way. I hope no more new sections will be added. I would greatly prefer striking out some that are already in the Bill of Rights; for instance, all that are literally from the Constitution from the United States. The people know where to find them if they desire to refer to them. There is no occasion to have them in the Constitution of California.

Mr. Norton. The fact that this is in the Constitution of the United States does us no good here; for it has been decided by the Supreme Court of the United States that these provisions only apply in the United States Courts. It is necessary that we should adopt it here if we desire it to apply in our State courts. If we have adopted a number of sections that might as well have been left out, it is no evidence against this. They may be unnecessary—this may be necessary. I deem it of great importance that a provision of this kind should form a part of our fundamental law.

Mr. Hastings. The section just adopted contains all that is necessary. It has precisely the same provision in regard to a prisoner having counsel: "The party accused shall be allowed to appear and defend in person and with counsel, as in civil actions." It seems unnecessary to repeat that this important privilege is secured to the prisoner.

Mr. Norton. The section just adopted gives the prisoner the privilege of appearing in person and defending with counsel; that is to say, he may have counsel provided he is able to pay for it; but the section which I propose makes it obligatory to give him counsel.

The question was then taken on the proposed section, and it was rejected.

The section as reported was then adopted.

The question being on concurring with the report of the Committee of the Whole in striking out the 7th section of the report of the Select Committee, it was concurred in.

The 8th section as reported was then adopted.

Section 9, as reported, being under consideration, as follows:

Sec. 9. The people shall have the right freely to assemble together to consult for the common good, to instruct their Representatives, and to petition the Legislature for redress of grievances.

Mr. Lippitt. I move to strike out the words "instruct their representatives." I conceive that the effect of that clause transforms a republic into a pure democracy. The peculiar excellence of our form of government consists in the practical working of our representative system; so that, in point of practice, the doctrine of instruction is very seldom carried out. Representatives very seldom receive direct instructions as to any particular subject, from their immediate constituents. The best authorities concur in the opinion that this is the peculiar excellence of our republican system. What is the object of a representative assembly? It is to devise measures and deliberate for the good of the whole, not for the good of particular sections of the country. The different sections represented may be remote; some of them are very remote. The constituency in those remote sections are unacquainted with the wants of the more central portions of the country. They know their own wants, and what will be best for their own locality. If this doctrine of instruction is to be recognized formally by the Constitution, so as to justify a resort to it, and compel, by implication, an obedience on the part of the representative, what would be the result? That some particular locality might be opposed to some general measure intended for the good of the great mass of the people, and still, because it conflicts with some particular interest or locality, or because the people of that locality thought so, they would instruct their representatives to vote against it. In other words, if this doctrine is carried out, it would amount to a substitution of the understanding and will of the people scattered over the whole country, unacquainted with the wants of each other in different districts, for the understanding of the representatives in their collective capacity. When they are sent to meet together and form a legislature they are supposed to be a deliberative assembly, and they discuss fully every subject upon which they are to act. Each representative makes up his mind after the full discussion which takes place among the representatives from every part of the country, and after hearing all the views presented with regard to the different interests of the different portions of the country. By that means he is enabled thoroughly to understand what will best meet the wants of the whole community, and promote the interests of the State. If that representative is compelled by instructions from his own locality to vote in a particular manner upon this measure and that, after he reaches the capital, I ask you, sir, what is the good of this representative assembly? The representatives are turned into mere delegates. There are occasions when instructions are proper and necessary—when delegates are appointed as attorneys acting under special powers; but I conceive when a representative is sent to make laws for the good of the whole, he does not assume the position of a special attorney; he comes under a power of the most general kind, because a general power is necessary in order that he may give his vote on particular measures for the best interests of the whole country. If his constituents are unwilling to give him this discretion, then it is not proper that he should represent them. I hope, therefore, that whatever may be the opinions of gentlemen in this House as to the duty of representatives in obeying the instructions of their constituents when given, that they will not insist upon introducing or recognizing the doctrine in this Constitution.

Mr. McCarver. I hold a doctrine entirely averse to that of the gentleman who has just taken his seat; and I sincerely trust that this provision of the Constitution will be retained. I hold, sir, that the people of a particular district who elect a representative, are the proper judges of all measures; and that when the representatives from the various districts meet together in their legislative capacity, they have no right to take any course contrary to the will of their constituents. If they do, they cease to represent their constituents. I see no reason why we should exclude so wholesome a provision from the Constitution of the State; it is one of the great privileges which belong to the people, and which appropriately comes in our Declaration of Rights. Our system of government is a system of compromises; the members of our legislative assemblies have various interests to represent; they come together and compromise those interests; and as a representative is the servant of the people who sent him here, I believe the people have an unquestionable right to instruct him as to the extent to which he shall go in making those compromises; and I hold, sir, that he is bound to obey the will of his constituents, as avowed in those instructions.

Mr. LIPPITT. Will the gentleman allow me to ask him one question? If the representatives come bound by instructions from their constituents, how can they effect any compromise?

Mr. MCCARVER. It is their duty to make every compromise not inconsistent with the will of their constituents. If they cannot effect any compromise without violating the instructions under which they act, then they should throw the responsibility upon those who sent them there.

Mr. SHERWOOD. I regret to differ from my friend from San Francisco (Mr. Lippitt) on this point; but I do differ from him both as to the nature of government and the duty of the representative. If I understand him, he contends that this provision recognizing the right of instruction, makes us a pure democracy, while in fact, our government is a representative democracy. The term pure democracy, as I understand it, means a government where the people assemble together without any representation, and make their own laws. As I understand a representative democracy, it is that in which one stands instead of many, or represents the will of those who elect him. How he can be a representative or a portion of the representative democracy, and not be guided by the instructions of his constituents—those who made him a representative—I cannot see. If I am elected by a thousand votes, and that thousand votes meet after my election and say, almost unanimously, that I am to vote so and so, if it is not a violation of principle with me, I am bound to vote as they direct. If it is a violation of principle with me, as a man of honor, I am bound to resign. There can be no other construction to the duties of a representative.

Mr. BROWN. I am of opinion that it would be impolitic to place this clause in the Constitution. It may be susceptible of evil. The natural course of a representative is to obey the will of his constituents. He knows what they desire; but if this provision is introduced in the Constitution, he may receive a letter with perhaps twenty or thirty names attached to it, instructing him to take a particular course. He has no instructions from the mass of his constituents; nevertheless, he knows that they entertain a different feeling—that the great majority of them do not wish him to take that course. But by this provision he is compelled to obey the wishes of twenty or thirty, and to disregard the will of perhaps several hundred. No representative would feel authorized to exercise any discretion in the matter, and act contrary to the expressed instructions which he had received. When a new measure comes up, it may not be in his power to ascertain the will of a majority of the people, not having any recent knowledge of their views. Under such circumstances, it would be unjust to require him to act upon the representation of ten or a dozen persons who may think proper to address him a written communication. If he is at all qualified to be a representative, he should have the discretionary power to judge of what will best meet the interests of his constituents—the great mass of whom may be entirely ignorant of the reasons for and against the measure. It may be a measure not generally discussed in his district previous to the meeting of the Legislature. I think it unusual to have such a provision in a Constitution, and I conceive that it would place members of the Legislature in a very embarrassing position. For these reasons, I hope it will be stricken out.

Mr. MCDOUGAL. I differ from the gentleman last up, and I hope the House will not strike out this provision. I think the people have a right to instruct their representatives, and the representative has a right to refuse to obey those instructions. Both have rights. But if the representative cannot conscientiously obey those instructions, he should resign. I regard him as a mere machine, so far as he is instructed, or so far as the wishes of his constituents are known to him. Exclusive of these cases, he has a right to exercise his own discretion.

Mr. McCarver. We simply say here that the people have a right to assemble and instruct their representatives. We do not say whether the representatives shall obey or not.

Mr. Lippitt. Under that construction the case is altered. But I put it in this light. I am a representative of the whole of California; that is to say, it is my duty to consider the best interests of the whole. If, when a question comes up, I know my constituents are unacquainted with all its aspects, and if I have contrary instructions, knowing that these instructions are based upon a want of knowledge of the case, still I should vote for it.

Mr. Vermeule. I believe the people have a right to instruct their representatives, and I believe that right should be acknowledged in the Constitution.

Mr. Hastings. I have simply to say that this clause should be stricken out, and for the reason that the people have a right to instruct their representatives, and this declares nothing else, and the people know it as well as we do. If they have that right why assert it here; if you strike out the clause you do not deprive them of the right. They will instruct their representatives if they think proper; if they do not think proper they will do just as they please about it. Our Constitution ought not to be encumbered with unnecessary provisions of this kind.

Mr. Gilbert. I think the remarks of the gentleman from Sacramento, (Mr. Hastings,) would go to strike out the whole section. The people have a right to assemble freely together. It is an unquestionable right; it has never been disputed; whereas, the right of instruction has been disputed. I think if any portion of the section should stand it is that. If the arguments adduced against introducing anything in regard to the right of instruction have a single particle of force, they apply to the whole of the section; and to nearly all others in this bill of rights. Most of them are simply declarations of great principles. Why not begin at the beginning and strike it all out. I should be in favor of retaining the clause relative to the right of instructing representatives for this reason, if for no other, that it has heretofore been considered at least doubtful.

The question was then taken on Mr. Lippitt's motion to strike out the words "instruct their representatives," and it was decided in the negative.

The section, as reported, was then adopted.

The 10th and 11th sections were adopted as reported.

The 12th section being under consideration, as follows:

No soldier shall, in time of peace, be quartered in any house without the consent of the owner, nor in time of war except in the manner prescribed by law.

Mr. Vermuele moved to insert the words "to be" after the word "manner," and before the word "prescribed."

Mr. McDougal said the question was "to be or not to be," and he therefore hoped the motion would prevail.

The amendment was agreed to, and the 12th section, as amended, was then adopted.

The 13th section being under consideration, viz:

As all men are entitled to equal political rights, representation should be apportioned according to population.

Mr. Lippitt said he was opposed to this section. He did not think that all men are entitled to equal political rights. He conceived that all men are entitled to equal natural rights; but the rights which grow out of society—out of the assembling of men in communities—those political rights resulting from the position in which they were placed, did not, he thought, belong to all men. If such was the case any provision designating the qualifications of citizenship would be unconstitutional.

Mr. Steuart moved to amend the section by striking out these words: "As all men are entitled to equal political rights," preceding the word "representation."

Mr. HASTINGS moved to amend the amendment by inserting the word "citizens" instead of "men."

Mr. VERMUELE thought there would be a discrepancy in the section if that amendment was adopted: "As all *citizens* are entitled to equal political rights, representation should be apportioned according to population." There would be a portion of the population not citizens. He thought the first section of the bill of rights sufficiently defined the rights of man.

Mr. HASTINGS withdrew his amendment.

The question was then taken on Mr. Steuart's amendment, to strike out the first clause of the section, so as to read "representation shall be apportioned according to population," and it was adopted, by yeas 13, nays 10.

The 13th section, as amended, was then adopted.

The remaining sections of the bill of rights, as reported by the Committee of the Whole, were adopted without debate; and, on motion of Mr. HALLECK, the article was ordered to be engrossed for a third reading.

On motion of Mr. GWIN, the resolution offered some days ago by Mr. Vallejo was taken up, viz:

Resolved, That three Commissioners be elected by ballot to draft a code of laws for the government of California, to be submitted to the Legislature for their approval at the first session thereof.

Mr. HALLECK moved to amend by striking out the words "for their approval," and inserting after the word "thereof" the words "subject to its adoption and modification from time to time." He did not know that he would vote for the original resolution, but if it was to be adopted, he wished it to be in as perfect a form as possible.

Mr. NORTON. I have but a single word to say in regard to this matter. There is some doubt on my mind whether we have power in this Convention to appoint any such commission. We were sent here for a special object—to form a Constitution to be submitted to the people; and that is all the power that I think is delegated to us. I am satisfied that there is a necessity for the appointment of these Commissioners; a necessity for preparing a system or code of laws for the Legislature; and that it will expedite the action of the Legislature very much if that course is adopted; but unless some gentleman can satisfy me that we have the right and power to appoint these Commissioners, I shall be compelled to vote against it, believing at the same time that there is an evident necessity for it.

Mr. SHERWOOD. We have fixed one important principle at any rate. The Committee asked instructions from this House as to the time when this government should go into operation, and they have been instructed to bring in a provision in the schedule that it shall go into operation at an early day after the adoption of this Constitution. It seems to be admitted that the Legislature will meet some time in December; and now I ask, from our own experience here, if, in starting the wheels of government; in swearing in your officers; in fashioning out the duties of your departments; in presenting laws to govern your judges, to regulate trials, to administer justice; to secure the rights of individuals—I ask if you will not be obliged to have a book of three or four hundred pages; and I ask you, if the experience of this House has not shown us that neither one, nor two, nor four months of the sitting of a legislative body similar to the character of this, can bring out such a code of laws as will be necessary for this country. All experience in the older States shows that codes of laws must be studied with care, and that no legislative committee, called suddenly into existence, can digest a code for the action of the Legislature at its first session. Our experience here shows, that during the last month, one large Committee have been engaged in forming a Constitution of six or eight pages; how, then, can the Legislature, in two or four months, bring out a code of laws embracing four or five hundred pages? We have to make a beginning; we have to start without any pre-existing laws, and on the first of January, when your Governor, and Secretary of State, Comptroller, and other officers are sworn in, they will have no duties to perform unless you have a code of laws; your offices are sinecures; there are no duties to perform, and they will be an expense to the public, without any benefit. Of course it is not to be expected that the Legislature will adopt at once the material prepared by these Commissioners. They will reject what is bad, and confirm what is good. Suppose you leave it to the Legislature; they meet, perhaps, in the middle of December; they will be engaged in session three or four months, wrangling about different propositions, with no connected code before them. We have here found that in one month the sum of seventy-five thousand dollars has been necessary to bear our expenses. The expenses of the Legislature in four months would be three hundred thousand dollars, setting aside the necessary printing. The people of the State would save probably one or two hundred thousand dollars by having this code prepared previous to the meeting of the Legislature. We, in our deliberations, have been guided by the experience of thirty States. If we had not the book of Constitutions before us, how long would it have taken us? Perhaps many months; and then we would have had but an imperfect Constitution. The new Legislature will thank you for appointing a commission of able men to present them a code of laws from which they can select such as will suit the people of this State. The right I consider unquestionable. We, the representatives of the people of California, have formed a Constitution. We have said that legislative and State authority shall go into operation at a certain time; and yet we know, from our own experience, that they cannot adopt a code of laws within any reasonable period. Representing the interests of the people, we take three of the best legal gentlemen in California, and let them draw up such a code of laws for the Legislature either to adopt or modify. We do not assume the right to force these laws upon the people. I trust there will not be a dissenting voice in regard to this matter. When we have fixed the time, I trust we will not entail an expense of two or three hundred thousand dollars upon the people, simply from the fears of gentlemen that we have no direct and express authority. I conceive that our position is anomalous; we have started without even a territorial government; we have formed a Constitution which I hope will be ratified by the people; and now we ask to present to the Legislature a code of laws to guide them in the distribution of justice throughout the State. If we do not adopt some such course, I think it quite probable that there will be an extra session of the Legislature in June or July; and it will be perhaps a year hence before we have an efficient code of laws in operation.

Mr. Shannon. The gentleman did well not to touch far upon the right of this Convention to appoint such a commission; and much as I would desire to support the resolution for the convenience of having such a code of laws prepared, I consider that there is an insuperable obstacle in the absence of all right to do so, on the part of this Convention. New York here comes in to our aid. The resolution is taken from the Constitution of New York. Is the appointment of commissioners made by the Convention which formed the Constitution? Not at all. They had not the right, and they were not willing to assume it. The section says that the Legislature at its first session after the adoption of the Constitution, shall provide for the appointment of such a commission. I claim that we have no right here to make any appointment of the kind. We have come here, whether it be under the instructions of the people or under the proclamation of General Riley, to form a Constitution, not to appoint commissioners to form laws. That, sir, is the province of the Legislature. The State from which my colleague came, (New York,) acknowledges that right as belonging to the Legislature and not to the Convention that forms the Constitution. Suppose the Constitution that we adopt here is not adopted by the people. Suppose they in their sovereignty see fit to refuse to ratify that Constitution. In the meantime we have had commissioners at work forming the laws by the appointment of this Convention, whose action the people refuse to ratify. Yes, sir, the authority which forms this commission is rejected by the people; they refuse to ratify our labors. Where, then, is your commission, and what becomes of the laws they have framed? It strikes me that it would be assuming a right not delegated to us; and I feel constrained to vote against the resolution.

Mr. SHERWOOD. In regard to the action of New York, we started without any Legislature; New York had a Legislature both before and after the Convention. They had very good laws in operation at the time. We create the necessity for laws. In regard to the right, also, it may be a very doubtful matter whether we have the right to fix our own pay, and yet we have fixed it. The circumstances under which we are placed, must be taken into consideration, and it will not do to draw a parallel line between this territory and States in which the whole pre-existing political organization was different.

Mr. McCARVER. I hold that the right of this body to appoint commissioners to form a code of laws for the Legislature, is very questionable; and that it would be improper for us and impolitic to do it, on the grounds of expediency. I have lived in a country for the last five years, (Oregon,) that adopted at one single sweep, laws which answered all the purposes, from the judicial code of Iowa. We might do just the same. I do not see why the Legislature could not just as well take up the laws of New York or Iowa, or Virginia, or any other State, as the report of these commissioners.

Mr. SHANNON. I would be perfectly willing to require the Legislature to appoint this commission at its first session, to form a code of laws.

Mr. GWIN. The example of New York has not the slightest bearing on this country. The commission in New York was appointed to revise a code of laws that had been in operation for upwards of fifty years. There is not the slightest similarity between the case of New York and California. As to what my friend from Sacramento (Mr. McCarver) says about adopting a code of laws from the States, what suited Oregon with eight hundred votes for a member of Congress, would scarcely suit such a country as this. The gentleman got more than eight hundred votes in his own district to come here. In Oregon it does very well; but when you adopt laws for a territory like this, with such an immense population, it is quite a different thing. There are portions of Mexican laws that must be re-enacted here; and the representatives of thirty of the States of the Union are here, and no system from one State will suit them. We ought to have three of the ablest men in California to prepare and chalk out the work for the guidance of the Legislature. Comparing the position of California with any other of the States, is entirely erroneous; we have had no system of government here as the other States have had. We are called upon to put immediately into effect a code of laws. As to the adoption of this Constitution by the people, I fear not. The gentleman (Mr. Shannon) can scarcely urge that as an argument. It has no force whatever. I have no apprehension that our Constitution will not be sanctioned by the people. As to the right, we have as much right to do this as we have to make a government. If we make a government, we must make provisions for having laws made to carry it out. You cannot get books in California; you must have able men to prepare the material for the Legislature; they have the enactment of the laws. I look upon it as absolutely indispensable; it is a matter of necessity; the right is the right of necessity; the same necessity that called us here to form a government.

Mr. VERMULE. I also am in favor of the passage of the resolution. I believe the great objection to it is based upon our want of power to appoint such a commission. I agree with the gentleman that the history of New York furnishes no precedent for the guidance of California. California is a political anomaly; and being anomalous, you must deviate from the fixed usages of other States. Who is to question this want of right on the part of this Convention? I know of no other than the people; and it is my opinion, that instead of objection to the exercise of such a right on the part of this Convention, they will thank us for abridging the labors of the Legislature.

Mr. Hastings. No doubt the members of the Legislature will be very grateful to us for making laws for them, and leaving them nothing to do but sit in their seats and receive their sixteen dollars a day.

Mr. Gilbert. I rise to express my conviction of the expediency, necessity and propriety of this propostion; but I must say I have very great doubts as to our power to appoint such a commission. If I understand the directions under which we come here, all our actions must be submitted to the people. I apprehend this resolution is not to go into the Constitution, nor is it to be inserted in the schedule. If so, I think it is clear and positive that it forms no part of our duty, and that we have no right to pass such a resolution. All our acts should be submitted to the people for their ratification. If we deny that principle, I do not think we have a right to come here at all. I rise, therefore, simply to say that this doubt as to the right will force me to vote against a measure which I believe to be necessary and expedient.

The question was then taken on Mr. Halleck's amendment, and it was adopted.

The question then being on the adoption of the resolution, it was decided in the affirmative, by yeas and nays, as follows:

Yeas.—Messrs. Aram, Covarrubias, De la Guerra, Dimmick, Dominguez, Gwin, Hanks, Hoppe, Hollingsworth, Lippincott, Moore, McDougal, Pico, Snyder, Sherwood, Steuart, Stearns, Vallejo, Vermule, Walker, Wozencraft.—21.

Nays.—Messrs. Brown, Foster, Gilbert, Hill, Halleck, Hastings, McCarver, Norton, Pedrorena, Sutter, Shannon, President.—12.

Mr. Semple said he voted in the negative simply from the fact that the people might not ratify this Constitution, and the Commissioners would have no means of getting their pay.

Mr. Sherwood suggested that that was a very good reason why the Convention should have adjourned fifteen days ago, in order that the members might save themselves some expense.

On motion, the House then adjourned to 12 o'clock, to-morrow.

SATURDAY, SEPTEMBER 29, 1849.

The Convention was called to order at half-past 10 o'clock.

Prayer by Senor Padre Ramirez.

The journal of yesterday was read and approved.

During the reading of the journal, Mr. Gwin moved the following amendment, to come in before the vote taken upon the per diem allowance of the President:

"Mr. Gwin stated that he would vote for the compensation allowed the President, on the principle that had been established by all deliberative bodies with which he was acquainted, of giving the presiding officer twice the amount of the members; and as the Convention had determined to pay its members $16 per diem, he would vote to give the President $25, as reported by the Committee.

Messrs. Botts, McDougal, Lippitt and Vermeule opposed the motion, on the ground that it was out of order.

The Chair decided it to be in order.

Mr. Vermeule appealed from the decision of the Chair.

Mr. Gwin then stated that his motion was to amend the journal by the recording of his reasons.

Mr. Lippitt opposed the motion on the ground that it would be establishing a very bad precedent. It was enough for members to state their reasons, but it would not be proper to encumber the Journal with every member's reasons.

Mr. Vermeule withdrew his appeal.

The question on the motion to amend was then taken, and rejected.

Mr. Moore, Chairman of the Committee appointed to prepare a plan of enumeration for representation, presented a report, which was laid upon the table, subject to call.

Mr. NORTON, from the Select Committee on the Constitution, reported the schedule to the Constitution.

On motion of Mr. WOZENCRAFT, the matter was laid upon the table, subject to call.

Mr. GWIN gave notice that he should move sundry amendments to the schedule, or present them in the form of a minority report.

Mr. NORTON stated that the Committee on the Constitution, having completed their labors, begged to be discharged.

Mr. WOZENCRAFT hoped they would not be, as there might be other business for them to transact.

Mr. NORTON said that he would withdraw the request, as he recollected that the Committee had yet to make a preamble.

Mr. PRICE, Chairman of the Committee appointed to receive propositions and designs for a Seal for the State of California, reported that the Committee had received but one design, and that was presented by Mr. Caleb Lyons, of Lyonsdale. The Committee considered it peculiarly appropriate, and recommended its adoption by the Convention.

On motion, the report, with the design of the Seal and its explanation, were laid upon the table, subject to call.

Mr. SHERWOOD moved that the Convention proceed to the election of Commissioners to frame a code of laws to be presented to the next Legislature for their adoption.

Mr. BOTTS presented a resolution to render any member of the Convention ineligible for the office of Commissioner.

Mr. VERMEULE wished the resolution so modified as to provide that only two of the three should be members of the Convention. He had had but little time to become acquainted with the legal talent in the country, and was not able to say whether there were three gentlemen, not in the Convention, who were capable of filling the office.

Mr. BOTTS was utterly opposed to such a proposition. He was opposed to this Convention making fat offices for its members to fill. These offices had been created by the Convention in an extraordinary manner, without any right, and it was quite likely, as the precedent had been established, that other offices might be created also. As the members of the Convention were not numerous, it might be said that these offices were created simply for the purpose of providing themselves with good berths.

Mr. VERMEULE deemed the reasoning just, and withdrew his opposition to Mr. Botts' resolution.

Mr. HASTINGS was opposed to the proposition and in favor of at once going into the election of the Commissioners. Was it at all likely that the people would find fault with the actions of the members of the Convention whom they had selected to represent them? Not at all. They would certainly be satisfied with the acts of those in whose talents and abilities they had already shown their confidence.

Mr. TEFFT contended that Mr. Hastings had argued upon false principles. The people had not sent delegates to the Convention to form a code of laws, but to form a Constitution. It was presumptuous to contend that all the legal talent and ability was centred in the Convention—he saw no evidence of it; and he believed that if the Commissioners were appointed by the Convention, the Legislature would indignantly reject any code of laws they might present to them. It was necessary to have at least one member of the commission who was thoroughly acquainted with the Spanish laws, and of all of those whose names he had heard in connection with the subject, he had heard of no such person. It was evident the board had been created by gentlemen here for the purpose of being elected themselves, and he felt himself fully warranted in making that assertion. If the Convention entertained any desire that the code of laws reported by these Commissioners should be adopted by the Legislature, they should be extremely cautious who they selected. For his own part, he doubted whether the Legislature would recognize the right of the Convention to appoint Commissioners at all.

Mr. Shannon remarked that the question had been fully discussed last night, and the gentleman from San Luis Obispo, (Mr. Tefft,) was too late with his argument as to the right of the Convention. That question had been already decided. In order to cut off all further argument, he moved the previous question.

Mr. Lippitt requested the gentleman from Sacramento (Mr. Shannon) to withdraw his motion; but that gentleman declined.

The Convention then refused the call for the previous question.

Mr. Lippitt stated that he had been compelled to leave the previous evening under indisposition, before the question came up. He did not desire to make a speech, and would only say that he fully concurred with the gentleman from San Luis Obispo, (Mr. Tefft,) in his opinion.

Mr. Vermeule stated that he had voted for the resolution to appoint, purely from motives of political rectitude; but his opinion as to the propriety of appointing the Commissioners having undergone a change, he moved a reconsideration of the vote of last night.

The motion was adopted.

Mr. Lippitt then opposed the adoption of the resolution on several grounds. First, that it was exceeding the authority for which the people had sent the delegates here. Next, it was impossible, in his opinion, for three men or thirty men, to draw up a code of laws in time for the action of the next Legislature. It was a work of years to form a code of laws—and he had never known one to be formed in less than two years. Questions would arise, perfectly new, and which had never before been presented, and extraordinary skill and industry were required. It was the province of the Legislature to make laws—that body was elected for that purpose and none other; and the Convention had no business to abrogate to themselves their powers—either to make laws or appoint a commission to make them.

Mr. Sherwood moved that the Convention take a recess till half-past 2 o'clock; carried.

AFTERNOON SESSION, HALF PAST 2 O'CLOCK, P. M.

The debate upon the resolution last under consideration was resumed.

Mr. Botts opposed the adoption of the resolution as an assumption of power which would not, and should not, be recognized by the Legislature. It would impede and retard the passage of laws; for the Legislature would look with no favor upon any code reported by that commission, and would, in all probability, reject anything they might produce. Besides that, it was an unnecessary expense.

Mr. Vallejo was in favor of the resolution. He had no other motive than to provide for the rapid passage of laws by the Legislature. It was a matter of economy to pay the three Commissioners rather than an entire Legislature. The session of that body would not be near so protracted if their business was already prepared to their hands. If the Convention objected to paying $3,000 or $4,000 for Commissioners, he would pay it himself, willingly, though of slight importance to him in comparison to the State. He regretted that his limited knowledge of the English language prevented him from replying to all the arguments adduced by those gentlemen who did not speak in his own tongue.

This discussion was continued on the same grounds; Messrs. Sherwood, Hastings, and Price occupied the floor in favor of, and Messrs. Lippett, Halleck, and Botts, against the adoption of the resolution.

Mr. Price submitted the following as an amendment to the resolution, which, after debate, was rejected, by yeas 19, nays 20:

The Legislature, at its first session after the adoption of this Constitution, and from time to time thereafter, as may be necessary, shall pass laws regulating the tenure of office, the filling of vacancies therein, and the compensation of the said Commissioners.

Mr. SHANNON called for the previous question, which the Convention sustained.

The question being on the adoption of the original resolution, Mr. BOTTS asked the yeas and nays, which were ordered and resulted as follows:

YEAS.—Messrs. Covarrubias, De la Guerra, Dimmick, Gwin, Hobson, Jones, Lippincott, McDougal, Price, Rodriguez, Sutter, Sherwood, Steuart, Stearns, Vallejo, Vermeule, Walker, Wozencraft—18.

NAYS.—Messrs. Aram, Botts, Brown, Carillo, Crosby, Dent, Dominguez, Foster, Gilbert, Hanks, Hill, Hoppe, Halleck, Hastings, Hollingsworth, Larkin, Lippitt, McCarver, Norton, Pedrorena, Pico, Reid, Shannon, Sansevaine, Tefft, President—26.

Mr. WOZENCRAFT moved for the appointment of a committee of three to receive a design or device of a suitable coat of arms for the State.

Mr. PRICE said that was a matter for the Legislature to determine, and not for the Convention.

The motion was withdrawn.

Mr. PRICE moved that when the Convention adjourns, it adjourn till Monday morning; carried.

Mr. HALLECK, at quarter of 6 o'clock, moved for a recess till half-past 7 o'clock; carried.

EVENING SESSION, HALF-PAST 7 O'CLOCK.

Several unimportant motions were made, but withdrawn without discussion.

On motion of Mr. PRICE, the House took up the report upon the Great Seal of the State.

Mr. SHANNON inquired whether the design presented was for the Great Seal of the State or the coat of arms. He deemed the design a most happy one, but more appropriate for a coat of arms than for a seal. It was unusual for a seal to contain a motto, the seal commonly containing the main emblems and the words "Great Seal of the State."

The explanation accompanying the seal was then read, as follows:

THE SEAL OF THE STATE AND COAT OF ARMS.

EXPLANATION.

Around the bend of the ring are represented thirty-one stars, being the number of States of which the Union will consist upon the admission of California. The foreground figure represents the goddess Minerva having sprung full grow from the brain of Jupiter. She is introduced as a type of the political birth of the State of California, without having gone through the probation of a territory. At her feet crouches a grisly bear feeding upon the clusters from a grape vine, emblematic of the peculiar characteristics of the country. A miner is engaged with his rocker and bowl at his side, illustrating the golden wealth of the Sacramento, upon whose waters are seen shipping, typical of commercial greatness; and the snow-clad peaks of the Sierra Nevada make up the background, while above is the Greek motto "Eureka," (I have found,) applying either to the principle involved in the admission of the State, or the success of the miner at work.

CALEB LYON,
of Lyonsdale.

MONTEREY, *Sept.* 26, 1849.

After various amendments had been suggested, the whole matter was laid upon the table.

On motion of Mr. MORTON, Article III of the Constitution was taken up.

Section 1st being under consideration—

The PRESIDENT called upon Mr. Norton to take the chair, stating that he was too unwell to occupy it at present.

Mr. BOTTS. Mr. Chairman, it is Saturday night, sir. The President is broken down by hard work; the clerks are broken down; the reporter is broken down; and I believe the members are nearly all broken down. I therefore move an adjournment.

The Convention refused to adjourn, by a vote of 19 to 17.

The 1st section, as reported by the Committee of the Whole, was then taken up for consideration, as follows:

SEC. 1. Every white male citizen of the United States, and every male citizen of Mexico (Indians, Africans, and descendents of Africans excepted) who shall have elected to become a citizen of the United States under the treaty of peace exchanged and ratified at Queretaro on the 30th day of May, 1848, of the age of twenty-one years, who shall have been a resident of the State six months next preceding the election, and the county or district in which he claims his vote thirty days, shall be entitled to vote at all elections which are now or hereafter be authorized by law.

The question being on concurring in the amendment of the Committee of the Whole, an animated discussion sprung up, and the same points were re-argued in the House that had been so warmly discussed in the Committee.

Mr. HALLECK was opposed to the amendment, because he thought that it might be said to conflict with the conditions of the treaty. He would not say that it did do so, but that it might be so construed. If such was the case, several of the most worthy citizens of California would be excluded from exercising the right of franchise; and one of them was one of the members of this very Convention. He hoped that the section might be amended so as to remove this difficulty—he had sought so to modify it, but having failed, would leave the matter in the hands of others.

Mr. LIPPITT asked how it conflicted with the treaty.

Mr. HALLECK replied that he did not assert that it did; but it might possibly be so construed.

Mr. MCCARVER wished to know what class was excluded.

Mr. NORIEGO addressed the Convention through the interpreter. The Convention was now treating upon a point of very great importance to himself and to California—a question as interesting as it was important; and he should be doing a very great injustice to his constituents, did he not speak upon the subject. By the proposed amendment, all Indians were excluded, while at the same time it allowed all foreigners who might choose to come to California and reside for a few years, to become citizens. You allow the Kanaka to come within your territory and admit them to citizenship, when he is as ignorant and as foolish as any Indian in California. And yet you exclude the native Indians from enjoying equal privileges with him. It had been asserted by some members that Indians are brutal and irrational. Let those gentlemen cast their eyes back for three hundred years and say who were the Indians then. They were a proud and gifted race, capable of forming a government for themselves. If they were not so much enlightened as now, it was not for want of natural gifts, but because the lights of science were not then so bright as now, even in Europe; and they could fall but dimly upon the natives of the soil. And he would say to those gentlemen who had sneered at the Indian race, that there might still be Indians in the Territory of California who were equally as rational and gifted as highly by nature as those who had depreciated them. He would not carry their recollections back three centuries, but bid them look back but for half a century. All the work that was seen in California, was the work of Indians led by some foreigners. If they were not cultivated and highly civilized, it was because they had been ground down and made slaves of. They were intelligent and capable of receiving instructions, and it was the duty of the citizens to endeavor to elevate them and better their condition in every way, instead of seeking to sink them still lower. He regretted that he could not give full expression to his feelings through the services of an interpreter, but hoped he had made himself understood. If it was the will of the Convention to exclude the body of Indians, he hoped exceptions might be made, and that those who were the holders of property and had heretofore exercised all the rights and privileges of freemen, might still be permitted to continue in the exercise of those rights.

Mr. DIMMICK said that he had voted for the amendment, but upon sober second thought he had arrived at the conclusion that it was too exclusive. He accordingly submitted an amendment which, in effect, excluded only Indians not taxed, and Africans and their descendants.

20

Mr. Halleck moved an amendment, which, after modification, at the suggestion of Mr. Lippitt, was as follows:

Insert in the 1st section, after the words "United States," and before the words "of the age," the following:

"And every citizen of Mexico (Indians, not taxed as owners of real estate, and negroes excepted) entitled to the right of suffrage at the ratification of the treaty of Gaudalupe Hidalgo, and who shall have elected to become a citizen of the United States, under the provisions of said treaty."

Mr. Tefft supported the amendment, and was in favor of such a provision, if there was but one man in all California who could be benefitted by it.

Mr. Shannon was also in favor of it.

Mr. Steuart said that he could not vote for the amendment without further explanation from the mover. He could see nothing in the section, as amended in the Committee of the Whole, conflicting with the treaty. (*Mr. S. then read section* 8 *of the treaty.*) There was no gentleman in that Hall that recognized the Kanaka as any thing more than an Indian, or who pretended to do so. He did not deny that there had been Indians who had done honor to the legislative halls, but it was better to avoid an evil that we knew not of, than to adopt a loose course which might produce most unfortunate results and incalculable evils. It would compel researches in old edicts and musty records of by-gone days of foreign lands, and in a language of which we were ignorant.

Mr. Hoppe was in favor of the section as it stood. Was there a man, he would ask, who was willing to place himself on a level with the Indian or the negro? Not he, for one. The proposed amendment was loose in the extreme. Where were those Indians who were to be admitted by this amendment? They were along the Pacific coast, populating the *ranchos*.. There was not a *rancho* where you would not find fifty or a hundred buck Indians, and the owner could run these *freemen* up to the polls, and carry any measure he might desire.

Mr. Halleck interrupted to explain that only those Indians who were taxed were competent to vote.

Mr. Hoppe continued. There were ranchos in certain districts where the California proprietors could control at least two hundred votes in favor of any particular candidate; and these votes could be purchased for a few dollars, for the Indians knew no better.

Mr. Dent addressed the Convention in favor of the Indian race.

Mr. McCarver opposed Mr. Halleck's amendment.

Mr. Halleck advocated it.

Mr. Sherwood was opposed to the principle of any man voting who was not a white man. It had been said that if the amendment was not adopted a member of the Convention would be excluded from the right of franchise. He knew of no gentleman present who was not a white man; and he believed every one in the country who was entitled to vote was a white man. He knew that his constituents were in favor of excluding the Indians. With the gentlemen from California he agreed, when he argued that all endeavors should be used to elevate, and cultivate, and instruct the Indians; and that it was the duty of the State Government to adopt every measure in their power to produce such a result; but that had nothing to do with the question. If the amendment of Mr. Halleck was adopted he was sure that there was not a man in the mines who would vote for the Constitution. Under such a state of things, his friend Captain Sutter, if so disposed, if he desired to become a politician, and wished office, could, by simply granting a small portion of land to each Indian, control a vote of ten thousand.

Mr. Noriego said he could easily remove the fears entertained by the last speaker, that such an overflowing amount of Indians would vote. There was no such desire on the part of any member of that Convention. He did not at all desire that the mass of Indians should vote, and he had expressly said so. All the Indians in the entire Territory who owned land and were entitled to vote, under the laws of Mexico, were not more than two hundred; he was perfectly satisfied of it. For himself, he only proposed that those who were entitled to a vote by virtue of holding property, purchased under the Mexican laws prior to the cession of California, should still be permitted to exercise that right. There was no fear of two hundred votes having any serious effect in a population of 60,000.

Mr. BOTTS moved to amend the amendment by inserting after the words "real estate," the words "to the amount of $500, subjected to taxation;" but subsequently withdrew the same.

Mr. SHERWOOD moved to amend the amendment by inserting, as a substitute therefor, the section as originally reported by the Committee on the Constitution.

Mr. SHANNON moved the previous question, which motion was sustained by the Convention; and the question being taken on Mr. Sherwood's amendment, the yeas and nays were required and ordered, and resulted as follows:

YEES.—Messrs. Aram, Brown, Crosby, Gwin, Hobson, Jones, Lippincott, Moore, McCarver, McDougal, Price, Sutter, Sherwood, Vermeule, Walker, Wozencraft.—16.

NAYS.—Messrs. Botts, Carillo, Covarrubias, De La Guerra, Dimmick, Dominguez, Foster, Gilbert, Hanks, Hill, Hoppe, Halleck, Hollingsworth, Larkin, Lippitt, Norton, Ord, Pedrorena, Rodriguez, Reid, Sherwood, Shannon, Stearns, Sansevaine, Tefft, Vallejo.—26.

The question then being on Mr. Halleck's amendment—

Mr. STEUART moved to amend the same by substituting therefor the following:

Every white male citizen of the United States, and every white male inhabitant of California, as provided for under the treaty of peace exchanged and ratified at Queretaro, on the 30th day of May, 1848, of the age of twenty-one years, who shall have been a resident of the State six months next preceding the election, and the county and district in which he claims his vote thirty days, shall be entitled to vote at all elections which are now, or hereafter may be authorized by law.

The presiding officer (Mr. Norton) decided that, as the previous question had been sustained by the Convention, the amendment was not in order.

Mr. PRICE moved an adjournment, which motion the CHAIR decided to be not in order.

Mr. PRICE appealed from this decision, and the question being put, "Shall the decision of the Chair stand as the judgment of the House?" it was decided in the affirmative.

The question then again recurring on Mr. Halleck's amendment, the yeas and nays were required and ordered, and resulted as follows:

YEAS.—Messrs. Carillo, Covarrubias, De la Guerra, Dimmick, Dominguez, Foster, Gilbert, Hill, Halleck, Hollingsworth, Larkin, Lippitt, Ord, Pedrorena, Rodriguez, Reid, Shannon, Stearns, Sansevaine, Tefft, Vallejo.—21.

NAYS.—Messrs. Aram, Botts, Brown, Crosby, Gwin, Hanks, Hoppe, Hobson, Hastings, Jones, Lippincott, Moore, McCarver, McDougal, Norton, Price, Sutter, Sherwood, Steuart, Vermeule, Walker, Wozencraft.—22.

The question then recurring on concurring in the amendment of the Committee of the Whole, Mr. PRICE inquired of the presiding officer, (Mr. Norton,) what would be the effect of a rejection of that amendment, the original section of the article having already been offered as an amendment by Mr. Sherwood and voted down?

The presiding officer explained and decided that the amendment of Mr. Sherwood, and the vote thereon, had been irregular, and must be considered as not having taken place.

On motion, the Convention adjourned.

MONDAY, OCTOBER 1, 1849.

The Convention met pursuant to adjournment. Prayer by Rev. S. H. Willey. Journal of Saturday read and approved.

The House then, on motion, took took up the report from the Committee of the Whole, on the "Right of Suffrage," and the first three sections of said report was concurred in.

Mr. Gilbert. I have an amendment which I proposed in Committee of the Whole, and which I will read again for the consideration of the House. This section provides that no citizen who happens to be absent from the State on public business, shall be deprived of the right of voting. It is in the following words :

4. For the purpose of voting, no person shall be deemed to have gained or lost a residence by reason of his presence or absence while employed in the service of the United States; nor while engaged in the navigation of the waters of this State, or of the United States, or of the high seas; nor while a student of any seminary of learning; nor while kept at any almshouse, or other asylum, at public expense; nor while confined in any public prison.

Mr. Steuart. I would rather retain the 4th section and adopt that of the gentleman as an additional section.

Mr. Gilbert. I am sorry to detain the House, but I think that this section is much superior to the other, and covers the whole ground. It is a condensation of all that ought to be said on the subject in the Constitution. If there be other sections that conflict with it, I shall vote to strike them out at the proper time ; and if we can treat this subject fully in one section, why make two or three, or half a dozen.

Mr. Steuart. I am perfectly satisfied upon further examination of the two sections, that this is a condensation of all that is said in the report of the Committee, and I therefore withdraw all objection to it.

The question was then taken on the proposed substitute, and it was adopted by ayes 27, noes 20.

The 5th section was then adopted as reported.

The 6th section being under consideration, as follows :

All elections by the people shall be by ballot.

Mr. Botts moved to strike out the words "by ballot," and insert "viva voce," which amendment was rejected, and the section adopted.

Article II, as adopted, was then ordered to be engrossed for a third reading.

Article III on the Distribution of Powers, was then read as follows :

Sec. 1. The powers of government of the State of California shall be divided into three separate departments, the Legislature, the Executive, and the Judicial; and no person charged with the exercise of powers properly belonging to one of these departments, shall exercise any function appertaining to either of the others, except in the cases hereinafter expressly directed or permitted.

The section was adopted as reported ; and the second section being under consideration—

Mr. Halleck said that it properly came under the head of the Legislative Department. He therefore moved that the article on the Distribution of Powers be engrossed for a third reading, and that the words "Article III," be inserted at the head of Legislative Department, which was agreed to.

The 1st section of Article III being under consideration—

Mr. Botts moved to insert before it as the first section, the following :

The Legislature shall have power to enact all laws for the good of this State that do not conflict with the provisions of this Constitution.

Mr. Botts said his object in moving this amendment was, that the Legislature should exercise no power except what the people delegated to it ; and that the Constitution was the proper place to look for these delegated powers. He wished specially to enjoin that which was sometimes taken for granted. We do this in the Constitution, but declare that the Legislature have a great many special powers ; these special powers might be construed to include the general powers.

Mr. Lippitt did not agree with his friend from Monterey. He concurred with him as to the source of all power, but he did not agree with him that the channel through which that power flows, was through the Constitution. He had no objection to the proposed section ; it could do no harm. It might have the effect of preventing dispute if there should be a division of opinion on this subject. He thought it best, therefore, that such a provision should be inserted.

Mr. McCarver. It seems to be a principle so well established, that the power is in the hands of the people, that I cannot see the object of inserting this provision in the Constitution. It is the fundamental principle upon which our republican government is based. The American people need hardly be reminded that they possess this power.

Mr. Botts did not suppose the gentleman would confound the government with the people. The government derives its powers from the people; but it possesses only just as much power as the people choose to give it. He preferred specifying all powers that the people chose to give the government, and he offered this as a general rule where such powers were not specified.

Mr. McCarver. What is the connection between the government and the people? The power is in the people and the people constitute the government, and place the power in the hands of their representatives, under the restrictions imposed by the Constitution. Unless we place such restrictions on the law-making power in this Constitution, there is no check upon the Legislature; hence all power not specified comes back to its original source—the people. It cannot be brought under a general head, and transferred to a third party.

Mr. Botts contended that the object of the Constitution was to protect the minority, and that to omit this constitutional provision would be a violation of that principle.

The question was then taken on the proposed section, and it was rejected, by yeas 13, nays 14.

The question recurring on the adoption of the fourth section, viz:

Sec. 1. The legislative power of this State shall be vested in a Senate and Assembly, which shall be designated the Legislature of the State of California, and the style of their laws shall commence in the following manner: "The people of the State of California, represented in Senate and Assembly, do enact as follows."

Mr. Gilbert moved to strike out "style of" their laws, and insert "their laws." He deemed it unnecessary to say "style of."

The amendment was agreed to; and the section, as amended, was adopted.

The second section, as reported, being under consideration, as follows:

Sec. 2. The sessions of the Legislature shall be annual, and shall commence on the first Monday in January next ensuing the election of its members, unless the Governor of the State shall in the interim convene the Legislature by proclamation.

Mr. Gwin moved to insert after the word "Legislature" in the first line, the words "until otherwise provided by law." His object in moving this amendment was this; that it might after a few years become evident that there was no necessity for annual sessions; and in order that the people should not be put to the expense of calling another Convention to amend the Constitution, he desired to give the Legislature power to change from annual to biennial sessions. In some States the people were obliged to call a Convention to provide for this. No Legislature would make the change unless it was desired by the people.

Mr. McCarver said it appeared to him that this would not attain the object. He was in favor of the provision, but he was not certain that the amendment covered the ground. It did not make it obligatory on the Legislature that the change should be to biennial sessions.

Mr. Botts asked if it was the object that the Legislature should make the sessions semi-annual.

Mr. Gwin said the power was given to the Legislature, and they would not exercise it unless it was deemed expedient.

Mr. Dimmick said if this clause was altered it would be necessary to alter the next and succeeding sections.

Mr. Hill thought the object was a very good one, but that it would be desirable to define whether sessions should be biennial or semi-annual.

Mr. Lippitt agreed with the gentleman last up, and would ask the gentleman from San Francisco (Mr. Gwin) so to amend his motion.

Mr. NORTON was of opinion that in adopting this amendment the House would get into a great deal of difficulty. All this could be done by a vote of the people in the manner provided in the Constitution. It could be done under an act of the Legislature, without calling a Convention to form a new Constitution. Besides, he thought that if California should ever become the great State which all anticipated, it would be indispensably necessary to have annual sessions of the Legislature.

Mr. BOTTS was surprised to see any amendnent from the quarter from which this came. He recollected that the gentleman from San Francisco, (Mr. Gwin,) was struck with horror that any amendment should be proposed after the debates in Committee of the Whole; but he was most of all astonished that such an amendment as this should come from that gentleman. This amendment is fraught with evil. To what does it amount? That the Legislature may do this: they may provide, if they choose, that another Legislature shall not sit for twenty years, and you could not avoid that decision except by a revolution. Even to amend your Constitution you would be obliged to have a revolution, for there would be no Legislature to amend it according to the provisions of that Constitution. It was evident that the resolution should not pass as it is now worded. It seemed to him that this was a very important matter, and that the sessions of the Legislature should be annual, and not be altered except in the manner provided in the Constitution.

Mr. HILL was in favor of the provision, but wished to have it restricted to some definite time.

Mr. NORTON was opposed to any provision of the kind. It was not necessary now; and whenever the necessity that such a change should be made was apparent to the Legislature or the people, there was a very easy method pointed out in the Constitution of effecting the object.

Mr. STEUART said that, further than that, it carried along with it a *quasi* argument in favor of making such a change. He begged that gentlemen would not refer constantly to the action of the Committee. He did not consider it proper that the action of the House should be restricted by what was done in Committee. It was almost impossible to make a motion without being told that it was fully discussed and determined in Committee.

Mr. GWIN said it was very well known to all the members that this subject had been fully discussed in Committee of the Whole; it was no secret. If it was the gentleman's (Mr. Steuart's) misfortune not to be here during the proceedings of the Committee, it was not just that the House should, on his account, be detained by a repetition of all the arguments brought forward there. The gentleman from San Francisco (Mr. Norton) said it was a very easy thing to alter the Constitution. He (Mr. Gwin) did not regard it in that light. He thought the Constitution should be the permanent law of the land. The gentleman, if he read the papers, would see that in Michigan a Convention had been called for this very purpose—to change to biennial sessions, and that they were now engaged in an exciting controversy on the subject.

Mr. LIPPITT. I am opposed to the proposition because it places too much power in the hands of the Legislature. It might produce serious evil. A great political party object might be accomplished by making the sessions biennial.

Mr. NORTON, in answer to the remark of his colleague, (Mr. Gwin,) that they were having discussions and difficulty in Michigan in regard to such an amendment in the Constitution of that State, had only to say, that this very fact proved that there was a division of opinion among the people, and that there was no obvious necessity for the change.

Mr. SHERWOOD contended that biennial sessions of the Legislature would not shorten the time or diminish the expense of our Legislatures. If there are laws that are necessary for the government of the people, it will require two months of a biennial session to pass what require one month, at each session, in two annual sessions; that is to say, two months' legislation will be necessary in either case. You do not diminish the expense in that way. Another reason why the report of the Committee of the Whole should be adopted is this: it is a principle in all republican governments that the acts of the representative should come as immediately from his constituents as possible; and, if they are disputed, that they should be as immediately as possible altered. If the people feel themselves laboring under an unjust law, it should be repealed as soon as possible. Annual sessions will be necessary here to carry out the will of the people, and meet the progressive wants of the country. We have said in this Constitution, that the representation of the different districts shall be fixed, and that a certain census or enumeration of the inhabitants shall be taken. Now, suppose your session ends just the winter preceding the census; you have biennial sessions; your census is taken in June; a very great change in your population within the two or five years previous; several districts will contain an immense majority which they did not contain when the representation was fixed before; will you deny the people the right to have a change of representation for two years?

Mr. HASTINGS said we were now just commencing the organization of a new government, and annual sessions of the Legislature would be absolutely necessary for many years to come—perhaps for the next fifty years. An entire code of laws must be prepared; the Legislature could not, unless it met annually, present to the people of California such laws as the wants of the country required. He therefore preferred the section in its present form, and would oppose the amendment.

Mr. JONES, in order to meet the objections which had been urged against the proposition of the gentleman from San Francisco, by those who were friendly to the object, proposed to amend the amendment, by saying: "Until the Legislature shall have provided by law for biennial sessions."

Mr. GWIN accepted the amendment.

The question was then taken on Mr. Gwin's amendment, and it was rejected, by ayes 8, noes 25.

The 2d section, as reported, was then adopted.

Sections 3 and 4 were then adopted; and, on motion, the House took a recess till 7 P. M.

NIGHT SESSION, 7 O'CLOCK, P. M.

Section 5 of the Article on the Legislative Department being under consideration, as follows:

SEC. 5. Senators shall be chosen for the term of two years, at the same time and place as members of the Assembly. And no person shall be a member of the Senate or Assembly who has not been a citizen and inhabitant of the State one year, and of the county for which he shall be chosen six months next before his election.

The amendments of the Committee of the Whole to the 5th section being under consideration, they were amended on motion of Mr. GILBERT, by inserting after the word "county," the words "or district;" and the question being taken by yeas and nays on the first clause of the section, as amended, it was decided in the affirmative, as follows:

YEAS.—Messrs. Botts, Brown, Carrillo, Crosby, Dent, Dimmick, Dominguez, Foster, Hanks, Hill, Hoppe, Hastings, Hollingsworth, Lippitt, Lippincott, McCarver, Norton, Price, Pico, Reid, Shannon, Stearns, Steuart, Vermeule, Walker, Wozencraft, President—27.

NAYS.—Messrs. Aram, Gilbert, Gwin, Halleck, Moore, McDougal, Sherwood, Tefft—8.

Mr. GWIN was opposed to the qualification of twelve months' residence, and in favor of six. By the first section, six month's residence was necessary to acquire the privileges of citizenship. He was in favor of all citizens being eligible to the Legislature; and had contended for this principle in Committee of the Whole.

He now moved to strike out the entire section, with a view of proposing the section as originally reported by the Select Committee.

The yeas and nays being called, the motion was decided in the negative, as follows:

YEAS.—Messrs. Gilbert, Gwin, Moore—3.

NAYS.—Messrs. Aram, Botts, Brown, Carrillo, Covarrubias, Crosby, Dent, De La Guerra, Dimmick, Dominguez, Foster, Hanks, Hill, Hoppe, Hastings, Hollingsworth, Larkin, Lippitt, Lippincott, McCarver, McDougal, Norton, Price, Pico, Rodriguez, Reid, Sherwood, Shannon, Sansevaine, Stearns, Steuart, Tefft, Vermeule, Walker, Wozencraft, President—36.

The 6th section was amended, on motion of Mr. LIPPITT, by striking out the word "that" and inserting therefor the words "that of the."

The amendment of the Committee of the Whole was concurred in, and the section, thus amended, was adopted.

The 7th section, as reported, being under consideration, as follows:

7. When the number of Senators is increased, they shall be annexed to one of the two classes, so as to keep them as nearly equal as practicable.

Mr. PRICE moved to strike out the entire section and substitute the following, which was adopted:

SEC. 7. When the number of Senators is increased, they shall be apportioned by lot, so as to keep the two classes as nearly equal in number as possible.

The 8th section, as reported, being under consideration, as follows:

Each House shall choose its own officers and judge of the qualifications, elections, and returns of its own members. A contested election shall be determined in such manner as shall be directed by law.

Mr. BOTTS wanted to know if these two parts were not contradictory. Each House was to judge of the qualifications, elections, and returns of its own members. But contested elections are to be decided in such manner as may be prescribed by law. He desired to know if every legislative body was not the judge, and sole judge of the contested elections arising in that body. He maintained that it was not proper that one Legislature should determine by law the contested elections of the next Legislature. He presumed the intention was, that each Legislature should settle the elections of its own members; yet if the latter part of this clause meant any thing, it meant that one Legislature should have the power to say how a contested election in the next Legislature should be settled.

Mr. NORTON said that this matter was sufficiently explained in Committee of the Whole. The first part of the section provides what is always provided for in every Constitution, that each House shall choose its own officers and judge of the qualifications, elections, and returns of its own members. These are not the only election returns. There are also the returns for Governor and other State officers. The latter clause provides that contested elections in these cases shall be determined in such manner as the Legislature shall prescribe by law.

Mr. BOTTS had no objection to it, if the clause was made to read so.

Mr. LIPPITT said it appeared to him that it was not necessary to insert this latter clause. A court of law would be bound by the law of the land to settle these questions.

Mr. BOTTS proposed to amend the clause by inserting the words "But other contested elections shall be determined in such manner as may be provided by law." The clause might first be amended, and then, if it was deemed unnecessary by the House, it could be stricken out.

The question was then taken on Mr. Botts' amendment, and decided in the negative.

Mr. LIPPITT moved to strike out entirely the last clause of the section.

The motion was determined in the affirmative; and the 8th section, as amended, was adopted.

The 9th, 10th, and 11th sections were adopted, as reported by the Committee of the Whole.

The 12th section being under consideration, as follows:

Members of the Legislature shall in all cases except treason, felony, and breach of the peace, be privileged from arrest; nor shall they be subject to any civil process during the session of the Legislature, nor for fifteen days next before the commencement and after the termination of each session.

Mr. LIPPITT thought this section required a verbal alteration. It was certainly not the intention to extend the privilege to all time, and yet there was no restriction as to time in the first clause of the section. Why not begin the section by saying, "During the sessions of the Legislature, and for fifteen days," &c.

Mr. NORTON presumed that any body in the habit of reading English would say that the provision in the latter clause referred to the whole section. There could be no other meaning made out of it.

Mr. STEUART suggested that the difficulty could be remedied by striking out the words "from arrest, nor shall they be subject to any civil process," and inserting "from any process of law," and substituting the word "and" for the word "nor" before the words "for fifteen."

Mr. LIPPITT accepted the modification.

The question was then taken on the proposed amendment, and it was rejected.

Mr. LIPPITT then moved to strike out the entire section, and insert the following:

SEC. 12. During the session of the Legislature, and for fifteen days next before the commencement and after the termination of each session, members of the Legislature shall, in all cases, except treason, felony, and breach of the peace, be privileged from arrest and from any civil process.

The amendment was rejected, and the section, as reported, was adopted.

The 13th, 14th and 15th sections were then adopted, as reported.

The 16th section being under consideration, as follows:

Any bill may originate in either House of the Legislature; and all bills passed by one House may be amended by the other.

Mr. VERMEULE asked if there was any provision elsewhere in the case of money bills.

Mr. NORTON replied that there was not.

Mr. VERMEULE then moved to amend, by inserting the words, "except a bill for the appropriation of money," after the word "bill."

Mr. LIPPITT thought such a provision was very necessary where one branch was a popular branch, coming directly from the people, and where the other was not; but he could see no necessity for it here.

The CHAIR stated that it was the rule in the British Parliament, as also in the Congress of the United States, that all money bills should originate in the lower House.

Mr. LIPPITT said there was very good reason for it in England. The House of Commons was the popular branch. So, also, in the Congress of the United States. The members of the House of Representatives are the direct representatives of the people; they are the popular branch of Congress. Not so with the Senate. The Senators represent the States; they are the delegates from the States. In both of these cases there is very good reason why money bills should originate in the lower House. But in our case, both Houses are elected directly by the people, and both directly represent the people.

Mr. McCARVER fully concurred in the views of the gentleman from San Francisco.

Mr. VERMEULE said it was true that under the Constitution of California the Senate would be as popular a branch of the Legislature as the Assembly, with the exception that they served for double the length of time; but he presumed it would be admitted that the lower House would be the most numerous branch of the Legislature; and if that House passed the measure first, it would be most likely to receive the approbation of the body which was the least numerous.

Mr. McCarver contended that bills of this kind would have to pass through both Houses; that both emanated directly from the people; and it made no difference in which House such bills originated.

The question was then taken on the proposed amendment, and it was rejected, by ayes 11, noes 16.

The 16th section, as reported, was then adopted.

Sections 17, 18, 19 and 20 were adopted, as reported.

Section 21 being under consideration, as follows:

No person holding any lucrative office under the United States or this State, or any other Power, shall be eligible to the Legislature: *Provided,* That officers in the militia to which there is attached no annual salary, or local officers and postmasters whose compensation does not exceed five hundred dollars per annum, shall not be deemed lucrative.

Mr. Botts said he had an amendment to propose for the first part of the section. He was very well aware that it was very difficult to get an amendment through the House at this time of the night, and he knew the determination of gentlemen generally to support the report of the Committee of the Whole; but he thought there was a very apparent necessity for this amendment. He moved to strike out the first clause, from the word "no" to the word "legislative," inclusive, and insert in lieu thereof, "No person holding any lucrative office under the United States, or any other power, shall be eligible to any civil office of profit under this State." He desired that the provision should be general.

The question was taken, and the amendment was adopted.

Mr. Tefft did not think an office of $500 was lucrative in California. He would be in favor of inserting $1,000.

Mr. Gwin said it might be a lucrative office at some future day.

The 21st section, as reported, was then adopted.

The 22d section being under consideration, as follows:

No person who may hereafter be a holder of public moneys, shall have a seat in either House of the Legislature, or be eligible to any office of trust or profit under this State, until he shall have accounted for and paid into the treasury all sums for which he may be liable.

Mr. Price hoped this section would be rejected. He could see no good reason for retaining it in the Constitution. It was purely a legislative enactment. Our legislative department already extended to the thirty-eight sections. It was descending altogether too much into detail. Not only was it objectionable in that point of view, but to him it seemed inexpedient and improper to adopt it, because it might defeat the wishes and feelings of the people by depriving an individual whom they might choose to elect of a right to hold a seat in the Legislature. It was an unconstitutional provision. It fixed a penalty without any trial; it required no verdict against the accused in any competent court. Who was to be the judge of the liability under this clause? There was no provision for it. Perhaps a very honest man might be disfranchised under it—a man who, by a visitation of God, might be unable to settle his accounts at the proper time. He trusted that the provision would either be rejected or so amended as to meet these objections.

Mr. Lippitt agreed with his colleague, (Mr. Price,) that this was rather a legislative section than a constitutional one; and not only that, but even considered as a legislative provision, it was imperfectly drawn up. The last line says: "all sums for which he may be liable." Who is to determine that liability? The Legislature would necessarily be obliged to point out some means by which that liability should be determined. As the section stands, it is imperfect even as a legislative provision. It is not necessary, so far as I can see, to adopt it in the Constitution. The Legislature certainly is competent to pass laws punishing defaulters.

Mr. Botts had heard a great many Constitutions quoted here. He would now quote the Constitution of Mexico. It provides that no notorious gamblers shall be eligible; but it then goes on to make certain provisions—that he only shall be deemed a notorious gambler who shall be convicted in a court of justice. You ought to say here, he only shall be considered liable who shall be found guilty in a court of justice, and found guilty of embezzlement. That would be felony, and therefore it would not be necessary to insert any provision in regard to it in the Constitution.

Mr. TEFFT said that this matter was fully discussed in Committee of the Whole. He would only notice one or two of the objections urged against it. First, as to the length of the legislative department. Any person who reflected upon the peculiar circumstances and position of this country, and the absolute necessity for clear, full, and definite provisions, which would meet the great variety of circumstances, would see that it was not too long. In the next place these restrictions were made in regard to every officer created under this Constitution. The only valid reason he had heard urged, was that contained in the example cited from the Mexican Constitution by the gentleman from Monterey, but if the gentleman would refer to the defalcations in the old States he would find that his argument did not hold good. He (Mr. Botts) said that the guilt should be proved in a court of justice. But every person knew that certain men were guilty of embezzlement, yet how many of these could be proved guilty in a court of justice? He (Mr. Tefft) looked upon it as a most important provision, and hoped it would be retained in the Constitution.

Mr. McCARVER was astonished that legal gentlemen should urge the necessity of altering this, and allowing the Legislature to act upon it as it thought proper. This provision is to deprive a man of a constitutional privilege. What right has the Legislature to deprive a man of the power to hold office if the people elect him to it, unless it is made a constitutional provision. It is proper and right that no functionary under the State authority, who has not accounted for all the moneys in his hands, should wallow in office, and continue his system of embezzlement.

Mr. BOTTS said it was perfectly competent for the Legislature to provide that any man who was convicted of felony, should not be entitled to be elected to a seat in the Legislature.

Mr. McCARVER saw no evil, but a great deal of propriety in the section as reported. The system of fraud practised by public officers was such as to require this constitutional check.

Mr. SHANNON thought it most singular that there should be this eternal harping upon questions having been discussed in Committee of the Whole. He hoped no considerations of that kind would be allowed to restrict the action of the House. So far as the section was concerned, he regarded it as an encroachment upon the rights and privileges of the Legislature. It was not a matter that properly came within the province of a Convention forming a Constitution. You say here that a man shall be deprived of his rights; that he shall not be eligible to any office when charged with embezzlement; when in another section you declare that no man shall suffer punishment until he has first had the advantage and benefit of a trial by jury, and is convicted by the judgment of his peers. Is this consistent?

Mr. VERMEULE was in favor of disfranchising a thief whether he was an official functionary or private individual; and he was in favor of providing in this Constitution that a thief should not only be ineligible to office, but that he should be put in the penitentiary. He would therefore move to amend the section by substituting therefor, the following:

No person who shall be convicted of the embezzlement or defalcation of the public funds of this State shall ever be eligible to any office of honor, trust, or profit, under this State. And the Legislature shall, as soon as practicable, pass a law providing for the punishment of such embezzlement or defalcation as a felony.

Pending this amendment, the House adjourned to 10 o'clock, A. M., to-morrow.

TUESDAY, OCTOBER 2, 1849.

The Convention met pursuant to adjournment. Prayer by Padre Ramirez. Journal of yesterday read and approved.

Mr. McCarver submitted the following resolutions, viz:

Resolved, As the deliberate opinion of this Convention, that the public domain within the limits of this State in right and justice, belongs to the people of California, and the undisturbed enjoyment thereof ought to be secured in them.

Resolved. That the Legislature of this State, at its first session, be requested to take such steps as they may deem necessary to carry out the object of the foregoing resolution.

Mr. McCarver said: I conceive the object of these resolutions to be of vital importance to the citizens of California; and I hope the House will generally unite with me, at least so far as to take the matter seriously into consideration. These resolutions refer to the rights of the new States to the public domain within their limits. The question has been before the American people, and has been advocated by the people of the West especially, for many years; and the right of new States to the public domain within their borders, has been generally conceded throughout the United States. These resolutions are merely declaratory of the opinions of this Convention that the public domain within the limits of the State of right belongs to the State. It is not designed as a constitutional provision; it is a mere declaration of the people of California through their representatives in this Convention. If the House think proper to make any amendment, it can be done; but the main object I have in view, is that this subject shall be taken into full and favorable consideration. The object of the last resolution is to provide that the Legislature shall instruct our representatives on this subject, which I think would be proper. California has a vast quantity of the public land; and if sold for $1 25 an acre, it would be fifty years before the new State could derive any revenue from it. Here are these vast mineral regions; the policy of the General Government has heretofore been to come in and derive the benefit of the public lands; but I contend that we, as a State, have a right to derive some revenue from them for the support of our State Government. The General Government has not found this system of the sales of the public lands to be profitable; the State has the advantage in this respect. It can classify them and put them down at a moderate price, so that they may be speedily purchased, and a revenue be derived from them. Otherwise they are of no benefit either to the State or to the General Government. These are important considerations, and I hope the resolutions will meet with a favorable reception.

Mr. Botts. I shall vote against these resolutions; and I am compelled to give very briefly my reasons for doing so. As to the principle avowed by the gentleman from Sacramento, (Mr. McCarver,) that the public lands necessarily belong to the State, I am willing to acknowledge it; but I shall vote against any action of this Convention on that subject, simply because I think it is a proper subject of legislative action. I do not think we are here to instruct the Legislature as to what they shall do. It is for the people to give their instructions to the Legislature on this subject; and as one of the people, I am ready at the polls to instruct the representative for whom I may cast my vote, to take all proper measures to advocate, not I will say this right, but this matter of policy. That ground I am ready to take, but I will take it at the polls. I do not think this Convention has any thing to do with the matter at all. I do not object to the principle avowed in the resolutions, but to any action of this House on the subject.

Mr. McCarver. If the House does not think proper to ask the Legislature to do this, the resolutions may be shaped in some other way; but my main object is to assert the right on the part of the people of California, which is asserted by all the Western States. I think the subject comes very properly within this Constitution, in which we declare all our rights.

On motion, the resolutions were referred to the Committee of the Whole.

Mr. McDougal offered the following resolution:

Resolved, That in the opinion of this Convention, the moneys collected as duties on foreign goods in the ports of California after the ratification of the treaty of peace with Mexico, and before the revenue laws of the United States went into operation, of right belong to the people of California.

Mr. Botts. I shall oppose that resolution exactly for the same reason that I opposed the last.

Mr. Sherwood. We have made up our minds on this subject, and can vote without any discussion. I therefore move the previous question.

Mr. Price. The principle of the previous question as I understand it, under the rules of this House, has not been acted upon fully. I believe the rules require that a call for the previous question shall be seconded by a majority.

The Chair. The rule says one-fifth of the members present.

Mr. Wozencraft. I dislike this manner of moving the previous question before the House has considered the subject, and shall therefore vote against the motion.

Mr. Sherwood. I hope there will be a direct vote on this proposition. I want to see every man on record in regard to the right of the people of California to this money.

Mr. Lippitt. I shall state the reason of my vote.

Mr. Gwin. Is it not a rule of the House, that when a resolution is objected to, it shall lie over one day?

The Chair stated that it was, but the previous question was now pending.

Mr. Botts. Is it competent for any member to state the reasons why the previous question should not be put?

The Chair was of opinion that it was not.

Mr. Price. If I have a right, under the rules of the House, to ask that this resolution lie over one day, I make that motion.

Mr. Sherwood. No such motion can be made under a call for the previous question. That question must first be decided, and then the gentleman, if he pleases, can make his motion.

Further discussion took place in regard to the rules.

Mr. Botts asked the yeas and nays on Mr. Sherwood's motion, and they were ordered, and resulted as follows:

Yeas.—Messrs. Aram, Brown, Crosby, Dent, Dimmick, Ellis, Foster, Hanks, Hoppe, Halleck, Hastings, Larkin, Lippincott, McCarver, McDougal, Pedrorena, Pico, Sutter, Snyder, Sherwood, Shannon, Stearns.—22.

Nays.—Messrs. Botts, Carrillo, Covarrubias, De La Guerra, Dominguez, Gilbert, Gwin, Hobson, Hollingsworth, Lippitt, Price, Rodriguez, Reid, Vallejo, Walker, Wozencraft, President.—17.

So the Convention having thus determined that the main question should be put.

The question being on the adoption of the resolution,

Mr. Dent said: It is a principle of our Constitution, that no man can be taxed without his own consent; and as I believe the merchants who paid these duties were taxed by their own consent, I shall vote for the adoption of the resolution.

Mr. Noriego. In my opinion, the money belongs to the people of California; but as I conceive that we are not called upon here to express any opinion on the subject, I shall vote in the negative.

Mr. Larkin. I shall vote in the negative, because I do not believe the money belongs either to the United States or to the people of California. It belongs to the merchants from whom it was illegally collected.

The vote was then taken, as follows:

Yeas.—Messrs. Aram, Brown, Carrillo, Covarrubias, Crosby, Dent, Dimmick, Ellis, Foster, Gilbert, Gwin, Hanks, Hoppe, Halleck, Hastings, Hollingsworth, Lippitt, Lippincott, Moore, McCarver, McDougal, Pedrorena, Price, Pico, Rodriguez, Reid, Sutter, Snyder, Sherwood, Shannon, Stearns, Vallejo, Walker, Wozencraft, President.—35.

Nays.—Messrs. Botts, De La Guerra, Dominguez, Hobson, Larkin.—5.

Mr. Gwin. I voted in the affirmative on this question, and I claim the right to move a reconsideration, and for that motion I shall give my reasons. With regard to the right involved in this question, the only right that can be brought forward is, that the people of California not having had the advantage of a Territorial Government, should not be taxed by the General Government. Why does this resolution stop at the mere assertion of the right? Why does it not go on and say that the Government of the United States having failed to give to California the protection of government, the revenue laws should not have been extended here; that having been extended here, the money collected under them belongs to the people who paid it? If we have any right to the revenues collected here, we have a right to the whole of them. The revenue laws have committed a great wrong upon the people of this country; and, as such, I denounce any proposition emanating from this Convention which justifies any officer here in collecting money without law, and sanctions a law passed by Congress to tax us without giving us the protection of government. When we commence talking on this subject let us meet the whole issue. I say, sir, that the revenue law which passed Congress on the 3d of March last, was an act of usurpation; and I am ready to meet that question in its fullest and broadest sense. To gag members of this House, and force such a resolution through without affording any opportunity of putting it upon its proper footing, is an unprecedented proceeding. How was this money collected? Under the guns, sir, of the ships of the United States. It is a matter of record that the persons who brought in those goods, were notified that if they refused to pay the duty upon them, the guns of the American vessels of war would be brought to bear upon them. Who has this money? It is in the possession of those who collected it. Our simply passing the resolution will do no good. No man contends that this money belongs to the United States; no man will get up in the halls of Congress and say that this money belongs to the Government of the United States. It cannot and will not be contended that money which has been notoriously collected without authority of law, can by an *ex post facto* law of Congress be put into the Treasury of the United States. If it cannot go into the Treasury of the United States, where can it go? The only contest that can exist in regard to this money is between the people of California and the individuals who paid it. That question must go into a court of law. It is a domestic question entirely, and it can never be contended that it belongs to the public treasury. As to the question whether it belongs to the people who paid it or not, that is a matter which we cannot decide. Until we have our government organized here, in the absence of any government extended over us by the General Government, every dollar collected in the custom-house here, should go to the people of California, and not into the Treasury of the Union. But I look upon it as a matter of great importance that we should not make a declaration here, without being prepared to take ground in regard to it. It is a most unprecedented act, to force a resolution through the House in this manner. No person will deny that we have a right to all the money collected under the revenue laws extended over us by Congress.

Mr. Sherwood. If I understand the gentleman right, he is not only in favor of passing this resolution, but something further. But the argument he has made here would induce him, in my opinion, to vote in the negative on this resolution. The resolution says that the money collected after the treaty of peace, and before the passage of the revenue laws, of right belongs to the people of California. The gentleman, if I understand him, says it belongs to the merchants.

Mr. Gwin. I said no such thing. I said it did not belong to the General Government; and that it was a question of law to be decided in the courts, and not by this Convention, whether it belonged to the merchants or to the people.

Mr. Sherwood. I understand the gentleman's argument to be that this money was illegally collected, and ought to be paid back to the merchants. Now, I understand him to say that it is a matter to be decided by law. The Supreme Court of the United States is to decide whether the money was legally collected or not. Do I understand the gentleman as denying that this money ought to be paid back to the merchants?

Mr. Gwin. If the decision of the Supreme Court is in favor of the merchants they will get it.

Mr. Sherwood. I ask the gentleman's opinion.

Mr. Gwin. The gentleman has no right to ask my opinion, and I shall give no opinion on the subject.

Mr. Sherwood. Then the gentleman flinches. I believe it was perfectly proper that this money should be collected as it was; that these goods should not have been admitted without paying duties. We are a portion of the people of the United States. I admit, as the gentleman states, that Congress should have given us a government. But Congress has neglected to give us a government, and this money has been collected, not from the merchants, but from the people. It is a false position that it has been collected from the merchants. The merchant has received back his twenty per cent; it is the people of the State who paid the tax, and to them of right it belongs. If the gentleman desires to introduce a further resolution, that these revenue laws should not have been passed by Congress unless the protection of government had been extended over us also, I perfectly agree with him. I agree, that a revenue law, taking money out of the pockets of the people and putting it into the Treasury of the United States, without establishing any territorial government for our protection, was wrong. But the resolution, so far as it goes, tells the truth. I cannot consent to the doctrine that this money should, upon any pretext, go back to the merchants. They have no right to one cent of it. The people have already paid it to them. The gentleman does not express any opinion upon that point. He leaves it to the Supreme Court. I claim that it belongs to the people, and cannot be taken out of their pockets and paid again into the pockets of the merchants.

Mr. Botts. Mr. President: when Greek meets Greek then comes the tug of war. How glad I am, sir, to see the subtle gentleman from Sacramento floored in his own way by the old stager from the Halls of Congress. He knew how to open the debate when the gate had been shut down upon him. Gag laws will not answer for him; and he has given us all the advantage which he has taken himself. I thank him for it. I shall be in favor of the reconsideration of this question, because I want to see that vote recorded on its proper footing. I thought we had gone far enough in overstepping the proper bounds of a Convention after we had erected ourselves into a Legislature. We have passed legislative enactments enough to make us a legislative body in addition to that of a Convention. And now this proposition amounts to this: that we shall erect ourselves into a court, and if not instruct our judges how they shall decide this question, absolutely decide it for them. Our action here reminds me of a little boy, who at the head of a company, desires to carry the colors, play the drum, and act the part of captain himself. We are a Convention, a Legislature, and now we are a Court. I shall vote against the resolution, Mr. President, because it decides a judicial question, with which we have nothing at all to do. It may be a question for the courts to decide whether this money belongs to the United States, to the merchants who paid the duty, or to the people of California. That is purely a legal question. The gentleman from Sacramento (Mr. Sherwood) is anxious to obtain opinions on the subject. Does he want to know mine? If he does, I can tell him how he will get it. He can get any legal opinion from me by paying the money for it. That is all I have to say about the matter. This Convention has nothing to do with it; any decision made here would be ruled out of a court; it is totally incompetent to decide judicial questions.

Mr. Tefft. I have a few words to say on this matter; but I do not regard it in the same light as the gentleman from Monterey. We are not deciding a judicial question. It is a question of right between the people of California and the

Government of the United States, and we, on the part of the people, express our opinion that this fund belongs to the people. There is a diversity of interests in this House as well as a diversity of opinions as to this fund. We have a perfect right to say that, in our opinion, it belongs to the people. If the opinion is of no force, and not binding upon any party, it can do no harm to express it. It may do good; it may satisfy many who have doubts on their minds. If it can do no harm, and can, by any possibility, do good, it is our duty to express it. I believe this fund to be the property of the State of California.

Mr. Gwin then withdrew his motion for a reconsideration.

Mr. Botts offered the following resolution:

Resolved, That, as in the opinion of this House, the moneys collected on foreign goods in the ports of California, after the ratification of the treaty of peace with Mexico, belongs to the people of California, it ought to be paid over to the Treasurer of the State of California as soon as practicable after he is elected and qualified.

Mr. McCarver. I believe that Congress has the control of this matter, and will give it to the State of California without any action on our part.

Mr. McDougal. When I offered the resolution which has been adopted, it was simply to get an expression of opinion of this body as to the real owners of this money collected in our ports since the treaty of peace, and before the revenue laws went into effect. There was a great deal of doubt on the subject, and it was simply to get the expression of this House that I offered the resolution. The previous question was passed without my knowledge. The gentleman (Mr. Gwin) complains of the gag law. After the vote was taken, my worthy friend (Mr. Gwin) jumps up and moves a reconsideration; makes his stump speech, and then withdraws it without allowing the House to say any thing more. I wonder if that is not a gag law with a vengeance!

Mr. President, I believe this money belongs of right to the people of California; and it was to get the opinion of this House as to that right, that I offered the resolution. After establishing that right, I consider that we can make such a disposition of it as we may deem proper. I shall therefore vote in favor of the resolution of the gentleman from Monterey, (Mr. Botts.)

Mr. Halleck. I was very sorry when I first heard that this subject was introduced into this House. I believe with many members who have spoken on the subject, that it is beyond our province; but when the House had determined to act upon it, and it was brought to me to say whether I thought in justice this money belongs to the people of California or not, I could but say that it does belong to them. But I think this latter resolution is an injudicious one. The first merely expresses an opinion on this question of right; this makes an actual disposition of the fund. I believe that that course, if not forbidden by orders from Washington, will be pursued; if forbidden, this resolution can have no effect, for no one will talk of taking the money by force. It might place the existing civil authority here in a very embarrassing position, either of disobeying the orders from Washington, or the wishes of this House. A communication has been laid before the House, explaining the position in which this fund is. Of what avail can it be to throw embarrassments in the way of the authorities which have this matter in hand?

Mr. Gwin. Do I understand the gentleman to say that he speaks here *ex cathedra*, that if the present acting Executive of California does not receive instructions from the President of the United States or the Secretary of War, forbidding the payment of this money into the treasury of California, that he will pay it into the treasury of California under the order of the new Government?

Mr. Halleck. I merely give it as my individual opinion. I am not authorized to state what will be done, or what will not be done. I stated that I believed from what had already occurred on this matter, that that course would be pursued. I do not know that it will be done the moment this Government goes into operation; nor do I know what instructions will be received from Washington. I know that instructions have been asked for. What will be done, I have no authority to say. I give my opinion based upon the facts which are before the whole House. I move that the original resolution and amendment be laid on the table.

Mr. Botts. I do not doubt at all that the gentleman from Monterey (Mr. Halleck) speaks the opinions of the Executive; and it is also my opinion. I believe that the gentleman at the head of this government now, if he had a seat upon this floor, would vote for this resolution. I believe he thinks so; I believe he will do as a soldier ought to do. He will obey his orders from Washington, be they what they may. I believe he would do what the gentleman from Monterey (Mr. Halleck) would not do. What are we told? We are told that, in the opinion of the gentleman from Monterey, this resolution is unnecessary, because the powers here will do this thing if the authorities of the United States do not order otherwise. We were told a little while ago, about the other resolution: Express your opinion, it may have some influence upon the authorities at Washington. I say then, express your opinion here that this money ought to be turned over to the treasury; it may have some influence upon the authorities at Washington. Mr. President, I thought the feathers would fly when this resolution came up. I am going to insist upon it. I am going to do more. I call for the yeas and nays upon it. I want to see who it is that votes that this money belongs to the people of California, and are not willing to say that if it does it ought to be paid over to the Treasurer. I want to see who will say that this money, belonging to California, ought to be kept in the coffers of the United States.

Mr. Halleck. I renew my motion to lay the resolution on the table.

Mr. Hastings. If I am called upon to say whether I believe this money ought to be paid into the treasury of California, I must say that it ought to be. I have said it is ours; but, sir, if the motion is before the House to lay on the table, I shall sustain that motion. If this question is forced upon us, I am constrained to vote for the resolution; but I think it injudicious to compel the House to vote directly upon that question, and if I can avoid it I will do so. It appears to me that there is no indisposition to turn the money over to us; therefore I prefer not voting upon that subject. It would be liable to the inference that the authorities are unwilling to take that course. I voted for the resolution declaring that the money is ours. I believe there is every disposition to give it to us; and where the authorities are willing to pay the money into the treasury of the State, I am not willing to vote upon a resolution, the principle of which I agree with, but the passage of which by this House would convey the idea that there was not such willingness on the part of the authorities here.

Mr. Wozencraft. For the very same reasons just adduced by the gentleman from Sacramento, (Mr. Hastings,) I shall vote against laying on the table, and for the adoption of the resolution. The concurrence of this House with the presumed future action of the existing civil government, would be as little as we could give. I am willing to vote in concurrence with that presumed action. It will be a further justification, if any is necessary, why this should be done.

Mr. McCarver. I am in favor of laying this matter on the table. I come to my conclusions on somewhat different premises from my colleague. Those who hold this money in custody at present are governed by instructions. I do not wish to place the present Executive of the Territory, or those who have this money in charge, in the embarrassing attitude, either of disobeying their instructions from Washington, or disobeying the will of this Convention. I am decidedly of opinion that the money belongs to the people, as my colleague from Sacramento has expressed himself; and I believe that when the present authorities of California are satisfied that they can obey the wishes of the people without disobeying their instructions, that they will do so. Under these circumstances, I shall sustain the motion to lay on the table.

Mr. Dimmick. I am at a loss to determine in what attitude we are now. I had supposed our legitimate purpose here was to form a Constitution for adoption by the people ; but, sir, I find that at one time we are upon a point of legislation ; at another, we erect ourselves into a court ; and now, from the proceedings before the House, it seems we are but a popular assemblage of the people, passing resolutions appropriate for such an assembly, but not appropriate for a deliberative body like this. What effect can the action of this body have in regard to resolutions of this kind ? It is merely the opinions of men who have come here, on subjects upon which they are retained as lawyers in the defence of certain cases. It is drawing out an opinion here which they are giving as lawyers.

Mr. LIPPITT. In the absence of my friend from Monterey, (Mr. Botts,) I beg leave to make an explanation. The gentleman from Montery expresses no legal opinion whatever. He distinctly declines expressing any.

Mr. DIMMICK. I allude to no particular person. My remarks have reference to more than one. I was speaking of the uselessness of our spending the time of the people here upon questions which do not legitimately belong to us. Our decision can have no legal bearing upon this matter. We have already spent a great deal of time unnecessarily in debating questions of order. Most of the members are anxious to finish the business of the Convention and return to their homes. I trust that this resolution, and all other subjects foreign to our business, will be laid upon the table.

Mr. MOORE. I have merely to say that there has been a great deal of debate here for nothing. No man in the House doubts that the Government of the United States have collected money that they had no right to collect, and that the money is the hands of its officers. I can see no harm in claiming what belongs to the people of California.

The question being on Mr. Halleck's motion to lay the resolution on the table—

Mr. BOTTS called for the yeas and nays.

Mr. ELLIS. In voting for the original resolution, I merely understood it as expressing the opinion of this House that the moneys collected in the ports of California after the treaty of peace, and before the revenue laws were extended here, belongs to the people of California. I do not consider that we have any right to instruct the Executive of this Territory as to what he shall do with that money. I shall therefore vote in favor of laying the resolution on the table.

The question was then taken, and decided in the affirmative, as follows :

YEAS.—Messrs. Aram, Brown, Carillo, Dimmick, Dominguez, Ellis, Hanks, Hill, Hoppe, Halleck, Hastings, Hollingsworth, Lippincott, Pedrorena, Pico, Rodriguez, Reid, Sutter, Snyder, Sherwood, Shannon, Stearns, Walker, Wozencraft—24.

NAYS.—Messrs. Botts, Gilbert, Gwin, Larkin, Lippitt, Moore, Price, President—8.

Mr. SHERWOOD submitted the following resolution, but objection being made to its consideration at this time, it was laid over :

Resolved, That a commission, consisting of John B. Weller and Peter H. Burnett, be appointed by this Convention, whose duty it shall be to prepare a Code of Laws for the government of California, to be submitted to the Legislature for its adoption, at the first session thereof : *provided,* that the whole expenses of said commission, including compensation of commissioners, clerk hire, office rent, stationery, &c., shall not exceed four thousand dollars, and the amount thereof to be fixed at the first session of the Legislature.

On motion of Mr. PRICE, the report of the Select Committee, appointed to receive designs for a " Seal for the State of California," was taken up.

Mr. PRICE submitted the following resolution :

Resolved, That the design for a Seal for the State of California, reported by the Committee, be accepted, and that the explanation be entered upon the journal of this House.

Mr. WOZENCRAFT submitted the following as an amendment to Mr. Price's resolution, and the question being taken thereon, it was rejected :

Resolved, That the Seal be amended by striking out the figures of the gold digger and the bear, and introducing instead bags of gold and bales of merchandise.

Mr. VALLEJO submitted the following, as an amendment to Mr. Price's resolution:

Resolved, That the bear be taken out of the design for the Seal of California; or, if it do remain, that it be represented as made fast by a lazo in the hands of a Vaquero.

On motion, the Convention took a recess until 3, P. M.

AFTERNOON SESSION.

The consideration of the Report of the Select Committee, appointed to receive designs for a Seal for the State of California, was resumed; and, after debate, the question being taken on the resolution of Mr. Vallejo, it was rejected, ayes 16, noes 21.

The question recurring on Mr. Price's resolution, it was adopted. The explanation of the design was ordered to be entered on the journal.

Mr. SHERWOOD moved that the "Seal" just adopted be the "Coat of Arms" of the State of California, and the motion was decided in the affirmative, 21 to 16.

Mr. PRICE submitted the following, which was ordered to lie on the table:

Resolved, That Mr. Caleb Lyon be, and is hereby authorized, to superintend the engraving of the Seal for the State, and to furnish the same in the shortest possible time to the Secretary of this Convention, with the press and all necessary appendages; and that the sum of $1,000 be advanced to Mr. Lyon, in full compensation and payment for the design and seal.

Mr. LA GUERRA submitted a resolution, agreeably to previous notice, to reconsider the vote by which the Convention adopted the first section of Article II, on the "Right of Suffrage," with a view to offer the following, as a substitute:

"Every white male citizen of the United States, and every male citizen of Mexico, (Indians, negroes, and descendants of negroes excepted,) who shall have elected to become a citizen of the United States, under the treaty of peace exchanged and ratified at Queretaro, on the 30th day of May, 1848, shall be entitled to vote at all elections which are now, or may hereafter be authorized by law; but this section shall not be construed to prevent the Legislature from admitting such Indians to the elective franchise as they may in future deem capable thereof."

The resolution was laid over.

On motion, the consideration of the report of the Committee of the Whole on the Legislative Department, was resumed, the question being on Mr. Vermeule's motion to strike out section 22, and insert a substitute therefore.

The motion was decided in the affirmative, yeas 20, nays 12.

Mr. PRICE moved to amend section 23, by inserting at the close thereof, the following:

An accurate statement of the receipts and expenditures of the public money shall be attached to and published with the laws, at every regular session of the Legislature.

The amendment was agreed to, and the section, as amended, adopted.

The amendments of the Committee of the Whole to section 24, were concurred in, and the section, as amended, adopted.

Sections 25, 26, and 27, were adopted as reported by the Committee on the Constitution.

The amendments of the Committee of the Whole to section 28, were concurred in, and the section, as amended, was adopted.

Sections 29 and 30, were adopted as reported by the Committee on the Constitution.

On the question of concurring in the amendment of the Committee of the Whole to section 31, the yeas and nays were ordered, and resulted as follows:

YEAS.—Messrs. Aram, Botts, Brown, Carillo, Covarrubias, Crosby, Dent, De la Guerra, Dominguez, Ellis, Foster, Gilbert, Gwin, Hanks, Hoppe, Hobson, Halleck, Hastings, Jones, Larkin, Lippitt, Pedrorena, Price, Pico, Rodriguez, Reid, Shannon, Stearns, Sansevaine, Wozencraft, President—32.

NAYS.—Messrs. McDougal, Norton, Snyder, Sherwood, Vallejo—5.

The section, as amended, was then adopted by yeas and nays, as follows:

YEAS.—Messrs. Aram, Botts, Brown, Carrillo, Covarrubias, Crosby, Dent, De La Guerra, Dominguez, Ellis, Foster, Gilbert, Gwin, Hanks, Hoppe, Hobson, Halleck, Hastings, Jones, Larkin, Lippitt, Moore, McCarver, Norton, Pico, Rodriguez, Reid, Sherwood, Shannon, Stearns, Sansevaine, Tefft, Wozencraft, President.—34.

NAYS.—Messrs. McDougal, Price, Vallejo—3.

Mr. McDOUGAL submitted the following as an additional section, to come in after section 31:

Any one member of either House shall have liberty to dissent from and protest against any act or resolution which he may think injurious to the public, or any individual or individuals, and have the reason of his dissent entered on the journal.

The question being taken thereon, it was decided in the negative.

The 32d section was adopted as reported by the Committee on the Constitution.

Mr. LIPPITT moved to amend the 33d section by substituting in the last line thereof, the word "manner" for the word "cases."

The question was decided in the negative, and the section adopted as reported.

The 34th section as amended by the Committee of the Whole, being under consideration, as follows:

34. The Legislature shall have no power to pass any act granting any charter for banking purposes; but associations may be formed under general laws for the deposit of gold and silver. But no association shall make, issue, or put in circulation, any bill, check, ticket, certificate, promissory note, or other paper, or the paper of any bank, to circulate as money.

Mr. BOTTS said: I propose to offer a substitute for that section and amendment. I offered it in Committee of the Whole, and I offer it here more for the benefit of posterity than for the present. Nor am I going to make a speech, for I do not think this House at present would listen to Moses on the mountain. The question of currency is one of the most important that we have considered, or that can be considered here. The currency of the country should be taken under the guardiancy of the law; to leave it free to the action of individuals has been found to be attended with the greatest of evils; and to counterfeit the coin of the realm has always been punishable in the highest degree known to the law. Sir, it is one of the greatest objects of government to guard the currency and keep it pure; particularly is it necessary when that currency ceases to be gold and silver coin, and becomes a paper currency. I lay it down as a proposition hardly to be questioned that in every great commercial community, you must necessarily have a paper currency of some sort or other. I will relate to you a circumstance that occurred within my own knowledge, within the last four or five weeks, as illustrative of this fact—the necessity of a paper currency. I received a draft from a gentleman in San Francisco, drawn upon one of the most respectable and staunch houses in Monterey, and I received a note from my correspondent stating that i was extremely desirable to have the money remitted as soon as the draft wa paid. I drew at once; the person upon whom the draft was given said to me here is your money. He presented me with a bag of silver dollars; from tha time to this, I have not had an opportunity of transmitting the money to the gentleman to whom it belongs. If any individual here had issued notes, I should hav been induced to take them. Bank paper, or a circulating medium more portabl than gold or silver, will, in some way or other, get into circulation. You cannc transport gold and silver, especially where you have no railroads and steamboats You must have some substitute for it. The most I ask to do is to give you a goo substitute for it instead of a bad substitute, which you will inevitably have if yo attempt to prohibit the circulation of all kinds of paper. I believe this is the origi of all banks—the absolute necessity of a convenient and portable circulating medium. If you do not provide a good and wholesome currency, in spite of all you restrictions in the Constitution, you will have paper, you must have paper. Th substitute which I propose is this:

It shall be the duty of the Treasurer of the State to receive on deposit gold and silver, either coined or in bullion, and to issue certificates for the same, redeemable on demand at the Treasury in gold or silver coin, under such restrictions and upon such terms as the Legislature may prescribe. But no certificate of deposit shall be given for any sum less than five dollars.

The issuing of bills, checks, or promissory notes, or other paper to circulate as money, shall be taken to be a felony, and shall be punishable as such; and for any criminal or felonious act committed by a corporation, the President and Directors, or other managers, shall be held personally liable.

Another reason is this; you want a mint in California; you cannot have one; you cannot get it. As stated on the floor of Congress, it would take three years to prepare the machinery for a mint; you cannot have one in three years, nor can you have it at all, because the expense of labor required to conduct it would be too great in this country. That labor must be paid at California prices, and the Government of the United States, if it pays for it, will charge it to the individuals whose money it coins; that is the universal rule. To coin your money here will cost you so much more, that you will send your bullion to Philadelphia to be coined there, just as you send your hides to be manufactured where it is done cheapest. I say, then, you will not have a mint here, and I say this is the best substitute that you can devise for a mint. Now, sir, I want to see whether the gentlemen who were talking this morning about gold diggers, are willing now to adopt this to secure the working men from the sharpers and shavers of San Francisco. I disavow the application to any gentleman in this Convention.

Mr. Lippitt. I am so ignorant of this subject that I shall say but one word. It strikes me that the amendment just proposed by my friend from Monterey (Mr. Botts) is open to a constitutional objection. The object of it is, if I understand it, to give us a sort of State bank; to make the State Treasurer cashier of that bank; to allow any individual to go and deposit his bullion or money, and receive from the Treasurer a certificate of deposit. That gives us a much safer and better currency than we can get from irresponsible corporations or individuals; but the great difficulty that I have at present is, that it conflicts with that clause of the Constitution of the United States which prohibits States from emitting bills of credit; and I think the term bills of credit has already received judicial decision; that a bill of credit is anything that amounts to a promise to pay at any time, any paper which can circulate, which is negotiable, merchantable, and entitles the bearer or the present holder to receive the payment of a particular fund. That I believe the Supreme Court has decided to be the meaning of bills of credit in that clause of the Constitution. If so, it strikes me that the amendment proposed as a substitute is open to that objection. I go further; on the ground of expediency I think we had better not have even that kind of paper. I am so totally opposed to any paper currency whatever, that I am even opposed to the section as reported by the Select Committee, even with its amendment, which qualifies it. It appears to me, Mr. President, that the clause in the section which allows the creation, under general laws, of associations for the deposit of gold and silver, brings you at once to the very evil in another shape, which you wish to avoid in the shape of bank notes. Instead of having bank notes you will have certificates of deposit; and I want to know by what constitutional enactments you are going, after creating these certificates, to prevent them from circulating from hand to hand, as much as if they were United States bank bills. I shall, therefore, go against the whole section, as amended by the Committee of the Whole. I think the amendment that I have just referred to is nugatory. The depositor must have something to show for his deposit, and whatever he has must circulate as money.

On motion the House took a recess till half-past 7 P. M.

EVENING SESSION, HALF-PAST 7 O'CLOCK.

At 8 o'clock, the President called the Convention to order, when it was evident that there was not a quorum of members present.

Mr. Gwin moved for a call of the House, with the understanding that some measures should be taken to compel the attendance of the absentees, and inflict some punishment upon them. The Convention had nearly terminated its labors, and it was necessary that members should be punctually in their seats in order to expedite the transaction of business.

The roll was then called, when it was found that there were twenty-five members absent.

On motion of Mr. Gwin, the Sergeant-at-Arms was furnished with a list of the absentees, and directed to bring them into the Hall.

After a brief lapse of time the Sergeant-at-Arms returned with several members.

Mr. Gwin said, that as a quorum of members was then present, he would move that all further proceedings be suspended; which was agreed to.

The Convention then resumed the consideration of the Article on the Legislative Department, the question pending being on the amendment of Mr. Botts.

After some debate on the same grounds taken in Committee of the Whole, the substitute was rejected. The amendment adopted in Committee of the Whole, to the section, was then discussed at length.

Mr. Sherwood opposed the amendment, and maintained the necessity of adopting the original section as reported by the Select Committee. He contended, that in a community such as that of California, it was absolutely necessary to have some circulating medium, and that the certificates of deposite, as provided for by the original resolution, would be used as such, and were absolutely necessary. If the amendment was adopted this would be prevented entirely.

Mr. Gwin was astonished at the gentleman for wheeling round as suddenly as he had, advocating banking principles, and expressing himself in favor of creatng a circulating medium of paper—a paper currency. He thought the gentleman must have received some encouragement from some unknown quarter, to have induced him to go so far. It was very evident that there was a desire creeping into the Convention, to permit the issue and circulation of certificates of deposit, which was a banking system of the very worst character. He was astonished that he (Mr. Sherwood) should get up and say, that the commerce of the country could not be carried on without some such circulating medium, when it was known that the entire system was being rapidly rooted out in the United States. Iowa, New York, and Louisiana, had all done away with the entire banking system in their Constitutions, and he would ask if it was more necessary here than there. To give the Convention an idea what the opinion of one of the best and soundest financiers of the country was upon the subject of the simple issue of certificates of deposit—not from an association or corporate body as a paper currency—he would read the argument of Mr. Walker in favor of establishing a branch mint in the city of New York:

"With a branch mint at New York, the transactions of business would be undisturbed by the operations of the constitutional treasury. It is true, that even with such a branch there the collection of duties in specie would operate as a check, not upon the issues, but upon the over-issues of their banks; a gentle and most useful check, restraining their over-issues, and mitigating if not preventing those revulsions which are sure to ensue when the business of the banks, and as a consequence that of the country, is unduly extended. Credit is useful and most abundant only when it is based upon capital and specie and a legitimate business and commerce. But when it is stretched beyond those limits, it necessarily produces revulsions, disastrous not only to the parties involved, but to the commerce and business of the whole country. It is this fatal tendency to over-issues, and the too great and dangerous extension of their business, which constitute the greatest objection to our banking system; and those banks which are based on a sound capital, and desire to conduct their business advantageously to themselves and to the country, ought to rejoice that such others as would transcend these limits are checked and restrained by the demand for coin created by the specie receiving and specie circulating constitutional treasury. During the year 1847, when more than twenty-four millions of specie were brought into the country, and to a great extent paid in for duties and loans to the government, had this coin gone into the banks, as under the old State bank deposite system to a great extent it must, and have been made the basis of an inflated currency, far exceeding that of 1836, it would have been followed, upon the sudden fall of the price of our breadstuffs and staples, and the turn of exchange and flow of specie out of the country, by a revulsion more disastrous than that of 1837. The fall would have been from a greater inflation to a lower depression, the intensity of the disaster being augmented by the loans and expenses of a foreign war, by the drain of specie to sustain immense armies in foreign countries, by depreciation of government loans and the fall of the government credit. The public credit under that system being inseparably connected with that of the bank as its depositories, the government having no specie and depending upon their paper, its credit must have fallen with that of the banks, as happened in 1837, and during the war of 1812; and loans for specie (which were indispensable) could only have been obtained, as they were during that war, at ruinous discounts amounting to millions of dollars per annum. Instead of these sacrifices, the public credit was maintained throughout the war, and its stocks sold for high premiums instead of ruinous discounts, the total premium realized by me for the government being $545,511 39."

Mr. Botts said that gentlemen must do either one thing or the other—they could not be on both sides of the fence at the same time; they could not ride on two saddles at once. They must either take the clause of the original section as a banking clause or as an anti-banking clause. When the matter came up in Committee of the Whole, the gentleman from Sacramento said there was nothing like banking contemplated in the section—oh, no, nothing at all! Nothing of the kind was intended; it couldn't be so construed; there wasn't a squinting that way. They said, the whole Committee, chairman and all, there wasn't any banking contemplated; the chairman said so—he knew it; he swore to it. He hated all banking, could not bear the very idea; the Committee hated it. He (Mr. Botts) thought the chairman must have forgotten the gentleman from Sacramento. The Committee all had such a holy horror of banking that they interposed but very little objection to the restrictions imposed in the Committee of the Whole; but now gentlemen were compelled to show their hands, the cloven foot appeared. He was glad of it; there was now a chance of a fair fight. Gentlemen were disposed to come out now openly and say that banking was a very good thing, an excellent thing, and never could do the least possible harm in the world. He was afraid the members of the Committee had been imposed upon. The chairman had been imposed upon—they had taken advantage of his credulity. Good, easy soul, he had never dreamed that banking could creep in; and he (Mr. Botts) really felt for him. He was afraid the chairman had not investigated the matter thoroughly. To show how easily the bank monster could come in, he would read the section. The first sentence provided that no corporation should be allowed with banking priviliges. There he was afraid the gentleman had paused; but if he proceeded a little further, he would find that "associations" could be formed—"associations" which issue certificates of deposit.

Mr. Botts then continued his argument in opposition to the original section and in support of the amendment, urging the same points which he had offered in Committee of the Whole.

Mr. Norton said that he had not intended to say any thing upon the subject; but inasmuch as he had been alluded to, he would say a few words. The section as reported from the Select Committee, prohibited the Legislature from chartering corporations for banking purposes, and he had thought that amply sufficient at the time, and he thought so still. He was opposed to the banking system entirely. There were other sections in the report which declared positively that there should be no associations for banking purposes. He opposed the amendment because he then thought the section was strong enough, and he thought so still. It was necessary to permit the issue of certificates of deposit, and no law could be made to prevent it—it was illegal and unconstitutional. It could no more be done than could mercantile transactions be restricted—the issue of promissory notes prevented. Certificates of deposit issued by individuals were already in circulation, and they could not be stopped. If associations were not allowed to issue certificates by law, private individuals would issue them.

Mr. Jones said that he would not have said a word, if it had not have been said that this paper circulating medium could not be restricted—that the people had no right to destroy this great bank humbug. Such an idea was absurd—it could be destroyed; it had been, and he hoped it would be annihilated in California. He was also glad to see the bank men out. In Committee of the Whole, they had evinced a holy horror of banks and of paper as a circulating medium; now they had changed ground and come out boldly, and he would call for the yeas and nays when the question was taken, that they might be recorded in black and white. He would ask what was the object of these associations, if not for banking purposes? Would they do nothing more than receive the deposits and take their four or five per cent. for the purpose of keeping it safe, and counting it over and seeing that it was all right? No! These associations would be composed of small men of small means who required a special endorsement for the Legislature, that they were good and responsible men. They would take the money deposited with them and use it—they would loan it out—they would speculate with it—they would enrich themselves with its use. But suppose their speculations failed, what would become of the poor man, who, after months of hard toil in the mines, had deposited his little earning in the coffers of the association! Why the individual stockholders were held responsible, but unfortunately, he would find that these individuals were not exactly responsible, and that he would lose every thing. By the proposed section, unless taken with the amendment, there was not a single guard against banking. A private individual would be a much more safer reliance than these specially endorsed associations. The capitalist needed no such special act of the Legislature. The clause as proposed by the Committee was in its operation the most general, the most infamous clause that was ever penned; and he hoped no gentleman would come out in its favor who was not ready to say fairly he was in favor of a bank.

Mr. Tefft was in favor of the section as amended, as it was thought that the original section was not sufficiently strong.

Mr. Halleck had voted for the original section because he had supposed it strong enough; but when in Committee of the Whole it was suggested that it was not strong enough, he had himself proposed the amendment which was adopted, and the members of the Select Committee generally had voted for it. He merely made this statement because an imputation had been cast upon the motives of the Select Committee, in reporting a section which would admit banking.

Mr. Lippitt gave notice that in case the Convention rejected the original section and amendment, he should offer a substitute combining the original section and the amendment, rejecting the clause which would admit banks.

Mr. Price was opposed to banks and corporations, or associations with banking privileges, and thought too many restrictions could not be imposed. He spoke at some length in support of the section as amended, and concluded by hoping that the record would be kept free of anything that could be construed into a toleration of banking.

Mr. Wozencraft inquired whether it would be in order to move, before action on the amendment of the Committee of the Whole, an amendment to the original section; and being answered by the President in the negative, gave notice that he should move, after the vote had been taken on the amendment reported by the Committee of the Whole, to strike out of the original section the words "but associations may be formed, under general laws, for the deposit of gold and silver."

Mr. McCarver was in favor of the section as amended.

Mr. Sherwood spoke at some length to show that there was nothing like banking intended, but that it was necessary to have certificates of deposite legalized and permitted to circulate. He concluded by saying that a false issue had been raised, and that an attempt was made to humbug the Convention. That if any such frauds as those anticipated were practised, the perpetrators would be punished for felony.

Mr. Botts said that he had an indistinct recollection of an institution called the United States Bank which broke one day, but he did not recollect that Mr. Nicholas Biddle was arrested for felony, nor did he remember that many of our prisons and penitentiaries were filled with the stockholders and directors of that institution. The gentleman had said that an attempt was made to humbug the Convention; he thought the Convention would not be humbugged.

Mr. Ellis said his opinion was that the Convention was humbugged, and he would therefore move the previous question.

The motion was sustained by the Conventon.

Mr. Gwin asked if he could offer an amendment if the present one was adopted.

The Chair decided that it would not be in order.

Mr. Gwin appealed, but after some little discussion withdrew his appeal.

The amendment of the Committee of the Whole was then adopted as follows:

Yeas.—Messrs. Aram, Botts, Dent, Dimmick, Ellis, Foster, Gilbert, Gwin, Hanks, Hill, Hoppe, Hobson, Halleck, Hollingsworth, Jones, Larkin, Lippitt, Lippincott, Moore, McCarver, Ord, Pedrorena, Price, Reid, Sutter, Snyder, Shannon, Stearns, Tefft, Walker, Wozencraft, President.—32.

Nays.—Messrs. McDougal, Pico, Vallejo.—3.

The question then recurring on the section, as amended—

Mr. Gwin proposed to amend by striking out the section, as amended, and inserting in lieu thereof the following:

The Legislature shall have no power to pass any act granting any charter for banking purposes, and shall prohibit by law any person or persons, association or corporation, from making, issuing, or putting in circulation any bill, check, ticket, certificate, promissory note, or other paper, or the paper of any bank to circulate as money.

The Chair decided that no proposition to amend was in order, as the effect of the previous question had not been exhausted, but would continue in full force until the question had been taken on the section, as amended; when, if the section was rejected, it would be competent for any member to move to introduce any new matter.

Mr. Gwin appealed, contending that he had given notice of his intention to offer it, previous to the call for the previous question. He then proceeded to argue the appeal.

Mr. Shannon rose to a point of order, and called the attention of the President to the 18th rule.

The President called Mr. Shannon to order, and said he was acquainted with the rule.

The Chair explained its position, and decided that the appeal was debateable.

Mr. Gwin called upon Mr. Botts to say whether he had not stated that he would withdraw his amendment to allow him (Mr. Gwin) to offer one; and whether he did not understand the Chair to decide that he could offer it after Mr. Bott's resolution had been acted upon.

Mr. Botts said that he did so understand the decision of the Chair.

The Chair stated that when he gave that decision the previous question had not been demanded; but that since it had been called, Mr. Gwin's amendment was not in order.

Mr. Gwin then withdrew his appeal, but again renewed it.

Mr. Sherwood gave notice that if the motion for reconsideration prevailed he should move as a substitute for the section, the following:

The Legislature shall have no power to pass any act granting any charter for banking purposes.

The President explained that his statement to Mr. Gwin was made before the previous question had been moved and sustained, which act of the Convention had entirely changed the aspect of the proceedings.

The yeas and nays being ordered on the appeal, the decision of the Chair was sustained, by yeas and nays, as follows:

Yeas.—Messrs. Aram, Covarrubias, Dent, Dimmick, Dominguez, Ellis, Hanks, Halleck, Hastings, Larkin, Lippincott, McDougal, Norton, Pedrorena, Pico, Reid, Sutter, Snyder, Sherwood, Shannon, Stearns, Sansevaine, Tefft, Walker, Wozencraft.—25.

Nays.—Messrs. Botts, Brown, Foster, Gilbert, Gwin, Hill, Hoppe, Hollingsworth, Jones, Lippitt, Moore, McCarver, Ord.—13.

The question recurring on the adoption of the section, as amended by the Committee of the Whole, it was, by yeas and nays, decided in the affirmative, as follows:

YEAS.—Messrs. Aram, Brown, Dent, Dominguez, Foster, Gwin, Hanks, Hoppe, Hobson, Halleck, Hollingsworth, Jones, Lippincott, Moore, McCarver, McDougal, Ord, Pedrorena, Price, Reid, Sutter, Snyder, Shannon, Stearns, Sansevaine, Tefft, Walker, President.—28.

NAYS.—Messrs. Botts, Covarrubias, Crosby, Dimmick, Ellis, Gilbert, Hill, Hastings, Larkin, Lippitt, Norton, Pico, Sherwood, Wozencraft.—14.

Mr. GWIN moved a reconsideration of the vote just taken, and gave notice that if reconsidered he would offer, as a substitute for the section, the amendment which he had before proposed.

Mr. BOTTS moved an adjournment, but the question was decided in the negative.

The question being taken on the motion to reconsider, it was, by yeas and nays, decided in the negative, as follows:

YEAS.—Messrs. Botts, Covarrubias, Dimmick, Ellis, Gilbert, Gwin, Hill, Jones, Larkin, Lippitt, Moore, McCarver, Norton, Ord, Price, Pico, Sherwood, Wozencraft.—18.

NAYS.—Messrs. Aram, Brown, Crosby, Dent, Dominguez, Foster, Hanks, Hoppe, Hobson, Halleck, Hastings, Hollingsworth, Lippincott, McDougal, Pedrorena, Reid, Sutter, Snyder, Shannon, Stearns, Sansevaine, Tefft, Walker, President.—24.

The amendments of the Committee of the Whole to the 35th and 36th sections, were concurred in; and those sections were adopted as amended.

The 37th and 38th sections of the report of the Committee on the Constitution were adopted.

The 39th section, reported by the Committee of the Whole, being under consideration—

Mr. NORTON moved to strike out of the section the following words: "effectually prohibit free persons of color from immigrating to and settling in this State, and to."

He contended that this clause was contrary to the provisions of the Constitution. He would read article 4, section 2, of the Constitution of the United States. (Section read.) He would next read the definition of the word "citizen," from Walker's Dictionary. (Definition read.) He would then read the definition of the word "inhabitant." (Definition read.) Under these definitions, all free persons of color were citizens of the place where they dwelt. This was not the first time the question of free negroes had arisen in the formation of a Constitution. It was the same question which had prevented the admission of Missouri into the Union. They had a similar section in the Constitution, and when Congress admitted her, it was with the express condition that she should strike out this clause. The Legislature ultimately agreed to do so; and after two years delay, she was admitted into the Union. He did not wish that any bar to the speedy admission of California into the Union should exist, and therefore moved the amendment.

Mr. JONES opposed the amendment of Mr. Norton as inoperative, also. The section as it would stand if amended, would prohibit owners of slaves from bringing them into the country to set them free. This was already provided for by the section which prohibited involuntary servitude forever. The fear was not that owners of slaves would bring them here to manumit them, but that they would do this in the States and bring them here under bonds of servitude. He should vote for the section as it stood.

Mr. McCARVER moved to amend the amendment of Mr. Norton by striking out the last clause of the same, from the words "as will," to the words "and to," and insert the following:

The Legislature shall, at its first session, pass such laws as will effectually prohibit free persons of color from immigrating to and settling in this State, except such as have been previous to immigration hither, entitled to the right of citizenship in any one of the States of the United States, and to effectually prevent the owners of slaves from bringing them in to this State for the purpose of setting them free.

He contended that this overcame the difficulties which precluded the admission of Missouri into the Union.

Mr. NORTON objected to it as inoperative.

On motion of Mr. SHERWOOD, the Convention adjourned.

WEDNESDAY, OCTOBER 3, 1849.

In Convention. Prayer by the Rev. Mr. Willey. Journal of yesterday read, amended, and approved.

Mr. BOTTS offered a resolution to adjourn *sine die* at ten o'clock, to-morrow morning. He would mention, among other reasons, that the Spanish gentlemen had to labor under great difficulty, in consequence of having no interpreter. He thought the House could get through all the business before it by that time.

The question was taken, and the resolution was rejected.

On motion of Mr. MCCARVER, the House resumed the consideration of the 39th section of 4th article, being the section on the prohibition of free negroes.

Mr. MCCARVER then moved the following amendment to the amendment of Mr. Norton:

The Legislature shall, at its first session, pass such laws as will effectually prohibit free persons of color from immigrating to and settling in the State, and to effectually prevent the owners of slaves from bringing them to this State for the purpose of setting them free: *Provided*, That nothing in this Constitution shall be construed to conflict with the provisions of the first clause of the second section of the fourth article of the Constitution of the United States.

Mr. MCCARVER said: On yesterday evening after I had presented the first clause of the article now under consideration, I was shown the proviso which obviated the objections which had been made to the admission of Missouri, and which enabled her to become a State of the Union. I beg leave to read you the original article as proposed in the Constitution of Missouri, with the proviso which was subsequently attached to it, (see Constitution of Missouri,) which is almost identically the same words contained in the prohibition here.

It has been contended by my friend here, (Mr. Norton,) that negroes are citizens; that a resident is a citizen, and consequently is entitled to all the rights and privileges here enjoyed by citizens of the States generally. Now, we all know how this matter stands there; we are well aware that negroes are not regarded as citizens. The great principle in regard to the right of citizens of the United States, or of any of the States, to make a provision of this kind for their own protection, has been settled by the action of many of the States themselves; and the question as to whether negroes are citizens has been fully determined by the decisions of the Courts of the United States. I hold, sir, that we possess an undeniable right to protect ourselves against this class of population. If they are permitted to come here, they will be a burden to us, and a drain from our treasury, which every citizen of the State will feel in the increased taxation necessary to provide the means of keeping them in order. Now, as to the amendment which the gentleman (Mr. Norton) has offered to the report of the Committee, I wish to show the utter impracticability of it to carry out the object that the friends of this measure have in view. It provides against the introduction of negroes here for the purpose of setting them free; but where are the provisions prohibiting them from being set free by the States and brought here free; it allows men who have slaves in the States to set them at liberty on condition of working for so many years in the mines, and perhaps the negro does not know he is free until he is on his way here. All the evils that we wish to avoid will be left open, if we adopt the amendment of the gentleman from San Francisco; but this proposition which I offer embodies all the principles which caused Missouri to be admitted as a State of the Union. If the gentleman's proposition pass, I shall most unquestionably feel myself bound to place this matter directly before the people, so that they may place it in the Constitution. I feel this to be a solemn duty imposed upon me by the instructions of my constituents. I believe it the most popular measure that can go before the people, and if we cannot pass it here, I wish it to go before them. I ask the yeas and nays upon that subject. I believe it is a provision that is absolutely necessary to the success of this Constitution. It is not proper to leave it to the Legislature, which may vaccilate upon the subject. We want it to go to Congress in the Constitution; they will carefully watch its provisions, and if we here make it the duty of the Legislature to prohibit the emigration of free negroes, we stop the evil because the prohibition is seen upon the face of the Constitution.

Mr. SEMPLE. I merely wish to speak of a few facts in relation to the action of the older States of the Union on the subject of the admission of persons from other States. I was living in Alabama some years ago when a law was passed by the Legislature requiring that all the free negroes who were not residents in the State for a certain number of years antecedent to the law, should have a certain time to leave the State, and in the event of their not leaving by that time, they were liable to be seized upon by any person and sold as slaves. This has been the practice of a number of other States; and although it created in 1820, in Missouri, some difficulty, yet I am decidedly of opinion that since that time it has become universally conceded, that the States have a right to protect themselves from such an evil as that class of population. If, by an act of Congress, we are prohibited from protecting ourselves against free negroes, we will soon be completely overrun by them. Suppose an act was passed in Maryland turning all her negroes free, and setting them upon the shores of Massachusetts, do you suppose the people of Massachusetts would pay their expenses and sustain them. By no means, sir; it would be most unreasonable; the people could not sustain such a population. Massachusetts would have a right to protect herself against such an evil; and it is a right possessed by every State in the Union. The right is general, and the practice has been so frequent that it seems beyond all doubt. One other remark in relation to the effect that it would have in California. I am in favor of introducing this in its most stringent terms, and my reason is this, that I believe our union with the United States would be worse than useless; that it would be a curse to us, instead of a blessing, if we are to admit every class of people, and have no right to protect ourselves by keeping out such as are inimical to our interests. If we are to be restricted in this right, or any rights that naturally belong to us, then Congress might just as well say that those negroes shall come to our ballot boxes. It would be quite as constitutional. The other States, either in their individual or confederate capacity, have no rights over the local affairs of this State. For myself, I would prefer being kept out of the Union to all eternity, rather than acknowledge such a power on the part of Congress, or admit these herds of free negroes. I am as anxious to become one of the bright stars of the glorious Union as any gentleman upon this floor, or in California, or in the United States, but if we are to come in with a curse upon us, from which we can never be redeemed, from which the States of the Union have never been able to redeem themselves, and from which they can never redeem us, I would prefer remaining as we are. Aye, sir, and I would take my rifle and defend that right as freely as I did the flag of the United States when we achieved the right to this Territory.

Mr. JONES. I had supposed that this question was fully understood and argued; and I certainly should not in my present state of health trouble the House with any remarks, were it not that I stand upon this floor as a representative of a community of California which has a right to be heard upon this question—a part of California that is determined to carry this provision into effect. It is a question of immense importance to the mining districts of California; it is those districts that are threatened. It is not to the South, but it is to these mining districts where the money is to be made that these persons will go. There they will enter into competition with and degrade the white labor of the miners; it is they who desire to speak on this floor. It is useless to say that this question has not been discussed in those districts; I, who canvassed my own district, say that it was there discussed, and in all that district I saw but one solitary individual who was not anxious and determined to carry out such a measure, so far as his own vote was concerned. Then, as one of the representatives of the districts most prominently interested, I claim that they shall have the right to vote upon this question, either in the Constitution or as a separate article. It is a question whose importance seems to be but little appreciated by gentlemen from other districts. I know that even in the district of San Francisco, perhaps every vote, if it were put in the Constitution, would be cast against it. Every district is governed by its separate interests. I acknowledge that it is to the interest of gentlemen from San Francisco that they should have their body servants at the lowest possible price. But it is a question of vital importance to the people of the mining districts, not merely affecting their comfort and convenience, but involving the very foundations of their prosperity. They also have a right to have their interests consulted upon this floor. The question whether it would be politic to introduce this population within our borders and deluge this State with them, was most amply debated in Committee of the Whole; and I shall merely recall, as briefly as possible, a few of the arguments there adduced.

The peculiar position of this country, the vast advantage which labor has here over capital, will bring laborers from all parts of the world; and we know that in all parts of the United States there are these free negroes, oppressed, degraded, vilified at home, with no rights, no privileges—despised by society; they will see the advantage that they would have in this country; they will muster their little all and come out here, where they can gain ten or twenty times what they can at home. In the State of New York there are thousands of them—and in all the States of the Union. They will be rushing where labor is profitable. But this is not the greatest danger. The danger is, that the citizens of the Southern States, whose slaves are gaining nothing, will emancipate them under certain contracts of servitude here for one year or more. Slaves are worth from three to four hundred dollars in Mississippi; it would be a very good speculation to bring them here to serve either in the mines, or for a certain time as servants. We know that such is the intention, and that it has been made manifest to members of this House by private letters received from the States. Why should we not have the liberty of guarding against this evil? Sir, in the mining districts of this country we want no such competition. The labor of the white man brought into competition with the labor of the negro is always degraded. There is now a respectable and intelligent class of population in the mines; men of talent and education; men digging there in the pit with the spade and pick, who would be amply competent to sit in these halls. Do you think they would dig with the African? No, sir, they would leave this country first.

There is one view in relation to the constitutionality of this question which I believe has not been taken. There is nothing in my mind clearer than our constitutional right to put this restriction in our Constitution. There is no provision in the Constitution of the United States prohibiting it. It would be absurd; it cannot be. Every State has the right to determine the qualifications of its own citizens. By the Constitution of the United States, article 4, section 2, it is provided that "the citizens of each State shall be entitled to all the privileges and immunities of citizens in the several States."

Now, it is contended by gentlemen on this floor that, because New York, one of the States of the Union, sees fit to invest with the privileges of citizenship a class of citizens who, when that article was introduced into the Constitution of the United States, were not recognized by any of the States, that they are thereby invested with the rights of citizenship in every State in the United States, and that every State is bound to acknowledge them with all the privileges and rights of citizens. That construction would lead to the most absurd of absurdities. Sir, when that article was introduced into the Constitution of the United States, there was not one single State of the Union which endowed the African race with the rights of citizenship. The State of New York was then a slave State, and so was Pennsylvania, and so was New Jersey, and so were nearly all the old thirteen colonies. In no one of them was the negro entitled to the privileges of citizenship. But if that construction be true, it would lead to another absurdity. Suppose, for instance, that the State of Texas should admit negroes to the rights of citizenship; does the gentleman say that New York would not have the right to prohibit the introduction of these negroes, or remove them from her borders? Has Texas the right to declare what New York shall exclude from her boundaries? Shall Texas interfere with New York or Georgia, or any other State? Yet here is exactly a similar case. We, in view of the bad character of a certain population, attempt to exclude them from our borders. Gentlemen say that we cannot, because the Constitution of New York endows them with the privileges of citizenship, and the Constitution of the United States says that the citizens of each State shall enjoy the rights and privileges of the citizens of the several States; in other words, that the Constitution of New York determines the rights of citizenship in California. The article in the Constitution of the United States was designed to protect the citizens of each State in the enjoyment of those fundamental and inherent rights which it guaranties to all citizens of the Union. It was not designed to interfere with the local political regulations of the States. If such was the meaning of it, every State in the Union has violated the Constitution. The State of Iowa says that a man may be a Senator at the age of twenty-one; in New York it is fixed at thirty. The State of Virginia says that no man shall vote unless he is possessed of certain property; in Illinois this is not the case. Can a citizen of any one of these States go into the other States and claim the rights which he possessed in his own State? By no means, sir; such a construction of the Federal Constitution would destroy our entire system of State sovereignty.

I throw out these remarks more in the way of suggestion than any thing else, for I certainly have not had time to enter into this question at length. I will conclude by endeavoring to explain, as far as I remember, the action of Congress in relation to the Missouri question. The Constitution of Missouri contains an absolute and unconditional article. (See Constitution of Missouri.)

That article has been in the Constitution of Missouri from the first to the last. It has never been stricken out. It is true that, being then a very new question, and perhaps very little understood in the halls of Congress, some difficulty was made to this section. What was the consequence? They required the Legislature of Missouri to pass an explanatory act. That was the whole extent and effect of the action of the Missouri Legislature; and upon that action, President Madison issued his proclamation to incorporate Missouri as a State of the Union. The ordinance of the subsequent Convention of the people of the State of Missouri, says nothing whatever upon this subject. They go on and decide about certain propositions of the United States in relation to the public lands; but they carefully abstain from annulling that portion of their Constitution. The Legislature, after a preamble acknowledging its want of power to do any thing for the State of Missouri, goes on and says, that as Congress requires it, we will do it. I am not in favor of putting this clause absolutely in the Constitution, and for this reason; I am afraid that objections will be raised to one article and another article, and putting the objections on various grounds together, that a large vote will be brought to bear against it—some in favor of article one—others opposed to it and in favor of article two. I think it should be submitted to the people in the form of a separate article, so that it can be voted upon separately. If they desire it to be a part of our fundamental law, the Constitution of the United States says that they shall have it, and we grant it to them in this Constitution.

Mr. SNYDER. It is with a great degree of reluctance, Mr. President, that I enter into this discussion; but I feel constrained to make a few remarks. I oppose the introduction of the negro race as a matter of principle, not from any dislike to the race. I know that the state of affairs here will draw a large number of negroes into this country, provided they are not excluded. What are the evils resulting from it? There is one of vast importance and of sufficient magnitude to swallow up all others; the bare contemplation of it for one moment would convince any person. I have already stated that the negro and white man cannot associate in their labors, *particularly in this country*, and the admission of free negroes, I consider a greater injury than the admission of slaves. We want neither free men nor slaves of that particular dye in California. Let us make a calculation about the matter, for the yankees are a calculating nation, and they are making calculations every day on the other side of the snowy ridge. What is a negro worth in Missouri? that is, taking the average value—say $600. Well, what is the clear profit that a slaveholder in Missouri or Kentucky calculates to derive from the labor of each able bodied man per year?—one hundred and sixty dollars. Say two hundred. Then the slave will yield two hundred dollars a year from the time he is sixteen until he is fifty years of age, which will nett the owner $6,800 up to the time that he may be considered useless, to say nothing of sickness or death. Then we see that if the owner makes $6,800 from the labor of each slave, he is doing as much as can be expected in a general way.

Now suppose that the slaveholder will say, "Mose, if you will go with me to California, I will give you your freedom after working there for four years;" or I will give you your freedom now, and have indentures made for the fulfilment of the agreement. Do you suppose, Mr. President, that Mose would object? No, never!

Now what would the slaveholder make by the operation in three years? A working man in the mines by one year's labor will procure $4,000 at least in gold dust, which at the same rate for four years will be $16,000, leaving the handsome sum of $9,200, more by one half than what the negro would have paid by working his whole life in Missouri. And this is accomplished in the short space of four years.

Do you suppose that this will not be tried? It will, sir, and depend upon it, you will find the country flooded with a population of free negroes—the greatest calamity that could befall California. The evil effects of this may not be felt for a number of years, but should the door be left open, the evil will come, sooner or later.

I love ease and enjoyment as much as any man, but do you suppose that I would attempt to sacrifice the interest of California and her people for my own personal convenience? No, sir, no such narrow and contracted views ever actuated me. I go for the people—for all. This is no *buncombe*, for I ask no favors of any person or party. If they don't like me, they can draw their line; I will not encroach upon it. And as far as depending upon political favor, I would sooner depend upon my rifle in the midst of the wilderness.

It can hardly be worth my while to show the utter incapacity of the free negro to be of any general good, as a community of people. Have the intelligent gentlemen of which this Convention is composed, forgotten the negro riot in Philadelphia—in the district of Southwark? Have they forgotten the burning of Pennsylvania Hall at Philadelphia? Where the freest and most unlimited freedom, as my Sacramento friend said, was extended to the dusky gentlemen! Where the picture of bright and rosy morning was hung beside that of deep, black midnight! What a contrast! While the staid old puritan was watching the progress of his favorite scheme of engrafting the snow white rose upon the dark ebony, a cloud was slumbering below the horizon, and in the stillness of night the pent up wrath within its bosom broke forth; the sky was lit up by the fiery elements at work upon the temple of the enthusiast; and in a brief space of time the once magnificent pile was a mass of ruins. Long stood its bare and blackened walls—a warning to those who tamper with the rights and interests of a generous people.

I need not carry you to San Domingo to look upon another picture, to convince you of the evils of a large population of free negroes; you are all aware of the facts of the history of that country. And if not convinced, come with me to Jamaica; what is the condition of those people since their emancipation by the British Government? most miserable in the extreme, and the country ruined. Their condition since they have been freed has proved the utter impossibility of raising them to the standard of a white man.

If the people of the Sacramento district, or even the whole of California, were to oppose me, so long as I thought I was right, and convinced, in my own judgment, of the propriety and justice of my position, I would maintain it, *unless instructed otherwise.*

Mr. Lippitt. There seems to be some division of opinion on the constitutional question involved in this proposition. It is supposed by some that we are denied the right to introduce such a section by the provision of the Constitution of the United States, which declares that the citizens of each State shall enjoy all the privileges and immunities of the citizens of the several States. My opinion is that the proposed section does not conflict with this clause. In addition to the reasons by which I arrive at this conclusion, there is one which I do not think has been adverted to. What was the object of the Federal Constitution? It was to bind together the thirteen colonies in one Union—to give them one interest—so far as that there should be no conflicts or collisions between the sovereign and independent States. It was to prevent war between them, which would inevitably occur if they were distinct republics, in no way connected with each other. The design of this section is evidently to carry out that very object. What is the proper construction to be put upon this clause? "The citizens of each State shall be entitled to all the privileges and immunities of the citizens in the several States."

Certainly this; we must construe it that it was designed to prevent collisions between the States. To illustrate my meaning, I will suppose that the State of New York should pass an act levelled against the citizens of Virginia—an act to prevent the citizens of Virginia from coming into that State, would it not be a violation of this compact between the States? Most certainly; it would be a sort of declaration of war againt the citizens of Virginia, denying them the right to enter that State. But I think that if the State of New York finds it necessary for the peace or comfort or happiness of her citizens, to exclude men of a certain race, without reference to the State that they came from, upon considerations of policy, she certainly has the right of a sovereign and independent State to do so; nor does she in carrying this right into effect, violate this clause of the Constitution. Suppose the case of a religious sect, or a sect under the color of religion, carrying on licentious practices; it is clearly the right of the State of New York to exclude all members of this licentious sect from coming within her borders, no matter of what State or States they may be citizens. The prohibition of this class could not be considered as being an offence against any particular State, as in the case first supposed. It would not be a hostile act towards any one. So much for the constitutional question. In regard to the measure here proposed, I am of opinion, in the first place, that we have the constitutional right to exclude this class of population; and in the next place, I am of opinion that it would be on the whole perhaps better that they should be excluded. The two races cannot mix without degradation to the white race. I think, therefore, looking to the future, and to the happiness and prosperity of this whole people, that it would be better to exclude the African race; and if I were a member of the Legislature, I should vote in favor of that course. But, sir, I am opposed to inserting such a provision in the Constitution. I do not consider it absolutely necessary that it should be here, and the objections to it in our fundamental law are very great. It is clearly in the power of the Legislature coming directly from the people, to make any provision of this kind. If the people desire such a provision, they will so instruct their representatives. They have it in their own hands; and whenever they deem it expedient to enact a law of this kind, they will so instruct their representatives. They can do it if they please, at the first session of the Legislature. In the two or three months intervening, certainly no very great harm can come from the delay. But I shall vote against the section not only on the ground that it is unnecessary, and had better be left to the direct action of the people themselves, but on the ground that it may jeopard the acceptance of this Constitution in Congress. I understand that a provision of this kind did actually delay the admission of Missouri into the

Union in consequence of the non-acceptance of her constitution by Congress on that ground. If there is the slightest danger, therefore, of such a detention by Congress of our admission into the Union as a State, I think it certainly safer and better to leave it out of our Constitution. We may also endanger its acceptance by the people. We know there is a difference of opinion and feeling throughout this Territory among the people upon this subject; and I think it very desirable under all the circumstances, that nothing should appear in this Constitution which might, by possibility, prevent its unanimous approval by the people, and its acceptance in Congress.

Mr. Hastings. I give notice that I will introduce the following amendment at the proper time, as a substitute for the section under consideration:

The Legislature shall pass such laws as may be deemed necessary, either prohibiting the introduction and emigration of free negroes to this State, or prescribing the conditions upon which the introduction and emigrat.on of such persons may be allowed.,

I shall consequently oppose the amendment now before the House, as it stands. I oppose the resolution which I formerly sustained; and I do it, sir, because I have heard further from the people of California; not from my own immediate constituents, but from the people generally. If the people are opposed to this measure, and it is likely to meet with any considerable opposition, it seems to me that the Constitution should not contain any thing of the kind. When I voted before, I had heard no expression of opinion of my constituents in reference to it. The question as to the prohibition of slavery was unanimous, and the vote in this House, prohibiting the introduction of slaves was unanimous; and the vote will be unanimous among the people. But in this case we have nothing direct. The members of the Legislature will come direct from the people, and in the mean time the question will be agitated. Each member will know the feeling of his constituents on this subject. It appears to me, therefore, that the Legislature is the only competent power to act understandingly upon it. If the people desire such laws to be passed, they will pass them. At present we are undecided whether they desire it or not. It may be possible that a majority would prefer that a gentleman emigrating to this country should be allowed to bring with him his man and maid servant. They may entertain different views from this House on the subject, and since we are not in possession of these views we cannot with propriety introduce such a clause. I shall therefore oppose both the amendment and original resolution; and, at the proper time, introduce the substitute which I have just read.

Mr. Steuart. After the resolution which I had the honor to submit in Committee of the Whole, I deem it necessary to make a few remarks explanatory of the vote which I shall give upon this question. A great deal has been said here as to the views entertained upon this subject at home—and especially in the various parts of California. The election which took place in San Francisco was during my absence. I had no opportunity of making my own views known upon the subject, and certainly very little opportunity of knowing the views of my constituents. I say this, because I hold it due to myself, entertaining the opinions that I do, that every representative is bound by the will of his constituents when known to that representative; and, sir, upon a question involving principle, if I could believe that a majority were opposed to it, I would resign rather than, by my vote, carry that question against their will. I can say truly that I concur entirely with the views expressed by the gentleman from San Joaquin (Mr. Jones) and the gentleman from Sacramento (Mr. Hastings) that one universal feeling is entertained in that upper country—especially among those newly arrived, against the introduction of free negroes. I shall therefore vote against the reception of the resolution now presented to the House, and in favor of leaving the whole matter to be acted upon by the Legislature. I differ materially from the views which have been expressed here by gentlemen in regard to the rights given to any persons so named as citizens of the various States. Gentlemen will find that this question has been fully decided in two,

22

at least, of the most important States of the Union, New York and Pennsylvania. The term citizen, in the highest courts of those States, has been fully defined. But I have another reason why I am opposed to the adoption of this section. We ought to leave all matters which can properly be acted upon by the Legislature, free to the people. We are going on continually adding to this instrument when we ought to be cutting it down. Let us imitate the Constitution of the United States. We are here bringing in every thing that we can possibly force into the Constitution as an organic law of the State, when we should be omitting every thing that is not indispensably necessary.

Mr. BOTTS. I should vote for the amendment, because I prefer it to the original resolution, if it would be in my power afterwards to vote against striking out the whole clause. I consider this a mere matter of policy—an evil that is anticipated. I can see that it is much better that we should leave the people to instruct the Legislature to take such steps as they should take, than that we should do it for them. It will be fully competent for the Legislature to take that action. I think instructions to the Legislature come a great deal more appropriately from the people than from us. It is a right that belongs to the people. These distinctions, as to citizenship, exist throughout the Union. It has been done by other Legislatures in the States everywhere. In South Carolina it has been done. In New York distinctions have been made between the citizens of one State and another, and declared to be constitutional. It has been done in the State of Virginia, and, as the gentleman from Saçramento told you before, it has been done in every State of the Union. To the Legislature and to the people I wish to leave it.

Mr. ELLIS. I merely wish to state that I intend to oppose both the amendment and the original resolution; and for this reason, I consider that we have no right to place any restriction of the kind in our Constitution. Some members have stated that they have been instructed by their constituents to advocate such a measure, and procure its adoption in this Constitution, if possible. I can only say that my constituents were perfectly astonished when they heard that such a resolution had been proposed, and that it was actually adopted in Committee of the Whole. Having just returned from San Francisco, I know the state of feeling there. The excitement was general, and the people, without any exception, were decided in their opposition to such a measure. I am of opinion, sir, that in San Francisco, if such a provision is embraced in the Constitution, it will be unanimously rejected. I therefore hope that the whole subject will be left to the Legislature; and in order to prevent further waste of time in discussing it, I call for the previous question.

The question, "Shall the main question be now put?" was then taken, and decided in the negative, by ayes 16, noes 22.

The question being on the substitute proposed by Mr. McCarver—

Mr. HOPPE said: In Committee of the Whole, I was in favor of a clause prohibiting the introduction of free negroes. Since then, upon reflection, I have changed my mind completely upon that subject. Now, to obviate any feeling on the part of the citizens of California against the Constitution, I think it best to vote against any amendment, and finally against the adoption of the section, and to leave it entirely to the Legislature to decide this matter. They will get their authority directly from the people; and if the Constitution, as has been stated, be burdened with articles which should not be there, it may be rejected. The Legislature will be more competent to pass such laws as the mass of the people may desire. I shall therefore vote against the amendment, and finally against the adoption of the article.

The question was then taken on the proposed substitute, and it was rejected, by yeas 9, nays 33, as follows:

YEAS.—Messrs. Brown, Dent, Jones, Lippincott, Moore, McCarver, Shannon, Wozencraft, President.—9.

NAYS.—Messrs. Aram, Botts, Carrillo, Covarrubias, De La Guerra, Dimmick, Dominguez, Ellis, Foster, Gilbert, Gwin, Hanks, Hill, Hoppe, Hobson, Halleck, Hastings, Hollingsworth, Larkin, Lippitt, McDougal, Norton, Ord, Price, Pico, Rodriguez, Reid, Stearns, Sansevaine, Steuart, Tefft, Vallejo, Vermeule—33.

Mr. McDougal said: I now offer the following amendment as a substitute for Mr. Norton's:

The Legislature shall, at its first session, create such laws as will prohibit the introduction into this State, of any negro or mulatto who was previously a slave in any of the United States, or of any other country, and who is brought here under bonds of indenture; and any bond or indenture given and executed in this State, by any negro or mulatto who was previously a slave, shall be void.

I offer this simply for the purpose of stopping the emigration to this country of slaves who will be brought here under these bonds, if we prohibit slavery in this country. Unless we adopt such a restriction, thousands of that class will be brought from the States for the purpose of working in this country under bonds.

Mr. Dent. How is it to be determined whether these persons were formerly slaves or not?

Mr. Botts. I was in hopes that no more amendments would be offered. I think a test vote has been taken as to having any thing upon the subject in the Constitution at all. It is evident that a majority of the House are opposed to introducing any thing of the kind in the Constitution.

Mr. McDougal. My object in offering the amendment was to make it known in the States that there was such a feeling in California. If it is left to the Legislature to create such laws, the laws cannot get to the States in time to prevent the slaveholders from bringing their slaves here. I wish to stop them in time.

Mr. Halleck. I wish to know why a difference should be made between a free negro and one who was formerly a slave. If you want to keep them out, I say keep them all out. I am opposed to any such distinction.

The question was then taken on Mr. McDougal's amendment, and it was rejected.

The question being on the amendment offered by Mr. Norton, to strike out a portion of the section reported—

Mr. Norton said: For the purpose of having a direct vote on the proposition of the Committee of the Whole, I withdraw my amendment.

The question recurring on the adoption of the section as reported by the Committee of the Whole, it was rejected by yeas 8, nays 31, as follows:

Yeas.—Messrs. Carrillo, Dent, Hill, Larkin, McCarver, McDougal, Wozencraft, President—8.

Nays.—Messrs. Aram, Botts, Brown, De La Guerra, Dimmick, Dominguez, Ellis, Foster, Gilbert, Gwin, Hanks, Hoppe, Hobson, Halleck, Hastings, Hollingsworth, Jones, Lippitt, Norton, Ord, Price, Pico, Rodriguez, Reid, Stearns, Sansevaine, Steuart, Tefft, Vallejo, Vermeule, Walker—31.

Mr. Jones. I move a reconsideration of that vote for the purpose of presenting that article separately to the people.

Mr. Botts. I certainly cannot sustain that motion. I hope no such thing will be done. If this question is to be submitted to the people, I know of a dozen questions that could just as well be put in a separate article to the people.

Mr. McCarver. I can see no impropriety in submitting this question to the people, and leaving it to them to decide it. Illinois did it, and what did the people say? A majority of twenty thousand said it should be put in the Constitution. I want the people of California to have all the privileges of the people of Illinois or any other State in the Union.

Mr. Norton. I am opposed to this reconsideration, for the simple reason that I want this whole matter submitted to the Legislature. If the people desire such a clause, they can so instruct their representatives; and then an enactment of the Legislature can be made. That will prevent any discussion of this question in Congress, and the probability of our being thrown out of the Union.

Mr. McCarver. I want to see the yeas and nays upon this question, so that the people may know who was opposed to allowing this question to be submitted to them.

Mr. Botts. I hope the gentleman will go and tell them that I, for one, was opposed to it.

Mr. Vermeule. I think, by the action of the House, we rather reserve the right to the people than deny them that right. I do not, for myself, know the views of the people who sent me here, upon this subject. I think it far better to leave the exercise of that right to them, than make it imperative upon the Legislatnre, at its first session, to pass this law. In regard to the resolution offered as a suggestion to the people to elect their representatives who will pass such laws, the quertion will be before the people, and they can express such views as they please through their representatives.

The question to reconsider was then taken, and it was decided in the negative, by yeas 10, nays 27, as follows:

Yeas.—Messrs. Aram, Brown, Dent, Gilbert, Gwin, Jones, McCarver, McDougal, Wozencraft, President—10.

Nays.—Messrs. Botts, Carrillo, Covarrubias, De La Guerra, Dimmick, Dominguez, Ellis, Foster, Hanks, Hill, Hoppe, Hobscn, Halleck, Hastings, Hollingsworth, Larkin, Lippitt, Norton, Price, Pico, Rodriguez, Stearns, Sansevaine, Steuart, Tefft, Vallejo, Vermeule—27.

Mr. Hastings. I now propose to introduce a new section:

The Legislature shall pass such laws as may be deemed necessary, either prohibiting the introduction and emigration of free negroes to this State, or presenting the conditions upon which the introduction and emigration of such persons may be allowed.

I do not conceive that there has been a test question on this subject. The question involved in this proposition has not come before the House, whether any law shall be passed either prohibiting,or allowing the introduction of free negroes. I hold that it is an entirely new question.

Mr. Botts. I offer the following amendment:

Resolved, That the Legislature shall do just as they please on the subject of free negroes.

At the suggestion of a friend I withdraw it; but I really do hope the time of the House will not be consumed in discussing such propositions as this.

Mr. Hastings. I hope the gentleman will perceive the difference between directing the Legislature to do what they please, and directing them to pass laws which they must pass, according to the provisions of this Constitution, if this amendment is adopted.

Mr. Botts. I shall vote against it on the ground that it amounts to nothing.

The question was then taken, and the amendment of Mr. Hastings was rejected, by yeas 6, nays 27, as follows:

Yeas.—Messrs. Aram, Brown, Hastings, McDougal, Wozencraft, President.—6.

Nays.—Messrs. Botts, Carrillo, Covarrubias, De La Guerra, Dimmick, Dominguez, Ellis, Gilbert, Gwin, Hanks, Hill, Hobson, Halleck, Hollingsworth, Larkin, Lippitt, Norton, Ord, Price, Pico, Rodriguez, Stearns, Sansevaine, Steuart, Tefft, Vallejo, Vermeule.—27.

Mr. Wozencraft. I beg leave, Mr. President, to offer the following resolution, as an additional section. I have not much expectation, from the present condition of the House, that it will be adopted; but I offer it, nevertheless, for the benefit of posterity:

That the Legislature be instructed to enact such laws as shall effectually prevent convicts and paupers from being thrown into the State from abroad.

Mr. Botts. No doubt posterity will be very much incensed at me, but I am opposed to that resolution. It is altogether unnecessary. The Legislature will know what they are about as well as the members of this Convention.

The question was then taken, and the proposed section was rejected.

On motion, Articles III and IV were then ordered to be engrossed for a third reading.

Mr. Norton, from the Committee on the Constitution, made a report, submitting a Preamble to the Constitution, which was read and referred to the Committee of the Whole.

Mr. Gwin submitted a minority report on the same subject, which was similarly disposed of.

Mr. NORIEGO called for the consideration of his motion of yesterday, to reconsider the vote by which the first section of Article II, on the "Right of Suffrage" was adopted; and the question being taken on the proposition to reconsider, it was decided in the affirmative.

The question then recurring on the adoption of the first section, as amended by the Committee of the Whole, Mr. DE LA GUERRA submitted his amendment, as inserted in yesterday's proceedings, but withdrew the same to enable Mr. Botts to move to amend the original section, as amended, by inserting the word "white" before "males," and striking out the words "Indians, Africans, and descendants of Africans;" which amendments of Mr. Botts were adopted.

Mr. DE LA GUERRA then offered, as a further amendment to the section, as amended, the *proviso*, merely, of his amendment, as withdrawn.

Mr. VERMEULE moved to amend Mr. La Guerra's amendment, by striking out the same, and inserting in lieu thereof, the following:

Provided, That nothing herein contained shall be construed to prevent the Legislature, by a two-thirds concurrent vote, from admitting to the right of suffrage Indians, or the descendants of Indians, in such special cases as such a proportion of the legislative body may deem just and proper.

The amendment of Mr. Vermeule was unanimously agreed to, and the section, as amended, was adopted.

On motion, the Article, as amended, was ordered to be engrossed for a third reading.

On motion, the Convention took a recess until 7 o'clock, P. M.

NIGHT SESSION, 7 O'CLOCK, P. M.

On motion of Mr. GWIN, Article V of the Constitution, on the "Executive Department," as reported from the Committee of the Whole, was taken up.

The first section was adopted as reported by the Committee on the Constitution.

Mr. GILBERT moved to amend the second section by striking out all after the word "office" and before the word "and," and inserting therefor, the words "for two years from the first day of January next ensuing his election."

The amendment was rejected, and the section adopted as reported by the Committee on the Constitution.

Mr. WOZENCRAFT moved to insert, as an additional section, after the second section, the following:

A Governor who has served *two consecutive terms*, shall be, and is hereby so declared, *ineligible* for the *third* consecutive term.

The yeas and nays being ordered on this proposed section, it was decided in the negative, as follows:

YEAS.—Messrs. Brown, Crosby, Gwin, Hill, Hoppe, Hobson, Hastings, Moore, Ord, Steuart, Wozencraft.—12.

NAYS.—Messrs. Aram, Botts, Carillo, Dent, Dimmick, Dominguez, Ellis, Gilbert, Hanks, Halleck, Larkin, Lippincott, McCarver, McDougal, Norton, Price, Rodriguez, Sherwood, Shannon, Stearns, Vallejo, Vermuele, Walker, and President.—24.

Section 13 being under consideration, as follows:

The Governor shall have power to grant reprieves, commutations, and pardons, after conviction, for all offences except treason and cases of impeachment, upon such conditions and with such restrictions and limitations as he may think proper, subject to such regulations as may be provided by law relative to the manner of applying for pardons. Upon conviction for treason, he shall have power to suspend the execution of the sentence until the case shall be reported to the Legislature, at its next meeting, when the Legislature shall either pardon or commute the sentence, direct the execution of the sentence, or grant a further reprieve.

He shall communicate to the Legislature at the beginning of every session every case of reprieve, commutation, or pardon granted, stating the name of the convict, the crime of which he was convicted, the sentence and its date, and the date of the commutation, pardon, or reprieve.

Mr. BOTTS said: With the permission of the Chairman of the Committee, I would offer an amendment to this section. No objection being made, I propose to amend by striking from this clause the words "commute and commutations" where they occur, so as to leave to the Governor the pardoning power, and take away from him this more extensive and indefinite one of commutation of sentence. The law fixes one sentence and the Governor is allowed to commute it to another sentence. It has been said, and with a great deal of truth, that the power of reprieve is greater than the power of pardon. I wish to grant to the Governor the power of pardoning alone. That power carries with it a degree of responsibility that will compel him to interfere with the laws of the land only in those extraordinary cases in which such a power ought to be exercised at all; but when you give him the power of reprieve, or the opportunity of interfering with the decisions of your courts and the laws of the land, you give him a power that has no limit. It may be that he would commute from a greater to a lesser punishment; but you make him a judge of the lesser punishment; you put it in his power to decide what shall be the lesser punishment, and he may commute it to what the criminal esteems a greater punishment. There is a case, as I see by the papers, in Ireland, where the rebel and patriot Smith O'Brien is condemned to be hung for disputing the power of the government. The proposition is to commute his sentence to transportation. He denies the power because he knows this, that the public feeling will not permit his execution, but public feeling might possibly sanction his transportation. He finds, sir, that it is the greater power vested in the Crown; he sees what I wish you to see, that this power of commutation is a much greater and larger power than that of pardon. It is one that I am by no means disposed to grant to the Governor of this State. I therefore propose to strike out the words "commute and commutation," in each place in the sentence where they occur.

Mr. SHERWOOD. I think that the power of reprieve should be with the Governor. It may be, under some sudden excitement, that a person may be convicted; afterwards circumstances might be produced and brought before the Governor which would render proper the exercise of a power of reprieve, until further action should be had.

The question was then taken on Mr. Botts' motion, and it was adopted, by yeas 18, nays 15.

The question recurring on the section, as amended, it was adopted.

Sections 14, 15, 16, and 17 were then adopted as reported.

Mr. GILBERT moved to amend the 18th section by striking out the words "a Comptroller."

Mr. PRICE hoped the amendment would not prevail, for it appeared to him that it was one of the most important offices enumerated here. No system of financial accounts could be kept in the State without a Comptroller. He is the proper auditing officer, and is essential to the efficient transaction of the financial business of the State.

The question was then taken on the amendment, and it was rejected.

Sections 18 and 19 were then adopted.

Mr. NORTON moved to amend section 20th, by inserting the word "vote" instead of "ballot," which was agreed to; and the section, as amended, was then adopted.

Section 22 being under consideration, as follows:

22. The Governor may suspend from office the Secretary of State, Comptroller, Treasurer, Surveyor General, and Attorney General, during the recess of the Legislature, whenever it shall appear to him that such officer has in any particular violated his duty, and he shall appoint a competent person to discharge the duties of the office during such suspension, and within ten days after the meeting of the Legislature, or after such suspension; if made during the session, the Governor shall lay before that body his reasons for such suspension, and the Legislature shall determine by joint ballot whether the officer so suspended, shall be removed or restored to office.

Mr. GWIN said: I am not at all satisfied with that section; and I move to strike it out. It is an extraordinary power conferred upon the Governor, and when it was before the Committee, I thought it was too great a power to confer upon the Governor.

Mr. Botts. I like the proposition of the gentleman from San Francisco; and I am authorized to say that this section is so objectionable in its character, that a motion to strike it out would have been made by the chairman of the Committee himself, if it had not came from another quarter. I would like to ask the gentleman one question; I want to know if the case of death, resignation, or inability, is provided for?

Mr. Norton. All vacancies can be filled by the Governor. After having examined this matter, I am satisfied that this section gives too much power to the Governor. The Governor has power to impeach; that will cover the whole ground.

The question was then taken on Mr. Gwin's motion, and the 22d section was stricken out.

Article V was then ordered to be engrossed for a third reading.

On motion of Mr. Norton, Article VI on the Judiciary, was then taken up, and sections 1, 2, and 3, were adopted as reported.

Section 4 being under consideration, as amended, in Committee of the Whole—

The question was taken upon concurring with the Committee in the first amendment, and the amendment of the Committee was concurred in.

The question being on the second amendment—

Mr. Norton said: I am opposed to that amendment. It was very fully discussed on both sides in Committee of the Whole. I hold, sir, that the Supreme Court should have appellate jurisdiction in all cases, and that you cannot, in justice, limit them to any amount whatever. As was said here in Committee of the Whole, there are many cases where the amount in controversy may not exceed $25, where the principal involved is of far greater consequence than though the question involved property to the amount of $20,000. In all cases in the States, I believe the Supreme Court has jurisdiction whatever may be the amount in controversy.

The question was then taken, and the report of the Committee was concurred in; and the section, as amended, was adopted.

Section 6 being under consideration—

Mr. Ord. I move to amend by inserting after the words "issues of," the words "in all cases of law and fact."

I would state the object of this amendment, that the most important issues that would come before the Probate or County Court where issues are carried, would be issues of law. For instance, some question of law might arise as to which party would be entitled to the administration of an estate. That, by the wording of this article, is left to the county judge. I wish to give the jurisdiction to the district judge.

Mr. Norton. I think the difficulty in the way of this course would be much greater than the difficulty which the gentleman apprehends. If issues occur, they cannot be tried in the County Court, but must be sent to the District Court for decision. Issues of importance are very seldom cast in the Probate Courts. The party, if he is not satisfied with the decision of the Probate Court, has a right to appeal, and have his case brought up to the District Court.

The question was then taken on Mr. Ord's amendment, and it was rejected.

The 6th section, as reported, was then adopted.

Sections 7, 8, 9, 10, 11, 12, 13, 14, 15, 16, 17, and 18, were then adopted as reported.

On motion, Article VI was then ordered to be engrossed for a third reading.

On motion, the House then took up Article VII, on the Militia; and the first section, as reported, was adopted.

The House then adjourned.

THURSDAY, OCTOBER 4, 1849.

In Convention. Prayer by the Rev. Antonio Ramirez. Journal of yesterday read, amended, and approved.

Mr. Wozencraft, from the Committee on Printing, made a report, which was read and laid on table.

On motion, the House then resumed the consideration of Article VII on the Militia.

The 2d section being under consideration—

Mr. Norton said he did not think the section read very smoothly. One word was left out—the word "private." He thought the whole section required amendment.

Mr. Lippitt was of opinion that the first section covered the whole ground.

Mr. Steuart moved to strike out the 2d section.

Mr. Dimmick said that the section, as reported, makes it obligatory on the Legislature to provide for an *efficient* discipline. This might be a matter of impossibility for the Legislature. He hoped it would be stricken out.

Mr. Sherwood thought if any discipline at all was necessary, an efficient discipline was. He would be glad to see the first stricken out.

Mr. McCarver moved to strike out the words stating that the Legislature "*may* provide by law;" he thought the Legislature had a right to do it. It did not add any additional force to that right to insert it here.

The question was then taken on the 2d section as reported, and it was stricken out.

Mr. Wozencraft then offered the following as a substitute, which was rejected:

2. The Legislature shall encourage the organization of independent companies, and make suitable provision for the same.

Section 3 being under consideration—

Mr. Vermeule moved to strike out "appointment by the chief of the staff." Under the discretionary power provided under this first section, the Legislature may organize the whole militia into independent volunteer companies. Was it to be supposed that the individuals composing that corps, would surrender the right to elect their own officers?

Mr. Norton and Mr. Dimmick opposed the motion on the ground of the necessity of this provision.

Mr. Lippitt. I am very far from having made up my mind that it would not be better that this system of election of any troops, whether militia or regular, should be abolished entirely. But there is a class of militia officers that must be appointed by a higher authority. Staff officers must be selected by the chiefs of their staffs. The service could not get along without it. Inasmuch, therefore, as a certain class of officers must be appointed, and not elected by the men, I do not see any other way than by retaining the words "appointment by the chief of the staff," in this section. If we were a Legislature forming a law declaring in what way the officers should be elected, it would be very easy for us to say what officers should be elected by the men.

Mr. Vermeule. I am perfectly aware that the right is in the legislative body; but by this provision, the whole militia system would be nugatory.

Mr. McCarver. I am decidedly opposed to anything like taking away from the chiefs of the staffs this power of appointment. I should be glad to see a restriction that the Governor should appoint certain officers. It is dangerous to take away from the militia the right to elect their own officers.

Mr. McDougal. I am certainly in favor of giving the election of a certain portion of the officers—the company officers—to the people; but the appointment of higher officers of the service ought to be given to the Governor or to the head of the corps. We have seen in the recent war with Mexico, to our great regret, where this system has been established—leaving the election of field officers to the men—we have seen that they have appointed officers entirely incompetent to perform the duties. I hope there will be no provision leaving the power to the privates to select their own officers.

Mr. BOTTS. I rise for information, and I am sure there is no member of this House needs it more than I do upon this subject. The study of my life has been to preserve men's lives, and therefore it is that I want to understand more about this matter before I give my vote. Is it proposed, by any alteration in this section, to take from the Legislature that power which it seems to me is here given them to provide how officers of the militia shall be elected; because if it is so, I am in favor of it. There is certainly one proper way or another of electing these officers; and I think it is for us to provide that proper way. I do not pretend to say what it is. Nor is it a sufficient answer that the people can fix it through the Legislature. We do not say that a Governor shall be elected as the people may prescribe. We are here to fix great fundamental principles; we conceive one of these principles to be that he should be elected by the people. Sometimes we have usurped the powers of the Legislature, and here, it seems to me, that we permit the Legislature to usurp our powers. Now, sir, I do not know what a staff officer is. I think it has been said upon this floor that the Governor ought to appoint officers. Certainly that is not the case any where. What, sir, make a colonel by any dictate of a Governor! Such a power does not belong to the President of the United States. And as to this staff officer, he is a staff officer made under the United States Government. They have the largest kind of arrangements there, and one would suppose the best arrangements for purposes of this sort. Under this provision your Legislature may prescribe to the Governor who appoints all officers of whatever grade. It is evident to my mind that this is all wrong.

Mr. SHANNON. The suggestions thrown out by my friend from San Joaquin (Mr. Vermeule) in regard to this matter are correct, and I think it absolutely necessary that we should fix positively what should be the appointing powers of the militia of this State. But, sir, the amendment for striking out the word "appointed" will not meet it; and here the experience of New York foresaw this very matter. If you leave the word as inserted here it will leave the Legislature the power to place the appointment of all the officers of the militia of the State in particular hands, or their election to some other hands, or divide that election and appointment as they see fit. I think we ought to have something here which will positively point out the source from which these officers derive their authority, and the section, as contained in the Constitution of the State of New York, is, I think, the only one, and indicates the only manner in which this can possibly be remedied. It is in the following words:

SEC. 3. Militia officers shall be chosen or appointed, as follows: captains, subalterns, and non-commissioned officers shall be chosen by the written votes of their respective companies; field officers of regiments and separate batallions, by the written votes of the commissioned officers of the respective regiments and separate battalions; brigadier-generals and brigade inspectors by the field officers of their respective brigades; major-generals, brigadier-generals, and commanding officers of the regiments or separate battalions shall appoint the staff officers to their respective divisions, brigades, regiments, or separate battalions.

Mr. VERMEULE then withdrew his original amendment, and offered the following:

SEC. 3. Staff officers shall be appointed, and all other commissioned officers shall be elected, in such manner as the Legislature shall, from time to time direct, and shall be commissioned by the Governor.

Mr. VERMEULE said: With regard to the future militia of the State of California, I think there will be, so far as the volunteer principle is concerned, very few volunteer infantry. The greater portion will be militia of light-horse. I have not the slightest doubt that the members of these corps will be jealous of their right to appoint these inferior officers, and these inferior of their right to appoint the higher officers. I think the amendment which I have submitted will remove every objection.

Mr. McDougal. I hope if the House pass any law upon this subject that they will adopt that of my colleague, (Mr. Shannon,) from the Constitution of New York. I think it is certainly the best and the most complete—particularly as my great grandfather was born in New York.

Mr. Price. I am opposed to adopting any of the amendments presented, and in favor of the original section as it stands. I think the Legislature will be just as competent to regulate the election of militia officers as we are.

Mr. Vermuele. My own objection to this section, as reported, is that it gives to the Legislature the power to deprive the members of volunteer corps from electing their own officers. Perhaps the Legislature may not exercise it, but they will have the power to do it. They have the power to give that right to the members of the company, but they also have the power to deny it to them. In regard to the election of officers in New York, I know it has been a subject of great complaint. I know of more than one instance of officers being forced upon the militia who were entirely incompetent to perform the duties of their offices.

Mr. Hill. I would say to the gentleman that he might give the election to the people at large, throughout the State. I think myself that the proposition of the gentleman from Sacramento (Mr. Shannon) is better than that.

Mr. Ellis. I desire to ascertain how many amendments there are before the House. I wish to move another, if in order.

Mr. Lippitt. I wish to say a word which I think will be a reply to the objections to the section as it stands, that the Legislature may possibly take away from the militia the election even of their company officers. We do not provide in the section against possibility, but probability. I would submit to the Convention whether it is a power that would be at all likely to be exercised to that extent. The people appoint the members of the Legislature; the very militiamen themselves. The militia are the body of the citizens. It is not reasonable to suppose that these members appointed by them will abuse their trust by taking away any power which should be given to them.

Mr. Brown moved the previous question; which was sustained.

The amendment of Mr. Vermuele was then rejected.

The question recurring on Mr. Shannon's amendment, it was also rejected.

The section as reported was then adopted.

The article on the militia was then engrossed for a third reading.

On motion, Article VIII, on State Debts, was taken up and passed, as reported by the Committee of the Whole, and ordered to be engrossed for a third reading.

On motion of Mr. Ellis, Article IX, on Education, was then taken up, and the first section was adopted as reported.

The question then being on agreeing to the amendment of the Committee of the Whole, to the second section—

Mr. Sherwood said: I hope the House will not concur in that amendment of the Committee striking out the proviso. I think it ought to be evident to every one that, after giving all the landed property derived from the Government of the United States for the purpose of education, and also any per centage upon the sales of all the public lands belonging to the United States in this State, besides every other property which the Legislature may from time to time grant, that we should not now tie ourselves up, and deprive ourselves of the power of making use of this overplus when the exigences of the State require it. I think that if the revenue from this land is larger than is necessary at present for school purposes, it will be squandered, unless we make provision for its temporary application to the expenses of the State. It is true we will have many children here; but if you make your fund unwieldy, you offer inducements to men to put their hands in it. I trust the amendment of the Committee will not be adopted.

Mr. Lippitt. I am in favor of striking out the proviso, and of leaving a most munificent fund for the purpose of education, and especially for one reason. The very fact that California offers such a munificent fund for that purpose, will be an inducement to a most valuable class of population to come here—families having children. This inducement will be still stronger when it is known that, by the provisions of this Constitution, the Legislature cannot encroach upon the fund thus set apart for educational purposes. It will probably be sufficient to give us every advantage in the way of education. It will make our population a permanent one. So long as single men only come here without families, it will be a transient population, taking little interest in the progress and prosperity of the country. It is greatly to our interest to have a permanent population, which will identify itself with the prosperity of the State.

Mr. STEUART. I would go as far as any gentleman to provide for the most liberal means of education in California ; but, sir, I cannot consent, looking to the situation of California now, and what it may be in time to come, to tie up all the resources of the State for one special purpose. This country is peculiarly situated. A long time must elapse before landed property can be brought into such a position as will subject it to a sufficient tax for the support of the State Government. I wish to see other means besides loans provided for the support of this Government. If that proviso is stricken out, I shall be in favor of striking out the words "together with all the rest of the unsold lands." Considering the great extent of country over which the placers extend; the extraordinary manner in which nature has scattered her treasures over it ; the roving character of the operations now carried on in these mines, I consider it utterly impracticable for a long time, if not impossible, to parcel out that mining country into lots of convenient size for mining operations. It would take a long series of years, and the highest of surveyors, and an immense amount of capital, to carry out and maintain such regulations. I have drawn up, sir, and intend to offer when permitted, a series of resolutions bringing that subject before Congress. I believe that Congress, with great propriety, without interfering with any system for the collection of revenue for the support of the General Government, without infringing upon any constitutional provision, might very properly give to California that to which she is so justly entitled, and by that means not only show her generosity to the youngest State sprung into existence, but without detriment to the other States, or taking away from them any portion of the public revenue which could be properly divided among them. I read by way of argument, the following proposition, which I shall offer at the proper time:

Resolved, That the Congress of the United States be, and they are hereby respectfully, but earnestly solicited, to give up to the people of California for a series of years, or so long as may be deemed expedient, all the revenue which may be derived from the renting, leasing, or otherwise authorized occupation of the gold placers.

Resolved, That in order to secure to the people of California a certain, immediate, and abundant revenue from the working of the gold mines, it is hereby recommended—

1st. That the Congress of the United States throw open for a given time the whole placer country to the thousands who are pouring in by every ocean port, as well as inland communication, requiring by proper enactments, and under regulations to be established by law, every gold seeker to take out a license or permit for a given and stipulated time, from offices to be established for that purpose at convenient places, and further requiring every such operative, if not a citizen of the United States, to take the oath of allegiance so long as be shall be a resident of California. The fee or charge for such license or permit not to exceed five dollars per month, and the nett proceeds arising therefrom, to be paid into the Treasury of California.

2d. That the Congress of the United States establish an essay office at the most suitable place, where all gold dust intended for exportation shall be assayed, made into ingots or bars, and stamped with its lay or rate of purity, on payment of a charge not to exceed one per cent.; the holder of any such ingot, however, to have the right to have the same coined free of further charge, on presentation at any mint of the United States. The net proceeds or receipts of said office, to be paid into the Treasury of the State of California.

3d. That the Congress of the United States prohibit by law the exportation of gold dust from California, under the penalty of forfeiture of one-third to the informer, and the remaining two-thirds to the State of California.

Resolved, That in the opinion of this Convention, the establishment of a mint at this time in California, would not be made in time to meet the exigencies of the present and immediate wants of California, and would be burdened with far more expense than the establishment of an essay office, while it is believed such stamped ingots would not only answer all the purposes of exchange and currency, but would be a preferrable article of commerce in all countries of the Pacific, China seas, and Indian ocean, if not throughout the whole world.

Resolved, That these resolutions be signed by the President and Secretary of this Convention, and that the Senators and Representatives first elected under the Constitution of the State of California, be requested to lay the same before the Congress of the United States, and urge the adoption of the measures therein proposed.

I propose, if the proviso is stricken out of this article, to amend the section by striking out these words: all after the word "purposes" to the words "the rents," inclusive, and also the word "other" in the succeeding portion of the proviso.

Mr. SHERWOOD. I desire to offer an amendment. To insert after the word "legislative," "by a vote of two-thirds," so that the fund shall never be diverted from school purposes, except by a two-thirds vote of the Legislature.

Mr. McCARVER. I entertain the same views upon this subject that the gentleman from San Francisco (Mr. Lippitt) does, as to the propriety of collecting together for the State of California a large fund for educational purposes; and I never expect to live to see the time when that fund will be too large. As to the gentleman's proposition (Mr. Steuart's) in regard to the public lands, it is a matter well worthy of consideration. I hope it may go before the Committee of the Whole, and there receive proper examination. My colleague from Sacramento, (Mr. Sherwood,) frequently refers to what New York has done. I hope he will not consider it an encroachment, if I refer him to what the State of Iowa has done. She has nobly appropriated all this fund for the purpose of education; and if New York had a fund for education such as Iowa, I have no doubt she would as nobly appropriate for the same purpose. I can see no way in which it can be appropriated more beneficially to California.

Mr. HALLECK. I would say to the gentleman that New York has done what Iowa has done. She stated in her Constitution that that fund should be inviolably appropriated to school purposes. No Legislature can touch it in any manner whatever.

Mr. GWIN. I think it proper to state why I shall vote for striking out the proviso. I originally agreed to its introduction, but my colleague (Mr. Lippitt) gave very sufficient reasons why it should not be introduced. I agree with him that nothing can add so much to the permanent settlement and prosperity of this country as the establishment of a munificent school fund; and this, I trust, will prove to be one of the most munificent school funds known to the world. We have the privilege, whenever we become a State, of taking five hundred thousand acres of land out of any of the public domain within the State. As a matter of course we will select the best from the gold mines. The plan that has been proposed by my colleague, (Mr. Steuart,) requires very great consideration. I shall not allude to it further than this. If you take the five hundred thousand acres appropriated by Congress, it is an uncertain fund, which may fall upon bad land as well as good. Some of them may be covered by private land claims. Hence it is very important for us to have something over and above the school sections and the five per cent. that the gentleman alludes to. If we do this, we shall have to agree not to tax the land sold for five years. In a great many new States the 16th section has created a very small fund, but this plan will produce a splendid fund. I believe the people would rather be taxed than have this fund infringed upon to support the government. If we insert this, it will create a permanent population, and I hope the proviso will be stricken out.

Mr. STEUART. I had intended to have called the attention of the gentleman particularly to the situation of California, and to the absolute necessity that will be imposed upon Congress to adopt some other system of surveying and locating public lands in California, than has hitherto been adopted in the Territories of the United States. I think that every gentleman who has been through any portion of California, and who is at all acquainted with its topographical character, will concur in opinion with me that it would not only take a very long period of time for any number of surveyors to locate and mark the boundaries, as is done in the territories, by townships and sections. In the territory of California there is scarcely a plain, independent of the mountain regions, that is not divided and cut up in various ways by streams and rivers, and a large portion of the year by an immense overlay of water. This, of itself, would render this survey exceedingly onerous, and require a great length of time; and it would be the greatest injustice that could possibly be done to an individual offering to buy these lands not to give him an opportunity of seeing the character of the land that he has to purchase. The Congress of the United States, seeing the necessity of the case, will adopt some particular mode of locating and parcelling out the lands of California. I concur entirely with my colleague from San Francisco, (Mr. Gwin,) in regard to the five hundred thousand acres of land granted by Congress for the purpose of education. But I beg gentlemen to consider for a moment the position in which we are placed, and in their desire to do a great and magnanimous act, to show the whole world a most munificent fund, and make California a mark and model of the times, I hope they will not go so far beyond discretion as to rob themselves of the power of providing the ways and means for the support of the government.

Mr. Semple. I have taken a good deal of interest in this donation as connected with the subject of education. Now, in regard to the proposed amendment, what is it you propose to do? To give them, as the gentleman from San Francisco (Mr. Gwin) observed, a very uncertain and unlimited fund. The State of California will be sufficiently capable of sustaining her political institutions; and whenever you take away any portion of this school fund, or place it within the power of the Legislature, I would feel more secure if two-thirds of all the members were to appropriate it. Will any gentleman pretend to say that there ever has been too large a fund collected in any State for the purpose of education. I desire to record my vote against touching this fund for any other than its legitimate purpose. When gentleman tell us we shall not be able to raise funds to support the civil organization of the government, it is assuming what I deem altogether improbable. I hope, then, that every item mentioned in the proviso will be stricken out. I shall not detain the House upon the subject. I enter my protest against touching a single dollar of that fund.

Mr. McDougal moved a call of the House, but after some conversation, he withdrew the motion.

Mr. Sherwood. I am as fully in favor as the gentleman from Sonoma, (Mr. Semple,) or any other gentleman, of a large school fund, and in favor of appropriating it exclusively to school purposes, except where the necessity of applying any surplus temporarily to the exigencies of the State is so obvious as to be demonstrated by a two-thirds vote of the Legislature. It is under the supposition that this 500,000 acres, or a portion of it, may be located in the mining districts, and that from these lands, so located, a large revenue may be derived, which properly should go to defray the expenses of the government, that I think this proviso should stand. It is proposed by some that the miner, who is guarantied in his rights by the State Government, should pay a poll tax. That is uncertain. We cannot tell what the Legislature may do; whether they may not impose a poll tax as the entire tax, or the rent of a portion of these lands, or they may impose a certain per centage on the amount of gold extracted. It is a matter for future legislation. But I say that if you do collect one or the other of these taxes from the profit which the miner derives from the mines, and then appropriate it to the support of schools, it is making an unequal tax. You would make the whole burden of the expenses of the civil government fall upon the landholders, for you cannot impose a double tax on the people of the mining districts. It is not just or equitable. Our position is different from that of any other country. Miners have a separate occupation; they will form two-thirds, perhaps, of the whole population. It is not to be expected that they are to pay no part of the expenses of the government. They require no capital. A man with his own hands in the mines has a capital worth more to him than in the old States he would have with twenty-five thousand dollars capital. You have given him a capital in the material which makes his labor productive, and of course there must be some return. There is no indisposition on the part of the miner to pay a tax to support the government, but if these lands are so located, we have tied up that whole source of revenue, so that it shall all go for the purposes of education. I am in favor, if these lands are so located, of giving the Legislature the power, by a two-thirds vote, of appropriating a portion of the proceeds to the support of the civil government. The proviso also gives the Legislature power to appropriate the rents from the unsold lands. It may be that we shall have a further grant from Congress; that that grant may cover this mineral region; that it may give to the State all the lands upon the rivers where the mines are worked. In that case the rents should be appropriated to the support of the State government, but as we do not now know whether it will be embraced in the 500,000 acres of land, or bestowed as a separate grant, we should embrace both. We expect more, and I think we shall get more; but we have to ask a body where we have not the power to control, and it is not a matter of certainty that our expectations will be realized.

Mr. Botts. I will not, Mr. President, travel over the ground that has been occupied by gentlemen on the same side with myself. They have, I think, most conclusively shown the value and benefit that California will derive from devoting this munificent fund to educational purposes. What, I would ask you, is the great objection to California, at home—I mean that permanent and valuable sort of emigration that you want here? I believe there is but one, and that is the want of the opportunity of education. And remember this, sir; in bringing here this class of emigration, you bring additional sources of national wealth and national taxation. Muscular labor creates wealth, and wealth affords the subject of taxation; and this provision increases the muscular strength of California, and not only that but the mental strength. Therefore, I say, so far from depriving California of a source of taxation it gives her an additional source. I shall now advert to but a single argument that has been urged upon this floor, and that is in favor of the amendment. And here I wish to enter my objection against the use of the two-thirds vote of the Legislature whenever it can be avoided. I hold, sir, either that this is a proper subject of taxation by this Convention or by the Legislature. If it is proper that the people should act upon it at all through the Legislature, they should be permitted to decide it by the democratic principle of a majority. I think this proposition is the most objectionable of the three. Whom do you propose to leave this matter to? Two-thirds of the Legislature. Where does this new rule come from? The people are willing to enter into a government upon certain conditions, and these conditions they send us here to form, and I believe it will meet with their approbation that one of the conditions upon which they enter shall be that a munificent fund shall be devoted to the subject of education; that they will trammel themselves so far as that is concerned; but, sir, if they do not trammel themselves they will desire, I believe, to remain untrammeled, to decide the question for themselves by a vote of the majority. I object upon general principles to the two-third system, and I do not think this is one of the cases that form an exception to the general rule. The striking out of this proviso occurred upon a motion of my own in Committee of the Whole, and I am proud of it. I am proud that this attempt to enable the Legislature to divert this fund from this purpose was thwarted in Committee of the Whole; and I should be sorry and individually mortified if this House should refuse to sustain the action of the Committee. I wish I had the physical ability to discuss this question properly, but at present I feel so exhausted that I must here conclnde my remarks. The amendment of the gentleman from San Francisco (Mr. Steuart) I do not comprehend, and therefore will not say a word upon it.

Mr. Halleck. I think the question, without any reference to the mineral lands, comes down to this point. Whether we shall allow our Legislature to interfere with the lands set apart for educational purposes. In all the Constitutions, I find that all the States provide that these lands shall not be used for any other purpose.

Shall we do it? I think the proviso should be rejected, and that this fund should be left inviolate. The fund will not be wanted, in all probability, for the support of the government after a few years, and in the meantime, it will most likely be used unless we strike out this proviso; and that is the time we want it most for the purpose of education in California. It is known to the members of this House that families in California now who wish to educate their children, are obliged to send them to the United States, or Chili, or Peru; that there are no schools here suited to the higher branches of education. Let us make as large a fund as we can and as soon as possible. If we include this proviso, that fund will not be appropriated to purposes of education. We know well that there will be a difficulty in supporting the government for two or three years, and there is no doubt that there can be a vote got up in the Legislature to devote this fund to other than the legitimate purpose. We know from what we have seen in this Convention, that if we place at the disposition of the new government, moneys more than sufficient for her support, that it will be used very lavishly. Instead of having an economical government, we will have a most expensive one. Let us be careful not to produce that result. Suppose we place at the disposition of the Legislature these lands, and this fund, and also the civil fund, or what remains of it, and let us, if possible, get a further appropriation from Congress to support this government, what will be the result? Extravagance and bankruptcy. Let us lay the foundation here for an economical government; and if the new government is obliged to support itself by raising a fund out of the pockets of the people, it will be an economical government. They cannot get it from the General Government, or if they do, they will not get any too much. But if you place every source of revenue in the hands of the Legislature, the result will be extravagance and bankruptcy.

Mr. Hoppe. I think our object should be to provide a fund sufficient for the education of every child in California. In order to get that fund, and have it appropriated to its legitimate purpose, it is necessary that we should secure it by constitutional provision. If we, in this Constitution, say that the five hundred thousand acres of land set apart by the Congress of the United States for educational purposes, shall be given, or the interest arising therefrom, for the benefit of common schools, and then place it in the hands of the Legislature to use it for other purposes, I think we go entirely too far, and violate the trust reposed in us. I am decidedly in favor of the report of the Committee of the Whole. The fund that will be created by the donation of that land for school purposes will be a munificent one, and the system that will be established under it, will be such as to draw the attention of every part of the world to this State—especially that intelligent and permanent character of population which will add wealth to our country and stability to our institutions—those who have families, and who contemplate settling in California. The first question that every person in the States who desires emigrating to California with his family asks, is, what provision is there there for schools; he desires that his rising family shall be educated; he looks at the Constitution of California and sees that there is one of the most magnificent school funds that any State can boast of. The inducements for the emigration of this class of population will therefore be very great. Every person will see upon the face of the Constitution that means of education are most liberally provided, and that California is one of the most desirable States in the Union in this respect, as well as in others; that they can have their children as well educated here as in Europe. The consequence will be, that in place of the husband coming here to dig gold for his family and carry it home, he will not leave them, but will bring them here to reside in this country permanently, having assurance that he can have his children, however numerous, educated free of charge. It has been stated here that these school lands might be located in the mines. Now, sir, I do not believe they will. Our Government has always reserved the mineral lands, and we have every reason to believe that the mineral lands of California will also be reserved. But admitting that the five hundred thousand acres of land would be located in the mineral districts, covering the best lands we have, it would create a still greater revenue; and if we have more than we desire for educational purposes, we can loan it to the State for other purposes. But, sir, never let it be put in the hands of the Legislature. You know not who may constitute that Legislature. It may be constituted of men who are regardless of education; who are not sensible of the great advantages that must arise from an enlightened state of society, and the increased wealth and stability that must result from encouraging the emigration of families.

Mr. BOTTS. If I was sure the amendment was not likely to pass, I would not say another word; but I wish to show you that it is wholly inconsistent with the provision—as much so as the proviso itself. In the first part of the section you say that the proceeds of all lands that may be granted by the United States to this State, for the support of schools, &c., shall be inviolably appropriated to that object; and the proviso says that the Legislature may appropriate to other purposes, if the exigencies of the State require it, the revenue derived from these lands. The amendment says that the rents and profits of all unsold lands may be appropriated to other purposes. The original section says: "and also such per centage as may be granted by Congress on the sale of public lands in this State shall be and remain a perpetual fund, the interest of which, *together with all the rents of the unsold lands*, and such other means as the Legislature may provide," &c. Do you not see, sir, that this is a manifest contradiction—that the proviso is as objectionable after it is amended as before. The amendment is entirely inconsistent with the section, as much so as the proviso in its original form.

Mr. GWIN. I am in favor of striking out the whole proviso.

Mr. STEUART. I regret exceedingly that I have been misunderstood in the few remarks that I offered to this House, and I now rise for a word of explanation. I said before that I would go as far as any gentleman on this floor, to extend the benefits of education to the people of California, but I am averse to tying up all the revenues of this State to one special purpose, however praiseworthy that purpose may be in itself. I read, by way of argument, what I shall propose as a source of revenue, which might be provided by the Congress of the United States, for the support of the government. I endeavored to show the difficulty which this State would be under in supporting her government by taxation; and inasmuch as you have created a government which exceeds in expense that of any other State in the Union, from the number of officers, the salaries, &c., an expense which will be a burden to the people of California, I think it very desirable that we should take advantage of every legitimate source of revenue to provide for it. Whatever the views of gentlemen may be upon this subject, from what little examination I have made of the gold region, I am clearly of opinion that in less than two years from this time every bar upon every river now worked will be entirely exhausted; and unless great discoveries should be made, I believe that the gold will not be so inexhaustible as some gentlemen have supposed. The amendment which I proposed was intended to give full sway and scope to the Legislature, to provide by all constitutional means for the support of education; and in amending the proviso as I proposed, I merely wish to be able to bring in the proposition which I had the honor to submit to the House, and which I trust will be granted by Congress. I merely wish to provide that whatever revenue shall be derived from the mineral lands, or lands leased, rented, or given for a specified period, and not, as the gentleman from San Francisco (Mr. Gwin) argued, for an indefinite period, that all lands derived from that special purpose should go for the mitigation of the burden upon your citizens. I believe that the fund to be derived from the appropriation of lands granted by Congress for the support of schools will be ample and sufficient for the purpose of education; but at the same time, if there is anything remaining over and above, I propose that it shall be used to defray the necessary expenses of the government; that the revenue arising from the fund which I propose to create by the granting of these mineral lands for a specified period to the people of California, may be appropriated by the Legislature to the expenses of our State Government. I am perfectly willing to leave it to the Legislature, not having such a distrust of that body as some gentlemen. No man in California will go more zealously for the support of any measure for the purpose of education than myself.

Mr. McDougal. The matter under consideration is one so important that I scarcely believe myself capable of giving any views that will enlighten members of this body. The subject of education is one which has engrossed the minds of our own country and of the world for many years past. When this matter was up in Committee of the Whole, I voted to strike out the proviso which was attached to the original report, and I am still in favor of keeping that proviso out, or any amendment to it. I believe, as it is now reported by the Committee of the Whole, it is the best thing we can adopt. I care not how great that fund may be, it is our duty to appropriate it for the support of common schools. If we make a division of this splendid fund, we give the power to the Legislature to do just what they please with it; they may say that the people will not object to whatever they think proper to do. In some States they have been so profligate that the people have raised a protest against their action. The people, sir, are willing to be taxed for an economical support of government. I do not wish any power of this kind to be given to the Legislature. We can create no fund too large for the purpose of education. I call upon my old bachelor friends to support this if they want wives, for it will introduce families into this country.

Mr. Vermeule. I simply rise for the purpose of making a brief explanation in regard to my vote. The great principle which this provision of your Constitution embodies, seems to be assented to by the great majority of this House; the great advantages, nay, the absolute necessity, of a well based system of school education. It is admitted that such a system is the only platform upon which can be planted the great cause of progressive freedom. There is no necessity for declaiming on this floor with regard to it; all must assent to it. I believe the only difficulty in our way now is, whether the great landed interest of this State shall be devoted to the cause of general education, or whether a part thereof shall be devoted to the necessities of the State. I shall give my vote against the proviso, and in favor of retaining this fund for the cause of education; but lest the majority of the House might decide otherwise, then, notwithstanding the objections made by the gentleman from Monterey (Mr. Botts) to the general application of the two-thirds rule, I certainly shall vote for the retention of that feature in the proviso; that the exigencies when it would be proper to divert a portion of this fund from the purposes of education, should not be decided by a mere log-rolling majority. Such we know to be a frequent thing. If the cause of education be so important; if we, who are all united as to the necessity of such a system here, agree unanimously that it is of incalculable importance, we should certainly put it out of the power of the Legislature to divert it from its legitimate object. I am proud, sir, to be a member of this body when I see the general disposition to stamp upon the Constitution of California this feature which will make it a mark for the admiration of the civilized world, to provide the means of education for the present and for the generations yet to come.

Mr. Steuart desired to amend his amendment by introducing the word "mineral" before the word "lands."

Mr. Botts hoped he would not be allowed to do so, as there would be another debate on this subject.

Mr. Steuart said it was the first time such an act of courtesy had been refused in a parliamentary body.

The question was taken on granting permission to make the amendment, and it was decided in the affiirmative.

The question was taken on Mr. Steuart's amendment, and it was rejected, by yeas 5, nays 31, as follows:

Yeas.—Messrs. Gilbert, Hobson, Sherwood, Steuart, Wozencraft—5.

Nays.—Messrs. Aram, Botts, Brown, Covarrubias, Dimmick, Dominguez, Foster, Gwin, Hanks, Hill, Hoppe, Halleck, Hollingsworth, Larkin, Lippitt, Lippincott, McCarver, McDougal, Norton, Ord, Price, Pico, Reid, Sutter, Snyder, Stearns, Sansevaine, Tefft, Vermeule, Walker, President—31.

The question being next on the amendment of Mr. Sherwood, to insert "by a two-thirds vote"—

Mr. McDougal said: I regard this as one of the most arbitrary, despotic, and anti-republican clauses ever adopted by a free people; and I desire that we shall put down in black and white those who are in favor of such a rule which violates all the rights and principles of an American freeman.

The question was then taken on the amendment, and it was rejected, by yeas 10, nays 27, as follows:

Yeas.—Messrs. Brown, Gilbert, Gwin, Halleck, Lippitt, Norton, Ord, Sherwood, Steuart—10.

Nays.—Messrs. Aram, Botts, Covarrubias, Dimmick, Dominguez, Foster, Hanks, Hill, Hoppe, Hobson, Hastings, Hollingsworth, Larkin, Lippincott, McCarver, McDougal, Price, Reid, Sutter, Snyder, Stearns, Sansevaine, Tefft, Vermeule, Walker, Wozencraft, President.—27.

The question was then taken on striking out the proviso, and it was decided in the affirmative, by yeas 26, nays 10, as follows:

Yeas.—Messrs. Aram, Botts, Brown, Covarrubias, Gwin, Hanks, Hill, Hoppe, Halleck, Hastings, Hollingsworth, Larkin, Lippitt, Lippincott, McCarver, McDougal, Ord, Price, Reid, Sutter, Stearns, Sansevaine, Tefft, Vermeule, Walker, President—26.

Nays.—Messrs. Dimmick, Dominguez, Foster, Gilbert, Hobson, Norton, Pico, Sherwood, Wozencraft.—14.

The 2d section, as amended by the Committee of the Whole, was then adopted.

On motion, the House took a recess of one hour.

AFTERNOON SESSION, HALF-PAST 3 O'CLOCK.

On motion, the consideration of Article IX, on Education, was resumed, and sections three and four adopted as reported.

The article was then, on motion, ordered to be passed for a third reading.

On motion, Article X, on Amendments to the Constitution, was then taken up.

Mr. Jones moved to amend the first section by striking out the words "two-thirds" and inserting "a majority." For the reasons of this motion, he would refer members present to the action of the Baltimore Convention in 1844.

Mr. Lippitt. I think this is a very proper check against hasty action. The two-thirds rule is very necessary on such a subject as this.

Mr. McDougal. There certainly can be no premature action. If a majority of the Legislature propose any amendment to the Constitution, it has to be submitted to the people. It is three months before the people. The people come up to the polls after that consideration, and vote directly on the amendment.

Mr. Norton. I am opposed to striking out the words "two-thirds." In amending the Constitution every step should be well guarded, and nothing should be done hastily, or under the fluctuating influences of political excitement.

Mr. Jones. I hope I will be allowed to say a few words. I think there are sufficient guards upon the people in this section, without the adoption of the two-third rule. An amendment is to be proposed and passed through two separate Legislatures, and must meet with the assent of a majority of both Houses; not of a quorum present, but of the members elected. It must then be published three months next previous to the election of the next Legislature. That Legislature must pass again upon this same proposition, and it must again receive the assent of two-thirds of the Legislature. Now, sir, I do not think this proposition is democratic, I do not think it is republican. I think the true democratic rule is that the majority shall rule. In all States of the Union you will find no restrictions so stringent as these, for not only do you have two separate Legislatures to pass upon it, but the last Legislature must pass it by a two-thirds vote. If gentlemen preach that up as democratic or republican doctrine, I must say I do not know what the doctrine is. If they preach it up as a specimen of liberal principles, I know not what liberality is. Sir, the majority, under proper restrictions, should have the right to rule. If the majority are dissatisfied with their Constitution, let them, as they may deem fit, alter and amend it. Put your restrictions of two legislatures; let them be chosen from the bosom of the people, and let the majority of the people three separate times, and three separate years, decide that it can be done; but do not say that one-third of a political party shall tell the majority what they shall and shall not do.

Mr. Crosby. I hope the amendment will prevail, for if the majority can first create a Constitution, the same majority most certainly should have the right to change it.

Mr. Lippitt. That is just the difference between the Constitution, or fundamental law of the land, and an ordinary law of the Legislature. Let the will of a majority of the people always make and unmake laws; they are changing from year to year; but do not let these changes—these transient changes, which are brought about by politicians for party purposes, party majorities in favor of a particular measure—affect your fundamental law. It would greatly militate against the permanent prosperity of the people. The laws of the State can be repealed at any time if they work badly; but if an alteration made in your Constitution is found to work badly, it will take years to correct it. Whether it be democratic, or republican, or otherwise, I would not leave it to the mere transient majority of the people; I would not leave the future interests of the whole people dependent upon that majority.

Mr. Price. I hope this amendment will prevail. I can see no reason why we should allow two-thirds of the Legislature to say whether the people should alter or amend their Constitution. By the section as drawn up, we refer back a resolution which is passed by one Legislature, and after a publication of that resolution three months before the meeting of a new Legislature, we require a two-thirds vote to pass it, and after it is passed the Constitution is not even then amended, but the amendment is at last referred to the people. This very clause is copied nearly verbatim from the proviso of the Constitution of New York, which requires only a majority.

Mr. Halleck. It is copied verbatim from the Constitution of Michigan.

Mr. Price. But New York is as good authority as Michigan, or Virginia, or any other State.

Mr. Botts. I should not say a word on this subject, but if I am compelled to vote I want to talk about it till I comprehend it. If I understand the proposition it is to enable the majority of the people to alter the Constitution. Yes, sir; I am now in earnest; it is to permit the majority of the people to make a Constitution. Who is making this Constitution? Two-thirds? Who is going to tell the majority of the people that they shall not make a Constitution, when it is a majority here that is speaking? Can it be done by any other than the majority of the people themselves? Shall the majority making a Constitution say that another majority shall not make a Constitution? The whole question is, who shall make Constitutions when Constitutions are to be made, a majority or a minority? I think one of the greatest errors of the day is the popular one expressed by my friend from San Francisco (Mr. Lippitt) that Constitutions are not to be lightly altered. Sir, the progress of improvement has altered every where, and in nothing more than political liberty; and nothing is more desirable than that the people should have the liberty to amend their written Constitution according to the progressive improvement under the science of political liberty. I wish, sir, that more of these restraints were taken off; that the people may have the facility of putting it down in black and white, and making it a law of the land. I put this case to you, for the sake of convenience. I will suppose that the inhabitants of the State consist of no more than one hundred thousand. You have a Constitution that was made by thirty thousand, and seventy thousand desire to repeal it—to unmake it and make another Constitution, because of the new lights they have received. Do you tell me that thirty thousand can do it and seventy thousand cannot? Is the voice of thirty thousand to be omnipotent? When government is to be started it is to be done by thirty thousand, in opposition to the will of seventy thousand! and yet that is the doctrine. No man will go further than I will, in adopting a Constitution, in narrowing the bounds and limits of the government. I believe the world is over-governed; and I want to see the limits of government restrained within the narrowest compass, but as to what that Constitution shall be, I look alone to the voice of the majority. And why, sir? Because I am elected either by the voice of the minority or majority. The difference between me and my friend from San Francisco is, that he looks to the minority and I to the majority. There is but one way to determine in all republican countries what shall be the fundamental law of the country, and that is by the voice of a majority of the people. You say that all men shall be entitled to equal political freedom; you have said that one hundred thousand men in California shall be entitled to vote, and yet they cannot vote upon constitutional law; they may make municipal laws, but the great principles of constitutional law, when it is once made, it is at the nod and beck of the minority; and the majority can never alter or amend it, or have their political rights, except by consent of the minority. Now, sir, who proposes such a monstrous doctrine as this?

What is there about this Constitution that does not pertain to the next one or any one. I leave it to my friend (Mr. Lippitt) to explain away the doctrine which he maintains, but which I am sure he does not mean to support; and yet I will urge upon him that it comes to this, and to nothing else; that the whole question of remodeling your Constitution is the question of making a Constitution. It is not different from the original making of a Constitution—exactly as we are doing now. I shall vote in favor of the amendment.

Mr. Norton. I am not going to back out, notwithstanding the denunciations of my friend from Monterey, (Mr. Botts.) Let us see how this will operate. A majority of the members of both Houses say that, in their opinion, there shall be certain amendments to the Constitution—that it shall be revised in a certain way. It is done by yeas and nays entered upon the journal of each House. After that, and in three months previous to the next election, these amendments are severally submitted to the people, at the very same time that the people themselves elect another Legislature. Within that whole three months they have an opportunity of examining these amendments, and ascertaining for themselves whether they desire such amendments or not. If they do, at the same time that they pass upon these amendments they elect members to the Legislature, and of necessity instruct them to vote for these amendments; and can they not, if they choose, get a majority of two-thirds in the Legislature for the purpose of proposing these amendments, and then submitting them to the people again by instructions to their representatives? Sir, in the case of a political party in power, they have the majority in the Legislature, and amendments or revision of the Constitution might be made for political purposes. That is what it is necessary to guard against; that no amendment shall be made for merely political purposes; no amendment unless the people themselves say there is an absolute necessity for it. The gentleman says there is too much law in the world. I agree with him. The great evil of the day is too much legislation and too much constitution making. For this reason, after you have once adopted a Constitution, submitted it to the people, and it is ratified by them, you should abide by that Constitution. If it is necessary to amend it you will find two-thirds of the Legislature and the people ready and willing to make these amendments, but do not give to a mere political majority the right to make them. Let it be done by a sufficient number of the people to know what they are acting upon, and who will not make light and trivial amendments. When it is done, let it be done by such a majority of the people and the Legislature as will give full force to their action.

Mr. Tefft. Suicidal as the gentleman from Monterey (Mr. Botts) thinks this course, I think we will adopt it. I am as much in favor of referring all power to the people as any gentleman present, but this constant cry of the people too often assumes the aspect of demagogueism. Let political excitement run wild here as it has in every State of the Union, then you will find the absolute necessity of the two-third rule. It is of essential importance, that in amending the fundamental law of the land, men should return to their sober second thought—to that great balancing power by which questions so deeply concerning the interests of the whole people are decided. It has always been so in matters of so much importance, involving the welfare and prosperity of the State. And I think it is altogether unfounded to presume, after an expression of the will of the people, that a majority of two-thirds of both Houses of the Legislature will dare to say these amendments shall not be made. There are times, sir, when political excitement makes it absolutely necessary that the people should be restrained, and for the purpose of having this regulating check upon political parties, I shall certainly vote for the two-thirds rule.

Mr. Botts. I speak in answer to the first gentleman from San Francisco, (Mr. Lippitt.) I want to know, Mr. President, what the Legislature is after the people have said that it shall amend or re-make the Constitution, but a constant Convention. This way of amending the Constitution, avoids the usual mode of calling a Convention, and directs the Legislature by the determination of the people to have the Constitution altered. It becomes a Convention subject to the declared will of the people. A Convention is an assemblage of persons chosen to alter the Constitution; and the vote of the people asks that the Legislature shall be that Convention. The whole question then, comes to this: shall the Convention so formed, alter the Constitution by a vote of a majority or two-thirds? Now, if that question were put in its bare and naked form, who is there upon this floor who would vote for the two-thirds rule? If you provide, by the calling of this Convention to make a Constitution, who would propose that that Constitution should be made by a vote of two-thirds of the House only? Who would vote for it? And is not this Legislature a Convention to all intents and purposes? Mr. President, I charge, then, this thing; that your Constitution does not provide for the calling of a Convention in accordance with the will of the people.

Mr. Norton. The following section provides for it.

Mr. Botts. Very well. I do not care what the next section provides. This section provides that, under certain circumstances, the Legislature becomes a Convention; that is to say, it provides that the Constitution shall be passed upon by the members of the Legislature; and what reason is there for declaring that, in that Convention or Legislature, the Constitution shall not be altered except by a vote of two thirds, and in the next section, by a majority. Do you provide in the next section that a vote of two-thirds shall make a Constitution? The gentleman from San Francisco says if a majority of the people are in favor of it, they can always elect a Legislature to amend it. One hundred thousand here are in favor of curtailing the power of the Legislature. How are less than two-thirds of the people to instruct two-thirds of their representatives? If the gentleman had argued thus: that whenever two-thirds of the people are in favor of a thing, it would be proper that they should be able to instruct two-thirds of the Legislature, I would grant it; but less than two-thirds cannot instruct two-thirds of the Legislature. We have heard a great deal here about the necessity of restraining the will of the people during very exciting times. Who is to restrain the people? Angels from Heaven, coming down here free from all political excitement, or that body in which there is, of all others, the greatest political huckstering? Does the gentleman from San Luis Obispo, (Mr. Tefft,) suppose that a man who comes from the body of the people, is from the fact of being made a legislator, free from all the impurities of clay; does he not know that that man is still one of the people, even more unleavened than the mass from which he came, and that he is the last man on the face of the earth to restrain the improper action of the people. Now, Mr. President, as to republican doctrine. I thought the republican doctrine was, that the people, like the king, could do no wrong. Certainly when compared with a petty Legislature, they can do no wrong. The master can do no wrong in the eyes of the servant—that is my doctrine, and I have always maintained that principle, not that I mean to say that all mankind may not, even if they were unanimous, do wrong, but politically, the republican doctrine of the present day that the people can do no wrong; that is, that they are more right than individuals; that the majority are more likely to be right than the minority; and that it is not for these servants of the people, those who have sworn to obey them, to talk about putting a bridle in the mouths of their masters.

Mr. Lippitt. As I have been personally appealed to, I hope the House will not object to my saying a word or two in reply to the gentleman from Monterey. He says that under this first section the Legislature becomes a Convention, with delegated powers to adopt a Constitution. I maintain that they do not come there receiving instructions to form a Constitution; they come to pass laws; their constituents send them there to pass laws upon a variety of subjects. But when the people elect delegates to a Convention to form a Constitution, they elect them for that purpose and no other. The members coming from the people for that purpose are supposed to know what sort of provisions this people want incorporated in this Constitution, and what sort excluded from it; but where a particular amendment is given to a Legislature, that Legislature have other matters that conflict with the will of their constituents. Many of them must be supposed to be sent there with more direct reference to the laws that they are to pass, than with reference to the particular amendment proposed to the Constitution. The gentleman's doctrine would abrogate all distinctions whatever between the original law of the land and the mere statutes, which can be repealed from one year to another. Such a doctrine will not do. It gives, in all cases, to the transient majority of the people, the power to unmake or to make a Constitution. What more does he give to the Legislature? In other words, the same power which is to make an ordinary law is to make a Constitution. Sir, it is the wisdom of the people of every one of the States that has incorporated restrictions and checks of this kind, against the will of a temporary majority of the people. In our own Constitution, in the Executive department, this very Convention has incorporated the veto power. What is this but a restricting power upon the will of the people? If a bill is passed by a majority of both Houses of the Legislature, a majority which must be supposed to represent the will of the majority, we allow the Governor to come in with a veto to check that expression, and require a two-thirds vote to make it a law. Checks of this kind are introduced into the Constitutions of all the States. The whole American people, whether they be republican or monarchical, have sanctioned this provision. Take up any Constitution you please, and you will find these checks upon the will of the people. I ask whether we, the delegates in this Convention, have not, in representing the people, a right to say that we, the people, will impose upon the temporary will of the majority such and such restraints with respect to our Constitution, as we are doing with respect to our laws. This veto power is a restraint upon the law-making power—a power far more easy to restrain than the Constitution-making power. The majority of the people when they have met together, either by themselves or representatives, to make a Constitution, have always introduced such checks upon the Constitution-making and Constitution-altering power, as to put it upon a more permanent basis than mere laws enacted by the Legislature. The people want some security that their organic law shall not be left at the mercy of the dominant political party of the State. I take it, sir, that at all times a bare majority of the people are on one side or the other of the great political parties of the State; we know that the majority of each party is constantly changing from year to year. Every majority of the people when they come together to make a Constitution, know and consider that they themselves next year or the year after may be in the minority. They have their own interests to guard; they have the interests of the whole people to guard.

Mr. SHANNON. I have arisen merely on account of a dread I had. We all know the character of the representative from New York, (Mr. Sherwood,) and I feared my two friends, (Mr. Norton and Mr. Lippett,) had been advocating this so strenously that it might be in the Constitution of New York. But it is not. It has been stricken from the Constitution. The old Constitution requires a two-third vote, but the new one only requires a majority. Then comes Pennsylvania, then New Jersey, then Rhode Island, and half a dozen more, which do not require the two-third rule in any way. Some of them providing amendments to be made to the Constitution; others providing for conventions to be called by a majority of the Legislature, and a majority of the people. So much for New York. I would ask, Mr. President, what is the principle upon which our government is established? Is it not democratic that the majority shall rule; and what reason is there to put a restriction of this kind, denying the very first principle of our form of government? But this has been discussed here fully; and I would merely wish to state one idea that has occurred to me while listening to the gentleman from San Francisco, (Mr. Lippett,) and it is this: The fact that after giving the people the three months' notice in the first place, this amendment presented by a majority of the Legislature to the people, and then three months' notice given, and having this time to reflect upon it and make up their minds, and send back their instructions to the Legislature in favor of the amendments—that the same majority which elects them, and which approves of the amendments shall then cut itself off and defeat its own will. I think it is a most extraordinary doctrine.

Mr. ELLIS. In regard to this two-third vote which has been so highly deprecated here as being anti-republican, I beg leave to read what the Constitution of the United States says on the subject:

ART. V. The Congress, whenever two-thirds of both Houses shall deem it necessary, shall propose amendments to this Constitution, or, on the application of the Legislatures of two-thirds of the several States, shall call a convention for proposing amendments, which, in either case, shall be valid to all intents and purposes, as part of this Constitution, when ratified by the Legislatures of three-fourths of the several States, or by conventions in three-fourths thereof, as the one or the other mode of ratification may be proposed by the Congress; provided that no amendment which may be made prior to the year one thousand eight hundred and eight shall in any manner affect the first and fourth clauses in the ninth section of the first article; and that no State without its consent, shall be deprived of its equal suffrage in the Senate.

It required a two-third vote there; and I now move the previous question to see whether we can have a two-third vote here or not.

The previous question was ordered.

The question then being on the amendment of Mr. Jones, it was rejected by yeas 16, nays 21, as follows:

YEAS.—Messrs. Botts, Crosby, Dominguez, Dent, Hill, Jones, Larkin, McCarver, Ord, Price, Reid, Sutter, Shannon, Walker, Wozencraft, President—16.

NAYS.—Messrs. Aram, Brown, Carillo, Covarrubias, Dimmick, Ellis, Foster, Gilbert, Hanks, Hoppe, Hobson, Halleck, Lippitt, Norton, Pico, Rodriguez, Snyder, Sansevaine, Steuart, Tefft—21.

The first section, as reported, was then adopted.

Mr. BOTTS moved to strike out in the first line of the second section the words, "two-thirds," and to insert in lieu thereof the words, "a majority." The motion was, by yeas and nays, decided in the negative as follows:

YEAS.—Messrs. Botts, Crosby, Dent, Jones, Larkin, Moore, McDougal, Ord, Reid, Sutter, Snyder, Sherwood, Shannon, Walker, Wozencraft, President.—16.

NAYS.—Messrs. Aram, Brown, Carrillo, Covarrubias, Dimmick, Dominguez, Ellis, Foster, Gilbert, Gwin, Hanks, Hill, Hoppe, Hobson, Hollingsworth, Lippitt, McCarver, Norton, Price, Pico, Roderiguez, Stearns, Sansevaine, Steuart, Tefft—25.

Mr. Steuart moved to amend the section by adding thereto the following proviso:

Provided, That nothing herein contained shall be construed to deny to the people of the State the conservative right which belongs to every free people, to meet in Convention for the purpose of altering and amending the organic law of their Government, in such manner as a majority shall deem expedient.

Mr. Steuart. I am as much in favor, sir, of the rights of the people as any man, but I think it is necessary, in order to show our love for the rights of the people, that we should endeavor to show it for the whole people; for the minority as well as the majority. I think we should protect minorities against any factious majority got up for party purposes or political speculation. Without such a clause as my friend from San Francisco (Mr. Ellis) read from the Constitution of the United States, where would be the government which is our boast at the present day? Where, amid all the fluctuating influences of political parties, would be the rights of the minority of the people? I wish the rights of the minority in California to be protected. I would follow up the dictates of my own conscience even against friends and blood relations. I contend for the right of the people—whenever it shall be necessary to exercise that right—to amend the Constitution; but for the minority as well as the majority. Sir, when I look back to my own native State, it is not that I rejoice in her beautiful slopes and valleys, her waving fields and industrious population, but that in every period of our history they have stood foremost among the protectors of their country. They, sir, have this provision in their Constitution. When I go for the rights of the people I wish to go for the rights of the whole people, and in offering this proviso I claim that I offer nothing that is inconsistent with that position.

Mr. McCarver. The object of that amendment is in direct conflict with the vote which we have just given. It is clearly out of order.

The Chair will give an opinion if called upon.

Mr. McDougal. I hope the Chair will give us his opinion on this subject.

The Chair. At the proper time.

Mr. Wozencraft. I shall vote for that proviso for the simple reason that it stultifies the former action of the House.

Mr. Norton. I am opposed to any amendment giving to the people a legitimate way of effecting a revolution and overthrowing the Constitution.

Mr. Lippitt. I believe it is a rule of law that a man shall not be allowed to stultify himself. We have pointed out a way in which the people, without resort to revolution, can legally change their Constitution. What does this propose? It proposes to leave it open, in spite of all these restrictions; it says to the populace: You need not regard these constitutional provisions; call yourselves a majority of the people; meet in Convention, and make your Constitution just as you please. It gives the people the constitutional right to come together and make a revolution every day in the year. If the people to-day get together in that way, without reference to the mode pointed out in the Constitution, and establish a Constitution, the people the next day, if the majority happens to alter its mind, get up another meeting and establish another Constitution. In that way we may have three hundred and sixty-five Constitutions in one year.

Mr. Botts. I think if posterity is to be tied down by the action of a Convention of the present day, a revolution is a very good thing.

Mr. Ellis. I believe the Chair decides that the resolution is before the House. Does any gentleman appeal from the decision of the Chair?

Mr. McCarver. Look at the proposition. It is at direct issue with the last vote taken by the House. What would be the predicament of the House if we should adopt both? It would show a vacillation that would render us ridiculous wherever the Constitution is read.

Mr. Dimmick. I am in favor of a majority altering this Constitution at any time, but I consider that the proposition of the gentleman from San Francisco does no more than the section just passed.

Mr. SEMPLE. I have but one word to say on this subject. I am willing, if this proviso is adopted, to sign the Constitution as the will of the majority of this House, but I shall take the stump against the Constitution. I would prefer having it rejected by the people to having this provision incorporated in it.

Mr. STEUART. I thought if there ever had been a disposition manifested in favor of the rights of the people that it would be manifested on this occasion; and I was perfectly astonished at the opposition coming from the quarter that it does. Had I been over-anxious to have this proposition carried, I might possibly have sought the counsel of my honorable friend, (Mr. Wozencraft,) seeing how perfect he is in the phraseology of his resolutions, and how lucky he is in having them carried; but I did not suppose, in offering this proposition to secure to the people their favorite right, that I offered any thing contrary to that right. I might, if I had thought proper, have amplified upon this subject, but it has been my studious desire to deal as much as possible in abstract principle, and present my ideas as plainly as I could. It was far from my desire to stultify this House or any member of it. I think if gentlemen will calmly and deliberately examine the two they will find no inconsistency.

Mr. BOTTS. I believe the gentleman from San Francisco (Mr. Steuart) is perfectly honest in his intentions, and desires that the people shall possess all the power; but I call upon him to observe this: that the first section, as adopted, does provide unquestionably that a majority of the people shall alter the Constitution; but it provides, also, that that opinion shall not be expressed but at the will of the minority. When the question is submitted to them undoubtedly the gentleman is right; the section provides that a majority shall settle it; but how can it be submitted to the people except by a minority vote. They are prohibited by the minority from expressing any opinion about it.

Mr. SHANNON. I merely wish to read the 2d section of the Bill of Rights. I think it contains the substance of the proviso of the gentleman from San Francisco, (Mr. Steuart.)

All political power is inherent in the people. Government is instituted for the protection, security, and benefit of the people; and they have the right at all times to alter or reform the same, whenever the public good may require it.

The question was then taken on Mr. Steuart's amendment, and it was decided in the negative, as follows:

YEAS.—Messrs. Aram, Botts, Crosby, Hoppe, Jones, Moore, McDougal, Ord, Price, Snyder, Sherwood, Steuart, Walker, Wozencraft, President—15.

NAYS.—Messrs. Brown, Carrillo, Covarrubias, Dent, Dimmick, Dominguez, Ellis, Foster, Gilbert, Gwin, Hanks, Hill, Hobson, Halleck, Hastings, Hollingsworth, Larkin, Lippitt, McCarver, Norton, Pico, Rodriguez, Sutter, Shannon, Stearns, Sansevaine, Tefft, Vermeule—28.

On motion of Mr. MCCARVER, the vote by which the 1st section of Article X was adopted, was reconsidered.

Mr. JONES moved to strike out of the section the words "two-thirds," and insert "a majority."

The previous question was moved and sustained; and the yeas and nays being ordered on agreeing to the amendment, it was decided in the affirmative, as follows:

YEAS.—Messrs. Aram, Botts, Brown, Crosby, Dent, Dimmick, Gwin, Hoppe, Jones, Larkin, Lippincott, Moore, McDougal, Price, Reid, Synder, Sherwood, Steuart, Vermeule, Walker, Wozencraft, President.—22.

NAYS.—Messrs. Carrillo, Covarrubias, De La Guerra, Dominguez, Gilbert, Hobson, Halleck, Lippitt, McCarver, Norton, Pico, Rodriguez, Stearns, Sansevaine, Tefft—15.

The section, as amended, was adopted.

The 2d section was adopted as reported.

On motion, the House then took a recess till half-past seven o'clock.

NIGHT SESSION.

Mr. McDougal moved that the Convention go into Committee of the Whole upon the Schedule.

The Convention refused the motion.

On motion, the Convention took up the article entitled Miscellaneous Provisions, and proceeded to the consideration thereof.

Section 1st was read.

Mr. Halleck moved to amend by a provision that the first session of the Legislature should be holden at Monterey. He would inform the Convention that he was authorized to offer the use of the entire building in which the Convention was then holding its sessions, for the use of the Legislature as long as they might choose to occupy it.

Mr. Dimmick stated that he was authorized to offer, on the part of the people of the Puebla de San Jose, a house and accommodations equally as good as that in Monterey.

Mr. Botts called for the reading of the offer of the Town Council of San Jose.

Mr. Hoppe read the offer of the donation of thirty-two acres of Washington Square, and also an obligation of the San Jose delegates, under a forfeiture of $50,000, to furnish suitable buildings.

Mr. Botts desired that the House should consider this proposed donation well. It was a trammel upon the people from ever removing the capital if they so desired, without a heavy forfeiture. The cost of the State buildings would not be less than $700,000 or $800,000, and if in five or six years it was thought expedient to remove the capital, the good substantial buildings would be forfeited to San Jose, and a very pretty speculation they would make out of it.

Mr. Hoppe said that the town was willing to give a fee simple of the land to California, without any reservation whatever, and give any security necessary.

Mr. Dimmick supported his colleague.

Mr. Vermuele was fearful that they were going to enter into a sort of family war, a York and Lancaster affair—the people of San Jose vs. the people of Monterey. With him the only question was that of convenience. He thought the situation of San Jose was more central and more convenient, and that the climate was better.

Mr. Jones was in favor of San Jose.

Mr. McCarver was opposed to it.

Mr. Halleck contended that the Town Council of San Jose had no right to make grants of land except to individuals, and then only in single lots. If the State should accept the gift it would not be legal until confirmed by the Legislature.

Mr. Botts desired to know which proposition was before the Convention—that of the Town Council or that of Messrs. Hoppe and Dimmick? He did not doubt that those gentlemen were responsible men, but certainly their proposition was not before the Convention in a shape that could be acted upon. The only proposition was that of the Town Council. Let the matter rest upon its own merits. Don't make the President of this Convention an auctioneer to knock down the capital, with his hammer, to the highest bidder. If San Jose would give thirty-two acres of land, he was authorized to offer on the part of Monterey forty acres. Who would bid fifty?

After some further discussion, the amendment of Mr. Halleck was decided in the negative as follows:

Yeas.—Messrs. Botts, Carrillo, Dent, De La Guerra, Foster, Hill, Halleck, Larkin, Lippitt, McCarver, Ord, Pedrorena, Rodriguez, Reid, Stearns, Tefft, President.—17.

Nays.—Messrs. Aram, Brown, Covarrubias, Crosby, Dimmick, Dominguez, Ellis, Gilbert, Gwin, Hanks, Hoppe, Hobson, Hastings, Hollingsworth, Jones, Lippincott, Norton, Price, Pico, Snyder, Sherwood, Shannon, Sansevaine, Steuart, Vermeule, Walker, Wozencraft.—27.

The section was then adopted.

The amendments of the Committee of the Whole to the second section (on duelling) were concurred in; and the question being on the adoption of the section, as amended—

Mr. PRICE moved to strike out the section; and the yeas and nays being ordered, the motion was decided in the negative, as follows:

YEAS.—Messrs. Botts, Crosby, Dent, Ellis, Hill, Hobson, Hastings, Hollingsworth, Jones, Price, Shannon, Stearns, Steuart, Vermeule, Walker, President.—18.

NAYS.—Messrs. Aram, Carrillo, Covarrubias, Dimmick, Dominguez, Foster, Gilbert, Gwin, Hanks, Hoppe, Larkin, Lippitt, Lippincott, Norton, Ord, Pedrorena, Pico, Rodriguez, Snyder, Sherwood, Sansevaine, Tefft, Wozencraft,—23.

Mr. GWIN moved a reconsideration of the vote just taken, which was decided in the affirmative.

Mr. STEUART submitted the following as a substitute for the section:

SEC. 2. The Legislature shall, at as early a period as practicable, pass laws for the suppression and punishment of the practice of duelling within this State.

The previous question was moved thereon, and sustained; and the question being taken on the amendment, it was rejected, by yeas and nays, as follows:

YEAS.—Messrs. Botts, Crosby, Dent, Ellis, Hill, Hobson, Hollingsworth, Jones, Moore, McDougal, Norton, Pedrorena, Price, Shannon, Stearns, Steuart, Vermeule, Walker, and President.—19.

NAYS.—Messrs. Aram, Brown, Covarrubias, De La Guerra, Dimmick, Dominguez, Gilbert, Gwin, Hanks, Hoppe, Hastings, Larkin, Lippitt, Ord, Pico, Rodriguez, Snyder, Sherwood, Sansevaine, Tefft, Wozencraft,—21.

The question recurring on the original section, as amended by the Committee of the Whole, it was decided in the affirmative.

The amendment of the Committee of the Whole to section 3d was concurred in, and the section, as amended, was adopted.

Sections 4th and 5th were adopted, as reported by the Committee on the Constitution.

On motion of Mr. LIPPITT, section 6th, as reported by the Committee on the Constitution, was amended, by striking out all, from the commencement of the section to the word "purpose," inclusive; and by striking out the word "other," in the first line of the remaining portion. Thus amended the section was adopted.

The amendment of the Committee of the Whole to the 7th section was concurred in, and the section, as amended, was adopted.

Mr. PRICE moved to strike out of the 8th section the words "the political year shall begin on the first day of January," and to insert after "fiscal year" the words "shall commence." The amendment was agreed to, and the section, as amended, was adopted.

The 9th, 10th, 11th and 12th sections were adopted, as reported by the Committee on the Constitution.

The consideration of the new section reported from the Committee of the Whole, to be inserted after the 12th and before the 13th, was, at the request of Mr. De La Guerra, postponed until to-morrow.

The 13th section was adopted, as reported by the Committee on the Constitution.

On motion, adjourned to 10 o'clock, to-morrow.

FRIDAY, OCTOBER 5, 1849.

The Convention met pursuant to adjournment.

Prayer by Rev. Mr. Willey.

Journal of yesterday's proceedings read and approved.

Mr. BOTTS submitted the following resolution:

Resolved, That the compensation of $12 a day, allowed to the Doorkeeper, shall be increased by an additional allowance of $4 a day.

The resolution was adopted.

Mr. BROWN submitted the following, which was adopted:

Resolved, That the Secretary report to this House the amount of labor performed per day by each of the several Clerks of this House, and the amounts received and due for extra copying, and to whom.

On motion of Mr. WOZENCRAFT, the Report of the Committee on Printing, in reference to the printing of the Constitution, was taken up.

Mr. WOZENCRAFT moved that the proposal of Edward C. Kemble, ordered to be filed with the report, be accepted.

After debate, the report and accompanying papers were ordered to lie on the table.

The PRESIDENT asked for instructions from this Convention as to whether the per diem allowance of the Secretaries and Clerks should be paid from the commencement of the session, or from the days on which they were severally elected or appointed.

Thereupon Mr. HALLECK submitted the following resolution:

Resolved, That the pay of the officers of this House commence at the date on which they commenced their duties.

Mr. NORTON moved to amend the resolution by striking out all after the word resolved, and inserting the following:

Resolved, That the officers of this Convention, except the Doorkeeper, be paid from the com mencement of the session.

Mr. Norton's amendment was agreed to, and the resolution, as amended, was adopted.

On motion, the consideration of the "Miscellaneous Provisions" of the Constitution were resumed; the question being on concurring in the additional section reported by the Committee of the Whole, to be inserted between the 12th and 13th sections reported by the Committee on the Constitution, viz:

All lands liable to taxation in this State, shall be taxed in proportion to their value; and this value shall be appraised by officers elected by the qualified electors of the district, county, or town in which the lands to be taxed are situated.

Mr. GWIN moved, as a substitute for the proposed section, the following:

Taxation shall be equal and uniform throughout the State. All property in this State shall be taxed in proportion to its value; to be ascertained as directed by law.

Mr. JONES moved to amend the amendment of Mr. Gwin, by adding thereto the following:

But assessors and collectors of town, county, and State taxes, shall be elected by the qualified electors of the district, county, or town in which the property taxed for State, county, or town purposes, is situated.

Mr. SHANNON. There was a certain committee appointed by resolution of the House for the purpose of making a report upon the ways and means of defraying the expenses of the State Government, to be adopted by this Convention. I do not know the exact bearing of the resolution, but I have the report of the Committee before me. There is certainly nothing contained in the report which can properly come within the Constitution; and I wish to know, as we are now upon this question of taxation, in what position the report stands. I think it was referred to the Committee of the Whole; but it certainly has never come either before the Committee or the House since that disposition was made of it. The document is rather an important one, and as we are now on the subject of taxation, I think it proper that we should act upon it now, if any action is to be taken upon it.

Mr. HALLECK. I believe the amendment proposed by the gentleman from San Joaquin, (Mr. Jones,) is the question before the House. I would say with respect to it, that I prefer it by far to the provision passed by the Committee of the Whole, and I shall vote for it. I prefer it also to the substitute of the gentleman from San Francisco, (Mr. Gwin;) not that all of these propositions do not tend to the same object and produce precisely the same result, but I think the mode indicated in that amendment is the most judicious. There is no danger in leaving this matter to the Legislature; but as fears have been expressed, there can be no objection to putting a provision of this kind in the Constitution, saying that such a course shall be pursued, which has been provided by all the Legislatures, and which is engrafted in many of the Constitutions of the States. I have never heard of an instance of assessors being sent from one extremity of the State to assess lands and property in another. When the amount of tax to be raised is fixed, the assessors in the county or districts where the lands are situated, fix what the individuals are to pay. In the Constitution of Alabama, nearly the same words are used as in the section passed in Committee of the Whole. I prefer the words proposed by the gentleman from San Joaquin.

Mr. LIPPITT. I differ somewhat from my friend from Monterey (Mr. Halleck;) I hope to be enlightened by discussion; but as I look upon it at present, it strikes me that this subject of taxation is one that we must be careful how we interfere with by constitutional enactment. Everything pertaining to taxation should be left to the Legislature. The objects of the tax and the rule to be adopted in taxation, properly belong to the Legislature, and should be left to it; because on this very power of taxation may depend, in emergencies which we cannot foresee in this Convention, the welfare and the very preservation and existence of the State. The whole people, represented in their Legislature, should have their hands perfectly free on this subject. There is another difficulty about it. I agree with my friend from Monterey, (Mr. Halleck,) that there is not much danger of any Legislature sending assessors from one extremity of the country to another to assess real estate; but on the other hand, suppose in any one district where there is no property but real estate held in large amounts in the hands of one individual, how easy it would be, in such a state of things, where the district is made up principally of the lands belonging to this individual, where he would have the amount to fix, to influence the assessment; the proportion that he would have to pay for the support of the Government would be left entirely at his option. Those dependant upon him would, necessarily, be the assessors of his own property. The case would be the same if there were two or three large property holders—they would themselves have the power of fixing the property tax which they are to pay into the public treasury. Now I do not pretend that any of these gentlemen will be guilty of any bad faith in this matter; but we have, in forming this Constitution, to provide for human nature as it is, and as it may be; to provide against all possibility of abuse. We do not know but that this power which we leave in their hands may be abused; and I would therefore be opposed to incorporating in our Constitution any provision of that kind. I greatly prefer leaving the whole matter in the hands of the Legislature.

Mr. NORIEGO. I desire to make a few observations in regard to what the gentleman has said. He appears to be afraid that in some districts one or two large land owners may have the power of naming as assessors whatever persons they like; and that these being nominated by their influence would value the property as the owners would direct. That difficulty could easily be removed by requiring the assessors to take an oath that they will do justice in the valuation of the property. I am not acquainted with this means of appraising property for the purpose of taxation, for it has never been customary in California; but I understand that when a merchant is called upon, his oath is taken as to the value of his taxable property. If a merchant's oath is taken, why cannot a land-owner's be taken? I do not see why bad faith should be expected in one class of persons more than another. I think the argument of the gentleman from San Francisco, (Mr. Lippitt,) has been sufficiently answered; and I shall vote for the amendment of the gentleman from San Joaquin, (Mr. Jones.)

Mr. TEFFT. It is with a great degree of diffidence that I rise to advocate this article. I am in favor of the section as reported by the Committee of the Whole. I believe it accomplishes all that is necessary. I had much rather that this defence should fall to older and abler heads, and I trust that this provision may so far meet the approbation of such members, that they may take the burden of support from my hands.

It has been said that the position occupied by California at this time is an anomalous one. It is most truly so, and in more respects than one. A very few years since, California contained a population sparse in the extreme; a large portion proprietors of immense landed property, and yet poor; many of them destitute; the commerce of the country limited; the country itself unsought and uncared for. How strange the change, and how extraordinary in so short a space of time! This is one of those great events of the nineteenth century, that goes to prove that time should not be measured by years, but by events. The state of things existing here at present, is wholly unparalleled in the history of the world. California is the great idea of the present age, and she promises every thing for the future. Her position is strange, yet most promising.

Let us direct our attention for a moment, to the actual state of things in this country. We see here a population ranging from 70,000 to 100,000 persons, of whom, not to exceed 15,000, are natives of the country. The great majority are a mixed population, from every part of the world, possessing divers interests, and accustomed to various systems of government. And yet, strange as it may seem, we see this immense number of persons from every nation and clime, unknown to each other, unacquainted with each other's habits and customs, living together in harmony and peace. Notwithstanding the dreadful accounts with which the papers of the States have been filled for the past year of outrages and wrongs committed here—that murder was an amusement, and every species of crime a pastime—things as yet, almost entirely unknown to California; yet I say, we find this people uniting as in one family, all feeling that their interests are identical, and having for their only object, a desire to give to the State a Constitution and laws under which they may advance to that greatness which must follow in the natural course of events. This people, without distinction of class, have met together; and as an expression of their desire, have sent to this Convention their delegates from the farthest parts of the country, to form and present to them the organic law of a new State. Reasoning from experience, it is proper to assume that the people who create the State, are ready and willing to maintain and support it. Then from the anomalous position of the country in this respect as well in all others, the question naturally follows, "How is a revenue sufficient to defray the necessary expenses of our State to be raised?"

In this connection I do not wish to be misunderstood. It has been said that lines of distinction have been drawn upon this floor between the native Californians and Americans. And it has also been said that I have drawn these lines. I disclaim entirely any such intention. I believe, and ever have believed, the interests of all actual residents here are identical—one and inseparable. Would it not be very strange if I, an American born, with all the love of country, of family, and of name, implanted, I trust in the breast of every true American, should so far forget myself and my country, as to advocate greater freedom and greater rights for any other race of people than for my fellow-countrymen here? I have never done this. I have only said what I again repeat, that if from the circumstances the interest of any class of people here are to be protected at the expense of any other, common justice demands that those of the native Californians shall be protected. The magnanimous spirit which abides in the breast of every true American will sustain me in this position. Gentlemen may say, that I have no right to make a supposition of this sort. I maintain that the history of the world fully bears me out in the assertion, that there is a possibility, nay a probability, that such a contingency may arise here. Where, in any country, there are two races of men different by birth and education, it is impossible to avoid a clashing of interests; and in such a state of things the argument is not far-fetched to assert, that there is great danger that the interests of the minority will be overlooked, and merged in the interest of the majority.

In view of this possibility, I again assert what I have before asserted on this floor, that any proposition that in itself, or in its consequences, cannot work injury to any other class of persons, and yet is of vital importance to the native inhabitants of California, should receive a careful attention, and if found to be of that character, our unanimous approval. Such a proposition I consider the article under consideration to be.

That the native population of the country are willing to submit cheerfully to any imposition of taxes, within the bounds of justice, necessary to the support of the government of the State, is fully proven from the fact they are the supporters of this article. And I wish to be understood as believing that every class of inhabitants of California are equally willing to contribute to the support of the government which they themselves have formed. And I question very much whether any gentleman on this floor will assert, that any portion of the people in California, wherever located, or whatever their interests, are not willing to assist in the support of the Government in whatever form the necessities of the State may call for it.

It is a principle of equity that all persons should be taxed who in any manner are benefitted by the government imposing such taxes. "Consequently," says a very able writer, "those countries are best governed, in respect of taxation, where each class of inhabitants contributes proportionately to the benefit derived by it from the expenditure." In order to a more full understanding of the matter it becomes necessary to advert to the system of taxation in general. "It is the transfer of a portion of the national products from the hands of individuals to those of the government, for the purpose of meeting the public consumption or expenditure. Whatever be the denomination it bears, whether tax, contribution, duty, excise, custom, aid, grant, or free gift, is virtually a burden imposed on individuals, either in a separate or corporate character, by the ruling power for the time being, for the purpose of supplying the consumption it may think proper to make at their expense; in short, an impost in the literal sense."

Men may talk about the right of taxation. I say that it can only be considered as matter of expediency, and not of right; and nothing further is to be regarded than its nature, the source whence it derives its value, and its effects upon the interests of the country and individuals. And this fact, I maintain, we are called upon to examine most carefully, viz: the effect which unlimited power of taxation in the Legislature *might* work upon the interests of a certain portion of the people of this country—the proprietors of landed property. Gentlemen may urge that is improper to limit the power of the Legislature in regard to the levying of taxes—that it is difficult to discriminate in this matter, &c.

It is true that taxation may be, and often is productive of good when the funds thus raised are properly applied. Yet the act of levying taxation is always attended by abuses in the outset; and this very mischief, good governments have always endeavored to render as inconsiderable to the people as possible, by the practice of economy, and by levying, not *to the full extent of the people's ability*, but to such extent only as is absolutely necessary. Taxation in this country must be burdensome; and what I wish to urge particularly, is, that we should provide that that burden may rest as nearly equally upon the shoulders of all as possible. And knowing this fact, viz: that, from the necessities of the case, taxation must be burdensome for some years to come, I feel deeply interested in the adoption of this article, confining the power of the Legislature to certain judicious limits, and compelling them to resort to measures that will ensure an equality of taxation. Representing, as I do, a district of landed proprietors, I feel particularly interested in this matter, knowing that there is every reason to believe that unless the Legislature is restricted in its powers, that the demagogue cry against certain modes of raising revenue will be raised, restraining the Legislature and compelling them to impose taxes which, in their practical effects, will be unequal and unjust.

Gentlemen may suggest that financial projects will be devised, and ways and means employed for filling the treasury of the State without imposing a burden on the people. But no plan of finance can give to the government without taking either from the people or from the government in some other way. Something cannot be produced out of nothing by a mere touch of the wand, though California, in her present condition, seems to belie this axiom, yet in the collection of revenue I think it will be found to hold good.

"The best scheme of finance is to spend as little as possible, and the best tax is always the lightest;" and, I may add, the most equally divided. Admitting that taxation is the taking from individuals a part of their property for public purposes, it is impossible to deny that the best taxes, or, at least, those that are least objectionable, are:

1. Such as are most moderate in their rates.
2. Such as are attended with least trouble and expense.
3. Such as press impartially on all classes.
4. Such as are favorable to the morality of the people.

This first position no one will deny, and I will only advert to it to show what would be the result if the Legislature were allowed to impose more than a certain amount of tax upon the proprietors of this country. Under the existing state of things, should taxation be pushed to the extreme, it would certainly and most surely have this effect: it would impoverish the large proprietors without enriching the State.

We can plainly see how this can be, if we bear in mind the simple fact that each tax-payer's consumption, whether productive or not, is always limited to the amount of his revenue. No part of his revenue, therefore, can be taken from him without necessarily curtailing his consumption in the same degree. And this is particularly the case with the landholders in California, who possess large amounts of taxable property and very small revenue; impose heavy taxes, and you ruin them beyond a doubt.

Let us look at this in another light. I affirm that this article should be adopted in this country, of all others, not only as an act of justice to individuals, but as a matter of policy for the State. Let this government lean to the side of the tax-payer, and I venture to say that the future will show that lenity on the part of the government in the imposition and collection of taxes on landed property in California will prove advantageous to the interests, and consequently to the prosperity of the country.

I learn from good authority that in thirteen years from 1778, during which time Spain adopted a somewhat more liberal system of government in regard to her American dependencies, that the increase of the revenue in Mexico alone amounted to no less than one hundred millions of dollars. This is undoubtedly an extreme case, but the principle holds good everywhere; and the circumstances of this country most certainly demand a liberal system of taxation. I do not wish to be understood, Mr. President, as advocating the imposition of light taxes upon the landholders, or making them pay less than their proper share of the burden; not at all; they are willing to pay all they can, and only ask to be protected from excessive taxation. All citizens of California should enjoy the same exemption from onerous taxation.

Mr. President, with reference to the 2d head: Taxes which are attended with least trouble and expense in their collection. This refers particularly to the article regulating the collection of taxes in each county for the payment of county officers.

We come now, sir, to the important reason why this article should be adopted, viz: that taxation, in order not to be too burdensome, should be such as to press impartially on all classes. Admitting that taxation is a burden, it must necessarily weigh lightest on each individual when it bears upon all alike. When it presses inequitably upon one individual or branch of the community, it is oppressive; it is a direct incumbrance; for it prevents the particular branch or individual from competing on equal terms with the rest. Oppression to one branch of industry has often been the ruin of several others. Favor to one is most commonly injustice to all others.

Now, in view of these facts, what is the present situation of California, with regard to this most important question of taxation? There are now, or will be in this country at the time of the ratification of this Constitution, one hundred thousand people living under and enjoying the benefits of the government, and each individual of that number, because he receives the protection of the government, of right is subject to be taxed. Of this hundred thousand persons there may be fifteen thousand native Californians, and of the whole number, not exceeding five thousand are proprietors of landed property, and the great majority of the residue have neither real estate nor personal property that is taxable, and yet most of them with a competency, though it is not tangible. No man can assert that this vast majority of the citizens of California, possessing the greatest amount of wealth, should not contribute to the support of the very government which is founded for their protection and benefit. I do not for a moment, even in thought, do this class of citizens the injustice to believe that they are not only ready but willing to submit to any manner of taxation that is necessary, particularly when informed that the landed proprietors, who of necessity must be taxed heavily, are at the same time willing to submit to a similar tax for the support of government.

There is, Mr. President, probably $40,000,000 of taxable real estate, and as much more of moveable property in this country, at the present time; this, at the amount of taxation to which it is proposed to limit the Legislature, would yield a revenue of $200,000. It is asked, how are we to raise revenue sufficient for the expenses of the State? I answer, impose a capitation tax. I know that this is the most unpopular word that I can use. But I believe that, when it is shown clearly and beyond a doubt that the necessities of the State and the rights of individuals require it, no man but a demagogue will raise his voice against it. I am in favor of, and shall, if called upon, advocate the imposition here of a capitation tax for the very reason that the necessities of our country require it, and the rights and interests of very many of our citizens demand it. I have sufficient confidence in the honesty of the great majority of the people of California to believe that such a tax, instead of being considered a burden, would be cheerfully responded to. I believe that one man, with his census books, can go from San Diego to the most remote settlement on the Sacramento, and the Collector behind him, and that ninety-nine men of every hundred who place their names on the books will pay the tax demanded.

Mr. Sherwood. I was forcibly struck with the proposition, that the people taxed should elect the officers who taxed them. Since then, I have had doubts, from the peculiar condition of things and the population of this country, as to the propriety of saying any thing about it, leaving it to the Legislature to say what way the value of property shall be ascertained and a tax imposed; but, upon further reflection, I have come to the conclusion that there is nothing in the principle involved in either the section originally proposed by the gentleman from Monterey, (Mr. Halleck,) or in the amendment now proposed by the gentleman from San Joaquin, (Mr. Jones,) which should not be adopted in the Constitution. I prefer, however, the amendment of the gentleman from San Joaquin, because, in the first place, it establishes a principle which should be fixed, that property should be assessed and taxed according to its value. That is a fundamental principle. In the next place, it provides that the officers shall be elected by the people of the town, county, or district taxed. I am opposed at all times to the assessing of the value of property by men not acquainted with its value. It is a principle well settled in the old States, that no officer should be sent two or three hundred miles into a district to which he is a stranger, to fix the value of property upon which taxes are to be levied. It is not republican, and I am entirely opposed to it. There are difficulties which have suggested themselves to some members, on account of the position of property in one portion of this future State, which, upon further consideration, I think may be obviated by the reasoning of these gentlemen. There can be no injustice done in this way—no unequal burdens imposed in different parts of the country. When a State tax is imposed, it is so much upon the dollar. If we have to raise half a million of dollars, we observe the same rule; collect together and report to the Legislature the amount of real and personal property in the State, and that is the way in all the States of the Union. Having this basis, it being ascertained that we have to raise half a million of dollars for a State tax, we then are able to ascertain very nearly what amount of per centage upon the property is necessary to be raised. Now, suppose that upon the whole amount of property in the State assessed and returned to the State Department, it is necessary to levy a tax of five hundred thousand dollars. The Legislature fixes the per centage which will draw the five hundred thousand dollars from the whole amount of property in the State; and they therefore lay a tax of one mill or one per cent—whatever may be necessary—on all the taxable property; and the objection which occurred at first to my mind, and I suppose to the minds of other gentlemen, that property which was in fact valuable—say in the southern part of the State—might escape taxation, I think is groundless if this article is adopted. The assessors fix the value, for instance, of a ranche of a thousand acres, or eleven leagues, or any amount you please, and they may fix it at one dollar per acre, or fifty cents. Very well; if they assess equally throughout one district, no citizen is burdened beyond another. Now, so much money is to be raised. The State tax is apportioned around in the different districts, carrying out the assessment rules; and upon these lands so much money is to be raised, and if the lands are valued at one dollar an acre, and the sum amounts to ten cents an acre, that tax must be raised; if the lands are worth ten dollars an acre, then of course the sum will be larger, so that in fact there is no difficulty in the matter. They may lower the amount; they may in any portion of the State elect assessors who will bring down the assessed value of the property; yet they must bring in a certain amount. No portion of the State can elude taxation if this clause is adopted. Taking this view of the matter, which to my mind is clear and unquestionable; taking the ground, too, that men should be selected in the district where the property is located, and who know the value of the property, I am in favor of the amendment of the gentleman from San Joaquin. It says expressly that property shall be taxed according to its value, and the officers shall be elected in the town, county, or district where the property is located. Suppose these officers forswear themselves and do not give the true value of the property, then they violate that fundamental law which says that it shall be assessed according to its value; and will your Legislature, viewing the conduct of these officers—the complaints made that officers do not value the property at what it is worth—will they sanction it? They will punish offenders by penal enactment; they will provide that officers shall be elected, in the first place, to look over the assessment rules to see whether these officers did their duty or not. But I do not fear any such thing. All portions of the State are prepared to pay a just tax upon their property. I am willing, therefore, to take this clause, because it is republican in its character and right in its nature—that property shall be taxed according to its value, and assessments made by persons acquainted with its value.

Mr. Botts. I am somewhat like my friend from Sacramento (Mr. Sherwood) in one thing. When this clause was proposed in the Committee of the Whole I did not know that there was any material objection to it, and it was not until last evening that I began to consider it in its true and proper light. When the gentleman from San Luis Obispo (Mr. Tefft) called the attention of the House to the particular state of things existing in California, where there are divers local interests, according to the different sections, then it was that I saw that this provision might do harm. If the interests of all sections were alike, there would be no difficulty or danger in this proposition; but we are told, sir, from the best authority, that the gentlemen of the southern portion of this country do consider that their local interests upon the subject of taxation are directly opposite to the interests of another and much larger portion; and that they claim here, in this House, that they may be permitted to sit in judgment upon the amount of taxation that they shall pay. Mr. President, I do not believe even that the proposition they ask for is usual. We have been told, sir, by one gentleman—my colleague from Monterey (Mr. Halleck)—that this provision, as proposed by him, is just the provision of the Alabama Constitution. I thought it was somewhat remarkable that it should be so; that any person or any set of persons, by any Constitution, should be allowed to assess the value of their property to be taxed. If the bare proposition were before you that A, B, or C should be permitted to fix his own value upon his own property, who would entertain it for a moment? No one; and yet this proposition is this: that a particular county, sparse in its population, probably consisting wholly of landed proprietors, shall meet together and shall elect an individual for no other purpose than that of assessing and valuing these lands. We are told, sir, by the gentleman from Santa Barbara (Mr. Noriego) that they will act under the influence of an oath. An oath! Remember, sir, who that man is likely to be—elected by these individuals; remember the interest they have in selecting a particular individual, and that he will in all probability be one of the most extensive landholders himself. His interest is identified with theirs, and that interest is to put these lands at the very smallest value. Sir, I thought it was strange that such a provision should exist in the Constitution of Alabama, and I turned to it, and all I can see upon the subject is this: "All lands liable to taxation in this State shall be taxed in proportion to their value." That is a very short sentence. It is exceedingly strange that the gentleman should read that line and contend that it was the proposition of the gentleman from Monterey. It is exactly the proposition of the gentleman from San Francisco, (Mr. Lippitt,) except that it does not say, but leaves to inference, that the mode of ascertaining the value shall be ascertained by law. It implies exactly what the Constitution of Louisiana expresses, and so far from being identical with the one proposition it is exactly identical with the opposite proposition.

Mr. President, I was sorry to hear the gentleman from San Luis Obispo, although he disclaimed it, repeat the declaration that the object of this provision was to guard the original citizens of California from oppression by those who have come here, and who are the majority. Sir, is not the position that these gentlemen occupy here a sufficient guaranty that no such thing is intended? Do we not present here the noblest spectacle that the world has ever seen? It has been the custom of other nations, who were the conquerors, to trample to the dust the rights of the conquered; but what do you see here? You see these gentlemen admitted to exactly the same platform that you occupy yourselves—taken to your hearts as friends and brothers; and here, when they sit upon this floor, treated with a degree of deference and respect that no other members in this Convention can command. Is not that a guaranty—a sufficient guaranty—that they who have done this will never do them wrong? I say, sir, it is not to be permitted; if there be these local interests they ought to be restrained from doing injustice to others with contrary interests; if suspicions are raised against the majority, why may not the majority entertain suspicions against the minority, who were the first to raise suspicions? If the northern portion of the country is to be charged with a design to throw an undue burden of the taxation of the State upon the southern portion, why may not, upon the very same foundation, the charge be thrown back; and why may we not aver that these gentlemen, in assessing their own lands, may avoid their proportionate burden of taxation? Remember, sir, that there is a very important point involved in this question of assessed value. I have heard a gentleman lay down this doctrine, and probably a gentleman who would be a voter for it; he honestly entertains this opinion: that an individual who owns eleven leagues of land, for which he could at any day receive from others a hundred thousand dollars, that that land should be assessed not according to its worth in the market, but according to the income which he receives from it under the present circumstances of the country, which may not possibly be $500. Do you not know that this does frequently happen? It happens if property is not at all productive and yet exceedingly valuable. How would it work, for instance, in towns and villages, according to this rule of estimate?

Why, sir, the owners of untenanted houses would go scot free, whilst an individual with a much smaller amount of property would be liable for his proportion of taxes. This might be found to be the opinion of the assessor that is elected by these persons. This is one view of the question. What, on the other hand, is the proposition of the gentleman from San Francisco, (Mr. Lippitt,) which I advocate upon this floor? It is this: that the Legislature may have an opportunity of trying and testing this doubtful question, and seeing how these things will work; that the whole people of the country, who are interested in this matter, may have an opportunity of seeing how the arrangement for assessing this value proposed by one Legislature shall work; and if it works injustice, that they may have an opportunity of repealing it; and that is the great advantage of legislative instead of constitutional action. If ever it was politic to submit any question to the Legislature, it seems to be it is peculiarly so in the present extremely doubtful question. There is no other way of arriving at a just conclusion except that of trial; and with the Legislature resides the power of altering or amending, as circumstances may require. If it were proposed that the taxes for county purposes were to be raised by an assessment upon the value of that land, nothing could be more proper than that the assessors of the value of the land should be chosen alone by a vote of the county; but you do not mark the difference. This is not for the expenses of the county; it is a tax for the support of the State. Each county has to bear its general proportion of the burden of taxation for the whole country; and every individual is interested in this assessment, which in the other case would be confined to the particular voters of the county themselves. The distinction is marked and manifest. With these few remarks I dispose of the gentlemen who have preceded me, with the exception of the gentleman from Sacramento, (Mr. Sherwood,) and I have only one or two observations to make in answer to his argument. I very much have liked all my life the proposition of that gentleman—that the proper mode of raising taxation is by a per centage upon property, without regard to the character or quality of it. I hold nothing to be more true than that government is instituted for the preservation of life, liberty, and property, and that he who holds property ought to pay for the protection of that property in proportion to the amount that is protected; and that I say without any regard to the kind of property, because all men have an equal right to acquire any kind of property they please. I like the doctrine, but I do not see how the gentleman applies that doctrine to carry out his particular views or his support of this proposition. He tells you that, when that per centage is laid, no portion of the State can elude its proportion of the taxation. Why not, sir? Where is the difficulty? You have got, it is true, $100,000 to raise, and a per centage of one per cent. is to be paid upon all the wealth of the country; but if you will permit me to assess the value of my own property, I will pay a per centage on it and pay a very small portion of my burden of taxation. It does not alter the case at all. How will you ascertain the value of this property? Whether the ad valorem principle or direct principle be resorted to, it is equally important to fix the actual value in order to obtain the proper proportion of taxation. How would the gentleman under this principle ascertain the per centage? The Legislature is to fix the amount required, and proportion it among the several counties. You must know the amount of property in the State. How are you to get at it? I consider this proposition to be equivalent to this. Let every man send in his assessment of his property; let every county with these divers local interests choose their assessors, with instructions how they are to assess the property. It is but one remove from the odious principle that a man shall have a perfect right to fix his property at what he pleases.

It has been said here that we may well adopt this; that the Legislature never will send assessors from one part of the State to another. That may be true, but there are a good many other things that the Legislature may do. If an individual is to be elected as an assessor, it may take this precaution—that he be elected also for another purpose; that he be sheriff of the county. They may interpose a thousand guards and checks, which neither you nor I can think of in a minute's warning; and therefore it is that I propose to leave it to those who have more time—who have years and years of reflection—to determine how these evils on the one hand and on the other shall be avoided; how such assessments as will operate justly and equitably shall be fixed, and such as will prevent that wrong which gentlemen from below fear, whilst they may also avoid that wrong which other portions perhaps are justified in fearing from the suspicions raised.

With regard to a capitation tax, I, sir, who am not afraid to avow any thing on the face of the earth, who have been taught all my life just to think what I please and say what I think, I am in favor of a capitation tax. Go tell that to the people. I am in favor of taxing every man's head, but not laying the whole burthen of taxation there.

Mr. Tefft. That is not assumed here.

Mr. Botts. Then I am with the gentleman. This clause only provides how property shall be taxed; it leaves to the Legislature to fix a tax upon every man in the country as it chooses. Then there is no argument between us at all on the subject of taxation; no difference of opinion. Mr. President, I believe that, under the circumstances, I am through with what I have to say, although I am well aware that there is an infinite deal more to be said against the clause which has been reported by the Committee of the Whole, and which I hope will not be permitted to pass this House.

Mr. Snyder. I hold in my hand the report of the Committee of Ways and Means. At the time that report was introduced, I anticipated this discussion. I foresaw what the result would be, and last night, when the gentleman from San Luis Obispo (Mr. Tefft) addressed the House, the position he took did not astonish me. The report of the Committee is the basis of it; there is a line of distinction drawn in that report between the native and the American population of California. It is to that portion of the report that speaks of the poverty of the people of the southern portion of California that I will call your attention.

I have a great respect for the people of the south. I have known many of them personally for several years, and would be sorry to see any thing placed upon the records of this Convention lowering them in the estimation of our friends at home. As regards the poverty of these people, I will merely state that there are now some of their representatives in this House, and I have no doubt that they would treat with the greatest indignation any effort made by any person to look upon them as objects of charity. I therefore think, Mr. President, that is in bad taste, if not altogether superfluous, to hold them up in that light. First, I would ask you, sir, if any of the people from the south have ever been in the placers, and if they have ever obtained any of the gold that the report speaks of as having been obtained by the people of the upper districts? Secondly, I would ask whether any of the people of the south have ever driven their horses and cattle into the upper districts to be sold? I will answer the first question by asserting that I have seen many of the Southern inhabitants of this country in the mines, with numbers of their servants, obtaining immense quantities of gold. There is another part of the report from which we are to infer that the discovery of the gold mines has inflicted the deepest injury on this portion of the Territory, where but two years since were concentrated its wealth and population.

Now, sir, I would ask, from what the advantages of the people of the lower part of California were derived two years since, that made the wealth of that portion of the country so highly concentrated? What had they to sell? Hides and tallow, aguadiente and wine. The hides and tallow constituted the bulk of their trade.

As for the whisky and wine, we all know the amount that constituted that part of the trade. Even admitting that the market is now supplied with foreign wines, and probably at cheaper rates, does this argue that the people are now in a suffering condition? The report says that cattle, or the capital invested in stock for ranchos, has not paid over a certain per cent. and offers this as a reason why the people of the south are unable to bear the burden of taxation. In regard to the cattle, it is a well known fact that many cattle and horses have been driven into the mining districts and sold at a handsome profit. Why, sir, one of the members of this Convention has a partner now on his way to the mining districts from Santa Barbara with 1,500 head, and this is only one person. The report makes it a most singular state of affairs, and I presume it would require another Adam Smith to explain how such changes could be brought about.

Is there any man here that will tell me that the people of the south will suffer from the discovery of gold in the upper portion of California? Is it possible that, with the immense population that is flooding the country at all points of the compass, there are no beef eaters? Is it possible that, with this rapid influx, there should be no demand for beef? And, sir, if there is a demand for beef, is it possible that the people of the south cannot find a market for it? The argument made use of in the report is utterly at variance with all systems of political economy that I have ever read. There are no people in California richer than the cattle owners.

I am not in favor of heavy taxation, for I know that the Southern portion of the people of this country are large landholders, and I do not approve of any system of heavy taxation being imposed upon them.

The report goes on to say:

"In the towns that have sprung up something might be collected; but, like all new communities, they make the most of their *limited capital.*"

Mr. President, I would like to know where the gentlemen got their information in regard to the *limited capital* contained in the new towns that are springing up. I know, sir, that public works have been performed by individuals at their own expense, and I have not seen a person in the town that I have come from who would object to pay a tax for either Municipal or State support, although their capital is, as the report says, *limited.*

"In the opinion of the Committee the system of taxation might fail."

Now, sir, the only failure that some of the gentlemen of the Committee apprehend appears to be in the south, amongst the *poor people.* What does one of the southern gentlemen of this Committee say about the matter?

"The undersigned, a member of this Committee, finds great difficulty in organizing the ways and means best adapted to the present peculiar and unprecedented circumstances in which the State of California is placed, but would recommend, as the more eligible plan, that the Legislature be empowered to raise the proper revenue for defraying the State expenses by levying an income and property tax, which shall not exceed one quarter per cent., as likewise a poll tax, which shall be left entirely to the Legislature to decide upon, both in relation to the amount as well as the manner of carrying out the same. Signed, A. STEARNES."

This is the opinion of one of those poor men from the south.

A gentleman from the south, a member, a few days ago remarked that they were not in want of money but in want of wit. This is another voice from amongst the poor people from the south; and, as far as wit is concerned, I have no doubt he can be supplied with a certain kind now on hand in market, for sale cheap.

We have two reports on ways and means. I do not understand parliamentary rules, and would like to know if there can be two minority reports, as I believe the report was made by a Committee of two, and they differ in opinion. But I will vote for the proposition of the gentleman from Los Angelos, who seems to think that the poor people of the south are able to pay taxes.

Mr. STEUART said that, coming from a State where the burden of taxation had been very great, he could speak feelingly on the subject. It was a question of the most vital importance. He had endeavored already briefly to show the condition of the landed interests in California, and it was his opinion that for some time to come there could not be a sufficient revenue obtained from taxes levied upon the lands held by individuals to support the State Government. In view of the difficulty of obtaining means, he had submitted a plan for the consideration of the House, by which he thought additional revenue might be raised. With regard to the propositions before the House, he thought it was usual to appoint assessors from among those best acquainted with the character and value of the lands. He would vote for the section as reported by the Committee, because he believed it to be right and proper in itself.

Mr. GWIN. I will not detain the House long, for I believe there is a general disposition to get through with this subject. The proposition that I presented to the House this morning is copied from the Constitution of Texas, leaving out certain provisions which I do not think proper to introduce. Texas is very similarly situated to this country. There are there many landholders who have large estates which are not productive. I do not wish to do injustice to any portion of the people of this country; and this desire to do justice to all parts led me to examine for precedents where there were large landholders. Hence, I offered the proposition—not precisely as it is in the Constitution of Texas, but all I thought was necessary to cover the case. I want it distinctly understood, in advance, that the main argument urged here on the subject of assessors—that they should be elected in the county where the lands are situated—the argument brought forward that, by implication, my proposition contemplates that these elections shall be held in any other part of the State, is without foundation. I have never known that practice in any State of the Union. I want the assessors to live in the county where the property is. I am in favor of that; but I want the Legislature to have the power to form a system of taxation. I say that taxation should be equal and uniform throughout the State. "All property in this State shall be taxed in proportion to its value, to be ascertained as directed by law." Then, if gentlemen wish to be more specific on this subject, I am perfectly willing that the assessors shall be residents of the county or district in which the lands are situated.

In regard to the comments on the report of the Committee of Ways and Means, I shall only say a word or two. I do not look upon it that any argument has been brought against it. These paper missiles thrown upon the House may be laid aside to be used elsewhere. I have seen such things before, and I am not at all afraid of their effects. That the price of cattle has risen, I do not doubt; but so has every thing else, and the relative value is the same. We are assured by the southern people themselves, that the products of the farms in the southern part of the State have been diminished in value, because of the great difficulty of procuring labor. I know the people of California will sustain their Government by any tax put upon them. I am in favor of establishing a State Government, and asking as a matter of right that the expenses of this Government shall be paid by the Government of the United States until we are prepared to pay it ourselves; and if we do not get it from that source, I believe the people will sustain an equitable taxation, whatever it may be. They are prepared to go through with what they have started, and that is, to establish a government here. My only opposition to incorporating any specific plan of taxation in the Constitution is, that it may give rise to some inequality in its operation, owing to the different interests in the different parts of the country. For this reason, I prefer leaving the subject to the Legislature, with the general provision that taxation shall be equal and uniform, and property taxed according to its value—principles which nobody will deny. I have not the least apprehension that the property of landholders will be unfairly assessed. As members of this Convention, forming a fundamental law, we should be cautious how we introduce any thing to the disadvantage of one portion of the country or another. The whole object and scope of the report of the Committee of Ways and Means was to show that the people of this country were not prepared for taxation as yet, and that they ought not to be required to impose a burden upon themselves when it was the duty of the General Government to furnish them with means—not asking this in a spirit of humble solicitation, but as a matter of right.

Mr. PRICE. I offered an amendment to the original section as it was reported from the Committee of the Whole, to strike out what I considered a legislative provision, and I did it, sir, upon this principle; that the provision was restrictive in itself, and was a right that belonged peculiarly to the Legislature, and one which it would seem like aggression on our part to interfere with. I want to send this Constitution to the people with no insulting or aggressive provision, such as, in my opinion, is done by the section as it originally stood. I do not wish to see the landed proprietors of this country disproportionately taxed. I believe that by putting this provision in the Constitution it will be attended by results that all would deprecate. It might operate very injuriously upon the landholders of the south. I appreciate their position, sir, and I should be willing to put any guard or protection around them that is consistent with our duties here.

The question being on Mr. Gwin's amendment, as amended by Mr. Jones, it was adopted; and the report of the Committee of the Whole, as amended, was then concurred in.

On motion, the Convention took a recess till half-past three.

AFTERNOON SESSION.

The consideration of the "Miscellaneous Provisions" of the Constitution was resumed.

The amendments of the Committee of the Whole to the 14th section were concurred in, and the section, as amended, was adopted.

On motion of Mr. STEUART, the additional section reported by the Committee of the Whole, to follow the 14th section, was amended, by inserting at the close thereof the words, "except for eleemosynary purposes;" and thus amended the amendment of the Committee of the Whole was concurred in; and the section adopted, viz:

No perpetuities shall be allowed, except for eleemosynary purposes.

Section 16th was adopted as reported by the Committee on the Constitution.

On motion of Mr. SHERWOOD, the 17th section, as amended by the Committee of the Whole, was stricken out, and the following inserted in lieu thereof:

SEC. 17. Absence from this State, on business of the State or of the United States, shall not affect the question of residence of any person.

Section 18th was adopted as reported by the Committee on the Constitution.

The additional section, reported as section 19th by the Committee of the Whole, was taken up, viz:

All laws, decrees, regulations, and provisions, emanating from any of the three supreme powers of this State, which from their nature require publication, shall be published in English and Spanish.

Mr. NORTON moved to amend by striking out the word "supreme," and inserting in lieu thereof the word "several."

Mr. BOTTS moved to amend the amendment of Mr. Norton, so as to strike out of the section the words, "emanating from any of the three supreme powers of the State," which Mr. Norton accepted as a modification of his amendment.

The amendment, as amended, was agreed to; and, thus amended, the amendment of the Committee of the Whole was concurred in, and the section adopted.

Mr. ORD moved an additional section, as follows:

The Legislature shall have power to extend this Constitution, and the jurisdiction of this State, over any territory acquired by compact with any State, or with the United States, the same being done with the consent of the United States.

Mr. Norton. I have no objection to that, but I do not see the necessity of it.

Mr. McCarver. It is hardly probable that the Congress of the United States would consent to a provision of that kind. We are assuming enormous powers when we adopt such a provision as that.

Mr. Steuart. I will support the amendment. It is gravely agitated in Congress the propriety of annexing the Canadas and Cuba. It may be a very important provision to us. Probably the extent of California will be such as to call upon us in a short time to take under our protecting wing the Sandwich Islands.

Mr. McCarver. I expect to be a citizen of Oregon, and, if I were a citizen, I should object to the Legislature of your State fixing a Constitution upon me.

Mr. Hastings. Notwithstanding the protest of my colleague, I am disposed to favor the section. It may soon become necessary to annex the Sandwich Islands or Oregon. We will find it very difficult to make room for the immense population pouring in here.

Mr. Botts. I would not say a word but for the fear that this clause might possibly creep into the Constitution. What is that you propose to do? After fixing the right of suffrage, excluding negroes and the descendants of negroes, you introduce a clause by which you may extend this Constitution to the Sandwich Islands, and make citizens of the Kanakas.

Mr. McCarver. We are getting to be an almighty people here. Who knows but we may have a resolution presented to annex China? If the Congress of the United States and California will assent to it, the Chinese may enjoy the benefit of the wisdom of this Convention in having our Constitution extended over them. As a citizen of California and of the United States, I protest against such a measure.

Mr. Sherwood. If we should chance at any time to annex a portion of the territory south of us by consent of the people, I do not see why we should deny ourselves that right with the consent of Congress, to extend our Constitution over them. Being citizens of the western coast, it becomes us, if possible, to extend our power. As my friend from San Francisco (Mr. Gwin) said the other day, I hope we will have six or more States upon this coast; I hope, if I live forty years, to see the whole coast populated, and a vast empire on it, so that our power on the east and west will be the greatest in the world.

Mr. Ord. I do not think the meaning of this additional section is distinctly understood. Suppose it were found necessary or convenient to California that Oregon should dispose of a part of her territory to California by donation, finding that she could not govern it conveniently, and California was willing to accept it; it would be necessary before we could extend our laws over that territory to have the power in our Constitution. The Legislature could not extend our laws over that newly acquired territory, however small it might be. It would be necessary, without this provision, to call a Convention. It is for the purpose of anticipating any contingency of that kind that this section is offered.

Mr. Hill. I shall oppose the adoption of this provision. I think it is useless. If we should get a portion of Oregon, it becomes a part of California. The present Constitution would extend over it.

Mr. Ord. It cannot extend beyond the boundary which we fix in the Constitution.

Mr. Lippitt. I think there is some doubt whether this Constitution could be extended beyond the boundaries therein established. I can conceive the probability of such an instance as that mentioned by the gentleman from Monterey, (Mr. Ord.) I do not think the Legislature would have power to extend the jurisdiction of the State beyond what we have now marked in this Constitution. I would also remind gentlemen that, according to a provision already adopted, there is no way of calling a Convention of the people, so as to give that power to the Legislature, under two years; it will be two years before that constitutional power could be given; and if the case alluded to should arise, we can conceive very readily that it would be important that it should be acted upon immediately. If there is no power except by altering the Constitution, it would take two years to do it. I am therefore inclined to support the amendment.

Mr. Ellis. I merely rise to announce to the House that the previous question is around again.

Mr. McCarver. I wish to refer to this fact: that the only instance on record in which the set limits of a State were altered was that of Missouri. The Constitution of Missouri made no provision for that purpose. A simple act of Congress, with the assent of the Legislature, admitted an additional portion of territory into the State of Missouri. Now, if Oregon should be a State, and one of the parties should consent to make this donation, I have no doubt that the action of the two Legislatures and of Congress would be sufficient to accomplish the purpose.

Mr. Botts. I am astonished, sir, to hear gentlemen talk here about giving away human beings and selling human beings, without consulting them. Suppose Oregon, says the gentleman, should give away thirty thousand of her inhabitants to California; the Legislature would extend our laws over them. Do you mean to say, sir, that our Legislature shall assume this control over them, without consulting their wishes? I deny any such doctrine. The only way to accomplish the object, in such an event as that referred to, is to call a Convention to make a Constitution. Let it be the work of the whole population of California. I have no doubt that, when this Convention lays down the boundaries of this State, it is utterly impossible for the Legislature to alter a constitutional provision, the boundary being one. How can it be that, whilst the Constitution is there telling them what the boundary of this State is, the Legislature can violate that Constitution which every member must be sworn to support? You propose to leave to the Legislature the extension or contraction of this boundary question; that the Legislature shall make the boundary of this State precisely what they please; and without the consent of those persons that are so donated that you extend and force over them your laws and your government.

Mr. Shannon. I call the attention of the House to the 10th section of the 1st article of the Constitution of the United States.

Mr. Ellis. I move the previous question.

The yeas and nays being ordered, the result was as follows:

Yeas.—Messrs. Carrillo, Covarrubias, Crosby, Ellis, Gwin, Hoppe, Hobson, Hollingsworth, Lippitt, Ord, Pico, Rodriguez, Reid, Sutter, Stearns, Steuart, Wozencraft—17.

Nays.—Messrs. Aram, Botts, Dimmick, Dominguez, Gilbert, Hanks, Hill, Hastings, McCarver, McDougal, Norton, Pedrorena, Shannon, Vallejo—14.

Mr. Lippitt moved a reconsideration of the vote just taken; and the article and amendment was ordered to lie on the table for further consideration.

On motion of Mr. Gwin, the House then resolved itself into Committee of the Whole, Mr. Lippitt in the chair, on so much of the report of the Committee on the Constitution as relates to the preamble.

The majority report being under consideration, as follows:

We, the people of California, grateful to Almighty God for our freedom, in order to secure its blessings, do establish this Constitution.

The minority report was called up by Mr. Gwin, as follows:

We, the people of the Territory of California, by our representatives in Convention assembled, at Monterey, on the first day of September, A. D. 1849, and of the Independence of the United States the seventy-third, having the right of admission into the Union as one of the United States of America, consistent with the Federal Constitution, (and by the Treaty of Peace between the United States and Mexico, ratified on the 30th day of May, A. D. 1848,) in order to secure to ourselves and our posterity the enjoyment of all the rights of life, liberty, and the free pursuit of happiness, do mutually agree with each other to form ourselves into a free and independent State, by the name and style of the "State of California," and do ordain and establish the following Constitution for the government thereof.

Mr. GWIN. All I have to say in favor of the minority report is, that it is the same precisely as the preambles of the Constitutions of Arkansas, Louisiana, and Florida, territories which were acquired under nearly the same circumstances as California, by treaty or purchase.

Mr. NORTON. I have but a single word to say in behalf of the report of the majority. It was desired by nearly all the members of the Committee, that we should adopt some preamble that would be short and expressive, and at the same time contain every thing that would be absolutely necessary. I do not think myself that it is necessary in a preamble to refer to the treaty of peace between the United States and Mexico. It should not be in the Constitution any more than any other part of the history of the State of California. Neither do I think we should put in anything in regard to the protection of life, liberty, and the pursuit of happiness—a long rigmarole which everybody knows. They are contained in our declaration of rights. For these reasons the majority of the Committee agreed upon the report which has been presented here; which I believe expresses all that need be said in a preamble.

Mr. GWIN. The gentleman's opinion may pass for what its weight may be. Three States have adopted the plan which I have presented in becoming members of the Union. The main point with the gentleman is, that the preamble which he presents is from the Constitution of New York.

Mr. NORTON. And a very good one it is.

Mr. SHANNON. We are told that the preamble of the majority is from the Constitution of New York. In my opinion it is the most butt-ended one that could be found. She commenced under the new Constitution as a State; we commence as a Territory, and we have no right to assume that we are a State until we are formed as such. I think both propositions are objectionable; and I offer the following as a substitute:

We, the representatives of the people of the Territory of California, in Convention assembled, at Monterey, on Saturday, the first day of September, A. D. 1849, and of the Independence of the United States the seventy-third, in order to secure to ourselves and our posterity the enjoyments of civil, religious, and political liberty, form a more perfect government, establish justice, ensure domestic tranquility, provide for the common defence, and promote the general welfare, do mutually agree to form ourselves into a free and independent State, by the style and title of the "State of California," and do ordain and establish this Constitution for its government.

Mr. HASTINGS. I cannot see the necessity of a preamble at all. I think it is quite enough to say "the Constitution of the State of California." Neither can I see the necessity of inserting in an instrument of this kind a prayer to Almighty God. I shall vote for any preamble that comes the nearest to being no preamble at all.

Mr. NORTON. I must protest against the gentleman from Sacramento, (Mr. Shannon,) calling this a butt-ended proposition. He does not show much reverence for the State from which he came. I have seen nothing from any of the States that exceeds this in beauty and simplicity. The other gentleman from Sacramento, (Mr. Hastings,) does not seem to think it necessary to be grateful to Almighty God. I hope some of the members of this House perceive that necessity. I think it is proper, doing so solemn an act, that we should make a due reference to the Supreme Being. This preamble I consider as appropriate as any that we could adopt. The gentleman (Mr. Shannon) says we have no right to call ourselves the people of the State of California. The argument will not stand. This Constitution is nothing until ratified by the people; but from the moment it is ratified we are the State of California.

Mr. McDOUGAL. I hope this House has originality enough about it to form a preamble of its own, without referring to New York, or any other State. I desire to see in this Constitution a few lines at least of our own manufacture.

Mr. McCARVER. The preamble of the gentleman from Monterey (Mr. Botts) suits me better than any I have seen, because it is the shortest. There is no necessity for a long preamble; neither is it necessary that we should go to the different States for a model. The very fact that the proposition of the Committee is from the Constitution of New York would induce me to reject it. If we sit here much longer we will have a resolution to annex New York, Constitution and all.

On motion, the Committee then rose and reported progress.

It appearing that a quorum was not present, on motion, the House adjourned till to-morrow at 10 o'clock.

SATURDAY, OCTOBER 6, 1849.

In Convention. Prayer by Padre Ramirez. Journal of yesterday read and approved.

On motion of Mr. GWIN, the House resolved itself into Committee of the Whole, Mr. Gilbert in the chair, on so much of the report of the Committee on the Constitution, as relates to the Schedule.

Section 1 being under consideration, as follows:

SEC. 1. All rights, prosecutions, claims, and contracts, as well of individuals as of bodies corporate, and all laws in force at the time of the adoption of this Constitution, and not inconsistent therewith, until altered or repealed by the Legislature, shall continue as if the same had not been adopted.

Mr. SHANNON moved the transposition of the third and first sections.

Mr. PRICE moved to strike out the first section. He could see no necessity for it.

Mr. DIMMICK thought there was a good deal of necessity for it. It was to provide that the present officers of the Government, prefects, alcaldes and others, should perform the duties of their offices until their places were taken, under the new Constitution.

Mr. MCCARVER did not think we should make laws with any reference whatever to the laws of Mexico. This was a Constitution for our own State. He was opposed to legalising the acts of any officers under the Mexican law. This Convention was not called upon to say whether there any such officers in existence.

Mr. DIMMICK said it was not to meddle with the existing form of government that this section was proposed. When this Constitution was adopted by the people, it would be the supreme law of the land. But under it, as it stands, the present officers of the Government have no power to act. Consequently, until these officers were susperseded, there would be no government at all, without such a provision. This only recognizes these officers until the Legislature shall meet and provide for the emergency.

Mr. HALLECK said that the first section was copied from the second section of the Schedule of the Constitution of Louisiana. Section 3d was copied with very slight alteration from the 4th section of the same schedule, (142 and 144, Constitution of La.) Both of these sections correspond very closely with the sections on the same subject in the first Constitution of Louisiana when she was in nearly the same situation with respect to former laws as California now is. It was a matter of great importance that they should be adopted.

Mr. MCCARVER said there was a marked difference between our Constitution and that of Louisiana. Louisiana was an organized Territory, and under territorial laws from 1803 to 1805. It was therefore necessary that the authority recognized by the Government of the United States should continue in existence until the State Government went into operation.

Mr. BOTTS. I have no objection to this section myself, except that it lays down just this proposition: two and two are four. It asserts a doctrine, sir, which I have never yet seen the man to controvert—that the municipal laws continue in existence until they are abolished by the competent authority. All rights, prosecutions, claims, and contracts, as well of individuals as of bodies corporate, and all laws in force at the time of the adoption of this Constitution that it does not repeal, are not repealed. Who, in the name of common sense, doubts that? If the question is upon the truth contained in this section, where can you find a negative vote? That these laws continue in force if they are not repealed; in other words, that a man lives till he dies. There is only one of two ways that they can cease to exist; by the enactment of this Constitution, or by the enactment of the Legislature.

Mr. Gwin. I think the gentleman from Monterey is entirely mistaken in one respect. There are some rights under the present laws that this Constitution takes away—those of individuals. The right of suffrage is one. It is proper that they should know it. This Constitution declares who shall vote in California. There were other individuals who could vote under the municipal law; there may be municipal laws that are in conflict with the Constitution. No possible harm can result from such a provision. It makes no declaration what the law is. It is designed to tell those who have lived under the existing municipal laws, of what rights they are deprived, and what privileges are conferred upon them.

Mr. Botts. If the object of the clause be what the gentleman from San Francisco says, to tell the inhabitants of this country that this Constitution is the law of the land from the time of its adoption, and that those who are excluded from voting are excluded from voting, I think I could form a section that would answer quite as well. Why, sir, the people know all this. It is not necessary to tell them.

Mr. Jones. I would ask the gentleman (Mr. Botts) to reflect and see if, in the recent history of California, he cannot pick out a spot where this principle has been doubted, and even denied. It may not have been so in Monterey. But, sir, I myself, even with my very limited knowledge of the history of this country, can very well see the importance of asserting this great principle in the Constitution which we have adopted. I have heard it doubted; I have heard it denied; and there is more than one gentleman in this House who has heard it doubted and denied, and perhaps the gentleman himself, (Mr. Botts,) if he reflects, will see the necessity of it.

Mr. Price. I cannot perceive that there is any principle contained in this section at all. It is a mere declaration that this Constitution goes into effect after its ratification by the people.

Mr. Jones. There is a very important principle contained in it; that the municipal laws heretofore in force in this country, are in force until they are properly repealed. Perhaps the gentleman from San Francisco (Mr. Price) has come from where the principle has been denied.

Mr. Steuart. If this section is to carry with it the interpretation which has been given to it by gentlemen who have addressed the House, that all laws not inconsistent with this Constitution shall continue in force if not repealed, then, sir, I think it comes in conflict with another section following soon after, which makes it depend upon the happening of another contingency—a contingency that may never occur. In the 7th section you make it the duty of the present Executive of this State, immediately after ascertaining that this Constitution has been so ratified, to make proclamation of that fact, and thenceforth this Constitution shall be ordained and established as the Constitution of California. Now, suppose the present Executive of this State does not choose to make this proclamation, what is going to be the result? I want information as to the effect.

Mr. Sherwood. If it conflicts the Constitution, it will not be enforced, as a matter of course.

The question was then taken on striking out the 1st section, and decided in the negative.

Mr. Shannon's motion to transpose the 1st and 3d sections, was also decided in the negative.

The section, as reported, was then adopted.

Section 2 was adopted as reported, viz:

Sec. 2. The Legislature shall provide for the removal of all causes which may be pending when this Constitution goes into effect, to courts created by the same.

Section 3 being under consideration, as follows:

SEC. 3. In order that no inconvenience may result to the public service from the taking effect of this Constitution, no office shall be superceded thereby; but the laws relative to the duties of the officers to be appointed under this Constitution, shall remain in full force.

Mr. BOTTS. I hardly know what to say about this section. I do not know if there are any officers in this government—if there be any such thing as a government here at all. If there be any officers I am perfectly willing that they should remain officers, but I have heretofore endeavored to show that, under the decision of the Supreme Court, the political offices created under the Constitution of Mexico have been abolished. I shall, perhaps, be compelled to vote against the section simply because I think, under the decision of the Supreme Court, there is no government in California. Most objectionable as the laws are, which define the powers of those officers, if there be such officers, I would rather have them than none at all. That is the alternative; but remember, sir, one of these laws is this, if I understand it, and one adopted by your judges in your Supreme Court: that the judge who sits upon a case of life and death shall be entitled to receive $100 if he can procure the conviction of the criminal. That is one of the principles under the Mexican law—a principle most odious and repugnant to the feelings of an American. I will not refer to others; I do not want now to show how objectionable many of these principles are, but I contend that the whole of them have been blotted out by the change of government, under the decision of the Supreme Court, and of common sense and common custom. There are no officers, and no laws in existence in California that define and determine the duties of officers. Government is what? It is that power which is authorized to make laws. Does any body pretend to say that there exists in California a power to alter, amend, or abolish any laws, other than that of the people themselves? No, sir, we are expressly told that no such power exists; and yet we are told that a government exists; a government which cannot amend—cannot reform the laws. Who ever heard of such a government? There are no officers, yet I wish there were, objectionable as are their powers. I would rather have them for the short space of time that intervenes, than have none. But I cannot support the doctrine contained in that section. I shall vote against the section, not because I have any objection to these gentlemen performing the functions of officers, if they had the right to do it, but because they have no such right, under the decision of the Supreme Court. We are required in this clause to run in direct opposition to that decision, and declare that the political law of this country has not been changed, and that their duties and powers are those that the political law of Mexico gave them. It is utterly impossible that I can recognize this doctrine.

Mr. SHERWOOD. I think I see the difficulty under which the gentleman labors, but if he looks over the section it will not prove liable to the objection which he names. We neither affirm nor deny the existence of any officers; the section says nothing about the legality of the exercise of these offices. Public custom has permitted them to exercise these duties, and the section merely provides that they shall continue to exercise them as before, until the laws are established. I do not think it would be proper in the Constitution either to affirm or interdict the discharge of these duties; but we say that no officer shall be superseded by the going into effect of this Constitution until the Legislature shall have passed laws and elected, or provided for the election, of officers to supersede those that may exist, if any do exist. I think the gentleman should vote for it, and that the objections which he makes to the exercise of the duties by certain officers under the Mexican law would be very well addressed to the Legislature, and would excite that body to speedy action. If $100 is offered to a judge as a bribe, the sooner he is out of office the better. The argument could very appropriately be addressed to the Legislature.

Mr. JONES. Either one of three things must exist: either there are no officers and none will be superseded, or there are certain offices which do legally exist, and certain others which do not legally exist, and a part will be superseded and a part will not be superseded; or they all legally exist, and none will be superseded. The article expresses nothing in regard to the legality of the offices. If an office is an office at all by the decision of the Supreme Court it certainly will not be superseded. But if the gentleman (Mr. Botts) will look to the law of nations he will see that this has always been the case. Such was the case in Louisiana; such when France conquered Italy; and such has been the case in all conquered countries; that there are certain offices which, from the necessity of the case, do exist until other offices are established to supersede them. It is necessary that there should be some administration of laws—some order and government. This usage is established by the law of nations. Now I apprehend that the decision of the Supreme Court of the United States does not extend to all the offices of this territory. There are certain offices which must be retained until other offices are created in their place. They have nothing to do, *per se*, with the political law of the land. But, sir, the question has been decided by the people of this territory; they have elected by their voice officers to fill certain stations. How could they elect officers to offices which do not exist? The gentleman from Monterey must see that his argument fails here. The law, as it exists, becomes the voice of the people of this territory; they have adopted it as a part of their municipal law. Then if these offices do exist, we, the Convention of the people of this territory, have no right to abolish and deny the will of the people who elected these officers. Upon the very same day that these officers were elected we were elected. The very same voters that elected the Supreme Judges and Alcaldes elected us their representatives. What power have we to deny this right to the people? I say we have none.

Mr. Hastings. I am willing to admit that the gentleman from Monterey (Mr. Botts) understands his own position, but I hope he will admit that he is entirely wrong. The officers alluded to here are officers that may be created under municipal law.

Mr. Botts. I admit it.

Mr. Hastings. Then it alludes to some officers whose election is authorized by law. But the gentlemen who sustain this question are more out of the way than the gentleman from Monterey. It seems to me that they do not understand what the purport of this section is. It declares, that "in order that no inconvenience may result to the public service from the taking effect of this Constitution, *no office shall be superseded thereby.*"

It expressly states that no office shall be superseded thereby. At the same time, in their argument, they tell you that these offices shall be superseded. The section does not say so; perhaps there is a mistake in the copy. But, Mr. Chairman, here I think is where the difficulty arises; the section adds: "but the laws relative to the duties of the several officers shall remain in full force until the entering into office of the new officer"—the new officer to be appointed under this Constitution. But is it at all said, either here or in the first part of the section, that any officers shall be superseded. We are superseding officers now of Prefect, Sub-Prefect and Alcalde, yet we declare positively that no officers shall be superseded, but the laws shall remain in full force regulating the duties of these officers. Now either the section is wrong or the gentlemen are wrong. I shall vote against it as it stands.

Mr. Steuart. I agree entirely with the views expressed by my friend from Monterey (Mr. Botts) upon this occasion, as well as upon a former occasion. I shall not attempt to add anything to an argument which has been so ably and fully presented as this. I merely rise to offer an amendment, without which I cannot vote for that section. I move to substitute for the word "office" the word "officer," and to insert after the word "shall" the following, "officer appointed by the existing government," &c.

Mr. Botts. Perhaps I was too broad in the statement I made a little while ago that no offices were in force in California. I yield entirely to the statement made by the gentleman from San Joaquim, (Mr. Jones,) because I think it is undeniable that there are some offices which the people have created by election. I never hesitate to admit an error when I discover it; but most unquestionably the gentleman from Sacramento (Mr. Hastings) is right in the reading of this clause; and it is very plain to see how this error has crept into the Convention. It came from the Committee. Do you not see, sir, what the Committee has done? Have they ever presented you with an original idea since they have been acting here? They admit it themselves; they have gone to other Constitutions and presented them to you, without any regard at all to California, and the peculiar circumstances under which California exists. What have they done? In their haste they have grabbed up a provision out of a Constitution, where, no doubt, the offices that were brought into existence under the new Constitution were exactly the same that existed under the old, and therefore that Constitution very wisely inserted this provision, that no inconvenience might result from the change of government. They were offices that were not inimical to the people, and to which the people did not object. Has not the gentleman from Sacramento shown you that offices must be superseded thereby—are bound to be superseded thereby? The very offices created by the people themselves it is intended shall be superseded by the Constitution. If the gentleman wishes to effect what the Committee thought they had effected, he must alter this clause so as to read that they shall not be superseded thereby, until the laws of this Constitution shall go into operation. In one part of the sentence they say no office shall be superseded; in another part they tell us about new officers entering upon their duties.

Mr. Sherwood. I think the gentleman is entirely mistaken. The section is clear enough. It simply says that upon the going into operation of this Constitution no office is superseded, nor the duties of this office, until the new officers are installed into office under this Constitution. These officers remain until they are superseded. I would leave the question as to the legality of these offices entirely open, to be decided by those who have a right to decide it.

Mr. Halleck. I rise merely to call attention to this fact. It was said that this section was taken from some Constitution that did not supersede any office. I have looked over the Constitution from which it is taken, and I find that it supersedes a good many offices. It entirely changes the organization of the courts, and puts out of office innumerable judges. Now it would be rather strange if these officers continue yet in Louisiana, notwithstanding this clause, under the new Constitution. I agree perfectly with the gentleman from Sacramento, (Mr. Hastings,) in regard to the inconsistency which he points out in this section. I think myself that it requires amendment.

Mr. Shannon. I think this difficulty can very easily be removed, and I shall move an amendment to the amendment of the gentleman from San Francisco, as follows: to strike out the word "but" after the word "thereby," and insert the word "nor;" strike out the words "several offices shall remain in full force" and insert the words "same be changed."

Mr. Halleck proposed to amend Mr. Shannon's amendment, so as to strike out all after the word "thereby," and insert "nor the laws relative to the duties of the several officers be changed, until the entering into office of the new officers to be appointed under this Constitution;" which Mr. Shannon accepted as a modification of his amendment.

Mr. Gwin offered the following, which Mr. Halleck said was precisely the same as his:

Strike out the words "but the laws relative to the duties of the officers to be," and insert in lieu thereof the words, "nor the laws relative to the duties of the several officers be changed until the entering into office of the new officers to be."

Mr. SHANNON then withdrew his amendment, as amended, and the question being on Mr. Gwin's amendment it was agreed to; and the section, as amended, was adopted.

Section 4th of the report being under consideration, as follows:

SEC. 4. The provisions of this Constitution concerning the inability of persons to hold certain offices therein mentioned, shall not be held to apply to officers chosen by the people at the first election, or by the Legislature at its first session.

Mr. BOTTS said: There are certain things provided with respect to the inability of certain persons, which I think require amendment. For instance, no person holding an office under the Government of the United States, shall be eligible to office under this Government. Is it intended that the effect of this section shall be, that officers who hold these offices may also hold office under the election held at the first election for officers of this State Government. I think, sir, although that might suit me, it would not suit other gentlemen in this House. I think, for instance, that there is the office of Governor, a very snug little place, and there is the offices of member of Congress and Senator, and there are State officers, judges of the Supreme Court, Attorney General, &c. I think we said a little while ago that no person holding the office of naval storekeeper should be eligible to these offices. I feel personally interested in that matter, and I want to know whether the naval storekeeper can be judge of the Supreme Court or Attorney General.

Mr. JONES. I move to strike out the words "inability of," and insert the words "term of residence necessary to enable."

Mr. GWIN. I certainly, when this question was before the Committee, never saw any other bearing to it than this: that it was to enable every person who was an elector under this Constitution, to be a candidate for the Legislature, and that members of the Legislature should be eligible to offices under the first Legislature that they are afterwards excluded from by this Constitution. The reason that influenced my mind was, that the members elected to the first Legislature might be the best qualified to fill offices that were to be provided by the Legislature. In the Constitution of Louisiana which has recently gone into operation, there is this provision, Article 146 of the Schedule:

The provisions of Article 28, concerning the inability of members of the Legislature to hold certain offices therein mentioned, shall not be held to apply to the members of the first Legislature elected under this Constitution.

This 28th article of the Constitution of Louisiana, excluded members of the Legislature from holding certain offices, and all the important offices of the State were to be filled. All the important offices of California are to be filled by the Legislature; Judges of the Supreme Court, Attorney General, Surveyor General, Treasurer, Secretary of State, &c. It was intended that the members of the first Legislature should not be excluded from holding these offices. There are certain qualifications as to residence; and it was intended that it should not apply in the first election; that any man who could vote at the first election, could be a candidate for the Senate and House of Representatives. That was the bearing of the section in my mind when it was before the Committee. If the gentleman (Mr. Botts) offers any amendment providing for what he deems the difficulty, I am willing to vote for it.

The question was taken on laying the section on the table for future consideration, and decided in the negative.

Mr. JONES inquired in what section of the Constitution the provision in relation to the inability of members of the Legislature was contained. He thought by comparing that and the section under consideration the House might be able to arrive at some satisfactory result.

Section 20, of the Legislative Department was then read, as follows:

SEC. 20. No Senator, or member of Assembly, shall, during the term for which he shall have been elected, be appointed to any civil office of profit, under this State, which shall have been created, or the emoluments of which shall have been increased, during such term, except such office as may be filled by elections by the people.

Mr. HALLECK explained the object of the section under consideration, (sec. 4.) It was intended to obviate questions in regard to the eligibility of existing officers of the country. He thought it should be so amended as to include all. A judge could not be elected to the Legislature if the amendment of the member from San Joaquin prevailed.

Mr. BOTTS would simply remind the gentleman that although there might be some difficulty about excluding so good a man as a judge from the Legislature, that evil was more than counterbalanced by admitting the navy agent to hold office under this Constitution, which he would be if the clause was adopted as it stood. He thought, however, that it was best to exclude both judge and navy agent.

Mr. HASTINGS. I am aware that in our vicinity here, and perhaps throughout the whole House, there is a great disinclination to make any invasion upon the report of the Committee; therefore, being afraid that perhaps this may be voted down, I will say a word. Most certainly every member of the House will see that the section as it now stands would not at all accomplish the object that the Committee had in view, and that the Committee committed a great oversight. "The provisions of this Constitution concerning the inability of persons to hold certain offices therein mentioned, shall not be held to apply to officers chosen by the people at the first election, or by the Legislature at its first session."

Now, the laws in this Constitution relative to the inability of persons to hold office are not to apply at the first election. It is provided in this Constitution, that any person guilty of bribery, or a man who fights a duel, is thereby rendered incompetent to hold any office of trust or honor. But he may receive a bribe, or fight a duel, with impunity, previous to the first election. This section gives him that privilege. If he has been convicted of any infamous crime it amounts to the same thing.

Mr. GWIN. I second the amendment of the gentleman from San Joaquin, (Mr. JONES,) which I think covers the whole ground, with the further amendment—"or the office."

Mr. STEUART. I really think this is a very important matter. I do not see that either of the amendments covers the whole ground. I move that the section be laid by for a little while in order that it may be properly considered and acted upon.

The question was then taken on Mr. JONES's amendment, and it was adopted, and the 4th section, as amended, was adopted.

Section 5 was then adopted, as reported, viz:

SEC. 5. Every citizen of California, declared a legal voter by this Constitution, and every citizen of the United States, a resident of this State on the day of election, shall be entitled to vote at the first general election under the Constitution.

Section 6, as reported by the Committee, was then taken up as follows, viz:

SEC 6. This Constitution shall be submitted to the people for their ratification or rejection, at the general election to be held on Tuesday, the sixth day of November next. The Executive of the existing government of California shall issue a proclamation to the Prefects of the several districts, or, in case of vacancy, to the Sub-Prefects, requiring them to cause such election to be held on the day aforesaid, in their respective districts. The election shall be conducted in the manner which was prescribed for the election of the delegates to this Convention, except that the Prefects or Sub-Prefects ordering such election in each district, shall have power to designate any additional number of places for opening the polls, and that in every place of holding the election a regular poll list shall be kept by the judges and inspectors of elections. It shall be the duty of these judges and inspectors of elections, on the days aforesaid, to receive the votes of the voters qualified to vote at such election. Each voter shall express his opinion by depositing in the ballot-box a ticket whereon shall be written "For the Constitution," or "Against the Constitution," or some such words as will distinctly convey the intention of the voter. These judges and inspectors shall also receive the votes for the several officers to be voted for at said election, as herein provided. At the close of the election the judges and inspectors shall carefully count each ballot, and forthwith make duplicate returns thereof to the Prefect (or Sub-Prefect, as the case may be) of their respective districts, and said Prefect or Sub-Prefect shall transmit one of the same by the most safe and rapid conveyance, to the Secretary of State. Upon the receipt of said returns, or on the 7th day of December next, if the returns be not sooner received, it shall be the duty of a Board of Canvassers, to consist of the Secretary of State, one of the Judges of the Superior Court, the Prefect, Judge of First Instance, and an Alcalde of the district of Monterey, or any three of the aforementioned officers, in the presence of all persons who choose to attend, to compare the votes given at said election, and to immediately publish an abstract of the same in one or more of the newspapers of California.

Mr. Botts. I think this section has been taken again at random from some Constitution where the state of things is altogether different from that which exists in California. To say that the Executive of the existing government shall issue a proclamation, may be a very proper way for the people of Louisiana or New York to talk to their Governor, whom they make, and who is under their control, and it would be a very proper way for us to talk to our Governor if he was under our control; but I do not feel authorized here to give any directions to the Executive of this Territory, nor do I think such an order would come with much propriety from this body. The Executive of the existing government of California has proclaimed to the people of California that he is instructed to prevent the existence of a government here under the circumstances that we propose to have this government. Such a proclamation is issued from him—I do not know how much, as an individual, he is with us in this matter, but he tells us, that as an officer of the Government, the action of Congress is necessary to render this a government. There is a great want of delicacy in asking that gentlemen under these circumstances to take any hand at all in this matter; but, sir, I think it is an unheard of impropriety to *command* him to do it. I therefore, at least, propose to amend the words of the section by saying that the Executive of the existing government of California "shall be *requested* to issue a proclamation." Unless I have evidence on this floor that he is willing to issue such a proclamation, I will not even request him to do it. But if he is willing, there is no man in the land of whom I would sooner ask a favor than of that gentleman, for it is certainly a fav r. You have no right to make such an application to an individual in this land, not known to this Constitution; you have not a Governor at all under this Constitution. If he is a Governor, he is a Governor by other authority than that created by you. I move, therefore, to amend by saying "the existing Governor *shall be requested* to issue a proclamation.

Mr. Halleck. I think the amendment of the gentleman from Monterey is a very proper one; but whether you say shall do it, or shall be requested, I can assure him that the gentleman to whom he refers, will do it.

Mr. Gwin. I think it very important that we should leave nothing to contingencies here. I have heard General Riley say in private conversation, that he will issue such a proclamation; but I think there should be no doubt on the subject. By some contingency that we know not of, he might refuse to do it, and this is what I think should be provided against.

Mr. Hastings. Suppose the Executive should decline to issue this proclamation, or another Executive takes the place of this one, and he is not willing to acknowledge our right to make this order. These are contingencies that we must provide for. We have no certainty that in November the same Executive will be here, or that the feelings of the present Executive will be the same. Now, to *request* the Executive, whoever he may be, is still leaving the matter entirely doubtful. Although we have assurance that General Riley will do it, we have no assurance that any other Governor will do it, should there be another placed in the office. If gentlemen will provide for that contingency, I will be in favor of the motion.

Mr. Sherwood. If such casualties should occur, of course the election would nevertheless be held, because we say expressly such an election shall be held on the 7th of November. It would be precisely the same case of interregnum that is always provided for. The prefects would go on as if there was a Governor.

Mr. Gwin. I move to insert the following:

That the President of the Convention shall issue a proclamation in the event of the Governor refusing to do it.

Mr. Botts. I would rather not anticipate such an event. I therefore prefer not accepting the amendment.

Mr. Jones. If the election should take place on the 7th day of November, it would not give time to print the Constitution and send it down to Los Angeles and San Diego. Even if they had time at Los Angeles to consider the effect of this Constitution, here is another difficulty. Upon the 7th day of December, if the returns are not received sooner, the Secretary must count them, and upon the 15th day of December, the Legislature must hold its session. That will give only seven days for the members from Los Angeles to arrive at the seat of Government; and if it be necessary for the Secretary to issue certificates of election to the persons elected, he will have no time. In the districts of San Joaquin and Sacramento where the difference between the precincts is great, and the means of communication limited, it would be very difficult for a member to know whether he was elected or not, and perhaps some intimation from the Secretary might be necessary. At all events, the members from Los Angeles have only seven days to come to the place of the Legislature. I think they ought to have at least two weeks.

Mr. Tefft. I think if the gentleman will look at that section he will see that the difficulty is provided for in requiring the duplicate returns of the election to be returned to the Prefect, so that the candidate elected can ascertain as to his election from the Prefect.

Mr. Jones. That avoids the difficulty.

Mr. Botts. I rise simply to suggest a modification of the words which I originally moved. I think it better than the original. Strike out the words "shall issue a proclamation to," and insert "is hereby requested to issue a proclamation to the people of California, directing," and further to amend, by striking out the words "to" and "requiring."

Mr. Gwin. Before we go into that, there is something more important which we ought to settle. Whether we hold this election on the 7th day of November or not, I think the gentleman from San Joaquin (Mr. Jones) is mistaken in regard to the difficulty. I do not object to the election on that day, because the sooner we put this government in operation the better, and I have received assurance that this Constitution can be printed and placed in the hands of the people in time for them to vote upon it by the 7th of November. I am satisfied with that, although I would prefer a longer time. But, sir, I wish to call the attention of the Committee to this fact: that if the election takes place on the 7th of November, the Legislature should meet at an earlier day than the 15th of December. It is absolutely necessary. I believe, sir, that it is a matter of the greatest importance to California, inasmuch as we have determined to put this government in operation forthwith, that the representatives from California should appear in the Congress of the United States at the earliest practicable period; and if we hold our election on the 7th of November, I believe that the Legislature ought to meet on the fourth Monday of November, which is the 27th. That gives three weeks; and the members can be notified of their election by the Prefects in the several districts, giving sufficient time for them to attend at the seat of government. The reason why I conceive this to be so important is this: on the 7th of November we elect two members of Congress. It is well known, that on the 1st of December, before the steamer sails, it can be ascertained to a certainty that there are two members of Congress elected, and it would be the duty of these two members of Congress to proceed forthwith to Washington City. But, sir, that would be only half a representation of the State, unless the Senators should go on at the same time. I know that this section provides that the canvass of votes cannot take place till the 7th of December—so late that the members elected could not receive official notification in time to go on. It may not be generally known in this country that, in the appropriations made by Congress, it is a rule of Congress that the appropriation bills shall all be reported within sixty days after the meeting of Congress at the long session. If we send our Members and Senators there to take their seats on the 1st of January, they will be in full time to ask for appropriations for breakwaters, light-houses, and other purposes. But if the representation from this State do not get to Washington before the last of January, when these appropriation bills are reported, they will find the thirty millions of dollars apprcpriated, and California will find herself in the background. The statement of the Senators and Members, even if they were not admitted officially, would be listened to, and would have a beneficial influence. Hence, sir, it is a matter of the greatest importance that, if we can possibly organize our government, and send on our Senators and Representatives on the 1st day of December, we should do it; and if this Convention decides upon this course, I say there is plenty of time; and inasmuch as there are important interests of this State that can be promoted in the Congress of the United States by the advance of one month in the appearance of our Representatives there, I hope it will determine to elect these officers in time for the steamer of the 1st of December.

Mr. Hill. I think the time is too short from the 7th to the 27th of November.

Mr. Sherwood. By an oversight of the Committee the 7th was fixed upon. It should be the 6th of November.

The question was then taken on the amendment of Mr. Botts, and it was adopted.

Mr. Jones. I would now merely suggest to the House the difficulty which will necessarily attend this first date. In the first place, we cannot adjourn before the 10th; then it will take at least four days for this Constitution to be drawn up and the official copies made and sent to San Francisco. If it is to go to San Francisco to be printed, it will take eight days to get it printed, bound, and ready to be sent to the several districts; and it will take ten days to go from San Francisco to Los Angeles, and two or three days more to San Diego. That will bring it to the 3d day of November at Los Angeles, and the 5th of November at San Diego. Thus you cannot have it voted upon by the people on the 6th day of November, without even allowing for accidents.

Mr. Sherwood. If we adjourn here on the 9th of this month; say it takes three days to get it to San Francisco, that is the 12th; eight days to print it would be the 20th; ten days to send it to Los Angeles would be the 1st of November; that would leave six days there and four days at San Diego. But the members of this Convention who go down, will circulate the substance of this Constitution; they will take copies down with them, and submit them to the people in advance. Besides, the rainy season is coming on, and the longer you put off this election, the less voters you will get.

Mr. Hill. All I ask for the people of San Diego is, that they may have a chance of reading this Constitution before they vote upon it. If we adjourn upon the 9th, this Constitution has to be made up and sent to San Francisco. Taking into consideration the length of time that it will require to print and distribute it, I consider the time allowed altogether too short. If there were express horses on the road, it might do; but there are none. I think the shortest time that you can possibly make your Constitution reach San Diego, would be about the day of the election. There would not one in twenty have a chance of reading it. If the House order copies to be written and furnished to the District of San Diego, by the delegates when they leave here, I have no objection. I see the necessity of having this election take place as soon as possible, and I am not opposed to the 6th of November on any other ground than the impracticability of having it at so early a period. I would be very glad if it could be held on that day.

Mr. Gwin. I agree with the gentleman that these copies can and ought to be made out. I understand that the mail rider who was to have started yesterday morning is still here; and I think the Governor can keep him until these copies are written out. I have no doubt we have clerks here who can very soon make out such a number of copies as will be required, and have them ready in time.

Mr. Tefft. The members here themselves can take copies down to their respective districts. I have before me a perfect copy of the constitution, and I intend to take it home. Nearly every delegate has an entire copy lying on his table. He will have this ready to take with him as he starts. This is a matter of calculation, and I am well convinced that the constitution can be placed before the people of San Diego, even the printed copies, on or before the 1st day of November.

Mr. Price. I am in hopes the earliest day may be fixed for holding the election. I see no reason why the constitution cannot be sufficiently circulated in the most remote districts in proper time. The steamer of the 1st of November, will be at San Diego on the 4th or 5th, and there will be sailing vessels that will start before, and run down in a very short time. At this season of the year, a vessel will arrive there in four or five days.

Mr. Hill. All I ask is, that the constitution may be laid before the people of San Diego in time for them to read it, and make up their minds how they shall vote.

Mr. Noriego. In my opinion, the date fixed upon for the election is far too early. Even supposing you could finish your business by the 10th, it would be necessary to make out a revised and complete copy, have it translated, and revise the translation. It must be put in such language as will be fit to send to the press. The Interpreter has not as yet had any portion of the engrossed copies presented to him to make a clear and correct translation from. It will have to be revised by some of the Spanish members themselves; they wish to see that the language is correct. I do not see how it is practicable to have this prepared and sent down to the southern districts by that date. I think the earliest date should be fixed at the 20th instead of the 7th of November. It is a great evil that we should be delayed a single day; but I consider it absolutely necessary that the people should have a few days to examine the constitution submitted to them, before they determine upon it.

Mr. Botts. After hearing what has been said on this subject, I have changed my opinion very much about it. I am inclined to think I shall go for the latest day. We do, in this proposition of the 6th of November, hurry this thing in a most extraordinary manner. The people ought to have time not only to read, but to understand, to consider—yes, sir, and to discuss the provisions of this constitution. That is infinitely more important than an early day. The people of San Jose and Monterey want all and more than the time that is proposed under this section, to consider what their representatives have been doing here. It has taken us thirty days to consider this, and we tell the people of San Diego they must consider it in two days or one day—probably in thirty minutes. This is the previous question, sir; and the previous question brought to bear upon the people with a vengeance. It will not do. As to the consideration that has been urged here of sending down written copies, I do not think that subject has been properly considered. These manuscript copies must be certified copies; and the copies that gentlemen take from their tables are not the correct copies necessarily of this constitution. It is not a garbled constitution that ought to go to the people. You must send down certified copies. Remember, you have given an order for the printing of this Constitution, and probably your printed copies may cost you sixty cents a copy. What will your manuscript copies cost you? Sixty dollars, sir! I guarantee that you may write dollars for cents. To thrust this constitution down the throats of the people in this manner, whether they will or no, is not the way to receive their unanimous vote.

Mr. Stearns. I shall offer an amendment: to insert in place of Tuesday, the 7th, the 4th Tuesday of November. It would be impossible for the constitution to be circulatod before the 7th.

Mr. Shannon. I think the time between the adjournment of the Convention and the holding of the election, and between the day of the election and the day of canvassing the votes, is in rather bad proportion. We might very well extend the first time by limiting the latter. We might have the canvassing day on the 7th of December, and give the time thus gained to the time previous to the election; take a week from that, and add a week to the other. I do not think we will gain any thing by attempting to force this election at so early a day as the 7th of November. We ought to allow the people time to reflect and consider upon the constitution which we submit to them. While the time proposed by the gentleman from Los Angeles (Mr. Stearns) is too long, I think this is too short. I think it is of more importance that the Constitution should be well considered here, and receive the deliberate sanction of the people, than any of those considerations urged in reference to sending our representatives to Congress. I move to insert the 2d Tuesday of November.

Mr. Gwin. I believe the first question to be decided is whether we shall have this election on the 1st Tuesday in November. If the House determine to hold it on that day all the other motions fail. If it is stricken out, it will be the sense of the Convention that we should have a later day. In order to have a direct vote, I move to strike out that date, and leave the blank to be filled up.

Mr. Steuart. I rise to appeal to the gentlemen from Sacramento, who are familiar with the difficulties of communicating information through that region, whether these difficulties do not exist. I really and honestly believe that a vast number of persons who are coming in by that route, and hundreds of citizens of California here, do not know we are holding this Convention. It was not until the members had left Sacramento City that I was informed of it, even seven miles off. I know of hundreds who did not hear even that such a thing was proposed. It is utterly impossible—I do not care how many expresses you send—to disseminate this information throughout that region in time to hold the election at the time proposed. I hope, therefore, that we shall have a longer period.

Mr. Hill. So far as the time of holding the election is concerned, we are proceeding rather too fast in fixing that time. We may sit twenty days longer in this Convention. In reference to the express, I desire to state for the information of the House, that I was in Los Angeles, and the average time of the express was twenty days—sometimes thirty days. I hope the House will not force upon the lower districts this constitution, without giving the people time to consider it.

Mr. Sherwood. If this time is extended from the 6th to the 13th of November, I have no objection to its being so extended, but I certainly cannot vote to go beyond that date. I desire, with all other gentlemen, that sufficient time shall be given for the full consideration of this constitution. As to the adjournment of this Convention, I shall be for fixing, if possible, the very earliest day, in order to drive us to an adjournment. I cannot consent to sit here much longer than one or two days next week.

Mr. Stearns. I withdraw my amendment in order to let the gentleman (Mr. Gwin) move to strike out the 6th.

Mr. Gwin. I move to strike out the 6th of November.

Mr. Dimmick. I am in favor of having this left blank for the present, because it is uncertain how long a time will be spent in Convention, and if you fix the time now, it may be that that time may elapse before we get through with our business here. I understand that certain legal gentlemen are writing out speeches in regard to the decisions of the Supreme Court of the United States, and if we are to wait until they are prepared and delivered, I presume a month will be spent here before this Constitutian is completed.

The question was then taken on Mr. Gwin's motion to strike out the date in the section, and it was adopted.

Mr. Stearns then renewed his motion to insert the 4th Tuesday in November.

Mr. Hoppe. If it is in order, I should like to move an amendment.

The CHAIR stated that it was not in order, because there were two amendments pending.

Mr. HOPPE. If the amendments now pending are rejected, I shall move to insert the 20th of November. The members of this Convention have all admitted, that by the 5th day of November, the constitution can be sent to the farthest extremity of California. In that event, the people of the different districts would have fifteen days for reading, discussing, and digesting the articles therein proposed. I am in favor of having this election as soon as possible, but I am not willing to vote for a day that will compel a large portion of the people to take up the constitution and read it, and immediately vote upon it. No man can get the full sense of a constitution by a mere reading of it. The people should have an opportunity of assembling together, comparing their views, and discussing the subject fully. I believe fifteen days is the least time within which they can carefully read, digest, and come to a deliberate judgment upon the provisions of this constitution, and I would therefore move to insert the 20th of November.

Mr. JONES. I would suggest that the other blanks be filled with the words "December the 20th and December the 25th," thus giving ample time to the Legislature to elect Senators and Representatives to start in the steamer of the 1st of January. If you defer the election to the 13th of November, of course the Senators and Representatives cannot start before the first of January. This will give them ample time.

Mr. HALLECK. I shall vote for the second Tuesday in November. I think that will give us plenty of time, even including the long speeches on constitutional questions with which we are threatened. I was in favor of the 7th of November when reported by the Committee, because I then anticipated that the Convention would adjourn in time for that date; but as such is not likely to be the case, I think the second Tuesday will be the proper date to insert.

After further discussion, Mr. Stearns withdrew his motion.

Mr. HILL then offered the following resolution, which was adopted:

Resolved, That for the present, the blank shall not be filled fixing the day of election.

On motion, the Committee rose and reported progress.

On motion, leave of absence was granted to Mr. Sansevaine, in consequence of sickness in his family.

On motion, the House took a recess till half-past 3 o'clock, P. M.

AFTERNOON SESSION, 3½ O'CLOCK, P. M.

Mr. GWIN submitted the following resolution, which was adopted after a short debate, viz:

Resolved, That this Convention will adjourn *sine die* on Tuesday the 9th inst.

Mr. McDOUGAL moved a suspension of the rules, which being agreed to, he submitted the following resolution, which was adopted, viz:

Resolved, That no member shall speak longer than five minutes on any matter before this body.

The House then, on motion of Mr. GWIN, resolved into Committee of the Whole, Mr. Gilbert in the chair, on so much of the report of the Committee on the Constitution as relates to the "Schedule."

Section 6 of the report of the Committee being under consideration—

Mr. BOTTS moved to amend by adding at the end thereof the words: "And the Executive will also, immediately after ascertaining that the Constitution has been ratified by the people, make proclamation of the fact; and thenceforth this Constitution shall be ordained and established as the Constitution of California;" which was agreed to.

On motion of Mr. GWIN, the dates in the section were all stricken out.

On motion of Mr. WOZENCRAFT, the words "or printed" were inserted after the words "written;" and thus amended, the section was adopted.

Section 7 then being under consideration, as follows, viz:

SEC. 7. If this Constitution shall be ratified by the people of California, the Executive of the existing government shall immediately after the same shall be ascertained in the manner herein directed, cause a fair copy thereof to be forwarded to the President of the United States, with the respectful request of the people of California that it may be laid before the Congress of the United States. And the Executive will also immediately after ascertaining that this Constitution has been so ratified, make proclamation of that fact; and thenceforth this Constitution shall be ordained and established as the Constitution of California.

Mr. GWIN. Inasmuch as the latter clause of this section has been placed in the 6th section, I move the following substitute:

If this Constitution shall be ratified by the people of California, the representatives to Congress, elected as before provided for, shall immediately proceed to Washington, and laying a fair copy thereof before the Congress of the United States, request in the name of the people of California, the admission of the new State of California into the American Union.

I offer this, because the House has decided, by unanimous vote, that immediately upon the ratification of this constitution by the people, we will establish the State government; and when that is done, we are one of the sovereign States of this Confederacy, and as such we are entitled to our Senators and Representatives in Congress.

Mr. COVARRUBIAS. I am opposed to this amendment. It may be liable to great disadvantages. In case these representatives should not reach Washington the Constitution would not be presented at all. It is far safer to desire the present Executive of California to forward it. Then it would be sure to arrive.

Mr. HALLECK. The article, as reported by the Committee, shows the way pursued by other new States. It strikes me as a more legitimate way than that proposed by the gentleman from San Francisco, to bring it before the two Houses of Congress through the President of the United States. The Senators and Representatives going from here can carry certified copies with them. They are not received and recognized until after the constitution has been approved, and the State is admitted as a member of the Union. The article reported by the Committee takes the most appropriate course. It certainly will be more advantageous to the constitution to be laid before Congress through the President of the United States, than to have it go in by the back door, by Senators and Representatives who have not been, and will not be received by Congress until it is acted upon.

Mr. GWIN. Our situation, sir, is entirely different from that of any other State ever admitted into the Union. In the first instance we have had no territorial government; no delegates in Congress to represent our interests. Every other State admitted into the Union had its territorial representatives, and until they were admitted the government went on as before. In our case, it is altogether different. We have determined by the unanimous vote of this body, that as soon as our constitution is ratified by the people this government shall go into operation. We elect our Governor, and all the subordinate officers of the State; we are a State to all intents and purposes. Being a State, we send our Senators and Representatives to the Congress of the United States, not as a State going out of a territorial into a State government, but as a State that has sprung full grown into existence; and when we officially notify the Congress of the United States that we are a State, we do it through our duly elected Representatives, who appear there to demand admission into the Union. If the official notification of our formation of a State government, and going into existence as a State, is sent there by our Representatives, they make it at the bar of the House, and present this Constitution, and the Congress of the United States say then, that inasmuch as the people of California have formed a State Constitution which is republican in its character, therefore, according to the provisions of the Federal Constitution, we recognize them as a part of this Confederacy. Nothing else is to be done. We are then either a State, or our Representatives come back.

Mr. HALLECK. In reply to these remarks, it is only necessary to repeat what has come from the same source before—that we cannot bully the Congress of the

United States; and as for our Senators and Representatives going there, and forcing themselves into the halls of Congress, and saying: We come here to take our seats by force; you must receive us; you are compelled to receive us, and we will take our seats in defiance of your authority—I say that is bad policy. Let us pursue the moderate and usual course; let us do as the gentleman has urged heretofore—follow the beaten track; follow the examples of other States. It would be most unwise and improper to take the course last recommended by the gentleman. If our Senators and Representatives are going there to present this constitution to Congress, when they are not received within the bar I say they come in through the back door.

Mr. Gwin. Who ever used the word bully? Is it not the privilege of an American citizen to petition Congress in person as well as in writing? And are not these gentlemen the Representatives of one of the sovereign States of this Confederacy, presenting its claims for admission in a respectful form to that body? Is that bullying? Sir, was it ever known or declared before, that when an American citizen petitions Congress, or when one of the States of this Confederacy respectfully, through their Representatives, present their petition to be admitted into the Union, that it is bullying? These Representatives claim the privilege of representing on the floor of Congress why they should be received, if it is controverted at all. My own impression is that they might be received instantaneously. If not, they have the privilege of appearing there and urging the reasons why they should be received. But if it is sent through the President of the United States, the Representatives of the State have to stand outside, and wait until Congress decides the question whether the State is to come in at all. We assume the responsibility of establishing a State government at once, and as such we present our claims through our Representatives, under the most imposing aspect. We send our Constitution there, and lay it before that body; and we announce the fact, that having established a republican form of government, we ask admission as one of the States of the Confederacy. That, in my view, is the most imposing and respectful mode of doing it.

Mr. Botts. There was a word that came from that corner of the House that jarred harshly on my ear. This proceeding was designated as a back-door manner of getting into the Congress of the United States. Mr. Chairman, the Constitution of the United States provides for the admission of new States into the Union. You have declared that when this constitution shall be ratified, a new State is made; and, sir, when it is proposed that you shall send ambassadors, commissioners if you please, to treat with another high power for admission into the Confederacy, as the Constitution of the United States provides that you may do, we are told, sir, that it is not the way to carry out the provisions of the Constitution; that the proper way is that of humble solicitation; that you should humbly solicit the Executive department here, humbly to solicit the President of the United States, to lay the humble petition of the State of California before the Congress of the United States. Sir, I care not who your Representative is, he is your ambassador; and he should go in no form but that most potent one of an ambassador, presenting—I will not say your petition, as the gentleman has said—but his instructions. We who stand here, a new State, propose admission into the Union; we dictate the terms; and these terms and these instructions are the constitution that has received the sanction of the people. You send an ambassador then, and you send him with instructions as to the terms upon which you make this proposition to come into the Union. You say, moreover, that these terms must be accepted; that these are your terms, and none others. And is it not an honor, sir—is it not a high honor to be conferred upon any man, no matter how high his station—to act as the ambassador upon such an occasion. Is this going for such a purpose—is it an humble appeal that you are making?—is it to be degraded by the opprobious epithet of a back-door entrance? Sir, the man does not live who ever attained a higher honor than that which this resolution proposes to confer upon these persons; to take this Constitution from a great State to a great Confederacy of States, there to dictate the terms of her admission. He claims to be heard, sir, and he will be heard with respect and attention. He will be received, and his approach hailed with honors; he will be admitted to the bar of that House as the plenipotentiary of a great State desiring to be admitted into the Union.

Mr. McCarver. I see no impropriety in the present Executive giving notice of the adoption of this Constitution, and transmitting a copy to the President of the United States; but I think it also proper that the Representatives of this State, whoever may be elected, should also carry on copies. I think, then, the proposition of the gentleman from San Francisco (Mr. Gwin) is correct, if it be offered as an addition to the section. I am not certain, however, that it is best to put it in the hands of the Executive of this Territory, who holds his appointment under the General Government, and not under the State government. I think if these members are admitted on the floor of Congress, they will be admitted without any constitutional privileges. In the case of Michigan, the members had to wait a long time for admission. I have no doubt that the Representatives of this State would be permitted to be heard upon the floor of Congress, but not as a matter of right. If they were admitted at all before the ratification of the Constitution, it would be as a matter of courtesy.

Mr. Gwin. The very reason the gentleman gave in regard to Michigan is the reason why I offer this amendment; that our Representatives should not be kept waiting outside, but should be admitted at once to defend the claims of the new State. I want Congress to have no official notification of the formation of this government, until our Representatives present it to them in person, and are on the spot to maintain the interests of California. I do not desire that they shall have it before them in any shape until it is presented by the Representatives whom we send there, in order that we shall not be kept waiting, by sending it through the President of the United States, or any other agency, except that designated by the voice of the people.

Mr. Halleck. I give notice that if this substitute is rejected, I will introduce a provision that the Senators and Representatives be furnished with certified copies of the constitution.

Mr. Jones. If I understand the meaning and intention of the amendment, it amounts to kicking the door of Congress down, instead of knocking at it. Our Senators and Representatives are to go with the constitution in their hands and, *per se*, by virtue of this constitution alone, without its reception by Congress, are to demand admission. I think, sir, this is emphatically kicking the door down. Whether you call them ambassadors, or envoys to negotiate a treaty between California and the United States, I apprehend it must depend upon the action of Congress whether they shall be received or not.

(Here Mr. Jones gave notice of an amendment which he should move in case the substitute under consideration was rejected.)

Mr. Gwin. It is not knocking the door down to make a request. If that request is not granted, we do not expect to go and drive Congress out of its halls. I do not think this is a fair way of drawing off votes, offering this notice. The proposed substitute simply amounts to this: An independent State sends its Representatives to Congress, and they respectfully request in behalf of that State to be permitted to take their seats, and ask for its admission into the Union, having complied with all the requirements of the Constitution of the United States.

Mr. McDougal. I am opposed to pursuing the course indicated by my friend from San Francisco, (Mr. Gwin,) for this reason. Suppose our Members of Congress should by accident be taken sick here, or their business should keep them here a little longer than the time of departure proposed, we may not be admitted during the session of Congress. But if our Executive transmits a copy of the Constitution to the President of the United States, he (the President) lays it before Congress, and there will be no difficulty of that kind. Even if our Senators and Representatives carry it to Washington, they must transmit it to Congress through a third person. I see no possible advantage to be gained by that course.

The question was then taken on the substitute offered by Mr. Gwin, and it was rejected.

Mr. Jones. I now move the substitute which I read a few moments ago.

Mr. Gwin. I hope it will be rejected. It is one of those propositions not becoming a free and independent State.

Mr. McCarver. I was in hopes the amendment of the gentleman from Monterey (Mr. Halleck) would be offered here.

Mr. Halleck. I think that after providing for the election of Senators and Representatives, it would be the proper place to introduce it.

Mr. McCarver. Then I will vote against both this section and the proposed substitute, because I do not think they will be necessary.

The question was then taken upon the substitute offered by Mr. Jones, and it was rejected.

Mr. Semple moved to amend the original section by striking out the latter clause, and inserting the following amendment: To strike out all after the words "President of the United States," and insert in lieu thereof, the following:

And the Senators and Representatives elected under this Constitution, shall be the commissioners to present the same to Congress, and ask the admission of California as one of the States of the Union.

He did not think it proper at all that the constitution should be sent to the President of the United States. As to sending certified copies, it would be just as much to the purpose to send certified copies there by a Chilian, or an Englishman, or a Dutchman. If you want to send a commissioner to be clothed with authority, you must send him with the official copy of the constitution, by the authority of the State of California. It is vastly different from sending commissioners there with certified copies. Those who are sent with the constitution should have authority to defend it.

Mr. Sherwood. I have heard about commissioners to the Sandwich Islands, but never heard of one of the States sending commissioners to Congress. What would be the duties of these commissioners? Some of them are to carry a copy of this constitution to lay before Congress. It is not to be presumed that they are to be admitted as members of Congress before the constitution is received and acted upon. They will be commissioners to Congress, not members. I think the gentleman (Mr. Semple) if he was elected Senator, would prefer standing there as Senator, and not as commissioner.

Mr. Botts. I want these gentlemen—call them what you please—to be something more than four individuals to hold each corner of a piece of paper; that it should be their business to do this—to ask to be heard at the bar of that House upon this very subject. It may be one of doubt; it may be necessary that this constitution should be defended by able men sent there in behalf of the State; persons who will be able to explain to Congress why we desire to become a member of the Union, and what would be the effect of our not becoming a part of the Union. It is for this purpose, and not merely to bear a roll of parchment, that I want this House to pass such a provision. I do not object to the word commissioner. A commissioner is a man who has a commission to execute. I want these commissioners to take this constitution and ask to be heard at the bar of the House; to advocate it as the representatives of one contracting party, and endeavor to get the concurrence of the other party.

Mr. Sherwood. I would prefer, if they go to Congress, that they go in their proper capacity. If they are elected as members, they should go there and claim their seats, Congress having the right to receive or reject their claims; but if the question of admission comes up before Congress, then they should claim the right of being heard. I think, without passing any special provision in the Constitution, saying that they should go there with this parchment, if we say here that the Executive of this Government shall send this Constitution to the President of the United States so that he can at the first of the session lay it before Congress, it will accomplish the object.

Mr. Steuart. Under the definition of the gentleman from Monterey, (Mr. Botts,) you must provide for the commissioning of these commissioners before you can send them on that duty. I want to know if we give them any more power as commissioners than they would have as the Senators and Representatives of an independent State. I do not agree with the gentleman who supposes that we have to go there and beg admission. If we have any right at all under the Federal Constitution, we are secured in our right of demanding admission, and no other persons can so properly speak the voice of the people of California as her Senators and Representatives. We do not go to a royal power to ask for an exercise of clemency. We demand a right guarantied to us under the Constitution of the United States. I am in favor of sending to the Executive of the United States a certified copy of the constitution ; but I am also in favor of our Senators and Representatives presenting this constitution to Congress.

Mr. Halleck. I now give notice of a section which I intend to move between sections 11 and 12 :

The Senators and Representatives to the Congress of the United States, elected by the Legislature and people of California as herein directed, shall be furnished with certified copies of this Constitution when ratified, which they shall lay before the Congress of the United States, requesting, in the name of the people of California, the admission of the State of California into the American Union.

Mr. Semple. Upon the notification of that section, I withdraw my amendment.

Mr. McCarver. I am decidedly in favor of the proposition of the gentleman from Monterey, (Mr. Halleck,) but I cannot agree with the doctrine entertained by the gentleman from Sacramento, (Mr. Sherwood,) or my friend from San Francisco, (Mr. Gwin.) I do not agree with those gentlemen that when we elect Senators and Representatives, that they are in fact Senators and Representatives having a right to seats upon the floor of Congress. We are but one of the high contracting parties, and until the other contracting party agrees to our proposition, it is not binding upon that party. We say, in electing these officers, that we are willing they should be such, provided the other party agrees to receive them. We cannot defy Congress by claiming that they have a right to their seats, whether Congress is willing to acknowledge that right or not. If Congress is willing to admit them, then they will be entitled to their seats, but not otherwise.

On motion of Mr. Gwin, all after the words "United States," where they first occur in the section as reported, to the words "United States," inclusive, where they next occur therein, were stricken out.

After further discussion,

Mr. Gwin said that it was proper to send a copy to the President of the United States, but that the constitution should be presented to the Congress of the United States through our Senators and Representatives.

Mr. Sherwood asked what General Taylor would think if this Convention sent him a copy of the constitution, and said at the same time that it was to be presented to Congress through another channel.

Mr. Steuart thought the gentleman was mistaken on this subject. General Taylor, by the Constitution of the United States, would be obliged to present to Congress, in his annual message, a full exposition of the state of the country. This was emphatically connected with the state of the country.

Mr. Gwin said there were two branches of the Government—one the Executive, and the other the Legislative. It was due to both that we should send them copies of this Constitution.

On motion of Mr. Steuart, the word "shall" was stricken out after the words "Executive of the existing government," and the words "is hereby requested," substituted therefor.

Mr. De La Guerra moved to amend, by inserting after the words "President of the United States," the following: "For him to present it to Congress in the name of the people of California, asking to be admitted into the Union."

The amendment was modified, at the suggestion of Mr. Halleck, so as to read, "in order that he may lay it before the Congress of the United States," and was then agreed to.

The section, as amended, was then adopted.

On motion, the Committee rose, and reported progress.

On motion, the House took a recess till 7, P. M.

NIGHT SESSION, 7 O'CLOCK, P. M.

Mr. Shannon offered the following resolution, which was adopted:

Resolved, That an Engrossing Committee, of three members, on the engrossment of the Constitution in Spanish, be appointed by the President.

The Chair appointed Messrs. Pedrorena, Jones, and Vallejo such Committee.

Mr. McCarver then submitted the following, viz:

Resolved, That the Committee on the Engrossment of the Constitution, be instructed to prepare a copy on parchment, to be written in the English language.

Mr. Halleck moved an amendment, but withdrew the same, in favor of the following substitute, proposed by Mr. Ord, viz:

Resolved, That the Constitution be engrossed in English, and a translation of the same, by the Translator of this Convention, be made and placed in parallel columns, and certified by him as a true copy.

After some discussion, the following substitute for both the previous resolutions, was offered by Mr. Steuart, and adopted, viz:

Resolved, That the Committee on Engrossment be instructed to have the Constitution of the State of California engrossed on parchment, in the English language; and that a copy of the same be made by the Translator of this Convention, in the Spanish and English languages, which shall be engrossed in like manner on parchment, and be certified by him, and both be placed among the archives of the State.

On motion, the House then resolved itself into Committee of the Whole, Mr. Gilbert in the chair, on so much of the report of the Committee on the Constitution, as relates to the "Schedule."

Section 8 was then taken up, as follows, viz:

Sec. 8. At the general election aforesaid, viz: the 7th day of November next, there shall be elected a Governor, Lieutenant Governor, members of the Legislature, and also two members of Congress; it being uncertain whether two members of the House of Representatives of the United States will be received, and it being impracticable at the present time to divide California into Congressional Districts, the two members of Congress will be voted for on a general ticket, by all the electors of the State qualified to vote at this election; and in case only one shall be allowed by the act of Congress, admitting the State into the Union to take his seat in that body, the one for whom the highest number of votes was cast shall be declared elected.

Mr. Hill moved to strike out "7th," so as to leave the date blank.

Mr. Semple remarked that there was an act of Congress requiring that members of Congress should be elected by districts in all the States. It had been the custom for some time to elect by general ticket, so as to give the dominant party the entire delegation. Congress saw the difficulty, and provided that each district should vote independent of the others. He thought, therefore, that it would be necessary to make two districts, and have them altogether independent of each other. The two members of Congress could then be elected in accordance with the act of Congress, one coming from each district.

Mr. Gwin said he was aware of an act of that kind having been passed by Congress, but it was never regarded in the States. Mississippi, New Hampshire, South Carolina, all elected members of Congress without reference to this act. He (Mr. Gwin) intended to vote against the election of members of Congress if the constitution adopted by this Convention was to be brought before the Congress by the Chief Magistrate. He did not think, if such a course was pursued, that there would be any need of members of Congress.

The question was then taken on Mr. Hill's motion to strike out the date, and it was adopted.

Mr. Gwin moved to strike out all after the words "members of Congress," which amendment was agreed to, and the section, as amended, was adopted.

Section 9 being under consideration, as follows;

Sec. 9. If this Constitution shall be ratified by the people of California, the Legislature shall assemble at the seat of Government on the fifteenth day of December next; and in order to complete the organization of that body, the Senate shall elect a President *pro tempore* until the Lieutenant Governor shall be installed into office.

On motion of Mr. Halleck, the date was stricken out, and the section, as amended, was adopted.

Sections 10 and 11, were adopted without debate, as follows:

Sec. 10. On the organization of the Legislature, it shall be the duty of the Secretary of State to lay before each House a copy of the abstract made by the Board of Canvassers, and if called for, the original returns of election, in order that each House may judge of the correctness of the report of said Board of Canvassers.

Sec. 11. The Legislature at its first session shall elect such officers as may be ordered by this Constitution to be elected by that body, and within four days after its organization, proceed to elect two Senators to the Congress of the United States. But no law passed by this Legislature shall take effect until signed by the Governor after his installation into office.

Mr. Botts said he was requested to state, on the part of the Spanish gentlemen, that they could not understand what was going on, and would be obliged to leave tbe room without intending the slightest disrespect to the Convention, unless furnished with an interpreter. The official interpreter was absent on account of illness; and it was unjust to require these gentlemen to vote without affording them an opportunity of understanding what they were to vote upon.

Mr. Hoppe said that Dr. Ord understood the Spanish language better than any gentleman of his acquaintance, and he moved that he be requested to act as interpreter during the remainder of the session.

Mr. Ord stated that his brother (Dr. Ord) declined acting as interpreter.

Mr. Botts knew of no other course than to let the gentlemen themselves select some interpreter, and trust to the courtesy of the House to reconsider any section passed in the meantime that might be objectionable to them.

Mr. Gwin did not see how the business of the Convention was to progress in that way. The only way was to rise and report progress, rescind the resolution to adjourn on Tuesday, and wait until an interpreter could be procured.

Mr. Halleck moved the following as section 12:

12. The Senators and Representatives to the Congress of the United States elected by the Legislature and people of California, as herein directed, shall be furnished with certified copies of this Constitution when ratified, which they shall lay before the Congress of the United States, requesting, in the name of the people of California, the admission of the State of California into the American Union.

Mr. Gwin hoped this section would be rejected. It seemed to him that it would be trifling with the subject to send two certified copies in two different channels. There was only one proper course to pursue; either to transmit it through the President, or through the Representatives of the State. If the Convention was determined to transmit it through the President, then he could see no necessity for sending these certified copies through the Representatives.

Mr. Botts advocated the proposition.

Mr. Halleck explained its object.

The question was then taken, and the additional section was adopted.

The 12th section of the Committee's report was then taken up, as follows:

Sec. 12. All officers of this State, other than members of the Legislature, shall be installed into office on or immediately after the first day of January next, as provided in this Constitution.

On motion, the date was stricken out, and the section then adopted.

Section 13 coming up, as follows:

SEC. 13. Until the Legislature shall divide the State into counties and senatorial and assembly districts, as directed by this Constitution, the following shall be the apportionment of the two Houses of the Legislature, viz: The districts of San Diego and Los Angelos, shall jointly elect two Senators, the districts of Santa Barbara and San Luis Obispo, shall jointly elect one Senator, the district of Monterey one Senator, the district of San Jose one Senator, the district of San Francisco two Sen. ators, the district of Sonoma one Senator, the district of Sacramento four Senators, and the district of San Joaquin four Senators; and the district of San Diego shall elect one member of assembly, the district of Los Angelos two members of the assembly, the district of Santa Barbara two members of assembly, the district of San Luis Obispo one member of assembly, the district of Monterey two members of assembly, the district of San Jose three members of assembly, the district of San Francisco five members of assembly, the district of Sonoma two members of assembly, the district of Sacramento nine members of assembly, and the district of San Joaquin nine members of assembly.

Mr. BOTTS said he was requested by one of the gentleman on the other side, (a member of the native California delegation,) to state that that portion of the House would be extremely sorry to throw any obstacle in the way of the proceedings of this Convention. They generally had very little objection to any of the provisions adopted by the Convention, but as this section was one in which they felt interested, and as they could not understand it without having it translated, and the arguments explained to them through an interpreter, they hoped at least that they would be allowed the privilege of a reconsideration, if it was deemed necessary.

Mr. GWIN moved that the section be passed over for the present.

Mr. SHERWOOD was opposed to passing over the section. If any amendments should be deemed necessary they could be presented when the subject came up for consideration in the House.

Mr. HALLECK read a proposition which he desired to offer here in regard to the boundaries of some of the southern districts. They were found to be very indistinctly laid down in the old archives, and it was necessary that they should be clearly determined. After some conversation, he agreed that the consideration of his proposition should be postponed until this section came up for final action.

The 14th section being consideration, as follows:

SEC. 14. Until the Legislature shall otherwise directs in accordance with the provisions of this Constitution, the following shall be the salaries and pay of the several officers and members of the Legislature of this State, viz: The Governor, eight thousand dollars per annum; the Lieutenant Governor, double the pay of a State Senator; Secretary of State, four thousand dollars per annum; the Treasuer, four thousand dollars per annum; the Attorney General, three thousand dollars per annum; the Surveyor General, —— thousand dollars per annum; Justice of the Supreme Court, five thousand dollars per annum; District Judges, five thousand dollars per annum; and the members of the Legislature, —— dollars per diem while in attendance, and —— dollars for every twenty miles by the usual route from their residences to the place of holding the session of the Legislature, and in returning therefrom.

Mr. STEUART. I find that in the article entitled Executive Department, which provides for the appointment of Secretary of State, very onerous duties are imposed upon that officer—more than upon the Secretary of State of any other State in the Union. These are his duties:

SEC. 19. The Secretary of State shall be appointed by the Governor, by and with the advice and consent of the Senate. He shall keep a fair record of the official acts of the legislative and executive departments of the government, and shall, when required, lay the same and all matters relative thereto, before either branch of the Legislature, and shall perform such other duties as shall be assigned him by law.

Now, sir, I consider that these are very onerous duties. I move, therefore, in consideration of this fact, an amendment which shall make the compensation of the Secretary of State $5,000 per annum.

Mr. GWIN. I think my colleague is entirely mistaken in regard to the duties imposed upon that officer. He is required to keep these records, but they are prepared for him. He is only resposible for them. I look upon it as a very light duty. I think it is our true policy in the organization of this State to make the salaries of the officers as low as possible. I now move that the salary of the Governor shall be $6,000 instead of $8,000.

Mr. PRICE. I move the question be divided, and that the vote be taken upon each of these questions separately.

The CHAIR was of opinion that the Committee could act upon any of the salaries separately.

Mr. PRICE moved to amend Mr. Gwin's motion by inserting $10,000.

Mr. SHANNON. If the gentleman from San Francisco (Mr. Price) had not made that motion, I certainly should have done it. I think the report of the Committee is rather a singular one. Certain blanks here are filled;—the pay of the officers of State is fixed; everything beyond that is left blank. I see no reason why the Committee should have reported any particular sum for these officers, and left other portions of the report so lame and impotent as this. I shall certainly sustain the motion of the gentleman from San Francisco, (Mr. Price,) because it increases the amount. I think you cannot obtain the talents requisite to fill these offices as they should be filled without paying a liberal price. Every body knows that in the present condition of California, not even six or eight thousand is sufficient to pay any man for the expenditure of his time in serving the public; nor will that amount clothe or feed his family, and sustain him in the position which he occupies.

Mr. McCARVER. I would suggest, if gentlemen are determined to pay very high salaries in California—and I admit that nothing but high salaries would command the requisite talent—that the Legislature, which comes directly from the people, have power to determine this matter.

Mr. BOTTS. I want to present a single view to your consideration. These salaries are all too low. When you were voting upon the pay of the members of this House, you voted each member at the rate of $5,840 a year, and you said it was nothing like what a man got in the exercise of his profession, and you fixed it at that rate as a mere nominal pay. It was stated by the Committee on Finance that they did not deem it by any means an appropriate remuneration for the expense sustained in coming here, and the sacrifices made. Now I undertake to say that these officers of the State will receive less than a nominal pay if you fix it at the proposed rate. Your Attorney General will receive about one half of what was the nominal pay of a member of this House. I think they are all much too low; but I do pretend to be a judge of what ought to be the salary of the last mentioned officer, the Attorney General. Your Attorney General, if you remember, should be of the best talent in the land; he is necessarily excluded from the entire practice in your criminal courts; where the State prosecutes he cannot appear, because that very case may come up before the Appellate Court, where he is bound to appear for the State. You give him $3,000 to buy him off from all the criminals in the land, when it is well known that one criminal in California will pay that much for his defence. Now, sir, who do you calculate to get to exclude himself from the whole criminal practice in California for the petty sum of $3,000? For the other officers you must get the talent and ability of ten thousand dollars for five. If you want a good article, sir, you must pay a good price. Not only are the salaries of the other officers too low, but the salary of this officer is too low in proportion to them.

Mr. GWIN. I do not intend to argue this question, because the blanks will have to be filled up in the House. I am clearly of opinion, however, that if we do not establish low rates of salaries, the expenses of the government will be so enormous that it will be very difficult to keep it operation without oppressing the community. I have never know an office of honor in the United States where the incumbent makes anything out of it, or even sustains himself upon the salary. There are no money-making offices under the Government of the United States. I find the judges of the Supreme Court there are very willing to accept four thousand dollars a year. As to the Attorney General, he is not obliged to attend to the State business alone; he attends to civil practice in addition to that. This is merely a temporary provision; and if the future condition of the country should render it desirable, the Legislature, which is more directly responsible to the people than we are, can, if we fix the salaries at too low a rate, raise them. I think there are many gentlemen who would be willing to take these offices—gentlemen fully capable of filling them—at these rates.

Mr. BOTTS. I know the idea is rather prevalent that this thing of low salaries would be a very popular thing to electioneer with. Now, sir, I proclaim publicly and openly that I am a candidate for the office of Governor, Senator of the United States, member of Congress, and Attorney General. I am ready to go out upon the stump and meet those gentlemen there with low salaries. I will tell them this: that there are honorable places which are kept for the rich of the land, and that a poor man cannot afford to accept them; that it requires a man of other means to accept an office which will not of itself sustain him; that the Governor could not sustain himself on $6,000 a year, but if he is worth millions there is no difficulty about it; he can then hold the highest office of state in the gift of the people.

Mr. GWIN. If the gentleman should be equally as successful in attacking all of those candidates who run for offices on this principle of low salaries, as he is in most of the measures which he advocates here, he will be very apt to accomplish the object I have in view. As to putting the salaries of officers so low that none other than rich men can hold them, I have this to state: that in starting all new governments it is exceedingly difficult for the revenue of the country to be equal to the expenditures. In Texas the President of that Republic lived in a log cabin, and slept on the floor. His house was not secure from the weather even, and he lived in a style almost too bad for this country. Sir, I want this distinctly understood, that I have no wish to put these salaries so low that none but rich men can hold office; but I do desire to fix them at such a reasonable and moderate standard that we can pay the expenses of the government without imposing burdensome taxes on the people; and inasmuch as this is merely temporary, and many competent men are ready and able to fill these offices, I think we might venture to put them at a rate lower than would meet the wishes of the country. If they are deemed too low they can very easily be made higher. I do not desire to fix the salaries below what is proper, nor have I any wish to make a political hobby in connexion with this matter.

The question was then taken on Mr. Price's amendment to make the salary of the Governor $10,000, and it was adopted.

Mr. STEUART. The next is the salary of the Lieutenant Governor, who has here double the pay of State Senator. Now, acting in the capacity of President of the Senate, I can readily see why his pay should be double that of a member of the Senate; but what is to be the salary of the Lieutenant Governor, acting as Governor, in the absence of the Governor.

Mr. GWIN referred the gentleman to the case of the Vice President of the United States, who holds the same position in regard to the President, as the Lieutenant Governor holds to the Governor.

Further discussion on the same grounds took place, when

On motion, the Committee rose and reported progress.

On motion, the House adjourned till 10 o'clock on Monday morning.

MONDAY, OCTOBER 8, 1849.

Met pursuant to adjournment. Prayer by Rev. Mr. Willey. Journal of Saturday read and approved.

On motion of Mr. GWIN, the article on "Miscellaneous Provisions" of the Constitution was taken up.

The question being on the motion of Mr. Lippitt to reconsider the vote by which the additional section submitted by Mr. Ord as the last section of the article was adopted,

Mr. Ellis moved the previous question, which was sustained; and the motion to reconsider, prevailed.

The question then recurring on the adoption of the section, it was, by yeas and nays, decided in the negative, as follows:

Yeas.—Messrs. Carrillo, Dominguez, Ellis, Gwin, Hobson, Moore, Ord, Pico, Reid, Sherwood, Stearns, Steuart, Vallejo, Wozencraft—16.

Nays.—Messrs. Aram, Botts, Brown, Dent, Dimmick, Foster, Gilbert, Hanks, Hill, Halleck, Hastings, Larkin, Lippincott, McCarver, McDougal, Pedrorena, Price, Sutter, Snyder, Shannon, Vallejo, Vermeule, Walker, President—24.

On motion of Mr. Gwin, the article, as amended, was ordered to be engrossed for a third reading.

The House then, on motion of Mr. Gwin, resolved itself into Committee of the Whole, Mr. Gilbert in the chair, on the Schedule.

Section 14 being under consideration—

Mr. Botts asked who, by the previous provisions of this Constitution, were to be elected by the Legislature at the first session. He had never seen any reason why all these officers that were to be elected by the people, should not be elected at the first election.

Mr. Jones offered a resolution providing that the Legislature shall fix the salaries of all officers other than those elected by the people at their first election.

Mr. Botts argued in favor of having all officers that were to be elected by the people, so elected at the first election.

Mr. Sherwood contended that where so large a majority of the population were strangers to each other, and unacquainted with the best men to fill these offices, that it was absolutely necessary that they should be appointed in the beginning by the Legislature.

Mr. McCarver was in favor of these officers being elected at all times by the people. He thought the people were the proper judges of their own officers. With them rested the responsibility of choosing proper and efficient officers. It was not for this Convention or the Legislature to take the choice of these officers out of their hands. He was opposed to all log-rolling in a legislative body, which would inevitably be the case, if this matter was left to the Legislature. He had seen too much political corruption of that kind. It would be much easier to corrupt the Legislature than to corrupt the whole community.

The question was then taken on the resolution, and it was adopted.

The question being on filling the blanks in the 14th section—

Mr. Hoppe moved to insert $3,000 as the salary of the Lieutenant Governor. The duties were nothing more than to act as President of the Senate, which would occupy probably about fifty days in the year. This would make sixty dollars a day, which he thought was amply sufficient to compensate that officer for his services. At $6,000, it would be $120 a day. It was necessary to pay these officers a good price, but he was opposed to paying $120 a day. If the office of Governor should be vacated, and the Lieutenant Governor should take his place, he considered it perfectly proper that he should receive the pay of Governor.

The motion to insert $6,000, was then withdrawn; and the question recurring on the original section so far as relates to the pay of Lieutenant Governor, it was adopted.

Mr. Halleck moved to strike out the remaining portion of the section.

Mr. Botts said that the salary of the Governor was fixed; but the salary of the Lieutenant Governor was first fixed and then unfixed. By this motion it would be left altogether depending upon a contingency. It was not to be provided what the pay of Senators should be. His pay was to be double that of Senators, but their pay was to be left undetermined. He would like to know what reason there was for adopting a course of this kind.

Mr. SHANNON was of opinion that the salaries should all be fixed now, and proceeded to explain his views.

Mr. HALLECK said if the gentleman was going to make a speech, he would withdraw his motion.

Mr. JONES remarked, that the Legislature, coming directly from the body of the people, would be the best judges of what their pay ought to be.

Mr. STEUART offered the following as a substitute:

14. Until the Legislature shall otherwise direct, in accordance with the provisions of this Constitution, the salary of the Governor shall be ten thousand dollars per annum; the salary of the Lieutenant Governor shall be double the pay of a State Senator; the pay of members of the Legislature shall be sixteen dollars per diem while in attendance, and sixteen dollars for every twenty miles travel by the usual route from their residences to the place of holding the session of the Legislature, and in returning therefrom. And the Legislature shall fix the salaries of all officers other than those elected by the people at the first election.

Mr. ELLIS moved to amend by inserting $10 as the pay of the members, instead of $16.

Mr. JONES opposed the motion as a libel upon this Convention.

Mr. CROSBY suggested that if we were to go in for cheap legislation, it would be better at once to put up the members of the Legislature at auction, and take the lowest bidders.

Mr. SHERWOOD referred to his motion made some days since, for the appointment of a commission to codifying the laws as the best mode of reducing the expenses of the Legislature. He was in favor of paying the members of the Legislature the ordinary wages of daily laborers throughout the country, which was sixteen dollars. The Convention had voted itself below the pay which would afford an adequate renumeration, and he was opposed to making the pay of members of the Legislature less.

The question was then taken on Mr. Ellis's motion, and it was rejected.

The question recurring on Mr. Steuart's amendment,

Mr. GWIN moved to strike out all that portion of it referring to the compensation of members of the Legislature.

The question was then taken, and the motion was decided in the negative.

Mr. STEUART's substitute was then adopted.

Section 15 being under consideration, as follows:

SEC. 15. The limitation of the powers of the Legislature contained in article 7th of this Constitution shall not extend to the first Legislature elected under the same, which is hereby authorized to negotiate for such amount as may be necessary to pay the expenses of the State government.

Mr. GWIN said it would be recollected that there was a restriction upon the Legislature in regard to State debts, in the 7th article, which prohibited the borrowing of more than $300,000. Inasmuch as since that article was adopted, it had been determined by the Convention that this government should go into immediate operation, it might be necessary to raise a larger sum, and hence this section was reported.

The 15th section as reported, was then adopted.

The 13th section, (being the section on the apportionment,) which had been laid aside for further consideration, was then, on motion of Mr. GWIN, taken up.

Mr. PRICE said he would suggest a very slight alteration to this section. To reduce the number proposed here of Representatives from Sacramento and San Joaquin, so as to make a representation of eight Members and three Senators from each of those districts.

Mr. BOTTS said that if he were not satisfied with the report of the Committee, he would move to increase the representation from Sacramento and San Joaquin. He believed those districts were better entitled to ten Representatives than Monterey was to what it was allowed in the report.

Mr. WOZENCRAFT observed that when the Convention first assembled here, that was taken as a fair apportionment. Since that time he was satisfied that the immigration into these two districts was tenfold that of any and all the other districts in the country. He could bring evidence of the fact if required. He concurred with the gentleman from Monterey, that if any change was made the representation from those districts should be increased; but he, as one of the delegates from San Joaquin, would not go beyond the report of the Committee. When it came to reducing the number of Representatives from the district which he represented it was a different matter, and would meet with his most decided opposition.

Mr. Hill said that the report of the Committee was only adopted as a basis for the action of the House. When it came up in Committee it was voted down; the majority were against it; but to save time and let the discussion come up in the House many of them changed their votes, and it was finally adopted with the understanding that it was merely a basis for the action of the House, and that the Chairman was to state that fact to the House.

Mr. Price urged the adoption of his proposed amendment as the best means of arriving at a satisfactory result.

Mr. Gwin hoped the House would vote down the motion of his colleague. He agreed with the gentleman from Monterey (Mr. Botts) that so far as population was concerned, those districts were entitled to a larger representation than any other portion of the country. If the members from those two districts were willing to let the apportionment take one-half of the Legislature, he thought it was best to give it to them.

Mr. Vermeule. The short period of time left to the labors of this body, Mr. President, is drawing rapidly to a close; and I submit it to you, sir, and to the House, whether that time should be further absorbed by the much longer discussion of a subject, which is well settled, I think, in the minds of a large majority this House. But, sir, as I consider that I have not immodestly, on any occasion, trenched upon the time or patience of the Convention, I shall ask its indulgence in presenting my views upon the question before us, and the question itself in what I believe to be its naked colors. Sir, this land of California was acquired to the American people—how? Why, sir, to use the least offensive form of speech, it was acquired by military occupation; in more glowing phrase, it is a rich gift bequeathed to the American people by the valor of their soldiers, their volunteers, and their sailors.

Well, sir, before the proclamation of the treaty of peace, which formally affixes the fortunes and destinies of California to those of the United States, gold is discovered in the gorges of her mountains, and upon the margins of her rivers; and gold in such abundance as to challenge credulity, and render the pursuit of avarice but little more than a romantic gratification. As the tidings spread upon the wings of the wind, and the American public are aroused to a just appreciation of the value of the territorial legacy they have acquired, it is not to be wondered at that a people as wide awake as themselves to the value of money, and as alert in its acquisition, should cross a continent, or nearly circumnavigate a hemisphere, in pursuit of the El Dorado—the great home of wealth—sealed hermetrically to other eyes, and as it would almost appear, consecrated by destiny as a guerdon to the most energetic and adventurous of modern races.

Within the past six months the population of California has augmented by tens of thousands, and the four thousand diggers of last year are transformed into a mining and trading interest which now embraces, according to a safe estimate, I think from 70,000 to 100,000 souls. That California which but little more than a year ago was looked upon as a sparsely populated land, destined to drag on a slow territorial existence of years, now rises in her populous might and demands admission to the great American Confederacy, as one equal star of the galaxy—though she intrinsically bear the rank of a planet, new risen in the occident.

A confiding people absorbed themselves in the great pursuit of gold-getting, but ever mindful of the importance of a just and equitable system of government, based on the radical principles of their republican creed, have sent here ourselves (farmers, lawyers, merchants, mechanics, and men of business,) to form for them a constitution—the organic law of a new State—and the terms of contract with the American Union. Here also, assembled in brotherly conjunction, sit the highly respectable delegates who represent the older inhabitants of California—the former Mexican citizens, who, by treaty and their own choice, have become citizens of the United States. This class of citizens, however seeming now may be the hardship attending the introduction of a new polity, new rules of political conduct, and a new language, it is my hope and belief will be abundantly reconciled to the new order of things when its strangeness shall have somewhat worn away. The quick flight of time smooths the keen asperities of war—the rude shocks of battle will be remembered as great, perhaps, but as by-gone events, and the blood of old Spain shall commingle in the vein of the Anglo-Saxon to strengthen and to unite.

One of the most important points of difference between the two great classes is that involved in the subject before the House—the apportionment of representation. The location of the mines in the more Northern districts of Sacramento and San Joaquim, has converged the principal tide of emigration thitherward; while the great commercial advantages accruing to the port and harbor of San Francisco, have caused a populous city to arise where but two or three years ago was little more than amphitheatre of naked hills. And at many of the prominent points on the great bay, and of the waters leading thereto, have been formed the *nuclei* of towns—perhaps of cities.

These causes, in addition to the fact that this constitution, in its unavoidable conformity to American principles, restricts from the right of suffrage numbers of Indians, descendants of Africans, &c., whom it is asserted possessed that right under the Mexican supremacy, must give a material preponderance in the Legislature of the State to the northern over the middle and southern districts. This result, though it may be deplored, naturally enough, by the people of the latter districts, cannot be combatted, unless it be demanded that we should forego a fundamental American principle, namely, representation in the ratio of population; and to this demand, if made, there is but one answer—it *cannot* be granted. Nine-tenths of the people of California would repudiate this constitution at a blow, if so daring an innovation were attempted to be engrafted upon it.

Mr. President, I shall support by my vote the entire report of the Committee on Apportionment, because from what I have been able to gather of the subject-matter, I believe it to be well based upon the actual population of the respective districts, and therefore to be just and equitable. To the districts of Sacramento and San Joaquin, the Committee have apportioned four Senators and nine Assemblymen each—being in each House half of its representation, and of course in joint ballot half of the entire Legislature. Now, I presume it will not be denied upon this floor that three-fifths of the entire present population of California are actually resident within these two districts, and the proportion, in my opinion, might without exaggeration be exalted still higher. Therefore, when your Committee assign to *three-fifths* (beyond dispute) of the entire people, *one-half* of the representation in the Legislature, have they exceeded their duty? I think not; and such I believe will be the judgment of the House, ratified by the people of California. The assertion that the people to whom this representation is assigned are migratory, and may be elsewhere in the winter or in the spring, I hold to be no valid argument. We cannot entertain the question of where a citizen *will* live *in future*, in assigning to him the place for the exercise of his right of suffrage, but where *does* he live, under certain restrictions imposed by law as to the time such residence has existed.

I shall not, sir, consume more time by entering into detail, with regard to other districts, but believing that the Committee have presented as fair an apportionment as the nature of the peculiar circumstances of California at this time will admit, shall give to the report my hearty concurrence and support.

Mr. Hill. So far as the basis of the plan reported by the Committee goes, I have no objection to it, except in relation to the apportionment which it fixes in the lower districts. It allows the Districts of San Diego and Los Angeles two Senators jointly. I object to that. If in order, I propose to amend the report so that the District of San Diego shall elect one Senator, and the District of Los Angeles one Senator. Let the report stand as it now is, so far as it regards the upper districts. The interests of Los Angeles and San Diego are distinct and separate. They have separate seaports. I want this representation divided.

Mr. Wozencraft had no objection to that and would vote for it. He did not see why those districts should not have a separate representation.

Mr. Hoppe did not see how San Diego could have one Senator, when the whole Senate was only allowed one-half of the popular Assembly, which was sixteen.

Mr. Carrillo said he regarded the proposition of the gentleman from San Diego as very unjust; that San Diego, which had only about a thousand inhabitants, should have the same representation as Los Angeles, which had eight thousand. He could not perceive any fairness in such a proposition; nor did he see any justice in the comparison which had been made between the population of Los Angeles and Sacramento and San Joaquin. The inhabitants of those two districts were migratory; they had no settled locality; nobody knew where to find them; they did not reside there; whilst in Los Angeles the people were permanent residents; they had property, and were not constantly moving about from one part of the country to another. He wished also to impress upon the House that the great population in the two upper districts did not consist altogether of American citizens; there were foreigners there from all parts of the world, who contributed greatly to the imposing appearance of the population. They had no right to vote, whilst nearly the entire population below had that right. Although great numbers were arriving in San Francisco, a large portion of them were women and children and foreigners. He requested that this subject would be taken into consideration again, and that a Committee would be appointed to give a just representation, which he did not conceive this to be.

Mr. Shannon. The gentleman from Los Angeles (Mr. Carrillo) asks where the population of the upper districts is to be found; he inquires who knows where it is, and states that it is a transient, migratory population. I can give him a different account. If he goes to the city of Sacramento, he will find there splendid buildings, not tents. They have grown up as if by magic, within the last few months; all solid, permanent buildings of every character and description. You find a beautifully laid out city, with its eight or nine thousand industrious inhabitants, all busy in promoting the prosperity of the place; you hear the hammer and the saw at all times. There you start, and you can find below another busy, thriving town, containing a large number of inhabitants—how many I do not know; but I believe my friend (Mr. McDougal) can tell what the city of Sutterville contains. All along in both places, you can see the river covered with shipping; forests of masts cover the water. Go on further up, and you find numerous large ranches; go to each of the branches and tributaries of the Sacramento, and you find a great many permanently established towns. My friend from Vernon (Mr. Crosby) can tell you what the city of Vernon was when he left there. Such is the extraordinary improvement of these places; such the additions from day to day to the population, that in one week they may be doubled and trebled. You find numerous towns scattered all over this district, permanently established; a large number of the inhabitants fixed, not in tents, but in well constructed houses, and these are daily on the increase. You can go to the little interior town of Columna, and there you find a permanent population of fifteen hundred or two thousand. Go beyond that to what is called the old Dry Diggings, and there you find from a hundred and fifty to two hundred well built houses. Go beyond that to the settlement of Weaver's Creek, and there you find some sixty or a hundred good houses; but it is not in these places that the population lies alone. Every glen, every ravine, every canon, almost every hill top, is lined and covered with the thousands and tens of thousands that are scattered over the whole country. The entire district to the northern part of it, swarms with an immense population. Neither is that population so migratory as the gentleman seems to imagine. What is the character, and what are purposes of those people? They do not go there simply to dig gold from these canons and river beds, and be off. They dig from these mines a sufficient capital to enter into other business, and they come back to the towns and invest their capital in property. That, so far as my observation extends, has been the almost uniform practice. Every business man who has been able to acquire in the mines a capital sufficient to start any kind of business upon, or invest it in a manner which will create additional capital for him, invests it in the permanent property of these towns, and that contains the secret of their immense and rapid increase. Then I claim that not only is there an immense population and wealth there, but I contend that there is a permanency in the population and in the establishment of the twons, exceeding that of any other district in California; that there is not the mutability among the miners which has been so frequently represented here. But it is not confined to that district alone. The same wealth which is drawn from the mines of Sacramento, assists in building up and adding wealth and permanency to the property of Los Angeles, San Diego, and every other district in the State. For these reasons, I shall certainly be obliged to oppose the proposition of the gentleman from Los Angeles.

Mr. Carrillo. When I spoke of Sacramento and San Joaquin, I did not intend to compare their population with that of Los Angeles; but I did wish to have it understood that however large that population may be, they never had near the landed interest that they have down below. If you take into consideration the immense agricultural interests of the southern portion of the country, there is no comparison whatever between San Joaquin at least, and Los Angeles. In regard to Sacramento, I regard it as possessing great agricultural interests, but San Joaquin can bear no comparison. The population of San Joaquin is completely migratory; and it is doing great injustice to give Los Angeles so small a representation compared with that district. I am perfectly willing that San Joaquin should have a representation equal to that of Los Angeles, but not more.

Mr. McDougal. From the last source in the world that I should expect an objection to come to the report of the Committee is San Francisco. The representation given by this Committee to that district, is greater in proportion to its inhabitants than any other district. It may be, perhaps, that the gentleman has got some of the southern notions in his head about property representation; and that he claims for San Francisco, which is a land of stock-jobbing, a reduction of the number of representatives in the populous districts, with a view to increasing the number in San Francisco.

Mr. Steuart. I hope the gentleman does not apply his remarks to me.

Mr. McDougal. I am very happy to relieve the gentleman. I will confine myself to the other gentleman from San Francisco, (Mr. Price.) When this report was made, I thought if there was any district in the territory that had a right to complain, it was the San Joaquin and Sacramento districts. If we undertake to have the representation of this State upon population, this is certainly a very unfair distribution of the members. If the population is to be considered, I contend that the apportionment is unjust; and we certainly have some data to guide us. These two districts ought to have at least three-fourths in the next assembly, instead of one-half, and that is a liberal apportionment to the other districts. I have some data here, Mr. Chairman, which I respectfully submit for the benefit of those liberal members who are at least willing to give a representation in proportion to population. By a careful estimate, emigrant parties have started, amounting to 36,600, and parties from other portions of the country, amounting to as much more. That population comes direct into Sacramento and San Joaquin. I put it down at the least calculation at forty thousand. We take then the number that come by sea, ten thousand, which is a very low calculation, and no one will dispute it. For the last four or five months could be seen from one to fifteen or twenty vessels sailing up the Sacramento, laden with passengers just arrived in the country. My colleague states that twelve hundred came by sea in one day. That will make our district fifty thousand. Add to that the large population emigrating from Oregon, say ten thousand, and we have sixty thousand; and by the other overland routes—by the Gila—some fifteen or twenty thousand, all coming direct to the mines.

Now I have given our district but five thousand, while we have a population at once of sixty thousand people. Upon that, you have a representation of nine members. I presume the gentleman (Mr. Price) will not claim for San Francisco over six or ten thousand at most, which is a very liberal estimate. The report gives him five representatives for ten thousand; and Sacramento, nine for sixty-five thousand. Who has a right to complain? I presume, when the gentleman rose to make his amendment, that he had but one objection; if he had other objections he would have embraced them in his amendment. He can see no objection to the very large representation allowed to San Francisco, the land of stock-jobbers; but when he comes up to the main population of the country, he can see very great disproportion. I understand the population of San Diego to be one thousand, and they have one Senator and one Representative. By that principle, if we apportion the number of Senators and Representatives according to the population, we ought to have sixty Senators and sixty Representatives in the next Legislature. But I do not rise for the purpose of making any complaint against the report of the Committee. I am satisfied with the number that they have given us, and I shall vote for it; and I think if we are satisfied, other members who have largely over us, in proportion to their population, ought certainly to be satisfied. And now, sir, I presume if the gentleman from San Francisco (Mr. Price) is at all liberal, allowing the representation to be in proportion to population, he will rise in his seat, apologise to the representatives from Sacramento and San Joaquin, and withdraw his motion. I trust in his honesty and integrity to rise and withdraw his amendment, or decrease the representation as given by the Committee to San Francisco.

Mr. Price. There is no gentleman in this Convention for whom I have a higher regard than for my friend who has last addressed the House. He seems to be wonderfully given to figures. Now, sir, I have a penchant for arithmetic myself, but I work out entirely different results from those produced by the gentleman from Sacramento. Sir, I was brought up in a democratic school, and I never yet assumed that property should be represented. I have always taken the broad ground that representation should be according to population; that has always been my creed, and I do not mean to depart from it now. The gentleman, in supposing that I had property in view when I moved my amendment, is entirely mistaken. I moved it with this view. There is one principle incorporated here which I rather object to, and that is the representation in both Houses being in accordance with numbers. In the State from which I came, and in most of the States of the Union, one branch—the upper branch—of the Legislature is represented equally by districts or counties, without regard to numbers. In the Congress of the United States the same principle is observed, by the representation in the Senate. This has always been considered a very wholesome restraint upon majorities, in protecting the rights and interests of minorities. Under this Constitution, as we have shaped it, we give a large district the same power in both branches of the Legislature; and in moving this amendment my object is to provide for the protection of minorities—a principle which is so generally recognized under our system of government. I have reduced one member in Sacramento and one in San Joaquin. I have no doubt at all, sir, in regard to the great extent of the population in those districts. Probably at this time they can justly claim all that the Committee have asked for; but it is only for the first Legislature that we are fixing this apportionment. The census will be taken next year, and then the respective districts will be represented according to the official data. Those districts according to my amendment have twenty-two votes in forty-eight, in the first Legislature. They are districts whose interests are essentially the same, and those interests are opposed to the agricultural interests of the south. It would be unjust without some authentic data, to give them a larger representation in the first Legislature. Gentlemen may assume that they contain sixty or eighty thousand inhabitants, but we have nothing definite on that subject. The population of the lower districts has been fixed for a number of years, and may be estimated with some approach to accuracy. I considered this amendment rather more fair than the report of the Committee, but I have no material objection to that report. As to the gentleman's remarks in relation to the population of San Francisco, I place the population at thirty thousand instead of ten thousand, and I think the House will sustain me in that estimate.

Mr. McCarver. If there is any portion of the country that has been dealt with unjustly by the report of the Committee, San Francisco certainly has no cause to complain. That district has a larger representation in proportion to the number of inhabitants than any district in California. I propose to offer an amendment, for several different reasons. I have been a witness of the powerful influence that has been exercised over this body by members on their return from San Francisco, and I consider it an alarming position when San Francisco can come in a convention like this and defeat one of the best measures ever introduced into a State Convention. I should look with more alarm upon any increase in San Francisco than in any other section. She has already exercised more than her share of influence in this body. The rest of the country is composed of the working and laboring men, who have an interest in the permanent welfare of the State. The representation of San Francisco comes from amongst men who have no interest in the country. If the gentleman thinks that we have an unfair representation from the Sacramento district, I move to place it upon a just principle, and in acccordance with the statement of my colleague, (Mr. McDougal,) base our calculation not upon capital or wealth or influence, but upon actual population. According to this calculation, and I believe it to be founded upon correct data, the mining districts have sixty thousand inhabitants. If that be the case, sir, we have not had justice done to Sacramento; but, like my colleague, situated as we are at present, without any means of ascertaining exactly the population, I am willing to rest content even if we do not get at the first session of the Legislature a sufficient number. I do not believe that the report of the Committee gives us that number; but I am willing to acquiesce in it under present circumstances. I am happy to see that this movement is not a general thing among the members from San Francisco—that it was only made by one gentleman, (Mr. Price.)

Mr. Price. I claim the full responsibility of the act.

Mr. Ellis. I hope the gentleman from Sacramento (Mr. McCarver) will not make any further allusions to the negro question. If it comes up again I will be ready to head him with the previous question.

Mr. McCarver said his proposition was to cut down the District of San Francisco to its proper proportion, if the motion of the gentleman (Mr. Price) prevailed. He thought the Districts of Sacramento and San Joaquin should not be cut down, and San Francisco be allowed a representation already too large.

Mr. Jones claimed to say a few words for San Joaquin. He stood here as the representative of living cities and full houses—not empty ones; as the representative of a district into which people were going, not one from which they were coming; a district filling up—he might say already filled up—in a most extraordinary manner. (Here Mr. Jones went into a calculation to show the rapid increase of population in the District of San Joaquin.) There were people there that he knew nothing about—thousands pouring in from all quarters that he had never heard of. He received sixty-nine votes in one precinct, and had not been able to find out where the poll was. He objected to any cutting down of that district. Gentlemen had said that it was a fluctuating population. This was not the case. There were villages, and towns, and cities in almost every gulch and ravine. If there was a floating population, then these towns and cities must float. The report provided a representation of four Senators and nine Members of Assembly for the District of San Joaquin. He was willing to abide by the report, in the belief that although the apportionment was too low, the Legislature would provide for it. Gentlemen would see what the vote was when the election came on. Those who advocated the cutting down of this district, if they came there as candidates for any public office, would find out where the votes were. He was surprised at the statement of the gentleman from San Francisco (Mr. Price) that the interests of the miner were in conflict with, or opposed to, the agricultural and commercial interests of the country. He (Mr. Jones) would like to know upon what the interests of San Francisco depended. What built up the commercial interests of that place? How did the gentleman earn his bread if not from the mining districts?

Mr. Botts. I am not going to advocate the interests of Sacramento or San Joaquin; they can take care of themselves; nor am I going to attack my friend from San Francisco, (Mr. Price,) for I think he has been so torn to pieces that there is not a particle of him left; but there has been a principle avowed upon this floor that I mean to attack, and that principle is, that the ratio of population is not the proper ratio of representation. That principle the gentleman (Mr. Price) laid down, and said it was a democratic principle; that the ratio of representation in the Senate should not be in proportion to population. Why did not the gentleman, when that provision of our constitution came before the House—"representation shall be according to population"—why did he not rise in his seat and say that this great principle was only half true; true in the lower house, but not true in the upper? I know there are men who have a tendency towards democratic principles who avow the principle that the gentleman avows; but, sir, they are babes and sucklings in democracy. Such I apprehend is my friend. They find that by the Constitution of the United States the Senate is constituted without regard to numbers. It was battled against in the Convention that framed the Constitution as an aristocratic feature; but it was put in there for a most wholesome and useful purpose—to preserve the sovereignty of the individual States, and place them upon an equal footing. In the one case, it is an imperfect government, consisting of limited powers delegated to it by a Confederacy of States; in the other, it is a perfect government, originating directly from the people. Those who, like my friend, do not look at this fact are misled, and endeavor to introduce the principle where it does not belong. It is a law maxim—*cessante ratione lex ipsa cessat*—when the reason of the rule ceases, then the rule itself ceases. If the gentleman wants to maintain that doctrine he must go back to the Bill of Rights and amend the short clause which declares the popular doctrine that representation shall be in proportion to population. He should declare that it is only half true—true in the lower House, but not true in the upper.

I have one remark more to make, not in defence of San Joaquin, but of the population of San Joaquin. If he was rightly interpreted, the gentleman from Los Angeles (Mr. Carrillo) said that he admitted that there was a greater amount of population in that district than in Los Angeles; but he said there was no comparison between the kind of population. I know, sir, that that district is called "Los Angeles;" perhaps it may be his idea that the people of Los Angeles are the people of "the Angels," and consequently a very superior kind of population. When I came to this country I was told that Los Angeles was a place fit for the angels; but without denying that, or going into that branch of the subject, I will remark while I am up, that the gentleman's argument with respect to a division of the apportionment of two Senators between Los Angeles and San Diego is irresistible in my mind, and I shall vote against the proposition of the gentleman from San Diego, (Mr. Hill,) unless the facts stated by the gentleman from Los Angeles (Mr. Carrillo) are disproved.

Mr. Steuart. If there is any thing which has met my approbation more than another in this Convention, it has been the exceeding courtesy shown by every member towards his associates; and especially, that in all their deliberations there has been a manifest disposition on the part of the whole Convention to act in that spirit of concession and compromise which is so necessary in forming a constitution for a people scattered over such an extent of territory as this. I regret exceedingly that any thing like sectional feeling should have been introduced by the resolution offered by my colleague from San Francisco, (Mr. Price.) I regret exceedingly that the resolution did not come under the observation of the other members from San Francisco before it was offered. For my own part, when I heard the report of the Committee read, I was entirely satisfied with it. I thought that justice had been done to every portion of the proposed State, and injustice to none. Sir, there is a great deal to be said upon both sides of this question if we get into this sectional discussion. Although a citizen of the district of San Francisco, it has been my lot to be perhaps as much through other portions of the territory as any gentleman upon this floor; and while I admit that there is a vast influx of population daily pouring in from every avenue of inland communication into the upper districts, and that a large number of those who arrive in our seaports go up the Sacramento and San Joaquin and disperse through that wide extent of country, I will also affirm that there are vast numbers continually returning to the port of San Francisco and other seaports. I deny that the population of the District of San Francisco has not been fairly stated. There is not a vessel that comes down which does not bring crowds of persons from the mines, disappointed, sick, or satisfied with their success and otherwise disposed to return. I know in one single instance of sixty individuals belonging to a single company. In less than one week the whole of that party were dispersed, and there were but two left upon the waters of the Juba. When I left San Francisco, many of them were engaged there in commercial or other pursuits. They were chiefly hard working mechanics. But this is not the only case. The same I affirm to be the case in other portions of the mining districts. A large portion of them return to San Francisco and become permanent residents. I do not believe that either of these districts, San Joaquin, or Sacramento, has one single Senator or member in the report less than it is entitled to; I believe that the future census will give them more; but at the present time I believe that the apportionment allowed them will meet with the approbation of the people throughout the country. I do not intend to enter into a discussion of sectional rights and privileges; but I will merely observe, that while gentlemen from these districts are so positive as to the population there, if they had similar knowledge of the facts in regard to San Francisco, it would not be stigmatized as a mere land of stock-jobbers and money lenders.

Mr. McDougal. I rise merely to say that the gentleman from San Francisco (Mr. Steuart) is certainly laboring under a delusion when he states that the people who are flocking back from the mines, go to San Francisco for the purpose of becoming residents. I know from my own observation that such is not the fact. I have frequently this summer been up and down that river from San Francisco to Sacramento, and each time on my return to San Francisco, the vessel was crowded with persons coming down from Sacramento; but they were coming down to purchase goods, and expected to return as soon as they completed their purchases. There might be some few on their way back to their native States, who stopped there a short time, but finding themselves fleeced of their gold, they had to return to the mines to resucitate their pockets.

Mr. Wozencraft. I regret that the gentleman from Los Angeles (Mr. Carrillo) is not in his seat, as I wish to say something in relation to the remarks that he made relative to the population of that and the mining districts. It is well known that the interests of the California population lie in the mining districts. I venture to assert that there are more native Californians engaged in mining and commercial pursuits in the District of San Joaquin, than in any other part of the country. It is of as much importance that they should be represented as the southern portion of the native population. The gentleman's argument militates against his own brethren who reside there. He further remarked that there were a great many foreigners in the mining districts who had not the right to vote, and that the numercial population was thus vastly increased. I would remark that these foreigners of whom he speaks, are not permitted to reside there, and the fact of their being there, does not increase the vote. In calculating the resident population, they are not taken into consideration at all. I hope the resolution of the gentleman from San Francisco (Mr. Price) will be withdrawn. I am willing to vote for the report of the Committee.

Mr. Sherwood. Believing that we have had sufficient discussion on this subject, I move the previous question.

Mr. Tefft. Will the gentleman withdraw his motion for a moment? I have but a word to say upon this matter. I am fully convinced that there is a general disposition to make a fair and equitable apportionment. In the absence of all statistical information, and believing that gentlemen have stated facts as to the population of the mining districts, without any interested motives; believing that the district of Sacramento is an immense mining district, and entitled to the full representation reported by the Committee, I should have said nothing if the gentleman from San Joaquin (Mr. Wozencraft) had not made a most unfortunate statement in regard to the population there. He says a large portion of them are composed of the native population; that that they are the brethren of the southern people here. If this is so, and I do not doubt it, where is their property? It is in the southern districts where their homes are, and where they will vote at the coming election. I do not wish to take the vote from the district of San Joaquin that she is entitled to; but I think it is due to the member from Los Angeles, (Mr. Carrillo,) to say that the statement he made is a fair one. As to the remarks of the gentleman from Monterey, (Mr. Botts) in regard to "the Angels," he misconstrued the remarks of the gentleman from Los Angeles. He (Mr. Carrillo) merely said that the people in Los Angeles were a permanent, fixed population—that they were owners of the soil; but that in the upper districts the population was migratory.

Mr. McCarver. I wish to withdraw my amendment, if the gentleman from San Francisco (Mr. Price) will withdraw his.

Mr. Ellis. I hope he will withdraw it. I have not discovered that the feeling of any member from San Francisco is in favor of it.

Mr. Carrillo. Some gentleman has stated that in the district of San Joaquin there is a large number of inhabitants of Los Angeles, who being there would have the right to vote there. I understand from a provision of the constitution which we have adopted, that no individual of one district is allowed to vote in another district. The reason is very obvious; that the judges of the election must qualify those who are allowed to vote and those who are not. If a person from one district is in another he is not allowed to vote. Therefore, I consider that that argument is completely refuted by the facts as they exist.

Mr. Vermuele. I rise to say a single word. If, unfortunately for the district of Los Angeles, it be true that a considerable number of actual residents in San Joaquin be persons owning landed property in the district of Los Angeles, what are we to do with them? They cannot live in San Joaquin and vote by deputy in Los Angeles. Does the gentleman wish to deprive them of their franchise altogether? They cannot vote in Los Angeles. Does he mean to say that they should not vote at all?

The Chair explained that the law in relation to residence would not apply at the first election.

Mr. CARRILLO said he was perfectly satisfied with that explanation.

Mr. PRICE then withdrew his amendment.

Mr. McCARVER also withdrew his; when the question recurring on Mr. Hill's amendment—

Mr. NORIEGO said he was extremely sorry he could not coincide in opinion with the gentleman from San Diego (Mr. Hill.) He thought that gentleman's proposition would be very far from meeting the approbation of the southern pueblos. It would be very unfair that San Diego, with only a thousand inhabitants, should have a larger representation than Santa Barbara and San Luis Obispo.

Mr. HILL. So far as the population is concerned, I do not think any body here can tell the exact population. I only ask to divide the two Senators. Los Angeles has two and San Diego none. All I ask is that San Diego shall have one of the Senators, so that we may have a representation in the Senate.

Mr. BOTTS. I always bow to the decision of this House, especially when that decision is in unison with my own views. The House has decided that representation ought to be in proportion to population. According to this principle the united districts of Los Angeles and San Diego ought to have two Senators and no more; and now the proposition comes to split the two Senators. All I can say is this. If that district is to be separated, I would desire to separate it on the principle laid down by this House; and I would run the line so as to have as much population in the district of San Diego as in Los Angelos, but that is impossible; consequently I cannot vote for such a disproportionate arrangement as the gentleman proposes.

The question was then taken on Mr. Hill's amendment, and it was rejected.

Mr. HASTINGS moved to amend by inserting "And the District cf the Great Salt Lake fifteen Senators and thirty Members of Assembly." This he desired to add to the latter clause of the section. He was opposed to including the Salt Lake settlement in the State of California; he thought this Convention had nothing to do with it; but inasmuch as they were included by the boundary adopted in Committee of the Whole, he deemed it just and proper that they should be represented. Was there a gentleman here who would assert that this population of thirty thousand souls should have no representation—that no district should comprehend them?

Mr. McDOUGAL said they were comprehended in the District of Sacramento.

Mr. HASTINGS said that the representation of Sacramento was not based upon that calculation, nor were the boundary lines of that district so laid down. Here was a large population positively included within the limits of the State, and compelled to become amenable to the laws, and that, too, by force if necessary; and yet no provision was to be made to give them a representation in the Legislature. This was the doctrine of those who insisted upon including the entire territory. He offered this amendment for the purpose of providing for every human soul within the limits of the State, in case this boundary should be fixed by the final action of the House. It was not reasonable, it was not just; it was in conflict with the spirit of our Declaration of Rights to include them, and not give them the benefit of representation. It was a mockery to pretend to give them the benefit of government, and refuse to give them the benefit of representation. Even if they had their proper representation in the Legislature, justice would not then be done them, for they had not enjoyed the benefit of representation in this Convention.

Mr. JONES was of opinion that when the people of the Salt Lake thought proper to apply for the admission of their representatives into the Legislature of the State, every facility would be afforded them.

Mr. BOTTS hoped the gentleman would withdraw his amendment. He would not make a speech. He preferred seeing this whole subject laid aside until the boundary question was fixed. Much had been said about the population of the District of Sacramento; and yet it was not determined what that district should be. The whole action of the House was founded upon that district being fixed; but it was not fixed; it might include the settlements of the Salt Lake. If, in laying off that district, the population of the Salt Lake should be included, he would vote for giving Sacramento eighteen members. He trusted that the gentleman would withdraw his motion to amend. Until the boundary was fixed it would not be expedient to act upon it; and he thought that by the final action of the House this Salt Lake country would be excluded.

Mr. Gwin said that the proposition of the gentleman from Sacramento (Mr. Hastings) was evidently intended to get in an argument on the boundary question. That gentleman and the gentleman from Monterey (Mr. Botts) both knew very well that the Committee had gone to the extreme limit of representation; that it had gone to thirty-six representatives. The proposed amendment was only intended to forestall the action of the House in an indirect manner on the boundary question. The gentlemen were well aware that when this question came to be considered in the House they would be under the operation of the five minutes rule, and they took advantage of this fact to introduce the subject here, where they could have long speeches to sustain their own particular views.

Mr. McCarver had no doubt that the House would fix a permanent eastern boundary, and that by that action his colleague's amendment would be rendered null and void. If that portion of the country was to be included, he thought they were equally as well entitled to a representation as other districts. But at present, as it was not positively known to what conclusion the House would come, he thought it better that the proposition should not be acted upon.

Mr. Hastings wished to say a single word. Those who contended that the Salt Lake was included within the District of Sacramento labored altogether under mistaken views. That district did not extend beyond the Sierra Nevada. He could adduce the proclamation of General Riley to prove it.

Mr. Wozencraft did not know that it was obligatory to district the entire territory until after the census was taken. He thought there was no impropriety in excluding any portion which was not within the districts now known and established.

Mr. McDougal agreed with his colleague, (Mr. Hastings,) that if the people of the Salt Lake were included in the boundaries of this State, they ought to have a representation in the General Assembly, but he could not agree with him in regard to the number. He moved to amend the amendment so as to make it read: "Four Senators and nine Members of Assembly."

Mr. Jones said it was related of the inhabitants of some city of the East, that they met together and petitioned the Deity that each man should have the sentiments of his soul written upon his forehead. Now he did know whether any of the inhabitants in this part of the world had the word Buncombe written upon their foreheads, but certain it was, that it would be a very strikingly visible inscription upon the foreheads of certain members of this Convention, if the sentiments of their souls were written there. Here was a resolution introduced to get up an excitement upon a question not connected with what was before the House at all. The gentleman from Sacramento (Mr. Hastings) stated that there were twenty-five or thirty thousand inhabitants at the Salt Lake. While in Committee of the Whole, and while this subject was up, he would ask that gentleman, who knew infinitely more about the population of that region than any gentleman on this floor, if he considered this to be a settled and permanent population?

Mr. Dimmick wished to know whether this was a deliberative body sitting here to form a Constitution, or a mere debating society. This sort of discussion was children's play; it was a useless expenditure of the people's money. What was the object of this Convention? What were the members doing? He appealed to them to trifle away their time no longer; he trusted they would turn to their work in earnest, and confine themselve to the business before the House.

Mr. Sherwood did not think it advisable that the vote should be taken now. He would therefore move to rise and report progress.

The motion was adopted, and the Committee rose and reported progress.

Mr. Gwin gave notice of an ordinance to be attached to the Constitution, which was laid upon the table, subject to call.

The Convention then took a recess of one hour.

AFTERNOON SESSION, 3 O'CLOCK, P. M.

On motion, the House resolved itself into Committee of the Whole, Mr. Gilbert in the chair, on the "Schedule."

The question being on the amendment of Mr. Hastings to the 13th section, it was rejected.

Section 13 was then adopted as reported.

After a short discussion on the same grounds already taken in Committee, the first blank in the 6th section was filled with "thirteenth," and the second blank with "tenth." The blank in the 8th section was filled with "thirteenth." The blank in section 9th was filled with "twentieth." The blank in section 12th was filled with "fifteenth day of December."

The "Schedule" was then, on motion, laid aside, and the "Preamble" taken up.

The Preamble, as reported by the Committee, with the substitute as proposed by Mr. Gwin and Mr. Shannon, being under consideration—

Mr. Gwin withdrew his amendment, to allow

Mr. Lippitt to present the following, viz:

We, the people of California, in the exercise of the right of self-government which belongs to the people under the Constitution of the United States, for the purpose of organizing a State Government, do hereby ordain and establish this Constitution.

Mr. Shannon then withdrew his proposition, to allow

Mr. Botts to offer the following, viz:

In order to institute a government, the free and independent people of California do ordain as follows:

Mr. Botts said that if this preamble was to be rejected, he should prefer the one nominally offered by the Select Committee; he said nominally, for the Committee had never seen it. It was the preamble of the New York Constitution, and that was one of the greatest objections to it. It was not the report of the Committee. The report read in this way, after the first clause: "do establish this Constitution by order of the Select Committee." But there was also this objection to it. He (Mr. Botts) had always been opposed to the abuse of the language of prayer and thanksgiving on occasions of this kind. He thought there was an inappropriateness in it. Gentlemen should consider the circumstances under which this Constitution was to be made. It was to be made by the votes of the people at the polls. They are supposed to adopt the language of that instrument. But it is well known that no such feeling or sentiment prevails at a political meeting. The voter may be a religious man and may pray at other times, but he is not in the proper frame of mind to utter prayers at the polls. There has always been, in my mind, an hypocricy in making him say what he does not intend to say, and what he does does not even think of saying. The closet is the proper place for devotion—not the ballot-box.

Mr. Norton. I have but a single word to remark in regard to this reference in the preamble to the Supreme Being. I think it is very appropriate; and although we may not (some of us at least) be in the habit of praying, where an opportunity occurs when it would be not only appropriate but proper to do so, that we should do it. The gentleman's remarks that the voters at the polls in making this Constitution, are supposed to adopt its language, and therefore make such a prayer to the Supreme Being, only show how desirable it is to insert this clause.

If we can, by supposition, get a prayer out of those who are not in the habit of praying, we should by all means do it.

Mr. Steuart. I think the gentleman from Monterey has rather forgotten his remarks made some short time since, in which he quoted from the Constitution of his native State an article which, if I mistake not, was worthy the pen of the recording angel. That clause read something in this manner: that religion or the duty which we owe to our Creator and the manner of discharging it, can be directed only by reason and conviction, not by force or violence; therefore, all men are equally entitled to the free exercise of religion, according to the dictates of conscience; and that it is the mutual duty of all to practise christian forbearance, love, and charity towards each other. I acknowledged the full force of the remark made by the gentleman at the time; and for one, I do not hesitate to avow, upon this floor, that I should have been well pleased to have adopted in our constitution a similar provision. I think we should make a due reference to the Supreme Being in performing a work of such magnitude and importance as this.

Mr. Hastings. I am really in hopes that the preamble suggested by my friend from Monterey will be adopted, for this reason: that it is original. Another reason, is, that it is brief; if it had been still briefer, it would have been still better. The nearer it approaches to nothing, the better is the preamble. A preamble is altogether unnecessary. If gentlemen will turn to the Constitution of Mississippi, they will find that there is no preamble at all. "The Constitution of Mississippi" is all we find there. In reference to the prayer, we find that there is nothing like a prayer in it except the President's name, which is Pray.

Mr. Wozencraft. There is a preamble and a very appropriate one, to the Constitution of Mississippi: "That the general, great, and essential principles of liberty and free government may be recognized and established, we declare."

The question was then taken on Mr. Botts' substitute, and it was adopted.

The proposition of the Committee, and the substitute offered by Mr. Lippitt, were rejected.

Thereupon, the Committee rose and reported the "Schedule" and the "Preamble" to the House, with sundry amendments, which report was received and laid upon the table.

The House then adjourned to 7 o'clock, P. M.

NIGHT SESSION, 7 O'CLOCK, P. M.

The Convention met pursuant to adjournment.

On motion of Mr. Gwin, the report of the Committee of the Whole on the Preamble was taken up, and the amendment of the Committee was non-concurred in.

The question recurring on the adoption of the report of the Committee on the Constitution, the words "the State of" were by unanimous consent, stricken out, and thus amended, the Preamble, as reported by the Committee, was adopted.

On motion of Mr. Dimmick, the Preamble was ordered to be engrossed for a third reading.

On motion of Mr. Ellis, the report of the Committee of the Whole on the "Boundary," was then taken up, and

Mr. Hastings moved the following substitute therefor, viz:

Resolved, That the boundary of the State of California be as follows: Commencing at the intersection of the 42d parallel of north latitude and the 118th meridian line; thence south upon the said meridian line to the point where it intersects the 38th parallel of north latitude; thence southeasterly in a direct line, to the point where the 114th meridian line intersects the Rio Colorado; thence southerly down the said river following the main channel thereof to the boundary line between the United States and Mexico, as established by the treaty of peace, ratified by the said Governments at Queretaro on the 30th day of May, A. D., 1848; thence west upon said boundary line to the Pacific ocean; thence northerly, bounded by the said ocean, to the said 42d parallel of north latitude, including all the bays, harbors, and islands adjacent to, and in the vicinity of the said coast; and thence east upon the said 42d parallel of north latitude to the place of beginning.

Mr. SHANNON called the attention of the House to the amendment which he had offered in Committee of the Whole.

Mr. McCARVER recapitulated some of the arguments which he had advanced in Committee in favor of fixing a permanent eastern boundary.

Mr. GWIN explained the nature of the proposition adopted in Committee of the Whole.

Mr. BOTTS said there was a sort of tacit understanding that the vote was to be taken upon this question without further debate. He desired either one thing or the other—either no debate at all, or full debate.

The question was then taken on the substitute of Hastings, and it was adopted, by yeas 23, nays 21, as follows:

YEAS.—Messrs. Aram, Botts, Brown, Crosby, Dent, Dimmick, Ellis, Hanks, Hill, Hoppe, Hastings, Larkin, McCarver, McDougal, Norton, Ord, Price, Reid, Sutter, Snyder, Steuart, Walker, President.—23.

NAYS.—Messrs. Carrillo, Covarrubias, Dominguez, Foster, Gilbert, Gwin, Hobson, Halleck, Hollingsworth, Jones, Lippincott, Moore, Pedrorena, Pico, Rodriguez, Sherwood, Stearns, Shannon, Tefft, Vallejo, Wozencraft.—21.

On motion of Mr. DIMMICK, the article was ordered to be engrossed for a third reading.

On motion of Mr. PRICE, the Schedule was then taken up for consideration.

The 1st section was adopted as reported from the Committee of the Whole.

Mr. GWIN moved that the Schedule be laid aside, and that the House proceed to the third reading of the constitution.

The CHAIR observed that it would be necessary to suspend the rule requiring the third reading on a separate day.

Mr. McDOUGAL said he had voted in the affirmative on the boundary question, with a view to moving a reconsideration for the purpose of introducing a substitute. He now moved that the vote on the engrossment of the article on the boundary be reconsidered.

Mr. SHERWOOD. On the question of reconsideration, Mr. President, I beg leave to say a few words. I said upon this floor once before, that I thought the natural boundary for the State of California was the ridge of the snowy mountains. Although I conceive that to be the natural boundary, I think a parallel of longitude may be taken for convenience near those mountains. But the consideration which has governed my vote and action here, in regard to the boundary, has not been simply what might ultimately be the boundary of this State. I have been governed by other motives, somewhat distinct from the propriety of fixing any permanent boundary at the present period. We have several States now much larger than they ultimately will be. When by compact Texas was annexed to the United States, that compact embraced over a hundred thousand square miles—enough for two or three States. It is not, and was not assumed, on the annexation of Texas, that it would be the only State formed out of that immense territory. It is now a settled opinion that when Texas receives population sufficient to entitle her to a division, a new State will be formed; and so, if we embrace larger limits than ultimately may be the desire of the people, a new State can be formed, or two or three States if it be desirable. According to the present boundary north and south, we extend some eight or nine hundred miles. East and west our extent of territory is still greater, as stated in the amendment of the Committee of the Whole. I have no doubt in ten or twenty years from this time, if we fix upon the Sierra Nevada, still we shall be divided into two or three States west of that line; but that is a matter for us to determine hereafter—perhaps for our descendants. So that in now fixing a permanent boundary, we cannot, as the gentleman from San Francisco well said, attempt to fix the one which we fixed by a close vote a short time since. There are questions connected with this boundary which agitate not only the people of this territory, but the people throughout the whole Union. If it had not been for that one question of slavery, we should have had last winter a

Territorial Government; if that question had not produced such dissension in Congress, we should not now probably be sitting in Convention within these halls. We should have rested satisfied with a Territorial Government, which Congress then would have granted us. But that question—I might say that demon question—which has disturbed Congress, has disturbed the people of the North and South. The people of the United States are an excitable people; the question of slavery is an exciting question. It was made by demagogues—perhaps, to some extent, by honest men—a leading question before and among the people—shall the new territory, acquired by the treaty of peace between Mexico and the United States, prohibit slavery or not? A party called the Free-Soil party was raised upon that question in the North. It counted about two hundred thousand votes. And what were the principles of that party? They proclaimed as their standing principles the Wilmot proviso. That proviso was an exclusion by Congress of slavery from the territory thus acquired, whether the people wished it or not. It was preached in evening meetings—in primary assemblages of the people—in every State, county, district, and town throughout the North; and this Free-Soil party sent out their agents in every direction to agitate this question. Many of the Northern people, actuated by honest motives, voted for President of the United States in favor of a candidate professing these principles. They voted with the Wilmot proviso on their ballots. At least twenty thousand Whigs in the State of New York, who had formerly reviled and vilified Mr. Van Buren in previous contests between the two political parties, were brought together with the democratic party on this question of slavery, and they voted for Mr. Van Buren because he was the head and front of the Free-Soil party. In the State of New York alone they counted a hundred thousand votes. The other sections of the Democratic party voted for General Cass. It was nothing but the military popularity of Gen. Taylor, acquired in Mexico, that carried strength sufficient to elect him in that State, and gave him the electoral vote. If his name and popularity had been out of the way, and nothing but Northern and Western, or Southern men in the field, the result would have been almost unanimously in favor of the Northern man—simply because of this question. The two great parties were thus divided. Now, it is a matter of very little importance to us whether, for a year or two, we possess that barren desert between the Sierra Nevada and New Mexico, but it is a matter of great importance to the people of the United States, and to the perpetuity of the American Union and its institutions, that we should settle this question. If by a vote of this Convention we can keep it from discussion hereafter; if by extending our government over this territory for a year or two, we can forever prevent discussion in Congress on this subject—prevent a settled division between the North and South, it is our bounden duty to do so.

[Here Mr. Hastings interrupted the gentleman from Sacramento to say that he hoped the House would either rescind or observe the five minutes rule.]

Mr. Sherwood said he would detain the House but a few moments longer.

Mr. McDougal moved to rescind the rule, which was adopted.

Mr. Sherwood then proceeded: I have no motive in making these remarks other than those indicated in the remarks themselves. I have said before that I do not desire this territory east of the Sierra Nevada as a portion of the State permanently; but it is on account of the discussion of this question, which to the knowledge of every man upon this floor has prevented our having a government here up to this period, that I wished our boundary to comprise what was and what is California. If this question is not kept out of Congress, if you barely go to the snowy mountains, or to a parallel of longitude beyond that, you leave the whole tract beyond that entirely open to discussion. It was for naught that we said to the Northern States last fall, in the presidential contest, that the people here did not want slavery. It made no difference. The fire had got among them; they were determined by their votes to settle the question. Men were not there disposed to reason upon a question of this character; they were not willing to leave it to the people of California. Although assured through the only organ in California, that the people of that territory did not desire the existence of slavery within its limits, yet they would not trust it to them. They wanted Congress to pass a resolve that slavery should be forever excluded from California. Upon that question they polled two hundred thousand votes in the Presidential election. Both before and since I came to California, I heard a general expression from among those who did not vote for Mr. Van Buren—those who voted for General Cass and General Taylor, that when this question would come up four years after, none but a Northern man could receive their votes—a Northern man in favor of the Wilmot proviso. No other could sustain himself among his constituents in the North. Politicians saw that the people were against slavery, and for having a Congressional enactment against its extension, and all men of all parties four years from last fall will vote for and sustain a Northern man. I firmly and sincerely believe this; and, as I said the other day, the moment the question reaches such an issue—the moment the North, which is the strongest, vote for their own Presidential candidate, and the South for theirs—that moment your Union is dissolved. We may come in now as a State, under the constitutional limits, by a close vote; but if the Union is to be cut asunder by this one question, we shall regret for years, that having it in our power, with no cost to ourselves, we did not settle it forever. It is this that governs my vote, and not any desire that I have to embrace that territory within our limits as a State. I want to see it forever kept out of the halls of Congress. The people of Mexico have said by their action that they do not want slavery; we have said by our action that we do not. Now if we extend our limits to what was and what is California throughout all the territory, by the action of the people themselves, slavery is excluded. I wish this territory to go to Congress in the shape adopted in Committee of the Whole, with the proviso, that if they choose to cut us down, if they have become convinced (I fear they have not) that slavery will ever exist east of the Sierra Nevada and west of the New Mexico line, then of course they will put our boundary where we all want it to be—the crest of the Sierra Nevada—extending from our northern to the southern line, and thence adopting the boundary as fixed by the United States and Mexican commission.

Mr. Botts. I want to make a few remarks on this subject, if I can keep cool. I want to bring to your notice the history of this transaction here tonight. This agitating question of the boundary, as I said before, had been tacitly agreed upon so far as this: that it was not to be discussed here; that a vote was to be taken on it without discussion. I think my friend from San Francisco (Mr. Gwin) so far recognized that that was his understanding and agreement that when he inadvertently made a few remarks upon the subject, he even came forward and withdrew them. But the vote is taken and carried in a particular way; then, indeed, the floodgates of discussion are opened, and that stringent five minutes rule is rejected at once. Why is this? Because discussion, and discussion of more than five minutes becomes necessary to effect the objects of gentlemen. Who made that five minutes rule, a few days ago, when it suited their purpose not to discuss this question? Those who now object to it because it conflicts with their present position. Now, Mr. President, I will enter upon the merits of the question, and there are no five minute rules to interdict me.

The gentleman who has last taken his seat (Mr. Sherwood) has made his strongest appeal in behalf of this extreme eastern boundary; that it will be the only means of getting you into the Union. Sir, I can tell you this will not be the means of your admission; you will never get into the Union with this boundary. If you do, it will be only to sit among its ruins, like Marius among the ruins of Carthage.

Let me relate to you the history of this question, and I will relate it perhaps a little different from the gentleman who has taken his seat.

There has been for some years in the United States a most violent party, who have waged war against the rights of the Southern people with respect to their domestic institution of slavery. They have become known by what among us is the hated name of abolitionist, and they are as much deprecated by the good men of the North as by all men of the South. They are not only the men who are opposed to slavery in the abstract—for of such a large majority of the Southern people themselves consist—but of such who, in spite of the Constitution, ask to thrust their views and opinions into our homes and firesides; these are the people and this is the faction who, in the Congress of the United States, contend that it does not become, and does not belong to any people living in a territory acquired by conquest, to decide for themselves the local question of slavery; they contend that the power resides in the Congress of the United States, and that they might inhibit it or admit it whenever they pleased. Against this faction, sir, appeared a faction on the other extreme, headed by Mr. Calhoun, of the Southern party, who contended also that it does not belong to the people of the territory to settle this question for themselves, but that Congress could not prohibit the Southern portion of the country from introducing their institutions into a territory achieved by the common blood and treasure of all the States of the Union. These were the two extreme factions, sir; the one contending that the power remained in Congress to exclude slavery, and the other contending that the power was retained by the North and South equally to bring all their institutions into a conquered country. Well, sir, between these two violent extremes appeared the mediating portion of the wisdom, both of the North and South, and they agreed thereupon to a great compromise principle. It was this: that the people of the territory should be allowed to settle the matter for themselves; and this proposition, sir, was hailed with general acclamation. When it was proposed, it received the unanimous vote, except of these extreme factions, one of which I believe is represented upon this floor. There was a general shaking of hands between the North and South; between the middle men, the wise and moderate men of both parties. This proposition was acceded to, and they said: we have established a principle that puts this question of slavery at rest forever, because the territory of the United States will be either organized into Territories or States, and slavery will exist or not, as the people in the Territory or State shall choose. It was thus supposed that California would immediately erect herself into a State, and that she would settle this question for herself. Now, sir, all we ask is that she shall do it. Is that the proposition here? Is the proposition of this eastern boundary based upon any such principle as that? No, sir, the people of California have gone into Convention, and declared through their representatives that they will settle this question for themselves, Congress having already agreed to the proposition. Now, whom do we, the delegates in this Convention, represent? Do we represent the people east of the Sierra Nevada? If the country east of that range of mountains had been called into this Convention, is any man prepared to say that this constitution is the same as it would have been had they been represented? Is it not evident then, sir, that you are evading those directions under which you are acting; that compromise principle under which you are called upon to act; and that you are settling this question not for yourselves, but for others; others, sir, who have never been heard, and who it is not intended shall ever be heard upon this floor? Why, sir, if the member from the Salt Lake had been here this morning, while gentlemen have been swearing to the number of their constituents, what do you suppose he would have sworn to? To one hundred thousand, I suppose; and yet, sir, the great sixty thousand people in Sacramento would scarcely have exceeded this portion that you propose entirely to leave out and settle the question for them without their consent. I ask you what will be said when you go to Congress with this constitution; not what the extreme faction of the South, headed by Mr. Calhoun, will say; not what every man of the South will say, but I ask you what the wise and moderate men of the North will say? I do not speak of the old story brought up in Committee of the Whole. You recollect what a gentleman here said a gentleman from Congress said; you may possibly remember the letters which had always just been received from the States. The gentleman from Sacramento (Mr. Sherwood) does not read letters, but he has just come from the abolitionist section of New York.

Mr. Sherwood. No, sir; I came from no such section.

Mr. Botts. The gentleman, however, certainly did not come from the Southern portion of the State; and I apprehend that when he tells you what he knows to be the feelings of the North he means the comparatively small circle in which he moved. I speak more largely; I speak of the great men of the North and South, as exhibited upon the floor of the Congress of the United States. I say, then, that when you come with this constitution in your hand, and demand admission into the Union, your Representative will be asked: Has this constitution, formed in this Convention, been ratified by the voice of the people; was it submitted to the people over whom it extends? What will be his answer? Can you find the man, can you buy him with money, that will go there, and say, yes? Can you for gold—all the gold of California—purchase the man who will go there and tell the barefaced lie that the people within this territory were represented in this Convention, and that this constitution has been submitted to them, and has been ratified by them. No, sir; he is obliged to hang his head and say, no!—in this republican government that we have proposed, we have avoided the first principle of republican liberty; we have made a constitution for a people who were not represented, and we have forced upon them, without their consent, this constitution. I said the other day, sir, that it would be an honor high enough for any man to go to the Congress of the United States as a commissioner to ask for admission into the Union, but it will not be an honor if he has to advocate such a cause as this. I know no man within the range of my acquaintance so low who would not be degraded by this office. Mr. President, let me put you this case in a clear light. A little community in San Francisco some months ago elected a local legislature, and in the absence of other and perhaps a better government erected a government for themselves. The legality of that government was much questioned. It was defended upon this ground: that they pretended to extend their laws, rules and regulations over no other persons than those that were there represented. Suppose they had for a moment entertained the idea, or declared that these laws and regulations which they made, should extend not only over the persons who had sent them there, but over one hundred freemen of these limits, where is the man who would have stood it? Not one. And yet is not this precisely what you you propose to do, when you make this eastern boundary extend to the Rocky Mountains? You call a Convention. In that call you define the object. Who do you call together to settle this question of slavery for themselves? Look at the proclamation, sir; you call the people west of the Sierra Nevada; it is they who form this constitution, and it is beyond all question their right and privilege to settle the question of slavery, and every other question for themselves, but not for others.

Mr. President, the gentleman from San Francisco, (Mr. Gwin,) how eloquent he was a day or two ago, when he was speaking of the passage of the revenue law in the Congress of the United States to be extended over this territory; over a people that had never been represented there. With what face can that gentleman now propose to do to others that which he so strenuously objected to when applied to himself? Does he not propose that a Legislature shall be called together here in a little while that shall have the power of taxing this very people that have never been represented here in this Convention? If you want to increase the bounds of your State, sir, extend your laws and impose your taxes over a territory beyond that which is represented here; if you wish to do it in conformity with the republican principles which you have avowed, you should dissolve this Convention, call a new Convention from all parts of the country which you propose to include in your State; then it will be legal and proper, and then there will be no Southern man found to dispute your principles. Yes, sir; call your

Convention from every portion of the country west of the Rocky Mountains; let them appear here in this hall; let them exclude for themselves slavery from this territory; let the constitution which does so be submitted to them; let them ratify it, and I will guarantee that there is no true Southern man or Northern man that will offer the least resistance to that boundary. That is the only way to do it; the only way that any republican can propose to do it.

Mr. President, I urge then, as a matter of policy, that you should not extend this boundary to the Rocky mountains. If you do, you cannot come into the Union; you must be opposed by every compromise man in the House; you must be opposed by every man who avows the doctrine that all men are free and equal, and that government can only be instituted by the consent of the governed; and that, sir, in the United States, is a very large party. Both of these classes, sir, the extreme factionist and the moderate men, are pledged to oppose you on this ground. But, Mr. President, this is not the only light in which this question is to be viewed. Has any gentleman—and I have heard many talk about the enormous expense of sustaining this Government—has any gentleman calculated the actual expense and the taxation that will be necessary to keep it up. Remember, sir, that you extend your laws over it; an individual rides eight hundred miles to make a complaint that these laws have been violated, in his person, and swears to the fact that A. B. and C. did commit such an act of violence. Must not your warrant issue; can you withhold from an individual within the limits of your laws the benefit of these laws? Will you not be compelled to arrest the accused and bring him before some tribunal; must not tribunals be established? If tribunals are established, must not the people be taxed to pay for the expense of them; and if the people are taxed, must they not in turn be represented? Do not these conclusions follow from each other as directly as a conclusion in any problem in Euclid. And then, sir, what an insignificant item is the expense of paying the members of the Legislature, compared with the expense of such a magnificent government as you propose. The lands of the south would hardly pay it at a hundred per cent., because you must remember that you are to give a government to probably six hundred square miles, where there are not more than probably thirty or forty thousand souls; much too large to be excluded from their share of the burden—much too scattered to pay their own expenses.

Then, Mr. President, I say briefly, upon every ground of policy and convenience, and every ground of right and justice, you cannot extend the eastern boundary of California beyond that portion that is represented here. I say that, in effect, you have already designated the eastern boundary; that General Riley proclaimed the eastern boundary of California in his proclamation, and the people said amen. I say that he, in his proclamation, called upon the people of California in pursuance of instructions, if you please—California as laid down in certain described lines—to form this Convention, and they, through their representatives, have excluded slavery for themselves; and is it for you, sir, now to reverse that decision. No, sir, you cannot do it; the people themselves cannot do it; the people themselves, within certain limits, cannot make rules for people without those limits. A line has been laid down for you already; you have adopted it; and, sir, I only voted for the other line because I was told that it probably included no other additional human being than those included in the true and proper lines; but the true and proper line to which we would be legally bound, is the line laid down in that proclamation under which we make laws for those whom we represent, and for no others. Why, sir, is it necessary at this day, in this enlightened country, to stand here and argue and prove that people can make laws only for themselves? I am ashamed of the position that I am compelled to occupy. Sir, you may ask me why I voted for the other line—for other than the line laid down in the proclamation. I have already stated the reason; it was because I was informed that there were none, or so few, that they were perhaps hardly worth mentioning, and I was compelled to yield something of my own opinions to the opinions of others; to compromise upon something, and I came as near my own opinions on that subject as I possibly could.

I hope then, Mr. President, if the object be to reconsider this vote to extend the line to the extreme eastern limits of the territory, from the most contracted line, that it will not be reconsidered for any such purpose.

Mr. Tefft. The gentleman from Monterey has argued long upon a question which is without any foundation whatever. He assumes that we have no right in this House of Delegates, to extend this constitution beyond the limits which are here presented; and that has been his chief and principal argument upon the floor here. I think a simple statement of facts, founded upon circumstances much more striking than this, will have a greater weight than any arguments based upon an assumption of that kind. When the Convention for the formation of the constitution of Wisconsin was called, the large district of Saint Croix was not represented at all in that Convention. That constitution was adopted and the lines extended so as to include the district of Saint Croix within the State. Not only was that district unrepresented in that Convention, but a protest was sent to Congress requesting that they should not be included in those boundaries, but should become a part of what was afterwards the Territory of Minesota.

Mr. Botts. And that Convention acted most foully in doing it.

Mr. Tefft. They did it nevertheless. The district of Saint Croix was made a part of the State, and the people are now represented in the State Legislature. I believe that is a precedent that warrants us, with other strong reasons, in taking the extreme eastern boundary. I had formed the conclusion when this matter was agitated before, that from all the circumstances, the extreme eastern line was the proper line. My views have not as yet been changed, and I have been open to conviction on this subject, for I go for policy and principle in all cases, whether they accord with my own feelings or not. I have listened carefully to every argument urged against it, with a sincere desire to cast my vote in such manner as would best promote the interests of California, and I must say that I have as yet seen no cause why I should come to a different conclusion from that which I before expressed. I must confess it was with great surprise that I saw certain members of this House whose minds I thought had been made up, vote in Committee of the Whole one way, and in the House completely change their votes.

I profess to have come recently from the States. I have not received any letters; but I can corroborate the statement of the gentleman from Sacramento (Mr. Sherwood) in regard to the feeling there. I do say, sir, that there is a grand combination of the North and West, the extreme West, against the South in this question of slavery. It is a question in comparison with which, every thing else that has been argued here, is trifling. I believe gentlemen will see when our constitution comes to be considered in the halls of Congress, that it is a matter of vital importance, not to California alone, but to our whole Confederacy. I do not wish to assume for this House of Delegates any greater degree of importance than it bears; but I do firmly believe, that for the past fifty years, no body of men have met together under circumstances of greater responsibility—circumstances which place it in their power to work greater weal or woe, not only to themselves and those whom they represent, but to the whole Confederacy of which they form a part, than this Convention. It is now in their power to mark out the ground and provide the effectual means of quieting this agitating question of slavery. Without reference to party feeling at home, let us look at what is right and fair in the premises; and then if we find that it coincides with views of good policy, and will have a beneficial influence in the Congress of the United States, let us proceed and adopt it. The Senate of the United States have said, in an official map, that such and such are the bounds of California; let us take those boundaries and say that they are the limits of the State of California. There is no doubt whatever in my mind that this extreme eastern boundary will meet with the entire approbation of the Southern party; every free-soil man of the North and West, and that is a great majority of both parties. It is a grand combination, comprising a large majority of both parties and Benton's entire western faction; if that will not take this constitution through the Congress of the United States, I know not what countenance the representatives of the people there can expect at home. I say, however, that the question is not whether this eastern boundary is going to expedite the admission of the State or not. We should look to right and justice in the premises, and to the greatest good for the greatest number, whether we can settle the question of slavery or not. If we find this to be not only right and just, but politic, then it is our duty to consider the expediency and let it have its additional weight. If, by the mere vote of this Convention, we can keep from discussion the question of slavery in this entire territory between the New Mexican line and the Sierra Nevada, as well as in that portion of the territory along the shores of the Pacific, is it not proper that we should take that course. Sir, it is our duty; and I hope that every member of this House will, in the vote which he may cast, remember the solemn trusts confided to him by the people, and weigh well the consequences of that vote.

Mr. Hastings. We have just passed upon this question, and, in my opinion, settled as it should be; but it is again raised by a reconsideration, and the object in raising it seems to be to again extend the boundary over this entire territory. For what purpose, Mr. President, is this to be done? It is stated boldly and publicly that the object designed to be accomplished is this: first, to settle the question of slavery for a vast extent of territory—an extent as large as all the non-slaveholding States of the Union. Now, sir, I assume this ground, and I believe it to be incontrovertible, that we neither settle the question of slavery, nor can we get into the Union if we include this entire territory. Instead of settling that question we raise it. No man, if he reflects, can arrive at any other conclusion. If we fix a reasonable and moderate boundary the question of slavery is forever settled; but if we include territory enough for thirteen or fourteen States the question is raised. The Congress of the United States will have no occasion to refer to that question if we include only sufficient territory for a single State. They have agreed by compromise that we have the right to determine it for ourselves. Would the South raise the question? No, sir; they have agreed that we have a perfect right to settle it for ourselves. Will the North raise it? That would be very singular, when they have a new free State added to the Union. Nobody can raise the question.

In reference to leaving an open boundary, it is objectionable precisely on the same ground; we neither settle the question of slavery nor the boundary; nor can we get into the Union with such a proviso. The South will forever insist upon limiting us to the smallest possible extent of territory; the North will oppose the position taken by the South; and North and South will contend for years to come, as they have contended for years past, and meantime we are left without a government.

In consideration of these facts, sir; in consideration of the population of forty or fifty thousand in the region proposed to be included, and who are not represented here, I trust no such course will be pursued. One gentleman has remarked upon this floor, that there are other portions of California not represented here; that perhaps not one-half of the people in certain districts have been represented; that perhaps not one-third of the people have voted. But, sir, observe the difference. These people have had notice that a Convention was to be held. It was optional for them to vote or not; and now they have their option to vote or not upon the constitution. But the people east of the Sierra Nevada, whom you propose to include, have no such option.

I think, sir, that the sentiment of this House is now decided; and I think there is no probability that a proposition so monstrous will ultimately be adopted. Whether the House may think proper to narrow the boundary proposed by the

Committee down even to the Sierra Nevada, I do not know nor do I much care; provided we have a certain definite boundary, not including too much territory. Let it be determined, sir; let it be fixed at once, and then there will be no question to be decided hereafter. We are at once admitted into the Union upon the ratification of our constitution.

Mr. Halleck. I do not intend at the present time to enter into any discussion of the different propositions of boundaries which have been made to the House. I shall, however, vote for a reconsideration; not that I am wedded to the proposition of the gentleman from San Francisco, (Mr. Gwin,) in favor of which I voted before, with the proviso offered by myself, but for this reason: that of all the boundaries which have been proposed by this House, I think the one last adopted is the most objectionable. I, sir, certainly prefer next to the one first mentioned that of the gentleman from Sacramento, (Mr. McDougal.)—I prefer it to the proposition of the other gentleman from Sacramento, (Mr. Shannon,) and even to the original report of the Committee on the boundary. But of all the boundaries proposed, I think the one just passed is the most awkward and objectionable, and I do hope the House will reconsider that vote; and if they are determined not to adopt the boundary with the proviso, as passed in Committee of the Whole, that they will take one of the other propositions. If they still adhere to the proposition just passed, I trust that they will fix a proviso to it so as to render it less objectionable than it now is. I do not intend to discuss the main question, as to which of the provisos is best, but I really think we jeopard our admission unless we adopt some provision of that kind, leaving Congress, with the consent of the Legislature, to fix upon any other line to the westward that may be desirable.

Mr. McDougal. When I moved a reconsideration of this matter I had no idea that we would have had anything like the discussion that we have had. I supposed that all like myself were very desirous that we should get through the business before us, that we might return to our respective places of residence; and I was somewhat surprised when I heard a long speech from my colleague, (Mr. Sherwood,) and another from the gentleman from Monterey, (Mr. Botts,) entering into a discussion of the whole question. I gave my vote for the measure just passed, and I gave it for the purpose of reconsidering it, for I consider it very objectionable—more objectionable than any yet proposed. I fully agree with the gentleman from Monterey, (Mr. Halleck,) in the opinion which he has expressed of this boundary.

Nature, sir, has marked out for us the boundary line of California. God has designated her limits, and we ought not to go beyond the line traced by the Omnipotent hand. The snowy range of the Sierra Nevada separates two communities of this country; one community living upon the eastern side and the other upon the western; they can have no connexion, either social or political. I therefore am opposed to any line which proposes to connect the two, or bring them under the same government and the same laws. When the Committee reported, they made their boldest and strongest argument upon that very ground; that there was a line forbidding any social or political union between the communities residing upon either side of that range of mountains. They set forth in that report this argument as perfectly conclusive; and it struck me at the time as the most forcible argument that they brought forward. But when they drew their line, I was surprised to find that they had included two hundred and fifty miles of the country beyond this natural division, which they said was an interminable barrier to any political connexion beyond one side and the other. The measure just passed takes in some three or four hundred miles east beyond the Sierra Nevada, running from the north to the south; and the Chairman of that Committee urges as the reason why he takes it in that it possesses some valuable lands for agricultural purposes; at the same time he states that it is impossible for any political association to be had with that part of the country thus included. I say, sir, that Nature has drawn the line for us, and we ought to take it; it is the ridge from which the waters flow eastward and westward.

When this subject was up in Committee of the Whole, I had the honor of introducing an amendment taking in that line as the true boundary of this State. But we were told by men, who probably knew something of the political movements of the country in the United States, that they wanted the people of California to include the whole territory, in order to silence the agitating question of slavery, which is now almost rending this Union asunder. That was the argument maintained here; and being a young man, sir, not so well versed in the political movements at Washington as some other gentlemen, I inserted a proviso including that country, but leaving it to Congress either to take the whole if it should settle the question of slavery, or adopt that fixed upon the Sierra Nevada in the first instance. I am willing now, sir, to include the entire territory, but only upon that ground. The country west of the Sierra Nevada contains an area of land double that of any other State in the Union, and I think if the people of the United States would be satisfied with that, we certainly ought to be. I think, sir, that under the present excited state of the Union in respect to the subject of slavery, if we can settle that matter, and create a harmonious feeling in Congress and throughout the Union, we ought to do it; but if Congress should not think proper to adopt it—if we have mistaken their feelings on this subject, and they have not sent their emissaries here to proclaim such doctrines, then let us settle the question ourselves, for such territory as we intend shall constitute our State. But take a line marked by Nature—one that you can extend your laws over; that you can hold both social and political union with; and if this question of a proviso is sustained, I shall certainly introduce an amendment similar in effect to that which I introduced in Committee of the Whole.

Mr. Shannon. The question I presume before the House is simply upon the reconsideration. I do not desire to discuss the merits of the different propositions any more than is absolutely necessary, and I shall endeavor to make but few observations. I am glad, sir, that although we are fighting against each other, as we were before, for the mode of attaining the object, yet we are now fighting together for a reconsideration—though we entertain different conclusions. In my opinion the most distant line is less objectionable than the one adopted by the House this evening. The argument of the gentleman himself (Mr. Hastings) against including the entire territory east of the Sierra Nevada will apply with almost equal force to the very boundary line contained in his proposition. The great argument which he has presented is the immense extent of territory. I put it back upon him, and it places his proposition directly in the position of that which he assails. What benefit does that line afford us? None, sir; every gentleman upon this floor who is acquainted with that country asserts that it is a perfect barren waste. The argument of the gentleman himself, sir, when he introduced his report as chairman of the Committee, of the total division that must exist between that portion to the east of the Sierra Nevada and to the west of it, and the utter impracticability of holding communication with it during a great portion of the year, is another strong reason why that line should not be adopted.

My object in sustaining and voting for this reconsideration is, that we shall, if we fix upon a permanent boundary line, as I desire, fix it as near as practicable to the eastern base of the Sierra Nevada, so that all those objections which can be urged against a useless extent of territory can be removed when our constitution is presented to Congress. I think, sir, that whatever boundary we agree to—let us fix it where we may, we should carry it, not by one or two votes, but by a majority which will carry with it all the influence that can be produced by unanimity of opinion.

Mr. McCarver. I wish to notice some few remarks made by my colleague from Sacramento, (Mr. Sherwood.) The whole question is narrowed down to this point: whether we shall extend our territory to the full extent of what heretofore has been considered California, for the express purpose of settling a great question that exists in the United States, or confine ourselves to a proper boundary that will probably admit us into the Union. My colleague (Mr. Sherwood) says that this is a waste country, not desirable, and that our only object in adopting it, would be to settle a question that the Congress of the United States is unable to settle. Why, sir, we are only one of the contracting parties; and the same party that refused to give us a Territorial Government last winter, may, upon the same grounds, refuse to give us a State Government now. We can determine what questions we shall settle for ourselves, as one party, but we cannot settle questions for both the contracting parties. They kept us out of the Union last session, and may keep us out if they choose this session. It is true the South admits that a State may decide whether it shall have slavery or not before it comes into the Union; but is it true that the South would permit one State to settle that question for all the States of the Union? The idea is preposterous. I think, sir, instead of facilitating our admission into the Union, we are placing fetters upon our constitution that will effectually prevent our admission.

Mr. Jones moved the previous question, which was sustained.

The main question being on the motion of Mr. McDougal to reconsider the vote on the engrossment of the article on the boundary, it was taken and decided in the affirmative, as follows:

Yeas.—Messrs. Aram, Brown, Carrillo, Covarrubias, Crosby, De La Guerra, Dimmick, Dominguez, Ellis, Foster, Hanks, Hobson, Hollingsworth, Jones, Lippincott, McCarver, McDougal, Pedrorena, Pico, Rodriguez, Reid, Stearns, Tefft, Vallejo.—24.

Nays.—Messrs. Botts, Gilbert, Gwin, Hastings, Larkin, Moore, Norton, Ord, Price, Sherwood, Shannon, Steuart, Walker, Wozencraft, President—16.

So the vote on the engrossment was reconsidered; and on motion, the proposition itself (being the substitute offered by Mr. Hastings) was reconsidered.

Mr. Gwin. Having got back to where we started some time ago, I desire, Mr. President, to give my views in favor of the plan as reported by the Committee of the Whole. I do not intend, sir, to blink this question at all. I am in favor of the plan adopted in Committee of the Whole, because it is my honest conviction that it is the only plan that will secure our immediate admission as a State. I thank the gentleman from San Luis Obispo (Mr. Tefft) for stating the fact, which I was not aware of before, in regard to the admission of Wisconsin into the Union. He showed conclusively that this principle of representing every portion of the people included within the limits of the State, could not be maintained; and that it was no act of usurpation to extend this Government over the people of the Salt Lake; that the principle is not so regarded by Congress, or by the States of this Confederacy. It was a case in point, where a portion of the people of Wisconsin were not only not represented, but they entered their protest against the constitution that was formed without their having a voice in its formation.

When this subject was up for discussion in Committee of the Whole, I referred to another State that was admitted under circumstances not similar to our own—under the proposed boundary of the Committee—but much stronger; the State of Michigan. If you look at the head of their Constitution you will see that it commences "We, the people of the Territory of Michigan," &c., "do by our delegates in Convention assembled, mutually agree to form ourselves into a free and independent State, by the style and title of the State of Michigan, and do ordain and establish the following Constitution for the government of the same." Yet there was a large portion of the population who not only took no part in the formation of that constitution, but actually protested against it. Nevertheless, it was adopted by the majority; the State was admitted, and they were as much bound to obey that constitution as those who had taken part in its formation. It was a constitution formed by a political party. So much for this bugbear in regard to the settlements on the Salt Lake. Suppose these people are not represented here? Are they any worse off with this government than they were before? Have they any government at all now? Do we propose to send the tax collector among them? Do we propose to put any of the burdens of this government upon them? Does not this proposition put it in the power of the Congress of the United States to exclude all that portion of the territory? Sir, no man can contradict it. It is the very words of the proposition, with the proviso of the gentleman from Monterey, (Mr. Halleck.) As to its being an outrage committed upon the Mormons, they would certainly be no worse off under this constitution than they are now. I cannot perceive in what light it can be regarded as an outrage. If they complain, it is time to remedy their grievances. I am surprised to hear the gentleman from Sacramento (Mr. Hastings) so urgent about representation here. Why, sir, three-fourths of the population that this gentleman represents here never went to the polls, and one-half of the population of Sacramento knew nothing about this Convention.

Mr. Halleck. I was on the American river near Cullumna when the first portion of the American emigration came in, and not one of them had heard of this Convention.

Mr. Gwin. Not one-half of that population knew of this Convention, and still we are forcing this government upon them, and upon the thousands and tens of thousands who have come in since that election. What are we to do in regard to them? Gentlemen talk about the enormous expense of this government. Do they expect that we are going to send beyond the Sierra Nevada our officers, and establish our courts there? When they are ready to assume the burdens of government, and apply for representation, they can get it.

Mr. Gwin continued his argument on the different points presented in the proposition before the House, on the same grounds as in Committee of the Whole.

Mr. McDougal wished to explain why he objected to the boundary reported from the Committee of the Whole. He objected to the proviso which referred the subject back from Congress to the Legislature. It would keep California out of a representation in Congress for some time. He desired to propose a boundary the same as that of the Committee of the Whole, but with this difference, that if Congress should not adopt it, then to have a positive line which should be adopted immediately by the action of Congress alone; and upon that, to rest our admission as a State. He gave notice of this amendment to the House, and would offer it at the proper time.

Mr. Price. I regret exceedingly that this question has been reconsidered. I was satisfied with the boundary as it passed the House; and I cannot but look upon this reconsideration as unfortunate, particularly when I consider the debate that it has opened. And, sir, if it were in my power, I would blot from the pages of the report that has been written down of the proceedings of this Convention, all allusion to that agitating question which has so inappropriately been brought up in this discussion—a question which might have been permitted to exercise its due influence upon the minds of the members out of doors, but which I had hoped would never have been brought up in this hall.

I desire, Mr. President, to say a few words in regard to the manner in which I shall vote on this boundary question, and give the reasons that dictate the course which I intend to pursue. Sir, one of the first reasons that controlled my mind upon this subject, was the fact that I believed, by extending our boundary to the greatest limit which has been here proposed, that we would do a manifest act of injustice to the South. I am not a Southern man; I am from New Jersey—one of the middle States; I do not belong to the class of canting abolitionists, nor to the hot-brained slaveholders of the South; and I believe I have a right to speak and can speak on this subject boldly and without prejudice. Now, sir, our desire is to become a State of the Union; it is the first object that we wish to accomplish; and we want to accomplish it in the shortest possible time. But by the adoption of this extreme limit, we totally defeat that object. We do a wrong to the South which will produce contention and discord in Congress, and prevent our admission into the Union. It will be utterly impossible to go into the Union with that boundary. On the other hand, by contracting our limits to the boundary that we have just reconsidered, we do no injury to the North. There is no party that can justly complain of our act. Who can say we have wronged either North or South? Not one, sir. We have the right of a free people to establish this constitution, and we have put upon the face of it that slavery shall not exist within the bounds of this State. This we have an undeniable right to do; and this we have done unanimously.

But, sir, we have no right to extend our boundary over an unlimited extent of territory, and establish our institutions over it, without the consent of the inhabitants. The moderate men of the South, whilst they maintain that we have the right to settle among ourselves this slavery question, will never admit that we have the right to extend our government over the unlimited space contemplated in the boundary adopted in Committee of the Whole. It is a question in my mind of policy alone; and it was policy that dictated my vote upon this question. I believe we are better off as a people with the limited boundary than we would be with the other. I am not particular as to natural boundaries. I do not regard it as indispensable that we should designate the line proposed by some gentleman here, the summit of the Sierra Nevada. Sir, we know no natural boundaries; the American people know no natural boundaries. They think as Napoleon did. When a general of his spoke of the difficulty of crossing the Alps, his reply was, "Sir, the Alps don't exist." I say the Sierra Nevada sinks before the genius and enterprise of the American people. I am willing to extend our line to the eastern slope of the Sierra Nevada; I am willing to take in that great region of mines which I believe exists there, and which will contribute to the wealth of this country. You will see, sir, what difficulties are to the American people, if you include that region. You will see them creeping up the gulches of the west and meeting with their brothers on the eastern side; and they will be one community, bound by the same social and political compact. But I consider the boundary that we have adopted in the House the best that we could fix as the limits of California. The Committee proposed a proviso leaving it discretionary with Congress to give us the greatest extent of limit, or to contract that limit, with the consent of our Legislature. I believe we should present ourselves to Congress with a distinct and definite boundary; one that is acceptable to us, and not leave it to the discretion of Congress to say where that boundary shall be. We are the best judges of what is good for us. If Congress does not see fit to accept us with the boundary which we think proper to adopt, we can exist as an independent State, and we want that State to be a compact one. The people of California have an undoubted right to say what their boundary shall be, and this boundary will be just what they say. They are the sovereigns, sir; we do not want to hear another voice on the subject; we want to leave it to no other power. The line passed here to-night I believe embraces just sufficient territory to make us a compact, happy, and glorious State.

On motion, the House then adjourned.

TUESDAY, OCTOBER 9, 1849.

The Convention met pursuant to adjournment. Prayer by Padre Ramirez.

The journal of yesterday was read and approved.

Mr. Jones submitted the following resolution:

Resolved, That in the opinion of this Convention, it will be practically impossible to survey and sell to private purchasers the public lands in California. That the comparatively small space valuable for mining purposes would inevitably fall into the hands of a few speculators, and the vast body of the mining population would either be compelled to cease their labors, or violate a right and a monopoly which would have neither force nor opinion to protect them. That the Congress of the

United States is therefore most earnestly requested, should the General Government retain its dominion over the said lands, to allow the free use and enjoyment of the same to all American citizens.

Mr. McCarver said he offered a resolution some days since on the same subject. He hoped if any proposition was to be considered now, that his would be taken up, as it had the preference.

Mr. Steuart. I should be very unwilling to offer anything which had been prejudged by the action of the House. Upon looking at the report of the Committee of Ways and Means, I find that it proposes that a memorial should be addressed to Congress on the subject of the public lands. In the remarks which I made in Committee of the Whole on the subject of the appropriation for purposes of education, I endeavored to point out the difficulties which this Convention would bring itself into, if it carried out the munificent plan of education, as proposed in the section to which the proviso was attached. I am clearly convinced that the funds from the mineral lands is your only salvation; the only means by which you can redeem the State from the onerous burdens which you have imposed upon her by your votes here. I may be wrong in these views—they are my individual opinions; but I am happy to find that they are concurred in by a great number of persons out of the House, and sustained by a great many in the House. I gave notice in Committee that I would offer the resolution which I hold in my hand. I have, sir, upon all occasions avoided consuming the time of the House in debate; I have endeavored to present my views in the most succinct manner. In consequence of this desire to forward the business of the Convention, I proposed to take this matter up at a convenient time, and what has been the consequence? A gentleman who had heard the argument which I advanced in support of such a measure has come forward and submitted an ordinance to cover in a great degree the very plan which I had proposed. Another gentleman comes forward this morning and presents a series of resolutions on the same subject. If it is the pleasure of the House not to give an expression of their opinion on a question of such vital importance, I for one shall not object; but I do insist upon it that I have a right to offer any proposition which, in my opinion, is germain to the question. If this question therefore is to be considered at all, I submit the resolutions of which I gave notice several days since. (See debate September 27th.)

Mr. Dimmick objected to both the resolutions of the gentleman from San Joaquin (Mr. Jones) and the gentleman from San Francisco (Mr. Steuart,) and under the rule they were laid over.

On motion, the consideration of the report of the Committee of the Whole on the boundary was resumed; the proposition before the House being the substitute proposed by Mr. Hastings for the report of the Committee of the Whole.

Mr. Ellis moved the previous question, which was sustained; and the question being taken on the substitute of Mr. Hastings, it was rejected, as follows:

Yeas.—Messrs. Aram, Botts, Brown, Crosby, Dent, Hill, Hoppe, Hastings, Larkin, McCarver, Ord, Price, Reid, Sutter, Steuart, Walker, President—17.

Nays.—Messrs. Carrillo, Covarrubias, De la Guerra, Dimmick, Dominguez, Ellis, Foster, Gilbert, Gwin, Hobson, Halleck, Hollingsworth, Jones, Lippincott, Moore, McDougal, Norton, Pedrorena, Pico, Rodriguez, Snyder, Sherwood, Shannon, Stearns, Tefft, Vallejo, and Wozencraft—27.

Mr. Shannon then submitted the following substitute for the report of the Committee of the Whole, viz:

That the boundary of the State of California be the following: commencing at the point where the 120th degree of west longitude, as laid down on the official map of John Charles Fremont, drawn by Charles Preuss by order of the United States Senate, intersects the 42d degree of north latitude (forming the southern boundary of the territory of Oregon); thence following said 120th meridian southerly to its intersection with the 38th degree of north latitude; thence in a southeasterly direction to the point where the 35th degree of north latitude crosses the river Colorado; thence southerly following high water mark on the east bank of said river, to the boundary line established by the late treaty between the United States and Mexico, dated at Queretaro, May 30th, 1848; thence westerly along and upon said line to the Pacific ocean; thence following the course of said

Pacific coast to the parallel of 42 degrees north latitude, extending one marine league into the sea from said coast, and including all the bays, harbors, and islands adjacent to said coast, to said 42d egree; and thence eastwardly along and upon said parallel of latitude to the place of beginning.

Mr. Hoppe. After the elaborate discussion which we have had upon this subject, it would seem useless to renew it; and I would not now trespass upon the attention of the House, but I think it a question of such vital importance, that if we do not properly understand it and come to a judicious decision upon it, we may jeopard the best interests of California. Many gentlemen, I think, are led astray on this subject; some are for taking in the whole of California; others for a more limited and definite boundary. A few days ago I was in favor of taking a certain boundary, as fixed by the Select Committee. Were it not for a portion of the population at the Great Salt Lake, I would now vote for taking in the whole of California; but, sir, taking the strict letter of the constitution, that representation shall be based upon population, I do not see how we are to be justified in taking this course. Shall we fix the line of the Sierra Nevada or the one just proposed here, and say that the Mormons there, a body of American people settled at the Great Salt Lake, numbering at least twenty-five thousand souls, shall not have a representation on the floor of the Legislature? Is it reasonable? According to the proclamation of the Governor, which has been adopted as the act of the people, the eastern boundary is fixed at the Sierra Nevada, unless the districts be altered and the apportionment be remodelled. We allow no representation to a body of American people, constituting one-fourth of the souls in California. I say then, if the whole of California is taken in, we must remodel the apportionment; and if the Salt Lake is included in the District of Sacramento, I am in favor of giving that district at least five or six additional delegates. If they are included in the District of San Diego, the same additional apportionment should be given to that district. Let us look, gentlemen, at the future before we go too far. It will be impracticable for the Mormons to have a representation in our Legislature; at any rate it will be attended by great inconvenience and enormous expense to the Government. The question of expense should be well considered, and it is highly desirable that we should not establish an extravagant system of government. Allowing a representation for the twenty-five thousand souls at the Salt Lake, they will be entitled to seven representatives in the Senate and Assembly. The distance is about nine hundred miles; allowing each member at the rate that we have fixed, it will be $14 40 for each, making the round sum of $10,080 for mileage alone for the representation of Salt Lake. Some members may regard it as very improbable that there should be such a body of people permanently located at the Salt Lake, and some are of opinion that there but few. But, sir, I beg leave to inform gentlemen that I know that place; I crossed it myself; I know that such is not the fact. There is already a large population of Mormons settled and permanently located there, with good houses, better than we have in California; good mills, fine farms, and flour now selling at ten dollars a hundred. But a few days ago I conversed with Captain Walker, the celebrated mountaineer, who knows that country better than any man that exists, and he states that it is absurd to think that there cannot be a populous State between the Salt Lake and the Colorada river. It is a fine valley, susceptible of supporting a valuable and flourishing State. Steamboats can ascend that fine river three hundred and fifty miles. With all these facilities, who will deny that there must and will be a large population equal to any of our States. For aught we know, there may be gold discovered in those mountains surrounding the Salt Lake; mineral wealth equal to what we possess on this side. There may be a larger population there than in this portion of California. With these considerations in view, how can gentlemen consent to exclude the Mormons and cut them off entirely from representation. It is not just; it is anti-republican and contrary to the provisions of our constitution. Shall we say in one part of the constitution that representation shall be according to population, and in another, that one-fourth of the population of California shall not have a representation? What will the world say? That we have done them gross injustice; that we have violated the first principles a of a republican government. Sir, if they have the hearts of freemen, they will rebel against it themselves. What! shall they be governed by laws forced upon them by people a thousand miles away, who give them no voice in the formation of those laws? No, sir, they will justly regard it is act of despotism which no free people could submit to. If the whole of California is to be admitted, I shall be in favor of dissolving this Convention, remodeling the apportionment, and giving them an equal representation with ourselves. Finally, Mr. President, I am decidedly of opinion that we should fix upon a definite boundary. I prefer that last proposed by Mr. Hastings; but of the others, I prefer Mr. McDougal's.

The question was then taken on Mr. Shannon's substitute, and it was decided in the negative, as follows:

Yeas.—Messrs. Aram, Botts, Brown, Crosby, Dent, Ellis, Hanks, Hill, Larkin, McCarver, Ord, Price, Reid, Sutter, Snyder, Shannon, Steuart, Walker, President—19.

Nays—Messrs. Carrillo, Covarrubias, De La Guerra, Dimmick, Dominguez, Foster, Gilbert, Gwin, Hobson, Halleck, Hastings, Hollingsworth, Jones, Lippitt, Lippincott, McDougal, Norton, Pedrorena, Pico, Rodriguez, Sherwood, Stearns, Tefft, Vallejo, Wozencraft—25.

Mr. Halleck. I beg leave to offer a few remarks on this boundary question before it is finally submitted to the vote of the House; the subject, however, has been so fully debated both in Committee of the Whole and in the House, that it is hardly necessary at the present moment to enter into any very detailed discussion.

After listening with attention to the various remarks of gentlemen on this floor my opinion is still decidedly in favor of the boundary reported by the Committee of the Whole: *i. e.* the plan of the gentleman from San Francisco (Mr. Gwin) to include within the State all that portion of California ceded to the United States by the treaty of Gaudalupe Hidalgo; with the proviso offered by myself, authorizing the Legislature to arrange, if desirable, with Congress, for a more limited boundary on the east; provided that such line be not drawn west of the crest of the Sierra Nevada and the mouth of the Gila River. My reasons for supporting this report of the Committee of the Whole may be summed up in a few words.

In the first place, we are assembled here to form a constitution for California, as she is recognized in the treaty of cession, in the official papers and despatches of our own Government, in the maps and memoirs published by order of the Congress of the United States, and in the maps and records of the Spanish and Mexican governments. Such, in my opinion, is the California for which we are now called upon to form a constitution. It is not for a mere corner or piece of this territory for which we are now organizing a government; nor for that little strip of country west of the snowy range; nor the more extensive territory west of the great desert or of the Salt Lake; but for California, as she was ceded to us by Mexico, and as she is recognized and marked out in the official acts of the Government of the United States. Such is the purpose for which our constituents sent us here, and we have no right to divide up the country, and to throw away such portion of it as, in our individual opinions, may be worthless in itself, or inconvenient to include within the limits of the new State. But while we organize a State Government for California, as she now is, we may, with propriety, provide in our constitution for forming (with the consent of Congress) a more limited boundary on the east, whenever the people, through their representatives in the State legislature, shall ask for such line of boundary.

In the second place, to form a constitution for California as she now is, without division or change, will facilitate the admission of the new State into the Union. It is a well known fact that at the last session of Congress the attempts to form a territorial government for a part of California received very little favor or support from any party; both the ultra free-soil men of the North and the pro-slavery men of the South voted against such division; while, on the other hand, the various projects for organizing a government for California, without division or limitation, were much more favorably received. Such will be the case when we present our constitution at the bar of Congress, and ask for admission as one of the States of our great Confederacy. If we present a constitution for all of California included within the limits of the United States, with the slavery question settled by the unanimous vote of the Convention, we shall unite all parties in favor of our admission. The administration will favor it, not only as a matter of right and justice, but on the score of policy, because it will relieve their party from the embarrassments of "Southern Addresses" and "Wilmot Provisos"; the Northern Free-Soil party will favor such admission because our constitution makes California a free State, and this removes all object or excuse for further agitation; the Southern pro-slavery and State-right party will be for us, because, by deciding for ourselves, without any intervention of Congress, we merely exercise the right which has always been claimed for us by the South. But if we divide this territory, and, while settling the slavery question for one portion of California, leave it open for all the remainder of this country, we shall satisfy no party, and very possibly may array against us large portions of all these political factions of the older States. Let us, therefore, act in this matter with great prudence and discretion.

The bitter feelings engendered by the discussion of this slavery question with respect to the territory acquired of Mexico, have, as is well known, almost sapped the foundations of the Union. The blind enthusiasm and feverish excitement of the North have been brought in conflict with the heated fancy and irrascible honor of the South, and the very pillars of the capitol have been shaken by the contest. Every attempt at arrangement and compromise has only tended to widen the breach. The States east of the Rocky Mountains cannot settle this question; the contending parties have advanced too far .o recede. All look to us to do for them what they cannot do for themselves; to hold out the olive branch of peace, to satisfy the sentiment and honor of both parties, and to enable both to retire with credit from the field. We in California *can* settle this question, and settle it, too, forever. We can soothe the wounded honor of the South, while at the same time we take from the Northern agitators the very aliment upon which they subsist. Let us not fail in the performance of the great and responsible part which has been alotted us in the drama of modern politics. While we act with calmness and discretion, let us fearlessly do our duty to our country. We are laying the foundation for a great empire; let it be broad and deep; let us be governed by no narrow or short-sighted policy. We are not legislating merely for a single day or a single generation, but for ages and generations yet in the womb of time. The position of California is unprecedented in history; she is already attracting the attention of the world; there is no spot on this continent which excites at the present time so much interest and concern. Men of intelligence and enterprise from the old and new States, and from the commercial cities of South America and Europe are already rushing in large bodies to this land of promise; every avenue of approach is crowded to excess, every vessel that reaches our ports is filled to overflowing. This new population will form a State of high public spirit, and of daring enterprise; no other portion of the globe will exercise a greater influence upon the civilization and commerce of the world. The people of California will penetrate the hitherto inaccessible portions of Asia, carrying with them not only the arts and sciences, but the refining and purifying influence of civilization and Christianity; they will unlock the vast resources of the East, and, by reversing the commerce of the world, pour the riches of India into the metropolis of the new State; while at the same time new avenues of communication will be opened between this and the older members of the Confederacy, connecting us together with new bonds of interest and union. We should, therefore, be careful, in laying the foundation of the new empire, not to contract within too narrow limits the circle of its action, nor to unnecessarily circumscribe the sphere of its usefulness.

A third reason for including all of California within the limits of the new State is, that we do not yet know where the eastern line ought to be drawn. Some say that the crest of the snowy mountains forms the best and most natural boundary; while others, who have visited and examined that portion of California, tell us that some of the most valuable mineral and agricultural lands in the territory lie on the eastern slope of the snowy range; gold, they say, is as abundant on that side as upon the face of the mountains looking into the great valleys of the Sacramento and San Joaquin. A third party contend that the middle of the Great Desert, between the Salt Lake and the Sierra Nevada, will form the most convenient boundary on the east; and that if that line be prolonged south till it meet the Gila river, it will include all the most valuable mineral lands within the limits of the State. They say that indications of coal have recently been discovered near the Rio Colorado, or between that river and the Rio Gila, and that this coal formation, if it really exist, would be excluded by a more limited boundary. Without entering into any examination of the correctness of these statements, is it not evident that we are yet too ignorant of the true character of the country east of the Sierra Nevada to determine positively where the eastern boundary of the State should be drawn? If the members of this Convention are so divided in opinion, ought we not to leave the question to the Legistature, to be decided by that body, when the proper information shall be obtained? Another strong reason for including all of California within the limits of the new State, is the necessity of giving a government to the people who are settling the country east of the Sierra Nevada. Congress, embarrassed as that body will be by the slavery question, (if we leave it unsettled for a large portion of the territory,) cannot organize a government for these people. In any new attempt to do this, the same questions of constitutional power will arise, and the same exciting discussions on sectional interests and domestic institutions. *We*, however, can give them a government. Under the constitution which we are now forming, that portion of country can be organized into counties and judicial districts, so as to secure the life and property of individuals. Large numbers of people annually cross that territory in order to reach the *El Dorada* of the west, and crimes of the darkest dye are committed on the road. If that territory be excluded from the limits of the State, there will be no legitimate mode of bringing these culprits to trial and punishment. Let us, therefore, settle this question of slavery for all of California, and extend the benefits of our constitution over the whole territory, till such time as Congress shall be able to organize a separate government for that part of it which we do not wish to include within the permanent boundaries of our State.

Let us now look for a moment at the various objections which have been urged against the boundary as reported by the Committee of the Whole. In the first place, it is said that this boundary includes too large an extent of country. To this it is replied, that the Legislature, as soon as it shall deem proper, can cede to the General Government any portion of this territory, and contract our boundary within limits as narrow as it may desire. In the second place, it is urged that we should, in our constitution, fix a definite boundary so as to leave nothing to the discretion of Congress and the State Legislature. This would be well if we knew precisely where to draw this boundary line, and if there was no extraneous questions calculated to impede our admission into the Union as a State formed out of only a *portion* of California.

Again, it is urged that as the people east of the snowy mountains are not represented in this Convention we have no right to include them within the limits of the State. This objection has been answered by a reference to numerous instances in the older States, where new settlements, not included within any organized district or county, have had no voice in State Conventions or legislative bodies. If there had been time for delegates to come from the great Salt Lake, no one would have objected to their taking seats in this body; and the fact that any district, or part of a district, or new settlement, not within any organized district, is unrepresented here, can form no serious objection to including such district or settlement within the boundaries of the State. Suppose no delegate had appeared in this Convention from one of the central districts of California, would that be any reason why the boundaries of the State should be so drawn as to exclude that district? The Constitution formed by this body can have no legal force till approved by the people; but when ratified by a majority of the legal voters, it will be binding upon the whole. No one will pretend for a moment that a majority of the people of California are not represented in this Convention, and the new settlers east of the snowy mountains have no more reason to complain of a want of representation here, than the great mass of emigrants who have entered the country since the election of the 1st of August. If they do not like our constitution they can vote against it, when it shall be submitted to them for ratification; and if they do not wish to be included in the State they can ask for a separation. But no such objection will be made; nor will such a separation be asked for. What they wish, and what they have already asked for, is a *government;* and as Congress cannot give them one, they will willingly embrace our constitution, and organize courts of justice in accordance with its provisions. Another objection, which has been urged with great warmth to the boundary as reported by the Committee of the Whole, is, that it includes the Mormon settlement upon the great Salt Lake. It is asserted that these are a disagreeable and dangerous people, who, if included, will be calculated to disturb the peace and quiet of the new State, and involve us in civil war; and in order to increase this feeling of local or personal prejudice, the most exaggerated statements have been made respecting their numbers and power. Let us look at this question cooly and dispassionately, and not be carried away by the excitement gotten up by these descriptions of imaginary dangers. During my residence in California, I have seen much of the Mormons, both as a military body and as private citizens, and I believe them to be an industrious and well-disposed people; and I am certain that, if not molested or persecuted for their religious opinions, they will prove themselves a peaceable and law-abiding community. The meanest and most inoffensive reptile on earth, when trodden under foot, will turn upon its destroyer. But even supposing the Mormons to be, as here represented, a dangerous and troublesome community, the report of the Committee provides for their exclusion whenever the State Legislature shall see fit to contract our boundaries to a more narrow limit. If the Mormons wish to conform themselves to our constitution, and to obey our laws, why not permit them to do so; and if, on the other hand, they wish a separate organization, why not leave it to Congress, with the concurrence of our Legislature, to give them such an organization. Under every view which has been taken of this question, the boundary reported by the Committee seems to me the most convenient and safe that can be adopted.

One more remark and I have done. It has been charged by one of the gentlemen who speaks against the report of the Committee, that this boundary proposition has been gotten up for political purposes; that it is intended to relieve the present general administration from the embarrassments of the slavery question. Nay further, that its very terms were dictated to this Convention by political emissaries of General Taylor, and that it was carried through the Committee of the Whole by the direct interference and "log-rolling" of such government emmissaries, now in the lobby of this House. Such charges are scarcely worthy of notice, and those who make them only lower themselves in the estimation of every respectable member of this body. The gentleman who first offered this article on the boundary, (Mr. Gwin,) can hardly be charged with being an emissary of an administration to which he is politically opposed, and the amendment submitted by myself, and accepted by that gentleman, was written by me at this table after he had offered his proposition, and without one word of consultation either with him or any other person, either in or out of this House. I offered it on my own responsibility, without knowing or wishing to know what were the opinions of others. Gentlemen give themselves a great deal of unnecessary trouble in dragging into every discussion here the bearing of political parties at home, and in tasking their ingenuity to discover some difference of opinion, with respect to affairs in California, between the past and present administration. When all the papers and correspondence connected with California are laid before the public, it will be found that no such difference of opinion or of policy ever existed. The instructions issued by General Taylor's cabinet correspond in every essential particular with those which came from the cabinet of Mr. Polk. General Riley's proclamation calling for a more complete organization of the existing government of California, and for the election of delegates to this Convention, was issued and sent to the press on the 3d day of June last, and the steamer which brought the first instructions from the present administration did not reach San Francisco till the 4th of June, and were not received by Gen. Riley till the 10th of that month. Those instructions, however, confirmed in every respect the course which General Riley had previously taken. I hope this explanation will be sufficient to satisfy gentlemen that there has been no essential difference of opinion at home with respect to the course pursued by the government here, and that these authorities have been uninfluenced in their course by any considerations connected with party politics. And if any emissaries of either political party are now in California attempting to dictate to this Convention what course it should pursue, I, at least, am ignorant of the fact. I know no such emissaries; and if there be any, I have no desire to know them, Nor, when this boundary question was proposed, did I know the opinion of a single individual out of this House. And I earnestly hope that for our own credit, and for the honor of those who sent us here, that we shall act upon this important question free from the trammels of party politics, and with reference solely to the interest and welfare of California.

Mr. McDougal then offered the following substitute, viz:

The boundary of the State of California shall include all the tract of country from or near the 107th degree of longitude west from Greenwich to the Pacific coast, and from the 32d to the 42d degree of north latitude, known as the Territory of California; also the harbors, islands, and bays adjacent, and along the Pacific coast; also to extend three English miles into said Pacific ocean, and along the coast thereof, from the 32d to the 42d degree of latitude north; but if Congress should not grant or adopt the boundary line herein set forth, then the boundary shall be as follows, viz: Commencing at the point of intersection of the 42d degree of north latitude with the 120th degree of longitude west from Greenwich, and running south on the line of said 120th degree of west longitude until it intersects the 39th degree of north latitude; thence running in a straight line in a southeasterly direction to the river Colorado, where the 35th degree of north latitude intersects said river; thence down the river in the middle of the channel thereof to the boundary line between the United States and Mexico, as is now being established under the treaty exchanged and ratified at Queretaro, May 30th, 1848; thence running west and along the boundary line to the Pacific ocean and extending therein three English miles; thence running in a northwesterly direction and following the direction of the Pacific coast to the 42d degree of north latitude; thence on the line of said 42d degree of north latitude to the place of beginning; also, all the islands, harbors, and bays along and adjacent to the Pacific coast.

Mr. Botts said that inasmuch as the report of the Committee of the Whole reserved a vote to the Legislature of California, and the plan of the gentleman from Sacramento, (Mr. McDougal,) left the final decision to Congress alone, he thought the original proposition, objectionable as it was, was not so objectionable as that, because it left some power to the people of California.

Mr. Hastings suggested a division of the two questions—the original proposition as offered by the gentleman from Sacramento, (Mr. Gwin,) and the proviso of the gentleman from Monterey, (Mr. Halleck.)

Mr. Steuart. I do not wish to discuss this question. The disposition manifested by this House warns me that any attempt of mine could add nothing to the arguments of the gentleman from Monterey, (Mr. Botts.) I regret, sir, as much as any man, that matters have been introduced in this discussion, which I had hoped would have been kept from it—especially that the gentleman from Sacramento (Mr. Sherwood) should have led off the debate, by giving his views as to the state of political parties in the United States. I rejoiced, sir, in the thought that we came here as Californians, not as party men. I deny the position which the gentleman assumes. I will never admit that the great statesmen of old Massachusetts will be so recreant to their ancestors as to go in favor of the proposition which the gentleman advocates—to settle the question of slavery for others than the people included within our natural limits. I do not believe there is any such combination between the Whigs and Democrats of the North. But, sir, if the contest which the gentleman predicts should come—much as I value the Union—I am ready to meet it upon the great platform of principle. If they do force us into that position, I am prepared to sustain the rights of the South against the fanaticism of the North. I had hoped that this question never would have been brought up here. It has been brought up, and we have been obliged to meet it. Look around this assembly and see who composes it. You have Southern gentlemen, delegates with principles which grew with their growth and strengthened with their strength; they have sacrificed these feelings and principles; they believe that it is their duty to California to avert that curse which has been inflicted upon their country, and aggravated day by day by the theories of fanaticism; and, sir, they have cast their unanimous vote against the institution of slavery in this country. Sir, if you go among the people from Tennessee and Kentucky and Louisiana, who are rapidly filling up this country, you will find that they are all anxious to avoid here the curse which has fallen upon their native States. If it had been a question here between the population from Louisiana, Kentucky, Tennessee, and other slaveholding States, and the people from the North, we might have had a different result. But they meet here in a spirit of compromise and concession. The prejudices of education and association are forgotten in their earnest desire to avert those collisions here which have proved so disastrous at home. But, sir, they claim to settle this question for themselves—not for others. They claim that this constitution is the constitution of the people who are represented in this Convention, and of no others; and that position I hold to be incontrovertible. I am opposed to any proviso being introduced; I think that the proviso itself is calculated, above all things, to throw a fire-brand into Congress. We give them there a theme for discussion the whole session. I am for fixing a settled and established boundary, one which will meet the approval of the people who are represented here. I deny the power of Congress to interfere with the rights of the people of any territory by imposing a government over them which may be objectionable to them.

Mr. Sherwood. I am sure the gentleman who last took his seat has not understood the views which I expressed to the House. If he understood me as attempting to draw a line in this country between different classes of men as to the political views that they entertained in the United States, or as attempting to get up any division here upon the platform that divides the people of the United States, he is entirely mistaken.

Mr. Steuart. I will do the gentleman the justice to say that I believe no man entertains purer feelings than he does. I only object to his views.

Mr. Sherwood. I think the House, and every Southern gentleman will bear me witness that I attempted to throw no firebrand into the Halls of Congress; I attempted to get up no question here between the North and South; but it was to avoid in Congress what the gentleman objects to here—the discussion of this question, that I urged the views which I have presented to the House. The gentlemen said that if it had been a question here between the people from Louisiana, Kentucky and Tennessee, against the North, we might have had a different result. I care not if the South form the majority here. Upon this question of slavery, I ask the gentleman if North and South were not all in favor of excluding slavery here? The gentleman intimates that if it had been made a question, he, as a Southern man, would have stood out against the Wilmot proviso. I object, sir, to any application of that argument to me. I have made no argument in favor of the Wilmot proviso. It was to prevent hereafter any such attempt in the United States to get up a discussion in regard to slavery here, where we have the right and the only right to settle it, that I urged the adoption of this whole boundary; it was to prevent the introduction of that firebrand into Congress. It was to exclude slavery by our own action. The gentleman acknowledges that his own constituents are in favor of excluding slavery. It is settled by unanimous consent that we do not want slavery here. The argument which I adduced was that if we covered the whole of what was originally designated and known as California, we would prevent that firebrand from exciting the same feeling in Congress which the gentleman has shown here. He says if the North turn fanatics upon this question, he, as a Southern man, will stand up for Southern rights. It was to prevent any such division in the States and in Congress; to settle the question here where there is no point of honor involved; no feeling except the practical feeling of expediency in regard to what institutions we shall have, that I used the argument to which the gentleman objects.

Should the whole boundary proposed be adopted, it will be time enough, when the people beyond the Sierra Nevada are able to bear the expenses of government, and ask for a division, to cut them off. Can it be said that Southern men, who regard the rights of the States to establish their own institutions, will object to the exclusion of slavery within our established limits! Mr. Calhoun cannot object to this question being settled by the people of the new State. If he does, it will be in conflict with his declared opinions. There can, therefore, be no objection; the South will be glad to have this question settled without discussion; they know they are weaker in numbers than the North. I, for one, wish to avoid any division on this agitating question. The feeling that exists in the Northern breast cannot be driven out. The South admit, themselves, that slavery is an evil; but entailed upon them, and difficult to be got rid of The feeling of every man, either North or South, is opposed to slavery of all kinds; it is a feeling instinctive in the human breast. It was to break the chains of slavery that the American Revolution broke out; to prevent unjust taxation, that the North and South united in that revolution. But this institution exists among the people of the South, and I am willing that they should sustain their own institutions; and let slavery be abolished, State by State, according to the supreme and sovereign power of the people.

Mr. Botts. With the consent of the House, Mr. President, I will tell you an anecdote. I was at a little party last night, and I met there a certain gentleman —a Northern gentleman; and after he had been excited by wine, (you know the old proverb—*in vino est veritas,*) he, this Northern gentleman, sir, said to me: "Suppose the Southern feeling had had the ascendancy in this Convention, and slavery had been permitted in our constitution; and then a proposition had been made to extend the line to the Rocky Mountains for the purpose of making that country a slave country, said he, what would Northern men have done? They would have put their hats upon their heads and left the House." I tell you, sir, that I believe if I had been a Northern man, and that course had been pursued— that illegal course to extend slavery over those whom I represented and those whom I did not represent, I would have left the house. Now, Mr. President, I have but one word to say in regard to the latter part of the argument of the gentleman from Sacramento (Mr. Sherwood.) He has come out now plainly and openly, and I understand that the Northern doctrine, so far as he knows, is this: that slavery shall not be permitted to exist in any of the territories of the United States; that the people shall do as they please, but they shall not introduce slavery; that if the free and independent people of California had in this Convention declared that they would entertain among themselves the local institution of slavery, that the Northern men would not have permitted it.

Mr. Sherwood. The gentleman does not state my argument correctly. I go for each State settling this question and all other questions for itself.

Mr. BOTTS. Whatever interpretation the gentleman may give to his own argument, he clearly maintains the doctrine of the Wilmot proviso. He insists that we should settle this question by extending our boundary over a people whose consent he does not ask. Yes, sir, against their will if necessary; and what more does the Wilmot proviso? Now, sir, as a Californian, not as a representative of North or South, but as a free and independent Californian, I denounce that doctrine. I will meet it and denounce it wherever it exists. North or South, sir, I care not whence it comes, I shall fight against it mentally and physically. What, sir! That the people of this territory are to go to New York and not only ask them for a constitution, but ask them if they may be permitted to include or exclude slavery! Such a doctrine need not be broached here. It will not be listened to. The people of California are free and independent; they have a right to form their own government; yet the gentlemen tells us that we are bought body and soul, and must be ruled by the North; that we must form just such a constitution as they like.

Mr. SHERWOOD. I denied any such doctrine; but I stated what I believed to be the feeling in the North.

Mr. BOTTS. My remarks apply to what the gentleman says is the Northern doctrine.

On motion, the Convention took a recess till 3 o'clock.

AFTERNOON SESSION, 3 O'CLOCK, P. M.

The CHAIR stated that the substitute proposed by Mr. McDougal, was before the House.

Mr. BOTTS moved a division of the question so that the vote should first be taken on the first clause of the proposition, and it was so ordered.

Mr. McDOUGAL withdrew the first clause of his amendment, confining it exclusively to the boundary last described therein, viz:

The boundary of California shall be as follows, viz: Commencing at the point of intersection of the 42d degree of north latitude with the 120th degree of longitude west from Greenwich, and running south on the line of said 120th degree of west longitude until it intersects the 39th degree of north latitude; thence running in a straight line in a southeasterly direction to the river Colorado at a point where the 35th degree of north latitude intersects said river; thence down and along the middle of the channel of said river to the boundary line as is now being established under the treaty with Mexico, exchanged and ratified at Queretaro on the 30th day of May, 1848; thence along said boundary line to the Pacific ocean, and extending therein three English miles; thence running in an northwesterly direction and following the direction of the Pacific coast to the 42d degree of north latitude; thence on a line of said 42d degree of north latitude to the place of beginning; also all the islands, harbors, and bays along and adjacent to the Pacific coast.

Mr. ELLIS moved the previous question, which was sustained.

The vote was then taken, and the amendment lost as follows, viz:

YEAS.—Messrs. Aram, Botts, Brown, Crosby, Dent, Ellis, Hill, Hoppe, Hastings, Larkin, McCarver, McDougal, Ord, Price, Reid, Sutter, Snyder, Shannon, Steuart, Vermeule, Walker, President.—22.

NAYS.—Messrs. Carrillo, Covarrubias, De La Guerra, Dimmick, Dominguez, Foster, Gilbert, Gwin, Hanks, Hobson, Halleck, Hollingsworth, Jones, Lippincott, Moore, Norton, Pedrorena, Pico, Rodriguez, Sherwood, Stearns, Tefft, Vallejo, Wozencraft.—24.

The question recurring on the adoption of the report of the Committee of the Whole, a division of the question was moved in order that the vote might be taken on the main proposition and on the proviso separately.

The CHAIR decided that the question was divisible.

From this decision Mr. TEFFT appealed, and the decision of the Chair was reversed by the House.

The question was then taken, and the report of the Committee concurred in, viz:

YEAS.—Messrs. Carrillo, Covarrubias, De La Guerra, Dominguez, Dimmick, Foster, Gilbert, Gwin, Halleck, Hanks, Hobson, Hollingsworth, Jones, Lippincott, Moore, Norton, Pedrorena, Pico, Rodriguez, Sherwood, Stearns, Tefft, Vallejo, Wozencraft—29.

Nays.—Messrs. Aram, Botts, Brown, Crosby, Dent, Ellis, Hill, Hoppe, Hastings, Larkin, McCarver, McDougal, Ord, Price, Reid, Sutter, Snyder, Shannon, Steuart, Vermeule, Walker, President—22.

Upon the announcement of this vote, several members rose to their feet under much excitement, and great confusion ensued.

Mr. McCarver. I now move we adjourn *sine die.* We have done enough of mischief!

Mr. Hoppe. I give notice that I will file a protest against this vote. Rest assured that the thirty-nine thousand emigrants coming across the Sierra Nevada, will never sanction this constitution if you include the Mormons.

Mr. Snyder. Your constitution is gone! Your constitution is gone!

Cries of "order!" "order!" from all from all parts of the house, and "the constitution is lost!" I will sign it under a protest!

Mr. McCarver. I insist upon my motion to adjourn *sine die!* This Convention has done harm enough!

Mr. Norton. There is a resoulution now before the House fixing the time of adjournment. It must first be rescinded.

Mr. Gilbert. I call for the yeas and nays on the motion to adjourn *sine die.*

Mr. Vermeule. I hope the motion will prevail, in order to give a safety-valve operation to this excitement.

Mr. Shannon. I appeal to my colleague to withdraw his motion.

Mr. Botts. The question is on the adjournment; I call for the question.

Cries of "the question!" "the question!" from all parts of the House.

Mr. Snyder. I shall vote against the House adjourning before the business before us is completed. I ask you one question. Have you completed the business that the people of California sent you here to perform? If you have not, can you go back to your constituents and say you have discharged your duty?

Mr. McCarver. I withdraw the motion to adjourn *sine die.*

The Chair having partially succeeded in restoring order, on motion, the resolution adopted on Saturday, to adjourn *sine die* on Tuesday, (this day) the 9th instant, was rescinded. The House then adjourned.

WEDNESDAY, OCTOBER 10, 1849.

In Convention. Prayer by the Rev. Mr. Willey. Journal of yesterday read and approved.

Mr. Jones. I am now going to recur, Mr. President, to a subject which has created a great deal of excitement among members of this House. I allude to the boundary question, upon which the vote was last night taken. I have not yet spoken upon it, and I trust I will be indulged in a few remarks. There is, sir, among members of this House, a great difference of opinion, and I believe an honest difference of opinion, in regard to the policy which we should adopt in determining this question; but I think that difference may be narrowed down to a very small point. A part of this House are anxious to create an absolute, definite, and determinate boundary for the State of California; another part are anxious to avoid the difficulty which they foresee may, and in all probability will, arise in the Congress of the United States on the settlement of this question. Both parties admit that it is our policy to avoid raising any question in Congress, which may endanger or delay our admission into the Union; and both agree that if we can be admitted with the boundary of the Sierra Nevada—which is conceded to be the natural boundary of the State—that it would be our best policy. I am willing for one to admit this proposition; but here comes the point of difference. Upon the one side, we are told that we must take this line absolutely and determinately, and make no provision for any difficulty in Congress; shape our action with no reference to the action of Congress; but if we cannot be admitted without difficulty, then we must defy the Government of the United States, and tell them that we are a sovereign and independent people, and have a right to fix our boundary. Upon the other hand, here is the difference. While we are willing to admit that the Sierra Nevada is the best boundary for California, we say that if any difficulty, in regard to our admission, should arise in Congress on this subject, we are willing to treat with that power, and, by the united action of Congress and our Legislature, determine it as much to our advantage as we can. The one wishes to avoid the difficulty; the other avoids it by running up against it. Sir, I hope we may come to a compromise. After we have reduced the question down to this small point, shall we avoid the difficulty or not? I hold in my hand a proposition, which I think accomplishes this object; and I will move a reconsideration of the vote of last night, for the express purpose of offering this proposition to the House. It is this: that we shall take the Sierra Nevada line; but if Congress will not admit us with that line—if it is an insuperable barrier to our admission—then we provide for this difficulty by saying, that if Congress absolutely refuse to admit us upon the smaller line, we will take a larger. The question then is clearly presented to the House: Will you avoid this difficulty or will you encounter it? Sir, it will be more than difficulty here; it will be a great difficulty there; it will raise dangerous and exciting questions in the Congress of the United States. Apart from our position here—a most anomalous position; a State and yet not a State; which claims to be an independent Government, and yet admits itself to be subordinate; apart from this anomalous position, look at the grave and exciting questions which will be raised in the Government at home;—questions, sir, upon which the parties of the United States are almost equally divided, and which haye caused dissension throughout the Union. One of those questions is, that a territory of the United States, until it is admitted as one of the United States, have no right to admit slavery into their own territory. This principle is advocated by a party in the North; it is denied by the South. It is the first question that will be raised, when we present our Constitution for ratification; and while we find such men as Soule of Louisiana, Foote of Missisisppi, and Calhoun, differing in opinion upon other points, yet they were all united upon this, and it will be one of the most exciting questions—a question that may may possibly lead to the dissolution of the Union itself. That all territory acquired by the common blood and treasure of the United States belongs equally to the North and South; and that by the provisions of the federal Constitution each State has an equal right to introduce its institutions into that terrrritory. There will be other questions connected with it, as to our right to fix a definite boundary. Do you suppose that the people of this territory would, upon some nice point of honor, agree to exist in this anomalous condition for years to come? Sir, I have heard gentlemen, inside of this House and out of it, say that they had rather remain out of the Union for five years, than come in with the whole of this boundary; that they would rather ruin and desolate this country by putting it in conflict with the Government of the United States for five years. Sir, I cannot agree to that position. I am willing to go before the people with the proposition which I hold in my hand, and I say there is hardly a sensible man in the land who will not agree with me, that our policy is to avoid difficulty with the General Government.

It has been said by a gentleman here—I don't know to what wing he belongs—that we are favoring the admission of slavery here. How are we doing it? By creating difficulties, says this gentleman, which will prevent our admission by Congress as a State into the Union, for some two or three years to come, and thereby give to the South a chance, while we are a territory, to bring in their slaves. How is it then that this proposition is supported by the North as well as the South? The argument is not worthy of consideration.

The question resolves itself to this, and I wish to place it in its true position before members of this House. If we can get in at all with the smaller line—the Sierra Nevada line—we can get in under this proposition. We tell the Congress of the United States what our choice is. We tell them what we want. If we cannot get in under that line, we say, in order to conciliate the opponents of the smaller line, you may admit us under the larger line. We give them no choice between the two. We do not give them the right to carve out the territory here as they please. We tell them precisely what the alternative is. There is nothing indefinite about it. Now, it is certain that those who contend that we should come in as a whole will agree to this; and those who favor the Sierra Nevada line cannot object; because if it is at all possible to get the smaller line, we have every chance by this proposition that is afforded by those which have no alternative. The question is then, shall we if possible avoid the difficulty, or shall this Convention say that they will not come into the Union upon these terms?—that they will not avoid any such difficulty—that if Congress will not admit us with the smaller line, we do not want to be admitted at all?

But if Congress does not refuse to admit us with the Sierra Nevada line; if they do contend that we cannot divide the territory; if they compel us to come in with the large boundary, where are the great and insuperable difficulties which will fall upon the inhabitants on the other side of the limited line. We could within one or two years, or even six months, divide them off, and put them into a separate State. If gentlemen see fit to maintain the doctrine that we should not take any means of avoiding the difficulty, but hold ourselves as a sovereign and independent State, I am willing to meet them before the people of California on that question. The compromise which I propose is in the following words:

The boundary of the State of California shall be as follows: Commencing at the point of intersection of the 42d degree of north latitude with the 120th degree of longitude west from Greenwich, and running south on the line of said 120th degree of west longitude until it intersects the 39th degree of north latitude; thence running in a straight line in a southeasterly direction to the river Colorado at a point where it intersects the 35th degree of north latitude; thence down the middle of the channel of said river to the boundary line between the United States and Mexico, as established by the treaty of May 30, 1848; thence running west and along said boundary line to the Pacific ocean and extending therein three English miles; thence running in a northerly direction and following the direction of the Pacific coast to the 42d degree of north latitude; thence on the line of said 42d degree of north latitude to the place of beginning; also all the islands, harbors, and bays along and adjacent the Pacific coast.

But if Congress should refuse to admit the State of California with the above boundary, then the boundary shall be as follows: Beginning at the point on the Pacific ocean south of San Diego to be established by the commissioners of the United States and Mexico, appointed under treaty of 30th May, 1848, for running the boundary line between the territories of the United States and those of Mexico, and thence running in an easterly direction on the line fixed by said commissioners as the boundary to the Territory of New Mexico; thence northerly on the boundary line between New Mexico and the territory of the United States previous to the year 1846, and California as laid down on the "Map of Oregon and Upper California, from the surveys of John Charles Fremont, and other authorities, drawn by Charles Preuss under the order of the Senate of the United States, Washington city, 1848," to the 42d degree of north latitude; thence due west on the boundary line between Oregon and California to the Pacific ocean; thence southerly along the coast of the Pacific ocean, including the islands and bays belonging to California, to the place of beginning. The said boundary to be subject to the approval of the Legislature of the State of California.

Mr. Wozencraft. It will be borne in mind by this House that the same identical proposition was submitted by me to the House several days ago, but there was no action taken upon it. The House did extend the courtesy to me so far as to say it might be read, but they went no further. I believe now, as I then did, that it would have been a peace-maker. I believed it would receive a more unanimous vote than any proposition which has been presented. The gentleman from San Joaquin claims the paternity of it. I have no objection, if the House will adopt it; but certainly this is my proposition. I for one, sir, am not willing to take any course which may tend to dissolve this confederacy. I consider that a clause, leaving an alternative, is absolutely necessary in order to avoid that difficulty; but I must admit that I prefer, if we can obtain it, the line marked out by nature. I am pleased to see this proposition brought up, because I think it will be the means of a compromise. I now move the suspension of the 30th rule, which requires that no rule shall be suspended without one day's notice, with the intention of moving the suspension of the 29th rule, which requires that the same subject shall not be reconsidered the second time.

The CHAIR decided that it was not competent, under the rules, to reconsider again a vote or subject that had been once reconsidered. There had been a vote taken here by which a certain boundary was fixed, and that vote was reconsidered, and it would be utterly impossible to reconsider it a second time if the same result had prevailed; but upon that reconsideration that vote was entirely destroyed, and another vote was given, which had never been reconsidered, and which therefore it was competent for the House to reconsider. This was a new subject and a new vote; the former reconsideration did not apply to it.

Upon this decision a long discussion, on parliamentary usages, ensued.

The CHAIR stated that inasmuch as there was considerable difference of opinion on this subject, the shortest way of testing the sense of the House would be an appeal from the decision of the Chair. Any member who objected to that decision was at liberty to take an appeal.

Mr. BOTTS. Suppose it were possible to throw some obstacle in the way of this reconsideration, is there any gentleman who desires to do it? What did we adjourn for yesterday afternoon? That we might coolly and dispassionately reflect upon this subject, and come to a decision which would be harmonious and satisfactory. Now, when an amicable proposition comes forward from the side of the majority, I had hoped that gentlemen here would meet it in the same amicable spirit, and endeavor to establish that good feeling that once existed, and that desire that always ought to prevail among the members of this body, to secure for this constitution such a vote as would give it an influence that it could not otherwise possess. When that is the object and may be the effect of such a reconsideration, I ask is any gentleman willing to place any obstacle in the way. I believe the Chair is correct in his decision; but I appeal to gentlemen not to raise any excited feeling upon this subject by attempting to thwart this proposition for amicable adjustment.

Mr. GWIN. I ask the gentleman from Monterey (Mr. Botts) one question. When he advocates the reconsideration, in order that the proposition of the gentleman from San Joaquin may be brought forward, does he intend to convey the idea, that this being an amicable proposition to settle the difficulty, he will support it?

Mr. BOTTS. Now, did you ever hear such a question? I will answer the gentleman. I am asked, sir, if I advocate the reconsideration, pledging myself to hear no debate, but to determine to support and vote for a certain proposition. No, sir, I go for a reconsideration for no such purpose. I go for a reconsideration to open this question again, and debate it, and compromise it if we can; to hear other gentlemen upon this floor besides the gentleman from San Joaquin, (Mr. Jones,) and to vote for any proposition that I consider the most advantageous and best calculated to secure a large vote of the people for this constitution.

Mr. GWIN. I merely asked the question in order to know what to expect from this reconsideration. I think we have discussed this question sufficiently. Further discussion will produce no effect upon this House. If a new plan is brought forward and both sides of the House would determine to sustain that plan, then there is some reason for a reconsideration. Otherwise I cannot see what is to be gained by it. The whole subject has been before the House for some time, and fully discussed. I do not want to bind any gentleman to any proposition; but inasmuch as it was understood here that the gentleman from San Joaquin (Mr. Jones) had moved a reconsideration, for a specific object—to settle the difficulties of this House by a new proposition—I wanted to learn whether it would settle those difficulties. That is the avowed object of the reconsideration. Why then go into a reconsideration, if the manifest disposition of the House shows that it can produce no such effect? Gentlemen refuse to give any pledge. The question then presents itself, shall we open this question again for unlimited discussion? Is there a member of this body who has not made up his opinion? The great contest has been whether or not we will include within our boundaries the territory of California, giving the power to Congress and the Legislature of this State to reduce it if they think proper; or make a definite boundary, including only a portion of the territory. I now state most distinctly that if the boundary passed yesterday is not to be the boundary, I am in favor of the Sierra Nevada line. I do not wish to blink this question at all. I am in favor of the proposition as it passed yesterday, or the natural boundary—the Sierra Nevada. If the question is to be presented here in any other shape, I shall vote against it. The reason why I opposed fixing an absolute boundary, leaving no alternative, when this subject was up before, was that we would open the difficulties which gentlemen wish to avoid; that Congress having a supervisory power in this matter, might think proper, instead of giving us a definite boundary, to cut us down to an infinitely smaller extent of territory than we proposed in that definite boundary. I proposed that this should be the constitution of California, because we are the people of California. Look at the papers that we have just received, and you will find that we are only known as the people of California. I have advocated this line with the proviso simply on the ground of expediency. I believed and still believe it would be the best plan we could adopt to avoid future difficulty. I do not desire to include the whole territory; but Congress may desire to do it, and with Congress lies the discretionary power. I have stated again and again that we are sitting in Convention here because this matter could not be settled by the Congress of the United States. We know that Congress has the right to settle our boundary, and the boundary of all new States; it is a right which they will insist upon, and which they have always refused to surrender. Inasmuch as this territory and New Mexico have been bought from Mexico by the Government of the United States, and fifteen millions of dollars paid for it, they are clearly entitled to say where our boundary shall be; and hence I have thought that if we make the boundary of the Sierra Nevada, running to the mouth of the Gila, Congress might say to us: you have included too much for one State; we will limit you to the territory within which your population resides; we will cut off all south of 36° 30′. South of that must be a territorial government.

That will be the great battle-field. I confess I would greatly prefer a more restricted boundary. We have the natural boundary to make a greater State than any in this Union—the bay of San Francisco and its tributaries. If we had our choice we would thus shape our boundaries; but what do our brethren to the South say. "Although we prefer a territorial government to avoid the heavy expense of a State organization, yet we prefer enduring taxation rather than separate from you, and run the risk of getting no government at all from Congress."

The line of 36° 30′ is a great question on the other side of the mountains. Here it is nothing. If any portion of our population are opposed to slavery, *per se*, it is that portion south of that line. It is utterly unfitted for slave labor, being a grazing and grape country, with a few rich valleys and extensive arid plains. My desire is that we should not jeopard the admission of the State by committing a blunder about this boundary line. Let our State boundaries be the same as the territorial boundaries. If Congress does not like them, it can alter them without destroying the work we are assembled here to perform.

Mr. McCarver. I believe it is not usual to enter into a discussion of the merits of a question on a motion to reconsider. The object of the reconsideration may be explained, but I think it is digressing to go back to the main subject and enter into another debate upon it. I shall go for a definite boundary, and for this reason I am in favor of the reconsideration. It is for the purpose of getting a definite boundary that I advocate this course. The Chair, I think, is perfectly correct. This is entirely a different vote from the one reconsidered the other day.

Mr. Hill. I hope the motion to reconsider will prevail. I am willing to vote for any proposition that brings our boundary this side of the Salt Lake—any proposition that will exclude the Mormons. As to the remarks of the gentleman (Mr. Gwin) upon a Territorial Government south of 36 deg. 30 min., the people of the South do not oppose a State Government; they were only of opinion that a State Government would bear heavily upon them at this time, but they greatly prefer a State Government to having a separate organization; and they are ready and willing to assume their proportionate share of its expenses.

Mr. Pedrorena. I am for a State Government, and I believe such is the will of my constituents.

Mr. Hill. I am authorized to say that the people of San Diego do not want a Territorial Government; they want a State Government.

Mr. Carrillo. It is necessary for me to go aside a little from the question before the House, on account of the example set by other gentlemen. It appears, as well as I have been enabled to learn the substance of the discussion, that some gentleman has said that the people of the South would prefer a Territorial to a State organization. This is a great mistake—I might almost say a falsity; and the best proof is, that they have hitherto contributed with you to form a State Government. It has likewise been asserted that the people of the southern part of the country are in favor of slavery; this is entirely false. They have equally as much desire as any portion of the people of California to avoid the curse of slavery. I do not propose to discuss the question of reconsideration. In my opinion, the proposition last adopted, that of Messrs. Gwin and Halleck, is the best, and I am opposed to the reconsideration; but should the motion prevail, I shall vote as may seem to me proper.

Mr. Tefft. When the question was originally taken in this House whether we should form a State or Territorial organization, certain delegates voted in favor of a Territorial Government, but not in favor of having a Territorial Government south and a State Government north. In the present case when it is proposed to established a State Government, the interests of the two portions of the country being identical, so far as regards the form of government, I do not think there is a man in the southern districts in favor of a separate organization—that is, of a State and Territorial Government. From the excited state of feeling manifested in this House yesterday, I am opposed to bringing up this boundary question again, without the assurance that there is now a spirit of conciliation in the House. I am opposed to having tables knocked down as they were yesterday in this madness of excitement.

Mr. McDougal. I hope the House will not forget the subject before them, the proposition of the gentleman from San Joaquin, which it appears has given rise to a discussion entirely irrelevant to the question which we are called upon to decide. I trust a decision will be had at once, and that all further debate will be checked. The issue is now, whether we can reconsider the vote of yesterday, under the 29th rule. That rule states positively that the same subject cannot be reconsidered twice without unanimous consent. The point to decide is, what is the subject. I conceive that we have not reconsidered the subject at all as yet.

Mr. Hoppe. I hope there may be a spirit of conciliation in this House; and certainly there is, so far as I am concerned. I am perfectly willing to bring this question to any final vote, which I conceive will be satisfactory to the people; but I do not believe any reconciliation can be effected, or that this satisfaction can be produced, unless we have a definite boundary. If we leave it open, it will lead to results that we would all deprecate; and gentlemen would find out these results in the halls of Congress. I say, Mr. President, let us exclude the Mormons, whatever we do. Their influence would be most injurious. They would make the taxes of this State burdensome to every man in it; no citizen of California desires that we shall have any social or political connexion with them.

The question was then taken, and the motion to reconsider adopted by ayes 32, noes 13.

Mr. PRICE. In a spirit of compromise, and with the hope that the resolution which I am about to offer to the House, may bring about the happy result of enabling the Convention to act upon this subject without any heartburning, I offer the following resolution, leaving the subject of the boundary to the people themselves. I believe it will be the most satisfactory course, and the best calculated to avoid that excitement which may jeopard the ratification of this Constitution.

Resolved, That the question of boundary be submitted to the people of California, at the first election, and two lines be proposed, to be defined by this Convention.

Mr. WOZENCRAFT. In moving the reconsideration of the vote on this question, my colleague (Mr. Jones) gave notice to the House that he did so for the purpose of submitting a certain proposition. He gave notice of that proposition at the time. I believe, in all courtesy, that it has the precedence, and should be considered first.

Mr. JONES. I had the particular good fortune, sir, to obtain the floor this morning before any other member of the Convention. I call it a particular good fortune, for I have no doubt if any member had known that I wished to obtain the floor, there would have been some difficulty in getting it. I made a motion, sir, to reconsider the last vote of the House on this subject; and I gave notice that if the reconsideration prevailed, I would offer the proposition which I hold in my hand. It was for that purpose that I moved the reconsideration; and after the motion prevailed, a gentleman jumps up with another proposition, and claims that it shall be considered. I can only say, in relation to that proposition, that whether the people establish the one line or the other, the whole object of this compromise is defeated; because, if this Territory is confined absolutely to one limit or the other, then we avoid no difficulty that may present itself in the Halls of Congress.

Mr. BOTTS. I was afraid, Mr. President, that we would have several very important but minor questions to settle—minor to the great question under consideration. A little while ago there was a dispute as to the paternity of the resolution offered by the gentleman from San Joaquin (Mr. Jones.) This I thought the House would have to sit in judgment upon as Solon did between the two mothers. Now, sir, I am afraid another question will arise as to whether the gentleman from San Francisco (Mr. Price,) or the gentleman from San Joaquin (Mr. Jones,) has the right to offer the first amendment. If that is settled, I come to the consideration of the question before the House, and it is first upon the proposition of the gentleman from San Joaquin (Mr. Jones.)

Mr. President, I assure you that I am not insincere when I say that I came here in a spirit of compromise and conciliation. I am not one to put my foot down upon a mark and say I will neither advance nor retrograde. I have even been twitted here from the fact that I have more than once changed my opinions; and what I had thought to be a virtue on the part of an honorable man, to confess the fact that he has been in error, has been thrown up in my teeth as a fault. Now, I will tell you why, with all this spirit of conciliation, I cannot vote for this proposition. There are some things, Mr. President, that cannot be compromised. It has been said that a principle can no more be compromised than chastity can be compromised. I cannot therefore give my sanction to the proposed compromise. I have maintained upon this floor, and I stand committed to this: that to institute a government, directly or indirectly, over a people, without their consent, is a violation of every principle of republicanism and justice. Sir, I have a debate in my pocket on this question; a debate between Mr. Calhoun and Mr. Webster. I wish I could read it. They are both right, putting the two together; one makes out one part of the argument, and the other makes out the other part. You arrive inevitably at the conclusion that the Constitution of the United States, according to the showing of Mr. Webster, does not extend to the people of California. Then you have the other great mind to prove that if it does not, there is no power in the Congress of the United States to legislate upon it at all. It is true Mr. Calhoun endeavored to show that Mr. Webster was wrong, but he failed to do it. He shows conclusively that it is not in the power of Congress to legislate in any manner for the people of California. The gentleman from San Joaquin in one breath admits the power of Congress to impose this government over the entire extent of this territory; over a people who have taken no part in its formation, and who may not desire it; but in another breath he says it cannot be done without the consent of our Legislature. I hold, sir, that Congress either has the power or has not the power—that the principle is either true or false; that the act of our Legislature cannot give to Congress any power which that Legislature does not possess, and that the two conjointly possess no power over a third party which is possessed by neither one of them individually. I should prefer a line, which I understand will be proposed here—the boundary marked in the proclamation of General Riley; but I will vote for any line that does not include a community of men not represented here.

Mr. Lippitt. I beg leave, Mr. President, to explain the reasons which will induce me to vote against the proposition of the gentleman from San Joaquin (Mr. Jones.) I am in favor of the Sierra Nevada line, and most decidedly against the proposition to extend the boundary to the Rocky Mountains. We have no right, sir, to extend our constitution and government over the inhabitants of the great Salt Lake, comprising some thirty or forty thousand Mormons, who have never been consulted in making this constitution—who have had no representation in this Convention. We have no legal right to impose a government upon these people. But I have another objection, which I do not think has attracted the attention of the House. Suppose they should afterwards accept and ratify our constitution, and consent to come in under our State government. I say, that even then we do not want this great desert. It would be perfectly impracticable to carry on our government over that immense territory. Nature herself has shut us up between the Sierra Nevada and the Pacific, and told us in strongest possible language—"thus far shalt thou go, and no further." Consider, sir, the expense and difficulty of carrying on a government over a vast desert, where the means of communication are so limited. The expense alone ought to be a sufficient objection, apart from every other consideration. It should be borne in mind that when our government goes into operation we will be a new State—a State just formed, without any previous territorial organization.

The expense of putting in operation for the first time an entire judicial system, together with the various branches of our State government, must necessarily be very great, even within the smallest limit proposed, where the difficulties of communication are less formidable. How much greater would be the expense over a vast wilderness, separated from us by snowy ridges of mountains, and hundreds of miles distant from the nearest point of civilization. But the chief ground of my opposition to this proposed extension of boundary is, that it opens a most dangerous and exciting question in Congress. Just so sure as we form an issue, to be tried between the two great parties of the North and South, our constitution goes by the board. I doubt very much, if such an issue is raised there, whether we shall have our constitution adopted and ourselves admitted into the Union for years. Now, sir, let us take this boundary of the Sierra Nevada. Let us shut ourselves within the limit which Nature has formed for us. Is there any issue, then, between the North and the South? When the question of admission comes before Congress what issue can there be? The question will be simply on the acceptance of this constitution, containing a certain and definite boundary. It is republican in its form, and that being the case, we are entitled to admission under the provisions of the Federal Constitution,

The South has laid down the principle that the people of the State are the sole judges of what shall be its domestic institutions. That has been the sole ground of conflict on the Wilmot proviso. The whole South will therefore take us as we are, with that boundary. Then how will it be with the North? Perhaps they will not be satisfied that we have not claimed the whole boundary. They would probably prefer having us extend our government over that territory. But, sir, there will be no issue joined between the North and the South. There is no battle to be fought in Congress between the two great parties. The issue, if any there should be, will be between the North and the people of California themselves. They will say, why did you not extend your limits to the Rocky Mountains? What will California reply? We have no right to extend our constitution over a people who have not been consulted—who have had no voice in our Convention—who are not to be represented in our Legislature. In the next place, the expense of such a government, even if the people of the Great Salt Lake were willing to accept our constitution and abide by our laws, would render it entirely impracticable for us to adopt such a boundary. Even if we did adopt it, the very next year we would be obliged to turn round and say—take back this territory; it is too much for us; we cannot afford to pay the expense of a government over it. And this would be a very sufficient reply. The North is reasonable. It would not be so unjust as to say: we will not adopt your constitution; we will not admit you into the Union, because you do not extend your jurisdiction over a people whom you have not consulted in the formation of your government. I repeat, then, that if we fix the Sierra Nevada as the line, the question goes before Congress uncomplicated and unembarrassed. There is no issue between the North and the South. The South agrees to it as a matter of course. If there is any dissatisfaction at all, it will be on the part of the North; and do you suppose, sir, that the North will be so unreasonable as to reject our constitution and refuse to admit us into the Union, because we do not, in establishing our boundary, do a thing which it is extremely doubtful whether we have a right to do, which it would be impracticable to carry out, and which would overwhelm us with debt, and probably ruin us, if we made the attempt?

Another consideration. The North, although she may express some dissatisfaction, will not refuse to accept us when it comes to the point. We give her two Senators from a non-slaveholding State. That addition turns the scale in the Senate of the United States. It gives her the command of the whole question hereafter. The existence of slavery in the vast desert east of the Sierra Nevada is a mere abstract question. A great part of the territory south of 36° 30′ is a desert that will never be inhabited by an American population. It will never, in reality, be a part of the State. But suppose it should be inhabited to some limited extent—suppose, even, that it should become a densely populated country, I ask you whether the North, by accepting our constitution with this boundary, does not get her two additional Senators? What more does she want?

And what will the South say? Certainly the South will not commit an act so suicidal as to refuse its assent to this Constitution, because we have not cut off all south of 36° 30′. There is not a member on this floor, who believes that slavery can ever exist there. Whatever desire the South might have to introduce slavery there, the fact that it is utterly impracticable to do so—that it can never exist in that region—is sufficient to preclude the idea. If the Territory is divided at all, it will, in accordance with the compromise agreed to between the two great parties, be erected into a free State by the action of the people themselves. There is no division of opinion between the northern and southern population of California on this subject. Consequently if it becomes a separate State, it will be a free State; and instead of one, there will be two free States.

If the other boundary is adopted, let us see what would be the consequences. It is a double proposition—a proposition with an alternative—to fix our boundary either on the Sierra Nevada, or include the whole of California, as Congress and the Legislature may hereafter determine. I ask you, sir, if that is not making an open question of it?—throwing down the glove between the two great parties? The very idea of such a question, not upon the adoption of the Constitution, not upon the local institutions of the new State, but upon the great conflicting and extraneous interests involved in this extensive boundary, will be the commencement of the battle. The question will be, whether slavery is to be excluded forever from that immense territory east of the Sierra Nevada, or only from the natural boundary of the new State. Is it possible that any member of this Convention does not see that this leaves the whole question open? that it has no tendency towards settling it? that the South will fight the same battle again, and on the same ground that it has fought it for years? Sir, I am a Northern man. I am as much opposed to slavery as any member of this Convention. I have lived in a slave State sufficiently long to witness the practical evils of this institution, and to learn that it is deemed a curse by the slaveholders themselves; but I cannot help looking at the inevitable result of this policy, as it will appear to the South. What is the proposition? That some few thousand inhabitants, shut up here behind the Sierra Nevada, shall undertake to say that slavery shall not exist within the limits of their own territory, over which they have a right to extend a government (for that the South is willing we should say); but we also say, for the hundreds of thousands that may inhabit the vast territory on the other side of that boundary—for a population of free Americans, in actual existence there, of thirty or forty thousand, who have had no part in framing this Constitution—that slavery shall not exist there. Sir, it would be very strange indeed if the South did not object to this proposition.

The point to which I desire particularly to call the attention of the Convention, is this. If you adopt at once a definite boundary, affording a reasonable extent of territory, you form no issue upon which a question can arise between the North and the South—an issue which every reasonable man wishes to avoid. But if you leave an alternative, which must necessarily open the question, you compel a conflict which must be determined in Congress before your constitution is adopted. The South never will yield on that point. Will the North yield? I doubt it very much. I admit she is more likely to yield than the South; but if she does it will be to the lesser boundary. But this proposition of a definite boundary, does not require her to yield; and suppose you fix it at the Sierra Nevada, I ask you whether it is not far more likely that the North will yield without any condition whatever, than if you adopt a boundary with an alternative which must inevitably compel a conflict with the South?

For these reasons, Mr. President, I am opposed to the proviso of the gentleman from San Joaquin, and shall vote in favor of any proposition making the Sierra Nevada the definite boundary line.

Mr. Shannon. I intended before this to have drawn the attention of the House to a certain fact, more for the purpose of obtaining information than any thing else. It is this: that there exists a Vice Royal decree published during the existence of the old Spanish Government, previous to the independence of Mexico, establishing a line which runs through the centre of the Great Desert, being an extension of the eastern boundary line of Lower California, running northerly from the Colorado river to the 42d degree of north latitude, or to the northern boundary of Upper California. All upon the eastern side of that line belonged to New Mexico, and was entirely under its jurisdiction; and all upon the western side belonged to and was under the jurisdiction of Upper California. I desire to get some definite information upon that subject, because if this is a fact, we include more in the large boundary proposed, than actually belongs to Upper California, and consequently it presents an insuperable objection to the extension of that boundary line so far eastward. I understand the document to which I refer is probably among the official archives. I ask for some information in regard to this from Mr. Hartnell or Mr. Halleck.

Permission being granted—

Mr. Hartnell said: I am not aware that there exists among the archives any such document, but I have been told that there has been one seen there. Perhaps Mr. Vallejo may be able to give the desired information.

Mr. Vallejo. I have myself formerly seen in the archives of the California Government, a document issued in the time of the Spanish Government, dated 1781, in which the boundary from the 32d deg. 30 min. to the 42d deg. 30 min. of north latitude divides the Great Desert, leaving one-half to the jurisdiction of New Mexico, and the other half to Upper California.

Mr. Covarrubias. I am of opinion that the gentleman (Mr. Vallejo) is mistaken in asserting that from the 32d deg. 30 min. to the 42d deg. 30 min. of north latitude, from the point at which that line strikes the Colorado river, belonged to New Mexico on the one side, and to California on the other. It is well known that the boundary of New Mexico never went up to the 42d deg. 30 min. of north latitude.

Mr. Vallejo. I do not say that this line was ever formally laid down by official surveys, but that such a line did exist, dividing the Great Desert in two, is, I think, sufficiently established by the document to which I refer. Col. Fremont, in his map, did not take in the exact boundary of California. I suppose his intention was, as it was not known whether the United States would take in New Mexico or not, and as all were determined to take in California, that the boundaries of California should include as much as possible.

Mr. Halleck. About a year ago, Mr. Hartnell and myself overhauled the old archives, and those that I considered of interest, relating to the history of California, were laid aside for future reference. We found among these old archives the first map that was ever drawn of California, and the manuscript journal of the priest who explored the Great Basin and a portion of the Sierra Nevada and Tulare Valley. From this map all the maps of the country have been made. It is stated in Greenhow's history that this map and journal were lost, but fortunately they were found among a collection of old papers in the custom house at Monterey. After this map was drawn, several decrees of the Viceroy were made with regard to the judicial districts, and judicial boundaries were laid down. The two Californias were united, and several times afterwards separated; they were sometimes under separate, and again united under one judicial district; at one time attached to Sonora, and afterwards to New Mexico. Lower California was finally separated in its judicial relation from Upper California, although the two until recently, were included in the same judicial department. The dividing line between Upper and Lower California—the final one fixed by a commission sent from Mexico, was not either the 32d or 32½ degree of north latitude; it was a line fixed by certain rivers and hills running between Upper and Lower California at a considerable distance below the line agreed upon the by the treaty of peace, so that we have given up a small portion of what was finally fixed upon as the limits of Upper California by the Mexican Government itself. That formal line ran up the Colorado river. There was a decree making a dividing line on the great caravan route that runs north of the Gila and north of the Colorado river. All criminals arrested for offences on that route to a certain point, were sent back to New Mexico for trial. All on this side were sent back to California. That line crossed the Great Desert somewhere near the Salt Lake; but it was merely a judicial regulation established for convenience. This is the only decree that I have ever seen in the archives in respect to any division of that kind. There certainly is nothing of the kind referred to in the archives at the present time, unless it has been overlooked; and I think it is scarcely possible that it can have been overlooked, for Mr. Hartnell and myself have examined every paper on that subject in the archives.

Mr. Foster. In relation to the line, as laid down in Fremont's map of California—that map embraces in California a part of New Mexico. The pueblo of Zunia, a village of civilized Indians, subject for a hundred and fifty years to New Mexico, is a hundred and fifty miles within the territory of California, according to the western line of New Mexico as laid down in Fremont's map. The Navejoe, Moquis, Apaches, and Utahs, have their treaty regulations with New Mexico, and are recognized as within her territory. I think there is no doubt that the boundary of California is too extensive, and that the actual boundary of New Mexico extends even to the westward of those tribes. The true line runs in a northeast and southwest direction through the middle of the Great Desert. Sonora has always claimed jurisdiction, to an indefinite extent, east of the Colorado and north of the Gila. I speak from knowledge obtained while a resident in New Mexico and Sonora, in which I believe I have the advantage of any member on this floor. The boundaries of the departments mentioned have always been very loosely defined, but the above I believe is the one recognized.

Mr. Halleck. In respect to that, the gentleman is perfectly right. Fremont's map includes, in my opinion, a portion of what properly belongs to New Mexico.

Mr. Shannon. We are coming to it at last. I now begin to see that this reconsideration was not entirely in vain. It is stated that this old line is a judicial line; what is a judicial line? Is it not a dividing line between two distinct counties or provinces? What do you call this line but the dividing line where the different laws of two distinct provinces meet?

Mr. Halleck. One word on that point. At that time there was no difference as to the laws. These provinces were all included under the Government of Mexico, and were under the same laws; but it was ordered by the government that a part should be within the jurisdiction of New Mexico and a part within the jurisdiction of California.

Mr. Shannon. Very well; this line was a judicial line, between two distinct countries, territories, or provinces. What is it but a boundary line between the two provinces? This view is sustained by the facts stated by the gentleman from Los Angeles (Mr. Foster.) Another very important fact that has come to light is this: that east of the Colorado, Upper California has not exercised jurisdiction; that the jurisdiction there has been exercised by Sonora for a certain distance north, or jointly by Sonora and New Mexico. As to this line starting from the 32d degree of north latitude, it is well known that the boundary line between Upper and Lower California has been disputed, and that it was never distinctly determined. Sometimes it was the 32d degree, and at others a lower line, and now it is the line established by the treaty.

Mr. Carrillo. I recollect perfectly well having seen a document among the archives of the government at Los Angeles, when I was alcalde of that place, and I examined it with great care, and I have no doubt myself that an order was sent from the Spanish Government in 1781, making this line from 32 or 32½ degrees north latitude to 42, cutting the Great Desert in two, and that the territory on the eastern side was thus divided from the territory on the western side. Part of the territory on the eastern side belonged to New Mexico, and part to Sonora. The whole territory on the western side belonged to California.

Mr. Foster. It appears to me that we can reconcile this difficulty. In order to do so, I would propose to run the line on the 113th parallel of longitude, due north to the 42d degree. That will remove the difficulty of the gentleman from Monterey, (Mr. Botts,) in regard to admitting the settlements east of that line. It is utterly unfit for agricultural, grazing, or other purposes, and there is no white person living in that country. I suggest it as a compromise.

Mr. Hill stated that he had drawn up a resolution to that effect, which he desired to offer to the House, and of which he now gave notice.

Mr. Shannon. We can now base the boundary upon facts. It is narrowed down in its eastern limit to the line recognized by the Spanish Government. Between that line and any line that may be agreed upon west, I leave the matter.

Mr. Jones. There is no member of this House, Mr. President, who is more willing to accept any proposition that we can in principle accept to compromise this vexed question, than myself. But, sir, here is a piece of news; new light upon the subject. It is true we have certain authorized maps—authorized by the Congress of the United States—certain conventions and agreements drawn up between the two high contracting parties, all having reference to these maps—all recognizing them—maps which have been before us and which are now before us; but we are told that they are all wrong! Yes, sir, we have been laboring in the dark on this subject. The boundaries of this territory have been incorrectly laid down; it has been discovered that a new boundary exists somewhere among the Spanish archives, ~~bordering~~ the Great Desert. Where are these maps, sir, that John C. Fremont knew not of? Where were these maps when he based his maps upon maps of Mexican authority? Did they know nothing of their own boundaries? Had they no knowledge of their own official archives? Suppose the Vice Royalty of Spain did fix this boundary, and the Mexican Government thought proper to fix another, am I to be told that the act of the Mexican Government could not legally change the Vice Royal decree of the old Spanish Government? Sir, we are not bound in any manner by the Vice Royalty of Spain. The boundary stands as fixed by the two contracting parties in the treaty of peace. Neither Mexico nor the United States can now assume any right to say that that boundary is different. The treaty of Guadaloupe Hidalgo took these boundaries, such as they are here represented. Now, if gentlemen could give me any assurance that this avoids all difficulty, and that these facts which they bring forth will be recognized by the Congress of the United States and the Congress of Mexico, I would be perfectly willing to accept the compromise. But, sir, I apprehend that the Congress of the United States would say, that the boundaries of California had already been determined by the maps of the Mexican Republic, the treaty of peace, and the official map drawn by J. C. Fremont.

Mr. President, there are certain propositions laid before this House which I must deny. The issue is, that the Congress of the United States have no right to establish the boundary that we propose: and rather than avoid the difficulty, that we should refuse to become one of the United States. That issue I am ready to take up. Sir, there is a great principle for which the gentleman from Monterey (Mr. Botts) contends upon this floor. I suppose that gentleman, as a man of sense, is ready to admit that a great principle will apply to a small matter as well as to a large matter. He says that that great principle is about to be violated here; that the Congress of the United States, by the ratification of this Constitution with the proposed boundary, would be forcing a government upon a people who do not want it, and who have had no part in its formation. I suppose if that principle will hold good in reference to the Mormons, that it will hold good in reference to the population of the Trinity River. If you take the proclamation of General Riley, and take the vote of every poll for the members of this Convention, you will find that it falls some hundreds of miles this side of the Sierra Nevada; and there are certain miners who are now digging out gold from the Sierra Nevada, who are not represented in this Convention. This is the great principle which the gentleman does not wish to see violated; but he violates it himself by taking in parts of the country which he does not pretend are represented upon this floor.

Sir, I have only supported this proposition for one reason. I profess to know something of the opinions of men in political life; I know something of the opinions of members of Congress; and when I tell you they have urged you to come in as a State of the Union, there is not one who tells you to come in as a part; they want you to come in as a whole. I only seek to avoid the difficulty with which we are threatened.

Mr. Botts. I merely rise for the purpose of correcting two statements of the gentleman from San Joaquin, (Mr. Jones,) and if he misrepresents his constituents as much as he misrepresents history, he ought to be discarded from their service. I say, sir, that in the treaty of peace between the United States and Mexico, Fremont's map is not mentioned at all; and the line that he puts down as the boundary between New Mexico and California, is never alluded to.

Mr. Jones. I did not say it was. I spoke of the Mexican maps used by J. C. Fremont.

Mr. Botts. The particular question under discussion here, the boundary between Mexico and California, is not touched at all. As to the fact that the Congress of the United States have adopted the line as laid down in Fremont's map, do you know what it amounts to? Col. Thomas H. Benton, upon the floor of the Senate of the United States, looking directly to the valuable character of the explorations made by his son-in-law, Col. Fremont, and according to him that credit to which he is so justly entitled, with the unanimous approbation of the Senate, proposed this: that Col. Fremont's explorations and maps should be printed for the use of the Senate, and I believe it was unanimously agreed to. The Senate ordered the printing of five thousand copies of this map of Fremont's explorations. That is the full extent to which this is an official map; and yet we are told that the Senate adopted this line between New Mexico and California; that is, that every Senator pledged himself, and the President of the United States pledged himself, to every line upon this map, printed by order of the Senate!

After some discussion as to the order of amendments,

Mr. Price withdrew his proposition, to allow Mr. Hill to propose the following:

The boundary of the State of California shall be as follows:—Beginning at the point on the Pacific Ocean, south of San Diego, to be established by the Commission of the United States and Mexico, appointed under the treaty of the 20th February, 1848, for running the boundary between the territories of the United States and those of Mexico; and thence along said line, until it reaches the mouth of the Rio Gila; thence along the centre of the Rio Colorado, until it strikes the 35th degree of north latitude; thence due north, until it intersects the boundary line between Oregon and California; thence southerly along the coast of the Pacific, including all the islands and bays belonging to California, to the place of beginning.

Mr. Ellis moved the previous question.

Mr. McDougal said it was very important that every member of the House should be present to vote upon this question. He therefore hoped the question would not be pressed at present, and moved a recess till three o'clock.

The House then took a recess till 3 P. M.

AFTERNOON SESSION, 3 O'CLOCK, P. M.

The Chair stated that there was some doubt in regard to the question first in order. If the original report of the Committee on the Boundary was beyond the reach of the House, then the report of the Committee of the Whole would be the primary question.

Mr. Jones said that the proposition of the gentleman from San Francisco (Mr. Price) having been withdrawn, the proposition submitted by him would come next to the report of the Committee of the Whole, and that of the gentleman from San Diego (Mr. Hill) next to his.

Mr. Gilbert supposed the proper way of getting at the difficulty would be to have the House decide whether the report of the Committee on the Boundary or the report of the Committee of the Whole should be the main question.

Mr. Foster moved to suspend the rules, so as to enable the Convention to take up and decide upon the several propositions, without regard to the usual parliamentary order of proceeding.

The Chair stated that the question then would be which one of the reports should be taken up for consideration.

Mr. Sherwood moved to take up Mr. Jones's proposition, which was agreed to.

Mr. Gilbert. A question of order was yesterday raised in regard to the divisibility of a question of this kind, with a proviso attached to it. The Chair decided that it was divisible, and that the question would first fall upon the main proposition, preceding the proviso. It is my opinion that the question should first have been taken upon the proviso. That, I believe, when a division is made, is the parliamentary usage.

If I understand this question, one party are for a definite and limited boundary, claiming it as an ultimatum, and leaving it to Congress to adopt us with that boundary or reject us entirely. To prevent any difficulty in claiming the whole of this territory, the other party are in favor of a proviso, leaving the boundary to be determined by Congress in conjunction with the Legislature of this State, in case of objection to the line proposed in our constitution. It strikes me that the test question is this: shall we have an unconditional and definite boundary, claiming it as our right, or shall we fix a boundary, also claiming it as our right, but leaving it to Congress to settle it with the consent of our Legislature. Now, I shall move to strike out the proviso of the gentleman from San Joaquin, (Mr. Jones,) which will settle the point in dispute, although I am not favor of the proposition. If we cannot have the whole of California, if we cannot present an undivided front on the Sierra Nevada, I am not for going into the middle of the Great Desert and making our dividing line there. If we cannot claim the whole, let us claim only that which we have a right to claim, and that which we can extend our institutions over and do justice to the people who live within it. It is for this reason that I make the motion. While I am with those who claim the whole territory; while I believe, by adopting that policy, we can settle forever the question that is likely to divide the Union, still, when a majority of this Convention say that they cannot go with us, then I wish to limit the State to the most compact boundaries. If we cannot include the whole of the Great Desert, let us say we do not want any part of it. Matters were brought up here to-day about the exact lines of that boundary, which in my view are considerations of no importance. It makes very little difference to me whether they take a few Indian villages from New Mexico, or give a few to New Mexico. I contend that, by taking the larger boundary, we settle the question of slavery over the territory included within it, and that every man who wishes well to the Union would wish that question settled. I desire the proposition to come distinctly on this point, and I think my motion accomplishes the object.

While I am upon this subject, Mr. President, allow me to notice one of the arguments advanced against the proposition to include the whole territory. It is urged upon this floor that it is not republican or democratic to include within the boundaries of this State the Mormons; that they have no representation in this Convention; no voice in the formation of this constitution; and that they could have none in our Legislature. Admitting these facts, sir, I say it is still another and perhaps a greater principle of republicanism that the majority should rule; and does any gentleman here pretend to say that, if this constitution is adopted by the whole people of California west of the Sierra Nevada, they will not constitute a majority of the people of California, Mormons and all. We are told that there are thirty thousand Mormons in the valley of the Great Salt Lake. Now, from the best information, I do not believe that there is half that number. But admitting that there are thirty thousand, how many voters will they have? Five thousand voters. If this constitution does not get more than double that number of votes, it ought not to be the constitution of California. I think then, if gentlemen will insist upon one principle, that they ought not to forget that there are others, and that they will find this perhaps a better test of republicanism than the principle first stated. As a test question, therefore, I would suggest that all after the words fixing a definite boundary be stricken out.

Mr. Botts. I believe every gentleman knows that I am in favor of the Sierra Nevada; but I said to-day, and mean to adhere to it, that for a compromise I would go as far as the middle of the desert. I now rise to a question of order. The gentleman from San Francisco (Mr. Gilbert) is out of order. His proposition to amend by striking out the proviso is an amendment to an amendment to an amendment. It is also out of order on another ground. It leaves you the original proposition, (Mr. McDougal's,) which has already been voted down.

Mr. Gilbert. I would simply state to the gentleman from Monterey (Mr. Botts) that I was aware that my motion was out of order, and that I only gave notice of it for the information of the House; but in regard to the gentleman's statement that the proposition of Mr. McDougal would be out of order, I think that, upon a reconsideration of the whole question, he (Mr. Botts) will admit himself to be mistaken. Under the reconsideration the original motion of Mr. McDougal could be moved as a new proposition. I merely suggested by my motion to make it a test question. So far as I know, the gentlemen who voted for taking in this whole boundary are anxious not to divide the Great Desert, but take the limits of the Sierra Nevada.

Mr. McCarver here rose to speak, but was interrupted by calls for the question.

Mr. McCarver. If the gentleman from San Francisco is to have a privilege which I am denied upon this floor—— [Cries of question! question! let us have the question!] I protest against it as an outrage. If you deny me any privilege, you deny the rights of my constituents. I have never occupied the time of the House upon this question. I deny your right to put me down in this manner. Gentlemen have spoken twice, or three times, and I am to be debarred from the privilege of speaking once! If the District of Sacramento is to be cut off from her proper representation in this Convention, whilst San Francisco is allowed to be heard on all occasions, I want to know it—I want the people of Sacramento to know it. [Great confusion, and repeated calls for the question.] I will not be insulted—my constituents shall not be insulted. If this House is to stamp me down and allow other individuals to speak as often as they please, I shall no longer remain here. [Mr. McCarver thereupon left the Hall.]

Mr. McDougal. I hope my colleague, Gen. McCarver, may be excused. It is a matter of personal feeling with him ever since the sad fate of his free negro project. The news brought down from San Francisco on that melancholy occasion has made him very sore in regard to anything coming from that district.

Mr. Sherwood moved a call of the House; it was ordered, and 39 members answered to their names. The Sergeant-at-arms was furnished, by order of the President, with a list of the absentees, with directions to require their attendance forthwith; when, a quorum being present, on motion of Mr. Sherwood, further proceedings under the call were suspended.

A division of the question was moved, on Mr. Jones's proposition, so that the vote should be taken on the first and second clauses separately.

The President decided that the question was divisible. From this decision an appeal was taken, and the decision of the Chair was reversed.

The question recurring on the adoption of Mr. Jones's proposition, the yeas and nays were ordered, and resulted as follows:

Yeas.—Messrs. Aram, Brown, Dimmick, Gilbert, Hanks, Hoppe, Hobson, Hollingsworth, Jones, Moore, Reid, Sherwood, Stearns—13.

Nays.—Messrs. Botts, Carrillo, Covarrubias, Crosby, Dent, Dominguez, Ellis, Foster, Gwin, Hill, Halleck, Hastings, Larkin, Lippitt, McDougal, Norton, Ord, Pedrorena, Price, Pico, Rodriguez, Sutter, Snyder, Shannon, Steuart, Tefft, Vallejo, Vermeule, Walker, Wozencraft, President—31.

Mr. Steuart moved to take up the proposition of the gentleman from San Diego, (Mr. Hill,) which was agreed to.

Mr. Jones said his reason for voting against this proposition was that it was not less objectionable than any proposition which had come before the House.

Mr. Carrillo remarked that so much had been said on this subject that he supposed the Convention was heartily tired of it. He, therefore, against his own opinion, and, perhaps, against the interests of California, felt constrained to vote in favor of the proposition of the gentleman from San Diego, (Mr. Hill,) so as to put an end to this question, and have some boundary.

Mr. Covarrubias said he held an entirely different view from that just stated. This Convention was assembled here for the purpose of performing certain duties, and whatever debate might arise on questions presented to the consideration of the House, he thought it was the duty of every member to hear everything that was said, especially on a question of so much importance as this, and therefore he did not approve of the sentiments expressed by his friend from Los Angelos (Mr. Carrillo.)

Mr. Carrillo said the reasons which he had avowed for the vote which he intended to give on this proposition was a matter for which he alone was responsible. The gentleman (Mr. Covarrubiás) should keep his personalities to himself and vote as he thought proper, without undertaking to hold other members accountable for their votes.

Mr. Lippitt gave notice, that in the event of all the amendments now before the House being rejected, he would move the first part of the proposition of the gentleman from Sacramento, (Mr. McDougal,) adopting the Sierra Nevada as the definite boundary line.

Mr. Halleck gave notice, if the House came to the determination not to adopt any of the propositions, he would move that the constitution go without any fixed boundary, leaving the question to be decided by the Congress of the United States.

Mr. Tefft thought this compromise had turned out to be a perfect farce. Many members were compelled to vote for a proposition which they were opposed to, from the fear of getting no boundary at all.

The question was then taken on Mr. Hill's proposition, and it was adopted, as follows:

Yeas.—Messrs. Aram, Botts, Brown, Carrillo, Crosby, Dominguez, Foster, Hill, Hoppe, Hastings, Jones, Larkin, McCarver, Ord, Pedrorena, Price, Reid, Sutter, Shannon, Steuart, Vallejo, Vermeule, Walker, President.—24.

Nays.—Messrs. Covarrubias, Dent, Dimmick, Ellis, Gilbert, Gwin, Hanks, Hobson, Halleck, Hollingsworth, Lippitt, Lippincott, Moore, McDougal, Norton, Pico, Rodriguez, Snyder, Sherwood, Stearns, Tefft, Wozencraft,—22.

Mr. McCarver here asked to be excused from further attendance, inasmuch as he considered that himself and the district which he represented had been treated with disrespect by the interruption of his remarks this morning.

Several members disclaimed, on the part of the House, any intention of disrespect or want of courtesy towards the gentleman from Sacramento; whereupon, Mr. McCarver expressed himself satisfied.

Mr. Gwin moved that the article on the boundary be engrossed for a third reading, and stated that inasmuch as he would prefer having no boundary at all to the one just adopted, he would vote against the engrossment.

Mr. Halleck said he would suggest one other remedy in regard to this boundary: to put in a proviso that the Legislature and Congress might fix upon the Sierra Nevada.

Mr. Price said he was confident a majority of the members of this House were in favor of the Sierra Nevada line. If the last vote could be reconsidered, he had no doubt that line would be adopted.

Mr. Botts was opposed to the line adopted, and greatly preferred the Sierra Nevada; he would therefore vote against the engrossment.

Mr. Dent gave the same reasons for his vote.

Mr. Halleck thought the object could be attained in this way. The Chair had put the question, and it had been decided by yeas and nays, as to this amendment; but the question had not yet been put upon the report of the Committee of the Whole, as amended. The House could reject that report, as amended by this proposition.

Mr. Jones said he would vote against the engrossment, in the hope that a line which would please him better might be proposed.

Mr. Lippitt stated, as the reason of his vote, that if this line was rejected, he desired to offer the proposition of which he had given notice.

Mr. Tefft said he would vote against the engrossment, for the purpose of getting the original report of the Committee as the boundary.

Mr. SHERWOOD would also vote against the same for the same reason.

Mr. VERMEULE said that the proposition of the gentleman from San Joaquin, (Mr. Jones.) having been lost and another adopted, he would vote against the engrossment, in the hope that the Sierra Nevada line would be adopted, as it seemed to be the only compromise left.

The question was then taken on the engrossment, and it was decided in the negative as follows:

YEAS.—Messrs. Aram, Botts, Brown, Crosby, Dominguez, Ellis, Foster, Hill, Hoppe, Hastings, Larkin, Ord, Pedrorena, Price, Reid, Shannon, Steuart, Vallejo, Walker, President—20.

NAYS.—Messrs. Covarrubias, Dent, Dimmick, Gilbert, Gwin, Hanks, Hobson, Halleck, Hollingsworth, Jones, Lippitt, Lippincott, Moore, McCarver, McDougal, Norton, Pico, Rodriguez, Sutter, Snyder, Sherwood, Stearns, Tefft, Vermeule, Walker—29.

Mr. JONES then moved the adoption of the first branch of his proposition.

Mr. SHERWOOD moved as an amendment, the report of the Committee of the Whole.

The question being taken on the proposition of Mr. Sherwood, it was rejected as follows:

YEAS.—Messrs. Covarrubias, Dimmick, Dominguez, Foster, Gilbert, Gwin, Hobson, Halleck, Hollingsworth, Moore, Norton, Pedrorena, Pico, Rodriguez, Sherwood, Stearns, Vallejo, Wozencraft.—18.

NAYS.—Messrs. Aram, Botts, Brown, Crosby, Dent, Ellis, Hanks, Hill, Hoppe, Hastings, Jones, Larkin, McDougal, Ord, Price, Reid, Sutter, Snyder, Shannon, Steuart, Vallejo, Vermeule, Walker, President—24.

Thereupon, the question recurring on the proposition of Mr. Jones, it was adopted by the following vote, viz:

YEAS.—Messrs. Aram, Botts, Brown, Covarrubias, Crosby, Dent, Dominguez, Ellis, Gilbert, Gwin, Hanks, Hastings, Hoppe, Hollingsworth, Jones, Larkin, Lippitt, Lippincott, McCarver, McDougal, Norton, Ord, Price, Rodriguez, Reid, Sutter, Synder, Shannon, Steuart, Vermeule, Walker, President.—32.

NAYS.—Messrs. Dimmick, Foster, Hill, Hobson, Pedrorena, Vallejo, Wozencraft—7.

On motion of Mr. SHANNON, the article just adopted, was ordered to be engrossed for a third reading.

The House then adjourned to 7 o'clock, P. M.

NIGHT SESSION, 7 O'CLOCK, P. M.

The Preamble to the constitution was read the third time and passed.

On motion of Mr. HALLECK, it was ordered that the article on the Boundary be inserted in the constitution immediately preceding the schedule.

Article I of the constitution on the "Declaration of Rights," was taken up, read the third time, a few verbal errors corrected, and then passed.

Article II on the "Right of Suffrage," was then taken up, read the third time, and passed.

Article III on the "Distribution of Powers," was taken up, read the third time, and passed.

Article IV on the "Legislative Department," was taken up, read the third time, several errors in phraseology corrected, and then passed.

Article V on the "Executive Department," was taken up, read the third time, one or two verbal errors corrected, and the article then passed.

Article VI on the "Judiciary," was then taken up, read the third time, and passed.

Article VII on the "Militia," was taken up, read the third time, and passed.

On motion, the report of the Committee of the Whole on the "Schedule," was taken up, the amendments proposed by that Committee concurred in, and the article, thus amended, ordered to be engrossed for a third reading.

Article VIII on the "State Debt," was taken up, read the third time, and passed.

Article IX on "Education," was taken up, read the third time, and passed.

Article X on the "mode of amending or revising the constitution," was taken up, read the third time, and passed.

The "Miscellaneous Provisions" of the constitution, were taken up, read the third time, and passed.

On motion, adjourned to 10 o'clock, A. M., to-morrow.

THURSDAY, OCTOBER 11, 1849.

In Convention. Prayer by Rev. Padre Antonio Ramirez. Journal read and approved.

The Secretary submitted a report in reference to the duties and pay of the clerks, asked for by Mr. Brown's resolution, which was read, and ordered to lie on the table.

Mr. Steuart called for the consideration of the resolutions in relation to the mineral lands of California, submitted by him on the 9th inst.

Mr. Crosby. I should like to know what authority we have to pass such a resolution as this? As I understand it, it is merely recommendatory.

Mr. Steuart. I shall not detain the House by any argument in support of the resolutions. I believe they carry on their face a sufficient argument to induce every gentleman to vote for them. I will only say that, in bringing forward these resolutions, I was not influenced in any degree by the singular position in which this Convention is placed, but solely by the known desire of my constituents, and the people in the gold mines. I will further say that, in conversation with some of the most intelligent merchants, the views expressed in these resolutions as regards the advantage of the gold dust being cast in ingots or bars, so as to form an article of commerce, were fully concurred in. I could also present to the House, but it must be a subject familiar to the minds of every one, some arguments as to the time and cost that it would require to establish a mint in California. It would require several years, if we look to the time required for the establishment of mints in other parts of the United States. The establishment of an assay office is preliminary to the establishment of a mint. But the chief object I have in view is to save to the people of California this source of revenue. There is one general feeling among all that class of persons who are engaged in mining operations, to make every person pay for the privilege of working the mines. They go further; they would exclude all classes who would refuse to pay. I have put this proposition in its simplest form. I ask merely an expression of opinion of this Convention as individual members. I believe that such an expression of opinion of the gentlemen now present here, known to be possessed of the best information as regards the sources of revenue of California, will have a very important bearing upon the action of Congress. I believe it is a measure so reasonable and so well grounded that Congress will not refuse to grant what we desire. They can do it without infringing any of the existing laws of the General Government for the collection of revenue. I leave it to the consideration of the House, with this single remark—that by the adoption of the article with respect to the public lands granted to California, you have tied up every source of revenue, and the whole burden of supporting the government—a burden very onerous in itself is thrown immediately, and as soon as taxation can be laid, upon the people. You have to resort to a measure more pregnant with mischief—more calculated to shackle the energies of the State than any other you could possibly adopt—I mean the exercise of that authority given to the legislature to borrow money to pay the expenses of the government.

Mr. McCarver. I rise to a point of order. There was a resolution offered here a few days ago declaratory of the views of this House in relation to the public lands; claiming from Congress the right to these lands on the part of the people of California. This resolution, it seems to me, should have the precedence, having been referred to the Committee of the Whole. I do not know that the proposition of the gentleman from San Francisco, (Mr. Steuart) comes directly in conflict with it; but the resolution proposed by me covers the ground of the mining country. I rise to inquire whether it is not entitled to the precedence?

Mr. Steuart. I was not aware that any proposition of the kind had been offered. Why did not the gentleman make a motion to have his resolution taken up? I asked the House to take up the resolutions which I had offered on the subject of the mineral lands, and they are now the subject before the House.

The Chair. It seems to the Chair that these resolutions come before the House as a memorial, to be signed by the members.

Mr. McCarver. I move to lay them upon the table. Mine certainly has the preference. The object of the two is very nearly the same.

Mr. Botts. The gentlemen are disputing about the preference of their resolutions. I hope the House will give neither the preference by postponing both of them indefinitely. As to the principle, which is necessarily involved in the proposition of the gentleman from Sacramento, (Mr. McCarver,) I am much in favor of it in the right place; but I hope we will go on to make a constitution, and I hope that the Legislature, at its very first session, will pass a resolution requesting the members of Congress from California and instructing the Senators to introduce such a plan, and vote for it, in the Congress of the United States. That course is infinitely more efficacious, sir; the Legislature can do what we cannot do; they can instruct those whom they elect; and they can at least do all we can do—request others. We have usurped very many of the powers of the Legislature, but none to such an extent as this. To pass such a resolution here would be simply a petition to Congress signed by forty-six individuals. There is another objection. The Congress of the United States cannot prohibit the exportation of gold from California, without prohibiting it from every State in the Union. I certainly would not like to sign a paper to send to Congress recognising the right of Congress to pass a law prohibiting the exportation of gold from this State. If they can pass a particular law for our benefit, remember, sir, they can pass a particular law for our oppression also. I think we had better lay all these matters on the table, never to be raised from it.

Mr. Steuart. It was a principle established in the formation of the constitution, and held from that time to the present, as regards the public lands, that they were held in trust by the General Government for the benefit of the whole United States. Congress is the guardian of that public property. This principle holds good in regard to any public property acquired at the expense of the blood and treasure of the United States. I thought the gentleman from Monterey, (Mr. Botts,) looking to the State from which he came, would be the last to deny such a principle. I do not propose to ask Congress to give us in perpetuity these public lands; but for a short period and for a specific object. Congress having failed to give us the benefit of a territorial government, the least that we can expect is that she will grant us this source of revenue for the support of our State governmen until we can adopt some system of taxation that will not be onerous to our citizens. The gentleman says that this will merely be a petition. Sir, he rather overlooks the fact that it proposes to be a series of resolutions adopted by this Convention, representing the people of California. We ask that a copy of these resolutions be placed in the hands of our Senators and Representatives, that they may be laid before Congress and receive the early hearing and speedy action of that body.

Mr. McCarver. I beg leave to differ materially from my friend from Monterey (Mr. Botts.) The matter contained in both of these resolutions is a subject which I think the members of this Convention should take into consideration, and which comes very appropriately within their province. It is right and proper that the delegates of the people here assembled should declare their opinion that they believe this to be a portion of the public domain that they ought to have. We do not do it in an official capacity, but as the representatives of the wishes of the people, on our own responsibility. We know what the wishes of the people are on this subject, and if by the influence of this Convention we can carry out those wishes it is unquestionably our duty to do so.

Mr. McDougal. The proposition of the gentleman from San Francisco, (Mr. Steuart,) as I heard it read, struck me very forcibly as one of great interest and importance; but inasmuch as the House is very anxious to get through with the constitution, I hope the gentleman will postpone his resolutions till to-morrow, when their minds will not be so much burdened with other matters.

Mr. Steuart. I called up the resolutions this morning at the request of a number of gentlemen. There was nothing else before the House that we could act upon. I would make one explanation in regard to the objections of the gentleman from Monterey (Mr. Botts.) There is not one word in all these resolutions about taxes or duties. The Constitution of the United States well provides that "Congress shall have power to lay and collect taxes, duties, imposts, and excises; to pay the debts and provide for the common defence and general welfare of the United States; but all duties, imposts and excises shall be uniform throughout the United States."

Mr. Botts. I call the gentleman's attention to the 5th article to the 9th section, which says:

No tax or duty shall be laid on articles exported from any State. No preference shall be given by any regulation of commerce or revenue to the ports of one State over those of another; nor shall vessels bound to or from one State be obliged to enter, clear, or pay duties in another.

Mr. Steuart. I am ready to meet the gentleman on that ground. I say it is not proposed to lay any tax or duty upon any article exported from this State. There is nothing of the kind in the resolutions. As well might the gentleman say that Congress has no right to establish a mint and make persons pay for having their gold assessed and coined. It is nothing more than the inspection laws of the State.

Mr. Botts. The gentleman says there is no duty laid upon the exportation of any article. I say there is a duty of one hundred per cent.; a forfeiture of the whole amount—the largest duty I ever heard of.

Mr. Aram. So far as relates to the leasing of the mines, I recollect in the old mines of the northwest, the United States endeavored to collect revenue from the mines situated there, and established agencies from the year 1826 up to 1844. But from the report of the Secretary of War on that subject, it appears that the expense of keeping up these agencies has overrun the income. That satisfied Congress that it was utterly impracticable for the General Government to make anything out of the public mines, and in compliance with memorials from the people of those districts the lands were sold. I think myself that Congress would willingly relinquish all claim to the gold regions; at least give the State the privilege of drawing an income from the working of the mines. It would be a source of very considerable revenue to the State. Those who worked them could be obliged to take out licenses at so much a month; and they would be very willing to pay for the privilege, which would at the same time secure to them the protection of a good government.

On motion, the resolutions were laid upon the table.

The Schedule was then taken up, amended in the 5th section, by adding at the close thereof the words, "and on the question of the adoption thereof;" and thus amended, the article was passed.

The article on the Boundary was taken up, read a third time, and passed.

Mr. Gwin moved to take up the ordinance heretofore submitted by him; but the motion was decided in the negative.

On motion, the Convention took a recess till 3 o'clock, P. M.

AFTERNOON SESSION, 3 O'CLOCK, P. M.

On motion of Mr. WOZENCRAFT, the Committee on Printing were discharged from further duty in relation to that subject.

Mr. TEFFT offered the following resolution, which, after some discussion, was adopted:

Resolved, That certified copies of this constitution in English and Spanish, be presented to the present Executive of California, and that 8,000 copies in English, and 2,000 copies in Spanish, be ordered to be printed and circulated.

Mr. STEUART then called up his resolutions relative to the mineral lands of California.

Mr. MCDOUGAL said he was opposed to that portion of the resolution fixing a penalty; and also to that portion relating to the establishment of an essay office instead of a mint. While he was in favor of obtaining revenue from this source, he did not entirely approve of the mode proposed by the gentleman from San Fracisco. He thought if these lands could be obtained from Congress, the necessary regulations in relation to them should be made by the Legislature.

Mr. STEUART recapitulated his former remarks in defence of the resolutions.

Mr. SEMPLE. The most important objection I have to these resolutions, is in reference to the establishment of an essay office instead of a mint. It is said here that we do not want a mint; that it would be impracticable for the Government of the United States to get one up and put it in operation short of three or four years. Now, sir, I contend that we could get a mint almost as soon as we could get an assay office. It will take no such time to erect one as the gentleman supposes. I judge from the private mints established here by individual enterprize; if they can get up mints in a few weeks, the Government of the United States certainly can in a few months. What object is there in getting an assay office? What protection will it afford the community? Every gold digger knows what gold is, and there are very few, if any in California, who have not seen enough of gold dust to tell it at a glance. There is no danger of imposition. Again, you require a forfeiture of the entire amount of gold to prevent smuggling. If any man undertakes to carry off his own bag of gold dust because he does not choose to pay a duty of one per cent. to have it cast in ingots, or because he may be ignorant of the law of Congress upon the subject, he is compelled to forfeit the entire sum, which may be all he possesses. This seems to me to be a very improper restriction, and I think it would be very inexpedient for us to ask Congress to pass such a law. I think, instead of having cause to be grateful to the Government at Washington for such protection, we would find it to be a curse.

I see no objection to the first resolution, soliciting Congress to give up for a series of years, all the revenue which may be derived from the renting, leasing, or otherwise authorized occupation of the gold placers. That, I think, we are entitled to, and I believe the unanimous opinion of the Convention is in favor of obtaining from Congress, as a matter of justice, what revenue can be derived from these lands, though there may be some difference of opinion as to the mode.

Mr. STEUART. I do not know, sir, what kind of mints the gentleman refers to; but we have only one reliable way of judging of these things, and that is, by reference to operations at home. We well know that the establishment of a mint in North Carolina and in Louisiana, has been attended with immense expense, and they are not yet in as successful operation as the mint in Philadelphia. We all know that for years and years back, with all the commercial influence of the great emporium of the United States, they have in vain sought to obtain from Congress the establishment of a mint at the city of New York. I have no doubt that the Congress of the United States will establish a mint in California. But this will not interfere with it. An assay office is part and parcel of it. The establishment of a mint will require much time, and will be very expensive in such a country as this where every species of labor is so high. We want something in the meantime. An assay office can be set in operation in a short time. In regard to the advantage of having the gold cast in ingots, I have only to say this: that in conversation with the most intelligent merchants, they all concurred in the opinion that the ingots so cast, would be a much better article of commerce than either the gold dust or the coin of the country. We all know the vacillating character of the coin of the country. When I left the United States, two years ago, the ounce was $15 45; in Panama, $19; in Lima, $18; and at Valparaiso, $17 25. This is the case all over the world. I am perfectly persuaded that the plan proposed in the resolution would be the means of a large commerce directly into the country.

Mr. Sherwood. I am in favor of the mines being left free for everybody to work under certain regulations; but I am not in favor of the United States owning them. I want the State of California to own them. I am in favor of a mint, and I am opposed to bars or ingots or any thing of the kind. I want the round dollar, sir, or the $5 or $10 or $20 gold pieces to circulate here. I want the coin of the United States. In regard to the penalty of forfeiture fixed by the gentlemen, I am opposed to determining the fine here for any infraction of the laws regulating this matter. I think we should pass a general resolution in regard to opening these mines for everybody, asking Congress to grant them to the State of California, and then making such regulations in regard to them as we may deem proper. Believing, therefore, that the gentleman is entirely mistaken as to the ground which this Convention and the people of California should take, I shall vote against the resolutions, and I hope they will not receive the sanction of the House.

Mr. Wozencraft. I do not think it would be at all proper to throw open the mines to everybody. The American population should be protected in their right to the profits resulting from these mines. The gentleman himself (Mr. Steuart) does not design that they shall be thrown open to foreigners, without restriction, nor do I believe such is the desire of any person here. The resolution provides that they shall first become naturalized. It is very proper that they should be thrown open to all American citizens; but we see already that thousands are coming from Europe, to draw wealth from these mines and carry it out of the country. They have no right to do it; they contributed in no measure to the acquisition of this territory, and they have no permanent interest in its welfare.

Mr. Gilbert. As this is a question of considerable importance, and as I agree in part with the gentleman from San Francisco, (Mr. Steuart,) I will endeavor to state in what I disagree with him. He says in the first resolution:

That the Congress of the United States be, and they are hereby respectfully but earnestly solicited to give up to the people of California for a series of years, or so long as may be deemed expedient, all the revenue which may be derived from the renting, leasing, or otherwise authorized occupation of the gold placers..

Now, sir, if I understand the gentleman, by that, he means that the United States shall give up the mines to the State of California; but he goes on to say:

That in order to secure to the people of California a certain, immediate, and abundant revenue from the working of the gold mines, it is hereby recommended,

1st. That the Congress of the United States throw open for a given time the whole placer country to the thousands who are pouring in by every ocean port, as well as inland communication, requiring by proper enactments and under regulations to be established by law, every gold-seeker to take out a license or permit for a given and stipulated time, from offices to be established for that purpose at convenient places; and further requiring every such operative, if not a citizen of the United States, to take the oath of allegiance, so long as he shall be a resident of California. The fee or charge for such license or permit not to exceed five dollars per month, and the net proceeds arising therefrom to be paid into the treasury of California.

I apprehend, sir, that if the Congress of the United States should consent to give to California these mines, they would at the same time be willing to give us the whole control of them; that we and not the Congress of the United States should say who shall work them; upon what conditions they shall be worked; if we are to derive the revenue from them, that we should take such steps as we deem best calculated to make that revenue what it should be. On that ground I am opposed to the first provision that follows the resolution. The next says that the Congress of the United States shall establish an assay office. I have no objection to an assay office, only that it seems to preclude the establishment of a mint.

Mr. Steuart. Not at all. It is recommended as a preliminary measure. There is no prohibition against the establishment of a mint.

Mr. Gilbert. I think, however, that if an assay office be established—especially if you take up the succeeding resolution, which says that a mint cannot be established at the proper time—that it would have the effect of precluding the establishment of a mint. Now, Mr. President, I am in favor of the establishment of a mint in California. I think the country requires it; and the sooner we can get it the better; not that I am opposed to an assay office, except that it would preclude the speedy establishment of a mint.

This is substantially all the objection I have to the plan. I have no objection to the first or to the last resolution. I therefore move that they be voted upon *seriatim*.

Mr. Steuart. In asking Congress to give us the entire revenue and benefit of the mines for a number of years, it is all I thought we probably could get; as Congress would not be likely to give in perpetuity these mines to California, or entangle them with such regulations as might give rise to difficulty hereafter. As regards the gentleman's objections on the subject of a mint, I am as much in favor of the establishment of a mint in California as any gentleman here. But it has been urged upon me by gentlemen acquainted with the subject, that an assay office must precede the establishment of a mint, and I desired that, until we could get a mint, the establishment of which would be more expensive, and require much more time, that we should have an assay office. It would not preclude the establishment of a mint. It would rather be an auxiliary. We must have an assay office, if we get a mint. I am willing that the House should take up these resolutions *seriatim* and vote upon them. I am not particularly wedded to any particular form of words or any set of resolutions. All I desire is an expression of the opinion of this Convention on the main subjects embraced in the resolutions. I would prefer, however, that they should go as a whole.

Mr. Gilbert. I believe the gentleman will admit that I am as anxious to have a mint in California as he is; but inasmuch as I do not think this the best plan to get it, I am opposed to that portion of the resolutions. If he prefers that they should go as a whole, I shall withdraw my motion; but I shall be compelled to vote against the proposition as a whole.

Mr. McCarver. I would call attention to my resolution, offered in relation to the public lands. That resolution gives the Legislature the power to do all that Congress is required to do in these resolutions, provided Congress agree to it. It covers the whole subject included in the proposition of the gentleman. I am in favor of any proposition that asks that the gold mines shall be granted to California; but I do not at the same time believe that Congress would be so likely to relinquish the gold mines as they would the public lands in any other part of the country.

Mr. McDougal. I regard this as a very important matter, and I hope the gentleman (Mr. Steuart) will revise his proposition so as to leave out all the objectionable matter, which is not material, and then it will probably pass.

Mr. Ellis. I am also of opinion that this is a very important subject; but I cannot think that any gentleman here can vote for it as it stands, without violating an oath which he took to support the Constitution of the United States. The same objection has been urged by the gentleman from Monterey, (Mr. Botts.) It is contained in the 5th article of the 9th section: "No tax or duty shall be laid on articles exported from any State."

Mr. STEUART. The gentleman entirely mistakes the nature of the resolution. If the United States have the right to make an individual pay for the coining of gold at the mint, they have a right to make him pay for having it assayed. This right has never been denied. A tax has always been laid by the inspection laws. This is nothing more than an inspection of the gold of California.

Mr. DENT. I am in favor of many of the provisions of these resolutions, but as they now stand, I shall be obliged to vote in the negative.

Mr. MCDOUGAL. I should vote in the affirmative if the objectionable clauses were stricken out; but I cannot vote in favor of the resolutions as a whole.

The question was then taken, and the resolution was rejected.

Mr. MCCARVER's resolution in relation to the public lands was then, on motion, taken up.

Mr. SHERWOOD. I shall vote against this resolution. I think these lands belong to the Government of the United States. They cost the General Government fifteen millions of dollars; and although it may be very well for us to ask Congress to grant them to the State of California, inasmuch as she has had no appropriation for the support of a government, I think we cannot say that of right they belong to California.

Mr. STEUART. I certainly cannot vote for the resolution. It is a doctrine broached some twenty or thirty years ago—a doctrine which can never prevail in the Congress of the United States. It may be popular in the Western States; but it is in open violation of the Constitution of the United States.

The question was then taken, and the resolution was rejected.

On motion of Mr. NORTON, Mr. Steuart's resolution, submitted on the 27th of September, for the appointment of a Committee to draft an Address to the people of California, was then taken up.

Mr. STEUART said he had offered the resolution because he thought it important to send out with the constitution, as adopted by this Convention, a short address to the people of California, upon the importance of an early consideration of the constitution, and also the importance of attendance at the polls, in order that a full expression of the public voice might be had, not only to show the sense of the people of California in regard to this constitution, but to show the Congress of the United States the imposing attitude that we assume, and the array of votes which we can produce in the formation of our State government.

The question was then taken, and the resolution was adopted.

The CHAIR (Mr. Botts) appointed Messrs. Steuart, Halleck and Vermeule.

Mr. HALLECK asked to be excused, as other duties would render it very difficult for him to attend upon this Committee.

Mr. SHERWOOD thought it would be proper to have one delegate from each district

Mr. VERMEULE was also of that opinion.

On motion, the vote on the resolution was reconsidered; and, on motion, it was so amended as to provide that the Committee should consist of one from each district, and thus amended, the resolution was adopted.

The CHAIR appointed as such Committee, Messrs. Steuart, McDougal, Vermeule, Larkin, Hoppe, Walker, Tefft, De La Guerra, Stearns and Pedrorena.

Mr. MCDOUGAL offered the following resolution:

Resolved, That Mr. Howe, a clerk of this House, be allowed the sum of five dollars per day additional to his present salary.

Mr. MCDOUGAL said he would merely state that Mr. Howe was a most faithful and efficient clerk; that his duties had been very laborious, and he had discharged them with great credit to himself and advantage to the Convention.

Mr. STEUART fully concurred in the opinion expressed by his frind from Sacramento.

Mr. GWIN thought it an act of justice to state that he had never seen duties more faithfully performed. Those duties had been very laborious; and he hoped the House would unanimously adopt the resolution.

Mr. STEUART moved to amend, by adding thereto the following:

And that he be authorized to continue the record of the proceedings at the same per diem allowance, *provided* he shall not be employed more than ten days from the adjournment of this Convention.

The amendment was agreed to, and the resolution adopted, as amended.

Mr. MOORE offered the following resolution:

Resolved, That William H. Richardson is entitled to receive mileage and per diem while prosecuting his claim to a seat in this House, as a delegate from the District of San Diego.

Mr. MOORE said he considered that inasmuch as Mr. Richardson had come here with a certificate of election, he was entitled to his per diem and mileage.

Mr. MCDOUGAL stated that Mr. Richardson was duly elected under the call of the people of San Diego, and they gave him a certificate of election, as a delegate from that district. He came here with that certificate. When he arrived here, he found that this Convention had resolved to admit but a certain number, and they decided that he could not be admitted. He (Mr. McDougal) thought it was but simple justice that Mr. Richardson should at least have his allowance for travelling expenses.

Mr. SHANNON was of opinion that there was a good deal of doubt upon this matter. It was known to the House that if Mr. Richardson could have been at all admitted he could have been admitted only as a supernumerary. He (Mr. Richardson) then came here at his own risk; but further than that, he came here under pay from the United States Government, and at public expense.

Mr. PEDRORENA stated that Mr. Richardson resigned his office under the Government of the United States, before he left for this Convention.

The question was then taken on the resolution, and it was adopted.

Mr. SHERWOOD offered the following resolution, which was adopted unanimously:

Resolved, That J. S. Houston be recommended to Gen. Riley as a suitable person to circulate the constitution in the Districts of San Francisco, Sonoma, Sacramento and San Joaquin.

On motion of Mr. PRICE, the resolution submitted by him on the 27th of September, relative to the Seal of State of California, was taken up.

Mr. DIMMICK moved to amend the resolution by adding at the end, "press and materials."

Mr. NORTON wanted to know what this $1,000 was for? Whether it was for the payment of the design and execution of the work, or to enable Mr. Lyon to go up to San Francisco and superintend the work.

Mr. MCDOUGAL said it was for the design, the engraving of the seal, and press, all included. He hoped no gentleman would think the sum too much. He was authorised to say that if the House thought it too extravagant, that Sacramento herself would pay the $1,000.

Mr. MCCARVER stated that the mechanic's bill for the press for the State of Iowa was $500. If the Committee had said $2,000 he would not have thought it out of the way.

Mr. NORTON said he had made no objection whatever to the thousand dollars. All he wanted to know was what it was for. He did not know but that it was to pay Mr. Lyon for going to Sacramento, and merely superintending the work. He moved to insert at the end of the resolution, "press and all appendages."

Mr. DIMMICK said this was his amendment.

Mr. HALLECK suggested that this thousand dollars could not be advanced, because the work was not for the existing government, and could not be paid for except by the new State government, for which the seal was intended.

Mr. NORTON then offered the following substitute, which was adopted:

Resolved, That Mr. Caleb Lyon be, and is hereby, authorised to superintend the engraving o the Seal for the State, and to furnish the same in the shortest possible time to the Secretary of the Convention, with the press and all necessary appendages, to be by him delivered to the Secretary of State appointed under this Constitution; and that the sum of $1,000 be paid to Mr. Lyon in full compensation and payment for the design, seal, press, and all appendages.

Resolved, That the words "The great Seal of the State of California," be added to the design.

Mr. HALLECK inquired if any gentleman present knew what had become of the original design. The gentleman by whom it was designed* requested that it should be found, if possible, and handed to the gentleman who occupied the Chair.

Mr. SHERWOOD believed that this seal was not the entire production of the gentleman who was authorized to have it engraved, and he (Mr. Lyon) did not claim it as such. The original design was given to Mr. Lyon by a gentleman who did not wish his name to be made public, but expressed a desire in a confidential letter to Mr. Lyon that he (Mr. Lyon) might be known as the author of the design. Some additions were made to it by Mr. Lyon, and it was adopted by the House in its present form.

Mr. HALLECK did not wish to throw the slightest censure upon Mr. Lyon, but after the matter was all settled and disposed of, he was requested to ascertain if the original paper laid before the House could be found.

On motion the Convention took a recess until 7 o'clock P. M.

NIGHT SESSION, 7 O'CLOCK, P. M.

The Convention met pursuant to adjournment.

On motion of Mr. GWIN, the ordinance heretofore submitted by him, was taken up, as follows, viz:

ORDINANCE.

Be it ordained by the Convention assembled to form a constitution for the State of California, on behalf and by authority of the people of said State, that the following propositions be submitted to the Congress of the United States, which, if assented to by that body, shall be obligatory upon this State:

1. One section of land for every quarter township of the public lands; and when such section has been sold or otherwise disposed of, other lands equivalent thereto, and as contiguous as may be, shall be granted to the State for the use of schools.

2. Seventy-two sections of the unappropriated lands within this State, shall be set apart and reserved for use and support of a University, which, together with such further quantities as may be agreed upon by Congress, shall be conveyed to the State and appropriated solely to the use and support of such university in such manner as the Legislature may prescribe.

3. Four sections of land, to be selected under the direction of the Legislature, from any of the unappropriated public lands belonging to the United States, within this State, shall be granted to the State for its use in establishing a seat of Government, or to defray the expenses of public buildings at the same.

4. Five hundred thousand acres of the unappropriated public lands in this State, belonging to the United States, in addition to the 500,000 acres granted to the new States under an act of Congress distributing the proceeds of the public lands among the several States of the Union, approved A. D., 1841, shall be designated, under the direction of the Legislature, and granted to the State for the purpose of defraying the expenses of the State Government, and for other State purposes. And five per cent. of the net proceeds of the sale of all lands lying within the State which shall be sold under the authority of the United States, after deducting all expenses incident to the same, shall also be appropriated for the encouragement of learning.

5. All salt springs within this State, and the lands reserved for the use of the same, at least one section including each spring, shall be granted to the State, to be used or disposed of as the Legislature may direct.

6. The first Senators and Representatives elected to Congress from this State, are hereby authorized and empowered to make or assent to such other proposition, or to such variations of the propositions herein made, as the interests of the State may require; and any such changes when approved by the Legislature shall be as obligatory as if the assent of this Convention were given thereto; and all stipulations entered into by the Legislature in pursuance of the authority herein conferred, shall be considered articles of compact between the United States and this State; and the Legislature is hereby further authorized to declare in behalf of the people of California, if such declaration be proposed by Congress, that they will not interfere with the primary disposal, under the authority of the United States, of the vacant lands within the limits of this State.

Mr. GWIN. I find appended to most of the Constitutions of the new States an ordinance, guaranteeing to the United States the exclusive right to dispose of the

* Major Garnett.

vacant land within the State, and agreeing to certain propositions, made by Congress, or when the Constitution has been formed without previous authorization by Congress, making propositions to that body.

An ordinance of this kind may not be indispensible to the admission of California into the Union, but the want of it might seriously embarrass if not postpone the admission. With the limited means at hand I have not been able to make a thorough examination into these ordinances, but I find Ohio had no ordinance. Louisiana had one agreeing to the requirements of the act of Congress relinquishing the right to the public domain: so also with Alabama and Mississippi. Indiana has an ordinance, without guaranteeing the right of the vacant lands to the United States. The same with Illinois and Missouri, and Florida merely gave the power to two-thirds of the Legislature to agree to such propositions as might be made by the United States; while Arkansas passed no ordinance. These two latter States formed constitutions without the authority of a previous act of Congress. One gave limited power to the Legislature to agree to propositions Congress might make, while the other gave none at all. Yet we see no difficulty between this State and the United States in regard to the primary disposal of the vacant lands within their borders.

In looking over these ordinances, I have seen none that seems so well adapted to our situation as that of Michigan; and I have accordingly adopted it as the basis of the one I hold in my hand and propose for adoption by this body. I have varied it in some of its provisions, For instance, I ask for a section of land for schools for every quarter township instead of one for each township. I earnestly hope this proposition will be acceded to by the United States. It will give us a munificent school fund, and bring the school-house within reach of every house in the State. Congress has already in part adopted this policy with Oregon, giving them two sections to each township instead of one, as was formerly the case. May we not hope that, influenced by the liberal and enlightened spirit of an age when the schoolmaster is abroad, we may get a section to each quarter township, and thus, as I said before, bring the residence of every citizen within reach of the school-house?

There is another slight alteration in the third clause, where we ask for four sections of land upon which to establish a seat of government, or to be appropriated towards erecting public buildings. In the fourth clause, instead of asking for seven hundred sections for roads and canals, we ask for half a million of acres to assist us in starting our State Government. This is but just and proper, and I hope will be acceded to without hesitation by Congress. We have been forced into the organization of a State Government, to prevent confusion and anarchy, by the failure of Congress to give us a Territorial Government. We have had no territorial pupilage, with large appropriations to build court houses, jails, and other necessary buildings. All of this has to be done by us, by a tax upon the people, unless Congress gives us a portion of the public domain for that purpose, or allows us, what is nothing but just, right, and proper, all the moneys collected prior to the admission of our State into the Union.

I conceive it to be of the utmost importance that this ordinance should be adopted by the Convention. It may prevent serious difficulties, and can do no possible harm; for not a member of this body supposes or proposes that the United States should not have the exclusive disposal of the vacant lands within our borders, although some of us hope that the General Government may relinquish to the State authorities the control of the mineral lands, upon the payment of a very moderate sum into the National Treasury. But this is a subject for future action between the State authorities and the General Government, and I will not consume the time of the House by giving my views on it, but submit the ordinance without further remark.

Mr. Steuart. I had hoped, sir, from hearing this resolution or ordinance read, that some proposition would have been presented to this House upon which we could base a calculation for the support of this government; but I have heard none, nor have I heard any very strong argument in favor of the adoption of the ordinance, except that it is found in the Constitution of Michigan. After the violent objections that the gentleman made to the reports of the Select Committee, because of the free use they made of the Constitution of New York, I hardly expected to be told that this ordinance was specially recommended to our consideration because it had been adopted by Michigan and other new States. I think, however, sir, that in looking at the article already adopted on the subject of education, that the House will find itself in some difficulty in adopting this. That article carries with it no meaning at all, or a palpable inconsistency; a distinct and absolute appropriation of all the proceeds of all the unsold lands of the State; and then comes the proviso, which, if it means anything, is in conflict with the inviolable pledge already adopted.

Mr. Jones. That proviso has been stricken out.

Mr. Botts. It seems to me that the fact that it was stricken out is a still greater reason against the adoption of this ordinance. It proposes to do something else with the proceeds of the public lands than what the constitution provides. I am opposed to the whole ordinance, for it amounts, in my view, to a dictation to Congress to pass a law; it is a proposition that this Convention shall prescribe a law which the Congress of the United States shall adopt. It seems to me that such a recommendation would come much better from the Legislature, which is the legitimate and customary source of all such action. But if this is to be adopted at all, hastily passing my eye over the 6th section, I see a difficulty which I hope will be remedied. It reads:

> The first Senators and Representatives elected to Congress from this State are hereby authorised and empowered to make, or assent to, *such other propositions*, or to such variations of the propositions herein made, as the interests of the State may require; and any such changes, when approved by the Legislature, shall be as obligatory as if the assent of this Convention were given thereto; and all stipulations entered into by the Legislature, in pursuance of the authority herein conferred, shall be considered articles of compact between the United States and this State; and the Legislature is hereby further authorised to declare in behalf of the people of California, if such declaration be proposed by Congress, that they will not interfere with the primary disposal, under the authority of the United States, of the vacant lands within the limits of this State.

Then the Congress of the United States and our honorable Representatives in Congress, and our Legislature, may together make us a new Constitution. This only shows that although a thing may be in the constitution of Michigan or New York, it may be faulty; and as we have so many gentlemen here who no doubt were very able at home to make these constitutions, both for Michigan and New York, I see no reason at all why we may not correct the errors into which they have fallen, or their forefathers. I propose to amend this section so far as to dispossess these gentlemen of the power to make or unmake a constitution for us. We have absolutely prohibited a majority of our own people from altering it at their polls. You remember how hard I contended on this floor for that power; but I did not succeed. I object to the two-third principle; the majority were however, by the Select Committee, denied the right to alter this Constitution. But now, sir, the Legislature, two Senators, and the Congress of the United States may change this Constitution. I have not had time to examine the rest of this ordinance in detail, but I am afraid there may be equally objectionable provisions in the other sections. I therefore propose that the Legislature shall take the subject in hand, and if any such action on the part of Congress is needed for this State, that the Legislature shall take such action as is necessary upon it. I move the indefinite postponement of the ordinance.

Mr. McCarver. I have exactly the same objection that the gentleman (Mr. Botts) has; and only to that section. It is to me a most serious objection. We have already fixed a plan by which the constitution shall be altered, and now it is proposed to adopt a different plan. Our boundary lines may be altered under that provision, with barely the sanction of the members of Congress and the Legislature of this State, without even consulting the people. It seems to me that it renders perfectly nugatory the existing provision of the constitution on that subject. We are opening a door to Congress to make various propositions. The reasons why such a provision was adopted in the constitution of Michigan were very obvious, and if we had left open this boundary question it might have been done here. In Michigan there was a difficulty, as to the extent of her territory, between that State and Ohio, and it was presupposed that the Congress of the United States was going to make some proposition to give her the disputed territory. It does not apply to California in any way, and should not be considered here.

Mr. Sherwood. I am in favor of the proposition, and I regret that my friend from Monterey, (Mr. Botts,) who is opposed to almost everything, should have made objections to a portion of the proposition, the propriety of which I think is evident to all. The gentleman objects to the power given to the Representatives of the State of California in the Senate and Lower House to make a different arrangement with Congress; to accede to a different proposition from what is offered. The ordinance which was passed in Michigan was passed not by the Legislature but by the Convention that framed its organic law. It claimed so much land from Congress; it asked Congress to concede so much; it did not say that they should not grant more. The result was that they obtained what they asked; and the object of passing this ordinance is to place something before Congress expressive of our wishes as a State as to what we should receive of the public domain. Now suppose Congress should grant us the seventy-two sections, as she did to Michigan, and the sections for school lands, and any portion of the public lands for the capital of the State, which everybody knows must cost several hundred thousand dollars; suppose the majority in Congress should say, we are perfectly willing to grant an additional five hundred thousand acres of land; the very proposition that the gentleman objects to is, that the Representatives of California shall be authorized to receive this additional grant. I say, if Congress should grant us more than the additional half million, let our Representatives receive it. We are not there as a body in Convention; we cannot negotiate with Congress; it is a matter of negotiation, and every one knows who knows anything about legislation, either in this body or a legislative body, that propositions come up different from anything that can be foreseen. Any proposition before a body which may be much more acceptable to the people of California than any we may here present to Congress, it is our desire to accept, and for this purpose we introduce this provision; but suppose, on the other hand, that Congress were willing to grant us four hundred thousand instead of five hundred thousand acres of land, should we not grant the power to our Representatives to conform to the wishes of Congress? Shall we say that we will take five hundred thousand acres, and not half an acre more or less? If the people, represented in the Legislature, elect two Senators; if the people by their vote elect two Representatives to the lower branch of Congress, shall we not trust them? That is the point. If you confine them to one specific quantity of land and they cannot get it, you do not, unless you pass this provision, give them any power to take anything. If Congress is willing to give us three or four hundred thousand you reject the grant, and you do the same if they are willing to give us more. It is a discretionary power that should be left to our Senators and Representatives, and to them only; for they are the only Representatives of the free people of California in Congress, and after we have elected them we should trust them in regard to any gifts that the National Legislature should wish to grant to us.

Mr. McCarver. I am extremely sorry to see my colleague (Mr. Sherwood) take a position which seems to me so absurd. It is singular that any gentleman should question the right of the Government of the United States to make this donation to the people of California, without its being received in this way; or that the Legislature should not have power to acquiesce in it. It is done in many of the States. Congress appropriates it in whatever way they think proper. It is just as absurd as to say that I could not receive a gift that the gentleman would tender me. The Legislature is competent to receive anything that the Congress of the United States may give to the State. It is a right that the representatives of the people possess without any constitutional authority. I am afraid the friends of the large boundary are trying to get that measure through in another shape.

Mr. SHERWOOD. I am very sorry that the phantom of the boundary should trouble the gentleman. I think that matter is pretty well settled here. Nothing of the kind ever entered my head. I admit that Congress has the right, if we do not say a word, to grant us what they please; but all men who hear me know that Congress is very apt to regard the wishes of the people of the State rather than the wishes of one Representative in Congress, who may bring in a bill upon a certain subject. If the gentleman himself was in Congress, and was to introduce a bill to grant us a half million, you would find fifty objections made; but if he brought in an ordinance adopted by the people through their Convention, Congress would listen to it. We are willing to receive all we can get. Our Representatives may go there, without any wish expressed by this Convention or by the people, and say that we do not want any addition to the five hundred thousand acres granted by the law of 1841. It is for us to say that we require or ask more; and for this purpose we instruct our Representatives to make known through this ordinance our wish; and if Congress is willing to grant more, we give them the power to receive it. Other States have come into the Union without any such ordinance, and they have never got as much as Michigan did. Let us ask to receive this additional grant, and ask it in such a manner that our request will have the greatest weight. It does not prevent Congress from granting the whole of the public lands to us if they think proper. Besides in this ordinance, if they get five hundred thousand acres in addition to the five hundred thousand granted under the law of 1841, without any proviso, it allows the State to select these lands; to locate them in the mining districts—giving the State the choice of selection. Inasmuch as, under the article upon education, we appropriate all that to the support of schools, we certainly ought to have something for the support of Government. We might then sustain our State Government partially at least, from these mineral lands, or from a tax imposed upon those who extract gold from these mineral lands.

Mr. JONES. I do not profess to be very profoundly versed in this question, and I shall not say a great deal about it; but I should be at a loss to account for the many objections that have been raised to what I conceive to be a plain proposition, if it were not for certain writings that I saw at the front door as I came in; and it strikes me that as there is to be a meeting of certain gentlemen, perhaps of the whole Convention—for a purpose about which we all know something, that there may be a little advantage gained in the race. As I want to go before the people with a fair face, I do not want to vote against a proposition which I consider so reasonable, so just, and necessary as this. We are told as a great objection to this proposition, that Michigan claimed the same thing and got it. I consider that a recommendation. If we have the precedent in Congress of the successful action of Michigan, it is surely a strong argument in favor of our adopting the same policy. I do not think our own originality here would be any great recommendation in Congress. I believe we could originate here as well as they could in Michigan; but as long as we have a successful precedent, I think we had better follow it. That article as to the lands granted by Congress for the purpose of education, should be held sacred for that purpose, and the rents should also be applied to the same purpose. We do not talk here of revenues or rents; we talk of a specific appropriation by Congress for a specific purpose. I do not see a word in this constitution against it. But we are told that Congress and our Representatives, together with the Legislature, are given, by this ordinance, the power to alter the constitution. Here is an ordinance for a particular purpose. It gives a power merely to accept an appropriation. The Legislature might open the boundary, gentlemen say. Why, sir, gentlemen seem to be afraid of ghosts. One gentleman thinks that the Legislature ought to go before Congress with its petition. Sir, we want it now; it is always demanded and granted upon the admission of a State; it is most properly demanded by the constitution which demands the admission of the State. We have just as much right to present this matter for the action of Congress as a majority of the Legislature. But we have rendered absolutely necessary some action of this sort by the very act of this Convention in giving up the whole revenue from the school lands. We must go before Congress with a demand for revenue from additional lands, otherwise we may be scarcely able to bear the expenses of government. I must say, finally, that I have seen nothing more proper presented to this body than these resolutions. I go for them heart and hand. If I were one of these gentlemen who oppose such a measure, I should hesitate to go before the people on the yeas and nays.

Mr. SHANNON. I move as an amendment, to strike out the last section. I do it for these reasons: It seems that there is considerable objection to this section on account of the possibility of its interference with Congress and the boundary question, as established by this Convention. Grant that it is so, and I think, since my attention has been called to it, that it may be so. It appears to me that the reading of that section conveys a most distinct and separate idea. Probably from the imperfection of the language used, it may be that the whole section refers to those which precede; but if that be so, then the language used, does not convey the true meaning of the section. It refers to some other sections beyond it contained in the body of the ordinance. The reference is most decided and direct; and most surely I do not wish, nor do I think any member wishes that any thing contained in an informal instrument appended to this constitution, should conflict with its provisions, which we have here so deliberately and unanimously passed. Either one thing or the other is certain; if it has no reference to any thing without or beyond that contained within the ordinance, then the wording is most incorrect and improper. If it is so, I think it should be striken out. Moreover, if we wish any of the benefits to be accrued from this ordinance, those benefits are to be obtained by every section and part of the ordinance preceding this section.

Mr. HASTINGS. I would sustain the motion made by my colleague to strike out the entire section. I will read the section. The word "other" applies to any thing at all; whether it is conducive to the interest of the State or not, is left entirely to the judgment of our Representatives in Congress.

Mr. SHERWOOD. To save all discussion on this subject, I will move to insert "such other propositions touching this ordinance."

Mr. HASTINGS. It appears to me that this is too general, and leaves an unlimited power to our Representatives in Congress. I would suggest, "not inconsistent with this constitution."

Mr. GWIN. If we do not retain something of this kind in the ordinance, we may be kept out until the people assemble in Convention and pass a new provision.

Mr. SHANNON then moved to strike out of the 6th section the clause "to such other propositions or" which Mr. Gwin accepted, and thus amended, the ordinance was passed.

Mr. JONES called for the consideration of the resolution submitted by him on the 9th instant; which being taken up, and the yeas and nays ordered thereon, it was rejected, as follows:

YEAS.—Messrs. Aram, Brown, Crosby, Dent, Gilbert, Hoppe, Hollingsworth, Jones, Larkin, Moore, McCarver, McDougal, Pedrorena, Sherwood, Steuart, Vermeule, Walker, Wozencraft—16.

NAYS.—Messrs. Botts, Dimmick, Dominguez, Ellis, Gwin, Hill, Hobson, Halleck, Hastings, Lippincott, Norton, Ord, Price, Sutter, Snyder, Shannon, Stearns, Tefft, President—21.

On motion of Mr. SHERWOOD, the report of the Committee on the Census was taken up, viz:

The committee to whom was referred the subject of taking an enumeration of the inhabitants of California, under the instructions of the Convention, beg leave to report:

It is a fact well known to all, that there are no statistics to which we can refer in order to determine the number of inhabitants in this Territory. Such has been the immense imigration to this country by sea and land within the past six months, that no man can obtain a basis upon which to estimate the number. The North and the South, the East and the West, the Old and the New Worlds have been sending their thousands of enterprising and industrious men into California. We cannot doubt that the present population (exclusive of Indians) amounts to 80,000. We are aware that the number has been placed higher, by many intelligent men, well acquainted with the various districts into which the tide has flown. At all events we hazard nothing in saying that on the 1st of January next the population may be set down at 100,000. But after all, when this State applies for admission into the Federal Union, it may be said that this is mere conjecture, and those who are called upon to vote for our admission, may demand better evidence than our opinions on this subject. In order to prevent delay, and secure at once a State Government capable of giving security to our persons and property, it is in our opinion necessary that steps should be taken to have immediately the census taken. Our Representatives at Washington will then be armed with *official* evidence of our right to ask admission into the Union.

Your Committee, entertaining these opinions, recommend that an enumeration be taken of the inhabitants of California, specifying:

1st. Number of white Males over the age of 21 years.
2d. " Females " 18 "
3d. " Males under 21 "
4th. " Females " 18 "

To effect this object as speedily as possible your Committee recommend the appointment of a Marshal, who shall have power to select deputies, who shall proceed at as early a day as possible to take the census, and report to the first session of the Legislature.

2d. That there be allowed to the said Marshal the sum of dollars per day for each day actually employed, and his necessary traveling expenses.

3d. That the deputies appointed by the Marshal shall receive for their salaries cents for each name returned by them on their separate rolls.

4th. That said Marshal and his deputies shall, before entering on the duties of their offices, subscribe an oath before some competent authority to discharge their duties faithfully, and make a true and accurate report of the population of the respective districts assigned to them.

(Signed) B. F. MOORE, *Chairman.*

Mr. STEUART moved that the report be indefinitely postponed.

The motion was decided in the affirmative.

Mr. SHANNON moved to take up the report of the Committee of Ways and Means, but the motion was decided in the negative.

Mr. HILL moved that the Convention adjourn until Saturday at 10 o'clock, but the motion was decided in the negative, by yeas and nays, as follows:

YEAS.—Messrs. Gilbert, Hill, Tefft—3.

NAYS.—Messrs. Aram, Botts, Brown, Covarrubias, Crosby, Dent, Dimmick, Ellis, Gwin, Hoppe, Hobson, Halleck, Hastings, Jones, Larkin, Lippincott, Moore, McDougal, Norton, Ord, Pedrorena, Price, Rodriguez, Sutter, Snyder, Sherwood, Shannon, Stearns, Steuart, Walker—30.

On motion, the Convention then adjourned until 10 o'clock, A. M., to-morrow.

FRIDAY, OCTOBER 12, 1849.

The Convention met pursuant to adjournment.

Journal of yesterday read and approved.

Mr. Norton submitted the following resolution, which was unanimously adopted, viz:

Resolved, That the thanks of this Convention be presented to the Honorable Robert Semple, for the faithful and impartial manner in which he has discharged the arduous and responsible duties of the Chair; and that in retiring therefrom he carries with him the best wishes of this Convention.

On motion of Mr. Ellis, it was unanimously

Resolved, That a committee of three be appointed to transmit a copy of the Constitution of the State of California to General Riley, acting Governor of California, with an accompanying letter signed by the President of this body, requesting the Governor to forward the same to the President of the United States by the earliest opportunity.

The Chair appointed Messrs. Ellis, Hastings, and McCarver as such committee.

The President announced to the Convention that he had received official notice from General Riley, that a national salute would be fired by his order, on the signing of the Constitution adopted by this Convention.

SATURDAY, OCTOBER 13, 1849.

The Convention met pursuant to adjournment.

On motion (the President being absent on acount of sickness) Mr. Sutter was called to the chair.

The Journal of yesterday was read and approved.

Mr. Botts submitted the following resolution, which was unanimously adopted, viz:

Resolved, That the thanks of this Convention be tendered to Brevet Brigadier General Riley, acting as Governor of California, for the kindness and courtesy which has marked his intercourse, private and official, with the members of this body.

Mr. Steuart, from the committee appointed to prepare an Address to the People of California, presented the following, which was unanimously adopted:

TO THE PEOPLE OF CALIFORNIA.

The undersigned, Delegates to a Convention authorized to form a Constitution for the State of California, having to the best of their ability discharged the high trust committed to them, respectfully submit the accompanying plan of government for your approval. Acknowledging the great fundamental principles that all political power is inherent in the people, and that government is instituted for the protection, security, and benefit of the people, the Constitution presented for your consideration is intended only to give such organic powers to the several departments of the proposed government as shall be necessary for its efficient administration; and while it is believed *no* power has been given which is not thus essentially necessary, the Convention deem individual rights, as well as public liberty, are amply secured by the people, still retaining not only the great conservative power of free choice and election of all officers, agents, and representatives, but the inalienable right to alter or reform their government, whenever the public good may require.

Although born in different climes, coming from different States, imbued with local feelings, and educated perhaps with predilections for peculiar institutions, laws and customs, the delegates assembled in Convention, *as Californians*, and carried on their deliberations in a spirit of amity, compromise, and mutual concession for the public weal.

It cannot be denied, that a difference of opinion was entertained in the Convention, as to the policy and expediency of several measures embodied in the Constitution; but looking to the great interests of the State of California, the peace, happiness, and prosperity of the whole people, individual opinions were freely surrendered to the will of the majority, and with one voice we respectfully but earnestly recommend to our fellow-citizens, the adoption of the Constitution which we have the honor to submit.

In establishing a boundary for the State, the Convention conformed, as near as was deemed practicable and expedient, to great natural landmarks, so as to bring into a union all those who should be included by mutual interest, mutual wants, and mutual dependence. No portion of territory is included, the inhabitants of which were not or might not have been legitimately represented in the Convention, under the authority by which it was convened; and in unanimously resolving to exclude slavery from the State of California, the great principle has been maintained, that to the people of each State and Territory, *alone*, belongs the right to establish such municipal regulations, and to decide such questions as affect their own peace, prosperity, and happiness.

A free people, in the enjoyment of an elective government, capable of securing their civil, religious, and political rights, may rest assured these inestimable privileges can never be wrested from them, so long as they keep a watchful eye on the operations of their government, and hold to strict accountability, those to whom power is delegated. No people were ever yet enslaved, who knew and dared maintain the co-relative rights and obligations of free and independent citizens. A knowledge of the laws, their moral force and efficacy, thus becomes an essential element of freedom, and makes public education of primary importance. In this view, the Constitution of California provides for and guarantees in the most ample manner, the establishment of common schools, seminaries, and colleges, so as to extend the blessings of education throughout the land, and secure its advantages to the present and future generations.

Under the peculiar circumstances in which California becomes a State—with an unexampled increase of a population, coming from every part of the world, speaking various languages, and imbued with different feelings and prejudices, no form of government, no system of laws, can be be expected to meet with immediate and unanimous assent. It is to be remembered, moreover, that a considerable portion of our fellow-citizens are natives of Old Spain, Californians, and those who have voluntarily relinquished the rights of Mexicans, to enjoy those of American citizens. Long accustomed to a different form of government, regarding the rights of person and property as interwoven with ancient usages and time-honored customs, they may not at once see the advantage of the proposed new government, or yield an immediate approval of new laws, however salutary their provisions or conducive to the general welfare. But it is confidently believed, when the government as now proposed, shall have gone into successful operation, when each department thereof shall move on harmoniously in its appropriate and respective sphere; when laws based on the eternal laws of equity and justice shall be established; when every citizen of California shall find himself secure in life, liberty and property—all will unite in the cordial support of institutions, which are not only the pride and boast of every true-hearted citizen of the Union, but which have gone forth, a guiding light to every people groping through the gloom of religious supertition or political fanaticism. Institutions, which even now, while all Europe is agitated with the convulsive efforts of nations battling for liberty, have become the mark and model of government for every people who would hold themselves free, sovereign and independent.

With this brief exposition of the views and opinions of the Convention, the undersigned submit the constitution and plan of government for your approval. They earnestly recommend it to your calm and deliberate consideration, and especially do they most respectfully urge on every voter to attend the polls.

The putting into operation of a government which shall establish justice, ensure domestic tranquillity, promote the general welfare, and secure the blessings of civil, religious and political liberty, should be an object of the deepest solicitude to every true-hearted citizen, and the consummation of his dearest wishes. The price of liberty is eternal vigilance, and thus it is not only the privilege, but the duty, of every voter to vote his sentiments. No freeman of this land who values his birthright, and would transmit unimpaired to his children an inheritance so rich in glory and in honor, will refuse to give one day to the service of his country. Let every qualified voter go early to the polls, and give his *free* vote at the election appointed to be held on Tuesday, the 13th day of November next, not only that a full and fair expression of the public voice may be had, for or against a constitution intended to secure the peace, happiness and prosperity of the whole people, but that their numerical and political strength may be made manifest, and the whole world see by what majority of freemen California, the bright star of the West, claims a place in the diadem of that glorious Republic, formed by the union of thirty-one sovereign States.

Joseph Aram,
Charles T. Botts,
Elam Brown,
Jose Anto. Carrillo,
Jose M. Covarrubias,
Elisha O. Crosby,
Lewis Dent,
Manuel Dominguez,
K. H. Dimmick,
A. J. Ellis,
Stephen G. Foster,
Pablo De La Guerra,
Edward Gilbert,
William M. Gwin,
Julian Hanks,
Henry Hill,
J. D. Hoppe,
Joseph Hobson,
H. W. Halleck,
L. W. Hastings,
J. McH. Hollinsworth,
James McHall Jones,
Thomas O. Larkin,
Francis J. Lippitt,
Benjamin S. Lippincott,
M. M. McCarver,
John McDougal,
Benjamin F. Moore,
Myron Norton,
P. Ord,
Miguel De Pedrorena,
Rodman M. Price,
Antonio M. Pico,
Jacinto Rodriguez,
Hugh Reid,
J. A. Sutter,
Jacob R. Snyder,
Winfield S. Sherwood,
William C. Shannon,
Pedro Sansevaine,
Abel Stearns,
W. M. Steuart,
R. Semple,
Henry A. Tefft,
M. G. Vallejo,
Thomas L. Vermeule,
Joel P. Walker,
O. M. Wozencraft.

Mr. Norton submitted the following resolution, which was adopted, viz:

Resolved, That Mr. Hamilton, employed by this Convention to enroll the constitution upon parchment, be paid for his services the sum of five hundred dollars.

Mr. Shannon moved a suspension of the rules to enable him to move a reconsideration of the vote by whieh the resolution of Mr. Jones, submitted on the 9th instant, was rejected; but the motion was decided in the negative—yeas 16, nays 23.

On motion of Mr. SHERWOOD, it was

Resolved, That the ten days additional services authorized by a resolution of this Convention to be performed by Mr. Howe, after its adjournment *sine die*, in completing the journal of the Committee of the Whole, and arranging the papers and reports necessary to a perfect understanding of the whole proceedings of this Convention, be performed by him, as customary in such cases, under the supervision of the Secretary of the Convention.

On motion, the Convention adjourned to 2 o'clock P. M.

AFTERNOON SESSION, 2 O'CLOCK P. M.

The Convention met pursuant to adjournment. The President, though in feeble health, resumed the Chair.

Mr. SHERWOOD, submitted the following resolution, which was unanimously adopted, viz:

Resolved, That Bvt. Brig. Gen. Riley should, in the opinion of this Convention, representing, as it believes, the wishes of the people, receive during his continuance in office as the Executive of the existing government in California, at the rate of $10,000 per annum, for his salary; and that Bvt. Capt. H. W. Halleck, Secretary of State, should receive at the rate of $6,000 per annum, for his salary.

On motion of Mr. McDOUGAL, it was unanimously

Resolved, That the members of this Convention will wait on Governor Riley in a body, after the signing of the constitution.

Mr. ORD submitted the following resolution, which was unanimously adopted:

Resolved, That the thanks of this Convention be tendered to the Secretary, the Assistant Secretaries, the Engrossing Clerk, and other officers, for the able and efficient discharge of their duties.

On motion of Mr. GWIN, Mr. J. A. Sutter was requested to address Gov. Riley on behalf of this Convention, when it shall wait upon him in a body after the adjournment *sine die*.

On motion of Mr. McCARVER, the thanks of the Convention were tendered to the Trustees of Colton Hall for the use of that building during the sessions of the Convention.

The Convention then, on motion of Mr. McDOUGAL, proceeded to sign the enrolled constitution.

After which the President addressed to the Convention a few remarks, thanking them for the honor they had done him, and the courtesy they had always exhibited, and wishing them a safe and speedy return to their several homes.

And then, on motion of Mr. McCARVER, the Convention adjourned *sine die*.

The members thereupon proceeded in a body to General Riley's house.

Captain SUTTER, in behalf of the Convention, addressed General Riley as follows:

GENERAL: I have been appointed by the delegates elected by the people of California to form a Constitution, to address you in their names and in behalf of the whole people of California, and express the thanks of the Convention for the aid and co-operation they have received from you in the discharge of the responsible duty of creating a State Government. And, sir, the Convention, as you will perceive from the official records, duly appreciate the great and important services you have rendered to our common country, and especially to the people of California, and entertains the confident belief that you will receive from the whole people of the United States, when you retire from your official duties here, that verdict so grateful to the heart of the patriot: "Well done, thou good and faithful servant."

General RILEY replied as follows:

GENTLEMEN: I never made a speech in my life. I am a soldier—but I can *feel*; and I do feel deeply the honor you have this day conferred upon me. Gentlemen, this is a prouder day to me than that on which my soldiers cheered me on the field of Contreras. I thank you all from my heart. I am satisfied now that the people have done right in selecting delegates to form a constitution. They have chosen a body of men upon whom our country may look with pride; you have formed a constitution worthy of California. And I have no fear for California while her people choose their representatives so wisely. Gentlemen, I congratulate you upon the successful conclusion of your arduous labors; and I wish you all happiness and prosperity.

[Here Gen. Riley was interrupted by three cheers from the members, "as Governor of California," and three more "as a gallant soldier, and worthy of his country's glory."]

He then concluded in the following words: I have but one thing to add, gentlemen, and that is, that my success in the affairs of California is mainly owing to the efficient aid rendered me by Captain Halleck, the Secretary of State. He has stood by me in all emergencies; to him I have always appealed when at a loss myself; and he has never failed me.

Members of the Convention of California.

Names.	Age.	Where born.	Of what State last a resident.	District in California.	Town or Post Office in California.	How long a resident of California.	Profession.
J. D. Hoppe	35	Carroll County, Md	Missouri	San Jose	Pueblo de San Jose	Three years	Merchant.
Joseph Aram	39	Oneida County, N. Y	Illinois	San Jose	Pueblo de San Jose	Three years	Farmer.
Elam Brown	52	Herkimer County, N. Y	Missouri	San Jose	Bencia	Three years	Farmer.
Jacob R. Snyder	34	Philadelphia, Pa	Pennsylvania	Sacramento	Sacramento City	Four years	Surveyor.
Winfield S. Sherwood	32	Sandy Hill, Washington Co	New York	Sacramento	Mormon Island	Four months	Lawyer.
H. W. Halleck	32	Oneida County	New York	Monterey	Monterey	Three years	U. S. Engineer.
L. W. Hastings	30	Knox County	Ohio	Sacramento	Sutter	Six years	Lawyer.
J. A. Sutter	47	Switzerland	Missouri	Sacramento	Sutter	Ten years	Farmer.
John McDougal	32	Ohio	Indiana	Sacramento	Sutter	Seven months	Merchant.
E. O. Crosby	34	Tompkins County, N. Y	New York	Sacramento	Vernon	Seven months	Lawyer.
M. M. McCarver	42	Madison County, Kentucky	Oregon	Sacramento	Sacramento City	One year	Farmer.
Julian Hanks	39	Tolland County, Conn	Connecticut	San Jose	Pueblo de San Jose	Ten years	Farmer.
Kimball H. Dimmick	34	Chenango County, N. Y	New York	San Jose	Pueblo de San Jose	Three years	Lawyer.
Thomas O. Larkin	47	Charlestown	Massachusetts	Monterey	Monterey	Sixteen years	Trader.
Lewis Dent	26	St. Louis County	Missouri	Monterey	Monterey	Three years	Lawyer.
Rodman M. Price	30	Orange County, N. Y	New Jersey	San Francisco	San Francisco	Four years	U. S. Navy.
Ch. T. Botts	40	Spotsylvania County, Va	Virginia	Monterey	Monterey	Sixteen months	Attorney at Law.
M. G. Vallejo	42	Monterey, (U. C.)	California	Sonoma	Sonoma	All my life	Military.
Manl. Dominguez	46	San Diego	California	Angeles	Angeles	All my life	Banker.
Antonio M. Pico	40	Monterey	California	Pueblo de San Jose	Pueblo de San Jose	All my life	Agriculturist.
Jacinto Rodriguez	36	Monterey	California	Monterey	Monterey	All my life	Agriculturist.
Henry A. Tefft	26	Washington County, N. Y	Wisconsin	San Luis Obispo	Nipomo	Four months	Lawyer.
Pedro Sansevaine	31	Bordeaux	Bordeaux	San Jose	Pueblo de San Jose	Eleven years	Negotiant.
Hugo Reid	38	Cardross	Scotland	Angeles	San Gabriel	Sixteen years	Farmer.
Stephen C. Foster	28	East Machias, Me	Missouri	Angeles	Pueblo de Los Angeles.	Three years	Agriculturist.
J. McH. Hollingsworth	25	Baltimore	Maryland	San Joaquin		Three years	Lieut. Volunteers.
Joseph Hobson	39	Baltimore	Maryland	San Francisco.	San Francisco	Five months	Merchant.
Pacificus Ord	34	Allegany County, Md	Louisiana	Monterey	Monterey	Eight months	Lawyer.
O. M. Wozencraft	34	Clermont City, Ohio	Louisiana	San Joaquin	San Francisco	Four months	Physician.
J. P. Walker	52	Goochland County, Va	Missouri	Sonoma	Sonoma	Thirteen months	Farmer.
W. E. Shannon	27	Ireland, (Mayo)	New York	Sacramento	Columa	Three years	Lawyer.
Abel Stearns	51	Massachusetts	Massachusetts	Angeles	Angeles	Twenty years	Merchant.

Thos. L. Vermeule	35	New Jersey	New York	San Joaquin	Stockton	Three years	Lawyer.
Benj. S. Lippincott	34	New York	New Jersey	San Joaquin	Stockton	Three years and-a-half.	Trader.
Myron Norton	27	Birmington County, Vt.	New York	San Francisco	San Francisco	One year	Lawyer.
W. M. Steuart	49	Montgomery County, Md.	Maryland	San Francisco	San Francisco	One year	Attorney at Law.
B. F. Moore	29	Florida	Texas	San Joaquin	Stockton	One year	Elegant leisure.
A. J. Ellis	33	Oneida County	New York	San Francisco	San Francisco	Two years and-a-half.	Merchant.
Edw. Gilbert	27	Dutchess County, N. Y.	New York	San Francisco	San Francisco	Two years and-a-half.	Printer.
J. M. Jones	25	Scott County, Ky.	Louisiana	San Joaquin	San Francisco	About four months	Attorney at Law.
W. M. Gwin	44	Sumner County, Tenn.	Louisiana	San Francisco	San Francisco	Four months	Farmer.
Jose Anto. Carrillo	53	San Francisco	California	Angeles	Angeles	Toda la vida	Labrador.
Francis J. Lippitt	37	Rhode Island	New York	San Francisco	San Francisco	Two years seven m'ths	Lawyer.
Henry Hill	33	Virginia	Virginia	San Diego	Monterey	One year five months	U. S. Army.
Miguel de Pedrorena	41	Spain	California	San Diego	San Diego	Twelve years	Merchant.
R. Semple	42	Kentucky	Missouri	Sonoma	Benicia	Five years	Printer.
P. N. de la Guerra	36	California	California	Santa Barbara	Santa Barbara		
J. M. Covarrubias	40	California	California	San Luis Obispo	San Luis Obispo		

APPENDIX.

APPENDIX.

CONSTITUTION OF THE STATE OF CALIFORNIA.

PROCLAMATION TO THE PEOPLE OF CALIFORNIA.

The delegates of the people assembled in Convention, have formed a Constitution, which is now presented for your ratification. The time and manner of voting on this Constitution, and of holding the first general election, are clearly set forth in the Schedule; the whole subject is therefore left for your unbiased and deliberate consideration.

The Prefect (or person exercising the functions of that office,) of each District will designate the places for opening the polls, and give due notice of the election, in accordance with the provisions of the Constitution and Schedule.

The people are now called upon to form a government for themselves, and to designate such officers as they desire to make and execute the laws. That their choice may be wisely made, and that the government so organised may secure the permanent welfare and happiness of the people of the new State, is the sincere and earnest wish of the present Executive, who, if the Constitution be ratified, will, with pleasure, surrender his powers to whomsoever the people may designate as his successor.

Given at Monterey, California, this 12th day of October, A. D., 1849.

B. RILEY,
Bvt. Brig. Gen'l U. S. A. and Governor of California.

OFFICIAL: H. W. HALLECK,
Brev. Capt. and Secretary of State.

WE, the People of California, grateful to Almighty God for our freedom, in order to secure its blessings, do establish this Constitution.

ARTICLE I.

Declaration of Rights.

Sec. 1. All men are by nature free and independent, and have certain inalienable rights, among which are those of enjoying and defending life and liberty, acquiring, possessing, and protecting property: and pursuing and obtaining safety and happiness.

Sec. 2. All political power is inherent in the people. Government is instituted for the protection, security, and benefit of the people; and they have the right to alter or reform the same, whenever the public good may require it.

Sec. 3. The right of trial by jury shall be secured to all, and remain inviolate forever; but a jury trial may be waved by the parties, in all civil cases, in the manner to be prescribed by law.

Sec. 4. The free exercise and enjoyment of religious profession and worship, without discrimination or preference, shall forever be allowed in this State: and no person shall be rendered incompetent to be a witness on account of his opinions on matters of religious belief; but the liberty of conscience, hereby secured, shall not be so construed as to excuse acts of licentiousness, or justify practices inconsistent with the peace or safety of this State.

Sec. 5. The privilege of the writ of *habeas corpus* shall not be suspended, unless when, in cases of rebellion or invasion, the public safety may require its suspension.

Sec. 6. Excessive bail shall not be required, nor exeessive fines imposed, nor shall cruel or unusual punishments be inflicted, nor shall witnesses be unreasonably detained.

Sec. 7. All persons shall be bailable, by sufficient sureties: unless for capital offences, when the proof is evident or the presumption great.

Sec. 8. No person shall be held to answer for a capital or otherwise infamous crime, (except in cases of impeachment, and in cases of militia when in actual service, and the land and naval forces in time of war, or which this State may keep with the consent of Congress in time of peace, and in cases of petit larceny under the regulation of the Legislature) unless on presentment or indictment of a grand jury; and in any trial in any court whatever, the party accused shall be allowed to appear and defend in person and with counsel, as in civil actions. No person shall be subject to be twice put in jeopardy for the same offence; nor shall he be compelled, in any criminal case, to be a witness against himself, nor be deprived of life, liberty, or property, without due process of law; nor shall private property be taken for public use without just compensation.

Sec. 9. Every citizen may freely speak, write, and publish his sentiments on all subjects, being responsible for the abuse of that right; and no law shall be passed to restrain or abridge the liberty of speech or of the press. In all criminal prosecutions on indictments for libels, the truth may be given in evidence to the jury; and if it shall appear to the jury that the matter charged as libellous is true, and was published with good motives and for justifiable ends, the party shall be acquitted; and the jury shall have the right to determine the law and the fact.

Sec. 10. The people shall have the right freely to assemble together, to consult for the common good, to instruct their representatives, and to petition the legislature for redress of grievances.

Sec. 11. All laws of a general nature shall have a uniform operation.

Sec. 12. The military shall be subordinate to the civil power. No standing army shall be kept up by this State in time of peace; and in time of war no appropriation for a standing army shall be for a longer time than two years.

Sec. 13. No soldier shall, in time of peace, be quartered in any house, without the consent of the owner; nor in time of war, except in the manner to be prescribed by law.

Sec. 14. Representation shall be apportioned according to population.

Sec. 15. No person shall be imprisoned for debt, in any civil action on *mesne* or final process, unless in cases of fraud; and no person shall be imprisoned for a militia fine in time of peace.

Sec. 16. No bill of attainder, *ex post facto* law, or law impairing the obligation of contracts, shall ever be passed.

Sec. 17. Foreigners who are, or who may hereafter become *bona fide* residents of this State, shall enjoy the same rights in respect to the possession, enjoyment, and inheritance of property, as native born citizens.

Sec. 18. Neither slavery, nor involuntary servitude, unless for the punishment of crimes, shall ever be tolerated in this State.

Sec. 19. The right of the people to be secure in their persons, houses, papers and effects, against unreasonable seizures and searches, shall not be violated; and no warrant shall issue but on probable cause, supported by oath or affirmation, particularly describing the place to be searched, and the persons and things to be seized.

Sec. 20. Treason against the State shall consist only in levying war against it, adhering to its enemies, or giving them aid and comfort. No person shall be convicted of treason, unless on the evidence of two witnesses to the same overt act, or confession in open court.

Sec. 21. This enumeration of rights shall not be construed to impair or deny others retained by the people.

ARTICLE II.

Right of Suffrage.

Sec. 1. Every white male citizen of the United States, and every white male citizen of Mexico, who shall have elected to become a citizen of the United States, under the treaty of peace exchanged and ratified at Queretaro, on the 30th day of May, 1848, of the age of twenty-one years, who shall have been a resident of the State six months next preceding the election, and the county or district in which he claims his vote thirty days, shall be entitled to vote at all elections which are now or hereafter may be authorized by law: Provided, that nothing herein contained, shall be construed to prevent the Legislature, by a two-thirds concurrent vote, from admitting to the right of suffrage, Indians or the descendants of Indians, in such special cases as such a proportion of the legislative body may deem just and proper.

Sec. 2. Electors shall, in all cases except treason, felony, or breach of the peace, be privileged from arrest on the days of the election, during their attendance at such election, going to and returning therefrom.

Sec. 3. No elector shall be obliged to perform militia duty on the day of election, except in time of war or public danger.

Sec. 4. For the purpose of voting, no person shall be deemed to have gained or lost a residence by reason of his presence or absence while employed in the service of the United States; nor while engaged in the navigation of the waters of this State, or of the United States, or of the high seas; nor while a student of any seminary of learning; nor while kept at any almshouse, or other asylum, at public expense; nor while confined in any public prison.

Sec. 5. No idiot or insane person, or person convicted of any infamous crime, shall be entitled to the privileges of an elector.

Sec. 6. All elections by the people shall be by ballot.

ARTICLE III.

Distribution of Powers.

The powers of the Government of the State of California shall be divided into three separate departments: the Legislative, the Executive, and Judicial; and no person charged with the exercise of powers properly belonging to one of these departments, shall exercise any functions appertaining to either of the others, except in the cases hereinafter expressly directed or permitted.

ARTICLE IV.

Legislative Department.

Sec. 1. The Legislative power of this State shall be vested in a Senate and Assembly, which shall be designated the Legislature of the State of California; and the enacting clause of every law shall be as follows: "The people of the State of California, represented in Senate and Assembly, do enact as follows."

Sec. 2. The sessions of the Legislature shall be annual, and shall commence on the first Monday of January, next ensuing the election of its members, unless the Governor of the State shall, in the interim, convene the Legislature by proclamation.

Sec. 3. The members of the Assembly shall be chosen annually, by the qualified electors of their respective districts, on the Tuesday next after the first Monday in November, unless otherwise ordered by the Legislature, and their term of office shall be one year.

Sec. 4. Senators and Members of Assembly shall be duly qualified electors in the respective counties and districts which they represent.

Sec. 5. Senators shall be chosen for the term of two years, at the same time and places as Members of Assembly; and no person shall be a member of the Senate or Assembly, who has not been a citizen and inhabitant of the State one year, and of the country or district for which he shall be chosens six months next beforo his election.

Sec. 6. The number of Senators shall not be less than one-third, nor more than one-half, of that of the Members of Assembly; and at the first session of the Legislature after this Constitution takes effect, the Senators shall be divided by lot as equally as may be, into two classes; the seats of the Senators of the first class shall be vacated at the expiration of the first year, so that one-half shall be chosen annually.

Sec. 7. When the number of Senators is increased, they shall be apportioned by lot, so as to keep the two classes as nearly equal in number as possible.

Sec. 8. Each house shall choose its own officers and judge of the qualifications, elections, and returns of its own members.

Sec. 9. A majority of each house shall constitute a quorum to do business; but a smaller number may adjourn from day to day, and may compel the attendance of absent members, in such manner, and under such penalties, as each house may provide.

Sec. 10. Each house shall determine the rules of its own proceedings, and may, with the concurrence of two thirds of all the members elected, expel a member.

Sec. 11. Each house shall keep a journal of its own proceedings, and publish the same; and the yeas and nays of the members of either house, on any question, shall at the desire of any three members present be entered on the journal.

Sec. 12. Members of the Legislature shall, in all cases except treason, felony, and breach of the peace, be privileged from arrest, and they shall not be subject to any civil process during the session of the Legislature, nor for fifteen days next before the commencement and after the termination of each session.

Sec. 13. When vacancies occur in either house, the Governor, or the person exercising the functions of the Governor, shall issue writs of election to fill such vacancies.

Sec. 14. The doors of each house shall be open, except on such occasions as, in the opinion of the House, may require secrecy.

Sec. 15. Neither house shall, without the consent of the other, adjourn for more than three days, nor to any other place than that in which they may be sitting.

Sec. 16. Any bill may originate in either house of the Legislature, and all bills passed by one house may be amended in the other.

Sec. 17. Every bill which may have passed the Legislature, shall, before it becomes a law, be presented to the Governor. If he approve it, he shall sign it; but if not, he shall return it, with his objections, to the house in which it originated, which shall enter the same upon the journal, and proceed to reconsider it. If, after such reconsideration, it again pass both houses, by yeas and nays, by a majority of two-thirds of the members of each house present, it shall become a law, notwithstanding the Governor's objections. If any bill shall not be returned within ten days after it shall have been presented to him, (Sunday excepted,) the same shall be a law, in like manner as if he had signed it, unless the Legislature, by adjournment, prevent such return.

Sec. 18. The Assembly shall have the sole power of impeachment; and all impeachments shall be tried by the Senate. When sitting for that purpose, the Senators shall be upon oath or affirmation; and no person shall be convicted, without the concurrence of two-thirds of the members present.

Sec. 19. The Governor, Lieutenant Governor, Secretary of State, Comptroller, Treasurer, Attorney General, Surveyor General, Justices of the Supreme Court and Judges of the District Courts, shall be liable to impeachment for any misdemeanor in office; but judgment in such cases shall extend only to removal from office, and disqualification to hold any office of honor, trust or profit, under the State; but the party convicted, or acquitted, shall nevertheless, be liable to indictment, trial, and punishment, according to law. All other civil officers shall be tried, for misdemeanors in office, in such manner as the Legislature may provide.

Sec. 20. No Senator, or member of Assembly, shall, during the term for which he shall have been elected, be appointed to any civil office of profit, under this State, which shall have been created, or the emoluments of which shall have been increased, during such term, except such office as may be filled by elections by the people.

Sec. 21. No person holding any lucrative office under the United States, or any other power, shall be eligible to any civil office of profit, under this State: provided, that officers in the militia, to which there is attached no annual salary, or local officers and postmasters whose compensation does not exceed five hundred dollars per annum, shall not be deemed lucrative.

Sec. 22. No person who shall be convicted of the embezzlement, or defalcation of the public funds of this State, shall ever be eligible to any office of honor, trust, or profit under this State; and the Legislature shall, as soon as practicable, pass a law providing for the punishment of such embezzlement, or defalcation, as a felony.

Sec. 23. No money shall be drawn from the treasury but in consequence of appropriations made by law. An accurate statement of the receipts and expenditures of the public moneys, shall be attached to and published with the laws at every regular session of the Legislature.

Sec. 24. The members of the Legislature shall receive for their services, a compensation to be fixed by law, and paid out of the public treasury; but no increase of the compensation shall take effect during the term for which the members of either house shall have been elected.

Sec. 25. Every law enacted by the Legislature shall embrace but one object, and that shall be expressed in the title; and no law shall be revised, or amended, by reference to its title; but in such case, the act revised, or section amended shall be re-enacted and published at length.

Sec. 26. No divorce shall be granted by the Legislature.

Sec. 27. No lottery shall be authorized by this State, nor shall the sale of lottery tickets be allowed.

Sec. 28. The enumeration of the inhabitants of this State shall be taken, under the direction of the Legislature, in the year one thousand eight hundred and fifty-two, and one thousand eight hundred and fifty-five, and at the end of every ten years thereafter; and these enumerations, together with the census that may be taken, under the direction of the Congress of the United States, in the year one thousand eight hundred and fifty, and every subsequent ten years, shall serve as the basis of representation in both houses of the Legislature.

Sec. 29. The number of Senators and members of Assembly, shall, at the first session of the Legislature, holden after the enumerations herein provided for are made, be fixed by the Legislature, and apportioned among the several counties and districts to be established by law, according to the number of white inhabitants. The number of members of Assembly shall not be less than twenty-four, nor more than thirty-six, until the number of inhabitants within this State, shall amount to one hundred thousand; and after that period, at such ratio that the whole number of members of Assembly shall never be less than thirty, nor more than eighty.

Sec. 30. When a congressional, senatorial, or assembly district, shall be composed of two or more counties, it shall not be separated by any county belonging to another district; and no county shall be divided, in forming a congressional, senatorial, or assembly district.

Sec. 31. Corporations may be formed under general laws, but shall not be created by special act, except for municipal purposes. All general laws and special acts passed pursuant to this section may be altered from time to time, or repealed.

Sec. 32. Dues from corporations shall be secured by such individual liability of the corporators, and other means, as may be prescribed by law.

Sec. 33. The term corporations as used in this article shall be construed to include all associations and joint-stock companies, having any of the powers or privileges of corporations not possessed by individuals or partnerships. And all corporations shall have the right to sue, and shall be subject to be sued, in all courts, in like cases as natural persons.

Sec. 34. The Legislature shall have no power to pass any act granting any charter for banking purposes; but associations may be formed, under general laws, for the deposite of gold and silver, but no such association shall make, issue, or put in circulation, any bill, check, ticket, certificate, promissory note, or other paper, or the paper of any bank, to circulate as money.

Sec. 35. The Legislature of this State shall prohibit, by law, any person or persons, association, company, or corporation, from exercising the privileges of banking, or creating paper to circulate as money.

Sec. 36. Each stockholder of a corporation, or joint-stock association, shall be individually and personally liable for his proportion of all its debts and liabilities.

Sec. 37. It shall be the duty of the Legislature to provide for the organization of cities and incorporated villages, and to restrict their power of taxation, assessment, borrowing money, contracting debts, and loaning their credit, so as to prevent abuses in assessments and in contracting debts by such municipal corporations.

Sec. 38. In all elections by the Legislature, the members thereof shall vote *viva voce*, and the votes shall be entered on the journal.

ARTICLE V.

Executive Department.

Sec. 1. The supreme executive power of this State shall be vested in a Chief Magistrate, who shall be styled the Governor of the State of California.

Sec. 2. The Governor shall be elected by the qualified electors, at the time and places of voting for members of Assembly, and shall hold his office two years from the time of his installation, and until his successor shall be qualified.

Sec. 3. No person shall be eligible to the office of Governor, (except at the first election) who has not been a citizen of the United States and a resident of this State two years next preceding the election, and attained the age of twenty-five years at the time of said election.

Sec. 4. The returns of every election for Governor shall be sealed up and transmitted to the seat of government, directed to the speaker of the Assembly, who shall, during the first week of the session, open and publish them in presence of both houses of the Legislature. The person having the highest number of votes shall be Governor; but in case any two or more have an equal and the highest number of votes, the Legislature shall, by joint vote of both houses, choose one of said persons, so having an equal and the highest number of votes, for Governor.

Sec. 5. The Governor shall be commander-in-chief of the militia, the army and navy of this State.

Sec. 6. He shall transact all executive business with the officers of Government, civil and military, and may require information in writing from the officers of the executive department, upon any subject relating to the duties of their respective offices.

Sec. 7. He shall see that the laws are faithfully executed.

Sec. 8. When any office shall, from any cause become vacant, and no mode is provided by the Constitution and laws for filling such vacancy, the Governor shall have power to fill such vacancy by granting a commission, which shall expire at the end of the next session of the Legislature, or at the next election by the people.

Sec. 9. He may, on extraordinary occasions, convene the Legislature by proclamation, and shall state to both houses, when assembled, the purpose for which they shall have been convened.

Sec. 10. He shall communicate by message to the Legislature, at every session, the condition of the State, and recommend such matters as he shall deem expedient.

Sec. 11. In case of a disagreement between the two houses, with respect to the time of adjournment, the Governor shall have power to adjourn the Legislature to such time as he may think proper; provided, it be not beyond the time fixed for the meeting of the next Legislature.

Sec. 12. No person shall, while holding any office under the United States, or this State, exercise the office of Governor, except as hereinafter expressly provided.

Sec. 13. The Governor shall have the power to grant reprieves and pardons after conviction, for all offences except treason and cases of impeachment, upon such conditions, and with such restrictions and limitations, as he may think proper, subject to such regulations as may be provided by law relative to the manner of applying for pardons. Upon conviction for treason he shall have the power to suspend the execution of the sentence until the case shall be reported to the Legislature at its next meeting, when the Legislature shall either pardon, direct the execution of the sentence, or grant a further reprieve. He shall communicate to the Legislature, at the beginning of every session, every case of reprieve or pardon granted, stating the name of the convict, the crime of which he was convicted, the sentence, and its date, and the date of the pardon or reprieve.

Sec. 14. There shall be a seal of this State, which shall be kept by the Governor, and used by him officially, and shall be called "The great seal of the State of California."

Sec. 15. All grants and commissions shall be in the name and by the authority of the people of the State of California, sealed with the great seal of the State, signed by the Governor and countersigned by the Secretary of State.

Sec. 16. A Lieutenant Governor shall be elected at the same time and places, and in the same manner as the Governor; and his term of office, and his qualifications of elegibility shall also be the same. He shall be President of the Senate, but shall only have a casting vote therein. If, during a vacancy of the office of Governor, the Lieutenant Governor shall be impeached, displaced, resign, die or become incapable of performing the duties of his offiee, or be absent from the State, the President of the Senate shall act as Governor, until the vacancy be filled, or the disability shall cease.

Sec. 17. In case of the impeachment of the Governor, or his removal from office, death, inability to discharge the powers and duties of the said office, resignation, or absence from the State, the powers and duties of the office shall devolve upon the Lieutenant Governor for the residue of the term, or until the disability shall cease. But when the Governor shall, with the consent of the Legislature, be out of the State in time of war, at the head of any military force thereof, he shall continue commander-in-chief of the military force of the State.

Sec. 18. A Secretary of State, a Comptroller, a Treasurer, an Attorney General, and Surveyor General, shall be chosen in the manner provided in this Constitution; and the term of office, and elegibility of each shall be the same as are prescribed for the Governor and Lieutenant Governor.

Sec. 19. The Secretary of State shall be appointed by the Governor, by and with the advice and consent of the Senate. He shall keep a fair record of the official acts of the legislative and executive departments of the Government, and shall, when required, lay the same, and all matters relative thereto, before either branch of the Legislature; and shall perform such other duties as shall be assigned him by law.

Sec. 20. The Comptroller, Treasurer, Attorney General, and Surveyor General, shall be chosen by joint vote of the two houses of the Legislature, at their first session under this Constitution, and thereafter shall be elected at the same time and places, and in the same manner as the Governor and Lieutenant Governor.

Sec. 21. The Governor, Lieutenant Governor, Secretary of State, Comptroller, Treasurer, Attorney General, and Surveyor General, shall each at stated times during their continuance in office, receive for their services a compensation, which shall not be increased or diminished during the term for which they shall have been elected; but neither of these officers shall receive for his own use any fees for the performance of his official duties.

ARTICLE VI.

Judicial Department.

Sec. 1. The judicial power of this State shall be vested in a Supreme Court, in District Courts, in County Courts, and in Justices of the Peace. The Legislature may also establish such municipal and other inferior courts as may be deemed necessary.

Sec. 2. The Supreme Court shall consist of a Chief Justice and two Associate Justices, any two of whom shall constitute a quorum.

Sec. 3. The Justices of the Supreme Court shall be elected at the general election, by the qualified electors of the State, and shall hold their office for the term of six years from the first day of January next after their election; provided that the Legislature shall, at its first meeting, elect a Chief Justice and two Associate Justices of the Supreme Court, by joint vote of both houses, and so classify them that one shall go out of office every two years. After the first election the senior Justice in commission shall be the Chief Justice.

Sec. 4. The Supreme Court shall have appellate jurisdiction in all cases when the matter in dispute exceeds two hundred dollars, when the legality of any tax, toll, or impost or municipal fine is in question, and in all criminal cases amounting to felony or questions of law alone. And the said Court, and each of the Justices thereof, as well as all district and county judges, shall have power to issue writs of *habeas corpus* at the instance of any person held in actual custody. They shall also have power to issue all other writs and process necessary to the exercise of their appellate jurisdiction, and shall be conservators of the peace throughout the State.

Sec. 5. The State shall be divided by the first Legislature into a convenient number of districts subject to such alteration from time to time as the public good may require, for each of which a district judge shall be appointed by the joint vote of the Legislature, at its first meeting, who shall hold his office for two years from the first day of January next after his election; after which, said judges shall be elected by the qualified electors of their respective districts, at the general election, and shall hold their office for the term of six years.

Sec. 6. The District Courts shall have original jurisdiction, in law and equity, in all civil cases where the amount in dispute exceeds two hundred dollars, exclusive of interest. In all criminal cases not otherwise provided for, and in all issues of fact joined in the probate courts, their jurisdiction shall be unlimited.

Sec. 7. The Legislature shall provide for the election, by the people, of a Clerk of the Supreme Court, and County Clerks, District Attorneys, Sheriffs, Coroners, and other necessary officers; and shall fix by law their duties and compensation. County Clerks shall be, *ex officio*, clerks of the District Courts in and for their respective counties.

Sec. 8. There shall be elected in each of the organized counties of this State, one County Judge, who shall hold his office for four years. He shall hold the County Court, and perform the duties of Surrogate, or Probate Judge. The County Judge, with two Justices of the Peace, to be designated according to law, shall hold courts of sessions, with such criminal jurisdiction as the Legislature shall prescribe, and he shall perform such other duties as shall be required by law.

Sec. 9. The County Courts shall have such jurisdiction, in cases arising in Justices Courts, and in special cases, as the Legislature may prescribe, but shall have no original civil jurisdiction, except in such special cases.

Sec. 10. The times and places of holding the terms of the Supreme Court, and the general and special terms of the District Courts within the several districts, shall be provided for by law.

Sec. 11. No judicial officer, except a Justice of the Peace, shall receive, to his own use, any fees or perquisites of office.

Sec. 12. The Legislature shall provide for the speedy publication of all statute laws, and of such judicial decisions as it may deem expedient; and all laws and judicial decisions shall be free for publication by any person.

Sec. 13. Tribunals for conciliation may be established, with such powers and duties as may be prescribed by law; but such tribunals shall have no power to render judgment to be obligatory on the parties, except they voluntarily submit their matters in difference, and agree to abide the judgment, or assent thereto in the presence of such tribunal, in such cases as shall be prescribed by law.

Sec. 14. The Legislature shall determine the number of Justices of the Peace, to be elected in each county, city, town, and incorporated village of the State, and fix by law their powers, duties, and responsibilities. It shall also determine in what cases appeals may be made from Justices' Courts to the County Court.

Sec. 15. The Justices of the Supreme Court, and Judges of the District Court, shall severally, at stated times during their continuance in office, receive for their services a compensation, to be paid out of the treasury, which shall not be increased or diminished during the term for which they shall have been elected. The county Judges shall also severally, at stated times, receive for their services a compensation to be paid out of the county treasury of their respective counties, which shall not be increased or diminished during the term for which they shall have been elected.

Sec. 16. The Justices of the Supreme Court and District Judges shall be ineligible to any other office, during the term for which they shall have been elected.

Sec. 17. Judges shall not charge juries with respect to matters of fact, but may state the testimony and declare the law.

Sec. 18. The style of all process shall be "The People of the State of California;" all the prosecutions shall be conducted in the name and by the authority of the same.

ARTICLE VII.

Militia.

Sec. 1. The Legislature shall provide by law for organising and disciplining the militia, in such manner as they shall deem expedient, not incompatible with the Constitution and laws of the United States.

Sec. 2. Officers of the militia shall be elected, or appointed, in such a manner as the Legislature shall from time to time direct, and shall be commissioned by the governor.

Sec. 3. The governor shall have power to call forth the militia, to execute the laws of the State, to suppress insurrections, and repel invasions.

ARTICLE VIII.

State Debts.

The Legislature shall not in any manner create any debt or debts, liability or liabilities, which shall singly, or in the aggregate, with any previous debts or liabilities, exceed the sum of three hundred thousand dollars, except in case of war, to repel invasion or suppress insurrection, unless the same shall be authorised by some law for some single object or work, to be distinctly specified therein, which law shall provide ways and means, exclusive of loans, for the payment of the interest of such debt or liability, as it falls due, and also pay and discharge the principal of such debt or liability within twenty years from the time of the contracting thereof, and shall be irrepealable until the principal and interest thereon shall be paid and discharged; but no such law shall take effect until, at a general election, it shall have been submitted to the people, and have received a majority of all the votes cast for and against it at such election; and all money raised by authority of such law, shall be applied only to the specific object therein stated, or to the payment of the debt thereby created; and such law shall be published in at least one newspaper in each judicial district, if one be published therein, throughout the State, for three months next preceding the election at which it is submitted to the people.

ARTICLE IX.

Education.

Sec. 1. The Legislature shall provide for the election, by the people, of a superintendent of public instruction, who shall hold his office for three years, and whose duties shall be prescribed by law, and who shall receive such compensation as the Legislature may direct.

Sec. 2. The Legislature shall encourage, by all suitable means, the promotion of intellectual, scientific, moral and agricultural improvement. The proceeds of all land that may be granted by the United States to this State for the support of schools, which may be sold or disposed of, and the five hundred thousand acres of land granted to the new States, under an act of Congress distributing the proceeds of the public lands among the several States of the Union, approved A. D. 1841; and all estates of deceased persons who may have died without leaving a will, or heir, and also such per cent. as may be granted by Congress on the sale of lands in this State, shall be and remain a perpetual fund, the interest of which, together with all the rents of the unsold lands, and such other means as the Legislature may provide, shall be inviolably appropriated to the support of common schools throughout the State.

Sec. 3. The Legislature shall provide for a system of common schools, by which a school shall be kept up and supported in each district at least three months in every year, and any school neglecting to keep and support such a school, may be deprived of its proportion of the interest of the public fund during such neglect.

Sec. 4. The Legislature shall take measures for the protection, improvement, or other disposition of such lands as have been, or may hereafter be reserved or granted by the United States, or any person or persons to the State for the use of a University; and the funds accruing from the rents or sale of such lands, or from any other source for the purpose aforesaid, shall be and remain a permanent fund, the interest of which shall be applied to the support of said University, with such branches as the public convenienee may demand, for the promotion of literature, the arts and sciences, as may be authorised by the terms of such grant. And it shall be the duty of the Legislature, as soon as may be, to provide effectual means for the improvement and permanent security of the funds of said University.

ARTICLE X.

Mode of Amending and Revising the Constitution.

Sec. 1. Any amendment, or amendments to this Constitution, may be proposed in the Senate or Assembly; and if the same shall be agreed to by a majority of the members elected to each of the two houses, such proposed amendment or amendments, shall be entered on their journals, with the yeas and nays taken thereon, and referred to the Legislature then next to be chosen, and shall be published for three months next preceding the time of making such choice. And if, in the Legislature next chosen as aforesaid, such proposed amendment or amendments, shall be agreed to by a majority of all the members elected to each house, then it shall be the duty of the Legislature to submit such proposed amendment or amendments to the people, in such manner, and at such time as the Legislature shall prescribe; and if the people shall approve and ratify such amendment or amendments, by a majority of the electors qualified to vote for members of the Legislature, voting thereon, such amendment or amendments, shall become part of the Constitution.

Sec. 2. And if, at any time two-thirds of the Senate and Assembly shall think it necessary to revise and change this entire Constitution, they shall recommend to the electors, at the next election for members of the Legislature, to vote for or against the convention; and if it shall appear that a majority of the electors voting at such election have voted in favor of calling a convention, the Legislature shall, at its next session, provide by law for calling a convention, to be holden within six months after the passage of such law; and such convention shall consist of a number of members not less than that of both branches of the Legislature.

ARTICLE XI.

Miscellaneous Provisions.

Sec. 1. The first session of the Legislature shall be held at the Pueblo de San Jose; which place shall be the permanent seat of government, until removed by law: Provided, however, that that two-thirds of all the members elected to each house of the Legislature shall concur in the passage of such law.

Sec. 2. Any citizen of this State who shall, after the adoption of this Constitution, fight a duel with deadly weapons, or send, or accept a challenge to fight a duel with deadly weapons, either within this State or out of it; or who shall act as second, or knowingly aid or assist in any manner those thus offending, shall not be allowed to hold any office of profit, or to enjoy the right of suffrage under this Constitution.

Sec. 3. Members of the Legislature, and all officers, executive and judicial, except such inferior officers as may be by law exempted, shall, before they enter on the duties of their respective offices, take and subscribe the following oath or affirmation:

"I do solemnly swear (or affirm, as the case may be,) that I will support the Constitution of the United States, and the Constitution of the State of California, and that I will faithfully discharge the duties of the office of ———, according to the best of my ability."

And no other oath, declaration, or test, shall be required as a qualification for any office or public trust.

Sec. 4. The Legislature shall establish a system of county and town governments, which shall be as nearly uniform as practicable, throughout the State.

Sec. 5. The Legislature shall have power to provide for the election of a board of supervisors in each county; and these supervisors shall jointly and individually perform such duties as may be prescribed by law.

Sec. 6. All officers whose election or appointment is not provided for by this Constitution, and all officers whose offices may hereafter be created by law, shall be elected by the people, or appointed as the Legislature may direct.

Sec. 7. When the duration of any office is not provided for by this Constitution, it may be declared by law, and if not so declared, such office shall be held during the pleasure of the authority making the appointment; nor shall the duration of any office not fixed by this Constitution ever exceed four years.

Sec. 8. The fiscal year shall commence on the 1st day of July.

Sec. 9. Each county, town, city, and incorporated village, shall make provision for the support of its own officers, subject to such restrictions and regulations as the Legislature may prescribe.

Sec. 10. The credit of the State shall not, in any manner, be given or loaned to or in aid of any individual, association, or corporation; nor shall the State directly or indirectly become a stockholder in any association or corporation.

Sec. 11. Suits may be brought against the State in such manner, and in such courts, as shall be directed by law.

Sec. 12. No contract of marriage, if otherwise duly made, shall be invalidated for want of conformity to the requirements of any religious sect.

Sec. 13. Taxation shall be equal and uniform throughout the State. All property in this State shall be taxed in proportion to its value, to be ascertained as directed by law; but assessors and collectors of town, county, and State taxes, shall be elected by the qualified electors of the district, county, or town, in which the property taxed for State, county, or town purposes is situated.

Sec. 14. All property, both real and personal, of the wife, owned or claimed by marriage, and that acquired afterwards by gift, devise, or descent, shall be her separate property; and laws shall be passed more clearly defining the rights of the wife, in relation as well to her separate property, as to that held in common with her husband. Laws shall also be passed providing for the registration of the wife's separate property.

Sec. 15. The Legislature shall protect by law, from forced sale, a certain portion of the homestead and other property of all heads of families.

Sec. 16. No perpetuities shall be allowed, except for eleemosynary purposes.

Sec. 17. Every person shall be disqualified from holding any office of profit in this State, who shall have been convicted of having given, or offered a bribe, to procure his election or appointment.

Sec. 18. Laws shall be made to exclude from office, serving on juries, and from the right of suffrage, those who shall hereafter be convicted of bribery, perjury, forgery, or other high crimes. The privilege of free suffrage shall be supported by laws regulating elections, and prohibiting, under adequate penalties, all undue influence thereon from power, bribery, tumult, or other improper practice.

Sec. 19. Absence from this State on business of the State, or of the United States, shall not affect the question of residence of any person.

Sec. 20. A plurality of the votes given at an election shall constitute a choice, where not otherwise directed in this Constitution.

Sec. 21. All laws, decrees, regulations, and provisions, which from their nature require publication, shall be published in English and Spanish.

ARTICLE XII.

Boundary.

The Boundary of the State of California shall be as follows:

Commencing at the point of intersection of 42d degree of north latitude with the 120th degree of longitude west from Greenwich, and running south on the line of said 120th degree of west longitude until it intersects the 39th degree of north latitude; thence running in a straight line in a south easterly direction to the River Colorado, at a point where it intersects the 35th degree of north latitude; thence down the middle of the channel of said river, to the boundary line between the United States and Mexico, as established by the Treaty of May 30th, 1848; thence running west and along said boundary line to the Pacific Ocean, and extending therein three English miles; thence running in a northwesterly direction, and following the direction of the Pacific Coast to the 42d degree of north latitude, thence on the line of said 42d degree of north latitude to the place of beginning. Also all the islands, harbors, and bays, along and adjacent to the Pacific Coast.

SCHEDULE.

Sec. 1. All rights, prosecutions, claims and contracts, as well of individuals as of bodies corporate, and all laws in force at the time of the adoption of this Constitution, and not inconsistent therewith, until altered or repealed by the Legislature, shall continue as if the same had not been adopted.

Sec. 2. The Legislature shall provide for the removal of all causes which may be pending when this Constitution goes into effect, to courts created by the same.

Sec. 3. In order that no inconvenience may result to the public service, from the taking effect of this Constitution, no office shall be superceded thereby, nor the laws relative to the duties of the several officers be changed, until the entering into office of the new officers to be appointed under this Constitution.

Sec. 4. The provisions of this Constitution corncerning the term of residence necessary to enable persons to hold certain offices therein mentioned, shall not be held to apply to officers chosen by the people at the first election, or by the Legislature at its first session.

Sec. 5. Every citizen of California, declared a legal voter by this Constitution, and every citizen of the United States, a resident of this State on the day of election, shall be entitled to vote at the first general election under this Constitution, and on the question of the adoption thereof.

Sec. 6. This Constitution shall be submitted to the people, for their ratification or rejection, at the general election to be held on Tuesday, the thirteenth day of November next. The Executive of the existing Government of California is hereby requested to issue a proclamation to the people, directing the Prefects of the several districts, or in case of vacancy, the Sub-Prefects, or senior Judge of first Instance, to cause such election to be held, the day aforesaid, in the respective districts. The election shall be conducted in the manner which was prescribed for the election of Delegates to this Convention, except that the Prefect, Sub-Prefect, or senior Judge of first Instance ordering such election in each district, shall have power to designate any additional number of places for opening the polls, and that, in every place of holding the election, a regular poll-list shall be kept by the judges and inspectors of election. It shall also be the duty of these judges and inspectors of election, on the day aforesaid, to receive the votes of the electors qualified to vote at such election. Each voter shall express his opinion, by depositing in the ballot-box a ticket, whereon shall be written, or printed "For the Constitution," or "Against the Constitution," or some such words as will distinctly convey the intention of the voter. These Judges and Inspectors shall also receive the votes for the several officers to be voted for at the said election as herein provided. At the close of the election, the judges and Inspectors shall carefully count each ballot, and forthwith make duplicate returns thereof to the Prefect, Sub-Prefect, or senior Judge of first Instance, as the case may be, of their respective districts; and said Prefect, Sub-Prefect, or senior Judge of first Instance shall trsnsmit one of the same, by the most safe and rapid conveyance, to the Secretary of State. Upon the receipt of said returns, or on the tenth day of December next, if the returns be not sooner received, it shall be the duty of a board of canvassers, to consist of the Secretary of State, one of the Judges of the Superior Court, the Prefect, Judge of first Instance, and an Alcalde of the District of Monterey, or any three of the aforementioned officers, in the presence of all who shall choose to attend, to compare the votes given at said election, and to immediately publish an abstract of the same in one or more of the newspapers of California. And the Executive will also immediately after ascertaining that the Constitution has been ratified by the people, make proclation of the fact; and thenceforth this Constitution shall be ordained and established as the Constitution of California.

Sec. 7. If this Constitution shall be ratified by the people of California, the Executive of the existing government is hereby requested immediately after, the same shall be ascertained, in the manner herein directed, to cause a fair copy thereof to be forwarded to the President of the United States, in order that he may lay it before the Congress of the United States.

Sec. 8. At the general election aforesaid, viz: the thirteenth day of November next, there shall be elected a Governor, Lieutenant-Governor, members of the Legislature, and also two Members of Congress.

Sec. 9. If this Constitution shall be ratified by the People of California, the Legislature shall assemble at the seat of government on the fifteenth day of December next, and in order to complete the organization of that body, the Senate shall elect a President *pro tempore*, until the Lieutenant-Governor shall be installed into office.

Sec. 10. On the organization of the Legislature, it shall be the duty of the Secretary of State, to lay before each house, a copy of the abstract made by the board of canvassers, and if called for, the original returns of election, in order that each house may judge of the correctness of the report of said board of canvassers.

Sec. 11. The Legislature, at its first session, shall elect such officers as may be ordereded by this Constitution, to be elected by that body, and within four days after it organization, proceed to elect two Senators to the Congress of the United States. But no law passed by this Legislature shall take effect until signed by the Governor after his installation into office.

Sec. 12. The Senators and Representatives to the Congress of the United States, elected by the Legislature and People of California, as herein directed, shall be furnished with certified copies of this Constitution, when ratified, which they shall lay before the Congress of the United States, requesting, in the name of the People of California, the admission of the State of California into the American Union.

Sec. 13. All officers of this State, other than members of the Legislature, shall be installed into office on the fifteenth day of December next, or as soon thereafter as practicable.

Sec. 14. Until the Legislature shall divide the State into counties, and senatorial and assembly districts, as directed by this Constitution, the following shall be the apportionment of the two houses of the Legislature, viz: the districts of San Diego and Los Angelos, shall jointly elect two senators; the districts of Santa Barbara and San Luis Obispo, shall jointly elect one senator; the district of Monterey, one senator; the district of San Jose, one senator; the district of San Francisco, two senators; the district of Sonoma, one senator; the district of Sacramento, four senators; and the district of San Joaquin, four senators. And the district of San Diego shall elect one member of assembly; the district of Los Angelos, two members of assembly; the district of Santa Barbara, two members of assembly; the district of San Luis Obispo, one member of assembly; the district of Monterey, two members of assembly; the district of San Jose, three members of assembly; the district of San Francisco, five members of assembly; the district of Sonoma, two members of assembly; the district of Sacramento, nine members of assembly; and the district of San Joaquin nine members of assembly.

Sec. 15. Until the Legislature shall otherwise direct, in accordance with the provisions of this Constitution, the salary of the Governor shall be ten thousand dollars per annum; and the salary of the Lieutenant-Governor shall be double the pay of a State senator; and the pay of members of the Legislature shall be sixteen dollars per diem, while in attendance, and sixteen dollars for every twenty miles travel by the usual route from their residences, to the place of holding the session of the Legislature, and in returning therefrom. And the Legislature shall fix the salaries of all officers, other than those elected by the people, at the first election.

Sec. 16. The limitation of the powers of the Legislature, contained in article 8th of this Constitution, shall not extend to the first Legislature elected under the same, which is hereby authorised to negotiate for such amount as may be necessary to pay the expenses of the State Government.

R. SEMPLE,
President of the Convention, and Delegate from Benicia.

Wm. G. Marcy, *Secretary.*

J. Aram,
C. T. Botts,
E. Brown,
J. A. Carrillo,
J. M. Covarrubias,
E. O. Crosby,
P. De la Guerra,
L. Dent,
M. Dominguez,
K. H. Dimmick,
A. J. Ellis,
S. C. Foster,
E. Gilbert,
W. M. Gwin,
H. W. Halleck,
Julian Hanks,
L. W. Hastings,
Henry Hill,
J. Hobson,
J. McH. Hollinsworth,
J. D. Hoppe,
J. M. Jones,
T. O. Larkin,
Francis J. Lippitt,
B. S. Lippincott,
M. M. McCarver,
John McDougal,
B. F. Moore,
Myron Norton,
P. Ord,
Miguel Pedrorena,
A. M. Pico,
R. M. Price,
Hugo Reid,
Jacinto Rodriguez,
Pedro Sansevaine,
W. E. Shannon,
W. S. Sherwood,
J. R. Snyder,
A. Stearns,
W. M. Steuart,
J. A. Sutter,
Henry A. Tefft,
S. L. Vermule,
M. G. Vallejo,
J. Walker,
O. M. Wozencraft.

MEMORIAL.

To the Honorable the Senate and House of Representatives of the United States of America in Congress assembled:

The undersigned, Senators and Representatives elect from the State of California, have the honor, in pursuance of a requirement in the Constitution recently adopted by her people for her government as a State, to lay before your honorable bodies certified copies of said Constitution, together with their credentials, and to request "in the name of the people of California, the admission of the State of California into the American Union."

In performing this duty, the undersigned deem it but just to state that they have learned with astonishment and sincere regret, since their arrival in the City of Washington, of the existence of an organized, respectable, and talented opposition to the admission of the new State which they have the distinguished honor to represent. This opposition is so unexpected, so important in numbers and ability, and so decided in its sectional character, that they feel they should do injustice to their constituents, to the cause of good government, and to the progressive advance of freedom and civilization, did they not at least attempt an answer to the many arguments urged against the admission of California.

The undersigned, therefore, fully aware that much ignorance, misapprehension, and misconception exists in the public mind of the Atlantic States relative to their country, its citizens, and the proceedings by which a State Government has been recently formed there, and deeply sorrowful that false charges should have been made against the character, intelligence, and virtue of their constituents, have deemed it obligatory upon them, in presenting in a formal manner the request of the State of California for admission into the American Union, that they should, by a narration of facts, at once and forever silence those who have disregarded the obligations of courtesy and all the rules of justice, by ungenerous insinuations, unfair deductions, false premises, and unwarranted conclusions. They believe that in so doing they will carry out the wishes of those who have commissioned them, and contribute to the true history of this important political era; while they ardently desire and hope that they may thereby be enabled to exert a happy influence in allaying that intense excitement which now menaces the perpetuity of the Republic, and all the dearest hopes of freedom.

In pursuance of this determination, the undersigned have thought it proper to present, as briefly as possible, an outline of the history of the country, from its conquest by the American forces to the adoption of her present Constitution and the erection of a State Government. In order to do this satisfactorily, it is not believed to be necessary to dwell at length upon the details of the early history, but simply to state that the first emigration of Americans into California in any considerable numbers, occurred during the summer and fall of the year 1845. This emigration, which is believed not to have exceeded 500 persons, constituted the basis from which sprung the train of causes which led to the ultimate subjugation of the country. The particulars of those events are presumed to be familiar to the members of each of your honorable bodies, and generally understood by the public at large, and the undersigned therefore pass over the history of the revolutionary and military operations which resulted in the establishment of Col. Richard B. Mason as the military, and *ex officio* civil, Governor of the Department of Upper California, on the 31st day of May, 1847.

At that time the American forces held possession of the whole of what was then denominated Upper California, and were posted at different points, in small detachments, from Sutter's Fort in the north to the town of San Diego in the south. The Pacific squadron of the Navy of the United States, under the command of Commodore Shubrick, was then upon the coast, and its vessels were at anchor in the different harbors of the country. The country was quiet, and the population orderly, industrious, intelligent, and enterprising. From the time that the united forces of American emigrant volunteers under Col. Fremont, and the United States naval forces under Commodore Sloat had raised the American standard throughout the country, the supreme authorities had collected in all the ports of California a revenue from imports. This, with other slight cases of individual severity and infringement by the military and naval commandants during the war, upon what was regarded by the American emigrants as the inherent rights of the citizen, together with a natural jealousy of military rule, which is believed to be a national characteristic, could not fail to make the military authority, which had now devolved upon Col. Mason, a source of suspicion, disagreement, and discontent. This was more particularly the case in regard to the American inhabitants, who had now become quite numerous by continued arrivals of emigrants, both by sea and land; but the feeling was also participated in, to a great extent, by the native citizens of the country, who were further influenced by the chagrin, hatred, and uncertainty which is sure to fill the breasts of a subjugated but courageous people.

Even at this early day the subject of the establishment of a *Civil Territorial Government* had found advocates; but as the war was not yet ended, and as the country could not be regarded in any other light than that of a military conquest, and as such, subject to the government of the military power, and as the majority of the people felt that self-reliance which convinced them there was little danger of any serious attempt at usurpation on the part of the military authority, the matter was not seriously pressed, though generally approved. Nevertheless, it was becoming daily more and more a pervading sentiment, that the civil government, as then organized under the almost obsolete laws of Mexico, was totally inadequate to the changed circumstances of the country; and, as the undersigned believe, none were more fully convinced of that fact, than the executive officers of that Government. This sentiment finally became general; and the errors and difficulties that every day occurred, from the ignorance of Mexican law, or its inapplicability, induced the Governor to make a compilation and translation of all such Mexican regulations as could be found in the archives of the State Department at Monterey, with such additions as were thought advisable and necessary. These were printed in both the English and Spanish languages; but, unfortunately for the country, they were not quite ready for publication at the time news of peace reached California, and the Governor, therefore, never proclaimed nor issued them.

In the month of October, 1847, the Military Contribution Tariff, promulgated by the then President of the United States, was established in the ports of California. The custom-houses, which theretofore had remained in the hands of citizens who accounted to the Military Governor, or the Commodore of the Pacific Squadron, were now filled by army or navy officers. This tariff was justly but rigorously enforced; and, though its provisions bore so oppressively upon the country as to add slightly to the causes and feeling of discontent, no opposition was manifested. Indeed, during this whole time, although the evils and difficulties under which the country suffered were manifold, we believe no single instance can be found of unlawful or riotous resistance to the constituted authorities.

But the desire for a more congenial government went on steadily increasing in that portion of the country lying around and north of the district of San Francisco. To this feeling the arrival of the overland emigration in the fall of 1847 greatly contributed. In the meantime, the original citizens of California had become in a measure satisfied with their position, and as the conduct of the American officers and citizens was of a courteous and upright character, they gradually became assured that there rights, property, and happiness were not likely to be destroyed by the conquerors. Still, a degree of solicitude and suspicion preyed upon the public mind. An uncertainty seemed to pervade the whole country, exercising a chilling and depressing effect upon its agricultural, commerce, mechanic arts, and general business relations The military government had continued the collection of duties under the military contribution tariff, and as a parsimonious policy of expenditure was maintained, the whole circulating medium of the country was gradually locked up in the military chest. This exerted a paralyzing effect on the industrial and business pursuits of the whole community, and gave rise to complaints that the military power was taxing the people without allowing them a voice in the matter, and that at the same time they failed to give to the country a government in consonance with its wishes or commensurate to its wants; in other words, that after taxing the inhabitants of the country in contravention of all right, they committed the greater injustice of refusing or neglecting to expend the money so obtained in such a manner as would provide a government that would give protection to the citizen and security to his property. California, however, went on steadily increasing in population, wealth, industry and commercial and political importance.

Such was the condition of California in April, 1848. In that month was made the extraordinary discovery of the gold mines, and instantly the whole territory was in a blaze. The towns were deserted by their male population, and a complete cessation of the whole industrial pursuits of the country was the consequence. Commerce, agriculture, mechanical pursuits, professions—all were abandoned for the purpose of gathering the glittering treasures which lay buried in the ravines, the gorges, and the rivers of the Sierra Nevada. The productive industry of the country was annihilated in a day. In some instances the moral perceptions were blunted, and men left their families unprovided, and soldiers deserted their colors. The desire for gold was not regulated by any of the ordinary processes of reasoning, and such was the disastrous effect of the discovery of the precious ore upon the social, business, and political interests of the country, that the high hopes which the far-seeing and patriotic had entertained of the future progress and greatness of California, were dashed at once to the ground. A pall seemed to settle upon the country; and even the bewildered miners wondered as the result.

But the peculiar energy and the utilitarian predisposition of the American character could not long be diverted from its natural and accustomed channels, even by the glitter of gold. Commerce slowly revived, and mechanical and professional pursuits began to assume their wonted importance, as the novelty of gold digging was dispelled by a correct understanding of the difficult and laborious nature of the pursuit. The large emigration which was now pouring into the country from Oregon, Mexico, and the Sandwich Islands, though it added to the number of miners, contributed to the necessities which had made a diversion in favor of the sober pursuits of every day life, and a more healthy and staid condition of public opinion and business ensued.

At about this time (on the 7th of August, 1848) the news of peace between the republics of the United States and Mexico reached the country, and was communicated to the people in a proclamation by Governor Mason. This proclamation, after reciting so much of the treaty as applied to California, stated that the existing laws would remain in force, and the existing officers would administer them as heretofore; and it did not fail to express the confident hope that the Congress of the United States, which was in session at the time of the ratification of the treaty, had already organised a Territorial Government, which might be expected to arrive at any moment. Governor Mason then abolished, in pursuance with treaty stipulations, the military contribution tariff; but not deeming it advisable to abandon the collection of revenue entirely, and yet having no authority either in executive orders, law, or precedent, he declared the revenue laws of the United States in force throughout the Territory, appointed civilians to the post of collector, and received the duties into the military treasury of the department, under the distinctive appellation of the "civil fund of California."

There were those in the country at this time, and they were not few in numbers, who believed that it was the duty of Governor Mason, immediately after the reception of the news of peace, to have called upon the people to elect delegates to a Territorial Convention for the purpose of forming a *Civil Provisional Territorial Government* for California; and that it was his duty, so soon as such form of government was ratified by the people of the Territory, to have delivered up to the appointed agent the powers he possessed as Civil Governor, and left to such appointee of the people the entire discharge of the duties appertaining to a civil Executive. It may be imagined then, that when, instead of doing this, the existing order of things was preserved and the United States revenue laws enforced, that great dissatisfaction ensued. To add to the general discontent, the daily arrival of large importations created so great a demand for coin with which to meet the custom house charges, that gold dust was depreciated so much in value as to be sold as low as seven dollars per ounce, at one time; and finally such became the utter barrenness of the San Francisco money market, that the collector at that port was authorised to receive gold dust on deposit as collateral security for duties, at the rate of ten dollars per ounce. Other difficulties of a perplexing and serious character grew out of this sudden substitution of a new revenue system, by which foreign vessels were denied the privileges which they would have had under the military contribution tariff. But, suffice it to say, that again the public mind was disturbed and excited by taxation without representation, and by that falsely economical policy which continued to take money from the people without law, and yet would not appropriate the funds so obtained to the purpose of securing them a good government.

But the unsettled and unstable order of things which had ensued upon the discovery of the gold mines still existed; and the dissatisfaction and discontent of the people, though quite general, failed, for this reason, to assume an organized or imposing form. The fact that four-fifths of the male population of the country were eagerly engaged in the mines, greatly contributed to this result, and the almost universal belief that the United States Congress had before its adjournment passed a law establishing a Territorial Government, satisfied the public mind that no action on its part was then necessary. So passed the summer and fall of 1848.

Upon the coming on of winter, the great majority of the miners returned to their homes in the towns. They came rich in gold dust; but a single glance at the desolate and unthrifty appearance of the Territory convinced them that other pursuits than that of gold-digging must receive a proportion of their care and labor, if they wished to be really happy, and promote the true interests of the country. They felt, as all Americans feel, that the most important step they could take, and that most imperatively called for by the wants of the inhabitants, was the establishment of a stable system of government, which would command the respect and obedience of the people whose property it protected, and whose rights it preserved. Congress had adjourned without providing a Territorial Government, and the public had settled into the firm conviction that the *de facto* Government was radically defective and incapable of answering the public wants. The large increase in the emigration during the past year, the still greater prospective increase in the year to come, the increased wants which were daily growing from a rapidly rising and extending commerce, and the growing demands of an enterprising and progressive people, all required a new and compatible system of government. Recent murders, highway robberies, and other outrages in various portions of the country, had convinced the honest and the orderly that anarchy, misrule, and wrong were abroad in the land. For a moment doubt, fear, uncertainty and indecision seemed to paralyze the public energies; but that love of order and justice which ever springs from the "still small voice," soon triumphed, and terrible indeed, was the retribution meted out to the offenders.

The opinions of the people, accelerated by the combined causes just enumerated, now, for the first time in the history of the country, assumed an organised form. On the 11th day of December 1848, a large meeting of the inhabitants of the district of San Jose was held at the town of that name, at which speeches were made, committees appointed, and resolutions unanimously adopted in favor of holding a convention for the purpose of forming a *Provisional Territorial Government*, to be put into immediate operation, and to remain in force until Congress should discharge its duty, and supersede it by a regular Territorial organization. The proceedings of this meeting were published and disseminated as rapidly as the means of communication would allow; and its action met with the unanimous approval of the people of the northern and middle portions of California. On the 21st and 23d of December, 1848, two of the largest public meetings ever held in California convened at San Francisco, and unanimously declared their concurrence in the course of action recommended by the citizens of San Jose. On the 6th and 8th of January, 1849, meetings at Sacramento City were held concurring in the same purpose. In the district of Monterey a similar meeting was held on the 31st of January, 1849, and in the district of Sonoma a meeting of approval and concurrence was held on the 5th of February, 1849. These five districts elected delegates to the proposed convention, viz: The district of Sacramento 5, Sonoma 10, San Francisco 5, San Jose 3, Monterey 5. These districts comprised at that time more than three-fifths of the entire population of the country. But the five other districts, viz: San Joaquin in the north, and San Luis Obispo, Santa Barbara, Los Angelos, and San Diego in the south, failed to concur in this movement for the establishment of a Provisional Territorial Government. The reasons of this non-concurrence were substantially the following:

The meeting held at San Jose recommended that the Convention for forming a Provisional Government should assemble at San Jose, on the second Monday of January, 1849. The San Francisco meeting believing that day much too early to allow communication with the remote Districts—and deeming it of paramount importance that the whole Territory should be represented in the proposed Convention, recommended that it should meet on Monday, March 5. In this recommendation of the District of San Francisco the Disrricts of Sonoma and Sacramento concurred, as did tacitly the District of San Jose. The District of Monterey, also concurred therein, but constituted its elected Delegates a Committee to confer with the other Districts to obtain, if possible and advisable, a still further extension of the time of holding the Convention.

The Corresponding Committee appointed by the San Francisco meeting had taken great pains to spread the intelligence of the action of the people there and in San Jose, and to request that measures be adopted to promote the cause of Provisional Government in the surrounding Districts; but the inclemency of the weather and the impassable condition of the roads and streams in consequence of the severe winter rains, had, up to January 24, 1849, prevented all communication with the five Districts above named. The Committee received many letters and much verbal information from different sections, which finally decided them in issuing to the public on January 24, 1849, a recommendation "that the time for the proposed assembling of the Provisional Government Convention be changed from Monday, the 5th day of March, to Tuesday the 1st day of May, 1849."

As was to have been expected, this recommendation, though generally concurred in, and though the reasons by which it was supported were never attempted to be controverted, had a tendency, by creating an impression of uncertainty, to cool the ardor of those interested in the cause. In addition to this, the recent intelligence from the Atlantic coast had given some assurance that Congress would not again adjourn without the adoption of a Territorial Government for California, and the arrival of Gen. P. F. Smith, on the 28th day of February, at San Francisco, to assume the command of the Pacific Division of the U. S. Army, was considered a favorable omen of what might be expected from the action of the cabinet and the law-givers at Washington.

Notwithstanding all these obstacles, the cause of Provisional Government still progressed; and though it was now feared and foreseen that the attempt to assemble a Convention on the first of May would probably fail, yet twelve of the Delegates elected to that body met at San Francisco early in the month of March, 1849, and issued an address to the people of California. That address, after recounting the reasons which prevented the assembling of the Convention, as originally proposed, on the 5th of March, and after reasserting the truth, that the action of a Convention which did not consist of representatives from each and every district would not be likely to meet with approval or respect from the public at large, concluded with the suggestion that "new elections should be held in the several districts for delegates to meet in convention at Monterey, on the first Monday in August next;" and that those delegates "should be vested with full power to frame a State Constitution to be submitted to the people of California; and further staing their belief that the circumstances and wants of the country were "such as to requre the immediate formation of a State Constitution, and entitle us to a right to be admitted into that Union of sovereign States, which we trust will ever be 'distinct as the billows, but one as the ocean.'" There is no doubt that this was then the prevailing sentiment of the people of the Territory.

In order to provide for the immediate wants of their respective districts, the citizens of Sonoma and Sacramento had elected, early in the year 1849, District Legislative Assemblies. The district of San Francisco, in consequence of difficulties between their Alcalde and two Town Councils claiming jurisdiction, resorted to the same method, and elected a Legislative Assembly. These acts on the part of the people of the respective districts brought about various collisions between the people and the *de facto* government of which Gen. Riley, who arrived on the 13th of April, 1849, was now the head. It is not necessary for us to enter into details of these matters, further than to say that a very excited and bitter feeling of hostility to this *de facto* government was quite universal, and that this feeling was strengthened by the failure of Congress to pass a bill establishing a Territorial government in California, and the passage of a law for the collection of revenue. The intelligence of this failure to act in the one case, and action in the oth-

b

er, on the part of Congress, reached San Francisco on the 28th May, 1849, by the U. S. propeller Edith, which vessel had been despatched to Mazatlan by order of Gen. Smith, on the preceding 10th of April. No sooner was this intelligence disseminated throughout the country, than it became evident to all men that the political complexion which a great question had assumed in the Atlantic States had prevented Congress from establishing a Territorial government, or even authorizing the people of California to form a State government; and there grew up at once a unanimous desire in the hearts of the citizens of the Territory, to adopt the only feasible scheme which promised them a government—that of a State organization. This sentiment daily gained ground until the beginning of June, 1849, when the Legislative Assembly of the District of San Francisco published an address to the people of California, asserting that they "believed it, to be their duty to earnestly recommend to their fellow-citizens the propriety of electing at least twelve delegates from each district to attend a general convention to be held at the Puebla de San Jose on the third Monday in August next, for the purpose of organizing a government for the whole Territory of California;" such "*conditional* or *temporary* State government to be put into operation at the earliest practicable moment" after "its ratification by the people," and "to become a *permanent* State government when admitted into the Union." This recomendation met with universal approval.

Simultaneous with this action on the part of the Legislative Assembly of the district of San Francisco, though without any knowledge thereof, Gov. Riley issued at Monterey, (130 miles distant,) on the 3d day of June, 1849, a proclamation recommending the election of delegates to a convention for forming a State Constitution, said body to convene at Monterey on the 1st day of September following. He also evinced a disposition, which had not been manifested before, to put in immediate, complete, and fair operation, the whole machinery of the *de facto* government, of which he claimed to be the head; he assured the people of his patriotic desire to accomplish his duty and their welfare by recommending them to elect all such officers as the existing laws authorized, whether it were provided that such officers should be elected by the people or appointed by the executive; and he convinced them of his good faith by at once coming forward and appropriating the "civil fund of California," which had been collected upon the imports of the country without law or authority, to the payment of the current expenses of the *de facto* government, which he had determined to put fully into operation. Notwithstanding all this, however, the majority of the people of the Territory denied his right to issue a proclamation calling a convention, contending that in the default of the action of Congress, the right to pursue such a course was inherent in the people.

But the opposition of the people to the *de facto* government had sprung from patriotic motives and from experimental conviction that it was insufficient for the exigencies of the country. This opposition was confined in its public manifestations entirely to the American born population. The Californians proper, as a whole, had never participated in any of the popular exhibitions of discontent; and the emigration that was now daily arriving in large numbers did not, of necessity, enter into the spirit of the grievances which were complained of by the older residents, nor espouse either side of a quarrel of which they could not distinctly comprehend the nature. All men, though, ardently desired a settled, Constitutional form of government; and it became the duty of the patriotic to yield their prejudices and abstract opinions, and to unite in one common effort to promote the public good. Congress had abandoned the Territory to its own resources—had oppressed it by the passage of an unjust law—a large portion of its population were in determined and open hostility to the *de faato* government—petty governments had been established in several districts—and anarchy and civil discord impending over the land. It was a moment of uncertainty and fear for California; but American patriotism and American love of law and order were superior to all other considerations, and the present and future prosperity of California was secured by a unanimous combination to form a State government

On the 7th of June, 1849, the citizens of San Jose, in a public meeting, concurred in the recommendations of Gen. Riley; and on the 11th of the same month the citizens of Monterey agreed thereto in a similar manner. On the 12th day of that month the largest mass meeting of the citizens of San Francisco ever held convened in Portsmouth square in that city. That meeting was addressed by Hon. T. Butler King, Wm. M. Gwin, Edward Gilbert, and other gentlemen; but such was the excited state of feeling in that district that the meeting, by a direct vote, refused to concur in the recommendation of Gen. Riley's proclamation. A corresponding Committee was, however, appointed, which, on the 18th of June, in an address to the public, used the following language, viz:

"The Committee, not recognizing the least power, as matter of *right* in Brev. Brig. Gen. Riley to '*appoint*' a time and place for the election of delegates and the assembling of the convention, yet as these matters are subordinate, and as the people of San Jose have, in public meeting, expressed their satisfaction with the times mentioned by Gen Riley, and as we are informed the districts below will accede to the same; and as it is of the first importance that there be unanimity of action among the people of California in reference to the great leading object—the attempt to form a government for ourselves—we recommend to our fellow citizens of California the propriety, under existing circumstances, of acceding to the time and place mentioned by Gen. Riley in his proclamation, and acceded to by the people of other districts."

This is believed to have been the general sentiment.

In all the other districts of the Territory, public meetings of concurrence in Gen. Riley's proclamation were subsequently held. The election followed on the 1st of August, and the convention assembled at Monterey on the 1st of September, 1849.

The undersigned have not presumed to weary your patience by laying before you in full the proceedings and action of the public bodies to which they have made allusion ; nor have they thought it neccessary to enter into a detail of minor particulars of difference and disagreement between the people and the *de facto* government. They, however, deem it their duty to assure you, that the persons who figured most conspicuously in the whole undertaking, enjoyed a high share of the public confidence and esteem ; and we believe that the best tribute to their worth and respectability is to be found in the fact that many of them were members of the convention which framed the Constitution, and now enjoy responsible and honorable positions under the government whose basis they so patriotically contributed to establish.

Such, in the opinion of the undersigned, is a brief and impartial history of the causes which have resulted in the formation of the present State government of California, and the presentation of her request for admission into the American Union. And the undersigned firmly and religiously believe that a perusal of the foregoing pages must lead irresistibly to the following conclusions, viz :

1. That a Territorial government, under the revisory power of Congress, would, so far from promoting the interests of California, so circumscribe its energies, prevent the development of its capacities, and impede its general advancement, as to be a source of discontent, difficulty, and ultimate ruin, either to the government or governed.

2. That the wonderful increase of the country in population, in wealth, and consequently in commercial, social, and political importance, renders imperatively necessary the adoption of such a system of measures as can only be enacted by a State Legislature and enforced by a State government.

3. That the neglect and oppression of the United States Congress, forced California to form a State goverment, if she desired to avoid civil strife and anarchy.

And, 4. That the people of that country did not adopt such form of government in obedience to dictation from the executive here, through Gen. Riley there ; but on the contrary, actually took the initiative in the movement, and only concurred in the suggestions of the *de facto* Governor as a matter of convenience, to save time, and with a patriotic resolution to merge all minor differences of opinion in one unanimous effort to avert impending ills and remedy existing evils.

Much misapprehension appears to have obtained in the Atlantic States relative to the question of slavery in California. The undersigned have no hesitation in saying that the provision in the Constitution excluding that institution, meets with the almost unanimous approval of that people. This unanimity is believed to result not so much from the prejudices against the system, which are quite general in the northern portion of the United States, as from a universal conviction that in no portion of California is the climate and soil of a character adapted to slave labor. Since the discovery of the mines, the feeling in opposition to the introduction of slavery is believed to have become, if possible, more unanimous than heretofore. The relation of master and slave has never existed in the country, and is there generally believed to be prohibited by Mexican law, consequently the original California population is utterly opposed to it. Slavery is a question little discussed in California, so settled appears the public mind relative thereto. Public meetings have scarcely ever considered it. The opinion put forward, that the decision of this question has been forestalled, has no foundation in truth. And no more conclusive proof of this can be found than the simple facts, that fifteen of the forty-eight members composing the convention which *unanimously* inserted the prohibtory clause in the Constitution, were from slaveholding States, while twelve were Californians proper, and twenty one northern men. Further than this, there is no doubt, that two-fifths of those who voted in favor of the Constitution were recent emigrants from slaveholding States, while it is known that many of the votes given against the instrument were so given in consequence of the failure of the messengers to distribute the printed copies in several mining localities. No debate upon the subject was had in the convention, though some "conversation" ensued upon a proposition to submit the provision to the people for a separate vote. This was suggested by northern men, and did not prevail.

Objections have been urged against the boundaries of California, as fixed by her Constitution. The convention which settled upon the proposed boundary, was engaged during three days in debate upon that subject. There were two parties, or rather two propositions : 1. To take in the whole of California as it existed when a department of Mexico ; but with a proviso that Congress and the State Legislature might limit the bounds of the State to the summit of the Sierra Nevada, and leaving it to Congress to establish Territorial governments over such portions of the country as it might see fit. 2. To divide the whole Territory on the 116th degree of west longitude, from the southern boundary of Oregon to the northern boundary of Mexico, that portion of said Territory lying west of the one hundred and sixteenth degree of West longitude, and between that line and the Pacific Ocean, to constitute the State of California. The opinion of the convention was so nearly divided between these two propositions, that both were supported by a majority at different times during the informal stages ; and on the final passage the present boundary was adopted as a species of compromise. This question called out the most vehement and angry debate which was witnessed during the sitting of the convention. The project of fixing the southern boundary of the State on the parallel of 36° 30′ was never entertained by that body. Indeed, when it is recollected that eleven of the delegates sitting in the convention, represented a large constituency south of that line, it is at once apparent that it would have been a most unjust and discourteous act to have listened to such a proposition, unless it came from them. The people of that southern portion of California most certainly did not wish, and probably never would consent to such a separation. In former years they constituted the great majority of the population—they have always been governed by the same laws—and they would be the last to sanction a division of California as they have always known it. In a political point of view, too, it would seem desirable that these original Mexican citizens should become as speedily as possible Americans in sentiment and language, and there certainly can be no more effectual mode of accomplishing this than by bringing them into that daily contact which an existence under the same laws and the same social, political, and commercial regulations must inevitably produce. In the extreme north, also, the adventurous miners had crossed the coast range, and penetrated to the head waters of the Trinity river, which finds its way through an unexplored and dangerous Indian country to the Pacific Ocean. As the abundance of gold found there rendered it probable that a large community would soon become permanently established in that region, the convention felt that it could not refuse them the benefits and protection of a government by circumscribing the limits of the State in that direction. The eastern boundary of the State, so far as explored and known, runs through a desert A small portion of the eastern slope of the Sierra Nevada is said to be adapted to agricultural and grazing purposes, and as that country, when settled, must necessarily find an outlet across the mountains into the valleys of the Sacramento and San Joaquin Rivers, and as it could never have any natural connection with the country to the eastward of it, by reason of the great desert, it was thought advisable and proper to include that strip of territory within the bounds of the State. That portion of the State lying to the southward and eastward of the Sierra Nevada and the coast range, and between those mountains and the Colorado river, is believed to be an arid desert. So much as lies upon the usual emigrant trail from the Colorado to San Diego and that further north in the vicinity of the explorations of John Charles Fremont, is known to be of that character. The general impression therefore is, that that part of the Territory included in the State boundaries is of little or no value. The superficial area of the State of California, according to the boundaries prescribed in her Constitution, is 155,550 square miles, or 99,552,000 square acres, exclusive of the islands adjacent to her coast. A glance at the map prepared by order of the United States Senate, from the surveys of John C. Fremont and other authorities, upon which the above calculation is based, will at once satisfy all that the topographical characteristics of that country are peculiar and novel. Two great chains of mountains, the Sierra Nevada, and the coast range, traverse it in nearly its whole extent from north to south. The large valleys that lie between these two ranges, and the small lateral valleys that pierce their rugged sides in every direction, are the valuable arable portion of the land of California. Assuming then, that two-fourths of the whole superficial area of the State is covered by mountains, that another fourth is a desert waste, and we have left one fourth as useful for agricultural purposes, that is, 38,887½ square miles, or 24,888,000 square acres of arable and productive land. This estimate, in the opinion of the undersigned, is fully borne out by the topographical surveys of the country ; but anxious as they are to avoid misstatement, they do not hesitate to assert their belief that it is quite apparent, after all due allowances, three-fifths of the whole Territory embraced in the State of California will never be susceptible of cultivation or useful to man. This, then, would give, as the remaining two-fifths, 62,220, square miles, or 39,820,800 square acres, which would constitute the sum total of valuable arable and grazing land embraced within the boundary fixed by the Constitution of the State of California, and distributed at intervals over the whole surface of the country, from its extreme northern to its extreme southern limit. The foregoing are believed to be substantially the reasons which led to the present proposed boundary of California.

The qualifications prescribed for voters by Gen. Riley's proclamation were carried out at the election of delegates to the convention. These qualifications were generally approved, and believed to be correct. By that proclamation, after requiring the voter to be twenty-one years of age and an actual resident of the district where he offered his vote, three classes of voters were declared eligible, viz: 1. American citizens ; 2. Mexicans who had elected under the treaty to become American citizens ; and 3. Mexican citizens who had been forced to leave their country in consequence of giving aid and succor to the American arms during the recent war. These requirements were faithfully complied with, beyond all doubt. Such would seem to be the undeniable fact, as no complaint was ever made of illegal voting.

Under the provision relative to the right of suffrage in the Constitution of California, white male American citizens twenty-one years of age, and white male citizens of Mexico of the same age, who had elected to become citizens of the United States under the treaty of peace, were permitted to vote, in the districts of their residence, upon the ratification of the Constitution, and for the various officers to be elected under it. No other persons were allowed to vote—no other persons did vote. The allegation, therefore, that foreigners, aliens, and adventurers adopted the Constitution, of California is not warranted by facts. That Constitution was ratified by over 12,000 votes in its favor, of which, it is firmly believed, not a single one was that of a foreigner, and from the best information, it is past doubt that there were only about some 1,300 Californian votes, while the remaining 10,700 were totally American.

The undersigned believe that they would fail to fulfil their duty if they did not, in connection with this subject, express the regret which they so strongly feel at the unjust attacks which have thus been made upon their constituents. They regard such assaults as not only ungenerous toward the citizens of California, but as direct offences against the nobility and sacredness of the American character itself. They look upon such insinuations as hurtful and injurious to the last degree, to a population than which none nobler and truer ever existed. You will search history in vain for an example of order under excitement like that which California has presented for the last two years. And it is the proud boast of every American, that to the republican education which that people has received, is due the extraordinary state of things which has heretofore rendered life and property secure where there was no law but the law of force. Yet this people, whose conduct has excited the admiration of every portion of the civilized world where their course is understood, are disparaged by a portion of their American brothers!

The Convention which formed the Constitution of California assembled at Monterey on the 1st day of September, 1849. Under the apportionment fixed by the Proclamation of General Riley, it would have consisted of 37 Delegates. This apportionment was based upon the Mexican law applicable to the country when it was a Department of Mexico; but inasmuch as the recent large immigration had changed the relative importance of the Districts in regard to the number of population, Gen. Riley had recommended the election of such number of supernumerary Delegates from each District as the inhabitants thereof might deem proper. Most of the Districts acted on this suggestion; and one of the first acts of the Convention was the settlement of the rights of membership, and the adoption of a new apportionment. Under the rule thereupon passed, the number of Delegates was fixed at 73, of whom 48 appeared, took their seats, and participated in the deliberations and action of the body. The Convention was in session from the 1st day of September till the 13th of October 1849. Its proceedings were characterized by order and a correct understanding and application of legislative rules. Every subject upon which diverse opinions were entertained was fully and ably debated; and though the action of the body was unanimous to an extraordinary degree, it was a unanimity springing from reasoning and conviction, and not the effect of sycophancy, truckling, or fear. The men composing it were highly and justly esteemed among their immediate constituents for their independence, republican principles, ability, and honesty; and it is confidently believed that the great and good qualities displayed by them in their action in the Convention have not only endeared them the more to their old and devoted friends, but have given them an enviable reputation and a flattering name coextensive with the boundaries of the State and perhaps of the American Union. Known among their fellow-citizens by their social qualities and virtues; appreciated for their industry, enterprise, and devotion to the interests of the massess, to liberty and law, they were elected without distinction of party; and the Constitution which they prepared for the government of the new State in which they have cast their lot, and on whose soil many of them were born, and most of them have resided for several years, is an instrument which cannot fail for ever to bear testimony to the integrity, the capacity, and the patriotism of those who framed it. The insinuation that those men were awed or influenced by Gov. Riley, is an unjust assault not only upon their character and that of their constituents, but upon the fame and integrity of as brave a soldier and as good a man as the annals of American glory can boast.

The result of the labors of the Convention was submitted to the People of California for their consideration on the 13th day of October, 1849, on which day the Convention adjourned *sine die*. The Constitution was printed in the English and Spanish languages, and extraordinary efforts were made to circulate it in every portion of the Territory. In order that as full a vote as possible might be had both upon the Constitution and for the election of the officers under it, it was deemed absolutely necessary that the election should be fixed at a time anterior to the setting in of the winter rains. The impassable condition of the roads and rivers during the winter, it was well known, must inevitably detain large numbers of voters from the polls, if the election were too long postponed. Beside, it was deemed important that the admission of the State should be secured as speedily as possible, in order that her Senators and Representatives might early take their seats in Congress, and devote their energies to the promotion of the national legislation of which the country was so much in need. Accordingly the 13th of November, 1849, was fixed upon as the day of the election, and the 15th of December, 1849, as the day of the assembling of the State Legislature.

The anticipations which had caused the election to be held at an early day, proved not to be unfounded. The winter rains commenced several days before the 13th of November, and on that day one of the worst storms ever experienced raged throughout the whole country. The consequence was, notwithstanding the personal exertions of the friends of the different candidates for popular favor, that only about fifteen thousand votes were polled. Of these 12,061 were for the Constitution, 811 were against it, and from 1,200 to 1,500 were blanks, in consequence of the failure of the printer to place the words "For the Constitution" at the head of the ballots. It is believed that there never was an election attended with less excitement. The sentiment in favor of the Constitution was nearly unanimous, and was entirely the result of the unbiassed and deliberate opinions of those who were most interested in it. No attempt was made to mislead or control public opinion in relation to the Constitution. No candidate sought success by either an ardent advocacy of its merits, or a broad denunciation of any of its provisions. The three newspapers published in the Territory did not feel called upon to aid it, further than to publish it with a simple recommendatory paragraph, and no member of the Convention urged its adoption with improper zeal. The truth is, that no political result in the history of any nation is more surely the honest expression of a public opinion founded in reason, reflection, and deliberate judgment, than the ratification afforded by the People of California to their Constitution.

The Legislature elected in November, assembled at San Jose, the Capitol of the State, on the 15th December last. The Governor elected by the People, PETER H. BURNETT, Esq. was inaugurated according to the requirements of the Constitution; and on the 20th of the same month, Gen Riley, by proclamation, delivered the Civil Government into the hands of the duly-elected agents of the newly-organized State. That State Government, complete in all its elemental parts, is now exercising the powers and performing the duties prescribed by the Constitution of the State of California. The legislation that is likely to ensue will be of such a character as is demanded by the public interests, but always in conformity to the Constitution of the United States and the laws of Congress. The intelligence and patriotism of those composing the State Government, are a warranty that no conflict of authority or interests is likely to occur, either from ignorance or design, between the Government of the United States and the Government of the State of California; and while it cannot be denied that the position of affairs is anomalous, it is not doubted that the legitimate channels of the two powers are so widely different that, running in a parallel direction, they never can come into collision. Such is believed to be the settled opinion of the People of California and of their Legislative and Executive authorities.

It was not from any desire to establish a State Government in opposition to or regardless of the wishes and rights of the people of the United States, that the people of California pursued this course. No improper motives, no ambitious impulses, no executive influence prompted their action. They believed that their brethren on the Atlantic appreciated their sufferings, admitted their patriotism, and would hail their action with joy. They thought that the Congress of the United States would instantly open its doors to their delegated representatives, and that the State would be immediately and gladly admitted. To this impression the tone of the public press, the dispatches of executive officers, and the speeches of distinguished statesmen in Congress had contributed in a very great degree; and as nothing of a contrary character had ever reached the Pacific shores, it is not surprising that the sentiment became a general one. The daily arriving emigration added their corroborative evidence to the already general belief, and it finally came to be credited that the great public of the Atlantic States were as ardently and unanimously in favor of the admission of California as were her own citizens. They did not anticipate delay, and consequently could not perceive or guard against a contingency arising from such a state of things They believed their action to be eminently right and necessary, and sanctioned by the approving voice of the American people.

The population of California on the first day of January, 1850, is supposed to have been about 107,000 souls There are no means of ascertaining with certainty the number and character of the large immigration which has poured into the country since the discovery of the gold mines, but the undersigned, having taken much pains to arrive at correct conclusions on this subject, submit the following estimates:

The population of California, exclusively of Indians and Africans, is supposed to have been, on the first day of January, 1849, as follows, viz:

Californians	13,000
Americans	8,000
Foreigners	5,000
Total	26,000

From that time down to the 11th day of April, 1849, the arrivals by sea at the different ports is believed to have exceeded 6,000, and the arrivals by land from Sonora, Mexico, is estimated at 2,000. One-half of this increase, it is presumed, were Americans.

The following statistical table, compiled from the records of the Harbor-Master's Office at San Francisco, presents a more reliable and satisfactory account of the immigration which arrived there by sea from the 12th of April to the 31st of December, 1849, viz:

Months.	Americans.	Foreigners.	Males.	Females.	Totals.
April, May, June	3,944	1,942	5,677	209	5,886
July	3,000	614	3,565	49	3,614
August	3,384	509	3,806	87	3,893
September	4,271	1,531	5,680	122	5,802
October	2,655	1,414	3,950	119	4,069
November	1,746	490	2,155	81	2,236
December	3,069	500	3,436	133	3,569
Totals	22,069	7,000	28,269	800	29,069

In addition to the immigration thus arriving by sea at the port of San Francisco, it is believed that not less than 1,000 persons landed at other ports in California, during the same time. By the way of Santa Fe and the Gila the immigration was estimated at 8,000. From Mexico by land, from 6,000 to 8,000 were supposed to have arrived, of which only about 2,000 were believed to have remained in the country. Adding to these amounts the 3,000 sailors who have deserted from ships arriving in the country, and computing the great overland immigration (which was variously estimated from 30,000 to 40,000,) at 25,000, the following totals result, viz:

	Jan. 1, 1849.	Jan. 1, 1850.
Americans	8,000	76,069
Californians	13,000	13,000
Foreigners	5,000	18,000
Totals	26,000	107,069

The foregoing figures and estimates though known not to be strictly accurate, are thought to be a near approximation to the actual numbers of the inhabitants. The round numbers are presumed, in every case, to be below the mark.

The undersigned do not deem it their duty or province to urge upon your honorable bodies the many cogent reasons which in their opinion might be justly presented in favor of the admission of California as a State. Nor do they feel assured that it would be proper for them to lay before you any impressions which they may have of the history of the admission of new States, or the prescriptions, regulations, or laws of Congress relative thereto. Neither would they wish to overstep the bounds of true propriety by indelicately requesting a speedy decision of this question. Yet they cannot refrain from saying that great interests—inserests of the highest importance to the Republic and to California—are suffering incalculably for want of action on the part of Congress. They will not attempt to particularize them, confident that the intelligent statesmen who compose your honorable bodies will at once understand to what they allude, and properly appreciate the suggestion.

The people of California are neither rebels, usurpers, nor anarchists. They have not sought to sow the seeds of revolution, that they might reap in the harvest of discord. They believe that the principles that guided them are true—they know that the motives which actuated them are pure and just—and they had hoped that their action would be acceptable to every portion of their common country. They did not expect that their admission as a State would be made the test question upon which would hang the preservation of the American Union, nor did they desire such a result; but urged by the imperative and extraordinary necessities of their country, they united in such action as they believed would secure them a government under and in conformity to the Constitution of their country.

In thus presenting the certified copies of their State Constitution and their credentials, and asking the admission of the State, and that they may be permitted to take their seats in your respective bodies, the undersigned feel that they would neglect an important duty if they failed to assure you of the anxious desire for the perpetuity of this Union which animates all classes of their constituents. Born and reared under its protecting influences, as most of them were, their patriotism is as broad as the Republic—it extends from the Atlantic to the Pacific—it is as deep as the current of their mighty rivers—as pure as the never-melting snows which crown their mountains, and as indestructible as the virgin gold extracted from their soil. Coming as they nearly all do from the different States composing the Union, deeply impressed, as most of them have been by passing through foreign lands, with the immeasurable superiority of American institutions and American character, it would be strange, indeed, if they did not turn with reverence and affection toward their country, its institutions, and its people. Possessed, too, in a remarkable degree, of intelligence, enterprise, and ability, rich in high moral qualities, industrious, energetic and honest, firm in their devotion to order and justice, they compose a community which has no superiors in the elements which constitute a citizen's glory, and a nation's greatness.

This people request admisssion into the American Union as a State. They understand and estimate the advantages which will accrue to them from such a connection, while they trust they do not too highly compute those which will be conferred upon their brethren. They do not present themselves as suppliants, nor do they bear themselves with arrogance or presumption. They come as free Americans citizens—citizens by treaty, by adoption, and by birth—and ask that they may be permitted to reap the common benefits, share the common ills, and promote the common welfare, as one of the United States of America!

WILLIAM M. GWIN,
JOHN C. FREMONT,
GEORGE W. WRIGHT,
EDWARD GILBERT.

WASHINGTON, D. C. March 12, 1850.

DIGEST OF LAWS.

Translation and Digest of such portions of the Mexican Laws of March 20th and May 23d, 1837, as are supposed to be still in force and adapted to the present condition of California; with an Introduction and Notes, by J. Halleck, *Attorney at Law, and* W. E. P. Hartnell, *Government Translator.*

Executive Department of California,
Monterey, *July* 2, 1849.

The following pages have been examined in manuscript and compared with the original text, and are believed to be essentially correct. As it is thought that their publication at this time will be useful and advantageous, three hundred copies are ordered for distribution among the officers of the existing Government, to be paid for out of the "Civil Fund."

[Signed.] B. RILEY,
B'vt. Brig. Gen'l U. S. Army,
and Governor of California.

INTRODUCTION.

In 1828 the Supreme Court of the United States, in a case concerning the then Territory of Florida, made the following decision:

"The usage of the world is, if a nation be not entirely subdued, to consider the holding of conquered territory as a mere military occupation until its fate be determined at the treaty of peace. If it be ceded by the treaty, the acquisition is confirmed, and the ceded territory becomes a part of the nation to which it is annexed, either on the terms stipulated in the treaty of cession, or on such as its new master shall impose. On such transfer of territory it has never been held that the relations of the inhabitants with each other undergo any change. Their relations with the former sovereign are dissolved, and new relations are created between them and the Government which has acquired their territory. The mere act which transfers their country, transfers the allegiance of those who remain in it; and the law which may be denominated political, is necessarily changed, although that which regulates the intercourse and general conduct of individuals *remains in force* until altered by the newly created power of the State.

"The treaty (by which Florida was ceded) is the law of the land, and admits the inhabitants of Florida to the enjoyment of the privileges, rights, and immunities of the citizens of the United States. It is unnecessary to inquire whether this is not their condition, independent of stipulation. They do not, however, participate in political power; they do not share in the government till Florida become a State. In the mean time, Florida continues to be a territory of the United States, governed by virtue of that clause of the Constitution which empowers Congress to make all needful rules and regulations respecting the territory or other property belonging to the United States.

"Perhaps the power of governing a territory belonging to the United States, which has not by becoming a State, acquired the means of self-government, may result necesssarily from the fact, that it is not within the jurisdiction of any particular State, and is within the power and jurisdiction of the United States. The right to govern may be the inevitable consequence of the right to acquire territory. Whichever may be the source whence the power is derived, the possession of it is unquestioned."

This decision shows plainly and conclusively what is the present legal condition of things in California. The laws which were in force in this country previous to its conquest, and which do not conflict with the Constitution, Treaties and Laws of the United States, constitute the existing laws of California, and the government recognised in those laws is the only one which can be recognised in any legal court, and these laws and this government must continue until changed by or with the consent of Congress.

During the military occupation of California, the commanding officer here, under the general authority conferred on him by the laws of war, could suspend or change any of the laws of Mexico affecting the people of this Territory; but all such suspensions and changes were only of a temporary character, and ceased with the war.

The relations which formerly existed between this government and Mexico were dissolved by the transfer of the territory, and it may be a question how far these relations have been transferred to the Government of the United States. Some of the powers of the General Government of Mexico over this country we know have never been transferred to the Government of the United States, because the Constitution of the United States forbids certain powers to our Government which by the Constitution of Mexico are given to its Government; while, on the other hand, the Government of the United States possesses certain powers over the Territory of the United States which Mexico did not possess over even her frontier department. For example, the Government and Legislature of California, under the Mexican laws, could on certain conditions make and confirm grants of public lands; but no one will pretend that the Government and Legislature of California can now make or confirm such grants, Congress alone having power to dispose of the public domain. Again, the people of California could participate in a limited manner in the General Government of Mexico; but now they cannot participate in the Government of the United States till Congress gives them that right. Formerly, the peeple of California had only such rights as were given them by the Constitution and laws of Mexico; now they have all the rights, privileges, and immunities given by our Constitution and laws to the people of the United States. This is a great and important distinction, which cannot be too highly appreciated, and which compensates more than a thousand fold for what little we have temporarily lost in political power.

As some months will necessarily elapse before the existing government and laws of California can be changed, it is important to know the powers and responsibilities of the several political and judicial officers of the present Government. The following pages have been prepared to assist in furnishing this information. The laws of March 20th and May 23d, 1837, are regarded as the laws in force in California up to the time of the conquest. The Mexican Constitution of 1844, partially adopted in Mexico, was never regarded as in force in California, nor was it known here that these laws were materially modified by any decrees or orders of the Mexican Congress. It will be a question hereafter for the decision of courts, what modifications were legally made by Mexico, and how far they are actually in force under the existing circumstances of the country. It is not pretended that all the provisions of the laws of 1837, actually in force in California, are embodied in the following pages, nor that all the articles which have been selected are applicable in their full extent to the existing state of the country. This little work is merely intended as a temporary guide and assistance to the inferior officers of Government, till more complete treaties can be prepared by competent persons. Most of the articles in the following pages are nearly literal translations of the Spanish text, consequently new words and awkward expressions are frequently introduced. This was deemed preferable to attempting a more liberal rendering. The translator will not vouch for the perfect correctness of his translation in every instance, for he does not himself understand the exact meaning of some of the terms and phrases used in the Spanish laws. Where doubts arise respecting the meaning of these phrases, it will be neceasary for the court to critically examine the words of the original text.

In putting in practice the existing laws of California important assistance will be derived by consulting the "Febrero Mejicano," "Alvarez' *Instituciones de derecho real de Castilla y de Indias,*" "Gutierres' *Practica Criminal,*" the work of "Salas," &c. The codes of Louisiana, which are almost identical with the Spanish codes, will also be found applicable in most of the cases which may arise in the courts of California. The following brief sketch of the history of the jurisprudence of that State by an eminent American writer will be read with interest at the present time:

Louisiana was ceded by France to Spain in 1762, and was taken possession of by this latter power in 1769, when the Spanish law was introduced. The great body of this law, called the *Siete Partidas*, was compiled as early as 1263. The *Recopilacion de Castilla*, published in 1567, was intended to clear up the confusion of the previous codes, but it leaves the authority of the *partidas* generally unimpaired. The cession of Louisiana to the United States necessarily introduced the trial by jury in a modified form, and the writ of *habeas corpus*, which were unknown to the pre-existing laws. The legislative council of the territory of Orleans borrowed largely from the common law, but principally those forms of proceedings necessary to confer efficient powers on the courts organized under the authority of the union. But, in the adjudication of suits between individuals, the Spanish jurisprudence was the sole guide, except in commercial questions. In 1806 the legislative council ordered two able jurists to prepare a civil code for the use of the territory on the groundwork of the civil laws which governed the territory. It was reported in 1808 and adopted, but was not allowed to supersede the previous laws, except as far as those laws were inconsistent with its provisions. The "Digest of the Civil Code now in force in the territory of Orleans," as it was called, though termed a code, is, in fact, little more than a synopsis of the jurisprudence of Spain. It continued in operation for fourteen years without any material innovation. In 1822 Messrs. Derbigny, Livingston, and Moreau Lislet were selected by the legislature to revise and amend the civil code, and to add to it such of the laws still in force as were not included therein. They were authorized to add a system of commercial laws and a code of practice. The code which they prepared, having been adopted, was promulgated in 1824, under the title of the "Civil Code of the State Louisiana;" and the legislature resolved, that "from and after the promulgation of this code, the Spanish, Roman, and French laws, which were in force when Louisiana was ceded to the United States, and the acts of the legislative council of the legislature of the territory of Orleans, and of the legislature of the state of Louisiana, be, and hereby are, repealed in every case for which it has been specially provided in this code." It would seem that where the code is silent on any subject, any pre-existing laws on that subject, whether of French or Spanish origin, or of native growth, would be considered as still in force. The new code, independently of the great changes which it has introduced, is much more full and explicit in the doctrinal parts than the former digest. The theory of obligations particularly deserves to be mentioned, as comprising, in a condensed and even elegant form, the most satisfactory enunciation of general principles. The jurisconsults appear to have profited much by the great work of Toublier, entitled *Le Droit civil Francais*. The code contains 3,552 articles, numbered from the beginning for convenience of reference. The most striking and material changes introduced by the new code relate to the rules of succession, and the enlarged liberty of disposing of property by last will, by curtailing the portions which must be reserved for forced heirs. The new order of succession conforms to that established in France by the Code Napoleon, and will be found to be copied almost precisely from the 118th novel of Justinian, from which the Spanish rules of descent had deviated in some essential particulars. The legislature of Louisiana provided also for the formation of a penal code, by an act passed in 1820, and entrusted the charge of preparing it to Mr. Edward Livingston.

A plan of a penal code was accordingly drawn up by him, and presented to the legislature in 1822. This code has since been published, and is regarded as one of the most elegant and learned legal works extant.

PART FIRST.

POLITICAL.

LAW OF MARCH 20TH, 1837.

The interior Government of the Department shall be under the charge of the Governor, Departmental Legislature (Juncta,) Prefects and Sub-Prefects, Ayuntamientos, Alcaldes, and Justices of the Peace.

SECTION I.

Of the Governor.

ART. 1. His term of service and the necessary qualifications for election are specified in the sixth constitutional law. (1)

It shall be his duty,

1st. To take care of the preservation of public order in the interior of the department;

2nd. To dispose of the armed force which the laws assign to him for this purpose, and in default thereof, or where it may not be sufficient, to ask the necessary force from the military commandant, who cannot refuse it;

3d. To publish without delay, execute and cause to be executed, the laws and decrees of Congress, and circulate them through the Department;

4th. To execute also, and cause to be executed, the decrees and orders of the General Government and the resolutions of the departmental legislature, previously approved, when necessary, by Congress;

5th. To remit to the General Government, with his report, all the resolutions of the departmental legislature;

6th. To appoint the Prefects, approve the appointment of Sub-Prefects of the department, confirm that of the Justices of Peace, and to remove any of these functionaries, having first the opinion of the departmental legislature respecting such removal;

---

(1) These qualifications are no longer necessary, nor even admissible, for by the transfer of this Territory to the United States our relations with Mexico were dissolved.

7th. To apppoint likewise the other officers of the Department, whose appointment is not reserved to some other authority ;

8th. To suspend the officers of the Department for a term not exceeding three months, and even deprive them of half of their salary for the same period ;

9th. To suspend the Ayuntamientos of the Department with the consent of the departmental legislature ; (1)

10th. In case of exercising either of the two foregoing attributes, he shall immediately report to the general government ;

11th. To grant permission with a just motive, for a period not exceeding two months in each year, to government officers to be absent from their stations ;

12th. To decide executively and without appeal the doubts which may arise respecting the elections of Ayuntamientos, and admit or not the renunciations of the members elected ;

13th. To exercise, in union with the departmental legislature, with a casting vote in case of a tie, the rejecting power (esclusiva) referred to in Article 22nd, Attributes 8th of the fifth constitutional law ; (2)

14th. To incite the tribunals and magistrates to the prompt and correct administration of justice, and report to the respective superior authorities the faults of the inferior ones ;

15th. To watch over the revenue officers of the Department in the manner which shall be prescribed by law ;

16th. To watch over the public health of the Department, taking, in concert with the legislature, the necessary measures for its preservation ;

17th. To take particular care that there be no want of elementary schools in any of the towns of the Department, and that the masters and mistresses, as far as the circumstances of the place will admit, possess good moral character and the necessary qualifications.

Art. 2. He may in his executive capacity, and without appeal, impose fines not exceeding two hundred dollars, which shall be paid into the municipal funds (propios y arbitrios) of the place to which the person fined belongs ; or he may sentence the inhabitants of the Department who shall disobey him or be wanting in respect, or who in any other manner disturb the public tranquillity, to one month at public works, or double the time of arrest, conforming himself to the circumstances of the individuals, and allowing them a summary and verbal hearing, in case they should request it. But with respect to faults for which the law has provided a penalty, the existing regulations must be observed.

Art. 3. He shall hear complaints against the functionaries of the departmental government, and for faults cognizable by government he may impose executively and without appeal a fine not exceeding fifty dollars, to be likewise paid over to the municipal funds ; but said functionaries shall also be heard in a summary and verbal manner in case they desire it.

Art. 4. He may send vagabonds, idle persons, and such as have no known occupation, to the establishment dedicated to this object, or to such workshops or agricultural establishments as may choose voluntarily to admit them ; but the persons so to be disposed of shall have the choice of the two latter destinations.

Art. 5. When the public tranquility shall require it, he may give a written order to search houses and to arrest persons ; and even without this requisite he may command the arrest of any delinquent caught in the act : but in either case the persons arrested must within three days be put at the disposal of the competent magistrate, to whom he will make a written report of the motives of the arrest. (3)

Art. 6. On the report of the Prefect (the opinion of the departmental legislature being obtained) he may grant permission to the Ayuntamiento or authorities in charge of the administration and expenditure of municipal funds, to defray such extraordinary expenses as may be required for objects of necessity or common utility.

Art. 7. In cases of necessity or for motives of public utility, he may, in concert with the departmental legislature, grant permission to said authorities to alienate certain property belonging to the municipal funds (proprios y arbitrios ;) and any cession, donation, or contract made without this requisite, will be null and void.

Art. 8. He will issue the respective commissions to the officers whom by law he is entitled to appoint. (4)

---

(1) Where there is no departmental legislature organized it has always been held that the power of removal and suspension rests with the Governor, who is responsible for his acts to the general government.

(2) This has reference to the appointments of certain subaltern officers.

(3) It may be a question whether this clause is not slightly modified by Art. IV. amendments to the Constitution of the United States.

(4) The original text also states how he shall sign his name to different documents, when his family name, and when his mere flourish is sufficient. With us one and the same signature is always used.

Art. 9. At public meetings he will take precedence of all the authorities of the department.

Art. 10. He will also preside at the departmental legislature when he shall attend the sessions; but he shall only be entitled to vote in case of a tie, or in such cases as are or may be provided for by the Constitution and the laws.

Art. 11. Should he be in any town of the department, he may preside without vote at the sessions of the ayuntamiento thereof.

Art. 12. He shall nominate and remove at pleasure the Secretary of the Departmental government, but he cannot appoint to this office, or to that of prefect, any public officer, without the consent of the authority who named him.

13. His ordinary residence shall be in the capital of the department, and in order to remove therefrom, he will require the permission of the President.

Art. 14. He shall be the ordinary channel of communication between the supreme powers of the nation and the departmental legislature, and between the latter and the authorities of the department.

Art. 15. In all official matters, the Governor, whether regularly appointed, or acting as such *ad interim*, shall be entitled to the appellation of "Your Excellency."

Art. 16. The salary of the Governor is regulated by the General Government, but can never exceed five thousand dollars per annum.

Art. 17. In temporary default of the Governor, another shall be named *ad interim*, in the same manner as the proper one. If the default should be of short duration, the senior (mas antiguo) lay member of the departmental legislature shall take charge of the government, as he shall in like manner do, during the interval which may take place between the default of the Governor proper and the appointment of his successor *ad interim*. (1)

SECTION II.

Of the Secretary.

Art. 1. There shall be a Secretary's Office in the Department for the transaction of the affairs of its interior government.

Art. 2. The Secretary shall be the immediate head of the office and shall form regulations for the interior government of the same, which must be submitted to the Governor for him to approve or reform as he may see fit.

Art. 3. The Secretary shall authorize under his signature the publication and circulation of the laws, decrees and orders of the Supreme powers, the determinations of the departmental legislature, the municipal ordinances of the Ayuntamientos, the interior police regulations of the Department and the titles or despatches issued by the Governor.

Art. 4. He shall carry on the Governor's correspondence with the inferior authorities under his signature, restricting himself to what is directed by the Governor, and he shall be answerable for any deviation therefrom.

Art. 5. He shall likewise be answerable for the want of the *espedientes*, laws, decrees, orders, and other papers, which ought to be on file in the office.

Art. 6. Neither the Secretary or any of the Clerks of the office shall ask or accept any fees or emoluments for the despatch of any kind of business.

Art. 7. He shall be officially entitled to the appellation of "Honorable" (Senoria.)

Art. 8. The salary of the Secretary is fixed by the Governor (with the approbation of the General Government,) but can never exceed two thousand five hundred dollars per annum.

SECTION III.

Of the Departmental Legislature.

Art. 1. In this Department there shall be an assembly denominated the "Departmental Legislature," composed of seven individuals.

(1.) In the older Departments of Mexico the Legislature nominated several persons from which the President selected the Governor, but in California and the other frontier Departments, no such right was vested in the Legislature, the President having power to select any person for Governor without a previous nomination. In the present instance, the commanding officer of this military department is designated by the President of the United States, as Governor of California, which power is exercised in accordance with the former laws of the country; it is therefore unnecessary to examine whether this power could not have been exercised (any laws of this country to the contrary notwithstanding) under the new relations, created by the trausfer of the territory, between its inhabitants and the General Government of the United States.

ART. 2. These persons shall be elected by the same electors who choose the deputies to Congress, and the election must take place precisely on the day following that of said deputies.

ART. 3. Seven substitutes shall likewise be named in the same manner as the foregoing, who shall fill vacancies that may occur, according to the order of their nomination.

ART. 4. The Departmental Legislature shall be entirely renovated every four years, and they will commence their functions on the first day of January following their election.

ART. 5. It belongs to the Departmental Legislature:—

1st. To pass (iniciar) laws relative to taxes, public education, industry, trade and municipal administration.

2d. To establish common schools in all the towns of the Department, and assign to them competent donations, out of the municipal funds, where there are any, and when not, to impose moderate contributions.

3d. To order the establishment and repairs of the interior roads of the Department, establishing moderate tolls for the payment of the expenses.

4th. To dictate all regulations proper for the preservation and improvement of the establishments of public instruction and benificence, and such as tend to the encouragement of agriculture, industry and commerce: but if such regulation should in any way be burdensome to the towns of the department, they must not be put in execution until they be previously approved by Congress.

5th. To promote by means of the Governor whatever may be conducive to the prosperity of of the Department in all its branches, and to the well being of its inhabitants.

6th. To form, in union with the Governor, the Municipal Ordinances of the Ayuntamientos, and the regulations of the interior police of the Department.

7th. To examine and approve the accounts which are to be rendered of the collection and expenditure of the municipal funds (propios y arbitrios.)

8th. To advise with the Governor in all affairs in which he may require it.

ART. 6. The Legislature will form its own regulations for its interior government, and elect its own subordinate officers.

ART. 7. Four members present are necessary to form a quorum.

ART. 8. The acts of the Legislature must be signed by the senior member present and by the Secretary.

ART. 9. Each one of the members of the Legislature shall be responsible for the opinion said Legislature may give to the Governor against an express law, and particularly if it be constitutional, or for bribery or subornation.

ART. 10. The Legislature shall be styled "Excellency;" their members "Honorable" (Senoria) in their official capacity; and they shall receive $1,500 per annum.

ART. 11. The Governor shall administer the oath of office to each member of the Legislature, in case that body be present it shall be administered in their presence, to keep and cause to be kept the constitutional laws, and faithfully to fulfil the obligations of their situations, being responsible for the infractions which they may commit or not impede.

ART. 12. The Legislature shall have a Secretary with a salary not to exceed $1200 per annum.

ART. 13. The Restrictions of the Governor and Departmental Legislature:—

1st. They shall impose no illegal contributions, nor apply any contributions to other than those objects pointed out by law.

2d. They shall not adopt any measures for raising armed forces except in such cases wherein they are expressly authorized by law, or when they may be ordered so to do by the General Government.

3d. They shall not make use of any other authority than that granted to them by law.

ART. 14. The members of the Departmental Legislature cannot renounce their situations without a legal motive, to be approved by the Legislature itself, and sanctioned by the Governor.

SECTION IV.

Prefects and Sub-Prefects.

ART. 1. In each district there shall be a Prefect named by the Governor and confirmed by the General Government, who shall remain in office four years, and may be re-elected.

ART. 2. It belongs to the Prefects:—

1st. To take care of public order and tranquility in their district, with entire subjection to the Governor.

2d. To publish without delay, enforce and cause to be enforced, the laws and decrees of Congress which they may receive from the Governor, and circulate them in the towns of the district.

3d. To observe, and cause to be observed, the decrees and orders of the General Government, the resolutions of the Departmental Legislature and of the Governor.

ART. 3. In order to carry out the foregoing powers and duties (atribuciodes,) they may in their district impose by their own authority, fines to the amount of one hundred dollars, to be delivered to the municipal fund of the place where the person fined belongs, or they may sentence to fifteen days of public works, or arrest for double that period, those who disobey or are wanting in respect towards them, or who in any other way disturb the public tranquility ; attention being paid to the circumstances of the individuals, and a trial being allowed them in case they should require one. But with respect to such faults as have penalties assigned to them by law, the existing laws must be observed.

Art. 4. They will hear complaints against the functionaries of the government of the district, and they may in their own authority impose upon them a fine of the amount of thirty dollars, to be applied to the municipal fund of the place to which the person fined belongs, for faults cognizable by government ; but in case they should consider that said functionaries should be suspended, they will inform the Governor for him to determine what may be convenient.

Art. 5. They will resolve on their own authority the doubts which may occur respecting the election of Ayuntamientos, and accept or not the resignations of the members thereof, and the Justices of the Peace ; but the parties interested will nevertheless have the right to appeal directly to the Governor.

Art. 6. Should any one consider himself wronged in any of the three foregoing cases, he may appeal to the Governor, who will definitively decide what he may consider just.

Art. 7. When public tranquility or the investigation of some crime makes it necessary, they may give a written order to search certain houses, and to arrest any person ; and without this requisite they will order the culprit *in fragante* to be secured, but in both cases they will within three days place the person arrested at the disposal of the competent judge, to whom they will manifest in writing the cause of the arrest.

Art. 8. With the consent of the Governor they may order idle vagabonds who have no known occupation, for the time necessary for their correction, to the establishments destined to that object, or to such manufactories or agricultural establishments as may choose to receive them voluntarily ; the person sentenced being allowed to choose to which of the last two establishments he wishes to go.

Art. 9. They will incite the tribunals to render prompt and upright justice, informing the Governor of the defects they may note in the magistrates ; but without intermeddling in their functions.

Art. 10. They will take particular care that common schools be not wanting in any of the towns of the Department.

Art. 11. They will scrupulously take care that the masters and mistresses not only possess the necessary instruction, but they also be of good moral character, the circumstances of the place being taken into consideration.

Art. 12. Should the want of funds prevent the establishment of schools, they will apply to the Governor that he may make it known to the Departmental Legislature.

Art. 13. They will propose to the Governor whatever measures they may judge proper for the encouragement of agriculture and all the branches of industry, instruction, and public beneficence, and for the execution of new works of public utility and for the repairs of the old ones.

Art. 14. They will by their own authority and agreeable to the laws, regulate the distribution of *common* lands in the towns of the district, provided there be no law suits pending in the tribunals respecting them ; the parties interested having the right to appeal to the Governor, who in concert with the Departmental Legislature, will decide definitively what may be most convenient. (1.)

Art. 15. They will cause the Sub Prefects, Ayuntamientos, and Justices of the Peace to comply faithfully with their respective obligations, and see that they do not exceed their authority.

Art. 16. In the administration and expenditure of the funds of the towns, they will exercise the supervision which may be granted to them by the ordinances of the Ayuntamientos.

Art. 17. They will appoint the Sub-Prefects, sending the appointments to the Governor to obtain his approval.

Art. 18. Should not the Governor's answer arrive in time, owing to the loss of the mail or any other cause, the person appointed will take his situation on the 1st of January in which the periodical renovation takes place, without prejudicing what the Governor may resolve.

Art. 19. They will also name the Justices of the Peace of the District, to be proposed to them by the Sub-Prefects of the different towns, observing what is ordered in the two preceding articles.

Art. 20. The Prefects will communicate their appointments to the new Sub-Prefects in an official letter, of which they will also send a copy to the former ones, that they may likewise officially inform the authorities of the towns.

Art. 21. In the same manner they will communicate the appointments to the new Justices of the Peace and to those who have ceased, that these latter may inform all whom it may concern.

(1.) This distribution has reference only to temporary use and occupation. *Common* lands cannot be sold without legislative authority, but *municipal* lands, with certain restrictions, may be sold by the Town Councils.

Art. 22. They will require from the military commandant the necessary force for the preservation or re-establishment of public tranquility and for the security of the roads.

Art. 23. The Prefects on taking possession of their situations will receive by inventory all the documents, laws, decrees, orders and other papers belonging to the Prefect's office, and will in the same manner deliver to their successors, they being responsible for any loss of said documents.

Art. 24. They shall be the ordinary channel of communication between the Governor and the Subaltern authorities of the District; and whatever representations may be made by the latter to the former must be accompanied with their remarks (information.) Their ordinary place of residence shall be the chief town of the district, unless under particular circumstances, the Governor may determine otherwise with the consent of the Departmental Legislature.

Art. 25 Whenever they may think proper they will consult with some competent judge, (Juez de letras) who is bound to give his advice.

Art. 26. The Governor in concert with the Departmental Legislature, and bearing in mind the different circumstances of the districts, will propose to the President of the Republic the salary which each Prefect ought to enjoy, but this must not exceed $2500 per annum.

Art. 27. Each Prefect shall have a Secretary, which he may appoint and remove at pleasure, who shall have a salary of $700 per annum. Neither the Prefects nor their Secretaries can ask or receive any emolument or fee for any kind of business connected with their offices.

Art. 28. The Prefects on entering on their duties will make oath in presence of the Ayuntamiento of the chief town of their district, or if there be no Ayuntamiento, then before a Justice of the Peace.

Art. 29. The Secretaries will take a similar oath before their respective Prefects.

Art. 30. The Sub-Prefects have the same faculties and are subject to the same obligations of the Prefects in their respective localities, but in all their official duties they are subject to the direction of the Prefect of their District. They can however of their own authority impose a fine of $50 or sentence to eight days labor on the public works in the same manner and under the same restrictions as the Prefects. On entering upon the duties of their office they take a similar oath, and are allowed $365 per annum for stationery &c., which is the only salary they receive; they however are not prohibited from receiving fees.

SECTION V.

Of the Ayuntamientos.

Art. 1. The Capital of the Department, Ports with a population of 4000 inhabitants, Interior Towns of 8000 inhabitants, Towns which had Ayuntamientos previous to 1808, and those to whom this right is given by special law, shall be entitled to Ayuntamientos or Town Councils.

Art. 2. In order to form a quorum for the transaction of any business, more than one half of the members must be present.

Art. 3. The number of Alcaldes, Regidores, and Sindicos will be fixed by the Departmental Legislature in concert with the Governor, but the first must not exceed six; the second, twelve; and the third, two.

Art. 4. The Alcaldes are to be removed every year, half of the Regidores the same, and when there are two Sindicos one of them, the first appointed to be first removed; when there is only one Sindico he must be changed every year.

Art. 5. The Alcaldes, Regidores, and Sindicos may be re-elected indefinitely, and no one can refuse to serve without a just cause, approved by the Governor or Prefect, or in case of re-election, when two years have not expired, or if within the same period they have acted in any other municipal situation, or as Sub Prefect, or Justice of the Peace.

Art. 6. In case of the death or incapacity of any of the members of the Ayuntamiento, others may be elected to supply their places, unless the vacancy should occur within less than three months of the close of the year; in which case the periodical time must be waited for.

Art. 7. If the newly elected should be an Alcalde, he will take the place that was vacant; if a Regidor or Sindico, he will occupy the lowest place, and the others will ascend according to the order of their appointment, until the vacancy be filled up.

Art. 8. In case of the suspension of an entire Ayuntamiento, or part of one, the Ayuntamiento of the preceding year will take its place in the whole or in part as it may happen.

Art. 9. The following persons cannot be members of Ayuntamiento: Officers appointed by Congress, by the General or Departmental Governments, the Magistrates of the Supreme tribunals, the legal judge of the lower court (de primera instancia;) Clergymen, Directors of Hospitals, or other chartible institutions.

Art. 10. The Ayuntamientos, under subjection to the Sub-Prefects, and through them to the Prefects and Governor, will have charge of the police, health, comfort, ornament, order and security of their respective jurisdictions.

Art. 11. They will consequently take care of the cleanliness of the streets, market places and the public squares.

ART. 12. They will see that in each town there be one or more burying grounds conveniently located.

ART. 13. They will watch over the quality of all kinds of liquors and provisions, in order that nothing unsound or corrupted be sold.

ART. 14. They will take care that in the Apothecary shops, no rancid or adulterated drugs be sold, to which end they may appoint intelligent persons of the faculty to examine them.

ART. 15. They will see that marshes be drained, and that stagnant and unhealthy waters be made to run off, and that everything which tends to injure the health of men or cattle be removed.

ART. 16. They will likewise take care of prisons, hospitals, and establishments of public benificence which are not of private foundations.

ART. 17. The moment that any prevailing sickness makes its appearance in the district of the Municipality, the Ayuntamiento will inform the Sub-Prefect, or should there be no Sub-Prefect, the Prefect, in order that through his means, the necessary assistance may be administered, but this will not prevent the Ayuntamiento from taking in the mean time the necessary steps to cut off or restrain the evil in its commencement.

ART. 18. With this laudabe object, they will name a committee of charity, composed of a Regidor or Alcalde, a Sindico, a Physician should there be one in the place, and two residents or more, should the Ayuntamiento think it necessary, according to the extent of the place and the duties to be performed.

ART. 19. The Ayuntamiento will remit semi-annually, to the Sub-Prefect, or in default of him to the Prefect, that he may forward it to the Governor, an account of the births, marriages and deaths in each of these periods, which must embrace all its district, and mention the sex, age, diseases of which they may have died, keeping in its records a copy of this document.

ART. 20. In order to obtain these data, they may ask them of the parish curates, the Justices of the Peace, the municipality, or any other persons or corporation capable of furnishing them.

ART. 21. In order to attend to the ornament and comfort of the towns, they will see that the market places, be well distributed, and that every obstacle, tending to hinder them from being sufficiently provided be removed.

ART. 22. They will take care of the preservation of the public fountains, and see that there be abundance of water for men and cattle.

ART. 23. They will likewise endeavor as far as possible, to have the streets straight, paved and lighted, and that there be public walks and abundant plantations, for the beauty and health of the towns.

ART. 24. It belongs to them to procure the construction and repairing of bridges, causeways and roads, and to encourage agriculture, industry, trade and whatever they may consider useful to the inhabitants.

ART. 25. At the junction of different roads, they will place inscriptions pointing out the respective directions and distances to the nearest towns.

ART. 26. It belongs to the Ayuntamientos, to make contract for all kinds of diversions, licence having previously been obtained from the first local political authorty.

ART. 27. The products from these contracts must be paid into the municipal funds.

ART. 28. If the regulations of police and good government should not embrace all the measures which the Ayuntamientos may consider necessary for the preservation of order and the security of persons and property, they may propose to the Governor whatever others they may deem convenient, in order that those which may appear just may be adopted.

ART. 29. They will see that in every town there be a safe and commodious prison, that in said prisons different departments be found for persons arrested and for prisoners, and they will take care that the latter be usefully employed.

ART. 30. They will pay careful attention to the establishment of Common Schools in every town, the masters and mistresses of which must be paid out of the municipal fund, and they will not only be careful to appoint proper persons, but to see that at all times they continue to be of good conduct and sound morals.

ART. 31. They will distribute with all possible impartiality, the municipal duties imposed upon the citizens, guiding themselves by the existing laws, or by such as may hereafter be made.

ART. 32. They will watch over the arrangement of the weights and measures, agreeable to the laws on the subject.

ART. 33. The Ayuntamientos, and every one of their members, whenever they may be called upon by the Prefect, Sub-Prefect, and Alcaldes, will render every assistance towards carrying into execution the laws, decrees and orders, and the preservation of public order.

ART. 34. They will have the administration and expenditure of the municipal funds to manage, being guided by the ordinances relating thereto, and having in view the expenses approved by the Government. Within the first two months of the year, they will remit to the Sub-Prefect, or in default of him, to the Prefect, that he may send to the Governor, an account with vouchers, of the total amount of municipal funds, and of the direction given them during the preceeding year.

ART. 35. The municipal funds will be deposited with such person or persons as the Ayuntamiento may appoint, under its responsibility.

ART. 36. The mal administration of the funds and the expenditure thereof in expenses not designated by the ordinances of the Ayuntamientos, or which have not obtained the approbation of Government, involve the pecuniary and personal responsibility of each of its members, who may prove to be culpable in its management, or who may have given their votes in the resolutions of said corporation; but those who may not have voted for such resolutions will be free from responsibility.

Art. 37. The Ayuntamientos may appoint at their pleasure a Secretary, and assign him with the approbation of the Governor, who will act in concert with the Departmental Legislature, the salary that may be considered just; but he cannot be removed from his situation without the same approbation.

Art. 38. Should the municipal funds not be sufficient to pay the salary of a Secretary, the Regidores by monthly turns will perform his duties, and they will only be allowed stationery.

Art. 39. The members of the Ayuntamientos on taking office will take the same oath as other political authorities; the Alcalde, or the first one, should there be two or more, will take it at the hands of the Prefect or Sub-Prefect, or in defect of both, at the hands of the former Alcalde; and the other members of the corporation, as likewise the Justices of the Peace of the Municipality will also be sworn in by the Alcalde.

Art. 40. The Secretaries will take the same oath before their Ayuntamientos.

SECTION VI.

Of the Alcaldes.

Art. 1. The Alcaldes in the places of their usual residence, will take care of good order and public tranquility.

Art. 2. They will watch over the execution and fulfilment of the police regulations, laws, decrees, and orders which may be communicated to them by the Sub-Prefects, or in their defect, by the Prefects, and they will duly circulate them to the Justices of the Peace of the Municipality.

Art. 3. For the fulfilment of the objects mentioned in the preceding articles they will ask for the necessary force from the Military Commandant.

Art. 4. In defect of such force, or if it should not be sufficient, and any citizens should ask assistance in order to secure their persons or property when they are in danger, and in general for the security or apprehension of criminals within their jurisdiction, and for the preservation of public order, they will call upon the citizens, who are strictly obliged to obey them, the same as any other public authority.

Art. 5. They will cause the culprit, *in fragante*, to be secured and within three days will put him at the disposal of the competent Judge.

Art. 6. They will see that the residents of the place live by useful occupations, and they will reprimand the idle, vagabonds, persons of bad conduct, and those who have no known occupation.

Art. 7. Those who through drunkenness or any other motive, disturb the public tranquility, or who disobey them, or are wanting in respect to them, they may on their own authority fine to the amount of $25, to be applied to the municipal funds, or they may sentence to four days of public works, or double the time of arrest, taking into consideration the circumstances of the individuals, and giving them a trial in case they may require it; but with respect to crimes designated by law the existing regulations must be observed.

Art. 8. Should any one consider himself aggrieved in the case of the preceding article he may appeal to the immediate superior, who will definitely determine what he may esteem just.

Art. 9. They will assist and have a vote at the session of the Ayuntamientos, and they will preside over them according to the order of their appointment when neither the Prefect nor Sub-Prefect assist, and when they do preside their vote shall be decisive.

Art. 10. The temporary absence of the Alcaldes will be supplied by the Regidores according to the order of their appointment. The same will be practised in case of death, &c., until the person be elected who is to succeed them.

SECTION VII.

Of the Justices of the Peace.

Art. 1. The Departmental Legislature and the Governor, having previously heard the opinion of the respective Prefects and Sub-Prefects, and bearing in mind the different circumstances of all the towns and villages of the Department, will determine the number of Justices of the Peace which there should be in each of them; but they must not neglect to establish them in every ward and populous rancheria distant from a town.

Art. 2. The Justices of the Peace are to be named by the Prefect of the District on the recommendations of the respective Sub Prefects.

Art. 3. In every place of one thousand inhabitants or more, the Justice of the Peace shall have, under subjection to the Sub Prefect, and through him to the superior authorities, the same faculties and obligations as the Ayuntamientos; but in the management or supervision of the municipal funds, they will restrict themselves to what may be established in the ordinances to be made by the Departmental Legislature.

Art. 4. These Justices of the Peace, as well as those of places which do not contain one thousand inhabitants; those of the suburbs and rancherias at a distance from towns, and those of the quarters and wards of every populous town, shall have the faculties and obligations granted to and imposed on the Alcaldes in Section VI, Art. 1—6.

Art. 5. In the suburbs and rancherias distant from towns, and in such towns where only a Justice of the Peace is established, a substitute shall also be named in the same manner as the real one, to take his place in case of temporary absence. In other places where there are several Justices of the Peace, they shall during the present year 1837 mutually supply the places of each other. In future this shall be done by the former Justices of the Peace, according to the order of their appointment, beginning with those of the last year.

Art. 6. The Justices of the Peace of those places in which the Ayuntamientos are to cease, will receive, by means of correct inventory, all the documents, books of acts, and whatever may belong to those corporations, and they will remit a copy of it to the Governor that he may send it to the Departmental Legislature.

Art. 7. The Governor, in concert with the Departmental Legislature, will dictate convenient regulations relative to securing the municipal funds until the ordinances fix the rules for their good management and expenditure.

Art. 8. The situation of the Justices of the Peace is a Municipal office which cannot be refused except for a legal cause approved by the Governor or Prefect, after hearing the opinion of the authority that named or proposed him, or in the case of re-election, if two years have not transpired, or if an equal time has not passed since he served as Sub-Prefect.

Art. 9. The Justices of the Peace on entering into office will make the same oath as the other authorities, at the hands of the Sub-Prefect, or in default of him, before the last Justice of the Peace or before the first one appointed, should there be several.

SECTION VIII.

General Observations.

Art. 1. The channels of communication established by this law cannot be deviated from except in extraordinary circumstances, or in case of complaint against some functionary through whose hands the communications ought to be forwarded.

Art. 2. The fines imposed by the functionaries mentioned in this law shall not be collected by themselves, but they shall order them to be delivered to the Treasurer or depository of the municipal funds, who will give the corresponding receipt, so that the person fined may satisfy the authority by which he was fined.

Art. 3. If those elected for Governors, Members of the Departmental Legislature, Prefects, and persons employed in their Secretaries' offices, should receive a higher salary or pension from the public funds than the salary designated by this law, they shall continue to enjoy it, and to that end the excess shall be credited to them.

Art. 4. The laws which organized the economic-political government of the Department are abolished.

PART SECOND.

JUDICIAL.

LAW OF MAY 23d, 1837.

SECTION I.

Of the Superior Court—(Tribunal.,

ART. 1. The Superior Tribunal of California shall consist of four Judges, (ministros,) and one Attorney General, (fiscal;) of which Judges the three senior ones shall compose the first bench, (sala,) and the junior one the second.

ART. 2. The Tribunal shall have a President, who will remain in office two years, and may be re-elected; he shall be appointed by the Tribunal itself, from its own magistrates. In defect of the President, the senior Judge shall preside.

ART. 3. The Judges and Attorney General shall each receive a salary of four thousand dollars per annum.

ART. 4. The superior Tribunals in a body shall be addressed with the title of "Your Excellency." The same title shall be given to each of the benches thereof, and the President, Judges, and Attorney General shall officially be styled "Your Honor," (Senoria.)

ART. 5. Whenever the number of Judges necessary to complete the benches shall be defective, through absence, recusation, vacancy or any other cause, such deficiencies shall be supplied with primary Judges, (Jueces de primera instancia.)

ART. 6. Within the three first months after the installation of the superior Tribunal, it shall form a tariff of the fees and dues to be collected in the Department by the primary Judges, Alcaldes, Advocates, Clerks, and other judicial officers.

ART. 7. The second bench of the superior Tribunal (1) shall take cognizance of the first appeals (en segunda instancia) in the civil and criminal causes of the Territory mentioned in the first attribution of Art. 22d, 5th Constitutional Law; and the first bench shall take cognizance of the second appeals, (en tercera instancia.) (2.)

ART. 8. In the same manner shall causes instituted against Magistrates and Subalterns as mentioned in the second attribution (3) be dispatched; and the second appeal mentioned in said attribution shall belong to the first bench. This bench shall also take cognizance of the right of appeal (recurso) mentioned in the 3d and 4th attributions. (4.) In order to carry out the objects comprehended in the 7th, 8th, and 9th attributions, (5) a full tribunal of all the Judges shall sit, in which the Attorney General shall also have a vote.

ART. 9. The superior Tribunal, including the President, all the Judges and the Attorney General, shall, in the capital of the Department, perform a general examination of prisons, including all places where prisoners may be detained subject to the ordinary jurisdiction, and make a report of said examination to government, that it may publish the same and take the necessary measures in virtue of its powers. At these examinations two members of the Ayuntamiento shall attend (without any vote) with the Magistrates of the Tribunals, next to the senior one; and the Ayuntamiento shall be previously informed of the appointed hour, in order that it may appoint those who are to attend.

ART. 10. Public examinations shall likewise be made by two of the Judges, acting by turns, and commencing with the junior ones. The President shall not be included; the Attorney Gene-

---

(1) The powers of the superior Tribunals, as originally organized, are given in Law 5th, Art. 22d, of the Constitution of Mexico, but the transfer of this Territory to the United States has annulled or limited some of the powers so conferred.

(2) The causes referred to in the latter part of this Article are those against the superior Magistrates of the Territory.

(3) This has reference to causes against inferior Magistrates and the Subalterns and dependents of the Tribunal.

(4) These have reference to appeals from the Judges of first instance, and the adjustment of competences of jurisdiction arising between subaltern Judges.

(5) These have reference to the nomination of Judges, subalterns and dependents of the Courts.

ral and Secretaries shall attend, and likewise the Judges of first instance in criminal cases, with their respective clerks.

Art. 11. At both of these examinations all the prisoners shall present themselves. The Magistrates, besides the customary examination, shall personally inspect the habitations and scrupulously inquire into the treatment given to the prisoners, the food and attention bestowed upon them, and if they are loaded with more irons than the Judge has commanded, or are kept in solitary confinement (incomunicados) without orders. But if there should be prisoners of another jurisdiction in the public prisons, they shall confine themselves to examining how they are treated, correct the abuses and defects of the jailors, and report to the respective Magistrates whatever further they may observe.

Art. 12. Whenever a prisoner shall ask to be heard, one of the Judges having cognizance of the cause shall go and hear what he has to say, and report to the corresponding bench.

Art. 13. The reports or notices of the institution of suits or causes, which the inferior Judges have to address to the superior Tribunal, shall be presented to the bench of second instance, for it to take the necessary measures for the speedy conclusion of the same, according as the nature and enormity of the crimes may require.

Art. 14. The superior Tribunal shall see that the primary Judges in criminal cases remit to it, quarterly, circumstantial lists of the causes finished during that period, and of those still pending, expressing the dates on which they commenced and their actual state of forwardness; which shall be submitted to the bench of second instance, in order that in view thereof, and after hearing the Attorney General, the necessary steps may be taken towards the speedy and exact administration of justice.

Art. 15. The Attorney General shall be heard in all criminal and civil causes in which the public interests or the ordinary jurisdiction are concerned. When he acts as plaintiff, (actor,) or pleads his own rights (coadyuvare sus derechos,) he shall speak in Court before the attorney of the criminal, and may be constrained (apremiado) at the instance of the parties the same as any of them. His replies, whether in civil or criminal cases, shall never be concealed so that the parties interested cannot see them, and he cannot be recused. (recusado.)

Art. 16. To constitute a sentence in a bench of three judges, two perfectly coinciding votes are requisite.

SECTION II.

Of the Courts of First Instance—(Primeria Instancia.)

Art. 1. The Governor and Legislature, on the recommendation of the superior Tribunal, shall designate the number of Judges of this Court in the chief town (cabecera) of each district, in conformity with the laws.

Art. 2. Where there is but one Judge of first instance to a district, he shall have both civil and criminal jurisdiction; if more than one, these are separate.

Art. 3. Each Court shall have a Clerk and Recorder, (Escribano y Escribiente,) and an Executive officer, (Comisario.)

Art. 4. The salaries of the Judges and subalterns of this court is fixed by the Governor and superior Tribunal, in concert with the Departmental Legislature, to be afterwards approved of by the General Government. (1.)

Art. 5. The Clerks or Notaries (Escribanos) of this Court are appointed by the superior Tribunal, on the recommendation of the Judges of the Court; the other subalterns are named by the Judges themselves, due notice of these appointments being given both to the Governor and superior Tribunal.

Art. 6. These Judges, on entering upon their duties, must take the usual oath of office. In case of sickness, absence, death, &c., their places may be supplied *ad interim* by persons appointed by the superior Tribunal, with the approbation of the Governor.

Art. 7. No Judge of first instance can act in a civil or criminal case without the Clerk of the Court, (Escribano,) except in case there be no such Clerk, or where the case is too urgent to wait for his presence, in which case two witnesses must be called in, and the papers so witnessed must be afterwards turned over to the custody of the Clerk.

Art. 8. The cognizance and jurisdiction of these Judges are limited to the judicial subjects of their territory.

Art. 9. All law suits and civil or criminal causes, of whatever description, shall be brought forward and carried on before the respective Magistrate of first instance, excepting in cases wherein clergymen and military persons are privileged by the constitutional or other laws in force.

---

(1) The salary of the Judge of Civil Courts was fixed at $1,500, with the stipulated fees of fice. Governor Riley, in his Proclamation, has signified his intention to pay this salary to the Judge of first instance in each political district of California.

ART. 10. No complaint, either civil or criminal, involving simply personal injuries, can be admitted without proving, with a competent certificate, that conciliatory measures have been attempted, (viz : by means of arbitrators or *hombres buenos.*)

ART. 11. From the preceding Art. are to be excepted, verbal processes; those of contest respecting chaplaincies, (capellanias colativas,) and other ecclesiastical causes of the same description, in which the parties interested cannot come to a previous arrangement; the causes which interest the public revenue, the municipal funds of towns, public establishments, minors, those deprived of the administration of their property, and vacant inheritances. In the same manner, no conciliation is to be attempted for the recovery of any kind of contributions or taxes, whether national or municipal ones, nor for the recovery of debts which have the same origin. Neither is it necessary in the trial of summary and very summary interdictions of possession, the denouncement of a new work, or a retraction; nor in promoting the faculty of inventories and distribution of inheritances, nor in other urgent cases of the same nature; but should a formal complaint have to be afterwards made which would cause a litigious process, then conciliation ought first to be attempted, but it must not take place in cases of bankruptcy where creditors sue for their dues; but it shall take place when any citizen has to demand judicially the payment of a debt, although it may arise from a public writing.

Note.—The translator cannot vouch for the correctness of the translation of the foregoing Art., as he does not himself fully understand the original, on account of the many law terms used therein.—W. E. P. H.

ART 12. In the trial of causes which exceed one hundred dollars but do not exceed two hundred dollars, the Judges will take cognizance by means of a written process according to law, but without appeal; nevertheless the parties may take advantage of the appeal of necessity before the superior Tribunal, should the laws have been violated which regulate the mode of proceeding. This appeal shall be referred to the same Judge, in the terms and for the purpose mentioned in Art. 20 of Sec. iv.

ART. 13. Any person who may be despoiled of or disturbed in his possessions, whether the aggressor be an ecclesiastic, a layman, or a military character, will apply to the legal Judge for restitution and protection; and cognizance of these matters are to be taken by means of the corresponding very summary process, or even by means of the plenary one of possession if the parties should desire it, with appeal to the respective superior Tribunal; the judgment of property (juicio de propriedad) being reserved to the competent Judges.

ART. 14. The Judges of the first instance, in their respective districts, will take cognizance, by way of precaution, with the Alcaldes, in the formation of inventories, justifications, *ad perpetuam*, and other judicial matters of this kind, in which the parties have yet made no opposition.

ART. 15. They will likewise take cognizance of such civil and criminal causes respecting common crimes as may arise against the Alcaldes of their district.

ART. 16. Every sentence of first instance in criminal causes must be immediately notified to the person who entered the suit and to the culprit, and if either of them shall appeal, said causes must, without delay, be remitted to the superior tribunal, the parties being previously summoned.

ART. 17. If both the accused and culprit agree to the sentence, and the suit should be respecting trivial crimes for which the law imposes no corporeal punishment, the judge will execute the sentence. But if the cause should be one respecting crimes which have such a punishment assigned to them. the process shall be remitted to the superior tribunal, the time for appealing having passed, although the parties themselves should not appeal, they being previously cited.

ART. 18. In all civil causes, in which according to law the appeal should take place in both effects, and be clearly admitted, the original acts of the process shall be remitted to the superior tribunal at the costs of the appellant, the parties being previously cited, that they may make use of their rights. But if said appeal be merely admitted in the devolutive effect and not in the suspensive one (*efecto devolutivo y* (*no en el*) *suspensivo*) [the former of which means, the cognizance which a superior judge takes of the determinations of an inferior one without suspending the execution of them; and the latter, the same thing together with the suspension of the execution—*the Translator*,] the remission must not take place until after the execution of the determination, whatever practice there may be to the contrary.

ART. 19. The Judges of first instance, in the place of their residence, if there be no superior tribunal there, will in public make the prision examinations required by law; two members of the Ayuntamiento will also be present at the general ones, but without a vote; and every month a report of said examinations will be rendered to the superior tribunal. They will likewise go to the prison when any culprit asks for audience, and they will hear whatever he may have to say.

ART. 20. The inferior magistrate will also report to the superior tribunal, at furthest within the three days after commencing the causes, all such as they may be forming for crimes committed in the respective jurisdictions. They will likewise send to said tribunal quarterly, a general list of those that they may have concluded in that time, and of such as still remain unfinished in their respective courts, expressing the state in which they may be and the dates of their commencement.

SECTION III.

Of Alcaldes and Justices of the Peace.

Art. 1. It belongs exclusively to the Alcaldes of the Ayuntamientos and to the Justices of the Peace, in places whose population consists of one thousand or more inhabitants, to exercise in their jurisdiction, with respect to all classes of persons, the office of conciliators.

Art. 2. It likewise belongs to such Alcaldes and Justices of the Peace to take cognizance of, and decide in their respective towns, all verbal processes which may occur, except those in which ecclesiastics and military persons are sued.

Art. 3. It belongs likewise to them, to dictate in litigious cases the very urgent measures that will not admit being taken before the primary judges; and to take, under similar circumstances, the first steps in criminal causes, and also such others as they may be commissioned to do by the respective tribunals and primary courts.

Art. 4. Of the attributions comprehended in the three foregoing articles, the Justices of Peace of such places as do not contain one thousand inhabitants shall only exercise that of taking (whether in civil or criminal cases) such steps as from their urgency do not give time to apply to the nearest respective authorities.

Art. 5. In order to verify the judgment of conciliation, whosoever may have to institute any civil suit, the value of which does not exceed one hundred dollars, or any criminal one respecting serious injuries, purely personal, shall make his complaint to the Alcalde or competent Justice of the Peace, demanding verbally to have the accused party summoned in order to commence the trial of conciliation, and said Alcalde or Justice of Peace will immediately have the summons made out, which must mention the object of the complaint, and fix the day, hour, and place, in which the parties have to appear, and both the accuser and the accused are to be told to bring each his arbitrator (hombre-bueno), who must be a citizen in the exercise of his rights, and completed his 25th year of age—[with us 21 years is the legal age.]

Art. 6. The accused party is bound to concur in obedience to the summons of the Alcalde or Justice of Peace, but should he not do so, a second summons must be sent to him to appear at some newly appointed time, under a penalty of from two to ten dollars fine; and should he still not come forward, it shall be considered that the means of conciliation have been attempted, and that the trial is at an end, (*i. e.* the trial of conciliation,) and the fine imposed upon the accused party shall be irremissibly exacted.

Art. 7. It shall likewise be considered that the means of conciliation have been tried, and that the trial is concluded, if the person summoned appear before the Alcade or Justice of Peace in obedience to the first or second summons, and say that he renounces the benefit of conciliation.

Art. 8. In the two cases treated of in the two foregoing articles, the corresponding record must be made in the respective book, and be signed in the first case by the Alcalde or Justice of Peace, the Plaintiff and Clerk, (Escribano,) if there be one, and if not by two assisting witnesses; and in the second case, by the Alcalde or Justice of Peace, the Plaintiff and Defendant; and whenever the latter does not make his appearance, but renounces the aforesaid benefit, he must necessarily do it in writing.

Art. 9. When the parties do come forward, either personally or by means of their lawful representatives, to proceed with the trial of Conciliation, the Alcalde or Justice of Peace and the Arbitrators will make themselves acquainted with what the parties have to expose respecting the matter in dispute, and when the said parties retire, the Alcalde or Justice of Peace will hear the opinion of the Arbitrators, and will immediately, or within eight days at farthest, give the sentence which he may consider most fitting to avoid a law suit, and to bring about the mutual conformity of the parties.

Art. 10. Each Alcalde or Justice of Peace shall have a book entitled "BOOK OF CONCILIATIONS," in which he shall note down a concise account of what occurs in the trials of Conciliation, agreeably to what is ordered in the preceding article and in continuation of the Conciliatory Sentence dictated by the Alcalde or Justice of Peace, which must be notified to the parties interested in presence of the Arbitrators, in order that they may say whether they agree to it or not, which must also be noted down and be signed by the Alcalde or Justice, the Arbitrators, and parties interested.

Art. 11. When the parties agree to the Sentence, the certified copies of the proceedings which they may ask for shall be given to them in order that the corresponding authority may carry it into effect, and if either of the parties should not agree, the Alcalde or Justice of Peace will give him a certificate that the means of Conciliation have been attempted, but without success; the parties interested merely paying the costs of said certificates in the accustomed form.

Art. 12. In the same Book of Conciliations must be entered the record mentioned in Art. 8, and this Book must remain in the archives when the Alcalde or Justice of Peace conclude the time of their appointment.

Art. 13. The fines mentioned in Art. 6 must be delivered to the respective Treasurers of the Ayuntamientos, in order that the amount of them may go towards paying the expenses of the books which are to be given to the Alcaldes and Justices of Peace.

Art. 14. These Alcaldes and Justices will decide by verbal process the civil complaints which do not exceed one hundred dollars, and the criminal ones respecting trifling injuries and other similar faults that do not merit any other punishment than a slight reprehension or correction.

Art. 15. The plaintiff or complainant who enters any suit of this kind, will apply to the competent Alcade or Justice, and make his complaint verbally, and this authority will cause the defendant to appear, ordering each party to bring his respective arbitrator with him, who must have the requisites mentioned in Art. 5.

Art. 16. In verbal processes, also, the Clerk (if there be one) will concur, or in his defect two assisting witnesses; and after the Alcalde or Justice of Peace and the arbitrators have made themselves acquainted with the complaint of the one party and the defence of the other, these parties shall retire and the Alcalde or Justice of Peace will hear the opinion ot the arbitrators, and immediately or within eight days at farthest pronounce his definitive sentence or decision, which shall be ordered to be carried into execution by the same Alcalde or Justice of Peace, or by any other authority to which a proper certificate of said sentence be presented.

Art. 17. A concise account of the proceedings of these processes shall be entered in a book called "Book of Verbal Processes," and in continuation, the definitive decision or sentence dictated on the subject, and this instrument must be signed by the Alcalde or Justice of Peace, the arbitrators, the parties interested and the Clerk or acting witnesses. This book shall also be placed in the archives when the Alcaldes or Justices of Peace conclude their term of office.

Art. 18. Against the definitive sentences given in verbal processes, no other appeal can be admitted than that of the responsibility of the Alcaldes and Justices of Peace to the superior tribunal; and in said processes no fees are to be recovered, but merely the costs of the certificates that may be given.

Art. 19. The attributions mentioned in Arts. 4 and 5 must necessarily be exercised by the Alcaldes or Justices of Peace in presence of the Clerks, if there be such, and if not, before two assisting witnesses.

Art. 20. When the subject brought before the Alcaldes or Justices of Peace relates to the retention of the goods of a debtor who wishes to make away with or conceal them, the prohibition of a new work, or other matters of like urgency, the Alcaldes or Justices of Peace will themselves take such necessary steps as may be required to avoid the evils consequent on delay, and they will order the parties interested then to try the means of conciliation.

SECTION IV.

General Laws.

Art. 1. In every criminal suit, the sentence of first appeal (segunda instancia) shall cause execution when it is perfectly agreeable to the first sentence, or if the parties agree to it.

Art. 2. In criminal causes there cannot be less than one appeal (dos instancias) even when the accuser and the culprit agree to the first sentence.

Art. 3. All witnesses to be examined in any civil or criminal cause must necessarily be examined by the proper tribunals or magistrates which have cognizance of said causes, and if they should reside at other places, they must be examined by the Magistrate or Alcalde where they live. (1)

Art. 4. Every person, of whatever class, privileges, or condition he may be, when he has to give his declaration as a witness in a criminal cause, is obliged to appear for this purpose before the Magistrate who has cognizance thereof, without the necessity of previous permission from his chiefs or superiors.

Art. 5. The confrontation of witnesses with the culprit shall only be practised when the Magistrate considers it absolutely necessary in order to find out the truth.

Art. 6. Both the confrontation mentioned in the preceding article and the ratifications, are to be made in the process immediately after having examined the witness; the culprit being made to appear in order that he may know him, and the witness summoned in the act of ratification, which must take place immediately after the culprit retires.

Art. 7. If the first steps of the process (information sumaria) take place before the culprit be apprehended, as soon as he is apprehended and his preparatory declaration shall have been taken, the witnesses which have to be examined must be summoned for the purposes mentioned in the preceding article.

Art. 8. No summons shall be sent which has not some relation to the crime, or which is judged to be useless or of no weight in the business as regards the eliciting of truth.

---

(1) It may be a question whether this and some of the following articles are not modified by Arts. V. and VI. of the amendments to the Constitution of the United States.

Art. 9. When the pleas alleged by the culprit have no relation to the crime, or cannot in any way diminish its enormity, or are unlikely or improbable, they shall be left out altogether without receiving the cause on proof (a'prueba;) in which case the trial (sumaria) being concluded, the culprit having been previously cited, and the Attorney General in the superior tribunal, it shall be delivered to the attorney or defender of the culprit for him to answer to the charges in the term of three days, which having taken place the definitive sentence shall be given.

Art. 10. When any criminal escapes he shall not be summoned by edicts or by the public crier; but requisitory letters shall be made out for his apprehension and the necessary steps taken for his recovery: in the mean time the trial shall be postponed, except as to collecting proof of the crime and its circumstances: but it shall be resumed when the apprehension takes place.

Art. 11. In cases where the plenary judgment has to be renewed, the cause shall be received on proof for a short time, to be postponed, according to its circumstances, as far as forty days; and only in the case of having to examine witnesses or to receive some other proof at such considerable distances as to make that term not sufficient, it may be postponed for sixty days, without any restitution or other recourse taking place in these terms.

Art. 12. When the criminals interpose an appeal against any interlocutory proceedings, or any other appeal that has to go to the tribunal of second or third instance, the continuation of the cause shall not be suspended; and, therefore, if the original acts which caused the appeal can not be forwarded, certified copies must be sent.

Art. 13. In all civil and criminal causes the interlocutory sentences must be pronounced within the precise term of three days; and the definitive ones shall be dictated by the superior tribunals within fifteen days after the first stage of the suit (vista) be concluded; and by the judges of first instance within eight days after finishing the causes.

Art. 14. In trials of property, plenary ones of possession, and any other civil trial wherein the amount disputed shall exceed $4,000, appeal may be made to the tribunal of the third instance if the parties wish it, although the second sentence agree with the first.

Art. 15. In the same trials, if the amount in question be less than $4,000, the sentence of the tribunal of second instance will cause execution, if it correspond exactly with the first, that is if the second sentence neither adds nor takes away anything which alters the substance or intrinsic merit of the first instance; so that neither the condemnation to pay costs, nor any other demonstration of a similar nature, can be called in opposition to said agreement.

OFFICIAL CORRESPONDENCE.

Executive Department of California,
Monterey, September 11, 1849.

Gentlemen: I have the honor to acknowledge the receipt of your communication of yesterday, respecting the mode of providing for the payment of the expenses of the convention now in session.

I consider myself authorized by the Executive of the United States to use the "civil funds" now in my hands for defraying the necessary expenses of the civil officers of the existing government.

The necessary expenses of the convention will be paid by me from this fund, as far as I may have the means at my disposal; but, as these means may be limited, and as I am held responsible to the government of the United States for the expenditure of the money, I cannot say beforehand whether I shall feel authorized to pay all, or, if not all, what proportion of the expenses incurred by the convention.

Very respectfully, your obedient servant,
B. RILEY,
Brevet Brig. Gen. U. S. Army, and Governor of California.

Messrs. C. T. Botts, E. O. Crosby, T. O. Larkin, Elam Brown, R. M. Price, *Committee.*

Executive Department of California,
Monterey, September 13, 1849.

Sir: I have the honor to acknowledge the receipt of your note, (without date,) with a copy of a resolution of the committee, asking if I can place at the disposition of the convention, on or before the first day of October next, the sum of $70,000. I have no authority to place any of the public money now under my control at the disposition of any other person; but, as stated in my letter of the 11th instant, I shall consider it my duty to pay, so far as my means will allow, all the necessary expenses of the convention. I cannot, however, now say positively whether I shall have money enough at my disposal for the accomplishment of this object. In order that your committee may judge of this contingency for yourselves, I enclose a copy of my letter of August 30 to Lieutenant Colonel Hooker.

Very respectfully, your obedient servant,
B. RILEY,
Brevet Brig. Gen. U. S. A., and Governor of California.

Hon. C. T. Botts, *Chairman, &c.*

Executive Department of California,
Monterey, August 30, 1849.

Colonel: I have the honor to acknowledge the receipt of your letter of the 12th instant, communicating the views of General Smith respecting my acts and duties as governor of California.

I must beg leave to dissent from some of these views, and to offer a few remarks in defence of the course which I have pursued in the administration of civil affairs in this country.

In the instructions issued from Washington to General Kearney in 1846, for his guidance in California, the establishment of port regulations was assigned to the commander of the Pacific squadron, while it was said "the appointment of temporary collectors at the several ports appertains to the civil governor of the province." It was also directed that the duties at the custom-houses should be used for the support of the necessary officers of the civil government. This division of duties and this disposition of the proceeds of the customs were continued during the whole war, except that for a part of one year the duties of collectors in some of the ports were performed by army and navy officers, while in others the civil collectors appointed by the governor of California were retained. On the reception of the treaty of peace, Governor Mason, for reasons which have been communicated to government, determined to continue the collection of revenues in this country, on the authority which has been given him, until Congress should act in the matter, or orders to the contrary should be received from Washington. He, therefore, as Governor of California, again appointed collectors in the ports where military officers had performed those duties, and collected the customs on all foreign goods as directed in the tariff of 1846—the commodore of the Pacific squadron continuing the direction of all matters relating to port regulations.

A double necessity impelled the governor to this course: the country was in pressing need of these foreign goods, and Congress had established no port of entry on this coast; the want of a more complete organization of the existing civil government was daily increasing; and as Congress had made no provision for supporting a territorial government in this country, it was absolutely necessary to create a fund for that purpose from duties collected on these foreign goods. It is true there was no law of Congress authorizing the collection of those duties, but at the same time the laws forbade the landing of the goods till the duties were paid. Congress had declined to legislate on the subject, and both the President and Secretary of the Treasury acknowledged the want of power of the Treasury Department to collect revenue in California. The Governor of California, therefore, assumed the responsibility of collecting this revenue for the support of the government of this country—a responsibility which he was fully justified in assuming by the necessity of the case, by the instructions which he had received from Washington, (and which had never been countermanded,) and by the existing laws of the country. It is not pretended that the Governor of California could derive any authority, either from the laws of this country or the instructions of the President, to collect revenue here, *after Congress* assumed the control of it. But in the interim between the signing of the treaty of peace and the extension of the revenue laws over this country, it is a fair presumption that the temporary regulations established here by executive authority respecting foreign commerce continued in force, so far as they conflicted with no provision of the constitution, treaties, or laws of the United States; at any rate, such was the course which Governor Mason determined to pursue, and, as this determination was immediately communicated to Washington, and the receipt of his despatch acknowledged, without one word of dissent being expressed, it is to be presumed that his action in the case met the approval of the government. The executive departments, though well informed of the course which the governor of California was pursuing in reference to the collection and disposition of this money, refrained from any interference, and, in all their orders, letters, and circulars, they most carefully avoided expressing the slightest disapprobation, or even doubt, as to the propriety of that course. Congress was fully aware that Governor Mason was collecting revenue here for the support of the civil government, and yet that body declined passing any laws for appointing collectors on this coast till the very close of the session, and even then no cognizance was taken of the moneys which had been or might be collected previous to the appointment and due instalment of these officers. The reason of this is obvious: as Congress had failed to organize a territorial government here, all were aware that the existing government must continue in force, and that it must have some means of support; such means were found in the neglected revenues of this coast, and employed for that object, and no one felt disposed to interfere or turn these revenues into the general treasury, until a fund was established sufficient for the more immediate and urgent wants of California. On no other supposition can we account for the action of Congress and of the authorities at Washington. It cannot for a moment be supposed that they would direct the continuance of a government here without the means of defraying its expenses; nor that they would tax, through the custom-houses, the people of this infant colony, and at the same time deprive them of all the benefits of a government. Such a course might accord with the policy of the despotic powers of the Old World, but it would never be attempted with impunity in our country.

On assuming command in this country as civil governor, I was directed to receive from Governor Mason all his instructions and communications, and to take them for my guidance in the administration of civil affairs. Upon an examination of these instructions, and a full consultation with Governor Mason, I determined to continue the collection of the revenue till the general government should assume that power, and to add the proceeds to the "civil fund"—using that fund for the necessary expenses of the civil government. Indeed, I had no other course left for me to pursue. This fund formed my only means of defraying the expenses of the government, which were already great. These expenses are daily increasing, and, as I have no power to impose taxes in this country, I cannot carry on the government without the moneys belonging to this "civil fund." Under existing circumstances, the necessity of employing civil officers, and paying them the full salaries allowed by law, is too obvious to require comment. I have pledged myself to pay these salaries from that fund, unless forbidden to do so by direct orders from Washington; and I shall redeem my pledge.

This "civil fund" was commenced in the early part of 1847, and has been formed and used in the manner pointed out in the early instructions to the governor of this Territory. The money has been collected and disbursed by the "Governor of California," and by those appointed by him in virtue of his office. He is, therefore, the person responsible for this money, both to the government and the parties from whom it was collected; and it can be expended only on his orders. Not a cent of this money has been collected under the authority of any department of the army; nor can any such department, or any officer of the army, simply in virtue of his military commission, have any control, direct or indirect, over it. It is true, some of this money has, from time to time, as the wants of the service required, been transferred to the different military departments; but this transfer was in the form of a *loan*; and the money so transferred is still due to the "civil fund," and should be returned. The increased expenditures for the support of the civil government as it is now organized, and the pressing necessity of constructing prisons for the security of civil prisoners, will soon render this restoration absolutely essential in order to carry on the government, especially as the transfer of the custom-houses to the regular collectors appointed by the general government will now cut off all further means of supplying the civil treasury.

Entertaining these views of the correctness of the course which has been pursued by my predecessor and by myself respecting this "civil fund," I was not a little surprised at the ground assumed in your communication, that the collectors in California "are agents of the *military* authority of the department," and that "disbursing officers [of the army] are allowed to draw on this deposite [the civil fund] for all expenses for which there are appropriations by law."

No collectors in California now hold, or have ever held, any appointments, commissions, or authority from any military department; nor have they ever received any orders or instructions from such sources.. All their powers have been derived from the Governor of California, and they have been subject to his orders only. No disbursing officer of the army or of the general government has ever been allowed to draw upon this "civil fund," except in character of civil agent, or as a *loan* to a military department. And I am both surprised and mortified to learn that, at this late hour, an attempt is to be made to remove this money from my control, and to place it at the disposition of officers who have had no responsibility in its collection, and who of right can exercise no authority over it. Under the peculiar situation of the country, with an immense floating population collected together from all parts of the world, I thought my position as Governor of California sufficiently embarrassing without having new obstacles placed in my way by any attempts to deprive me of the only means at my disposal for carrying on the government.

If I mistake not, the opinion that the Governor of California has no control over the "civil fund" is of recent origin. I am told that the civil order of General Mason, as *Governor of California*, dated February 23, to the collector at San Francisco, was shown to General Smith on that day, and received his approbation; and that division orders No. 2, of the same date, were issued at the request of Governor Mason, for the purpose of showing the people of California that the course which had been adopted respecting the revenue on this coast accorded with the views of the general of the division. Moreover, that when informed that all the temporary collectors in California held their authority from the *governor*, the General expressed no wish or desire that the system should be changed. Granting that the military authorities here had a right to assume entire control of the revenue on this coast, although the President of the United States (if I mistake not) has clearly asserted that no such powers could be exercised by officers of the general government without the authority of Congress, it is nevertheless plain that no such power *has* ever been exercised. If such a course was intended by General Smith's orders of February 23, these instructions were never properly carried into execution; nor until the receipt of your letter had I any intimation that such a course was at all desired. The commanding general of the division was certainly aware that this whole revenue matter was managed by officers holding their authority from me as Governor of California, and that when money was wanted by the military departments, application was made to me to authorize the loan or temporary transfer from the "civil funds." If, however, it now be the General's wish to assume a military control of the collection of duties on imports into California, I will immediately discharge the collectors appointed by the Governors of California, and surrender the entire direction of the matter to such military department or military officers as he may direct. But for the money which *has already been collected* by the civil officers under my authority, I alone am responsible; and until further instructions from Washington, I shall continue to hold it, subject to my orders only, and to expend, as heretofore, such portions of it as may be required for the support of the existing civil government. No military officer or military department will be allowed to exercise any control over it. Let me not be understood as claiming for California any authority whatever over the duties on imports *after* that power was assumed and exercised by the general government. But I do say, that when the general government declined exercising that power, and voluntarily and knowingly permitted the proceeds of such duties to be devoted to the support of the existing civil government, it would be both unjust and ungenerous for military officers to attempt to embarrass the civil authorities by taking from them their only means of carrying on that government.

I have but a few words to add respecting that part of your letter which refers to the relations of the civil government with Indian affairs and the public lands.

General Kearney, some two years and a half ago, in virtue of his authority as Governor of California, appointed two sub-Indian agents, and immediately communicated these appointments to Washington. The general government was also informed that these agents were paid from the "civil fund," and would be retained in office until the arrival of agents appointed by the proper authority at Washington.

No military officer has any control over these agents of the civil government, nor can they interfere in any way with the duties of the military officers. I have never claimed to exercise any authority as civil governor over lands properly belonging to the public domain; it, however, is a question still undecided, whether the missions of California belong to the general government, to the government of California, or to the church. The direction and preservation of this property have for many years been vested in the Governor of California, and this system will be continued till the general government shall see fit to assume control over it. The rents of these missions are paid into the "civil fund," and expended as directed by the laws of California ; but the leases are so conditioned as to cease whenever the agents of the United States shall be authorized to take possession of this property in the name of the general government. The authorities at Washington have been informed of this course ; and as no dissent has ever been expressed, it is presumed it meets their approbation.

I beg leave to remark, in conclusion, that while I shall always be most happy to receive the advice and suggestions of the commanding general of the division respecting my duties as civil governor of California, I must nevertheless be permitted to decide upon the measures of my own government; for as no military officer can be held accountable for my civil acts, so no such officer can exercise any control whatever over those acts.

Very respectfully, your obedient servant,

B. RILEY,

Brevet Brig. Gen. U. S. Army, and Governor of California.

Brevet Lieutenant Colonel J. Hooker,

Com'g. Department, Ass't. Adj. General Pacific Division.

EXECUTIVE DEPARTMENT OF CALIFORNIA,
Monterey, September 19, 1849.

GENTLEMEN : I have the honor to acknowledge the receipt of yours of the 17th, asking for information respecting the mode of making out the accounts of the affairs of the convention. Such accounts should in all cases be certified by the president of the convention *as just and true, and authorised by the convention;* then, on receiving my written approval, they will be paid by the civil treasurer, or his agents. Captain Kane will furnish you with blank form of accounts.

Very respectfully, your obedient servant,

B. RILEY,

Brevet Brigadier General United States Army,
and Governor of California.

Messrs. E. O. Crosby, J. P. Walker, E. Brown, T. O. Larkin, J. Aram, *Committee &c.*,

---

STATE DEPARTMENT OF CALIFORNIA,
Monterey, October 12, 1849.

MAJOR : I send you herewith a copy of the governor's proclamation of to-day, and of the constitution just formed by the convention. They will be printed together, in pamphlet form, for general circulation among the people. No effort should be spared to have them printed and circulated with the least possible delay.

I enclose you a copy of proposals for printing by the proprietors of "Alta Californian;" but, if you can get it done with equal expedition and at less expense by any other press, you will do so. These proposals were made with the understanding that the constitution would be printed in the two languages in parallel columns; but it was afterwards determined to print them separately, viz : 8,000 copies in the English and 2,000 in the Spanish language. You may therefore be able to expedite the printing by contracting with separate presses for the printing, that is, with one for the English and the other for the Spanish. Mr. Tefft has been employed by Captain Kane to take this to San Francisco, and to assist you in superintending the printing. As soon as the work is completed, you will deliver to him the copies intended for the districts south of San Jose, including that district. In distributing the printed copies of the Constitution, you will be guided by the ratio of representation as fixed in the schedule ; but in dividing the Spanish and English copies, a larger proportion of the latter should be sent to the northern districts, and most of the former to the south. Extra copies should be retained, on the first distribution, at San Francisco, to be sent south by the steamer, and north by other conveyances, so as to provide for the contingency of the loss of any of those first sent out. Every care should be taken to make the distribution as general as possible, previous to the time of hold the first election.

The Spanish translation will leave here on the 14th by express. You can make your contract accordingly for the printing. I will write you again by the express.

Very respectfully, your obedient servant,

H. W. HALLECK,

Brevet Captain, and Secretary of State.

Major R. Allen, *Civil Treasurer, San Francisco, California.*

EXECUTIVE DEPARTMENT OF CALIFORNIA,
Monterey, October 31, 1849.

GENERAL; The convention which assembled at this place on the 1st of September has completed its labors, and the constitution formed by that body was submitted on the 12th instant to the people for their approval, and I have no doubt of its being ratified by the almost unanimous vote of the qualified electors of this country. A printed copy of this constitution is enclosed herewith. You will see by examining the schedule that it is contemplated to put the new government into operation on or soon after the 15th day of December next; and I shall then surrender my civil powers to whosoever may be designated under the constitution as the executive of the new State. Whatever may be the legal objections to putting into operation a *State* Government previous to its being acknowledged or approved by Congress, these objections must yield to the obvious necessities of the case; for the powers of the existing government are too limited, and its organization too imperfect, to provide for the wants of a country so peculiarly situated, and of a population which is augmenting with such unprecedented rapidity.

I have deemed it my duty to pay from the "civil fund" the current expenses of the convention, and also the salaries of officers as authorised by that body. In the absence of any legislative assembly, I have regarded this convention as representing the wishes of the people of California in the matter of public expenditures. It is true that the salaries and payments authorised by the convention were high, and by some may be considered extravagant; but in deciding upon their justice, we must take into consideration the peculiar state of the country, and the high prices paid here for every thing, even including the necessaries of life. It, however, will continue to be my aim, as it has been heretofore, to keep the expenditures from the "civil funds" within the limits of the strictest economy; nevertheless, the expenses of a civil government in this country are now, and will be for years to come, very large.

The whole country remains remarkable quiet, and the civil officers encounter no serious difficulties in enforcing the laws. It is therefore hoped and believed that the powers of the existing government will be found sufficiently ample to preserve the public tranquillity until it shall be replaced by a more perfect organization under the constitution.

For my views with respect to the proper disposition to be made of the mineral and agricultural lands in this country, with respect to the importance of immediately establishing a mint in California, and the use which should be made of the "civil funds" which have accrued from the customs collected here by the Governor of California previous to the assumption by the general government of the control of this matter, I would respectfully refer you to my former civil despatches. The attention which I have given to these subjects since writing those despatches has only tended to confirm the opinions there expressed.

This despatch and the accompanying papers will be delivered to you by Mr. J. McHenry Hollingsworth, late lieutenant of the regiment of New York volunteers disbanded in this country. He has, in accordance with the instructions of the Secretary of War, been furnished by the quartermaster's department with transportation to the place of his enlistment. Mr. Hollingsworth has proved himself a faithful and trustworthy officer, and merits in every respect the confidence of the government.

Very respectfully, your obedient servant,

B. RILEY,
Brevet Brig. Gen. U. S. A., and Governor of California.

Major General R. Jones, *Adjutant General of the Army, Washington, D. C.*

EXECUTIVE DEPARTMENT OF CALIFORNIA,
Monterey, October 1, 1849.

GENERAL: Enclosed herewith are copies of all civil papers issued since the date of my last civil despatch.

The convention called by my proclamation of June 3, assembled at this place on the 1st ultimo, and has nearly completed its labors in forming a constitution to be submitted to the people for their ratification. It has been determined by the unanimous vote of this convention (at least I am so informed) that the new government organized under this constitution, should it be ratified by the people, shall go into operation as soon as may be convenient after such ratification, and without waiting for the approval of Congress and the admission of California into the Union. I have strong doubts of the legality of such a course, under the decision of the Supreme Conrt of the United States; but if it should be the wish of the people of California to put the new government into operation without awaiting the action of Congress, I shall deem it my duty, under the circumstances, to surrender my civil powers into the hands of the new executive, unless special orders to the contrary are received from Washington.

In my civil despatch of August 30, I explained the character of the "civil funds" now in my hands, and the use which would be made of them in defraying the expenses of the existing government; and I now ask for instructions as to the disposition to be made of such portions of these funds as may be left when this government shall be superseded by that organized by the constitution now forming by this convention. Many have expressed the opinion that these funds should be turned over to the new government to enable it to go immediately into successful operation. However strongly of the opinion that this money belongs, in justice, to the people of California, I nevertheless shall not deem myself authorized to turn over this money till instructed to do so by direct orders from Washington. I hope that the views of the government touching this matter may be sent to me without delay.

I send herewith a copy of a report of Brevet Captain Wescott respecting the missions of San Jose and Santa Clara. The temporary arrangement made for the care and management of this property, will be seen in the copies of civil papers transmitted with this despatch.

Very respectfully, your obedient servant,

B. RILEY,

Brevet Brig. Gen. U. S. Army, commanding Department, and Acting Governor of California.

Major General R. Jones,

Adjutant General U. S. Army, Washington, D. C.

THE MILITARY AND CIVIL GOVERNMENT.

PROCLAMATION.

To the People of California.

A new Executive having been elected and installed into office, in accordance with the provisions of the Constitution of the State, the undersigned hereby resigns his powers as Governor of California. In thus dissolving his official connection with the people of this country, he would tender to them his heartfelt thanks for their many kind attentions, and for the uniform support which they have given to the measures of his administration. The principal object of all his wishes is now accomplished—the people have a government of their own choice, and one which, under the favor of divine Providence, will secure their own prosperity and happiness, and the permanent welfare of the new State.

Given at San Jose, California, this 20th day of December, A. D. 1849.

B. RILEY,

Brevet Brig. Gen. U. S. A., and Governor of California.

By the Governor: H. W. HALLECK,

Brevet Captain and Secretary of State.

HEADQUARTERS 10TH MILITARY DEPARTMENT,
SAN JOSE, *California*, Dec. 20, 1849.

(Orders No. 41.)

1. The Brigadier General commanding the Department has this day relinquished the administration of civil affairs in California to the execution of the government organized under the provisions of the Constitution ratified by the people of California at the recent general election.

2. Brevet Captain H. W. Halleck, Corps of Engineers, is relieved from duty as Secretary of State.

By order of GENERAL RILEY.

Ed. U. S. Canby, Ass't. Ad't. General.

CONTENTS.

www.ingramcontent.com/pod-product-compliance
Lightning Source LLC
LaVergne TN
LVHW021309110826
845150LV00003B/533

* 9 7 8 1 4 2 5 5 5 8 6 0 4 *